The Princeton Encyclopedia of American Political History

The Princeton Encyclopedia

ADVISORS

Richard R. John

Ira I. Katznelson

Jack N. Rakove

Julian E. Zelizer

# of American Political History

Volume I

EDITOR

Michael Kazin
Georgetown University

ASSOCIATE EDITORS

Rebecca Edwards
Vassar College

Adam Rothman
Georgetown University

PRINCETON UNIVERSITY PRESS

PRINCETON AND OXFORD

Published by Princeton University Press, 41 William Street, Princeton,
New Jersey 08540

In the United Kingdom: Princeton University Press, 6 Oxford Street,
Woodstock, Oxfordshire OX20 1TW

Library of Congress Cataloging-in-Publication Data

The Princeton encyclopedia of American political history / Michael
Kazin, editor . . . [et al.].
     v. cm.
   Includes bibliographical references and index.
   ISBN 978-0-691-12971-6 (hardcover : alk. paper)   1. United
States—Politics and government—Encyclopedias.   2. Political
science—United States—History—Encyclopedias.   I. Kazin,
Michael, 1948–   II. Title: Encyclopedia of American political
history.
   E183.P85 2010
   973.03—dc22   2009032311

This book has been composed in Adobe Garamond and Myriad Pro
Printed on acid-free paper.

press.princeton.edu

Printed in the United States of America
10 9 8 7 6 5 4 3 2 1

Contents

Preface

What is political history? The answer may seem obvious. In everyday language, "politics" in a democratic nation like the United States is the subject of who gets elected to office and what they do with the powers granted to them by voters, laws, and constitutions. It is an endless contest of speech making, lawmaking, fund-raising, and negotiating in which ambitious actors spend their lives struggling to come out on top.

This definition may seem like common sense, but it does not capture what most political historians actually do. Many authors who engage in the serious study of past politics try to understand the larger forces that propel changes in governments, laws, and campaigns. The most influential historians, in particular, have always framed the narrative of legislative give-and-take and winning and losing office within a context of grand historical themes and developments. In the 1890s, Frederick Jackson Turner argued that the frontier experience shaped American democracy. For him, regional identities and cultures drove political development. Early in the twentieth century, Charles and Mary Beard contended that the clash of economic interests was at the root of every turning point in U.S. history—from the drafting of the Constitution to the Civil War. At mid-century, Richard Hofstadter used the psychological concept of "status anxiety" to explain the fervor of both Populist and Progressive reformers. In recent decades, leading scholars have sought to illuminate evolving tensions within the body politic by focusing on intersecting differences of religion and cultural taste, race and ethnicity, gender and class.

This encyclopedia also assumes an expansive definition of politics: the meaning and uses of power in the public sphere and the competition to gain that power. The word *politics* derives from the Greek word for "citizen," and the rights, powers, and obligations of citizens and their governments have been at the core of the subject since the days of Aristotle, Plato, and Herodotus.

Another tradition has been with us since the building of the Acropolis: history is a constant debate. In this spirit, our contributors offer interpretations of their topics, not merely a factual record or a summary of views held by others. Each article ends with a bibliography meant to guide the reader to some of the most significant works on that topic.

――

The study of politics in the United States has featured several interpretive approaches since the first serious histories of the subject were published in the middle of the nineteenth century. First, at a time when universities were just beginning to train historians, such self-taught, eloquent writers as George Bancroft and Henry Adams wrote multivolume narratives of presidents and diplomats. Their prose was often vivid, and their judgments had a stern, moralizing flavor.

By the early twentieth century, such grand personal works were being supplanted by a rigorously empirical approach. This was a style of history pioneered by disciples of the German academic scholar Leopold von Ranke, who declared that the past should be studied "as it really was." Rankean scholars wrote careful monographs which piled fact upon fact about such subjects as the decisions that led to independence and the making of new state constitutions. They believed a "scientific" approach could produce a political history with the opinions of the historian left out.

At the same time, however, a new group known as the "progressive" historians was garnering controversy and a large readership outside academia as well as among scholars. Such leading progressives as Turner, the Beards, and Vernon Parrington described a long-standing division between, on the one hand, the makers of elite, urban culture and big business and, on the other hand, small farmers and self-taught, self-made men from rural areas and the frontier. These historians were sympathetic toward the reform movements of their day—from the Populists in the 1890s to the New Dealers of the 1930s—which portrayed themselves as fighting for "the people."

By the 1940s, a reaction to the progressive scholars was gathering force. Such historians as David Potter, Daniel Boorstin, and the political scientist Louis Hartz joined Hofstadter in arguing that politics in the United States had long been characterized more by a consensus of values than by a conflict over economic interests. Such "counterprogressive" scholars argued that most Americans had always embraced liberal capitalism and rejected any politicians and movements that aimed to do more than tinker with the existing system.

This sober, often ironic sensibility was challenged head-on in the late 1960s by historians—most of them young—who were inspired by contemporary movements for African American freedom, feminism, and against the war in Vietnam. These "New Left" scholars revived the progressive emphasis on sharp, ongoing conflict but located its wellsprings among workers, racial and ethnic minorities, and women—groups that had previously received little attention from political historians. Influential scholars like Eric Foner, Gerda Lerner, Nathan Huggins, Eugene Genovese, and Alan Brinkley embedded their narratives of power in a rich context of class relations, racial identities, and cultural assumptions. Arguing that ordinary people were as much agents of change as were national politicians and government officials helped to democratize understanding of the past, even as it deemphasized such durable institutions as the courts, Congress, and the major political parties.

More recently, an increasing number of scholars have turned away from focusing on American politics in isolation from similar developments occurring elsewhere in the world. Their "transnational" perspective challenges patriotic vanities by chipping away at the notion that the United States ever stood apart from ideas and social movements that shook other lands and peoples. Thomas Bender interprets the North's victory in the Civil War as producing a newly potent national state much like those emerging at the same time in Japan, Italy, Argentina, and Germany. Similarly, Daniel Rod-

gers describes how American reformers in the early twentieth century tried to apply policy ideas they had picked up on visits with fellow progressives and moderate socialists in Europe.

Whatever the individual approach, nearly every contemporary historian implicitly applies a broad definition of politics to her or his work. Historians are interested not only in such traditional topics as presidents, bureaucratic institutions, and constitutions but also in popular ideology and consciousness, social movements, war, education, crime, sexuality, and the reciprocal influence of mass culture on political thinking and behavior. At the same time, scholars in fields outside of history—especially in political science and law—have demonstrated a growing interest in the American past. Meanwhile, best-seller lists routinely include one or more skillful narratives about past presidents, diplomacy, and the politics of war. This is an exciting time to be a political historian in the United States.

To convey that excitement and the breadth of the subject, the encyclopedia includes 187 essays in the following areas—some traditional, some exemplifying the creative changes that mark the discipline.

Periods

Which issues, parties, institutions, events, and leaders were dominant in different spans of time? In chronological order, these essays include the era of a new republic (1789–1827), the Jacksonian era (1828–45), sectional conflict and secession (1845–65), Reconstruction (1865–77), the Gilded Age (1870s–90s), progressivism and the Progressive Era (1890s–1920), the conservative interregnum (1920–32), the New Deal Era (1933–52), the era of consensus (1952–64), the era of confrontation and decline (1964–80), and the conservative ascendancy (1980–2004). The essays provide an overview of pivotal elections, political developments, policies, and policy makers, and the rise and fall of major party coalitions.

Institutions

This category includes the presidency, the House of Representatives, the Senate, and the Supreme Court; as well as the cabinet departments; the Electoral College; local, state, and territorial governments; and civil service. But it also includes such nongovernmental institutions as party nominating conventions, think tanks, interest groups, and public opinion polls, as well as such topics as citizenship, whose legal and political history is critical to understanding the politics of ethnicity, immigration, and gender.

Movements

Mass movements have had a major impact on political change in the United States. This category includes both long-lived movements that still exist—such as labor and pacifism—and ones of great historical significance that now exist only in memory, such as abolitionism and Prohibition.

Political Parties

This category includes lengthy articles on the Democrats and Republicans in different periods as well as shorter essays about defunct major parties, such as the Federalists and Whigs, and a variety of other political parties that have had a national presence. The essays on the major parties discuss the impact of key elections, leaders, events, and social changes on the fortunes and evolution of these organizations whose competition has done much to structure the political order from the 1850s to the present.

Ideas, Philosophies, and Religions

This category includes such hotly contested and undeniably significant concepts as conservatism, liberalism, republicanism, radicalism, Americanism, feminism, and democracy. It also includes articles about how American Protestants, Catholics, Jews, and Muslims have influenced politics and vice versa.

War and Foreign Policy

The rest of the world has been a major influence on the development of the American polity and on a variety of related subjects—from the growth of the military, to the Fourteenth Amendment, to the rise of the African American freedom movement in the 1940s and 1950s. The essays about the nation's wars discuss the effect of military operations on domestic debate and policy as well as the role of military leaders and battles in shaping electoral outcomes.

Founding Documents

This category includes the Articles of Confederation as well as the Declaration of Independence, the Constitution, and the initial amendments to it, the Bill of Rights. Articles in this category discuss the genesis of these docu-ments as well as debates about their meaning and application over the next two centuries and beyond. The full text of these documents can be found in the appendix (volume II).

Regions

In wide-ranging essays, authors focus on the major issues, dominant institutions, and pivotal actors in the politics of New England, the Middle Atlantic, the South since the end of Reconstruction, the Midwest, the Great Plains, the Rocky Mountains, the Pacific Coast, and Alaska and Hawai'i. These contributions examine how the expansionist, regionally diverse character of U.S. history has shaped its political evolution.

Ethnic and Racial Groups

Tens of millions of people immigrated to the United States voluntarily, and many others came as slaves. The articles in this category discuss the ideas and political activities of immigrant clusters from different parts of the world and their descendants—European, African, Latino, Asian, Caribbean—and how ethnic and racial diversity have influenced larger social changes. There is also an article on Native Americans, the original immigrants, and separate contributions on the changing role of race in politics.

Issues

This category includes subjects and actors whose significance has been perennial in U.S. history, as in the political history of every modern nation: the economy (banking policy, agrarian politics, consumers, taxation, transportation), cities and suburbs, class and crime. These are the "issues" that—since the beginning of the republic—politicians, movements, and voters have debated, and that have spurred major pieces of legislation and court rulings.

Mass Culture

Anyone who follows politics knows how important the culture of image making and performance is to framing and winning contests for office. But the engagement of mass culture and politics stretches back to the beginnings of the nation. This category includes essays about cartooning, the American novel, film, music, radio, television, political advertising, and the Internet. These essays offer provocative interpretations about how art and artful technology have influenced the world of politics.

Biographical directories abound, in print and on the Internet. So we decided that even short sketches of the 44 presidents would take up space better devoted to major themes and contexts in which each chief executive won office and governed. Of course, nearly every article mentions prominent individuals and the decisions they made, and the index can help readers follow significant historical figures through the book.

The best political histories teach readers a good deal that is new to them but do so in clear, direct, evocative prose. This work is intended to help readers at all levels of knowledge to understand patterns and connections in U.S. history, from its colonial origins to the present day, and to serve as a first step to further research. All our contributors combine expertise with an ability to write for a broad audience.

We hope you find this encyclopedia both instructive and a pleasure to read.

Recommended Reading

For excellent surveys of historical scholarship about U.S. politics, see Richard J. Jensen, "Historiography of American Political History," in *Encyclopedia of American Political History*, edited by Jack P. Greene (New York: Scribner's, 1984), 1–25; Meg Jacobs and Julian E. Zelizer, "The Democratic Experiment: New Directions in American Political History," in *The Democratic Experiment: New Directions in American Political History*, edited by Meg Jacobs, William J. Novak, and Julian E. Zelizer (Princeton, NJ: Princeton University Press, 2003), 1–19; Sean Wilentz, "American Political Histories," *OAH Magazine of History* (April 2007), 23–27. For excellent essays on significant individuals, see *American National Biography* (New York: Oxford University Press, 2002). The latter is also available online (with a subscription). A bracing history of the historical profession in the United States is Peter Novick's *That Noble Dream* (Cambridge, UK: Cambridge University Press, 1989).

Acknowledgments

Three names appear on the covers of these volumes, but the encyclopedia is really the work of hundreds of people and could not have been conceived, edited, or produced without them. Since Anne Savarese, reference editor at Princeton University Press, asked me to join this daunting project, she has been a paragon of wisdom and efficiency. I quickly learned that when Anne makes a suggestion about a topic, an author, or anything else, the only wise choice is to take it. Claire Tillman-McTigue, her assistant, was equally sensible and resourceful. I have learned a great deal about editing from both of them. And my agent, Sandy Dijkstra, continued to give me lessons about the complicated business of publishing.

Terri O'Prey managed the production of the encyclopedia with great skill and unfailing enthusiasm. She had a fine team to help her. It included Tracy Baldwin, who is responsible for the elegant design; Dimitri Karetnikov, who handled the illustrations; the copyeditors Joseph N. Reilly and Brian Bendlin; the proofreader, Jeanette Nakada; and the indexer, Richard Comfort.

The title of "associate editor" does not really convey what Rebecca Edwards and Adam Rothman contributed to this work. As distinguished scholars, Rebecca and Adam used their deep knowledge and lists of contacts to find the right authors for dozens of topics and then helped make those essays both more probing and more precise. And their own entries are models of concision and analysis.

Finally, I am grateful to the over 150 people who agreed to write entries on a remarkable variety of topics in U.S. political history. Most are academics who teach history, political science, or a related discipline; some are journalists, and a few are advanced graduate students. But each took on the difficult task of synthesizing what is known about a vital subject and produced a thoughtful essay that makes sense of it. This is their encyclopedia, most of all.

MICHAEL KAZIN
Editor in Chief

Alphabetical List of Entries

Topical List of Entries

Contributors

Sean Adams
History Department, University of Florida

    energy and politics

Patrick Allitt
Department of History, Emory University

    religion and politics since 1945

John Ashworth
*School of American and Canadian Studies,
University of Nottingham*

    Democratic Party, 1828–60

Dean Baker
Center for Economic Policy and Research, Washington, D.C.

    economy and politics since 1970

Paula Baker
Department of History, Ohio State University

    campaign law and finance to 1900;
    campaign law and finance since 1900

James M. Banner Jr.
National History Center

    Federalist Party

Lois Banner
Department of History, University of Southern California

    feminism

Kyle Barbieri
*Hillsborough Community College and
Polk Community College, Florida*

    Republican Party, 1968–2008 *(coauthor)*

Stephen Bates
*Hank Greenspun School of Journalism and Media Studies,
University of Nevada–Las Vegas*

    political advertising

David H. Bennett
*Department of History, Maxwell School,
Syracuse University*

    nativism

Edward D. Berkowitz
*Elliott School of International Affairs,
George Washington University*

    Social Security

Frederick J. Blue
*Department of History (emeritus),
Youngstown State University*

    Free Soil Party

Stuart M. Blumin
Department of History, Cornell University

    antiparty sentiment

Matthew Bowman
Department of History, Georgetown University

    conservative third parties since the New Deal;
    Electoral College; inaugural addresses of U.S.
    presidents; Libertarian Party; party nominating
    conventions

Amy Bridges
*Department of Political Science,
University of California–San Diego*

    cities and politics

Contributors

Stephen Brooks
Department of Political Science, University of Windsor
foreign observers of U.S. politics

Joshua Brown
American Social History Project/Center for Media and Learning, Graduate Center, City University of New York
cartooning

W. Elliot Brownlee
Department of History, University of California–Santa Barbara
taxation since 1913

Frank M. Bryan
Department of Political Science, University of Vermont
New England

Richard Buel Jr.
Department of History (emeritus), Wesleyan University
War of 1812

Paul Buhle
Departments of History and American Civilization, Brown University
anarchism

Charles W. Calhoun
Department of History, East Carolina University
Republican Party to 1896

Christopher Capozzola
Department of History, Massachusetts Institute of Technology
World War I

Daniel Carpenter
Department of Government, Harvard University
regulation

Robert W. Cherny
Department of History, San Francisco State University
the Great Plains; the Pacific Coast

Elisabeth S. Clemens
Department of Sociology, University of Chicago
interest groups

Dorothy Sue Cobble
Department of Labor and Employment Relations, Rutgers University
women and politics, 1920–70

Michael Cornfield
Graduate School of Political Management, George Washington University
Internet and politics

Edward Countryman
Department of History, Southern Methodist University
colonial legacy

Matthew J. Countryman
Department of History, University of Michigan
race and politics since 1933

Douglas Craig
School of Social Sciences, Australian National University
radio and politics

Joe Creech
Lilly Fellows Program and Christ College, Honors College of Valparaiso University
religion and politics, 1865–1945

Joseph Crespino
Department of History, Emory University
South since 1877, the

Donald T. Critchlow
Department of History, Saint Louis University
conservatism *(coauthor)*

Elliott Currie
Department of Criminology, Law, and Society, University of California–Irvine
crime

John Patrick Diggins, deceased
Graduate Center, City University of New York
liberal consensus and American exceptionalism

John Dinan
Department of Political Science, Wake Forest University
state constitutions

Ellen Carol DuBois
Department of History, University of California–Los Angeles

woman suffrage

Gerald Early
American Culture Studies, Washington University in St. Louis

popular music and politics

Max M. Edling
Department of History, Uppsala University

Constitution, federal

Rebecca Edwards
Department of History, Vassar College

gender and sexuality

Robin L. Einhorn
Department of History, University of California–Berkeley

taxation to 1913

Richard E. Ellis
Department of History, University at Buffalo, State University of New York

Democratic Party, 1800–28

Nicole Etcheson
Department of History, Ball State University

Midwest, the

Michael W. Flamm
Department of History, Ohio Wesleyan University

conservative ascendancy, 1980–2008

Maureen A. Flanagan
Department of History, Michigan State University

progressivism and the Progressive Era, 1890s–1920

Anne L. Foster
Department of History, Indiana State University

Spanish-American War and Filipino Insurrection

Steve Fraser
New York University

business and politics

Kevin Gaines
Department of History, University of Michigan

African Americans and politics

Michael A. Genovese
Department of Political Science, Loyola Marymount University

presidency to 1860

Michael Gerhardt
School of Law, University of North Carolina–Chapel Hill

impeachment

Steven M. Gillon
Department of History, University of Oklahoma

Democratic Party, 1932–68

Marcia Tremmel Goldstein
Department of History, University of Colorado

Rocky Mountain region *(coauthor)*

Lewis L. Gould
Department of History (emeritus), University of Texas–Austin

Gilded Age, 1870s–90s; Republican Party; Republican Party, 1896–1932

Amy S. Greenberg
Department of History, Pennsylvania State University

Mexican-American War

Eric Allen Hall
Department of History, Purdue University

sports and politics *(coauthor)*

Richard F. Hamm
Department of History, University at Albany, State University of New York

Prohibition and temperance

Stanley Harrold
Department of Social Sciences, South Carolina State University

abolitionism

D. G. Hart
Intercollegiate Studies Institute

religion and politics to 1865

David C. Hendrickson
Department of Political Science, Colorado College

Articles of Confederation

Contributors

Williamjames Hull Hoffer
Department of History, Seton Hall University

 Supreme Court

Susan Hoffmann
Department of Political Science, University of Western Michigan

 banking policy

David A. Horowitz
Department of History, Portland State University

 anti-statism

Jane Armstrong Hudiburg
Annapolis, Maryland

 Senate

Andrew Hunt
Department of History, University of Waterloo

 pacifism

Sarah E. Igo
Department of History, University of Pennsylvania

 public opinion polls

Maurice Isserman
Department of History, Hamilton College

 communism; era of confrontation and decline, 1964–80; New Deal Era, 1932–52

Meg Jacobs
Department of History, Massachusetts Institute of Technology

 consumers and politics

Dennis W. Johnson
Graduate School of Political Management, George Washington University

 campaign consultants

Robert D. Johnston
Department of History, University of Illinois–Chicago

 class and politics since 1877

Jeffrey P. Jones
Department of Communication and Theatre Arts, Old Dominion University

 television and politics

Stephen Kantrowitz
Department of History, University of Wisconsin–Madison

 Reconstruction Era, 1865–77

Michael B. Katz
Department of History, University of Pennsylvania

 welfare

Michael Kazin
Department of History, Georgetown University

 Americanism; Democratic Party, 1800–2008; populism

Alexander Keyssar
John F. Kennedy School of Government, Harvard University

 voting

Michael Kimmage
History Department, Catholic University of America

 politics in the American novel

Michael J. Klarman
Harvard Law School

 segregation and Jim Crow

Jennifer Klein
Department of History, Yale University

 economy and politics, 1945–70

James T. Kloppenberg
Department of History, Harvard University

 liberalism

Gary J. Kornblith
Department of History, Oberlin College

 class and politics to 1877

J. Morgan Kousser
Division of the Humanities and Social Sciences, California Institute of Technology

 race and politics, 1860–1933

Alan M. Kraut
Department of History, American University

 European immigrants and politics; health and illness

Kathleen Smith Kutolowski
Department of History, College at Brockport, State University of New York

 Anti-Masonic Party

David E. Kyvig
Department of History, Northern Illinois University

 amendment process

Matthew D. Lassiter
Department of History, University of Michigan

suburbs and politics

Mark Lause
Department of History, University of Cincinnati

Greenback-Labor Party

Steven F. Lawson
Department of History, Rutgers University

civil rights

Allan J. Lichtman
Department of History, American University

elections and electoral eras; presidency, 1860–1932; presidency, 1932–2008

Patricia Nelson Limerick
Center of the American West, University of Colorado

Rocky Mountain region *(coauthor)*

James Livingston
Department of History, Rutgers University

economy and politics, 1860–1920

John Majewski
Department of History, University of California–Santa Barbara

economy and politics to 1860

Chandra Manning
Department of History, Georgetown University

Civil War and Reconstruction; sectional conflict and secession, 1845–65

Glenna Matthews
Independent Scholar, Laguna Beach, California

women and politics since 1970

Joseph A. McCartin
Department of History, Georgetown University

labor movement and politics

Stuart McConnell
History, Pitzer College

veterans

Lisa McGirr
Department of History, Harvard University

conservative interregnum, 1920–32

Alan McPherson
School of International and Area Studies, University of Oklahoma

foreign policy and domestic politics, 1865–1933

Yanek Mieczkowski
Division of Social Sciences, Dowling College

Republican Party, 1932–68

David Montejano
Department of Comparative Ethnic Studies, University of California–Berkeley

Latinos and politics

Kathleen M. Moore
Religious Studies Department, University of California–Santa Barbara

Muslims and politics

James A. Morone
Department of Political Science, Brown University

political culture

Kevin P. Murphy
Department of History, University of Minnesota

homosexuality

Teresa Murphy
Department of American Studies, George Washington University

women and politics, 1828–65

Mark A. Noll
Department of History, University of Notre Dame

Protestants and politics

James Oakes
Graduate Center, City University of New York

race and politics to 1860

David O'Brien
History Department, College of the Holy Cross

Catholics and politics

Peter S. Onuf
Department of History, University of Virginia

federalism

Jeffrey Ostler
Department of History, University of Oregon

Native Americans and politics

Contributors

Meredith Oyen
Department of History, Georgetown University

   Asian immigrants and politics

Jeffrey L. Pasley
Department of History, University of Missouri

   era of new republic, 1789–1827

William Pencak
Department of History and Religious Studies,
Pennsylvania State University

   Middle Atlantic, the

Michael Perman
Department of History, University of Illinois–Chicago

   Democratic Party, 1860–96

Elisabeth Israels Perry
Department of History, Saint Louis University

   women and politics, 1865–1920

Christopher Phelps
School of American and Canadian Studies, University of
Nottingham

   radicalism

Sarah T. Phillips
Department of History, Columbia University

   economy and politics, 1920–45

Kim Phillips-Fein
Gallatin School, New York University

   era of consensus, 1952–64

Dan Plesch
Center for International Studies and Diplomacy, University of
London

   United Nations

Charles L. Ponce de Leon
Department of History, California State University–Long Beach

   press and politics

Kevin Powers
Department of History, Georgetown University

   cabinet departments; labor parties; Progressive parties

Richard Gid Powers
College of Staten Island, and Graduate Center,
City University of New York

   anticommunism

Jack N. Rakove
Department of History, Stanford University

   Bill of Rights

Donald J. Ratcliffe
Faculty of History, University of Oxford

   National Republican Party

Eric Rauchway
Department of History, University of California–Davis

   assassination, presidential; globalization

William J. Reese
Departments of Educational Policy Studies and History,
University of Wisconsin–Madison

   education and politics

Brian Holden Reid
Department of War Studies, King's College London

   armed forces, politics in the

Joanne Reitano
Social Science Department, La Guardia Community College,
City University of New York

   tariffs and politics

Leo P. Ribuffo
Elliott School of International Affairs,
George Washington University

   Democratic Party, 1968–2008

Andrew Rich
Franklin and Eleanor Roosevelt Institute

   think tanks

Randy Roberts
Department of History, Purdue University

   sports and politics *(coauthor)*

Adam Rome
Department of History, Pennsylvania State University

   environmental issues and politics

Steven J. Ross
Department of History, University of Southern California

   politics in American film

Doug Rossinow
History Department, Metropolitan State University

   New Left

Adam Rothman
Department of History, Georgetown University

Liberty Party; slavery

Andrew J. Rotter
Department of History, Colgate University

Vietnam and Indochina wars

Mark Rozell
School of Public Policy, George Mason University

Republican Party, 1968–2008 *(coauthor)*

Anne Sarah Rubin
History Department, University of Maryland–Baltimore County

Confederacy

Leonard J. Sadosky
Department of History, Iowa State University

Declaration of Independence; foreign policy and domestic politics to 1865

Nick Salvatore
Industrial and Labor Relations School and Program in American Studies, Cornell University

socialism

Elizabeth Sanders
Department of Government, Cornell University

agrarian politics

David Sarasohn
The Oregonian

Democratic Party, 1896–1932

Gregory Schneider
Department of Social Sciences, Emporia State University

conservatism *(coauthor)*

Robert Schulzinger
Department of History, University of Colorado–Boulder

Korean War and cold war

Carlos A. Schwantes
Department of History, University of Missouri–St. Louis

transportation and politics

William G. Shade
Department of History (emeritus), Lehigh University

Whig Party

Robert E. Shalhope
Department of History, University of Oklahoma

republicanism

Michael Sherry
Department of History, Northwestern University

war and politics

John Shy
Department of History, University of Michigan

war for independence

David J. Siemers
Political Science, University of Wisconsin–Oshkosh

anti-Federalists

Stephen Skowronek
Department of Political Science, Yale University

presidency, the

Jason Scott Smith
Department of History, University of New Mexico

patronage

Bartholomew H. Sparrow
Department of Government, University of Texas–Austin

territorial government

Jeremi Suri
Department of History, University of Wisconsin–Madison

transnational influences on American politics

Jon C. Teaford
Department of History, Purdue University

local government; state government

Daniel J. Tichenor
Department of Political Science, University of Oregon

immigration policy

Anand Toprani
Department of History, Georgetown University

Iraq wars of 1991 and 2003

Frank Towers
History Department, University of Calgary

American (Know-Nothing) Party

Contributors

Gil Troy
Department of History, McGill University

  campaigning

Cyrus Veeser
Department of History, Bentley College

  Caribbean, Central America, and Mexico, interventions in, 1903–34

Penny M. Von Eschen
Department of History, University of Michigan

  foreign policy and domestic politics since 1933

Samuel Walker
School of Criminology and Criminal Justice, University of Nebraska–Omaha

  civil liberties

Irma Watkins-Owens
Department of History, Fordham University

  Caribbean immigrants and politics

Harry L. Watson
Department of History and Center for the Study of the American South, University of North Carolina–Chapel Hill

  Jacksonian era, 1828–45

Robert Westbrook
Department of History, University of Rochester

  democracy

Richard D. White Jr.
Public Administration Institute, Louisiana State University

  civil service

John S. Whitehead
Department of History, University of Alaska Fairbanks

  Alaska and Hawai'i

Stephen J. Whitfield
Department of American Studies, Brandeis University

  Jews and politics

Allan M. Winkler
Department of History, Miami University

  World War II

Rosemarie Zagarri
Department of History, George Mason University

  women and politics to 1828

Julian E. Zelizer
Department of History, Princeton University

  House of Representatives

Aristide R. Zolberg
Department of Political Science, New School for Social Research

  citizenship

The Princeton Encyclopedia of American Political History

abolitionism

A major reform movement during the eighteenth and nineteenth centuries, abolitionism sought to end slavery and free millions of black people held as slaves. Also known as the antislavery movement, abolitionism in the United States was part of an international effort against slavery and the slave trade in the Atlantic World. Its historical roots lay in black resistance to slavery, changing interpretations of Christian morality, eighteenth-century ideas concerning universal human rights, and economic change. Some of slavery's opponents advocated gradual abolition and others immediate abolition. By the 1830s the term *abolitionism* applied only to the latter.

Early Development

Race-based slavery, whereby people of European descent relied on the forced labor of Africans and their descendants, began on a large scale during the sixteenth century as a result of European colonization in the Americas. By the middle of the seventeenth century, slavery had reached the portion of Great Britain's North American colonies that later became the United States. In the American form of slavery, the enslaved lost customary rights, served for life, and passed their unfree condition on to their children. From the start, those subjected to slavery sought freedom through self-purchase, court action, escape, or, more rarely, rebellion. There were major slave revolts in New York City in 1712 and Stono, South Carolina, in 1739.

The first white abolitionists in America were members of the Society of Friends (Quakers), who—like their coreligionists in Britain—held slavery to be sinful and physically dangerous to slave and master alike. During the 1740s and 1750s, Quaker abolitionists John Woolman of New Jersey and Anthony Benezet of Pennsylvania urged other American members of the society to end their involvement in the slave trade and gradually free their slaves. With the American Revolution (1775–83), abolitionism spread beyond African Americans and Quakers. Natural rights doctrines rooted in the European Enlightenment and endorsed by the Declaration of Independence, black service in Patriot armies, black petitions for emancipation, evangelical Christianity, and the activities of the earliest white abolition societies encouraged the American North to lead the world in political abolitionism. Starting with Vermont in 1777 and Massachusetts in 1783, all the states north of Delaware had by 1804 either ended slavery within their jurisdiction or provided for its gradual abolition. Meanwhile, Congress in 1787 included a clause in the Northwest Ordinance banning slavery in the Northwest Territory. During the 1780s, states in the Upper South eased restrictions on masters who wished to free individual slaves, and small, Quaker-dominated, gradual abolition societies spread into Delaware, Maryland, and Virginia.

Revolutionary-era abolitionism peaked during the 1780s. Thereafter, several developments stopped and then reversed the southward advance of antislavery sentiment. The invention of the cotton gin in 1793 and resulting expansion of cotton cultivation into the Old Southwest reinvigorated slavery. The brutal Haitian slave revolt that began in 1791 and culminated in the creation of an independent black republic in 1804 led white Southerners—who feared they could not control free African Americans—to believe that slavery had to be strengthened rather than abolished. An aborted revolt conspiracy led by the slave Gabriel near Richmond, Virginia, in 1800 bolstered this belief. As a direct result of increased white defensiveness, antislavery societies in the Upper South disbanded or declined. Meanwhile, in the North, a new scientific racism encouraged white residents to interpret social status in racial terms, restrict black access to schools, churches, and jobs, and regard enslavement as suitable for black Southerners.

White gradual abolitionists came to accept a contention that emancipation must be linked with expatriation of former slaves to avoid the formation of a dangerous and uncontrollable free black class. The American Colonization Society (ACS), organized by prominent slaveholders in 1816, claimed its objective was to encourage gradual abolition by sending *free* African Americans to Africa. It became the leading American antislavery organization of the 1820s and established Liberia as a black colony in West Africa. For a time black leaders, facing increasing oppression in the United States, agreed with this strategy. Best represented by black sea captain Paul Cuffe, they cooperated with the ACS during the 1810s, hoping that a homeland beyond America's borders would undermine slavery there and throughout the Atlantic World. Yet, by the 1820s, most free African Americans believed the ACS's real goal was to strengthen slavery by removing its most dedicated opponents—themselves.

Immediate Abolitionism

Three factors led to the emergence, during the late 1820s and early 1830s, of a more radical form of abolitionism dedicated to immediate emancipation and equal rights for African Americans in the United States. First, black abolitionists convinced a small minority of white Northerners that the ACS was a proslavery fraud. Second, signs of black unrest inspired urgency among white abolitionists who wished to avoid a race war in the South. In 1822 a free black man named Denmark Vesey organized a major slave conspiracy in Charleston, South Carolina. Seven years later in Boston, black abolitionist David Walker published his revolutionary *Appeal to the Colored Citizens of the World*. Slave preacher Nat Turner in 1831 led a slave revolt in Southampton County, Virginia, which left nearly 60 white residents dead. Third, the convergence of northern economic modernization with a massive religious revival known as the Second Great Awakening encouraged increasing numbers of white people to regard slavery as a barbaric, outmoded, and sinful practice. They believed it had to be ended if the country were to prosper and avoid God's wrath.

All these factors influenced the extraordinary career of William Lloyd Garrison, a white New Englander who began publishing his weekly newspaper, *The Liberator*, in Boston in 1831. Late in 1833 Garrison brought together in Philadelphia a diverse group—including a few black men and a few white women—to form the American Anti-

Slavery Society (AASS). Rejecting all violent means, the AASS pledged to rely on "moral suasion" to achieve immediate, uncompensated emancipation and equal rights for African Americans in the United States. White men dominated the organization's leadership, but thousands of black men and thousands of women of both races lent active support. A few African Americans, including former slaves Frederick Douglass, Henry Highland Garnet, and Sojourner Truth, emerged as leaders in this biracial abolitionist movement. As they became antislavery activists, such white women as Susan B. Anthony and Elizabeth Cady Stanton grew conscious of their own inequality and initiated the women's rights movement.

Although members of the AASS comprised a tiny, despised minority, the organization spread rapidly across the North. In 1835 and 1836 its members sent thousands of antislavery petitions to Congress and stacks of abolitionist propaganda into the South. Their efforts, combined with Turner's revolt and the 1833 initiation of gradual abolition in the British West Indies, produced another fierce proslavery reaction. Abolitionists could not safely venture into the South. In the North, mobs beat abolitionist speakers and destroyed abolitionist meeting places, schools, and printing presses. They also attacked black communities.

A More Aggressive Abolitionism

Antiabolitionism and the failure of peaceful agitation to weaken slavery split the immediatist movement in 1840. Garrison and his associates, centered in New England, became social perfectionists, feminists, and anarchists. They denounced violence, unrighteous government, and organized religion. They refused to vote and embraced dissolution of the Union as the only way to save the North from the sin of slavery and force the South to abolish it. Known as Garrisonians, they retained control of the AASS and, until the Civil War, concentrated on agitation in the North.

The great majority of abolitionists (black and white) insisted, however, that church and government action could end slavery. They became more willing to use violent means, rejected radical assertions of women's rights, and formed aggressive organizations. The American and Foreign Anti-Slavery Society (1840–55), led by New York City businessman Lewis Tappan, concentrated on converting churches to immediatism and continued to send antislavery propaganda into the South. The Liberty Party (1840–48) employed a variety of political strategies. The more radical Liberty abolitionists, centered in upstate

New York and led by Gerrit Smith, maintained that slavery was always illegal, that immediatists had an obligation to go south to help slaves escape, and that Congress could abolish slavery in the southern states. The more conservative—and by far more numerous—Liberty faction depended on two Cincinnati residents, Gamaliel Bailey and Salmon P. Chase, for intellectual and political leadership. It accepted the legality of slavery in the southern states, rejected abolitionist aid to help slaves escape in the South and sought to build a mass political party on a platform calling not for abolition but removing U.S. government support for slavery.

Meanwhile, black abolitionists led in forming local vigilance associations designed to protect fugitive slaves, and most of them supported the AFASS and the Liberty Party. In 1846 they joined church-oriented white abolitionists in the American Missionary Association, an outgrowth of the AFASS that sent antislavery missionaries into the South. Douglass, who in 1847 began publishing the *North Star* in Rochester, New York, remained loyal to Garrison until 1851, when he joined the radical wing of the Liberty Party.

In 1848 members of the Liberty Party's conservative wing helped organize the Free Soil Party, dedicated to preventing the spread of slavery into American territories. By then they had essentially ceased to be immediatists. In 1854, when Congress opened Kansas Territory to slavery, they worked with antislavery Whigs and Democrats to form the Republican Party, which nominated its first presidential candidate in 1856. The Republican Party formally aimed only at ending slavery within the national domain. Many of its leaders claimed to represent the interests of white Northerners against the domination of slaveholders. But members of the party's "Old Liberty Guard" and such former Free Soilers as Charles Sumner of Massachusetts and Joshua R. Giddings of Ohio held Republicans to a higher standard. As Radical Republicans, they pressed for abolition and equal rights for African Americans.

After 1848 the more radical members of the Liberty Party—known as radical political abolitionists—maintained their tiny organization. They excelled in Underground Railroad efforts and resistance in the North to the Fugitive Slave Law of 1850. More than any other abolitionist faction, the radical political abolitionists supported John Brown's raid at Harpers Ferry in 1859. Brown and his biracial band had hoped to spark a slave revolt but were easily captured by Virginia militia and U.S. troops. Brown's actions, nevertheless, angered and frightened white Southerners; after his capture and prior to his ex-

ecution that December, his elegant appeals for racial justice aroused sympathy among many Northerners.

Abolitionism during the Civil War and Reconstruction

Brown's raid and the victory of Republican candidate Abraham Lincoln in the presidential election of 1860 precipitated the secession movement among white Southerners, which led to the Civil War in 1861. As the war began, Lincoln, who advocated the "ultimate extinction" of human bondage, believed former slaves should be colonized outside the United States and promised not to interfere with slavery in the South. He feared that to go further would alienate southern Unionists and weaken northern support for the war. Abolitionists, nevertheless, almost universally supported the war because they believed it would end slavery. Garrison and his associates dropped their opposition to forceful means, and church-oriented and radical political abolitionists rejoined the AASS. As the organization's influence grew, Garrison's friend Wendell Phillips emerged as the North's most popular orator. Phillips, Frederick Douglass, Sojourner Truth, and other prominent abolitionists joined Radical Republicans in lobbying Lincoln in favor of making emancipation and racial justice Union war aims. Abolitionists—especially black abolitionists—led in urging the president to enlist black troops.

When, in January 1863, Lincoln issued the Emancipation Proclamation, declaring slaves in areas under Confederate control to be free, abolitionists worried that—by resting emancipation on military necessity rather than racial justice—he had laid an unsound basis for black freedom. But they recognized the proclamation's significance, particularly its endorsement of enlisting black troops. Young white abolitionist men became officers in the otherwise segregated black regiments. Abolitionists advocated voting rights, education, and landownership for African Americans as compensation for generations of unrequited labor. These, they maintained, were essential to black economic and political advancement. In this regard abolitionists were similar to Radical Republicans, but they were much more insistent on involving African Americans in rebuilding the Union. They reacted negatively to Lincoln's December 1863 Reconstruction plan that would leave former masters in control of the status of their former slaves. As a result, in 1864 a few abolitionists joined a small group of Radical Republicans in opposing Lincoln's renomination for the presidency. However, Garrison, Douglass, and most leaders of the

AASS believed they could influence Lincoln and continued to support him.

During the summer of 1861, abolitionist organizations had begun sending missionaries and teachers into war zones to minister to the physical, spiritual, and educational needs of the former slaves. Women predominated, in part because younger abolitionist men had enrolled in Union armies. The most ambitious effort occurred in the South Carolina Sea Islands centered on Port Royal, which Union forces captured in 1861. There, and at locations in Virginia, Kentucky, and Louisiana, abolitionists attempted to transform an oppressed people into independent proprietors and wage laborers. Their efforts encouraged the formation of black churches, schools, and other institutions but had serious shortcomings. Northerners did not understand southern black culture, tended toward unworkable bureaucratic policies, and put too much faith in wage labor as a solution to entrenched conditions. When the former slaves did not progress under these conditions, most abolitionists blamed the victims.

Nevertheless, with the end of the Civil War in May 1865 and the ratification that December of the Thirteenth Amendment, making slavery illegal throughout the United States, Garrison declared that abolitionism had succeeded. He ceased publication of the *Liberator* and urged the AASS to disband. He believed the Republican Party could henceforth protect black rights and interests. A majority of immediatists, including Douglass, Phillips, and Smith, were not so sure and kept the AASS in existence until 1870. Black abolitionists became especially active in lobbying on behalf of the rights of the former slaves and against the regressive policies of Andrew Johnson, Lincoln's successor as president. In 1866 and 1867 most abolitionists opposed ratification of the Fourteenth Amendment, contending that it did not insufficiently protect the right of black men to vote. Thereafter, they supported the stronger guarantees the Fifteenth Amendment provided for adult black male suffrage, although a minority of feminist abolitionists—led by Stanton—objected that enfranchisement of white women should take precedence.

When the Fifteenth Amendment gained ratification in 1870, the AASS declared that abolitionism had achieved its ultimate objective and disbanded. The organization was too optimistic. During the 1870s and 1880s, southern states—having rejoined the Union—curtailed black rights and the white North acquiesced. The abolitionists bear some responsibility for this tragic outcome. Nevertheless, they played a crucial role in ending slavery, in creating black institutions in the postwar South, and in placing protections for minority rights in the Constitution.

See also slavery.

FURTHER READING

Essig, James D. *The Bonds of Wickedness: American Evangelicals against Slavery 1770–1808*. Philadelphia: Temple University Press, 1982.

Friedman, Lawrence J. *Gregarious Saints: Self and Community in American Abolitionism, 1830–1870*. New York: Cambridge University Press, 1982.

Harrold, Stanley. *American Abolitionists*. Harlow, UK: Longman, 2001.

———. *The Rise of Aggressive Abolitionism: Addresses to the Slaves*. Lexington: University Press of Kentucky, 2004.

Horton, James Oliver, and Lois E. Horton. *In Hope of Liberty: Culture, Community, and Protest among Northern Free Blacks 1700–1860*. New York: Oxford University Press, 1997.

Jeffrey, Julie Roy. *The Great Silent Army of Abolitionism: Ordinary Women in the Antislavery Movement*. Chapel Hill: University of North Carolina Press, 1998.

Mason, Matthew. *Slavery and Politics in the Early American Republic*. Chapel Hill: University of North Carolina Press, 2006.

McPherson, James M. *The Struggle for Equality: Abolitionists and the Negro in the Civil War and Reconstruction*. 1964. Reprint Princeton, NJ: Princeton University Press, 1992.

Sewell, Richard H. *Ballots for Freedom: Antislavery Politics in the United States 1837–1860*. New York: Oxford University Press, 1976.

Stewart, James Brewer. *Holy Warriors: The Abolitionists and American Slavery*. 2nd ed. New York: Hill and Wang, 1997.

STANLEY HARROLD

advertising

See political advertising.

African Americans and politics

In its most common sense, African American politics refers to the active participation of African Americans in U.S. electoral and party politics and the nation's domestic and foreign policy. But given America's historical denial of basic human rights and the rights of citizenship to African Americans, any definition must also take into account the responsiveness of American political institutions to African American interests and the group's quest for universal freedom.

This expanded definition requires one to consider the myriad ways in which African Americans have struggled to realize the nation's founding ideals of freedom and equality. Their struggle has expanded the constitutional definition of national citizenship and transformed the nation as a whole. Yet the persistence of racial inequity at the start of the twenty-first century highlights the limitations of the formal equality achieved through civil rights legislation. In particular, despite the historic election of Barack Obama as the first African American president of the United States, the ascendancy of the conservative movement after 1980 has steadily eroded political support for African American civil rights and universal freedom.

Strangers in Their Own Land

An understanding of the history of African American politics begins with the question of how to define the political behavior of a group that has traditionally been excluded from freedom, citizenship, and personhood— the basic rights that, under normal conditions, would make political participation possible.

Enslavement limited the range of political options available to people of African heritage in British-controlled America. Political action and agitation were their most important tools in pursuit of universal freedom and equality. As crown and colony institutionalized slavery into law during the seventeenth century, the responses of the enslaved ranged from individual acts of resistance and rebellion to full-blown conspiracies and violent insurrections. Colonial legislatures reacted by asserting military control over the enslaved population, particularly in colonies like South Carolina, where there were three times as many blacks as whites in 1724. During the Revolutionary War, the British offered freedom to any slaves who fought alongside them against the colonists. Many enslaved persons seized this opportunity, and joined the ranks of the British. After their emancipation, most settled in Nova Scotia.

Meanwhile, slavery remained essential to the agricultural export economy of the southeastern states. This dependence led the framers of the Constitution to enact several proslavery ordinances, even in the face of northern qualms about the institution: Congress could not

ban the slave trade before 1808; slaves would be counted as three-fifths of a person for the purposes of taxation and political representation; and the federal government would assume responsibility for the rendition of fugitive slaves and the maintenance of internal security against slave and other insurrections.

Throughout the Revolutionary era, slaves and free blacks decried the moral contradiction of upholding slavery amid Patriots' cries for universal liberty. During the early years of the republic, free and enslaved blacks petitioned for general emancipation, sued for their own freedom, and demanded equal access to education, an end to the slave trade, and support for those seeking emigration to Africa. In 1783 an aged former slave in Boston named Belinda petitioned the Massachusetts legislature for an annual pension to be paid by her former master, a loyalist. The legislature ruled in Belinda's favor (the former master's executor, however, paid the pension only sporadically). Belinda was just one of dozens of ex-slaves in the early republic who sought compensation from former masters, sometimes successfully. Historians have seen these early suits as evidence that the notion of reparations for slavery long predated Reconstruction.

Slavery was largely domestic in the North, as opposed to the plantation system of the South. But like its southern counterpart, it was hereditary and permanent. Postrevolutionary idealism, which inspired a transatlantic evangelical movement for the abolition of the slave trade, contributed to the gradual demise of slavery in the northern states. Connecticut and Rhode Island passed laws in 1784 that freed the children of slaves born after that date. But northern antislavery sentiment—even when it took the form of law—did not temper the racism directed against free blacks. Out of necessity, and as a buffer against this stark prejudice and discrimination, free blacks in the North and many areas of the South developed vibrant communities of their own, replete with churches, schools, and mutual aid institutions. By 1830, America's free black population had grown to almost a quarter of a million. An outspoken leadership emerged from these communities that condemned slavery and the exclusion of blacks from northern white churches, schools, and civic organizations, laying the foundation for the abolitionist and civil rights movements of later years.

These "black founders" of the early republic aired their demands for equality through petitions, pamphlets, legal challenges, literary societies, and public orations, claiming American citizenship as the birthright of African Americans. The black founders and abolitionists of the antebellum era insisted that America was their homeland, built and enriched by their toil, tears, and blood. They equated literacy with the pursuit of freedom and cultivated a "dreaded eloquence" that enabled them to oppose slavery and contest antiblack stereotypes.

Black religious leaders became forceful exponents of abolition, reform, and racial uplift. These ministers, abolitionists, writers, and orators fused elements of Judeo-Christian liberation theology, drawn from the biblical story of Exodus, with natural rights ideas from the Declaration of Independence. In 1797 the Masonic leader Prince Hall cited the Haitian revolution and the abolition of slavery in the French colonies when he condemned the public harassment of blacks in Cambridge, Massachusetts. He disputed the pessimistic and disparaging views of racial difference and black citizenship offered by such authorities as Thomas Jefferson and Benjamin Franklin. Like Hall, the African Methodist minister Richard Allen, the writer Lemuel Haynes, the scientist Benjamin Banneker, and others considered slavery an affront to republican ideals of freedom and liberty and called for the redemption of the American nation. Some, including the shipping magnates Paul Cuffee and James Forten, supported emigration to Africa in protest against slavery and discrimination.

Though largely excluded from electoral politics—free blacks could vote in only five northern states before 1860—African Americans established abolitionist strongholds in several northern cities, including Boston, Newport, Philadelphia, and New York. Their efforts attained national prominence with the founding of *Freedom's Journal*, the first African American–owned newspaper, in New York in 1827. *Freedom's Journal* established the African American press as the voice of group aspirations—a role that it continued to play through the modern civil rights movement. The paper exposed the abuses of chattel slavery and discrimination against free blacks in the North. Like many antebellum black newspapers, it also exhorted free blacks to redouble their commitment to self-help, education, moral reform, and group advancement.

In 1829, David Walker, a Boston-based clothing merchant, journalist, and abolitionist born free in North Carolina, published his *Appeal to the Colored Citizens of the World*, an incendiary call for armed resistance by slaves. Walker denounced slavery as a threat to the republic, attacked religious proslavery arguments as avaricious propaganda, and derided the colonization movement, which encouraged emancipated blacks to emigrate to Africa, as a proslavery plot to rid America of abolitionist free blacks. Walker's seafaring customers covertly distributed his pamphlet up and down the Atlantic seaboard. But southern states put a price on his head and made possession of his book a capital offense. The author died under mysterious circumstances in his shop in 1830.

Walker's incitement heightened the southern authorities' fears of slave uprisings and insurrections. They responded to news of the conspiracies led by the slave Gabriel in Virginia in 1800 and the free black Denmark Vesey in Charleston, South Carolina, in 1822 by restricting the rights of free blacks to assemble, worship, and own guns. Southern states also outlawed public debate of antislavery ideas and prohibited the circulation of abolitionist literature. After scores of whites were slain in a revolt led by Nat Turner in Southampton, Virginia, in 1831, the white population organized itself into informal patrols, creating a formidable deterrent for large-scale revolts.

With the armed revolt option foreclosed, slave resistance took other forms, including spontaneous flights north into free territory, the more concerted efforts of the Underground Railroad to assist fugitive slaves, and the reinterpretation of Christianity as a liberation theology. While many slaveholders used religious indoctrination to enforce the tenets of slavery, the slaves themselves insisted that all persons were equal in the sight of God. African American Christians identified with the Israelites, to whom God sent Moses to deliver them from bondage. They came to see the God of the Old Testament and a fighting "King Jesus" as sympathetic to their aspirations for freedom. Such beliefs and practices sustained African Americans throughout slavery, the Civil War, and the segregation of the Jim Crow era. Religious leaders continued to provide political, as well as moral, leadership for many African Americans throughout the twentieth century and to this day. Their churches, independent institutions not entirely beholden to white power, became a cradle of political socialization and a source of mass support for the modern civil rights movement.

The era of Jacksonian democracy was, from the standpoint of free blacks, a democracy for whites only. Free blacks were routinely met with intolerance and even violence, as when white mobs attacked them and their abolitionist supporters in Philadelphia in 1838. Such antiabolitionist violence was commonplace in the North.

As the conflict between the North and South over the expansion of slavery intensified, free blacks came under renewed assault. The 1850 Fugitive Slave Act empowered federal marshals to summon ordinary citizens, regular troops, and militias to capture escaped slaves, and subjected those who aided fugitives to fines and imprisonment. Slave hunters cited the need to capture alleged fugitives as a pretense to invade abolitionist offices in Massachusetts and New York. The Supreme Court decision in *Dred Scott v. Sandiford* (1857) further jeopardized black freedom by affirming the legitimacy of slave property in all territories and declaring that African Americans could not be citizens of the United States. The Court's decision left many blacks feeling that they had no future in America, and African American leaders such as abolitionist Martin Delany began to argue for emigration to Africa.

Support for emigration among disaffected blacks differed from the colonization movement, which remained one of the most popular solutions for whites who believed racial equality was impossible, including *Uncle Tom's Cabin* author Harriet Beecher Stowe and President Abraham Lincoln. As president, Lincoln supported the removal of emancipated blacks to Haiti and Liberia. Blacks who espoused emigration did so from a pragmatic conception of self-determination, which was quite different from whites' dismal estimate of the capacity of black people to be free and equal citizens. Emigration's appeal waned for many blacks, however, once Lincoln responded to the pressures of the Civil War by issuing the Emancipation Proclamation and opening Union Army recruitment to African American soldiers. Delany himself soon became a commissioned officer.

Reconstruction and Electoral Politics

The Civil War and Reconstruction revolutionized both the status of African Americans and the nation's politics. The Thirteenth Amendment to the Constitution outlawed slavery, and the Fourteenth and Fifteenth Amendments affirmed African Americans as citizens of the United States, ending their exclusion from the body politic. Black men voted and ran for and won office in substantial numbers, serving in Congress as well as state legislatures and municipal governments throughout the South. Because the Democratic Party remained hostile to their interests, African American voters generally heeded the counsel attributed to Frederick Douglass: "The Republican Party is the deck, all else the sea." African American political representation in this period was indeed almost exclusively the result of pro–civil rights laws and Constitutional amendments passed by "radical" Republicans.

In the face of white attempts to reassert economic and political dominance, former slaves struggled to define freedom on their own terms. Yet, for all their efforts, the period of black office holding and political participation proved brief in most of the South. It ended by the 1890s with the rise of segregationist Jim Crow laws and customs, the amendment of state constitutions to deny the vote to African Americans, and the rampant use of violence to oust blacks from politics.

Still, black Americans maintained their commitment to the electoral system, despite being rejected by one or the other political party throughout most of the nation's history. Between 1865 and the 1930s, the Republicans were the only party somewhat responsive to black interests and rhetorically committed to equal rights. Choices did open up once other parties started to vie for black support in the 1930s, but the change proved fleeting. Since 1964, when the conservatism associated with Arizona senator and Republican presidential nominee Barry Goldwater first gained influence, large majorities of African Americans have voted Democratic, at least in national elections.

However fleeting, the Reconstruction period was a time in which African Americans forged an abiding sense of collective interests and linked fate. The aspirations for economic independence and redistributive justice sparked by Reconstruction still loom large in cultural memory a century and a half later. But the readiness of so many whites to engage in lynching and other forms of violence against blacks has also indelibly stamped the political imagination of African Americans. Although post–civil rights class differences may be eroding the idea of a cohesive black identity, many African Americans still view politics through the prism of their history of oppression and the continuing use of antiblack racial imagery in the nation's electoral politics—and vote accordingly.

Reconstruction also profoundly affected the southern political landscape. As former slaves and others of humble station replaced elite slaveholders in political office, the new leadership class redefined the scope and responsibilities of government for the South and the entire nation. After all, the federal government had intervened against southern claims of states' rights in order to affirm the national citizenship of African Americans. Federal power had also established the Freedman's Bureau to provide relief for ex-slaves and destitute whites, and to create schools for freed people. (African Americans also committed their own resources in order to build schools and hire teachers.) Reconstruction state governments supported free universal public education and generally broke with the laissez-faire politics propagated by the masters of the antebellum slave economy.

With the end of Reconstruction, political violence waged by forces sympathetic to the Democratic Party drove the majority of the region's black officials from electoral office. Meanwhile, the national Republican Party retreated from its support for equal rights to become an advocate for business interests. Many of the same U.S. Army troops that had recently defended Reconstruction governments were now redeployed to suppress a nationwide railroad workers' strike. Well into the twentieth century, historians of Reconstruction echoed the white supremacist portrayal of the immediate postwar period as an era of "Negro domination" and condoned the rampant use of violence by such vigilante groups as the Ku Klux Klan. When the Supreme Court upheld a Louisiana law segregating railroad travel in *Plessy v. Ferguson* (1896), its assertion of the "separate but equal" principle decisively restored the concept of states' rights federalism to its pre-Reconstruction dominance.

Voting with Their Feet

Denied the rights and protections of federal citizenship, African Americans were once again left to their own devices. Besieged by debt peonage, lynching, concubinage, and wholesale violations of human rights hardly distinguishable from slavery, they came to see internal migration as one of the only remaining paths to freedom. The

1878 "exodus" of some 5,000 African Americans from Louisiana and Mississippi to Kansas is one such case, and it exemplifies how black political behavior found expression outside of mainstream white channels.

The exodus began with desperate calls among rural black masses for migration to Liberia, a West African nation established by former slaves in 1847 with the aid of the U.S. government and the American Colonization Society. Although mass emigration to Liberia ultimately proved impractical, many African Americans considered it a viable option up through the 1890s as they struggled to cope with impoverishment and the brutality of southern racism. The former Georgia Reconstruction politician Henry McNeal Turner was moved by the pervasive violence against blacks to join those advocating this solution.

The calls for migration also exposed internal group conflicts in the black leadership of the time. On one side were leaders who doubted that the movement would lead to freedom; on the other were those who felt that "voting with one's feet" was the only way to better African Americans' situation. Having rejected Liberia as a haven, a number of enterprising grassroots black leaders from the promigration group, including Benjamin "Pap" Singleton, organized transportation to land they had purchased in Kansas. These migrants to Kansas became known as the "Exodusters."

Journalist Ida B. Wells became another prominent advocate of migration, although with her own characteristic take on the issue. Thrust into leadership by her eloquent account of the lynching of three black businessmen in Memphis, Tennessee, in 1892, Wells advocated the mass migration of African Americans as retaliation against the

The twentieth annual session of the National Association for the Advancement of Colored People (NAACP) took place June 6, 1929, in Cleveland, Ohio. (Library of Congress)

city's white elite for their condoning of extralegal violence. Wells also promoted armed self-defense, declaring that a Winchester rifle should have a sacred place in every black home. Reviving an antebellum tradition of transatlantic speaking tours by black abolitionists, Wells brought her antilynching campaign to audiences in England, marshaling international condemnation of mob rule. Like other outspoken southern black leaders, she was eventually forced into exile in the North, where she became a leading agitator for equal rights.

Wells eventually joined the National Afro-American Council, which, along with the Niagara Movement, was formed almost exclusively by northern African American male professionals who opposed the relatively conservative leadership of Booker T. Washington. She was also a founding member of the National Association for the Advancement of Colored People (NAACP), an interracial group that lobbied Congress, the president, and persons of influence to support the cause of civil rights and oppose lynching. As a highly visible and effective black woman activist, Wells combated not only the racist practices of whites but also, on occasion, the sexism of male "race" leaders.

Foreign Wars as Engines of Change

Military service has provided African Americans with many of their most important opportunities for material and political gain. The need to respond quickly and decisively to foreign wars has encouraged and sometimes forced the federal government to recognize African American demands for freedom and equal rights, in exchange for their support as citizens and soldiers.

Foreign wars have heightened the stakes for African Americans in their quest for freedom and equal citizenship. Blacks who served in wars of imperial expansion waged against racialized enemies, such as the Spanish-American War and the U.S. war in the Philippines, were reminded of their own inferior status as African American troops bearing arms alongside many white racists on behalf of a nation hostile to their own rights and well-being. The question of black participation in World War I was hotly contested within African American leadership, coming as the war did in the wake of the administration of Woodrow Wilson's segregation of the federal bureaucracy.

In retrospect, the "Great War" also catalyzed African Americans' admission into the industrial working class. The labor shortage created by the war's disruption of European immigration led northern defense industries to actively recruit African American workers from the South. The black-owned *Chicago Defender*, which was covertly distributed below the Mason-Dixon Line by African American Pullman porters, encouraged southern blacks to abandon dehumanizing conditions in the South for opportunity and a better life in the North.

The wartime migration of almost a million African Americans to northern cities transformed black politics. African American migrants entered electoral politics, voting first for Republican and then Democratic urban machines. Oscar De Priest of Chicago was elected to Congress in 1928, the first black representative since 1901. The postwar emergence of vibrant urban black communities fostered a newly militant and ideologically diverse black leadership, as well as a new group assertiveness that was celebrated in the person of the "New Negro." The New Negro made his (or her) presence felt by organizing self-defense and retaliation efforts in response to the urban race riots of the Red Summer of 1919; by joining the NAACP in record numbers in response to the organization's antilynching campaign; and by supporting Marcus Garvey, the Jamaican immigrant whose formidable but short-lived Universal Negro Improvement Association inspired West Indian immigrants and native-born southern blacks alike with its message of self-reliance and black pride.

The ideological diversification of black politics continued throughout this period, fueled by interactions with other radical movements, including the Communist and Socialist parties. In 1926 black socialist and labor leader A. Philip Randolph broke the Pullman Company's alliance with probusiness African American ministers by organizing the Pullman porters (an occupation restricted to black and Filipino men) and winning American Federation of Labor support for the Brotherhood of Sleeping Car Porters.

Until the 1940s, no U.S. president since Ulysses S. Grant had actively supported the cause of civil rights (with the partial exception of Benjamin Harrison, who did support legislation to reverse the Supreme Court's 1883 ruling outlawing the Civil Rights Act of 1866). This neglect of civil rights was even true of Franklin D. Roosevelt, the Democratic president who broke the Republican Party's traditional monopoly over the African American vote. Despite the entreaties of civil rights advocates—including his wife Eleanor—Roosevelt refused to jeopardize the support of southern Democrats by endorsing efforts to make lynching a federal crime. He was convinced that he needed the support of the white supremacist southern wing of the Democratic Party in order for his New Deal economic reform programs to succeed.

The New Deal did, however, lend indirect support to civil rights efforts. Federal relief programs challenged the states' rights ideology of the South, energizing civil rights challenges to the disenfranchisement of black voters. Blacks benefited from the New Deal's public works and relief programs, as well, even though these were administered in a discriminatory manner. Cognizant of his party's need for black votes, Roosevelt set aside his concerns about white southern voters long enough to appoint African Americans to the federal bureaucracy, and to name William Hastie the first black judge to serve on a federal court.

In 1941, with war looming, the threat of labor unrest eventually forced Roosevelt to make a more significant concession to civil rights demands. As America prepared to enter World War II, A. Philip Randolph threatened to bring 150,000 people to march on Washington against racial discrimination in the defense industries. Hastening to avoid this spectacle, Roosevelt issued Executive Order 8802, banning employment discrimination in defense jobs. Such reforms boosted Roosevelt's popularity with African American voters and led to increased Democratic support from northern blacks.

Because FDR's support for civil rights was tempered by his continued reliance on segregationist Democrats, freedom advocates turned to the courts. The NAACP Legal Defense Fund was founded in 1939; under the guidance of Thurgood Marshall, it developed a winning strategy of well-researched challenges against educational discrimination, with the goal of invalidating the *Plessy v. Ferguson* doctrine of "separate but equal." Marshall's strategy culminated in the 1954 *Brown v. Board of Education of Topeka* decision, which found segregation in all forms to be inherently unequal and thus a violation of the Fourteenth Amendment's equal protection clause.

Brown was a triumph for Marshall and all those associated with it. Indeed, women's rights and other interest groups would adopt a similar strategy with great success in subsequent decades. But the Court's decision in *Brown* included no provisions for enforcing desegregation, essentially leaving it up to the states to desegregate themselves. It became apparent to blacks that mass activism would be necessary to effect real change.

Civil rights leaders embraced the cold war struggle against communism as an opportunity in this regard, arguing that desegregation was vital for national security.

The tactic proved effective in influential circles. After Roosevelt's death, his successor, Harry S. Truman, supported civil rights out of a concern for national security and America's continued influence in global affairs. With an eye toward gaining crucial African American support for his 1948 reelection campaign, Truman also became the first president in the twentieth century to publicly endorse civil rights and to submit reform legislation to Congress, although none of his proposed laws passed. That same year, Truman issued Executive Order 9981, banning discrimination in the armed forces.

Truman's successor, Dwight D. Eisenhower, had opposed the *Brown* decision but nonetheless felt bound to respond to international pressures by ordering the National Guard to enforce the desegregation of Central High School in Little Rock, Arkansas, in 1957. For presidents Truman, Eisenhower and, later, John F. Kennedy—who, like Roosevelt, was reluctant to antagonize segregationists by supporting civil rights—the imperatives of the cold war were paramount. Indeed, Kennedy had once regarded civil rights demonstrations as injurious to America's image overseas. But after the brutal repression of nonviolent demonstrators led by Dr. Martin Luther King Jr. in Birmingham, Alabama, in 1963, Kennedy proposed a civil rights bill and began describing racial equality as a moral issue. After Kennedy's assassination, President Lyndon Johnson fulfilled Kennedy's vision by securing the passage of the 1964 Civil Rights Act and the 1965 Voting Rights Act. But as presidents from Roosevelt to Kennedy had foreseen, Johnson's decision came at a political cost. Upon signing the Civil Rights Act, Johnson is reported to have said, "We [the Democratic Party] have just lost the South for a generation."

The Post–Civil Rights Era

The ideological diversity of African American politics was a significant factor during the turbulent years of the civil rights movement. While Martin Luther King Jr. led nonviolent direct-action campaigns in the South from the mid-1950s until 1965, northern African American spokespersons, including Nation of Islam minister Malcolm X and African American writer James Baldwin, aggressively challenged the nation's conscience over institutionalized racism. Malcolm X and Baldwin expressed a growing impatience with the Kennedy administration's cautious approach to civil rights, and gave voice to African Americans' fury and helplessness as bombings, shootings, and assaults claimed the lives of black activists. For many, the goodwill of the massive August

1963 March on Washington was shattered just a month later, when the bombing of the Sixteenth Street Baptist Church in Birmingham claimed the lives of four young girls. Meanwhile, seeing that civil rights reforms had failed to address the socioeconomic roots of discontent among urban blacks, Dr. King shifted his movement northward to a campaign for economic and racial justice in 1966; the following year he added his voice to the growing opposition to the Vietnam War. These stands made him a pariah in the eyes of a once admiring U.S. mass media. But for a younger generation of black activists, nonviolence had ceased to be a viable strategy well before King's murder in April of 1968.

During the late 1960s and 1970s, African Americans celebrated the election of black mayors in major American cities. But the timing of these gains—and indeed, of desegregation overall—coincided with the collapse of the industrial economy that had underwritten much black social mobility. Black urban populations struggled against the loss of capital and jobs, "white flight" to the suburbs, and a shrinking tax base. The declining fortunes of central cities, combined with the enormous cost of the Vietnam War, undermined efforts to expand on the reforms of President Johnson's War on Poverty.

Ironically, given his pursuit of southern white racist voters in the election of 1968, President Richard Nixon's Republican administration arguably achieved a stronger record on civil rights than the two Democratic administrations that followed his. Nixon presided over the desegregation of southern public schools, the 1970 renewal of the Voting Rights Act, and the implementation of Executive Order 11246, which established affirmative action. Nixon also appointed blacks to a number of high-level government posts. Even more intriguing was his proposal for the Family Assistance Plan, which, if approved, would have guaranteed an income to all families with children and would have substantially raised the income of poor households of all races.

Democratic president Jimmy Carter supported affirmative action but opposed an antipoverty program proposed by his African American housing secretary Patricia Roberts Harris. Arkansas governor Bill Clinton, a complex figure widely perceived to be free of racial prejudice, nevertheless distanced himself from African Americans during his presidential campaign in pursuit of right-leaning Democratic voters. After winning the White House, Clinton defended affirmative action against right-wing opposition but also capitulated to conservatives by withdrawing his nomination of Lani Guinier, a strong advocate of civil rights, as Assistant Attorney General for Civil Rights.

Clinton also proposed a comprehensive plan that would have guaranteed health care to all Americans—a plan that, if passed by Congress, would have benefited African Americans. But the bill failed. And in July 1996, during his reelection campaign, Clinton signed a welfare bill that included a GOP-authored provision abolishing the New Deal guarantee of welfare as a universal, federally mandated right.

Clinton had appointed more black officials than any previous president, but also left intact executive orders by Republican presidents Ronald Reagan and George H. W. Bush that undercut federal antidiscrimination provisions. Many of his own regulatory reforms ignored civil rights as well.

The nation's judiciary described a similar arc of hope and disappointment. From roughly 1940 until the 1970s, the Supreme Court under Chief Justice Earl Warren staunchly defended civil rights reforms and civil liberties. But in its more recent iterations the Court has tended to reject calls to remedy discrimination. Indeed, the Court's 2007 ruling under Chief Justice John G. Roberts against race-conscious admissions policies in public schools in Seattle, Washington, and Louisville, Kentucky, construed remediation itself as discriminatory. Since the late 1980s, the Court has eroded affirmative action in contracting for minority-owned businesses, school desegregation, voting rights and redistricting, often with the support of conservative black justice Clarence Thomas.

One notable exception to this trend was the Court's decision in *Grutter v. Bollinger* (2003), which reaffirmed the 1978 *Regents of the University of California v. Bakke* decision upholding the use of race-conscious admissions policies in higher education. The hope inspired by the *Grutter* decision was short-lived, however: opponents of affirmative action, led by African American businessman Ward Connerly, launched a campaign to overturn the policy through a series of state ballot initiatives. To date, such initiatives have succeeded in outlawing affirmative action in public institutions in California, Washington, Florida, and Michigan. This post–civil rights trend, in which African Americans lend legitimacy to an anti–civil rights agenda, recalls Thurgood Marshall's statement upon his resignation from the Court in 1991 when asked if he believed an African American should be appointed to replace him. No, Marshall replied with his characteristically earthy wit: "There's no difference between a black snake and a white snake—they'll both bite."

Back in 1962, Attorney General Robert Kennedy had speculated that the United States would elect a black president in 40 years, infuriating James Baldwin, who felt that Kennedy was not doing enough to secure equal rights for his own time. The next four decades did see a significant number of successful black candidacies at the state and national levels. Traditionally, black elected officials have been "race men" whose electoral constituencies are predominantly African American and who have an image as staunch, if not defiant, champions of black interests. Representative Adam Clayton Powell, elected to Congress in 1944 from his position as pastor of Harlem's largest church, was a well-known example, as were black mayors Coleman Young (Detroit, 1974–93) and Harold Washington (Chicago, 1983–87), although both Young and Washington also depended on the votes of white liberals.

In recent years, scholars have debated whether black politicians for statewide and national office can forge winning coalitions by moving beyond their (presumed) African American base to attract white voters. Only a few have done so in significant numbers. On the state level, Douglas Wilder, a grandson of slaves, was elected governor of Virginia in 1990 and served until 1994. In national politics, Edward Brooke, a Republican from Massachusetts, served in the Senate from 1966 to 1979. Brooke, who did not fit the "race man" mold, was the first black elected to that house since Reconstruction—and the last until Carol Moseley Braun, a Democrat from Illinois, followed him in 1992. And the civil rights leader Jesse Jackson, in some respects a "race man" par excellence, attracted enough white support with his message of economic populism to win several primaries and caucuses during his 1984 and 1988 presidential campaigns.

Racial antagonisms are still used to attempt to derail black candidates. As recently as 2006, a political advertisement evoking the South's miscegenation taboo may have helped defeat the Senate run in Tennessee of U.S. representative Harold Ford Jr. At the same time, the Republican Party's reputation for racial scapegoating has drastically limited the prospects for a dwindling number of black GOP candidates overall. Republican racial policies also helped the Democratic Party gain some 90 percent of the African American vote in national elections during the 1980s and 1990s.

Barack Obama, an Illinois Democrat elected to the Senate in 2004, represented a younger generation of black politicians—including Newark Mayor Cory

Booker; Deval Patrick, the first African American governor of Massachusetts; Harold Ford Jr.; and Governor David Paterson of New York—whose perceived cross-racial appeal seemed to offer an alternative to the "race man." In 2008 Obama became the first person of African heritage to win a major party's presidential nomination, besting Hillary Clinton in a hard-fought primary campaign. In defeating the Republican Party nominee, Arizona senator John McCain, Obama defied the doubts of many in the United States and abroad, to become the first African American elected to the presidency.

Obama did so by consistently downplaying the issue of race. In their apparent disavowal of the "race man" model, Obama and his peers may be younger and more liberal analogues to Colin Powell, the African American former chairman of the Joint Chiefs of Staff and secretary of state in the administration of George W. Bush. Like Powell, who rose through the military (and who broke from the Republican fold to endorse Obama), Obama and his counterparts (all Democrats) claimed to represent an alternative to black leaders shaped by the civil rights movement, even as they have undoubtedly benefited from that movement and absorbed its influences and legacy (Obama had been a community organizer and his campaign prevailed in large part on the strength of a massive 50-state voter registration effort).

But the real story is more complex. Obama's 2008 campaign brought attention to the so-called Bradley effect, named for African American Los Angeles mayor Tom Bradley, who was defeated in the 1982 California gubernatorial election despite a strong lead in preelection polls. In the Bradley effect, significant numbers of whites claim in polls to support a black candidate, only to later cast their votes for the white opponent. While scholars will continue to debate the validity of the Bradley effect, Obama's campaign highlighted African American candidates' continuing need to overcome the fears of a substantial segment of the white electorate.

See also abolitionism; civil rights; race and politics; Reconstruction era, 1865–77; segregation and Jim Crow; slavery; voting.

FURTHER READING

Berry, Mary Frances. *Black Resistance, White Law: A History of Constitutional Racism in America*. New York: Penguin, 1994.

Dawson, Michael. *Black Visions: The Roots of Contemporary African American Political Ideologies*. Chicago: University of Chicago Press, 2001.

Foner, Eric. *Freedom's Lawmakers: A Directory of Black Officeholders during Reconstruction.* Baton Rouge: Louisiana State University Press, 1996.

Newman, Richard S., and Roy E. Finkenbine. "Black Founders in the New Republic: Introduction." *William and Mary Quarterly* 64, no. 1 (January 2007), 83–94.

Painter, Nell. *Exodusters: Black Migration to Kansas after Reconstruction.* New York: Knopf, 1977.

Walton, Hanes, Jr., and Robert C. Smith. *American Politics and the African American Quest for Universal Freedom.* New York: Pearson Longman, 2008.

KEVIN GAINES

agrarian politics

Agrarian politics describes the strategies, tactics, and values of the farmer-based political movements that played a prominent reform role in American political history. Its purest manifestation came in the Populist movement of the 1880s and 1890s, but its language, goals, and methods persisted, in a more subdued way, in the New Deal Era and beyond.

Agrarian politics played an important role in the evolution of American democracy and the construction of public institutions to regulate business without diminishing its productive energies. Indeed, the regulatory goal of agrarian politics after the Civil War provided the confidence that consumers, service users, and investors needed to buy, sell, and ship in a market economy. Agrarian politics—egalitarian, rights-based, inclusive, electoral, and targeted at the legislature where the most numerous classes presumably have their best shot—produced important structural reforms of national institutions, at least those not won by war: the Bill of Rights, direct election of senators, antimonopoly laws, an income tax, regulation of big business (starting with railroads), a monetary system controlled by public officials and not based on gold, the right of workers to organize and bargain collectively (and of agricultural cooperatives to similarly operate without being charged as "conspiracies in restraint of trade" under the Sherman Act), and the lowering of tariffs (the most prevalent and burdensome taxes) on goods consumed and used by ordinary people, to name just a few.

The term *agrarian* is virtually synonymous with *republican*, denoting a mode of politics and political thought nurtured by British and French Enlightenment philosophy that flowered in eighteenth-century North America. It was no doubt encouraged by the immigration of dissenters and the mode of settlement in what became (in 1789) the United States—a nation of independent landowners who belonged to diverse religious communities, themselves permeated by democratic demand, in contrast to the hierarchical denominations prevalent in the Old World.

Agrarianism's central tenets were galvanized by the struggle for independence from Great Britain. Its foremost philosopher was Thomas Jefferson, the apostle of sturdy yeoman farmer democracy (or, more accurately, *self-government*), whose creed came together in the cauldron of revolution and who provided the revolutionary language of that struggle. Agrarianism's principal antagonist was Alexander Hamilton, the foremost intellectual advocate of economic industrialism, commercialism, and political elitism.

In Jefferson's philosophy, the hand of government should be as light as possible, keeping opportunities open without favoritism, exploitation, or needless constraints on human affairs; and that hand's guidance should be in the legislature, the popular branch of the people's elected representatives. If its public officials became unresponsive to the sufferings of their constituents, the spectacle of a passionate people rising up in arms against its government (as in Shays's Rebellion in 1787) was not for Jefferson the nightmare it was for Hamilton.

Popular mobilization *against* bad, and *for* better, government, with wide participation by citizens and guaranteed commitment not to infringe on the personal rights on which good government depended—these were the tenets of Jeffersonian republicanism that shaped the rhetoric and action of agrarian politics. Individual rights, but a strong role for collective action; decentralized power, but enough governmental authority to protect the people from private exploitation—these became the central tensions of agrarian republicanism. This may sound like the rosiest statement of an American creed. But while an American creed without Alexander Hamilton, business politics, and a powerful presidency is possible to imagine, an American political history without Jeffersonian republicanism is not.

Yet agrarian reformers had to struggle for decades to achieve their political goals; their successes were episodic, concentrated in reform periods like the Populist and Progressive eras, and the New Deal. Their opponents had far greater material resources and the deference of many elected officials (as well as the federal courts, historically skeptical of regulation and redistribution).

The first national manifestation of agrarian politics came in the battle over the Constitution itself. Given the elite composition and Hamiltonian persuasion of many delegates at Philadelphia, the small farmers of the interior and less-developed regions who had constituted the left flank of the Revolution would not accept this ominous concentration of power in a national government without the guarantees of the Bill of Rights, and only its promise got the new Constitution ratified.

In the next decades came the spread of yeoman settlement at the expense of the native population, to whom few of the agrarian democrats would grant equal citizenship rights. For white Americans, the Jacksonian era brought a broadening of suffrage to all adult white males, the moving of presidential nominations to a large meeting of partisan delegates from local jurisdictions (the party-nominating convention), the war with a national bank seen as serving only elite interests, and the democratizing of government service in the partisan spoils system later reviled by the well educated (who saw their own placement in those jobs as a matter of natural right and governmental efficiency). Though the new national government had been conceived without partisanship (and in fear of it), it was the fundamental agrarian republican vehicle of popular government.

Bureaucracy would inevitably expand, but the notion of autonomous and expert bureaucratic governance never achieved legitimacy in an agrarian republic where universal suffrage preceded any significant growth of executive power. Nor has it today, despite the dramatic expansion of the executive branch in the New Deal, cold war, and Great Society eras. Agrarian politics cherishes collective action at the grass roots, and hails laws that tax the rich and restrain the powerful, but prefers to accomplish those goals with minimal bureaucratic discretion. Agrarian movements press for clear and specific laws, powerful in their precision and automatic sanctions, leaving little to presidential or bureaucratic imagination. "Thou shalt not, on penalty of a hefty fine and jail term, do the following" is the favored preamble of an agrarian statute.

The practice of slavery was the shame of one region in the agrarian heartland, and of elites elsewhere who tolerated it—including Jefferson himself. Racism was a system of elite social control in the South, and was not implicit in agrarian republicanism. To the contrary,

the disfranchising and segregation laws developed in the South at the end of the nineteenth century were a response to the threat that agrarian populism would succeed and confront the Democratic Party elite with a biracial, class-based reform coalition.

Beginning in the late 1860s, a sequence of agrarian movements—the Grange, antimonopoly and greenback movements; the Farmers' Alliance; the Agricultural Wheel, an important farm organization that began in Arkansas and ultimately merged with the Farmers' Alliance; the Populist Party; and the Farmers' Union—had put democratic demands on the agenda of national politics. In demanding expansion of government powers, they abandoned the Jeffersonian-Jacksonian antipathy to big government and affirmed the faith that an aroused populace with universal (male) suffrage could seize and purify the state, turning it away from elite privilege and toward the common good. Agrarian radicals won few legislative victories in the Gilded Age— the Sherman Act, the Interstate Commerce Act, and the first postwar attempt at an income tax were greatly weakened or, in the latter case, struck down by the Supreme Court—though the agrarians did accomplish a considerable radicalization of the Democratic Party in 1896.

The defeat of the Populist Party in the South, and the contraction of the electorate that followed it, sapped the promise of agrarian reform, however. Thereafter, agrarians relied on an alliance of white farmers and workers within a Democratic Party tainted with racism and less committed to reform than their forebears in the Populist and Greenback-Labor parties had been.

While the agrarians could not elect their most popular leader, William Jennings Bryan, to the presidency, the Democratic Party he presided over lost most of its elite wing and strengthened its farmer and labor base after 1896. Dissident agrarian Republicans in the Midwest and the mountain states joined the mostly southern Democratic agrarians to accomplish the key economic and political reforms of the Progressive Era, and to oppose President Woodrow Wilson's war preparedness program in 1915–16.

Critically expanded with the influx of millions of urban lower-middle-class voters, the agrarian-labor coalition put through many reforms of the New Deal: the Agricultural Adjustment Act, the Tennessee Valley Act, the Silver Purchase Act, the Glass Steagall (banking regulation) Act, the Securities Act, the National Labor Relations Act, the Public Utility Holding Company Act, the

Farm Security Act, and the Huey Long–inspired Income Tax Act of 1935.

After World War II, agrarianism waned with the industrialization of the South and the West, and the rise of the civil rights struggle. In the southern heartland of agrarian politics, race had always been an enormous hurdle to class politics. It was, nevertheless, still possible to identify the occasional agrarian political style among southern Democrats. Texas representative Wright Patman fought the banks and the Federal Reserve over credit, interest rates, and the supply of money until he lost his House Banking Committee chair to a more urbane and conservative Democrat in the 1970s. In the early 1980s and as late as the early 1990s, congressional representatives of farm states and districts battled those same antagonists in one of the most serious threats to Federal Reserve Board autonomy that the agency had ever experienced. Former Texas commissioner of agriculture Jim Hightower was a radical agrarian critic of the administrations of Ronald Reagan, George H. W. Bush, and George W. Bush.

Yet agrarian politics was born in a yeoman agricultural society and the thick web of community self-help activities and movement-readiness of that past America. Whether it could continue in a thoroughly urban era was always open to question. The city, for Jefferson and his followers, was a place where citizens lost their independence, dignity, and virtue, in a polity dominated by the wealthy and a politics naturally inclined toward Hamiltonianism. Early agrarians saw the city as a place of weaker cultural strictures that people confused with freedom.

The greenback-populist transformation of the Jeffersonian creed in the late 1870s and 1880s acknowledged that most Americans had lost their independence to the powerful forces of the emerging industrial and commercial marketplace. It would take a much more powerful government to level the playing field, and so the Jeffersonian animus against government was abandoned as a matter of practical necessity. Vulnerable workers (who had lost their artisanal autonomy decades before the farmers had to confront the railroad and the commodity market) could sometimes be recruited to farmer-labor politics, as demonstrated fitfully in the greenback and populist movements and the Progressive Era, and more successfully in the New Deal.

The Republican Party's "Reagan Revolution" of 1980 revived the Gilded Age assault on government, using populist language without the populist class base or policy impetus. But the Democratic Party also did its part to bury agrarianism by adopting a new form of cultural liberalism. Agrarians were radical on economics and conservative on morals, which President Franklin Roosevelt had recognized when he led the repeal of Prohibition and pushed that hotly contested social issue back to the states and localities. Supreme Court decisions in the 1960s and 1970s that outlawed prayer in public schools and public functions and nationalized abortion rights took away that structural dodge, and thus contributed to the defeat of the agrarian impulse in American politics. The agrarians who remained would have to choose between their moral and religious passions and their agrarian economics. Each of the two major political parties offered half, but only half, and the agrarian soul was clearly torn.

Of course, fewer and fewer rural and small town people existed in the early twenty-first century. Despite some protection in the Senate, the steady dwindling of farm and ranch populations and the towns and businesses they once supported had weakened rural political clout. The results of earlier political successes and the rise of agribusiness also made farmers much more conservative than they once were.

Nevertheless, cultural norms were imbedded and perpetuated in memory and in institutions, and the legacy of agrarian politics may be, to some extent, self-perpetuating. However, one imagines that it would take a serious economic downturn, and perhaps a revolt against a Hamiltonian presidency, to induce a genuine revival of agrarian republican politics.

See also populism.

FURTHER READING

Appleby, Joyce, and Terrence Ball, eds. *Thomas Jefferson: Political Writings*. New York: Cambridge University Press, 1999.

Goodwyn, Lawrence. *Democratic Promise: The Populist Movement in America*. New York: Oxford University Press, 1976.

Graham, Otis L., Jr. *An Encore for Reform: The Old Progressives and the New Deal*. New York: Oxford University Press, 1967.

Hild, Matthew. *Greenbackers, Knights of Labor, and Populists*. Athens: University of Georgia Press, 2007.

Kazin, Michael. *A Godly Hero: The Life of William Jennings Bryan*. New York: Knopf, 2006.

McMath, Robert. *Populist Vanguard*. Chapel Hill: University of North Carolina Press, 1975.

Palmer, Bruce. *Man over Money: The Southern Populist Critique of American Capitalism*. Chapel Hill: University of North Carolina Press, 1980.

Sanders, Elizabeth. *Roots of Reform: Farmers, Workers, and the American State, 1877–1917*. Chicago: University of Chicago Press, 1999.

Williams, T. Harry. *Huey Long*. New York: Vintage, 1981.

ELIZABETH SANDERS

Alaska and Hawai'i

Alaska and Hawai'i, the forty-ninth and fiftieth states, may be considered a political region when viewed from the mainland United States. The two share a number of historical and political characteristics that are decidedly different from those of the contiguous 48 states. They were both part of an American expansion into the Pacific in the nineteenth century, and each experienced a prolonged territorial period in the twentieth century. Alaska and Hawai'i saw direct military action in World War II and joined forces in a 15-year period after the war to achieve statehood. In the early twenty-first century, both still discuss the relative success that they hoped statehood would bring but which still seems unfulfilled. Each state contains a mix of indigenous and settler populations with a greater political prominence of native minorities than on the mainland. These similar experiences differentiate Alaska and Hawai'i from the mainland more than unite them in a common region. Each sees itself as a political area separate from the contiguous states.

In the first half of the nineteenth century, Alaska—then known as Russian America—was a European colony, governed by the commercial Russian-American Company. Hawai'i was an independent kingdom. American entry into the China trade in the 1790s brought American ships into ports in both Russian America and Hawai'i. American commercial contact increased with the expansion of the Pacific whaling industry. American missionaries, many of whom became permanent settlers, arrived in Hawai'i in the 1820s. With the admission of California as a state in 1850, U.S. commercial presence in the Pacific swelled. Overtures for the annexation or purchase of Russian America and Hawai'i were widespread.

The outbreak of the Civil War turned mainland attention away from the Pacific. The end of the war reignited dreams of Pacific expansion. Secretary of State William Seward negotiated the purchase of Alaska for $7.2 million in less than a month in early 1867 from a Russian government ready to divest its North American holdings. A predicted a rush of settlement to the north did not occur. Uncertain of what Alaska's political form should be, the United States left the northern region in a nebulous condition as a customs and military district, not as an American territory with any form of elected government. Alaska's population remained low until gold discoveries in the late 1880s revived interest in the north.

Though overtures of annexation were made to Hawai'i after the war, the monarchy sought to distance itself from the United States and kindle relations with Britain.

The United States issued this check for the purchase of Alaska from Russia, in the amount of $7.2 million, dated August 1, 1868. (National Archives)

The island kingdom, however, drew closer to the United States in trade relations when a reciprocity treaty, first signed in 1875 and renewed in 1887, allowed raw sugar grown in the islands to enter the United States duty free. The ensuing boom in sugar production created the need for an ever increasing labor supply. The plantations recruited substantial numbers of Chinese, Japanese, Portuguese, and later Filipino workers. By the mid-1890s, the newly arrived workers outnumbered native Hawaiians and the smaller Caucasian commercial community of Americans and Europeans (locally called *haoles*) in an overall population of 100,000.

In the late 1880s and early 1890s, tensions increased between the *haoles,* many of whom were now third-generation settlers, and the monarchy. In 1893 the *haoles*, with the aid of a U.S. Marine contingent in Honolulu, staged a revolution against Queen Lili'uokalani. The revolutionaries asked for U.S. annexation but were initially turned down because James Henderson Blount, an investigator sent by President Grover Cleveland, concluded that Hawaiian natives did not support the revolution. The revolutionaries then created the independent Republic of Hawai'i. Finally, in 1898, under the euphoria of U.S. victory in the Spanish-American War, Congress agreed to annex Hawai'i. The subject of the Hawaiian Revolution and the annexation remains controversial more than a century later. Was the annexation spearheaded by local settlers who manipulated Congress to annex Hawai'i, or was the annexation an act of mainland imperialists who found a group of willing settlers to help execute their plan? Nearly all modern interpretations agree that native Hawaiians did not support the overthrow of their kingdom. Hawai'i became an American territory in 1900. It differed from previous territories in the western United States in that the native population had full voting rights and representation in the territorial legislature.

The Twentieth-Century Territorial Period

During the first four decades of the twentieth century, Alaska and Hawai'i followed quite different paths of political and economic development. Hawai'i functioned much like earlier American territories. It had an elected legislature and an appointed governor, who was selected from island residents. As an American territory, it came under federal anti-Asian immigration legislation. Chinese immigration ended immediately, while Japanese immigration was halted for men in 1907–8 and women in 1924. Asian immigrants were forbidden naturalization by federal precedent. Their children born in Hawai'i were American citizens under the Fourteenth Amendment. Thus, in the early decades of territorial life, resident Asians were not a part of Hawai'i's political process. In the late 1920s and early 1930s, local-born Asians came of voting age and entered the territorial legislature. By 1940 the Hawai'i territorial legislature was one of the most racially diverse in the nation, containing Hawaiian, Causcasian, Chinese American, Japanese American, and African American members.

In the pre–World War II period, sugar continued to be the economic mainstay of the islands. The companies dominating the industry, known locally as the Big Five, were owned predominantly by island residents. Local companies successfully bought out both Californian and German interests between 1900 and 1920. Hawai'i's economy was characterized by hierarchically managed plantations, but Hawai'i differed from other Pacific plantation cultures in that the territory maintained a tax-supported public school system for children of all races.

Hawai'i's economy and population were also influenced by the growth of military installations built between 1900 and 1940. The federal government saw Hawai'i as the centerpiece for its Pacific military presence. By 1940, the naval installation at Pearl Harbor as well as army installations at Schofield Barracks and Hickam Field gave the islands a military population of approximately 25,000 to 30,000, out of a total population of 423,000.

While territorial Hawai'i grew economically and in population, Alaska followed a different path of development. Gold strikes at Juneau in southeastern Alaska in the 1880s brought a modest increase in population. The Klondike gold strike of 1896–98, though technically in Canada, brought a rush of mainland settlers into Alaska, where gold was then discovered at Nome in 1899 and Fairbanks in 1902. Alaska's population, which stood at 32,000 (mostly indigenous natives) in 1890, doubled to 63,000 in 1900. Such a population increase, which remained stable over the next decade, led to the creation of a full territorial government with a small elected legislature in 1912. Hopes for economic expansion increased with the growth of the canned salmon industry and further discoveries of gold and copper. During World War I, Alaska canned salmon became a staple for American soldiers in Europe, and Alaska copper became a main source of supply for war munitions.

The economy of Alaska was absentee controlled. The canned salmon industry was owned by firms in San Francisco and Seattle, and the metals industry was controlled

Workers stack sugar cane on the island of Oahu, Hawai'i. (Department of Special Collections, University of Chicago Library)

by outsiders, including the New York–based Guggenheim/Morgan conglomerate known as the Alaska Syndicate. Local residents increasingly resented the grip of the "outside interests," whom they accused of controlling the small, 24-member territorial legislature.

Unlike Hawai'i, where the federal government built a substantial military infrastructure, Alaska was left relatively unfortified until 1940, when Congress made appropriations to increase airfields and troop levels as a guard against both a Japanese naval or air attack and an "over the pole" aerial attack from German-occupied Norway. In 1940 Alaska, with a population of 72,000, was still an underdeveloped territory. It had seemingly little in common with its more prosperous Pacific neighbor 2,500 miles directly south.

World War II and the Statehood Movement

But American entry into World War II in late 1941 brought the two territories closer together. The bombing of Pearl Harbor in December 1941, followed by the bombing of Dutch Harbor in the Aleutians in June 1942 and the ensuing battles of Attu and Kiska in 1943, united Alaska and Hawai'i in the American consciousness as centers of the Pacific campaign. Hundreds of thousands of military personnel and civilian workers from the mainland flooded both territories. Hawai'i's population doubled to 860,000 by 1944; Alaska's more than tripled to 230,000 at the same time. Though the military infrastructure of Hawai'i was solidly in place by 1941,

the military buildup of Alaska, which had begun only in 1940, increased dramatically and helped the cities of Fairbanks and Anchorage to emerge from their earlier status as small towns, if not villages. The most dramatic infrastructure improvement was the building of the 1,500-mile Alaska Highway in only nine months from March to November 1942.

Each territory had a different political experience during the war. Hawai'i was placed under martial law a few hours after the Pearl Harbor attack and remained so until 1944. Though about 1,000 Japanese and Japanese Americans in Hawai'i were arrested and interned for supposedly subversive activities, the massive relocation and internment of that population, which occurred so dramatically in the western United States, did not occur in Hawai'i, largely through the cooperation of the business community and Army commander Delos C. Emmons. The tricky question of the service of Japanese Americans in the military was resolved through initiatives in Hawai'i and Washington to create the 100th Infantry Battalion and the 442nd Regimental Combat Team. Both groups were highly decorated by the end of the war.

Alaska escaped the imposition of martial law, though Japanese Americans in the territory were interned, and Aleuts were relocated to southeastern Alaska. The political development of the northern territory was heavily shaped during the war by the extended governorship of Ernest Gruening, an easterner and New Deal civil servant, who served from 1939 to 1953. Gruening created territorial reserve guard units to include Alaska natives (Indians and Eskimos) in the war effort and then encouraged natives to run for political office. One native, William Paul, had served in the territorial legislature from 1925 to 1929, and in 1944 the election of two natives, Frank Peratrovich and Andrew Hope, started a tradition of native representation unbroken to the present day. In 1945 Gruening championed the passage of the Alaska Equal Rights Act, which ended racial discrimination against natives in public accommodations.

The end of World War II in 1945 spelled changes and common causes for Alaska and Hawai'i. Though there was an initial demobilization of military forces in 1946, national decisions for a permanent cold war military presence in both territories were made by 1947. In both territories, 1946 also marked the emergence of statehood movements. World War II convinced residents of both territories to shed their second-class status and gave them hope that Congress would grant statehood.

A plebiscite in Hawai'i in 1940 endorsed statehood, but Congress delayed hearings until 1946. Initial signs pointed to quick congressional action, but delay ensued when Senator Hugh Butler of Nebraska feared that the islands' largest labor union, the International Longshoremen's and Warehouse Union, was under Communist influence. Meanwhile, Alaska held a plebiscite in 1946 that endorsed statehood. Congressional statehood hearings soon began in the northern territory. While concerns over Communist influence delayed action on Hawai'i, fears that Alaska did not have a sustainable economy, except for its military defense role, stymied the northern region. During the early 1950s, Congress was narrowly split between Republicans and Democrats. Each party feared that the admission of one state might tip the balance, as Hawai'i was considered Republican and Alaska Democratic.

To attract national attention in the 1950s, each territory sought to convince Congress of its fitness for statehood. Both states wrote and ratified new constitutions. Alaska had been politically underdeveloped, so it eliminated counties in the proposed new state and established one unified state court system. Both states increased the size of their legislatures, and Hawai'i lowered the voting age from 21 to 20 and Alaska to 19. While waiting for statehood, Japanese Americans increased their representation in the Hawai'i territorial legislature. In 1952 Congress passed the McCarran-Walter Act, which ended the prohibition of naturalization for Japanese and Korean

immigrants. (The prohibition of Chinese naturalization had been ended during World War II.) Thus, all of Hawai'i's residents now could become citizens and vote.

In the late 1950s, the congressional delegates from Alaska and Hawai'i (Bob Bartlett and John Burns) co-coordinated their statehood initiatives to ensure congressional passage for both. In 1958 Congress finally voted to admit Alaska as the forty-ninth state. Alaska's statehood bill was significant because it made a grant of 103 million acres (out of 365 million acres in the territory) directly to the state to help spur economic development. In 1959 Congress voted to admit Hawai'i as the fiftieth state. Residents then ratified statehood in local plebiscites with substantial majorities, 8 to 1 in Alaska and 17 to 1 in Hawai'i. Both states officially joined the union in 1959.

In the 50 years since statehood, Alaska and Hawai'i have retained certain common characteristics but have rarely worked together on any particular issue such as they did for statehood. Both continue to be major bastions of America's Pacific military presence. Internally, each state has pursued different objectives. Alaska's quest for economic sustainability was advanced by oil discoveries in the late 1960s on portions of the lands (Prudhoe Bay) granted to the state in 1959. Other land issues have also been in the forefront. Native land claims, acknowledged but held in limbo by the federal government since 1867, were finally settled in 1971 with the passage of the Alaska Native Claims Settlement Act (ANCSA), which apportioned some 44 million acres of land and $962 million in cash to 13 native corporations. A final settlement of most of the remaining federal lands was made in 1980 with the passage of the Alaska National Interest Lands Conservation Act (ANILCA), which placed 131 million acres of wilderness lands in the National Park Service and National Wildlife Refuge System.

In Hawai'i issues of economic development were not so pressing, but the new state grew substantially, with tourism replacing agriculture as a mainstay of the economy. Asian Americans continued to advance politically in the state, and Hawai'i elected both Chinese and Japanese Americans to Congress for the first time. On the other hand, many native Hawaiians perceived that their influence in the islands, politically and culturally, declined in the years since statehood. As a result, there was a Hawaiian Movement in the last decades of the twentieth century to revive traditional Hawaiian culture and, in some cases, to call for political independence.

Debates over the proper disposition of native lands, held originally by the monarch but transferred to the United States after annexation, have yet to be resolved.

As a political region in the twenty-first century, Alaska and Hawai'i are more different from the mainland than they are alike. Native issues have been a common concern, but the natives of the two states have not made a common cause. Both states are in the mid-Pacific, distant from the mainland, but 2,500 miles from each other. Still, the common memory of their wartime heritage and joint battle to join the union as the last two states should keep them united in the American mind for some time to come.

See also territorial government.

FURTHER READING

Coffman, Tom. *Nation Within: The Story of America's Annexation of the Nation of Hawai'i*. Honolulu: Epicenter, 1998.

Fuchs, Lawrence. *Hawaii Pono: A Social History*. New York: Harcourt Brace, 1961.

Haycox, Stephen. *Alaska: An American Colony*. Seattle: University of Washington Press, 2002.

Trask, Haunani-Kay. *From a Native Daughter: Colonialism and Sovereignty in Hawai'i*. Monroe, ME: Common Courage Press, 1993.

Whitehead, John S. *Completing the Union: Alaska, Hawai'i, and the Battle for Statehood*. Albuquerque: University of New Mexico Press, 2004.

JOHN S. WHITEHEAD

amendment process

The creation of a mechanism to formally alter the terms of the U.S. Constitution provided a means of bridging the gulf between the conflicting goals of stability and adaptability in the basic principles, structure, and functions of American national government. From the time that effective legal instruments to define and limit governmental powers began to appear, a question persisted as to how such arrangements could be altered short of a revolution or coup d'etat so that a government would perform those tasks, and only those tasks, that political society desired of it. The British solved the problem through sweeping parliamentary declarations at moments of crisis to refine the original instrument of articu-

lated and confined royal power, the Magna Carta of 1215. The 1628 Petition of Rights, the 1689 Bill of Rights, and the 1701 Act of Settlement further confined the ruler and led to a multipart and not entirely consistent framework for government. This collection of legislative acts came to be referred to often, if somewhat inaccurately, as an unwritten constitution.

Operating under royal charters or other instruments laying out quite specifically the terms for their rule, the British North American colonies functioned as subordinates of the mother country but with more coherent written frameworks of government. In their quest for independence in the 1770s, the rebellious colonies demonstrated their commitment to the concept of constitutionalism and their resistance to British-imposed changes in fundamental arrangements that lacked popular sanction.

Creating an Amendable Constitution

The initial U.S. state and federal constitutions put into effect after the Declaration of Independence usually contained specific provisions for their own amendment. The federal Articles of Confederation were no exception, stipulating that a majority of the Congress could initiate changes in constitutional arrangements, but these would only take effect if the legislatures of every state endorsed the provision for reform. As the first U.S. government began to function in the midst of ongoing war with Britain, various deficiencies in the Articles of Confederation became apparent, especially in matters of finance. Efforts to amend the articles failed repeatedly, however, when they failed to win the unanimous support of the states.

The need to devise satisfactory amendments for the articles propelled the convening of a convention of the states in Philadelphia in 1787. The framers' decision to construct an entirely new basic instrument for their federation, submit it for the approval of the Confederation Congress, and stipulate that it would go into operation if ratified by conventions in at least 9 of the 13 states was a radical approach to the process of amending the Articles of Confederation. If the states initially embraced the new instrument, they would subsequently be bound to accept altered arrangements lacking their unanimous consent. The founders thus set a bold standard that amendment could fundamentally reconfigure a government, not merely make modest revisions in its terms.

Discussion of a proper constitutional amending process continued throughout the Philadelphia convention, intertwined with considerations of federal versus state authority, large state versus small state power, and majority preference versus a higher consensus for fundamental commitments. Contemplation of an amending process was entangled with discussion of how the Constitution itself could be legitimately ratified. The convention reached a Lockean conclusion that the sovereign people had the right to constitute a new government when previous arrangements proved wanting and when their representatives specifically chosen for the purpose agreed to the new Constitution. Moreover, once approved, the new fundamental instrument could then be amended if such a proposal came from two-thirds of each house of Congress, or, in the absence of congressional action, if two-thirds of the states summoned another constitutional convention. In any case, amendments proposed by either means would take effect only if ratified by three-fourths of the states through conventions of popularly elected delegates or decisions of states' legislatures—whichever method the Congress chose. These multiple avenues to amendment were incorporated into the new Constitution's Article V and submitted with the rest of the document to the Confederation Congress. Swift approval there, however, was not an indicator of certain ratification by state conventions, which proved to be a greater test.

The frame of government that 55 men produced in Philadelphia between May and September 1787 met a mixed reception, not only from the convention's members, a few of whom refused to sign it, but also from the politically alert public. The principal objection to the proposed Constitution was its lack of rights guaranteeing individual protections against abusive conduct by the new government. Faced with stiff and potentially fatal resistance to ratification in, first, the Massachusetts conventions and, subsequently, in Maryland, Virginia, New York, and elsewhere, the Constitution's proponents narrowly carried the day by calling attention to the availability of the amending process and agreeing to submit proposals for a Bill of Rights. The reassurance provided by the existence of Article V was crucial to the ratification of the Constitution by the requisite number of states.

Fulfilling the pledge to provide a Bill of Rights through constitutional amendment became the highest priority of James Madison, one of the Constitution's most influential framers and one of its leading protectors in the first House of Representatives. Insistent that the pledge to enact a Bill of Rights not be neglected in the face of other pressing needs in establishing a functioning government, Madison refined a long list of proposals from the various state ratifying conventions. His efforts in the House and those of colleagues in the Senate achieved adoption of a package of 12 amendments during the first session of Congress in 1789. Two years later, 10 of the 12 measures, subsequently referred to as the Bill of Rights, were ratified by enough state legislatures to put them into effect. Anti-Federalist criticism of the Constitution was undercut by this effective first employment of the amending process, and thereafter confidence in the new national government grew steadily.

Reshaping American Government in the Nineteenth Century

As the Constitution began to function, flaws in the document soon became evident. The Eleventh and Twelfth Amendments were easily adopted in 1798 and 1804 to remedy problems involving suits of state governments by citizens of other states and the lack of clarity in the Electoral College's process for selecting presidents and vice presidents, a matter that became clear during the election of 1800. Thereafter, given the cumbersome nature of the amending process and its requirement of supermajority consensus, a preference soon emerged for resolving most constitutional disputes through judicial review. Prior to 1860, Congress approved only one more amendment, a measure forbidding grants of foreign titles to American citizens, and it failed to win ratification. As the sectional crisis came to a head following the election of Abraham Lincoln, Congress made a desperate effort to avert conflict by approving an amendment to preserve slavery in states where it existed. This first effort at a Thirteenth Amendment came too late to avert southern secession and gained ratification by only two northern states.

The Civil War led to a fundamental reformulation of the Constitution through three amendments. All were designed by the Congress to confirm the Union victory. Southern state acceptance was required as the price of regaining full participation in national affairs. The Thirteenth Amendment, adopted in 1865, not only abolished slavery but also demonstrated that the amending process could reverse, not merely modify, previous constitutional arrangements. The Fourteenth Amendment (1868) bestowed the privileges and immunities of citizenship as a birthright, regardless of race or previous condition of servitude, and also promised equal protection and due process of law to all citizens. In essence, this amendment asserted the dominant authority of the national government over the states in the federal relationship. The Fifteenth Amendment (1870) took the further step of guaranteeing adult male citizens suffrage regardless of race. Although southern grumbling about coerced ratification of the Reconstruction Amendments would persist, the process of making these amendments met the Article V standard and represented a choice made by the South to accept its loss on the battlefield and take the necessary steps to regain its place in national government.

Accelerated Amending in the Twentieth Century

The amending process would not be employed again for more than 40 years, stirring new doubts that it could function in ordinary circumstances. However, the Supreme Court's 1895 rejection of an income tax and the Senate's repeated refusal to accept the principle of popular election (instead of state legislative selection) of its members led to public demands for fundamental reform. The House and a majority of state legislatures embraced both proposals, and the Senate finally capitulated, fearing that if it did not, states would employ the alternative Article V process of demanding a constitutional convention that would be beyond congressional control. The adoption and ratification of the Sixteenth (income tax) and Seventeenth (direct election of senators) Amendments were completed in 1913, encouraging a belief that amendment was possible and stimulating successful campaigns for nine amendments in little more than a half century.

In 1913 long-standing temperance and women's rights campaigns turned their attention to quests for amendments to prohibit alcoholic beverages and grant woman suffrage. Mobilizing public pressure on Congress and benefiting from the crisis of World War I, both crusades achieved success by the end of the decade. Congressmen who did not favor Prohibition but hoped to make the issue go away agreed to vote for the amendment if a provision was added requiring ratification within seven years, something they thought unlikely. This first effort to frustrate amendment by placing a time limit on the Article V process failed miserably. The Eighteenth Amendment was ratified in 1919, 13 months after Congress proposed it. The Nineteenth Amendment encountered more resistance, but ratification of woman suffrage was completed shortly before the 1920 election.

Both amendments proved disappointing, however; the Eighteenth because many Americans did not wish to abandon drinking alcohol and the Nineteenth because suffrage neither changed the partisan balance nor brought full equality for women. Within a few years, a campaign was underway to repeal national Prohibition, based in part on the belief that it was undermining respect for the Constitution. Perceiving that state legislators had succumbed to pressure from temperance advocates rather than that they reflected majority will, the anti-Prohibition movement insisted that a repeal amendment be sent for ratification to popularly elected state conventions. After the 1932 election seemed to show that the electorate wanted repeal by favoring wet Democrats over dry Republicans, the convention ratification process, unused since the endorsement of the original Constitution, functioned smoothly and quickly, bringing Prohibition to an end in December 1933 with the Twenty-First Amendment. That a constitutional provision could be repealed a mere 14 years after its implementation revealed an unanticipated flexibility in the amendment process. Whereas the Civil War amendments had demonstrated that original constitutional provisions could be overturned, the repeal of national Prohibition made it clear that amendments could be toppled if public and legislative opinion changed direction substantially.

The amending process was used repeatedly during the twentieth century to make technical changes in the Constitution that seemed far less consequential than alcohol control, income taxation, or suffrage expansion, but subtly reshaped the functioning of government. The Twentieth Amendment of 1933 reset the calendar to initiate presidential and congressional terms more promptly after a national election. It ended lengthy postelection periods, during which discredited lame ducks continued to exercise power and serve rejected interests. The Twenty-Second Amendment of 1951, limiting a president to two terms, represented a reaction of Republicans and conservative southern Democrats to the four electoral victories of Franklin D. Roosevelt. The measure had the unexpected consequence of politically weakening second-term presidents unable to run again. The Twenty-Third Amendment (1961), granting the District of Columbia three electoral votes, and the Twenty-Fourth (1964), eliminating the poll tax, were small steps toward civic participation for African Americans, symbolic victories for proponents of major civil rights reform, but so modest that even congressional opponents did not strenuously object. The Twenty-Fifth Amendment (1967), establishing procedures to deal with presidential disability and fill vice presidential vacancies, was expected to be rarely needed. Within a decade, however, it was used twice in a single term as both Spiro Agnew and Richard Nixon resigned: their replacements, Gerald Ford and Nelson

Rockefeller, were presidential selections, confirmed by Congress rather than the choice of voters. The Twenty-Sixth Amendment (1971), lowering the suffrage age from 21 to 18, was, like the preceding technical amendments, quickly ratified once adopted by Congress.

The steepest hurdle in the amending process appeared to be obtaining congressional approval, with more than 10,000 proposed amendments failing that test in the Constitution's first two centuries. Some came close but failed to win congressional approval, such as measures requiring a national referendum on a declaration of war; limiting executive agreements with foreign nations; overturning Supreme Court rulings requiring equal-sized legislative districts, forbidding school prayer, protecting flag burning as symbolic free speech; and requiring an annually balanced federal budget. A few measures obtained the required two-thirds congressional approval but fell short of ratification by three-fourths of the states. The child labor amendment of the 1920s languished in state legislatures at first, then appeared unnecessary after adoption and judicial acceptance of the New Deal's Fair Labor Standards Act. The equal rights amendment (ERA) and District of Columbia amendment, adopted in the 1970s with ratification time limits, likewise succumbed, the ERA falling only three states short of the necessary 38.

The importance of state ratification in the overall system was underscored in 1992, as the process was completed for an amendment approved by Congress in 1789 as a part of the original package of 12 that had no time limit on ratification. After 203 years, words drafted by James Madison were added to the Constitution in a Twenty-seventh Amendment that prohibited a Congress from raising its own salary. Despite doubts regarding the amendment's viability after such a long time, as well as unhappiness with its limitation on congressional prerogatives, Congress chose not to challenge the stark language of Article V as to the bounds of the amending process.

A Difficult but Manageable Method for Constitutional Change

As its repeated use over more than two centuries has shown, the Constitution's Article V amending process provides a workable mechanism for altering the basic terms of government when a supermajority consensus to do so can be achieved. The failure to bring the process to a successful conclusion often reflects a general unwillingness to tamper with the framers' design, widely regarded

as a work of genius. At times, an inability to achieve the required federal and state supermajority consensus in the face of sectional, ideological, and partisan divisions has also been involved. Yet the successful operation of the amending process provides fundamental confirmation of a living, evolving Constitution, one whose unamended features gain reendorsement whenever its other terms are altered, and thus one whose legitimacy no longer rests simply on the original intent of the framers.

See also Articles of Confederation; Bill of Rights; Constitution, federal.

FURTHER READING

Ackerman, Bruce. *We the People.* 2 vols. Cambridge, MA: Harvard University Press, 1991–98.

Bernstein, Richard B., with Jerome Agel. *Amending America: If We Love the Constitution So Much, Why Do We Keep Trying to Change It?* New York: Times Books, 1993.

Grimes, Alan P. *Democracy and the Amendments to the Constitution.* Lexington, MA: Lexington Books, 1978.

Kammen, Michael. *A Machine That Would Go of Itself: The Constitution in American Culture.* New York: Knopf, 1986.

Kyvig, David E. *Explicit and Authentic Acts: Amending the U.S. Constitution, 1776–1995.* Lawrence: University Press of Kansas, 1996.

———. *Repealing National Prohibition.* Chicago: University of Chicago Press, 1979.

———, ed. *Unintended Consequences of Constitutional Amendment.* Athens: University of Georgia Press, 2000.

Levinson, Sanford, ed. *Our Undemocratic Constitution: Where the Constitution Goes Wrong (and How We the People Can Correct It).* New York: Oxford University Press, 2006.

———. *Responding to Imperfection: The Theory and Practice of Constitutional Amendment.* Princeton, NJ: Princeton University Press, 1998.

Vose, Clement E. *Constitutional Change: Amendment Politics and Supreme Court Litigation since 1900.* Lexington, MA: Lexington Books, 1972.

DAVID E. KYVIG

American (Know-Nothing) Party

In 1854 and 1855 the American Party, nicknamed Know-Nothings because of their secretive origins, won hundreds of elections by campaigning against immigration, political corruption, and sectional extremism. In 1856 the party collapsed when conflict over slavery overshadowed its signature issue of nativism, or hostility to foreigners.

Political nativists reacted to a wave of immigration between 1845 and 1854 that brought 3 million foreigners to the United States, most of whom fled hard times in Ireland, Germany, and England. Foes of immigration argued that foreigners were ignorant of how America's republican government worked. Protestant bigots went further, claiming that Catholic immigrants, who comprised a majority of the newcomers, acted as Vatican foot soldiers in a plot to subvert American liberty. Moral reformers believed that immigrants drank to excess, committed crime, and disrespected American cultural values. Workers feared job competition. Know-Nothings addressed these concerns with proposals to curb immigration, extend naturalization to 21 years, restrict foreign-born voting and officeholding, teach Protestant values in public schools, disband immigrant militia units, and investigate allegations of sexual abuse committed by Catholic priests and nuns.

The American Party traced its origins to the short-lived American Republican Party of 1844–45. American Republicans fared poorly because although underway, the full impact of the 3-million strong wave of German and Irish immigration had yet to materialize. It would take until the mid-1850s, when all these immigrants had arrived, for their presence to become highly visible. Another factor limiting the American Republicans' success was enduring voter loyalty to the established Whig and Democratic parties. Although defeated, American Republicans created the Order of United Americans, a semisecret nativist society that, in 1853, merged with the Order of the Star Spangled Banner, which limited membership to American-born Protestants sworn to vote for men of the same status.

In 1854 these secret societies fielded candidates for the newly minted American Party in elections across the country. Know-Nothings won votes by capitalizing on nativist concerns that the established parties had largely ignored and by exploiting discontent with the Kansas-Nebraska Act, a measure that opened to slavery territories north of the old Missouri Compromise line should settlers vote to allow it. Popular criticism of Whig and Democratic corruption intensified voter alienation. In response, Know-Nothings promised to combat immigration, safeguard the Union from extremists, and clean up government.

Because of the irregular schedules of nineteenth-century elections, most of the 1854 contests occurred in the North. The American Party performed best in the populous northeastern states of Massachusetts, New York, and Pennsylvania. In one year, Know-Nothings doubled their membership to 1 million people organized into more than 10,000 lodges. Seeking to build on that surge, the American Party abandoned secrecy, which many voters disliked. In the 1855 elections, most of which were held in the South, Know-Nothings polled the strongest in Kentucky, Maryland, and Louisiana, where Whigs had been dominant and where large cities provided a base of nativist workers. Although both Whigs and Democrats switched to the Know-Nothings, the collapse of the Whigs after the 1852 elections made their former partisans more receptive to the new Know-Nothing and Republican parties.

Seeking the White House in 1856, the American Party nominated former president Millard Fillmore, a New York Whig. While he tried to appeal to the party's nativist base, Fillmore hoped to win votes on his conservative Unionist credentials derived from his support for the Compromise of 1850. Although they wanted to preserve the Union, Know-Nothings both North and South disagreed on what the other side should concede on the slavery question. Southern nativists were proslavery but unwilling to back the proimmigrant and more sectional Democrats. Northern Know-Nothings generally opposed the Kansas-Nebraska Act, but their support for nativism kept them out of the Republican Party, a new organization committed to excluding slavery from federal territory rather than nativism.

The presidential election of 1856 forced Know-Nothing supporters to choose between the pro-Union nativist Fillmore and more sectional, non-nativist alternatives. At the American Party's February nominating convention, a united southern delegation aided by a northern minority endorsed existing proslavery laws. That stand alienated most of the northern delegation, which quit the convention and formed a rival North American Party that endorsed John C. Frémont, the Republican nominee.

Fillmore's remaining hopes to win on a platform that emphasized nativism and sectional comity disappeared in May 1856, when proslavery vigilantes rampaged in Kansas, and South Carolina Democratic congressman Preston Brooks caned Massachusetts Republican senator Charles Sumner in retaliation for an inflammatory speech. This violence convinced many Northerners to back the Republicans and drove Southerners to the Democrats, who not only had a better record of sup-

porting slavery but also appeared more likely to beat Frémont. On Election Day, Fillmore won 22 percent of the
ballots and the Electoral College vote of only one state
(Maryland).

Although dead at the national level and in much of
the North, the American Party survived in some southern states and cities. In the presidential election of
1860, many southern Know-Nothings supported constitutional unionist John Bell and opposed secession
during the ensuing crisis that culminated in the Civil
War.

Despite their quick fall, Know-Nothing victories in
1854–56 were impressive. They elected seven governors,
eight U.S. senators, and 104 members of the House of
Representatives and took majority control of eight state
legislatures. Know-Nothings were particularly influential
in cities where they won votes from workers concerned
about immigrant job competition. In cities, election
rioting by nativist gangs often accompanied Know-
Nothing victories. Because the American Party never
held a congressional majority and rarely controlled all
three branches of any state government, it failed to enact
most of its anti-immigrant agenda.

In states where Know-Nothings held legislative majorities, such as Connecticut, Maryland, and Massachusetts, they banned immigrant militias and restricted
public works employment to the native born. The
Know-Nothing stronghold of Massachusetts enacted a
delay on voting rights for naturalized citizens, but the
law was quickly repealed by the next Republican administration. A more extreme proposal to outlaw Catholic
convents also failed.

Beyond nativism, the American Party combined the
public investment policies of the defunct Whig Party
and good government measures advocated by nonpartisan reformers. Massachusetts, with a Know-Nothing
majority in the statehouse and a Know-Nothing governor, illustrated this tendency. American Party legislators
increased social welfare spending via poor hospitals and
expanded public schooling. Workers benefited from the
elimination of imprisonment for debt and state regulation of industry. Massachusetts Know-Nothings also
advanced women's legal equality by protecting married
women's property rights; liberalizing divorce law; and
giving wives the right to sue, make business contracts,
and work without their husband's consent. In the North,
Know-Nothings generally opposed slavery and its expansion, and in Massachusetts the party passed a personal liberty law protecting runaway slaves and ended

racial segregation in public schools. While Massachusetts
had perhaps America's most progressive Know-Nothing
regime, it also had one of the most anti-Catholic ones.
The same legislature that promoted the rights of blacks,
women, and workers investigated convents, mandated
reading of the Protestant King James version of the Bible
in public classrooms, and banned state aid to Catholic
schools. Unlike civil rights liberals of a later day, northern Know-Nothings saw no contradiction between promoting Protestant nativism while breaking down other
categories of social exclusion.

At the municipal level, Know-Nothings managed to
deliver on many of their promises to native-born workers. American Party administrations in cities increased
municipal spending on public works, created more
working-class jobs in government by professionalizing
police and fire departments, extended city services to
newer, cheaper neighborhoods on the edges of growing
cities, and permitted unions to wage strikes free of police interference. In a few places—such as New Orleans,
where a stevedore won the mayoralty—Know-Nothings
placed wage earners in positions of power, but most leaders belonged to the same class of lawyers and business
professionals who traditionally predominated in high
party offices.

The American Party combined nativism with antipartisan reform and a commitment to preserving the
Union. It briefly used these issues to win elections across
the country, but it fell apart when its leaders failed to
resolve sectional conflicts within their own party.

See also Free Soil Party; nativism.

FURTHER READING
Anbinder, Tyler. *Nativism and Slavery: The Northern Know
Nothings and the Politics of the 1850s.* New York: Oxford
University Press, 1992.
Gienapp, William E. *The Origins of the Republican Party, 1852–
1856.* New York: Oxford University Press, 1986.
Holt, Michael F. *The Rise and Fall of the American Whig Party:
Jacksonian Politics and the Onset of the Civil War.* New York:
Oxford University Press, 2001.
Levine, Bruce. "Conservatism, Nativism, and Slavery: Thomas R.
Whitney and the Origins of the Know-Nothing Party."
Journal of American History 88 (Sept. 2001), 455–88.
Mulkern, John R. *The Know-Nothing Party in Massachusetts: The
Rise and Fall of a People's Movement.* Boston: Northeastern
University Press, 1990.
Towers, Frank. *The Coming of the Civil War in the Urban South.*
Charlottesville: University of Virginia Press, 2004.

Voss-Hubbard, Mark. *Beyond Party: Cultures of Antipartisanship in Northern Politics before the Civil War.* Baltimore, MD: Johns Hopkins University Press, 2002.

FRANK TOWERS

Americanism

Americanism has two different meanings: it signifies both what is distinctive about the United States (and the colonies and territories that formed it) *and* loyalty to that nation, rooted in a defense of its political ideals. Those canonic ideals—self-government, equal opportunity, freedom of speech and association, a belief in progress— were first proclaimed during the era of the Revolution and early republic and have developed more expansive meanings since then. Thanks to a powerful civil rights movement, *social* equality, for example, fully entered the canon only in the decades after World War II. But the bundle of ideals associated with Americanism has proved remarkably supple over time, which helps to account for its enduring appeal to people in other lands as well as at home.

Its shifting content is not the only thing that distinguishes Americanism from the patriotisms generated by other powerful nation-states. Love of any country requires attachment to its supposed virtues, past and present. Affection for "Holy Russia"—its fields and forests and Orthodox Church—long predated the Soviet Union and easily survived it. Traditional Japanese patriots revere the uniqueness of their national tongue and of Shinto, a pantheistic faith linked closely with an unbroken imperial house. Americanism, by contrast, has been rooted less in a shared culture than in shared political ideals.

Like Americans, French patriots may pay homage to the Enlightenment-born ideals of their revolution— liberty, equality, fraternity—but French patriotism includes a stronger cultural component than does America's national creed. Americans have always fought more over how to define and apply the national ideals than about the merits of their language or cuisine. As the historian Richard Hofstader wrote, "It has been our fate as a nation not to have ideologies but to be one." The resulting battles to define Americanism have alternately divided the nation and unified it, producing both

internal strife and solidarity against foreign enemies. These two tendencies have often crested together during wartime. Americanism's propensity to generate both conflict and cohesion continues in the early twenty-first century, when the United States has no rival on the world stage but when "Americanism" is fought about nearly everywhere.

From the Puritans to the Pledge of Allegiance

The concept itself is nearly as old as the first European settlements to endure on the land mass of North America. John Winthrop was thinking about his church, not a nation, when in 1630 he told those fellow Puritans who sailed with him to a New World that "we must consider that we shall be as a city upon a hill, the eyes of all people are upon us." But Winthrop's notion that America ought to be a model for Christendom and beyond soon transcended the intra-Protestant dispute that had led to the founding of the Massachusetts Bay Colony. In 1763 another New Englander, John Adams, wrote that America's settlement was "the Opening of a grand scene and design in Providence." Adams believed his young land was destined to break the grip of feudal laws and customs, thus showing how individuals could free themselves from an irrational, often tyrannical past. During and just after the war for independence, such thinking was commonplace in sermons, pamphlets, and even in the diaries of ordinary men and women. The new nation had the potential to be more than what Tom Paine called "an asylum for mankind." It had a mission to liberate the world.

For many Americans, that messianic ambition was fused with religious meaning. The Second Great Awakening of the early nineteenth century spawned thousands of new Protestant churches and made the passion of evangelicalism the common discourse of most inhabitants, whether free or slave. Since that spiritual upsurge, the idea that anyone, regardless of learning or social background, can "come to Christ" has dovetailed with the belief in equal rights emblazoned in the Declaration of Independence. This synthesis of evangelical Protestantism and republicanism was found in no other nation—at least not with such passionate conviction and for such a long period of time.

Over the past two centuries, Americanism has been put to a variety of uses, benign and belligerent, democratic and demagogic. During the first decades of the nineteenth century, the quasi-religious ideal took luxuriant, imperial form. It inspired the notion of Manifest

Destiny, which legitimized the conquest of lands occupied by Native American tribes as well as by Mexicans in the Southwest. It was omnipresent among both Jacksonian Democrats, who defined it as the gospel of rough hewn, self-made men in conflict with "the rich, the proud, [and] the privileged," and their Whig opponents, whose "American System" called for higher tariffs and a national bank. It also animated, in the 1850s, the attempt by the new American Party (the Know-Nothings) to drive Irish immigrants from political power wherever the "papists" had established a foothold.

At the same time, the national faith was provoking an equally prophetic critique. In the forefront were abolitionists, both black and white, who scored the hypocrisy of a slave-holding republic. In 1829 David Walker demanded that white citizens "compare your own language" in the Declaration of Independence "with your cruelties and murders inflicted … on our fathers and on us—men who have never given your fathers or you the least provocation ! ! ! ! !" In the 1850s, William Lloyd Garrison called the Constitution "a covenant with hell," and Frederick Douglass asked, "What to the slave is the Fourth of July?"

Yet few radicals rejected the ideals themselves. At the end of his famous Independence Day speech in 1852, Douglass predicted the abolition of slavery in his lifetime. He drew his optimism from "the great principles" of that same Declaration of Independence "and the genius of American institutions" as well as from an enlightened spirit he believed was swelling on both sides of the Atlantic. Such figures initiated a vital countertradition. Since the antebellum era, dissidents have routinely cited the gap between America's utopian promise and its disappointing reality.

The Civil War brought two contending versions of Americanism into a bloody conflict, the terms of which were not finally settled until Reconstruction had run its course in the mid-1870s. In many ways, the war's "new birth of freedom" renewed the national faith. Yet no sooner had Reconstruction begun to wane, than anxiety grew about the weakness of Americanism in the fast-growing, culturally fragmented land. On the eve of the war, Carl Schurz, a German-born reformer and foe of slavery, had confidently predicted, "True Americanism, tolerance and equal rights will peacefully overcome all that is not reconcilable. . . ." By the 1870s it seemed that jagged splits along lines of region, race, religion, class, and immigrant status could tear the industrializing society apart.

For national leaders, it thus became essential to Americanize the population if Americanism were to prosper. Never before had patriots made so self-conscious an attempt "to make a religion out of citizenship," as the political theorist Michael Walzer puts it. The massive Grand Army of the Republic created the ritual of Memorial Day to associate love of country with selfless loyalty in battle. Veterans, ministers, and teachers urged that the flag be displayed in every public building and many private ones.

In 1892 Francis Bellamy, a devout Christian attracted to socialism, wrote a short pledge to the Stars and Stripes that he hoped would bind American children to a shared set of beliefs. An admirer of the French Revolution, Bellamy mused about including "equality and fraternity" in the pledge but decided that would be too controversial in a society riven by differences of race and ideology. So he restricted himself to a single line: "one nation indivisible, with liberty and justice for all." His Pledge of Allegiance was quickly adopted by schools throughout the land (Congress added "under God" in 1954).

As that example suggests, a reassertion of Americanism was not always intended to produce political conformity at the turn of the twentieth century. Dissenters could appropriate the national faith as readily as conservatives. Three years after the pledge was drafted, Eugene Debs, the railroad unionist who would soon become leader of the Socialist Party, emerged from jail to greet a throng of his supporters. "Manifestly the spirit of '76 still survives," he declared, "The fires of liberty and noble aspirations are not yet extinguished."

The Armoring of Americanism

Yet as the United States grappled with a flood of new immigrants and became an imperial power, the most aggressive promoters of Americanism were eager to prop up the established order. These figures weren't necessarily conservative, as we now define the term. But Theodore Roosevelt's praise of the melting pot and of martial virtues stemmed from his fear that immigrants who retained even a shred of loyalty to their native countries weakened America's resolve in a dangerous world.

Inevitably, such fears intensified during World War I. All but ignoring the First Amendment, the federal government jailed radicals who opposed the war and looked the other way when vigilantes forced German Americans to prostrate themselves before the flag. The new American Legion crafted a "100 per cent Americanism" that stressed only the self-protective, coercive aspects of the creed. In the 1920s, this defensive style of Americanism merged with the desire for cultural homogeneity to produce a spate of restrictive immigration laws. Throughout this period, racists had little difficulty rationalizing racial segregation as an essential component of the "American way of life."

The armoring of Americanism in the early twentieth century produced some unexpected consequences. Wartime service in uniform or in defense industries allowed immigrants to legitimize their struggles for justice by draping them in the mantle of Americanism. Those struggles were further validated during World War I as federal officials enticed ethnic workers with the promise of "industrial democracy" and the idea that, in America, "The People ARE the Government." Even the immigration restrictions of the 1920s, by weakening ties between immigrants and their countries of origin, fostered an Americanization from below that set the stage for a new regime of cultural pluralism.

Patriots Left and Right
in the Twentieth Century

During the 1930s and World War II, New Deal liberals managed to daub Americanism with a tolerant, populist hue. The federal government hired artists to paint historical murals in post offices that highlighted the exploits of farmers and workers. It also published guides to every big city and region that documented the riches of local histories and cultures. In the new National Archives building next to the Capital Mall, the founding documents of the United States were displayed as if they were the relics of secular saints. Meanwhile, such filmmakers-turned-wartime-propagandists as Frank Capra depicted America as one big friendly house for ordinary people of all religions and races (even if, in most of their productions, the minorities politely kept to their own rooms).

Yet the Left's attempt to marry class-consciousness to nationalism did not fare as well. During the Great Depression, CIO organizers described their nascent unions as expressions of "working-class Americanism," while pro-Soviet radicals portrayed communism as "Twentieth-Century Americanism." But domestic opponents ridiculed these leftist twists on a common theme, and they all but vanished during the cold war. The new global conflict recast Americanism as the antithesis of communism and identified the national creed as the last best hope of a world threatened by totalitarianism and yearning for freedom.

The subsequent hunt for "un-American activities" brought to a close the long period during which no single political faction controlled the meaning of the national canon. The civil rights struggle of the late 1950s and early 1960s did reinvigorate the dissident tradition, for a time. But by the late 1960s, Americanism had become virtually the exclusive property of the cultural and political right.

The politics of the Vietnam War played a critical role in this change. In a decisive break with tradition, leading activists in the protest movements of the era took issue not just with government policies but also with the ideals from which those policies were supposedly drawn. Young radicals did not seek to draw attention to the distance between America's promise and its reality as much as to debunk the national creed itself as inherently reactionary and destructive.

That cynical view held firm among dissenters through the remainder of the twentieth century and beyond, despite a sprinkling of anti-war posters declaring that "peace is patriotic." In 2001 Noam Chomsky, one of the most popular writers on the left, dismissed patriotism as the governing elite's way of telling its subjects, "You shut up and be obedient, and I'll relentlessly advance my own interests."

Meanwhile, conservatives redoubled their efforts to claim Americanism as their cause. They successfully yoked such rituals as saluting the flag, honoring the Founding Fathers, and singing patriotic songs to their larger purposes. But their success occurred largely by default.

How Exceptional a Nation?

The conflict of words and symbols drew new attention to an ongoing debate about the degree to which, in the context of world history, America has been an "exceptional" nation. From Alexis de Tocqueville to Louis Hartz, leading interpreters, whether admirers or critics, focused on what seemed distinctive about the character and ideology of Americans and viewed the development of the nation as unique. The list of exceptional qualities is a lengthy one. It includes the primacy of individual identity over communal ties, belief in almost unlimited social mobility, absence of an established state church and the consequent flourishing of both diverse denominations and grassroots piety, and a potent tradition of antiauthoritarian and anticentralist politics. One should also add the remarkable self-confidence of most Americans, particularly white ones, that they live in a nation blessed by God that has a right, even a duty, to help other nations become more like the United States. Over the decades, the exceptionalist argument was repeated so often—by scholars, journalists, and politicians—that it hardened into cliché.

Perhaps some exceptionalisms, some nationalist ideologies, are more equal than others. For over 200 years, the idea of America—as new Jerusalem or new Rome or something in between—has had a uniquely potent meaning for a broad variety of people outside the United States: from French aristocrats like Tocqueville to European Communists like Antonio Gramsci to Islamic terrorists like Mohammed Atta to teenagers all over the world. Recently, non-American scholars have joined U.S. historians in concentrating on the fragmented, disputatious nature of American society and the influence of those factors on the development of nationalist ideology. But there remains a persistent inclination by academics as well as ordinary citizens in other lands to view America as a whole—to examine how "it" uses and abuses its ideology both within the nation's borders and outside them.

What makes *Americanism* exceptional is thus its confluence with the realities of historical development itself. Ultimately, Americanism demands understanding on its own terms because of the unrivaled power for good or ill that the United States wields in the world. As the historian David Hollinger wrote in 2002, the United States is "the most successful nationalist project in all of modern history. . . . Its significance is measured by its sheer longevity, its influence in the world arena, and its absorption of a variety of peoples through immigration, conquest, and enslavement and emancipation."

The success of the American nation has, in turn, bestowed tremendous power on the notion of Americanism, with all its contradictions and silences. It allows Mormons from Utah and Pentecostalists from Missouri to go into the world, converting people to a faith marked by the material success of its adherents as much as by the appeal of their doctrines and ceremonies. It has also given dissident groups in the United States the ability to inspire analogous movements in other parts of the globe. The U.S. movement for black freedom helped galvanize the antiapartheid struggle in South Africa, and the radical feminist movement (although indebted to texts by non-Americans like Juliet Mitchell and Simone de Beauvoir) to spark like-minded insurgencies on every continent. The same is true of the gay and lesbian rights movement, spawned in the United States at the end of the 1960s.

The recent rise of anti-Americanism notwithstanding, one cannot neglect the worldwide appeal of Americanist ideology in the laudable desire to internationalize the study and teaching of U.S. history. The very perception that such a distinct set of "values" exists was greatly boosted, particularly from World War II on, by the unmatched power and allure of the American nation itself. Of course, no "civilizing mission" proceeds by discourse alone. Yet without a well-developed, internally persuasive ideology, no national mission, whether civilizing or barbarous, ever gains much sway.

See also conservatism; liberalism; republicanism.

FURTHER READING

Gerstle, Gary. *American Crucible: Race and Nation in the Twentieth Century*. Princeton, NJ: Princeton University Press, 2001.

Hartz, Louis. *The Liberal Tradition in America: An Interpretation of American Political Thought since the Revolution*. New York: Harcourt, 1955.

Hobsbawm, Eric. *Nations and Nationalism since 1780: Programme, Myth, Reality*. Cambridge, UK: Cambridge University Press, 1990.

Hollinger, David. *Postethnic America: Beyond Multiculturalism*. New York: Basic Books, 1995.

Lieven, Anatol. *America Right or Wrong: An Anatomy of American Nationalism*. New York: Oxford University Press, 2004.

O'Leary, Cecilia Elizabeth. *To Die For: The Paradox of American Patriotism*. Princeton, NJ: Princeton University Press, 1999.

Tuveson, Ernest. *Redeemer Nation: The Idea of America's Millennial Role*. Chicago: University of Chicago Press, 1968.

Walzer, Michael. *What It Means to Be an American*. New York: Marsilio Publishers, 1992.

MICHAEL KAZIN

anarchism

Often described as having exhausted its historical mission—or at least its political significance—anarchism has come back repeatedly in U.S. political history. With the collapse of the Soviet model in 1989 and growing public distaste for its corporate capitalist alternative in the decades since, the anarchist dream found newer generations of disciples, newer projects in ecology, and decentralized political-economic models.

Anarchism first grew to considerable numbers in the United States among the German immigrant community of the 1870s–80s. Its visionaries opposed all forms of class society, all political and economic hierarchies, capitalists and state authorities alike. Their influence reached a high point in Chicago in the mid-1880s, with newspapers, schools, athletic societies, and militia, all crushed by authorities in the aftermath of an 1886 bombing incident in the city's Haymarket Square on May Day. Repression spread rapidly across German American communities, the labor movement's radical cutting edge was demobilized, and an anarchist era ended. Individual immigrant anarchists, notably Johann Most, retained a following and helped bring about a new generation of mostly Jewish immigrant anarchists, notably Alexander Berkman and Emma Goldman. A more individualistic and cultural-minded Yankee anarchist trend also formed around issues like women's rights and birth control. An attempt to form utopian colonies of cooperative labor, inspired by Edward Bellamy's 1888 novel *Looking Backward*, brought a fresh wave of perfectionists into a type of anarchist politics little appreciated by immigrant radicals fixed on ideas of class struggle.

In 1901 the assassination of President William McKinley by the anarchist-influenced Leon Czolgosz seemed to end the movement's prospects in another wave of repression, but the founding of the Industrial Workers of the World (IWW) four years later revived it gloriously. Drawing heavily from European immigrant traditions, the "Wobblies" made anarcho-syndicalist ideas of workers' councils substituting for political and economic government seem poetic as well as genuinely American. The Lawrence, Massachusetts, textile strike of 1912 united more than a dozen nationalities under Wobbly banners, and songster Joe Hill wrote famous and hilarious ballads before being executed by authorities in Utah in 1915. The IWW did not officially oppose U.S. entry into the World War I, but its unwillingness to support the war brought horrendous attacks upon the Wobblies, including long prison sentences for their leaders. The Communist movement that grew out of the war drew upon anarchist traditions but also swallowed or crushed anarchist movements everywhere: Bolshevism seemed to be a philosophy of action, rather than patient education of workers, and a global movement uniting the world's oppressed, including the colonized peoples, but one linked to decisive state force.

A largely cultural movement with anarchist sympathies remained. Before their exile to Europe, avant-garde

Dadaists breathed anarchist sentiment into nascent modern art during the late 1910s. Meanwhile, small cooperative colonies with nude swimming and free thought survived in some places; likewise free-spirited schools for children, pacifist and non-English language (mainly Yiddish) publications held on. The defense of Italian American anarchists Nicola Sacco and Bartolomeo Vanzetti, executed by the state of Massachusetts in 1927, became a cause for embattled immigrant radicals at large, with a strong sense of martyrdom that passed from anarchist to Communist sensibilities.

Not until the later 1940s did anarchists have a larger public influence, mostly but not entirely cultural in form. In the wake of the Holocaust, the horror of atomic warfare and the saber rattling of the world's two surviving superpowers, a new generation of anarchist sympathizers began to gather on both coasts. Dwight Macdonald's *Politics* magazine (1944–49)—the most important anarchist publication after the aging Yiddish *Fraye Arbeter Shtimme* (Free Workers' Voice)—sparkled, then faltered and disappeared. In the San Francisco Bay area, KPFA, first station of what would become the Pacifica radio network, offered thousands of listeners anarchist-flavored politics and avant-garde culture.

The religious anarchist-pacifist Catholic Worker group, established during the 1930s and barely tolerated by Church authorities, joined with a post-Marxist Ban the Bomb sentiment in resisting nuclear weapons testing and the staging of government drills in preparation of war. Allen Ginsberg, Lawrence Ferlinghetti, and others loosely called "Beats" added a decisive cultural flavoring to these antiwar, antigovernment sentiments. These latter savants presaged the movements of the 1960s and imprinted upon them a sense of radicalism far exceeding old notions of a future rational, worker-run economy. *Liberation* magazine, absorbing an eclectic opposition to the state and a generous spirit, was the paper bridge to the New Left.

The Students for a Democratic Society (SDS), ideologically uncertain until its sudden takeover by factions of Marxist-Leninists in 1969, discovered an identity for itself as "student syndicalism," an IWW-like belief in student autonomy, self-direction, and resistance to the corporate control of campus. Able to synthesize antidraft sentiment, youth revolt, and insistence on wider democracy than older generations would accept, SDS was hugely popular for a few years among millions of young people. Not since the immigrant brigades of the 1880s had so many rebels shaped by roughly anarchist doctrines exerted themselves so successfully against state-imposed rules (such as Selective Service and drug laws) and social norms (premarital sex, heterosexuality, unmarried cohabitation, and most of all, women's passivity). Nothing was quite so anarchist or short-lived as Hippiedom, and nothing so quickly rendered avant-gardism into popular culture.

But, once again, by 1980, this time through absorption and political reversion, anarchism seemed dead and beyond revival. When the first strains of the globalized economy began to reveal the depths of ecological devastation and the deteriorating condition of populations in the global South, Wobbly-like themes of a global people's movement against capitalist globalization returned to anarchist doctrines. State socialism having failed, decentralization became fashionable among rebellious sections of the young. And so, a new Students for a Democratic Society suddenly came back to life in 2006. No ideology could be described as dominant in the new SDS, but some form of anarchism was the overwhelming favorite of emerging activists.

Two other, apparently dissimilar phenomena had been hidden within the political culture of the late twentieth century and early twenty-first. During the 1980s, Liberation Theology, a vision and practice of egalitarian, anti-imperial, and anticorporate religiosity, encouraged and embraced the landless and their supporters on several continents. It owed so little to any centralized authority that, in effect, it embraced anarchist principles. Its influence was mainly among younger activist clergy and idealists of a dwindling liberal Christian community in the United States. Meanwhile, a DIY, "do it yourself," impulse flourished among young people in the former factory districts of large cities, where cheap rents or "squats" offered space to artists and musicians seeking their own versions of community. With each technological shift, the possibilities of self-created art by masses of youngsters inspired the restless and creative-minded.

How much did such diverse impulses owe to historic anarchism? It is a difficult question to answer. It seems that the belief in a self-created community against the power of the state and its economic partners lived on more in spirit than in doctrine. But it could not die.

See also communism; labor movement and politics; labor parties; New Left.

FURTHER READING

Avrich, Paul. *Anarchist Voices: An Oral History of Anarchism in America*. Princeton, NJ: Princeton University Press, 1994.

Buhle, Paul, and Nicole Schulman, eds. *Wobblies: A Graphic History*. New York: Verso Books, 2005.

DeLeon, David. *The American as Anarchist: Reflections on Indigenous Radicalism*. Baltimore, MD: Johns Hopkins University Press, 1996.

Nelson, Bruce. *Beyond the Martyrs: A Social History of Chicago Anarchism, 1870–1900*. New Brunswick, NJ: Rutgers University Press, 1988.

Wechsler, Alice. *Emma Goldman in America*. Boston: Beacon Press, 1984.

PAUL BUHLE

anticommunism

Under close analysis, political movements sometimes turn out to be coalitions of antagonistic groups brought together for a time by a common antipathy that overcomes their enmity toward each other. Such was the case with American anticommunism, an activist movement distinct from the passive anticommunism sentiment that was the common reaction of almost all Americans to communism, to the extent that they thought about it. This coalition included Jews, Protestants, and Catholics in an age of religious and ethnic tensions. It included white racist anti-Communists and black anti-Communists during the Jim Crow era. There were socialist, liberal, and conservative anti-Communists; there were ex-Communist anti-Communists and former fellow traveler anti-Communists. There were soberly realistic experts on communism and the Soviet Union, and there were conspiracy theorists in thrall to paranoid fantasies that saw all American reform as a "red web" with Moscow at the center. It should come as no surprise, then, that American anti-Communists expended at least as much energy fighting one another as they did the common enemy.

Some historians have seen American anticommunism as simply the twentieth-century manifestation of nineteenth-century nativism and antiradicalism. Nativists and antiradicals, the countersubversive anti-Communists, *were* among the first to mobilize opposition to the Russian Revolution and its American supporters, and remained a noisy and generally disruptive presence throughout the history of anticommunism. But while anticommunism's opponents often succeeded in making the countersubversive part stand for the anti-Communist whole, that was not the whole story.

The Bolshevik Revolution of November 1917 produced three political reactions in the United States: liberal internationalists (whose views were summarized in Woodrow Wilson's Fourteen Points of 1918 with his vision of a world organization of liberal democratic nation-states); the progressive left, which agreed with Lenin that world revolution and an international workers' state were the only solution to militarism, imperialism, and the injustices of capitalism; and, finally, anti-Communists, who believed that communism was such a threat to American values that it could not merely be contained, as the liberal internationalists advocated, but had to be actively opposed by exposing the activities of American Communists and their supporters. Liberal internationalists, who ran American foreign policy for the rest of the century, generally regarded both the progressive left and their anti-Communist opponents as dangerous extremists and pests who made it difficult to pursue a rational foreign policy. For their part, anti-Communists saw themselves as a protest movement on the defensive against a power structure of liberal internationalists who failed to understand the Communist threat.

The Beginning

The history of anticommunism passed through five stages from its beginnings in 1917 until communism's collapse as an international movement at the end of the 1980s. The first period began with the Bolshevik takeover in Russia that touched off a series of Communist revolutions in Europe. When these were followed by a general strike in Seattle in February 1919 and a wave of political bombings that spring, many Americans and much of the press feared that America was also on the brink of a revolution. The government formed an antiradical division of the Justice Department, led by the young J. Edgar Hoover, who led a roundup of alien anarchists and Communists in December 1918 and January 1919, intended as a prelude to an attack on the entire American radical movement.

A disorganized movement of more responsible and knowledgeable anti-Communists, motivated by communism's threat to their own group interests, included Jewish anti-Communists like Louis Marshall of the American Jewish Committee, who tried to protect American Jews from the Jewish-Bolshevik stereotype, and socialists like Abraham Cahan, editor of the *Jewish Forward*, who was dismayed by the fate of Jewish social-

ists in Russia. Among Catholic anti-Communists Father Edmund A. Walsh of Georgetown University (founder of its Foreign Service School) saw communism primarily as an enemy of the Roman Catholic Church, while Patrick Scanlan of the *Brooklyn Tablet* saw anticommunism as a way to advance Catholics at the expense of the Church's rivals.

There were black anti-Communists, like George Schuyler, Harlem editor of the *Pittsburgh Courier*, who targeted black Communists for denunciation and satire. There were disillusioned ex-Communists and ex-fellow travelers. After Stalin's repression of his rivals in the late 1920s, ex-Communists such as Ben Gitlow, Jay Lovestone, Isaac Don Levine, Bertram Wolfe, and Eugene Lyons, and ex-front members such as J. B. Matthews (whose *Memoirs of a Fellow Traveler* became classic reading for right-wing anti-Communists) became anti-Communist activists. Labor anti-Communists like Samuel Gompers and David Dubinsky worried about Communist attempts to subvert the unions. But there were also countersubversive anti-Communists concocting fanciful red web smears, among them Attorney General Harry Daugherty, Blair Coan, Richard Whitney, Nesta Webster, Ralph Easley, and Hamilton Fish, who held the first congressional investigations of communism in 1930 and 1931.

Anti-Fascism Versus Anti-Communism

The second chapter in the history of anticommunism began in 1933, when Hitler came to power in Germany. Anti-Communists now had to choose which of the two evils, Nazism or communism, was the more immediate threat. Some, notably right-wing countersubversives and many Catholics, saw Hitler as the lesser of two evils, even an ally. In the 1930s, charismatic radio preacher Father Charles Coughlin used his newspaper *Social Justice* and his nationwide broadcasts to give voice to an anti-Semitic Catholic anticommunism, although he was opposed by anti-Communist liberal Catholics who were themselves terrified at losing the allegiance of the working class and who fought Communists in the labor unions. Once again the irresponsibility of countersubversives discredited all anti-Communists. Martin Dies of the House Un-American Activities Committee, whose staff director was J. B. Matthews, convulsed the country by "exposing" the actress Shirley Temple for lending her name to a front group. Dies also gave lunatic countersubversives like Elizabeth Dilling (who wrote *The Red Network* and *The Roosevelt Red Record*) a respectful hearing.

Left anti-Communists came to regard the Hitler-Stalin pact as a litmus test separating true anti-Nazis from supine Communists following the Moscow party line. Sidney Hook led the drive against the fronts and helped found the anti-Communist American Committee for Cultural Freedom in 1939. He also organized the Dewey Commission of Inquiry into the Truth of the Moscow Trials. Anti-Communist union leader John L. Lewis took his mine workers out of the Congress of Industrial Organizations (CIO), charging it was Communist dominated, while Matthew Woll, David Dubinsky, and George Meany fought Communists within the CIO and hired Jay Lovestone as the CIO's liaison with anti-Communist unions in Europe.

During this 1939–41 period, anti-Communists were subjected to what historian Leo Ribuffo called the "brown scare," in which the entire movement was blamed for the Nazi sympathies of a few. A serious body of writing emerged that exposed the reality of Communist subversion and espionage, such as Eugene Lyons's *The Red Decade*, 1941; Walter Krivitsky's *In Stalin's Secret Service*, 1939 (edited by Isaac Don Levine); and Jan Valtin's *Out of the Night*, 1939. Former Soviet espionage agent Whittaker Chambers took his revelations about Soviet spy networks to the State Department in 1939, but they were ignored until after the war, when Chambers became an icon of countersubversive anticommunism.

Perceived opposition to or half-hearted support for the war effort weakened anticommunism during World War II. The government staged a show sedition trial of notorious right-wing anti-Communists in 1944 to expose their Nazi sympathies, as alleged in John Roy Carlson's *Undercover*. Catholic anti-Communists also resented Franklin D. Roosevelt's war policy and judged the success of the war by the outcome in Poland and Lithuania, where pro-Soviet governments reigned. By the end of the war, anticommunism stood discredited for skepticism about the good intentions of Stalin and American Communists, who were, respectively, America's most important ally and the war's most vigorous supporters.

The Domestic Cold War

The third stage of anti-Communist history began with the end of World War II and the Russian occupation of Eastern Europe. The American Catholic community was galvanized by the Communist takeover of Catholic Poland, Hungary, Romania, and the rest of Eastern Europe. Bishops led protest parades in cities across the country and commissioned a study of the influence of Communists in the government, which they saw as blocking aid to the captive nations. Father John Cronin, a labor priest from Baltimore, wrote the report with the assistance of the FBI, and the Chamber of Commerce gave it national circulation during the 1946 congressional elections.

President Harry Truman, a liberal internationalist, was deeply suspicious of domestic anticommunism, likening it to witch-hunting, and actually commissioned a report to support this conclusion. This perspective led Truman to agree with a reporter's characterization of the Communists-in-government issue as a red herring. That all but ceded the security issue to countersubversive Republicans and to J. Edgar Hoover's FBI, paving the way for the emergence of Senator Joseph R. McCarthy as the new face of the anti-Communist movement.

The great spy cases of the late 1940s seemed at last to prove that a vast Communist conspiracy reached to the highest levels of the government and penetrated secret defense installations. Hoover's FBI rode a wave of popularity from its success in the spy and Smith Act cases that imprisoned the leadership of the American Communist Party. To create public support for the internment of Communists and their sympathizers in the event of hostilities with the Soviet Union, Hoover launched a mass media campaign to indoctrinate the public in anti-Communist ideology.

Liberal anti-Communists mobilized to fight Communist influence in culture and politics. With the help of the CIA, they organized the Congress for Cultural Freedom, founded by Arthur Koestler and Sidney Hook, to combat the Soviet peace offensive against the Marshall Plan and the Truman Doctrine, and sponsored anti-Communist intellectual journals like *Preuves* and *Encounter*. Anti-Communist liberals like Eleanor Roosevelt, Hubert Humphrey, Walter Reuther, Arthur Schlesinger Jr., and David Dubinsky launched the Americans for Democratic Action to combat communism in the Democratic Party and opposed Henry Wallace's progressive campaign for president in 1948.

McCarthyism and the Collapse of the Anti-Communist Consensus

The fourth stage of anti-Communist history began with the rise of Senator McCarthy in 1950, bringing to an end this uneasy coalition of conservative, left, and liberal anti-Communists, and leaving the movement nearly totally discredited and with little influence in

American politics. McCarthy's indiscriminate smearing of liberals during his notorious Senate hearings conjured up images of anticommunism as the new face of American fascism, and his incredible Senate speech accusing George Marshall of being a Communist traitor raised questions about his sanity. His reign between 1950 and 1954 demolished whatever fragile consensus had bound together liberal, socialist, and conservative anti-Communists in the early cold war years.

Their support for McCarthy pushed conservative and countersubversive anti-Communists outside the respectable mainstream of American politics. Liberal and left anti-Communists were wary of anything that might associate them with such pariahs. That reluctance was reinforced with the emergence of Robert Welch's John Birch Society, built around its leader's theory that Dwight D. Eisenhower himself was a "conscious, deliberate agent of the Soviet conspiracy." A vigorous liberal counterattack against Welch succeeded in branding all ideological anticommunism as "extremist," the kiss of death in American politics. The Kennedy administration used the extremist issue against right-wing anti-Communists, as did Lyndon Johnson in his 1964 campaign against Barry Goldwater, another anti-Communist icon. The Kennedy administration ended anti-Communist indoctrination programs in the armed forces, claiming they fueled dangerous extremism. By this time it was inadvisable for anti-Communists to bring up the subject of communism as an ideological justification for the cold war without being (self)-caricatured as belonging to the lunatic anti-Communist right.

Meanwhile, developments in the Roman Catholic Church were carrying the mass of American Catholics out of the anti-Communist movement. Anticommunism had been a vehicle to social respectability for American Catholics because it allowed them to demonstrate their patriotism. McCarthy's disgrace had been a serious setback, but with the election of Kennedy, American Catholics felt they could dispense with the tainted crutch of anticommunism. Pope John XXIII opened the Church to a dialogue with the left, and the Kennedy administration's equation of anticommunism with extremism provided more motivation for Catholics to discard the movement, to the dismay of true believers like William F. Buckley Jr.

One of the paradoxes of the Vietnam War was that it was an essentially anti-Communist conflict in which there was little discussion of the anti-Communist ideological basis for the war, leaving by default the liberal internationalist domino theory as its justification. Nevertheless, the disastrous course of the war, the publication of the *Pentagon Papers*, the Watergate scandal, and the Church Committee investigations of government security agencies in 1975 resulted in anticommunism being blamed not only for Vietnam but, by implication, for a misguided cold war foreign policy. By the end of the 1970s, the United States had a president, Jimmy Carter, who decried the nation's alleged "inordinate fear of communism." Anticommunism had achieved the dubious status of national scapegoat for much of what had gone wrong at home and abroad, a point driven home by a library of revisionist histories about the cold war and McCarthyism.

Rebirth and Redemption?

Now began the fifth and final chapter in the story of American anticommunism: its improbable and vigorous rebirth during the Ronald Reagan administration. By 1976 anticommunism was, in the opinion of Norman Podhoretz, the editor of *Commentary* (sponsored by the anti-Communist American Jewish Committee), a taboo term in American political discourse. Meanwhile, Soviet dissidents like Andrei Sakharov and Alexander Solzhenitsyn scolded Americans for abandoning anticommunism. Podhoretz revived the discussion of communism and helped organize the Committee on the Present Danger (along with Paul Nitze and Eugene Rostow), populated with surviving members of the Jewish, Socialist, and labor union anti-Communist movements along with big business conservatives, retired military officers, and old-time architects of cold war foreign policy.

The Committee launched a withering attack on Carter's arms negotiations strategy and furnished the Reagan campaign with its foreign policy expertise. Almost all its members were appointed to powerful positions in the Reagan administration.

Reagan was arguably the nation's first and only truly anti-Communist president, a product of labor union anticommunism of the late 1940s and early 1950s. He appointed the anti-Communist William F. Casey as director of central intelligence. Casey convinced Reagan that the time was ripe to roll back communism, and the administration began funneling arms, money, and moral support to anti-Communist insurgencies and dissidents around the world. Reagan's Evil Empire speech of 1983 unabashedly made the anti-Communist critique of the Soviet Union the moral basis for American foreign policy, and he used Catholic and AFL-CIO anti-Communists to aid the Polish Solidarity movement that opened the first fatal crack in the iron curtain.

With the collapse of the Soviet Union in 1991, American anticommunism had achieved its main goal. Outside of the movement itself, it got little credit. Because it is identified with the most intolerant elements of American politics, its worthwhile contributions have been generally ignored, though commentators from Russian and Eastern Europe have been more generous in giving American anticommunism some share of the credit for communism's demise. But the American anti-Communist remains, and probably will remain, a prophet without honor in his own country and in his own house.

See also communism, nativism.

FURTHER READING

Heale, M. J. *American Anticommunism: Combating the Enemy Within, 1830–1970.* Baltimore, MD: Johns Hopkins University Press, 1990.

Powers, Richard Gid. *Not without Honor: The History of American Anticommunism.* New York: Free Press, 1995.

Schrecker, Ellen. *Many Are the Crimes: McCarthyism in America.* Boston: Little, Brown, 1998.

RICHARD GID POWERS

anti-Federalists

Anti-Federalists opposed the proposed Constitution's ratification in the late 1780s. Many current scholars prefer to hyphenate the term and write it as "anti-Federalist." While this changes the label that has described this group for 200 years, it clarifies that they did not necessarily oppose Federalism, the division of governmental powers between multiple geographic levels. Instead it emphasizes that they opposed the group that championed the Constitution, who called themselves Federalists and who probably pinned the name Antifederalists on their critics to discredit them. Though the anti-Federalists represented many different views, the great majority of them objected to the amount of power the Constitution would shift to the national government. Their criticisms forced the Federalists to explain how the new government would work. They possessed sufficient strength to pass recommended amendments in five states, and they

prevented ratification for a time in two others. Many of their suggestions were incorporated into the Bill of Rights. The anti-Federalists' influence and arguments are of enduring importance in the United States, where the relationship between levels of government is frequently contentious and always evolving.

The Anti-Federalist Movement through Time

When the American colonies revolted in 1776, they did so together but as independent political states. Each of these states retained its sovereignty, or ultimate decision-making power. Most who favored revolution wanted self-government by each state because they identified with their state more than they did with America as a whole. They were also convinced that self-government was more likely to work in a small territory, a point made by political philosopher Baron de Montesquieu in the 1750s. The colonists' experience with the British government seemed to prove Montesquieu right. The British Empire did not allow colonists representation in Parliament, and King George III had come to dictate colonial policy. In opposing the Constitution, the anti-Federalists believed that they were preserving the individual rights and popular rule that had been vindicated by the American Revolution from a dangerous attempt to recentralize government on a continental scale.

Those who wanted to preserve state power were wary of calls for a constitutional convention in the mid-1780s. Rhode Island decided not to send delegates to the Philadelphia convention in 1787 and others, like Virginia's Patrick Henry, refused to attend. When it became clear that the convention would exceed its authority to revise the Articles of Confederation and propose a new sovereign national government, New York's Robert Yates and John Lansing left it, never to return. After serious fights over many provisions, there was no one fully satisfied with the final document, although most of the delegates were sufficiently satisfied to back the proposed government. However, seven delegates were so concerned about the Constitution that they did not support it when it became public in September 1787.

They were joined by numerous newspaper editorials and pamphlets objecting to the Constitution, most written by people employing pseudonyms. Some of these authors, like "Brutus," "Centinel," and the "Federal Farmer," wrote series of letters in late 1787 and into 1788 explaining why adopting the Constitution unamended would be problematic. Some of their commentary was shrill and alarmist. Other commentary was measured and sober. Some authors fanned popular prejudices. Others employed arguments borrowed from respected political thinkers like Montesquieu. Despite differences in style and tone, together the anti-Federalists ensured that the Constitution was thoroughly examined. Through this ratification debate, Federalists were made to articulate how the Constitution would work and to explain its benefits.

The ratification debate was longer and more contentious in some states than others. Delaware, Georgia, Connecticut, and New Jersey ratified the document quickly and without much opposition. Pennsylvania's ratification occurred quickly, but its critics were silenced in the state convention, prompting them to circulate a petition objecting to the convention's actions and articulating their objections to the Constitution. In most of the remaining states, anti-Federal forces were strong enough to prevent a straightforward ratification. Federalists in Massachusetts responded by agreeing to a list of recommended amendments. Four of the next five states, including the large and politically powerful states of Virginia and New York, ratified with recommended amendments.

Many anti-Federalists advocated holding a second constitutional convention that would consider these proposals. Federalists objected, thinking that a second convention would threaten what had been accomplished in Philadelphia. Ratification was secured only after enough states had approved of the document for it to go into effect. Some anti-Federalists in New York's convention had to vote for ratification to secure its passage. They did so, probably to keep the national capital in New York City.

As believers in the rule of law, the vast majority of anti-Federalists pledged to abide by the new government as the nation prepared for its implementation. Promises from Federalists that the national government possessed only limited powers and the expectation that amendments would be considered allowed them to think that their worst fears would not be realized. Federalists won a landslide victory in the first federal elections, ending a number of anti-Federalist political careers as a result. With anti-Federalist strongholds North Carolina and Rhode Island still not part of the new national government, it was up to the Federalists to formulate amendments, but most were willing to ignore the anti-Federalists' concerns.

However, during the First Congress, James Madison convinced his colleagues that they should frame amendments to bolster the legitimacy of the new government.

Madison wrote 15 amendments that guaranteed individual rights and assured Americans that the national government possessed only limited power. By 1791 ten of these amendments had become part of the Constitution, protecting such fundamental freedoms as the right to worship without government interference, the guarantee of a free press, and the right to peaceably assemble and petition the government. Additionally, the Tenth Amendment codified the Federalists' reassurance that the "powers not delegated to the United States by the Constitution . . . are reserved to the States respectively, or to the people." In other words, the national government's power was to be limited to the responsibilities outlined in the Constitution itself.

Most anti-Federalists opposed the policies formulated by the Federalist Congress and implemented by the Washington administration in the early and mid-1790s. They forged an alliance with Thomas Jefferson, James Madison, and other like-minded supporters of the Constitution who came to feel that the national government was exercising too much power. This coalition became the Democratic-Republican Party. They used the Federalists' ratification arguments against them, insisting that the national government had limited powers and that the Federalists were exceeding them in many cases.

The Federalists continued to denigrate their opponents as "Antifederalists" throughout the 1790s, wanting to link their opponents with their losing battle against the Constitution. But the Democratic-Republican Party swept the elections of 1800 and this coalition, including most of the former anti-Federalists, attempted to roll back many Federalist policies to restrict the national government to what they thought was proper.

Anti-Federalist Views
Anti-Federalists often disagreed with each other about why the Constitution was problematic and how its flaws should be remedied. The most ardent opponents of the Constitution wanted the states to retain their sovereignty. They preferred the weak alliance of states that already existed under the Articles of Confederation to any national government. Even an amended Constitution would not have satisfied them because it would still have set up a stronger national government.

Among the critics of the Constitution representing this view were New York's delegates to the Philadelphia convention, Robert Yates and John Lansing. They suggested that the policies formulated by a national government would differ fundamentally from their own states' preferences and interests. While their argument fit with the widely accepted view that sovereignty could not be divided, in practice the United States was already more than a confederation of independent states. Most citizens also recognized that the United States was disadvantaged by its weakness and that centralizing reforms were necessary.

The largest group of anti-Federalists was willing to lodge more power in a national government but thought that the Constitution granted the nation too much power or that it would render the states powerless over time. These figures stressed that the "necessary and proper clause" and the "supremacy clause" of the Constitution might be used to allow the national government to do whatever it wished. Among them was Brutus, a middle-class pamphleteer who stressed that the state governments were more representative than the national government would be.

Early in the ratification debate, a prominent Federalist, James Wilson, suggested that the Constitution granted only enumerated powers to the national government. The U.S. Congress could only make laws on the subjects listed in Article I, Section VIII of the Constitution, Wilson said. His argument was repeated by many Federalists, and it was a major concession to this group of anti-Federalists. They may have doubted the sincerity of these Federalist pledges, but after ratification they did their best to hold the Federalists to this promise, and the Tenth Amendment helped them to make their case. This group came to work fairly comfortably within the Constitution's bounds, using its language and logic to oppose Federalist initiatives.

A few other anti-Federalists objected narrowly to the lack of popular representation in the new government. Their objection was rooted in a philosophical preference for a "mixed republic," where each institution of government represents a different interest in society, a view not shared by many who criticized the Constitution. These elite figures were comfortable with the Senate being few in number so it could represent property, or a "natural aristocracy," but they felt that the House of Representatives should be expanded to represent average citizens. Initially, the House was slated to have just 65 members. People like Elbridge Gerry, a wealthy Boston merchant who refused to sign the Constitution, suggested that the House should be significantly expanded to represent people from various walks of life.

The anti-Federalist coalition was formidable, perhaps even encompassing a majority of the politically literate

and empowered citizenry. Yet their differing philosophies and interests hurt their ability to win politically. There was no clear, constructive alternative to the Federalist proposal, because the Federalists had set the agenda by proposing the Constitution and because there was no single alternative to it that appealed to all the anti-Federalists. The anti-Federalist cause was also hurt by its geographical distribution. Some northern anti-Federalists objected to the Constitution because it accepted slavery. Some southern anti-Federalists were angered that it did not sufficiently protect that institution. Merchants were predominantly Federalist because the Constitution promised to break down trade barriers. The anti-Federalists were concentrated away from the mercantile hubs of the nation, and many of their strongholds were inland. This harmed their ability to communicate with each other. Additionally, most of the nation's newspapers were printed in the coastal areas that tended to be Federalist strongholds, a major benefit to the Federalist cause.

Nevertheless, there was a consensus among the anti-Federalists that representation would be inadequate in the new national government. The Federalists intentionally made each person elected to national office represent many people. They believed that the more people citizens would have to choose from for an office, the more likely a quality individual would be chosen. Most senators would represent over 100,000 people, and their selection was not given to the public but to state legislators. The average representative in the House would have more than 30,000 constituents. The only individuals known by enough people to get elected would be those who were already rich and famous. Anti-Federalists thus predicted that the House of Representatives would not be a representative cross section of the American electorate. Few anti-Federalists had confidence that these patrician representatives would write legislation favoring the average citizen.

Legacy

The anti-Federalists cannot be simply dismissed as losers in the fight over the Constitution. Ratification was a process that clarified how the Constitution would be implemented. It forced the Federalists to reassure their doubters and to consider adopting amendments, even though it did not alter the institutions set up by the Constitution, as many anti-Federalists had hoped. The safeguards on individual rights that resulted have had an enduring effect on American law. Most of the cases before the Supreme Court involve language from the Bill of Rights. Often, one of the litigants before the Court asks that the national government's actions be limited, reflecting anti-Federalists' hopes.

Having multiple layers of government is perhaps the most distinctive feature of the American system. This federal relationship is both cooperative and contentious. Many anti-Federalists noted the tendency of centralized government to expand its reach and eclipse the power of state and local governments. American history seems to vindicate these predictions. Additionally, their actions, both during the ratification debate and afterward, served to put a brake on the extension of national power and helped to preserve state autonomy. Some find this effort worthy and others find it problematic, yet there is little doubt that they helped preserve the states as the main locus of government action in their time.

Among the anti-Federalists were individuals who later became powerful figures in the national government. They took their experience from the ratification fight into a variety of political offices. Presidents James Monroe and John Quincy Adams had expressed their opposition to the Constitution, as did vice presidents George Clinton and Elbridge Gerry. A host of the Constitution's critics were elected to Congress and state legislatures, the last of them serving into the 1820s.

Ironically, the anti-Federalists must also be credited with helping to legitimate the Constitution itself. Their acquiescence to the ratified document helped to move it beyond a contentious document weakened by the divisive ratification fight. In the 1790s, when they employed James Wilson's argument and the Constitution's language to suggest that Federalist policies were unconstitutional, they cemented the Constitution's central position in American political culture. Almost all politicians, the former anti-Federalists included, quickly came to argue that the Constitution set definitive bounds for American politics, even though they did not agree on what those bounds were.

Recently the anti-Federalists have enjoyed something of a renaissance, with many scholars rediscovering their thinking and several presses issuing compilations of their writings. Various political movements have also gained inspiration from the critics of the Constitution. Many conservatives admire the anti-Federalists for their attempt to limit national power. They suggest that a more faithful reading of the Constitution would restrict national policies and restore the independent

prerogatives of the states. A very different group, participatory democrats, wish to see a more active and engaged citizenry. They echo the anti-Federalist view that the sheer size of the national government prevents average citizens from participating and having an impact on American politics. Like many of the original critics of the Constitution, they argue that politicians would be more responsive if governmental power were more localized. The anti-Federalists' thinking should continue to be attractive to those who are not fully satisfied with U.S. politics and who wish to contemplate alternatives not fully explored in American political history.

The ratification process created a hybrid regime. No individual or group was entirely successful, including the Federalists. Their coalition was fragile, proving that the Constitution could be interpreted and administered in several different ways. The anti-Federalists learned to live with the Constitution and helped to administer it after 1800. This was not a result of them being convinced of its benefits. Rather, it was due to the respect they accorded to what had been made legal by the American people and the reassuring clarification that it sanctioned a limited government at the national level.

See also federalism; Federalist Party.

FURTHER READING

Cornell, Saul. "The Changing Historical Fortunes of the Anti-Federalists." *Northwestern University Law Review* 84 (1989), 39–73.

———. *The Other Founders: Anti-Federalists and the Dissenting Tradition in America, 1788–1828.* Chapel Hill: University of North Carolina Press, 1999.

Duncan, Christopher M. *The Anti-Federalists and Early American Political Thought.* DeKalb: Northern Illinois University Press, 1995.

Finkelman, Paul. "Turning Losers into Winners: What Can We Learn, If Anything, from the Antifederalists?" *Texas Law Review* 79 (2001), 849–94.

Jensen, Merrill, John P. Kaminski, Richard Leffler, and Gaspare Saladino, eds. *The Documentary History of the Ratification of the Constitution*, 19 vols. plus microfiche supplements. Madison: State Historical Society of Wisconsin, 1976– .

Kenyon, Cecelia. "Men of Little Faith: The Anti-Federalists on the Nature of Representative Government." *William & Mary Quarterly* 3rd series, 12 (1955), 3–43.

Lienesch, Michael. "In Defense of the Anti-federalists." *History of Political Thought* 4 (1983), 65–87.

———. *Ratifying the Republic: Antifederalists and Federalists in Constitutional Time.* Stanford, CA: Stanford University Press, 2002.

Siemers, David J. *The Antifederalists: Men of Great Faith and Forbearance.* Lanham, MD: Rowman & Littlefield, 2003.

DAVID J. SIEMERS

Anti-Masonic Party

The transformation of American political culture in the second quarter of the nineteenth century cannot be understood without reference to America's original third party. The Anti-Masonic Party sprang from western New York in response to the 1826 disappearance of William Morgan, an obscure artisan kidnapped and apparently murdered by Freemasons to stop his publication of Masonic rituals. Spreading quickly throughout the Northeast and parts of the Old Northwest, the party marshaled voters by the tens of thousands behind populist evangelical and egalitarian appeals. Anti-party in rhetoric though not in practice, Anti-Masons pioneered new techniques of organization and persuasion. Placing religion and republican ideology center stage in partisan debate and insisting on the centrality of public opinion via the ballot box, this ephemeral party shaped mass politics in lasting ways.

How could Morgan's disappearance from a small village, no matter how dramatic the circumstances, trigger physical and verbal violence, divide families, churches, and communities, and create a powerful political movement? Freemasonry, a prestigious fraternal order that included founders and leaders of the new nation, expanded rapidly after the Revolution, spreading south as far as Georgia and Louisiana and west to Kentucky and Michigan Territory. Brothers exerted great political influence in many locales, initially as Federalists but increasingly as Republicans. Growth was particularly spectacular in New York, where Masons in frontier communities spearheaded local development and held elected and appointed offices out of all proportion to their numbers in the population. Masonry's emphasis on virtue, merit, and hierarchy resonated with republican values and attracted upwardly mobile men. The addition of higher degrees and new oaths to post-Revolutionary Masonry raised no red flags until "the Outrages."

Anti-Masonry began a citizens' protest against vigilantism, followed by the thwarting of justice and stonewalling by unapologetic Masons. Particularly noticeable to incipient Anti-Masons were the many public officials and jurors associated with the earliest trials of the accused in Genesee and Ontario counties in New York. Religious concerns took hold first, but early in 1827 public meetings began resolving to bar Masons from town offices. Fifteen Republican-Anti-Masons won New York Assembly seats (one-eighth of the total) in September, and Anti-Masonic slates swept some counties. Voter realignment presaging the Second Party System had begun. In 1830 Anti-Masons held the nation's first national political convention, and one year later, delegates from 12 states convened the first presidential nominating convention. Jacksonian Democrats followed suit immediately.

As a third party that split the anti-Jackson vote in most states, the Anti-Masons enjoyed mixed success. Their presidential nominee William Wirt won only Vermont, where Anti-Masons controlled the governorship and legislature for four years, but the party also briefly played pivotal roles at the state level in Pennsylvania, New York, Massachusetts, and Rhode Island. Three states prohibited extra-judicial oaths, but none abolished Freemasonry. However, the party so faded, in part, due to its success. In northern electoral strongholds Anti-Masonry kept Masons from public office for a generation, and the movement devastated Freemasonry everywhere. Lodges surrendered their charters or went underground, and membership dropped by some two-thirds nationally. Even in southern states, where Anti-Masonry did not organize politically, lodges experienced sharp declines in membership. The fraternity revived in the 1840s but never regained its earlier public influence.

Historians have struggled to explain this firestorm, debating Anti-Masonry's left-wing or right-wing tendencies, its mix of religious and political-ideological motivations, and partisans' social characteristics. In places studied systematically, Anti-Masons came from all socioeconomic strata and especially from the rising middle class of towns and villages. Some New England Anti-Masons seemed anxious about market-inspired changes. But, in the party's western New York heartland, the most economically developed or rapidly developing towns supported Anti-Masonry overwhelmingly. There, party leaders co-operated with other local boosters to spur internal improvements and banking. Everywhere, Anti-Masonry politicized evangelical Protestants, with some churches barring loyal Masons.

A bottom-up party, the Anti-Masons harnessed a tradition of popular protest and politicization dating from the Revolution to an innovative means of persuasion. Anti-Masons, along with Jacksonian Democrats, constructed the new mass politics of the "party period." Organizers utilized the communications revolution to tell and re-tell the Morgan narrative through newspapers, including some 100 new ones; almanacs; broadsides; public inquiries; traveling lecturers, and dramatization of lodge rituals. Appealing directly to "the people" with stirring calls for "equal rights and equal privileges," the party enlisted thousands of activists, including many new to politics, for a hierarchy of delegate conventions and grassroots Anti-Masonic committees which sometimes extended to the school district level. And some women, as well as men, entered an expanding public sphere to embrace Anti-Masonry. In at least one instance "Anti-Masonic ladies" passed resolutions condemning Masonry, among its other dangers, as a threat to family life.

Anti-Masons had responded to an immediate local situation and to existing powerful currents of political egalitarianism, religious revivalism, economic optimism, moral reform, and domesticity. Along New York's booming Erie Canal and across "the universal Yankee nation," a secret, closed, oath-bound, all-male society that privileged its members seemed to threaten economic and political opportunity, piety, family life, and a republic of laws controlled by the people. When Anti-Masonry turned political, organizers such as Thurlow Weed made the most of this perfect storm of circumstances and the populist passions it aroused. As Masonry waned, leaders broadened the party's appeal, backing other reforms, such as abolition of imprisonment for debt (accomplished in New York in 1831), and government-supported economic development.

With few exceptions, Anti-Masons moved into the Whig Party as it took shape in the 1830s. They provided Whiggery with leaders like Weed, William H. Seward, and Thaddeus Stevens and with a large, persistent evangelical voting block and reformist wing. Subsequently they helped shape political insurgencies emerging from the sectional crisis, including the Free Soil movement and the Republican Party. The Anti-Masonic Party, albeit short-lived, had contributed to the new political culture of the mid-nineteenth century, and its former

partisans continued to inject a moralistic and egalitarian dimension into American politics.

See also antiparty sentiment; Whig Party.

FURTHER READING

Bullock, Steven. *Revolutionary Brotherhood: Freemasonry and the Transformation of the American Social Order, 1730–1840.* Chapel Hill: University of North Carolina Press, 1996.

Formisano, Ronald P. *For the People: American Populist Movements from the Revolution to the 1850s.* Chapel Hill: University of North Carolina Press, 2008.

Goodman, Paul. *Towards a Christian Republic: Antimasonry and the Great Transition in New England, 1826–1836.* New York: Oxford University Press, 1988.

Holt, Michael F. "The Antimasonic and Know Nothing Parties." In *History of U.S. Political Parties,* edited by Arthur M. Schlesinger Jr., 575–620. New York: Chelsea House, 1973.

Kutolowski, Kathleen Smith. "Antimasonry Reexamined: Social Bases of the Grass-Roots Party." *Journal of American History* 71 (September 1984), 269–93.

Vaughn, William Preston. *The Anti-Masonic Party in the United States, 1826–1843.* Lexington: University Press of Kentucky, 1983.

KATHLEEN SMITH KUTOLOWSKI

antiparty sentiment

Hostility toward the political party has been an important dimension of American culture from the earliest days of the republic. During the first three or four decades following the adoption of the Constitution, antiparty sentiment derived primarily from the central tenets of classical republican theory, as this ancient body of thought was developed and reshaped by British political philosophers during the seventeenth and eighteenth centuries. Particularly important were two related concepts: that effective and just government flows from the decisions of virtuous leaders pursuing the public good rather than their own or others' private interests; and that the political influence of those interests and interest groups that do emerge within society must be transitory and contained, so that no single interest acquires enduring power over all others and over the republic as a whole. The notion of party was antithetical to these concepts and was universally condemned by the Founding Fathers (who used the terms *party* and *faction* interchangeably), even before anything resembling an institutionalized political party appeared on the American landscape.

To be sure, some of the most prominent spokesmen for the republican creed—Thomas Jefferson, James Madison, Alexander Hamilton, John Adams, and even George Washington, whose Farewell Address of 1796 remains the classic American warning against the dangers of party—quickly behaved in accordance with the first system of enduring alignments that could be identified as partisan. But the Federalists and Republicans of the early republic did not develop the elaborate institutional structures of later political parties, and their leaders perpetuated antiparty principles, in public discourse at least, by claiming that they and their allies worked for the common good while their opponents threatened good government by representing a specific constellation of interests. As the historian Richard Hofstadter has pointed out, neither party accepted the legitimacy of the other, while in power or as a formal opposition. Both sought to eradicate the other, and when the Republicans succeeded in doing this in the aftermath of the War of 1812, they were able to interpret their success as the fulfillment of classic republican principles.

The factionalism that soon bedeviled the triumphant Republicans gave way during the 1830s and 1840s to a fully institutionalized and enduring two-party system, and to a new set of ideas that legitimated the party as necessary to the functioning of a viable democracy. In this era of mass voter mobilization by Democrats and Whigs (the latter replaced by Republicans before the Civil War), well-organized parties linked themselves not only to new theories of power and legitimate opposition but also to popular ideas and symbols intended to establish each party as truly national and fully American, and therefore less worrisome as ongoing representatives of specific programs and interests. Antiparty sentiment, in this new environment, was deliberately weakened; yet, it survived not merely as an old-fashioned idea but discovered a new foundation in the very success of political parties as institutions.

As the parties grew, they developed professional roles and a set of cultural and behavioral codes that emphasized institutional loyalty and reward. Perhaps more than party platforms supporting or opposing one or another interest-based program, professionalism and patronage undermined each party's republican charac-

ter. Increasingly, Americans defined partisan activists as "politicians," driven by the quest for power and for private reward in the form of government jobs or contracts rather than by service to the public good, even when that good was loftily declared in the party's specific program. And in the pursuit of power and its spoils, politicians debased the electoral process with vulgar campaign practices and widespread bribery and intimidation at the polls. The corruption that followed from self-interest was now to many Americans—including regular voters and avid partisans—the concrete property of the party system.

Even before this system was fully formed, antiparty sentiment helped fuel a number of dissenting movements, including several that put themselves forward as alternative political parties, freer from the corruption inherent in routine partisan activity. The Know-Nothings of the 1850s, for example, attracted some of their adherents by portraying themselves in this way. Such dissent could emerge, too, from within the parties, as it did in the decades following the Civil War, when groups of mostly well-to-do Republicans, and somewhat later their counterparts in the Democratic Party, urged civil service reform, educational campaigns, voter registration, secret balloting, and other changes to a party system increasingly perceived as disreputable.

These reforms may have succeeded in elevating the reputation of the political system, but they did not prevent a general weakening of partisan identity during the course of the twentieth century. Traditional antiparty themes such as political careerism, corruption, and the pursuit of interests opposed to the general good continued and still remain persuasive in political discourse. They have manifested themselves in a long trend toward independent voter registration (by the end of the twentieth century, independents were as numerous as either Democrats or Republicans among registered voters), toward the elevation of nonpartisanship as apolitical ideal, and toward more personalized political campaigns, stressing the qualities of the candidate rather than his or her party affiliation and in many cases portraying the candidate as a political outsider transcending mere partisanship. Even third-party movements have been more frequently organized around highly visible and often charismatic leaders, from Theodore Roosevelt and Robert La Follette to Ross Perot and Ralph Nader.

Parties remain central to the American political process. But they continue to function within a culture long suspicious about partisan methods and motives and newly inclined to reduce the role of parties in the shaping of public affairs.

See also republicanism.

FURTHER READING

Altschuler, Glenn C., and Stuart M. Blumin. *Rude Republic: Americans and Their Politics in the Nineteenth Century.* Princeton, NJ: Princeton University Press, 2000.

Formisano, Ronald P. *The Transformation of Political Culture: Massachusetts Parties, 1790s–1840s.* New York: Oxford University Press, 1983.

Hofstadter, Richard. *The Idea of a Party System: The Rise of Legitimate Opposition in the United States, 1780–1840.* Berkeley: University of California Press, 1969.

McCormick, Richard L., ed. *Political Parties and the Modern State.* New Brunswick, NJ: Rutgers University Press, 1984.

Silbey, Joel H. *The American Political Nation, 1838–1893.* Stanford, CA: Stanford University Press, 1991.

Voss-Hubbard, Mark. *Beyond Party: Cultures of Antipartisanship in Northern Politics before the Civil War.* Baltimore, MD: Johns Hopkins University Press, 2002.

Wallace, Michael. "Changing Concepts of Party in the United States: New York, 1815–1828." *American Historical Review* 74 (December 1968), 453–91.

STUART M. BLUMIN

anti-statism

Although conservative Austrian economist Friedrich A. Hayek first employed the term *statism* in 1944 as part of a critique of modern governance, hostility to centralized political power has profound roots in the American experience. Borrowing notions from liberal theorists John Locke and Adam Smith, American Revolution leaders contrasted natural property rights with the privileges of political and market power. A concurrent republican ideology endorsed liberation from government coercion and freedom from the tyrannies of bureaucracy and standing armies. By the 1830s, the followers of President Andrew Jackson had codified such sentiment into a campaign against government-licensed monopolies like the Second Bank of the United States. Free market advocates of nineteenth-century producer democracy continued to celebrate the perceived advantages of a government whose laissez-faire policies left corporations and individual enterprisers freed from state interference. Not surprisingly, Congress and the federal courts viewed regulation of business and the workplace as violations of constitutional rights of property.

As a complex industrial order convinced Progressive-era reformers like educator John Dewey and economist Richard T. Ely to advocate government use of scientific expertise to serve the general welfare, small business and independent farming interests increasingly took exception. In Wisconsin, the Democratic Party contested rule by reform-minded Republicans in 1912 and 1914 with charges that "tax-eating commissions" and remote bureaucrats had imposed paternalistic rule on ordinary people. A similar cry characterized the protests of Idaho Republican Senator William E. Borah in the 1920s. "The remorseless urge of centralization" and "the insatiable maw of bureaucracy," complained Borah, deprived "more and more the people of all voice, all rights touching home and hearthstone, of family and neighbor."

Suspicion of government rule accelerated in the later stages of President Franklin D. Roosevelt's New Deal. Employing a "brain trust" of academic advisers and planning consultants to fashion a consumer-oriented revival of the economy, Roosevelt came under fire for a lack of political accountability to constituencies beyond his electoral coalition. As producer interests attacked the administration's judicial and executive reorganization plans, deficit spending, ties to organized labor, and sponsorship of social experimentation, critics began to picture Washington, D.C., as a hotbed of "strangers" to the American way. During World War II, when domestic agencies like the Office of Price Administration (OPA) and the National Resources Planning Board (NRPB) sought systemic solutions to wartime inflation and prospects of postwar unemployment, congressional critics of government concentration closed down New Deal agencies and welcomed a spate of polemics about the dangers of excessive bureaucracy.

Hayek's anti-statist treatise, *The Road to Serfdom*, was one of five such works published in 1944. The unitary economic power of the managerial state was a threat to human freedom and personal liberty, insisted the author, because it sought to control productive output and distribution. Behind government collectivism, Hayek saw the shadowy hand of technical specialists who used their expertise to advance an agenda that furthered their own role in the administrative machinery. By focusing on the political intelligentsia's ties to state power, Hayek anticipated Milovan Djilas's descriptions of the New

Class. A former official in Communist Yugoslavia imprisoned for dissenting views, Djilas contended that socialized economies allowed managers and officials to serve their own class interests by administering collectivized property.

Speculation over the policy-making influence of New Class intellectuals prompted a number of social scientists in the United States to apply such a model at home. Sociologist Alvin W. Gouldner's *The Future of Intellectuals and the Rise of the New Class* (1979) suggested that knowledge elites were often responsible for policies involving state regulation of production and the provision of social welfare services. Beginning in the late 1960s, a more critical portrait emerged from a group of neoconservatives including economist Milton Friedman, sociologist Daniel P. Moynihan, social commentator Michael Novak, and editor Norman Podhoretz. These critics condemned a powerful cabal of collectivist bureaucrats and planners who consolidated a hold on power by providing social services to the poor and administering an antibusiness regulatory structure.

As federal involvement in civil rights placed Washington, D.C., in a controversial light in the South and elsewhere in the 1950s and 1960s, antigovernment discourse broadened. The first politician to exploit such hostility was Alabama governor George C. Wallace. Running in several Democratic presidential primaries outside the South in 1964, Wallace abandoned rhetoric about white supremacy and focused on the social engineering of a federal government that ruled by executive or judicial edict. Arizona's Republican Senator Barry Goldwater made a similar case in the general election campaign. Centralized planning, bureaucracy, and regimentation, charged Goldwater, had produced a government of "easy morals and uneasy ethics." Although Republican Richard Nixon occasionally embraced conservative critiques of big government and the liberal establishment, Ronald Reagan proved to be the twentieth century's most successful inheritor of the anti-statist mantle. Campaigning for Goldwater in 1964, Reagan warned that "government can't control the economy without controlling the people." Two years later the popular Republican sailed into the California governor's chair by directing conservative critiques of state power to exposure of the seemingly wasteful welfare programs of President Lyndon B. Johnson's Great Society. Similar approaches energized Reagan's election to the White House in 1980. Promising to "take the government off the backs of the people," the populist conservative heralded "an

era of national renewal" freed from federal bureaucracy and excessive taxation. Accordingly, Reagan cut taxes, reduced corporate regulation, trimmed welfare spending, and limited federal civil rights enforcement.

Following the election of President George H. W. Bush in 1988, Republican strategists boasted of a "new paradigm" that rejected rule by experts and bureaucrats. By the early twenty-first century, however, increasing concerns about health care, social security, pension viability, and federal responses to the threats of terrorism and natural disasters profoundly complicated the conversation about state power. After more than two centuries of heated debate over the proper place of government in a democratic society, Americans seem as uncertain as ever over the legitimate role of knowledge professionals, human service practitioners, and administrative specialists who have ruled in their name.

See also conservatism.

FURTHER READING

Brinkley, Alan. *The End of Reform: New Deal Liberalism in Recession and War*. New York: Vintage, 1995.

Edsall, Thomas Byrne, with Mary D. Edsall. *Chain Reaction: The Impact of Race, Rights, and Taxes on American Politics*. New York: Norton, 1991.

Hayek, Friedrich A. *The Road to Serfdom*. Chicago: University of Chicago Press, 1944.

Horowitz, David A. *America's Political Class under Fire: The Twentieth Century's Great Culture War*. New York: Routledge, 2003.

DAVID A. HOROWITZ

armed forces, politics in the

In considering the connection between politics and the American armed forces, three features are most noteworthy: first, the political attitudes and relations that develop within the services; second, the political connections that develop with civilians, notably political leaders, outside the services; and third, the role of the armed forces as a political lobby—not just in terms of their role in promoting debates over national security but in relation to their place and function in society. Such an approach was pioneered in Samuel P. Huntington's book *The*

Soldier and the State (1957). Soldiers in particular have played a significant part in American politics even before independence. The glamor and heroism implicit in military service have proved alluring. Electoral competition at every level could be promoted if the candidate had been in earshot of what George Washington described as the "charming sound" of bullets. The American republic shared one important feature with the Roman republic of antiquity: both witnessed a large degree of interpenetration between military and political institutions, with politicians eager to become military men, and vice versa. But American military heroes, unlike their Roman counterparts, have not sought to overthrow the U.S. Constitution and set up a dictatorship. They have preferred advancement within strict constitutional boundaries and have rarely sought to overstep them.

The Legacy of the Revolution

The emphasis on political supervision of military affairs before 1783 reflects the revolutionary character of the revolt against the British crown. Ironically, discontent with British rule and agitation for self-government and then independence in the former colonies underlined the degree to which they had inherited British military attitudes. Occupation by small numbers of British troops provoked a latent suspicion of and hostility toward regular, standing armies and a disinclination to pay for them. Americans came to believe that standing armies were a source of tyranny, a threat to the values of popular freedom eventually expressed as liberal democracy. Here lay a source of perpetual distrust that runs throughout American history. Civilians suspected soldiers of harboring antidemocratic tendencies, and soldiers believed that civilians were prepared to indulge their prejudices to the degree that they might endanger American security itself.

In 1775 George Washington's commission as commander in chief and those of all his senior generals were issued by a Continental Congress responding to the interests of the various states and the level of commitment of each to the Revolution. "Political generals"—leaders who could exert influence over important areas of the home front—could be found in all American wars. But whether these were professional politicians or not, they unleashed disenchantment with the system of promotion and, in turn, stirred up political agitation against the leaders who had appointed them. Throughout the Revolution, Washington shrewdly ensured that civilians always remained in control. In his official relations with the Continental Congress and the state governments,

Washington chose to overlook lethargy, ignorance, and inexperience—although he inveighed against these in private—and treated them with deference, conscious of the precedents he was establishing. Civilians have been attacked in all American wars for failure to understand how to wage war and treat military men. In 1783 such discontent threatened to get out of control during the Newburgh Conspiracy, an attempt by Continental Army soldiers to secure back pay by threatening a military coup. Washington acted energetically to thwart any military intervention in politics and ensure that legitimate grievances over back pay were brought before Congress in a respectful manner.

The image of Cincinnatus, the successful Roman general who laid aside his command to return meekly to agricultural pursuits, lacking either ambition or a thirst for power, remained a potent element of the American military tradition for 150 years. It continued to exert influence after the rise of military professionalism, stimulated by the 1802 founding of the United States Military Academy at West Point. The professional ethos came to embrace discipline, duty, physical fitness, and manly virtue. Soldiers believed themselves expert; they evinced a sense of superiority in relation to civilians; they felt a more powerful patriotism, were singular and devoted, moderate and rational by comparison with their selfish, grasping, and often unscrupulous political masters. From such attitudes grew the myth that soldiers avoided political entanglements. Winfield Scott boasted that he never voted; George B. McClellan admitted to doing so only once, in 1860; so, too, did Ulysses S. Grant, in 1856. Yet all these men sought the presidency. Only Grant was successful, serving two terms and desirous of a third. McClellan served as governor of New Jersey (1878–81). Many other military officers engaged in politics. In 1858 P. G. T. Beauregard ran for mayor of New Orleans, and the later General Montgomery C. Meigs thought nothing of building up congressional alliances to aid him in a dispute with the secretary of war, John B. Floyd.

Civilian Control and the Two Party System

The presumption of political "innocence" among regular officers arose partly from resentment at the failure of American leadership from the War of 1812 onward to distinguish between high political and military rank. During the Mexican-American War (1846–48), the tensions between President James K. Polk and his generals Winfield Scott and Zachary Taylor resulted not from a clash of values but from the Democratic president's justified fear that Scott and Taylor, as Whigs, would exploit any military success in subsequent runs for the presidency. Polk briefly considered placing Democrat senator Thomas Hart Benton as a lieutenant general over both of them before abandoning the idea. However, throughout the nineteenth century the nonregular soldier appeared to fit the Cincinnatus model more closely. In Andrew Jackson's first inaugural address on March 4, 1829, he declared that "the bulwark of our defence is the national militia." High rank in volunteer service proved a path to the presidency not just for Jackson, but also for William Henry Harrison, Franklin Pierce, Rutherford B. Hayes, James A. Garfield, Benjamin Harrison, and William McKinley.

In 1861 many Americans blamed the outbreak of the Civil War on selfish partisanship that had inflamed passions. Abraham Lincoln thus treated the enlistment of northern Democrats in support of the war effort as a high priority. He offered many of them senior commissions, including Benjamin F. Butler, Daniel E. Sickles, John A. Logan, and John A. McClernand. James G. Blaine, later a Republican presidential candidate and secretary of state, contended in his *Twenty Years of Congress* (1884–86) that the war could not have been won without them. War Democrats also included Secretary of War Edwin M. Stanton and Judge Advocate General Joseph Holt. Indeed, disappointed Republicans calculated that 80 out of 110 brigadier generals' commissions and 80 percent of all generals' commissions had gone to the Democratic Party opposition. In 1861–62, the three most important commands were held by Democrats: George B. McClellan, who presided as general in chief; Henry W. Halleck, who in July 1862 succeeded him; and Don Carlos Buell.

All these generals were West Point graduates. Professional soldiers tend to be conservative in politics, and before 1861 West Point had been criticized for nurturing an "aristocratic" elitism among regular officers. For years afterward Republicans accused it of having sheltered a treasonous "slave power" conspiracy, as over 26 percent of West Point graduates resigned and sought commissions in the armies of the Confederacy. The leading Democratic generals were spokesmen for military professionalism, and thus made claims for their superior knowledge of military science. They argued that they should be able to make decisions free of "political" harassment. McClellan, who admired the code of the southern gentleman, and Buell, who had southern relatives through marriage, gained a reputation for being slow, overly cautious, and incapable of making the most

of their opportunities. Their Republican critics on the Congressional Joint Committee on the Conduct of the War equated their reluctance to engage southern armies in "vigorous" operations to their conservative political views. Such critics as Senator Benjamin F. Wade of Ohio, ridiculed McClellan's use of military jargon—especially "lines of retreat"—as an excuse for moral cowardice. One War Democrat, Senator Andrew Johnson of Tennessee, joined in such denunciation because he saw McClellan as a rival for the 1864 Democratic nomination, which he eventually won after leaving the service.

Few of the antebellum regulars among the senior officers of the Union Army were opposed to slavery. In 1861 outright abolitionists, like David Hunter, were a beleaguered minority. After McClellan's removal in November 1862, the influence of Democrats waned. A growing number, like Henry W. Halleck, Ambrose E. Burnside, and Joseph Hooker, came to embrace the Emancipation Proclamation. In 1863 an aggrieved Abner Doubleday still complained that proslavery "cliques" ran the army and that "anti-McClellan men" were held back. Nonetheless, under the Grant-Sherman regime of 1864–65 most of the significant commands were held by West Pointers, though Grant evinced a skill at handling "political generals" like Butler. The soldiers in the ranks—especially in the East—who had previously adored McClellan did not vote for him in the presidential election of 1864. Lincoln and the Republican Party won 77.5 percent of the soldiers' vote.

After the Civil War, the powerful support offered to the Republican Party by the veterans' organization, the Grand Army of the Republic, foreshadowed the political sway of such twentieth-century successors as the American Legion.

The partisanship of 1861–65 had also bequeathed a bitter legacy. The sense that the regular army was "apart" from American society probably dates from the 1840s, but it came to assume greater symbolic importance after 1877. Such disillusionment had less impact in the U.S. Navy, which expanded rapidly after the 1880s. Democratic societies, in any case, have felt less antipathy toward navies, as they represented a lesser direct threat to liberty.

Resentment of the army's marginal role at the conclusion of the Indian Wars diminished respect in the ranks for the Constitution and popular democracy. Brevet Major General Emory Upton became the mouthpiece for such views. Upton argued that volunteers were invariably ineffective and that civilian control remained the central reason for American military failures. Henceforth, he argued, all decision making should be the monopoly of military professionals.

The U.S. triumphs in both world wars revealed these claims to be misguided. The role of military men in policy making worked smoothly, especially from 1941–45. Harmony prevailed because to work effectively civilian control requires trust, not sulky acquiescence. The chief of staff during World War II, George C. Marshall, spoke out candidly when he disagreed with President Franklin D. Roosevelt, but he never made any disagreements public. The basic system continued to work well after 1945 despite interservice squabbling over budgets. Most differences could be subsumed in pursuit of the common goal of winning the cold war. But the dramatic dismissal of General Douglas MacArthur in 1951 for colluding with a Republican congressman while criticizing President Harry S. Truman's policy in the Korean War (1950–53) was a portent of the tensions that would develop after 1989 with the collapse of the cold war consensus.

MacArthur's dismissal led to a revival in interest in civil-military relations, especially after the publication of Arthur M. Schlesinger Jr. and Richard H. Rovere's book on the controversy, *The General and the President and the Future of American Foreign Policy* (1952). Yet MacArthur's political record before the Korean War, in which he acted prudently and democratically as supreme commander of the Allied Powers (1945–51) in postwar Japan, belies the fear that he hankered for the military's dominance in politics.

The postwar détente smiled favorably on younger candidates for political office who fought in "the good war." All the victorious presidential candidates from 1960–92, with the exception of Ronald Reagan, had respectable service records in the U.S. Navy: John F. Kennedy, Lyndon B. Johnson, Richard Nixon, Gerald Ford, Jimmy Carter, and George H. W. Bush. Service records or the lack of them would continue to be controversial in President Bill Clinton's relations with the U.S. Army, especially, and would resurface in the 2004 presidential election in the exchanges over the relative merits of the incumbent president, George W. Bush, who did not serve in Vietnam, in comparison with that of the Democratic Party candidate, Senator John Kerry, a decorated Vietnam War veteran.

Given the importance of military service to candidates, it was hardly unexpected that the Second World War's higher commanders—mostly generals—would pursue political careers. Former Army Chief of Staff Marshall served as secretary of state (1947–49), setting a precedent whereby, after 1945, retired military men were often preferred candidates for this office, and as secretary of defense (1950–51) in the Truman administration. Dwight D. Eisenhower served two terms as president (1953–61); at the beginning of his political career, Eisenhower appeared ideologically ambiguous, and could have gained either the Democratic or Republican nomination. His instincts proved to be more conservative, however. He was committed to fiscal conservatism and "small government," suspicious of the civil rights movement, and hostile to high defense expenditures. Eisenhower's policies were subject to scathing criticism by some generals, most notably Maxwell D. Taylor in his *The Uncertain Trumpet* (1959). In 1961 John F. Kennedy summoned Taylor from retirement to become chairman of the Joint Chiefs of Staff.

Civil Military Relations since Vietnam

Compared with the MacArthur controversy during the Korean War, a civil-military consensus held up to the strain of conducting the Vietnam War reasonably well—until it was clear the conflict could not be won. By December 1969, however, the notion became popular that the errors of the war were due, as *Time* magazine explained in a feature exploring the army's "stab-in-the-back complex," to civilian leaders forcing military men to fight with "one hand tied behind their back." Another popular scapegoat was the media, which was accused of corroding support for the war by mischievous reporting, although most news agencies (both print and television) had been consistent supporters of the war. By the 1980s, however, the military had changed its tack and drew very different lessons that advised less, rather than more, force.

The reaction of all three services to the humiliation of defeat in Vietnam ushered in a new period of civil-military tensions. An initial solution was expressed in the Powell Doctrine, which resolved that the United States should never again intervene militarily unless victory was virtually guaranteed, and should always plan an "exit strategy"—a euphemism for retreat. Its author, General Colin Powell, then chairman of the Joint Chiefs of Staff, seemed to demand a right of veto over policy which echoed McClellan's practice and Upton's complaints.

At the same time, the armed services had given ground to technically minded civilian think tanks and the private sector. Many tasks were contracted out to private firms and such business techniques as management models and systems analysis were increasingly employed. Under Robert S. McNamara, secretary of defense from 1961–67, the value of military experience had been subordinated to earlier, similar, techniques, advanced by "whiz kids" equipped with slide rules. But, from the 1990s onward, civilianization represented a major assault on the military ethos; in short, the military could be treated as "just another profession." Other armed forces with comparable traditions, like the British, faced similar threats.

The Future of Civil Control

The armed forces reacted to such challenges with a politically alert response that exploited unprecedented levels of public support evident since the Gulf War of 1991. Senior officers did not hesitate to express partisan political opinions. The habit of endorsing presidential candidates began with Admiral William J. Crowe for Clinton in 1992. Powell and General Norman Schwarzkopf, former commander in chief of the U.S. Central Command and overall commander in the Gulf War of 1990–91, supported Robert Dole in 1996; the majority of the senior military supported George W. Bush in 2000 (and Powell served as his first secretary of state). In December 2007, more than 100 retired admirals and generals (with 54 of them at four-star rank) endorsed Senator John McCain for the Republican nomination.

It is therefore ironic that the most bitter recent political tussle between the armed forces and a presidential administration should be with that of the party that the military supported at the polls. Opposition to Secretary of Defense Donald H. Rumsfeld escalated as the 2003 invasion of Iraq touched off a long war. In April 2006, a group of retired senior officers launched a scathing attack on Rumsfeld, violating the principle laid down by George Marshall that disputes should never be made public until the administration concerned has left office.

Such events pose serious questions for the future of civilian control. The military risks being seen as just another political lobby that invites purges of its senior ranks. In 2007–8, criticism of the role of General David Petraeus as the "front man" of the Bush administration's policy in Iraq hinted that the neutrality of the armed forces, and especially the U.S. Army, had become suspect. Scholars have detected a rise in the "militarization" of American society, and fear that the army again stands apart from the mainstream of American society. Officers frequently voice hostility to what they see as a hedonistic society that contrasts unfavorably with their own ethos.

This shift to increased politicization, Richard H. Kohn has argued, can only be arrested when civilians especially regard the armed forces with renewed knowledge and sympathy. Such knowledge cannot be assumed to exist among the members of any one political party. Donald Rumsfeld provoked more hostility than any other secretary of defense for 40 years. Servicemen and women must also reflect on the price paid for forfeiting political neutrality.

See also war and politics.

FURTHER READING

Blaine, James G. *Twenty Years of Congress.* 2 vols. Norwich, CT: Henry Bill, 1884–86.

Cunliffe, Marcus. *Soldiers and Civilians: The Martial Spirit in America, 1775–1865.* New York: Little, Brown, 1968.

Feaver, Peter D., and Richard H. Kohn, eds. *Soldiers and Civilians: The Civil Military Gap and American National Security.* Cambridge, MA: MIT Press, 2001.

Higginbotham, Don. *George Washington and the American Military Tradition.* Athens: University of Georgia Press, 1985.

Huntington, Samuel P. *The Soldier and the State: The Theory and Politics of Civil-Military Relations.* Cambridge, MA: Belknapp Press, 1957.

Kohn, Richard H. "The Danger of Militarization in an Endless 'War' on Terrorism." *Journal of Military History* 73 (January 2009), 177–208.

———. "The Erosion of Civil Control of the Military in the United States Today." *Naval War College Review* 55 (Summer 2002), 9–59.

———. "Using the Military at Home: Yesterday, Today and Tomorrow." *Chicago Journal of International Law* 4 (Spring 2003), 165–92.

Loveland, Anne C. *American Evangelicals and the U.S. Military, 1942–1993.* Baton Rouge: Louisiana State University Press, 1996.

Reid, Brian Holden, and Joseph G. Dawson III, eds. "The Vistas of American Military History, 1800–1898." Special issue, *American Nineteenth Century History* 7 (June 2006), 139–321.

Rovere, Richard, and Arthur M. Schlesinger Jr. *General MacArthur and President Truman: The Struggle for Control of American Foreign Policy.* 1952. Reprint, New Brunswick, NJ: Transaction Books, 1992.

Taylor, Maxwell D. *The Uncertain Trumpet.* New York: Harper, 1959.

Upton, Emory. *The Military Policy of the United States.* 1904. Reprint, New York: Greenwood, 1968.

Weigley, Russell F. "The American Military and the Principle of Civilian Control from McClellan to Powell." *Journal of Military History* 57 (October 1993), 27–58.

———. "The Soldier, the Statesman and the Military Historian." *Journal of Military History* 63 (October 1999), 807–22.

BRIAN HOLDEN REID

Articles of Confederation

The Articles of Confederation and Perpetual Union, drafted in 1776, formed the first written constitution of the United States, in which the 13 newly independent states entered "into a firm league of friendship with each other, for their common defense, the security of their liberties, and their mutual and general welfare, binding themselves to assist each other, against all force offered to, or attacks made upon them, or any of them, on account of religion, sovereignty, trade, or any other pretense whatever." Known to history as the unfortunate predecessor of the federal Constitution of 1787, the articles have generally had a bad reputation, for on the eve of the 1787 convention the Congress they created had virtually ceased to function. In the estimation of Federalist critics, the articles provided for a system of federal government that was "radically vicious and unsound," requiring not amendment but "an entire change in its leading features and characters."

Despite these failures, which even the friends of state sovereignty were often willing to concede, the Articles of Confederation are nevertheless highly significant. Until the Civil War, and even in some measure thereafter, the articles were frequently invoked to justify contending interpretations of the nature of the union and the powers allocated to state and national governments by the 1787 Constitution. Many aspects of the articles found their way into that constitution—the change, as James Madison insisted, consisted "much less in the addition of new powers to the Union, than in the invigoration of its original powers." In the drafting of the Articles of Confederation, Americans confronted for the first time the great promise—and problems—entailed by the construction of their federal union. The idea that 13 independent sovereignties could elaborate an effective system of cooperation on a virgin continent was inspiring, and

augured a new ordering of state relations utterly unlike the European system, with its war-prone and clashing sovereignties.

The drafting of the articles and the subsequent experience of union, however, also showed how difficult it would be to actually establish such a system. From the beginning the union was surrounded, and nearly submerged, by contentious disputes among its states and sections. It was widely believed in Great Britain that no such system of cooperation among the American states could possibly succeed. In 1776, as David Ramsay of South Carolina recalled two years later, "Our enemies seemed confident of the impossibility of our union; our friends doubted it; and all indifferent persons, who judged of things present, by what has heretofore happened, considered the expectation thereof as romantic."

Origin and Purpose

The committee of the Continental Congress charged with drafting articles of confederation first met in May 1776, pursuant to the critical decisions in the first two weeks of May pointing toward a declaration of independence, the pursuit of foreign recognition and assistance, the establishment of new state governments, and the making of the union. Delegates to Congress, conscious that they would be setting vital precedents, had divided on which of these momentous acts should come first, if come they must, but they finally decided in the rush toward independence to do all four things together and at once.

Our understanding of the articles is hobbled by the absence of anything approaching a full record of the debates in either the drafting committee or the Congress. Unlike 1787, when James Madison resolved to take detailed notes of the proceedings, only fragmentary records remain of these debates, though we are assured they were voluminous.

The committee charged with devising terms of confederation issued its report on July 12, 1776, based on a draft in the hand of John Dickinson. Historians differ on the question of how much the initial conception of confederation changed over the next year, as debate over the terms continued in confidential sessions of the Congress. Some argue that the change was substantial, with a decided shift away from national control toward state sovereignty; others insist that the basic character of confederation changed very little between the first and final drafts. Though the finished product lost the provision granting Congress the authority to cut off the extravagant claims of the states with land claims beyond the Appalachians, the initial and final draft each provided for a league of states rather than a centralized government. Neither proposed that Congress be vested with the all-important power of taxation. Each established the dependence of the federal government on the state governments for the requisition of troops and revenues, and each made clear that the rights not surrendered by compact to the federal authority were retained by the states.

The promise of confederation was most eloquently conveyed by John Witherspoon, delegate from New Jersey. Witherspoon saw the union as the working out, under the novel conditions and circumstances of North America, of the "peace plan" tradition in European thought, and he expressed the hope that "a well planned confederacy among the states of America" might "hand down the blessings of peace and public order to many generations." Europe had progressed from its former "disunited and hostile situation" to the "enlarged system called the balance of power." It lay with America to take a step beyond the balance of power "to a state of more perfect and lasting union."

The paradigm shift that Witherspoon described—from balance of power to federal union—conveys a world of meaning and experience intensely relevant to his generation. But it was one thing to state in words this grand and glorious vision, quite another to bring it to fruition. As Witherspoon and others recognized in 1776, and which would be repeatedly echoed thereafter, Americans had a serious security problem, one represented by the likely interaction of the ambitions of foreign powers and internal divisions among the American states. In the absence of lasting confederacy, Witherspoon warned, the peace to follow the achievement of independence would raise the certain prospect "of a more lasting war, a more unnatural, more bloody, and much more hopeless war, among the colonies themselves." Given the profound regional differentiation of the colonies, that grim prospect was a much pondered outcome, and it profoundly conditioned attitudes toward the union.

"The colonies," as John Adams recalled in 1818, "had grown up under constitutions so different, there was so great a variety of religions, they were composed of so many different nations, their customs, manners, and habits had so little resemblance, and their intercourse had been so rare, and their knowledge of each other so imperfect, that to unite them in the same principles in theory and the same system of action, was certainly a very difficult enterprise." The most serious division was between the New England and the southern states. Neither region wished for a separate national identity; but forming a durable union out of these heterogeneous materials often seemed, from 1776 to 1787, to be a virtually hopeless enterprise.

Provisions

The articles, as finally submitted to the states, allowed one vote for each of the 13 states. The compact also allocated burdens according to the value of all land within each state. Both provisions provoked intense disagreement, though, together in the same document they formed something of a compromise. The one-state one-vote provision was disadvantageous to the southern states, led by Virginia, and the provision for dividing the burdens of the war fell most severely on New England. It would allow the southerners, wrote one New Englander, "by their negroes being left at home, [to] till their lands and git Bread & Riches, while some other States may be greatly distressed." The formula assessing burdens according to land value had been resorted to in preference to the more obvious criterion of population because the delegates were unable to reach agreement over how to count slaves, the discussion of which had disclosed the fundamentally incompatible perspectives of North and South.

A key provision, adopted at the urging of Thomas Burke of North Carolina, held, "Each state retains its sovereignty, freedom, and independence, and every power, jurisdiction, and right, which is not by this Confederation expressly delegated to the United States, in Congress assembled." By the same token, the United States did enjoy authority over those matters imparted to it by the confederation. Despite the absence of a clause empowering Congress to use force against recalcitrant states, some Americans believed that such a power was implicit in the confederation. Thomas Jefferson, a later apostle of nullification, noted in 1786, "When any one state in the American Union refuses obedience to the Confederation by which they have bound themselves, the rest have a natural right to compel them to obedience."

The articles provided that 9 out of 13 states were necessary in order to reach decisions on important matters, a provision adopted in order to ensure "a due Balance" among the states and sections. Without the agreement of nine states, Congress could not "engage in a war, nor grant letters of marque or reprisal in time of peace, nor enter into any treaties or alliances, nor coin money, nor regulate the value thereof, nor ascertain the sums and expenses necessary for the defense and welfare of the United States, or any of them, nor emit bills, nor borrow money on the credit of the United States, nor appropriate money, nor agree upon the number of vessels of war, to be built or purchased, or the number of land or sea forces to be raised, nor appoint a commander in chief of the army or navy."

Perhaps the most unusual feature of the Articles of Confederation is the resemblance it had to the "constitution of the British empire," as the Americans had come to understand it. That mixture of executive, judicial, and "federative" powers that, in the American theory, had belonged to king and council, were basically given to "the United States in Congress assembled"; those powers that belonged to the legislatures of the provincial colonies passed to the newly founded states. In the traditional theory of the British constitution, the king enjoyed the powers of war and peace and of leagues and alliances that John Locke had identified with the "federative power." This authority went to the Continental Congress under the articles, which excluded the states from everything touching on foreign relations. By the same token, the arrangement the Americans made among themselves displayed the same dependence on the provincial legislatures that, in their view, had characterized the imperial constitution. While Congress was to propose, the states were to dispose. Unlike the Congress established by the 1787 Constitution, which was undoubtedly a legislative body, the Congress of the Confederation is best thought of as a "plural Executive" or "deliberating Executive assembly" that would be the agent rather than the master of the states.

Controversy and Crisis

When independence was declared, the expectation among many congressmen was that Articles of Confederation would be rapidly drafted and ratified. In fact, it took 16 months, until November 1777, for the articles to be submitted to the states for approval, and it was not until 1781 that consent was received from all 13 states (with the last hold-out, Maryland, succumbing to pressure from the French minister to the United States).

This sequence of events created an anomalous constitutional situation for the American states and, both at the time and subsequently, aroused much disagreement over what it meant. In effect, the American states had agreed to get hitched in 1776 but experienced grave difficulties and delays in reaching agreement on the

terms. What was their constitutional relationship during this time of declared mutual love but not yet fully licit union? Until March 1781, the Articles of Confederation were not binding on the American states, but the states were nevertheless bound together by the sacred promises of the Declaration of Independence, which Jefferson would later call "the fundamental act of union of these states." Nationalists in later years argued that Congress from 1776 to 1781 actually enjoyed its authority from a revolutionary grant given to it by the American people; states' righters countered that no such people were recognized in the formal terms of union and that Congress before 1781 could scarcely be thought to have more authority than it enjoyed after ratification.

Another great debate in which the Articles of Confederation and Perpetual Union figured was just how permanent the union really was. In arguing that the union preceded the states, nationalists sought to counter any assumption that the states might enjoy a right to nullify federal laws within their jurisdiction or to secede from the union. The union, in their view, was perpetual. This perspective, however, was complicated by the fact that when the Federal Convention proposed revised terms of union, it violated the amendment procedures of the Articles of Confederation. Instead of requiring unanimous consent, as the articles had done, the federal Constitution would enter into operation and allow for amendments with the consent of three-fourths of the states. This was either a flagrant violation of constitutional propriety or a stark admission that the old union had ceased to exist. It was on the latter ground that the Federalists rested their case for the Constitution, but that, in turn, implied that the union was not perpetual and could be changed or dissolved by the acts of the states.

These now somewhat obscure controversies were once of commanding interest to Americans, and indeed formed part of the preliminaries to the Civil War. Whatever conclusion might be reached as to the validity of the contending cases in theory, little disagreement exists that, in practice, the Articles of Confederation institutionalized a huge gap between what Congress was responsible for doing and what it could actually accomplish. In the artful summary of one historian, Congress "could ask for money but not compel payment; it could enter into treaties but not enforce their stipulations; it could provide for raising of armies but not fill the ranks; it could borrow money but take no proper measures for repayment; it could advise and recommend but not command." It was the paralysis in government produced by that gap that provided the chief impetus on the road to the Philadelphia convention. Despite these acknowledged deficiencies, the 1783 Treaty of Paris securing American independence was achieved under the government provided by the articles; so, too, was the 1787 Northwest Ordinance establishing the terms under which western territories would be settled and admitted into the union.

A Distant Mirror

The 1787 federal Constitution had many imitators in foreign lands, but it is the "weak" and "defective" version of American federal union that most resembles international organization in the twentieth century. The boast sometimes heard in American history that America's federal union would be the model and beginning of the federation of the world proved only half right: modern international organizations (such as the United Nations, the North Atlantic Treaty Organization, and the European Union) are saddled with allocations of power and authority that mimic the articles in their bold aims and weak structures, leaving these associations always in danger of either disintegration or ineffectiveness. In the 1990s, the American political philosopher Benjamin Barber held that the Articles of Confederation had surprising relevance in dealing with the world of globalization, with its contending forces of profound interdependence and fanatical tribalism. The dilemma of modern governance—of nation-states that are too large for the small things in life and too small for the big things—shows that the generic problem the Articles of Confederation were intended to address remains very much with us. Repelled by visions of both international anarchy and a universal state, the contemporary world seems fated to experience all over again the trials and tribulations of states that bind themselves in "firm leagues of friendship" while reserving to themselves the maximum degree of autonomous action.

See also Bill of Rights; Constitution, federal.

FURTHER READING

Barber, Benjamin R. *Jihad vs. McWorld.* New York: Times Books, 1995.
Forsyth, Murray. *Unions of States: The Theory and Practice of Confederation.* New York: Holmes and Meier, 1981.
Henderson, H. James. *Party Politics in the Continental Congress.* New York: McGraw-Hill, 1974.

Hendrickson, David C. *Peace Pact: The Lost World of the American Founding.* Lawrence: University Press of Kansas, 2003.
Marston, Jerrilyn Greene. *King and Congress: The Transfer of Political Legitimacy, 1774–76.* Princeton, NJ: Princeton University Press, 1987.
Morris, Richard B. *The Forging of the Union, 1781–1789.* New York: Harper and Row, 1987.
Nagel, Paul C. *One Nation Indivisible: The Union in American Thought, 1776–1861.* New York: Oxford University Press, 1964.
Onuf, Peter S. "Anarchy and the Crisis of the Union." In *To Form a More Perfect Union*, edited by Herman Belz, Ronald Hoffman, and Peter J. Albert, 272–302. Charlottesville: University of Virginia Press, 1992.
———. "The First Federal Constitution: The Articles of Confederation." In *The Framing and Ratification of the Constitution*, edited by Leonard W. Levy and Dennis J. Mahoney, 82–97. New York: Macmillan, 1987.
Rakove, Jack N. *The Beginnings of National Politics: An Interpretive History of the Continental Congress.* New York: Knopf, 1979.

DAVID C. HENDRICKSON

Asian immigrants and politics

Asian immigrants and Asian Americans only became visible as a force in U.S. electoral politics in the last decades of the twentieth century, but they have a long history of political and legal activism in the United States. Asian immigrant and citizen activism have taken several forms over the years, including protests against substandard wages and working conditions and harsh immigration laws that limited options for entry to the United States, revolutionary activities aimed at the homeland, and engagement in local and national electoral politics. The development of Asian activism in each area was intrinsically linked to domestic and international factors that created the transpacific migration of Asians and the laws governing their movements and activities.

Early Immigration

The earliest Asian immigrants came to the United States from China, Japan, Korea, the Philippines, and India. Chinese merchants reached the American East Coast by the late eighteenth century, but the first large influx of Chinese arrived in California in the 1850s. There, Chinese not only panned for gold but also built railroads and filled gaps in the service industry in a predominantly male society by opening restaurants and laundries. In response to complaints by white workers about Chinese laborers putting in longer hours at lower wages, California considered laws to protect Americans from competition with the Chinese. As anti-Chinese sentiment and violence increased, Congress passed the first Chinese Exclusion Act in 1882, which barred Chinese laborers from entry for ten years. Economic arguments intersected with regional politics to create the first law restricting immigration to the United States and the only immigration act to single out a particular ethnic group. The Exclusion Acts—the laws renewed repeatedly over several decades—also had the effect of preventing Chinese from acquiring naturalized citizenship. Although the Supreme Court ruled in *United States v. Wong Kim Ark* that Chinese were eligible for birthright citizenship, Chinese women were barred from legal immigration to the United States, and antimiscegenation laws prevented many Chinese men from marrying outside their race.

The Chinese Exclusion Acts became the model for excluding Asians from the United States for decades, but they did not go unchallenged. Chinese immigrants organized mutual aid societies, and, through them, questioned the legality of the Chinese Exclusion Acts in lawsuits such as *Chae Chan Ping v. United States* and *Fong Yue Ting v. United States*. These efforts ultimately proved unsuccessful, as anti-Chinese sentiment trumped their careful legal arguments. But Chinese claiming the right to enter the United States so flooded the courts with cases suing for habeas corpus that the U.S. Department of Justice responded by creating a separate system for hearing immigration appeals. Chinese were also active in defending their rights as laborers, leading strikes against railroads and other employers and demanding equal pay and treatment.

Beginning in the 1890s, Japanese immigrants arrived in significant numbers after labor recruiters from California sought workers to help with backbreaking farm labor, and Hawaiian plantation owners began using Japanese to diversify their workforce. Unlike imperial China, the Japanese government was a strong power internationally and in a much better position to protect the rights and interests of its citizens abroad. Anti-Asian sentiment in

the United States included prejudices against Japanese migrants, however, so immigration was limited through the Gentlemen's Agreement of 1907. Like the Chinese, the Japanese contested poor treatment. In Hawai'i Japanese organized a mass strike in 1904 that involved some 1,200 workers; a second movement in 1909 mobilized an impressive 7,000. In both cases, the Japanese laborers sought better working conditions and more equitable wages. But concessions from their American employers proved hard to win as strike funds dwindled and the protests dragged on. Over time, employers in Hawai'i continued to diversify their labor forces, combining laborers from across Asia so that linguistic differences would make organization more difficult.

The question of whether Japanese were eligible for citizenship was highly contested, as more Japanese arrived intending to become permanent residents. After a series of inconsistent court rulings that allowed some Japanese to become naturalized citizens and denied others, the Supreme Court finally decided in the 1922 decision *Takao Ozawa v. United States* that Japanese were ineligible for naturalization.

Asian immigrants to the United States also came from three other locations: Korea, the Philippines, and British India. As with early Japanese arrivals, Korean immigrants first came as a result of American labor recruiters visiting their country. The window for early migration—only opened in 1905—closed by 1910, however, as Japanese colonial control over the peninsula solidified. South Asians, mostly from Punjab, also came in small numbers, many entering the United States after Canada began to place restrictions on their entrance in 1908. Beginning in 1917, U.S. laws restricted immigration from anywhere within the "Asiatic Barred Zone," and the national origins quotas created in 1920 further limited immigration to groups that already had a large presence in the United States. The 1924 Immigration Act succeeded in banning most remaining immigration from Asia. The sole exception to these legal restrictions on Asian immigration was that of the Philippines, because its citizens were U.S. nationals of an American colony. In 1934, the Tydings-McDuffie Act created a procedure for granting the Philippines independence. In the process, it restricted Filipino immigration to a mere 50 new arrivals each year.

During the Exclusion Era—the period between the advent of Chinese exclusion in 1882 and the revision of U.S. immigration laws to allow widespread Asian natu-

Persons of Japanese ancestry arrive at the Santa Anita Assembly Center in Arcadia, California, from San Pedro on April 5, 1942. Evacuees lived at this center before being moved inland to relocation centers. (Clem Albers/ National Archives)

ralization in 1952—ineligibility for citizenship barred most Asian immigrants from participation in the American political system. But Chinese, Korean, and Indian reformers took advantage of U.S. freedoms to call for changes in their homelands. In Hawai'i in 1894, Sun Yat-sen, later a leader of the Chinese republican revolution and the first elected leader of China, created a political party to promote the revolution. Koreans and Indians also sought independence from colonial rule for their homelands. Koreans founded the Korean Nationalist Association in 1909, while Indians created the revolutionary Ghadar Party in 1913.

Asian Immigration and Activism at Midcentury

World War II marked a beginning of major changes for Asian immigrant communities. Following the attack on Pearl Harbor in 1941, many Japanese Americans were labeled "enemy aliens." Suspected to be Axis collaborators by many Americans, Japanese American residents on the West Coast, most of whom were citizens, were rounded up and placed in camps to wait out the war. Some exceptions to the general internment found work inland or joined the U.S. armed forces, but thousands lost their homes, possessions, and jobs. At the same time, the once

reviled Chinese were given a new life as American allies and heroes of the East; they were rewarded for their homeland's long and difficult struggle against the Japanese with the repeal of the Exclusion Acts in 1943. After repeal, 105 Chinese immigrants were allowed to immigrate to the United States each year, but more important, Chinese nationals became eligible for naturalization for the first time since the 1882 Exclusion Acts. The repeal also paved the way for postwar acts permitting both Indian and Filipino migrants to naturalize and immigrate in small numbers. In 1952 the McCarran-Walter Act finally replaced the Asiatic Barred Zone with an Asia-Pacific Triangle in which minimum quotas of 100 were granted for each Asian nationality. The inclusion of Asian—primarily Chinese and Japanese—veterans in the privileges granted by the War Brides and War Fiancées acts of 1945 and 1946 also brought major changes to Asian American communities. Bachelor immigrants were able for the first time to marry or bring over their wives and began to build families and permanent homes in the United States.

In spite of these reforms, the era between the immigration laws passed by Congress in 1952 and 1965 is known as the era of de facto exclusion. Although McCarran-Walter opened the door for annual quotas and naturalization, it kept extremely low limits on new entries. The 1965 Immigration Act finally did away with national origins quotas altogether, creating in their place a series of preferences based on special skills and family ties and overall hemispheric quotas. As a result of this act, significant immigration began that fundamentally changed the nature of Asian America, created a quickly growing minority population, and sowed the first seeds of Asian American political activism. Not only did Chinese, Japanese, Korean, Indian, and Filipino immigrants arrive in greater numbers, but the new law opened the door for immigration from Asian countries not previously represented in the United States, such as Thailand, Pakistan, Indonesia, or Malaysia. U.S. involvement in the Vietnam War and the refugee acts that passed as a result of its withdrawal also created new migration from Vietnam, Cambodia, and Laos after 1975.

This new influx of Asian immigration created the impetus for increased engagement in U.S. politics. Long denied the vote, Asian Americans had earned a reputation for political apathy sometimes fed by those trying to prove that their immigration posed no threat to U.S. institutions. But as numbers increased, so did political involvement. In the postwar era, the first Asian American politicians were elected to U.S. political bodies. Arizona state representative Wing F. Ong became the first Asian American to be elected to a state assembly in 1946. In 1956, Dalip Singh Saund was elected to Congress from California. After Hawai'i achieved statehood in 1959, its large population elected Asian American Hiram Fong was to the U.S. Senate in 1959, followed three years later by Daniel K. Inouye. In 1964, Patsy Takemoto Mink became the first Asian American woman elected to Congress. Japanese and other Asian Americans in Congress proved critical to passing legislation in 1988 that compensated loyal Japanese Americans for their unlawful incarceration during World War II.

Asian Pride and Pan-Asian Organization

Although Asian American politicians from the U.S. mainland remained rarer than from Hawai'i, Asian Americans increasingly took part in the civil rights and antiwar movements that contributed to a breakdown in the domestic cold war consensus. Asian American students at San Francisco State University went on strike in 1968 to demand that the school create ethnic studies programs. At the same time, Asian and Asian American students also joined the movement calling for an end to American involvement in Vietnam; some claimed solidarity with the beleaguered citizens of Southeast Asia.

As such activism increased, however, so did the idea of Asians as a U.S. "model minority." With high rates of educational and occupational success and low levels of crime, Asian Americans were held up in political circles and the media as the ideal minority group, the model for African Americans and Latinos to follow. The reality proved more complicated: while many Asian Americans of Chinese and Japanese descent were high achievers, income levels for unskilled Asian American workers lagged behind those of white Americans. Meanwhile, the diversity of the Asian American population meant that generalizations that applied to second- or third-generation Chinese families were not valid for recent migrants from Vietnam or Cambodia.

The tendency of the American public at large to generalize about Asian American identity has had both tragic and useful consequences. For example, the murder of Vincent Chin in 1982 became a basis for greater cooperation among Asian American communities. Chin was a Chinese American two white attackers mistook for a Japanese foreigner complicit in the loss of their jobs in the auto industry. They beat him to death, but neither man was sent to jail. The failure of the courts to bring justice to Chin's killers energized Asian American organizers, and the result was the first real movement that crossed ethnic and national boundaries to organize Asian Americans to address their shared interests. Organizations like Chinese for Affirmative Action, the Japanese American Citizens League, the Organization of Chinese Americans, and the Filipino American Community Council worked together to help Chin's mother file a civil suit against the two men. The incident sparked mobilization to prosecute and raise awareness of hate crimes against Asian Americans; it was the start of a new push for civil rights.

However, the diversity between and within Asian American groups meant that they rarely formed a voting bloc that could influence the outcome of elections. Organizations like the nonpartisan 80/20–Initiative seek to change this reality and to form Asian Americans into an important constituency. The organization tries to get 80 percent of voting Asian Americans to vote for the same candidate in each race, chosen on the basis of how well that individual addresses issues of importance to the Asian American community. Though not yet united on issues, Asian Americans were more visible in the 2008 presidential primaries, as a political force than at any time in their long history of activism in the United States.

See also immigration policy.

FURTHER READING

Chan, Sucheng. *Asian Americans: An Interpretive History.* Boston: Twayne, 1991.

Chang, Gordon H., ed. *Asian Americans and Politics: Perspectives, Experiences, Prospects.* Washington, DC: Woodrow Wilson Center Press, 2001.

Fawcett, James T., and Benjamin V. Carino, eds. *Pacific Bridges: The New Immigration from Asia and the Pacific Islands.* Staten Island, NY: Center for Migration Studies, 1987.

McClain, Charles. *In Search of Equality: The Chinese Struggle against Discrimination in Nineteenth-Century America.* Berkeley: University of California Press, 1994.

Ng, Franklin, ed. *Asian American Interethnic Relations and Politics.* Asians in America: The Peoples of East, Southeast, and South Asia in American Life and Culture. New York: Garland, 1998.

Takaki, Ronald. *Strangers from a Different Shore: A History of Asian Americans.* Boston: Little, Brown, 1998.

Zhou, Min, and James V. Gatewood, eds. *Contemporary Asian America: A Multidisciplinary Reader.* New York: New York University Press, 2000.

MEREDITH OYEN

assassination, presidential

According to Secret Service research, between 1949 and 1996, 25 people tried to assassinate the president of the United States (and one of them succeeded). Thus, on average, someone tries to kill the president somewhat more often than every two years; or to put it another way, holders of the office stand vulnerable to such attacks perhaps twice in each of their four-year terms. Only four presidents have fallen prey to murderers, and the results of these killings do not explain why someone might wish to kill the president. But based on the frequency with which the Secret Service must prevent assassinations, presidential murder clearly occupies a larger place in the minds of violent Americans than the number of successful efforts suggests. It also sparks more extensive and complex political consequences than its perpetrators imagine.

In 1835 a painter named Richard Lawrence met President Andrew Jackson at the Capitol and tried to shoot him with two pistols. Both misfired. Jackson and some of his allies believed the assault came from his political opponents. Lawrence had a history of confinement for insanity in his family and, at his trial, indicated his belief that he was rightful ruler of Great Britain and the United States, declaring, "It is for me, gentlemen, to pass upon you, and not you upon me." The jury found him not guilty by reason of insanity, and he received a life sentence. In 1861 he died at the Government Hospital for the Insane in Washington, D.C.

The Lawrence incident established patterns that persist in discussions of presidential assassinations. Foremost among them was the evident readiness, particularly among the political class, to see murder as an extension of political conflict. Presidential politics requires a degree of devious anticipation, and the mind of a skilled and jaded practitioner can see the hand of a defeated opponent behind any effort to strike at one's position, even attempted murder. Close behind the assumption that assassination attempts result from political conspiracy came the alternative explanation: they result from delusion. As the Lawrence case also shows, it is often difficult to untangle the two. Someone who demonstrates madness in one way may nevertheless plan rationally and choose a target for reasons entirely in keeping with mainstream political assumptions: Lawrence appears to have been exercised about the Bank of the United States, like many Americans of the Jacksonian era. Even delusional assassins do not generally choose their targets at random, so an assassination or its attempt becomes an occasion to consider the role of political discourse in defining enemies.

Of the four presidential assassinations, that of Abraham Lincoln in 1865 resulted most clearly from political causes and entailed dramatic political consequences. Lincoln's murderer, John Wilkes Booth, took part in a conspiracy meant to achieve by personal violence the vengeance that the Confederate armies could not win on the battlefield. Not only did the conspirators kill the president, they also wounded (though not fatally) Secretary of State William Seward.

In murdering Lincoln, Booth put Andrew Johnson into the presidency, setting in motion a clash between president and Congress that culminated in Johnson's impeachment and produced a disastrous peace policy. Johnson's immediate lenience toward the recently rebellious white Southerners, coupled with his inability to craft and execute a successful plan for Reconstruction with the Republican Congress, assuredly rates as one of the greatest political catastrophes in American history. The consequences of the Johnson presidency—and thus of the Lincoln assassination—lasted for decades. Lincoln might not have wrung a triumphant peace and racial justice from the bloody shirt of Reconstruction politics, but it is hard to imagine that had he lived (and, say, had Seward died), he could have done considerably worse than Johnson. In the longer term, Lincoln's martyrdom became a powerful symbol for the forces opposing the Confederacy and its legacy, and was used to promote the cause of civil rights for African Americans a hundred years after his death.

Charles Guiteau shot President James Garfield in 1881 because, he said, he wished to "unite the Republican Party and save the Republic." Guiteau had spent time at the Republicans' New York headquarters during the 1880 campaign and claimed to have played a pivotal role in the election, though this was difficult to prove. He repeatedly asked officials of the new administration for a patronage position, which he believed he had earned through his support—perhaps, he suggested, he could have a diplomatic post in Paris. When Secretary of State James G. Blaine told Guiteau that he would not deliver this plum, Guiteau became convinced of Blaine's malign influence on Garfield, believing the two were pulling the Republican Party away from its traditions— and from men who would appoint him to the office he deserved.

Upon Guiteau's imprisonment, he poured forth justifications for his actions. They ranged from the political— "the President, under the manipulation of his Secretary of State . . . has wracked the Republican Party"—to the historic—"I shot the President as I would a rebel"—to the intermingled divine and commercial—"The President's nomination was an act of God. The President's election was an act of God. The President's removal is an act of God. I am clear in my purpose to remove the President. . . . it will create a great demand for my book, 'The Truth.' This book was written to save souls and not for money, and the Lord wants to save souls by circulating the book."

Guiteau's trial took 72 days, during which he took full opportunity of the epic stage thus afforded him. His brother-in-law defended him by claiming he suffered from an insanity that ran in the family, which Guiteau's brother denied, declaring "masturbation and self-abuse is at the bottom of his imbecility." Guiteau himself agreed

that, in the legal sense, he should enjoy the defense of insanity because he was not responsible for his actions— God was. He spoke confidently of his certain acquittal, frequently of his fan mail, and hopefully of his prospects in the presidential election of 1884. Found guilty, he read at the gallows a poem of his own in the voice, he said, "of a child babbling to his mamma and his papa," in which he declared repeatedly his certainty that "I am going to the Lordy."

Garfield's murder brought political consequences rather different from those his assassin intended. After the shooting and before the president's death, Senator George Pendleton delivered a speech in which he analyzed the crime: "This is the brutality of our politics. The desire for office is what made this crime possible. We must by law abolish the whole system of office-giving and office-seeking." In 1883 Congress passed a law bearing Pendleton's name, laying the basis for an independent civil service in which office seekers won places by competitive examination.

Twenty years later, the murder of William McKinley by Leon Czolgosz in Buffalo, New York, also entailed consequences the assassin would have been unlikely to predict. Upon his arrest and interrogation, Czolgosz said, "I killed President McKinley because I done my duty. I don't believe in one man having so much service and another man having none." He told police and attorneys, "I am an anarchist. . . . I fully understood what I was doing when I shot the President. I realized that I was sacrificing my life. I am willing to take the consequences." The district attorney tried to ensure Czolgosz would get little publicity and decided "suppress all that was possible," on the ground that "any writing or talking on this matter only kept it before the public." In other words, Czolgosz would not enjoy the spotlight that had shone on Guiteau. His trial came soon and passed swiftly, his jury deliberated briefly, and his execution followed shortly afterward. Just before his death, he claimed, "I shot the President because I thought it would help the working people, and for the sake of the common people. I am not sorry for my crime." As his guards strapped him into the electric chair, he added, "I am awfully sorry because I did not see my father." Afterward the prison staff poured sulfuric acid into his grave to ensure the swift dissolution of his remains.

Despite the speed with which the legal system dispensed justice to Czolgosz, his prosecutors could not prevent a painful rehearsal of the key political problem that presidential assassination presented. This problem was evident in the Lawrence case and was cast into cartoonish relief in the case of Guiteau: to acknowledge the sanity of the assassin was to acknowledge a logical case for a murderous assault on the president and a symbolic attack on the nation itself, while to deny the assassin's sanity was to deprive the community of its rightful revenge. Czolgosz cited as his motives the widespread inequality in America—which was real enough—and the cold logic of anarchism, which held that regimes perpetuating such inequality were subject to the same rationale that governed total war: there are, as one anarchist terrorist declared, no innocents. One of Czolgosz's defense lawyers argued at his trial that it would be much easier to find his client mad than to confront the implications of his sanity: "If our beloved President had met with a railroad accident coming here to our city and had been killed, we should all regret very much, we should mourn over the loss of a just man, but our grief would not compare to the grief that we have now. . . . [I]f you could find that he met his fate by the act of an insane man, it would amount to the same as though he met it accidentally." This the jury could not support.

In all that Czolgosz said or was supposed to have said, he did not appear to have anticipated the greatest consequence of his actions: the presidency of Theodore Roosevelt. Although some historians have claimed that Roosevelt only continued McKinley's policies, this is difficult to credit. McKinley may have pondered liberalization of the tariff and an antitrust prosecution or two, but he showed little desire or ability to champion progressive reforms as often, as loudly, and as memorably as Roosevelt did; Roosevelt "smote with many a message the money changers in the temple of his own party," as Charles Beard wrote. Roosevelt gave the most radical reforms of the day a place in the most respectable political discourse and set himself up as a friend to the common people, taking their side against those whom he called "malefactors of great wealth."

Czolgosz represented a greater threat than he really posed: with the Eastern European diphthongs in his name and his professed radical politics, he seemed like the personification of foreign menace. As police noted, he was born in the United States—but a great many of his fellow citizens saw him instantly as, in one man's words, an alien "who, thank God, bears a name that can not be mistaken for that of an American." In the years after McKinley's assassination, the unwarranted assumption that murderous radicalism came from overseas found legal expression in a new authority to bar immi-

grants based on their political beliefs. McKinley's murder also gave rise to plans for presidential protection by the Secret Service, a law enforcement agency of the U.S. Treasury.

The assassination of John F. Kennedy sprang from motives that remain murky, because Lee Harvey Oswald met his end even sooner after the crime than Leon Czolgosz had: nightclub operator Jack Ruby shot and killed Oswald before he could stand trial. A former U.S. Marine, Oswald developed a discontent with capitalism and fled America for the Soviet Union, which in turn quickly disillusioned him. He returned to the United States and settled in Dallas, Texas. In the spring of 1963, Oswald tried to kill retired General Edwin Walker, who was promoting a more aggressive policy toward Cuba and whom Oswald believed to be a "Fascist." Then, on November 22, Oswald shot Kennedy from the sixth floor of the Texas School Book Depository in Dallas and was arrested a short time later.

The swirl of theories that followed Kennedy's assassination, the subsequent political murders of other public figures, including Robert F. Kennedy, and the well-known assassination attempts on Richard Nixon, Gerald Ford, and Ronald Reagan gave rise to various efforts to categorize assassins. The most motivated of researchers in this effort, the Secret Service, compiled, in the 1990s, a list of all known assassinations and attempted assassinations of public figures spanning about 50 years. Researchers examining the data concluded that no set of factors could identify a plausible threat: "There was no single profile," they wrote. Beyond what "seems obvious"—that "people who see themselves as doing well in life rarely attempt assassinations"—they could not say what might trigger a political murder. If assassins were doing poorly, they were not unique: "the kinds of problems experienced . . . were, with few exceptions, neither rare nor extreme." A diagnosis of mental illness did not serve as a useful indicator, nor did making threats: "Although some threateners may pose a real threat, usually they do not. . . . However, most importantly, those who pose threats frequently do not make threats." Apart from looking out for those who are evidently planning such a murder, the Secret Service could not specify a sure method of prevention. Assassins focused ordinary anxieties in extraordinary ways, and in their great diversity and disillusion they represented, as Stephen Sondheim and John Weidman suggested in their 1990 musical *Assassins*, the American multicultural dream of opportunity for everyone, reflected in a dark, nightmarish mirror.

See also presidency.

FURTHER READING

Ackerman, Kenneth D. *Dark Horse: The Surprise Election and Political Murder of President James A. Garfield.* New York: Carroll and Graf, 2003.

Bugliosi, Vincent. *Reclaiming History: The Assassination of President John F. Kennedy.* New York: Norton, 2007.

Clarke, James W. *American Assassins: The Darker Side of Politics.* Princeton, NJ: Princeton University Press, 1982.

Donovan, Robert J. *The Assassins.* New York: Harper, 1955.

Kauffman, Michael W. *American Brutus: John Wilkes Booth and the Lincoln Conspiracies.* New York: Random House, 2004.

Rauchway, Eric. *Murdering McKinley: The Making of Theodore Roosevelt's America.* New York: Hill and Wang, 2003.

Sondheim, Stephen, and John Weidman. *Assassins.* New York: Theatre Communications Group, 1991.

Steers, Edward. *Blood on the Moon: The Assassination of Abraham Lincoln.* Lexington: University Press of Kentucky, 2001.

ERIC RAUCHWAY

banking policy

Banking policy has been debated in the United States since Alexander Hamilton and Thomas Jefferson squared off in George Washington's cabinet over the first Bank of the United States. Banks are depository financial institutions: people and firms deposit money in these intermediaries, which, in turn, lend it to other people and firms. Banking policy aims to ensure safety for depositors and borrowers and the financial soundness of banks. But there is more at stake than the banking industry. Banks allocate capital among the competing claims of individuals and firms, industries and regions, pursuing social goals and economic development. Further, the banking process is closely related to the nature and availability of the money supply, thus banking policy has long been entangled with monetary policy.

The big issues at stake are pragmatic and political. What arrangements will *work well* to provide and allocate money and credit? What implications do alternative arrangements have for the *distribution of power*? When do banks have too much economic power or political influence? U.S. banking policy debates have been about the *structure* of banking organizations—banks and regulatory agencies—as well as about rules that constrain their *practices*. Some of the organizations launched or redesigned in those debates are gone, but most remain. In the twenty-first century, banking firms include commercial banks and savings banks, savings and loan associations (S&Ls), and credit unions. Three federal agencies regulate commercial banks: the Office of the Comptroller of the Currency in the Treasury Department attends to national banks; the Federal Reserve System has responsibility for state banks that are its members; and the Federal Deposit Insurance Corporation (FDIC) oversees nonmember state banks. Federal S&Ls are supervised by the Office of Thrift Supervision, also in Treasury, while credit unions are overseen by the independent National Credit Union Administration. Public agencies in the states supervise and regulate depository intermediaries chartered under state laws. The Deposit Insurance Fund in the FDIC insures deposits in banks and S&Ls, while credit unions have a separate deposit insurance fund. Two rediscount institutions—Federal Reserve Banks and Federal Home Loan Banks—lend to depository intermediaries of all types. How did we get here?

First Bank of the United States

The first Bank of the United States was chartered by Congress in 1791. Alexander Hamilton, secretary of the treasury, proposed the bank to provide credit for economic development and a reliable circulating medium and to assist the government as fiscal agent. At the time, and until establishment of the Federal Reserve System more than a century later, what should comprise the circulating medium remained at issue. Provisions in the new Constitution had ended issuance of paper money by the states. The national government had taken up the practice during the Revolution, but Hamilton wanted to stop it, arguing that the temptation to run the printing presses excessively would be irresistible in an emergency. Bank notes, on the other hand, issued in the process of commercial lending, would not be inflationary. In laying out the bank's design, Hamilton identified dimensions of bank structure and practice that policy makers have manipulated in pursuit of workable institutions throughout U.S. history: capitalization, ownership, governance, and permissible assets and liabilities.

Thomas Jefferson, then secretary of state, led the opposition. Jefferson championed an agrarian economy, and so rejected the importance of aggregating capital for the development of manufacturing and commerce. Neither did he see merit in increasing circulating medium with bank notes. As a "hard money" (gold and silver, also called specie) advocate, Jefferson viewed paper money as inflationary regardless of whether it was issued by a bank or a government. But in a letter to George Washington disputing the bank's constitutionality, he rested the weight of his objection on its evils as a corporation. Jefferson opposed corporations as artificially contrived entities for the private accumulation of wealth. The economic inequality they engendered would threaten political equality. Jefferson indicted the first Bank of the United States as a corporation, and because the new Constitution did not explicitly grant Congress the power to charter corporations, charged that it was unconstitutional. Nonetheless, Washington signed the statute establishing the Bank.

The Bank of the United States operated from 1791–1811, augmenting capital and the money supply and serving as the government's fiscal agent, as planned. But in response to the unanticipated increase in the number of state-chartered banks, from four to over one hundred, it developed the additional function of de facto state bank regulator. As its charter approached expiration, President James Madison supported renewal, but a majority of Jefferson's Republican Party defeated it in Congress in 1811.

Second Bank of the United States

Over the next five years, the number of state banks doubled; they issued paper notes used as currency and drove inflation. As specie disappeared from circulation and efforts to sell Treasury notes to fund the War of 1812 largely failed, the government accepted state bank notes but found it difficult to use them across the states to pay soldiers and buy supplies. In a pragmatic consensus, Congress chartered a second Bank of the United States in 1816 to provide for a "uniform currency," which meant adequate but not inflationary levels of currency and credit available throughout the United States. John Calhoun developed the positive argument for the bank's constitutionality on which centralized monetary policy rests into the twenty-first century: the Constitution gives Congress authority to "coin money" and "regulate the value thereof." Bank paper had become money, and though the founders had not foreseen this, they had intended to provide authority to regulate whatever served as money.

The second Bank of the United States performed poorly at first. It fed the boom that followed the War of 1812 and then contributed to the financial panic of 1818–19. But under Nicholas Biddle, who became bank

president in 1823, it was widely viewed by contemporary policy makers as effective. Andrew Jackson nevertheless vetoed the bill renewing its charter in 1832. He argued that the corporate charter provided a monopoly on banking with the government's deposits and that the bank's economic power resulted in political influence. Efforts to override the veto failed and the second Bank was wound down as its charter expired in 1836.

State Banks

In 1833 Jackson directed Treasury Secretary Roger Taney to transfer government deposits from the Bank of the United States to selected state banks. Some chroniclers have interpreted this as favoritism for "pet banks" or an example of Jackson's support for states' rights. But Jackson opposed incorporated banking in the states as well as at the national level. He believed that the mechanisms involved in using bank notes as money inherently robbed common people. Jackson's solution was to return to hard money. Accordingly, his administration used government deposits in state banks as leverage to prohibit bank issuance of small notes and to require payment in specie on demand.

By the eve of Jackson's bank veto, state legislatures had chartered some 400 banks. Like Congress, they used banks to aggregate capital and provide commercial credit, a circulating medium, serve as the state's fiscal agent, and regulate other banks. Pragmatic legislators also used banks to finance public improvements and state operations, and to ensure credit for agriculture. They initially responded to Jackson's bank veto by chartering more banks and enlarging existing banks. But following the Panic of 1837, a partisan rift opened. A majority of Democrats moved to Jacksonian opposition to all incorporated banking. Whigs insisted that banks were needed, at a minimum, to provide capital for economic development. The issue in the state banking debates changed from how to design banks to whether to charter them at all.

The institutional outcome of these debates was the "free bank." This model emerged in New York as a compromise among Jacksonian opponents of all incorporated banking, free enterprisers who objected to requiring legislative authority to bank, and supporters of regulated banking. To address charges of monopoly, New York's free banking law was a general law, permitting anyone to bank who met its requirements. To protect noteholders, a new bond-backed currency was devised. A bank deposited bonds of public jurisdictions with the state's comptroller. If the bank refused to pay hard money on demand for its notes, the comptroller was to sell the bonds and redeem the notes.

National Banks

With the Civil War, banking policy returned to the agenda in Washington. Treasury Secretary Salmon P. Chase sold bonds, mostly to banks, to finance the war, and insisted that they pay in specie. By late 1861, major banks had no more specie and the government was confronted—as in the War of 1812—with the need for a uniform currency acceptable across state lines. Chase requested and Congress passed the National Currency Act of 1863, repealed and replaced by the National Bank Act of 1864. The statute aimed in the short run to finance the war but ultimately to achieve a national currency without raising Jacksonian specters of private power run amok in a single national bank or a currency wildly over-issued by many state banks. Modeled on the states' free banking laws, the National Bank Act provided for privately owned banks that would issue bond-backed currency. Minimum capitalization of these banks depended upon size of place, but all were very small compared to the first and second banks of the United States. The statute established the Office of the Comptroller of the Currency in the Treasury Department to regulate national banks and issue the currency.

Banks chartered under the National Bank Act became significant actors in the U.S. economy, but the approach did not result in the unified national banking system that was expected. To motivate state banks to convert to national charters, Congress placed a prohibitive tax on their notes. But as state banks learned to make loans in the form of deposit credit, legislatures returned to chartering banks to meet needs not well served by national banks, notably credit for agriculture, real estate, and local business. The distinctive U.S. dual banking system emerged. The National Bank Act did not result in one currency either. State bank notes disappeared, but since national banks were not operational quickly enough to meet the government's need for Civil War cash, the Treasury issued notes, dubbed "greenbacks." Greenbacks circulated with national bank notes, short-term U.S. bonds, gold and gold certificates, silver and silver certificates.

Institutional arrangements framed by the National Bank Act served the expanding economy poorly in the decades following the Civil War. Farmers' interests were ravaged as commodity prices declined in a long deflationary trend. In the populist critique that developed, the problem was the return to the gold standard, which arbitrarily limited the money supply, in tandem with bank control of credit allocation. The National Bank Act's pyramiding reserve arrangements (country banks held reserves in city banks, which in turn held reserves in larger "reserve city" banks) were charged with channeling every community's money to big banks in the East—the "money trust"—which loaned it to stock market speculators. In a reversal of the Jacksonian anti-inflation stance, farmers called for expanding the money supply through means subject to government—not bank—control, including greenbacks and remonetizing silver. In the realigning election of 1896, Democratic presidential candidate William Jennings Bryan championed free coinage of silver against supporters of the gold standard. The Democratic Party became home to farmers in the West and South, while erstwhile Democrats who favored the gold standard moved into the Republican fold to form a party system that stood until the New Deal.

Business and banking interests also indicted the National Bank Act's currency and reserve provisions. In their critique, these arrangements provided no leverage for countering the debilitating business cycles and financial panics that plagued the economy. The bond-backed currency was inelastic. It should be replaced with currency backed by bank assets and issued in the process of extending short-term commercial credit; the supply was expected to expand and contract automatically in keeping with productive needs (the "real bills" doctrine). Reserve provisions, which required that each bank *keep* reserves, should be changed to facilitate *using* reserves.

Federal Reserve System

More than 40 years after the National Bank Act, the Panic of 1907 and the severe contraction that followed finally provoked the Federal Reserve Act of 1913. This statute reflected compromises of ideology and interest as policy makers tried to design arrangements that would work. Old Guard Republicans and eastern bankers proposed a privately owned central reserve bank with monetary policy discretion. Conservative Democrats and small business agreed with private ownership but feared Wall Street control; they called for decentralized reserve banks and believed that self-regulating asset currency made monetary policy discretion unnecessary. Bryan Democrats insisted on government control of any reserve system and government-guaranteed currency. Determined to achieve banking reform, President Woodrow Wilson brokered compromises. The Federal Reserve Act established 12 regional Federal Reserve Banks owned by commercial bankers, a Federal Reserve Board (the Fed) comprising presidential appointees to regulate reserve banks, and new Federal Reserve notes backed by the assets of the bank that issued them and guaranteed by the government. National banks were required to join the Federal Reserve System; state banks were permitted to join.

The Federal Reserve System did not prevent the Great Depression or widespread bank runs. Indeed, easy money policy in 1927 and 1928, deployed under leadership of the Federal Reserve Bank of New York, was a factor in the speculative boom in the stock market that ended with the crash of October 1929. Once retrenchment was under way, an indecisive Federal Reserve Board permitted the money supply to contract along with the economy, intensifying the downward spiral into Depression. The Banking Act of 1935, introduced at the insistence of President Franklin Roosevelt's Fed chairman Marriner Eccles, responded to these mistakes by strengthening the Federal Reserve Board and subordinating the Federal Reserve Banks. The statute empowered the Board to wield the known instruments of discretionary monetary policy. Bank reserve requirements, previously fixed in the Federal Reserve Act, could be adjusted by the Fed within a statutory range. The discount rate, which had been the purview of the separate Federal Reserve Banks, became subject to Board approval. Open market operations, unknown when the Federal Reserve Act was passed in 1913, had been "discovered" in practice by the Federal Reserve Banks. Resolving a tug of war between the reserve banks (banker control) and the Federal Reserve Board (public control), the legislation vested authority to use this tool in a newly constituted Federal Open Market Committee, effectively controlled by the Board.

Depression-Era Changes to Depository Institutions

In the Banking Act of 1933 (the Glass-Steagall Act), Congress took aim at banking practices which had contributed, along with the Fed's easy money policy, to the stock market crash. As the stock market boom gained steam, large banks had financed the underwriting of securities (stocks and bonds), thus reaping fees; made loans to insiders for speculation in securities; *and* peddled securities to the public. To address this conflict of interest, the statute erected the "Glass-Steagall wall" that prohibited commercial bank involvement with investment banking (securities dealers). To restore public confidence in bank safety, it required deposit insurance for commercial banks. Funded with premiums paid by banks and backed by a government guarantee, the Federal Deposit Insurance Corporation (FDIC) is a public corporation that pays depositors if a bank cannot.

Depression-era legislation also put home ownership finance on a firmer footing. Savings and loan associations (S&Ls) were community-based depository intermediaries, chartered under state laws, devised to provide fixed-rate, fully amortizing loans for home ownership. The bipartisan Federal Home Loan Bank Act of 1932 established 12 regional Federal Home Loan Banks to make loans to S&Ls so that S&Ls could meet depositors' withdrawal pressure and borrowers' credit demand. Legislation in 1933 created a federal charter, and a 1934 statute provided for S&L deposit insurance.

Credit unions moved onto the national policy agenda during the Depression as well. Underpinned by a populist philosophy, credit unions are cooperatives, mutually owned by depositors. The Federal Credit Union Act of 1934 authorized a federal charter, which made it easier to organize credit unions in states with nonexistent or unwieldy enabling laws. In 1970, federal legislation gave them deposit insurance and an independent regulator.

Deregulation

These Depression-era banking arrangements stood for decades but were increasingly challenged by macroeconomic dynamics, financial market innovations, and shifting ideology. Inflationary spikes in the 1960s and stagflation in the 1970s led to "disintermediation": bank and S&L depositors transferred money to new money market instruments in pursuit of higher interest, while big borrowers went elsewhere for loans. Advocacy for deregulation gained ground among elites. The rationale was that easing asset and liability constraints would facilitate soundness in individual depository institutions, and that unleashing competition in the industry would improve macroeconomic efficiency. In 1971, President Richard Nixon's Commission on Financial Structure and Regulation (the Hunt Commission), laid out a comprehensive deregulatory reform agenda which was largely implemented over the next two decades.

The bipartisan Depository Institutions Deregulation and Monetary Control Act of 1980 phased out interest rate ceilings on deposits and substantially eliminated states' usury ceilings, permitted S&Ls and credit unions to offer checking accounts, and expanded banks' asset powers. At the same time, to increase monetary policy leverage, the statute extended the reach of the Fed. All depository institutions became subject to the Fed's reserve requirements and gained borrowing privileges. In 1982 the Garn-St. Germain Act moved further in the direction of expanding depository institutions' asset and liability options.

Whether due to too much deregulation or too little, in the 1980s much of the S&L industry collapsed, and its insurance fund went bankrupt. Commercial banks got into trouble too: several large banks failed and the bank insurance fund dipped into the red. The Financial Institutions Reform, Recovery and Enforcement Act of 1989 resolved the S&L crisis. It replaced S&Ls' original deposit insurer with a new fund located in the FDIC, and S&Ls' independent regulator with a new agency located in the Treasury Department. These changes moved toward the Hunt Commission objective of consolidating S&L and commercial bank regulation. In 1991 the Federal Deposit Insurance Corporation Improvement Act recapitalized the bank insurance fund and established new risk-based deposit insurance premiums: banks could compete aggressively but would need to pay a commensurate price for deposit insurance. In 2006, the S&L and commercial bank deposit insurance funds were merged into a single Deposit Insurance Fund.

In addition to easing asset and liability constraints and standardizing regulation across classes of depository institutions, the deregulatory agenda called for easing barriers to entry into banking. State and federal bank regulators progressively undermined restrictions on interstate banking and branching rooted in the Jeffersonian-Jacksonian-populist fear of concentrated wealth. The Riegle-Neal Interstate Banking and Branching Efficiency Act of 1994 eliminated what was left of these restrictions. In 1999, Congress ticked off the last major item on the deregulatory agenda: ease barriers to entry across the lines between banking and other financial services. The Financial Institutions Modernization Act (Gramm-Leach-Bliley Act) demolished the Glass-Steagall wall between commercial banking and the securities industry and removed the prohibition, dating from 1956, on banks dealing in insurance.

Under the "modernized" regulatory framework, bank size increased dramatically, and organizations of nationwide and regional scope combined banking with securities underwriting and brokerage and insurance. These organizations would be tested in terms of the same fundamental issues that Hamilton and Jefferson debated: Do they *work well* to achieve the goals of banking policy? Are they *too powerful* in the economy or in democratic politics?

In the financial crisis of 2008, deregulated U.S. banking failed its first significant test. At the root of the crisis were the large volume of subprime residential mortgages originated after 2000 and resulting waves of defaults and foreclosures. These loans were extended with inadequate attention to borrowers' ability to repay and had features, like variable interest rates, which had been mostly eliminated by Depression-era regulatory moves but reappeared with deregulation. The loans were assembled into pools on the basis of which mortgage-backed securities were issued. Three large banks heavily involved in subprime mortgage lending failed in 2008. Most subprime mortgages, however, were originated not by banks but by mortgage brokers and mortgage bankers, their way paved by banking deregulation. Similarly, securitization was mostly provided not by commercial banks and S&Ls, but by Wall Street investment banks. Even so, commercial banks were major *buyers* of the mortgage-backed securities built on low-quality mortgages—and this is the link between inadequately regulated mortgage lending, even outside of banks, to the failure of banking in 2008. As commercial banks realized that they could not assess one another's safety and soundness due to exposure to mortgage-backed securities, interbank lending, and therefore lending to business customers in the real economy, ground to a halt. The open question in banking policy is whether policy makers had learned, this time, that unregulated financial capitalism will—sooner or later—undermine the real economy.

See also business and politics; economy and politics.

FURTHER READING

Cargill, Thomas F., and Gillian G. Garcia. *Financial Reform in the 1980s.* Stanford, CA: Hoover Institution Press, 1985.

Degen, Robert A. *The American Monetary System: A Concise Survey of Its Evolution since 1896.* Lexington, MA: Lexington Books, 1987.

Hoffmann, Susan. *Politics and Banking: Ideas, Public Policy, and the Creation of Financial Institutions.* Baltimore, MD: Johns Hopkins University Press, 2001.

Kettl, Donald F. *Leadership at the Fed.* New Haven, CT: Yale University Press, 1986.

Kuttner, Robert. *The Squandering of America: How the Failure of Our Politics Undermines Our Prosperity.* New York: Knopf, 2007.

Litan, Robert E., with Jonathan Rauch. *American Finance for the 21st Century.* Washington, DC: Brookings Institution Press, 1998.

Livingston, James. *Origins of the Federal Reserve System: Money, Class, and Corporate Capitalism, 1890–1913.* Ithaca, NY: Cornell University Press, 1986.

McFaul, John M. *The Politics of Jacksonian Finance.* Ithaca, NY: Cornell University Press, 1972.

Moody, J. Carroll, and Gilbert C. Fite. *The Credit Union Movement: Origins and Development, 1850–1980.* 2nd ed. Dubuque, IA: Kendall/Hunt, 1984.

Unger, Irwin. *The Greenback Era: A Social and Political History of American Finance, 1865–1879.* Princeton, NJ: Princeton University Press, 1964.

White, Lawrence J. *The S&L Debacle: Public Policy Lessons for Bank and Thrift Regulation.* New York: Oxford University Press, 1991.

Wilburn, Jean Alexander. *Biddle's Bank.* New York: Columbia University Press, 1967.

SUSAN HOFFMANN

Bill of Rights

On September 25, 1789, the first Congress sent a packet of 12 constitutional amendments to the states. Two years later, ten of these amendments became part of the Constitution after Virginia's ratification provided their necessary approval by three-fourths of the states. Over time, these amendments came to be known collectively as the Bill of Rights, and their adoption is generally portrayed as a critical concluding act in the story of constitutional reform that began with the Federal Convention of 1787. Since the early twentieth century, the interpretation of the rights enumerated in the first eight amendments, along with the equal protection and due process clauses of the Fourteenth Amendment (ratified in 1868), has emerged as the richest and most controversial realm of modern constitutional jurisprudence.

At the time of their adoption, however, the amendments were as much an anticlimax to the great constitutional debate of the late 1780s as its culmination. The major changes that the anti-Federalist critics of the Constitution sought in 1787–88 involved the structure of the new federal government and the division of power between the Union and the states. The limited scope of the amendments that James Madison introduced in the House of Representatives on June 8, 1789, hardly satisfied the anti-Federalists' deeper concerns. Nor did most of the Federalist supporters of the Constitution who dominated the new Congress agree that amendments were necessary. It took a fair amount of hectoring from Madison even to get his congressional colleagues to consider the subject of amendments. Once Congress sent the amendments out for ratification, it took the states much longer to approve the ten articles that were adopted than it had to act on the original Constitution.

Once ratified, the amendments were largely forgotten. The Bill of Rights imposed restrictions only on the national government, not the states. Well into the nineteenth century, most of the governance that affected the daily lives of Americans occurred at the level of the states and local communities, where the federal guarantees did not apply. As the scope of federal activity gradually expanded after the Civil War, the national Bill of Rights slowly began to develop its own constitutional jurisprudence. But the critical evolution came later, after the Supreme Court, developing what is known as the Incorporation Doctrine, construed Section I of the Fourteenth Amendment to apply the protections enumerated in the federal Bill of Rights against state and local governments. In the 1960s and 1970s, a slew of decisions extended this doctrine almost comprehensively.

The Tradition of Declarations of Rights

The belief that bills of rights were an essential safeguard of liberty occupied a prominent and venerable place in Anglo-American constitutional thinking during the seventeenth and eighteenth centuries. The classic example was Magna Carta, the famous agreement between the protesting barons of England and the domineering King John. Its negotiation in 1215 was thought to mark the moment when an English nation began to recover the ancient liberties it had lost in 1066, when William the Conqueror sailed from Normandy to impose the yoke of feudal rule on a free people. To this way of thinking, a bill of rights was a compact negotiated between a ruler and his subjects. It was not so much the source of the rights they claimed as proof and confirmation that they already possessed the liberties and privileges in question.

There were other helpful examples of such documents of more recent vintage. In 1628, at an early point in the great constitutional controversies between the Stuart monarchy and its opponents, Parliament had presented King Charles I with a Petition of Right meant to affirm fundamental rights dating to Magna Carta and beyond. In 1689 the new monarchs William and Mary accepted a Declaration of Rights framed by the so-called Convention Parliament as an implicit condition of their accession to the throne after the flight of Mary's father, James II. Once legally reenacted by Parliament later that year, it became formally known as the Bill of Rights. Closer to home, many individual colonies had their own declarations of rights, often reiterating the customary rights and liberties that they and their English countrymen claimed but also including other statements of special importance to particular provinces.

There is no simple way to categorize the statements these documents could contain. In contemporary usage, a declaration of rights could combine broad principles of governance and general affirmations of natural rights to life, liberty, and property with the specific protections of common law procedures of trial and adjudication. Equally important, constitutional thinking before the revolutionary era did not regard statements of rights as legally binding commands that formally limited the power of government. Instead they identified principles and procedures that rulers *ought* to respect and follow. But the leading principle of Anglo-American constitutionalism after 1689 was the idea of legislative supremacy, which meant that the Crown, the executive branch of government, could no longer be allowed to assert the power to make law unilaterally, as a mere expression of royal will. The best way to protect the rights and liberties of a people was to empower and enable their duly elected representatives to act as lawmakers. A second security lay in the power of juries to prevent royal judges from deciding cases on their own authority. The right to vote for representatives and to serve on juries offered the best political safeguards a free people could enjoy.

The Revolutionary Controversy

In the mid-eighteenth century, these views were commonly held in both Britain and its American colonies. The great imperial controversy that began with the parliamentary Stamp Act of 1765 and ended with Americans declaring independence a decade later exposed the limited utility of bills of rights as instruments for checking power. The controversy pivoted on the British claim that the legislative supremacy of Parliament trumped the colonists' belief that they could be taxed and governed only by the acts of their elected representatives. Appealing to their colonial charters and statements of rights was only one of many ways in which the colonists tried to prove they were exempt from the jurisdiction of Parliament. There were occasional suggestions that the dispute might be resolved by negotiat-

ing an American bill of rights to clarify the respective powers of empire and colonies. But the colonists could not overcome the dominant principle of British authority: that Parliament was the supreme source of law within the empire. If the colonists were loyal subjects of that empire, they must ultimately acknowledge its sovereignty over them.

The Americans would not acknowledge such sovereignty, and war came in April 1775, followed by the decision for independence 15 months later. During this final crisis, legal government effectively collapsed in most of the colonies, replaced by a network of extra-legal committees, conventions, and congresses. By early 1776, many Americans recognized that independence was inevitable, and individual colonies began petitioning the Continental Congress for permission to create new legal governments to replace both the revolutionary committees and the old colonial institutions. That would require writing constitutions to establish institutions grounded on republican rather than monarchical principles.

In the process, eight states adopted declarations of rights to accompany the new constitutions they were drafting. In three states (Pennsylvania and North Carolina in 1776, Massachusetts in 1780), these declarations became integral parts of the new constitutions. In others, they remained independent documents of uncertain authority. Some states, like New York, while not adopting distinct declarations, did include articles specifying particular rights in the constitutional text.

Whatever form these statements took, they were not initially regarded as firm commands that the new governments were fully obliged to obey. Their original purpose was more political than legal. In a literal-minded way, Americans in 1776 saw themselves emerging from the condition known as a "dissolution of government," a situation well described by John Locke a century earlier. In that condition, a people exercising their natural right to form a compact of government were entitled and indeed expected to state the principles on which they were acting. By stating their rights, a people could remind themselves, their descendants, and their rulers of the basic purposes of the government they were forming. Hopefully, the rulers would not overstep the just boundaries of their power. But if they did, the existence of such declarations would enable a people to judge their ruler's behavior and oppose or resist the encroachments of the power of the state upon the liberty of society.

In adopting these constitutions and declarations, the revolutionaries did not immediately abandon the assumptions of legislative supremacy they had inherited from the Anglo-American constitutional tradition. Historically, the major threat to rights was perceived to lie in the unchecked power of the Crown and the great purpose of identifying and protecting rights was to secure the people as a whole, conceived as a collective entity outside of government, from its arbitrary will. The idea that a legislative assembly composed of the people's own representatives could also threaten their rights was not easy to conceive. These early statements of American constitutionalism sometimes included articles affirming the principle of separation of powers, as laid down by the Baron de Montesquieu in his influential treatise *The Spirit of the Laws*. A republican people had a right not to be subjected to a government in which the three forms of power (legislative, executive, and judicial) were concentrated in the same hands. But that did not make all three departments of power equal in authority. The legislature was the dominant branch, and its dominant role included protecting the rights of the people.

Developments after 1776

That inherited understanding was severely tested in the first decade after independence was declared. The war forced the legislatures to unprecedented levels of activity. The measures they adopted to keep the military struggle going intruded on people's lives and liberties in novel and costly ways, through economic dislocations that affected the property rights that Anglo-American thinking had long deemed almost sacred. Inevitably, these laws had a differential impact on various sectors of society, driving criticism of the elected legislatures that faced unpleasant choices in distributing the burden of waging a prolonged and difficult war. As Americans grew more critical of the performance of these governments, it also became possible to think of a bill of rights as a potential restriction on the authority of the people's own representatives.

A second, closely related development at the state level of governance also had a profound impact on American ideas. Calling a written charter of government a constitution did not by itself make such documents into supreme fundamental law. The constitutions drafted in 1776 were not only written in haste but also promulgated by the provincial conventions that drafted them, and not submitted to the people for ratification. In this sense, they did not embody a form of law higher than ordinary legislation, but were merely statutes, admittedly of exceptional importance, but still potentially subject to revision by later sessions of the legislature. They were not,

in other words, constitutions in the exalted sense of the term: supreme law that would set benchmarks against which ordinary acts of government could be measured.

The movement to find a way to distinguish constitutions as supreme law began in Massachusetts and led to an important procedural breakthrough. Two conditions had to be satisfied, several Massachusetts towns argued, for a constitution to become fully constitutional. First, it had to be drafted by a special body elected for that purpose alone. Second, it then had to be ratified by the sovereign voice of the people, assembled in their town meetings. This doctrine took hold with the adoption of the Massachusetts Constitution of 1780, and marked a milestone in American constitutional theory and practice. Thomas Jefferson, among others, elaborated on this idea in his *Notes on the State of Virginia*, first published in France in 1784.

These developments raised provocative questions about the value and authority of bills of rights. How could a declaration or bill of rights operate as an effective restraint on the people's own representatives? If constitutions were regarded as fundamental law, unalterable by ordinary acts of government, could the authority of bills of rights also be enhanced by following the precedent of the three states that integrated their statements of rights into the text of the constitution proper? If that happened, declarations of rights could operate less as statements of principle and more as legal commands, leaving open the possibility of their enforcement by the independent judiciaries the new constitutions had also created.

James Madison's Reformulation of the Problem of Rights

When Jefferson sent copies of his *Notes on Virginia* back home, he also asked James Madison whether the work would be appropriate for an American audience. One of Jefferson's concerns was that his adverse comments on the Virginia constitution would be taken amiss. After reading the work closely, Madison agreed with Jefferson's charge that the constitution had no greater authority than a statute. Madison also took the leading role in persuading the Virginia legislature to enact the Bill for Religious Freedom that Jefferson drafted in the late 1770s. Among other things, that bill affirmed that freedom of conscience—the right to believe whatever one wished about religious matters—was a fundamental natural right that no state could legitimately abridge. But the concluding paragraph of the bill also restated the constitutional dilemma that Jefferson had addressed in *Notes on Virginia.* A right recognized only by statute could also be repealed by statute, because one legislature had no power to bind its successors.

Jefferson and Madison had first met in 1776, while serving on the committee on religion in the lower house of the new Virginia legislature. Both were products of the eighteenth-century Enlightenment that regarded the previous centuries of religious persecution and warfare as a blight on European and Christian civilization. Their shared commitment to the principles of freedom of conscience and separation of church and state formed one basis of their deep personal friendship. But to Madison, even more than Jefferson, the idea of protecting an individual right to believe whatever one wished in matters of religion contributed to a broader rethinking of the problem of protecting rights in a republican society.

The basis for this rethinking came from Madison's experience in the Virginia legislature (1784–86). Notwithstanding his success in securing passage of the Bill for Religious Freedom, his three terms of legislative service convinced him that representative assemblies could not be relied upon to act as guardians of the people's rights. Too many recent acts seemed designed to promote one set of interests over another, without giving due attention to the rights of the losing minority. This was especially the case when matters of property were at stake. Madison was responding to the enormous upsurge in economic legislation that the war had made necessary, and which still plagued Americans in the mid-1780s as they wrestled with the public debt the war had created and other economic problems that accompanied the return of peace.

For Madison, as for most Anglo-American thinkers of the age, the protection of property was a fundamental purpose of society, as John Locke had made clear a century earlier in his *Second Treatise of Government.* But Madison combined his original commitment to freedom of conscience with his new appreciation of the problem of economic legislation to recast the problem of protecting rights in republican terms. The traditional problem under monarchical governments had been to protect the people against the arbitrary power of the Crown. But in a republic, where executive power seemed weak and derivative, the greater danger would come from a far more powerful legislature. Moreover, the real force driving the adoption of unjust laws would come not from the ambitions of the legislators but from the people themselves—or rather, from majorities among the people that would use legislative power to act unjustly to-ward disfavored minorities. Coming as he did from the upper stratum of Virginia's ruling class of landed slave owners, Madison was thinking of the interests of his own class. But his insight remained a profound one. In a republican government, unlike a monarchy, one could not naively assume that the people would unite to protect their collective rights against the concentrated power of the state. Historically, bills of rights had been seen as instruments negotiated between the people's representatives and their monarchical rulers. What use would they be when representatives and rulers were one, and when the people were the very source of the problem?

One other critical conclusion followed from this analysis. If the people themselves could threaten private rights, at which level of government would they pose the greater danger: national or state? Here Madison first formulated his famous argument about the problem of the "factious majority"—that is, a majority of citizens claiming democratic authority to rule but acting in ways inimical to either the "public good" or "private rights." The smaller the society, Madison reasoned, the easier it would be for such mischievous majorities to form. It followed that such majorities could coalesce more easily within the limited confines of the states than would be the case in the "extended republic" of an expansive and expanding federal union. National government should prove less "factious" than state government, and rights more secure at the national level than within the smaller compass of the states or localities. Moreover, Madison also understood that the states would remain the real locus of daily governance. If, then, one hoped to make rights more secure, a way had to be found to enable the national government to check or correct the unjust misuse of power at the state level. As he prepared for the Federal Convention that would meet at Philadelphia in May 1787, Madison reached the radical conclusion that the best way to protect rights would be to give the national legislature a negative on state laws, akin to the detested veto the British crown had enjoyed over colonial legislation.

The Convention's Great Oversight

In somewhat diluted form, Madison's proposal for a negative on state laws was part of the Virginia Plan that formed the basic agenda for the deliberations at Philadelphia. By mid-July, that proposal was dead, and with it, Madison's hope that the adoption of a federal constitution would provide a means for dealing with the problem of protecting rights within the individual states.

Ten days after the convention rejected the negative, it adjourned to allow a Committee of Detail to convert the resolutions adopted thus far into a working draft of a constitution. In its own deliberations, that committee briefly considered prefacing the constitution with some statement of principles akin to the state declarations. But as one of its members, Edmund Randolph, noted, the situation of 1787 was not the same as that of 1776. "We are not working on the natural rights of men not yet gathered into societies," Randolph observed, "but upon those rights, modified by society, and *interwoven with* what we call the rights of states."

The convention did include a few clauses protecting specific rights in the completed draft of the Constitution: the right to trial by jury in criminal cases; a prohibition on the suspension of habeas corpus except "in Cases of Rebellion or Invasion"; the guarantee that "Citizens of each State shall be entitled to privileges and Immunities of Citizens in the several States." A prohibition on religious tests for office-holding would open the right to participate in government to all, but the fundamental right to vote was left a matter of state, not federal, law. Similarly, a prohibition on state laws impairing the obligation of contracts was consistent with Madison's desire to prevent the states from enacting legislation inimical to vested rights of property (since such laws would advantage debtors over creditors).

Important as these individual provisions were, they did not amount to a comprehensive statement of fundamental rights. On September 12, five days before the convention adjourned, Elbridge Gerry and George Mason (the author of the Virginia Declarations of Rights of 1776) moved to correct that omission by proposing the adoption of a general bill of rights. By that point, most delegates knew that the two men would refuse to sign the completed Constitution. After cursory debate, their motion was rejected. The delegates apparently did not believe that the absence of a bill of rights would impair the prospects for ratification.

The convention's Federalist supporters (as they soon became known) quickly realized this was a major political miscalculation. Anti-Federalists almost immediately made the absence of a declaration of rights a rallying point against the Constitution. This was hardly their sole objection, nor even the most important. But the convention's failure to protect rights seemed to confirm the charge that the Constitution was in reality designed to consolidate all effective power in one supreme national government, leaving the states to wither away and the people's liberties at the mercy of distant institutions they could not control.

An early speech by James Wilson, a framer and leading Pennsylvania Federalist, inadvertently reinforced the opponents' concerns. Speaking outside the statehouse where the Constitution was written, Wilson argued that it would actually have been dangerous to provide explicit protection for such cherished rights as freedom of press or conscience. Properly understood, the Constitution vested only specific, explicitly designated powers in the new government. Providing for the protection of rights whose exercise the Constitution did not in fact threaten, Wilson argued, would imply that such a power had indeed been granted.

This was a lawyer's argument, and politically it proved counterproductive. By Wilson's logic, there was no need for the Constitution to protect the Great Writ of habeas corpus either; yet it did. By being too clever by half, Wilson only reinforced anti-Federalist suspicions that the Constitution was a lawyer's document that skillful politicians could exploit to run roughshod over the people's liberty.

With Wilson's October 6 speech serving as a lightning rod, the omission of a bill of rights became a staple theme of anti-Federalist rhetoric. Drawing on the provisions found in the state declarations, they argued that the Constitution should be amended to provide explicit protection for an array of rights, ranging from freedom of conscience and press to the "liberty to fowl and hunt in seasonable times, on the lands they hold" and "to fish in all navigable waters." Most Federalists remained unpersuaded. The convention might have miscalculated, but that did not mean that a constitution lacking such articles was truly defective.

In arguing for the adoption of rights-protecting amendments, anti-Federalists straddled a line between the traditional ideas of 1776 and the new constitutional norms that had emerged since. On the one hand, they did not fully imagine that a bill of rights, if adopted, would create a set of commands or rules that citizens could enforce at law, for example, by asking a court to provide a specific remedy when a right was infringed. Bills of rights were still regarded as *political* documents, a device for enabling the people to act in their political capacity to check abuses by government. This was a very traditional understanding. But many anti-Federalists also embraced the new way of thinking about written constitutions that had developed since 1776. By arguing that rights would remain insecure unless they were explicitly included in the constitutional text, they abandoned the older view that rights derived their authority from multiple sources, such as nature or custom. A right that was not incorporated in the text of a constitution might cease to be either a constitutional or a fundamental right.

The decisive fact making the adoption of a bill of rights more likely, however, was not the force of anti-Federalist reasoning. It was, rather, that narrow divisions in several key states—most notably Virginia and New York, the tenth and eleventh to ratify—inclined Federalists to agree to *recommend* the consideration of an array of amendments to the first Congress to meet under the Constitution. This concession was the price of ratification. To portray it as a firm bargain, as many histories have done, probably goes too far. It was more an expectation than a deal, and since Federalists successfully insisted that the states should ratify the Constitution without conditions or contingencies, they got the better of the deal.

Madison Again

Madison left the federal convention believing that its rejection of his proposed negative on state laws would leave the protection of individual and minority rights in the same vulnerable position as before. Though his disappointment eased over time, he shared the general Federalist misgivings about the utility of bills of rights. "Experience proves the inefficacy of a bill of rights on those occasions when its controul is most needed," Madison wrote Jefferson in October 1788. "Repeated violations of these parchment barriers have been committed by overbearing majorities in every State." Those majorities that concerned him were more popular than legislative, for in Madison's analysis, the problem of how best to protect rights required that one first identify where "the real power in a Government lies." In a republic, that power resided with "the majority of the Community," and he simply doubted that such popular majorities would allow a mere declaration of rights to deter them from pursuing their violations of "private rights."

This analysis of rights was, again, political rather than legal. But political considerations of a different kind were driving Madison to accept the idea of adding rights-protecting amendments to the Constitution. He had taken that position in the Virginia ratification convention in June, and he soon repeated it publicly during a tough race for election to the House of Representatives. Yet even then, Madison thought that the chief value of a declaration of rights would lie in its effect on public opinion. As the rights declared gradually acquired "the

character of fundamental maxims of free Government" and were "incorporated with the national sentiment," they would work to "counteract the impulses of interest and passion" that would still drive most citizens. It took a suggestion from Jefferson, writing from France, to prod Madison to concede that such articles might also enable the independent judiciary the Constitution would create to act as a "legal check" against abuses of power.

Consistent with his public statements, Madison assumed the burden of convincing the new Congress to take up the subject of amendments. This proved an uphill struggle. Federalists had gained easy control of both houses in the first federal elections, and few of them believed they were obligated to take up the question of amendments. For their part, anti-Federalists knew they would be unable to secure the structural changes to the Constitution they desired most, and without those, a mere statement of rights did not seem so important. Thus it fell to Madison to push what he privately called "the nauseous project of amendments."

In preparing for this task, Madison reviewed all the amendments that the various state ratification conventions had proposed. From this list of over 200 proposals, he culled the 19 clauses he introduced in the House of Representatives on June 8, 1789. Two of his proposals related to congressional salaries and the rule for apportioning House seats among the states. The rest were concerned with identifying constitutional rights. They would not appear as separate, supplemental articles but rather be inserted at those points in the Constitution where they seemed most salient.

In drafting these clauses, Madison avoided the principle-propounding language of 1776. He did include one set of articles that would have added a second preamble to the Constitution, this one affirming the fundamental right of a sovereign people to form and reform governments designed to secure "the enjoyment of life and liberty, with the right of acquiring and using property; and generally of pursuing and obtaining happiness and safety." The House eliminated this familiar language. The Senate subsequently rejected another article that Madison called "the most valuable amendment on the whole list": a proposal to prohibit the states from violating "the equal right of conscience, freedom of the press, or trial by jury in criminal cases." This proposal was consistent with Madison's belief that the greatest dangers to rights would continue to arise within the states.

The remaining proposals formed the framework for the amendments that Congress ultimately sent to the states nearly four months later. One major change in format came at the repeated urging of Roger Sherman of Connecticut, who insisted that Congress must not tamper directly with the original Constitution that he, like Madison, had helped to draft. Rather than interweave the amendments in the existing text, as Madison had proposed, they should be treated as supplemental articles. Sherman, a dogged politician, had some difficulty getting his suggestion accepted, but eventually it prevailed. Turning the amendments into additional articles rather than interwoven ones made it easier over time to think of them as a bill of rights, each of whose separate articles addressed some distinct or integral realm of civil liberty or governance.

Records of the House debates on the amendments suggest that few members regarded their approval as an urgent priority. They did not discuss how the amendments, if ratified, would be enforced, nor did they speculate about the ways in which the constitutional entrenchment of rights might lead to an expanded judicial role in their protection. Mostly, they tinkered with Madison's language before sending the amendments on to the Senate in August. The Senate did some editorial work of its own, and final revisions were made in a conference committee.

One especially noteworthy change occurred here. Madison had originally proposed a religion article, stating, somewhat awkwardly, "The civil rights of none shall be abridged on account of religious belief or worship, nor shall any national religion be established; nor shall the full and equal rights of conscience be in any manner, or on any pretext infringed." The House changed the second clause to read, more simply, "Congress shall make no law establishing religion." The Senate then narrowed that language to a mere prohibition on "laws establishing articles of faith or a mode of worship." The conference committee on which Madison sat took a much simpler tack still, rejecting these efforts at precision with a broad ban holding, "Congress shall make no law establishing a Religion, or prohibiting the free exercise thereof."

That broader and simpler wording has left ample room for continuing interpretation and controversy, but its original significance should not be overlooked. Religion was one realm of behavior that governments had always believed should remain subject to state support and public regulation. By approving the dual principles of nonestablishment and freedom of conscience, the adopters of the religion clause were endorsing the far-reaching principle that matters of religious organi-

zation and belief should henceforth fall entirely within the sphere of private activity, where individuals, acting freely for themselves or in free association with others, could be counted upon to decide what was best. Here was the most telling example of what the broader American commitment to individual liberty and private rights could mean in practice.

Beyond Ratification

For well over a century after its ratification, the Bill of Rights was not a significant element in American constitutional jurisprudence. The "Congress shall make no law" formula of the First Amendment did not prevent the enforcement of the Sedition Act of 1798, which criminalized seditious speech directed against the administration of John Adams. In 1833, the Supreme Court held, in *Barron v. Baltimore*, that the numerous protections of the first eight amendments applied only against acts of the national government, not those of the states. One noteworthy doctrinal development did take place in 1878. In *Reynolds v. U.S.*, a case involving the Mormon practice of plural marriage, the Court held that the free exercise clause of the First Amendment covered matters of religious belief but not all practices that followed from religious doctrine. In reaching this decision, the Court relied on the writings of Jefferson and Madison, the two Revolutionary-era leaders who had written most eloquently on the subject.

That decision came at a time, however, when the Court was blunting the potential reach of the Fourteenth Amendment, framed as the Reconstruction of the South was just getting under way. Section 1 of the amendment declared, "No state shall make or enforce any law which shall abridge the privileges or immunities of citizens of the United States." It was entirely plausible to read "privileges or immunities" to include the clauses of the federal Bill of Rights. Some of the amendment's leading authors and supporters believed that the *Barron* case of 1833 had been wrongly decided, and if their views were accepted, the amendment could have been read as a basis for enforcing the federal guarantees against the states generally. But in the early 1870s, with support for Reconstruction visibly waning, the Court began adopting a more restrictive approach, and the promise of the Fourteenth Amendment remained unfulfilled.

Only after World War I did the Court gradually begin to develop the so-called Incorporation Doctrine, under which it held that many, though not all, clauses of the original Bill of Rights could act as restraints on the actions of state governments. Freedom of speech was arguably the first right to be nationalized in this way, beginning with the 1925 ruling in *Gitlow v. New York*. The leading proponent of a wholesale incorporation of the Bill of Rights was Justice Hugo Black, the former Alabama senator and New Deal supporter who became the mid-century Court's leading libertarian. Although his brethren on the Court initially shied away from adopting his broad views, by the 1960s, the animus to apply most of the protections of the Bill of Rights against the states became one of the defining features of the jurisprudence of the Warren Court. Decisions on a whole array of subjects, from school prayer to the "revolution in criminal justice" brought about by expansive interpretation of the numerous procedural rights enshrined in the Fourth, Fifth, and Sixth Amendments, helped make the Supreme Court a lightning rod for political criticism.

The Court's most controversial modern decisions were those promoting desegregation (beginning with *Brown v. Topeka Board of Education* in 1954) and a woman's right to abortion (*Roe v. Wade* in 1973). But the nationalization of the Bill of Rights also played a critical role in the denunciations of "judicial activism" that have resonated so deeply in American politics since the 1960s, and that show no sign of abating. Whether debating school prayer or the right to bear arms or the unusual cruelty of the death penalty, Americans treat the clauses of the Bill of Rights as subjects for political discussion as well as judicial definition and enforcement. This is a different notion of the political value of bills of rights than the one that Federalists and anti-Federalists disputed in the late 1780s. But it helps to explain why "rights talk" remains so prominent an element of our political discourse.

See also Articles of Confederation; civil liberties; Constitution, federal.

FURTHER READING

Amar, Akhil Reid. *The Bill of Rights: Creation and Reconstruction.* New Haven, CT: Yale University Press, 1998.

Conley, Patrick T., and John Kaminski, eds. *The Bill of Rights and the States: The Colonial and Revolutionary Origins of American Liberties.* Madison, WI: Madison House, 1992.

Levy, Leonard. *Original Intent and the Framers' Constitution.* New York: Macmillan, 1988.

Rakove, Jack N. *Declaring Rights: A Brief History with Documents.* Boston: Bedford Books, 1997.

Schwartz, Bernard. *The Great Rights of Mankind: A History of the American Bill of Rights.* Madison, WI: Madison House, 1992.

JACK N. RAKOVE

bureaucracy

See regulation.

business and politics

For generations the United States has nourished the world's most potent capitalist economy. The United States is also the longest-lived democracy. Their coexistence would seem to suggest that capitalism and democracy, at least in America, go together like love and marriage. But their union has been far from harmonious. At critical moments, relations have deteriorated to the breaking point. Yet for even longer stretches of time, popular sentiment has tacitly endorsed President Calvin Coolidge's 1925 adage that "the business of America is business."

Faith in the inherent virtue of market society is less strictly mercenary than Coolidge's aphorism might suggest. From the origins of the republic to the present day, the free market has promised freedom, in particular, the liberty of the individual to pursue happiness, to dispose of his or her own powers and talents, and to amass private property unencumbered by government or other forms of social restraints. The conviction that the market is the passway to liberty has deep roots in American culture.

But some Americans have always dissented from this faith. Henry Demarest Lloyd, a widely read critic of the country's new plutocracy during the late nineteenth century, observed that "liberty produces wealth and that wealth destroys liberty." Lloyd was worried about the power of great industrial combines and financial institutions to exterminate their competitors, snuffing out the freedom the market pledged to offer to all. He was also bothered by the inordinate influence of these economic behemoths over the country's political institutions.

Capitalism and democracy, by their very natures, establish two rival sources of power and authority: one private, the other public. Large-scale corporations control and dispose of vast resources upon which the whole of society depends. The liberty associated with market society provides the rationale for this otherwise extraordinary grant of private empowerment over decisions that carry with them the greatest public import. Democracy operates according to a contradictory impulse, namely, that matters affecting the public welfare ought to be decided upon by popularly delegated and publicly responsible authorities.

It might be assumed that, in any showdown, democracy would trump capitalism, if only by virtue of sheer numbers. Quite the opposite has often been the case. Market society presumes the privileged position of private property as the vessel of liberty. Even a thoroughgoing liberal democracy like the United States has been reluctant to challenge that axiom. Precisely because business is so vital to the well-being of society, government has tended to bend over backward to encourage and promote the same business institutions that Lloyd cautioned were driven to destroy liberty.

Business and the Birth of the Nation

The fundamental question about the relationship between capitalism and democracy has been asked since the beginning of the nation. One of the most famous controversies about U.S. history was ignited by the historian Charles Beard in his 1913 book, *An Economic Interpretation of the Constitution of the United States*. Beard argued that the architects of the new nation who gathered in Philadelphia in 1787 were chiefly motivated by a desire to protect and further the interests of the country's dominant economic classes: merchants, bondholders, plantation owners, and the like. The Constitution they authored established a central government empowered to regulate interstate and foreign commerce, to secure the credit worthiness of the infant republic, to levy taxes, to implicitly legitimate chattel slavery, and to ward off overzealous assaults on the rights and prerogatives of private property—the sort of democratic upheavals, like Shays's Rebellion, that had made life under the Articles of Confederation too precarious for the well-off.

Beard's interpretation echoed a primal antagonism about the future of America that began with the country's birth and raged with great intensity all through the 1790s, turning founding fathers into fratricidal enemies. Alexander Hamilton, the first secretary of the treasury, envisioned a formidable commercial future for the new republic. He imagined a nation fully engaged in international trade, one with thriving manufacturing establishments and cosmopolitan urban centers where high culture and high finance would mingle. All this would happen thanks to the catalytic role of the federal government and under the guidance of the country's rich and well-born.

Three proposals in particular embodied the secretary's bold plan for the country's future: a "Report on the Public Credit," which called on the new federal government to assume at face value the nearly worthless revolutionary and postwar debt obligations of the Continental Congress and the states; the creation of a Bank of the United States; and a "Report on Manufacturers" that pledged the national government to help jump-start industrialization. Each in its own way was designed to mobilize the capital resources and active participation of the country's wealthier classes (as well as to attract foreign investment) in turning an underdeveloped country into a rival of the great European powers. Hamilton's view prevailed during the administrations of Washington and Adams.

But some old comrades from the war for independence, men with whom Hamilton had jointly conceived the Constitution, detested the secretary's policies. Thomas Jefferson and James Madison were convinced his proposals would incubate a new moneyed aristocracy that would subvert the democratic accomplishments of the Revolution. They feared precisely what Hamilton desired, namely, a commercial civilization like the one characteristic of the Old World. For all its cultural sophistication and economic vigor, such a society, they argued, was also a breeder of urban squalor and of vast inequalities of wealth and income. It fed a mania about money-making and self-seeking that incited moral and political corruption and an indifference to the public welfare.

Jeffersonians, however, did not comprise some eighteenth-century version of back-to-the-land romantics. They too recognized the advantages, even the necessity of trade and commerce. Hardly hostile to the free market, they instead wanted to widen its constituency beyond those circles favored by Hamilton. The most notable accomplishment of Jefferson's presidency was the Louisiana Purchase, which enormously enlarged the potential territory open to freeholder agriculture.

Nor did Jefferson or his successors imagine these pioneering agrarians living in splendid, self-sufficient isolation. Every subsequent administration through the presidency of James Monroe sought to buttress the nation's agricultural foundation by opening up the markets of the world to the produce of American farms. This meant breaking down the restrictions on trade with the rest of Europe and the Caribbean imposed by the British Empire, a policy that led first to Jefferson's embargo on trade with European belligerents during the Napoleonic Wars and eventually to the War of 1812. These drastic measures indicated that the Jeffersonians considered international trade a vital component of a flourishing agrarian republic.

Over time, the infeasibility of the old Jeffersonian persuasion became apparent. Even its most dedicated proponents reluctantly grew to accept that a modern market economy would inevitably bring in its wake dense commercial networks and a complex division of labor, industries, and cities. What nonetheless kept the temperature of political animosity at fever heat for the rest of the nineteenth century was how these warring parties envisioned the role of the government in promoting economic development and keeping the channels of economic opportunity open to all. Even as agrarian republicanism faded from view, its profound suspicion of finance and industrial capitalism remained very much alive, a living indictment of big business as the defining institution of American civilization.

The Age of Jackson

Andrew Jackson, "Old Hickory," seemed the natural inheritor of the Jeffersonian tradition. Jackson waged a dramatic and protracted struggle against an institution that seemed to embody every Jeffersonian nightmare about the rise of a counterrevolutionary moneyed aristocracy. The Second Bank of the United States was better known during the 1830s as "the Monster Bank." It was run by Nicholas Biddle, a blue-blooded Philadelphian. He presided over a quasi-public institution that exercised decisive influence over the country's monetary resources but without a scintilla of public accountability. The president set out to the kill the Monster. Because the bank aroused enormous popular resentment, he eventually succeeded.

Yet it would be a mistake to conclude from the so-called Bank War that antebellum Americans, especially in the North, were hostile to the commercial development of the country in the same way their Jeffersonian ancestors were. On the contrary, they were men on the make. What they most resented about the Monster Bank was the way it limited commercial opportunity rather than opening it up to every man. While they remained wary of ceding the government too much power, they also believed it could and should help to nourish their entrepreneurial ambitions.

Beginning in the antebellum years, government at every level was dedicated to the promotion, not the reg-

ulation, of business. The country's whole transportation and communications infrastructure—its roads, turnpikes, canals, wharves, dockyards, bridges, railroads, and telegraph system—were, practically without exception, quasi-public creations. Governments granted them franchises, incorporated them, lent them money, invested in them, provided them with tax exemptions and subsidies and land grants, and even, at times, shared in their management.

Such leaders of the Whig Party as Henry Clay and Daniel Webster sought to make this practice of state-assisted business development the policy of the national government. For this reason, the party commanded the allegiance of the rising business classes, as did the newly created Republican Party, into which the Whigs dissolved. Clay's "American system" of internal improvements and a protective tariff to nurture infant industry also enjoyed significant support among Jacksonian Democrats, but only in the North. Most Southern planters cared strictly about the cotton trade and were hostile to a protective tariff, which could only increase the costs of manufactured necessities and invite retaliation from its trading partners abroad. Because the slave South held the whip hand in the Democratic Party, the American system remained stillborn until after the Civil War. But the general proposition that government ought to be a helpmate to business was already widely, if not universally, accepted.

The Gilded Age

No myth about American history has demonstrated greater durability than the belief that the late nineteenth century was the golden age of laissez-faire. It was then, so the story goes, that a hands-off policy by the government allowed the impersonal operations of the free market to work their magic and turn the United States into an industrial goliath. But actually all branches of the federal government were deeply implicated in that process. Not only did they actively promote the development of a national capitalist economy; they did so in a way that favored the interests of industrial and financial corporations. Thus, the rise of big business was due less to impersonal economic laws and more to man-made ones.

Railroads epitomized how the system worked. Without the land grants, loans, tax exemptions, and subsidies provided by the federal government, it is hard to imagine the extraordinary transcontinental network of rail lines that provided the skeletal framework of the national marketplace. Railroads were to the mid-nineteenth century what the steel industry was a generation later or the auto industry was during the mid-twentieth century: the engine of the national economy driven by the country's dominant business institutions. America's emergence as the world's foremost economy began in this hothouse relationship between business and government.

However, accompanying government largesse were well-documented instances of cronyism and corruption. During the Grant administration, a scandal involving the Crédit Mobilier company, responsible for helping construct the transcontinental railroad, implicated congressmen, cabinet members, and even the vice president in schemes to defraud the government. Similar outrages occurred locally, as with the Erie Railroad in New York, where city councilmen, state legislators, and judges were bought and sold by rival railroad speculators. Such transgressions, however lurid and even illegal, were exceptional. Still, they signaled a more general disposition on the part of the country's political class to align itself with the country's most powerful business interests.

The Republican Party pursued this course most single-mindedly and commanded the loyalty of the emerging class of manufacturers, who particularly applauded the party's staunch support for the protective tariff—a barrier against industrial imports that grew steadily higher as the century drew to a close. The promotion of business, however, was a bipartisan policy. New York merchants and financiers engaged in the export trade tended to be Democrats because they favored free trade rather than a protective tariff. But the leadership of the party, and its two-time president Grover Cleveland, were of one mind with their Republican opponents when it came to defending the gold standard as essential for economic stability.

The late nineteenth century witnessed the emergence of trusts and other forms of industrial combinations all across the economy, from steel and sugar production to the drilling and distribution of oil. These firms exercised extraordinary power over the marketplace and, inevitably, posed a dire threat to the American dream of entrepreneurial independence, inspiring a fierce resistance.

Beginning during the Gilded Age and lasting well into the twentieth century, the antitrust movement was a major influence on American politics. It enjoyed the support of small and medium-sized businessmen and of the growing class of urban middle-class consumers and white-collar workers. It also inspired the political mobilization of the nation's farmers, especially in the South and the Great Plains, who particularly resented the life-threatening power of eastern financiers, the owners of the great railroads that crisscrossed the country, and the commercial middlemen (grain elevator operators, wholesalers, and the like) who dictated terms of credit as well as the costs of shipping, storing, and distributing farmers' produce.

Together, these groups turned to the government for help. During the 1870s and 1880s, they were moderately successful, especially in state politics. Laws were passed regulating and restraining the operations of interstate corporations, particularly the railroads. But all three branches of the federal government were hostile to reform. In a series of landmark cases, the Supreme Court ruled that these regulatory attempts by state governments violated the rights of corporations to due process under the Fourteenth Amendment (which was originally passed to protect the civil rights of emancipated slaves) and also trespassed on the exclusive powers delegated to the federal government to regulate interstate commerce. At the same time, the Senate came to be known as "the Millionaires Club," because its members seemed far more solicitous of the needs of major corporations than they did of their ordinary constituents.

Finally, the executive branch made its most formidable resource—the coercive power of the armed forces—available for the protection of corporate property. In addition to the antitrust and farmer movements (most famously the Populist or People's Party of the 1890s), the other great challenge to the profits and preeminence of big business came from the labor movement. The main battle took place on the factory floor, where workers were subjected to a ruthless regime of wage cutting, exhausting hours, and a draconian work discipline. Strikes, some local, some nationwide, in dozens of industries swept across the country in several waves, beginning in the mid-1870s and continuing to the end of the century. Again and again, businesses were able to count on state and federal judges to issue injunctions that outlawed these strikes, and on governors and even the president of the United States to send in state militias and federal troops to quell them when they continued. President Cleveland's decision in 1894 to use the army to end the strike of the American Railway Union against the Pullman Company is the most famous instance of the latter; it convinced many people that big business had captured the government.

Ironically, most leading businessmen of the Gilded Age initially had no serious interest in politics. They were content to turn to the government for particular favors when needed but otherwise kept aloof from party politics. All that began to change, however, when antitrust, Populist, and labor resistance grew so sizable it could not be ignored.

In the end, the groundswell of popular sentiment in favor of some form of regulation proved irresistible. Frustrated at the state level, reformers redoubled their efforts to get some redress from the federal government. The Interstate Commerce Act was passed in 1887 to try to do away with rebates and other forms of railroad market abuse. And, in 1890, Congress approved the Sherman Anti-Trust Act. But in both cases business interests used their political influence to dilute the effectiveness of these laws. By necessity, the nation's commercial elite became more practiced in the arts and crafts of democratic politics.

Indeed, as the century drew to a close, the business community mobilized to defeat its enemies in the electoral arena as well. In 1896 the Democratic Party was captured by elements sympathetic to populism and to antitrust reform and nominated the charismatic William Jennings Bryan as its presidential candidate. But the victory of Republican William McKinley, lavishly supported by leading industrial and financial interests, seemed to put an end to the immediate threat to the economic and political supremacy of big business and to bury along with it the vision of an alternative political economy and social order.

Business and the Progressive Movement

Yet in the early twentieth century, the axis of American politics shifted direction. Once devoted to the promotion of business, government in the Progressive Era turned to its regulation. Odder still, important segments of business and finance welcomed this turn of events as often as they had resisted it. No longer indifferent to or contemptuous of the democratic process, the business community increasingly grew to believe its fate would be decided in that arena.

The presidencies of Theodore Roosevelt and Woodrow Wilson especially marked the era as progressive. Roosevelt was feared by the Republican old guard—figures like the industrialist and politician Mark Hanna and financier J. P. Morgan. And the president was not shy in making known his disdain for such "malefactors of great wealth." His administration initiated the first antitrust lawsuits against such major corporations as Northern Securities (a gigantic railroad holding company) and Standard Oil.

Antitrust prosecutions comprised only a small portion of his attempts at regulating business. Roosevelt's regime achieved such legislative milestones as the Pure Food and Drug Act, the Meat Inspection Act, and the Hepburn and Mann-Elkins laws strengthening the hand of the Interstate Commerce Commission to rein in the railroads. Meanwhile, municipal and state governments in dozens of big cities and states—egged on by muckraking journalists like Lincoln Steffens and Ray Stannard Baker—took on public utility and urban mass transit companies that had been looting government budgets for years.

Woodrow Wilson, elected in 1912, promised to extend the scope of business regulation. He and a chief adviser, future Supreme Court justice Louis Brandeis, were convinced that the rise of big business and finance had worked to choke off opportunity for would-be entrepreneurs, had aborted technological innovations, and, by blocking the pathways of economic mobility, had undermined the institutions of political democracy as well. Wilson took office amid a widely publicized congressional investigation of the so-called money trust, a purported clique of Wall Street investment banks that controlled not only a host of other financial institutions but also many industrial corporations, including United States Steel and General Electric. Soon after the hearings ended, the president signed into law the Federal Reserve Act. It established a quasi-public institution to oversee the nation's monetary system and presumably break the stranglehold of the money trust.

The Wilson administration and a Democratic Congress accomplished other notable reforms of the business system as well. The Clayton Act tried to strengthen the antitrust provisions of the Sherman Act and exempted labor unions from prosecution as conspiracies in restraint of trade, which had been the main use of the earlier law. The new Federal Trade Commission (FTC) broadened the powers of the national government to regulate interstate commerce. The Adamson Act established the eight-hour day for railroad employees. However, the reform momentum stalled when the United States entered World War I in 1917.

Many businessmen and some consumers viewed corporate consolidation of the economy at the turn of the century as a godsend rather than a curse. It would, they assumed, end the competitive anarchy that had produced numerous booms and busts and two severe and protracted depressions during the Gilded Age. Businesses had tried, on their own, to impose some order over the marketplace by forming pools and other informal agreements to control prices, limit production, and share the market among the chief competitors. But such private arrangements to rein in the free market failed as firms could not resist taking advantage of any shift in the market to get a jump on their competitors.

Thus, some industrialists began to look to the government as the only institution with enough authority and legitimacy to impose commercial discipline. The Interstate Commerce Commission and the Mann-Elkins Act drew support not only from smaller businessmen who hoped to get rid of rate discrimination but also from the railroads themselves—as long as they could exercise some control over what the commissioners did and forestall popular pressure for more radical reform. Similarly, major meatpacking corporations welcomed the Meat Inspection Act. By establishing uniform standards of hygiene that their smaller competitors would have to meet, they hoped the act would open up foreign markets that had grown increasingly leery of importing American beef.

All this signaled that businessmen were becoming more politically conscious and organized. Trade associations representing whole industries began lobbying in Washington. The National Civic Federation—organized by Mark Hanna, Andrew Carnegie, and other leading industrialists—tried to impart a more conciliatory mood into the brittle, often violent relations between labor and capital characteristic of the Gilded Age. Other national business organizations, including the United States Chamber of Commerce (USCC) and the National Association of Manufacturers (NAM), formed to represent the political desires of smaller business, especially to thwart legislation sympathetic to labor.

Thus, on the eve of World War I, many businessmen and politicians had come to accept the need for some degree of regulation to supplement government promotion of private enterprise. However, differences within the business community and between it and the government over the nature and extent of that regulation left many questions unresolved.

Then the war fatefully shifted the terrain on which this tense relationship unfolded. On the one hand, the country's need to mobilize its resources restored the social reputation of big business, which produced most of the munitions and other goods for the American Expeditionary Force and its European allies. On the other hand, such a massive mobilization of private assets demanded a level of coordination that only the govern-

ment could impose. The War Industries Board, created by President Wilson and run by financier Bernard Baruch, initiated a degree of state intervention into the private sector that would have astonished most of the radical critics of the previous century. Although this apparatus was quickly dismantled once the war ended, the experience with economic planning and supervision left a legacy many would turn to during the next national emergency.

More immediately, however, it was the political rehabilitation of big business that left its mark on the Jazz Age following the war. The Republican administrations of Warren Harding, Calvin Coolidge, and Herbert Hoover deferred to the corporate world. Businessmen were hailed as the nation's wise men who seemed to have solved the age-old problem of the business cycle, ushering in a new era of permanent prosperity.

Antitrust prosecutions virtually ceased. The Supreme Court severely restricted the power of the FTC to define methods of unfair competition. The regulatory vigilance of the government was relaxed in what turned out to be a tragic turn of events.

The Great Depression and the New Deal Order
No crisis in American history, save for the Civil War, presented as grave a national trauma as did the crash of 1929 and the Great Depression that followed. The economic wisdom, social status, moral authority, and political weight of the business community collapsed in a hurry. Until that moment business had generally prevailed in its tug of war with the government and the forces of democracy. But, for a long generation beginning in the 1930s and lasting well into the 1970s, the balance of power was more equally divided.

President Franklin Delano Roosevelt's New Deal never amounted to a single, coherently conceived and executed set of economic policies. It was in a constant state of motion, tacking first in one direction, then in another, pursuing courses of action that were often contradictory. One fundamental, however, never changed: the government must act because economic recovery could not be left to the impersonal operations of the free market. A return to the laissez-faire approach of the old regime was, once and for all, off the table.

Indeed, the Roosevelt administration found itself under relentless pressure from various social movements to challenge the power of big business. A new and militant labor movement spread through the industrial heartland of the country, taking on the most formidable corporations and mobilizing in the political arena to support the New Deal. Small farmers, tenants, and sharecroppers in the Midwest and South defied banks and landlords to stop foreclosures and evictions. Charismatic figures aroused populist emotions against financiers and the wealthy. Huey Long, the demagogic governor and later senator from Louisiana, led a Share the Wealth movement that called for taxing away any income over a million dollars a year. Father Charles Coughlin, the "radio priest" broadcasting from a suburban Detroit Catholic church, electrified millions of listeners with his denunciations of parasitic bankers.

Such democratic upheavals reverberated within the Democratic Party and helped heighten the tension between the Roosevelt administration and major sectors of the business and financial world. They inspired the President's denunciation in 1936 of "economic royalists." Without these upheavals, it is hard to imagine the basic reforms accomplished by the New Deal.

New Deal innovations covered four broad areas affecting the material well-being of Americans: (1) economic security and relief; (2) financial and industrial regulation; (3) industrial reform; (4) economic planning.

The most enduring legislative legacy of the New Deal is the Social Security system. Passed in 1935 by an overwhelmingly Democratic Congress, the Social Security Act, for the first time, established government responsibility for protecting against the most frightening insecurities generated by the free market: a poverty-stricken old age and unemployment. In fits and starts, the New Deal also initiated a series of federal relief measures to address the plight of the jobless and dispossessed in both urban and rural America.

This ethos of social responsibility for the economic security of all citizens continued well beyond the New Deal years. The welfare state continued to expand after World War II, most memorably through the GI Bill, which committed the federal government to subsidizing the education and housing of returning veterans. In the mid-1960s, President Lyndon Johnson's Great Society programs included various antipoverty and urban redevelopment measures—especially Medicare and Medicaid, which addressed the health needs of the elderly and some of the poor. However limited and flawed, such programs represented a major shift in the country's political orientation. They indicated a recognition that the free enterprise system could not be relied upon, by itself, to assure the economic security of the American people.

Rightly or wrongly, most people blamed the Depression on Wall Street, in particular on the reckless speculation, insider trading, and fraudulent practices that allegedly led to the crash of 1929 and to the economic implosion that followed. The resulting demand for the government to closely monitor the behavior of business naturally focused on the financial system. Therefore, the Roosevelt administration and Congress targeted the banking and securities industries. The Glass-Steagall Act of 1933 made it illegal for the same establishment to function both as an investment and as a commercial bank on the grounds that there was an inherent conflict of interest between those two functions—one that had undermined the credibility of the whole banking structure of the country.

The suspect and secretive practices of the stock market were addressed by two securities acts, the second of which established the Securities and Exchange Commission. These reforms demanded of Wall Street a far greater transparency about its operations, outlawed certain kinds of insider dealings, and subjected the nation's chief financial markets to ongoing public supervision.

Business regulation under the New Deal was hardly confined to the financial sector. New agencies like the Federal Communications Commission were created, and transportation and public utility companies found themselves under more rigorous scrutiny. The Public Utility Holding Company Act attempted, without much success, to dismantle corporate pyramids in the electrical power industry that had fleeced consumers and left the underlying companies saddled with insupportable debt. This assault, while abortive, reflected a revving up of antitrust sentiment.

While the politics of antitrust would lose energy in the years ahead, the regulatory momentum of the New Deal order would only grow stronger. By the late 1960s and early 1970s, its emphasis would shift from regulating the abuses of particular industries to policing business in general. New environmental and consumer protection movements inspired deep popular distrust of the business community. Largely composed of middle-class, college-educated professionals, these public interest organizations demanded that corporations be held not only responsible but accountable for their actions. The Occupational Health and Safety Act and the Environmental Protection Act of 1970 and the Consumer Product Safety Commission created in 1972—followed by legislation to clean up the air and water and the toxins of industrial waste—were all passed during the

Republican administration of President Richard Nixon, suggesting just how irresistible this regulatory impulse had become.

A third phase of New Deal economic intervention proved just as robust. It is hardly an exaggeration to describe the pre–New Deal system of industrial labor relations as a form of industrial autocracy, especially in heavy industry. Most workers endured long hours at low wages, conditions subject only to the unilateral whim of their employers, who could also hire and fire them at will. The rise of a militant labor movement and the growth of pro-labor sentiment within the Democratic Party during the early years of the Depression resulted in fundamental reform. The National Labor Relations Act (NLRA, or Wagner Act) of 1935 established a form of industrial democracy by inscribing workers' right to organize unions free of employer interference. It proscribed a range of employer behaviors as unfair labor practices and made companies legally obliged to engage in collective bargaining once a union had been established by government-supervised elections. The Wagner Act was supplemented in 1938 by the Fair Labor Standards Act, which set a national standard of minimum wages and maximum hours and outlawed child labor.

Many of those who supported the NLRA did so not just out of a sense of social justice. They believed that reforming the system of labor relations was part of a larger design for economic recovery in which the government would have to play a central role. Unions and minimum wages, they hoped, would restore the mass purchasing power of ordinary Americans and thereby spur production and employment. The idea that government had an overarching role to play in getting the economy moving again was hardly restricted to these areas, however. It inspired the fourth salient of New Deal innovation: economic planning.

The National Industrial Recovery Act (NRA) of 1933—the New Deal's first attempt at general economic recovery—created a form of federally sanctioned corporatism or cartelization, operating not unlike the old War Industries Board of World War I. The system effectively suspended antitrust laws so that big businesses in every industrial sector could legally collaborate in establishing codes of fair competition.

A similar form of government intrusion into the operations of the free market tried to address the depressed state of the agricultural economy. The Agricultural Adjustment Administration established government-sanctioned production controls and acreage allotments that were designed to solve the crisis of overproduction that had led to mass farm foreclosures and evictions all across the country.

At first, many businesses welcomed these forms of economic planning, because they amounted to a form of self-regulation that left big firms in effective control of the government machinery charged with doing the planning. But for just that reason, they were vociferously attacked by smaller businessmen and small farmers. In 1935, the Supreme Court ruled the NRA was unconstitutional. Its demise, however, gave life to different, more democratically minded strategies for government-directed economic recovery.

Members of the New Deal administration were convinced that only government intervention could restart the country's economic engine. The Tennessee Valley Authority (TVA) was created with an ambitious mission to transform the economic and social life of the deeply impoverished trans-Appalachian southeast region. Under the auspices of the TVA, the federal government itself entered the electrical power business, directly competing with private utilities and forcing them to make their own operations more efficient and cost effective. By making electricity available to millions of rural Americans, TVA planners hoped to bring them within the orbit of the modern economy, improving their standard of living and turning them into customers for manufacturers of electrical appliances.

Balancing the federal government's budget had been a central orthodoxy of the old order. In the face of this, the New Deal committed the sacrilege of deficit spending to help get the economy out of its protracted slump. Deficit finance was at the heart of a new economic policy associated with the famous British economist, John Maynard Keynes. Keynesianism located the origins of the Depression in the problem of insufficient demand and argued that this tendency was inherent in modern capitalism. To overcome it, the government had to resort to its powers over fiscal and monetary policy, especially the former. The government's tax policy would redistribute wealth downward, bolstering consumer demand. The "wealth tax" of 1935 was a first attempt to do this by raising taxes on corporations and the wealthy. The Roosevelt administration never fully committed itself to this strategic break with the past, but even its experiments in that direction were pioneering.

During World War II, a version of Keynesianism became the new orthodoxy. Much of the war economy operated under government supervision, was financed with federal loans and cost-plus contracts, and a sizable portion of the new plants and equipment was actually owned by the government. But by putting an end to the Depression, the war also restored the economic and political fortunes of the private sector. Consequently, after the war, the business community managed to rein in the more social democratic variant of Keynesian policy and replace it with a version friendlier to private enterprise. Commercial Keynesianism relied more on monetary policy, that is, on manipulating the money supply and interest rates in responding to the business cycle. The government backed away from any effective commitment to assuring full employment, grew more leery of deficit spending (except in the military sector) and investments in the public sector, and avoided—until the mid 1960s—a broad expansion of the social welfare state. Commercial Keynesianism relied on automatic stabilizers like unemployment insurance to stabilize the business cycle.

The New Deal's groundbreaking efforts at income redistribution and social welfare did inspire the early years of the Lyndon Johnson's Great Society during the 1960s. But the enormous financial burdens of the Vietnam War and America's other military commitments short-circuited those assaults on poverty. Inflation—always the latent danger of deficit spending—haunted the economy as the decade of the 1960s drew to a close. It was easier to cut budgets for poverty programs than to tackle the politically more potent military-industrial complex that President Dwight Eisenhower had warned about in his Farewell Address in 1961.

Business and the Rise of Modern Conservatism

Commercial Keynesianism made business first among equals in the postwar New Deal order. Moreover, some segments of American finance and business had always supported certain New Deal reforms, just as there were elements of the business community that had backed Progressive-Era legislation. Industries that relied on the consumer market and banks oriented to the small depositor were sympathetic to Keynesian approaches that bolstered demand. These businesses formed the Committee on Economic Development in 1942. There were also corporations that supported Social Security as politically inevitable and worked to make the program business friendly. Some northern-based manufacturers backed the Fair Labor Standards Act as a way of eliminating the wage differential that gave their southern-based competitors an advantage. Still, the main business lobbies—the NAM and the USCC—militantly opposed most New Deal reforms.

Then the Keynesian regime entered a terminal crisis at the end of the 1960s. It collapsed for many reasons: the costs of the Vietnam War; the inability of the government's economic managers to stem war-induced inflation; the unraveling of the postwar system of fixed international exchange rates in 1971; the emergence of powerful industrial competitors in Germany and Japan; the rise of foreign oil-producing nations that hiked energy costs. A protracted period of what came to be called "stagflation" in the 1970s seemed the final refutation of the Keynesian outlook. After all, its adherents had always maintained it was impossible for the economy to suffer simultaneously from inflation and unemployment. By the late 1970s, however, it indubitably was.

Commercial Keynesianism had been a bipartisan persuasion. The reaction against it, however, formed mainly within the Republican Party and culminated in the election of Ronald Reagan to the presidency in 1980. If big business had been the bete noire of the New Deal, big government played that role for champions of the free market counterrevolution to reverse the New Deal.

Restoration of the old order proceeded in several directions at once. Supply-side economics, which in contrast to Keynesianism focused on encouraging investment rather than demand, became the theoretical justification for cutting taxes on corporations and the wealthy and for trimming the social welfare budget and public spending on infrastructure. Both occurred during the two Reagan administrations.

Deregulation became a key watchword of the new regime. It entailed both capturing and dismantling the regulatory apparatus of the federal government. Agencies were increasingly run and staffed by people either directly recruited from the industries they were charged with regulating or by civil servants with decided sympathies for the business point of view. So, for example, presidential appointees to the National Labor Relations Board, beginning under Reagan and continuing during the administrations of George H. W. Bush and his son George W. Bush, ruled repeatedly in favor of businesses charged with unfair labor practices, or they at least tolerated long procedural delays that effectively stymied union organizing and collective bargaining.

Rules were relaxed or not enforced or eliminated entirely in a host of specific industries, including airlines, trucking, telecommunications, and the financial sector.

The lifting of rules governing the operations of savings-and-loan banks resulted in the collapse of the whole industry in the late 1980s and the largest government bailout of private enterprise in American history; until, that is, the massive rescue and partial nationalization of the country's leading financial institutions during the meltdown of the country's financial system in 2008.

The drive to deregulate was less successful in the arena of non-industry-specific social regulation, exemplified by the Environmental Protection Agency and the Occupation Health and Safety Administration. Here powerful middle-class constituencies resisted the deregulatory impulse. Still provisions of the Clean Air Act were weakened, the powers of the FTC reduced, and efforts to beef up consumer protections thwarted.

The Democrats put up little effective resistance to such changes. The influence of big business and finance within the Democratic Party had grown steadily after Reagan's 1980 victory. By the 1990s, leading elements within the Democratic Party also favored cuts in the welfare state, deregulation, and monetary and fiscal policies that were designed to please the business community.

Still, the politics of restoration went only so far; modern business had come to rely on the government in certain crucial respects. While paying lip service to the aim of a balanced budget, deficits grew under both Ronald Reagan and George W. Bush, sometimes enormously. In both cases this had to do with a considerable expansion of the defense budget. Even before the Republican counterrevolution, military spending had become big business and a permanent part of the country's political economy. Much of this military production is sustained by government-guaranteed, cost-plus contracts, insulated from the oscillations of the free market.

However, the assault on the New Deal order had accomplished a great deal. Substantial credit for its success must go to the remarkable ideological discipline, self-organization, and political savvy of the business community itself. Beginning in the 1970s, new organizations like the Business Roundtable (founded in 1972 and made up the country's top CEOs) worked with established ones like the USSC and the NAM not only to affect public policy but also the underlying values that shaped such policy. Together with such well-funded think tanks as the Heritage Foundation and the American Enterprise Institute, they denounced the profligacy of "tax and spend" liberalism, exposed the "culture of dependency" encouraged by the welfare state, and ex-

tolled the virtues of the free market. If the New Deal had been premised on the quest for economic security and a sense of social obligation, the business-sponsored literature of the Reagan and Bush eras help create a large constituency for older values of individualism, risk taking, and self-reliance.

The heightened activities of corporate lobbyists and think tanks were supplemented by an equally spectacular growth of business involvement in elections. A 1976 Supreme Court decision—*Buckley v. Valeo*—established the right of corporations to make unlimited financial contributions to political parties and political action committees. Increasingly, the viability of candidates for public office came to depend on how much money they could raise to wage their campaigns. No one had more money to offer than big business. Even without engaging in corrupt or illegal practices, the machinery of American democracy came to be more and more lubricated by cold cash.

The relationship between capitalism and democracy in American history has been a tumultuous one. It began in mutual suspicion, but then passed through a period when the governing classes considered it their mission to promote the development of business and the national market. The dilemmas of late nineteenth-century free market capitalism led to widespread demands for reform, ushering in the next phase of that relationship in which the government took up the responsibility of regulating business, culminating in the New Deal order. At least until the presidency of Barack Obama, the latest stage shifted the balance of power back in favor of the private sector, but the contemporary business system relies on government intervention and support far more than its nineteenth-century predecessor. Arguably, this latest phase in the relationship between capitalism and democracy was less a return to some imaginary laissez-fair utopia than it was a return to the kind of elitist financial system that Alexander Hamilton proposed at the birth of the republic.

See also banking policy; economy and politics; labor movement and politics.

FURTHER READING

Berkowitz, Edward, and Kim McQuaid. *Creating the Welfare State.* New York: Praeger, 1988.

Cochran, Thomas, and William Miller. *The Age of Enterprise.* New York: Macmillan, 1942.

Collins, Robert. *The Business Response to Keynes, 1929–1964.* New York: Columbia University Press, 1981.

Fraser, Steve. *Every Man a Speculator: A History of Wall Street in American Life.* New York: HarperCollins, 2005.

Galbraith, John Kenneth. *The Great Crash: 1929.* Boston: Mariner Books, 1997.

Lindbloom, Charles. *Politics and Markets: The World's Political-Economic Systems.* New York: Basic Books, 1977.

McCoy, Drew. *The Elusive Republic: Political Economy in Jeffersonian America.* New York: Norton, 1982.

Mills, C. Wright. *The Power Elite.* New York: Oxford University Press, 1956.

Phillips, Kevin. *Wealth and Democracy: A Political History.* New York: Random House, 2002.

Vogel, David. *Fluctuating Fortunes: The Political Power of Business in America.* New York: Basic Books, 1989.

Wiebe, Robert. *Businessmen and Reform: A Study of the Progressive Movement.* Chicago: Quandrangle Books, 1962.

STEVE FRASER

cabinet departments

The first three cabinet departments—the Departments of State, War, and the Treasury—were organized in 1789 by the U.S. Congress at President George Washington's urgent request. The addition of the Department of Homeland Security in 2002 brought to 15 the total number of cabinet departments created since then. Charting the emergence of cabinet departments provides a shorthand guide of sorts to American history. The westward expansion of settlement, the extension of agriculture into unfamiliar environments, industrialization, urbanization, the emergence of the United States as a world power, and the advent of twentieth-century social movements in pursuit of political equality and economic security for all American citizens—each of these trends in American history was eventually reflected in the president's cabinet. Indeed, in a nation with a political culture supposedly premised on a mistrust of "big government," the existence of 15 cabinet departments within the executive branch stands as a frank acknowledgment of reality: there are, in fact, matters that require oversight and management on the part of the federal government. The order in which the cabinet departments were created provides not just a rough indication of the general contours of American history, then, but also suggests how and when Americans arrived at a consensus that the role of the federal government ought to be expanded to address a particular problem.

Political scientists often refer to "inner" and "outer" cabinet departments. Inner cabinet departments are generally understood as those performing essential governmental tasks, including national defense, finance, and enforcement of the law. These were among the first cabinet departments formed. The outer cabinet departments, by contrast, emerged over the course of the nine-teenth and twentieth centuries as new and unforeseen problems surfaced. The creation of these cabinet departments often met with controversy and delay, but most Americans have come to accept the role of the federal government in these areas as well.

The Inner Cabinet Departments

The inner cabinet departments perform functions nearly universally recognized as essential for any successful nation-state. These functions include forging relations with foreign nations, providing for the national defense, ensuring a sound financial system, and enforcing the law. Accordingly, during the first months of 1789, George Washington lobbied Congress successfully for the establishment of the Departments of War, State, and the Treasury. President Washington also established the Office of the Attorney General, forerunner to the Department of Justice and the fourth inner cabinet department. The Department of Homeland Security, created in the wake of the September 11, 2001, terrorist attacks on the United States, has arguably been the only addition made to the inner cabinet since 1789.

The Department of State

The Department of State was the first cabinet department created by Congress and is the oldest department in the executive branch. President Washington signed the law creating a Department of Foreign Affairs in July 1789 in order to formulate and carry out the new nation's foreign policy. After Congress placed a number of domestic duties into the new department's portfolio—including the administration of the census and the management of both the U.S. Mint and the nascent Library of Congress—the department was renamed the Department of State in September 1789. Although these domestic obligations were shuttled to other departments during the nineteenth century, the name stuck. Since its inception, the State Department has served as the primary representative of the American government and its citizens in the international community. It assumes responsibility for maintaining diplomatic relations with other nations and assists and protects U.S. citizens traveling or living overseas.

The office of the secretary of state was a prestigious position during the early years of the republic—Thomas Jefferson, James Madison, James Monroe, and John Quincy Adams all used the State Department as a stepping-stone to the presidency. But given its emphasis on foreign policy, it is not surprising that the department itself grew slowly during the early nineteenth century, when isolationism and a focus on continental expansion prevailed. As the United States became a leading exporter of goods in the decades following the Civil War, however, the State Department's consular functions became more important. And as the United States became more involved in hemispheric and then world affairs beginning in the late nineteenth century, the department grew accordingly. State Department officials also took steps to professionalize the department. Written examinations— complete with foreign-language tests—began in 1895. Secretary of State Philander Knox (1909–13) introduced geographic divisions into the organization of the department and encouraged area expertise among its employees. The Rogers Act of 1924 unified the department's diplomatic and consular services, thereby creating the modern Foreign Service of the United States. By World War II, the department was on its way to developing a career-oriented foreign service complete with improved salaries, merit-based promotions, and an increased emphasis on language and cultural training.

The development of the State Department during the World War II and cold war eras was even more notable. The number of employees at the department increased from 1,100 to nearly 10,000 between 1940 and 1950. In 1949, moreover, the department reorganized into geographic bureaus focusing on inter-American, Far Eastern, European, Near Eastern, African, and international organization affairs, reflecting the geographic scope of postwar American foreign policy.

Other additions, such as the Bureau of Economic Affairs (1944), the Bureau of Intelligence (1957), and the Bureau of Cultural Affairs (1960), indicated the wide range of interests that the shapers of U.S. foreign policy had in the rest of the world. And whereas the secretary of state position in the nineteenth century proved to be a prestigious perch from which to launch a bid for the presidency, during these immediate post-

World War II years when State Department influence was at its apex, secretaries of state George C. Marshall (1947–49), Dean Acheson (1949–53), and John Foster Dulles (1953–59) pursued cold war policies that endured for more than a generation, profoundly affected the U.S. role in international affairs, and altered American domestic politics. Yet at the very height of its influence, the State Department lost its monopoly on foreign affairs. Three cold war era creations—the Defense Department, the Central Intelligence Agency, and the National Security Council—circumscribed the State Department's power to shape American foreign policy. Secretary of State Henry Kissinger (1973–77) wielded considerable influence in the administration of President Richard Nixon, for example, but this was due as much to his concurrent position as national security advisor as to the power inherent in the office of the secretary of state. Similarly, President George W. Bush's secretary of state, Colin Powell (2001–5), proved unable to restrain the administration's hawkish foreign policy in advance of the 2003 invasion of Iraq.

Nevertheless, the Department of State remains the primary agency in charge of implementing U.S. foreign policy, even if it now competes with other policy actors at the formulation stage. The State Department currently maintains relations with nearly 180 countries, and, in 2007, it had approximately 30,000 employees and a budget of $10 billion.

The Department of the Treasury

Established in September 1789, the Department of the Treasury is the second oldest cabinet department still in existence. The Treasury Department performs many different functions, unified by money. It functions as the chief manager of the nation's financial and economic policies and ensures the solvency of the U.S. government. Its domestic duties include overseeing the collection of taxes and tariffs, allocating budgeted funds, borrowing the money necessary to operate the federal government, safeguarding the integrity of the nation's banks, manufacturing the nation's coins and printing its currency, and advising the president on matters of domestic and international economics.

The Department of the Treasury has historically served as one of the largest law enforcement agencies in the federal government: it enforces federal tax laws and investigates counterfeiting and the evasion of taxes and customs. These responsibilities have remained relatively consistent since 1789, although the department's power to manage the nation's finances naturally increased commensurate with the increasing power of the federal government. The Treasury Department expanded considerably during the Civil War, for example, when secession led both to a precipitous drop in revenue and a costly war to reunite the Union. The Bureau of Internal Revenue (forerunner to the Internal Revenue Service) was established in July 1862 to ensure a steady stream of revenue during the war effort. Similarly, the increased role of the United States in world affairs in the aftermath of the World War II led to an expansion in Treasury Department activities. The department helped shape the 1944 United Nations Monetary and Financial (Bretton Woods) Conference and has remained one of the dominant influences on the International Monetary Fund and the World Bank.

On the other hand, more recent events have stripped the Treasury Department of many of its law enforcement functions. Heightened concerns surrounding national security in the twenty-first century led to the transfer of the U.S. Customs Service and the U.S. Secret Service to the new Department of Homeland Security in 2002; the law enforcement arm of the Bureau of Alcohol, Tobacco, and Firearms was transferred to the Department of Justice by the same Homeland Security Act. This reorganization left the modern Treasury Department with an $11 billion annual budget and 110,000 employees spread throughout the Alcohol and Tobacco Tax and Trade Bureau, the Comptroller of the Currency, the Bureau of Engraving and Printing, the Financial Crimes Enforcement Network, the Internal Revenue Service, the U.S. Mint, the Bureau of the Public Debt, and the Office of Thrift Supervision.

The Department of Defense

Perhaps the most readily identifiable cabinet department, the Department of Defense is responsible for training, equipping, and deploying the military forces that defend the security of the United States and advance the nation's interests abroad. The Defense Department is the largest cabinet department in terms of human resources. It manages 1.4 million active-duty military men and women and 1.2 million Army Reservists and National Guard members. The Defense Department also employs approximately 700,000 civilians. Its budget was $440 billion in 2007, although it remains unclear how much of the costs of the ongoing wars in Afghanistan and Iraq were included in that figure.

The Department of Defense is the direct successor to the War Department, which was originally established alongside the Foreign Affairs (State) Department in July 1789 and was in charge of all land military forces from 1789 until 1947. Concerns over disorganization and inefficiency grew as the Army, Navy, and Air Force developed into discrete military units and made coherent military planning increasingly difficult. Between 1920 and 1945, for example, over 50 bills called for the uniting of the armed forces into a single organization, and concerns about inefficiency and redundancy were only exacerbated by the nation's participation in World War II and the looming cold war.

These anxieties culminated in the National Security Act of 1947, which eliminated the War Department and subsumed the Departments of the Army, Navy, and Air Force under the newly created National Military Establishment (NME). A series of 1949 amendments to this National Security Act reconstituted the NME as the Department of Defense, stripped the service branches of department status, and centralized command and control of all branches of the armed forces under the secretary of defense.

The Department of Justice

Often described as "the largest law firm in the nation," the Department of Justice is charged with enforcing federal laws. As is the case with the Department of Defense, the Justice Department can be traced back to the events of 1789, even though the department itself did not come into existence until much later. In 1789 Congress established the office of the attorney general to represent the interests of the United States at the Supreme Court and to advise the president on legal matters. But the legal work of a growing nation quickly became more than the small office of the attorney general could manage. An avalanche of costly litigation during the Civil War era led to the creation of the Department of Justice.

As established by the Judiciary Act of 1870, the Department of Justice—led by the attorney general—was ordered to conduct the legal business of the federal government, including all civil and criminal cases in which the United States had an interest. The 1870 legislation also established the Justice Department as the primary agency responsible for the enforcement of federal law. This obligation to enforce federal laws has meant that as such laws have moved into new legal territory, so, too, has the department expanded: alongside the original Civil, Criminal, and Tax Divisions, the modern Justice

Department also houses Antitrust, Civil Rights, Environment and Natural Resources, and National Security Divisions—all legacies of legal developments in the twentieth and twenty-first centuries.

Also included in the current Justice Department are the Drug Enforcement Administration, the Federal Bureau of Investigation, the Federal Bureau of Prisons, and the U.S. Marshals Service. Since 2003 the department has housed the Bureau of Alcohol, Tobacco, Firearms, and Explosives. In 2007 the Department of Justice employed 110,000 people and had a budget of $23 billion.

The Department of Homeland Security

The Department of Homeland Security's purpose is to safeguard the homeland against catastrophic domestic events, including acts of terrorism as well as natural disasters. The product of the largest governmental reorganization since the National Security Act of 1947 and an amalgam of 22 agencies and bureaus—such as the U.S. Customs Service and the U.S. Secret Service (both from the Treasury Department), the Immigration and Naturalization Service (from the Department of Justice), the U.S. Coast Guard, and the Federal Emergency Management Agency—Homeland Security instantly became the third-largest cabinet department, upon its creation in 2002, with approximately 200,000 employees. Early signs suggest that this reorganization has not been seamless. The department's hapless response to Hurricane Katrina in 2005 raised many questions about its readiness to handle similar natural disasters or a major terrorist attack. The Department of Homeland Security budget was $46.4 billion in 2008.

The Outer Cabinet Departments: 1849–1913

The cabinet departments created during the nineteenth and early part of the twentieth centuries—the Departments of the Interior, Agriculture, Commerce, and Labor—reflected the demands of a nation in the throes of westward expansion and economic upheaval.

The Department of the Interior

The Department of the Interior has been one of the more enigmatic cabinet departments. Proposals for a "home department" or a "home office" to manage federal territories, Indian Affairs, and internal improvements surfaced as early as 1789, but the Department of the Interior was not created until 1849 when the present-day southwestern United States became part of the national domain as a result of the U.S.-Mexican War. Yet even though the heart of the new Interior Department was the General Land Office, transferred from the Treasury Department in 1849, the department's identity as the nation's primary manager of the nation's public lands and natural resources remained partially obscured by the other tasks during much of the nineteenth century. In addition to the General Land Office, the department was given so many other miscellaneous offices—the Patent Office, the Office of Indian Affairs, a Pension Office serving Army veterans, the nation's first Office of Education, the first Federal Bureaus of Agriculture and Labor—that it became known as "the department of everything else." There seemed to be little coherence in the department's early mission.

But the history of the Department of the Interior from the late nineteenth century to the present is one in which it cast off many of these miscellaneous tasks and focused more intently on land management, natural resource use, and conservation—so much so that Secretary of the Interior Harold L. Ickes (1933–46) fought to reconstitute it as the Department of Conservation. If anything, though, the increased specialization on natural resource management only made the department's mission more complex: at times the Interior Department facilitated the development—even rank exploitation—of the country's natural resources; at other times it enforced strict conservation and preservation measures. The U.S. Geological Survey, for example, was created within the Interior Department in 1879 to survey the lands and mineral resources in order to facilitate the development of the U.S. West. But between the 1870s and the 1890s, the department also preserved lands that would eventually become Yellowstone, Yosemite, Sequoia, and Rainier National Parks.

The pattern of exploitation and conservation continued into the twentieth century: the department's Bureau of Reclamation rarely encountered a river it would not dam for irrigation and hydroelectricity, but the National Park Service and the Fish and Wildlife Service walled off millions of acres of land from future development. When the Interior Department tried to strike a balance between preservation and use, it did so with predictably controversial results. The Bureau of Land Management, for example, has closed remaining public lands to entry and offered instead to allow western ranchers to lease access. But ranchers were quick to complain that the department needlessly "locked up" resources, while conservationists decried "welfare ranchers" determined to use public lands on the cheap. The struggle among developers, conservationists, and preservationists for the control of the nation's public lands and natural resources is woven into the Interior Department's history.

Today the Interior Department consists of the Bureaus of Indian Affairs, Land Management, and Reclamation; the Minerals Management Service and the Office of Surface Mining; the National Park Service and the Fish and Wildlife Service; and the U.S. Geological Survey. The department manages over 500 million acres of public lands and nearly 500 dams and 350 reservoirs; oversees 8,500 active oil and gas operations on 44 million acres of the Outer Continental Shelf; operates nearly 400 national parks, monuments, seashores, battlefields, and other cultural sites, and over 500 national wildlife refuges; and conducts government-to-government relations with over 500 recognized Native American tribes. The Interior Department has 67,000 employees serving at 2,500 locations at an annual budget of $16 billion.

The Department of Agriculture

Unlike the Interior Department, the Department of Agriculture (USDA) began as a department that catered specifically to one economic interest—farmers. But over its century and a half of service, the USDA's mission has widened considerably to include not only the original goal of higher farm incomes through the promotion of agricultural research, businesslike farm management, the efficient use of the latest machinery, and better marketing practices, but also the improvement of the overall quality of life in the nation's rural areas, the protection of agricultural ecosystems through soil and water conservation programs, the promotion of U.S. agricultural goods in overseas markets, ensuring the safety of the U.S. food supply for consumers, educating the public about proper nutrition, and administering food stamp and school lunch programs to low-income Americans.

It is no surprise that suggestions for a Department of Agriculture can be traced back to the 1780s—a time when the United States was truly a nation of farmers. But early federal aid to agriculture was limited to a small seed collection and distribution program established in 1839 in the State Department's Patent Office. As agricultural settlement proceeded westward, however, and after years of lobbying on the part of agricultural societies, an independent Department of Agriculture was established in 1862 in order "to acquire and diffuse . . . useful information on subjects connected with agriculture."

At first, the USDA did little more than continue the seed collection program run by the Patent Office. But with the elevation to cabinet department status in 1889, the USDA embarked on a period of professionalization and expansion, particularly under Secretaries James Wilson (1897–1913) and David Houston (1913–20). During these decades the USDA engaged in more scientific research. The U.S. Forest Service was created in 1905 to professionalize the management of the nation's forest resources, for example, while bureaus or offices of entomology, soil chemistry, roads, weather, and agricultural economics were also established. The Smith-Lever Act of 1914 created the Cooperative Extension Service in order to disseminate the department's scientific and technological know-how to the nation's farmers.

Under the Depression-era management of Secretary Henry A. Wallace, the USDA's mission continued to expand. The Soil Conservation Service made the conservation of soils and water one of the department's tasks, while the Rural Electrification Administration and the Resettlement Administration sought to foster a better quality of life in the nation's rural communities. During the post–World War II era, the USDA turned its attention to issues of consumer safety, ensuring the safety and quality of the nation's food system, fighting hunger, and promoting proper nutrition.

These accumulated duties are now divided among the USDA's many bureaus and services. The Agricultural Marketing Service helps farmers market their products in domestic markets, while the Foreign Agricultural Service seeks to improve overseas markets for U.S. farm products. The Agricultural Research Service and the Animal and Plant Health Inspection Service provide farmers with research and information to increase productivity, aided by the Cooperative Extension Service. The Economic Research Service and the National Agricultural Statistics Service keep agricultural statistics and provide farmers with economic information. The Natural Resources Conservation Service helps farmers follow sound environmental practices. The Forest Service ensures the conservation and wise use of the nation's forest lands. The Farm Service Agency and Rural Development programs extend credit and federal aid to farmers and rural communities. The Food and Nutrition Service and the Food Safety Inspection Service ensure the safety of the nation's food supply, administer the federal government's antihunger programs, and seek to educate American consumers on matters of health and nutrition. The USDA had a budget of approximately $77 billion in 2007. It employs 110,000 people.

The Department of Commerce

The mission of the Department of Commerce is "to foster, promote, and develop the foreign and domestic commerce" of the United States. In other words, the Commerce Department exists to promote the conditions necessary for economic growth. To this end, it creates and disseminates the basic economic data necessary to make sound business decisions. It promotes scientific and technological innovation; facilitates foreign trade and tries to ensure the competitiveness of American businesses in international markets; and grants patents and registers trademarks.

The framers of the Constitution discussed the idea of creating a secretary of commerce and finance, with many of these tasks ending up as part of the Department of the Treasury's domain. But the advent of industrialization, the increase in American exports, and the overall growth in the size and scale of the American economy during the late nineteenth century led to increased demands on the part of business organizations such as the National Association of Manufacturers and the U.S. Chamber of Commerce for a separate cabinet department devoted exclusively to the needs of American business.

The Panic of 1893 served to underscore the need for better coordination and management of business conditions. In 1903 President Theodore Roosevelt signed a law creating the Department of Commerce and Labor; the two were divided into two separate cabinet departments in 1913. At the outset, the Commerce Department was charged with overseeing domestic and foreign commerce, manufacturing, shipping, the nation's fisheries, and its transportation systems.

The department peaked early. In its defining era under the leadership of secretary Herbert Hoover (1921–28), the Department of Commerce expanded by thousands of employees; its annual budget grew from approximately $1 million to $38 million; and the Building and Housing Division (1922), the Bureau of Mines and the Patent Office (1925), the Aeronautics Division (1926), and the Radio Division (1927) were established.

These functions are currently divided among the department's many offices and bureaus. The Economic and Statistics Administration and the Bureau of the Census provide business with data about the state of the economy. The International Trade Administration facilitates international commerce. The Economic Development Administration and the Minority Business Development Agency promote economic growth and business opportunity in economically troubled regions and underserved communities. The National Institutes of Standards and Technology, the National Oceanic and Atmospheric Administration, the National Technical Information Service, and the National Telecommunications and Information Administration each, in their own way, promote technological and scientific innovation among U.S. businesses. The Patent and Trademark Office seeks to encourage innovation through the protection of intellectual property rights. In 2007 the Commerce Department employed approximately 40,000 employees and had a budget of approximately $6.5 billion.

The Department of Labor

The culmination of nearly half a century of vigorous agitation for a "voice in the cabinet" on the part of organized labor, the Department of Labor was created in March 1913 in order "to foster, promote, and develop the welfare of working people, and to enhance their opportunities for profitable employment." It enforces federal laws governing workplace conditions, attempts to uphold the principle of collective bargaining, seeks to protect the solvency of retirement and health care benefits through regulation and oversight, administers unemployment insurance, helps displaced workers through retraining and educational programs, and tracks basic economic data relevant to the American labor force (such as changes in unemployment, prices, wages, and productivity). The department is also responsible for ensuring compliance with federal labor laws in the workplace, including safety and minimum wage regulations and freedom from discrimination.

These basic tasks have evolved over time. At its inception, the Labor Department consisted of a new U.S. Conciliation Service to mediate labor disputes, the Bureau of Labor Statistics, the Bureau of Immigration and Naturalization, and a Children's Bureau. Almost immediately, the demands of World War I meant that the department's primary responsibility was in the mediation of potential labor disputes—and this in turn meant that the department emphasized organized labor's right to collectively bargain with employers. That is, the Labor Department at times pushed for the organization of the workplace. But as health and safety regulations and rules governing the minimum hourly wage and overtime proliferated, the department's energies have focused on enforcing these governmental standards in American workplaces, regardless of unionization. Education, retraining, and reemployment programs grew in importance as deindustrialization began to plague traditional industries in the post–World War II era. The Area Redevelopment Act of 1961, for example, targeted unemployed workers in regions particularly hard hit by deindustrialization. The Comprehensive Employment and Training Act of 1973 underscored the department's increased emphasis on helping American workers survive in the "postindustrial" economy.

These functions are carried out today by the Bureau of Labor Statistics, the Employee Benefits Security Administration, the Employment Standards Administration, the Employment and Training Administration, the Mine Safety and Health Administration, the Occupational Safety and Health Administration, the Veterans' Employment and Training Service, and the Women's Bureau. The Labor Department's annual budget sits at roughly $60 billion, and the department employs 17,000 people.

The Outer Cabinet Departments Established in the Post–World War II Era

Departments established during the postwar decades addressed broad structural problems in American life. Unlike the Departments of Agriculture, Labor, and Commerce, however, many of the outer cabinet departments established in this era enjoyed the support of no single interest group. Departments such as Health and Human Services, Housing and Urban Development, and Education served millions of Americans. But as the institutional embodiments of New Deal and Great Society liberalism, these departments also became a target of attack by small-government conservatives.

The Department of Health and Human Services

The Department of Health and Human Services (HHS) is the federal government's principal department working to ensure the health and welfare of all Americans, particularly those citizens least able to help themselves. HHS is by far the largest cabinet department in terms of budget—its 2007 budget was $707.7 billion.

In many ways, HHS embodied much of the economic reformism and the search for a basic sense of fairness and security that many historians argue was at the heart of New Deal liberalism. HHS began, in a sense, in 1939, when the Federal Security Agency was created to house the Public Health Service (from the Treasury Department), the Food and Drug Administration (from Agriculture), the Children's Bureau (from Labor), and the newly created Social Security Administration. The undeniable popularity of the New Deal state led Republican President Dwight D. Eisenhower to transform the Federal Security Agency into the cabinet-level Department of Health, Education, and Welfare in 1953. This department became the Department of Health and Human Services in 1979, after the Education Division was removed and sent to the new Department of Education.

Aside from its New Deal–era foundations, by far the most important development in HHS history was the expansion in departmental functions that occurred as a result of President Lyndon Johnson's Great Society programs, including Medicare, Medicaid, and the Head Start program for underprivileged preschoolers.

The department's 65,000 employees currently administer more than 300 programs that affect the lives of hundreds of millions of Americans. The National Institutes of Heath is the federal government's primary medical research organization. The Centers for Disease Control and Prevention works to prevent the outbreak of infectious disease. The Food and Drug Administration guarantees the safety of foods, pharmaceuticals, and cosmetics. The Health Resources and Services Administration provides basic medical care to Americans unable to afford health insurance. The Indian Health Service provides health care to nearly 2 million Native Americans and Alaskan Natives through a system of hundreds of health centers and village clinics. The department's Administration for Children and Families administers 60 programs designed to provide basic economic and social security for low-income families with dependent children. This administration also oversees Head Start. The Administration on Aging provides services to elderly Americans, including the Meals on Wheels programs that deliver food to the homebound.

The hallmark of HHS, though, is the Centers for Medicare and Medicaid Services, which provide health insurance to nearly 50 million elderly or disabled persons through the Medicare program, cover another 50 million low-income Americans through Medicaid, and insure millions of children through the popular State Children's Health Insurance Program. HHS is perhaps the cabinet department where ideological arguments against "big government" welfare programs collide most clearly with the reality that Americans now accept a role for the federal government in ensuring basic economic and health security for all Americans.

The Department of Housing and Urban Development

In addition to expanding the mission of HHS, Great Society initiatives also led to the creation of the Department of Housing and Urban Development (HUD) and the Department of Transportation (DOT). The establishment of HUD was an acknowledgment of the problems facing an increasingly urban nation during the 1960s.

The mission of HUD is to increase home ownership and provide access to affordable quality housing free from discrimination. Yet the department in many ways has been a house divided. During the mid-1960s, when HUD was created, the private housing construction and banking industries sought to restrict the new department's activities to the promotion of the construction of new housing. Urban reformers, civil rights activists, and planners, on the other hand, wanted to seize upon urban redevelopment as a way to promote broader social and economic change. But community development agencies such as Lyndon Johnson's Office of Economic Opportunity were not placed within HUD. And in 1968, HUD lost jurisdiction over urban mass transportation systems to the newly created Department of Transportation—a truly crippling blow to its ability to engage in comprehensive urban planning.

Today the Department of Housing and Urban Development oversees hundreds of programs and is divided into three broad offices. The Office of Community Planning and Development tries to integrate affordable housing with expanded economic opportunity for needy families; the Office of Fair Housing and Equal Opportunity oversees the Fair Housing Act and other civil rights laws designed to ensure that all Americans have equal access to housing; and the Office of Public and Indian Housing provides affordable public housing for needy individuals. In 2008 the Department of Housing and Urban Development's budget was $35 billion.

The Department of Transportation

The Department of Transportation (DOT) is responsible for designing and carrying out policies to ensure the safety and efficiency of the nation's transportation systems. The creation of the DOT was signed into law in October 1966, and it began operations in April 1967 as the fourth-largest cabinet department, bringing together 95,000 employees then working in more than 30 existing transportation agencies scattered throughout the federal government.

The DOT is divided into 11 administrations: the Federal Aviation Administration, the Federal High-way Administration, the Federal Motor Carrier Safety Administration, the Federal Railroad Administration, the National Highway Traffic Safety Administration, the Federal Transit Administration (urban mass transport), the Maritime Administration, the St. Lawrence Seaway Development Corporation, the Research and Innovative Technologies Administration, the Pipeline and Hazardous Materials Safety Administration, and the Surface Transportation Board. Its 2008 budget was $68 billion.

The Department of Energy

The Department of Energy (DOE) became the twelfth cabinet department in October 1977 in the midst of the protracted energy crisis of the 1970s and was designed to consolidate existing energy agencies in order to promote efficiency and facilitate the research and development of new energy sources. To this end, the department assumed the responsibilities of the Federal Energy Administration; the Energy Research and Development Administration; the Federal Power Commission; the Southeastern, Southwestern, and Alaskan Power Administrations (regional hydroelectric projects); and a handful of other energy-related programs previously housed in the Departments of Defense, Commerce, and the Interior.

Since its creation, the DOE has been responsible for energy research and development, oversight and regulation of interstate transmission of natural gas, oil, and electricity, promotion of alternative energy, and managing the nation's nuclear weapons development and the cleanup and disposal of nuclear waste from cold war programs. It also serves as the federal government's liaison with the International Atomic Energy Agency.

Yet not all of these goals have proven to be created equal. During the late 1970s, DOE emphasis was on research and development of new energy sources and on efficiency and conservation. During the 1980s, the DOE disproportionately focused on nuclear weapons development. During the late 1990s, a concern with renewable and alternative energy was again stressed. This interest in alternative energy has continued into the twenty-first century, although the conflation of energy and national security matters has set up a potential conflict within the DOE: Does national security mean all-out development of traditional sources of energy, or does it mean a long-term plan to develop alternative energy technologies? The Department of Energy employed 116,000 people in 2008, and its budget was $25 billion.

The Department of Education

Education in the United States has historically been the responsibility of state and local governments. The Department of Education notwithstanding, this remains the case. Even the 1979 enabling act that created the Education Department emphasized the fundamentally nonfederal nature of education in America, noting that "the establishment of the Department of Education shall not . . . diminish the responsibility for education which is reserved for the states and the local school systems." The Department of Education's primary contributions to education are the disbursement of money in the form of grants to states and school districts, funding student loan and grant programs for postsecondary education, and ensuring equal access.

The antecedents of the Department of Education go back to 1867, when an Office of Education was established in the Interior Department. With fewer than ten clerks on staff, the Education Office served as a statistical agency, although during the 1890s, it also assumed a supporting role in overseeing the nation's land-grant colleges and universities.

In 1939 the Office of Education was transferred to the Federal Security Agency before being incorporated into the Department of Health, Education, and Welfare (HEW) in 1953. But even within HEW the Office of Education led an austere existence until a dramatic increase in the federal presence in American education during the cold war. In an effort to compete with the Soviet Union, the 1958 National Defense Education Act provided support for college loans and also backed efforts to improve instruction in science, math, foreign languages, and area studies at all levels of the American education system.

The civil rights movement and the War on Poverty programs of the 1960s and 1970s also expanded the federal role in education. The 1965 Elementary and Secondary Education Act initiated programs for underprivileged children living in poor urban and rural areas. The Higher Education Act of 1965 provided financial aid programs for eligible college students. Civil rights legislation, such as Title IX of the Education Amendments of 1972, prohibited discrimination based on race, gender, and disability. Each of these responsibilities transferred to the Department of Education upon its creation in 1979.

The Education Department's elementary and secondary programs affect 56 million students in nearly 100,000 public schools and 28,000 private schools in 14,000 school districts across the nation. The department administers grant and loan programs that support 11 million postsecondary students. The Education Department has a staff of 4,100—45 percent fewer than the 7,500 employees in 1980, a testament both to the powerful tradition of local control in the American education system and to the fact that the Education Department has spent most of its life under the management of conservative Republican administrations generally opposed to the idea of a strident federal role in education. The department's 2008 budget stood at $68.6 billion.

The Department of Veterans Affairs

The mission of the Department of Veterans Affairs (VA), as taken from President Abraham Lincoln's second inaugural address, is "to care for him who shall have borne the battle, and for his widow and his orphan." With 58 regional offices, the VA's Veterans Benefits Administration distributes benefits to veterans and their dependents that include compensation for death or disability, pensions, educational and vocational training, and low-interest loans. The Veterans Health Administration oversees one of the largest health care systems in the United States, complete with over 150 hospitals and 350 outpatient clinics. The National Cemetery Administration offers burial and memorial services.

Although the nation has always made some provision for the care of veterans, it was not until 1930, in the aftermath of World War I, that the federal government created a Veterans Administration to bring order to the government services offered to the nation's veterans. This independent Veterans Administration was elevated to cabinet department status in 1988, in part due to the plight of disaffected Vietnam veterans. The annual VA budget is approximately $90 billion, and the department's 250,000 employees cause the department to be ranked second only to the Defense Department in number.

FURTHER READING

Bennett, Anthony J. *The American President's Cabinet: From Kennedy to Bush*. New York: St. Martin's Press, 1996.

Cohen, Jeffrey E. *The Politics of the U.S. Cabinet: Representation in the Executive Branch, 1789–1984*. Pittsburgh, PA: University of Pittsburgh Press, 1988.

Frenno, Richard F., Jr. *The President's Cabinet: An Analysis in the Period from Wilson to Eisenhower*. Cambridge, MA: Harvard University Press, 1959.

Hess, Stephen. *Organizing the Presidency*. Washington, DC: Brookings Institution Press, 2002.

Hoxie, R. Gordon. "The Cabinet in the American Presidency, 1789–1984." *Presidential Studies Quarterly* 14, no. 2 (1984), 209–30.

Warshaw, Shirley Anne. *Power Sharing: White House–Cabinet Relations in the Modern Presidency*. Albany: State University of New York Press, 1996.

KEVIN POWERS

campaign consultants

The United States is the land of elections. Over any typical four-year cycle, there are more than a million elections, everything from the presidency, U.S. senator, and governor to big-city mayor, city council, and local school board bond issue. Americans vote into office approximately 513,000 elected officials and decide on thousands of ballot initiatives. No other country comes close to the number and variety of elections that are held in American states, cities, counties, and other political jurisdictions.

Most elections are low-profile, low-budget contests. For many voters, the first time they learn that an issue or some minor office is even being contested is when they close the curtain in the voting booth and see the official ballot. Candidates seeking office in these low-profile contests usually rely on their own shoe leather, pay for their own election expenses, and rely on assistance from family, friends, and other volunteers.

But in contests for big-city mayors, governors, members of Congress, and other contests, professional political consultants are used to help guide candidates, political parties, and interest groups through the complexities of today's elections. These are the expensive, often high-profile contests, where candidates and interested parties will raise hundreds of thousands, even millions of dollars to fund their races. It is not unusual for candidates for the U.S. Senate to raise and spend $10 to $15 million. It was once a rarity for candidates for Congress to spend $1 million; now it is commonplace. In some jurisdictions, candidates who are elected to the state supreme court might spend $5 or $8 million, while some school board candidates in big cities have been known to spend well over $100,000. Statewide spending in California presents a special case. In 2005 alone, with no governor, no state legislators, and no other state officials to elect,

still over $500 million was spent by participants trying to defend or defeat ballot issues.

Where does the money go? Much of it, of course, goes to television advertising or direct-mail expenses, but a considerable portion goes to a battery of professionals who are hired by the campaigns to help win the public over to their side. Campaign consulting is a thriving business; no serious candidate in an important contest can do without consultants. Yet, campaign consulting is a relatively new business.

Through much of American electoral history, campaigns were run by political party machines and operatives. Parties recruited candidates, funded election drives, urged people to vote, and tried to generate excitement through mass rallies and torchlight parades. But by the middle of the twentieth century, the political party was no longer the focus of campaigning for many elections. Increasingly, the focus was on the individual candidate. The candidates relied on others to assist them, and increasingly, as campaigns became more complex and sophisticated, they turned to professionals skilled in public relations, survey research, media relations, and other specialties.

The Beginning of the Business of Political Consulting
The business of political consulting traces back to the mid-1930s, when a California husband-wife public relations team, Clem Whitaker and Leone Baxter, created a firm called Campaigns, Inc. Throughout their 25-year career, Whitaker and Baxter were enormously successful, providing public relations and communications services to a variety of candidates, ballot initiatives, and issue causes.

Others followed, but even by the early 1950s, most political consulting was still a sideline for public relations firms. One study showed that by 1957 some 41 public relations firms, located mostly in California, Texas, and New York, offered campaign services. But during the 1950s a new specialty was emerging: the professional campaign manager or political consultant. These were political activists who were making campaign work their principal business. By the 1960s the political consultant was becoming a fixture in presidential, gubernatorial, and U.S. Senate races.

The first generation of consultants included Joseph Napolitan, Walter De Vries, F. Clifton White, Herbert M. Baus, William B. Ross, John Sears, Stuart Spencer, and Joseph Cerrell. They tended to be generalists, who would handle a campaign's overall strategy, develop themes and messages, and run campaigns. Others were known for special skills. Louis Harris, Albert H. (Tad) Cantril, Oliver Quayle, William Hamilton, Richard Wirthlin, Robert Teeter were among those who focused on research; Matt Reese was known for his campaign-organizing skills. Media specialists Charles Guggenheim, Tony Schwartz, David Garth, Marvin Chernoff, and Robert Squier crafted television commercials for Democratic candidates, while Robert Goodman, Douglas L. Bailey, John D. Deardourff, and others worked on the Republican side.

The business of political consulting grew quickly in the 1980s through 2000, and in 2008 approximately 3,000 consulting firms specialized in political campaigns. A few political consultants have become widely known to the public, like Karl Rove, Dick Morris, and James Carville. But they are the rare exceptions. Most consultants work quietly, and comfortably, behind the scenes. Even at the presidential level, few Americans would recognize the names of principal consultants for 2008 presidential candidates Hillary Clinton, Barack Obama, Rudy Giuliani, or John McCain.

The Role of Political Consultants in Campaigns

What do consultants bring to the modern campaign? They bring skills, experience, and discipline to an essentially unruly process. Few events are as potentially chaotic, vulnerable, and unpredictable as a modern campaign. They are, by definition, contests, pitting one side (or more) against another. So much can go wrong. There is such a steep learning curve for the campaign, so many ways to make a mistake, an often inattentive public, and an opponent and allies doing their best to knock your candidate off track.

In some campaigns, no amount of skill or energy from a consultant would change the ultimate outcome. Winning (and losing) is contingent on a variety of factors, and many of those are beyond the control of consultants. But consultants can make the vital difference between victory and defeat when contests are close. Furthermore, consultants can help candidates avoid big, costly mistakes. They can bring order, discipline, focus, and consistency when things might otherwise be falling apart; they can keep a volatile situation from total meltdown and fire up a listless, drifting campaign that has lost its direction.

Campaign consultants come with a variety of skills and occupy different niches in campaigns. For an $8 million U.S. Senate race, a candidate might hire a bevy of consultants. The candidate will hire *strategists* (a general consultant, a campaign manager, pollster, direct-mail specialist, media expert) and *specialists* (candidate and opposition researchers, fund-raisers, lawyers and accountants with specialized knowledge of campaign finance law, speechwriters, television time buyers, electronic media specialists, telemarketers, micro-targeting specialists, and others). The campaign will also use campaign *vendors* (firms that supply voter files, campaign software, yard signs, and more).

Many consultants offer niche services, such as providing state and federal election law advice, buying time for radio and television advertising, providing voter and demographic databases, geo-mapping, and sophisticated targeting techniques, helping candidates in debate preparation, preparing their stump speeches, or providing that all-important cadre of fund-raisers who collect money that provides the fuel for the entire campaign.

New specialties have emerged just as new technologies have been introduced. No serious political campaign now would be without a Web site, e-mail, and blog. One of the newest job descriptions is that of director of electronic media: the person on the campaign responsible for maintaining the Web site, coordinating e-mails, and monitoring the campaign's blog. Particularly since the 2004 presidential campaign, candidates have found that online communications can be cost-effective and efficient ways to reach out to volunteers, collect campaign funds (usually in smaller denominations), and keep activists and others engaged in the campaign.

Campaign consultants provide services for more than the traditional candidate campaign, such as a gubernatorial race or big-city mayor's race. In fact, very few campaign consultants work on only election cycle campaigns. Many are involved in ballot issue campaigns, such as found in California and about 25 other states. Many too provide services in issue advocacy fights, such as the battle over national health insurance, immigration reform, gay marriage, and many other issues. Consultants will work for corporations, trade associations, and other business interests. Finally, American consultants have found a lucrative market during the past 30 years going abroad and working on campaign elections in other countries.

The Business of Political Consulting

The business of political consulting is just a small fraction of the commercial marketing world. Many of these firms have fewer than ten employees and generate $1 million or less in revenue. Private political survey research represents only about 2.5 percent (or $100 million) of the $4 billion annual revenues of the polling industry. Direct mail for political causes constitutes but 2 percent of the direct-mail commercial market, and political telemarketing is less than 1 percent of the overall telemarketing industry.

While citizens watching television during a heated presidential primary might think that there is nothing but political commercials dominating the airwaves, in fact, such commercials are just a tiny portion of the market. In recent presidential campaign years, for example, during the six months that preceded the general election, political commercials represented only about 1.0 to 1.5 percent of all commercials. In a typical presidential election year, mass-marketing companies like Procter & Gamble or General Motors will each spend about the same amount selling their own products as all presidential candidates combined.

In the early twenty-first century, political campaigns pose special problems for candidates, consultants, and their campaigns. It is so much harder to get people's attention. There has been a fundamental shift in where people get their news and how candidates can advertise. Newspaper readership is declining; weekly newsmagazines have become slimmer and less relevant in a 24-hour news culture; network television, which once dominated viewers' attention, has little of its former power. Communications outlets exploded with the advent of cable television in the 1970s, followed by the Internet, e-mail, mobile phones, and instant messaging. The communications marketplace is extraordinarily splintered, making it much harder for campaigns to reach voters with their messages. The mass market of three television networks has largely been supplanted by niche markets with hundreds of choices.

At one time, campaigns were much simpler: one candidate vying against another. Television, radio, and print advertising from one camp were pitted against the advertising from the other side. Since then, campaign communications have become much more complicated. Other voices added their messages and get-out-the-vote drives in the campaigns. For example, labor unions, political parties, trade associations, even private individuals have been willing to spend great sums of money to influence a contest. Then contests became nationalized. By the mid-1990s, congressional races that once were considered only local contests were seeing advertising campaigns from abortion rights, pro-gun control, anti-NAFTA, and English-only advocates—national groups,

all—trying to influence the outcome. On top of these influences has come the wide open, robust influence of citizen activists through blogs and Web sites, adding their voices to the mix. This makes it all the more necessary to have professional campaign help to fight through the clutter and competition in the contest and make the candidate's views and positions known.

Consultants often get blamed for the harsh, negative tone of campaign rhetoric, especially in television ads. They defend their craft by saying that they are providing useful information, albeit in stark and clear terms, about the differences between their candidates and the opponents. Academics and public citizen groups worry about the negative impact such ads might have on democratic behavior or voter turnout.

If anyone is to be blamed, it must be the candidate, who ultimately is responsible for the conduct of a campaign. An unfair, slash-and-burn campaign commercial, a "dirty tricks" stunt against the opponent, an embarrassing photo digitally pieced together, a cruel, salacious comment by a campaign staffer—all these unfair or unethical practices redound against the campaign and the candidate.

The negativity and the harsh words found in contemporary campaigns will likely only get worse. New voices, without the constraints of professional responsibility, have entered the picture. We should expect campaigns to get uglier and louder. Particularly with online campaigning, there are so many more voices filling cyberspace, from bloggers to e-mail rumors, to the online posting of sound bites and video clips. Professional media consultants, knowing they have reputations to uphold and are working for a candidate and a party or interest group, will use some semblance of caution. The really wild, outrageous comments or videos posted on the Web will come from outsiders, often anonymous, unfettered by constraints. The early twenty-first century may become the Wild West period of campaigning.

Challenges and Opportunities of Online Campaigning

Particularly since Howard Dean's run for the Democratic presidential nomination in 2003–4, we have seen a challenge to the dominant form of professional campaigning. Dean and his campaign manager touted a new approach to campaigning. That approach was to listen to the voices expressed on Dean's blog and other online sources and emerge with a bottom-up campaign, gaining ideas from the people, listening to (and presumably acting on) their concerns, rather than imposing a command-and-control, top-down campaign (with the implication that it did not listen to the people).

While the approach sounded promising, it was less than what it appeared. A critical ingredient in any successful campaign is top-down control: message discipline, a fixed but flexible strategy, the ability to cut through all the noise (electronic and otherwise) of a campaign, set a firm, clear direction, and plan to beat the opponent. This is what traditional, professional campaigning does best: it brings order out of chaos. But at the same time, successful campaigns are not out of touch with what voters want or feel. They conduct polls, run focus groups, and monitor blogs; candidates engage in "listening tours," greet voters in malls, coffee shops, and private homes. In short, they listen very carefully to what people think.

In recent election cycles, a thriving blogging community, both on the liberal/Democratic and conservative/Republican sides, has emerged. These bloggers, self-appointed activists, are also claiming a stake in the nature, content, and direction of campaigning. Bloggers, particularly from the progressive or liberal side, like to tout that they will break down the barriers between the people and the candidates. They boast that they are the future of campaigns and will invariably supplant the activities of campaign consultants.

Electronic democracy, citizen activism, and Web advocacy, however, have not supplanted old-fashioned, professionally run campaigns. Professional campaign consultants, above all, want their clients to win. They adapt to new circumstances, and increasingly have added electronic communications to their arsenal of tools. No current professionally run campaign would be without an e-communications team to run the Web site, monitor the campaign blog, and produce online versions of campaign videos, fund-raising appeals, and other tricks of the trade. Consultants will adapt, endure, and prosper. They are indispensable to modern American campaigns, and, increasingly, in campaigns throughout the world.

See also campaigning; Internet and politics; political advertising; radio and politics; television and politics.

FURTHER READING

Dulio, David A. *For Better or Worse? How Political Consultants Are Changing Elections in the United States*. Albany: State University of New York Press, 2004.

Faucheux, Ronald A., and Paul S. Herrnson. *The Good Fight: How Political Candidates Struggle to Win Elections without Losing Their Souls*. Washington, DC: Campaigns & Elections, 2000.

Herrnson, Paul S. *Congressional Elections: Campaigning at Home and in Washington*, 4th ed. Washington, DC: CQ Press, 2007.

Jamieson, Kathleen Hall. *Packaging the Presidency: A History and Criticism of Presidential Campaign Advertising*. New York: Oxford University Press, 1984.

Johnson, Dennis W. *No Place for Amateurs: How Political Consultants Are Reshaping American Democracy*, 2nd ed. New York: Routledge, 2007.

Johnson, Dennis W., ed. *Routledge Handbook on Political Management*. New York: Routledge, 2008.

Medvic, Stephen K. *Political Consultants in U.S. Congressional Elections*. Columbus: Ohio State University Press, 2001.

Newman, Bruce I. *The Mass Marketing of Politics: Democracy in an Age of Manufactured Images*. Thousand Oaks, CA: Sage Publications, 1999.

Shea, Daniel M., and Michael John Burton. *Campaign Craft: The Strategies, Tactics, and Art of Political Campaign Management*, 3rd ed. Westport, CT: Praeger, 2006.

Thurber, James A., and Candice J. Nelson, eds. *Campaign Warriors: The Role of Political Consultants in Elections*. Washington, DC: Brookings Institution Press, 2000.

DENNIS W. JOHNSON

campaign law and finance to 1900

Financing candidates' campaigns was simple and uncontroversial in the absence of mass parties and a complex economy. But with the demise of the relatively hierarchical, elite-driven politics of the eighteenth and early nineteenth century, men of limited means who had made politics their profession needed financial help to reach an expanded electorate. Through the nineteenth century, campaign finance raised questions about who should pay for politics and whether those who paid got an unfair return on their investment. Those questions, asked with both public spiritedness and partisan advantage in mind, remain with us.

In the early years of the republic, many campaigns were straightforward. Men of prominence and wealth "stood" for office, ideally approaching the exercise as a somewhat unwelcome civic duty, akin to jury service in the twentieth century. The rituals of electioneering—

voice voting for the (usually) white propertied men who made up the electorate and the candidates treating the voters with food and drink—illustrated the hierarchical relationships. Voter turnout tended to be low. Costs were, too, and they were usually borne by the candidates.

Contentious elections required more desperate activity and more extensive methods. Newspapers devoted to parties and to factions, such as those organized around personal followings in the Middle Atlantic states, promoted candidates. The Federalists financed Noah Webster's *American Minerva* (later renamed *The Commercial Advertiser*); the Democratic-Republicans responded with Philip Freneau's *National Gazette*. So it went around the new nation: from 1790 to 1808, the number of newspapers, most of them partisan, more than tripled. Backed by wealthy patrons or government printing contracts, newspapers put out the partisan line, denigrating the godlessness of the Democratic-Republicans or the monarchical aspirations of the Federalists.

The party press remained an important cost of doing political business with the rise of mass parties in the 1830s. There were additional expenses: printing and distributing ballots, holding rallies, dispensing campaign paraphernalia, and getting out the vote of an electorate expanded to include most white men. Party activities were now nearly constant, reaching down from presidential campaigns to an expanded number of state and local races. All this exertion required a regular stream of funds, particularly since a new generation of men who made politics their profession lacked the means of more elite predecessors.

Part of a solution to the problem of funds emerged from the "spoils system" or "rotation in office," which followers of Andrew Jackson touted as a more democratic way to distribute government positions than the creation of a class of permanent officials. Replacing public employees, minor as well as major, with partisans of a new presidential administration—a practice repeated at the state and city levels—gave the executive branch loyal men to carry out the government's work. These workers could also be tapped for funds. The party in power expected the men holding patronage jobs—from upper-level administrators to postmasters—to show their gratitude and fealty by paying a percentage (generally 2 to 5 percent) of their salaries to their party. Such assessments became an alternative system of taxation or after-a-fashion public financing, in which those who benefited or hoped to benefit from the result of an election paid for it.

The assessment system generated controversy almost from the start, and like every attempt to regulate campaign finance to follow, proposed reforms were both partisan and principled. In 1837 Whig congressman John Bell of Tennessee introduced a bill that would have banned assessments and electioneering on the part of federal employees. This measure, as well as a hearing concerning abuses at a customs house, took aim at the Democrats. Proponents argued that the executive branch was using patronage to build a machine that interfered with legislative elections; they decried a system in which "partisan service is the required return for office, as office is to be the reward for public service." Opponents countered that everyone, including federal employees, had the right to participate in politics. The bill failed. But constituents received free copies of the debate and the hearing: the franking privilege was an important perk of incumbency.

Strains on the assessment system grew. Businessmen who relied on customs houses for import and export trade resented the sometimes inefficient service, which improved greatly with payoffs, provided by partisan employees. Workers who performed professional tasks increasingly wanted to be treated like professionals, rather than as patronage hacks. They came to resent paying taxes to their party. The cost of the Republican Party's effort to build party infrastructure in the South after the Civil War encouraged the GOP to nag public employees more tirelessly than usual. Democrats naturally grumbled, as did some Republicans. Appalled by the corruption of the Ulysses S. Grant administration and weary of Reconstruction, African Americans, and the South, Liberal Republicans offered civil service reform as a new issue and purpose for the party and a cure for corruption.

They felt strongly enough about the issue to form their own party in 1872; President Ulysses Grant responded by creating a civil service commission. Meaningful reform came with the passage of the Pendleton Act in 1883, given a final push by the mistaken idea that President James Garfield had been assassinated by a "disappointed office seeker," driven mad by patronage.

The campaign work and dollars of public employees continued to be a target of reform into the twentieth century, but assessments ceased to be a major source of funds for national party organizations by the late nineteenth century. Wealthy partisan individuals had pitched in throughout the nineteenth century, but as assessments dried up, business increasingly paid for elections. This money quickly sparked more controversy than assessments.

We know some of the names of the big spenders of the late nineteenth century—August Belmont, Jay Cooke, and Tom Scott, for example—and their interests in what government did in banking, tariffs, railroad subsidies, and regulation. The assumption of many, especially supporters of third parties, was that money blocked the path to reforms that were in the interests of those without huge wealth. Yet, business interests generally did not seek out political fund-raisers—rather it was the reverse, except perhaps for cases like the 1896 election, when fear of what William Jennings Bryan would do if elected, inspired businessmen to give William McKinley more money than his campaign could possibly use. The question of what businessmen bought with their contributions would be central to the campaign finance debates of the twentieth century.

See also campaign law and finance since 1900.

FURTHER READING

Baker, Paula, ed. *Money and Politics.* State College: Pennsylvania State University Press, 2002.

Mutch, Robert E. "Three Centuries of Campaign Finance Law." In *A User's Guide to Campaign Finance Reform,* edited by Jerold Lubenow, 1–24. Lanham, MD: Rowman and Littlefield, 2001.

Overacker, Louise. *Money in Elections.* 1932. Reprint ed. New York: Arno Press, 1974.

Yearly, Clifton K. *The Money Machines: The Breakdown and Reform of Governmental and Party Finance in the North, 1860–1920.* Albany: State University of New York Press, 1970.

PAULA BAKER

campaign law and finance since 1900

Concerns about campaign finance—the amount of money candidates and political parties raise and spend and the sources of those funds—have persisted through the twentieth and into the twenty-first century. The issue's appeal was and remains rooted in many Americans' suspicion of the influence of money on policy and fears for democracy itself. Anxiety has not produced satisfactory solutions. In contrast to the European model, American parties have no tradition of dues-paying members who support their activities, and American campaigns are long and require the purchase of increasingly expensive publicity. As campaign finance regulations have expanded, parties, candidates, and interest groups have adapted nimbly to the constraints, which they also helped to write. Regulations that control contributions and spending have been limited by constitutional protections of free speech. The structure of American politics and Supreme Court guidelines have allowed campaigns to raise and spend the funds they believe they need within each regulatory regime reformers have built, which leads inevitably to the next try at reform.

While fears about the impact of money on politics have been constant, the issue rarely has risen anywhere near the top of public concerns. The particular targets for reform have been driven by scandal and partisan politics. In the early twentieth century, large, secret corporate contributions, the mainstay of party fund-raisers in the 1890s, were the evil that most excited reformers' interest. The first federal legislation stemmed from Democratic presidential candidate Alton B. Parker's charges that his opponent, Theodore Roosevelt, collected big corporate contributions while threatening to regulate many of the same firms. Roosevelt successfully deflected the accusations, although his campaign had accepted substantial sums from financier J. P. Morgan ($150,000), Henry Clay Frick of U.S. Steel ($50,000), and railroad operator H. L. Harriman ($50,000, plus $200,000 raised from his contacts). A series of widely publicized scandals between 1904 and 1908—detailing campaign contributions and payoffs New York Republicans received from life insurance companies in return for favorable legislation, and benefits to utilities and railroads from legislators in the West and Midwest, among many others—appeared to confirm the suspicion that politicians catered to moneyed interests that made big contributions.

Federal Campaign Finance Legislation to 1970

The Tillman Act (1907) made it "unlawful for any national bank, or any corporation organized by authority of any laws of Congress, to make a money contribution in connection with any election to any political office." Corporations or their officers or board members who violated the law were subject to fines and up to one year in prison. While the final bill did not require the parties to disclose the sources of their funds, the Republican National Committee and Democratic National Committee began to voluntarily release financial records for the 1908 presidential election. The Tillman Act prevented firms from using stockholders' funds for campaign purposes but changed little in how campaigns raised money. There is record of only one prosecution, for a gift from the United States Brewers' Association to a House candidate.

Reformers were disappointed that the Tillman Act did not provide for the disclosure of contributions, and Congress responded with the 1910 Federal Corrupt Practices Act (FCPA) and amendments to it in 1911. The law required every House and Senate candidate and "political committee" to report the sources of their contributions and capped spending at $5,000 for a House seat and $10,000 for the Senate. Committees that operated in single states were excepted. The 1911 amendments required reports both before and after elections and extended spending limits to primary elections. The measure contained no enforcement mechanism; violators would have to be taken to court, where they would be subject to fines and up to two years in prison. The 1910 bill passed the House without much debate; the 1911 amendments were adopted unanimously by the House and passed the Senate with only seven no votes, all from southern Democrats who opposed any extension of federal power over state election procedures.

The legislation had minimal effect on campaigns, due to loopholes and upward pressures on campaign costs. A close reading suggested that the spending limits applied to candidates, not committees formed to advance their campaigns, so only the most naïve candidates indicated that they had spent anything more than a nominal sum while "independent" committees raised the real money. Campaigns spent it because of Progressive Era changes in how the parties operated required that they do so. Primary elections could double campaign costs in competitive states. Nineteenth-century parties had controlled their own newspapers, but twentieth-century campaigns could not count on free fawning press coverage. Purchased advertising filled the gap. Advertising totaled between 25 to 50 percent of campaign budgets, depending on the expense of the market (in 1920, a full-page ad in the *New York Times* cost $1,539 and the *Chicago Tribune* $1,708). Election Day expenses, including hiring the workers who once had been patronage-hungry volunteers, were also substantial.

If the wish embodied in legislation could not control costs, the FCPA still had its uses. Congressional Democrats hoped spending limits might frighten wealthy Republican donors and lessen the GOP's fund-raising advantages. An opponent's spending could be made into a campaign issue. And a losing candidate could take a

big-spending opponent to court or to Congress, in the hope of denying a seat to the winner. A few losing House candidates challenged the seating of winners, usually coupling charges of excessive spending with more traditional accusations of corruption. As the party balance in the Senate tightened in the 1910s and early 1920s, it became the site of numerous election challenges. The most consequential was Henry Ford's challenge to Republican Truman H. Newberry's 1918 victory in a close, nasty Michigan Senate race. The committee that promoted Newberry spent $190,000, almost all of it from his family and close friends, well above the apparent FCPA limits for candidates. The money bought the advertising deemed necessary to defeat the rich and famous automaker. Nearly four years of wrangling followed, including two grand jury hearings and one federal trial orchestrated by Ford that found Newberry guilty; a trip to the Supreme Court that reversed the conviction; and a Senate investigation that rehashed the legal proceedings. Newberry finally resigned in 1922 when that year's election brought in enough new Democrats to make a rehearing and his expulsion likely.

The Supreme Court had found fault in both Newberry's trial and the FCPA, but the majority opinion focused on the unconstitutional reach by Congress in regulating state primary elections. The 1924 and 1925 revisions of the FCPA removed coverage of primaries and increased the amounts candidates could spend, but otherwise left the law's vague provisions intact. The Senate could still refuse to seat members-elect it deemed to have spent too much. A coalition of progressive Republicans and Democrats succeeded in denying seats to Frank L. Smith, Republican of Illinois, and William A. Vare, Republican of Pennsylvania, who were elected in 1926 by the voters of their states in expensive races.

Attempts to deny seats to candidates over excessive spending disappeared when the Democrats gained solid control of Congress in the 1930s. But the campaign finance issue persisted, now with Republicans taking the lead. A coalition of southern Democrats and Republicans struck at some of the Franklin D. Roosevelt administration's sources of campaign labor and funds. The 1939 Hatch Act prohibited political activity by government workers, eliminating the threat of Works Progress Administration (WPA) recipients turning into the president's personal political workforce. Because of the prohibition against all but high-ranking federal officials participating in conventions, the president could not stack a convention. (In 1936 about half of the delegates were federal employees.) The law set spending and contribution limits of individual political committees at $3,000,000 per year and capped individual contributions at $5,000. Sure enough, numerous "independent" committees sprung up, each able to spend to the limit.

In 1940 Republicans spent five times the limit and the Democrats double, all the while staying within the letter of the law. Beginning with the 1936 election, organized labor became an important source of funds for Democrats, and southern Democrats and Republicans aimed to restrict its ability to fund campaigns. The Smith-Connally Act (1943) contained a provision that temporarily banned union contributions in the same language that the Tillman Act used against corporate donations; the 1946 Taft-Hartley Act made the restriction permanent. The Congress of Industrial Organizations responded by setting up the first political action committee (PAC) in 1944 that legally funneled money to pro-union candidates. Not until the 1960s did business PACs follow the labor model.

Although the Supreme Court had opened the way for Congress to regulate primary elections in 1941 and the cost of elections outstripped the nominal limits, the FCPA remained the basic, if ineffective, campaign finance law of the United States. The issue had not disappeared. New actors dedicated to campaign finance reform, including a handful of academics and foundations, tried to fire public concern and to sell Congress on new policies. In 1956 Senator Francis Case of South Dakota admitted he had been the target of an oil company deal offering cash in exchange for his vote on a pending bill. This scandal refocused enough interest in campaign finance reform to inspire an investigation headed by Senate Democratic liberals but not to generate new legislation.

The problem was conflicting goals and interests. Organized labor, one important Democratic constituent group that favored restrictions that might curb the advantages of business donors and their Republican recipients, opposed legislation that targeted PACs; many Republicans insisted on controls on PACs; television networks rejected proposals that required them to provide free time for short "spot" advertisements; some sitting officeholders worried about assisting challengers; and a number of powerful members of Congress, backed by public opinion, blocked proposals for public funding of campaigns. Meanwhile, campaign costs ballooned, a trend carefully tracked by new "public interest" groups such as the Citizen's Research Foundation and, by the late 1960s, Common Cause. Spending on the presidential elections of 1968 was up by 25 percent compared to that of 1964. Candidate- (rather than party-) centered campaigns, television, the consultants to coordinate the message, and fund-raising itself drove up the costs of congressional and statewide campaigns as well as presidential races.

Campaign Finance Legislation Since 1970

Rising costs got the attention of members of Congress, especially senators who could easily imagine facing well-financed challengers. With this prod, the logjam broke in 1971. The Federal Election Campaign Act (FECA) imposed much stronger disclosure requirements than those of the FCPA: candidates for federal office had to file quarterly reports detailing receipts and expenditures, with names, addresses, occupations, and businesses attached to each contribution over $100. It limited the contributions of candidates and their immediate families, spending on publicity and outreach, and the proportion of campaign budgets spent on radio and television advertising. The law thus treated media costs as the core problem and contained sufficient incumbent protection provisions to pass. But the FECA did not control overall costs. Richard M. Nixon's 1972 reelection campaign spent twice as much as his 1968 run; Democratic nominee George McGovern's race cost four times as much as Hubert H. Humphrey's 1968 campaign. That, together with the Watergate scandal, brought a major overhaul of the FECA in 1974, creating the current framework of campaign finance law.

Arguing that a renewed effort to divorce money from politics would revive American's sagging confidence in government (and, for Democratic liberals, promote their stalled policy agenda), the Senate bill provided public funds for primary and general election campaigns for federal offices and limits on what candidates could spend, even if using their own money. Restricted too were contributions to political parties and from independent groups, individuals, and PACs. The final bill kept the 1971 disclosure requirement and created the Federal Elections Commission, with commissioners evenly divided between the parties, to monitor compliance. It provided public funding for presidential elections, enabled by a $1 voluntary taxpayer checkoff, but no public support for congressional races. Even the most ardent champions of reform considered the bill not much better than a good first step toward clean elections.

The new regulations were immediately litigated. The major challenge came in *Buckley v. Valeo* (1976). A combination of left- and right-wing groups claimed that many of the FECA's provisions violated constitutional rights to free speech and association. The Court agreed, in part. Large contributions given directly to a campaign might be corrupt or create the appearance of corruption. Therefore, the FECA's $1,000 limit on individual donations and $5,000 for PACs to a single candidate fell within the federal government's interest. But spending was protected speech. "The First Amendment denies government the power to determine that spending to promote one's political view is wasteful, excessive or unwise," according to the Court. The decision struck down the restrictions on candidates' contributions to their own campaigns, mandatory spending limits (unless candidates voluntarily participated in the public financing system), and restrictions on expenditures by independent groups.

The FECA never succeeded in controlling campaign costs; it is doubtful that it would have done so even if the Court had ruled differently in *Buckley*. The law has required reams of paperwork but has only redirected the channels through which money reaches candidates. Raising enough money in small sums to run a credible campaign is expensive and time consuming. Internet fund-raising might lower the costs of finding small donors in future campaigns, but traditionally, only the most finely targeted and best maintained mailing and phone lists justified the considerable investment. Congressional and presidential candidates devote much more of their time to fund-raising than before the FECA. To lessen their load, they use "bundlers," who locate caches of $1,000 contributions and PACs. The number of PACs grew from 608 in 1974 to 4,180 in 1990. Many of these were business PACs, which were responding to the expansion of federal regulations through the 1960s and 1970s by making sure they had access to both Democratic and Republican policy makers. New ideological PACs as well as officeholders' PACs also emerged to encourage candidates who mirrored their agendas. A 1978 FEC ruling allowed state parties to follow state rather than federal disclosure and contribution guidelines. This had the effect of strengthening party organizations badly weakened by the FECA, but it also opened the way for unlimited "soft money" contributions. Democrats have relied more heavily than Republicans on "soft money," since the Republicans constructed an effective database to generate "hard" money.

Soft money was the target of the next round of reform, which followed revelations about questionable donations to the Democratic National Committee and some unseemly fund-raising by President Bill Clinton and Vice President Al Gore. The Bipartisan Campaign Reform Act, commonly known as McCain-Feingold, blocked some of the soft money channels; others, especially the independent "527" groups (named after their place in the Internal Revenue Service code) remain. The FECA system continues to demand time and effort to ensure compliance, but since 1996 many presidential aspirants have opted out of the restrictive federal financing system. The American system of campaign finance remains tangled, intrusive, and complex, while reformers await the next scandal.

See also campaign law and finance to 1900; interest groups.

FURTHER READING

Corrado, Anthony, et al. *The New Campaign Finance Sourcebook.* Washington, DC: Brookings Institution Press, 2005.

Ervin, Spencer. *Henry Ford vs. Truman Newberry: The Famous Senate Election Contest.* New York: Richard R. Smith, 1935.

Heard, Alexander. *The Costs of Democracy.* Chapel Hill: University of North Carolina Press, 1960.

Overacker, Louise. *Money in Elections.* New York: Macmillan, 1932.

Pollock, James K. *Party Campaign Funds.* New York: Knopf, 1926.

Urofsky, Melvin I. *Money and Free Speech: Campaign Finance and the Courts.* Lawrence: University Press of Kansas, 2005.

PAULA BAKER

campaigning

Campaigning for office is one of American democracy's most defining acts—yet many citizens find campaigns unruly, distasteful, demeaning. Most elections are shrouded in some mystery; even in the age of polling, surprises sometimes occur. But, especially in presidential campaigns, the complaints about campaigns being too long, expensive, demagogic, and frilly come as regularly as America's distinctive, scheduled election days, albeit more frequently.

The word *campaign* originated in the seventeenth century from the French word for open field, *campagne*.

With contemporary soldiers fighting sustained efforts, often on the wide country terrain, the term quickly acquired its military association. The political connotation emerged in seventeenth-century England to describe a lengthy legislative session. In nineteenth-century America "campaign" was part of the barrage of military terms describing electioneering: as the party *standard bearer*, *a war horse* tapping into his *war chest* and hoping not to be a *flash-in-the-pan*—a cannon that misfires—*mobilized* the *rank-and-file* with a *rallying cry* in *battleground states* to vanquish their enemies.

American politicians needed to conquer the people's hearts because popular sovereignty has been modern Anglo-American government's distinguishing anchor since colonial days. In elitist early America, the ideal candidates stood for election; they did not run. Wooing the people was considered too ambitious, deceitful, undignified; passivity demonstrated the potential leader's purity. This posture lingered longest at the presidential level, and it continues to feed the national fantasy about disinterested, virtuous candidates wafting into the presidential chair by acclamation, rather than the stereotypical grubby, aggressive, blow-dried, weather vane politicians slithering into office today.

There are more than 500,000 elected offices in the United States, ranging from tree warden to president. Most are elected directly to serve locally. While senatorial, gubernatorial, and presidential campaigns require "wholesale" campaigning to mobilize blocs of voters, the typical campaign is a "retail," mom-and-pop, door-to-door operation pressing the flesh. This contact enables American citizens to meet, assess, scrutinize those who aspire to lead them. Even in today's high-tech, television-saturated age, the July Fourth meet-and-greet county picnic or the Election Day get-out-the-vote drive by carpooling neighbors more typifies campaigns than big-budget multistate advertising buys during presidential elections.

While presidential campaigning commands most Americans' attention, often setting the tone for campaigns at all levels, the presidential election remains indirect. As many Americans only first realized in 2000, when Al Gore won more popular votes than George W. Bush but lost the presidency, voters choose slates of electors, organized state by state, and pledged to vote for particular candidates when the Electoral College meets. This filtering of the people's voice reflects the Founding Fathers' fears of "mobocracy." The Electoral College today orients campaign strategy toward a few

voter-rich, swing states. In 1960 Vice President Richard Nixon vowed to campaign in all 50 states. He lost, narrowly. Many Republicans grumbled that Nixon wasted precious resources fulfilling that imprudent pledge.

Campaigns are legitimizing and unifying democratic rituals, linking the leader and the led in a historic, tradition-rich rite of affirmation. Ultimately, campaigns involve the mystical alchemy of leadership and the practical allocation of power, cleanly and neatly. America's winner-take-all elections designate one winner, with no power sharing or booby prizes for losers. Campaigns also offer a clear narrative trajectory, with all the plots and personalities culminating on one day, when the people speak. As a result, the history of campaigning, on all levels, is a history of vivid clashes, colorful personalities, defining moments. Presidential campaigning history includes President John Adams clashing with his own vice president, Thomas Jefferson, in 1800; Republican Wide Awakes marching through northern cities before the Civil War; Grover Cleveland winning despite the mockery of "Ma, Ma, Where's my pa, gone to the White House, Ha, Ha, Ha" in 1884; William Jennings Bryan's valiant, superhuman speechifying in 1896; John Kennedy's elegance during the 1960 televised debates; Ronald Reagan's stirring Morning in America 1984 campaign; the geysers of baby boomer idealism that the honey-smooth Bill Clinton tapped in 1992; George W. Bush's Karl Rove–engineered, play-to-the-base strategy in his 2004 reelection; and Barack Obama's 2008 mix of redemptive "Yes We Can" uplift and an impressive ground game mixing old-fashioned grassroots politics with cutting edge netroots outreach.

The First Three Historical Phases: The Republican, Democratic, and Populist Campaigns

Just as earth scientists debate whether humans evolved gradually or through occasional leaps called punctuated equilibrium, political scientists debate how campaigns developed. Historians traditionally focused on breakthrough campaigns pioneering particular techniques, celebrating 1840 as the first popular campaign that mobilized the masses and 1896 as the first mass merchandising effort organized bureaucratically. Historians also identified critical elections that realigned power, especially the 1800 revolution that empowered Thomas Jefferson's Democratic-Republicans, the 1828 Democratic Jacksonian revolution, the 1860 Republican antislavery revolution, the 1896 corporate Republican realignment, the 1932 Democratic New Deal ascension, and the 1980 conservative Republican Reagan Revolution.

In fact, campaigns evolved slowly, haphazardly, sometimes fitfully, responding to changing communication and transportation technologies, shifts in population and society, the parties' rise and fall, and the growth of the presidency. Technological innovations, including the railroad, telegraph, radio, television, and even the Internet, created necessary but not sufficient conditions for change. Sometimes, traditionalists resisted: throughout the 1800s, editorialists and opponents repeatedly denounced candidates who stumped—mounted speaking tours—claiming they acted in an undignified—and unprecedented—way. Sometimes, innovations failed until politicians figured out how to adapt the technology. Citizens in a democracy get the campaign they deserve; interested, overall, in winning strategies, successful candidates offer unsentimental reflections of what works, despite what people wish worked or imagine worked in the past.

The history of presidential campaigning can be divided into four phases: the republican, democratic, populist, and electronic. The republican phase, reflecting the founders' republican ideology, trusted the wisdom of the few and feared the passion of mobs while rooting government's legitimacy in consent of the governed. Politics' gentlemanly tone reflected the search for virtuous candidates who would neither conspire with cabals nor rabble-rouse demagogically. Campaigns emphasized the candidate's suitability, as candidates functioned as icons, ideal representations of the perfect gentleman and leader.

Candidate, from the Latin word for white, *candidus*, evoked the white togas that represented Roman senators' supposed purity. In that spirit, candidates were to stand for election and not run. Local campaigns were not always as sober as the group conceit hoped. Decades before the Populist and Progressive movements instituted the secret, "Australian" ballot, Election Day was a raucous occasion. On this day, grandees, sitting at the polls as people voted, asked their social inferiors for help, thanking them with libations. This momentary egalitarianism reflected the essential links between equality, liberty, and democracy.

Still, the ideal republican candidate was George Washington. Reflecting his reluctance, he stayed on his farm in humble repose, awaiting the people's call, before being elected president unanimously. In 1792, he was re-elected without touring around begging for votes.

Embodying national virtue, Washington was a demigod who set the bar unrealistically high for Americans—and his successors. As parties developed and as local candidates began campaigning, Washington's passive silence became a straitjacket his successors tried wriggling out of, campaign by campaign.

The rise of political parties, the lifting of voting restrictions on white males, and the move from farms to factories triggered a democratic revolution. Local campaigns became increasingly hard fought. In 1824, 1828, and 1832, Andrew Jackson, the charismatic, controversial war hero who became an assertive president, brought a new personality-based mass excitement to the campaign. Jackson's elitist Whig opponents copied, perfected, and outdid the Jacksonian Democrats' mass appeal tactics in their 1840 campaign for William Henry Harrison. This Whig hijacking proved that the democratic sensibility had become all-American.

The nineteenth-century democratic campaign mobilized the masses through their partisan identities. Politicking became the national pastime. Election days were mass carnivals, culminating months of pamphleting, marching, orating, editorializing in party newspapers, and bickering neighbors. The party bosses dominating the system sought loyal soldiers more than virtuous gentlemen. The primary ability parties prized was "availability," seeking pliant, appealing, noncontroversial candidates. Rather than lofty, passive icons, candidates were becoming actors, sometimes speaking, sometimes stumping, always following the party script. During this time, acceptance letters became increasingly elaborate policy statements, fitting the candidate's views to the party platform, rather than simple republican expressions of virtuous reluctance to plunge into politics.

While party bosses picked most local candidates, the national parties mounted elaborate quadrennial conventions to nominate a standard-bearer and define the party platform. These colorful, often rollicking affairs were way stations between republican elitist politics and today's popular politics. Party bosses lobbied behind the scenes to select candidates and set agendas, but the conventions' deliciously democratic chaos reflected America's drift away from hierarchical politics.

Seeking loyalists, these conventions nominated last-minute dark horses, like James Knox Polk or James Garfield; undistinguished party hacks like Millard Fillmore and Franklin Pierce; war heroes like Lewis Cass, deemed a "doughface" because he could mold himself to appear sympathetic to the North or the South; and relatively uncontroversial, compromise candidates like Abraham Lincoln. A one-term Whig congressman in a party dominated by the antislavery titans William Henry Seward and Salmon Chase, Lincoln followed the textbook strategy during this phase: "My name is new in the field, and I suppose I am not the first choice of a very great many. Our policy, then, is to give no offense to others—leave them in a mood to come to us if they shall be compelled to give up their first love."

As democratization, urbanization, industrialization, and the communications revolution intensified, American politics became more populist, and the presidency became more central. In this populist phase, candidates were more independent of party and more nationalist in orientation. The quaint gentlemanly postures vanished as candidates stumped, whistle-stopped, and prop-stopped on trains, planes, and automobiles. Candidates needed to demonstrate their popularity and their potential to lead the nation. The best candidates were master orators with just a tinge of demagoguery who could move thousands listening in person and millions of newspaper readers and, eventually, radio listeners. After Franklin Roosevelt made America into a superpower and 1600 Pennsylvania Avenue America's central address, Americans no longer sought mere actors but superheroes who could dominate their parties, the campaign, the presidency, and the national news cycle.

Presidential candidates stumped more and more intensely throughout the nineteenth century, and the acceptance letter developed into an elaborate notification ceremony featuring a candidate's address. In the 1880s and 1890s, torn between the tradition of passivity and pressures to be more active, James A. Garfield and other candidates mounted Front Porch campaigns, staying at home but greeting huge delegations of supporters from across the country who came to pay homage. Still, the 1896 campaign became one of those historical moments that consolidated and advanced various innovations. William Jennings Bryan's elaborate 18,009 mile, 600-speech, 27-state rear-platform campaign ended the charade that candidates did not stump for themselves. William McKinley's front porch campaign, whereby he greeted over 300 delegations consisting of 750,000 visitors from 30 states at his Ohio home, genuflected toward the past. Meanwhile, McKinley's campaign manager,

Mark Hanna, mounted a modern campaign. Recognizing the growing overlap between consumerism and politics, he organized dozens of special-interest groups, deployed hundreds of speakers, raised millions of dollars, and distributed hundreds of millions of pamphlets.

Subsequently, the charismatic, candidate-centered campaigns of Theodore Roosevelt, Woodrow Wilson, and Franklin Roosevelt presented the candidate as poised to master what Theodore Roosevelt called the "bully pulpit." By 1948, even the mild-mannered Harry Truman felt compelled to run an aggressive, "Give 'em hell" Harry campaign crisscrossing America, despite the fact that he, following Franklin Roosevelt, was also dominating the airwaves thanks to radio's spread in the 1920s and 1930s.

By 1952, the heroic Dwight Eisenhower also campaigned actively and cut campaign commercials on the new medium of television. "Eisenhower Answers America" offered short, staged televised interactions between the general and "the people"—all-American types Eisenhower's advertising wizards selected from the queue at New York City's Radio City Music Hall. Between takes, Eisenhower muttered: "to think that an old soldier should come to this."

The Fourth Phase: The Electronic Campaign

The television revolution ushered in campaigning's electronic era. Most local candidates could not afford to broadcast television commercials, but the need for state, national, and some local candidates to raise big money favored entrepreneurial candidacies. Party discipline and loyalty faded as state primaries nominated most candidates. At all levels, outsiders could defy the bosses. Independent gunslingers with enough popularity could win the nomination and inherit the party apparatus. Movie stars could become California governors, billionaires could become New York City mayors. Losers then frequently faded into the sunset and winning candidates emerged less beholden to party powers. Media mastery, rather than virtue, loyalty, or oratory became prized, as candidates frequently traded on celebrity. Campaigns were no longer quests to emphasize a candidate's iconic virtue but to project an appealing image. In this electronic era, smooth-talking salesmen such as John Kennedy, Ronald Reagan, and Bill Clinton dominated.

Television debates offered some of the turning points in presidential campaigns, including when a tanned, confident John Kennedy bested a sweaty, shifty Richard

Nixon in 1960, when Gerald Ford stumbled and declared Eastern Europe "free" even though Soviets still dominated in 1976, and when Ronald Reagan laughed off Jimmy Carter's criticisms in 1980, chuckling, "There you go again." Television commercials offered equally powerful defining moments: 1964's pro-Lyndon Johnson "Daisy" commercial suggesting Republican Barry Goldwater might blow up the world, 1984's "Morning in America" commercial praising Ronald Reagan's America as paradise recovered, and 1988's "Willie Horton" commercial maligning Michael Dukakis for furloughing a murderer who then raped and murdered again.

Most recently, some politicians welcomed the computer age as heralding a fifth, virtual era of campaigning. But in the first few national election cycles, the Internet and blogosphere extended the reach of the electronic campaign without yet fully transforming it. In 2008, Barack Obama exploited the Internet as a fundraising and friend-raising tool, raising unprecedented amounts from a huge base of small donors. Still, most of his $600 million war chest came from big money sources. The revolution will happen, gradually, haphazardly.

Meanwhile, many of the historic conundrums surrounding campaigning persist. Are voters fools, do they make what scholars called "low information rationality" decisions like choosing a toothpaste brand, or are they seriously assessing a job applicant's potential to lead in the world's superpower? Why is voter turnout so low: does it reflect America's stability or Americans' disgust with politics? What is the role of money in politics: are campaign costs and donor influence out of control, or are costs reasonable, considering that Procter & Gamble's advertising budget of $6.8 billion in 2006 puts into perspective the estimated $4.3 billion spent during the 2008 campaign to select the leader of the free world? Do Americans seek a president who can be king or prime minister, or could the criteria for those two different jobs be combined? And do America's greatest leaders win campaigns—or if not, why not?

Questions and grumbling continue—and will continue, considering how important the process is, and how messy. Still, American campaigns remain magical, from the contest for the most common to the highest office in the land. Leaders trying to converse communally with thousands, millions, or even hundreds of millions face daunting challenges. But the lack of violence during campaigns, their remarkable regularity through prosperity and depression, peace and war reveal the system's buoyancy. And the fact that even after the contested presidential election of 2000, most Americans accepted the declared winner as legitimate speaks to the Constitution's continuing power. That a document cobbled together hastily in the horse-and-buggy age of the 1780s still works today is a miracle most Americans take for granted, but that every campaign affirms, no matter how much mudslinging, grandstanding, and promiscuous promising there may be.

See also campaign consultants; campaign law and finance; elections and electoral eras; Internet and politics; political advertising; radio and politics; television and politics.

FURTHER READING

Boller, Paul. *Presidential Campaigns: From George Washington to George W. Bush*, revised ed. New York: Oxford University Press, 2004.

Cramer, Richard Ben. *What It Takes: The Way to the White House*. New York: Vintage, 1993.

Jamieson, Kathleen Hall. *Packaging the Presidency: A History and Criticism of Presidential Campaign Advertising*, 3rd ed. New York: Oxford University Press, 1996.

Keyssar, Alexander. *The Right to Vote: The Contested History of Democracy in the United States*. New York: Basic Books, 2001.

McCormick, Richard P. *The Presidential Game: The Origins of American Presidential Politics*. New York: Oxford University Press, 1984.

McGinniss, Joe. *The Selling of the President*. New York: Penguin, 1988.

Polsby, Nelson, and Aaron Wildavsky, with David A. Hopkins. *Presidential Elections: Strategies and Structures of American Politics*, 12th ed. Lanham, MD: Rowman and Littlefield, 2007.

Troy, Gil. *See How They Ran: The Changing Role of the Presidential Candidate*, revised ed. Cambridge, MA: Harvard University Press, 1996.

White, Theodore H. *The Making of the President 1960*. New York: Signet, 1967.

GIL TROY

Caribbean, Central America, and Mexico, interventions in, 1903–34

In the first two decades of the twentieth century, the United States intervened in the Caribbean, Central America, and Mexico with a frequency and purpose that made earlier policy in the region seem haphazard. The interventions ranged from outright military occupations in Mexico, Haiti, and the Dominican Republic to less bellicose, but still coercive, efforts to control the finances of Honduras and Nicaragua. Despite their differences, the actions all aimed to force stability on the poor, weak, and politically volatile nations of the South while protecting U.S. security and promoting American economic interests. The wave of interventions gave U.S. foreign policy a formal new doctrine—the Roosevelt corollary to the Monroe Doctrine—as well as the informal, and at first pejorative, title "dollar diplomacy." While less dramatic than U.S. participation in the Spanish-American War and World War I, the interventions were highly controversial and had repercussions that echoed through the twentieth century and into the twenty-first.

U.S. Expansion in Global Context

The projection of American power in the Western Hemisphere in the early twentieth century was part of a larger global process by which advanced industrial nations—above all Great Britain and France, but also Germany, Italy, Belgium, and Japan—took direct or indirect control of less developed societies in Africa, Asia, and the Middle East. Many factors contributed to this New Imperialism, as it was called: the vast new military and technological power that the industrial revolution bestowed on a handful of advanced nations, the competition for raw materials, foreign markets and geopolitical advantage among these same powers, and the belief, supported at the time, that most non–European peoples were unfit for self-rule and thus needed to pass under the tutelage of one or another "civilized" nation—what Rudyard Kipling called the "White Man's Burden."

Similar factors encouraged the extension of American hegemony, or domination, over the Caribbean and Central America. The growing wealth, military power, technology, and trade of the United States meant that "more or less meddling on our part with the political affairs of our weaker neighbors seems inevitable," as one newspaper editorial put it in 1912. American leaders also looked over their shoulders at the relentless growth of Europe's colonial empires. They worried most of all that Germany, a powerful industrial nation with few colonies, would ignore the Monroe Doctrine and make a grab for territory in the New World.

Creating Panama

Those fears increased after the first American intervention of the twentieth century brought the nation of Panama into existence in 1903. This came about when Colombia refused to accept an American offer of $10 million for the right to build a canal across the isthmus of Panama, that nation's northernmost province at the time. In November 1903, with the U.S. warship *Nashville* in place to keep Colombian troops from interfering, rebels in Panama declared their independence. Soon after, the tiny new nation leased the Canal Zone to the United States, and work on the great project began the next year. When the Panama Canal opened in August 1914, it channeled a significant share of world trade through Caribbean waters and allowed the United States to move warships quickly from the Atlantic to Pacific theaters. Given the economic and strategic importance of the canal, American policy makers feared that the "weak and tottering republics" of the Caribbean would emerge as the soft underbelly of the United States. As signs grew clearer that a major European war was imminent, U.S. officials fretted that the European powers would pressure one or another country near the canal to grant them coaling stations or naval bases. "The inevitable effect of our building the Canal," Secretary of State Elihu Root noted in 1905, "must be to require us to police the surrounding premises."

The Panama intervention gave the United States a 99-year lease on the Canal Zone, and American officials did not seek to acquire more territory in the region. Few Americans of the time favored creating a formal empire on the European model, especially after the United States resorted to brutal tactics to suppress the Filipino independence movement in the wake of the Spanish-American War. Anti-imperialists like Senator Carl Schurz of Ohio argued that the United States did not need to own the countries it wished to trade with, since American products could compete with the best industrial goods made. Racial prejudice also worked against creating a formal empire. Historically, Americans had allowed new territories to become states, granting full political rights to their inhabitants. If the United States annexed the Dominican Republic or Haiti, eventually those overwhelmingly nonwhite peoples might gain the right to vote, an abhorrent idea to most Americans in the early 1900s. Thus, while policy makers wished to impose stability in the Caribbean and Central America, they did so through what William Appleman Williams called "non-colonial but nevertheless imperial expansion"—the policy of dominating the region without the cost or political headaches of outright ownership.

Noncolonial Expansion: The Dominican Receivership

President Theodore Roosevelt developed the centerpiece of this nonterritorial imperialism in the Dominican Republic, which shares the island of Hispaniola with Haiti. By 1904 the Dominican government had defaulted on millions of dollars in loans from both European and American creditors. At first the State Department worked to ensure that American investors got their money back, but when European foreign ministries threatened to force repayment by seizing Dominican custom houses, Roosevelt ordered U.S. Navy officers to broker a deal. In January 1905, Dominican president Carlos Morales agreed to accept U.S. control of his government's finances. Under the customs receivership, as it was called, American officials took over the Dominican Republic's custom houses—the source of nearly all government revenue—and then paid 45 percent of the money to the Dominicans, with the rest going to foreign creditors. The plan followed from the view that the frequent Latin American revolutions were nothing more than squabbles over money. Roosevelt believed that, by denying Dominicans control of their own national treasury, he had hit on the perfect mechanism to end political instability and financial chaos.

As a complement to the customs receivership, Washington officials brokered a $20 million loan from American banks to help the Caribbean nation build the roads, wharves, and other infrastructure needed for economic growth. Thus, the receivership and loan had the added, and not accidental, benefit of transferring Dominican financial dependence from Europe to the United States. Historian Emily Rosenberg has argued that, by linking a loan agreement to financial supervision, the Dominican plan was a prototype for public-private development partnerships that in the post–World War II period would be "enshrined in the International Monetary Fund."

The Roosevelt Corollary

The Dominican intervention was also the occasion of Roosevelt's famous corollary to the Monroe Doctrine. The original doctrine, first announced in 1823, warned European powers not to try to carve colonies from the newly independent but feeble nations of Latin America. Through the corollary, Roosevelt now forbade European powers to bombard or occupy nations anywhere in the Americas, even to collect legitimate debts. In return, Roosevelt promised that "the United States, however reluctantly," would itself exercise "an international police power" to ensure that each nation "keeps order

and pays its obligations." When Democrats and some progressive Republicans in the U.S. Senate objected to the extension of American power over the Caribbean republic, Roosevelt skirted their treaty-making power and had the U.S. Navy implement the receivership by executive fiat.

American leaders saw the customs receivership as an ideal solution to the problem of instability in the Caribbean and, for the first few years, the receivership seemed to live up to their hopes. The *New York Times* cheered that "Uncle Sam has waved the wand that produces National transformation, and lo! a republic has appeared where government is of the people, peace is assured, prosperity is perennial." Although the term would not be coined until a few years later, the Dominican receivership embodied the new policy of "dollar diplomacy," which promised to deploy financial control rather than troops to bring stability to the Caribbean region.

Dollar Diplomacy in Central America

American officials saw the Dominican receivership as such a success that they tried to replicate it elsewhere. After Roosevelt left office, President William Howard Taft and Secretary of State Philander C. Knox pressured Honduras to accept a receivership on the Dominican model, supplemented by loans from American banks. Honduran president Miguel Dávila waffled, fearing a nationalist outcry if he voluntarily gave control of his country's finances to a foreign power. At last, in 1911 he agreed to the plan—only to be driven from office a few months later. That same year, American diplomats pressed a similar arrangement on neighboring Nicaragua, where President Adolfo Díaz, formerly an employee of a U.S. mining company, fearfully accepted the receivership plan.

Both treaties ran into trouble in the U.S. Senate, however, where Democrats and some progressive Republicans objected to what they saw as an unholy alliance of Wall Street bankers and an overreaching president. Opponents worried that Taft would put the receiverships in place without Senate approval, as Roosevelt had done in the Dominican Republic. "They are trying to use the army and navy of the United States to accomplish that which we have specifically refused to give them authority to do," Senator Augustus Bacon, Democrat of Georgia, fumed in 1912. In the end, neither treaty won Senate approval.

Dollar diplomacy, conceived with the goal of ending military interventions, sometimes precipitated them. In

Nicaragua, President Díaz faced an armed insurrection by opponents of the U.S. receivership and the American loans that came with it. To keep Díaz in power, the United States landed over 2,000 marines in Nicaragua in what newspapers at the time noted was a clear setback to dollar diplomacy. Once the revolt was quelled, some marines remained, ostensibly to guard the U.S. embassy but really as a tripwire—if violence broke out again, American boots would already be on the ground, justifying the dispatch of reinforcements. U.S. soldiers would return to Nicaragua in force in the late 1920s to crush the rebellion led by Augusto Sandino, who declared, "I want a free country or death."

The Haitian and Dominican Occupations

Even more disappointing to U.S. policy makers was the fate of the "model" receivership in the Dominican Republic. In 1911 an assassin took the life of President Ramón Cáceres, a popular leader who had cooperated with the United States. The death of Cáceres unleashed several years of precisely the kind of instability that the receivership had supposedly ended. As Dominican presidents rose and fell, the United States began to interfere in day-to-day politics on the island, sending 750 marines to "protect" the U.S. embassy, ordering warships to cruise Dominican waters, and cutting off the receivership's payments to leaders that American diplomats disliked. It is noteworthy that these strong measures were taken by President Woodrow Wilson and his secretary of state, William Jennings Bryan, Democrats who had denounced the Latin American adventures of Republican presidents Roosevelt and Taft. Bryan, three times the Democratic candidate for president from 1896 to 1908, was indeed the symbol of anti-imperialism, once calling dollar diplomacy "a repudiation of the fundamental principles of morality."

It was, nevertheless, under Wilson that U.S. Marines invaded and occupied the Dominican Republic in 1916 (Bryan had resigned in mid-1915 over Wilson's increasing belligerence toward Germany). After repressing scattered resistance, the marines established a military government—no Dominican leader would give the occupation the fig leaf of local support—that imposed martial law, censored the press, and began confiscating arms from the local population.

The occupation lasted eight years. In that time, the American occupiers had some success improving infrastructure, education, and public health, despite unrelenting hostility from the Dominican people that grew into an armed resistance. In 1919 the Dominican president deposed by the U.S. Marines three years earlier traveled to the Versailles peace conference and called for an end to the occupation based on Wilson's pledge in the Fourteen Points to support "justice for all peoples . . . whether they are strong or weak." The Dominican plea had little effect beyond embarrassing American officials at the conference.

The Dominican intervention was not unique. Even before U.S. Marines landed in Santo Domingo, they had occupied the neighboring country of Haiti. Political instability in that country fed American fears of German intervention as World War I raged in Europe. Future secretary of state Robert Lansing justified the occupation of Haiti and other Caribbean nations as essential to "prevent a condition which would menace the interests of the United States . . . I make no argument on the ground of the benefit which would result to the peoples of these republics." The American occupation of Haiti lasted from 1915 until 1934. As in the Dominican Republic, it triggered violent popular opposition in the form of strikes, riots, and guerrilla warfare.

Wilson and Mexico

Wilson and Bryan also used military force to try to steer the course of the Mexican Revolution. The overthrow of Porfírio Díaz, the dictator who had ruled Mexico for over 30 years, led to a violent civil war in Mexico that began in 1911. By 1914 General Victoriano Huerta had defeated his opponents and taken the oath as Mexico's president, yet Wilson withheld official U.S. recognition and pressed for new elections.

When Huerta refused to resign, Wilson seized on a minor incident—Mexico's arrest of several American sailors—to force a showdown. Wilson ordered U.S. Marines to seize the port city of Veracruz, assuming there would be scant resistance and that the occupation would humiliate Huerta and force him to resign. Instead, the marines found themselves fighting street to street with Mexican forces while Huerta clung to power. Despite the casualties, Wilson would not abandon his plan "to help Mexico save herself and serve her people." Wilson at last withdrew the marines from Veracruz in November, after Huerta's rival Venustiano Carranza forced him from power. American meddling in Mexico was not over, however. After revolutionary leader Pancho Villa raided a border town in New Mexico, Wilson sent a 6,000-troop "punitive expedition" across the border in 1916. Wilson, the "anti-imperialist," intervened in Latin America more than any earlier U.S. president.

The receiverships, incursions, and occupations that characterized U.S. policy in the region left a bitter legacy of anti-Americanism throughout Latin America. Leading literary works of the early twentieth century, including Uruguayan intellectual José Enrique Rodó's essay *Ariel* and Nicaraguan poet Rubén Darío's bitter ode "To Roosevelt," cast the United States as a materialistic bully out to crush the romantic spirit of Latin America. In the wake of U.S. interventions in the region, many Latin Americans came to accept this view of their northern neighbor.

Political Repercussions of Intervention

The interventions in the Caribbean, Central America, and Mexico launched between 1903 and 1916 coincided with the high tide of progressivism in the United States. Political debate at home focused on critical economic issues, such as corporate power and labor unrest, in addition to perennial topics like the protective tariff. Those and other domestic issues, as well as the outsized personalities of Theodore Roosevelt, William Jennings Bryan, William Howard Taft, and Woodrow Wilson, dominated the presidential campaigns of 1904, 1908, and 1912. Although many Democrats and some Republicans objected to the way Roosevelt had "taken" Panama, a majority of voters favored building the canal and forgave the president's methods, returning him to the White House in 1904. By 1908, despite Bryan's efforts to make Republican foreign policy a campaign issue, the *New York Times* declared that "anti-imperialism is not an issue in this country, it is only a whine."

After Democrat Woodrow Wilson became president in 1913, Republicans accused him of "vacillating" in his defense of American lives and property in revolutionary Mexico. By 1914, however, World War I had dwarfed the issue of Mexico, and voters reelected Wilson in 1916 in large part for keeping the country out of what Democrats called the "carnival of slaughter" in Europe. While they never became decisive electoral issues, the U.S. interventions in Panama, the Dominican Republic, Nicaragua, Honduras, and Mexico triggered vigorous debate in the Senate, which was called on to approve treaties in the first four cases. The interventions thus became episodes in the long struggle between the executive and legislative branches over control of U.S. foreign policy.

The interventions in the Caribbean, Central America, and Mexico are arguably more relevant to U.S.

foreign policy in the twenty-first century than larger conflicts like the two world wars, Korea, and Vietnam. The interventions raised stark questions about the constitutional limits of presidential power in foreign affairs, the effectiveness of using the military to promote stability, democracy, and nation building in less-developed regions, and the unanticipated consequences of overthrowing hostile leaders in manifestly weaker nations. The occupations of the Dominican Republic and Haiti ended by 1934, and Franklin D. Roosevelt formally abandoned dollar diplomacy and pledged to be a "good neighbor" to Latin America after he took office in 1933. Even so, in the second half of the twentieth century the United States resorted to overt and covert intervention in the greater Caribbean, with the Central Intelligence Agency's destabilization of the elected government of Guatemala in 1954, the U.S.-sponsored Bay of Pigs invasion of Cuba in 1961, military intervention in the Dominican Republic in 1965, and the invasion of Panama in 1990.

See also foreign policy and domestic politics, 1865–1933; presidency 1860–1932; progressivism and the Progressive Era, 1890s–1920; Spanish-American War and Filipino Insurrection; territorial government.

FURTHER READING

Calder, Bruce J. *The Impact of Intervention: The Dominican Republic during the U.S. Occupation of 1916–1924.* Austin: University of Texas Press, 1984.

Green, Julie. *The Canal Builders: Making America's Empire at the Panama Canal.* New York: Penguin, 2009.

Hannigan, Robert E. *The New World Power: American Foreign Policy, 1898–1917.* Philadelphia: University of Pennsylvania Press, 2002.

Hart, John Mason. *Empire and Revolution: The Americans in Mexico since the Civil War.* Berkeley: University of California Press, 2002.

LaFeber, Walter. *Inevitable Revolutions: The United States in Central America.* New York: Norton, 1984.

Langley, Lester D. *The Banana Wars: United States Intervention in the Caribbean, 1898–1934.* New York: SR Books, 2002.

Rosenberg, Emily S. *Financial Missionaries to the World: The Politics and Culture of Dollar Diplomacy, 1900–1930.* Cambridge, MA: Harvard University Press, 1999.

Schmidt, Hans. *The United States Occupation of Haiti, 1915–1934.* New Brunswick, NJ: Rutgers University Press, 1971.

Schoultz, Lars. *Beneath the United States: A History of U.S. Policy toward Latin America.* Cambridge, MA: Harvard University Press, 1998.

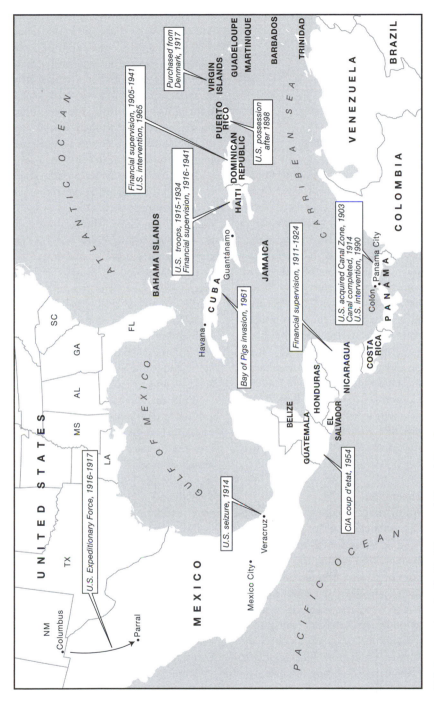

U.S. Interventions in the Caribbean and Central America

Veeser, Cyrus. *A World Safe for Capitalism: Dollar Diplomacy and America's Rise to Global Power.* New York: Columbia University Press, 2002.

Williams, William Appleman. *The Tragedy of American Diplomacy.* New York: Dell, 1959.

CYRUS VEESER

Caribbean immigrants and politics

Immigrants of African descent from the Caribbean have played important political roles in the United States, whether they arrived on American shores as slaves, as free men and women of color, or in the migration waves of the early and late twentieth century. The nature of their political activities has varied over time, but claims to a common African heritage and experience of enslavement often shaped a common political agenda with African Americans. Most black immigrants, with the exception of New Orleans Creoles, long shared common residential spaces with African Americans and generally shared membership in the same black civil society. Yet strong ties to the Caribbean and a commitment to transnational politics as well as civil rights have long characterized the politics of Caribbean immigrants. In addition, immigrant intellectuals contributed to a range of political ideas and joined with like-minded African Americans in promoting a diasporic and less nation-based political agenda.

Slavery and Post-Emancipation

The first Caribbean immigrants to contribute to transnational as well as black political goals in America were enslaved people who had been "seasoned" in the islands before being sold to the North American mainland. During nearly four centuries of slavery, immigrants became part of communities of Africans—seamen, runaways, and free people of color—who circulated along trade routes that connected port cities of the American mainland to various islands of the Caribbean. Vagrancy dockets and prison records of U.S. port cities from Philadelphia to Baltimore document the presence of long-distance runaways, a virtual maritime underground railroad that suggests a more fluid relationship between enslaved societies of the Caribbean and North America than historians had previously recognized.

The Haitian Revolution (1793–1804) was the first and one of the most lasting political contributions of the African Caribbean to African America. While the rhetoric of the American Revolution had asserted ideals of liberty and equality, the Haitian revolution actually demanded that enslaved people share in the liberty that the Enlightenment claimed as natural law. By challenging the political economy of slavery in the New World, embracing all escaped slaves as citizens, and abolishing racial distinctions in its constitution, the revolution inspired the oppressed everywhere in the hemisphere.

The Haitian Revolution also produced the first major immigration of African Caribbean people not connected with the international slave trade. Approximately 15,000 refugees fled the island between 1791 and 1804, and some 10,000 arrived in New Orleans in 1809 after having been expelled from Cuba. The 1809 wave doubled the size of the free population in New Orleans and helped make the city the largest urban community of black immigrants in the United States. Hundreds of refugees arrived in several other port cities, from Philadelphia to Savannah, in the summer of 1793 alone. In the southern ports, especially, the presence of enslaved or formerly enslaved Haitian immigrants, reluctant refugees from a successful revolution carried out by slaves, represented an immediate threat to the slave system and an inspiration to the enslaved and free alike.

While many of the Afro-Haitians maintained distinct cultural communities for generations, most black immigrants became well integrated into African American life. The number of free foreign-born black immigrants remained small throughout the nineteenth century. In 1850, only 4,067 foreign-born black immigrants lived in the United States. Most had been born in the Caribbean, were predominantly male, and belonged to a highly select group with the means to emigrate and the ambition and skills to compete in America. A significant number of the English-speaking immigrants were educated seamen, students, teachers, and ministers; some attended historically black colleges where they received training in professional occupations. In the nineteenth century, especially, their ties to the native-born African American community were reinforced through marriage and leadership in black civil society.

A number of free immigrant men founded major African American institutions before the Civil War. Prince Hall (probably from Barbados), a self-educated leather dealer and outspoken advocate for black rights, formed the first African Masonic Lodge in Boston in 1784.

Another immigrant, Peter Ogden, a Jamaican sailor and steward, formed the first African American branch of the Odd Fellows in New York City in 1842. (The Odd Fellows, like the Prince Hall Masons, became one of the largest and politically influential fraternal societies among African Americans in the nineteenth and twentieth centuries.)

Other immigrant men made their mark as intellectuals and activists. The Jamaican-born John Russwurm (1799–1851), one of the first three black graduates of an American college, cofounded with native-born Samuel Cornish the first black newspaper in the United States, the New York–based *Freedom's Journal*, in 1827. Russwurm left the United States in 1829 to join the Liberia settlement project in West Africa, where he became governor of the colony of Maryland. Another future Liberian, Edward Wilmot Blyden (1832–1912), a native of the then Danish Virgin Islands, spent only a short period in the United States in 1850, when he was denied admission to two theological seminaries because of his race. Blyden emigrated to Liberia, where he completed his secondary education. From Liberia and later Sierra Leone, Blyden—a prolific writer and passionate African nationalist—became one of the most influential figures of the nineteenth century among African Americans and others in the diaspora.

After the Civil War, a small number of first- and second-generation Caribbean immigrant men became active in the Republican Party. Two descendents of Charleston's Afro-Haitian immigrant community, Jacob Alonzo Ransier and Robert Carlos De Large, were elected to Congress from South Carolina and worked on the Civil Rights Act of 1875. Both also cultivated ties to Haiti in their official capacities. Two English-speaking black immigrant South Carolinians were elected to Congress. Robert Brown Elliot, a native of Liverpool, England (probably of Caribbean ancestry), a lawyer and graduate of Eton College, was elected to the House of Representatives from South Carolina in 1868. Barbados-born David Augustus Straker (1842–1908), an 1871 graduate of the Howard University School of Law, was elected to the South Carolina state legislature in 1876. The violent disruptions of Radical Reconstruction shortened Straker's career as a legislator, but he became prominent in South Carolina and later in Detroit, Michigan, as a lawyer and outspoken civil rights advocate. In the 1890 *William W. Ferguson v. Edward G. Gies* case he argued successfully before the Michigan Supreme Court that separation by race in public places was illegal in the State of Michigan.

That same year, several Haitian Creole civil rights lawyer activists began plans to challenge segregation in Louisiana. In New Orleans, Rudolph Lucien Desdunes, along with fellow Creoles and other African Americans, organized the Comité des Citoyens (Citizens Committee) to challenge segregation on the state's streetcars. Homère A. Plessy, a friend of Desdunes, agreed to test the constitutionality of the Louisiana Separate Car Act and was arrested in 1892 after he boarded a railroad car reserved for whites. Desdunes and his legal team fought the case all the way to the U.S. Supreme Court, which legalized the "separate but equal" doctrine in *Plessy v. Ferguson* on May 18, 1896. In the 1890s, Desdunes also edited a daily newspaper, the New Orleans *Crusader*, which aggressively promoted black rights.

While Straker, Desdunes, and other first- and second-generation immigrants were among the postemancipation era's most outspoken activists, Antigua-born William B. Derrick (1843–1913) took a more moderate path to leadership. Derrick arrived in the United States as a seaman in 1860, joined the U.S. Navy, and, after the Civil War, settled in Washington, D.C., and Virginia, where he married into a prominent African American family. A talented orator, he began his public career as a circuit preacher for the African Methodist Episcopal (AME) church, eventually rising to leadership as pastor and then, by the 1880s, bishop of New York City's largest AME congregation. Affiliated with the Odd Fellows, Masons, Good Samaritans, and a trustee of Wilberforce University (the first historically black college in the United States), Derrick, a Republican, also became the party's "colored leader" in New York City in the 1890s and a confidant of the powerful African American leader Booker T. Washington. Still, Derrick maintained lifelong ties to Antiguans in New York and at home.

The Great Migration

Men like Derrick were succeeded by a new generation of immigrants swept in by the Great Migration from the Caribbean after 1900. The black foreign-born population numbered nearly 100,000 by 1930—a presence large enough to cause ethnic-based communities to form from it. In that year, New York City claimed nearly 40,000 foreign-born black people, mostly from the English-speaking Caribbean. Smaller but important communities formed in Boston and southern Florida. This residential concentration of the newest immigrants, which included almost as many women as men, sustained networks of family, friends, and benevolent associations.

In New York, immigrants could forge a small intellectual community as well. Some Caribbean immigrant intellectuals joined primarily African American fraternal societies and other civic organizations, but most, typically self-educated, remained outside such groups. Untutored by the old guard, they—along with New York's many other immigrant intellectuals—explored the Bolshevik Revolution and the rising discontent of the colonized around the globe. They interacted with a variety of intellectuals and radicals, including Jewish and Japanese immigrants, and seized a public voice on U.S. social justice issues while promoting a broader vision of the black struggle.

The premier intellectual among them was Hubert Harrison (1883–1927), a native of St. Croix who arrived in New York City in 1900. He was the first of the radicals to form his own organization, the Liberty League, and newspaper, the *Voice*, in 1917. He mentored a cadre of Caribbean immigrant intellectuals, including Richard B. Moore, a native of Barbados; Nevis-born Cyril Briggs; Jamaican W. A. Domingo; and Surinamese Otto Huiswoud. Harrison, who broke with the Socialist Party over its refusal to address the unique racial circumstances of the U.S. working class, also introduced nationalist Marcus Garvey (who founded the Universal Negro Improvement Association in 1914 and the newspaper *Negro World* in 1918) to Harlem audiences. Although Garvey's organization went on to eclipse Harrison's as the largest mass-based movement in the United States before the civil rights era, Harrison's street corner lectures, unfettered by party or pulpit, became the prototype for democratic political spaces in Harlem and a platform for divergent ideas.

Immigrant Politics: 1930–65

By 1930 the issue of self-government and universal suffrage in the Caribbean attracted support from Caribbean immigrant men and women alike in New York and other cities. A number of New York–based organizations, including the Caribbean Union (1930) and the Jamaica Progressive League (1936), were formed to address these concerns. By the 1940s, a younger generation joined these intellectuals, led by such men as Trinidadian C.L.R. James (1901–89), the writer and socialist theorist, who would link these concerns to civil rights and conflicts in the developing world. Their activities, which European and American authorities deemed "subversive," were subject to surveillance and led to the arrest, detainment, or deportation of many key activists, including Domingo. James, an advocate of the West Indian Feder-

ation, was forced to leave the United States under threat of deportation in 1953.

Within the Caribbean immigrant community, women were essential builders of community institutions. They helped organize and sustain benevolent and home associations, churches, and vast networks of family and friends. It was through this institutional base that first-generation women were more likely to gain a public voice, while their male counterparts more easily moved back and forth between their own ethnic groups and the larger African American community.

Still, Caribbean women's politics in New York City became associated with local community, civil rights, and labor struggles. In New York City in 1915, Virgin Islander Elizabeth Hendrickson and other female compatriots organized an association of American Virgin Island women, the American West Indian Ladies Aid Society. Key members of this benevolent association were also active in the struggle for first class citizenship in the U.S.-controlled Virgin Islands, as well as in Harlem tenant movements during the Great Depression and after. Claudia Jones (1915–64), a native of Trinidad, was well known in Communist politics in New York City but also nationally for her fiery speeches on civil and human rights during the 1940s and 1950s. A victim of McCarthyism, Jones was deported in 1955 but reemerged in Britain as one of the Caribbean community's most outspoken civil rights activists. Her grave sits next to that of Karl Marx in London's Highgate Cemetery.

Caribbean women, one of the first groups of black women employed in a unionized industry—garment work—emerged as local union leaders, initially because they were the most literate in English among immigrant workers. International labor leader Maida Springer Kemp (1910–2005), a Panama native of African Caribbean ancestry, began her career in International Ladies Garment Workers Union Local 22 in 1933 and eventually became active in international trade unionism, international worker education (especially of women), and the women's movement.

While many early-twentieth-century Caribbean women and men became radical activists, others participated in the mainstream political arena, and their names are prominent among the list of black "firsts" in New York Democratic politics after 1930. Finding few opportunities in local Republican politics in New York City, the newest immigrants began working for the Democratic Party in the late nineteenth century. They were sometimes rewarded with "colored" or city jobs, but when the struggle for black political autonomy in Harlem's election districts began in the late 1920s, prominent immigrant men led the fight and reaped the rewards. Similar struggles led by immigrants took place in Brooklyn and the Bronx from the 1940s to the 1960s. (New York governor David Paterson, the grandson of Caribbean immigrants, has political roots from that period as the son of former New York secretary of state Basil Paterson.)

Two of the most influential Democrats in New York in the interwar and postwar periods, Herbert Bruce from Barbados and J. Raymond Jones, a native of the Virgin Islands, started as redcaps (porters) in New York's Pennsylvania Station, political jobs obtained after they began working for the Democratic Party. Members of the "Penn Station Gang," a group of politically active redcaps and Pullman Porters, both men eventually financed and controlled their own political clubs in Harlem. Neither man relied on electoral politics at first but cultivated alliances and influence to broker favors. But in 1935, Bruce was elected district leader from the twenty-first Assembly District in Harlem, the first black official in New York Democratic politics to hold such a position. Respected for his maverick qualities and his ability to get out the vote, Bruce used his influence to gain nominations and political jobs for black candidates. Jones, known as the "Harlem Fox" for his club room strategies, was elected district leader from the twenty-second in 1944 and remained active in Democratic politics until 1967.

Well-educated and well-connected Caribbean immigrant women, mostly members of the second generation, emerged by the 1950s and 1960s. Important examples include attorney Carmel Carrington Marr, a Republican appointed by Eisenhower as legal advisor to the U.S. Mission to the United Nations in 1953, and civil rights attorney Constance Baker Motley, elected the first woman borough president of Manhattan in 1965. In 1968, representing Brooklyn's Twelfth District, Shirley Chisholm became the first black woman to be elected to the House of Representatives. Though she knew she would not win, Chisholm also made a bid for her party's presidential nomination in 1972. She retired from Congress in 1982.

Post-1965: Immigration and a New Political Generation

By the 1990s, a new generation of Caribbean politicians emerged from the second major immigrant wave after the passage of the Hart-Cellar Reform Act of 1965, which lifted national origins quota restrictions established in 1924. In the ten years after Hart-Cellar, Caribbean immigration exceeded that of the previous 70 years. In contrast to past immigrations, the newest wave tended to be predominantly female. By the 1980s, 50,000 English-speaking immigrants and 6,000 to 8,000 Haitian immigrants entered the United States each year, and these numbers continued to grow. By 1996, half of these immigrants had settled in New York City. These increasingly distinct ethnic communities have actively sought representation. In places with a high concentration of Caribbean immigrants, such as South Florida and Brooklyn, some politicians have sought to carve out political influence based on a multigenerational Caribbean constituency, not just an African American one. Campaign issues in Caribbean communities have included a more equitable immigration policy, voting rights in local elections for noncitizens, and a voice in shaping U.S. policy in the Caribbean basin. While such old line leaders as Jones, Bruce, and even Chisholm were more likely to emphasize racial solidarity, new immigrant politicians readily claim ethnicity as a unifying strategy.

Viewing Caribbean political activities over time illustrates the remarkable roles these immigrants played in shaping diverse public voices in America. Although they formed political alliances with African Americans over abolitionism, civil rights, and social justice in the United States, their voices from the Haitian Revolution forward have also represented a more international perspective. Russwurm, Blyden, Harrison, Garvey, and James represented political alternatives even as Elliot, Straker, Derrick, the "Penn Station Gang," and Chisholm, largely invisible in U.S. political history, made their mark within the American political mainstream. In promoting such ideas as voting rights for noncitizen legal residents, contemporary Caribbean immigrant political leaders are seeking (even if in their own self-interest) political identities with ties to both the United States and the Caribbean islands.

See also African Americans and politics.

FURTHER READING

Flowers, Violet. *The Other Bostonians: West Indians in Boston, 1900–1950.* Bloomington: Indiana University Press, 2007.

James, Winston. "Explaining Afro-Caribbean Social Mobility in the U.S.: Beyond the Sowell Thesis." *Comparative Studies in Society and History* 44, no. 2 (April 2002), 218–61.

Kasinitz, Philip. *Caribbean Immigrants in New York.* Ithaca, NY: Cornell University Press, 1991.

Laguerre, Michel S. *Diasporic Citizenship: Haitian Americans in Transnational America*. New York: St. Martin's Press, 1998.

Logan, Rayford W., and Michael R. Winston, eds. *Dictionary of American Negro Biography*. New York: Norton, 1982.

Perry, Jeffrey B. *A Hubert Harrison Reader*. Middletown, CT: Wesleyan University Press, 2001.

Phillips, Glenn. "The Response of a West Indian Activist: D. A. Straker, 1842–1908." *Journal of Negro History* 66, no. 2 (Summer 1981), 128–39.

Rogers, Reuel R. "Race-Based Coalitions among Minority Groups: Afro-Caribbeans and African Americans in New York City." *Urban Affairs Review* 39 (January 2004), 283–317.

Scott, Rebecca. *Degrees of Freedom: Louisiana and Cuba after Slavery, 1862–1914*. Cambridge, MA: Harvard University Press, 2005.

Turner, Joyce Moore. *Caribbean Crusaders of the Harlem Renaissance*. Champaign: University of Illinois Press, 2005.

Watkins-Owens, Irma. *Blood Relations: Caribbean Immigrants and the Harlem Community*. Bloomington: Indiana University Press, 1996.

IRMA WATKINS-OWENS

cartooning

Political or editorial cartooning has been a ubiquitous feature of American politics since the eighteenth century. Usually characterized by a single image supplemented by or juxtaposed to text, cartoons comment on events, ideas, people, policies, and social mores, framing their observations with humor, derision, or irony. While the term *cartoon* did not gain its current meaning until 1843 (via a reference in the British satirical weekly *Punch*), the form had long made a regular appearance in election campaigns as a partisan tool and as a popular form of visual commentary on local and national politics in general. Cartoons introduced many of the enduring symbols and terms in American politics, including the Republican Party elephant and the manipulative redistricting term *gerrymander*.

The form emerged out of the transatlantic print culture of the eighteenth century and London's vibrant pictorial market of political prints commenting on British politics and colonial policy. The few American contributions by the likes of Philadelphia printer Benjamin Franklin and Boston silversmith and engraver Paul Revere, published either as small woodcuts in newspapers or as single-sheet copper engraving broadsides, were cruder in appearance than their British counterparts. But such images as Franklin's 1754 "Join or Die" snake, calling on Britain's colonies to form a unified defense as war with France approached—often cited as the first American political cartoon and reissued during the 1765 Stamp Act Crisis and again in 1774—and Revere's 1770 fanciful depiction of the Boston Massacre were effective expressions of the Patriot cause and were widely disseminated on both sides of the Atlantic. The broadside form of cartoon continued to make an appearance, albeit infrequently, during the early electoral contests and presidential administrations of the young republic (one authority counted only 78 political prints before 1828).

Jacksonian Prints

The cartoon finally became a staple of political commentary and a weapon in the arsenals of political campaigns with the 1828 presidential contest between incumbent John Quincy Adams and Andrew Jackson. Cartoons became ubiquitous during the campaign, fueled by the expansion of male suffrage and the unusual bitterness of the election. Their rise as a popular form of political expression also resulted from the introduction of lithographic prints, which were substantially cheaper to produce and purchase than other visual print media of the time. While newspapers eschewed publishing cartoons via the more expensive process of engraving (which

Benjamin Franklin's warning to the British colonies in America to unite shows a snake in segments, each named for a colony or region. Published in the *Pennsylvania Gazette*, May 9, 1754. (Library of Congress)

permitted the publication of illustrations within the columns of type), lithography houses such as H. R. Robinson and, subsequently, Currier and Ives sprang up in New York and other northeastern cities, producing affordable single-sheet political prints in the thousands for a picture-hungry electorate.

Artists such as Edward William Clay and David Claypool Johnston established commercial careers as creators of political pictorial commentary during the antebellum period. Johnston, in particular, created many stark and original images, such as his 1828 caricature of Andrew Jackson as "Richard III," his face composed from the dead bodies of Seminole Indians. But the standard antebellum political print featured flat, theatrical tableaux in which stiff figures—their faces rendered in expressionless portraits—were depicted performing absurd acts in incongruous situations, with gobs of pun-infested text emanating from their mouths into balloons overhead.

Despite its representational limitations, the print remained the dominant form of political pictorial commentary for more than three decades, extending into the presidential administration of Abraham Lincoln. Yet historians continue to speculate about how these often raucous and highly partisan images were actually used and where they were displayed. Too topical and unedifying to conform to the sentimental or didactic goals prescribed for lithographs that decorated genteel parlors, the prints may have found a place on kitchen walls; they were most likely to be appreciated in male-dominated institutions such as taverns, barber shops, and political clubs.

The Political Cartoon Comes of Age

By the 1840s, topical cartoons were a regular feature in weekly illustrated newspapers in Europe and England, including publications devoted entirely to satirical commentary, such as the French *Le Charivari* (1832), which inspired the British *Punch: The London Charivari* (1841). Meanwhile, pictorial publication remained anemic in the United States until midcentury, when improved transportation, innovations in printing—especially in the process of wood engraving, which was compatible with movable type—and public concern about the growing sectional crisis created the conditions for a viable commercial illustrated press. With the rise of weekly pictorial newspapers, particularly *Frank Leslie's Illustrated Newspaper* in 1855 and *Harper's Weekly* in 1857, political cartooning entered a new phase that spelled the end of the long, comparatively tepid reign of the individual political print.

Although the pictorial press was centered in New York City, these publications relied on a broad readership and regularly featured cartoons that addressed national issues, printed in the crisp black and white linear codes of engraving. Cartoons often appeared on the weeklies' covers, complemented by a full- or double-page cartoon inside, and followed by more modest cartoons, usually commenting on social mores, among the ads in the back. The number of cartoons and their vituperative tone increased every election cycle, and the cartoonist whose name was synonymous with this mode and medium of expression was the German immigrant and ardent Republican Thomas Nast.

Nast became *Harper's Weekly's* leading cartoonist in his early twenties during the Civil War, and subsequently sealed his position at the publication, and his reputation in the broader field, with a series of brilliantly reductive, savagely caricatured cartoons attacking the "ring" of the corrupt Tammany Hall Democrats that controlled New York City's government. The only cartoonist able to rival Nast was another German immigrant, Joseph Keppler, whose Democratic-leaning satirical weekly *Puck* made its English-language debut in New York in 1877 (after a brief phase as a German-language magazine). What set *Puck* apart, and inaugurated another phase in editorial cartooning, was his introduction of chromolithography to U.S. magazine publishing. Each issue featured skillful caricatures of the illustrious and notorious rendered in full color against lavish, elaborate settings. As both *Puck's* publisher and chief artist, Keppler cultivated a host of younger cartoonists; some left his employ in 1881 to start *Judge*, a rival Republican satirical weekly.

The work of Nast, Keppler, and other Gilded Age artists established and, through repetition, institutionalized many of the symbols and pictorial conventions of political cartoons. Nast, in particular, excelled at devising figures that would become enduring iconographic political symbols. Figures embodying the nation, such as Liberty and Uncle Sam, had evolved and gained purchase in U.S. political culture since the eighteenth century; Nast introduced new symbols, including the Republican elephant, the Democratic machine Tammany tiger, and the bloated, diamond-bedecked urban political boss—epitomized in his rendition of Tammany Hall's William M. "Boss" Tweed. As that encapsulation of corruption demonstrated, both Nast and Keppler were masters of caricature—the exaggeration and distortion of the features and figures of individuals—in itself a

In his cartoon "The Tammany Tiger Loose," Thomas Nast depicts the Tammany Hall Democrats as a vicious tiger attacking the law, the ballot, the republic, and power. Published in *Harper's Weekly*, November 11, 1871. (American Social History Project, Center for Media and Learning at The City University of New York Graduate Center)

sharp departure from antebellum cartoons' presentation of relatively accurate countenances. By midcentury, caricature received a big boost from the invention of photography and the corresponding rapid proliferation of official photographic portraits. The public quickly grew familiar with the faces of the famous and infamous, giving cartoonists license to offer contorted versions that were intended to reveal the true motives and morality of their subjects. But these cartoonists' devotion to physical distortion was most fervently directed at groups. While racial stereotypes had a long presence in U.S. cartooning (dating back to E. W. Clay's 1830s "Life in Philadelphia" series lampooning northern free African Americans), Nast and Keppler reveled in grotesque ethnic portrayals to attack political opponents, especially simian Irish Americans for whom, along with Catholicism, both artists expressed antipathy.

Cartoons and the Daily Press

The true popularity of the Gilded Age cartoonists remains difficult to determine. The readership of the comparatively expensive illustrated weeklies rarely exceeded the hundreds of thousands. Nonetheless, the weeklies continued to dominate editorial cartooning. With the exception of the short-lived *New York Daily Graphic*, newspapers remained underillustrated. Then on October 30, 1884, Joseph Pulitzer published a cartoon by Walt McDougall (assisted by Valerian Gribayedoff) on the front page of his *New York World*. "The Royal Feast of Belshazzar Blaine and the Money Kings," which portrayed a poor family begging at a sumptuous feast attended by notorious robber barons and presided over by Democratic presidential candidate James G. Blaine, was later cited as a factor in Blaine's loss to Grover Cleveland. After the publication of McDougall's picture, political cartoons became a regular front-page feature in daily newspapers across the country.

Political cartoons were part of the larger visual extravaganza of Sunday supplements, comic strips, celebrity portraits, color, news illustrations, and eventually photojournalism that became crucial to the success of the mass-circulation press. For the first time, editorial cartoons became a truly popular medium reaching millions of readers daily. In turn, cartoonists became part of the celebrity culture the newspapers helped foster, gaining greater prestige and commensurate salaries.

By the turn of the twentieth century, every major newspaper across the country published political cartoons, usually on the front page. Amounting to some 2,000 professional editorial cartoonists, the ranks were notable for their absence of the generation that had dominated the era of the newsweeklies. And, in contrast to their often obstreperously independent predecessors, newspaper cartoonists were in thrall to their publishers and the latter's political party allegiances (as well as to the newspapers' increasing reliance on advertising revenue).

The transition to the newspaper phase of cartooning also marked a significant change in the medium's form. Now on daily rather than weekly schedules, required to address a broader range of readers and hampered by cruder newspaper reproduction, the new generation of cartoonists adopted a simpler pen-and-ink drawing style and briefer captions, relinquishing the laborious detail, baroque compositions, text-heavy messages, and classical and Shakespearean references that characterized the Gilded Age cartoons. Soon that form became even more streamlined when Robert Minor convinced the *St. Louis Post-Dispatch*'s pressmen to let him draw using a blunt grease crayon on textured paper; the more sketchlike technique quickly caught on.

The cartoonists of the mass-circulation press, along with their professional predecessors, were not the only artists publishing editorial cartoons. From the Gilded Age onward, immigrants, African Americans, trade unionists, feminists, and radicals published alternative and oppositional periodicals. Often limited in circulation and resources, these publications included visual commentary offering their constituencies perspectives that countered or supplemented those in the commercial press. The number of these publications—and their cartoons—increased at the turn of the century with the great wave of immigration, a burgeoning reform movement, an increasingly militant labor movement, and the rise of the Socialist Party and other third parties, all assisted by decreased costs in the reproduction of illustrations.

America's entry into World War I starkly demarcated alternative from mass-circulation cartoons. Few newspapers (and consequently, cartoonists) criticized the mobilization for war. Recognizing the popularity of political cartooning and capitalizing on the press's war enthusiasm, President Woodrow Wilson's administration established a Bureau of Cartoons as an arm of the propagandistic Committee on Public Information. The Bureau issued a weekly *Bulletin for Cartoonists* with instructions about appropriate subjects and how to illustrate them. While absorbing cartoons into the war effort, the government also targeted dissenting images. After passage of the 1917 Espionage Statute and the 1918 Sedition Act, publications alleged to engage in "obstruction of recruitment" were banned from the U.S. mail, effectively eliminating most alternative publications. In the case of the New York–based *The Masses*, a radical monthly with a small circulation but a big reputation for featuring cartoons by some of the outstanding artists of the era, the government went further and, citing the cartoons, prosecuted the editor and several artists. Two trials resulted in hung juries but also ultimately spelled the end of the magazine.

Uniformity, Decline, and Experimentation

Isolationism, complacency, and suspicion of reforms characterized commercial editorial cartooning after the war. Significantly, most of the women who had breached the walls of the male cartoonist club (and were limited to drawing only cartoons about suffrage) lost their jobs in the wake of passage of the Nineteenth Amendment. National syndication of cartoons only exacerbated uniformity as local cartoonists were replaced by more celebrated practitioners located in major cities. Public interest in editorial cartoons lagged: they were removed from their long-standing front-page perch and relocated to the interior editorial page in reduced size.

Over the course of cartooning's long history, commentators and scholars have contemplated its influence on public opinion. Stories abound about its impact on presidential contests such as the 1884 election, where the wide circulation of the *World*'s "Belshazzar" cover and *Puck*'s corruption-covered "Tattooed Man" cartoon purportedly undermined Blaine's chances. There is strong evidence that multitudes were entertained by such energetic cartoon assaults but little indication that the medium actually changed minds. Moreover, some of the most notorious campaigns, such as the assault on Republican William McKinley's candidacy by Hearst cartoonist Oliver Davenport in 1896, did not avert their victims' electoral triumphs.

Indeed, Franklin D. Roosevelt's New Deal is a signal example of a time in which mainstream political cartoons misrepresented popular political sentiments. Influenced by their overwhelmingly Republican publishers, most commercial political cartoons in the 1930s denounced the administration's policies and tirelessly depicted the

MEN WANTED for the ARMY MEASUREMENTS

Army Medical Examiner: "At last a perfect soldier!"

Robert Minor's cartoons, like this one published in *The Masses*, July 1916, set the precedent for short captions and sketch-like drawings. (American Social History Project, Center for Media and Learning at The City University of New York Graduate Center)

country in the grip of an unpopular dictatorship. In contrast, cartoons in the alternative press provided greater insight into the attributes that contributed to Roosevelt's political longevity.

The post–World War II era saw little change in political cartoons' overall lackluster and conservative performance. Most newspaper cartoonists avoided controversy, which the larger profession implicitly applauded in a run of Pulitzer Prizes awarded to uninspired (and subsequently forgotten) work. Postwar conservatism and political repression, coupled with the rise of television, the triumph of syndication, and the start of what would be a long death roll of newspapers and cartoonist jobs further undermined originality and fostered conformity. The aging cohort of cartoonists saw their ranks diminish, and few registered surprise when the *New York Times* decided not to replace its cartoonist Edwin Marcus when he retired in 1958. Herbert Block in the *Washington Post* and Walt Kelly in his politically inflected comic strip

Pogo took on imposing figures such as Senator Joseph McCarthy; but the most promising cartoonist of the war generation, Bill Mauldin (creator of the irreverent *Up Front* cartoons eagerly read by GIs in *Stars and Stripes*), weary of attacks on his postwar cartoons about domestic problems and political repression, quit the profession for almost a decade.

Only when the Vietnam War reached its height in the late 1960s did many political cartoonists emerge from their torpor to take the unprecedented step of criticizing U.S. government foreign policy during wartime. But these visual commentaries—which found even greater purchase during the Watergate scandal that eventually undermined President Richard Nixon's administration—paled compared to the work of "antiestablishment" cartoonists such as Jules Feiffer, Edward Sorel, and David Levine. These and other polemical and innovative cartoonists were published in periodicals directed at younger and more liberal readers (complemented by Gary Trudeau, whose *Doonesbury* reinvigorated the otherwise moribund newspaper comic strip).

At the close of the first decade of the twenty-first century, the fate of editorial cartoons seemed entwined with the rapid decline of newspapers. Only some 70 full-time professional cartoonists continued to work in the commercial realm. Yet once again the introduction of a new medium, the Internet, signaled a change in the field—at least in the number of practitioners whose work is available. In the realm of print, a period of experimentation was under way, exemplified by the recent work of "graphic journalists" such as Joe Sacco, who created extended, first-person investigatory narratives about Bosnia, the Gaza Strip, and Iraq. Published serially in magazines and as books, these and other "long form" projects defied the constraints of the time-tested single-panel format and marked yet another new phase in the history of the political cartoon.

See also press and politics.

FURTHER READING

Dewey, Donald. *The Art of Ill Will: The Story of American Political Cartoons.* New York: New York University Press, 2007.

Fischer, Roger A. *Them Damned Pictures: Explorations in American Political Cartoon Art.* North Haven, CT: Archon Books, 1996.

Hess, Stephen, and Milton Kaplan. *The Ungentlemanly Art: A History of American Political Cartoons.* Revised ed. New York: Macmillan, 1975.

Hess, Stephen, and Sandy Northrop. *Drawn and Quartered: The History of American Political Cartoons.* Montgomery, AL: Elliott and Clark, 1996.

Kemnitz, Thomas Milton. "The Cartoon as a Historical Source." *Journal of Interdisciplinary History* 4 (Summer 1973), 81–93.

Leonard, Thomas C. *The Power of the Press: The Birth of American Political Reporting.* New York: Oxford University Press, 1986.

Reilly, Bernard F., Jr. *American Political Prints, 1766–1876: A Catalog of the Collections in the Library of Congress.* Boston: G. K. Hall, 1991.

JOSHUA BROWN

Catholics and politics

Religion has always played an important role in American political life, as a factor in shaping popular understanding of citizenship, as a moral force shaping debates about important public issues, and sometimes as the basis of organized efforts to shape public policy. The Catholic Church and its members have shared that experience of having a distinctive role as participants, and sometimes problems, in American political life.

The few Catholics in the early republic were heavily invested in American politics. Centered on a highly successful but politically excluded planter community in Maryland, they actively supported the Revolution and enthusiastically welcomed religious freedom. After two centuries of exclusion from English politics, America's Catholics could now participate in public life and practice their faith openly. Led by America's first bishop, John Carroll, Catholic leaders shaped a conservative style of Catholic politics marked by acknowledgment of civic duties, emphasis on the public interest, and care to avoid antagonizing the Protestant majority. The Carrolls and many of their native-born successors were sincere patriots, always alert to the need to avoid even the appearance of being outsiders or foreigners. Contending with anti-Catholicism at home and the antirepublican zeal of revived Catholicism in Europe, they consistently affirmed religious liberty and church-state separation, and never favored the formation of the clerically dominated Catholic political parties so common in Europe. Placing no religious barriers in the way

of their people's political participation, Catholic leaders sought a secure and respected place for the church in American society.

This moderate, republican style of Catholic politics was overwhelmed by the arrival of thousands of European Catholic immigrants between 1820 and 1920. Irish and German Catholics made their church America's largest denomination by the middle of the nineteenth century. Increasing numbers of Catholics aroused nativist movements, blending hostility to immigrants with a long-standing tradition of anti-Catholicism. In the 1840s and 1850s, local, state, and national nativist parties tried to control education and limit immigrant political participation, leading immigrant leaders to make more assertive claims to their rights as Americans. These conflicts, often articulated in religious language, tended to unite Catholics, despite their ethnic diversity, and solidify their support for the Democratic Party, which often championed their cause. Archbishop John Hughes of New York defended his people against attacks, used the conflicts to strengthen Catholic loyalty, and tried unsuccessfully to persuade them to become more politically independent, throwing their support only to parties and politicians who would support their interests.

Catholic immigrants proved skillful in building networks of mutual support that found expression in voluntary associations, ethnic parishes, parochial schools, and a bewildering array of social service institutions. First Irish and Germans, and then French Canadians, Poles, Italians, and many eastern Europeans dotted the urban landscape with Catholic churches, all built by working-class families. The same bottom-up, self-help approach informed immigrant politics as community leaders brokered relationships with elites and, in some cases, took control of urban party organizations. Machine politics meeting popular needs mirrored the self-interest behind ethnic societies and America's nonideological trade unions. Such political realism, with group interests shaping public actions in America's political, religious, and economic marketplaces, was at odds with the disinterested concern for the common good that informed republican Catholicism.

From the Civil War on, Catholics tended to support the Democratic Party in many urban areas, while voting patterns often reflected state and local conflicts over education, temperance, and language. Yet these same urban Catholics were not attracted to the populist message of William Jennings Bryan, three-time Democratic nominee for president, and that urban-rural, Catholic-evangelical

Protestant split came to dominate the party during the 1920s. Catholics also came into conflict with progressives, whose educational and social reforms were sometimes aimed at ethnic groups and local political machines. Although they tended to be supportive of reforms aimed at greater safety and security for working people, Catholics often were conservative on civil liberties and suspicious of liberal proposals dealing with education, the family, and sexuality. During the New Deal, President Franklin Roosevelt overcame these divisions, in part by paying respect to the Catholic Church while supporting policies attractive to working-class voters of all religions. From that point until 1972, Catholics remained a fairly reliable component of the Roosevelt coalition that enabled the Democratic Party to dominate national politics.

Three important things can be noted about the political history of immigrant Catholics. First, the church placed no barriers in the way of full participation in American political life. Indeed, as pastors worked to build institutions to serve community needs, they often lent their support to independent, nondenominational parties, unions, and community organizations. Backed by papal encyclicals, church leaders in America supported unions; "bread-and-butter" reforms of wages, hours, and working conditions; and, later, social welfare legislation implemented through decentralized public-private partnerships in which church-related agencies participated.

Second, Catholics' faith and practice gave legitimacy to immigrant and working-class aspirations. Churches and schools built by the people were designed in part to preserve "folk memories" and defend communal values, but also to pursue new aspirations, especially for children. In the United States, pastors and teachers restricted countercultural condemnations of modernity to personal, especially sexual, morality. They not only affirmed efforts for economic and social mobility but also accompanied their people as they moved from urban neighborhoods to automobile suburbs, where the social cement of ethnicity and minority status no longer reinforced Catholic solidarity. Freedom, education, economic security, and social status were real goals whose pursuit was assisted by parishes, schools, and networks. Their achievement was, for many families, an experience of liberation.

Third, Catholic practice helped shape American working-class politics, where concern for family interests and respect for group values were as important as economic interests. For the immigrant generations, democratic politics turned on power, which in turn required

organization, without which markets and those with the resources to dominate them would control the conditions of life. That heritage continues to be found in the congregation-based community organizing so strong in urban coalitions and Latino communities.

After World War II, Catholics became more divided in their partisan loyalties, but older patterns remained surprisingly persistent. At least since the 1890s, Catholics and their bishops had been progressive on economic issues, conservative on cultural issues, and divided on foreign policy. Similarly, they had combined participation in the politics of a democratic and religiously pluralist society, a republican approach like that of John Carroll, with promotion of their own distinctive interests, including moral interests, an interest-group approach practiced by John Hughes. The republican approach emphasized the shared responsibility of American citizens. The interest-group model, grounded in the immigrant working-class experience, also served as a form of identity politics, allowing civic action that was clearly Catholic and clarifying boundaries in the pursuit of power and respect in the public square.

The republican approach found support in the aspiring Catholic middle class of the twentieth century. John F. Kennedy, the nation's first Catholic president, exemplified it. Participation was a civic responsibility, the common good was a genuine good, and the community of faith was a community of conscience. Interest-group politics found its sources in the experience of urban, ethnic, working-class Catholics and in the concrete needs of the institutional church. Its staying power is associated with bottom-up community building and renewed concerns about the unity and integrity of the faithful.

The tension between citizenship and self-help, between shared responsibility, interest-group participation, and specifically Catholic concerns, long shaped the history of the American Catholic subculture. These tensions exploded in the 1960s, when the second Vatican Council at last affirmed religious liberty and the separation of church and state, opening the door to a strong renewal of the republican tradition. The American church claimed to have no political agenda of its own but to engage the public with a moral voice affirming human dignity and defending human rights. On that basis, the bishops condemned racism and supported civil rights, offered a sharpening moral critique of the Vietnam War and the nuclear arms race, and advocated economic and social policies giving first priority to the poor. A series of impressive pastoral letters on controversial topics sought to affirm the duties of citizenship, focus on the demands of the common good, and speak for those without a voice.

Events of the period encouraged another side of American Catholic politics, dissatisfied with the republican approach and no longer comfortable with the self-interest orientation. Some Catholics were convinced that racial injustice, endless war in Vietnam, nuclear weapons, and a right to abortion, affirmed by the Supreme Court in 1973, all required a principled response and evangelical witness. A Catholic peace movement took dramatic action against war and weapons, while a broad-based pro-life movement challenged the country on abortion. This evangelical approach was a Catholic version of the social Gospel, and it challenged the standard political approaches that had dominated American Catholic history.

The evangelical style took a stand on issues regarded as fundamental to the community's integrity and required a discipleship that places Christian commitments beyond the claims of citizenship and group self-interest. It involved a move from religious judgment to political prescription; practicing, at least in language, what Max Weber called a "politics of ultimate ends."

Three developments since the 1980s have dominated Catholic politics. First, the decline of unreflective Catholic Americanism and the rise to dominance of subcultural and countercultural language and strategies associated with the right-to-life movement drained the republican approach of its strength and support.

Second, the abortion issue and related life questions have strengthened the position of those concerned primarily about the integrity of the American church. The coalition around a new agenda of "nonnegotiable" moral issues included key figures in the Vatican, evangelical Catholics of the left, and pro-life Catholics inclined to conservative positions on domestic and foreign policy questions. For those who love their church, countercultural advocacy on the life questions became an expression of commitment and evidence of integrity.

Third, the decline of moderate, republican Catholicism was the product of success as well as failure. Positions on war, poverty, capital punishment, international development, and even peace that were once considered liberal or progressive were now incorporated into the Catechism of the Catholic Church.

During the 2004 presidential campaign, the Catholic question was back in an entirely new form. For John F. Kennedy in 1960 the question was about overcoming America's deeply rooted suspicion of Catholics. In 2004 the question for presidential nominee Senator John F. Kerry was not whether he would be accepted by non-Catholics but whether he would be denied communion by priests. In 2003 the Vatican had encouraged bishops to call pro-choice Catholics to account; one bishop, James Burke of LaCrosse, Wisconsin, denied communion to a prominent Catholic politician, Congressman David Obey, drawing intense media interest. Democrats never figured out how to deal with their Catholic question.

The Republican Party, in contrast, made an unprecedented bid for Catholic votes. Advised by Catholic conservatives, President George W. Bush mastered a Catholic friendly "culture of life" and "compassionate conservatism." The GOP also built its religious outreach strategy around evidence that Christians who went to church regularly were apt to vote Republican. The party developed a superb organization for reaching Catholic voters in key states, while independent Catholic groups blanketed the country with the message that "nonnegotiable" issues of human life should define political responsibility. The bishops issued their usual nonpartisan voter guide, in which they gave clear priority to the abortion issue but did so amid a broad range of peace and social justice issues that also merited consideration. But, the American church's silence on the war in Iraq made the bishops' text seem indecisive, and it was widely ignored.

The 2004 campaign was marked by unprecedented attention to the Catholic vote and by equally unprecedented attention to the relationship between Catholic politicians and their bishops. In the election's aftermath, it was clear that Catholics constituted a crucial swing bloc, and that the politics of American Catholicism—its internal relationships and external engagements—would be an important factor in determining the nation's future.

See also religion and politics.

FURTHER READING

Cochran, Clarke E., and David Carroll Cochran. *Catholics, Politics and Public Policy.* Maryknoll, NY: Orbis Books, 2003.

———. *Readings on Catholics and Political Life.* Washington, DC: United States Conference of Catholic Bishops, 2004.

Martin, George J. *The American Catholic Voter: 200 Years of Political Impact.* South Bend, IN: St. Augustine Press, 2004.

O'Brien, David J. *Public Catholicism*. New York: Macmillan, 1986.

DAVID O'BRIEN

cities and politics

City politics in the United States has a distinctive trajectory, characteristic competitors, and institutions different from national politics. Cities have been the entryway for immigrants to the United States and the destination of domestic migrants from the countryside; their arrivals have discomfited some and thus challenged local politicians to manage their accommodation into local politics. For most of U.S. history, the characteristic antagonists of city politics have been machine politicians and municipal reformers. Machine and reform politicians argued about the purposes and institutions of city government from the mid-nineteenth century until well after World War II. Over the same period, machine and reform politicians adapted their styles and organizations to the expanded purposes of governing the city and the changing demands of urban voters. In the last quarter of the twentieth century, local institutions were again changed to accommodate diverse and politically sophisticated constituents.

From Echo to Urban Politics

In the first decades after independence, city politics were largely an echo of national politics. When Whigs and Democrats debated internal improvements and small government, for example, local party leaders in the cities voiced the same arguments. Two sets of issues interrupted that debate. In the 1840s, and again in the 1850s, nativist politicians argued that the central problem in local politics was the presence of immigrant voters. In the late 1820s and the mid-1850s, organized workingmen campaigned for legal reforms and for assistance during hard times. Each of these challenges left its mark on city politics.

Nativists argued that recent immigrants, mostly Irish and German Catholics, did not fit well into American cities. Immigrants were costly to city government, as evidenced by their presence in local poorhouses and prisons. Worse, since they came from countries that did not enjoy republican government, they were new to political participation, and did not have the skills to bear the burdens of U.S. citizenship. That deficit was amplified by their religion, as Catholicism, nativists claimed, discouraged independent thinking. Nativists were organized into local "American" parties. In most places, Whigs were more receptive to nativist arguments, while Democrats were more likely to defend immigrants. In the 1850s, nativists came together in Know-Nothing parties, which elected representatives to city, state, and federal governments. Like the Whigs, the Know-Nothings foundered on the political divisions that led to the Civil War. Party politicians who defended immigrants denounced nativists as "traitors to the Constitution" and "bigots and fanatics in religion."

Workingmen's parties appeared in cities in the late 1820s and had a long political agenda. The "workingmen" for whom they spoke were artisans, skilled craftsmen working in small shops. The parties called for the abolition of imprisonment for debt, compensation for municipal office holders, improved public schools, and easing the obligations of the militia system. Some of these issues were also supported by farmers and small businessmen; as a result, the parties succeeded at abolishing imprisonment for debt, reform of militia systems, and enacting democratizing reforms. Issues peculiar to wage laborers—a legal limit to the workday, abolition of prison labor—found few supporters beyond their natural constituency and failed. By the 1850s, there were fewer artisans in the cities and many more wage workers. Workers organized in mutual aid societies, unions, and federations of unions; these functioned in prosperous times but could not survive the periodic "panics" (depressions) that plagued the nineteenth-century economy. During the depression of the mid-1850s, mass demonstrations loudly demanded "work or bread" from city halls in New York, Philadelphia, Baltimore, and Pittsburgh, as well as some smaller cities like Newark, New Jersey, and Lynn, Massachusetts. Although the protests briefly convinced some members of the elite that revolution was imminent, the same demands provided an opportunity for major party leaders to demonstrate their sympathy and support for workers. Party leaders in Boston, Philadelphia, New York, Philadelphia, and Trenton, New Jersey, responded with public works to provide employment, established soup kitchens, and endorsed many of labor's demands. In this decade, the first political bosses appeared in big cities. They led party organizations to which working class voters, especially the foreign-born, were fiercely loyal. Their opponents called the parties "machines" because they stamped out election victories as uniformly as machines created identical products.

Hardly had bosses appeared when municipal reformers challenged their rule. In the 1850s, municipal reform slates appeared in elections in Boston, Philadelphia, Baltimore, New York, and Springfield, Massachusetts. Reform politicians had good reasons for their discontent. First, party politics in the cities was corrupt. Second, as cities grew rapidly in the nineteenth century, their budgets grew with them. Even leaving aside the costs of corruption, the burgeoning cities needed streets, sewers, lighting, water, schools, and parks, and these required major investments. Given the incidence of municipal taxes in the nineteenth century—the rich could escape them and the poor were not taxed—growing municipal budgets rested squarely on the shoulders of a small, beleaguered urban middle class. Their disgruntlement provided followers and votes for municipal reform. Third, wealthy and middle-class citizens were not comfortable with the working classes, especially the immigrants, who were the foundation of party politics. Reformers denounced the reliance of party politicians on the unwashed, insisting that cities should be ruled "by mind instead of muscle." Reformers were united by a belief that machine politicians and their immigrant constituents had corrupted democratic institutions in the cities; and they were united in their desire to upset the status quo and create order in city government. Thus, by midcentury, city politics had developed its own political antagonists and political arguments. Municipal reformers led small groups of activists and put forward candidates to compete in elections, but they rarely won. Party leaders defended workers as "the bone and sinew of the Republic," denounced nativists, and insisted that parties were the best defense of the many against the few. Like extended families or married couples, they repeated these arguments over and over again in the century to follow.

Twentieth-Century Reform

Over the last half of the nineteenth century, the antipathies and discontents of municipal reformers coalesced into an agenda for change. Reformers' opposition to the dominant parties led to a more general antiparty sentiment, and reformers endorsed nonpartisanship. Arguing that the concerns of national parties, necessarily focused on national issues, were irrelevant to city life, reformers were fond of saying that there was no Republican way to lay a sewer, no Democratic way to pave a street. Cit-

ies, reformers argued, should be run as businesses; they required fewer politicians and more management. For reformers, urban budgets called for retrenchment, city governments should be frugal, and tax rates should be cut. In addition, municipal reformers opposed cronyism and patronage, called for competitive bidding for city contracts and, toward the end of the century, for merit-based appointments (civil service) for government jobs. Party leaders rejected the reform agenda. Cities were not like businesses, they argued, but communities in which government had obligations to citizens. Party leaders claimed that meeting needs for relief, public health, building codes, "make-work" during recessions, and accepting differences of religion and even affinity for drink were all in the legitimate province of politicians.

Seth Low, mayor of Brooklyn (1882–85) and then New York (1902–3), was an exemplary municipal reformer of this sort. Low made every effort to bring business-like efficiency to city government, and succeeded at reforming New York's tax system and reducing its municipal debt. He opposed cronyism and patronage and argued for merit-based appointments to city jobs. Low did not attend to tenement reform and assistance to needy citizens.

At about the time Low was elected, another type of reformer appeared in the nation's cities: the social reformer. Social reformers agreed with other advocates of municipal reform that corruption and cronyism were destructive of city finances and city government but also saw that corruption took its toll on all citizens. These views soon became widespread. Muckraking journalists brought shocking revelations to the public in newspapers and magazines. Lincoln Steffens's essays, later published in the collection *The Shame of the Cities* (1904), exposed corruption across the country. He traced it not to the low character of immigrant voters but to the malfeasance of large interests and calculated its many costs to city coffers, ordinary citizens, and the moral standard of urban life.

Hazen Pingree, mayor of Detroit from 1890 to 1897, was a businessman transformed by his election. Once in office, Pingree became one of the nation's leading social reformers. Detroit, like many cities, suffered from high prices set by its utilities. Of these, the most costly to working-class residents was the street railway; for workers, even a slight increase in fares might devastate a family budget. Pingree led a campaign to maintain the three-cent fare and free transfers. Resistance by the company led to riots not only of workers but also by middle-class patrons. Pingree vetoed renewal of the company's franchise. Well before that, his efforts became a national crusade, followed in the press, to keep the three-cent fare. There were other social reform mayors, including Tom Johnson (Cleveland, Ohio) and Mark Fagan (Jersey City, New Jersey), who served their cities in similar ways.

In 1894 municipal reformers and leading progressives, including Theodore Roosevelt, founded the National Municipal League. In 1899 the league published its first model city charter, which proposed commission government for cities. In this innovation, citizens elected commissioners who individually served as administrators of city departments (streets, parks, etc.) and collectively served as both the legislative and the executive branch of city government. Although briefly popular, commission government was problematic, and in 1919 the National Municipal League endorsed a different model charter for city manager government.

The charter embraced nonpartisan, citywide elections for city council and the mayor. The council and mayor together appointed the city manager, a professional administrator who served as the chief operating officer of city government. The manager appointed the leaders of municipal agencies and monitored their performance. In addition, the manager was expected to advise the council about both its choice of policies and their implementation. The National Municipal League promoted the model charter in its journal, and supplied public speakers, pamphlets, advice, and boilerplate for newspaper editorials. By 1923, 240 cities had adopted city manager charters.

The changes endorsed by the National Municipal League were important for a second round of reform in the middle of the twentieth century. The Great Depression, and the U.S. effort in World War II, meant that cities across the country were neglected for almost a generation. Housing was not built, roads and other infrastructure not maintained, government conducted without change. After the war, one response to urban stagnation was the federal Urban Renewal program. Urban Renewal funds were eagerly sought by mayors and their city governments and drew support from downtown and real estate interests, construction workers, and low-income residents who hoped for better housing. Urban Renewal revitalized the downtowns of many cities but also displaced communities and did not fulfill the promise of increased housing for low-income families. Displacement provoked the tag "Negro removal" for the program, evidence of the bitterness left in its wake. Lingering black resentment at urban renewal

joined demands for the integration of schools, anger at police brutality, resentment of job discrimination in the private sector, increased pressure for more candidates and public officials of color, and greater equity in law enforcement.

In the Southwest and the West, city governments responded to postwar challenges with a fresh campaign to reform city government. The goals of this latter-day reform movement were both to create new institutions and to staff them with new leaders. Between 1945 and 1955, charter change worked its way across the South and the West. This generation's efforts brought municipal reform to towns that grew to be among the nation's largest cities and mid-sized cities: Dallas and Austin, San Diego and San Jose, Phoenix, Albuquerque, and Toledo. In addition to renewed city manager governments, reformers in these cities created a counterpart to the political party, the Nonpartisan Slating Group (NPSG), which nominated candidates for office, agreed on a platform, placed advertisements in newspapers, and worked to get out the vote. In time, the local NPSGs were as successful as the political machines of earlier decades at winning elections, often without effective opposition. In the 20 years that followed World War II, the leaders of big-city reform governments achieved a great deal. They planned and oversaw unprecedented growth, recruited industry, and presided over enormous efforts to build housing, parks, roads, and schools for their cities' growing populations. NPSGs led governments unblemished by scandal or patronage and governed without effective opposition.

Civil Rights

As popular as big-city reform governments were, they had problems and failures alongside their great successes. The failures were not reported in the press and, in some cities, even politicians were blind to them. Two problems in particular could not be fixed without dramatic change. The first was fiscal. A central promise of reform governments was low taxes. Yet for a generation and more after World War II, cities in the Southwest enjoyed tremendous economic, population, and territorial growth. It was the territorial growth—aggressive annexation of outlying areas over many years—that sustained low taxes. As city government expanded to deliver services, annexation kept the taxable population growing even more rapidly, keeping taxes low. By 1970, however, the cities were reaching limits that could not be extended. Many could not annex more territory, as they bordered nature preserves, military installations, and Native American reservations. Municipal debt was on the increase as governments tried to maintain their level of services. Yet the size of these cities was so great that it was not possible to deliver adequate services to all the residents who had come to expect them.

The second problem was the restricted political communities big-city reform created. The institutions of reform—nonpartisan, citywide, and sometimes off-cycle elections, stiff voter registration requirements (sometimes required annually), and literacy tests, in some places well beyond the time they were declared unconstitutional, kept the electorate small. In Dallas, for example, fewer than 20 percent of adults over 21 voted in municipal elections from 1947 to 1963. Turnout in partisan cities was higher: in New Haven, the election with lowest turnout in the same years brought 51 percent of adults over 21 to the polls. Restrictions on voting particularly affected residents of lesser means and citizens of color. The candidates they supported were rarely if ever elected; city councils were remarkably uniform. Annexation of new communities almost always increased the Anglo population and electorate, but not the number of African American and Spanish-surnamed voters.

In 1975 San Antonio tried to annex an outlying suburb. Latino residents filed a suit to stop the annexation, claiming that its intent and consequence were to keep them a minority of the electorate just as Latinos were on the verge of becoming the majority. The U.S. Justice Department agreed with them, and gave San Antonio a choice: the city could annex the territory but had to elect city council members from districts rather than citywide, or the city could maintain citywide elections, but could not annex any more territory. The city chose the first option. San Antonio thus became the first in a long line of big-city reform governments toppled by civil rights activists and the Justice Department.

Big-city reform governments everywhere gave up citywide for districted elections to city councils. The most common consequence was a more equitable distribution of public services. In San Jose, San Diego, and Albuquerque, city council members have more authority assuring the delivery of services to their constituents. This is not trivial. Public services—libraries, roads, garbage collection, schools, police officers, and firefighters—are key to the quality of daily life, and they are what cities provide.

The legacies of political machines and municipal reform remain. The most important and widespread legacy of reform is the decline of patronage appointments for municipal employees, and their replacement by merit-based hiring and civil service. Civil service has delivered more competent city employees at the street level and in administration and in management, has increased the quality of services to citizens, and has created openness and fairness of employment opportunity for those seeking work in the public sector. The legacy of machine politics is the principles that the responsibilities of city government extend beyond business-like management, that urban governments are obliged to represent the interests and values of all of their citizens. At the beginning of the new millennium, U.S. cities were again host to many immigrants, and thus once again were required to rethink and revise municipal institutions, decide what is fair, and debate the appropriate functions and priorities of city government.

See also local government; suburbs and politics.

FURTHER READING

Bridges, Amy. *Morning Glories: Municipal Reform in the Southwest*. Princeton, NJ: Princeton University Press, 1997.

Erie, Steven P. *Rainbow's End: Irish-Americans and the Dilemmas of Urban Machine Politics 1840–1985*. Berkeley: University of California Press, 1988.

Holli, Melvin G. *Reform in Detroit: Hazen Pingree and Urban Politics*. New York: Oxford University Press, 1969.

Johnson, David R., John A. Booth, and Richard Harris, eds. *The Politics of San Antonio: Community, Progress, and Power*. Lincoln: University of Nebraska Press, 1983.

Steffens, Lincoln. *The Shame of the Cities*. New York: McClure Phillips, 1904.

Trounstine, Jessica. *Political Monopolies in American Cities: The Rise and Fall of Bosses and Reformers*. Chicago: University of Chicago Press, 2008.

AMY BRIDGES

citizenship

At the time of the founding, the American conception of citizenship was marked by two profound contradictions that influenced the new nation's constitutional and legal history.

First, the concept of citizenship, which we associate with freedom, was actually derived from the English tradition of subjecthood, anchored in the feudal notion of obligatory allegiance to the lord for all within his domain. This was formulated most prominently by Sir Edward Coke in *Calvin's Case* (1608). At issue was whether persons born in Scotland after 1603, when the Scottish king James VI became king of England, were to enjoy the benefits of English law as subjects of the English king. Coke argued that, by virtue of the divine law of nature, they indeed did so. Once established in common law, the principle of jus soli was applied to all persons born on the king's domain.

The residual importance of this element of domain is visible in American adherence to the overarching rule of jus soli, most prominently in the constitutional requirement of citizenship by birth on American soil as a qualification for the presidency, but also in the granting of citizenship to children of visitors and even illegal immigrants. However, well before the Revolution the colonists diverged from Coke, contending, in response to their special circumstances, that under the law of nature, subjecthood was modified by the wholly opposite principle of consent. They insisted that this transformed citizenship into an implicit contract whereby subjects could legitimately deny their allegiance to a tyrannical ruler. Accordingly, the concept of citizenship by consent is at the root of American constitutional documents and jurisprudence. By the same token, Americans proclaimed the right of the English and other Europeans to voluntary expatriation and the right of American citizens to shed their citizenship as well.

The second contradiction arose from the ambiguity of the concept of *person*. To begin with, the law of nature did not preclude the practice of slavery—whereby certain human beings were in effect property that could be owned, traded, and disposed of at will—nor the exclusion of persons of African origin born on American soil, even those legally free, from the benefit of jus soli. Although some of the colonies refrained early on from the practice of slavery, or even actively opposed it, the fact that American slaves were overwhelmingly of African descent extended the ambiguous legal status to all African Americans, even those legally free. This contradiction remained unresolved throughout the first half of the nineteenth century.

Eventually highlighted in the debates over the Dred Scott affair, it contributed to the escalation of tensions between the states. In the case formally known as *Dred Scott v. Sanford,* Scott was the slave of an army surgeon who was taken in 1834 from Missouri to Illinois, where slavery had been forbidden by the Ordinance of 1787, and later to the Wisconsin Territory, where slavery was also illegal. Scott sued for his and his wife's freedom on the grounds of their residence in those locations. The case reached the U.S. Supreme Court, which ruled that neither Scott nor any person of African ancestry could claim citizenship in the United States and therefore could not bring suit in federal court under the diversity of citizenship rules. Moreover, Scott's temporary residence in Illinois and Wisconsin did not affect his emancipation under the Missouri Compromise, as this would deprive Scott's owner of his property. This contradiction was not resolved until after the Civil War and the enactment of the Fourteenth Amendment.

Ironically, a similar contradiction pertained to the status of those we now call Native Americans, in acknowledgment of their ancestral roots on American soil. In colonial times, independent unconquered tribes were dealt with as foreign nations; tributary tribes were considered subjects of His Majesty, but within a subordinate jurisdiction and with a separate legal status. In the first half of the nineteenth century, the United States dealt with organized tribes through treaties executed by the Department of War, after which jurisdiction passed to civilian control under the Department of Interior. Tribes gradually encompassed by white settlements exhibited the contradiction most acutely. American leaders viewed the barring of Indians from citizenship as a concomitant of their "peculiar" status: they were either members of "foreign nations," ineligible for naturalization by virtue of the "free, white" requirement legislated in 1790, or—if living among whites—members of a "separate inferior race" in a "state of pupilage" resembling the relationship of a ward to his guardian (as pronounced by New York's Chancellor Kent in 1825 and reaffirmed later at the national level by Chief Justice John Marshall).

The contradiction persisted until 1924, when Congress passed the Indian Citizenship Act, the same year in which it firmed up the blatantly racist National Origins Quota system of immigration regulation. In 1921, the United States had imposed an annual limit on the admission of immigrants from the "Eastern Hemisphere" (meaning Europe, as Asians were already largely excluded) and allocated a quota to each country based on the putative number of persons of that national origin in the current population of the United States. The legislation was designed to reduce immigration from eastern and southern European countries (notably Poland, many of whose immigrants were Jewish; Italy; and Greece). The quotas were further reduced in 1924. By the end of the 1920s, the number of Poles admitted shrank to 8.5 percent of the pre-quota level.

One important source of contention between the settlers and England, featured among the grievances expressed in the Declaration of Independence, was disagreement over the granting of privileges and immunities of citizenship to aliens by way of naturalization. Whereas England jealously guarded this as an exclusive royal privilege, to be allocated sparingly and only under special circumstances, the colonial settlers eagerly adopted an acquisitive stance, asserting their own authority in the matter and establishing a much lower threshold of eligibility. One reason for this was economic: citizenship created attractive and lucrative opportunities to buy and sell land, as the status of national was traditionally required for holding real property. Under English common law and throughout much of Europe, aliens could not pass on property to their heirs; at their death, it reverted to the king. The ability to grant citizenship, therefore, was crucial for American land promoters.

The doctrine of citizenship by consent was reflected in all the founding constitutional documents, at both the state and national levels. However, constitutional doctrine failed to specify precisely what privileges and immunities citizenship conferred, and which Americans were citizens. Adult white women were undoubtedly citizens, but it did not follow that they shared in the voting rights of white *male* citizens. Moreover, a woman could lose her citizenship by marrying an alien. In retrospect, the concept of citizenship was, in effect, limited to the legal sphere.

Until the Civil War, citizenship matters were complicated by the U.S. constitutional structure, which established a distinction between the relationship of persons to the several states and to the central government. The most important aspect of this distinction was that an African American could be a citizen of New York or Illinois but not of the United States (as the *Dred Scott* decision established). This was eliminated by the Fourteenth Amendment (1868), which declared that "all persons born or naturalized in the United States . . . are citizens of the United States and of the State wherein they reside," and that "No State shall make or enforce any law which shall abridge the privileges or immunities of citizens of the United States." Two years later, the Fifteenth Amendment broadened legal citizenship to encompass the political sphere by specifying, "The right of citizens of the United States to vote shall not be de-

nied or abridged by the United States or any State on account of race, color, or previous condition of servitude." However, it took nearly a century for this amendment to move from prescription to practice. The struggle to extend political citizenship to women, launched in the final decades of the nineteenth century, was achieved only about half a century later with the ratification of the Nineteenth Amendment in 1920. Yet another half a century later, the Twenty-Sixth Amendment extended political citizenship to 18 year olds, down from the age of 21.

By the middle of the twentieth century, the concept of citizenship had expanded further in most western democracies to cover the social sphere, constituting what attorney Thurgood H. Marshall termed in 1950 "social citizenship." The United States made some important strides in this direction during the New Deal period, with the institution of unemployment compensation and Social Security. But after World War II it diverged significantly from the path followed by its European counterparts, as well as Canada and Australia, in the sphere of health insurance, the narrowing of income inequality, and the assurance of minimal means of subsistence to all citizens. In 1996 the United States did in effect acknowledge the broadening of the rights of citizenship to encompass the social sphere by enacting legislation to restrict important federal benefits, such as welfare, to U.S. citizens only and allow the states to do the same. In recent decades the concept of citizenship has begun to broaden further to encompass the cultural sphere: the acknowledgment of religious and linguistic diversity, as well as symbolic matters such as pictorial representations of "typical Americans" and references to their cultural heritage. However, in the United States this domain is largely relinquished to the private sector, leaving citizens to fend for themselves according to their varying resources.

Access to citizenship through naturalization figured prominently in the United States, as in other so-called immigrant nations. The dissolution of imperial bonds gave individual state governments the authority to admit members of the political community. Former British subjects were admitted without question on the basis of their participation in the revolutionary struggle. Beyond this, most of the states devised quite liberal rules for incorporating the foreign-born, either in their constitution or by statute. The northern states usually required good character, one year's residence, the renouncing of foreign allegiances, and the taking of an oath of allegiance to the state. Maryland required, in addition, an oath of belief in the Christian religion (which could be taken by either Catholics or Protestants). For anyone seeking appointment or election to public office, however, most of the states required a more extended period of residence, thereby introducing gradations of citizenship. The southern states usually specified, in addition, that the person be free and white. Initially, "national" citizenship was derived from membership in a state and, except for the racial qualification, the states generally accepted one another's acts of naturalization. Nevertheless, ambiguities arose and fostered a growing sense that citizenship was a national matter. The idea of a more unified state took shape in the Philadelphia Convention's proposed federation, which would have authority to implement a "uniform rule of naturalization." The coupling of naturalization with the authority to establish "uniform laws on the subject of bankruptcies" highlights the prominence of economic concerns in the Founding Fathers' view of citizenship and in the overall process of nationalizing governance.

President George Washington placed citizenship on the agenda in his very first message to Congress, which acted promptly on the matter. Pennsylvania and the western states advocated quick and easy naturalization, especially for prospective buyers of land, to whom citizenship would assure secure property rights. The stance would also serve the interests of ethnic minorities. In the national elections of 1788, for example, Pennsylvania's German community, which had hitherto shied away from politics, demanded representation in proportion to its weight in the population, thereby prompting both the Federalists and their opponents to nominate appropriate ethnic candidates. Voting as a bloc, the Germans sent three representatives to the new Congress, where they firmly supported what today would be called the liberal side in the naturalization debate, thereby demonstrating the feedback effect of political incorporation on immigration and naturalization policy. The other side consisted of a coalition of unlikely bedfellows: New Englanders, who reflected their region's narrower view of national identity, and Southerners who, although in favor of immigration, feared that most of the new citizens would oppose slavery.

Overall, naturalization appears to have been conceived originally as a first step toward Americanization, somewhat akin to a secular baptism, rather than as the capstone of a process of incorporation. The Naturalization Act of 1790 provided that free white persons of sat-

isfactory character would be eligible for naturalization after two years' residence in the United States, including one year within the state from which they applied. The qualifier *free* excluded numerous white immigrants bound in temporary servitude until their term expired. The requirement of satisfactory character, inspired by the Pennsylvania Constitution, was designed to exclude not only convicts and felons, but also "paupers," considered malefactors in need of discipline, much as with welfare cheats today. That said, the naturalization procedure was accessible: the law specified that it could take place in any common law court of record. The law also provided that the minor children of naturalized parents automatically became citizens by way of jus sanguinis and, conversely, that the children born abroad of American citizens be considered natural-born citizens.

Admission to the political community also required an oath of allegiance to the U.S. Constitution. Although applicants were not subject to political vetting, the Constitution did specify that foreign-born persons who had left the United States at the time of the Revolution could not become naturalized without the express consent of the states. Directed at repentant British-born Loyalists, this exclusionary provision constituted one more indication of the country's emerging assertiveness as a sovereign state and distinctive political régime.

Although the requirement of whiteness, which southern representatives insisted on, constituted a retreat from the inclusive notion of citizenship inscribed in the Northwest Ordinance enacted three years earlier, it evoked no debate whatsoever. Perennially restated in subsequent legislation down to the Civil War, this provision excluded not only persons of African descent, notably mulattoes from Saint-Domingue (now Haiti) who streamed into the United States as refugees from the island's revolution, but also American Indians, who could become citizens only by treaty. "White" clearly meant "white exclusively," and when Asians appeared on the scene in the 1840s, the courts quickly determined that they were ineligible as a matter of course. In the end, although the law confirmed the new republic's exclusionary racial boundary, the inclusiveness of all free Europeans of good character, regardless of nationality, language, religion, or even gender, constituted a unique assertion of republican universalism, no less remarkable for being driven by interests as much as principle.

Considered from an international perspective, the provision of routine access to American citizenship constituted a radical political innovation. It challenged the ruling European doctrine of "perpetual allegiance" and threatened to seduce subjects away from their sovereigns. Added to the marketing of land, the naturalization law encouraged immigration. As a counterpart of the naturalization procedure, Americans also insisted on the right to expatriation. At a time when Europe's population was still growing slowly and Europe adhered to Jean Bodin's mercantilist formula—"*Il n'y a richesse ni force que d'hommes*" (There is no wealth nor power but in men)—they actively recruited British subjects as well as foreign Europeans and intervened in the international arena to secure freedom of exit on their behalf. This entailed not only physical exit (i.e., emigration) but also political exit—those coming to America had to renounce their original nationality, thereby challenging the prevailing doctrine of perpetual allegiance. Indeed, Britain's insistence that British sailors who had become U.S. citizens remained under obligation to serve the king shortly emerged as one of the sources of conflict leading to the War of 1812.

Despite America's generally acquisitive stance, public opinion on immigration swung sharply after 1792, when the crisis triggered by the French Revolution flared into war. The United States attracted a variety of dissenting groups, including aristocratic Frenchmen and German Pietists seeking to evade military service. Most of all, the radicalization of the revolution in France triggered widespread fear of Jacobins. The Federalists, now in power, sought to restrict immigration altogether on the grounds that it constituted a threat to national security. The intrusion of security considerations into the sphere of immigration and citizenship prefigured similar movements in response to the threat of anarchism at the turn of the twentieth century, of Bolshevism in the wake of World War I and the Russian Revolution, and communism at the outset of the Cold War, as well as the fear of Jihad terrorism in the wake of 9/11.

The Federalists lacked constitutional authority to restrict immigration directly, however, because control over persons fell within the sphere of police powers that were reserved to the states in order to protect slavery. Instead, they sought to achieve such restrictions by passing the Alien and Sedition Acts, which subjected both aliens and their American associates to governmental surveillance and criminalized certain forms of political protest. Naturalization emerged as a secondary line of defense against undesirable immigration. In 1795 the ruling Federalists amended the naturalization law to require 14 years' residence and the filing of a declaration of intention five

years before undertaking naturalization proceedings. After the Jeffersonian Republicans gained power in 1800, they repealed the Federalist naturalization amendments: in 1802 the residency period for naturalization was set at five years, with a three-year delay for filing a declaration of intention.

These terms, founded on the notion that a substantial period of residence was necessary to infuse aliens with American values, marked a shift away from the idea of naturalization as a ritual starting point toward the notion that it constitutes the capstone of an apprenticeship. With the significant exception of the racial qualification, the terms of citizenship have changed little since 1802, with the addition of more or less demanding tests of language skills and political information to ascertain the candidate's qualification for naturalization. Although federal statutes excluded people of even partial African descent from ordinary naturalization (in keeping with the "one drop of blood rule"), the ruling doctrine of jus soli suggested they might claim citizenship by birthright. But this, in turn, threatened the founding's grand compromise that enabled the exemplary land of freedom to tolerate the existence of slavery. The resulting tension moved to the fore in the debates over the admission of Missouri in 1820 and remained unresolved throughout the first half of the century, culminating in the Supreme Court ruling in *Dred Scott v. Sanford* (1857).

At the end of the Napoleonic Wars in 1815, European emigration resumed quickly and encompassed a broader continental region, because the Congress of Vienna specifically authorized the departure of the inhabitants of the territory ceded by France, including most of present-day Belgium, for a period of six years, and also provided for free emigration from one German state to another, including the Netherlands. Once on the move, many "Germans" kept going until they reached the ports of embarkation for America. Numbers rose to at least 30,000 in both 1816 and 1817 and reached nearly 50,000 in 1818. The growing numbers found a warm welcome from America's budding manufacturing community hungry for labor as well as from land promoters. But they simultaneously stimulated public concern that the arrival of so many Germans, including numerous destitute persons and other undesirables that would burden state and municipal relief facilities, would dilute the nation's British heritage.

Lacking authority to restrict immigration directly, in January 1818 Congress adopted a motion to limit the number of persons carried by incoming ships according to the tonnage of the vessels. The proposal was modeled on the British Passenger Act of 1803, which had been designed to restrict emigration of sheepherders from Scotland. The measure prohibited ships of any nationality entering an American port from carrying more than two persons for every five tons of registry, and required them to deliver to the Department of State "a list or manifest of all the passengers taken on board," including each one's name, occupation, and place of origin. It further specified water and food requirements for Europe-bound ships departing from the United States.

The 1819 law, motivated by a combination of restrictionist and humanitarian concerns, stood as the sole federal enactment pertaining to European immigration until the late 1840s. In the broader perspective of American development, it can be seen as a block in the building of the "American system"—the ensemble of measures designed to promote the development of an autonomous American economy—in keeping with the continuing nationalization of major elements of economic policy. Five years later, the landmark 1824 Supreme Court decision in *Gibbons v. Ogden* granted Congress the power to regulate international commerce as well as immigration. Why 2.5 tons per passenger? Britain, it seems, had recently reduced the minimum from 5 tons per passenger to 3; therefore, 2.5 tons "would afford every necessary accommodation." This was in fact misinformation; Britain maintained a 5-ton requirement for U.S.-bound ships but had recently lowered it to 1.5 for the traffic to British North America. In any case, the regulation significantly reduced the passenger-carrying capacity of all U.S.-bound ships but simultaneously gave American ships an edge over their British competitors. Immigration restriction, yes, but business is business.

At the time of Alexis de Tocqueville's field trip to America in the 1830s, half a century after independence, his hosts did not think of themselves as a "nation of immigrants." Reflecting the prevailing self-image, the French statesman characterized them as a thoroughly formed Anglo-American people whose political culture was founded on a collective character molded in the course of many generations of shared existence. In effect, he saw white Americans making up a more unified nation than his native France, which, despite centuries of monarchical centralization, remained a country of highly diverse provinces and localities. Although he did observe some immigrants, the foreign-born then constituted at most 5 percent of the white population, a minimal level

not equaled again until the 1940s. However, in his second edition, Tocqueville added a last-minute footnote, undoubtedly inspired by information he received from his Whig friends, that deplored the undesirable impending changes likely to follow from the growing arrival of poor Europeans.

This was the first of the series of so-called immigration crises that have marked American history. Although the Know-Nothing Party and its sympathizers attempted to raise the residence requirement for naturalization to the Federalists' 14 years, or even 21 years—a symbolic term designed to subject newcomers to a thorough "re-maturing" process on American soil—they failed to achieve their goal, and had to satisfy themselves with the imposition of burdensome residence requirements for access to local elected and appointed offices. State and local measures of this genre were reenacted in the course of later crises as well, notably in the final decades of the nineteenth century and the first three decades of the twentieth, when they were supplemented by linguistic requirements, literacy tests, and demonstration of the candidate's knowledge of American history and governmental institutions. When these requirements were first imposed in the early decades of the twentieth century, public facilities existed to help applicants prepare. With the decline of immigration from the 1920s onward, however, these public facilities largely fell into disuse and were not fully revived when massive immigration resumed in the final third of the twentieth century.

When Asian immigrants appeared on the scene around 1850, the courts excluded them from naturalization by the long-standing statutory requirement of whiteness, ruling that this was in keeping with the Constitution. However, in the wake of the Civil War amendments, jus soli prevailed. In *United States v. Wong Kim Ark* (1898), a solid Supreme Court majority ruled that birth on American soil sufficed to make citizens of all people, even those of Chinese descent. Under the circumstances, the only way to prevent what many deemed the "racial pollution" of the citizenry was to minimize the likelihood of such births by redoubling efforts to exclude Chinese females, as well as by creating obstacles to miscegenation wherever possible. Consequently, the American population of Chinese origin declined steadily throughout the first four decades of the twentieth century, and Chinese and other Asians remained excluded from acquiring citizenship by naturalization. As a condition of China's participation in the war against Japan, Chinese were made eligible in 1943, but the last traces of racial qualifications for Chinese naturalization were eliminated only in 1952; ironically, the same law also reasserted the racist National Origins Quota system instituted in the 1920s. During World War II, the United States deliberately violated the rights of many citizens of Japanese descent by ordering them to move away from the West Coast on security grounds or interning them along with legally resident aliens.

Despite the doctrinal equality between native-born and naturalized citizens, in practice the naturalized were often subject to more demanding rules. For example, a citizen could lose his U.S. naturalization by returning to his native country and residing there for more than a year. Most of these discriminatory strictures were eliminated in the final decades of the twentieth century, restricting denaturalization to persons who engaged in willful misrepresentation in the filing process.

Not surprisingly, applications for naturalization rose steadily in the wake of the revival of immigration that followed the 1965 reform law. The average annual number of people who became naturalized American citizens increased from fewer than 120,000 during the 1950s and 1960s to 210,000 in the 1980s. Enactment of the Immigration Reform and Control Act of 1986, which provided an avenue to legalization for 2.7 million undocumented immigrants, stimulated an additional 1 million applications, boosting the annual average for the 1990s to 500,000. By 2005, the leading source country for newly naturalized citizens was Mexico, at 13 percent; followed by the Philippines, at 6.2 percent; India, at 6 percent; Vietnam, at 5.4 percent; and China, at 5.2 percent. Seventy-seven percent of immigrants were residents of ten states, with California in the lead, at 28 percent; followed by New York, at 14 percent; Florida, at 7 percent; and Texas, at 6 percent.

The growth of anti-immigrant sentiment from the 1990s onward, the denial of public benefits to noncitizens, and the costs of a newly imposed mandatory renewal of permanent residence permits ("green cards") prompted many eligible but hitherto unconcerned alien residents to apply for citizenship in order to be able to vote or to qualify for benefits. The swelling of applications quickly bogged down federal agencies and created lengthy delays.

Moreover, in the wake of 9/11, security concerns prompted U.S. authorities once again to tighten the borders and access to citizenship without resorting to statutory change. After the Immigration and Naturalization Service was relocated from the Department of

Justice to the newly created Department of Homeland Security, its officials reassessed established procedures and concluded that FBI checks on applicants for citizenship were insufficiently thorough. Consequently, in 2002 the agency resubmitted 2.7 million names to be checked further. Rather than simply determining if the applicants were subjects of FBI investigations, the bureau was charged with ascertaining if their names showed up in *any* FBI files, even as witnesses or victims. Because many old documents were not electronic and were scattered throughout the agency's 265 offices, the process could take months, if not years. Further confusion and delays arose from the difficulty of sorting out individuals with common non-European surnames. Some 90 percent of the names submitted for rechecking did not appear in the FBI records. The 10 percent whose names did appear faced further delays, because "deep checks" often require access to records of foreign governments. Many of those stuck in the backlog were from predominantly Muslim countries, as well as from Asia, Africa, and the former Communist countries of Eastern Europe.

According to the official rules as of 2006, to be eligible for naturalization: an alien had to be over 28 years of age, a legal permanent resident of the United States for at least five years (three if married to a U.S. citizen and only one if a member of the armed forces), with absences totaling no more than one year; reside in one state for at least three months; demonstrate the ability to read, write, speak, and understand "ordinary" English (with some exemptions); demonstrate knowledge and understanding of fundamentals of U.S. history and government (special consideration given to applicants with impairments or older than 65 with at least 20 years of residence); take an oath of allegiance that includes renouncing foreign allegiances (although dual citizenship with countries deemed friendly to the United States is permitted); and pay an application fee (plus an additional fee for fingerprints).

Grounds for refusal included certain criminal offenses and failure by the applicant to demonstrate that he or she is "of good moral character." Individuals were permanently barred from naturalization if they had ever been convicted of murder or of an aggravated felony since November 29, 1990. Moreover, a person could not be found to be of good moral character if he or she had "committed and been convicted of one or more crimes involving moral turpitude"; had been convicted of two or more offenses for which the total sentence imposed was five years or more; had been convicted under any controlled substance law, except for a single offense of simple possession of 30 grams or less of marijuana. Other grounds for denial of naturalization included prostitution, involvement in the smuggling of illegal aliens, polygamy, failure to support dependents, and giving false testimony in order to receive a benefit under the Immigration and Nationality Act.

The number naturalizing grew 12 percent from 537,151 in 2004 to 604,280 in 2005, with Mexico the leading country of birth and the Philippines in second place. At the end of that year, more than half a million applications awaited decisions. Growth accelerated further in 2006 with an increase of 16 percent to 702,589. Mexico remained the leading source country, but India overtook the Philippines for second place. A decline in the median number of years in legal permanent residence of the newly naturalized from a recent high of ten years in 2000 to only seven in 2006 confirmed that legal permanent residents who met the residence requirement had become more eager to avail themselves of the rights and privileges of U.S. citizenship. Despite a further increase in naturalization fees and the introduction of a new, more difficult civic test in 2007, the number of naturalization petitions doubled that year to 1.4 million. The backlog was so great that receipt of applications filed in July 2007 was acknowledged only four months later.

Although applicants for naturalization are still required to renounce their allegiance to foreign states, in practice, the United States has become more tolerant of multiple nationality, thus falling in step with the general movement of liberal democracies toward a more flexible concept of citizenship less bound to the world of mutually exclusive territorial sovereignties.

See also immigration policy; voting.

FURTHER READING

Aleinikof, Alexander, and Douglas Klusmeyer, eds. *Citizenship Today: Global Perspectives and Practices.* Washington, DC: Carnegie Endowment for International Peace, 2001.

Kettner, James. *The Development of American Citizenship, 1608–1870.* Chapel Hill: University of North Carolina Press, 1978.

Schuck, Peter H. *Citizens, Strangers, and In-Betweens: Essays on Immigration and Citizenship.* Boulder, CO: Westview Press, 1988.

Tichenor, Daniel J. *Dividing Lines: The Politics of Immigration Control in America.* Princeton, NJ: Princeton University Press, 2002.

Zolberg, Aistide R. *A Nation by Design: Immigration Policy in the Fashioning of America.* Cambridge and New York: Harvard University Press and Russell Sage Foundation, 2006.

ARISTIDE R. ZOLBERG

civil liberties

Civil liberties are defined as the rights enjoyed by individuals over and against the power of government. The idea of civil liberties originated in English history, with the Magna Carta in 1215, and developed over the following centuries. By the time of the American Revolution, the list of individual liberties included habeas corpus, freedom of speech, and religious liberty, among others. Specific guarantees were incorporated into the U.S. Constitution (1787), the Bill of Rights (1791), and the constitutions of the individual states.

Civil liberties have had an uneven history in America. The freedoms enshrined in the Bill of Rights were largely ignored for much of American history. In the late eighteenth century, political thinkers did not debate complex rights issues; discussions of free speech, for example, did not address obscenity or hate speech. Serious consideration of such issues did not begin until the modern civil liberties era in the twentieth century.

Civil Liberties in Early American History

The first great civil liberties crisis in American history involved the 1798 Alien and Sedition Acts. The Sedition Act prohibited virtually any criticism of the government, and the administration of President John Adams prosecuted and jailed a number of its critics under the law. The two laws provoked strong protests, most notably the Kentucky and Virginia Resolves in late 1798, which were secretly written by James Madison and Thomas Jefferson, respectively. Both resolves denounced the laws as threats to freedom of speech and challenged the power of the federal government to enact such laws. The principal focus, however, was on the respective powers of the federal government and the states, not on freedom of speech; the resolves contributed to the debate over states' rights rather to the theory of the First Amendment. The crisis over the Alien and Sedition Acts passed when Thomas Jefferson was elected president in 1800 and pardoned all Sedition Act victims.

In the years preceding the Civil War, a major free speech controversy erupted over efforts by proslavery forces to suppress advocacy of abolition, specifically by banning antislavery material from the U.S. mail and by restricting debates on slavery in the U.S. Congress. These assaults on free speech raised public concern to the point where the independent Free Soil Party in 1848 adopted the slogan "Free Soil, Free Labor, Free Speech, and Free Men." The new Republican Party adopted the same slogan in 1856.

Civil War and Reconstruction Era Crises

The Civil War produced two major civil liberties crises. President Abraham Lincoln, in a controversial move, suspended the right of habeas corpus in certain areas controlled by the federal government, fearing that opponents of the war would undermine the war effort. The Supreme Court declared Lincoln's action unconstitutional on the grounds that civil courts were still functioning in those areas. Military authorities in Ohio, meanwhile, arrested and convicted Clement Vallandigham, a prominent antiwar Democrat, for a speech opposing the war, charging him with interfering with the war effort. President Lincoln, however, deported Vallandigham to the Confederacy to avoid making him a martyr. Lincoln also directed military authorities to drop prosecution of an antiwar newspaper in Chicago, believing that such prosecution violated freedom of the press.

The Reconstruction era following the Civil War produced major changes in civil liberties law. The Thirteenth Amendment to the Constitution prohibited slavery, the Fourteenth Amendment forbade states from depriving persons of due process or equal protection of the law, and the Fifteenth Amendment guaranteed the right to vote. In practice, however, the Civil War amendments provided little actual protection to African Americans. The Supreme Court eventually interpreted the Fourteenth Amendment to invalidate social legislation to help working people, on the grounds that such laws violated individuals' right to freedom of contract (*Lochner v. New York*, 1905).

World War I and the Modern Era of Civil Liberties

The modern era of civil liberties began during the World War I years, when Woodrow Wilson's administration suppressed virtually all criticism of the war and also conducted massive illegal arrests of political dissidents. Such actions set in motion a national debate over the meaning of the Bill of Rights.

In the early twentieth century, the Supreme Court had issued a series of decisions on the First Amendment, all of which upheld the prosecution of antiwar critics. In the case of *Abrams v. United States* (1919), however, Justice Oliver Wendell Holmes, joined by Justice Louis Brandies, wrote a dissenting opinion arguing that the American experiment with democracy rested on the free expression of ideas. Holmes's dissent shaped the subsequent course of constitutional law on the First Amendment.

Another important development shortly after the war was the creation of the American Civil Liberties Union (ACLU) as the first permanent organization devoted to the defense of individual rights. The ACLU succeeded the National Civil Liberties Bureau, which had been created in 1917 to defend the rights of conscientious objectors and to fight violations of free speech during the war. Officially founded in 1920, the ACLU played a major role in advocating expanded protection for civil liberties in the decades that followed.

The legal and political climate in the United States was extremely hostile to civil liberties in the 1920s. The idea of free speech was associated with radicalism, and in the pro-business climate of the period, the freedom of speech and assembly rights of working people who sought to organize labor unions were systematically suppressed.

A 1925 controversy over a Tennessee law prohibiting the teaching of evolution in public schools had a major impact on public thinking about civil liberties. Biology teacher John T. Scopes was convicted of violating the law in a trial that received enormous national and international attention. Because Scopes's conviction was overturned on a technicality, there was no Supreme Court case on the underlying constitutional issues. Nonetheless, the case dramatized civil liberties issues for the general public and foreshadowed many subsequent battles over the role of religion in American public life.

The first important breakthrough for civil liberties in the Supreme Court occurred in the 1925 *Gitlow v. New York* case. The Court upheld Benjamin Gitlow's conviction for violating the New York State criminal anarchy law by distributing a "Left Wing Manifesto" calling for the establishment of socialism in America. In a major legal innovation, however, the Court held that freedom of speech was one of the liberties incorporated into the due process clause of the Fourteenth Amendment. By ruling that the Fourteenth Amendment incorporated parts of the Bill of

Rights, the Court laid the foundation for the revolution in civil liberties and civil rights law in the years ahead.

Four Supreme Court cases in the 1930s marked the first significant protections for civil liberties. In *Near v. Minnesota* (1931), the Court held that freedom of the press was incorporated into the Fourteenth Amendment. In *Stromberg v. California* (1931), meanwhile, it held that the Fourteenth Amendment incorporated the free speech clause of the First Amendment. Two cases arising from the celebrated Scottsboro case, where nine young African American men were prosecuted for allegedly raping a white woman, also resulted in new protections for individual rights. In *Powell v. Alabama* (1932) the Court overturned Ozie Powell's conviction because he had been denied the right to counsel, and in *Patterson v. Alabama* (1935), it reversed the conviction because African Americans were systematically excluded from Alabama juries.

The Era of the Roosevelt Court

International events also had a profound impact on American thinking about civil liberties in the late 1930s and early 1940s. The examples of Nazi Germany and the Soviet Union provoked a new appreciation of the Constitution and the Bill of Rights in protecting unpopular minorities and powerless groups. The American Bar Association, for example, created a special Committee on the Bill of Rights in 1938, which filed amicus briefs in several important Supreme Court cases. President Franklin D. Roosevelt, in his 1941 State of the Union address, argued that the "Four Freedoms," which included freedom of speech and freedom of worship, defined American democracy and promoted liberty in a world threatened by totalitarianism.

President Roosevelt appointed four justices to the Supreme Court who were strong advocates of civil liberties, and the so-called Roosevelt Court created a systematic body of constitutional law protecting individual rights. Some of the Court's most important decisions involved the unpopular religious sect known as the Jehovah's Witnesses. In *Cantwell v. Connecticut* (1940), the Court incorporated the freedom of religion clause of the First Amendment into the Fourteenth Amendment, thereby protecting the free exercise of religion against infringement by state officials. In the most famous controversy, the children of Jehovah's Witnesses refused to salute the American flag in public schools as required by the laws in several states on the grounds that it violated their religious beliefs. The Supreme Court upheld their right, holding that the government cannot compel a person to

express a belief contrary to his or her conscience (*West Virginia v. Barnette*, 1943).

World War II did not lead to the suppression of free speech that had occurred during World War I, but it did result in one of the greatest violations of civil liberties in American history. With Executive Order 9066, President Roosevelt ordered the internment of 120,000 Japanese Americans from the West Coast, 90,000 of whom were American citizens. They were held in "relocation centers" that were, essentially, concentration camps. Public opinion overwhelmingly supported the government's action, as did the Supreme Court. In *Hirabayashi v. United States* (1943) the Court upheld the constitutionality of a curfew on Japanese Americans, and in *Korematsu v. United States* (1944), it sustained the forced evacuation of Japanese Americans, although Justice Frank Murphy denounced the government's program as racist in his *Korematsu* dissent. In 1988 the federal government apologized for the Japanese evacuation and provided monetary damages to the surviving victims.

The Cold War Years

The anti-Communist hysteria of the cold war period resulted in sweeping assaults on civil liberties. Under President Harry Truman's 1947 Loyalty Program, a person could be denied federal employment for "sympathetic association" with a group or activities deemed subversive. The House Committee on Un-American

Following evacuation orders, this store was closed. The owner, a University of California graduate of Japanese descent, placed the "I AM AN AMERICAN" sign on the storefront on December 8, 1941, the day after Pearl Harbor. (Dorothea Lange/Oakland Museum of California)

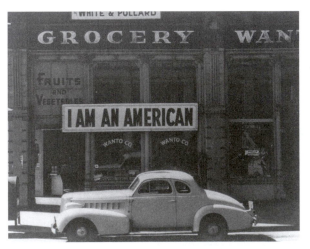

Activities publicly investigated individuals alleged to be Communists or Communist sympathizers. In the atmosphere of the times, people could lose their jobs or suffer other adverse consequences if the committee simply labeled them as subversive. States, meanwhile, required teachers and other public employees to take loyalty oaths. Senator Joseph McCarthy made reckless and unsupported claims that the government was filled with subversives, and "McCarthyism" became part of the American political lexicon. By the mid-1950s, Senator McCarthy was discredited, and the Supreme Court began to place constitutional limits on many anti-Communist measures.

Racial Equality and Other Advances in Civil Liberties

The post–World War II years also marked significant advances in civil liberties in several areas. The civil rights movement challenged racial segregation in all areas of American life. The high point of this effort was the landmark Supreme Court case *Brown v. Board of Education of Topeka* (1954), which declared racial segregation in public schools unconstitutional. The decision marked the advent of the Warren Court (1953–68), named after Chief Justice Earl Warren, which issued many decisions expanding the scope of civil liberties and defending individual rights.

In response to changing public demands for greater freedom of expression, the censorship of books, magazines, and motion pictures came under steady attack. In *Burstyn v. Wilson* (1952), for example, the Supreme Court ruled that motion pictures were a form of expression protected by the First Amendment. In a series of subsequent decisions, the Court by the late 1960s struck down censorship of virtually all sexually related material except for the most extreme or violent forms, although it never succeeded in formulating a precise definition of pornography or what kinds of expression were outside the protection of the First Amendment.

With respect to the establishment of religions, the Court in 1947 (in *Everson v. Board of Education*) held that the establishment of religion clause of the First Amendment created a "wall of separation" between church and state. In 1962 the Court held that official religious prayers in public schools violated the establishment clause.

The Supreme Court also imposed constitutional standards on the criminal justice system. It placed limits on searches and seizures (*Mapp v. Ohio*, 1961) and police interrogations, ruling in *Miranda v. Arizona* (1966) that the police are required to inform criminal suspects they

have a right to an attorney. The Court also held that all criminal defendants facing felony charges were entitled to an attorney under the Sixth Amendment. In *Furman v. Georgia* (1972), the Court held that existing state death penalty laws were unconstitutional as applied but did not declare the death penalty unconstitutional under the cruel and unusual punishment clause of the Eighth Amendment.

A New Rights Consciousness

The civil rights movement spurred a new consciousness about rights that affected virtually every aspect of American society and added a new and ambiguous element to thinking about constitutional rights. Although courts decided cases in terms of individual rights, the emerging rights consciousness increasingly focused on group rights. Decisions on equal protection and even the First Amendment rights of an African American, for example, became instruments for the advancement of African Americans as a group. As a consequence, political movements emerged in the 1960s to support the rights of women, prisoners, children, the mentally and physically disabled, and lesbian and gay people. Each group undertook litigation asserting an individual right as a device to advance the rights of the group in question and effect social change. The Supreme Court was sympathetic to many of these claims, and created a vast new body of constitutional law. The long-term result was the emergence of a new "rights culture" in which Americans responded to social problems by thinking in terms of individual and/or group rights.

The unresolved ambiguity between individual and group rights emerged in the controversy over affirmative action and other remedies for discrimination against particular groups. Traditional civil rights and women's rights advocates argued that group-based remedies were necessary to eliminate the legacy of discrimination. Their conservative opponents argued that group-based remedies violated the individual rights of groups who did not receive what they saw as preferential treatment.

The Vietnam War (1965–72) and the subsequent Watergate Scandal (1972–74) raised several important civil liberties issues. Some Americans argued that the Vietnam War was unconstitutional because Congress had never issued a declaration of war. After much debate, Congress enacted the 1973 War Powers Act, designed to reassert its constitutional authority over committing American military forces to combat. Most commentators, however, have argued that the law failed to achieve its objectives, and the war in Iraq in 2003 again raised difficult constitutional questions regarding the power of the president as commander in chief.

The Watergate scandal resulted in the first Supreme Court ruling on the concept of executive privilege. The Court ordered President Richard Nixon to turn over certain White House tape recordings (which quickly led to his resignation from office) but held that presidents could withhold material whose disclosure would jeopardize national security. The exact scope of this privilege remained a controversy under subsequent presidents. Watergate also brought to light the abuse of constitutional rights by the Federal Bureau of Investigation and the Central Intelligence Agency over many decades. Both agencies had engaged in illegal spying on Americans. To assert more effective legal control over the FBI, Attorney General Edward H. Levi in 1976 issued a set of guidelines for intelligence gathering by the Bureau. In 1978 Congress passed the Foreign Intelligence Surveillance Act (FISA) to control intelligence gathering related to suspected foreign spying or terrorist activities.

The most controversial aspect of the new rights culture involved abortion. In the 1973 *Roe v. Wade* decision, the Supreme Court held that the constitutional guarantee of a right to privacy included the right to an abortion. *Roe v. Wade* provoked a powerful political reaction that exposed a deep cultural division within American society over civil liberties issues related to abortion, prayer in school, pornography, and gay and lesbian rights. A powerful conservative movement led to the election of several presidents and the appointment of conservative Supreme Court justices who either took a more limited view of civil liberties or objected to particular remedies such as affirmative action.

The Supreme Court took a more conservative direction in the 1980s, backing away from the judicial activism on behalf of individual rights that characterized the Warren Court. The conservative orientation became particularly pronounced following the appointments of Chief Justice John Roberts in 2005 and Associate Justice Samuel Alito in 2006. Two important indicators of the Court's new orientation were the 2007 decisions disallowing race-based remedies for school integration (*People Involved in Community Schools, Inc. v. Seattle; Meredith v. Jefferson County*) and a 2008 decision striking down a Washington, D.C., gun control ordinance as a violation of the Second Amendment (*District of Columbia v. Heller*). Until the 2008 decision, the Court had ignored the question of whether the Second Amendment created an individual right to own firearms.

The War on Terrorism and Civil Liberties

The most significant development in civil liberties in the early twenty-first century involved the reaction to the September 11, 2001, terrorist attacks on the United States. The 2001 Uniting and Strengthening America by Providing Appropriate Tools Required to Intercept and Obstruct Terrorism Act (better known as the USA PATRIOT Act) included several provisions that critics argued threatened civil liberties. The law permitted secret searches of home or offices without a warrant (labeled "sneak and peek" searches) and authorized the FBI to collect information through "national security letters" that did not involve a judicial warrant and did not allow the person being investigated to reveal that the letter was even issued. President George W. Bush also authorized secret, warrantless wiretapping of American citizens by the National Security Agency, in violation of the 1978 FISA law. The administration also denied the right of habeas corpus to suspected terrorists held at the U.S. military base at Guantanamo Bay, Cuba. When the Supreme Court held that the president did not have constitutional authority to do this, Congress passed a law denying detainees the right of habeas corpus.

The controversies over habeas corpus, warrantless wiretapping, and other issues related to the so-called War on Terrorism represented what many observers regarded as the most serious constitutional crisis over civil liberties in American history, particularly with regard to the issues of separation of powers and presidential war powers.

See also anticommunism; civil rights.

FURTHER READING

Cole, David, and James X. Dempsey. *Terrorism and the Constitution: Sacrificing Civil Liberties in the Name of National Security.* 2nd ed. New York: New Press, 2002.

Larson, Edward J. *Summer for the Gods: The Scopes Trial and America's Continuing Debate over Science and Religion.* New York: Basic Books, 1997.

Murphy, Paul L. *World War I and the Origin of Civil Liberties in the United States.* New York: Norton, 1979.

Neeley, Mark E., Jr. *The Fate of Liberty: Abraham Lincoln and Civil Liberties.* New York: Oxford University Press, 1991.

Stone, Geoffrey. *Perilous Times: Free Speech in Wartime from the Sedition Act of 1798 to the War on Terrorism*. New York: Norton, 2004.

Walker, Samuel. *In Defense of American Liberty: A History of the ACLU*. 2nd ed. Carbondale: Southern Illinois University Press, 1999.

SAMUEL WALKER

civil rights

African Americans waged the civil rights struggle to obtain first-class citizenship, not just on an individual basis but for the entire group. Initially, historians situated the movement between 1954 and 1965, from the landmark Supreme Court decision in *Brown v. Board of Education* to passage of the Voting Rights Act. According to this version, national civil rights organizations led protests to win legal decisions and secure federal legislation. More recently, historians have questioned the validity of this interpretation, especially its focus on national politics and leaders, and have uncovered the origins of the civil rights struggle in earlier periods, such as Reconstruction, the turn of the twentieth century, the Great Depression and New Deal of the 1930s, and World War II. Revisionists also shift the spotlight from the national arena to local communities. More than a struggle for equal rights and racial integration, they argue the civil rights movement aimed to gain freedom for African Americans from all forms of white supremacy—economic, social, and cultural as well as legal and political.

The civil rights movement contained several components. It had a liberationist ideology; participants possessed a consciousness of oppression and the belief that something could be done to overcome it; and it offered a purposeful agenda. Consensus existed among civil rights activists, though the movement allowed for multiple and conflicting objectives and tactics. Although internal tensions weakened the unity of the movement, its diversity provided for a useful division of labor and creative energy.

Prelude to the Civil Rights Movement

Reconstruction laid the basis for black civil rights. Framed by the Republican Party, the Fourteenth Amendment (1868) conferred citizenship on African Americans and guaranteed due process and equal protection of the law, and the Fifteenth Amendment (1870) prohibited racial discrimination against citizens entitled to vote. However, black political participation gradually ended after the Republican Party abandoned Reconstruction in 1877. From 1877 to 1901, the Reconstruction amendments proved inadequate for protecting black citizenship rights. After Congress passed the Civil Rights Act of 1875, which guaranteed equal access to public accommodations regardless of race, the United States Supreme Court in 1883 struck it down as unconstitutional. Once Democrats regained power in the South, they circumvented the Fifteenth Amendment by passing literacy tests and poll taxes as voting requirements. Southern Democrats also adopted the all-white primary, effectively denying African Americans suffrage in that one-party region. In addition, in 1896 the Supreme Court in *Plessy v. Ferguson* ruled that the Fourteenth Amendment did not prohibit segregation in public accommodations, specifically on railroad cars, so long as separate meant equal, thereby opening up the way for the establishment of segregation, albeit without equality, in all aspects of southern life.

African Americans developed several strategies to deal with second-class citizenship. In the 1890s, the educator Booker T. Washington, the most powerful black leader in the nation, accepted the reality of segregation and urged black Southerners to improve themselves economically before seeking civil rights. Opposition to this approach came from Ida B. Wells and W.E.B. DuBois. Wells campaigned against lynching, which had skyrocketed in the 1890s, and DuBois joined sympathetic whites to form the National Association for the Advancement of Colored People (NAACP) in 1909. The NAACP fought against racial discrimination primarily in the courts and in Congress. Headquartered in New York City, the organization was less a mass movement than a single-interest pressure group. It had branches in the South, but they were small in number because it was still too dangerous to challenge white supremacy there.

The Great Depression of the 1930s and President Franklin D. Roosevelt's New Deal stimulated the growth of black activism without tearing down segregation and disfranchisement. World War I had generated a great migration of African Americans from the South to the North in search of jobs and freedom. Though the majority of blacks still lived in the South, those relocating to northern cities now had the right to vote, and sometimes could wield as the balance of power in close local, state, and national elections. Since Reconstruction, the small percentage of African Americans retaining the vote had kept their allegiance to the Republican Party. However, the economic assistance offered by Roosevelt's New Deal persuaded the majority of black voters to switch to the Democratic Party starting in 1936. Roosevelt was no champion of civil rights, as he depended on southern white Democratic congressmen to support his economic programs. Nevertheless, mainly in response to labor organizing against the repressive treatment of industrial workers, the Roosevelt administration set up the Civil Liberties Unit (CLU) in the Justice Department, which focused on civil rights enforcement. From then on, civil rights advocates viewed Washington as an ally.

The New Deal also inspired the formation of interracial organizations in the South, such as the Southern Con-

ference for Human Welfare (SCHW) and labor unions affiliated with the Congress of Industrial Organizations (CIO), that fought racial injustice and poverty. Along with the Communist Party, which actively recruited black members, these groups expanded the definition of civil rights to include economic justice. Their efforts, while significant, did not produce a successful mass movement for civil rights in the South or eradicate segregation, disfranchisement, and poverty.

The Second Reconstruction
More than any other event, World War II set in motion the forces that sparked the modern civil rights movement. The political ideology of freedom, democracy, and antiracism associated with the Allied fight against the Nazis gave African Americans ammunition in chal-

Aerial view of marchers along the Mall at the March on Washington for Jobs and Freedom on August 28, 1963, showing the Reflecting Pool and the Washington Monument. (National Archives)

lenging repressive, undemocratic, and racist practices at home. In mid-1941, with U.S. participation in the war on the horizon, black labor leader A. Philip Randolph threatened to lead 100,000 African Americans in a march on Washington (MOW) to protest segregation in the armed forces and racial discrimination in industries receiving federal government contracts. Seeking to build a national consensus in favor of going to war and recognizing the political transformation of blacks from Republicans to Democrats, Roosevelt issued an executive order creating the Fair Employment Practice Committee (FEPC) to investigate complaints of racial discrimination by military contractors. Although nothing was done to integrate the armed forces, Randolph called off the march.

Wartime militancy among blacks increased as civil rights groups proclaimed a "Double V" campaign— victory abroad and victory at home against white supremacy. Membership in the NAACP increased tenfold, and the organization won an important Supreme Court victory in 1944 against the white primary, which chipped away at southern disfranchisement. Returning from the war instilled with pride, black veterans lined up to battle domestic forces that continued to deny them freedom. They received moral and political support from the large numbers of black migrants who had journeyed to northern and western cities during the war.

President Harry S. Truman responded to the political reality of the augmented northern black vote. Looking ahead to the 1948 presidential election, Truman set up a committee on civil rights and used its findings to introduce congressional measures to abolish employment discrimination and the poll tax. Truman recognized the balance of political power held by black voters, and in 1948, when his civil rights proposals fell into the deadly clutches of southern congressmen, the president issued an executive order desegregating the armed forces. Truman was also responding to the cold war confrontation with the Soviet Union. As the United States embarked on military preparedness, Randolph threatened demonstrations against the draft if the military remained segregated. Furthermore, in the propaganda war with the Communists, Truman needed all the foreign allies he could get, including newly emerging nonwhite nations in Africa and Asia. However, the cold war was a double-edged sword. It provided a stimulus for racial equality, but repression of domestic Communists and their sympathizers curtailed the contribution of radicals to the civil rights struggle.

Anti-Communist repression ensured the civil rights movement would be black-led, as African American ministers and secular organizations of black men and women formed the vanguard of the movement. Following *Brown v. Board of Education*, which overturned *Plessy*, black citizens in Montgomery, Alabama, launched a boycott against segregation on municipal buses. Beginning in December 1955, it lasted until November 1956, when the Supreme Court ruled in their favor. The boycott thrust its leader, the Reverend Dr. Martin Luther King Jr., into the limelight. He became the most charismatic leader in the civil rights movement and founded the Southern Christian Leadership Conference (SCLC), consisting of black ministers who mobilized African American communities in nonviolent protests against Jim Crow and disfranchisement.

In 1957 the NAACP and other liberal and labor organizations lobbied for passage of the first civil rights law enacted since Reconstruction. The Civil Rights Act of 1957 gave the federal government authority to seek injunctions against discriminatory voter registration officials in the South and created two new agencies to advance civil rights: the Civil Rights Division of the Justice Department (the heir to the CLU) and the U.S. Commission on Civil Rights. President Eisenhower, a lukewarm supporter of government action to promote civil rights, endorsed the measure for several reasons. He believed in the right to vote, saw it as tactic in waging the cold war, and hoped blacks would return to the Republican Party. This measure and another passed in 1960 did not remove all hurdles to black enfranchisement, but they persuaded civil rights proponents that the federal government was prepared to carry out a second reconstruction.

The Civil Rights Movement at High Tide
In the 1960s the civil rights struggle became a genuine mass movement and leaped to the forefront of domestic politics. Following sit-in protests by college and high school students against segregated lunch counters in Greensboro, North Carolina, in February 1960, young people who participated in these and subsequent demonstrations formed the Student Nonviolent Coordinating Committee (SNCC). This interracial group used nonviolent tactics to confront directly all forms of racial discrimination, not only in public accommodations but with respect to the right to vote. The group believed in community organizing and sent its field staff into some of the most resistant areas in Mississippi, Alabama, and

Georgia to recruit local people to mount their own challenges to white supremacy. In addition, in 1961 the Congress of Racial Equality (CORE), originally formed in 1942, conducted freedom rides from Washington, D.C., to Mississippi, which ignited white brutality against the participants. President John F. Kennedy, fearing unfavorable publicity, tried to get the riders to call off their protests. When they refused, his administration persuaded the Interstate Commerce Commission to enforce existing desegregation decrees. Kennedy owed his presidential victory in no small part to black voters, who contributed to his margin of less than 1 percent of the popular vote. He had cemented the loyalty of black voters during the campaign by arranging the release of Dr. King from a Georgia jail.

However, Kennedy hesitated to propose antisegregation legislation for fear of alienating southern Democratic allies in Congress. Then, in June 1963, following civil rights demonstrations in Birmingham, Alabama, which led to bloodshed, the Kennedy administration proposed a comprehensive civil rights bill against segregation in public accommodations, schools, and employment. Before the measure became law in 1964, Kennedy was assassinated and replaced by Vice President Lyndon B. Johnson, a former segregationist lawmaker from Texas who had converted to the civil rights cause. In 1965,

in response to demonstrations directed by the SCLC in Selma, Alabama, Johnson signed the Voting Rights Act. The measure finally gave the federal government adequate weapons to destroy the chief instruments of disfranchisement: literacy tests and poll taxes.

Civil rights activists had orchestrated the transformation of American politics in another significant way. A year before passage of the landmark Voting Rights Act, the civil rights coalition of SNCC, CORE, and the NAACP, known as the Council of Federated Organizations (COFO), sponsored Freedom Summer in Mississippi, the state with the lowest percentage of black voter registrants (6 percent). During June, July, and August of 1964, COFO recruited some 800 volunteers, mainly white and from the North, to encourage blacks to register to vote, expose brutal white opposition in the state to the rest of the country, and persuade officials in Washington to take action on behalf of Mississippi blacks. After coordinated suffrage drives and the creation of freedom schools, black Mississippians, along with a few white supporters, formed the Mississippi Freedom Democratic Party (MFDP). At the 1964 Democratic National Convention, the MFDP challenged the credentials of the regular state Democratic Party delegates, whose organization barred blacks from participation. Seeking to keep southern white delegates

Civil rights leaders march from the Washington Monument to the Lincoln Memorial, August 28, 1963. (National Archives)

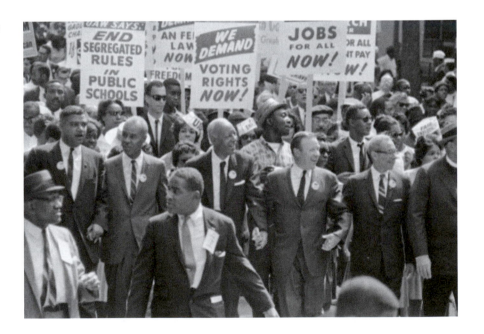

from walking out, President Johnson supported a compromise that gave the MFDP two at-large seats and recognized the Mississippi regulars who swore allegiance to the national Democratic Party. The compromise satisfied neither side, but it called for reforms to wipe out racism within party ranks. Keeping their promise at their next national convention in 1968, Democrats seated integrated delegations from Mississippi and other previously all-white state parties. Subsequently, the national party opened up representation to women and young people, demographic groups also underrepresented in state delegations.

Along with these reforms, Democratic Party identification with the civil rights movement initiated partisan realignment in the South. The once-solid Democratic South became the two-party South, with conservative voters drawn to the Republicans. The civil rights movement increased African American political clout, but it also turned the Democratic Party into a minority party in Dixie. This shift had national consequences. Since 1968, four of eight presidents have come from the South, but no Democratic candidate has won a majority of southern white votes. In addition, the party's identification with the cause of African Americans, especially after race riots and the rise of Black Power in the mid-1960s, pushed some traditionally Democratic groups in the North into Republican ranks. Many blue-collar workers and ethnic Americans of European origin viewed the party of Roosevelt as having abandoned them by favoring such programs as school busing and affirmative action, which they considered reverse racism. Some liberals became neoconservatives, dismayed with civil rights advocates for their apparent abandonment of color-blind principles in identity politics.

Civil Rights Legacies
The civil rights movement transformed politics for other exploited groups, such as women, Chicanos, Native Americans, the disabled, and homosexuals, who also demanded first-class citizenship. Each of these groups created its own freedom movement in the 1960s, benefiting from the ideology and tactics of the civil rights struggle. The feminist movement, in particular, profited from the black freedom movement. Young women working as freedom fighters in southern communities were inspired by older black women, such as Fannie Lou Hamer and Unita Blackwell in Mississippi, who constituted the backbone of grassroots organizing networks. Once Black

Power pushed whites out of SNCC and CORE, white women civil rights veterans applied the emancipationist ideology of the black freedom struggle to the formation of the women's liberation movement. In addition, the 1964 Civil Rights Act, with its provision against racial and sexual discrimination in employment, provided one of the main weapons women's groups used to combat occupational and educational bias.

By the end of the 1960s, the coalition of civil rights groups had collapsed. Yet the civil rights movement continued in new forms, such as the election of black officials (an estimated 9,000 by 2007). Two generations after the heyday of the civil rights movement, black politicians and their white allies still had not solved all the problems of racial and sexual discrimination embedded in the economic, political, and social structures of the United States. But they had transformed southern and national politics by opening up decision making at the highest levels to African Americans and other suppressed groups. This achievement of first-class citizenship and erosion of white male supremacy constitute the greatest legacies of the civil rights movement.

See also African Americans and politics; homosexuality; race and politics; voting; women and politics, 1920–70.

FURTHER READING
Auerbach, Jerold. *Labor and Liberty: The La Follette Committee and the New Deal.* Indianapolis: Bobbs-Merrill, 1966.
Dittmer, John. *Local People: The Struggle for Civil Rights in Mississippi.* Urbana: University of Illinois Press, 1994.
Dudziak, Mary. *Cold War Civil Rights: Race and the Image of American Democracy.* Princeton, NJ: Princeton University Press, 2000.
Fairclough, Adam. *Better Day Coming: Blacks and Equality, 1890–2000.* New York: Viking, 2001.
Lau, Peter. *Freedom Road Territory: The Politics of Civil Rights Struggle in South Carolina during the Jim Crow Era.* Lexington: University of Kentucky Press, 2002.
Lawson, Steven F. *Running for Freedom: Civil Rights and Black Politics in America since 1941.* 2nd ed. New York: McGraw-Hill, 1997.
Payne, Charles M. *"I've Got the Light of Freedom": The Organizing Tradition and the Mississippi Freedom Struggle.* Berkeley: University of California Press, 2007.
Sullivan, Patricia. *Days of Hope: Race and Democracy in the New Deal Era.* Chapel Hill: University of North Carolina Press, 1996.

Weiss, Nancy J. *Farewell to the Party of Lincoln: Black Politics in the Age of FDR.* Princeton, NJ: Princeton University Press, 1983.

STEVEN F. LAWSON

civil service

In most modern administrative states, the *civil service* consists of those nonpartisan and tenured civilian government employees who have been hired based on merit and technical expertise. Civil servants are the public administrators of government and, though not expressly responsible for making policy, they are charged with its execution. They are expected to be politically neutral. In the United States, civil servants work in a variety of fields such as teaching, health care, sanitation, management, and administration for the federal, state, or local government. As a rule, the civil service does not include elected officials, judicial officers, military personnel, or employees selected by patronage.

Most civil service positions are filled from lists of applicants who are rated in descending order of their passing scores on competitive written civil service examinations. The tests measure aptitude to perform a job. Promotional competitive examinations screen eligible employees for job advancement. Veterans of the armed services may receive hiring preference, usually in the form of extra points added to their examination scores, depending on the nature and duration of service. Legislatures establish basic prerequisites for employment, such as compliance with minimum age and educational requirements and residency laws. Once hired, an employee may have to take an oath to execute his or her job in good faith and in accordance with the law. Employees enjoy job security, promotion and educational opportunities, comprehensive medical insurance coverage, and pension and other benefits often not provided in comparable positions in the private sector.

The Early Civil Service Movement
The establishment of the modern civil service parallels the growth of centralized bureaucratic government and the decline of feudalism. Civil service systems probably originated in the earliest known Middle Eastern societies where rationalized administrations carried out the increasingly complex tasks of government. One of the oldest examples of a merit-based civil service existed in the imperial bureaucracy of China. Tracing back to 200 B.C., the Han dynasty adopted Confucianism as the basis of its political philosophy and structure, which included the revolutionary idea of replacing the nobility of blood with one of virtue and honesty, and thereby calling for administrative appointments to be based solely on merit. Later, the Chinese adopted the nine-rank system, which created a formal hierarchy based on power and expertise. Around A.D. 100, and about the same time paper was invented, the Han dynasty used competitive examinations to select civil officials. This system allowed anyone who passed an examination to become a government officer, a position that would bring wealth and honor to the whole family.

In part due to Chinese influence, the first European civil service did not originate in Europe but rather in India by the British-run East India Company during the early seventeenth century. Company managers hired and promoted employees based on competitive examinations in order to prevent corruption and favoritism. Indeed, today's Indian civil service attracts the best talent in that country, with officers selected through a tough examination system.

The modern European civil services date from seventeenth-century Prussia, when Frederick William and the electors of Brandenburg created an efficient public administration staffed by civil servants chosen competitively. In France a similar bureaucracy preceded the French Revolution and formed the basis for the Napoleonic reforms that converted the royal service into a professional civil service. Across Europe during the early nineteenth century, reformers established regulations intended to minimize favoritism and ensure a wide range of knowledge and skills among civil service officers.

The British Experience
In 1855 the British Parliament established the Civil Service Commission, which instituted a system of competitive examinations. After World War II, the influential Whitley Councils, representing both government employees and administrators, were created to deal with conditions in the civil service. In the British Civil Service, career employees are recruited and promoted on the basis of administrative skill and technical expertise. Civil servants are expected to be politically neutral and are prohibited from taking part in political campaigns or being members of Parliament.

The British Civil Service was at its largest in 1976, with approximately three-quarters of a million people employed. After falling to a record low of 459,600 in April 1999 due to privatization, outsourcing, and downsizing, the number of civil service employees has again risen. While it has been criticized for lack of flexibility and elitism in its upper ranks, the British system remains extremely powerful because of its permanency, extensive grants of power from Parliament, and a reputation for honesty.

The Civil Service Reform Movement in the United States

The history of civil service in the United States is dominated by the struggle between a completely politicized spoils system and a predominantly merit-based system, a struggle spanning more than a hundred years and still being waged in some state and local jurisdictions. During the Federal period under President George Washington and his successors through John Quincy Adams, the civil service was stable and characterized by relative competence, efficiency, and honesty, although it was somewhat elitist and, over time, superannuated. After 1829 and the election of Andrew Jackson, however, the increasingly strong pressures of grassroots democracy abruptly transformed the civil service of the Founding Fathers. For more than a half century federal, state, and local public services were governed by a spoils system that gave little consideration to competence. During this period, the political party in power dominated the patronage, and changes in party control resulted in a wholesale turnover of government employees. In 1831 New York Senator William Marcy best characterized this chaotic period with his oft quoted adage, "To the victor belong the spoils."

Because the spoils system spawned widespread corruption, inefficiency, and incompetence during the Jacksonian era, the United States lagged far behind European nations in standards of civil service competence and integrity. Agitation for reform began soon after the Civil War, when unprecedented corruption and political chicanery generated calls for a professional, merit-based civil service. In 1871 Congress created the first Civil Service Commission and authorized the president to prescribe regulations for admission to the public service and to utilize examinations in the appointing process. However, Congress refused subsequent appropriations for the commission and allowed it to expire in 1874.

The civil service movement continued to gain momentum after the scandals of President Ulysses Grant's administration, and especially after the assassination of President James Garfield in 1881 by a disappointed office seeker. Spurred by efforts of the National Civil Service League and other reformers, Congress passed the Pendleton Act in 1883, which reestablished the Civil Service Commission after a nine-year lapse. The act remains the federal government's central civil service law and provides the rulemaking process for governing examinations for civil service positions. Successive presidents, requiring increasing professional expertise to carry out congressional mandates, continued and consolidated the reform. Significant expansions of the merit system occurred during the presidencies of Grover Cleveland, Theodore Roosevelt, and Herbert Hoover. By 1900 the proportion of the federal civil service under the merit system reached nearly 60 percent. By 1930 it had exceeded 80 percent, and in the early twenty-first century, there were fewer than 15,000 patronage posts of any consequence in a federal civil service of 3 million.

In 1940 the Hatch Act attempted to divorce the civil service from politics by prohibiting federal civil service employees from participating in elections or making campaign contributions. A 1993 relaxation of the act allowed most civil servants to engage in political activity on their own time. Unlike workers in private employment, civil service employees may be prohibited from certain acts that would compromise their position as servants of the government and the general public. This is especially true of government employees involved in national defense activities or law enforcement and those holding security clearances.

Civil service reform took place in many state and local governments beginning in the late nineteenth century, although more slowly and less completely than in the federal government. In 1883 both New York and Massachusetts adopted the first state civil service acts. Many states followed after 1939, when the federal government ordered that merit systems be extended to those sections of state administration receiving federal grants. By the 1970s, over a million state and local positions fell within personnel systems closely monitored by the federal government. The proportion of states with comprehensive merit systems grew to one third by 1940 and to two thirds by 1970.

Civil service reform spread to large cities as well, beginning when New York City and Boston set up civil service commissions in the 1880s and followed by Chicago in 1895. Most large metropolitan centers and many smaller cities now have modern merit systems, especially for police and fire departments. In most jurisdictions, a bipartisan civil service commission provides administrative leadership, although the single personnel director has become an increasingly popular model.

The Modern Civil Service in the United States

In 1978 Congress passed the Civil Service Reform Act, one of the major domestic accomplishments of the Carter administration. The act instituted a wide variety of management reforms, including the creation of the Office of Personnel Management, the Merit Systems Protection Board, and the Federal Labor Relations Authority. These new agencies replaced the former Civil Service Commission. In addition, the act established the Senior Executive Service (SES), composed of 8,000 top civil servants having less tenure but greater opportunity for productivity bonuses than under previous classification arrangements. This was seen as a step toward the creation of a senior management system allowing recruitment and compensation of top managers on a basis competitive with the private sector. The act also established a system of productivity-related merit pay for senior federal employees just below the SES levels and provided explicit protection for whistle-blowers and employees who call attention to government malpractices.

The Civil Service Reform Act expanded the functions of federal personnel management, which had consisted mainly of administering examinations and policing the patronage. Consequences included improved pay and fringe benefits, training and executive development, a search for first-rate talent, new approaches to performance rating, equal employment opportunity, improved ethical standards, loyalty and security procedures, incentive systems, and special programs for the handicapped. These developments and a system of collective bargaining between unions and managers characterize the transformation of the nineteenth-century merit system into an advanced public personnel regime.

The federal civil service has grown from an institution of a few hundred employees in 1789 to nearly 3 million. During major wars, the federal civil service doubled and even quadrupled. Its peak occurred in 1945, when civil service employees numbered nearly 4 million. There has been a similar growth in state and local services. By the 1970s, federal civil employees functioned almost entirely under merit system procedures, as did some 75 percent of those in state and local governments.

But since the 1980s civil service systems have come under increasing criticism. Critics charge that government has become too big and costly. In response, state legislatures have proposed and implemented significant budget reductions in many civil services. As a result, civil service officers at both the state and federal levels face the challenge of meeting growing obligations with declining resources. Critics also complain that the civil service has outlived its usefulness, stifles flexibility and creativity, and creates unresponsive, out-of-touch government bureaucrats who put their own narrow interests ahead of those of the American people. As calls for the modification or abolition of civil service systems have grown louder, the federal government and some states have adopted an incremental approach in relaxing the strictures of civil service by streamlining recruiting and testing, simplifying job classifications, and building more flexibility into compensation systems. The federal government also made it easier for states to relax civil service requirements when it modified a longstanding requirement that federally paid state workers be covered by a formal merit system. Instead, federal law now asks that state agencies with federally funded employees follow "merit principles" in their personnel management practices.

Modern Civil Service Reform

Three southern states abandoned their civil service systems outright. In 1985 Texas became the first state to cast aside its traditional civil service when its legislature abolished the Texas Merit Council. As a result, agencies hire and promote as they see fit, most written exams are eliminated, and supervisors have more discretion over employee pay. In 1996 Georgia removed merit system protections for all new employees and decentralized hiring authority to agencies and departments. Florida followed in 2001 with the most dramatic reform. Overnight, thousands of merit-protected employees were reclassified into at-will status. The state eliminated seniority and no longer allowed longstanding employees to "bump" newer staff members during downsizing. Florida collapsed thousands of job categories into a few dozen occupational groups and assigned each group a wide pay band that allowed management great discretion in determining individual employee compensation. Between 2000 and 2002, Florida reduced its state workforce by 24,000 positions.

Notwithstanding budget concerns and retrenchment, civil service in the United States remains a uniquely open system, in contrast to the closed career system common to other nations, where one enters at a relatively early age and remains for a lifetime, in a manner similar to a military career. The Pendleton Act of 1883 established this original approach, providing that the federal service would be open to persons of any age who could pass job-oriented examinations. Employees can move in and out of public service, from government to private industry and back again, through a process known as lateral entry. U.S. civil service policy provides a viable route for upward mobility, especially for women and minorities. The federal civil service, in particular, continues to serve as the "model employer" by setting high standards for employee health and safety, amenable labor relations, equal opportunity for women and minorities, and open access to persons with disabilities. Thus, the U.S. civil service has reflected the open, mobile nature of an American society that values individual employees' rights and, in turn, has done much to support it.

FURTHER READING

Hoogenboom, Ari. *Outlawing the Spoils: A History of the Civil Service Reform Movement, 1865–1883.* Urbana: University of Illinois Press, 1961.

Ingraham, Patricia W. *The State of the Higher Civil Service after Reform: Britain, Canada, and the United States.* Paris: OECD, 1999.

Johnson, Ronald N. *The Federal Civil Service System and the Problem of Bureaucracy: The Economics and Politics of Institutional Change.* Chicago: University of Chicago Press, 1994.

Schultz, David A. *The Politics of Civil Service Reform.* New York: Peter Lang, 1998.

Van Riper, Paul. *History of the United States Civil Service.* Evanston, IL: Row, Peterson, 1958.

RICHARD D. WHITE JR.

Civil War and Reconstruction

The Civil War (1861–65), in which Northerners and Southerners fought over the federal government's relationship to slavery and with the states, destroyed slavery and replaced constitutional ambiguity about secession with an understanding of the United States as an indivisible nation. Reconstruction (1863–77) readmitted seceded states to the Union and redefined American citizenship to include African Americans. The Civil War and Reconstruction reshaped American government and politics by ending slavery, expanding federal power, inventing presidential war powers, establishing precedent for civil liberties in wartime, solidifying Republicans and Democrats as long-term players in a revitalized two-party system, and enlarging the American polity via constitutional amendment.

Collapse of the Two-Party System and the Coming of the War

Sectional conflict intensified in the 1840s and 1850s, leading to the collapse of the national two-party system, which for decades had discouraged secession and contained conflict over slavery. The question of slavery's extension into U.S. territories reconfigured political fault lines from partisan ones, in which Whigs opposed Democrats chiefly over economic issues, to sectional ones, in which Northerners and Southerners sparred over whether slavery should spread and what the federal government's relationship to slavery should be. In the 1850s, the slavery extension issue contributed to the downfall of the Whigs and the rise of the Republicans, an exclusively northern party opposed to slavery's expansion. In 1860 slavery split the Democratic Party between northern Democrats, who rallied behind Illinoisan Stephen Douglas and popular sovereignty (in which territorial voters, not Congress, determined slavery's status), and southern Democrats, who called for stronger federal commitment to slavery expressed through measures like formal recognition of slavery as a national (not local) institution, a federal slave code obligating federal forces to protect the extension of slavery into territories, and congressional invalidation of state personal liberty laws passed by some northern states to exempt individuals from helping recapture runaway slaves.

Four candidates ran for president in 1860. Southern Democrat John Breckinridge ran on a platform calling for increased federal commitment to slavery and a federal slave code. Stephen Douglas advocated popular sovereignty. John Bell ran as the candidate of the new Constitutional Union Party, which appealed to southern moderates by supporting slavery where it existed but avoiding the expansion question. Abraham Lincoln ran on a platform opposing slavery's extension. Lincoln won with 39 percent of the popular vote (none from southern states) and 59 percent of the electoral vote.

In the absence of national party organizations to temper sectional anger, Deep South states rejected the election results. The South Carolina legislature called a secession convention, which, on December 20, 1860, dissolved the Union between South Carolina and the United States. Mississippi, Alabama, Florida, Georgia,

Louisiana, and Texas seceded by February. Delegates from the seceded states met in Montgomery, Alabama, to select Jefferson Davis as president and Alexander Stephens as vice president of the Confederate States of America, and to draft a Constitution of the Confederate States, which echoed the U.S. Constitution in most places but added firmer protections for slavery. Davis's inaugural address compared the Confederacy to the 13 colonies declaring their independence when Great Britain no longer represented their interests, and he noted the need to prepare for war. The provisional Confederate Congress authorized 100,000 troops. As the new Confederate government formed, conventions in upper South states declined to secede but passed "coercion clauses" pledging to side with the seceded states if the U.S. government attempted to coerce them.

Northern public opinion split between those who called for compromise and those who advocated preserving the Union by whatever means necessary. Lame-duck president James Buchanan did not respond to secession, while Congress considered compromise measures. Most important was the Crittenden Compromise, which permitted the spread of slavery into territories south of the 36° 30′ north latitude line promised federal noninterference with slavery in Washington, D.C., and with the slave trade; and proposed an unamendable amendment to the Constitution that protected slavery. Denounced by Republicans who opposed the extension of slavery and the unalterable amendment, and by southern Democrats who objected to the lack of a federal slave code, the compromise failed.

As support for compromise faded, the Confederate seizure of forts and customs houses contributed to growing northern anger at the seceded states. In addition, many Northerners emphasized the international impact of the dissolution of the Union. Convinced that the American republic stood as an example to the world of self-government based on the egalitarian ideals stated in the Declaration of Independence, Northerners worried that to dissolve the Union over election results would doom the fate of self-government everywhere because other nations would conclude that republican government had failed.

Lincoln hoped to employ a strategy of "masterly inactivity," in which the federal government patiently waited until white Southerners renounced secession. But events intervened. Lincoln's inaugural address stressed the perpetuity of the Union, pledged not to provoke the seceded states, and vowed to preserve the Union. The following day, Major Robert Anderson informed the president that soldiers at Fort Sumter in Charleston Harbor were nearly out of food and other supplies. Lincoln notified Jefferson Davis and South Carolina officials that a U.S. ship with food but not arms would reprovision the fort. On April 12, 1861, acting on orders from Davis, General Pierre G. T. Beauregard and his troops shelled Fort Sumter, which surrendered on April 14. Lincoln called for 75,000 troops to put down the rebellion. Interpreting the call as coercion, Virginia, Tennessee, Arkansas, and North Carolina seceded to create an 11-state Confederacy.

Emancipation

Emancipation freed 4 million people, destroyed one of the country's greatest sources of wealth, upset the social order of the South, and, by transforming the United States from a slaveholding to a free nation, altered the interests that dictated foreign policy. For these reasons, emancipation was the most important result of the Civil War alongside the survival of the Union. But in 1861, several factors made abolition appear unlikely. For its entire existence, the U.S. government had sanctioned slavery. The Constitution did not permit federal interference with slavery and protected the property rights of slaveholders. The border slave states (Delaware, Kentucky, Maryland, Missouri) stayed in the Union, but close decisions in Kentucky, Maryland, and Missouri meant that retaining the border states would require assurances for the protection of slavery. Moreover, Lincoln and many white Northerners initially believed that most white Southerners were loyal to the Union at heart and would return peacefully if assured that slavery would be safe.

At first, President Lincoln and Congress supplied such assurances. In his July 1861 message to Congress, Lincoln emphasized that he had "no purpose, directly or indirectly to interfere with slavery in the States where it exists." That same month Lincoln endorsed the Crittenden Resolutions, in which Congress claimed that Union war aims did not include abolition. In August, when Union General John C. Frémont sought to pacify portions of Missouri by emancipating secessionists' slaves, Lincoln overturned the proclamation; he also revoked General David Hunter's similar proclamation in South Carolina in May 1862. When New York abolitionist Horace Greeley harangued Lincoln for his apparent reluctance to emancipate, Lincoln answered, in a public letter, that his primary purpose was to save the Union, and any decisions about slavery would be made in service to that goal.

The actions of African Americans and the course of the war led to dramatic changes in Union policy. In May 1861 a Confederate officer demanded the return of three slaves who had fled to Fortress Monroe, Virginia, an encampment under the command of General Benjamin F. Butler. Butler refused, declaring that the rules of war gave him the right to confiscate enemy property as "contraband of war." As word of Butler's actions spread, "contrabands" throughout the seceded states flocked to Union camps, where their labor sustained the Union war effort and their physical presence demonstrated that ending the war would require the Union to face the issue of slavery. Meanwhile, as Northerners realized that the Confederacy would fight a prolonged war, civilians, soldiers, and political leaders warmed to policies designed to rob the South of the valuable resource of slave labor. In August 1861 and July 1862, Congress passed Confiscation Acts permitting Union Army officers to confiscate and emancipate slaves owned by Southerners who supported the Confederacy. Also in 1862, Congress overturned the Crittenden Resolutions; abolished slavery in Washington, D.C., and U.S. territories; and passed the Militia Act, which authorized the enlistment of black Union soldiers and promised freedom to their families. In July of that year, Lincoln met with border state congressmen to urge the slaveholding Union states to emancipate within their own states.

When Lincoln's appeals to the border states failed, he made new plans. On July 23 the president announced to his cabinet that in his role as commander in chief, he would emancipate slaves in the rebelling states as an act of military necessity. Because Union armies had recently suffered setbacks (most notably, the failure of the army of the Potomac's elaborate Peninsula Campaign to capture Richmond), Secretary of State William H. Seward convinced Lincoln to wait for military victory to issue the proclamation so that the move did not appear to be an act of desperation. On September 22, 1862, five days after the Union Army repulsed a Confederate invasion of Maryland at the Battle of Antietam, Lincoln issued the preliminary Emancipation Proclamation, vowing to free slaves in areas still in rebellion on January 1, 1863. On January 1, Lincoln's final Emancipation Proclamation realized the promise. Though restricted in geographic scope and limited in moral fervor by its emphasis on military necessity, the Emancipation Proclamation nonetheless expanded the aims of the war to include abolition.

President Abraham Lincoln visits the battlefield at Antietam, Maryland, October 3, 1862. (Alexander Gardner/ National Archives)

Because the Emancipation Proclamation's status as a war measure meant that, in peacetime, its authority might be questioned, Lincoln and a growing number of antislavery advocates looked to a constitutional amendment to permanently end slavery throughout the nation. A proposed amendment abolishing slavery got the necessary two-thirds vote to pass the Senate in June 1864 and the House in January 1865. By December 1865, enough states had ratified the Thirteenth Amendment to make it part of the U.S. Constitution. The document that had protected slavery now outlawed it.

Centralization, Civil Liberties, and Dissent

Constitutional abolition of slavery was just one of many ways in which the national government's power grew during the Civil War. To pay for the war, Congress authorized the first national paper currency with the Legal Tender Act in February 1862. The following month, Congress passed a progressive income tax and empowered the federal government, rather than state governments, to collect it. The Confederacy enacted military conscription for the first time in the nation's history in April 1862, but the U.S. Congress also passed a conscription bill in March 1863 to take effect in July. Unlike the Confederate draft, which mandated the enlistment of every white male of arms-bearing age, the Union draft consisted of a lottery system that placed a percentage of men into the ranks, but even the Union draft expanded the central government's ability to affect the lives of its citizens.

With Democratic representation reduced by the secession of solidly Democratic southern states, Republicans used their newfound congressional majority to increase government involvement in the economy. In 1862 the Homestead Act made public lands in the West available to settlers for a nominal filing fee, the Pacific Railroad Grant subsidized the construction of a transcontinental railroad, and the Morrill Land-Grant College Act used government land grants to increase access to higher education. After decades of low tariffs, Congress raised protective tariffs to promote domestic industry and, supporters argued, to raise workingmen's wages. In short, the Civil War Congress laid the foundations for a distinctly national economy and a view of capitalism as inherently democratic that would come to be seen as a mainstream American (rather than partisan) view in the late nineteenth and twentieth centuries.

The role and power of the president expanded even more significantly, especially with the creation of presidential war powers. Lincoln first used the term *war power*

in his July 4, 1861, message to Congress. Since April, Lincoln had taken actions, such as blockading Confederate forts and expanding the armed forces, that seemed to violate Article 1 of the Constitution, which reserves to Congress the right to declare war and support armies. Lincoln's message argued that, with no Congress in session, the president's oath to preserve the Union and the Constitution necessitated that he "call out the war power of the Government." To detractors, the expansion made Lincoln a despot. To his supporters, and in his own mind, Lincoln's obligation to preserve the nation kept his actions aligned with the spirit of the Constitution, if not always its letter. Congress affirmed the idea of the president's war power when it ratified all of Lincoln's actions in July 1861, and the judicial branch gave tacit assent in March 1863, when the Supreme Court narrowly approved the president's blockade in the *Prize* cases. But precisely what "war power" meant would develop over the course of the conflict.

Lincoln used the concept of presidential war powers to take vigorous measures to keep the border states in the Union. Although Missouri and Kentucky remained in the Union largely due to Lincoln's hands-off approach, which respected Kentucky's initial "neutrality" and left matters in Missouri in the hands of state leaders, Maryland required more direct and immediate action because of its proximity to Washington, D.C. In April 1861, when Confederate sympathizers in Maryland effectively cut off the U.S. capital by destroying telegraph and rail lines and attacking a Washington, D.C.–bound Massachusetts regiment as it passed through Baltimore, Lincoln responded by suspending the writ of habeas corpus from Philadelphia to Washington. Because habeas corpus requires an arrested citizen to be promptly charged with and tried for a specific crime, its suspension permitted the indefinite imprisonment of suspected Confederate sympathizers without specific charges. A clear curb on individual liberty, the suspension was immediately tested when John Merryman, a wealthy Marylander and officer in a Confederate cavalry unit that cut telegraph lines, was imprisoned at Fort McHenry and petitioned for a writ of habeas corpus. The Union officer who imprisoned Merryman refused, citing the suspension of the writ; his refusal gave the federal circuit court judge Roger B. Taney (who also served as chief justice of the Supreme Court) the opportunity to rule the suspension unconstitutional because Congress, not the president, could suspend the writ. Lincoln ignored Taney's ruling and Congress later ratified the president's actions.

Lincoln also used the concept of presidential war powers, sometimes at the expense of civil liberties, to recruit and retain soldiers. As the number of men volunteering for military duty waned, Congress adopted measures to raise soldiers, at first by assigning enlistment quotas to states and later by delivering control over recruitment to the national government in the 1863 Conscription Act. Federal officials such as provost marshals and boards of enrollment oversaw the registration of men between ages 25 and 45 in communities throughout the North, and Lincoln issued several calls for troops to be filled by draft in 1863 and 1864. In areas where protesters threatened to interfere or where adversarial newspaper editors encouraged draft resistance, Lincoln suspended habeas corpus and limited freedom of the press. In the fall of 1862, when the requisitioning of troops from the states coincided with the announcement of the preliminary Emancipation Proclamation, Secretary of War Edwin Stanton issued an order subjecting "all persons discouraging volunteer enlistments, resisting militia drafts, or guilty of any disloyal practice affording aid and comfort to the rebels" to martial law, and Lincoln reinforced the order by suspending the writ of habeas corpus throughout the Union. Over the course of the war, about 5,000 civilian arrests were made under the suspension (the total number of individuals affected was smaller because many were arrested more than once), with most individuals released in a matter of weeks.

Emancipation, the expansion of federal power, and the abridgement of civil liberties generated fierce dissent. Antiwar Democrats decried federal overreaching on legal, constitutional, and racial grounds. Editors of some antiwar Democratic newspapers, such as Brick Pomeroy of the *La Crosse Democrat* in Wisconsin, railed against encroaching tyranny. In the fall 1862 elections, Democrats scored key victories in congressional and state contests in midwestern states, New York, and Pennsylvania. Ohio congressman Samuel Cox introduced a resolution denouncing Republican "usurpation of power," and Governor Horatio Seymour of New York chastised the administration for ignoring constitutional liberties. Outspoken antiwar Democrat Clement C. Vallandigham of Ohio lost his bid for reelection to Congress in 1862 but persevered as a vocal war opponent. Antiwar militancy divided the Democratic Party between "War Democrats," who supported the war effort, and "Peace Democrats," denounced by their detractors as "Copperheads"; the divide would not heal until after the war.

Dissent raged all over the North (the most dramatic outburst was the 1863 New York City Draft Riot), but it was particularly concentrated in southern Indiana, Illinois, and Ohio. In Indiana and Illinois, antiwar state legislatures clashed with Republican governors as secret organizations like the Knights of the Golden Circle were rumored to be plotting to overthrow governors, seize federal arms, and launch rebellions. Clement Vallandigham continued to militate against emancipation and the draft. In May 1863, when Vallandigham delivered a speech denouncing the administration and discouraging enlistment, Department of the Ohio Commander General Ambrose Burnside utilized Lincoln's suspension of habeas corpus to punish him. After Burnside ordered the arrest and trial of Vallandigham by military tribunal, Lincoln commuted the sentence to banishment to the Confederacy. Vallandigham escaped to Canada, then ran for governor of Ohio and lost decisively to War Democrat John Brough.

The presidential election of 1864 presented the Union with the biggest test of its ability to withstand dissent, as Lincoln faced challenges within his own party and from Democrats. Radical Republicans believed Lincoln had moved too slowly on emancipation and wanted to replace him with a stauncher abolitionist. Some Democrats portrayed Lincoln as an irresponsible radical intent on either elevating blacks over whites or, according to a pamphlet entitled *Miscegenation*, advocating racial mixing. Other Democrats focused their opposition on the president's conduct of the war. The convention adopted an antiwar and anti-emancipation platform and nominated General George McClellan for president. While party operatives hoped that McClellan's war credentials would mute charges of insufficient patriotism, vice presidential candidate George Pendleton's Copperhead reputation gave the Democratic ticket a decidedly antiwar cast. As the spring and summer of 1864 brought setbacks to Union arms and necessitated more drafts, McClellan and the antiwar platform grew so popular that Lincoln predicted his own defeat.

But the capture of Atlanta by General William Sherman in September 1864 shifted the military momentum of the war and the momentum of the presidential campaign. Aided by the fall of Atlanta and a resounding vote of confidence from Union soldiers, nearly 80 percent of whom voted for the incumbent, Lincoln defeated McClellan. The presidential contest was especially significant because its very existence in the midst of civil war helped quell doubts about the viability of self-government in wartime, validated the legitimacy of two-party politics, and so firmly embedded the Republican and Democratic parties in voters' consciousness that they would remain the dominant parties in a two-party system long after the initial issues that defined them had faded. More specifically, Lincoln's victory dashed Confederate hopes for a negotiated peace and contributed directly, though not immediately, to the conclusion of the war. The passage of the Thirteenth Amendment outlawing slavery temporarily reignited the Confederates' will to fight, but the relentless pressure of the Union Army eventually forced the Confederacy to capitulate in the spring of 1865.

Presidential and Congressional Reconstruction

After the war the United States needed to restore seceded states to the Union and determine the status of former slaves. Both tasks would proceed without the leadership of Abraham Lincoln. Shot by the actor John Wilkes Booth, Lincoln died on April 15, 1865. Struggles ensued between the president and Congress, and between former slaves and former Confederates, for control of Reconstruction.

The first stage, Presidential Reconstruction, in which control rested mainly with the president and the southern states, began in 1863. Aiming to turn internal southern disaffection with the Confederacy into pro-Union sentiment, Lincoln proposed the Ten Per Cent Plan, which offered lenient terms for readmission to the Union. Under Lincoln's plan, once 10 percent of the number of eligible state voters who had voted in the 1860 election took an oath of allegiance to the United States, the state could be readmitted to the Union upon drafting a state constitution abolishing slavery. Confederates, except for very high-ranking political and military leaders, would receive full amnesty and restoration of property except for slaves. Radical Republicans objected that the lenient terms offered insufficient safeguards for the rights of former slaves and would restore the prewar power structure that led to secession. Instead, they proposed the Wade-Davis Bill, which required a majority of eligible voters to take a loyalty oath and which prevented Confederate officials and soldiers from voting for delegates to the state constitutional conventions. Congress passed the bill, but Lincoln pocket-vetoed it. By April 1865 Lincoln recognized the need for a new approach and publicly supported voting rights for at least some African Americans, but he died before articulating a plan.

Lincoln's successor, President Andrew Johnson, shared his predecessor's determination to retain presidential control of Reconstruction but lacked Lincoln's political skill or sense of obligation to black Americans. In May 1865 Johnson outlined a plan that restored full political, legal, and property (except slave property) rights to all Confederates, except for members of specific exempted groups, including very high-ranking political and military leaders and planters owning more than $20,000 in taxable property, who were required to apply personally to the president for amnesty. Johnson also recognized state governments in Arkansas, Louisiana, Tennessee, and Virginia, thereby approving the rights of those states to send delegations to Congress, and he established easy terms for the readmission of all remaining states as soon as conventions drafted constitutions nullifying secession, repudiating Confederate debts, and recognizing the end of slavery. Encouraged by Johnson's leniency, states asserted the legitimacy of secession, slavery, and white supremacy by repealing rather than nullifying secession and by passing Black Codes that reduced former slaves to conditions close to servitude. Meanwhile, voters elected staunch Confederates to state constitutional conventions.

Alarmed that growing white southern intransigence threatened both genuine restoration of the Union and the rights of former slaves, members of Congress began to maneuver for control of Reconstruction. In December 1865 congressional Republicans refused to seat southern delegations and established a Joint Committee on Reconstruction to review policies for readmission to the Union. Despite divisions between moderate Republicans (who aimed to prevent secessionists from regaining power and sought to protect basic civil rights for blacks with minimal social change) and Radical Republicans (who desired disfranchisement of rebels, full civil rights for former slaves, and the restructuring of southern society), congressional Republicans united to pass two important pieces of legislation. The Freedmen's Bureau Bill established the Bureau of Refugees, Freedmen, and Abandoned Lands, a government agency whose official mission included ministering to civilian war refugees white and black, but in practice the Bureau concentrated on easing former slaves' transition to freedom. The Civil Rights Act explicitly defined national citizenship as applying to black Americans and protected all citizens' rights to make contracts, sue in court, and hold property. The Civil Rights Act was a moderate bill in that it left enforcement primarily to the states, but it still marked an important shift in delineating citizenship rights and linking them to the federal government.

When Johnson vetoed both bills, Congress passed the Fourteenth Amendment in June 1866. The amendment defined all white and black native-born Americans and all naturalized immigrants as citizens of the United States and barred states from denying equal protection under the law to any citizen. It did not guarantee voting rights, but it reduced congressional representation for any state that withheld suffrage from male citizens. To achieve ratification, the Fourteenth Amendment required the approval of three-fourths of the states, which meant it needed the approval of at least some former Confederate states.

Johnson's reaction to the Fourteenth Amendment tipped the balance of power to Congress. The president publicly reiterated his own white supremacist convictions, encouraged white southern hostility toward former slaves, and urged southern states to reject the Fourteenth Amendment. Johnson also embarked on the "Swing Around the Circle" tour of the northeastern and midwestern states to urge Northerners to oppose the amendment and support his approach to Reconstruction. Before large crowds, Johnson harangued Congress, portrayed himself as a persecuted martyr, and taunted audience members. Alienated by Johnson's behavior, northern voters blamed the president when every former Confederate state except Tennessee rejected the Fourteenth Amendment and when race riots erupted in Memphis and New Orleans. They overwhelmingly elected Republicans in the 1866 congressional elections, giving them a veto-proof congressional majority, yet power remained divided between radicals and moderates.

Congress passed the Military Reconstruction Acts and in so doing ushered in a new phase, Congressional Reconstruction, which neither restructured southern society nor redistributed property, but it did prevent former Confederates from dominating state constitutional conventions and did provide some protection for freed people's most basic civil rights. Because Tennessee had ratified the Fourteenth Amendment and reentered the Union, it was exempt, but the remaining ten Confederate states were divided into five military districts by the First Military Reconstruction Act, passed March 1867 over Johnson's veto. Each district fell under the command of a major general who would supervise the registration of eligible voters, including blacks and excluding high-ranking former Confederates. Registered voters would elect delegates to state constitutional conven-

tions. Once a state's convention framed a constitution that enfranchised blacks and barred the highest-ranking ex-Confederates from office, Congress would approve the constitution and the state could hold elections for state officials and members of Congress. Following the ratification of the Fourteenth Amendment by the newly elected state legislature, the state would be fully restored to the Union. Three additional Military Reconstruction Acts clarified ambiguous provisions. By June 1868 Alabama, North Carolina, South Carolina, Arkansas, Louisiana, and Florida had rejoined the Union under the terms of the Military Reconstruction Acts. Georgia, Texas, Virginia, and Mississippi followed by 1870.

The power struggle between Congress and Johnson over the Military Reconstruction Acts resulted in the nation's first presidential impeachment. Johnson replaced Republican generals in charge of military districts with conservative generals sympathetic to former Confederates and hostile to former slaves, and he dismissed cabinet officials until only Secretary of War Stanton remained from Lincoln's cabinet. Radicals pushed to impeach the president in early 1867, but moderates balked and instead Congress passed two laws. The Command of the Army Act, a provision of the Army Appropriations Act, required all orders to army commanders to be issued through General Ulysses S. Grant. The Tenure of Office Act prevented the president from removing federal officials, including cabinet members, without congressional approval until one month after the term of office of the appointing president had expired (April 1869 for officials appointed by President Lincoln).

Johnson tested both laws by removing Generals Philip Sheridan and Daniel Sickles and also by removing Stanton when Congress was not in session. Moderates still rejected impeachment, since by dismissing Stanton when Congress was unable to grant approval, Johnson technically had not violated the Tenure of Office Act. Congress reinstated Stanton, only to have Johnson remove him in February 1868, when Congress was in session. On February 24 the House of Representatives voted along strict party lines (126 to 47) to impeach the president. Johnson would stand trial in the Senate on eleven charges, nine concerning narrow violations of the Command of the Army Act and Tenure of Office Act and two concerning Johnson's broader obstruction of Reconstruction.

Moderate Republicans in the Senate faced a dilemma: they despised Johnson, but worried about the impact of impeachment on separation of powers, and distrusted the Radical Benjamin Wade, who would replace Johnson.

After striking a deal in which Johnson pledged to enforce the Reconstruction Acts, stop criticizing Congress, and appoint the well-regarded general John Schofield as secretary of war, seven moderate Republicans joined twelve Democrats to vote against removing the president from office. The final vote, 35 to 19, fell one short of the two-thirds necessary to oust Johnson, who remained in office for the remainder of his term, embittered and unrepentant but with little power to prevent Congress from overriding his vetoes.

The election of 1868 laid the groundwork for a third constitutional amendment. Republican Ulysses S. Grant defeated Democrat Horatio Seymour, but by narrower margins than party operatives anticipated. Concerned that restored southern state governments would abridge black rights, and also looking to bolster their party's base, Republicans drafted the Fifteenth Amendment guaranteeing black men's right to vote. Congress passed the amendment in February 1869.

Following passage of the Fifteenth Amendment, northern white interest in Reconstruction waned, and former Confederates reclaimed power and reasserted white supremacy through violence. Semisecret groups such as the Ku Klux Klan terrorized all southern Republicans but especially former slaves to prevent them from voting or exercising civil rights. Congress passed and President Grant vigorously administered the Enforcement Acts of 1870–71, which succeeded in paralyzing the Klan and protecting at least some black Southerners' right to vote in the 1872 election. Grant won reelection, and Republicans held their own in Congress, paving the way for a final Reconstruction measure, the Civil Rights Act of 1875, which outlawed segregation.

An economic depression in 1873 deflected white Northerners' attention from Reconstruction toward economic issues, and scandals within the Grant administration soured voters on Reconstruction politics. A splinter within the Republican Party, the Liberal Republicans, steered the party away from racial issues toward concerns like governmental corruption and economic recovery. As Democrats regained control and curtailed gains made by black Southerners in the former Confederate states, northern voters and the Republican Party looked the other way.

The election of 1876 brought Reconstruction to an official close. Democrat Samuel J. Tilden won the popular vote, but the Electoral College remained contested because of disputed tallies in South Carolina, Florida, and Louisiana. Republican and Democratic operatives agreed to concede all three states, and thus the presidency, to the Republican candidate, Rutherford B. Hayes, in exchange for Republicans removing the last federal troops enforcing Reconstruction measures and withdrawing national support from southern state Republican Party organizations. Hayes was inaugurated, Republican state governments in the South crumbled, and "Redemption," or the return of southern state governments to the Democratic Party, ensued. Over the next decade, conservative Democrats consolidated power, and by the turn of the twentieth century, an era of solid white Democratic state governance in the South had begun, with poll taxes, literacy tests, and intimidation effectively robbing black Southerners of many civil rights, including the right to vote.

Expansion and Contraction

While the Civil War enabled the expansion of federal power, citizenship rights, and the American polity, the aftermath of Reconstruction reversed significant aspects of wartime expansion, leaving a mixed legacy. The invention of presidential war powers had an ambiguous impact. Some of Lincoln's actions inhibited civil liberties, but he exercised relative restraint, using the authority mainly in areas of Confederate guerrilla activity rather than to punish political enemies. For example, newspaper editor Brick Pomeroy was never arrested despite his calls for Lincoln's assassination. After the Civil War, the Supreme Court trimmed presidential wartime powers with rulings like *ex Parte Milligan* (1866), which found that trying civilians in military courts when civilian courts were operational was unconstitutional. Further, despite growth in Lincoln's power, the impeachment of Andrew Johnson in 1868 and consistent overriding of his vetoes by Congress restricted presidential authority.

The aftermath of Reconstruction also curtailed the expansion of civil rights, particularly through a series of Supreme Court decisions limiting the impact of the Fourteenth and the Fifteenth Amendments. The *Slaughterhouse Cases* of 1873 identified most civil rights as state rights, rather than national rights, and concluded that the Fourteenth Amendment prevented states from depriving citizens of only a few national rights, such as access to ports. *United States v. Cruikshank* (1876) and the *Civil Rights Cases* (1883) determined that the constitutional amendments and the Civil Rights Act of 1875 prevented only states, not individuals, from infringing on citizens' rights. Most famously, *Plessy v. Ferguson* (1896) asserted the constitutionality of state-mandated racial segregation.

The Civil War and Reconstruction did resolve the questions of secession and slavery. Union military victory kept the southern states in the Union, and in *Texas v. White* (1869) the Supreme Court declared secession unconstitutional. The Thirteenth Amendment outlawed slavery. Further, the Fourteenth Amendment and the Fifteenth Amendment extended citizenship and voting rights to black men, and established scaffolding on which the civil rights movement of the twentieth century would build. Yet the precise relationship between federal and state governments and the exact meaning of former slaves' freedom would remain contested long after the era ended.

See also Reconstruction era, 1865–1877; slavery; South since 1877.

FURTHER READING

Benedict, Michael Les. *The Impeachment and Trial of Andrew Johnson*. New York: Norton, 1973.

Berlin, Ira, et al. *Slaves No More: Three Essays on Emancipation and the Civil War*. New York: Cambridge University Press, 1992.

Carter, Dan T. *When the War Was Over: The Failure of Self-Reconstruction in the South, 1865–1867*. Baton Rouge: Louisiana State University Press, 1985.

Foner, Eric. *Forever Free: The Story of Emancipation and Reconstruction*. New York: Knopf, 2005.

———. *A Short History of Reconstruction*. New York: Harper and Row, 1990.

Gienapp, William E. *Abraham Lincoln and Civil War America*. New York: Oxford University Press, 2002.

Guelzo, Allen C. *Lincoln's Emancipation Proclamation: The End of Slavery in America*. New York: Simon and Schuster, 2004.

Hahn, Steven. *A Nation under Our Feet: Black Political Struggles in the Rural South from Slavery to the Great Migration*. Cambridge, MA: Harvard University Press, 2003.

Klement, Frank L. *Lincoln's Critics: The Copperheads of the North*. Shippensburg, PA: White Mane Books, 1999.

McPherson, James M. *Battle Cry of Freedom*. New York: Oxford University Press, 1988.

Neely, Mark E. *The Last Best Hope of Earth: Abraham Lincoln and the Promise of America*. Cambridge, MA: Harvard University Press, 1995.

———. *The Union Divided: Party Conflict in the Civil War North*. Cambridge, MA: Harvard University Press, 2002.

Oakes, James. *The Radical and the Republican: Frederick Douglass, Abraham Lincoln, and the Triumph of Anti-slavery Politics*. New York: Norton, 2007.

Rable, George. *But There Was No Peace: The Role of Violence in the Politics of Reconstruction*. Athens: University of Georgia Press, 1984.

Richardson, Heather Cox. *The Greatest Party of the Earth: Republican Economic Policies during the Civil War*. Cambridge, MA: Harvard University Press, 1997.

Ross, Michael A. *Justice of Shattered Dreams: Samuel Freeman Miller and the Supreme Court during the Civil War Era*. Baton Rouge: Louisiana State University Press, 2003.

Scott, Rebecca J. *Degrees of Freedom: Louisiana and Cuba after Slavery*. Cambridge, MA: Harvard University Press, 2005.

Simon, James F. *Lincoln and Chief Justice Taney: Slavery, Secession, and the President's War Powers*. New York: Simon and Schuster, 2007.

Trefousse, Hans L. *The Radical Republicans: Lincoln's Vanguard for Racial Justice*. New York: Knopf, 1969.

Vorenberg, Michael. *Final Freedom: The Civil War, the Abolition of Slavery, and the Thirteenth Amendment*. New York: Cambridge University Press, 2001.

Weber, Jennifer L. *Copperheads: The Rise and Fall of Lincoln's Opponents in the North*. New York: Oxford, 2006.

CHANDRA MANNING

class and politics to 1877

Since the nation's founding, Americans have sought to reconcile the principle of equal rights for all (at least for all white men) with the reality of significant social differences based on wealth with occupation. To the Founding Fathers, there appeared no inherent contradiction. The Declaration of Independence famously asserted that "all men" possessed "certain unalienable rights," including "Life, Liberty, and the pursuit of Happiness." Yet just because everyone enjoyed the same right to pursue happiness did not mean that everyone would achieve the same level of success, material or otherwise. The founders envisioned the United States as a meritocracy where individuals' social and economic standing would reflect their relative talents, industriousness, and virtue. But they also recognized that differences in wealth and occupation could undermine popular faith in the legitimacy of American government if they hardened into enduring class divisions passed along from one generation to the next. Much of American political history has revolved around the issue of what role government should play both in promoting equal rights and in protecting the unequal results that meritocratic processes can produce over the long term.

The Federal Constitution

Class proved a controversial topic at the Constitutional Convention in 1787. Charles Pinckney of South Carolina argued that America was essentially a classless society and destined to remain so for the foreseeable future. Perhaps because the gap between free whites and enslaved blacks in his home state was so immense, he viewed differences among whites as negligible. "The people of the United States are more equal in their circumstances than the people of any other Country," he affirmed. "The genius of the people, their mediocrity of situation & the prospects which are afforded their industry in a country which must be a new one for centuries are unfavorable to the rapid distinctions of ranks." Virginian James Madison disputed Pinckney. "It was true," he conceded, "we had not among us . . . hereditary distinctions, of rank . . . nor those extremes of wealth or poverty" that plagued European countries. "We cannot however be regarded even at this time, as one homogenous mass." In the future, tensions between rich and poor were bound to grow. "An increase of population will of necessity increase the proportion of those who will labour under all the hardships of life, & secretly sigh for a more equal distribution of its blessings," Madison predicted. New Yorker Alexander Hamilton agreed. "It was certainly true that nothing like an equality of property existed," he declared, "that an inequality would exist as long as liberty existed, and that it would unavoidably result from the very liberty itself. This inequality of property constituted the great & fundamental distinction in Society."

To contain the threat of an impoverished and jealous majority in a republican polity, the Founding Fathers designed a national government that would be dominated by men of substantial property and social distinction. Given the large size of federal electoral districts, only persons of prior renown—for the most part members of established elites—were likely to win election to the House of Representatives, the most democratic branch of the new regime. Both sides in the struggle over ratification of the Constitution grasped this logic. New York anti-Federalist Melancton Smith warned that the new system would award too much power to "the natural aristocracy of the country." He did not wish to keep all men of high achievement and reputation out of government, but he wanted the new Congress to be open as

well to members of "the middling class." Although the campaign to block ratification of the Constitution failed, Smith framed a question that would recur periodically in American political history: what class of men should rule in a republic—the better sort or ordinary citizens?

Federalists, Republicans, and the "Revolution of 1800"

During the 1790s, political debate raged over the proper relationship between the populace at large and their representatives in the national government. Federalist leaders believed that natural aristocrats like themselves possessed a near monopoly on the wisdom necessary to identify the public good and guide the country in the right direction. When members of Democratic-Republican societies, many of them middling artisans and farmers, challenged administration policies on the grounds that they favored the rich and well-born, President George Washington denounced the societies as illegitimate "self-created" organizations bent on subverting the American republic. According to Federalists, qualified voters had a right and responsibility to elect virtuous gentlemen to Congress, but once elections were over, the common people should quietly abide by the policies prescribed by their social superiors.

Yet the natural aristocracy failed to consolidate into a cohesive ruling class under Federalist auspices. Soon after the new federal government got under way, a fierce quarrel broke out within the nation's upper echelons. Hamilton, as secretary of the treasury, sought to build a financial system modeled on the British example. He hoped to tie wealthy investors to the national project and to fuel economic development by establishing a national bank and by funding at par the combined public debt of the nation and the separate states. Hamilton's proposal deeply alienated his erstwhile ally Madison and Madison's good friend Thomas Jefferson. They feared that Hamilton meant to turn over control of the government to unscrupulous speculators and to prepare the way for a return to monarchy. In response, they formed the Republican Party and deployed class rhetoric to mobilize the middling sort against Hamilton's policies. The Federalists, Madison charged, "are more partial to the opulent than to the other classes of society; and having debauched themselves into a persuasion that mankind are incapable of governing themselves, it follows with them . . . that government can be carried on only by the pageantry of rank, the influence of money and emoluments, and the terror of military force."

The Republican triumph of 1800–1801—what Jefferson later called the "Revolution of 1800"—signaled an important shift in the class dynamics of American politics. Especially in the northern states, the Republican coalition challenged the political dominance of long-standing local elites. Jefferson, though by any measure a natural aristocrat, believed that, in a republic, sovereignty should reside actively in the people at large, with government—especially the federal government—interfering as little as possible in the "natural" processes of a free society. Yet Jefferson's policies as president proved more interventionist than his principles. By acquiring the huge Louisiana Territory, Jefferson safeguarded the economic opportunities of westward-heading farmers for generations to come. And by imposing the Embargo of 1807–9, he weakened New England commerce, stimulated American industrialization, and reenergized the partisan conflict between Federalists and Republicans. The result was a deepening sectional divide between the elites of the North and the South and a general rise in popular political participation. Despite the failure of Jefferson's embargo and the subsequent outbreak of the War of 1812, the Republicans succeeded in isolating northern merchants and financiers by consolidating their political base in the South and by attracting enough support among artisans and farmers in the middle states to dominate national politics. By 1820 the Federalist Party was moribund, and the eighteenth-century conception of rule by a natural aristocracy seemed passé.

The Missouri Crisis and the Rise of Jacksonian Democracy

Yet the uproar over Missouri's application for admission to the Union in 1819 revealed a serious cleavage within the Republican coalition. The most obvious line of division was sectional. Northerners opposed the extension of slavery while Southerners supported it. Underlying this difference were the parallel yet conflicting class dynamics of North and South. Even as the northern economy grew more diverse and many farmers' sons and daughters migrated to urban centers, other northern progeny sought to maintain an agricultural way of life by moving west. Their model of enterprise was the family farm, and they deeply feared competition from slaveholders whose ability to exploit black bondsmen made plantation agriculture more efficient. Southern farmers likewise looked westward for opportunity, especially as global demand for cotton soared in the early nineteenth century. Some large planters moved west, where land was compara-

tively cheap and the soil quite fertile, but the majority of southern whites who migrated were less affluent, including aspiring yeomen whose strategy for success was to climb into slaveholding ranks. The social goals of middling farmers in North and South had much in common, but their engagement in different labor systems tended to drive them apart.

During the late 1820s and 1830s, Andrew Jackson and his supporters were nonetheless able to build a Democratic Party composed mainly of northern and southern agriculturalists. To achieve this goal, Jacksonians muffled the debate over slavery as best they could. They also wooed middle-state manufacturing interests and disgruntled northern artisans, including veterans of short-lived Working Men's Parties based in the Northeast. Much of Jackson's appeal was personal: he was a self-made man and military hero whose rise from anonymity to fame and from rags to riches depended on his strength of will. He was not a natural aristocrat in the traditional sense, with its genteel connotations. He embodied a new variant of meritocracy, where those at the top of the social order were expected to resemble the middle class in temperament and opinion, only on a grander scale. As Alexis de Tocqueville observed in *Democracy in America*, "The men who are entrusted with the direction of public affairs in the United States are frequently inferior, both in point of capacity and of morality, to those whom aristocratic institutions would raise to power. But their interest is identified and confounded with that of their fellow citizens." In the public imagination, Andrew Jackson was the common man writ large.

Jackson's "war" on the Second Bank of the United States solidified the Democratic Party as a national organization. Like Jefferson, Jackson feared that an alliance between the federal government and large-scale financial interests—the so-called money power—would subvert the liberty of the American people. In his 1832 veto message aimed at the national bank, Jackson portrayed a situation in the United States bordering on class warfare. "It is to be regretted that the rich and powerful too often bend the acts of government to their selfish purposes," he wrote. "When the laws undertake to add to . . . natural and just advantages artificial distinctions, to grant titles, gratuities, and exclusive privileges, to make the rich richer and the potent more powerful, the humble members of society—the farmers, mechanics, and laborers—who have neither the time nor the means of securing like favors to themselves, have a right to complain of the injustice of their Government."

Jackson's opponents rejected his analysis root and branch. Calling themselves Whigs, they viewed the Second Bank of the United States as an economic engine that benefited all Americans. Whigs believed in class cooperation, not class conflict, and they thought a republican government, properly led, could and should maximize the public good by promoting balanced capitalist development. Unlike the Federalists before them, the Whigs did not believe in government by a natural aristocracy ruling the hoi polloi with aloof condescension. They celebrated self-made men as fervently as the Democrats and adopted modern forms of mass politics with enthusiasm. Yet they never fully escaped the charge that they cared more about business interests than the interests of ordinary people. Though studies of voting patterns have found significant variations from place to place and have demonstrated that factors such as ethnicity and religion were often as important as wealth and occupation, it appears that the Whigs drew their support mainly from those best positioned to gain directly from capitalist growth, while the Democrats drew their support primarily from those who feared they were losing out in a rapidly commercializing economy.

The Coming of the Civil War

While Democrats attacked federal intervention in the economy as an insidious plot to make the rich richer at the expense of everyone else, their laissez-faire policies served another, less egalitarian purpose: to protect slavery and the interests of southern slaveholders. The weaker the national government, the less chance it would interfere with the "peculiar institution"—an institution potentially at political risk as the proportion of slaveholders within the American population declined during the first half of the nineteenth century. In 1800 the demographic balance between free and slave states was roughly 50:50; by 1850 it was closer to 60:40. Moreover, within the slave states, slaveholders were a shrinking minority among the white population. Yet by leveraging their influence within the national Democratic Party, slaveholders captured a disproportionate share of high federal offices and exercised virtual veto power over congressional legislation. Between 1789 and 1850, slaveholders held the presidency four-fifths of the time, and, notwithstanding northern opposition to slavery's expansion, they greatly increased the amount of American territory open to human bondage. But when slaveholders demanded the repeal of the Missouri Compromise in 1854 and pushed for the introduction of slavery into Kansas—until then "free" territory under the Missouri accord—they overreached. In response to the Kansas-Nebraska Act, middle-class northerners turned against the so-called slave power with a vengeance and rallied with greater intensity than ever before to the antislavery appeal of "free soil" and "free labor."

Significantly, it was not New England's industrialists who led the campaign to end the slaveholders' control over national policy. Abolitionists angrily denounced the unholy alliance of the "lords of the lash" and the "lords of the loom." Nor did leading New York merchants wish to undermine the intersectional and trans-Atlantic trade in cotton that yielded them hefty profits. The new Republican Party of the mid-1850s found its strength elsewhere: among northern farmers, small-scale manufacturers, middling merchants, and a subset of wage earners. The Republicans cared less about the plight of southern slaves than the prospects of northern whites, but they earnestly deemed the slave power a font of evil.

Against the backdrop of Bleeding Kansas, the *Dred Scott* decision, and southern calls for a federal slave code, the Republican Party persuaded a majority of northerners that Democrats could not be trusted to safeguard northern rights. Likewise, against the backdrop of the Republicans' antisouthern rhetoric and John Brown's raid on Harpers Ferry, proslavery "fire-eaters" persuaded a large proportion of whites in the Deep South that the elevation of a Republican to the presidency would endanger their equal rights as American citizens. When Abraham Lincoln won the presidential election of 1860 with a clear-cut majority of the electoral vote, albeit only 40 percent of the popular vote, the stage was set for southern secession and the outbreak of civil war.

The Outcome of the Civil War and Reconstruction

After four years of bloodshed and devastation, the Union Army, helped by emboldened southern blacks and disaffected southern whites, defeated the slave power. Union victory opened the way for the liberation of America's most thoroughly exploited working class. Slaves were not the passive recipients of freedom but active agents in securing it. When peace came, they were eager to exercise their newly recognized rights, both as human beings and as American citizens.

The Thirteenth, Fourteenth, and Fifteenth Amendments to the federal Constitution promised an extraordinary transformation of the American social and political order. Not only would former slaves be guaranteed their freedom, they would enjoy the same civil rights as their former masters and voting rights on par with their fellow Americans regardless of "race, color, or previous condition of servitude." Although the postwar settlement did not include a large-scale transfer of land ownership from planters to the freed people, for a brief period in the late 1860s and early 1870s it looked like southern blacks might be able to rise out of poverty with the help of sympathetic Republican administrations at the state and national levels. Except for Haiti, no other country in the Western hemisphere experienced such a dramatic shift in class relations as the result of slavery's abolition. "The black man is free, the black man is a citizen, the black man is enfranchised, and this by the organic law of the land," exclaimed the ex-slave and radical leader Frederick Douglass in 1870. "One of the most remarkable features of this grand revolution is its thoroughness. Never was revolution more complete."

Unfortunately, this postwar settlement did not endure. Although some ex-slaveholders accepted the legitimacy of Union victory and the principle of black participation in the reconstructed polity, many more turned to terror and intimidation in order to regain control over local and state governments. They found collaborators among poor and middling southern whites whose social identities rested on their sense of racial superiority over blacks. This interclass racist alliance not only quashed the civil and political rights of black Southerners but also broke the will of middle-class white Northerners who had sought to impose a "free labor" vision on the South.

Abraham Lincoln had eloquently sketched the free labor vision in his annual message to Congress in 1861. "Labor is the superior of capital, and deserves much the higher consideration," he declared. Yet he emphasized, "A large majority belong to neither class—neither work for others, nor have others working for them." The epitome of success was the independent proprietor: "Men, with their families—wives, sons, and daughters—work for themselves on their farms, in their houses, and in their shops." The promise of America was that all free men could realistically aspire to this level of independence. "The prudent, penniless beginner in the world, labors for wages awhile, saves a surplus with which to buy tools or land for himself; then labors on his own account another while, and at length hires another new beginner to help him," Lincoln observed. "This is the just, and generous, and prosperous system, which opens the way to all—gives hope to all, and consequent energy, and progress, and improvement of condition to all."

But, in the aftermath of the Civil War, the chances of rising from wage labor to independent proprietorship seemed to diminish in the North. Mammoth capitalist enterprises—many of them corporations enjoying limited liability and legal immortality—came to dominate the fast-growing industrial sector, and small producers denounced the power that major railroad companies exercised over their livelihoods. While magnates like Andrew Carnegie of Carnegie Steel and John D. Rockefeller of Standard Oil were self-made men, their aggressive business strategies and huge fortunes set them far apart economically and socially from those in the middle and working classes. A new American aristocracy began to coalesce—one based mainly on capitalist calculation and the determination to corner markets by whatever means necessary. The new aristocrats did not boast formal titles, and unlike natural aristocrats of the late eighteenth century, they did not hold public office. But with unprecedented wealth at their disposal, they greatly influenced government policies. The muckraker Henry Demarest Lloyd wrote acerbically of Rockefeller's political machinations, "The Standard has done everything with the Pennsylvania legislature, except refine it."

As Northerners lost faith in the free labor vision, they also grew tired of the seemingly endless task of reconstructing the postwar South. Soon after taking office in 1877, President Rutherford B. Hayes, a Republican, removed federal troops from statehouse guard in Louisiana and South Carolina, thereby enabling ex-slaveholders to complete the "redemption" of former Confederate states. Over the next quarter century, the South, with little interference from Washington, would evolve into an apartheid social order. Yet while federal officials refused to intervene on behalf of blacks in the post-Reconstruction South, they proved eager to intervene on behalf of business interests in the North. Hayes established the precedent. When railway workers nationwide walked off their jobs in July 1877, he dispatched federal troops to break the strike and restore economic and social order. A decade and a half after Abraham Lincoln told Congress that "labor is the superior of capital, and deserves much the higher consideration," Hayes acted on a very different assumption: that the rights of workers to pursue their happiness were inferior to the rights of corporations to protect their property and to accumulate capital. A century after the nation's founding, there persisted a profound tension between the American ideal of equal rights and the reality of class inequities sustained by governmental power.

See also agrarian politics; business and politics; economy and politics; Free Soil Party; labor movement and politics; labor parties.

FURTHER READING

Ashworth, John. *"Agrarians" and "Aristocrats": Party Political Ideology in the United States, 1837–1846.* Cambridge, UK: Cambridge University Press, 1987.

Foner, Eric. *Free Soil, Free Labor, Free Men: The Ideology of the Republican Party before the Civil War.* New York: Oxford University Press, 1970.

———. *Reconstruction: America's Unfinished Revolution, 1863–1877.* New York: Harper and Row, 1988.

Fraser, Steve, and Gary Gerstle, eds. *Ruling America: A History of Wealth and Power in a Democracy.* Cambridge, MA: Harvard University Press, 2005.

Freehling, William W. *The Road to Disunion.* 2 vols. New York: Oxford University Press, 1990–2007.

Hahn, Steven. *A Nation under Our Feet: Black Political Struggles in the Rural South, from Slavery to the Great Migration.* Cambridge, MA: Belknap Press of Harvard University Press, 2003.

Oakes, James. *The Ruling Race: A History of American Slaveholders.* New York: Knopf, 1982.

Richardson, Heather Cox. *The Death of Reconstruction: Race, Labor, and Politics in the Post-Civil War North, 1865–1901.* Cambridge, MA: Harvard University Press, 2001.

Sellers, Charles Grier. *The Market Revolution: Jacksonian America, 1815–1846.* New York: Oxford University Press, 1991.

Wilentz, Sean. *The Rise of American Democracy: Jefferson to Lincoln.* New York: Norton, 2005.

GARY J. KORNBLITH

class and politics since 1877

Mainstream pundits and politicians have long proclaimed the absence of class in modern American politics. Leftist scholars have responded by proclaiming the centrality of the working class in the political realm. Both sides have compelling claims. The United States has indeed been distinctive in the way that class has influenced politics, with—at times—a striking lack of a classical European conflict between bourgeoisie and proletariat. As German sociologist Werner Sombart famously put it, referring to the relatively prosperous standard of living for ordinary Americans, radical working-class politics in America have often foundered on "roast beef and apple pie." Yet said proletariat has, at critical moments, been a crucial player in American public life, whether by means of Gilded Age anarchist bomb throwing, Depression era sit-down striking, or the simple act of being a collective electoral presence.

The standard debate about class between mainstream editorial writers and leftists, however, obscures more than it illuminates. What is truly distinctive about American class politics is the strength of that great beast, the middle class. That said, "the middle class" is a creature easy to caricature but difficult to pin down because of its demographic and ideological complexity. And the moral of the story is not, as so many scholars have claimed, that the middle class means the end of "class"; rather, that entity is the crucial starting point for understanding the foundational significance of class in modern American politics.

The Gilded Age

The year 1877 was a time of intense class polarization that witnessed some of the most violent class conflicts in all of American history. With the close of Reconstruction, federal troops moved from South to North to patrol the powder keg that many industrial cities had become as the result of a national railroad strike. Dozens of workers were killed, and millions of dollars' worth of property was damaged from Baltimore to St. Louis, before federal troops ended the 45-day melee.

The display of railroad employees shot down in the street by what many believed were rapacious corporate elites and the minions provided a dramatic opening act to the Gilded Age. And the gilding of the period was indeed quite thick. A self-conscious national elite formed, perhaps for the first time in American history, as merchants and manufacturers, Northerners and Southerners, united across divides of political economy and region to unleash a world historic wave of corporate growth sponsored by both major political parties. Armed not only with guns but with the proud ideology of social Darwinism, these elites were intent on politically marginalizing those outside their charmed circle, particularly an increasingly immigrant-based working class. In turn, workers responded with the most impressive drive for unionization to date. The Knights of Labor organized upward of 700,000 workers, often across the divides of race, gender, and job skills, and appeared poised to move the political economy in a more small-scale and worker-friendly direction.

As the battle between workers and elites lurched toward a momentous bombing at Haymarket Square in Chicago on May 4, 1886 (where seven police officers and an unknown number of citizens were killed in the melee caused by a bomb of unknown origin), it seemed that intense class conflict would be the defining axis of social and political life in the late nineteenth century. Yet matters were not so simple. The Knights of Labor, for example, were as intent on defining themselves as hardworking—and middling—"producers" as they were in forging a proletarian consciousness. (It was actually members of the more cautious and conservative American Federation of Labor, founded by Samuel Gompers in 1886 as a response to the Knights, that articulated a hard-core identity as "workers," set apart from small business owners and other "nonworkers.") Similarly, the Populist Party—the chief expression of rural rebellion during the 1890s—also claimed to stand for those in the middle. Protesting banking, transportation, and monetary policies, the Populists argued in their 1892 Omaha Platform that "from the same prolific womb of governmental injustice we breed the two great classes—tramps and millionaires." During their brief limelight, the Populists elected (sometimes on a fusion ticket with Democrats or Republicans) ten governorships and 45 members of Congress and placed a number of measures, such as that of income tax, firmly on the national agenda.

The middling nature of American politics showed up even more powerfully in mainstream politics. While many voters continued to vote in an "ethnocultural" way, with religion in particular a key point of conflict, the presidential campaigns of candidates from James Garfield to Grover Cleveland were able to assume a fairly moderate middle-class consensus, even amid the class tumult of the period. William McKinley appealed more directly to workers in the 1896 election against William Jennings Bryan, but still did so as an upholder of self-conscious middle-class and Middle American values—the beginnings of a tradition that would hold considerable sway over American electioneering up to the present day.

The Progressive Era

That small farmers like the Populists, as well as exploited workers like the Knights of Labor, were claiming the mantle of *middle class* meant that an important part of the structure of political conflict going into the early

twentieth century was a vigorous ideological battle over who should be included in that term and what it meant. Moreover, professions traditionally associated with the upstanding middle class—business owners, lawyers, doctors, and other white-collar workers—greatly expanded during the era of corporate modernization that lasted from 1877 to 1929. With such a wide range of occupations and experiences making up a culturally contested middle class, it is no surprise that those in the middle did not act in political unity.

This is especially important to recognize when reckoning with the politics of the early twentieth century—the period traditionally known as the Progressive Era. Scholars for more than a half century have argued that the middle class provided the impetus for progressive reform. Whether the anxious and antidemocratic middle class of Pulitzer Prize–winning Richard Hofstadter's *The Age of Reform* (1955) or the confident and modernizing middle class of Robert Wiebe's *The Search for Order* (1967), the middle class latched on to reform not just to stand with Theodore Roosevelt at Armageddon, battling for the Lord, but also to forge their own class identity against ethnic workers and old moneyed elites. Historians such as Hofstadter and Wiebe viewed the middle class as acting in lockstep, with "its" politics flowing out of a monolithic unity. Yet, in both local and national arenas, middling folks acted in quite disparate ways. In some cities, especially in the West, non-elite business owners formed the shock troops for a vigorous and often successful open shop and antiradical movement. In contrast, in places like San Francisco and Portland, Oregon, middling shopkeepers, printers, lawyers, and housewives joined with workers to forge a political culture that upheld the rights of unions and pressed for radical measures of direct democracy and economic equality.

Indeed, no matter how broadly the term is stretched, *middle class* does not cover a good portion of Progressive Era politics. It is applicable to a reformer like Jane Addams, who grew up in privileged circumstances in a small Illinois city but who was not a member of Chicago's upper class, no matter how much she associated with elites during her crusades for worker and immigrant rights. Yet the term cannot encompass one of the two most prominent political figures of the period, the ultra-upper-class Theodore Roosevelt, and it does not fit easily upon the shoulders of the other, Woodrow Wilson. The elite presence within progressive reform, and within Progressive Era politics more generally, was substantial. And, at the other end of the spectrum, the extreme class conflicts characteristic of the Gilded Age by no means disappeared in the generally more prosperous era before World War I. Poor and middling farmers, and their agrarian-oriented representatives in Congress, were a major reason for the rise of national regulatory power over business during the years 1910–20. Union membership also increased substantially with conflict intensifying to such peaks as a general strike in Seattle in 1919; workers also played an important role in campaigns such as those for accidental injury insurance. In tandem, a socialist movement, led by the charismatic (and middle-class) Eugene V. Debs, gained considerable strength. Debs twice gained close to a million votes in his race for the presidency, and Socialists took seats in Congress and plenty of political offices in cities ranging from Schenectady, New York, to Milwaukee, Wisconsin.

Despite the complexities of class politics during the Progressive Era, there was a substantial connection between the middle class and the politics of this period of reform. Middle-class outrage against corporate corruption helped fuel changes from limits on campaign contribution to the regulation of food and drugs. Middle-class concern about economic polarization also led to the passage of minimum wage and maximum hours laws (especially for women). Despite their support for the right to hold private property, ordinary Americans displayed considerable ambivalence about some of the basic structures of capitalism, ranging from the inequality of wealth to the exploitation of labor. Presidents Roosevelt and Wilson often expressed the same concerns as they engaged in a creative debate about the fate of the national economy; the result was the first systematic federal regulation of corporations and financial markets. Middling morality became a hurricane force in American politics, particularly in campaigns for Prohibition and against vice. And middle-class support was crucial for passage of the constitutional amendments of the period—regarding the income tax, the direct election of U.S. senators, Prohibition, and woman suffrage. The middle class never did any of this alone; in particular, much of the working class was attracted to "middle-class" political reform. Yet the middle class was clearly the star of the early twentieth-century political show.

From World War to World War

The period from 1914 to 1945 was an era in which American politics seemed to leapfrog rapidly between liberalism and conservatism. The glow of reform remained in the air from 1914 until the United States entered World War I in the spring of 1917. Immediately afterward, an intense period of reaction gripped the country, subsiding into a period of conservative "normalcy" until 1933—when Franklin D. Roosevelt abruptly switched gears and marched the country through the most sweeping moment of liberal reform in the nation's history.

A good portion of this leapfrogging can be explained by events that were related to but in many ways transcended issues of class: the rise of the United States to the status of a superpower, the greatest economic depression in world history, the growing threat of totalitarian powers in Europe and Asia. Yet part of the turbulence of American politics was also the result of the temporary decentering of the middle class. With the reform impulse of the Progressive Era stifled—even strangled—by the political consequences of World War I, middle-class concerns took a backseat as, first, elites took charge of American politics during the 1920s and then workers asserted power during the 1930s.

Woodrow Wilson feared that war would kill the spirit of reform, and he was right. While scholars have correctly pointed out that liberal and leftist politics survived during the war and into the 1920s, Wilson himself launched a devastatingly effective campaign against any perceived radicalism, with the net cast quite widely. Socialists and other labor radicals were jailed, and leaders of organized labor had little choice but to announce a suspension of strikes during the course of the war—a war that, at home, was in many ways run by corporate elites. A massive strike wave immediately followed the war, and the birth of bolshevism in the United States led to ardent fears of the overturning of the social order. Yet the strikes were, in the main, put down—often violently—and unions hemorrhaged membership throughout the 1920s.

Workers played a role in politics during this decade, particularly in their successful advocacy of what was arguably its most important piece of legislation—the Immigration Act of 1924, which strictly limited migration from countries outside of northern and western Europe. Also, Protestant workers joined avidly with their middling and elite counterparts to form the backbone for the brief but troubling rise to power of the Ku Klux Klan in the North during the early 1920s. Yet, overall, the period saw a remarkably strong consensus that, in the words of President Calvin Coolidge, "the chief business of the American people is business." Corporate chieftains such as Andrew Mellon were major players during the Republican administrations of Warren Harding, Coolidge, and Herbert Hoover. While Hoover, in particular, had creative ideas about how to bring government and business leaders together, few in the 1920s mainstream questioned the primary purpose of politics: the nurturing of corporate growth.

The start of the Great Depression in 1929 did not immediately change that purpose, but the inauguration of Franklin Roosevelt did. Roosevelt was no radical, and indeed his own elite pedigree was as blue-blooded as it gets. Moreover, Roosevelt made no bones that his ultimate goal in reforming the economic system was to save capitalism. Still, Roosevelt, who by 1936 was denouncing "economic royalists," transformed the political system and became a symbol for the hopes of ordinary Americans that the national government could work for them.

The capstone of this effort to transform American society was, arguably, the National Labor Relations Act of 1935, or Wagner Act, which officially recognized the rights of most workers to organize unions and established federal machinery to uphold workers' right to representation. The national government went from its Gilded Age role of often violently repressing to becoming, in many ways, the chief enforcer of workers' rights. Of course, Roosevelt and other national politicians responded to labor out of more than a sense of patrician obligation. They recognized the newfound power of workers, many of whom were attracted to radical ideas and needed to be convinced that mainstream politics could serve their needs. Nor did these workers simply rely on the benevolent power of Washington, D.C. The Wagner Act unleashed a historic set of strikes, with autoworkers taking over factories in Michigan and textile workers in South Carolina mobilizing their rural communities in support of unions. Employer response was often violent, but (at least in the North) just as often accommodating, and by the end of the 1930s, a markedly different political economy—one that actively incorporated unionization—had been born.

There were significant limits to this new New Deal order. The continued failure of unions in the South—the function of the power of white southern elites who skillfully wielded their economic as well as political power over disenfranchised African Americans—provided a substantial regional obstacle to the extension of liberalism. Even within successful New Deal legislation, there were significant restrictions to the empowering of "the working class." The Social Security Act of 1935— arguably the most important piece of New Deal legisla-

tion—provided pensions for millions of workers but left out the most exploited (and, not coincidentally, heavily nonwhite) laborers: in particular, agricultural workers and domestic servants.

The (Short) American Century

Class politics did not take a holiday during World War II, but they were generally suppressed in the global fight against fascism. They returned with a vengeance in the war's immediate aftermath, however, with another postwar strike wave accompanying an attempt by procorporate politicians to reverse the New Deal. The chief symbol of such reaction was the Taft-Hartley Act of 1947, which put significant restrictions on labor organization and required union officials to take loyalty oaths. Yet, despite the newly conservative legal and political environment, the overall pattern of class politics from the 1940s to the 1970s was far from traditional. Rather, at the height of "the American Century," many workers became so prosperous and secure that in many ways the divide between "the working class" and "the middle class" threatened to dissolve.

If Taft-Hartley symbolized the dreams of the most conservative of Republicans, the so-called Treaty of Detroit best epitomized the new class order. In 1950, United Auto Workers president Walter Reuther negotiated a five-year contract with the "big three" car manufacturers. Workers gave up hopes of control over the shop floor along with their rights to strike during the term of the contract. In exchange, they received generous benefits in areas ranging from health insurance to pensions, unemployment to vacations. Cost-of-living wage adjustments ensured that workers would remain prosperous in times of inflation. As a result of such contracts, union membership reached an all-time high during the postwar period. While this broad treaty left out plenty of workers, overall economic inequality declined substantially as the economy went through a prolonged expansion, driven in large part by mass demand for consumer goods.

As factory workers prospered, they increasingly moved to the suburbs. And while those who labored at manual and semiskilled tasks in gargantuan factories never stopped thinking of themselves as "workers" while on the job, they increasingly took on self-conscious identities as part of the "middle class" while living as homeowners, taxpayers, and members of neighborhood associations. Indeed, many contemporary intellectuals argued that all genuinely ideological problems were off the table, as the American political economy had produced the most inclusive middle class in world history. With the simultaneous rise of the civil rights movement, and the promise of a triumphant "color-blind" liberalism, it appeared that the American Dream was nearing fulfillment.

Deindustrialization, Globalization, and the Continuing Significance of Class

All too quickly the bottom fell out of this dream of a classless utopia. During the 1960s, the nation discovered that poverty, whether among whites in Appalachia or blacks in Watts, had not disappeared. A persistent strain of inflation, originating in President Lyndon Johnson's attempts to feed a war machine while also significantly expanding social programs, turned virulent in the late 1970s. Deindustrialization hit the Northeast and Midwest particularly hard during the 1960s and 1970s and was followed in succeeding decades by a globalization that moved much of American manufacturing outside the nation's borders. Union membership, particularly in the private sector, declined dramatically, with President Ronald Reagan (himself a former union chief) by 1981 taking on the mantle of proud union buster.

The promise of racial egalitarianism fell away as issues of class became increasingly intertwined with those of race. These abstractions had always been connected, and one popular argument among scholars holds that working-class revolution never came about primarily because of white workers' long-standing investment in their racial privilege. Yet it was not until the dismantlement of structures of legal racism that class became so visible within racial conflicts. The busing crises of the 1970s, which largely pitted white working-class ethnics against the black poor and working class in cities such as Boston, best symbolized a class conflict that took on the surface complexion of simple racial struggle. White workers who had previously been loyal to the New Deal order defected from the party of Roosevelt, becoming first "Reagan Democrats" and then volatile swing voters. In turn, members of a small but growing African American middle class joined their class brethren in a flight to the suburbs, where schools remained largely (and legally) segregated because of neighborhood residential patterns based on inequalities of wealth and income.

As the politics of prosperity and liberalism fell away, middle-class and working-class Americans began to increasingly practice the politics of populism. One of the longest-standing traditions in American civic life, populism could take many different forms, from Alabama governor George Wallace's and Pat Buchanan's implicit appeals to race when defending hard-working (white) "little" people against liberal elites and immigrants, to Ralph Nader's attempts to embrace racial egalitarianism while focusing on the depredations of big business. While some commentators have remarked that the language of populism in its invoking of "the people" has meant the abandonment of a hard-edged rhetoric of class, the opposite in fact seemed to be the case. When Democrats such as Bill Clinton and Al Gore spoke out on behalf of a neglected and forgotten middle class, for example, Republicans went to great lengths to charge their colleagues across the aisle with "class warfare."

These Republicans were more right than they knew. While much of this ideological battle played out as cynical and even duplicitous campaign rhetoric, the struggle over the middle class was the real thing, the authentic version of American class politics. And with the decline in socialism and social democracy in Europe, it now appears that the United States has not been "deficient" in the way that class has played out in its political history. Rather, with their own appeals to a populist middle class, politicians in the rest of the world may now be catching up to us.

See also business and politics; conservatism; labor movement and politics; populism; race and politics; socialism.

FURTHER READING

Beckert, Sven. *Monied Metropolis: New York City and the Consolidation of the American Bourgeoisie, 1850–1896*. New York: Cambridge University Press, 2001.

Cohen, Lizabeth. *Making a New Deal: Industrial Workers in Chicago, 1919–1939*. New York: Cambridge University Press, 1990.

Dubofsky, Melvyn. *The State and Labor in Modern America*. Chapel Hill: University of North Carolina Press, 1994.

Fraser, Steve, and Gary Gerstle, eds. *Ruling America: A History of Wealth and Power in a Democracy*. Cambridge, MA: Harvard University Press, 2005.

Hofstadter, Richard. *The Age of Reform: From Bryan to FDR*. New York: Knopf, 1955.

Johnston, Robert D. *The Radical Middle Class: Populist Democracy and the Question of Capitalism in Progressive Era Portland, Oregon*. Princeton, NJ: Princeton University Press, 2003.

Kazin, Michael. *The Populist Persuasion: An American History*. 2nd ed. Ithaca, NY: Cornell University Press, 1998.

Lassiter, Matthew D. *The Silent Majority: Suburban Politics in the Sunbelt South*. Princeton, NJ: Princeton University Press, 2006.

Lukas, Anthony. *Common Ground: A Turbulent Decade in the Lives of Three American Families.* New York: Knopf, 1985.

"The Omaha Platform" Downloadable from http://history matters.gmu.edu/d/5361/.

Wiebe, Robert. *The Search for Order, 1877–1920.* New York: Hill and Wang, 1967.

ROBERT D. JOHNSTON

cold war

See Korean War and cold war.

colonial legacy

At first glance, the colonial legacy for the political history of the United States seems obvious. Schoolbooks tell of the gathering in 1619 of Virginia's earliest representative assembly, which developed into the House of Burgesses, and of the Mayflower Compact two years later, establishing government among the settlers of Plymouth by mutual consent. Fast forward to the eve of independence, and it seems that the legacy of Virginia's gathering and the Pilgrims' agreement was fully worked out.

By the third quarter of the eighteenth century, each of the mainland British colonies south of newly founded Nova Scotia had its assembly. In all save Pennsylvania there was a council, which served as upper legislative house, court of appeals, and advisory body. Each colony had a governor, appointed by the king in most cases, named in Pennsylvania and Maryland (and formerly in New York, New Jersey, and the Carolinas) by the province's hereditary "proprietor," and locally chosen in Connecticut and Rhode Island. Election intervals and units of representation varied enormously: Massachusetts chose a new assembly every year, with all towns having the right to send a delegate if the town meeting chose. In neighboring New York, assembly elections could take place at intervals of up to seven years, and three of the province's quasi-feudal manors had the right to send their own delegates, which meant sending the landlord's choice. But there were elections everywhere from Georgia to New Hampshire, and those elections could be fought ferociously.

Above it all loomed the vaunted British government of king, lords, and commons, acting together as the king-in-Parliament. Colonials acknowledged the sovereign authority of the British monarch. In practice, they also acknowledged that Parliament could legislate for them, if the larger British good required it. Until 1763 neither Britons "at home" nor Britons in the American "dominions" gave serious thought to what Parliament could or could not do about America. Rather than worry, colonials basked in the half-formed thought that their local institutions served them well, protecting their "British liberties," much as Parliament served the realm. If anything, they placed greater trust in the crown than did metropolitan Britons.

Neither in Britain nor in the colonies could the king rule by decree. Louis XIV boasted that in France "l'état, c'est moi" (the state is myself) and a Spanish monarch could impose the royal will with the simple formula "yo, el rey" (I, the king). But the young Prince of Wales who was to become George III rejoiced that in Britain the king-in-Parliament, not the king alone, made laws, imposed taxes, and spent public money. This, thought the student prince, was the glory of the British crown and the secret of British liberty. His subjects-to-be agreed, in the metropolis and the colonies alike. So did envious continental Europeans, most notably the highly respected French political thinker Charles de Secondat, Baron de Montesquieu.

Fast forward again, this time a mere three decades, and the legacy of colonial political experience seems obvious. In place of a king named George, there was a president, also named George, whose public demeanor seemed kingly. He worked with two new institutions, a U.S. House of Representatives that clearly owed a great deal to Britain's House of Commons, and a U.S. Senate that resembled the House of Lords. The provinces had become states, with governors, state senates, and state assemblies. The continuity appears clear.

But Britain's North American empire had foundered on that very legacy. Had the colonial institutions existed "of right," fundamentally independent of Parliament's power and its will? Or had they been mere conveniences, to which Parliament could give orders and alter if it chose to do so? That question bedeviled colonial political thinkers after 1764, when Parliament began to assert its power over colonial life. When it proved to have no acceptable answer, the empire fell apart.

By 1790, the old order's fatal problems seemed resolved in two ways. One was that both the U.S. government and the separate state regimes drew their power directly from "the people" as codified in formal constitutions. No longer was there was any question of state institutions deriving power from the sovereign central government and being subject to its veto or its requirements, as Parliament had claimed to be the case with their colonial forebears. Federal and state governments were creatures of their respective peoples, where sovereignty lay.

The other issue that seemed settled was that the United States had its own colonial problem, including rebellion. Vermont declared its independence from New York in 1777, which called it a "pretended state" and its people "revolted subjects" until 1791. For a few years the "State of Franklin" tried to break free from North Carolina. Meanwhile settlers and enslaved black people were spilling west into country that they were seizing from its Indian owners. Like the original East Coast colonists, they required order and structure. But rather than form permanently subordinate colonies, they established "territories." These could win full statehood, with self-government and full participation in national politics. Except for Vermont, Kentucky, Tennessee, Texas, California, and West Virginia, all of the states from Ohio to Hawaii went through the process, which transformed what had been a major British problem into an American public ritual.

The Larger Politics of Colonial America

Despite these points, the legacy of colonial political life is neither simple nor straightforward. Historians have devoted a vast amount of energy to the study of East Coast, Anglophone, white, male institutional political life. The greatest political legacy of the colonial era was the creation of a robust, white, male-dominated republic that rapidly spanned the continent. But there is little point in simply updating previous writings that have dealt with it admirably. Let us start instead with the "continental turn" that historians have taken in understanding "colonial America." Current understanding no longer restricts the subject to the Anglophone East Coast.

Instead, different European communities and native peoples created a colonial social formation across much of the continent as early as 1700. Ultimately, all of that formation's people were linked to distant European centers of power. The elements that bound them to Europe and to one another included the emerging idea of race; the uncertain boundaries of empire; the justified belief by native peoples that the land belonged to them; hostility among tribes; conflicting ideas about the ownership and

use of land; enslavement; divergent religions; the damage wrought by unseen microbes; the impact of larger non-human species such as horses, swine, cattle, and wheat; and merchant-capitalist commerce that turned American products into commodities and introduced metallurgy, textiles, firearms, and alcohol to the American world. Colonial politics, including diplomacy and war, emerged from and dealt with all of these elements.

Politics is about the disposition of power, and of the resources, obligations, liabilities, and possibilities that power can command. From the very beginning of the permanent European presence, European "powers" that were becoming national states maintained that they could dispose of the American world and everything it contained, people and resources alike, all seeking to clothe their actions with legality.

The initial politics of empire was about turning a mere supposition of distant authority into a working imperial system, and it took two forms. One was to crush existing structures and impose new ones. That happened in the sixteenth century when the ruins of the Aztec capital Tenochtitlan became the foundation of Mexico City. It happened on a much smaller scale among the New England Indians who submitted to Puritan authority and became denizens of "praying towns." It happened, too, on Spanish missions in eighteenth-century California.

The other form was to link existing native ways to European ones in a hybrid fashion, which might be an informal but recognized pattern. Spaniards and Caddos in eighteenth-century Texas agreed that peace could come "in the form of a woman," meaning that women's presence at a parlay signified peaceful intentions in a world where war seemed to spread everywhere. Some arrangements congealed into de facto institutions, most notably the Covenant Chain. Developing out of the formal claims to neighboring spaces by the province of New York and by the Five Haudenosaunee (Iroquois) Nations, the Covenant Chain expanded from those two central links to include British provinces from Massachusetts to Virginia, together with many native groups. None of these arrangements was formal in the sense of being codified. All created some sort of "middle ground" between European and native ways. But exactly the same informality characterized the unwritten constitution of documents, usages, precedents, customs, and common law that set the rules of British political life.

The continent-spanning and culture-crossing politics of colonial America is apparent on the maps and other symbolic devices that imperial and provincial cartographers and native people produced. All of these were political in the sense that they expressed claims to power. None could display "definitive" lines in the manner of later political maps of the American republic and its separate states. Taken together, imperial, provincial, and native images show how geographical boundaries overlapped and how lines of political power tangled.

Perhaps the best-known case is the way that New France, Pennsylvania, and Virginia all claimed title to the forks of the Ohio River, where Pittsburgh now stands. To vindicate Virginia's claim, Governor Robert Dinwiddie sent the young Colonel George Washington there in 1754, instructing him to order the French to depart from their recently constructed Fort Duquesne. Virginia's northern boundary supposedly stretched indefinitely from the Potomac River to include the whole Ohio Valley, the western Great Lakes region, and beyond. On British maps, at least, the Old Dominion's southern boundary extended to the Pacific coast. So did the boundaries of the two Carolinas and Georgia. French, Spaniards, and native people of many sorts had other ideas. The politics of colonial empire emerged from those conflicting claims.

Within the supposedly British zone, Massachusetts, New Hampshire, and New York all claimed what is now Vermont. The Abenaki Indians disagreed. Massachusetts maintained that it overleaped New York's settled zone and had a claim to the Lake Ontario Plain, which the Iroquois nations understood to be their own. Writing to London in 1774, New York's final royal governor described how his province sprawled beyond Detroit, by virtue of an Iroquois deed to the Niagara Peninsula executed in 1702. But a very detailed map of the same province that was in preparation as the governor wrote his report placed New York's western boundary only a little west of Albany, where the country of the Iroquois Nations began.

Native people also tried to map the politics of American space. Their devices including Iroquois and Huron wampum belts and Catawba and Chickasaw maps traced on deerskin. The Iroquois Hiawatha Belt, now repatriated from the New York State Museum to the Onondaga Nation, shows the Five Nations linked to one another in a symbolic longhouse, with its eastern (Mohawk) and western (Seneca) doorkeepers. Hidden within its imagery is an elaborate pattern of relationships that the Iroquois had worked out before contact and which served them well. Some historians argue that what the Iroquois had wrought formed the original template for the U.S. Constitution. Others doubt the point, but nobody denies the magnitude of the Iroquois achievement.

Other belts identified the 51 holders of hereditary Haudenosaunee sachemships and the members of the Covenant Chain, colonies and tribes alike. Seventeenth-century Huron Indians used wampum to depict the relationship among their four nations, and, later, their confederacy's relationship with the French.

The Catawba deerskin map of 1723, traced on a paper copy that now is in Britain's Public Records Office, shows the detailed arrangements among the people who form its center and the world around them. It signifies their own villages with circles, and whites' communities with squares. Nearby South Carolina is divided into smaller squares, probably indicating city blocks in Charles Town, together with a simply drawn ship at anchor. More distant Virginia is just a box. Chickasaws used similar imagery. Wampum belts and native maps alike located the centers of affairs and power among native peoples, not in Quebec, Boston, Albany, Philadelphia, Williamsburg, Charles Town, New Orleans, San Antonio de Bexar, or Santa Fe, let alone Paris, London, or Madrid.

Throughout the colonial era, white scribes recorded conferences between their leaders and native peoples. These written observations rank among the fundamental documents of colonial political history. Though taken down in a European tongue, the records show growing sophistication on both sides about the language and ritual of negotiations and about the subjects under discussion. Ultimately, the participants attempted to resolve what is perhaps the most fundamental of all political problems, how various groups of people are to deal with one another without violence.

This intensely political conversation dealt increasingly with the most basic and intractable of colonial problems, which was the ownership, use, and disposition of land. Talk could and did collapse into warfare. During the late seventeenth and early eighteenth centuries, trouble broke out from Maritime Canada to New Mexico. Abenaki fought with northern New Englanders; lower New England Algonquians with Puritans; Iroquois with Algonquians' Abenaki, and French; Susquehannocks with Virginians; Yamasees and Tuscaroras with Carolinians; and, far to the west, Pueblo Indians with Spaniards. These people were not strangers. The New England Algonquians knew that befouling the Bible would infuriate the Puritans; the Pueblos understood the same point about the sacred vessels of the Catholic Mass.

A new pattern gradually emerged, as people worked out lasting accommodations. Iroquois and French did so in 1701 at Montreal, creating neutrality for the battered Indians, whatever British officials said about the Five Nations "depending" on them as de facto British subjects. In 1692, 12 years after the Pueblo Indians had driven Spaniards out of their country, they allowed them to return. But no longer did the Spaniards attempt total domination. Kivas, representing traditional ways, shared village space with missionary churches.

At the heart of the informal but enduring colonial situation was the reality that neither colonizers nor natives enjoyed full power over either their own lives or the lives of the people they encountered. Ultimately, all of them were linked to distant Europe—some tightly, others loosely. Everyone was "colonial" in a more meaningful and profound sense than conventional images of quaint costumes and imitation Parliaments. All of them took part one way or another in colonial politics.

Slavery and Freedom

Two major events took place in Virginia in 1619. One was the gathering of a representative assembly. The other was the arrival of a Dutch warship bearing 20 people who were sold to Virginians for labor in their burgeoning tobacco fields. The records described those people as "Negars."

There is more than coincidence to the events. The people sold from the Dutch vessel did not enter formal slavery when they stepped onto Virginia soil. Quite possibly, their shipboard slavery ended, because neither Virginia nor any other British possession recognized enslavement. Formal servitude did exist, in a debased, often brutal form from its English counterpart, and labor-hungry masters used many tricks and devices to extend their servants' terms. But some servants, both black and white, survived their terms, and at least a few of those survivors prospered.

Elsewhere in America those people would have been slaves. Spaniards simply transferred their law of slavery, codified under the medieval King Alfonso X "the Wise," to their American realms. After some debate, the Spanish Crown forbade the enslavement of Indians, but Bartholeme de las Casas, the Dominican priest who successfully argued for that outcome before the king, had no doubt that Africans could replace enslaved Indians. The Dutch brought both the law and the practice of slavery to New Netherland when they founded it. But English colonizers did not bring slavery with them—they had to create it themselves.

Barbadians did so first, establishing a slave law in 1636 to govern the Africans whom they were starting to import as sugar emerged as the West Indies cash crop. Three

decades later, the Barbadian founders of Carolina simply carried their island's slave law with them to the mainland colony. In 1641 Puritan Massachusetts created the earliest mainland slave law. The backhanded language in the statute read, "There shall never be any bond slaverie unles it be lawfull Captives taken in just warres, and such strangers as willingly selle themselves or are sold to us." They did enslave Indians, massively so after they defeated King Philip's forces in 1676. By that time, Carolina colonists were developing a sizable Indian slave trade that ultimately reached as far as the Great Plains. As late as 1776, South Carolina patriot leader William Henry Drayton was promising backcountry small farmers that they could seize Cherokee lands and enslave their former owners if the farmers joined the movement for independence from Britain.

Virginia, however, provides the most complex and probably most important case. Some evidence suggests that it treated black people unequally from the very start. In 1630 one Virginian was punished for "lying with a Negro." But we do not know the gender of that "Negro," so the punishment may have been for sodomy rather than a sign of black degradation. Virginia's slave law took shape slowly, as black servants lost such privileges as bearing firearms, intermarrying with whites, and owning personal property; as black escapees from servitude did not have their terms extended upon recapture, a clear indication that they already were serving for life; and as the condition of children came to follow the condition of their mothers, who were open to sexual exploitation.

What does seem clear is that, by 1700, Virginia slavery existed in both law and practice. It also seems clear that the emergence and consolidation of Virginia black slavery had a great deal to do with Virginia's transformation from a place where white colonists lived in mutual hostility to one where a local elite was able to rule through elected, representative institutions.

Perhaps this was aristocracy, since there was no question that the planter elite was in charge. Possibly it was democracy, since the elite ruled in the name of a larger population that gave its consent every time small-property-holding farmers and artisans gathered to elect a planter to speak for them in the House of Burgesses. Maybe the elite was secure, surrounded by rituals and customs that brought all white Virginians together. Conceivably, like its Carolina counterparts, the elite was beleaguered by discontented white folk as well as by native and black people with ample reason to be hostile.

Perhaps the real point is that Virginia's elite ruled through the House of Burgesses, not through outright force. Whatever the explanation, the creation and stabilization of racially defined plantation slavery went hand in hand with the eighteenth-century Virginia political settlement that eventually produced George Washington, Thomas Jefferson, and James Madison.

North of the plantation zone, New York developed the largest slave population. Unlike Virginia's increasingly cohesive eighteenth-century rulers, New York's elite was factious to the point of outright enmity. But when it appeared in 1741 that a major plot was taking shape among slaves and bottom-of-the-population white people in New York City, members of the elite turned the rumors to their political advantage. They launched a series of show trials that led to exile for some of the accused, hanging for others, and, for certain slaves caught up in the terror, burning at the stake. This, too, was political. Both in the North and South a pattern of enduring racial politics was taking shape. In some ways, that pattern's legacy endures today.

British Liberties in America
On both sides of the Atlantic, Britons took great pride in the belief that they enjoyed greater freedom than any other people on earth. Others might have argued with them, given the chance. Spaniards construed *liberdades* (liberties) as specific exemptions and privileges, not as absolute rights, a meaning close to what English colonists also thought. South Carolina slaves who sought to escape from the misery of the rice swamps invariably headed south, where they knew they would find a welcome from Florida's Spanish rulers. Nonetheless, in the formal political realm the Britons had reason for pride. British America, like Britain itself, possessed an electoral politics unlike anything seen in Quebec or Paris, Havana or Mexico City. Here lay the segment of the larger colonial political structure that developed into the civic life of the United States.

Historians have pored over the formal politics of the elections and legislation of the Anglophone provinces. Some have pondered whether colonial politics was "democratic" or "aristocratic." That question now seems badly posed. Proportionately, far more white, adult colonial males were able to vote than in any other place on earth, but the "better sort" remained in charge. Others have asked which colony's public life was most "American." Setting aside the quintessentially American tangle of slavery and race, does that mean that a colony

developed competitive, interest-group politics and perhaps even outright organized partisanship?

If so, Pennsylvania might qualify. Not happy about his province's politics, William Penn admonished its settlers, most of them fellow Quakers, to "be not so governmentish." The Penn family's hereditary proprietorship suggests that they were shopkeepers, but in reality they were lords, wielding more actual political power and enjoying greater potential wealth than any baron, viscount, earl, marquess, or duke in Britain.

Potentially, the Penns were the richest family on earth, thanks to their province's enormous resources of coal, iron ore, and oil. Southeastern Pennsylvania was so fertile that it, together with the northern Chesapeake Bay area, became the main supplier of wheat and flour to both the West Indies and Western Europe. Freehold farmers to whom the Penns sold the land—not rent-paying tenants—grew the wheat, and life among them could be good. But the farmers, together with many of Philadelphia's merchants, professional people, artisans, and ordinary laborers, came to resent Penn domination, as well as the Penns' refusal to allow the provincial assembly to tax the ruling family's own land, treating it instead as if it were sovereign property.

Tension mounted as religious and ethnic differences appeared. William Penn's sons left the Quaker faith for the Church of England, turning Quaker settlers from probable—albeit "governmentish"—allies into opponents. Attracted by Pennsylvania's reputation as "the best poor man's country" and a haven for religious dissenters, sectarian Protestants from Bohemia and Germany, and Scotch-Irish Presbyterians, migrated, together with a sprinkle of Catholics and Jews. Split by religion, ethnicity, and language; divided by the gulf between country and town; and broken again by issues of social class, Pennsylvanians were not a harmonious lot. Their public life was raucous and competitive from the province's founding until independence.

This was the milieu in which Benjamin Franklin emerged as a public figure. Franklin knew about elections in which armed mobs intimidated opponents and where Anglicans decried Presbyterians as "Piss-Brutearians." No fan of immigrants, Franklin dismissed German farmers (*Bauern*) as "boors." Aligning with the Quakers, he sought in 1765 to end the Penn family's rule and make Pennsylvania a royal province. Perhaps he had himself in mind for the office of governor. Indeed, his son William did become the final royal governor of neighboring New Jersey through the excellent connections that Benjamin Franklin had acquired as his own star rose. The father recovered from his faux pas of seeking direct royal government. In 1775, as the British Empire was collapsing, father and son found themselves bitterly emplaced on opposite sides. Their family tragedy, too, was a consequence of colonial political life, and the Franklins were not the only family to suffer such a split.

New York's political history under the English was even more vicious. After the Glorious Revolution, Captain Jacob Leisler seized power in 1689 in the name of the joint monarchs, William and Mary. But he could not consolidate his position, and a new royal governor had him tried and executed for treason. Years of partisan hatred resulted. The frequently told tale that Governor Edward Hyde, Lord Cornbury (in office 1701–8), was a public cross-dresser seems to be an urban legend. It developed out of hostile rhetoric about him "playing the Queen," a reference to his high-handed rule in the name of his cousin, Queen Anne. But Cornbury's political enemies jailed him the moment his successor arrived, and he lost the immunity that had gone with his office. Governor Danvers Osborne committed suicide within days of arriving in New York in 1753. The cause was a personal tragedy, but realizing what he had to govern could not have helped.

One of New York's enduring characteristics was its conquered Dutch population, which slowly adapted to English rule but which did not cohere as an ethnic bloc. Another of its qualities was great estates that legally possessed quasi-feudal standing. A third was New York City, with a public life that had been diverse, conflicted, and raucous from the very beginning. At the very least, New York was "factious," with no pretense of easy agreement among its elite or its various plebeians. At its worst, its public life could be lethal. The legacy of that public life was a disruptive, transforming revolution.

Was New England any more harmonious? Certainly its people were more homogeneous, being overwhelmingly English and largely Puritan in their ancestry and heritage. At the beginning, some Puritan villagers had cultivated harmony, showing by their behavior that they took seriously John Winthrop's advice to present a "model of Christian Charitie" to the world. But, from the start, Winthrop's own Boston was riven with division and it seems that, for every cohesive, placid village, there was another whose people seemed primed to argue with one another.

Connecticut, New Haven, and Rhode Island emerged from disputes as the supposedly unified Puritan founders of Massachusetts Bay found that they could not agree among themselves. As the founding generation was dying off in the mid-seventeenth century, Massachusetts disputed sharply about the requirements for church membership. Salem's notorious witchcraft trials have been so intensely studied that many explanations seem plausible. But the town of Salem failed completely to contain its internal tensions, spilling from what politics might have settled—had it worked—into bloodshed, particularly of its women.

Eighteenth-century New Englanders conflicted just as sharply. In town meetings and street gatherings alike, the wave of religious enthusiasm that historians call the "Great Awakening" broke congregations and whole towns open, on matters that emerged from Christian doctrine and practice and that had deep roots in social experience. Where non-Congregational churches emerged among New Englanders—be they Anglican, Presbyterian, Baptist, or Quaker—discord followed. The theory of town meetings was to create harmony, but Boston's town meetings turned raucous under popular leaders such as Samuel Adams. Prominent Bostonian Thomas Hutchinson, who spurned popularity for the sake of royal favor, became so disliked that when his elegant house caught fire in 1749, townsfolk tried to block volunteer firefighters, crying "Let it burn!" Sixteen years later, when Britain was trying to impose its Stamp Act, another Boston crowd invaded and wrecked Hutchinson's mansion, leaving it an empty, ruined shell.

"Regulators" in the North Carolina interior raised armed resistance to a provincial government that seemed not to serve them at all. In the mid-eighteenth century, land rioters wracked New Jersey, setting up a countergovernment with its own courts and "gaols" back "in the woods." Ethnic tensions among Protestant whites turned into racial hatred against Indians in central Pennsylvania. New York's Hudson Valley simmered with discontent between landlords and tenants and broke into a large rebellion of farmers in 1766. One reason was conditions on the great estates; another was belief that landlords had defrauded the river's Indians, a point with which the Indians agreed and on which they took a protest all the way to London. A third reason was the uncertainty of New York's boundary with New England. During the last ten years under British rule, similar problems led to outright insurgency in North Carolina and in the Green Mountain zone between Lake Champlain and the Connecticut River claimed by both New York and New Hampshire. Given the contentious future of American electoral politics, there were few places in the English colonies that could not claim to be among its starting places.

The Colonial Legacy

Half a century ago, Clinton Rossiter called the colonial era the "seedtime" of the Republic. At the time it seemed to historians that there was a fundamental consensus among the white English-speaking males who seemed to be the only people who counted. Now historians perceive that far more early Americans—and not just the people who did not speak English—who were not free, male, or white were somehow "present." We understand that such people participated in a colonial order that spread far beyond what the different sorts of settlers claimed were their boundaries.

Adding the elements of that order together, we can see that it bore more than a passing resemblance to the European ancien régime that had spawned it. French historian Fernand Braudel has called it "a mosaic of a hundred different colours: modern, archaic, primitive, or curious mixtures of all these." Like early modern Europe, colonial America had simply grown. It comprised a whole, but it had no coherence. A large part of the story of its politics was a constant struggle for mastery among tribes, empires, provinces, and settler communities, a struggle that nobody actually won in any "definitive" way. Another large part of that story was the emergence of a politics in which the supposed contrast between "savagery" and "civilization" melded into a politics of race, and in which race could justify the oppression of slavery and the driving back of the land's first peoples.

In the colonial era, those peoples possessed enough political, economic, and—if necessary—military power to resist, and so they were driven back only slowly or not at all. But the long thrust of colonial politics was to simplify the tangle of the American political map. Swedes in the Delaware Valley, Dutch from there to the upper Hudson, and the French from the mouth of the St. Lawrence to the mouth of the Mississippi all fell to the surging power of dynamic Britain and its East Coast provinces. But their relationship, too, is best understood as part of the ancien régime's unwieldy tangle. Britain's attempt to assert its mastery provoked another great struggle, this time among people who had agreed proudly that they all were Britons.

That struggle led to a sizable group of those people concluding that they were Britons no longer, and to giving themselves the means to assert and achieve a mastery that nobody in the old order had been able to maintain.

The republic they created completed the simplification that had long been under way. Its constitution established a "supreme law of the land." Its spreading political map gradually wiped out the overlapping, conflicting lines of possession and authority that colonial maps had shown. In this sense, the victorious revolutionaries were continuing a politics of expansion and consolidation that had run through the colonial era.

Colonial politics continued in two other ways. The American republican order only appeared to be similar to the British monarchical order that it overthrew and replaced. Washington was a president, not a king. Sovereign power in the United States lay among its people. But East Coast colonials had learned to compete in the public arena, and they carried what they had learned into their raucous republican future.

They also carried the colonial era's politics of race, reduced now to two propositions. The first, a direct continuation from colonial life, was that slavery was the normal condition in America of people whose ancestors had come, or who came themselves, from Africa. The second, different from colonial life, was that native people and their ways had no place in the new order, a point worked out in practice long before it became official public policy with the Indian Removal Act of 1830.

But there was another difference as well. The colonial version of politics had assumed human differences. John Winthrop, first governor of colonial Massachusetts, came close to theorizing the old order with his proposition that "God Almighty in his most holy and wise providence, hath soe disposed of the condition of mankind, as in all times some must be rich, some poore, some high and eminent in power and dignitie; others mean and in submission." In practice, that belief gave many sorts of people space in which to maneuver around one another, though it also meant that there was no intellectual problem with holding some people in the absolute meanness and submission that was slavery.

Theoretically, at least, the American Revolutionaries broke with that belief, asserting instead that "all men are created equal." Their practice, of course, fell far short of their theory. But the politics that their revolution inaugurated opened a new ground for contestation, a ground whose deep, continuing theme and enduring problem has been to resolve the contradictions between the theory and the harsh realities of American life.

See also era of a new republic, 1789–1827; Native Americans and politics; slavery; war for independence.

FURTHER READING

Anderson, Fred. *Crucible of War: The Seven Years War and the Fate of Empire in British North America, 1754–1766.* New York: Knopf, 2000.

Bailyn, Bernard. *The New England Merchants in the Seventeenth Century.* Cambridge, MA: Harvard University Press, 1955.

———. *The Ordeal of Thomas Hutchinson.* Cambridge, MA: Harvard University Press, 1955.

———. *The Origins of American Politics.* New York: Knopf, 1968.

Barr, Juliana. *Peace Came in the Form of a Woman: Indians and Spaniards in the Texas Borderlands.* Chapel Hill: University of North Carolina Press, 2007.

Becker, Carl Lotus. *The History of Political Parties in the Province of New York, 1760–1776.* Madison: University of Wisconsin Press, 1909.

Beeman, Richard R. *The Varieties of Political Experience in Eighteenth-Century America.* Philadelphia: University of Pennsylvania Press, 2004.

Bellesiles, Michael A. *Revolutionary Outlaws: Ethan Allen and the Struggle for Independence on the Early American Frontier.* Charlottesville: University Press of Virginia, 1993.

Blackburn, Robin. *The Making of New World Slavery: From the Baroque to the Modern, 1492–1800.* London: Verso, 1997.

Blackhawk, Ned. *Violence across the Land: Indians and Empires in the Early American West.* Cambridge, MA: Harvard University Press, 2006.

Bonomi, Patricia U. *A Factious People: Politics and Society in Colonial New York.* New York: Columbia University Press, 1971.

———. *The Lord Cornbury Scandal: The Politics of Reputation in British America.* Chapel Hill: University of North Carolina Press, 1998.

Boorstin, Daniel J. *The Americans: The Colonial Experience.* New York: Random House, 1958.

Bouton, Terry. *Taming Democracy: "The People," the Founders, and the Troubled Ending of the American Revolution.* New York: Oxford University Press, 2007.

Boyer, Paul, and Stephen Nissenbaum. *Salem Possessed: The Social Origins of Witchcraft.* Cambridge, MA: Harvard University Press, 1974.

Breen, T. H., and Stephen Innes, *"Myne Owne Ground": Race and Freedom on Virginia's Eastern Shore, 1640–1676.* New York: Oxford University Press, 1980.

Brooke, John. *The Heart of the Commonwealth: Society and Political Culture in Worcester County, Massachusetts, 1713–1861.* Amherst: University of Massachusetts Press, 1992.

Brown, Kathleen M. *Good Wives, Nasty Wenches, and Anxious Patriarchs: Gender, Race, and Power in Colonial Virginia.* Chapel Hill: University of North Carolina Press, 1996.

Brown, Robert E. *Middle Class Democracy and the Revolution in Massachusetts.* Ithaca, NY: Cornell University Press, 1955.

Brown, Robert E., and B. Katherine Brown. *Colonial Virginia 1705–1786: Democracy or Aristocracy?* East Lansing: Michigan State University Press, 1964.

Brückner, Martin. *The Geographic Revolution in Early America: Maps, Literacy, and National Identity.* Chapel Hill: University of North Carolina Press, 2006.

Bushman, Richard L. *From Puritan to Yankee: Character and the Social Order in Connecticut, 1690–1775.* Cambridge, MA: Harvard University Press, 1968.

Cayton, Andrew, and Fredrika Teute, eds. *Contact Points: American Frontiers from the Mohawk Valley to the Mississippi, 1750–1830.* Chapel Hill: University of North Carolina Press, 1998.

Cogley, Richard W., *John Eliot's Mission to the Indians before King Philip's War.* Cambridge, MA: Harvard University Press, 1999.

Countryman, Edward. "'Out of the Bounds of the Law:' Northern Land Rioters in the Eighteenth Century." In *The American Revolution: Explorations in the History of American Radicalism,* edited by Alfred F. Young, 37–69. Dekalb: Northern Illinois University Press, 1976.

———. *A People in Revolution: The American Revolution and Political Society in New York, 1760–1790.* Baltimore, MD: Johns Hopkins University Press, 1981.

———. "'To Secure the Blessings of Liberty:' Language, the Revolution, and American Capitalism." In *Beyond the American Revolution: Explorations in the History of American Radicalism,* edited by Alfred F. Young, 123–48. Dekalb: Northern Illinois University Press, 1993.

Davis, David Brion. *The Problem of Slavery in Western Culture.* Ithaca, NY: Cornell University Press, 1966.

Dayton, Cornelia Hughes. *Women before the Bar: Gender, Law, and Society in Connecticut, 1639–1789.* Chapel Hill: University of North Carolina Press, 1995.

Demos, John Putnam. *Entertaining Satan: Witchcraft and the Culture of Early New England.* New York: Oxford University Press, 1982.

Dennis, Matthew Dennis, *Cultivating a Landscape of Peace: Iroquois-European Encounters in Seventeenth-Century America.* Ithaca, NY: Cornell University Press, 1992.

Dunn, Richard S. *Sugar and Slaves: The Rise of the Planter Class in the English West Indies, 1624–1713.* New York: Norton, 1973.

Ekirch, A. Roger. *"Poor Carolina": Politics and Society in Colonial North Carolina 1729–1776*. Chapel Hill: University of North Carolina Press, 1981.

Fenton, William N. *The Great Law and the Longhouse: A Political History of the Iroquois Confederacy*. Norman: University of Oklahoma Press, 1998.

Foote, Thelma Wills. *Black and White Manhattan: The History of Race Formation in Colonial New York City*. New York: Oxford University Press, 2004.

Gallay, Alan. *The Indian Slave Trade: The Rise of the English Empire in the American South, 1670–1717*. New Haven, CT: Yale University Press, 2002.

Greene, Jack P. *The Quest for Power: The Lower Houses of Assembly in the Southern Royal Colonies, 1689–1776*. Chapel Hill: University of North Carolina Press, 1963.

———. "The Reappraisal of the American Revolution in Recent Historical Literature." In *The Reinterpretation of the American Revolution, 1763–1789*, edited by Jack P. Greene, 2–74. New York: Harper and Row, 1968.

Greven, Philip J. *Four Generations: Population, Land, and Family in Colonial Andover, Massachusetts*. Ithaca, NY: Cornell University Press, 1970.

Grinde, Donald J., and Bruce E. Johansen. *Exemplar of Liberty: Native America and the Evolution of Democracy*. Los Angeles: University of California American Indian Studies Center, 1991.

Gronim, Sara Stidstone. "Geography and Persuasion: Maps in British Colonial New York." *William and Mary Quarterly*, 3rd ser., 58 (April 2001), 373–402.

Gutierrez, Ramon A. *When Jesus Came the Corn Mothers Went Away: Marriage, Sexuality, and Power in New Mexico, 1500–1846*. Stanford, CA: Stanford University Press, 1991.

Hackel, Stephen W. *Children of Coyote, Missionaries of St. Francis: Indian-Spanish Relations in Colonial California, 1769–1850*. Chapel Hill: University of North Carolina Press, 2005.

Havard, Gilles. *The Great Peace of Montreal of 1701: French-Native Diplomacy in the Seventeenth Century*. Translated by Phyllis Aronoff and Howard Scott. Montreal: McGill-Queen's University Press, 2001.

Heyrman, Christine Leigh. *Commerce and Community: The Maritime Communities of Colonial Massachusetts, 1790–1850*. New York: Norton, 1984.

Higginbotham, A. Leon. *Shades of Freedom: Racial Politics and Presumptions of the American Legal Process*. New York: Oxford University Press, 1996.

Innes, Stephen. *Labor in a New Land: Economy and Society in Seventeenth-Century Springfield*. Princeton, NJ: Princeton University Press, 1983.

Isaac, Rhys. *The Transformation of Virginia, 1740–1790*. Chapel Hill: University of North Carolina Press, 1980.

Jennings, Francis. *The Ambiguous Iroquois Empire: The Covenant Chain Confederation of Indian Tribes from Its Beginnings to the Lancaster Treaty of 1744*. New York: Norton, 1983.

———. *Empire of Fortune: Crowns, Colonies, and Tribes in the Seven Years War in America*. New York: Norton, 1988.

Kammen, Michael G. *Deputyes and Libertyes: The Origins of Representative Government in Colonial America*. New York: Knopf, 1968.

Karlsen, Carol F. Karlsen. *The Devil in the Shape of a Woman: Witchcraft in Colonial New England*. New York: Norton, 1987.

Kars, Marjoleine. *Breaking Loose Together: The Regulator Rebellion in Pre-Revolutionary North Carolina*. Chapel Hill: University of North Carolina Press, 2002.

Katz, Stanley Nider. *Newcastle's New York: Anglo-American Politics, 1732–1753*. Cambridge, MA: Harvard University Press, 1968.

Klein, Milton M. *The Politics of Diversity: Essays in the History of Colonial New York*. Port Washington, NY: Kennikat, 1974.

Klein, Rachel N. *Unification of a Slave State: The Rise of the Planter Class in the South Carolina Back Country, 1760–1808*. Chapel Hill: University of North Carolina Press, 1990.

Knaut, Andrew. *The Pueblo Revolt of 1680: Conquest and Resistance in Seventeenth-Century New Mexico*. Norman: University of Oklahoma Press, 1995.

Koehler, Lyle. *A Search for Power: The "Weaker Sex" in Seventeenth-Century New England*. Urbana: University of Illinois Press, 1980.

Kulikoff, Allan. *Tobacco and Slaves: The Development of Southern Cultures in the Chesapeake, 1680–1800*. Chapel Hill: University of North Carolina Press, 1986.

Landers, Jane. *Black Society in Spanish Florida*. Urbana: University of Illinois Press, 1999.

Lemon, James T. *The Best Poor Man's Country: A Geographical Study of Early Southeastern Pennsylvania*. Baltimore, MD: Johns Hopkins University Press, 1972.

Lepore, Jill. *The Name of War: King Philip's War and the Origins of American Identity*. New York: Knopf, 1998.

———. *New York Burning: Liberty, Slavery, and Conspiracy in Eighteenth-Century Manhattan*. New York: Knopf, 2005.

Lockhart, James. *The Nahuas after the Conquest: A Social and Cultural History of the Indians of Central Mexico, Sixteenth through Eighteenth Centuries*. Stanford, CA: Stanford University Press, 1992.

Lockridge, Kenneth A. *A New England Town: The First Hundred Years, Dedham, Massachusetts, 1636–1736*. New York: Norton, 1970.

McConville, Brendan. *The King's Three Faces: The Rise and Fall of Royal America, 1680–1776*. Chapel Hill: University of North Carolina Press, 2006.

———. *Those Daring Disturbers of the Public Peace: The Struggle for Property and Power in Early New Jersey*. Ithaca, NY: Cornell University Press, 1999.

Merrell, James K. *Into the American Woods: Negotiators on the Pennsylvania Frontier*. New York: Norton, 1999.

Merritt, Jane T. *At the Crossroads: Indians and Empires on a Mid-Atlantic Frontier, 1700–1763*. Chapel Hill: University of North Carolina Press, 2003.

Morgan, Edmund S. *American Slavery, American Freedom: The Ordeal of Colonial Virginia*. New York: Norton, 1975.

Murrin, John M. "Political Development." In *Colonial British America: Essays in the New History of the Early Modern Era*, edited by Jack P. Greene and J. R. Pole, 408–56. Baltimore, MD: Johns Hopkins University Press, 1984.

Nader, Helen. *Liberty in Absolutist Spain: The Hapsburg Sale of Towns, 1516–1700*. Baltimore, MD: Johns Hopkins University Press, 1990.

Nadlehaft, Jerome J. *The Disorders of War: The Revolution in South Carolina*. Orono: University of Maine at Orono Press, 1981.

Narrett, David E. *Inheritance and Family Life in Colonial New York City*. Ithaca, NY: Cornell University Press, 1992.

Nash, Gary B. *Quakers and Politics: Pennsylvania, 1681–1726*. Princeton, NJ: Princeton University Press, 1968.

———. *The Urban Crucible: Social Change, Political Consciousness, and the Origins of the American Revolution*. Cambridge, MA: Harvard University Press, 1979.

Nobles, Gregory H. *Divisions throughout the Whole: Politics and Society in Hampshire County, Massachusetts, 1740–1775*. Cambridge, UK: Cambridge University Press, 1983.

Norton, Mary Beth. *Founding Mothers and Fathers: Gendered Power and the Forming of American Society*. New York: Knopf, 1996.

———. *In the Devil's Snare: The Salem Witchcraft Crisis of 1692*. New York: Knopf, 2002.

Onuf, Peter S. *The Origins of the Federal Republic: Jurisdictional Controversies in the United States, 1775–1787*. Philadelphia: University of Pennsylvania Press, 1983.

Pole, J. R. "Historians and the Problem of Early American Democracy." *American Historical Review* 68 (1962), 626–46.

Powell, Sumner Chilton. *Puritan Village: The Formation of a New England Town*. Middletown, CT: Wesleyan University Press, 1963.

Reis, Elizabeth. *Damned Women: Sinners and Witches in Puritan New England*. Ithaca, NY: Cornell University Press, 1997.

Richter, Daniel K. *The Ordeal of the Longhouse: The Peoples of the Iroquois League in the Era of European Colonization*. Chapel Hill: University of North Carolina Press, 1992.

Rink, Oliver A. *Holland on the Hudson: An Economic and Social History of Dutch New York*. Ithaca, NY: Cornell University Press, 1986.

Ritchie, Robert C. *The Duke's Province: A Study of New York Politics and Society, 1664–1691*. Chapel Hill: University of North Carolina Press, 1977.

Rossiter, Clinton. *Seedtime of the Republic: The Origin of the American Tradition of Political Liberty*. New York: Harcourt Brace, 1953.

Rutman, Darrett. *Winthrop's Boston: Portrait of a Puritan Town, 1630–1649*. New York: Norton, 1972.

Schwarz, Philip J. *The Jarring Interests: New York's Boundary Makers, 1664–1776*. Albany: State University of New York Press, 1979.

Seed, Patricia. *Ceremonies of Possession in Europe's Conquest of the New World, 1492–1640*. Cambridge, UK: Cambridge University Press, 1995.

Shklar, Judith N. *American Citizenship: The Quest for Inclusion*. Cambridge, MA: Harvard University Press, 1991.

Shoemaker, Nancy. *A Strange Likeness: Becoming Red and White in Eighteenth-Century North America*. New York: Oxford University Press, 2004.

Skemp, Sheila L. *William Franklin: Son of a Patriot, Servant of a King*. New York: Oxford University Press, 1990.

Taylor, Alan. *American Colonies: The Settling of North America*. New York: Viking, 2001.

Trigger, Bruce G. *The Children of Aataentsic: A History of the Huron People to 1660*. Montreal: McGill-Queen's University Press, 1976.

Tully, Alan. "Colonial Politics." In *A Companion to Colonial America*, edited by Daniel Vickers, 288–310. Malden, MA: Blackwell, 2003.

———. *Forming American Politics: Ideals, Interests, and Institutions in Colonial New York and Pennsylvania*. Baltimore, MD: Johns Hopkins University Press, 1994.

———. *William Penn's Legacy: Politics and Social Structure in Provincial Pennsylvania, 1726–1755*. Baltimore, MD: Johns Hopkins University Press, 1977.

Vickers, Daniel, ed. *A Companion to Colonial America*. Malden, MA: Blackwell, 2003.

Wallace, Mike, and Edwin G. Burrows. *Gotham: A History of New York City to 1898*. New York: Oxford University Press, 1999.

Waselkov, Gregory A. "Indian Maps of the Colonial Southeast." In *Powhatan's Mantle: Indians in the Colonial Southeast*, edited by Gregory A. Waskelov, Peter H. Wood, and

Tom Hatley, 292–343. Lincoln: University of Nebraska Press, 1989.

Washburn, Wilcomb E. *The Governor and the Rebel: A History of Bacon's Rebellion in Virginia*. Chapel Hill: University of North Carolina Press, 1957.

Weber, David S. *The Spanish Frontier in North America*. New Haven, CT: Yale University Press, 1993.

White, Richard. *The Middle Ground: Indians, Empires, and Republics in the Great Lakes Region, 1650–1815*. Cambridge, UK: Cambridge University Press, 1991.

Williams, Robert A. *The American Indian in Western Legal Thought: The Discourses of Conquest*. New York: Oxford University Press, 1990.

———. *Linking Arms Together: American Indian Visions of Law and Peace, 1600–1800*. New York: Oxford University Press, 1997.

Winthrop, John. "Christian Charitie, a Modell Hereof" (1630). Reprinted in *The Founding of Massachusetts: Historians and the Sources*, edited by Edmund S. Morgan, 191–204. Indianapolis, IN: Bobbs-Merrill, 1964.

Wood, Gordon S. *The Americanization of Benjamin Franklin*. New York: Penguin, 2004.

———. *The Creation of the American Republic, 1776–1787*. Chapel Hill: University of North Carolina Press, 1969.

———. *The Radicalism of the American Revolution*. New York: Knopf, 1992.

Wood, Peter H. *Black Majority: Negroes in Colonial South Carolina from 1670 through the Stono Rebellion*. New York: Knopf, 1974.

Wright, Esmond. *Franklin of Philadelphia*. Cambridge, MA: Harvard University Press, 1986.

Zuckerman, Michael. "Authority in Early America: The Decay of Deference on the Provincial Periphery." *Early American Studies* 1 (2003), 1–29.

EDWARD COUNTRYMAN

communism

Communism, a movement inspired by the 1917 Bolshevik Revolution in Russia, never attracted many adherents in the United States, peaking in the late 1930s with 75,000 members. Nonetheless, over the years Communists played significant roles in a number of social movements.

Communism came to the United States in the fall of 1919, a year of revolutionary upheaval. Vladimir Lenin and Leon Trotsky, the leaders of the precariously established Soviet government in Russia, looked abroad for aid, hoping sympathizers in Europe and elsewhere would open new fronts in the international struggle against capitalism. In March 1919, Russian Communist leaders presided over the founding in Moscow of the Communist International (also referred to as the Comintern), a federation of pro-Soviet revolutionary parties. The Comintern was intended to supplant the old Socialist International, scorned by Communists for its failure to prevent the outbreak of World War I.

A Party of a New Type

Lenin had long before decided that the Bolsheviks should be a "party of a new type," governed by the principle of "democratic centralism." After the success of the Bolshevik Revolution, these became the central organizational principles of the ideology known as Marxism-Leninism. Unlike the loosely organized socialist parties, the new Leninist parties would function as monoliths, whose members carried out decisions of their leaders without dissent. The Comintern's member parties were similarly required to carry out policies handed down from above.

No Americans attended the Comintern's founding meeting in Moscow, but there was strong sentiment within the left wing of the American Socialist Party (SP) and the radical labor federation, the Industrial Workers of the World (IWW), to affiliate. American journalist John Reed—who had been in the Russian capital of St. Petersburg during the revolution and whose 1919 account of the Bolshevik triumph, *Ten Days That Shook the World,* proved influential—was among those determined to create an American Communist Party. But faction fighting led in September 1919 to the creation of two rival Communist parties.

Soviet leaders regarded the Americans as squabbling amateurs, who would have to be taken in hand. Orders were dispatched from Moscow to end the division between the two Communist groups, but it was not until May 1921 that the merger was effected. Meanwhile, the Russian civil war drew to a close, and the Union of Soviet Socialist Republics (USSR) was founded, uniting most of the territory formerly part of the Czarist Empire. Another landmark event in Soviet history took place in 1922, when Joseph Stalin became general secretary of the Soviet Communist Party. Lenin suffered a stroke that year and played a diminished role in the affairs of the USSR until his death in January 1924.

Secrecy and Sectarianism

American Communists functioned as an underground movement in the early 1920s, partly in imitation of the prerevolutionary Bolsheviks and partly out of necessity. In 1917–18, the U.S. government cracked down on antiwar dissenters, sending hundreds to prison, including SP leader Eugene Debs. Attacks continued in the "Red scare" years after the war. Attorney General A. Mitchell Palmer launched a series of raids across the country on the second anniversary of the Bolshevik Revolution, November 7, 1919, resulting in the arrest of thousands of foreign-born Communists and anarchists, 200 of whom were deported to Russia aboard a ship dubbed the "Soviet ark."

American Communists began to emerge from underground in 1922, under the leadership of the Cleveland-born Charles E. Ruthenberg, with the formation of an open party, at first called the Workers Party, then the Workers (Communist) Party, and finally, in 1929, the Communist Party, USA (CPUSA). National headquarters were set up in Chicago but were moved to New York City, the center of the party's strength, in 1927. For the next two decades the party's activities were directed from the ninth floor of a building it owned at 35 East 12th Street. Secret financial subsidies from the Soviets helped pay for the CPUSA's operations.

Throughout the 1920s, factional struggles within the CPUSA mirrored those taking place among rival leaders of the USSR. In 1927 a group of American Communist leaders, including James P. Cannon, sided with Trotsky against Stalin. Trotsky was sent into exile, while the Trotskyists were expelled from the CPUSA.

Ruthenberg died in 1927 and was succeeded as general secretary (the party's leading post) by Jay Lovestone, a former student activist at the City College of New York. Lovestone's tenure in office was short-lived; he was deposed in 1929 on orders of the Comintern, having backed another soon-to-be-disgraced Soviet leader, Nicolai Bukharin. At the start of the 1930s, Stalin entrusted leadership of American communism to a hitherto obscure party functionary named Earl Browder, a former Kansas City bookkeeper. William Z. Foster, who in the 1920s headed the party's efforts to "bore from within" the American Federation of Labor (AFL) as leader of the Communist-organized Trade Union Education League (TUEL), had hoped to win the top spot for himself and became a bitter rival of Browder in the years to come.

In the 1920s most American Communists were foreign-born, with the largest groups coming from Finnish and Jewish backgrounds. The Communists launched a daily newspaper in Yiddish, the *Morgen Freiheit*, in 1922, two years before they started a daily newspaper in English, the *Daily Worker*. Although the party counted in its ranks some experienced labor organizers, like Foster, Communists had little influence in the broader union movement of the 1920s. In 1922 the party formed a youth affiliate, the Young Workers League, later renamed the Young Communist League (YCL), a group that gave Communists their first significant influx of native-born English-speaking members. Communists helped launch a monthly literary magazine, *New Masses*, in 1926 (which became a weekly in 1934); the magazine, along with a writers and artists organization called the John Reed Clubs, founded in 1929, began to give the Communists inroads among intellectuals and artists.

The Impact of the Great Depression

Stalin consolidated his control of the Soviet leadership in 1928, ending a period of relative moderation in the Soviet Union's political and economic life. He announced a crash industrialization program, to prepare the USSR for a new outbreak of "imperialist war." And he predicted a new wave of economic crisis and revolutionary activity in the capitalist world—a so-called third period. Communist parties around the world adopted this militant perspective, which seemed vindicated by the onset of the Great Depression of the 1930s. Instead of seeking united fronts with other radical parties around common aims, they denounced socialists as "social fascists." And they bitterly opposed the new reform-minded administration of President Franklin D. Roosevelt. Communist trade unionists in the United States abandoned attempts to "bore from within" the AFL, and formed their own openly revolutionary unions. Communist efforts to turn their Trade Union Unity League (TUUL) into a revolutionary alternative to the AFL proved futile. They were somewhat more successful in organizing Unemployed Councils to demand relief payments for laid-off workers.

This ultrarevolutionary stance hindered the party's growth and influence, compared to their rivals on the Left. The Communists started the decade with about 7,500 members. That number doubled in the next two years to about 15,000, but during the same period, the Socialist Party grew to 25,000 members.

But in the mid-1930s, American Communists saw their membership and their influence increase dramatically as they once again shifted their political line. Following the accession to power of Adolf Hitler in 1933, Stalin grew increasingly concerned about the threat to the Soviet Union posed by Nazi Germany. Hoping to negotiate collective security treaties with the Western democracies, Stalin ordered Communists around the world to build broad antifascist alliances.

"Communism Is Twentieth-Century Americanism"

In the United States the new policy, known as the Popular Front, led to the abandonment of the slogan "Towards a Soviet America," and its replacement with the less threatening "Communism Is Twentieth Century Americanism." Communists no longer denounced Roosevelt and even lent him backhanded support in the 1936 election, although they ran Browder as their presidential candidate that year. Communist-organized Popular Front organizations like the League Against War and Fascism, the American Youth Congress, the American Student Union, the League of American Writers, and the National Negro Congress, among others, attracted many non-Communist adherents. Much of this growing influence was a product of the party's staunch antifascism, particularly during the Spanish Civil War of 1936–39, when 3,000 American volunteers, about 80 percent of them Communists, went to Spain to fight against fascists and in defense of the Spanish Republic in the Comintern-organized International Brigades. In the later 1930s, for the first time, a majority of American Communists were native-born. About 10 percent of the party was made up of African Americans, attracted by the CPUSA's vigorous support for civil rights.

From 1935 on, Communists also played an important role in labor organizing. Mine union leader John L. Lewis broke with the craft-union-oriented AFL in 1935 to form the Committee (later Congress) of Industrial Organizations (CIO). Although staunchly anti-Communist, Lewis hired Communist organizers to help build new industrial unions in mass production industries like steel, auto, and electrical manufacturing.

By 1938 the CPUSA was ten times the size it had been in 1930. But for all its apparent adaptation to American political life, the party remained firmly under Soviet control. CPUSA leaders traveled to Moscow on an annual basis to consult about political strategy. In the era of the Soviet purges, when millions were rounded up for prison, exile, or execution, the CPUSA defended Stalin as a benevolent leader. Some American Communists were recruited into clandestine espionage rings in the United States.

Wartime Gyrations

The CPUSA proved its loyalty to the Soviet Union in August 1939, when in a stunning reversal of policy, Stalin signed a "nonaggression pact" with Hitler. Within days, the Nazis invaded Poland, setting off World War II. American Communists dutifully denounced both sides in what they labeled the "Second Imperialist War." The vast array of Popular Front organizations they had created over the past half-decade collapsed in disarray. In a "little Red scare," Communists found themselves under legal attack. Communist teachers were fired from the City College of New York, while Browder was imprisoned in 1940 on a passport violation charge. Congress passed the Smith Act in 1941, giving the federal government the power to prosecute those who conspired to advocate the overthrow of the government through force and violence.

When the Nazis invaded the Soviet Union in June 1941, Communists switched from being antiwar isolationists to prowar interventionists. With the United States and the USSR allied against Nazi Germany after American entrance into the war in December 1941, the Communists' pro-Soviet sympathies ceased to stigmatize them as disloyal. In 1943, as a goodwill gesture to his Western Allies, Stalin dissolved the Comintern. Browder, who had been released from prison, attempted a bold political experiment by dissolving the CPUSA and replacing it with a new and more loosely organized Communist Political Association (CPA). Despite such gestures, Communist loyalties to the Soviet cause remained undiminished; during the war, Soviet intelligence agents expanded their espionage efforts in the United States, recruiting American Communists to help penetrate the top-secret Manhattan Project in Los Alamos, New Mexico, where the atomic bomb was being developed.

During the war, Roosevelt met with Stalin on several occasions, and hopes for the continued postwar unity of the so-called Grand Alliance remained high through the spring of 1945. But tensions between the two countries were already rising when Roosevelt died in April. His successor, Harry Truman, was determined to stand up to Soviet expansionism in Europe and elsewhere. Before another year passed, the term *cold war* had come to describe the conflict between the United States and its allies, on the one hand, and the Soviet Union, its new Eastern European empire, and, after 1949, Communist China, on the other. Meanwhile, in June 1945 Browder was deposed as the American Communist leader for what was seen in Moscow as his heresy in dissolving the party. The CPUSA was restored with Browder's long-time rival Foster as chairman and Eugene Dennis as general secretary.

Cold War and McCarthyism

Under new leaders, the CPUSA veered leftward. The decision to launch a third-party campaign in 1948, with former vice president Henry Wallace as the presidential nominee of the new Progressive Party, would prove a disaster for the Communists. Wallace's Election Day showing was unimpressive and Truman was returned to the White House. Eleven Communist-led unions were expelled from the CIO in 1949 for breaking with the labor movement in endorsing Wallace. At the same time, the Communist Party was coming under fierce legal assault. The Truman administration initiated a loyalty review procedure for federal employees that resulted in the firing of several thousand suspected Communists. Private industries, including the Hollywood studios, fired or blacklisted hundreds of others for suspected Communist sympathies. The Federal Bureau of Investigation (FBI), under the directorship of J. Edgar Hoover, launched an intense campaign to infiltrate and disrupt the party. And federal prosecutors indicted 11 top Communists, including the party's general secretary Dennis, for violation of the Smith Act (between 1949 and 1956 over a hundred Communist leaders would be tried under the Smith Act and sentenced to lengthy prison terms). Sensational revelations about Soviet wartime espionage and the conviction and execution of Julius and Ethel Rosenberg for atomic espionage, reinforced public hostility to communism. Anticommunism provided the issue that launched the careers of some of the nation's most influential politicians, including Wisconsin senator Joseph McCarthy, and California congressman Richard M. Nixon.

By 1956 a battered Communist Party retained about 20,000 members. But that year the party was struck by two devastating blows from abroad. The first was the revelation in the spring of the text of a secret speech that Soviet premier Nikita Khrushchev had delivered to a Soviet Party congress in Moscow earlier in 1956 denouncing the bloody crimes committed by Stalin, who had died in 1953. The second was the outbreak of rebellion against Communist rule in Hungary in the fall of 1956, which was brutally suppressed by the Soviet Red Army. Thousands of American Communists resigned in disillusionment.

Fade to Irrelevance

The 1960s saw a minor revival of the CPUSA, under the leadership of Gus Hall, who became general secretary in 1959. The Communists' greatest asset in the 1960s was the young African American activist Angela Davis, who became famous for her fiery rhetoric and run-ins with the law. However, the CPUSA's decision to endorse the Warsaw Pact invasion of Czechoslovakia in 1968, overthrowing a reform-oriented Communist government, led to a new round of resignations. In an ironic twist, when reformer Mikhail Gorbachev took over the leadership of the Soviet Union in the 1980s, Hall and other orthodox Communists in the United States finally started to oppose Soviet policies. Following the collapse of the Soviet Union in 1991, the CPUSA split between the hard-liners and Gorbachev-influenced reformers, with the latter group, which included Davis, leaving to form the Committees of Correspondence for Democracy and Socialism. Hall remained the leader of the CPUSA until his death in 2000, when he was succeeded by Sam Webb.

See also anticommunism; radicalism; socialism.

FURTHER READING

Draper, Theodore. *The Roots of American Communism.* New York: Viking, 1957.

Haynes, John, and Harvey Klehr. *Verona: Decoding Soviet Espionage in America.* New Haven, CT: Yale University Press, 1999.

Healey, Dorothy, and Maurice Isserman. *Dorothy Healey Remembers: The Life of an American Communist.* New York: Oxford University Press, 1990.

Isserman, Maurice. *Which Side Were You On? The American Communist Party during the Second World War.* Middletown, CT: Wesleyan University Press, 1982.

Klehr, Harvey. *The Heyday of American Communism: The Depression Decade.* New York: Basic Books, 1985.

MAURICE ISSERMAN

Confederacy

The Confederacy refers to the Confederate States of America, the nation that existed between 1861 and 1865 and fought the United States of America during the Civil War. It encompassed 11 states (Virginia, North Carolina,

South Carolina, Georgia, Florida, Alabama, Mississippi, Louisiana, Texas, Arkansas, and Tennessee), though it laid claim to other, disputed, border states (Maryland, Missouri, and Kentucky). Although the Confederate state existed for scarcely more than four years, a sense of Confederate nationalism or identity persisted throughout the nineteenth century and, some might argue, well into the twentieth and twenty-first.

Politically, the Confederacy stood for several interrelated principles. First and foremost, its founders and citizens believed that their nation should be a slaveholding one, and they brooked no opposition to the "peculiar institution." Underlying that belief in the rightness of slavery were other ideas, including a staunch belief in states rights, a desire for a nonpartisan government, and a conviction that the Confederacy, not the United States, represented the perfection of the Founding Fathers' vision.

Creation

The Confederacy was born out of the secession of southern slaveholding states, but secession itself preceded the Confederacy. Abraham Lincoln's election in November 1860 gave longtime southern nationalists the excuse they needed to secede from the Union. South Carolina, long the home of the most fervent proslavery and states' rights ideologues, seceded first on December 20, 1860. The other Deep South states quickly followed, and by February 1, 1861, seven states had left the Union (in order: South Carolina, Mississippi, Florida, Alabama, Georgia, Louisiana, and Texas).

Secessionists were sensitive to criticism of their actions as illegitimate and were careful to provide constitutional justifications for their actions. They saw secession not as revolution but as an alternate and, in their minds, correct reading of constitutional provisions. Secessionists subscribed to the "compact theory" first elucidated in the Virginia and Kentucky Resolutions of 1798. According to this theory, the individual states delegated their authority to the federal government when they ratified the Constitution and could therefore withdraw it through another convention. In general, the secession ordinances passed at these conventions rescinded ratification of the Constitution. The secessionists believed themselves to be the true heirs of the Founding Fathers, and their rhetoric frequently hearkened back to 1776. They argued that the Republicans were the true revolutionaries, citing as evidence Lincoln's "A house divided" speech and William H. Seward's "irrepressible conflict" speech. Secession and its

rhetoric also took on an air of emotionalism and celebration, particularly in the lower South. Southerners had felt under siege for over a year, and secession provided a sort of catharsis or relief. Standard manifestations of nineteenth-century political culture, like parades, fireworks, and celebrations, accompanied each secession convention. Additionally, as each state seceded, it sent commissioners to sitting conventions, encouraging the slaveholding states still in the Union to jump on the bandwagon as well.

There were, however, opponents to secession within the slaveholding states and particularly in the border states of the upper South, the same regions that voted for the Constitutional Unionist John Bell in the 1860 election. These Unionists counseled moderation and urged their southern brethren to wait until Lincoln took overt action against them. Unlike in the lower South states, many of these conventions had Unionist majorities, until the firing on Fort Sumter and Lincoln's call for troops in April 1865. Many Unionists hoped to broker a compromise between the Lincoln administration and the new Confederacy.

The Confederate nation appears to have been born almost fully formed. On February 4, 1861, delegates from the seven seceded states met in Montgomery, Alabama, essentially to create their new nation. In large part because they believed themselves to be the heirs to the Founding Fathers, they drew heavily on the U.S. Constitution. This served a double function: first, it allowed them to create a nation quickly, without having to build everything from scratch. Second, and more importantly, it also gave the Confederate people a ready-made myth of national origin and eased the shifting of their allegiances from the United States to the Confederate States.

The Confederate Constitution adopted in March 1861 in Montgomery was almost identical to the U.S. Constitution, with a few differences that highlighted the Confederacy's shifts in ideological emphasis. In the preamble, it omitted the general welfare clause and added that each ratifying state was acting "in its sovereign and independent character," thus signaling that this was a true confederation of states. It prohibited protective tariffs and congressional appropriations for internal improvements, thus addressing a perennial source of southern resentment and complaint. Interestingly, the Confederate Constitution limited the president to one six-year term but gave him a line-item veto.

The greatest differences regarded slavery. The Confederate Constitution explicitly guaranteed slavery in both states and territories, charging that "no bill of attainder, ex post facto law, or law denying or impairing the right of negro property in slaves shall be passed." It did, however, ban the importation of slaves from outside the Confederacy. This may seem surprising, for many of the same men (especially South Carolinians) who had been agitating for secession during the 1850s had also been pushing for a reopening of the international slave trade. But the delegates to the Montgomery convention were also well aware that eight slaveholding states had not yet seceded and that the residents of these border states would not support the importation of slaves. Thus, banning the international trade was seen as a necessary measure to gain the support of the upper South states and ensure their eventual secession.

A similar impulse was at work in the selection of the Confederate president. The Montgomery convention was the site of considerable jockeying for political position, especially over the choice of president. The convention eventually selected Jefferson Davis, of Mississippi, a compromise candidate who was not even in attendance at Montgomery. Davis was clearly experienced in both foreign and domestic matters, as he had been secretary of war under Franklin Pierce as well as a senator and congressman. He was also more of a moderate, and this too appealed to the upper South. Extremists like William Lowndes Yancey of Alabama and South Carolina's Robert Barnwell Rhett were largely left out of the government. The vice presidential slot went to Alexander Stephens of Georgia, head of the Constitution-drafting committee. The process was also important to the Confederates: they liked the fact that Davis was chosen by consensus, no unseemly elections, no outright dissent. In this, they saw themselves returning to an earlier model, without dangerous factionalism. Whether a nation could survive based on states' rights and nonpartisanship remained to be seen.

On April 12, 1861, Confederate forces fired on Fort Sumter, a Union holdout on an island in Charleston Harbor. Thirty-four hours later, on April 14, the Union forces surrendered. On April 15, President Lincoln declared South Carolina in rebellion against the United States and issued a proclamation calling 75,000 state militiamen into federal service for 90 days in order to put down the insurrection. In the North, his call was answered eagerly, and a fever of excitement swept through the populace. Nearly every northern state sent more than its quota of men. The remaining slave states were placed in a more difficult position.

The eight slave states remaining in the Union (Delaware, Maryland, Virginia, Tennessee, North Carolina, Missouri, Kentucky, and Arkansas) were generally horrified by Lincoln's request that they take up arms against their "southern brethren." All but Maryland and Delaware rejected Lincoln's request. Most of the people in these border states had been conditional Unionists, and this was simply too much for them to accept. Within a matter of days, Virginia's convention voted to secede and offered Richmond as the new site of the Confederate capital. Within a matter of weeks, Arkansas, North Carolina, and Tennessee seceded from the Union, and the Confederacy was complete.

Nationalism

The vast majority of white Southerners, even those who had been Unionists throughout the winter of 1860–61, transferred their allegiance to the Confederacy with few backward glances. In large part, this transition was eased by the ways that Confederates drew on staples of American political culture and made them their own. Confederates carefully cast themselves as their heirs of the American Revolution and often drew explicit comparisons between the spirits of '76 and '61. George Washington's image adorned the Great Seal of the Confederacy and Confederate postage stamps. By drawing on the Revolutionary past, Confederates rejected antebellum bursts of southern sectionalism as exemplified in the nullification crisis and the debates over the Compromise of 1850, in favor of an image with more broadly based appeal. Discussions of Revolutionary antecedents rarely mentioned slavery, and Confederates seemed to like it this way. A war fought to protect the founders' values—however nebulously defined—would appeal to nonslaveholders and former Unionists as well as longtime fire-eaters.

Confederates also imbued their political culture and identity with a healthy dose of Christian rhetoric. They believed themselves to be God's chosen people, and they saw confirmation of that in their early victories of 1861–62. Of course, as the tide of battle increasingly turned against them in 1863–64, Confederates shifted their rhetoric, and believed that God was testing or chastening them.

As much as Confederates argued that their nation was based on constitutional principles, Revolutionary antecedents, and Christianity, it also included a potent mix of fear and rage. The fear was of the end of slavery, couched often in the language of so-called black rule or race-mixing; the rage was against invading Yankees, demonized to the point of dehumanization. White supremacy and the protection of slavery were integral to the Confederacy, and even nonslaveholders understood that benefits and status accrued to them by virtue of their white skin. Thus, discussions of slavery per se appeared only rarely in public forums. For the most part Confederates took slavery as a given, albeit a sometimes problematic one, subject to neither challenge nor discussion.

Confederates had a second reason to keep silent on the subject of slavery, for they worried constantly about how their nation would be perceived by foreign countries. The ever-present search for diplomatic recognition, a sort of national status anxiety, underlay Confederate calls for indigenous schoolbooks and literature and influenced the language in which Confederates framed their national aspirations. While hoping that the Confederate monopoly on cotton production would force Europeans to help the Confederacy, they were also sensitive to foreign, particularly British, opposition to slavery. By deemphasizing bondage as a cause of secession, stressing instead states' rights and political domination, Confederates were able to shift the terms of debate, thus making their cause more palatable to conditional Unionists, nonslaveholders, and foreign nations.

Collapse

The Confederacy struggled mightily as the war went on, pressured externally by the Union Army and internally by both slaves and its own structural instabilities. Confederates rather quickly discovered that states' rights (particularly when guarded jealously by state governors) was not a strong foundation from which to launch a nation and fight a war. Thus, each time President Jefferson Davis attempted to increase centralization—whether through taxation, impressment, or conscription, he faced considerable internal opposition. But because of the Confederacy's avowed anti-partyism (perhaps compounded by the six-year presidential term), there was no real channel for that opposition. Anger, resentment, and disenchantment became focused on Jefferson Davis personally. At the same time, while all Confederates struggled with shortages of foodstuffs and runaway inflation, lower-class whites were hit especially hard. Shortages and the perception inspired by the 20 slave exemption (a law that allowed one white man to stay home on plantations of over 20 slaves, ostensibly to help grow food and keep the peace) alienated even supportive yeomen. In 1863 there were bread riots in cities around the South, with the worst one in Richmond, as

working-class women stormed stores and government warehouses to get food for their families. Family interests might take precedence over national interests, as illustrated by letters from women begging their husbands and sons to desert. The South also had the problem of slaves who ran away or would simply refuse to work. A combination of labor unrest, slowdowns, and escape all rendered the southern economy much less efficient and contributed to a general sense that the Confederates' world was falling apart.

Some historians charged that the Confederacy ultimately lost the Civil War because of failures of will—essentially claiming that Confederate patriotism was not strong enough to sustain a viable nation and that a withdrawal of public support at home ultimately led to defeat on the battlefield. More recently, however, historians have discounted that view, arguing instead that the Confederacy was defeated by the North's superior resources, both material and personnel. These historians have sought to change the questions being asked from "Why did the Confederacy lose?" to "Why was the Confederacy able to exist for as long as it did?" The Confederacy, for all of its shortcomings, did possess the necessary apparatus of government—an executive, a legislature, a judiciary, a treasury, a postal service, a state department. Most importantly, for the Confederacy had no real existence apart from war, it raised and kept an army in the field. These may not have always functioned well or efficiently—indeed in many cases they barely functioned at all—but they did exist.

Furthermore, while the Confederate nation-state ceased to exist in April 1865 (although President Jefferson Davis was not captured by Union troops until May 10, 1865, and some Confederate troops remained in the field until late May 1865), a sense of allegiance to the Confederacy continued in the hearts of white Southerners for generations. During the late nineteenth and early twentieth centuries, veterans and descendants groups, most notably the United Daughters of the Confederacy, flourished. These groups helped to recast the Confederate experience into a noble "lost cause," from which slavery and white supremacy were almost entirely excised. Confederate flags, specifically the Army of Northern Virginia's battle flag, began to fly again throughout the South during the 1950s and 1960s in response to the civil rights movement. The 1990s and early 2000s saw renewed controversy over these flags and their meanings, demonstrating the degree to which the Confederacy, or

conservatism

at least an idealized, sanitized version of it, still holds a degree of cultural power in the United States.

See also Civil War and Reconstruction; race and politics; slavery.

FURTHER READING

Blight, David W. *Race and Reunion: The Civil War in American Memory*. Cambridge, MA: Harvard University Press, 2001.

Davis, William C. *"A Government of Our Own": The Making of the Confederacy*. New York: Free Press, 1994.

Escott, Paul D. *After Secession: Jefferson Davis and the Failure of Confederate Nationalism*. Baton Rouge: Louisiana State University Press, 1978.

Faust, Drew Gilpin. *The Creation of Confederate Nationalism: Ideology and Identity in the Civil War South*. Baton Rouge: Louisiana State University Press, 1988.

Rable, George C. *The Confederate Republic: A Revolution against Politics*. Chapel Hill: University of North Carolina Press, 1994.

Rubin, Anne Sarah. *A Shattered Nation: The Rise and Fall of the Confederacy, 1861–1868*. Chapel Hill: University of North Carolina Press, 2005.

Thomas, Emory M. *The Confederate Nation: 1861–1865*. New York: Harper, 1979.

ANNE SARAH RUBIN

conservatism

No coherent conservative political movement existed before the twentieth century. Until the late nineteenth century, the principles of laissez-faire and classical republicanism were integral to the American political tradition. Essential to this tradition was an inherent distrust of centralized government, and this distrust found its classic expression in the U.S. Constitution. Its famous beginning, "We the people," asserted that the source of its authority rested in the citizenry rather than in the state.

The tradition came under challenge in the late nineteenth century with the rise of corporations, mass manufacturing, international agricultural markets, and business malfeasance and exploitation of labor. Progressive reformers called for the federal government to expand its regulatory powers through legislation, the courts, and the marshaling of scientific expertise.

Conservatives developed two main responses to the changing political and social order. The first was social Darwinism, the application of Darwinian biology to promote laissez-faire ideas articulated by English author Herbert Spencer, Yale University professor William Graham Sumner, and steel mogul Andrew Carnegie. Social Darwinists supported laissez-faire capitalism, free trade, and anti-imperialism. The second response, conservative nationalism, drew upon long-standing Republican Party policies of high tariffs, government support for American business, the expansion of American economic interests abroad, and an adherence to strict constitutional interpretation. In the late nineteenth and early twentieth centuries, laissez-faire ideology was on the defensive. Conservative nationalism, however, remained crucial to Republican political success well into the 1920s in the presidential administrations of Warren Harding, Calvin Coolidge, and Herbert Hoover.

Conservatism in the early twentieth century was not a political movement per se. There was no self-identified political vehicle for conservative ideas. Many of the most important conservatives in the 1920s and 1930s were only peripherally concerned with politics; instead, they lamented what they saw as the cultural decline of Western civilization and criticized what Spanish political philosopher José Ortega y Gasset called "the revolt of the masses."

During the 1920s, the "new humanists," led by Irving Babbitt and Paul Elmer More, excoriated any literature published after the eighteenth century. The architect Ralph Adams Cram fought against the modern world in his own work designing Gothic cathedrals and buildings, and expressed a belief that human nature had not changed since the Neolithic era. Such views were hardly equipped to build a conservative political majority.

In the next decade, conservative commentators such as Garet Garrett and Albert Jay Nock condemned Franklin D. Roosevelt's New Deal for furthering the decline of individualism. Meanwhile, in 1934, businessmen hostile to the expanded power of the federal government founded the American Liberty League to challenge Roosevelt's view that "money changers in the temple of civilization" and the free enterprise system in general were responsible for the Great Depression, and that only government intervention could cure the broken economy. The Liberty League hoped to influence the midterm congressional elections, but the Democrats expanded their majorities in Congress; in 1936 Roosevelt won a landslide reelection, and the Liberty League soon disbanded.

Only in the late 1930s did conservatives in Congress from both parties succeed in opposing the New Deal

180

through such agencies as the House Committee on Un-American Activities, which investigated the influence of Communists in federal programs. Then, during World War II, a revitalized conservative coalition of Republicans and southern Democrats managed to terminate New Deal relief programs, although the most important liberal reforms—Social Security and the Wagner Act—remained impervious to change.

Groups like the National Association of Manufacturers, with individuals like Sun Oil chairman J. Howard Pew leading the way, revitalized the free enterprise message throughout World War II. Business recovered much of its damaged social authority during the war years by securing the economic and military power necessary to defeat Germany and Japan. Pew encouraged ideological combat against the New Deal, securing funds to help publish such seminal conservative works as Friedrich Hayek's *The Road to Serfdom* and Henry W. Wriston's *Challenge to Freedom*. The conservative weekly *Human Events* also began publishing in 1944. Initially critical of interventionist foreign policy—it was edited by former supporters of the antiwar group America First—*Human Events* would soon be a strong supporter of the cold war. After a long period in the political wilderness, conservatives had resurrected their ideas.

The Conservative Revival

Conservatism in the post–World War II period became intertwined with the Republican Party. This is not to say that all conservatives were Republicans: many conservatives, especially in the South, were aligned with the Democratic Party or voted, at various times, for third-party candidates. Nonetheless, in the postwar period, conservatives launched a movement to transform the Republican Party.

Many of the key intellectuals who reinvigorated conservatism in the postwar period were émigrés from Europe: Ayn Rand, from Russia; Friedrich Hayek and his fellow economist Ludwig Von Mises, from Austria; and the philosophers Eric Voegelin and Leo Strauss, from Germany. They were joined by such young American intellectuals as William F. Buckley Jr., who founded the conservative *National Review* in 1955; the historian Russell Kirk; the philosopher Richard Weaver; and the journalist Frank Meyer.

Fundamental philosophical differences separated these thinkers. Concern about communism intensified debate over an array of questions: Should the right compromise its principles of small government in support of the cold

war? Did the United States have the right to intervene militarily and politically in the affairs of another country to prevent a perceived Communist takeover? Should government restrict the civil liberties of Communists in the United States? These debates were largely philosophical and, until the 1960s, usually did not involve specific pieces of legislation. But they lent vitality to the right and appealed to a new generation of students and activists dissatisfied with the Freudianism and existentialism fashionable among liberal intellectuals of the day.

Much of this debate occurred in conservative journals, particularly the *National Review*. In founding the magazine, Buckley sought to present different perspectives on the right and to expand its readership beyond the only other mass-circulation conservative publication, *Human Events*, whose audience was mostly drawn from grassroots anti-Communists. Buckley gathered an impressive editorial board including James Burnham, former Communist Frank Meyer, Whittaker Chambers, Russell Kirk, novelist John Dos Passos, Buckley's brother-in-law L. Brent Bozell Jr., Yale University political scientist Willmore Kendall, corporate lawyer William Rusher, and libertarian Frank Chodorov.

The vitality of the conservative intellectual movement paralleled the growth of a mass grassroots anti-Communist movement organized primarily through local community, religious, and business groups. The movement reflected profound fears about the Soviet threat abroad and Communist subversion at home. Australian physician and evangelist minister Fred Schwarz organized the Christian Anti-Communist Crusade, which conducted seminars and lectures that drew tens of thousands of participants. In Texas, former Federal Bureau of Investigation agent Dan Smoot published a widely read newsletter and hosted a syndicated radio program. Leonard Read headed the Foundation for Economic Education, which promoted free enterprise and warned about the dangers of communism and socialism. In 1958 candy manufacturer Robert Welch founded the John Birch Society, which attracted a large national membership. Welch's accusation that Dwight D. Eisenhower was a conscious Soviet agent, however, stunted the growth of the society, and Welch later retracted his statement.

Within the Republican Party, conservatives sought to replace what they saw as the dominance of the eastern liberal wing, symbolized by Nelson Rockefeller, with an uncompromising anti–New Deal faction. Many conservatives had been disappointed by the failure of Ohio

Republican Robert Taft to win the GOP presidential nomination in 1948 and 1952. Conservative Republicans had generally supported Eisenhower's presidency, but discord within the party had increased.

Goldwater, 1964, and Civil Rights

As the 1960 election approached, conservatives hoped that Senator Barry Goldwater, a Republican from Arizona, would win the GOP nomination for president.

In 1959 Clarence Manion, former dean of the Notre Dame Law School, organized a Goldwater for President group. As part of the campaign, he arranged for Buckley's brother-in-law, Bozell, to write a political manifesto under Goldwater's name. Published in 1960, *Conscience of a Conservative* became a national best-seller, even though Richard Nixon secured the GOP nomination and went on to lose the election to John F. Kennedy. That same year, college-age supporters of Goldwater organized Young Americans for Freedom on the Buckley family estate in Sharon, Connecticut, proclaiming, "In this time of moral and political crisis, it is the responsibility of the youth of American to affirm certain eternal truths."

Conservatives believed that, if they could secure Goldwater's nomination in 1964, the GOP had a chance of winning the White House. The entire race changed, however, when President Kennedy was assassinated in Dallas, Texas, in November 1963. His successor, Lyndon Johnson, drew upon the tragedy to push an aggressive liberal agenda through Congress. Although Goldwater believed it would be impossible for any Republican to win in 1964, out of loyalty to his followers he remained in the race and defeated Nelson Rockefeller, the governor of New York, in a bitter fight for the GOP nomination.

Goldwater's vote against the Civil Rights Bill of 1964 as an unconstitutional interference in private matters drew heavy criticism from moderates within his own party as well as from northern Democrats. His acceptance speech, which contained the lines, "Extremism in the defense of liberty is no vice. Moderation in the pursuit of justice is no virtue," widened the gap even further.

The *National Review* did not help his cause. The magazine harshly criticized the civil rights movement and opposed federal enforcement of equal access to public accommodations and protection of black voting rights in the South, reinforcing perceptions that conservatives were racists. The magazine's editorial rhetoric often overstepped the bounds of civility and was racially offensive.

Years later Buckley would apologize for the tone the magazine had set.

Lyndon Johnson won by a landslide, and Democrats gained huge majorities in Congress. Conservatives found some signs of hope, however. Goldwater Republicans won Senate races in California with former movie star George Murphy and in Nebraska with Roman Hruska. Most significantly, the Republicans won most states in the Deep South for the first time since Reconstruction. This reversal of fortune persuaded southern Democrats to become more conservative and, often, more vocal in their support for segregation.

Nixon, Ford, and Frustration of Conservatives

In 1968, with the Democratic Party sharply divided over the Vietnam War, Richard Nixon narrowly won the presidency. Most conservatives had supported him, albeit reluctantly, in hopes of gaining influence over his policies. Few Republicans could stomach the third-party campaign of Alabama governor George Wallace, whose rage-filled populist message gained 13.5 percent of the popular vote. But Nixon came into office with big Democratic majorities in both houses of Congress. Even if he had wanted to move to the right, he would have been unable to do so. Instead, Nixon pursued a rather liberal agenda at home, expanding the welfare and regulatory state. He intensified the bombing in Vietnam, while his national security adviser, and later secretary of state, Henry Kissinger, opened negotiations with North Vietnam. At the same time, Nixon entered into a new arms-control agreement with the Soviet Union, the Strategic Arms Limitation Talks. Then, shortly before the 1972 election, Nixon announced he planned to open relations with mainland China.

These policies dismayed many GOP conservatives. But the primary challenge to Nixon mounted by the new American Conservative Union failed miserably. Nixon easily won renomination and went on to swamp George McGovern, his Democratic opponent. Two years later, Nixon's involvement in the Watergate scandal forced his resignation. New president Gerald Ford followed a moderate course that made him seem impervious to the rumblings of the right wing in his party.

In the mid-1970s, conservatives were a distinct minority within the Republican Party, but they were beginning to build an institutional foundation for their movement. They expanded the American Enterprise Institute, founded in the early 1940s, to provide conservative policy analysis. In 1973 conservative foundations such as the Scaife Fund, the John M. Olin Foundation, and the Bradley Foundation, and wealthy benefactors such as beer magnate Joseph Coors supported the establishment of the Heritage Foundation. These think tanks added intellectual firepower to the conservative resistance to the modern liberal state.

The founding of the magazine *Public Interest* by New York intellectual Irving Kristol in 1965 helped fuel the intellectual challenge to liberalism. Kristol viewed the *Public Interest* as an antidote to what he considered the increasing utopianism of leftist thinkers. The magazine attracted contributors who had become disgruntled with Johnson's Great Society, including Daniel Moynihan, Nathan Glazer, James Q. Wilson, Edward C. Banfield, and Aaron Wildavsky. These scholars, many of them social scientists, criticized programs devised by what they called the "new class" of fashionable leftists and government bureaucrats. Similar criticisms emerged in the Jewish opinion magazine *Commentary*, edited by Norman Podhoretz.

Although not uniformly conservative in their political outlooks, the most prominent writers for the *Public Interest* and *Commentary* became known as "neoconservatives," former liberals who rejected social experimentation, affirmative action, and moral relativism. They also supported a vigorous American foreign policy backed by a strong national defense to meet what they perceived as a heightened Soviet threat.

More traditional conservatives built a powerful movement to oppose the equal rights amendment (ERA) that Congress had passed in 1972—a victory for feminists. The ERA seemed to be headed toward easy ratification by the states until veteran right-wing activist Phyllis Schlafly organized a movement to stop it. She argued that the amendment would allow the drafting of women into the military, provide abortion on demand, legalize gay marriage, and weaken legislation protecting women in the workplace and in marriages. Schlafly organized a coalition of traditionalist Catholics, evangelical Protestants, Mormons, and orthodox Jews into a grassroots movement that helped stop the ERA from being ratified.

Other conservative activists—including Paul Weyrich, fund-raiser Richard Viguerie, Howard Phillips, and Republican strategist Terry Dolan—saw potential in Schlafly's success. They mounted a challenge to the GOP establishment through grassroots action on other "social issues," such as opposition to abortion and gay marriage, and support for school prayer. Calling themselves the

New Right, these activists brought new organizing and fund-raising prowess to the conservative cause.

With conservative activism growing, Ronald Reagan challenged Ford for the presidential nomination in 1976. He was unsuccessful, but Ford's narrow defeat by Jimmy Carter that year put Reagan in position to win the party's nomination four years later. White evangelical voters moved away from Carter, a southern Baptist Democrat, during his presidency; a key turning point was the Internal Revenue Service's 1978 ruling to deprive all private schools established after 1953 of their tax-exempt status if they were found guilty of discriminatory racial practices. Along with Carter's support for abortion rights, this decision rallied many evangelicals into supporting ministers Jerry Falwell and Tim LaHaye, who headed a new organization, the Moral Majority, that vowed to bring "traditional morality" back to government.

Conservatives exerted their influence in the 1978 midterm elections through the Committee for the Survival of a Free Congress and the National Conservative Political Action Committee. Although the South did not go fully Republican that year, history professor Newt Gingrich won election in Georgia, and, in Texas, Ron Paul won back a seat in Congress he had lost to a Democrat in 1976. At the same time, in California, voters ratified the Jarvis-Gann initiative, Proposition 13, cutting property taxes.

The Reagan and Bush Years

In 1980 Reagan won the Republican nomination and defeated Carter in the general election. The conservative standard bearer carried every region and every major constituency except Hispanics and African Americans. He won most southern states by 5 percentage points, and cut heavily into the blue-collar vote in the North. Republicans also won a majority of Senate seats for the first time in almost 30 years and made big gains in the House of Representatives. It was a significant victory for conservatives after 35 years of struggle.

During the next eight years, Reagan redefined the tone and nature of political discourse, although he had to compromise with a Democratic House throughout his term in office. Reagan failed to reshape the federal bureaucracy that sheltered liberal programs but did accomplish a good deal that delighted conservatives. The Economic Recovery Tax Act provided the largest tax decrease in history by reducing capital gains taxes and inflation-indexed tax rates. He continued Carter's policy of deregulation, enacting major monetary and banking reform. He ordered staff cuts in the Consumer Product Safety Commission, the Occupational Safety and Health Administration, and the Environmental Protection Agency. Reagan's administration supported efforts to restrict legalized abortion and to allow prayer in public schools, but these measures failed to pass in Congress. Reagan also initiated a massive increase in the defense budget and, in 1983, announced the Strategic Defense Initiative, an antimissile defense system based in outer space, which drew widespread protests from peace activists and liberal columnists.

The conservative president also waged what was, in effect, a proxy war against the Soviet Union. With the support of the AFL-CIO, the Vatican, and European trade unions, the United States assisted the anti-Communist labor movement Solidarity in Poland. The Reagan administration also aided "freedom fighters" in Central America, Southeast Asia, Africa, and Central America, and provided training and military assistance to Islamic forces opposed to the Soviet invasion of Afghanistan.

Reagan's policy toward the Soviet Union combined militant engagement and arms reduction. This policy, which appeared inconsistent to his opponents, followed a conservative strategy captured in the slogan "peace through strength." In pursuit of this aim, Reagan opposed calls by peace activists for a "nuclear freeze" on the development of new weapons and the deployment of Pershing II intermediate missiles in Europe. In a series of bilateral summit meetings from late 1985 through late 1988, Reagan and Soviet leader Premier Mikhail Gorbachev reached agreements that essentially brought an end to the cold war.

Conservatives found in Reagan an articulate and popular spokesman for their principles. While they sometimes criticized him as being overly pragmatic—raising taxes in 1983 and 1984, and failing to push for antiabortion legislation—he still left office as the hero of their movement. Reagan had succeeded in making conservatism a respectable political ideology in the nation as a whole.

Reagan's successor, George H. W. Bush, sought to turn the Republican Party to the center while maintaining his conservative base. This proved to be a cumbersome political act that betrayed a lack of principle. Bush seemed more involved in foreign than domestic policy: he ordered a military incursion in Panama to overthrow a corrupt dictatorship and then mobilized international support for military intervention in Iraq following its invasion of neighboring Kuwait. At home, Bush supported such Democratic measures as a ban on AK-47 assault rifles, the Americans with Disabilities Act, and a large tax hike for wealthy Americans. To fill two openings on the Supreme Court, he named David Souter, who turned out to be a liberal stalwart, and Clarence Thomas, a conservative whose nomination became controversial when a former employee, Anita Hill, accused him of sexual harassment.

The Clinton and George W. Bush Years

In the general election of 1992, Bush sought desperately to regain his conservative base. He invited conservative columnist Patrick Buchanan, who had challenged him in the primary campaign, to address the Republican convention. Buchanan's speech declared that the Democratic Party nominee Bill Clinton and his wife, Hillary Rodham Clinton, would "impose on America . . . abortion on demand, a litmus test for the Supreme Court, homosexual rights, discrimination against religious schools, women in combat. . . ." Buchanan's talk of a "culture war" was received enthusiastically by evangelical conservatives, but it alienated mainstream voters and probably helped defeat Bush's bid for reelection that fall.

Conservatives viewed Clinton as a baby boomer who had protested the war in Vietnam, repelled the military, and supported abortion. Conservatives seized on Clinton's proposal, as president-elect, to lift the ban on gay men and lesbians in the military, a quiet campaign promise he had to back away from under a barrage of criticism from the right. This proved to be the opening round in a well-orchestrated conservative assault that put the Clinton administration on the defensive and defeated the president's proposal for a universal health care system that the first lady had largely devised.

As the midterm election of 1994 drew near, conservatives led by Representative Newt Gingrich of Georgia organized a group of young Turks in the House to retake Republican control of that body for the first time since 1952. They drafted the Contract with America, which pledged 337 Republican candidates to a ten-part legislative program, including welfare reform, anticrime measures, a line-item veto, regulatory reform, and tax reduction. The contract notably ignored such emotional issues as abortion, pornography, and school prayer. The Contract with America drew enthusiastic response from the conservative media, especially Rush Limbaugh, whose radio program appeared on 600 stations with 20 million weekly listeners. On Election Day, Republicans captured both houses of Congress with a 230–204 majority in the House and eight new Senate seats.

Clinton nonetheless won reelection in 1996 against the weak campaign of Senator Robert Dole and survived a sexual scandal involving a White House intern that led the Republican House to impeach him. The Senate failed to convict, and Republicans lost seats in the 1998 election, shocking conservatives who had assumed that "immorality in the Oval Office" would benefit their cause. Many Republicans blamed Gingrich for the loss, and shortly after the election, he resigned from the House.

The Clinton scandal carried into the 2000 presidential race, in which Republican Texas governor George W. Bush defeated Democratic Vice President Al Gore in the closest election in modern U.S. history. Bush lost the popular vote, but he gained Republican support among observant conservative Christians, especially evangelical Protestants and Roman Catholics. Although Pat Robertson's Christian Coalition had waned in influence, a strong religious network made direct contact with voters through voter guides and pastoral commentary. Much of this strategy of targeting key voters was the brainchild of political consultant Karl Rove.

The world of politics—and the fate of Bush's presidency—was transformed by the terrorist attacks of September 11, 2001. Bush's resolute stance won him enormous popularity, and Congress passed a series of emergency measures, including the Combating Terrorism Act and the Uniting and Strengthening America by Providing Appropriate Tools Required to Intercept and Obstruct Terrorism (USA PATRIOT) Act, which expanded the surveillance powers of federal agencies. Civil libertarians worried that this legislation extended too much power to the federal government at a cost to personal liberties. But it underlined the Republican advantage on the issue of national security and helped the party gain seats in Congress in the 2002 election—and also gave the president the political support he needed to invade Iraq in early 2003. Although the war did not proceed as planned, Bush won a second term in 2004 against Democrat John Kerry, due in large part to his image as the leader of the so-called War on Terror. For the first time in decades, conservative Republicans were in firm control of the White House and Capitol Hill.

The triumph was brief, however. Soon after Bush's reelection, the continuing bloodshed in Iraq and the administration's fumbling of relief efforts following Hurricane Katrina led to the beginning of his steep decline in approval polls, and he never recovered. A series of lobby-ing and fund-raising scandals involving Republican leaders in Congress and a well-organized grassroots campaign allowed Democrats to regain control of the House and the Senate in 2006. The Republican decline continued in 2008, when Democrat Barack Obama was elected to the White House and Democrats retained control of Congress. Although Obama only won 1.5 percent more of the popular vote than George W. Bush had in 2004, Republicans were soundly defeated. Especially disturbing for the party was the defection of nearly 20 percent of Republicans who had voted for Bush. Moreover, Obama won among independents, women, and the young, while white males, white Catholics, and seniors barely supported the GOP presidential candidate, John McCain. No longer were the Republicans a majority party.

Conservatism in Defeat

Conservatism has been a dynamic political movement through most of the twentieth and early twenty-first centuries, continually shaped both by new ideas and ideological tensions. Before World War II, it consisted mainly of a defense of the cultural traditions of Western civilization and of laissez-faire and free markets. Pre–World War II conservatives staunchly defended localism, a strict adherence to the Constitution, and distrust of strong executive power in the face of profound technological and political change.

The cold war altered conservatism profoundly. Most conservatives supported cold war containment and extended the fear of communism into the domestic arena. In order to combat liberalism at home and communism abroad, it was necessary for conservatives to enter politics and not just to plead for their views in the intellectual realm. From the 1950s to the end of the cold war, conservatives constructed a political movement based on firmly opposing state-building tendencies at home while fighting communism abroad. There were inherent contradictions in such a policy, but conservatives focused on policies and programs designed to fulfill these two goals. The end of the cold war deprived conservatives of an enemy and left those critical of cold war conservatism, such as journalist Patrick Buchanan, to revive Old Right isolationism in the post-9/11 world.

Modern liberalism proved to be a formidable opponent; despite Republican victories, the modern welfare and regulatory states were not easily dismantled. Nonetheless, the conservative ascendancy within the Republican Party and in the electorate during the last half of the twentieth century led to significant political and policy changes. Conservatives were able to mobilize large number of voters to their cause. Even as late as 2008, when conservatives appeared to be in a downswing, nearly 35 percent of the electorate identified themselves as "conservative." More important, while conservatives acting through the Republican Party were not able to scale back Social Security, Medicare-Medicaid, education, or environmental protection, they won notable victories in strengthening national defense, reforming welfare policy, restricting reproductive rights, reinvigorating monetary policy, deregulating major industries, and appointing conservative federal judges.

As conservatives sought to regroup after the 2008 defeat, they could take little consolation in the historical reminder that Republican success often followed Democratic mistakes in office. Given the severity of the financial meltdown and the international threats of rogue nations, oil shortages, nuclear proliferation, and military involvement in the Middle East and Afghanistan, even the most partisan-minded Republicans hoped that their return to office would not be built on a failed Obama presidency. While partisan differences would not be ignored, Democrats and Republicans, progressive and conservatives alike, understood that above all else, as Abraham Lincoln said in 1858, "a house divided against itself cannot stand."

See also anticommunism; anti-statism; conservative third parties since the New Deal; economy and politics; liberalism; Republican Party.

FURTHER READING

Critchlow, Donald T. *The Conservative Ascendancy: How the GOP Right Made Political History.* Cambridge, MA: Harvard University Press, 2007.

Doherty, Brian. *Radicals for Capitalism: A Freewheeling History of the Modern American Libertarian Movement.* New York: Public Affairs, 2007.

Edwards, Lee. *The Conservative Revolution: The Movement that Remade America.* New York: Free Press, 1999.

Frohnen, Bruce, Jeremy Beer, and Jeffrey O. Nelson, eds. *American Conservatism: An Encyclopedia.* Wilmington, DE: ISI Books, 2006.

Hayek, F. A. *The Road to Serfdom.* Chicago: University of Chicago Press, 1944.

Hayward, Steven F. *The Age of Reagan: The Fall of the Old Liberal Order, 1964–1980.* New York: Prima, 2001.

Nash, George H. *The Conservative Intellectual Movement in America: Since 1945.* 3rd ed. Wilmington, DE: ISI Books, 2006.

Schneider, Gregory L. *The Conservative Century: From Reaction to Revolution.* Lanham, MD: Rowman and Littlefield, 2009.

Schoenwald, Jonathan M. *A Time for Choosing: The Rise of Modern American Conservatism.* New York: Oxford University Press, 2001.

Wriston, Henry M. *Challenge to Freedom.* New York: Harper, 1943.

DONALD T. CRITCHLOW AND GREGORY SCHNEIDER

conservative ascendancy, 1980–2008

In 1984 President Ronald Reagan cruised to reelection in the second largest electoral landslide in American history. The next year, before a cheering crowd of conservatives, Reagan declared, "The tide of history is moving irresistibly in our direction. Why? Because the other side is virtually bankrupt of ideas. It has nothing more to say, nothing to add to the debate. It has spent its intellectual capital." It was a bold proclamation by a leader who had proved beyond debate that conservative ideas could have mass appeal.

But was Reagan right? On the one hand, liberals had apparently lost the war of ideas. By the mid-1980s, conservatives had amassed an impressive stockpile of ideological weapons thanks to a well-financed and well-coordinated network of private foundations, policy journals, and think tanks. On the other hand, Reagan's explanation downplayed a host of other political, historical, economic, personal, and structural factors. And whether the "tide of history" was irresistible or irreversible was by no means a foregone conclusion.

Nevertheless, conservatives became dominant in the two decades immediately following 1984, at least in electoral terms. The Republicans won five of the seven presidential elections after 1980, when they also captured the Senate for the first time since 1952. The Democrats recaptured the Senate in 1986, but, eight years later, the Republicans reclaimed it and, for the first time since 1954, also took command of the House. For most of the next decade, the GOP had effective control of Congress. Moreover, by 2004 the party as a whole had veered sharply to the right, with conservatives in charge and moderates on the verge of extinction.

The conservative ascendance was not, however, preordained. Few could or would have predicted it in the wake of the Watergate scandal. An assassination attempt against Reagan in March 1981 dramatically boosted his popularity and contributed significantly to passage of his tax bill, the signature achievement of his first term. The terrorist attacks in September 2001 transformed the presidency of George W. Bush and restored national security as the preeminent issue in American politics. They also enabled the Republicans to extend their control of Congress in 2002 and made possible Bush's narrow reelection in 2004.

Nor was the conservative ascendancy complete by 2004. By some measures, public opinion had shifted to the right since 1980. President Bill Clinton, for instance, was the first Democrat since Franklin Roosevelt to win consecutive terms. But he also achieved his greatest popularity after he proclaimed "the end of welfare as we know it" and "the era of big government is over." By other measures, the country had remained in place or moved to the left. Even on controversial social issues like homosexuality, the data were mixed, with greater tolerance counterbalanced by strong opposition to gay marriage. On balance, the evidence suggests that while most Americans object to big government in principle, in practice they accept and approve of federal programs like Social Security that benefit the great majority. As a result, the bureaucracy has grown steadily, which in turn has led to a debate among conservatives between "small-government" purists, who are usually not elected officials, and "big-government" politicians like George W. Bush, who supported a major expansion in Medicare benefits.

By 2004 no mass or permanent realignment of partisan preferences had taken place. The conservatives had won many electoral victories since 1980, but the nation remained divided and polarized. In a sense, the situation was little changed from 2000, when Bush and Vice President Al Gore, the Democratic nominee for president, fought to a virtual stalemate, the Senate was split 50–50, and the Republicans retained a slim majority in the House. Nonetheless, the New Right had eclipsed the New Deal political coalition and brought the Democratic era in national politics to a clear end. What made the conservative ascendance possible, and what sustained it?

Immediate Causes

Scholars disagree as to whether the New Deal political coalition of white Southerners, urban workers, small farmers, racial minorities, and liberal intellectuals was inherently fragile or whether the 1960s was the moment of reckoning. But the immediate causes of Reagan's victory in 1980 are less debatable. Most important was the failure of the Carter presidency. At home, the "misery index" (the combined rates of inflation and unemployment) stood at more than 20 percent. Abroad, Soviet troops occupied Afghanistan, and American hostages were held captive in Tehran. The future seemed bleak, and the president appeared to be unable to provide confident or competent leadership. What the White House needed was a new occupant—the main question was whether Reagan was a conservative ideologue or capable candidate.

Reagan's personality proved critical during the campaign. A gifted and affable performer, he was able to cross the "credibility threshold" in the presidential debates and reassure Americans that he was a staunch anti-Communist, not an elderly madman bent on nuclear confrontation with the Soviet Union. On the contrary, Reagan appeared vigorous, warm, principled, and optimistic—he promised that America's best days lay in the future, not the past. He also asserted that the weak economy was the fault of the government, not the people. Above all, Reagan was the smiling and unthreatening face of modern conservatism.

A third cause of conservative ascendancy was the tax revolt of the late 1970s. As inflation mounted, the middle class was trapped between stagnant incomes and rising taxes. In 1978 California voters approved Proposition 13, which slashed property taxes and triggered a nationwide movement toward such relief. The tax issue helped unite a contentious conservative coalition of libertarians, traditionalists, and anti-Communists. It also crystallized opposition to the liberal welfare state and gave Republicans a potent weapon to aim at government programs previously viewed as politically untouchable. In the coming decades, tax cuts would become conservative dogma, the "magic bullet" for growing the economy, shrinking the bureaucracy, and harvesting the votes of disgruntled citizens.

A final cause was the emergence of religious conservatives as a significant bloc of Republican voters. Prior to the 1960s, many evangelical Christians either avoided the political world or divided their votes between the parties. But in 1962, the Supreme Court ruled in *Engel v. Vitale* that the First Amendment banned even nondenominational prayer in the public schools. Then the sexual revolution and the women's movement arrived amid the social upheaval of the decade. In 1973 *Roe v. Wade* made abortion an important issue, and in 1978 the Internal Revenue Service threatened to repeal the federal tax exemption for racially segregated Christian schools. The latter action outraged evangelicals, especially the Reverend Jerry Falwell, who in 1979 founded the Moral Majority, which quickly became a powerful force within the New Right. In 1980 Reagan received 61 percent of the fundamentalist vote; by comparison, Jimmy Carter (a born-again Christian) had received 56 percent in 1976. By 2004 the most reliable Republican voters were those Americans who went to church more than once a week.

Sustaining Factors

At first the conservative momentum continued under Reagan's successor, Vice President George H. W. Bush, who easily won election in 1988. But he lacked the personal charisma and communication skills that had enabled Reagan to attract moderates and bridge divisions on the right. The end of the cold war also removed a unifying issue from the right's repertoire and shifted the political focus from national security (a Republican strength) to economic security (a Democratic strength). The fall of the Soviet Union meant, moreover, that conservatives could no longer paint liberals as soft on communism—a deadly charge in American politics since the 1940s. Finally, Bush made a critical political error in 1990 when he broke his "read my lips" campaign pledge and agreed to a tax hike. According to most economists, the increase was not a significant factor in the recession of 1991–92. But many conservatives today trace the start of what they see as the betrayal or repudiation of the "Reagan Revolution" to that fateful moment.

In 1992 Clinton focused "like a laser beam" on the poor state of the economy and, thanks in large measure to the presence of independent candidate Ross Perot on the ballot, defeated Bush. Then the Democrat rode peace and prosperity to reelection in 1996. Clinton infuriated conservatives because he usurped what they saw as their natural claim to the White House, he seemed to embody the counterculture values of the 1960s, and was a gifted politician who co-opted many of their issues. In many respects, Clinton truly was a "New Democrat," who supported free trade, a balanced budget, and the death penalty. Nevertheless, even he was unable to reverse the conservative ascendance—at best, he could only restrain it after the Republicans took control of Congress in 1994.

In the 1990s, conservatives continued to set the political tone and agenda by demonstrating that they were masters of coordination and discipline. In Washington, they gathered every Wednesday at a breakfast sponsored by Americans for Tax Reform and a lunch sponsored by Coalitions for America to discuss issues, strategies, and policies. At the same time, the Club for Growth targeted moderates (deemed RINOs—Republicans in Name Only) and bankrolled primary challenges against them. And after 1994, members of Congress received committee chairs based on loyalty to the leadership, not seniority, a change spearheaded by House Speaker Newt Gingrich of Georgia. By 2000 conservative control and party discipline were so complete that Bush never had to employ the veto in his first term—a feat not accomplished since the presidency of John Quincy Adams.

The conservative movement was also flush with funds. Much Republican money came in small contributions from direct mailings aimed at true believers, but large sums came from two other sources. The first was corporate America, which in the 1970s found itself beset by foreign competition, rising wages, higher costs, and lower profits. In response, it created lobbying organizations like the Business Roundtable, formed political action committees, and channeled campaign contributions in ever larger amounts to conservative politicians, who in turn made government deregulation, lower taxes, and tort reform legislative priorities in the 1980s. The second source of funds was lobbyists, who represented many of the same corporations. After the GOP rout in 1994, House Majority Whip Tom DeLay of Texas initiated the "K Street Project," whereby lobbyists hoping to do business on Capitol Hill were pressured into making their hiring practices and campaign contributions conform to Republican interests.

At the same time, corporate boards and private foundations invested heavily in institutions like the American Enterprise Institute and the Heritage Foundation, which had immense influence in policy design, both domestic and foreign. These think tanks constituted a veritable shadow government for officials between positions or awaiting an opportunity. They also acted as incubators of ideas and command posts for policy research in the ideological war that conservatives fought against liberals.

The struggle was waged on several fronts. On the ground, conservatives proved expert at mobilizing their base, which became increasingly important to both parties as the number of undecided voters shrank in the highly partisan political climate of the 1990s. In 2004, for example, George W. Bush won largely because the Republicans recruited 1.4 million volunteers, who boosted the president's popular vote by 20 percent (including 4 million Christians who had voted in 1996 but not in 2000). By comparison, in 2004 the Democrats raised their vote totals by 12 percent over 2000, which was impressive but insufficient. On the air, the conservatives also exploited every advantage at their disposal. In 1987 the abolition of the Fairness Doctrine, which had required broadcasters to provide "equal time" to alternative views, opened the door to right-wing talk radio. Enter Rush Limbaugh, a disk jockey from Missouri, who by the mid-1990s had inspired countless imitators and was reaching 20 million devoted listeners (known as "dittoheads") daily on 660 stations across the nation. And, by 2000, FOX News, with a strong conservative slant, had surpassed CNN to become the most popular news channel on cable television.

Another source of strength for Republicans was the weakness of the Democrats, who lacked a clear vision or coherent set of core principles. The party was deeply divided between "upscale Democrats" (well-educated professionals who were more socially liberal) and "downscale Democrats" (economically marginal workers and minorities who were more socially conservative). Moreover, historical memories had faded—by 2002 less than one in ten voters could personally recall the Great Depression and New Deal. Labor unions, a pillar of the party, had also eroded in size and influence. In 1960, 40 percent of the workforce was unionized; by 2000, the figure was 14 percent and falling. In addition, the once Solid South was now reliably Republican. In the seven presidential elections between 1980 and 2004, Republican candidates lost a combined total of just five southern states to Democratic candidates.

Even the much touted "gender gap" provided little solace to the Democrats. Since 1980, when it first appeared, the party attracted women in growing numbers. By 2004, the Democrats were majority female and the Republicans were majority male. The problem for Democrats was that the exodus of men, especially working-class white Southerners, exceeded the influx of women. That was the real cause of the gender gap, which in 2004 was also a marriage gap (55 percent of married women voted for Bush, while 62 percent of single women voted against him). Nevertheless, if men and women had switched partisan allegiances at the same rate after 1980, Bush would have lost in both 2000 and 2004.

Future Considerations

After 2004 many Democrats were in despair. Bush, whom few experts had predicted would win in 2000, had again defied the odds by surviving an unpopular war, a weak economy, and soaring deficits. The Republicans had also extended their control of Congress and built a well-financed party structure. In the aftermath of the 2004 election, White House political adviser Karl Rove boasted that the United States was in the midst of a "rolling realignment." Eventually, the Republicans would become the dominant party, he predicted, as they had in 1896 and the Democrats had in 1932. It was merely a matter of time, especially if the terrorist threat continued to make national security a priority.

Some Democrats, however, were not disheartened. Both elections were close calls, and in 2004 Bush had a considerable advantage as an incumbent wartime president. Moreover, some long-term demographic and technological developments seemed to favor the Democrats. The Internet had filled their war chest with vast sums, and bloggers had reenergized intellectual debates among the party faithful, even if new groups like MoveOn.org and America Coming Together were less successful at mobilizing voters on election day. The increasing number of well-educated working women and Latino voters also seemed to bode well for the Democrats, as did the steady growth in unmarried and secular voters, who seemed to be more liberal in their outlook.

Nevertheless, the Republicans continued to have structural and ideological advantages. In the Electoral College, the less populated "red states" still had disproportionate influence, raising the bar for Democratic candidates. And in congressional districts, partisan gerrymandering kept most Republican districts intact. In 2004, for example, Bush carried 255 districts—almost 59 percent—compared with his popular vote total of less than 52 percent. In addition, the Republican Party's moral conservatism and entrepreneurial optimism seemed likely to appeal to a growing number of Latino voters, assuming that the immigration issue did not prove divisive in the long term.

But, in 2006, the Democrats surprised themselves and the pundits by retaking the House and Senate, as undecided voters punished the party in power and negated the base strategy of the Republicans by overwhelmingly blaming them for political corruption and the Iraq War. Then, in 2008, the Democrats solidified their control of Congress and recaptured the White House when Senator Barack Obama defeated Senator John McCain in a presidential race dominated by voter discontent with the Bush administration and the most serious financial crisis since the Great Depression. The tide of history that Reagan hailed in 1985 had ebbed. Republican hopes for a major realignment had faded. But it was too soon to tell whether the conservative ascendancy had come to a lasting end.

See also conservatism; Democratic Party, 1968–2008; Republican Party, 1968–2008.

FURTHER READING

Critchlow, Donald. *The Conservative Ascendancy: How the GOP Right Made Political History.* Cambridge, MA: Harvard University Press, 2007.

Edsall, Thomas B. *Building Red America: The New Conservative Coalition and the Drive for Permanent Power.* New York: Basic Books, 2006.

Hacker, Jacob S., and Paul Pierson. *Off Center: The Republican Revolution and the Erosion of American Democracy.* New Haven, CT: Yale University Press, 2005.

Micklethwait, John, and Adrian Wooldridge. *The Right Nation: Conservative Power in America.* New York: Penguin, 2004.

Schaller, Michael, and George Rising. *The Republican Ascendancy: American Politics, 1968–2001.* Wheeling, IL: Harlan Davidson, 2002.

Schaller, Thomas F. *Whistling Past Dixie: How Democrats Can Win without the South.* New York: Simon and Schuster, 2006.

MICHAEL W. FLAMM

conservative interregnum, 1920–32

The years between World War I and the New Deal are popularly known as the Roaring Twenties because of the era's tumultuous social and cultural experimentation and spectacular economic growth. The cultural upheaval—from the Harlem Renaissance to jazz, and from flappers to speakeasies—stands in contrast to the period's conservative politics. The decade witnessed a muting of the Progressive Era voices that had sought to end the abuses of unregulated capitalism through industrial regulation and reform. Presidents Warren Harding, Calvin Coolidge, and Herbert Hoover emphasized a limited role for the regulatory power of the federal government and the importance of efficiency, individualism, as well

as support for business. Calvin Coolidge summed up the dominant ethos in the White House with his statement, "The business of America is business."

Despite the support for business fostered in the halls of the White House and a broad segment of Congress, the 1920s did not simply represent a discontinuous period sandwiched between two eras of reform (the Progressive Era and the New Deal). Indeed, the decade opened with major victories for two important reform movements. With the passage of the Nineteenth Amendment in 1920, women's rights advocates had won their long battle for suffrage. The national electorate expanded dramatically with female citizens no longer excluded from the right to vote on the basis of gender. In the wake of woman suffrage, advocates for women's equality struggled to define their movement. Alice Paul and the National Women's Party battled for the passage of an equal rights amendment, while other activists pressed on for protective legislation, winning a victory in 1921 when Congress passed a bill providing funds for prenatal and child health care. A second reform movement, that of temperance, triumphed with the ratification of the Eighteenth Amendment, outlawing the sale, manufacture, and transportation of liquor, to take effect in January 1920. The radical experiment with national Prohibition, the law of the land until 1933, helped to lay the groundwork for the expansion of the federal government that took place during the New Deal. In addition, Hoover's conservative variant of progressivism included an important role for the federal government in providing knowledge, expertise, and information to business to shore up economic growth. Indeed, Franklin D. Roosevelt's first New Deal had much in common with Hoover's effort to utilize the state in cooperation with business to mitigate the severe economic crisis that shook the nation during the Great Depression.

After the upheavals of the "Great War," the tumultuous global ramifications of the Russian Revolution, and the defeat of Woodrow Wilson's postwar internationalism, Warren Harding's calls for a "return to normalcy" resonated with many voters. In November 1920, Harding won a lopsided victory over Democrat James M. Cox of Ohio, and the Republicans solidified the hold on Congress that they had won in 1918. Harding came to the presidency with a long record of public service but an undistinguished record as a senator. The policies of his administration, however, as well as those of the Supreme Court, demonstrated a strong orientation toward the business community. With the federal government's pro-business orientation, emboldened industrialists undertook a successful counterattack against the gains labor had made during World War I. The great labor strikes that rocked the nation in 1919 had ended in defeat. By 1923, union membership fell to 3.6 million from more than 5 million at the end of the war.

Falling union membership mirrored developments in political participation more broadly. Voter turnout rates were low throughout the decade, averaging around 46 percent. Progressive innovations such as nonpartisan elections undercut party organization and weakened party identification. The nonvoters tended to be the poor, and new voters such as women, African Americans, and naturalized immigrants. Only in 1928 did participation rise to 56 percent as the volatile issues of religion, ethnicity, and Prohibition mobilized the electorate.

With Harding's death on August 2, 1923, Vice President Calvin Coolidge succeeded to the presidency. His reserved New England demeanor marked a sharp break from Harding's outgoing midwestern charm, but their different personalities belied a common approach toward government. As Harding before him, Coolidge emphasized efficiency, limited government, and strong praise for capital. Coolidge summed up this ethos when he remarked, "The man who builds a factory builds a temple. The man who works there worships there." These notions seemed to resonate with large numbers of Americans in a period of economic expansion and growing affluence. While the decade had opened in recession, from 1922 to 1929, national income increased more than 40 percent, from $60.7 billion to $87.2 billion. Automobiles, construction, and new industries like radio fueled an economic boom. The number of passenger cars in the United States jumped from fewer than 7 million in 1919 to about 23 million in 1929. Radio, getting its start in 1920, was a household item for 12 million Americans by 1929. The availability of new products, installment buying, and an increasingly national advertising industry fueled a mass consumption economy just as increased leisure, radios, and movies generated a mass culture.

Economic growth and mass consumption went hand in hand, however, with the increasing maldistribution of wealth and purchasing power. Indeed, about one-third of families earned less than the minimum income estimated for a "decent standard of living." Those Americans working in what were then known as the "sick industries," such as textile and coal, along with the nation's farmers, failed to benefit from the economic

gains of the period. Progressive reformers continued to criticize the consolidation of private capital and the inequalities of income. Eugene Debs, sentenced to ten years in prison under the Seditions Act of 1918, ran as Socialist Party candidate for president in 1920 (from federal prison) and won close to a million votes. In 1924, Robert F. Lafollette, a senator from Wisconsin, led the third-party Progressive ticket, mobilizing reformers and labor leaders as well as disgruntled farmers. The Progressive Party called for the nationalization of railroads, the public ownership of utilities, and the right of Congress to overrule Supreme Court decisions. Lafollette won 5 million popular votes but carried only his home state of Wisconsin.

While progressives and radicals chipped away at the sanctified praise of business voiced by three Republican administrations, their criticisms were shadowed by far more powerful reactions against the tide of urbanization, secularization, and modernism. Protestant fundamentalist crusades against the teachings of Darwinism and modernism in the churches culminated in the *State of Tennessee v. John Thomas Scopes* trial (better known as the "Scopes Monkey Trial") in 1925. Riding a tide of backlash against urban concentrations of immigrants, Catholics, and Jews as well as militant Prohibitionist anger with the unending flow of illegal drink, the Ku Klux Klan mushroomed throughout the nation, becoming a significant force in politics in such states as Indiana, Ohio, and Colorado.

During its heyday in the mid-1920s, between 3 to 5 million people joined the ranks of the hooded Klan, making it one of the largest and most influential grassroots social movements in twentieth-century America. Systematically targeting African Americans, Catholics, Jews, and foreigners as threats to Americanism, the Klan drew from a broad group of white Protestant men and women throughout the Midwest, West, and South through its promises to stave off a drift away from the values of small-town Protestant America. The Klan sold itself as an organization devoted to "law and order" by promising to rid America of liquor. Prohibition intersected closely with the Klan's larger nativist, anti-Catholic agenda since many ethnic Catholic immigrants blatantly flouted the law. By organizing drives to "clean up" communities and put bootleggers out of business, the Klan became a popular means of acting on militant temperance sentiments.

Prohibition was a radical experiment and, not surprisingly, it sharpened key cultural divides of the era. The Eighteenth Amendment became effective on January 17,

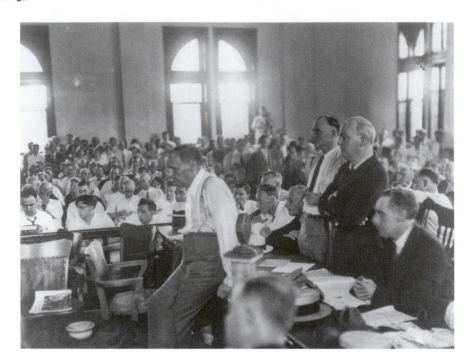

Clarence Darrow represented the defendant in the Scopes evolution trial, Dayton, Tennessee, July 1925. (Library of Congress)

1920, after ratification of all but two states (Connecticut and Rhode Island). Outlawing the sale, manufacture, and transport of alcohol, it was, one contemporary observed, "one of the most extensive and sweeping efforts to change the social habits of an entire nation in recorded history." It was an astonishing social innovation that brought with it the greatest expansion of federal authority since Reconstruction. While the Republican and Democratic parties had avoided taking official positions on the subject, during the 1920s, national Prohibition became a significant bone of contention, particularly for the Democratic Party, solidifying divisions between the Democratic Party's rural, "dry," Protestant wing and its urban, Catholic "wet" wing. The party's two wings fought over nativism, the Klan, and Prohibition at its 1924 Convention. And by 1928, the party's urban wet wing demonstrated its newfound strength when Alfred E. Smith became the Democratic presidential nominee.

For many of the nation's immigrants, Prohibition was an affront to personal liberty, particularly since their communities were the special targets of law enforcement efforts to dry up the flow of bootleg liquor. As a result, it ignited a growing politicization of ethnic immigrant workers. While Prohibition made immigrant, urban, and ethnic workers aware of the dangers of state power, it had the far greater effect of leading many of these workers into the national Democratic Party. Catholic immigrant and New York governor Al Smith carried the country's 12 largest cities, all rich in immigrants, and all of which had voted Republican in 1924. The Smith campaign forged an alignment of urban ethnic workers with the Democratic Party that was solidified during the New Deal. In their turn, the nation's rural Protestant and dry Democrats dreaded the specter of a Catholic and wet urbanite in the White House. Their disdain for Smith led many to abandon their allegiance to the Democratic Party to vote for Hoover. As a result, Hoover won in a landslide, receiving 58 percent of the popular vote and 447 electoral votes to Smith's 87. Hoover cut heavily into the normally Democratic South, taking the upper tier of the old confederacy, as well as Florida.

The third straight Republican to dominate the era's national politics, Hoover had won the support of many progressive reformers, including settlement house leader and international peace advocate Jane Addams. Hoover championed a conservative variant of progressivism that flourished in the 1920s. While he refused to countenance public authority to regulate business, he hoped to manage social change through informed, albeit limited, state action. He championed the tools of social scientific expertise, knowledge, and information in order to sustain a sound economy. His desire to organize national policies on a sound basis of knowledge resulted in a major study called *Recent Social Trends*, a 1,500-page survey that provided rich data about all aspects of American life. As this social scientific endeavor suggests, Hoover drew from a broad font of progressive ideas but remained firm in his commitment to what he called "American Individualism."

Hoover's strong belief in limited government regulation went hand in hand with his embrace of federal authority to shore up Prohibition enforcement. To make clear that the federal government would not tolerate the widespread violations apparent almost everywhere, Hoover signed the Jones Act in 1929, a measure strongly backed by the Anti-Saloon League. The act raised a first offense against the 1929 Volstead Act to the status of a felony and raised maximum penalties for first offenses from six months in jail and a $1,000 fine to five years and a $10,000 fine.

An outpouring of protest undermined support for the Eighteenth Amendment. William Randolph Hearst, once a strong backer of national Prohibition, now declared that the Jones Law was "the most menacing piece of repressive legislation that has stained the statute books of this republic since the Alien and Sedition laws." As the reaction to the Jones Act suggests, the "noble experiment" sounded a cautionary note about using the power of the state to regulate individual behavior.

But Prohibition's repeal did not signify a broad rejection of federal government regulation. Rather, the great debate over the merits of Prohibition throughout the decade helped lay the ground for a greater legitimacy of state authority: The debate did not challenge the government's right to regulate as much as it raised important questions over what its boundaries should be. Prohibition helped draw a thicker line between the legitimate arena of public government regulation and private behavior.

In the face of the increasingly dire economic circumstances at the end of the decade, the nation's preoccupation with moral regulation appeared increasingly frivolous. The stock market, symbol of national prosperity, crashed on October 29, 1929. By mid-November, stock prices had plunged 40 percent. The crash intensified a downward spiral of the economy brought about by multiple causes: structural weaknesses in the economy, unequal distribution of income, and the imbalanced

international economic system that had emerged from World War I.

Hoover put his conservative progressivism to the test during the downturn, and it proved inadequate for the scope of the crisis. He called on business to cooperate by ending cutthroat competition and the downward spiral of prices and wages. He proposed plans for public works to infuse money into the economy. And in 1932, he established the Reconstruction Finance Corporation to provide emergency loans to ailing banks, building and loan societies, and railroads. Hoover's embrace of government action was tethered, however, to his strong belief in voluntarism and, as a result, provided too little too late. His efforts, moreover, were directed for the most part toward business. While he did support federal spending to shore up state and local relief efforts, the sums were not enough. In 1932 a bitter and recalcitrant Hoover was trounced by the gregarious Franklin D. Roosevelt, whose declaration that the American people had "nothing to fear but fear itself" ushered in a new relationship of citizen to state and a new period of economic reform.

One of Roosevelt's first acts in office was to sign the Beer and Wine Revenue Act, anticipating the repeal of national Prohibition and effectively ending the radical experiment. The experience of national Prohibition had highlighted the real danger posed to personal liberty by the linkage of "morality" and politics. By the 1930s, the federal government's effort to dry up the nation and alter personal habits appeared increasingly absurd. Facing a grave economic crisis, the nation's chastised liberals now concerned themselves with using the state to regulate capitalism and provide a minimal security net for Americans against the vagaries of the marketplace. During the New Deal, state regulation focused on economic life, replacing an earlier era of regulation of public "moral" behavior that had marked the Roaring Twenties.

See also Americanism; conservatism; consumers and politics; New Deal Era, 1932–52; Prohibition and temperance.

FURTHER READING

Burner, David. *The Politics of Provincialism: The Democratic Party in Transition, 1918–1932*. Cambridge, MA: Harvard University Press, 1986.

Clark, Norman H. *Deliver Us from Evil: An Interpretation of American Prohibition*. New York: Norton, 1976.

Cohen, Lizabeth. *Making a New Deal: Industrial Workers in Chicago, 1919–1939*. 2nd ed. New York: Cambridge University Press, 2008.

Dawley, Alan. *Changing the World: American Progressives in War and Revolution.* Princeton, NJ: Princeton University Press, 2003.

Dumenil, Lynn. *Modern Temper: American Culture and Society in the 1920s.* New York: Hill and Wang, 1995.

Hawley, Ellis. *The Great War and the Search for a Modern Order.* New York: St. Martin's Press, 1979.

Kennedy, David. *Freedom from Fear: The American People in Depression and War, 1929–1945.* New York: Oxford University Press, 1999.

Kyvig, David. *Repealing National Prohibition.* Kent, OH: Kent State University Press, 2000.

LISA McGIRR

conservative third parties since the New Deal

Conservative third parties in the modern United States, like most minor parties in American history, have generally risen out of protest against the political establishment. Franklin Roosevelt's presidency established a political order that made the Democratic Party dominant in American politics from the 1930s through the 1980s. The expansive confidence in government action these New Deal Democrats espoused—initially in economic policy but by the 1960s in social and cultural issues as well—incited the organization of several conservative third parties, impatient with the Democrats but also with a Republican Party that seemed, with few exceptions, unwilling to take a strong stand against New Deal liberalism.

The activists and energy that fueled the growth of many of these parties were part of a larger conservative movement that drove the Republican Party toward parity with the Democrats after 1980. This success did not, however, put an end to conservative third parties. At the same time that the New Deal Order itself was weakening, partisan identification and organization were also in a process of decay. For many conservative purists, the Republican Party in power betrayed the principles that got it there. Conservative third parties thus remained a viable option for these disenchanted loyalists, and they thrived in the traditional role of insurgent groups, gadflies to the establishment that vocalized and popularized varieties of conservative orthodoxy rather than gaining electoral success in their own right.

Activists disillusioned with one of the two major parties founded many of the conservative third parties after World War II. When conservatives split from the Democratic Party, the key issue was almost invariably race. Two third parties mobilized in protest of government policies that challenged traditional racial segregation in 1948 and again in 1968, drawing most of their strength from the Deep South. Indeed, both parties depended upon the leadership of southern politicians: Governor Strom Thurmond of South Carolina led a broad range of southern Democrats into the States' Rights Democratic Party in 1948; the American Independent Party of 1968 was entirely the creation of former Alabama governor George Wallace. Though racial politics provoked these insurgencies, their members proved to be out of step with Democratic political orthodoxy on a broad range of issues. In both 1948 and 1968, they complained about the ambitious social and economic programs that Democratic presidents embraced. Instead, they advocated states' rights and made clear their paramount concern lay with individual liberty. The fault lines these campaigns illustrated and inflamed proved essential to larger political developments; as the Republican Party began to embrace the rhetoric and positions of these parties, GOP presidential candidates like Barry Goldwater and Richard Nixon increasingly found themselves competitive in the formerly Democratic Solid South. Indeed, by the 1980s, the South had virtually realigned to the Republican Party in presidential campaigns, a tendency that had begun to drift down the ticket to state and local offices. Though they failed in their bids for the presidency, the insurgent conservative third parties of 1948 and 1968 paved the way for large-scale political change.

The States' Rights Democratic Party

In July 1948 Governor Strom Thurmond of South Carolina led a host of southern governors and activists to abandon the Democratic Party. President Harry Truman faced a tight reelection campaign, and in a bid to reclaim the left wing from the insurgent Progressive Party, led by Henry Wallace, Truman proposed a wide variety of liberal social programs—among them national health insurance, federal aid to education, and, most disturbing to Thurmond and his allies, a civil rights package, including an antilynching bill, the abolition of poll taxes, and various measures attacking segregation. He also ordered the desegregation of the military. Southern Democrats protested, but Truman, believing they would have nowhere else to go on election day, refused to compromise.

In response, Thurmond led several southern delegations out of the July Democratic Convention in Philadelphia. Soon after, in Birmingham, Alabama, first capital of the Confederacy, these delegates organized the States' Rights Democratic Party, nominating Thurmond for president and Fielding Wright, governor of Mississippi, for vice president. The Dixiecrat platform accused Truman of totalitarianism, invoked the small government philosophy of Democratic Party founder Thomas Jefferson, and called for a return to "home rule, local self government, and a minimum of interference with individual rights." It also declared support for segregation, rejected Truman's denunciation of discrimination in hiring practices, and called for "the racial integrity of each race."

Despite initial broad support for the Dixiecrats across the South, Election Day revealed that Truman held the loyalty of most southern party establishments. He carried Texas, Florida, and Georgia. Thurmond won only Louisiana, his home state of South Carolina, and Mississippi and Alabama, the two states whose delegations followed him from the floor in Philadelphia. He also gained a single electoral vote in Tennessee, for a total of 39 to the victorious Truman's 307. Thurmond attracted 1,169,021 popular votes, 2.5 percent of the total and only 11,849 more than Wallace, who failed to win a single state. Two years later, Thurmond was defeated in an attempt to unseat South Carolina's Democratic senator Olin Johnson. The next year, 1951, Thurmond's successor as governor, James Byrnes, declined to assume the party's mantle in the next presidential election. This blow meant the end for the Dixiecrats; the party dissolved that year, though its ethos persisted throughout southern democracy through the next two decades.

The American Independent Party: 1968 and After

Indeed, in 1968 the American Independent Party essentially revived the Dixiecrat platform, sharpening its rhetoric and tying old positions on segregation and small federal government to a populist political strategy. George Wallace had been the Democratic governor of Alabama from 1963 to 1967 (and would be reelected to that office in 1970), winning election on a rhetorically fiery platform calculated to appeal to pro-segregationist Alabama voters. During his time in office, he lived up to the rhetoric, memorably facing down federal officials in a university doorway to prevent desegregation of the school. In 1968 he mounted a massive and successful grassroots campaign to get on the presidential ballot of all 50 states under the title of American Independent.

Like Thurmond, Wallace railed at the major party establishments, raising millions from small, individual donations and denouncing the "pointy-headed pseudo-intellectuals" of the two major parties, between which he denied any real difference existed. In addition to his advocacy of segregation, Wallace's platform attacked high taxes and inflation, "war abroad and a loss of personal liberty at home." In a particular rhetorical innovation from Thurmond's campaign, he professed himself to be "mad as hell" about the spiraling crime rate. Wallace pinned responsibility for the unrest of the 1960s on "minority group rebellions" (a barely disguised jab at the civil rights movement) and the national parties that seemed to many Americans unable or unwilling to do anything about it. Confirming the aggressiveness of Wallace's politics was his selection of General Curtis LeMay, notorious for his advocacy of a belligerent foreign policy, for vice president.

Wallace in 1968 was the most successful third-party presidential candidate of the twentieth century, with the exception of Theodore Roosevelt's 1912 "Bull Moose" bid. He won 13.5 percent of the popular vote and 46 electoral votes, carried all the states Thurmond had won except for South Carolina (which Nixon, significantly, won). He also picked up Georgia and Arkansas. Although Wallace ran again for president in 1972, he then chose to compete in the Democratic primaries rather than return to the party he had founded.

The American Independent Party, however, survived; in 1969 a national convention renamed it the American Party, and in 1972 it nominated Congressman John Schmitz of California for president. Schmitz was a conservative Republican and a member of the isolationist John Birch Society; that the American Party could so easily move from the Democrat Wallace to Schmitz indicates the essentially conservative nature of Wallace's appeal. Schmitz won 1.1 million votes, 1.5 percent of the vote. In 1976 the American Party's presidential nominating convention deadlocked between the John Bircher Thomas Anderson and Lester Maddox, former Democratic governor of Georgia and, politically, a kindred spirit of Wallace himself. The party split along regional lines, and both Anderson and Maddox were nominated by rival wings. Neither gained more than marginal electoral success; Maddox, the more successful, won 170,274 votes. Nevertheless, he did better than any of his successors as nominee through the 1980s. In the 1990s, the remnants of the American Independent Party moved into closer and closer affiliation with the U.S. Taxpayers Party, the America First Party, and other tiny parties characterized by cultural conservatism, suspicion of the federal government, isolationism, and a powerful orientation toward grassroots organization. The inheritance of Thurmond and Wallace among American third parties, then, lies primarily in their combination of populist rhetoric with cultural conservatism—a formula that characterizes more recent conservative third parties as well.

The Constitution Party: The Rise of Social Conservatism

What is now called the Constitution Party is the largest of these. It was founded in California in 1992, primarily through the efforts of Howard Phillips, a Nixon administration official who left government service to found an advocacy group called the Conservative Caucus. While with the caucus, Phillips lobbied against social welfare programs, government regulation of industry, the income tax, and American involvement in international organizations. Increasingly, Phillips combined this political conservatism with his own evangelical Christianity, taking strong stands on moral issues such as abortion, gambling, and, in the words of the platform of the Constitution Party, "offensive sexual behavior." In espousing this combination, Phillips's new party was characteristic of broader patterns in American politics; an alliance between religious social conservatives and small-government advocates had propelled the Republican Party to success beginning with Ronald Reagan's triumph in the 1980 presidential election. However, Phillips and his allies were discontented with the Republicans; Phillips himself had grown disillusioned with the Nixon administration's broad interpretation of federal power, and after 12 years of a Republican presidency in the 1980s and early 1990s, he believed about the GOP what Thurmond and Wallace had about the Democrats—that the party in power did not hold to its principles. In 1992 Phillips named his new group the U.S. Taxpayers Party, invoking the populist mantle. In 1999, however, a convention renamed it the Constitution Party, a moniker its leaders believed more consistent with the broad scope of their platforms, beyond the mere economics implied in the old name and into cultural and foreign affairs. As of 2006, the Constitution Party was the largest third party in the United States, claiming 366,937 registered members.

Phillips carried the banner of his party into the presidential race in 1992, 1996, and 2000. The second campaign was the most successful; Phillips then won 184,820 votes—a total neither he nor the 2004 candidate, Michael Peroutka, have come close to matching.

Several state branches of the American Party—most vocally, that of California—endorsed the U.S. Taxpayer/Constitution nominee in some or all of these elections. This gradual convergence reflects the similarity of the ideological paths the two groups have traveled. Both infuse small-government philosophy with a populist moralism drawn increasingly from evangelical Christianity, advocating a nearly belligerent patriotism, isolationism, and limited government in economic, political, but not social, policies. The opening years of the twenty-first century demonstrated how distinct from Republicanism this philosophy made these parties; in the 2004 presidential campaign, Peroutka vigorously attacked the security policies of the Bush administration as intrusive and unconstitutional and joined with Democratic activists to denounce the Iraq War. To date, the Constitution Party has managed to elect one state representative, Rick Jore, who won a seat in the Montana state legislature in 2006. In 1999 the Republican senator from New Hampshire, Bob Smith, briefly affiliated with the U.S. Taxpayers Party in order to seek its presidential nomination. However, he reaffiliated with the Republican Party after only a month.

The Conservative Party of New York

This populist, culture-oriented third-party genealogy was paralleled by another group. It grew not from the middle-class and lower middle-class culture warriors who supported Wallace but from one wing of the intellectual elite of the burgeoning conservative movement. Less concerned with cultural issues than with economic and political freedom, these conservatives first took a stand in the Conservative Party of New York, organized in 1962 in response to a series of frustrations: Democrat John Kennedy carried the state in the 1960 presidential election; the New York Republican Party, led by Governor Nelson Rockefeller, showed persistently liberal inclinations; and more broadly, these conservatives shared a discontent with the general support for large government. They advocated small government and a genteel cultural traditionalism (distinct from the more virulent, law-and-order cultural populism of Wallace and other agitators). The early leadership of the party included academics like legal scholar Charles Rice and attorney J. Daniel Mahoney; it soon attracted the support of the wealthy conservative Buckley brothers, James and William. William F. Buckley Jr., the editor of the *National Review* and a leading conservative thinker, served as the party's protest candidate in the 1965 New York City mayoral election, running primarily in an attempt to deny election to liberal Republican John Lindsay. In 1970, James Buckley won a surprise victory in a three-way race for the Senate and served one term, losing a reelection bid to Democrat Daniel Patrick Moynihan despite securing the Republican nomination.

Notwithstanding some initial successes, the Conservative Party of New York has recognized the historically marginal position of third parties on the American political landscape. Thus, it has primarily sought to influence the two-party system rather than win election in its own right. It strategically endorses or denies support to Republican Party candidates, hoping to influence that party's nomination process. Indeed, no Republican has won statewide office without Conservative support since 1974. The party has become increasingly concerned with social and cultural issues over time; it withheld endorsement of Republican Rudolph Giuliani for mayor of New York City in all three of Giuliani's campaigns—1989, 1993, and 1997—because of Giuliani's liberal stands on social issues such as abortion and gay marriage. Giuliani's only nominal association with the Republican Party had gained him the endorsement of the state Liberal Party. The party also suffered some internal dissent over its endorsement of Governor George Pataki's bid for a third term in 2002, some members complaining that Pataki had grown too liberal while in office.

The Libertarian Party exhibits similar concern with ideological purity. It was founded in 1971 by Republican activists disillusioned with the Nixon administration—origins similar to the later founders of the Constitution Party. The Libertarians are notable for their particular orthodoxy; unlike most other conservative third parties, which meld desire for economic and political freedom with some degree of cultural conservatism, the Libertarians support a reduction in government authority across the board and do not share the isolationist impulses of the Constitution Party, their closest competitor in the race for largest conservative third party in the United States. The Libertarians are currently fifth overall, boasting 235,500 registered members, behind the Constitution Party and the Green Party.

Ross Perot and the Reform Party

In 1995 the Texas businessman H. Ross Perot, who had won 19 percent of the popular vote as an independent candidate in the 1992 presidential election, founded the Reform Party and ran for president again as its nominee in 1996. He won only 8 percent of the vote that year and was widely criticized for using the party as a tool for his personal interests rather than allowing it to develop an independent political identity. Nevertheless, Perot's political views, and those of his initial followers, reflected a variety of populist conservative impulses: he endorsed a nationalist and isolationist trade and foreign policy, having opposed the 1991 Gulf War and the North American Free Trade Agreement. Similarly, he advocated a small government that held strictly to a balanced budget and engaged in limited welfare programs. He also supported conservative social policies. In 2000 and 2004, however, the Reform Party splintered all along the political spectrum, nominating the former Nixon administration figure Pat Buchanan after a bitter convention battle in 2000. Buchanan shared Perot's isolationism and cultural conservatism. However, he won the nomination without the support of followers of the semi-libertarian governor of Minnesota Jesse Ventura, the party's highest elected official, or the camp of John Hagelin, candidate of the Natural Law Party, who also sought the Reform nomination and advocated a political philosophy based on transcendental meditation. In 2004 the state of the party grew even more confused, as supporters of the left-wing Green Party activist Ralph Nader seized control of the Reform Party convention and nominated Nader for president. The Reform Party remains divided, crippled by multiple lawsuits over its legitimate leadership and lacking a coherent ideology. Its future is cloudy.

Under Perot, however, the Reform Party served a function similar to the Dixiecrats or the Conservative Party of New York or any other conservative third party. It was a party of protest, a forum for grievances, and a crucible in which issues neglected by the political mainstream gained resonance and influence. Though these parties have rarely gained electoral success, they have influenced American politics by forcing the Republican and Democratic parties to confront issues they would just as soon ignore, and providing the electorate a means of signaling where the future of American politics might go.

See also conservatism; Libertarian Party.

FURTHER READING

Frederickson, Kari. *The Dixiecrat Revolt and the End of the Solid South*. Chapel Hill: University of North Carolina Press, 2001.

Gillespie, J. David. *Politics at the Periphery: Third Parties in Two Party America*. Columbia: University of South Carolina Press, 1993.

Sifry, Micah. *Spoiling for a Fight: Third Party Politics in America.* New York: Routledge, 2002.

Wattenberg, Martin. *The Decline of American Political Parties, 1952–1992.* Cambridge, MA: Harvard University Press, 1994.

MATTHEW BOWMAN

Constitution, federal

The oldest of the world's effective written constitutions, the U.S. Constitution was designed in a convention in the summer of 1787, made public on September 17, and formally adopted with the ratification of New Hampshire on June 21 of the following year. It serves as the fundamental law determining the scope and limits of the federal government. But its origin lies in a perceived need to reform the "firm league of friendship" that held together the 13 original colonies in one nation, with "a more perfect Union."

Union and Liberty

The Articles of Confederation, drafted during the opening stages of the war for independence, had established the first American Union. Less than a decade later, they were widely regarded as a failure. In the 1780s, the United States faced a number of critical international and interstate issues arising from the Revolution and the ensuing separation of the colonies from the British Empire. State governments refused to adhere to the peace treaty with Britain; Britain refused to give up military posts on U.S. territory; public creditors went unpaid; Indians attacked settlers and squatters occupied public lands; Spain closed the Mississippi to American commerce; and Britain banned American ships from trading with the West Indies and the British Isles.

Congress—the central government established by the Articles of Confederation—was unable to address these issues. It had neither money nor soldiers, only minimal administrative departments, and no court system. The Constitution aimed to change this situation. It was therefore a practical solution to immediate problems. But this should not detract from the achievement of the founders, for the difficulties were pressing and the stakes were high. In the minds of the reformers, the American Union had become so weak that the future of the nation as an independent confederation of republics was in doubt. Because republican rule on the scale attempted in the United States was a novel political experiment, the outcome of the American crisis had global significance. The success or failure of the reform would decide whether republican government—that is, popular self-rule for the common good—was viable. Ultimately, therefore, the framing and ratification of the Constitution should be understood as an attempt to secure republican government by means of a stronger union.

The reform of the Union was based on two fundamental premises: first, that the civic liberties and rights that Britain had threatened and the American Revolution defended could only be safeguarded under a republican form of government; second, that the American states could only be guaranteed a republican form of government by union. Union and liberty were therefore intimately linked in the political imagination of the founding generation as the preservation of liberty was the raison d'être of the Union.

In the present world of stable democracies and superpower republics, the notion that republics are inherently weak and unstable, and therefore difficult to maintain, does not come naturally. Early modern political theory, however, taught that republics were prone to internal dissension and foreign conquest. Republican citizens were freer than the subjects of monarchs, but this freedom made them hard to control and made it difficult for the government to command the social resources and popular obedience necessary to act forcefully against foreign enemies and domestic rebellion. Monarchies were therefore held to be better equipped than republics for securing the survival of the state. But the strength of monarchical rule rested on centralization of power at the cost of popular liberty. Political theory also taught that republican rule could be maintained only in states with a limited territory and a small and homogeneous population. Thus, the republic's weakness came both from a necessary small size and the form of government.

Confederation provided a way out of this predicament. In the words of eighteenth-century French writer Baron Montesquieu, by joining together, republics could mobilize and project "the external force of a monarchy" without losing "all the internal advantages of republican government." Confederation also provided protection against internal dissension, the other great threat to the republic. "If sedition appears in one of the members of the confederation," noted Montesquieu, "the others can pacify it. If some abuses are introduced somewhere, they are corrected by the healthy part." In important respects, the U.S. Constitution is the practical application of Montesquieu's lesson.

The American states assumed independence and entered into union in a single political process. Work on an act of union was already under way when the states declared independence, but the Articles of Confederation were not finished until 1777 and took effect only with ratification by the thirteenth straggling member, Maryland, in 1781. Like the Constitution, the articles were both an agreement of union between the states and a charter for the central government created to realize the purposes of union. They aimed to provide the states with "common defense, the security of their Liberties, and their mutual and general welfare" (Article III). To this end, the states delegated certain enumerated powers to the central government. These powers were those that the English political philosopher John Locke termed "federative" and which he defined as "the Power of War and Peace, Leagues and Alliances, and all the Transactions, with all Persons and Communities without the Commonwealth." These powers had been invested in the imperial government under the colonial system, and, under the articles, the central government was to assume them.

Although in theory, the state governments would not exercise the powers they had vested in the central government, in practice, they retained complete control over the application of these powers. This was a reflection of the fear of central power that to a great extent had inspired the American Revolution. Thus, Congress possessed neither the right to collect taxes nor to raise an army, and it had neither a judiciary nor an executive. Therefore, the central government could declare and conduct war but not create or supply an army; it could borrow money but not provide for its repayment; it could enter into treaties with foreign powers but not prevent violations of international agreements. On paper, its powers were formidable, but in reality, Congress depended completely on the cooperation of the states.

Historians have emphasized the many conflicts during the reform process, first in the Constitutional Convention and later during the ratification struggle. Nevertheless, there was, in fact, a widely shared consensus on the essential features of the reform. Most Americans agreed on the necessity and ends of union; on the propriety of investing federative powers in the central government; and on the need to strengthen Congress. There was relatively little debate on the purposes of the union.

Commentators agreed that the central government was intended to manage interstate and international affairs. Congress should provide for the defense against foreign nations; prevent violations of international law and treaties; regulate interstate and international commerce; appoint and receive ambassadors; preserve peace among the states by preventing encroachments on states' rights; and ensure domestic peace and republican liberty by providing for defense against sedition in the states. The last of these duties has occasionally been interpreted as an undue involvement in the internal affairs of the states in order to quell popular movements. In fact, it originated in the need to maintain stability and republican government in the composite parts in order to guarantee the strength of the Union as a whole. In addition to these duties, some reformers had a more expansive agenda and wanted the central government to take an active role in governing the states. Chief among them was James Madison, who wanted Congress to guarantee "good internal legislation & administration to the particular States." But this was a minority view that had little influence on the final Constitution.

If there was consensus on the Union's objectives, there was also agreement that the Articles of Confederation had not met them. Three issues in particular needed to be addressed: Congress had to have the right to regulate trade; it needed a stable and sufficient income; and it had to possess some means by which it could ensure that the states complied with Congress's requisitions and resolutions.

Economic recovery after the war for independence was hampered by discrimination against American trade. The most serious restrictions were the closing of the Mississippi River and the exclusion of American ships from the British West Indies and British Isles. In order to retaliate against these measures, Congress needed the right to regulate commerce, including the right to tax imports and exports.

The Articles of Confederation had not entrusted Congress with power over taxation. Instead, the central government was expected to requisition money from the states, which would handle the administration of taxation. The system never worked, making it difficult to pursue the Revolutionary War efficiently and provide for the postwar debt. If states neglected or ignored Congress's legitimate demands, it had no way to enforce compliance. It was therefore necessary to reform the articles so as to provide the central government with power to enforce congressional resolutions.

The framing and adoption of the Constitution had been preceded by several reform initiatives originating in Congress, which sought to correct deficiencies by amending the Articles of Confederation without modifying the organization of the Union. One after another these attempts failed, however, and the reform initiative passed from Congress to the states. In 1785 Virginia negotiated an agreement with Maryland over the navigation of the Chesapeake Bay, and in the following year, Virginia invited all the states to a convention to meet in Annapolis, Maryland, to consider the Union's commerce. The convention adjourned almost immediately because of insufficient attendance (only five state delegations were present). But the convention also issued a report that spoke of "important defects in the system of the Foederal Government" a political situation that was serious enough "to render the situation of the United States delicate and critical." The report recommended calling a new convention with a broadened mandate to "take into Consideration the situation of the United States, to devise such further Provisions as shall appear to them necessary to render the constitution of the Foederal Government adequate to the exigencies of the Union." Congress and the states agreed to the proposal and a convention was called to meet in Philadelphia on May 14, 1787, "for the sole and express purpose of revising the Articles of Confederation."

The Constitutional Convention

In all, 55 delegates from 12 states attended the Constitutional Convention (only Rhode Island did not send delegates). They belonged to the political leadership of their respective states; many had served in Congress or held a commission in the Continental Army. A majority of delegates were lawyers (34), and almost half were college educated (26). If they were not the assembly of demigods they have sometimes been made out to be, they were nonetheless a group highly qualified to address the ills of the American union.

The convention did not reach a quorum until May 25, 1787, and the delay allowed the Virginia delegation to prepare a set of opening resolutions that set the agenda for the convention. The acceptance of these resolutions on May 30 was the most important decision of the convention, because it superseded its mandate to revise the Articles of Confederation in favor of establishing "a national government . . . consisting of a supreme legislative, judiciary and executive." The novelty of the Virginia Plan, as the resolutions are known, lay not in an expan-

sion of the powers delegated to the central government but in a reorganization of the structure of the union that would make it possible to use those powers effectively. According to the plan, the projected government would inherit all "the Legislative Rights vested in Congress by the Confederation." In addition, it would have the right "to legislate in all cases to which the separate States are incompetent, or in which the harmony of the United States may be interrupted by the exercise of individual Legislation"—a broad grant that included both the power to tax and to regulate trade. The plan did not question the aims of the Union, however, stating that like the Articles of Confederation it was created for the "common defence, security of liberty and general welfare" of the member states.

The Virginia Plan was largely the brainchild of James Madison, who came to Philadelphia best prepared of all the delegates. Madison was disappointed with important aspects of the finished Constitution, and his reputation as "Father of the Constitution" rests on his success in determining the basic thrust of the convention's work by means of the Virginia Plan. Madison had thoroughly analyzed the shortcomings of the Union under the Articles of Confederation and had identified the crucial defect to be the reliance on voluntary compliance of state governments to Congress's resolutions and the lack of "sanction to the laws, and of coercion in the Government of the Confederacy." Rather than providing Congress with an instrument of coercion, however, Madison suggested a reorganization of the central government. It would no longer be a confederated government that depended on state governments for both its upkeep and the implementation of its decisions, but a national government legislating for individuals and equipped with an executive and a judiciary to enforce its laws. It was a simple and ingenious solution to a critical problem: how to enable the central government to exercise its powers efficiently.

The basic idea of the Virginia Plan was to create two parallel governments that were each assigned a separate sphere of government business. As was the case under the Articles of Confederation, the business that would fall on the lot of the central government was foreign politics and interstate relations, whereas the state governments would manage their own internal affairs. The two governments would both derive their legitimacy from popular sovereignty and be elected by the people. Each government would be self-sufficient in the sense that it could provide for its own upkeep, legislate on individuals, and have its own governmental institutions for implementing its legislation.

If the line of demarcation that separated the central government from the state governments seemed clear enough in theory, there was a risk that each would encroach on the other. Madison and his supporters in the convention were convinced that the only real risk was state encroachment on the central government, and the Virginia Plan thus provided for its extensive protection. Other delegates were more concerned with the danger of central government encroachment on state interests and rights. In the course of the Constitutional Convention, such critiques of the plan led to important modifications intended to safeguard state interests.

Opposition to the Virginia Plan first came from the delegations of New York, New Jersey, Delaware, and Maryland, which, at critical points, were joined by Connecticut. During the convention and afterward, these delegations were called "small-state members." Gradually, concern for the protection of state interests came to be a common concern for almost all the delegates.

At times, objections to the Virginia Plan were so strong that the convention came close to dissolution, and only compromises and concessions saved it. Opposition first arose over the plan's provision that the "National Legislature" be elected by the people rather than the states and that "the rights of suffrage" in the legislature "ought to be proportioned to the Quotas of contribution [i.e., taxes], or to the number of free inhabitants." The "small-state" men were not ready to accept this change in the principle of representation but struggled to retain the rule of one state, one vote, as was the case under the Articles of Confederation. Concern for state interests reappeared in demands for protection of specific state rights and disagreement over the mode of electing the president. Conflicts over the status of the states dominated the convention's business and have tended to overshadow the consensus that existed on the fundamentals of the plan. Thus, the need for stronger central government was not challenged, nor were the concepts of separate spheres of government business and of two self-sufficient governments acting on the same citizens.

The small-state men first offered an alternative plan to that of the Virginia delegation. Presented by William Paterson of New Jersey (on June 14, 1787), the New Jersey Plan agreed to many of the provisions of the Virginia Plan, but left the principle of representation in Congress untouched. Had the plan been accepted, Congress would have continued to be an assembly appointed by and representing states in which each state had one vote. When the convention rejected the New Jersey Plan on June 19, the small-state members fell back on their second line of defense: demand for state appointment to, and state equality in, one of the two branches of the legislature. They secured this goal in the so-called Connecticut Compromise on July 16, whereby the states were to appoint the members of the Senate and have an equal number of representatives in this branch. Senators were to vote as individuals and not as state delegations, however. After this victory, the small-state opposition dissolved.

It was replaced by concern for specific state interests, chiefly emanating from southern delegations. State equality in the Senate meant that the southern states would now be outnumbered eight to five, which made encroachment on southern interests a distinct possibility. Whereas the small-state men had spoken in general and abstract terms of state rights, state interests now took concrete form. As Pierce Butler of South Carolina commented, "The security the Southn. States want is that their negroes may not be taken from them which some gentlemen within or without doors, have a very good mind to do." Eventually, several demands of the southern states made it into the finished Constitution, among them the Three-Fifths Compromise (which counted three-fifths of the slave population toward representation in the House of Representatives); the prohibition on interference with the slave trade before 1808; the Fugitive Slave Clause (which required that escaped slaves be apprehended also in free states and returned to slavery); and the ban on federal export duties. Concern for state interests also influenced the intricate rules for the election of the president, which were intended to balance the influence of small and large states, both in the North and the South.

Opposition to the Virginia Plan reveals much about conceptions of the Union at the time of its founding. Proposals to create new jurisdictions by means of a subdivision of the states were not seriously considered. Despite their recent and contingent history, the existing states had become political entities whose residents ascribed to them distinct interests arising chiefly from economic and social characteristics. The delegates to the convention further believed that the interests of different states were sometimes conflicting, something that had been repeatedly demonstrated in the 1780s when congressional delegations fought over western lands and commercial treaties. The founders grouped the states into sections of states sharing basic interests, the most important of which were the slave states in the South and the non-slave states in the North. Concern for protection of state interests grew not so much from a fear that the central government would pursue its own agenda to the detriment of the states collectively as from fear that the central government would come under the control of one section that would use it as an instrument to promote its own interests at the expense of another.

State interests were a reality in the minds of the American people and could hardly have been transcended, even if the delegates had wished to do so. Opposition to the Virginia Plan provided a necessary correction to the purely national government first envisioned by Madison. States were now protected from central government encroachment on their interests by state representation in the Senate and by guarantees for specific state interests. The central government was protected from state government encroachment primarily by being made self-sufficient and therefore able to act independently of the states, but also by making the Constitution and federal laws and treatises the supreme law of the land. All state officers and state courts were now bound to obey and uphold the Constitution and federal legislation.

It is often said that the Constitution was the result of a compromise that created a government, in Oliver Ellsworth's words, "partly national, partly federal." In comparison to the Virginia Plan, this seems accurate enough. But compared to the Articles of Confederation, the Constitution created a government much more national than federal, able to act in almost complete independence of the state governments. When Madison reflected on the Constitution in *The Federalist* he remarked, "If the new Constitution be examined with accuracy and candor, it will be found that the change which it proposes, consists much less in the addition of *New Powers* to the Union, than in the invigoration of its *Original Powers*." This is the best way to understand the achievements of the convention. By a radical reorganization of the Union that provided for a separate and self-sufficient central government acting on individuals rather than states, the Constitutional Convention had correctly diagnosed the Union's fundamental malady and provided for its cure.

The Struggle over Ratification

The finished Constitution was signed on September 17, 1787, and in a dramatic gesture, three of the delegates—Elbridge Gerry, George Mason, and Edmund Randolph—refused to sign the document. Gerry and Mason feared that the convention had gone too far in creating a strong central government and had failed to safeguard basic civic rights and liberties. Their objections foreshadowed a prominent critique that would soon be directed against ratification of the Constitution.

Framing the Constitution was only the first step toward re-forming the Union. An important part of the reorganization was the establishment of the federal government by an act of popular sovereignty, whereby it would be placed on par with the state governments. It had therefore to be accepted by the people and not the states. To this end, the Constitutional Convention had proposed that the states call ratifying conventions, whose delegates would be chosen by the electorate in each state. Despite some complaint in Congress and some of the states that the convention had exceeded its mandate, ratifying conventions were eventually called in all states except Rhode Island.

The ills arising from the defunct Union had been widely experienced, and the new Constitution stirred enormous interest. Within a few weeks, 61 of the nation's 80 newspapers had printed the Constitution in full; it also was printed in pamphlets and broadsides. The public debate that followed is impressive in scope, even by modern standards. The Federalists, who supported the Constitution, controlled most of the newspapers and dominated the debate. Yet the opposition, branded Anti-Federalists by their opponents, was nevertheless distinctly heard in both print debate and ratifying conventions.

Although states' rights comprised an important theme in Anti-Federalist rhetoric, the opposition was even more concerned with the dangers to republican liberty that would flow from an overly strong federal government. Apart from the last-minute objections by Gerry and Mason, such fear had not been a marked feature of the deliberations in the Constitutional Convention. The majority of Anti-Federalists accepted that the central government had to be strengthened, but also believed that the Constitution had gone too far in creating a government with unlimited power to raise armies and taxes, regulate the militia, borrow money, and to pass any law "deemed necessary and proper." By establishing a strong president, a small House of Representatives, and a Senate with a six-year mandate, the convention had set up a government that would be unresponsive to the wishes of the common people and beyond the effective control of the citizens. It was bound to fall under the control of the rich and "wellborn," who would use the new government to oppress the people and to increase their own

Table 1
Delegates Appointed to the Constitutional Convention (with Signers in Italics)

State	Name	Comment	State	Name	Comment
New Hampshire	*John Langdon*		Pennsylvania (*continued*)	*James Wilson**	
	Nicholas Gilman				
	John Pickering	Did not attend		*Gouverneur Morris*	
	Benjamin West	Did not attend	Delaware	*George Read**	
Massachusetts	*Nathaniel Gorham*			*Gunning Bedford Jr.*	
	Rufus King			*John Dickinson*	
	Elbridge Gerry*	Nonsigner		*Richard Bassett*	
	Caleb Strong	Left before adjournment		*Jacob Broom*	
			Maryland	*James McHenry*	
	Francis Dana	Did not attend		*Daniel of St. Thomas Jenifer*	
Connecticut	*William Samuel Johnson*			*Daniel Carroll*	
	*Roger Sherman**			Luther Martin	Left before adjournment
	Oliver Ellsworth	Left before adjournment		John Francis Mercer	Left before adjournment
	Erastus Wolcott	Declined appointment		Robert Hanson Harrison	Declined appointment
New York	*Alexander Hamilton*			Charles Carroll of Carrollton*	Declined appointment
	John Lansing Jr.	Left before adjournment		Thomas Sim Lee	Declined appointment
	Robert Yates	Left before adjournment		Thomas Stone*	Declined appointment
New Jersey	*William Livingston*			Gabriel Duvall	Declined appointment
	David Brearley				
	William Paterson		Virginia	*George Washington*	
	Jonathan Dayton			*John Blair*	
	William C. Houston	Left before adjournment		*James Madison*	
	Abraham Clark*	Declined appointment		Edmund Randolph	Nonsigner
				George Mason	Nonsigner
	John Nielson	Declined appointment		George Wythe*	Left before adjournment
Pennsylvania	*Benjamin Franklin**			James McClurg	Left before adjournment
	Thomas Mifflin			Patrick Henry	Declined appointment
	*Robert Morris**				
	*George Clymer**			Thomas Nelson*	Declined appointment
	Thomas FitzSimons				
	Jared Ingersoll				

(continued)

Table 1
Delegates Appointed to the Constitutional Convention (with Signers in Italics) (Continued)

State	Name	Comment	State	Name	Comment
Virginia (*continued*)	Richard Henry Lee*	Declined appointment	South Carolina	*John Rutledge*	
North Carolina	*William Blount*			*Charles Pinckney*	
	Richard Dobbs Spaight			*Charles Cotesworth Pinckney*	
	Hugh Williamson			*Pierce Butler*	
	Alexander Martin	Left before adjournment		Henry Laurens	Declined appointment
	William R. Davie	Left before adjournment	Georgia	*William Few*	
				Abraham Baldwin	
	Richard Caswell	Declined appointment		William Pierce	Left before adjournment
	Willie Jones	Declined appointment		William Houston	Left before adjournment
				George Walton*	Did not attend
				Nathanael Pendleton	Did not attend

*Signer of the Declaration of Independence
Sources: Farrand 3, 557–59, 596–90; Jensen et al., 1, 76, 230.

riches and prestige. Although the federal government would be able to act with energy against foreign nations, this ability would come at the price of a centralization of power that would eventually put an end to liberty.

Federalists never accepted that analysis of the Constitution. They maintained that representation would work and government would be exercised for the benefit of the people. They also argued that reorganization of the Union was necessary for the preservation of liberty. The main strategy of Federalist rhetoric was to contrast the blessings of union with the horrors of disunion. The choice before the American people was presented as a choice not between different ways to reform the Union but between adopting the Constitution or inviting certain disunion. According to the Federalists, disunion would result in the creation of mutually antagonistic regional confederacies. These confederacies would build up their military strength and enter into alliances with Europe's great powers. War was certain to follow, and in its train, political centralization and the decline of liberty. Wars gave rise to standing armies, heavy taxes and large public debts, a "trinity of evil"

that Madison once described as the bane of republics and the maker of monarchies. Adoption of the Constitution, in contrast, promised to secure the future of the Union and thereby to banish war from the North American continent.

Federalists also urged critics of the Constitution to accept that the American republic existed in a world of predatory monarchies. If the self-rule of the American people was to be maintained, their government had to be able to defend the independence and interests of the United States. Ultimately, this defense rested on the ability to project military power, which required the federal government to have unlimited powers of mobilization. If left to themselves, the states could only mobilize sufficient resources to defend their interests by exerting a heavy pressure on their citizens. By joining forces, however, states could establish enough strength to warn off hostile powers with a minimum imposition on the people. Thus, the Constitution promised the benefits of government with little cost.

Despite control over the press and support from the majority of the social and political elite, ratification of the Constitution was not a foregone conclusion. From the Federalist perspective, the ratification process began well: Delaware, Pennsylvania, New Jersey, Georgia, and Connecticut ratified the Constitution between December 7, 1787, and January 9, 1788, and only Pennsylvania's ratifying convention witnessed any real opposition. Although outnumbered, Pennsylvania Anti-Federalists were influential in shaping critical responses to the Constitution in other states. With the meeting of the Massachusetts convention in January, easy Federalist victories came to an end. Massachusetts finally ratified with a narrow margin of 187 to 168. Even this slight majority could be secured only after the Federalists had accepted that the Constitution be adopted with amendments. This practice was followed in all of the remaining states save Maryland. The next convention to meet was that of New Hampshire, where the Federalists avoided defeat only by securing a four-month adjournment before voting on the Constitution. Momentum seemed lost and ratification uncertain. However, Maryland and South Carolina ratified in April and May 1788 with solid majorities in favor of the Constitution. Eight out of the nine states required for the Constitution to take effect had now accepted the new compact of union. On June 21, New Hampshire became the ninth state to adopt the Constitution.

Without acceptance by Virginia and New York, the Union nevertheless had slight chance of success. In Virginia Anti-Federalism was strong, and in New York, it was overwhelming. Eventually, both states ratified the Constitution by narrow margins, ten votes in Virginia and only three in New York. Their acceptance can be explained by the late hour of their conventions. When the Virginia and New York conventions met, eight states had already ratified the Constitution and the two states' conventions were still in session when the news came of New Hampshire's vote. Rejecting the Constitution in this situation would have meant separation from the other states in the Union. With Virginia and New York in favor, it mattered little that North Carolina and Rhode Island at first rejected the Constitution and adopted it only in 1789 and 1790, respectively. Three years after the Philadelphia Convention adjourned, all of the states had accepted the new Constitution.

A Federal Republic

The new federal government convened in the spring of 1789. As had been universally anticipated, George Washington was elected the first president, and both the House of Representatives and the Senate had Federalist

majorities. The first Congress continued the work begun in the Constitutional Convention by transforming the clauses of the Constitution into government institutions and policies that would address the Union's problems. Only when these were in place would the Constitution truly be "adequate to the exigencies of the union" and the promise of the framers and the Federalists be fulfilled. For this reason, the first Congress may also have been the most important, and, overall, it was remarkably successful. It created three administrative departments to deal with foreign affairs, finances, and defense. It set up a postal service, an Indian Department, and a Land Office responsible for selling federal lands. The Judiciary Act of 1789 organized the federal judiciary and further specified its jurisdiction. Within six years under the new federal government, the United States had achieved a number of political successes. The Indian nations in the Ohio territory had been defeated and neutralized and the government earned revenue from public land sales. The fiscal apparatus was remodeled to secure a steady income from customs duties. Public finances were reformed and public credit restored. In 1795, major commercial treaties were entered into with Britain and Spain.

In the short run, the clearest evidence of the Founding Fathers' success in reforming the Union is that their

Table 2
Ratification of the Constitution by the States

State	Date	Vote	Amendments
Delaware	7 Dec. 1787	30–0	No
Pennsylvania	12 Dec. 1787	46–23	No
New Jersey	18 Dec. 1787	38–0	No
Georgia	31 Dec. 1787	26–0	No
Connecticut	9 Jan. 1788	128–40	No
Massachusetts	6 Feb. 1788	187–168	Yes
Maryland	26 Apr. 1788	63–11	No
South Carolina	23 May 1788	149–73	Yes
New Hampshire	21 June 1788	57–47	Yes
Virginia	25 June 1788	89–79	Yes
New York	26 July 1788	30–27	Yes
North Carolina	2 Aug. 1788	84–184	Yes
	21 Nov. 1789	194–77	Yes
Rhode Island	29 May 1790	34–32	Yes

rebuilt ship of state managed to sail unharmed, if not altogether untroubled, through the storm of the French Revolution and the ensuing quarter century of world-wide war. This period brought down kings and empires on both sides of the Atlantic, and it placed great stress on the Union, not the least of which came during the War of 1812. But the Union endured. The founders' work did not eliminate the tension that resulted from conflicting sectional interests; to the contrary, the Constitution facilitated the articulation of sectional interests through the representation of the states in the Senate and the guarantee to protect state interests such as the preservation of slavery. Eventually, internal tension came close to dissolving the Union during the Civil War. Yet despite such conflicts, the Constitution provided the institutional basis on which the nation would grow in territory, population, and riches. In the long run, therefore, the framers of the Constitution demonstrated that republics were not forever destined to weakness and in-stability but could become powerful and achieve world domination.

See also anti-Federalists; Articles of Confederation; Bill of Rights; federalism.

FURTHER READING

Banning, Lance. *The Sacred Fire of Liberty: James Madison and the Founding of the Federal Republic.* Ithaca, NY: Cornell University Press, 1995.

Cooke, Jacob E., ed. *The Federalist.* Middletown, CT: Wesleyan University Press, 1961.

Edling, Max M. *A Revolution in Favor of Government: The U.S. Constitution and the Making of the American State.* New York: Oxford University Press, 2003.

Farrand, Max, ed. *The Records of the Federal Convention of 1787.* 4 vols. New Haven, CT: Yale University Press, 1937.

Gibson, Alan. *Understanding the Founding: The Crucial Questions.* Lawrence: University Press of Kansas, 2007.

Hendrickson, David C. *Peace Pact: The Lost World of the American Founding.* Lawrence: University Press of Kansas, 2007.

Hutchinson, Willam T., and William E. Rachal, eds. *The Papers of James Madison.* 17 vols. Chicago: University of Chicago Press, 1962–91.

Hutson, James J., ed. *Supplement to Max Farrand's Records of the Federal Convention of 1787.* New Haven, CT: Yale University Press, 1987.

Jensen, Merrill, John P. Kaminiski, and Gaspare J. Saladino, eds. *The Documentary History of the Ratification of the Constitution.* 20 vols. Madison: State Historical Society of Wisconsin, 1976–.

Levy, Leonard W., and Dennis J. Mahoney, eds. *The Framing and Ratification of the Constitution.* New York: Macmillan, 1987.

Onuf, Peter S. *The Origins of the Federal Republic: Jurisdictional Controversies in the United States.* Philadelphia: University of Pennsylvania Press, 1983.

Onuf, Peter, and Nicholas Onuf. *Federal Union, Modern World: The Law of Nations in an Age of Revolutions, 1776–1814.* Madison, WI: Madison House, 1993.

Rakove, Jack N. *Original Meanings: Politics and Ideas in the Making of the Constitution.* New York: Knopf, 1997.

Wood, Gordon S. *The Creation of the American Republic, 1776–1787.* Chapel Hill: University of North Carolina Press, 1969.

MAX M. EDLING

consumers and politics

The history of consumers and American politics dates back to the founding of the country and has three distinct strands. First, since the American Revolution, Americans have used the boycott of consumer goods as a political tool. Second, beginning in the late nineteenth century, Americans have made political demands as consumers for a higher standard of living. Finally, in the twentieth century, especially in the postwar period, an organized movement has pushed for greater regulation of the quality and safety of consumer products.

From the Revolution to the Gilded Age
The American Revolution traced its origins, in part, to a consumer boycott, the famous Boston Tea Party on December 16, 1773, when rebelling colonialists dumped British tea in the harbor to protest the crown's imperial policies. This was not an isolated event. Before the American Declaration of Independence in 1776, colonists boycotted British goods to demonstrate their displeasure with England's tax policies. After the Seven Years' War, the British government sought to raise money to pay war debts by taxing its colonial subjects. At the time, the North American mainland purchased 25 percent of English exports. In that context, the colonialists' nonimportation strategy was a powerful political tool, one intended to put economic pressure on the British government to repeal the Stamp Act of 1765, the Townshend duties, and

the Tea Act as unconstitutional violations of the principle of no taxation without representation. Colonial merchants organized boycotts, which led to a decline in British exports by two-thirds. This strategy gained support from ordinary colonists, from the Daughters of Liberty who held spinning bees and encouraged the wearing of homespun clothes to crowds who mobilized to intimidate customs officials and importers. This new kind of mass politics based on organized popular resistance and everyday political participation culminated in the Boston Tea Party. At stake were fundamental questions of Britain's public power over its colonial subjects that led to the American Revolution. Colonialists not only achieved independence but also created a new notion of direct representation premised on popular participation in politics.

In the century that followed independence, Americans based their participation in politics on their producer identity as hardworking, virtuous independent farmers, small merchants, or artisans. As more Americans became wage earners, trade unions emerged to represent their collective interests and preserve a sense of autonomy and freedom at the workplace.

In the late nineteenth century, however, Americans began to embrace a consumer identity as the basis of political action. Between 1870 and 1920, the number of Americans living in cities doubled to over 50 percent. By 1920 more people worked in factories than on farms, and less than one-quarter of the workforce was self-employed. At the same time, people were now purchasing basic necessities, from prepared food to ready-to-wear clothing to store-bought tools and furnishings, rather than producing them at home. Moreover, the emergence of department stores, mass retailers, and mail-order catalogs, along with the rise of brand-name goods, created a new consumer ethos of satisfaction guaranteed. Amusement parks, nickelodeons, and commercial dance halls arose as forms of cheap amusement. In that context, Americans started to make demands as consumers entitled to a higher standard of living.

With a rise in productivity, organized labor insisted on a shortening of the workday and the right to leisure time. "Eight hours for work, eight hours for rest, eight hours for what we will!" was the slogan. In 1886 hundreds of thousands of workers staged an unsuccessful general strike to demand the eight-hour day. The eight-hour movement won a victory in 1916 with the passage of the Adamson Act, which limited hours for railroad workers. But only in 1938 did labor succeed in getting Congress to pass the Fair Labor Standards Act to make the eight-hour day the national standard.

In the late nineteenth century, organized labor also demanded higher wages as another crucial aspect of a sense of entitlement to an "American standard of living." Workers began to abandon their critique of wage labor as an extension of slavery. Becoming less critical of capitalism, instead they argued they had a right to earn a "living wage," by which advocates like American Federation of Labor (AFL) president Samuel Gompers meant enough money to buy a home of at least six rooms with indoor plumbing, furniture, pictures, carpets, and books. Rather than dulling political activism, the prospect of better living standards propelled labor agitation. As Gompers explained in an 1887 political speech, "Continual improvement, by opening up new vistas, creates new desires and develops legitimate aspirations. It makes men more dissatisfied with unjust conditions and readier to battle for the right."

From the Progressive Era to the 1920s

As nineteenth-century deflation gave way to twentieth-century inflation, a preoccupation with the cost of living led to an activist consumer politics. Between 1897 and 1916, the cost of living rose 30 percent. New sites of consumption, from streetcars to storefronts, became sites of protests with slight fluctuations in price. The early twentieth century witnessed countless rent strikes, beef boycotts, and other fights over the "high cost of living," led by housewives who understood their actions in the marketplace as the counterpart to their husbands' wage campaigns at the union hall and factory. For example, Pauline Newman, who became well known as a leader of the 1909 "uprising of 20,000," when tens of thousands of teenage New York garment workers went on strike, first cut her teeth by leading rent strikes around the city.

A consumer identity could cross class lines and be a unifying force in the Progressive Era fight against corporations. Contemporary Americans understood rising prices as the product of a conspiracy by big trusts. President Woodrow Wilson captured that antimonopoly sentiment when he said, "The high cost of living is arranged by private understanding." The fight against rising prices united workers and the growing segment of the white-collar middle class on fixed salaries, who shared the belief that trusts were to blame. Progressive journalist Walter Lippmann identified what he saw as a rising "consumer consciousness." In his 1914 book *Drift and Mastery*, he explained, "The real power emerging today in democratic politics is just the mass of people who are crying out against the 'high cost of living.'" That consumer sensibility was especially true for women, who were thought to be responsible for the vast majority of purchasing. "The mass of women do not look at the world as workers," said Lippmann. "In America, at least, their primary interest is as consumers."

Playing on that sentiment, reformers founded the National Consumers League (NCL) in 1898 as a lobbying group of middle-class women who would push for greater regulation of consumer goods and the conditions under which they were made. Under the leadership of Florence Kelley, the NCL led union-label campaigns to persuade women to purchase garments made only in union factories under safe and fair labor conditions. Kelley argued, based on germ theory, that consumers should be concerned about the health of workers and the potential spread of diseases like tuberculosis. Through boycotts, Kelley sought to transform women's purchasing power into a political force for labor reform. The NCL also pushed, sometimes successfully, for state-level minimum-wage legislation for women workers. Massachusetts passed the first law for minimum wages for women in 1912. Several other states followed until the U.S. Supreme Court declared such legislation unconstitutional in 1923.

Protests over high prices came to a head in World War I, when the cost of living doubled. The Wilson administration worried that high prices would trigger labor unrest as the cost of living outpaced wages. Indeed, organized labor justified its strikes by claiming the right to a living wage. Wilson appointed Herbert Hoover to head the Food Administration and lead the campaign to restrain inflation—or war profiteering, as it was popularly known. Hoover appealed to Americans for patriotic conservation with requests for "meatless Tuesdays and wheatless Wednesdays"; at the same time, he engaged in a massive propaganda effort that legitimized notions of "fair prices" and the rights of consumers and put pressure on businessmen to moderate price increases. In the absence of price controls, which ultimately doomed his efforts, Hoover mobilized housewives to investigate local prices as a way to keep inflation in check.

The notion that shoppers had rights in the marketplace evolved in the 1920s when America became a modern consumer society. The publication of Upton Sinclair's *The Jungle* (1906), with its description of the horrible conditions in packinghouses, had earlier led to the passage of the Pure Food and Drug Act and the Meat Inspection Act, bringing the government into the business of regulating product standards for the safety and health of consumers. But the number of mass-produced products and the advertising of those products vastly expanded in the 1920s and were largely unregulated. In the 1920s, Stuart Chase and F. J. Schlink published scathing critiques of the tactics used by manufacturers to produce and sell their goods in books with titles like *Your Money's Worth* and *100,000,000 Guinea Pigs*. Without standardization of weights, sizes, and materials, and without sufficient product information, consumers could not judge value. In addition, these reformers worried about adulterated and even harmful products and called for stiffer government regulation of production and advertising. Their books became best sellers and led them to form Consumers' Research as an agency to test branded goods.

Reformers like Chase worried not only about consumer safety but also about inadequate consumer income. In the 1920s, the gross national product increased by 40 percent as a result of the application of mass production techniques to many industries, from automobiles to appliances. Reformers argued that the new economy required a better distribution of income so that more Americans could actually afford to purchase the new consumer goods. Organized labor claimed that living wages were not only morally and politically necessary but also essential to sustaining a mass consumption economy. Edward Filene, the department store magnate, articulated this vision best at a 1925 meeting of progressive reformers: "Mass production can live only through mass distribution, and mass distribution means a mass of people who have buying power." As he put it, "Production cannot be profitable unless it produces, first of all, consumers." In 1926, at an AFL annual convention, AFL president William Green explained, "If America's prosperity is to be maintained, it must be possible for the masses of workmen to buy and use the things they have produced." Henry Ford had argued for the importance of working-class consumption when he introduced the five-dollar day and cut the prices of his cars. But the labor movement and their allies believed that only unions and federal regulation of wages would enable sufficient redistribution of income to sustain the economy.

The New Deal and World War II

This argument gained traction in the 1930s, when reformers pointed to the problem of underconsumption to explain the Great Depression. Though capital spending fell far more than consumption, the idea of underconsumption as the major economic problem had widespread appeal. In his Commonwealth Club speech in September 1932, Franklin D. Roosevelt said, "Our task now is . . . meeting the problem of underconsumption, of adjusting production to consumption, of distributing wealth and products more equitably." Once in office as president, Roosevelt used the language of consumers and consumption to justify a range of measures, often even contradictory, that would boost the purchasing power of Americans and thereby restore prosperity.

When Roosevelt introduced the New Deal in 1933, he promised an expansion of governmental authority to increase purchasing power: "The aim of this whole effort is to restore our rich domestic market by raising its vast consuming capacity." But the National Industrial Recovery Act (NIRA) and the Agricultural Adjustment Act (AAA), the two key measures of the early New Deal, were necessarily inflationary, enabling producers to cut production and raise prices as a way of restoring profits. Section 7a of the NIRA was intended to increase wages by legalizing collective bargaining, but industry noncompliance rendered this measure ineffective. Both the NIRA and AAA led to higher prices without substantially increasing national income. Those higher prices threatened to undermine public support for the New Deal. As a result, Congress created new bodies to look out for consumers' interest and to contain protest. In the spring of 1935, housewives across the country formed "high cost of living committees," demanding price cuts on meat, milk, and bread.

The Great Depression led to the creation of new governmental agencies dedicated to protecting consumers. The National Recovery Administrations's (NRA) Consumer Advisory Board and the AAA's Consumers' Counsel pushed for three programs. First, they sought to organize county consumer councils to create a grassroots consumer movement. These local groups distributed new government publications like *Consumers Guide* that listed average prices of basic goods like meat, milk, and bread and urged consumers not to pay more. Second, consumer advocates pushed for an end to price fixing in NRA codes. Finally, they called for a government system of quality standards to provide consumers with essential product information. Their efforts culminated in the Food, Drug, and Cosmetic Act of 1938.

The key moment of injecting a consumer rationale into New Deal legislation came with the passage of the National Labor Relations Act in 1935. New Dealers looked to organized labor as the way to challenge corporate power and redistribute income. When Roosevelt took office, only 10 percent of the industrial workforce was organized. In introducing his measure to Congress in 1935, Senator Robert Wagner of New York explained that unionization of workers was essential for economic recovery: "When employees are denied the freedom to act in concert, . . . they cannot participate in our national endeavor to coordinate production and purchasing power." The solution was to let workers organize and bargain collectively for higher wages.

By the election of 1936, Roosevelt cemented his coalition of farmers, workers, and middle-class voters, often using consumer rhetoric to justify his programs. Farm supports boosted agricultural purchasing power, unionization boosted labor's purchasing power, and Social Security would boost purchasing power for millions of unemployed and retired Americans. When the economy declined in 1937–38, Roosevelt announced a Keynesian deficit spending measure, saying that the government had a responsibility to increase national purchasing power during a recession. In the postwar period, politicians would continue to use Keynesian fiscal tools to stabilize the economy.

World War II ended the Depression, and inflation returned as the key economic problem. To fight it, the government created the Office of Price Administration (OPA). As in World War I, the wartime administration mobilized the nation's housewives to prevent profiteering. But this time Congress passed mandatory federal price controls and rationing. Influenced by the New Deal, the wartime government was committed to preserving mass purchasing power by an expansion of state power. By setting ceilings on millions of products, the OPA successfully restrained business; simultaneously, it got 20 million women to sign the Home Front pledge not to pay more than ceiling prices. Hundreds of thousands volunteered for "little OPAs" in each county, and millions more reported price violations. The OPA remained in place more than a year after the war ended, with broad popular support, including that of organized labor. Having agreed to no-strike pledges and wage freezes, labor supported price controls to protect its members. The war, with a strong activist state, was the high point of a public policy committed to protecting mass purchasing power by regulating prices and wages.

The Postwar Years

In 1962 President John F. Kennedy announced his commitment to a "consumers' bill of rights." But unlike during the first two-thirds of the twentieth century, consumer issues now had little to do with prices or income. Instead of regulating wages and prices, government relied on taxing and spending to stabilize the economy. In the 1960s and 1970s, the modern consumer movement led by activist Ralph Nader focused on health and safety issues. In 1962 Congress passed the Truth in Lending Act to protect credit borrowers and the Truth in Packaging Act to require better labeling, and created the Consumer Protection Safety Commission. Nader's *Unsafe at Any Speed* (1965) led to the National Traffic and Vehicle Safety Act of 1966. Nader launched the public interest movement in which lawyers pushed for greater government regulation of safety and health in the environment and at the workplace.

By the 1970s, liberals no longer saw greater consumption as the solution to the nation's ills but pointed to abundance and an ethos of indulgence as the problem. President Jimmy Carter made that point of view clear during the energy crisis. "In a nation that was proud of hard work, strong families, close-knit communities, and our faith in God," said Carter in his famous 1979 "malaise" speech, "too many of us now tend to worship self-indulgence and consumption. Human identity is no longer defined by what one does, but by what one owns. But we've discovered that owning things and consuming things does not satisfy our longing for meaning. We've learned that piling up material goods cannot fill the emptiness of lives, which have no confidence or purpose."

Since the energy crisis of the 1970s, critics have taken sharply different views about consumption. Most liberals have called for restraint and conservation, whereas the business community and conservatives have pushed for relaxing regulations to make it easier to exploit the country's natural resources and productive potential. During the 1980s, while the left condemned displays of conspicuous consumption and ridiculed the "yuppie" lifestyle, the right took up the consumer mantle, using arguments about consumer choice to call for an end of government regulation and a return to free-market policies. President Ronald Reagan signed the largest tax cut in the nation's

history in 1981, claiming that a reduction in taxes would unleash the nation's creative genius and result in greater economic growth. While the number of jobs in the high-tech and service industries grew, income inequality also increased. To maintain consumer lifestyles and make ends meet, Americans took on unprecedented amounts of consumer debt made possible by the explosion of the credit card industry.

At the beginning of the twenty-first century, the largest corporation in the United States is Wal-Mart. The company appeals to American consumers by offering everyday low prices, which it stocks through a global supply chain. Whereas reformers a century earlier sought to regulate sweatshops in American cities, most production of consumer goods is now located in "third world" countries, especially China. There are periodic campaigns to prevent Wal-Mart stores from expanding into neighborhoods, spearheaded either by unions who fear the corporation's low wages and nonunion workforce or by local retailers who fear the retail giant's low prices. The success and proliferation of global corporations like Wal-Mart have largely undercut the century-long effort for government regulation of prices and wages. But as long as America remains a consumer society, political struggles about the means and meaning of consumption will occur.

See also business and politics; economy and politics; labor movement and politics; New Deal Era, 1932–52.

FURTHER READING

Cohen, Lizabeth. *A Consumers' Republic: The Politics of Mass Consumption in Postwar America.* New York: Knopf, 2003.

Creighton, Lucy Black. *Pretenders to the Throne: The Consumer Movement in the United States.* Lexington, MA: Lexington Books, 1976.

Cross, Gary. *An All-Consuming Century: How Commercialism Won in Modern America.* New York: Columbia University Press, 2002.

Glickman, Lawrence B. *Buying Power: A History of Consumer Activism in America.* Chicago: University of Chicago Press, 2009.

———. *Consumer Society in American History: A Reader.* Ithaca, NY: Cornell University Press, 1999.

Jacobs, Meg. *Pocketbook Politics: Economic Citizenship in Twentieth-Century America.* Princeton, NJ: Princeton University Press, 2005.

MEG JACOBS

conventions, political

See party nominating conventions.

crime

The United States has long been distinctive among industrial societies for both its high level of violent crime and the harshness of its criminal justice systems. The paradox of great reliance on penal coercion to ensure social order in a society founded on the idea of individual liberty was noted early on by Gustave de Beaumont and Alexis de Tocqueville, who wrote in the 1830s that while society in the United States "gives the example of the most extended liberty," its prisons "offer the spectacle of the most complete despotism." In the late twentieth century, this difference became magnified, as the United States increasingly diverged from other advanced societies in the degree to which its citizens suffered from interpersonal violence and, simultaneously, in the degree to which it imprisoned an ever growing proportion of its citizens. By the turn of the twenty-first century, the United States stood as an outlier among advanced societies, with both the highest rates of homicide in the advanced industrial world and the highest proportion of its population behind bars of any country, advanced or otherwise.

At the start of the twenty-first century, the United States incarcerated its population at a rate five times that of its closest Western European counterpart, England; eight to nine times that of more typical European countries like Germany, France, or Sweden; and twelve times that of Japan. Yet the American death rate from homicide was six times that of Germany, eight times that of the United Kingdom, and ten times that of Japan.

Measured by the risks of death by violence, the United States more closely resembles some countries of the former Soviet bloc and the third world than it does other advanced societies. Measured by levels of incarceration, only Russia now comes close, among major countries, to the United States. One of the world's richest societies is also one of its most violent: one of the most militantly individualistic of nations also has more of its people under state confinement than any country in the world.

Moreover, at the turn of the twenty-first century, the United States stood almost alone among industrial democracies—and indeed among many less-developed countries—in continuing to use the death penalty on a regular basis. (Some other industrial democracies, including Japan and Taiwan, have also maintained the death penalty, though on a smaller scale.)

These patterns, however, have varied considerably across different regions in the United States. In some ways, it is misleading to speak of an "American" crime problem—or an "American" response to crime. Imprisonment rates have been especially high in some of the southern states in recent years, and far lower in parts of New England and the Midwest—a pattern that partly reflects differences in the underlying rate of serious crime, but also long-standing regional differences in political culture and social policy. In the early twenty-first century, Mississippi imprisoned its citizens at a rate nearly four times that of Minnesota. The use of the death penalty varies even more sharply: the vast majority of executions have taken place in a handful of southern states, with Texas alone accounting for more than a third of all executions in the United States since the mid-1970s.

Entrenched Problems, Failed Reforms

This situation would have been hard to predict from the nature of American approaches to criminal justice at the nation's beginnings. American attitudes toward crime and justice were diverse in the seventeenth and eighteenth centuries, but they were often shaped by a reaction against the harshness of British policy. The colonies used the death penalty relatively sparingly by English standards, for example, and Enlightenment ideas stressing the reformability of offenders flourished, at least in some places in the eighteenth and early nineteenth centuries (notably in Pennsylvania, center of a Quaker-inspired reform movement to prevent crime and rehabilitate criminals), American reformers invented the penitentiary (in Pennsylvania in the 1830s) and probation (in Massachusetts in the 1840s).

Yet, in what was to become an enduring pattern, early efforts at reform were generally short-lived and confined to certain states. Moreover, the reformers' vision was problematic—and doomed to failure—from the start. The belief that hard labor, religious instruction, and strict discipline—the foundations of the penitentiary system—could tame the unruly and desperate products of an unequal and disruptive society lent itself to extraordinary harshness in the best of times, and many of the "reformed" institutions ultimately devolved into places of routine official brutality and inmate rebellion. By the middle of the nineteenth century, the United States had built many prisons, but the reform impulse was hard to discern: the prisons generally warehoused offenders under conditions of sometimes horrific brutality.

Those conditions sparked another reform movement in the years just after the Civil War. Once again, reformers argued that a combination of severe discipline with industrial training (or domestic training for female offenders) could transform the volatile (and heavily immigrant) "dangerous classes" into productive and docile citizens of the emerging industrial order. There were some enduring changes in this period—notably the creation of the first juvenile court at the turn of the century. But on the whole, the reform movement again failed, as the belief that a divided and dangerous society could be held together through its penal institutions ran up against social and economic realities. Offenders turned out to be far more intractable than the reformers had hoped: urban crime remained rampant (and far worse than in foreign cities; New York's homicide rate was several times higher than London's throughout the nineteenth century). By the turn of the century, the reformers' emphasis on the malleability of offenders was increasingly replaced by a more pessimistic view, informed by the biological determinism of Cesar Lombroso and other European theorists, whose ideas found considerably greater traction in the United States than in their countries of origin.

Throughout this period, the South presented a different pattern, both with respect to crime and the response to it. The economics of slavery worked against the widespread use of incarceration in southern states: corporal punishment, supplemented by both formal and informal strategies of terror, was more appealing to slaveholders as a means of social control, since they stood to lose the labor of slaves if they went behind bars. The post–Civil War years brought a shift toward a peculiarly southern blend of state and private control of offenders, based on the leasing of convicts to private employers—a system that destroyed the bodies and lives of thousands of convicts but did nothing to lessen the stunningly disparate levels of violent crime in much of the South. (Journalist H. V. Redfield wrote in 1880 that "the number of homicides in the Southern states is proportionately greater than in any country on earth the population of which is rated as civilized.")

Explaining the American Exception

The distinctive American pattern of unusual harshness toward offenders coupled with unusually high levels of violence is sometimes attributed to the nation's "frontier" history. But other settler societies show a very different trajectory when it comes to crime and punishment. Australia, another nation with a long frontier tradition (and one settled partly by convicts), had an average homicide death rate roughly one-fourth that of the United States throughout the second half of the twentieth century, and, by the twenty-first, had an incarceration rate one-sixth that of the United States.

The growing gap in crime and punishment between the United States and other advanced societies is rooted in a broader set of developments in political culture and public policy that have increasingly distinguished the nation from its counterparts in the developed world. These differences had been apparent at least since the industrial revolution but sharpened after World War II, and particularly after the 1960s. The central difference is the degree to which the United States hewed to a Darwinian vision of social policy with minimal attempts to narrow social and economic inequalities. In contrast to many other industrial societies, political movements to challenge the dominance of market principles were relatively weak. This had a twofold impact on crime and punishment in America, simultaneously aggravating the conditions that breed violent crime and constricting the range of politically feasible responses to it.

Social and economic policies driven by market principles contributed to the distinctive American pattern of crime and punishment in several mutually reinforcing ways. These policies widened economic inequalities, deepened poverty, and fostered community disintegration—all conditions that are known to breed violent crime—and also produced a massive trade in illicit drugs that, particularly after the 1980s, became inextricably entwined with the problem of violence. (Hard drugs were illegal in other developed countries as well, but in none of them was drug abuse as severe as in the United States, or the illegal drug trade as extensive.) The same principles simultaneously crippled the ability of public authorities to address those conditions by minimizing preventive public social spending and by fostering an ideology that placed the blame for crime and other social ills on the shoulders of individuals.

In contrast to other advanced societies, too, the sale of firearms remained largely unregulated in the United States. While some nations—including England and Australia—moved toward even tighter restrictions on gun availability in the late twentieth century, the United States moved, on the whole, in the opposite direction—relaxing already minimal restrictions on the individual right to own and carry firearms. The gap between the United States and other advanced industrial societies in homicide is notably higher than the gap for other violent crimes or property crime, and the wide availability of guns is an important part of the explanation.

The Eclipse of Alternatives

During a pivotal period in the 1960s, a movement for reform challenged the traditional reliance on the criminal justice system to maintain order in the face of these structural pressures toward violent crime. It was widely argued among social scientists, as well as many criminal justice practitioners, that relying on an expanded prison system to control crime was inherently ineffective, as well as costly. There was increasing criticism of the drift toward warehousing offenders while neglecting their rehabilitation and ignoring the social conditions that predictably bred crime, especially in the inner cities. There were calls for limiting the scope of the criminal law and for reducing the role of the prison as a first line of defense against crime—particularly by removing nonviolent offenders and juveniles from confinement. But with the partial exception of the reform of juvenile justice, most of these tentative efforts were derailed in the 1970s and 1980s and replaced by a new insistence on deterrence and incapacitation as the only effective strategies against crime.

While many countries in Europe and Asia kept rates of incarceration within a relatively narrow historical range (and a few enjoyed actual declines in imprisonment rates), the United States saw a relentless increase beginning in the 1970s, which continued even during periods when crime rates fell overall. The American prison and jail population increased sevenfold during the last three decades of the twentieth century, a rise that was unprecedented in U.S. history and, in terms of sheer size, unparalleled anywhere in the rest of the world. Prison populations also rose significantly in some other countries—including England and, especially, the Netherlands—after the 1990s. But in no country did the expansion of the penal system take place on such a massive scale as in the United States.

The reasons why this shift took place when it did, and why it was maintained through every national administration—whether Democratic or Republican—since then are complex. The Vietnam War diverted public resources from the domestic social programs and promising criminal justice alternatives that could have made a difference in crime rates. Simultaneously, the 1970s and 1980s saw the growing dominance of conservative views stressing the limits of government intervention in addressing the problems from which urban violence grew. The argument that "liberal" solutions like fighting poverty or providing job programs had failed were widely accepted, not only among the right but across much of the political spectrum. Influential conservative scholars began to argue that the liberal belief in the potential for rehabilitation of criminal offenders was an illusion, and that argument became widely influential among legislators, criminal justice practitioners, and the media. Many factors fed this ideological shift, including the very real stubbornness and persistence of violence, particularly in the cities, and, from another angle, the relative weakness of expert opinion in influencing public policy, which tended to be driven to a degree unusual in advanced societies by specific political interests and popular fears.

By the 1980s, both major parties shared a self-consciously "tough" approach to crime that included support for the death penalty, stiffer sentences, and increased investment in incarceration. The tendency for party positions on crime to become blurred was accelerated during the administration of President Bill Clinton, which worked energetically to pass legislation expanding the number of crimes eligible for the death penalty and to use federal authority (and federal money) to coerce state governments into keeping offenders behind bars for longer periods.

By the early twenty-first century, indeed, crime and the state of the criminal justice system had nearly disappeared from national political debate and from presidential election campaigns—in sharp contrast to the 1960s, when concern over "crime in the streets" helped elect Richard Nixon to the presidency. This was not because the problems had receded: after a period of decline in the 1990s, violent crime had stabilized at a level that remained extraordinarily high by international standards—and in many places was increasing (especially among the inner-city young), despite the unprecedented growth in imprisonment during the past several decades. The criminal justice system had swollen to the point where maintaining it cut deeply into other public expenditures and, arguably, lowered the quality of life for much of the population. Rather, the near disappearance of these issues from the national political stage reflected the fact that the major parties no longer differed significantly in their approach to them; therefore no political advantage could be gained by invoking the continuing crisis of violence in the streets or the social and fiscal strain of an increasingly dysfunctional correctional system.

Paradoxically, this has meant that the United States, despite the pervasive rhetoric about "getting tough" on crime, routinely tolerates a degree of public fear and insecurity that does not exist in other advanced societies. Part of the reason for this paradoxical acceptance of violence, as well as the lack of broad social or political concern with the consequences of a swollen penal system, is that both violence and incarceration have become increasingly concentrated in low-income minority communities with little political influence or public voice. The most serious forms of street violence, as well as violence in the home, had always been more severe among the poor and became more so in the late twentieth century. High levels of homicide death among the poorest fifth of the population, for example, were a key reason why the overall gap in life expectancy between affluent and poor Americans widened after the 1960s.

The racial dimension of this concentration is inescapable: at the beginning of the twenty-first century, 17 percent of black men then living (more than one in six) had spent some time in a state or federal prison, versus less than 3 percent of whites. Moreover, the growing army of the formerly incarcerated came disproportionately from a relatively few neighborhoods in the inner cities. But this pervasive presence of prison in the lives of black men did not make them safer. Homicide death rates among young black men in some states exceeded those of their counterparts in many of the most violent countries in the third world: young black men in Louisiana were more likely to die by violence than young men in Brazil or El Salvador. The continuing danger of everyday life had not diminished for inner-city minority residents, especially the young, but inner-city minority residents had little influence on the preoccupations of national politics.

There have been a number of recent exceptions to the generally punitive drift of American criminal justice policy—most of them launched at the state (and some-times local) levels. In the early years of the twenty-first century, certain states moved, with some success, to divert minor drug offenders from incarceration; others explored a variety of strategies to remove some of the least dangerous offenders from prison. These developments were often driven by the fiscal burden placed on state budgets by increased spending on prisons. But on the national level, where debate on criminal justice policy was shaped less by hard fiscal realities and more by ideology, there was little change in almost 40 years of reliance on criminal sanctions to deal with social ills.

In the absence of a sustained set of policies to address the roots of violent crime, the criminal justice system in the United States has, by default, come to take on an unusually pervasive role—in effect becoming the social policy instrument of first resort for dealing with the multiple troubles of low-income communities. The tacit commitment of both major political parties to this general strategy—with occasional exceptions—means that there is little to suggest that the shape of American crime policy will change much anytime soon, or that the United States will relinquish its place as both the most violent and the most punitive of advanced societies.

FURTHER READING

Banner, Stuart. *The Death Penalty: An American History*. Cambridge, MA: Harvard University Press, 2003.

Beckett, Katherine. *Making Crime Pay: Law and Order in Contemporary American Politics*. New York: Oxford University Press, 1999.

Currie, Elliott. *Crime and Punishment in America*. New York: Henry Holt, 1998.

Friedman, Lawrence M. *Crime and Punishment in American History*. New York: Basic Books, 1994.

Mauer, Marc. *Race to Incarcerate*. Revised and updated ed. New York: New Press, 2006.

Monkkonen, Eric. *Murder in New York City*. Berkeley: University of California Press, 2001.

Simon, Jonathan. *Governing through Crime*. New York: Oxford University Press, 2007.

Western, Bruce. *Punishment and Inequality in America*. New York: Russell Sage Foundation, 2007.

Whitman, James Q. *Harsh Justice; the Widening Divide between America and Europe*. New York: Oxford University Press, 2003.

ELLIOTT CURRIE

Declaration of Independence

The Declaration of Independence, issued by the Second Continental Congress on July 4, 1776, publicly proclaimed 13 of Great Britain's colonial provinces in North America to be independent, sovereign states, and formally styled their union "The United States of America." In justifying the act of separation, the Declaration enumerated numerous grievances the 13 colonies had against King George III of Great Britain while it appealed to natural law, corporate and individual liberty, and the right to revolution—concepts widely accepted in the eighteenth-century European world generally and the Anglophone world in particular. The Declaration marked the end point of a debate in the American colonies over the pursuit of independence from Britain. After the American Revolution, the Declaration became one of the most important American state papers, cited repeatedly by political leaders, activists, and commentators in the United States and in the wider world.

Prelude to the Declaration

The Declaration of Independence resulted from two overlapping political discussions in the North American colonies of the British Empire, one beginning in 1763, the other in 1775. The first discussion was the series of debates that took place in the colonies and in Britain itself over various measures Parliament had passed after the conclusion of Seven Years' War in 1763—debates historians collectively refer to as the "imperial crisis." Between 1764 and 1774, Parliament passed numerous laws designed to raise revenue in the American colonies. The Sugar Act (1764), the Stamp Act (1765), the Townshend Duties (1767), and the Tea Act (1773) all met with protests, each increasingly widespread. The leadership in the colonies disputed Parliament's right to levy taxes on the colonial population for a variety of reasons. At the beginning of the crisis, many colonists disputed Parliament's right to enact taxes on commerce or activities within a colony's borders (so-called internal taxes), but supported Parliament's right to regulate imperial commerce (so-called external taxes). Other colonists disputed Parliament's right to collect any taxes or enact any laws affecting the colonies. Although the latter was a minority viewpoint in the mid-1760s, it gained an increasing number of supporters by the early to mid-1770s. Parliament consistently asserted its right to legislate for the colonies (and all of the British Empire), doing so explicitly in the Declaratory Act (1766) and implicitly in subsequent revenue legislation, as well as in its response to the colonial protest that became known as the Boston Tea Party, the punitive Coercive Acts (1774). The Declaration of Independence came at the end of this long constitutional discussion: Parliament's insistence on legislating for the colonies drove the colonial leadership to abandon hope for compromise and to seek recognition of their independence as sovereign states.

At the same time, the Declaration of Independence came at the end of a shorter but just as heated discussion that marked the final phase of the imperial crisis. After the military confrontation between British regulars and Massachusetts militia at Lexington and Concord in April 1775, the debate among the colonists increasingly focused not on whether to declare independence but on when and how. The Second Continental Congress convened on May 10, 1775. Almost immediately it began to consider how it and the colonies should respond to the violence at Lexington and Concord. While a vocal minority believed that the colonies should seek independence from Great Britain immediately, a majority of delegates hoped to improve the situation through the existing mechanisms of the British government—appealing to Parliament and the ministry of Lord Frederick North or to King George III. At the same time, a majority of delegates also believed that the colonies should coordinate their resistance to measures of the North Ministry. On July 6, 1775, the Continental Congress issued the Declaration of the Causes and Necessity for Taking Up Arms, a justification for the Continental Army created just weeks earlier. The tone of this declaration was strident and uncompromising. Yet two days later, the Congress issued a petition to King George III, colloquially known as the "Olive Branch Petition," that identified the North Ministry and Parliament as the parties responsible for the controversy and called on the king to mediate the dispute. George III rejected the "Olive Branch" as soon as it arrived in Britain, refusing to officially receive or respond to the document. Even months after Lexington and Concord, however, the desire in the colonies to pursue independence was not unanimous.

With many members of the Continental Congress and a large segment of the colonial population lukewarm on the prospect of American independence, the Congress enacted a series of measures that quietly moved the colonies toward a position where independence became tenable. In mid-June, the Congress had created the Continental Army to coordinate the colonial siege of Boston. Congress also created continental currency and issued £4 million of it by the end of 1775. On July 6, Congress not only issued the Declaration of Causes but also created a continental post office and appointed Benjamin Franklin as postmaster. In October, George III, during his speech opening the new session of Parliament, declared the American Congress to be leading "a desperate movement" to "establish an independent empire." At the end of November 1775, Congress created the Committee of Secret Correspondence to communicate independently with foreign powers, the precursor to the Committee on Foreign Affairs. Congress was thus performing many activities of an independent sovereign. In December, Congress rejected allegiance to Parliament, while still claiming allegiance to the crown. Weeks later, on December 22, Parliament issued the Prohibitory Act, which closed off British trade with the colonies. It was in this environment, in January 1776, that Thomas Paine published *Common Sense*. Paine's plainspoken argument against monarchy and in favor of American independence proved very popular; within a month more than 100,000 copies had been published. Circulated throughout the colonies, *Common Sense* did more than any other publication to put American public opinion squarely on the side of independence. In the months that followed the publication of *Common Sense*, groups of Americans

at the town, county, and state levels issued petitions and resolutions calling on the Continental Congress to declare American independence from Britain. In March, Congress dispatched a secret diplomatic agent, Silas Deane, to France; in April, Congress opened American ports to foreign commerce; and on May 10, Congress issued a resolution, written by John Adams, calling on the individual colonies to draft new constitutions. It was not surprising when, just three weeks later, Congress found itself pondering a declaration of independence.

Proposal and Drafting

The Continental Congress began formal discussion of a declaration of independence on June 7, 1776, when Richard Henry Lee, speaking on behalf of the Virginia delegation, declared, "That these United Colonies are, and of right ought to be, free and independent States." He called on Congress to proclaim that reality, to formulate a plan for contracting foreign alliances, and to prepare articles of confederation to bind the 13 independent states together. Congress resolved itself into the Committee of the Whole and took up discussion of Lee's resolution the following day. Again, the sentiment for American independence was far from unanimous; a group led by delegates John Dickinson, Robert Livingston, Edward Rutledge, and James Wilson held fast to the notion that the time was still not right for a declaration, that the public needed more time to come around, and that the questions of confederation and foreign alliances should be resolved *before* Congress issued a declaration. But a majority of delegates favored independence at this point, and on June 11, 1776, Congress appointed a committee composed of John Adams (Massachusetts), Benjamin Franklin (Pennsylvania), Thomas Jefferson (Virginia), Robert Livingston (New York), and Roger Sherman (Connecticut) to draft a declaration of independence. As is well known, the primary responsibilities of drafting the declaration fell to Jefferson, who wrote at least three drafts during the 17 days he devoted to the declaration's composition. Franklin and the rest of the committee made only minor alterations before sending the draft of the declaration to the Congress on June 28.

An initial vote in the Committee of the Whole found nine colonial delegations in favor, South Carolina and Pennsylvania opposed, Delaware deadlocked, and New York abstaining. After a series of eleventh-hour reconsiderations by South Carolina, the last-minute arrival of Delaware's Caesar Rodney to break the tie in his delegation, and the abstention of Pennsylvania's two anti-independence delegates (Dickinson and Robert Morris), the vote on July 2 was 12–0–1 in favor of independence. (The New York legislature subsequently approved independence later in the month, making the decision unanimous.) Congress spent the next two days debating and revising the text of the declaration, agreeing to a series of changes, and approving a final version on the evening of July 4.

The president of Congress, John Hancock, signed the declaration immediately, and it was quickly printed and then reprinted throughout the now independent United States. The parchment copy of the Declaration of Independence that modern Americans recognize as the official Declaration of Independence (the copy on display at the National Archives in Washington, D.C.) was completed on August 2, and the delegates signed it when they could, as they moved in and out of Philadelphia during the remainder of the summer. Answering the other two elements of Lee's resolution, as well as the concerns of critics, in September, Congress resolved on a "plan of treaties" that would guide American diplomats during the Revolution. The drafting of the Articles of Confederation would continue into 1777. The 13 colonies declared independence as a united whole, but left the exact nature of their union (a singular sovereignty? a confederation? an alliance?) unresolved at the moment of the Declaration. (The lack of capitalization of the term "united" in certain parts and copies of the Declaration likely has more to do with the vagaries and idiosyncrasies of eighteenth-century penmanship than any attempt by the framers at a definitive statement on American federalism.)

Contents and Influences

When asked about the Declaration of Independence late in his life, Thomas Jefferson told one correspondent that its contents were "the genuine effusion of the soul of our country at that time." In other words, in drafting the Declaration, Jefferson attempted to express the conventional wisdom of the majority of Americans at that moment. Politically, the Continental Congress needed to issue a document that would justify the movement to independence using language and ideas that most Americans would support. The Declaration thus lists a multitude of grievances against King George III that would have appealed to Americans from all sections of the union and orders of society. The Declaration was also couched in language designed to appeal to the public in Britain and the British Empire, and also to the publics and governments in other European states. The Declaration is beholden to several overlapping currents of early modern political thought, although historians and political scientists continue to debate which political philosophers and schools of thought most influenced the Declaration.

The Declaration is structured into three major parts: the preamble or introduction, which lays out the principles under which the United States are issuing their declaration; the body, which lists the grievances against King George III that have compelled the declaration; and the conclusion. The preamble has become the most famous and oft-quoted section of the Declaration, although the body arguably was the most crucial section for contemporaries, as the revolutionaries were quite sensitive about justifying so drastic an action as breaking with king and country. The body is of note in that it was the part of the Declaration in which the Committee of the Whole committed one of major pieces of editing—removing the entire clause in which Jefferson had blamed the king of England for the institution of the slave trade, a passage that has been construed as an attack on the institution of slavery by Jefferson (although this is a subject of debate). The conclusion contains the actual declaration (from Lee's resolution) that the colonies are now "Free and Independent States," as well as several phrases that are also often quoted during American patriotic celebrations.

The Declaration's preamble lays out in broad strokes the political theories under which the Americans were justifying their action of declaring independence. The preamble presents the framework within which political society had come into being, the circumstances under which overturning an established political authority was justified, and the assertion that British North Americans had found themselves in such a position.

The preamble blends two major strains of early modern Anglophone political thought: Enlightenment-era natural law and Lockean contractualism. Eighteenth-century British political thinking was defined by a consensus that emerged from the English revolutions of the seventeenth century that human beings possessed rights innately, as a product of their existence in nature as created beings. These rights were known as natural rights, and the system that supported them was known as natural law. While the idea of natural law traced its antecedents to antiquity and to medieval scholasticism, Enlightenment-era natural law writers downplayed or outright rejected the theological implications of rights and laws rooted in nature and took the mechanistic cosmos of the scientific revolution as a model. The notion was that natural rights—the rights of human beings—conformed to the same inherent set of principles that Isaac Newton's laws of motion did, and thus could be studied, articulated, and understood.

Natural law served as the fundamental building blocks for human governments and polities. This was the message of John Locke's *Second Treatise of Government*, in which he described how "Governments are instituted among men"—human beings labored in the earth, creating property, and then surrendered most of their total and absolute freedom to a government in order to protect that property and their remaining, unceded rights. Government relied on this implied contract between the governors and the governed, and Locke outlined, in the *Second Treatise*, justifications of when a people could undo the contract, abolish their existing government, and seek to establish a new one. It was to this conventional wisdom of British political thought that Jefferson and the Americans were appealing in the Declaration's preamble. It was almost the exact same form that English subjects had used in the 1689 Declaration of Rights that had overthrown James II, asserted Parliamentary supremacy, and set the stage for the installation of William and Mary on the English throne.

Most historians, political scientists, and commentators have pointed to the Declaration's origins in seventeenth- and eighteenth-century English Enlightenment thought. The classic modern statement of this interpretation was the scholarship of Carl Becker, particularly his 1922 book *The Declaration of Independence: A Study in the History of Political Ideas*. Becker's work remains the standard account of the Declaration's intellectual origins, although in recent years other historians have argued for emphasizing other potential intellectual antecedents to the Declaration. Essayist Garry Wills argued in *Inventing America* for locating the bulk of the intellectual history of Jefferson's Declaration of Independence in the writings and thinkers of the Scottish Enlightenment, such as Francis Hutcheson, Thomas Reid, David Hume, and Adam Ferguson. While few Jefferson scholars would argue with the notion that Jefferson was influenced by the Scottish Enlightenment, Wills controversially argued that Locke played a small role in shaping the Declaration as opposed to the Scots. Ronald Hamowy disagreed with Wills, pointing to the fact that Locke's writings influenced much of the Scottish Enlightenment, and that much of the thinking behind the Declaration can be observed in both Locke and Hutcheson. This insight

further demonstrates how Jefferson was working within a framework of British political conventional wisdom in laying out the intellectual framework for the American declaration.

As important as the preamble, if not more so, to contemporaries was the body of the Declaration. The list of grievances began with a set of general accusations accusing the king of poor governance and subverting the system of divided powers that characterized the English Constitution and then moved toward specific complaints about laws and policies that the British government had enacted. The first set of grievances accused King George of undermining the English Constitution. He was accused of being a bad executive, in that he refused to either enact or assent to laws designed to promote "the public good." The king was then accused of undermining the legislative and judicial bodies of government—suspending colonial legislatures, calling them at inconvenient times and in inconvenient places, or refusing to call them at all, while also making colonial judges "dependent on his will alone" for both their time of service and their salaries. The Declaration then moved from a general indictment to a list of more specific grievances. These included the placing of standing armies within the colonies and subordination of the civilian to the military power (a reference to Massachusetts, where General Thomas Gage served as both governor and commander in chief of the king's forces); the enactment of the punitive Intolerable Acts against Massachusetts in the wake of the Boston Tea Party; the Quebec Act, which expanded Quebec's boundaries and protected the rights of French Catholics; and the Prohibitory Act, which had suspended commerce between the 13 colonies and the rest of the British Empire. The final grievances referred to the recruitment and deployment of German mercenaries against the colonies, the recruitment of American Indian allies against the colonies ("the merciless Indian savages"), and the "excitement of domestic insurrections among us," which referred to the offers of freedom extended to slaves who would support the British cause.

The grievances were all directed at King George III, even though many of them were the responsibility of Parliament or the joint responsibility of both Parliament and the king. Congress had absolved itself of allegiance to Parliament in December 1775, so the king was the only person and office toward which the Americans could legitimately direct their complaints. While the Intolerable Acts and the actions of the king, ministry, and their officers since those acts—including the events at Lexington and Concord and Lord Dunmore's proclamation—formed most of the complaints, a number stretched back to the beginning of the imperial crisis. By and large, though, the Americans rooted their Declaration in the violations of their rights and liberties that had occurred in the previous two to three years. The grievances were important since they were the justification for the separation—something that required justification not so much for domestic consumption (where the violations were well known) nor for British consumption (where the Declaration would be dismissed outright by most), but for an international audience. As historian David Armitage has shown, the Declaration served as what diplomats referred to as a "general manifesto"—that is, a state paper issued by one government to others to justify a particular course of action. As the United States hoped to achieve equality with and recognition from the other European states ("to assume among the separate powers of the earth"), the justification for their separation from Britain and reasons for entry into the wider community of states were important, if for no other reason than to allow the other European states to justify future agreements with the United States.

The body of the Declaration was the place where Congress deleted the entire passage in which Jefferson accused the king of supporting the introduction of the slave trade into the American colonies and actively refusing its abolition. Congress not only found this statement inaccurate, but the antislavery tone of the complaint also was deleted in order not to offend the sensibilities of the southernmost states, especially South Carolina, which remained involved in the slave trade.

The Declaration's conclusion contains the actual affirmative declaration of the independence of the 13 states, their rejection of allegiance to Britain and the British, and their declaration that they could perform all the activities of independent, sovereign states.

Publication and Reception

Shortly after its approval on July 4, 1776, the Declaration was sent to Philadelphia printer John Dunlap. Official copies were printed as broadsides and sent by John Hancock, as president of the Congress, to the governors of each of the states and to General George Washington as commander in chief of the Continental Army. Washington ordered his officers to read the Declaration to their soldiers on July 9. Similar public readings were held throughout the United States. As historian Jay Fliegelman observed, Jefferson wrote the Declaration to

be read aloud, indicating on one of his handwritten drafts "reading marks" that indicated where readers should take pauses. These marks were transferred onto the first typeset proof that Dunlap prepared, and although they were removed from subsequent printings, the Declaration still became the publicly read document it was intended to be. Public readings usually were accompanied by celebrations that often included the defacement or removal of symbols of royal authority, such as portraits and statues of the king. The Declaration was subsequently reprinted in at least 30 American newspapers (including a German-language newspaper in Pennsylvania) by the end of July 1776.

While independence was greeted with enthusiasm in most of the states in the summer of 1776, the Declaration itself was met with a more lukewarm reception. Looking at declarations of independence, constitutions, and bills of rights enacted at state levels in the years following July 1776, historian Pauline Maier found that the rhetoric and particular phrasing of the Declaration of Independence were copied little, if at all, and other contemporary documents, such as George Mason's draft of the Virginia Declaration of Rights, proved to be more influential. In Great Britain, the Declaration was officially ignored, and American independence was not recognized until negotiations for the peace treaty to end the American Revolutionary War began in 1782. However, the North Ministry did silently commission a lawyer named John Lind to write *The Answer to the Declaration of the American Colonies*, which, after an initial round of revisions, was published in several editions by the end of 1776. Lind offered a point-by-point refutation of all the Americans' listed grievances. Lind, like many other Britons who opposed the American cause, criticized the Americans for issuing a declaration proclaiming that "all men are created equal" while they continued to hold African slaves. Criticisms of the Declaration, such as those by Jeremy Bentham, continued to appear in the British press through the end of the war. The Declaration was greeted with more enthusiasm in France, where American diplomats Silas Deane and Arthur Lee could point to the document as a sign of the seriousness of the American people and Congress to the cause for which they were seeking French support.

Legacy

The Declaration of Independence has become, along with the Constitution, the most important of American state papers. Its effects have been various. Most basically, the day on which the Declaration was published, July 4—and not the day on which the vote for independence was taken and approved (July 2)—is commemorated as Independence Day in the United States. The "Fourth of July" and "The Fourth" have become synonymous with Independence Day in the American vernacular, and it can be argued that the usage of these colloquialisms is more widespread and common than the official name, Independence Day. During the partisan battles of the 1790s, adherents to the Jeffersonian Republican Party began to emphasize the text of the Declaration, Jefferson's authorship of it, and the universality of its principles to distinguish their nationalism from the pro-British and anti-French leanings of the Federalist Party. Public readings of the Declaration took on a partisan tone, which faded in the aftermath of the War of 1812 along with the Federalists. Readings of the Declaration then became, and continue to be, the centerpiece of many public celebrations of Independence Day, and expressions of a desire for national unity. Beyond defining an American national holiday, the Declaration has served as a touchstone for American national identity, and the sentiments in its preamble are nearly universally regarded as an expression of the bedrock principles of American political organization.

Throughout the lifetime of the United States, groups or individuals protesting against a perceived injustice sanctioned by American federal, state, or local governments, and protestors have used the text of the Declaration to turn public opinion to their cause. One of the earliest and most famous examples was the publication of the "Declaration of Sentiments" by the Seneca Falls Convention for women's rights in July 1848. Authored principally by Elizabeth Cady Stanton, the Declaration of Sentiments rephrased the Declaration of Independence to include both men and women and went on to list rights that the established American political and legal order had denied to women—most important, the right to vote, the right to own property without qualification, and the right to equal citizenship. The Declaration of Sentiments and the Seneca Falls Convention marked what most historians consider to be the starting point of the modern American women's movement. One attendee at the Seneca Falls Convention, former slave and abolitionist Frederick Douglass, would argue in an 1852 Independence Day oration ("What to the Slave Is the Fourth of July?") that the Declaration's promise would remain unfulfilled as long as slavery existed in America. This was a theme President Abraham Lincoln seized on

as he implicitly referenced the Declaration as the starting point of the American ideal in the Gettysburg Address of November 19, 1863, when he located the birth of the American nation "four score and seven years ago." A century later, in one of the defining episodes of the civil rights movement, Martin Luther King Jr.'s "I Have a Dream" speech to the August 28, 1963, March on Washington for Jobs and Freedom quoted the Declaration to great effect. Historians regard that speech and march as a defining moment leading to the Civil Rights Act of 1964 and the Voting Rights Act of 1965.

The Declaration of Independence has also had a life beyond the borders of the United States. Issuing a declaration of independence became an important act for colonial peoples seeking to win independence from an imperial power. In his international history of the Declaration, historian David Armitage identified over a hundred declarations of independence issued by national groups between 1776 and the early 1990s. Many nations borrowed rhetoric or form or both from the American declaration in issuing theirs. Following the American actions against Britain, the Latin American colonies of Spain issued declarations of independence as either a prelude or part of their revolutions against colonial rule—beginning with Colombia and then including Venezuela, Mexico, Argentina, Chile, and Central America. Declarations of independence would proliferate in the wake of the First and Second World Wars as the European colonial empires were broken up. Among the most famous of the postcolonial declarations of independence was Ho Chi Minh's "Proclamation of Independence of the Democratic Republic of Vietnam," which was issued on September 2, 1945, in the wake of the collapse of the Japanese Empire and explicitly (and ironically, given later events) quoted the American Declaration of Independence. Following the collapse of the Soviet bloc between 1989 and 1991, many of the former republics of the Soviet Union issued their own declarations of independence. Thus, the influence and legacy of the Declaration of Independence continue into the twenty-first century.

See also Articles of Confederation; war for independence.

FURTHER READING

Ammerman, David. *Under the Common Cause: American Responses to the Coercive Acts of 1774.* Charlottesville: University Press of Virginia, 1974.

Armitage, David. *The Declaration of Independence: A Global History.* Cambridge, MA: Harvard University Press, 2007.

Becker, Carl. *The Declaration of Independence: A Study in the History of Political Ideas*. New York: Harcourt, Brace, 1922.

Fleigelman, Jay. *Declaring Independence: Jefferson, Natural Language, and the Culture of Performance*. Stanford, CA: Stanford University Press, 1993.

Hamowy, Ronald. "Jefferson and the Scottish Enlightenment: A Critique of Garry Wills's *Inventing America: Jefferson's Declaration of Independence*." *William and Mary Quarterly*, 3d ser., 36 (October 1979), 503–23.

Locke, John. *Two Treatises of Government*. 1690. Edited by Peter Laslett. Reprint, Cambridge, UK: Cambridge University Press, 1988.

Maier, Pauline. *American Scripture: Making the Declaration of Independence*. New York: Knopf, 1997.

Marston, Jerrilyn Greene. *King and Congress: The Transfer of Political Legitimacy, 1774–1776*. Princeton, NJ: Princeton University Press, 1987.

Wills, Garry. *Inventing America: Jefferson's Declaration of Independence*. Garden City, NY: Doubleday, 1978.

LEONARD J. SADOSKY

democracy

Democracy is one of the most significant of the essentially contested keywords of American politics—second only, perhaps, to "freedom." Any effort to define its meaning is bound to strike some as preemptory and partisan. The whole of American political history might well be narrated as a struggle, often bitter, over what democracy can and should mean. Since the early nineteenth century, few Americans have been so bold as to suggest that the nation should shelve democracy altogether, but this consensus has hardly quieted conflict over its meaning.

But one could do worse, by way of a helpful working definition, than Abraham Lincoln's lapidary formulation in his Gettysburg Address (1863): democracy is "government of the people, by the people, for the people." At least Lincoln's definition provides us with the critical questions at the heart of the American contest over democracy's meaning: Who are (and who are not) the sovereign people? How might the sovereign people govern themselves? And how might the interests of all citizens be given equal consideration by the policies of their government? That is, American contests over democracy have centered on matters of inclusion, participation, and distributive justice.

Those many Americans who have taken pride in their democracy over the last two centuries have, again and again, had to answer to other Americans who have objected that their democracy is not democratic enough. The adversarial edge to "democracy" lies in its tie to the ideal of political equality. Some of the most significant students of American democracy have, to be sure, pressed for an even more expansively egalitarian, less strictly political understanding of the term. Alexis de Tocqueville argued in *Democracy in America* (1838–40) for a conception of democracy as a "habit of the heart" grounded in an "equality of social conditions." John Dewey went even further, contending in *The Public and Its Problems* (1927) that, at bottom, democracy was a moral ideal that should govern "associated living" of all sorts, "a wider and fuller idea than can be exemplified in the state even at its best. To be realized, it must affect all modes of human association, the family, the school, industry, religion" (325). But even if we set aside the controversies engendered by these more expansive understandings of democracy, we are still left with a disruptive ideal.

As an ideal, political equality dictates that democracies manifest some common features. These include an equal and effective opportunity for all adult citizens to express their views in the making of public policy, to offer a vote of equal weight on public decisions, to inform themselves on matters of public moment, and to participate in determining the agenda of public decision. These common features prescribe for all citizens of democracies a set of fundamental political rights.

Before the late eighteenth century, the widespread assumption was that a strictly democratic government meant direct rule and face-to-face participation by an entire citizenry. It was a regime suitable, if at all, only to very small polities, such as the city-states of ancient Greece. The genius and the challenge of modern democracies, among which the United States has played a pivotal role, has been to pursue the ideals of political equality in large, populous nation-states by means of representative institutions, in which most political decisions are made not directly by citizens themselves but by their agents.

As a consequence of this ambition, modern democracies—despite a host of different constitutional arrangements—have developed some common institutions widely conceived to be necessary, if not sufficient, for a representative democracy. These include placing the making of public policy in the hands of officials subject to popular election; fair and fairly frequent elections in which all adult citizens are entitled to participate; the right of every citizen to seek election to public office, subject only to minimal requirements of age and residence; the right of every citizen to free expression on matters of public concern; the presence of independent and competing sources of information readily available to all citizens; and the right of all citizens to participate in relatively independent associations and organizations (such as political parties) through which they might pursue political interests. Each of these institutions is linked to one or more features of an ideal democracy: universal inclusion, effective participation in public decision making and agenda setting, voting equality, and equal opportunity for the development of informed views on public issues.

The regulative ideals of political equality are just that, regulative ideals against which to measure the political institutions and practices of putative democracies, none of which has yet to register a perfect score. Even if one doubts that any actual democratic polity could ever fully realize these ideals, they have set a horizon against which we may measure the history and momentum of each of them.

The Founding

The intention of American revolutionaries in 1776 was not to erect the world's first modern democracy but to launch a confederation of republics. Republics, as they saw it, were like democracies, governments "deriving their just powers from the consent of the governed." But unlike democracies, they held in check the destabilizing, anarchical effects of undue popular participation in politics. Ideally, republican government rested in the hands of virtuous elites capable of a disinterested discerning of the common good. The role of the people was periodically to hand over their power to some of their betters, who "virtually" represented them.

Nonetheless, as once-loyal British subjects, the revolutionaries believed that a measure of popular participation in government was necessary to prevent tyranny, and, for a century and a half, Americans had developed a taste for it. The ideal constitution was one, like that of Great Britain, that balanced or mixed a "democratical" element with those of monarchy and aristocracy. Although suffrage in both the metropole and the colonies was exceptionally narrow by modern democratic standards, Britons believed that in electing representatives to

bodies such as the House of Commons and the colonial assemblies, ordinary voters played an essential role in government as bulwarks for the protection of liberty. In the context of the controversies leading up to the Revolution, American patriots, outraged by imperial controls, argued that "virtual" representation in Parliament by legislators whom they had not elected was insufficient. Representation, they contended, must be "actual"—a decidedly democratic sentiment.

In writing their revolutionary state constitutions, Americans attempted to replicate the balanced government of the three social estates, even without the presence in the revolutionary polities of two of them. Most revolutionaries crafted state governments that, in the absence of a monarch or a hereditary aristocracy, attempted to mirror the British ideal by establishing the office of governor and an upper house of a bicameral legislature as expressions of the principles of monarchy and aristocracy, respectively, leaving popular representation to the lower house alone.

The portentous exception was Pennsylvania, where a largely plebian convention led by Thomas Paine and Benjamin Franklin argued in 1776 that, in the absence of a king and aristocracy, mixed government made no sense. "There is but one rank of men in America," they contended, "and therefore . . . there should be only one representation of them in government." Their constitution provided for a much simpler government: a single legislature of elected representatives with no governor or upper house. Although Pennsylvanians would replace this constitution in 1790 with a more typical alternative, the constitution of 1776, crafted just down the street from where a more genteel gathering was declaring independence, suggested the democratic ferment bubbling beneath the surface of the Revolution.

Critics of the first Pennsylvania Constitution were legion. It seemed to more conservative republicans a dangerously democratic deviation, a lurch beyond popular sovereignty to unconstrained popular rule. But these critics and defenders of balanced constitutions were hard pressed to meet the radicals' argument. Eventually, though, they arrived at an exceptionally original and immensely significant counterargument. They reconceived of American republican governments in their entirety as representative of the people—all elected officials, governors, and state senators as well as members of the lower houses were, by these lights, popular agents. The branches and divisions of the government were not the mirror of distinctive social estates but necessary *functional* divisions of a people's government, designed by virtue of the checks and balances among them to protect liberty (and property) from overweening power—including that of the people themselves.

As Gordon Wood has shown, "Because the so-called houses of representatives had lost their exclusive role of embodying the people in government, democracy as Americans had understood it in 1776 disappeared from their constitutions. The people ruled everywhere, or, from a different perspective, they ruled nowhere." The "true distinction" of American republicanism, James Madison wrote approvingly in *Federalist 63*, lay in its "*total exclusion of the people in their collective capacity* from any share" in government. Representation was the "pivot" on which American republicanism turned, and if it was "democratic" republicanism, it was so in a new sense that promised to address the shortcomings of popular rule and render it suitable for an expansive nation-state. Although many late eighteenth-century American republicans continued to regard democracy as little more than a synonym for mob rule, a decidedly less threatening reconstruction of its meaning had begun to emerge, one that, ironically, rested substantially on virtual representation.

This conceptual breakthrough guided Madison and other elite republicans in the drafting of the federal Constitution in 1787. The result was a framework for the national government that opened with a bold declaration of popular sovereignty and authorship ("We the People of the United States . . . do ordain and establish this Constitution for the United State of America"), and then proceeded to leave no constitutionally authorized space for the subsequent exercise of democratic citizenship.

Many are the ways that the original Constitution fell short of the ideals of democratic egalitarianism held by subsequent generations. It tacitly legitimated chattel slavery; it entrusted the election of the president in a body of worthies, the Electoral College, intended to be insulated from congressional or popular control; it entrusted the selection of senators not to the electorate but to state legislatures; it provided for the equal representation in the Senate of each state, whatever its population; and it opened the door to the review of legislation by the least democratic branch, the judiciary. Of particular note was the manner in which the Constitution left perhaps the most important attribute of full democratic citizenship, suffrage, to the states—authorizing exclusions that would leave American democracy long bereft of universal suffrage.

The constraints that the Constitution placed on popular participation did not go unremarked. The most democratic of the founders, Thomas Jefferson, was inclined to collapse the distinctions between republicanism and democracy, and he found early American constitutions troublingly undemocratic. As Jefferson saw it, a republic "means a government by its citizens in mass, acting directly and personally, according to rules established by the majority; and that every other government is more or less republican, in proportion as it has in its composition more or less of this ingredient of the direct action of citizens. . . . The further the departure from direct and constant control by the citizens, the less has the government of the ingredient of republicanism." By these lights, he concluded, "it must be agreed that our governments have much less of republicanism than ought to have been expected; in other words, that the people have less regular control over their agents, than their rights and their interests require."

The Course of American Democracy

If the original Constitution constrained the democratic impulses that the Revolution unleashed, it could not altogether contain them. In the longer term, the Revolution was a radical revolution of dramatic proportions, one that would invest considerable power in the hands of yeoman farmers, artisans, and other citizens of modest means once thought undeserving of a significant political role. American republicanism, as Gordon Wood has observed, "contained the seeds of its own transformation into democracy. The equality that was so crucial to republican citizenship had a permissive significance in America that could not be restrained, and ordinary people, whose meanness and need to labor had made them contemptible in the eyes of the superiors from the beginning of history, found in republican equality a powerful justification for their self-esteem and self-assertion. As a consequence, the important age-old distinction between leisured gentlemen and common working people, which the revolutionary leaders continued to try to honor, was repeatedly blurred and eventually dissolved."

In the wake of the Revolution, American democrats, like Jefferson, devised extraconstitutional means to inject a fuller measure of participatory democracy into the nation's politics. Chief among them was the political party.

In the face of the bitter conflict over the financial and foreign policy initiatives of Alexander Hamilton and other Federalists in the 1790s, Jefferson and his chief lieutenant Madison (ironically, the author of the oft-quoted denunciation of "factions" in *Federalist 10*) organized the opposition into the aptly named Democratic-Republican Party, the first political party to feature the organization of a grassroots electorate. Extraconstitutional democratic politics made further advances under the aegis of the even more aptly named Democratic Party of Andrew Jackson and Martin Van Buren. Jacksonians attacked the remaining property restrictions on suffrage, established widespread patronage networks that rewarded the loyalty of party workers, and lent vocal support to a popular constitutionalism that challenged judicial supremacy, if not judicial review.

From the 1830s through the 1890s, American political parties served as the basis for a vibrant, participatory public sphere. Mobilizing partisan "armies," they provided their "soldiers" with well-lubricated rallies, parades, and barbecues. They printed a vast array of campaign literature, dressed their supporters in buttons, ribbons, and hats, and armed them with banners and posters. Turnout was the key to victory in nineteenth-century elections, which were held year-round, and party members engaged in constant cajoling of the faithful. Between 1840 and 1872, turnout in presidential elections averaged 69 percent, and from 1876 to 1900, 77 percent.

This was, however, an exclusive and ritualized politics in which considerably less than half of the adult population and a bare majority of the free adult population could take part and in which participation was less deliberative than ceremonial. Although, by 1830, most states had committed to universal white male suffrage, women, slaves, many free blacks, and Native Americans were, to one degree or another, denied full citizenship. But for men enclosed within these exclusive boundaries, this period marked the height of participatory politics.

The course of American democracy since the mid-nineteenth century might be described as a bumpy, winding road toward the ideal of government *of* the people (inclusion), accompanied by a long and continuing detour away from government *by* the people (effective participation). In turn, the story of American democratic thought in this period can perhaps best be construed as a vigorous debate over whether this detour has best served the interests of government *for* the people.

The path toward a more inclusive and egalitarian representative democracy can be traced in the amendments to the federal Constitution. If it would be mistaken to characterize many of the anti-Federalists as radical democrats invested in widening and deepening political equality, they were responsible for the addition to the Constitution of the Bill of Rights, some provisions of which would subsequently serve the cause of political equality. The later Reconstruction amendments ended slavery and denied states the rights to limit suffrage on racial grounds. The most significant of these three amendments for the political equality of all Americans was the Fourteenth, which nationalized citizenship and guaranteed all citizens "the equal protection of the laws," a potentially powerful lever for extending democratic rights. Other later amendments provided for the direct election of senators, for women's suffrage, for electoral votes to residents of the District of Columbia, and for suffrage for citizens 18 years of age or older.

As the Twenty-Fourth Amendment abolishing the poll tax suggests, states and localities found a host of ways to make democracy less inclusive—so much has rested on the shifting interpretation of the Constitution by the courts. African American suffrage, supposedly authorized by the Fifteenth Amendment (1870), was not secured until nearly a century later with passage of the Twenty-Fourth Amendment and the Voting Rights Act of 1965. Today, the most significant exclusionary state laws are those that do not allow convicted felons to vote. These laws, which originated as part of the many late nineteenth-century Southern measures designed to disenfranchise African Americans (including poll taxes and literacy tests), continue to have a racially discriminatory effect, given the disproportionately African American percentage of the felon population. Estimates are that 31 percent of the black men who live in Alabama and Florida have been disenfranchised in this fashion. And, of course, some of the undemocratic provisions of the original Constitution remain in force. (As Robert Dahl observes, a resident of California on one side of Lake Tahoe can increase the worth of her senatorial vote by a factor of seventeen by moving to Nevada on the other side of the lake.)

If American democracy slowly became more inclusive in the twentieth century, at the same time it became decidedly less participatory. Presidential election turnout fell to an average of 65 percent from 1900 to 1916, and to only 52 percent in the 1920s. Behind these figures lay dramatic structural changes in American politics that, as Robert Wiebe put it, took shape as a simultaneous "sinking of the lower class" and the "raising of new hierarchies." That is, the period between 1880 and 1920 witnessed a steady constriction of popular political participation, particularly by the least advantaged Americans (including millions of new immigrants from eastern and southern Europe), and the rise of the elite, managerial rule by the modern industrial corporation. The growing hole in the electorate defined an emptied plebian space.

Democratic government, once intensely local, became increasingly centralized and insulated from popular scrutiny and control—much of it in the hands of unelected experts recruited from a new, college-educated middle class. The political party was first supplemented and then, to a large degree, supplanted by the specialized interest group as the extraconstitutional means of popular participation in government. Popular politics did enjoy a modest resurgence in the midst of the Great Depression, thanks in large measure to the prominence of labor unions in the councils of the Democratic Party. But the decay of union power after the 1960s again limited the collective political power of the working class, which lacked the clout and the resources available to other interests. Finally, the formidable national security state created to project American power overseas during the cold war shrouded in secrecy a host of exceptionally significant public decisions, not least the decision to go to war.

In this new context, democratic citizenship, once raucously collective, became increasingly atomized. An electorate once mobilized as active armies of partisan soldiers was now seen as individual consumers, targeted in the privacy of their homes with advertising that was guided by opinion polling and mediated by radio, television, and, of late, the Internet. "As the People dissolved," Wiebe observed, "the state thrived. . . . As the modern state solidified, it filled the spaces that a disintegrating People vacated, then rolled on to create empires of its own."

Market Capitalism and Political Equality

If American democracy began with a political revolution in the service of small property owners, it was thus transformed by an economic and social revolution led by large-scale manufacturers and finance capitalists, one that remade yeoman farmers and artisans into tenant farmers and industrial laborers. The relationship between market capitalism and American democracy has been particularly important in shaping the fate of political equality in the United States.

As Dahl has observed, the relationship between capitalism and democracy is one of "antagonistic symbiosis."

They are "like two persons bound in a tempestuous marriage that is riven by conflict and yet endures because neither partner wishes to separate from the other." All modern democracies have market-capitalist economies (though not all nations with market-capitalist economies are democracies). A market economy, which decentralizes control over production and consumption, has proven more accommodating to egalitarian politics than the centralizing alternatives, such as fascism and state socialism. A market economy, which diffuses economic power to a greater degree than state-managed command economies, seems necessary, if not sufficient, to political democracy.

Yet, at the same time, capitalism generates deep economic and social inequities that threaten democracy by producing enormous disparities in wealth, income, status, prestige, information, organization, education, and knowledge. As Dahl writes, "Because of inequalities in political resources, some citizens gain significantly more influence than others over the government's policies, decisions, and actions. . . . Consequently, citizens are not political equals—far from it—and thus the moral foundation of democracy, political equality among citizens, is seriously violated."

Dahl's concerns are hardly new. Anxiety about the effects of economic inequality on political equality date from the earliest days of the republic. In 1792 James Madison, who had moved closer since 1787 to his friend Jefferson's equation of republicanism and democracy, proposed that Americans could go a good way toward ensuring political equality "by withholding *unnecessary* opportunities from a few, to increase the inequality of property by an immoderate, and especially unmerited, accumulation of riches," as well as "by the silent operation of the laws, which, without violating the rights of property, reduce extreme wealth towards a state of mediocrity, and raise extreme indigence toward a state of comfort."

American citizens afflicted by political inequality have followed Madison's advice, often turning to the state for interventions and regulations to deter the inequitable effects of capitalism, seeking to sustain the benefits of a market economy while addressing the harm it does to political equality. The results have included not only reforms, such as campaign finance regulations that directly target the effects of economic inequities on political democracy but also measures such as public education, progressive income taxation, and social welfare legislation that do so indirectly.

In Theory

Since Jefferson's time, Americans have played a significant role in the history not only of democratic practice but of democratic thought. They not only provided raw material for Tocqueville's great meditation on democracy but have made important contributions to democracy's intellectual legacy, some of them fit to stand with his. The history of democratic thought would be much the poorer were it not for Jefferson, Madison, Frederick Douglass, Elizabeth Cady Stanton, Walt Whitman, Henry George, Jane Addams, Herbert Croly, Dewey, Walter Lippmann, Reinhold Niebuhr, Martin Luther King Jr., Hannah Arendt, Christopher Lasch, John Rawls, Richard Rorty, and Robert Dahl—to name but a few American democratic thinkers of distinction.

Not surprisingly, American democratic theory has been closely attuned to American democratic practice. For all its variety, much of American democratic thought, particularly since the late nineteenth century, can be construed as a debate in which the nation's practical detour from the ideal of robust and effective democratic participation is either a necessary accommodation to circumstance or a contingent and unhappy U-turn away from political equality. Pitting those who might be termed democratic realists against those who might be called democratic idealists, this debate remains important for the future of American democracy.

Walter Lippmann made the characteristic realist case in *Public Opinion* (1922). Most citizens, he wrote, were incapable of grasping the dynamics of a complex, interdependent, modern world, and should not be expected to do so: "the common interests very largely elude public opinion entirely, and can be managed only by a specialized class." Most democrats had erred in placing an emphasis on self-government. Men do not desire "self-government for its own sake. They desire it for the sake of results." Modern democracies were better served by a minimum of public participation in political life; too much participation gummed up the works, or worse. The criterion to assess a government was thus not the extent to which citizens were self-governing but "whether it is producing a certain minimum of health, of decent housing, of material necessities, of education, of freedom, of pleasures, of beauty." In sum, government *for* the people did not require much government *by* the people.

John Dewey responded with an idealist counter a few years later. He acknowledged that Lippmann's was "perhaps the most effective indictment of democracy as currently conceived ever penned." Yet in light of this indictment, he argued, the task for democrats was not to lower their sights, as Lippmann advised, but to figure out a way to rematerialize the "phantom public" and provide it with a much more substantial governing role in democratic politics. "The old saying that the cure for the ills of democracy is more democracy is not apt if it means that the evils may be remedied by introducing more machinery of the same kind as that which already exists, or by refining and perfecting that machinery," Dewey said. "But the phrase may also indicate the need of returning to the idea itself, of clarifying and deepening our sense of its meaning to criticize and re-make its political manifestations." And the "idea itself," as Dewey saw it, was in the broadest sense that of self-government. As he put it in 1888 at the outset of his long career as an oft-disappointed but never daunted democrat, "the ethical ideal is not satisfied merely when all men sound the note of harmony with the highest social good, so be it that they have not worked it out for themselves." Government *for* the people was inextricable from government *by* the people.

In the concluding pages of *Democracy in America*, Tocqueville suggested that "the kind of oppression with which democratic peoples are threatened will resemble nothing that has preceded it in the world." He imagined a democratic citizen oxymoronically invested largely in private life: "As for dwelling with his fellow citizens, he is beside them, but he does not see them; he touches them and does not feel them; he exists only for himself and for himself alone, and if a family still remains for him, one can at least say that he no longer has a native country." Such citizens would be subject to a state less tyrannical than protective:

> It would resemble paternal power if, like that, it had for its object to prepare men for manhood; but on the contrary, it seeks only to keep them fixed irrevocably in childhood; it likes citizens to enjoy themselves provided that they think only of enjoying themselves. It willingly works for their happiness; but it wants to be the unique agent and sole arbiter of that; it provides for their security, foresees and secures their needs, facilitates their pleasures, conducts their principal affairs, directs their industry, regulates their estates, divides their inheritances; can it not take away from them entirely the trouble of thinking and the pain of living?

This is not a scenario that cost democratic realists much sleep at night. They are minimalists, wedded to Joseph Schumpeter's definition of democracy as little more than "that institutional arrangement for arriving at political decisions in which individuals acquire the power to decide by means of a competitive struggle for the people's vote"—a return to strictly virtual representation by elite "deciders." But Tocqueville's vision is the specter that haunts the nightmares of democratic idealists who refuse to admit that the ideals of political equality have fallen over the horizon.

See also Constitution, federal; Declaration of Independence; liberalism; republicanism.

FURTHER READING

Dahl, Robert A. *How Democratic Is the American Constitution?* New Haven, CT: Yale University Press, 2001.

———. *On Democracy*. New Haven, CT: Yale University Press, 1998.

Hanson, Russell L. *The Democratic Imagination in America*. Princeton, NJ: Princeton University Press, 1985.

Keyssar, Alexander. *The Right to Vote*. Revised ed. New York: Basic Books, 2009.

McGerr, Michael. *The Decline of Popular Politics: The American North, 1865–1928*, New York: Oxford University Press, 1986.

Tocqueville, Alexis de. *Democracy in America*. Translated by Harvey Mansfield and Delba Winthrop. Chicago: University of Chicago Press, 2000.

Westbrook, Robert B. *John Dewey and American Democracy*, Ithaca, NY: Cornell University Press, 1991.

Wiebe, Robert. *Self-Rule: A Cultural History of American Democracy*. Chicago: University of Chicago Press, 1995.

Wilentz, Sean. *The Rise of American Democracy: From Jefferson to Lincoln*. New York: Norton, 2005.

Wood, Gordon S. *The Radicalism of the American Revolution*. New York: Knopf, 1992.

ROBERT WESTBROOK

Democratic Party, 1800–2008

Any party that endures for more than two centuries must learn to adapt to shifting historical circumstances. The Democratic Party has existed in some form since the 1790s, and its influence on American politics has been as long and profound as that of any private institution. That influence has always depended upon the party's ability to shift its ideology, policies, and leaders when necessary to win or hold power at every level of government.

Only 16 of the 43 presidents elected in competitive elections have been Democrats, but 5 of those chief executives—Thomas Jefferson, Andrew Jackson, Woodrow Wilson, Franklin Roosevelt, and Lyndon Johnson—altered the shape of American politics and of their party in lasting ways. One can trace those changes in three significant areas: *ideas, policies,* and *constituent groups.*

The Party of Jefferson and Jackson

Unlike most political organizations, the Democratic Party was not created on a specific date. Partisans of Andrew Jackson first adopted the name in the mid-1820s, but the seeds of "the Democracy" were planted in the 1790s. It was then that Democratic-Republican societies proliferated to support the views of Thomas Jefferson, who was engaged in conflict with Alexander Hamilton over what powers the new federal government should wield and whether it should take a friendly or hostile stance toward the French Revolution. By the time Jefferson won the presidency in 1800, most of his allies were calling themselves Democratic-Republicans as well. His victory and reelection relegated the opposition party, the Federalists, to the status of a permanent minority before it expired altogether during the War of 1812.

Into the 1820s, the Democratic-Republicans sought to keep faith with their founding leader's advocacy of states' rights and a weak federal role in the economy. As Jefferson had stated in his first State of the Union address, "the States themselves have principal care of our persons, our property, and our reputation . . . agriculture, manufactures, commerce, and navigation" are "most thriving when left most free to individual enterprise." He also left a legacy of informality in office—he sometimes greeted visitors in a dressing gown and slippers—and a creed of religious tolerance at a time when some states still had an established church to which all residents had to pay taxes.

But it took the partnership of Martin Van Buren and Andrew Jackson to transform the party now called the Democrats into an efficient electoral machine that competed successfully in a new era when most white men had the right to vote. This change began during the second half of the 1820s. In the election of 1824, Jackson lost the election for president, although he had received more popular votes than the victor, John Quincy Adams.

In the aftermath Van Buren, "The Little Magician" from New York State, secured the allegiance of influential politicians up and down the East Coast and helped establish pro-Jackson newspapers from New England down to Louisiana. In 1828 Jackson swept to victory, as voter participation more than doubled from the previous campaign.

From that watershed year until the eve of the Civil War, Democrats won all but two presidential elections and usually controlled both houses of Congress. They espoused policies that managed to please a broad coalition of white immigrants in the cities, southern planters, and Americans of every region who favored conquering and settling the entire continent. Democrats welcomed Catholic immigrants, opposed laws to prohibit alcohol or ban the use of languages other than English in public schools, and wanted to keep taxes, especially on imports, as low as possible. In vetoing a bill to recharter the (Second) Bank of the United States, Jackson aligned the party with anyone who resented powerful financial interests. Every Democratic president before the Civil War defended slavery on the basis of both states' rights and white supremacy. But party leaders had no solution to the deepening sectional crisis of the 1850s. In the election of 1860, Democrats split apart along the North-South divide and ran two opposing national tickets. Their rift virtually ensured the election of Abraham Lincoln, the first Republican president. It would be more than seven decades before the Democrats regained their status as the majority party.

Although the party elected just one president—Grover Cleveland, twice—during the remainder of the nineteenth century, Democrats were not without power. They remained strongly entrenched in the commercial metropoles of New York, Chicago, and San Francisco as well as in the South and most border states. The swelling of immigration from Catholic Europe to the urban North and fear of "Negro domination" in Dixie strengthened the party's appeal in both regions. One consequence was that the Democrats controlled the House of Representatives through much of the 1870s and 1880s and kept the GOP's majority in the Senate to a handful of seats.

The Gilded Age Democracy was a lively party indeed. Urban machines, while they made their bosses rich, also bestowed jobs and charity on working-class residents at a time when federal welfare payments went mainly to veterans of the Union Army and their nearest kin. Tammany Hall, the largest and most notorious of the machines, was a prodigious font of municipal jobs and contracts; in the late 1870s one of every twelve family men in New York held a position with the city. During each campaign, Tammany and its counterparts in cities across the nation held massive street parades, fireworks displays, and free banquets.

Democrats after the Civil War, however, had done little to alter their ideology or policies. With few prominent exceptions, they continued to preach a doctrine better suited to a decentralized, agrarian society than to a nation filling up with industries and big cities. Party stalwarts still tried to safeguard the powers of individual states, to curb federal spending, and to oppose agitators for such reform causes as prohibition, woman suffrage, and the redistribution of wealth. After helping to end Reconstruction, Democrats rebuilt a base in the Solid South, where ex-Confederates erected a "redeemed" social order that terrorized black voters it could not control and eviscerated funding for education and medical care. Critics of the party dubbed its leaders "Bourbons," a reference to the last kings of France, about whom a diplomat quipped that they "had learned nothing and forgotten nothing."

The Bryan-Wilson Shift

In the 1890s, the Democrats finally made a change. Across the South and West, movements of farmers and workers were demanding relief from what they saw as corporate domination of the economy and politics. They called on the government to protect union organizing, to create public works jobs for the unemployed, and to establish a flexible money supply that could give relief to debtors and small businesspeople. Some of the disgruntled joined the new People's Party which espoused this ambitious agenda. As the economy fell into depression, President Grover Cleveland, who had been elected to a second term in 1892, opposed all those demands and sent federal troops to break a national railroad strike. "Though the people support the government," Cleveland intoned, "the government should not support the people." In the midterm elections of 1894, the party lost 121 House seats, the worst drubbing in its history.

Many Democratic officeholders realized their survival was at stake, and they repudiated Cleveland and the laissez-faire tradition he was struggling to uphold. In 1896 the party nominated for president William Jennings Bryan, a 36-year-old former congressman from Nebraska who identified himself with the agrarian and labor insurgencies. In a dramatic speech at the party's national convention, Bryan claimed, "The Democratic idea" was to "legislate to make the masses prosperous" and "their prosperity will find its way up through every class which rests upon them." He lost the election that fall to William McKinley, a far better organized and financed candidate. But Bryan persuaded most Democrats to endorse a progressive, interventionist state, and the party never reverted to Cleveland's philosophy.

In 1912 the Republicans split into warring camps, allowing Woodrow Wilson to win the presidency and the Democrats to build large majorities in both houses of Congress. During his eight years in office, Wilson spearheaded passage of a legislative program, known as the New Freedom, which assumed the need for an active state to counterbalance the power of big business. The program included a new antitrust act, the creation of the Federal Reserve System, and some protection for unions—most of which had become part of the Democratic coalition.

Only in their ideas and policies about race did Bryan, Wilson, and most of their fellow Democrats remain true to the views of Jefferson and Jackson. In the South legislators rammed through Jim Crow laws that confined African Americans to a separate and unequal sphere of both public and private life and effectively disenfranchised millions of black citizens. One of Wilson's first acts as president was to segregate most jobs in the federal government, and he raised no objection to anti-Asian laws that Democrats on the West Coast were enacting. Most Democrats remained proud of belonging to a party for whites only.

Under Wilson, Americans also began to pay income taxes that made new federal programs possible, as well as raising funds for the troops who helped the United States and its allies win the World War I. In eloquent calls for a new democratic world order, the president also convinced his fellow Democrats that only international cooperation could stop future armed conflicts. However, many Americans resisted Wilson's demand that the United States join the new League of Nations he had proposed. They also feared the new immigrants from eastern and southern Europe, most of whom voted for Democrats. As a result, Republicans won three straight presidential elections during the 1920s, landslides every one.

FDR's Nation

Democrats returned to power with unprecedented force during the Great Depression of the 1930s. In winning four consecutive races for president, Franklin D.

Roosevelt established his party as the majority in every region of the country except for northern New England and the rural Midwest. To their older bases among white Southerners and urban Catholics, the Democrats under FDR added millions of workers in a booming labor movement as well as Jews and African Americans—the latter deserted the party of Lincoln in gratitude for public works jobs and the antiracist commitment of First Lady Eleanor Roosevelt. Most intellectuals also gave their allegiance to a party that welcomed their ideas and participation in policy making.

Their electoral dominance enabled the Democrats to institute a New Deal order that greatly expanded the power of the federal government in the lives of its citizens. The political scientist Samuel Lubell once wrote that the major parties in the United States are not "two equally competing suns, but a sun and a moon. It is within the majority party that the issues of the day are fought out; while the minority party shines in the reflected radiance of the heat thus generated." During the 1930s and early 1940s, the Democrats who ruled Congress wrangled constantly but ended up passing such landmark programs as Social Security, the National Labor Relations Act, the Wages and Hours Act, and the GI Bill—while their Republican opponents could only grumble from the cooler margins.

Even though Dwight Eisenhower twice won the presidency in the 1950s, he made no attempt to repeal these popular policies. Ike was in position to occupy the White House only because he had been one of the top military commanders during World War II—a conflict most Republicans had wanted the United States to avoid before the Japanese attack on Pearl Harbor. Although FDR died just before the war ended, he had ensured that Democrats would continue to uphold his Wilsonian vision. Under President Harry Truman, the party became an enthusiastic promoter of the United Nations, as well the creator of a multinational alliance that waged a cold war against communism everywhere in the world. In 1948 Democrats endorsed a civil rights plank at their national convention; in protest, white delegates from the Deep South walked out of the hall and ran their own States' Rights, or "Dixiecrat," ticket.

Kennedy, Johnson, and the Watershed of the 1960s
In the early 1960s, most liberals were confident they could lead the United States into a new era of sweeping change under the aggressive, idealistic leadership of President John F. Kennedy. Apart from those southern whites who

were hostile to the black freedom movement, the New Deal coalition held intact, and close to 60 percent of voters nationwide identified themselves as Democrats. Kennedy's assassination in 1963 helped Lyndon Johnson win reelection by a landslide the following year and give the Democrats majorities of 2 to 1 in both the House and Senate. Wielding the club of power like a wand, LBJ got Congress to enact a Great Society program as ambitious as the New Deal and one that, unlike in FDR's day, was committed to racial equality. Medicare, Medicaid, the National Endowment for the Humanities, the Voting Rights Act, a major change in immigration policy, and Head Start and other antipoverty initiatives all became law during Johnson's presidency. He also continued the cold war policies of JFK when he sent thousands of troops to combat a Communist-led insurgency in Vietnam.

But the new dawn of liberalism proved ephemeral. Beginning in 1965, events tore apart the coalition that had kept the Democrats on top during most of the years since the Great Depression. Riots in black communities scared white wage earners and convinced them to vote for candidates who promised to restore "law and order." Students on elite liberal campuses who protested the Vietnam War and reveled in drug taking and sexual promiscuity alienated many older Americans who revered the military and had not attended college. The enemy in Vietnam fought the United States to a standstill, while inflationary pressures and overseas competition began to stall the economy that had grown through most of the decade. Suddenly, Democrats appeared to be the party of failure. In 1966 they lost almost 50 seats in the House of Representatives; in 1968, after coverage of Chicago police beating up antiwar demonstrators on live TV, they also lost the presidency, as Vice President Hubert Humphrey received less than 43 percent of the popular vote.

During the next four decades, party activists struggled to accommodate themselves to a more conservative era. Republicans won all but three of the presidential contests held between 1968 and 2004. The Democratic exceptions—Jimmy Carter in 1976 and Bill Clinton in 1992 and 1996—did not call themselves liberals and triumphed in part because as Baptists from the South, they were able to win back a large number of white Protestants from that region who had deserted their ancestral political home. Clinton was also a leader of the Democratic Leadership Council, a group founded in 1985 that was determined to steer the party to the ideological center.

Nationally, from the 1970s through the 1990s, Democrats rarely descended to minority status and controlled Congress more often than did their Republican opponents. Most Americans continued to favor the limited welfare-state programs that Democrats had advocated throughout the twentieth century and enacted, whenever possible. Many citizens also gradually warmed to gender equality, environmental protection, and even homosexual rights—all of which liberal Democrats had helped to pioneer. Still, a majority of voters tended to give the benefit of the doubt to any politician who railed against big government and embraced "traditional values," and most of those were Republicans. As the percentage of union members in the workforce declined, well-educated professionals and African Americans became the most reliable elements in the Democratic coalition. Because those two groups were concentrated in just a few big states, it was difficult for the party's nominees to gain a majority in the Electoral College.

But during President George W. Bush's second term, Democrats again began to think that they could wrest control of the political agenda. Bush's perceived failures both at home and abroad made conservatism itself seem an ideology whose time had passed. Young people, in particular, had begun to register and vote Democratic in large numbers even before the party nominated Barack Obama for president in 2008. Latino Americans were increasingly rejecting the GOP as well, due in part to the nativist views of many Republican officeholders. In 2006 the Democrats regained control of both houses of Congress for the first time since the early 1990s. Loyalists in America's oldest political party seemed poised for another era in the sun.

Indeed, in 2008, the Democrats won their most impressive victory since the Johnson landslide of 1964. After a long and, at times, bitter primary campaign, Barack Obama won the presidential nomination and went on to gain an easy victory in the fall. Obama, the only African American ever to be nominated by a major party, outpaced his Republican rival, John McCain, by almost 200 electoral votes and close to 10 million popular votes. And he won three important states—Indiana, North Carolina, and Virginia—that no Democrat had carried since Lyndon B. Johnson 44 years earlier. Obama's triumph was one of party as well as personality. Democrats padded their majorities in both houses of Congress.

But the elation—in much of the world as well as at home—that followed Obama's victory was coupled with fear about the deep recession that had soured most voters in the United States on the probusiness Republican Party. The opportunity for Obama and his fellow Democrats to preside over a new New Deal probably depended on their ability to solve the economic crisis and to convince Americans that the federal government could once again be trusted to improve the fortunes of ordinary citizens.

See also elections and electoral eras; presidency.

FURTHER READING

Ashworth, John. *Slavery, Capitalism, and Politics in the Antebellum Republic*. 2 vols. New York: Cambridge University Press, 1995, 2007.

Gillon, Steven. *The Democrat's Dilemma: Walter F. Mondale and the Liberal Legacy*. New York: Columbia University Press, 1992.

Hofstadter, Richard. *The Idea of a Party System*. Berkeley: University of California Press, 1969.

Sarasohn, David. *The Party of Reform: Democrats in the Progressive Era*. Jackson: University Press of Mississippi, 1989.

Schlesinger, Arthur Jr. *The Age of Roosevelt*. 3 vols. Boston: Houghton Mifflin, 1957, 1958, 1960.

Wilentz, Sean. *The Rise of American Democracy*. New York: Norton, 2005.

MICHAEL KAZIN

Democratic Party, 1800–28

The Democratic Party, or Democratic-Republican Party as it first called itself, began to form early in George Washington's first administration (1789–93). Led by Thomas Jefferson in the cabinet and James Madison in the House of Representatives, the party opposed Alexander Hamilton's financial measures: the funding of the national debt in a way that benefited speculators, the assumption of state debts, the chartering of the first Bank of the United States, and the levying of numerous taxes. This division was further deepened by foreign policy and personality conflicts. Hamilton and his followers wanted the United States to align itself with Great Britain during the wars of the French Revolution, while Jefferson and Madison were anti-English and argued that the United States should live up to its treaty obligations with France, which dated back to 1778. By the end of the 1790s, the division had gone beyond specific policy issues to include differences over how to interpret the U.S. Constitution, the nature of the Union, and the kind of country America should become.

Actually, the Founding Fathers did not believe that political parties had any legitimacy or value. The Constitution made no provision for political parties. Moreover, they were generally viewed as dangerous to the stability of the Republic. The Federalists denounced the opposition associated with Jefferson and Madison as misguided, self-interested, obstructionist, and encouraging anarchy by opposing the authority of the government. The Democratic-Republicans portrayed the Federalists as essentially tyrants and monarchists intent on undermining the Republican principles of the American Revolution, and therefore determined to overthrow them. In the beginning of Washington's administration, the differences between the political combatants were confined to disputes within the government itself, to cabinet meetings and debates in Congress. But soon each side established newspapers to criticize its opponents and advocate its points of view to the broader public. When Washington left office in 1797, he denounced the development of political parties.

As the 1790s wore on, the Democratic-Republicans, especially in the Middle Atlantic states of Pennsylvania, New York, and New Jersey, increasingly resorted to public meetings, parades, demonstrations, and the establishment of various committees to direct their election campaigns by publishing addresses to the voters, circulating handbills and leaflets, and holding meetings. Following the Democratic-Republican victory in 1800 and the ascendancy of the Jeffersonians during the first few decades of the nineteenth century, many of these organizations remained active. Nonetheless, the Jeffersonians never fully embraced party development. Thus, when James Monroe was reelected president with only one vote cast against him, they celebrated it as an indication that the country had returned to the consensual ideal that had manifested itself in Washington's unanimous elections as president. Not until the very late 1820s and 1830s were political parties accepted as a development and a permanent fixture on the political scene.

With the exception of a brief period (1793–95) when the Democratic-Republicans captured control of the House of Representatives, they were a minority party throughout the 1790s. Following Washington's retirement from politics in 1796, the first contested election for the presidency took place, but the Federalist candidate John Adams defeated Jefferson by 71 electoral votes to 68. Since the Constitution at that time required the vice presidency to go the person with the second highest number of electoral votes, Jefferson assumed the position of presiding officer of the United States Senate, and while he had no influence on the making of policy, he continued to lead the opposition.

The Democratic-Republican Party finally gained control of both the presidency and Congress in the election of 1800. Geographically, its support was mainly in the Middle Atlantic and southern states, as well in large parts of northern New England (New Hampshire and Vermont; and what is now Maine, then still part of Massachusetts). It also had support in the new western states of Kentucky and Tennessee. The party included former Anti-Federalists, who called themselves Old Republicans because they strongly believed in a weak central government and limited executive power—the prevailing view at the time of the Revolution, but one the Old Republicans believed had been abandoned with the adoption of the U.S. Constitution in 1787–88. Support for the Democratic-Republican Party came from different classes that included slaveholding Virginia tobacco growers and South Carolina rice planters, but also most self-sufficient farmers and others who had at best only tenuous connection with the market. Also in the Democratic-Republican camp were most Baptists, Methodists, and members of other evangelical protestant denominations, along with Deists, Unitarians, and Universalists. Many of these people, unlike the Old Republicans, were not necessarily against the Constitution per se but objected to the specific policies implemented under its authority.

The Democratic-Republicans did not promulgate a formal platform in the election of 1800. But they did make their beliefs known by means of resolutions issued by the states of Kentucky and Virginia (1798) disputing the constitutionality of the Alien and Sedition Acts and arguing that the Constitution was a compact made by the states in which the powers not specifically granted to the federal government belonged to the states. They also found expression in pamphlets, essays in newspapers, campaign handbills, and private letters. In addition to strong support of states' rights, Democratic-Republicans advocated a frugal and simple central government, opposition to a standing army, and a reduction of the national debt.

The presidential election of 1800 turned out to be much more complicated than anyone anticipated. Jefferson defeated Adams's bid for reelection by eight electoral votes, 73 to 65. However, Jefferson's vice presidential candidate, Aaron Burr, also received 73 electoral votes. The tie meant that the election would be decided by the lame duck Federalist-dominated House of Representatives that had been elected in 1798, with each state having one vote. Although some Federalists failed to swing the election to Burr, they did manage to prevent Jefferson from getting the requisite majority. Jefferson was elected when a number of key Federalists withdrew their opposition, perhaps with the understanding that they would not be persecuted nor Hamilton's economic policies repudiated in a Jefferson administration.

Jefferson was sworn in as the third president of the United States on March 4, 1801. This was a particularly significant development because it was the first time under the U.S. Constitution that the out-party had peacefully assumed power with the cooperation of its defeated opponents. Equally significant, the Democratic-Republicans gained control of Congress, thus beginning a 24-year period of hegemony over the federal government that lasted through the administrations of Jefferson (1801–9), James Madison (1809–17), and James Monroe (1817–25).

Jefferson's assumption of the presidency raised important constitutional and even ideological issues. Was there simply to be a change in the personnel and policies of the new administration, or were changes to be made to the Constitution itself? To what extent was the Democratic-Republican victory in 1800 a popular mandate for the new administration to do whatever it wanted? Since the election had been particularly bitter, did the incoming administration need, in some way, to consider the interests and feelings of the defeated minority and make an effort to heal the wounds of the country? How, in particular, was Jefferson to reconcile his position as president of all the people with his position as a party leader?

In the quarter century that followed, not all Democratic-Republicans agreed on the answers to these questions. At the most important level, the Old Republicans wanted basic changes to the U.S. Constitution in order to weaken the powers of the central government and executive branch and to shorten the terms of office of senators. On the other hand, the more nationalist members of the Democratic-Republican Party, led by James Madison—who more than anyone else had helped create the Constitution—feared and opposed such changes. Sharp internal differences existed within the party over such issues as whether to repudiate Hamilton's financial measures and what to do about Federalist control of the national judiciary. Although Jefferson had some sympathy with the concerns of the Old Republican wing of the party, he opted for a policy of moderation and reconciliation.

But the Democratic-Republican Party, having achieved power, did not "out-Federalize" the Federalists. It reduced the size of the army and navy, significantly lowered internal taxes, and generally cut government spending to ensure the accumulation of surpluses that were used to pay off the national debt. Most important, the Democratic-Republicans acquired additional territory for the United States through wars and treaties with Native Americans, the Louisiana Purchase, and the buying of Florida. They encouraged settlement of the West by allowing people to buy land on credit.

During the first two decades of the nineteenth century the Democratic-Republicans effectively shifted the attention of the country from its involvement in the Atlantic economy to its own internal economic development. The most concrete manifestation of this was the number of new states admitted to the union between 1800 and 1820: Ohio (1803), Louisiana (1812), Indiana (1816), Mississippi (1817), Illinois (1818), Alabama (1819), Missouri (1820), and Maine (1820). This was also a period of rapid economic growth. Older urban areas like New York, Philadelphia, Baltimore, and New Orleans grew rapidly during these years, and various boomtowns like Pittsburgh, Pennsylvania; Lexington and Louisville, Kentucky; Cincinnati, Ohio; St. Louis, Missouri; Nashville, Tennessee; Rochester, New York; and Huntsville, Alabama, also emerged.

Madison's election to the presidency was a major victory for the commercial and national wing of the Democratic-Republican Party. He helped secure the independence of the federal judiciary by threatening to use force against Pennsylvania when it tried to resist a controversial Supreme Court decision, *United States v. Peters* (1809), compelling the state to back down. His appointments of Joseph Story and Gabriel Duvall to the high court were also important because the two men became firm allies of Chief Justice John Marshall. It is no accident that the most important economic and constitutional decisions made under Marshall's leadership occurred following Madison's assumption of the presidency.

At the same time, the numerous diplomatic problems created by the events that led to the War of 1812 brought difficulty and confusion to the Democratic-Republican Party. Jefferson's embargo policy proved controversial and unenforceable, and the drift and confusion that characterized Madison's foreign policy during his first term in office led to a temporary revival of Federalist strength in Congress. Madison also faced various personality and policy conflicts within his cabinet, and the failure of a measure he supported, the rechartering of the first Bank of the United States in 1811, created numerous economic problems and an unstable currency.

Madison was barely reelected president in 1812. The War of 1812 found the country unprepared militarily, and was characterized by chaos, inefficiency, and frequent military defeats, including the burning of Washington, D.C. Still, the results of the War of 1812 worked to Madison's and the Democratic-Republican Party's benefit: a spirit of nationalism prevailed in most parts of the United States, aided and magnified by Andrew Jackson's belated but significant victory at New Orleans.

As a result, during the last two years of his second administration, Madison and his followers were unusually popular and powerful. Significantly, the Federalists who had engaged in obstructionist activities during the war were now discredited as a national party, while the Old Republicans were also in disarray. As a consequence, a protective tariff and a second Bank of the United States were adopted in 1816, and a federal program of internal improvements failed when Madison opposed it for constitutional, not policy, reasons. These measures were later referred to as the American System because their purpose was to develop the domestic economy by making the nation less dependent on foreign trade.

The years immediately following the end of the War of 1812 were ones of agricultural prosperity in most parts of the country outside of New England. Following the Napoleonic Wars, bad weather in Europe created a heavy demand for American meat and grain products. At the same time, British manufacturing interests were willing to pay ever higher prices for American cotton. Within the United States, major transportation changes, which included the building of turnpikes and canals and the development of the steamboat, allowed goods to be shipped to market more quickly and cheaply than ever before and led to a quickening of communication among different parts of the country. During the early decades of the nineteenth century, a legal system that encouraged and protected the country's economic development also evolved. Perhaps most important, the United States underwent a major financial revolution built on the proliferation of banks, which made capital easily available and increased the money supply, lubricating the economy and replacing the older barter system used by small farmers in economic transactions.

James Monroe's presidency is frequently referred to as the "era of good feeling." At best, the term is misleading.

While no formal opposition party existed on the national level and the various constitutional and ideological struggles of the prewar period were muted, politics now involved struggles for power, the control of patronage, and special privileges on the local level. The result was that, with a few exceptions (mainly in New York and Pennsylvania) popular participation in politics tended to be low between 1815 and 1819.

This development did not disturb many Democratic-Republicans because they did not believe in a robust two-party system in which issues could be debated openly and the mass of the people could make the final decision at the polls. Most Democratic-Republicans believed political leaders were chosen because of their demonstrated superiority in education, experience, and achievement. They stressed consensus, compromise, and for the most part—at least outwardly—a harmony of interests. They also stressed a separation between the making of public policy by elites and participation in the development of a market economy by the mass of people that had been the object of their economic policies.

For the Democratic-Republicans, the congressional nominating caucus was the most important manifestation of how politics should operate. It consisted of members of the party from both houses of Congress, which selected the party's presidential candidate. The practice had started during the election of 1800 and continued through 1824. This nomination was the most important step in a presidential race because, with the exception of the election of 1812, selection by the caucus was tantamount to election during the first two decades of the nineteenth century. The caucus played a key role in 1808, selecting Madison over Monroe despite opposition by a number of important Old Republicans lead by John Randolph, John Taylor, Nathaniel Macon, and George Clinton, who were critical of Madison's constitutional nationalism and believed he had not been sufficiently extreme in his opposition to the Hamilton-inspired financial system after Jefferson's election. Madison was renominated in 1812, but DeWitt Clinton, an important Democratic-Republican from New York, openly aligned himself with a number of New England Federalists and other discontented Democratic-Republicans to oppose Madison's reelection. The election was extremely close, but Madison won. From that point, Clinton, who remained a major force in New York politics, was effectively barred from the national arena. In fact, Madison and Monroe used their control of the federal patronage to aid Clinton's opponents in New York. In 1816 Monroe received the caucus nomination, defeating William H. Crawford of Georgia by a vote of 65 to 54.

Unlike Clinton, Crawford accepted the caucus decision and supported Monroe, who went on to an easy victory. For his part, Crawford accepted an appointment as secretary of the treasury in Monroe's cabinet, and was generally considered to be his heir apparent: he was expected to receive the caucus nomination for president in 1824 after Monroe served his two terms in office.

But, by 1824, when Crawford did receive it, the caucus nomination meant little. The Democratic-Republican Party had begun to disintegrate under several pressures: the Panic of 1819 and the depression that followed, the states' rights reaction to the U.S. Supreme Court's nationalist decisions, the debate over the growth and expansion of slavery and the Missouri Compromise, and the emergence of Andrew Jackson as a national political figure. The Panic of 1819 was particularly important because it increased interest in politics among enfranchised white males who believed the making of economic policy should no longer be left in the hands of elites. As a consequence, the congressional caucus had become outdated by 1824, attended by less than one-third of its members. Instead, the various other candidates for the presidency (Andrew Jackson, John Q. Adams, Henry Clay, and John C. Calhoun) were selected by various state nominating conventions or by local resolutions.

The 1820s was also characterized by the development of sectionalism. It was linked in part to the growth of slavery, for the development of the cotton culture in the Old Southwest (Alabama, Mississippi, central and western Tennessee, and Louisiana) undercut the Jeffersonian view that slavery was a dying institution. But economic issues were the main focus of sectionalism. The struggle over a protective tariff and the push for a national bankruptcy law divided the country primarily along North-South lines, but the debate over a federal program of internal improvements and national land policy involved a contest between the East and West. As a consequence, the sectionalism of the 1820s tended to be kaleidoscopic, shifting from issue to issue and therefore different from the sectionalism that developed during the 1850s between the free and slave states.

In the ensuing presidential election of 1824, Jackson received a plurality of both the electoral and popular vote, but the House of Representatives chose Adams, who came in second in each category, on the first ballot. As president, Adams continued to espouse the American System and the older elitist view of politics, going so far at one point as to urge Congress not to be "palsied by the will of our constituents." During his administration, the Democratic-Republican Party divided into two groups. Adams and his supporters, led by Clay, became known as the National Republicans, which became the core of the Whig Party in the 1830s. Jackson's supporters became known as the Democratic Party and took most of their values from the Old Republicans.

There is no connection between the Democratic-Republicans and the Republican Party that emerged in 1854. There are, however, very real organizational ties between the Democratic-Republicans and the Democratic Party of today.

See also Republican Party to 1896.

FURTHER READING

Cunningham, Noble E., Jr. "The Jeffersonian Republican Party." In *History of U.S. Political Parties*, vol. 1, edited by Arthur M. Schlesinger Jr. New York: Chelsea House, 1973.

Ellis, Richard E. *Aggressive Nationalism:* McCulloch v. Maryland *and the Foundations of Federal Authority in the Young Republic*. New York: Oxford University Press, 2007.

———. "The Market Revolution and the Transformation of American Politics, 1801–1837." In *The Market Revolution in America: Social, Political, and Religious Expressions, 1800–1880*, edited by Melvyn Stokes and Stephen Conway. Charlottesville: University Press of Virginia, 1996.

Freehling, William W. *The Road to Disunion: Secessionists at Bay, 1776–1854*. New York: Oxford University Press, 1994.

Howe, Daniel Walter. *What God Hath Wrought: The Transformation of America, 1815–1848*. New York: Oxford University Press, 2007.

Peterson, Merrill D. *The Great Triumvirate: Webster, Clay, and Calhoun*. New York: Oxford University Press, 1987.

Sellers, Charles. *The Market Revolution: Jacksonian America, 1815–1846*. New York: Oxford University Press, 1991.

White, Leonard. *The Jeffersonians: A Study in Administrative History, 1801–1829*. New York: Macmillan, 1951.

Wilentz, Sean. *The Rise of American Democracy*. New York: Norton, 2005.

RICHARD E. ELLIS

Democratic Party, 1828–60

The Democratic Party was the dominant political organization of the antebellum republic. Although never entirely united and in fact prone to periodic schism and fracture, it commanded a degree of loyalty and reverence that made it more like a church than a political party. To its most dedicated supporters it was indissolubly linked to American democracy and freedom, and to the nation itself.

The party nevertheless presents the historian with some problems. As the splits and divisions that punctuate its history confirm, it was never monolithic. Moreover, it went through major changes in the generation between the election of Andrew Jackson and the republic's collapse in 1861: the issues of the 1850s were, for the most part, not those of the 1820s, and the party responded accordingly, despite continuities of personnel and policy and the ideological assumptions governing both.

Early Years

A sharp ideological focus was not apparent when the party came into existence in the 1820s. Andrew Jackson, its standard-bearer in that decade, first acquired fame not for the principles he propounded but for the triumphs he had secured on the military battlefield. As a slayer of Native Americans and the British (most conspicuously at the Battle of New Orleans in 1815), Jackson attracted public attention and—even more important—the attention of politicos who wished to find a winning candidate for the presidential election of 1824. Jackson was bolstered by disparate groups, with different motives in different sections and even states of the Union, but among his core supporters were some who feared that speculation and a newly emerging financial and political elite threatened the traditional values of the republic. Some had been disturbed by the Panic of 1819, which suggested that the commercial growth of the era had been purchased at the expense of the rural simplicity that Thomas Jefferson had extolled and that many believed essential to the preservation of American democracy. These groups and these perceptions would come to dominate the Democratic Party later, but they were merely one element among many in the party's earliest days.

In the presidential election of 1824, Jackson received a plurality of both popular ballots and votes in the electoral college. But with no outright winner, the election went into the House of Representatives and John Quincy Adams of Massachusetts, son of former president John Adams, was elected, thanks to support from a third group, the supporters of Henry Clay. When Adams then appointed Clay secretary of state, Jackson's supporters, together with the "Old Hero" Jackson himself, were outraged by what they believed had been a "corrupt bargain" that had cheated the American public of their rightful president. The election of 1824, together with the corrupt bargain charge, was of enormous importance to the Democratic Party. Partisans repeated the charge ad nauseam for the next four years while Jackson and his supporters identified their cause with that of American democracy itself. This identification would remain in place for a generation. The Democratic Party was confirmed, in the eyes of its members and even some of its enemies, as the party of American democracy.

As yet, however, Jackson was identified with few specific policies. He favored little more than "retrenchment" (a reduction in federal spending), and "reform" (the principle of rotation in office). On the issue of a protective tariff, he was largely uncommitted, and he had no specific policy toward the second Bank of the United States, which had been chartered in 1816.

The Jackson and Van Buren Presidencies

Having defeated Adams in 1828, however, the party of Jackson began to acquire a more distinctive identity. Four events in the 1820s and early 1830s were decisive. The first, the election of 1824, confirmed Jackson's majoritarianism (despite his failure to obtain a majority of the votes cast). Believing that the electorate had been cheated, he assumed a natural conflict between the people and the elites of the nation.

The second event that played a key role in the creation of a Democratic Party identity concerned Native Americans. By the time Jackson came to office, the Indians in the South and Southwest presented a barrier to the expansion of white America—or so men like Jackson believed. The new president accordingly suggested the "voluntary" removal of Indians in Georgia and elsewhere in the South to west of the Mississippi River. The scheme was tantamount to forced relocation, since the pressures on those who chose to remain would soon become unendurable. During his administration, Jackson and his officials signed dozens of treaties with Native Americans, obtaining in the process some 100 million acres of land. In its impact on the Indians this dispossession and forced relocation constituted one of the greatest tragedies of the antebellum era, such was the suffering endured by its alleged beneficiaries. For the Democratic Party, however, Indian removal contributed to the great strength that Jackson enjoyed in most of the states concerned. When combined with his personal popularity (resting in part upon his earlier military victories against Indians as well as Englishmen), it made his presidency almost unchallengeable in the states most directly affected. On balance, Indian removal was a tremendous vote winner for the Democratic Party in general and for Jackson in particular. Moreover, it reinforced a cardinal tenet of the Democratic creed: the party would advocate "equal rights"—but not for those whose skin was the "wrong" color.

The third major event of Jackson's presidential career concerned the politics of slavery. In the early and mid-1830s, the slavery controversy, relatively quiet since the early 1820s, entered a new era. Some agitators demanded immediate abolition; others insisted that slavery was perpetual in the Union, guaranteed by the Constitution, and, as such, deserving of special protection. The acknowledged leader of the proslavery forces was, by the early 1830s, John C. Calhoun, who had been elected Jackson's vice president but broke with his running mate. He argued that any state, within its own boundaries, had the right to nullify a federal law of which it disapproved. Clearly this was the principle of states' rights driven to its farthest reaches. Jackson's reply to the nullifiers was equally extreme. Unable to see any real threat to slavery, and concluding that Calhoun was driven by the basest of motives, the president condemned nullification as treason. He went further: insisting that the Union was perpetual, he refused to acknowledge that states possessed the right of secession. Indeed, he implied, secession—like nullification—was treason. To remove any ambiguity about his intentions, Jackson asked Congress for a "force bill" allowing him to use troops, if necessary, to collect the federal revenue.

The effect on southern opinion was immediate. Many of the president's supporters in the South balked at the Force Bill of 1833, and his previously unassailable position became vulnerable. His critics now came out into the open. Throughout most of the Middle and Deep South, where Jackson had run so strongly in 1828 and 1832, the results were similar. While most Southerners applauded Jackson's view of nullification, many were reluctant to endorse his view of secession, and, in some cases, the majoritarianism upon which it rested. Though the nullification crisis was soon over, in the next few years, abolitionists flooded the South with pamphlets, and controversy raged over the reception in Congress of antislavery petitions. The result was a new set of problems for Northerners and Southerners alike. In his presidential campaigns, Jackson had not had to contend with these difficulties, but in 1836, they would pose a severe test for all parties and for statesmen on both sides of the Mason-Dixon Line.

The fourth event to exercise a major influence on the Democratic Party was the war with the Bank of the United States. For many years, historians were reluctant to acknowledge the basic—and obvious—fact that Andrew Jackson disliked all banks on ideological grounds. These sentiments were not prominent in his election campaigns of the 1820s, but by the time of the Annual Message of 1829, Jackson was expressing serious misgivings about the bank. A year later, he proposed important modifications to any new charter it might receive. When its president, Nicholas Biddle, applied for a rechartering in 1832, Jackson not only vetoed the bill but expressed what would become classic Democratic hostility to "the rich and powerful," whose influence on government, he declared, posed an ever present threat to the well-being of the masses. In 1832 Jackson was triumphantly reelected; the masses seemed to have endorsed his view of the Bank of the United States.

Even more controversial was Jackson's next move in his war against the Bank of the United States: the removal of government deposits. In justifying this action, the president once again expressed his suspicion of the nation's elites, now both commercial and political. Here the ultimate goal of the president and those who shared his views could be glimpsed: he wanted to force smaller bills out of circulation entirely. Although paper money would continue to be used in larger commercial transactions, many Americans would encounter throughout their lives only specie—coins made of gold or silver. With the same goal in mind, Jackson in 1836 insisted that government agencies receive only gold and silver in payment for public lands. In his Farewell Message, he went far beyond attacks on a single commercial institution, however large. Excoriating the "money power" and the "paper system," the president warned that they engendered speculation, corruption, and inequality. Jackson posited an unending struggle between "the agricultural, the mechanical, and the laboring classes" on the one hand, and the "money power" on the other. Here was the pure milk of Jacksonian Democracy. By the time

of Jackson's Farewell Message, Democratic principles were as clear as they would ever be.

In the next few years, the bank war entered its most critical phase. No sooner had Old Hickory's chosen successor, Martin Van Buren, taken office than news of a financial crisis broke. By May a panic had set in, and banks across the nation suspended specie payments. The new president made a crucial decision. He would follow Jackson's lead and establish an Independent Treasury, an institution that would hold and disburse government funds but would not act like a bank in other ways. In effect, Van Buren was, as his supporters claimed, "divorcing" the government from the banks.

Still more important was the course of the bank war in the states. The late 1830s and early 1840s marked the high point of agrarian radicalism, not only in the Jacksonian era but in the entire history of the United States. They also signaled the eclipse of sectional hostilities. Banking overshadowed the slavery question throughout the nation. The hard-money Democrats, the heirs of Andrew Jackson, now brought the Jacksonian era to its culmination. In almost every state of the Union, the Democratic Party took action against the banks. In the West, where the financial turbulence had been most severe, hard money Democrats frequently aimed to destroy all banks; in the East, where the banking system was more mature and stable, reform was the order of the day. How successful were they? The configuration of political forces varied from state to state. A minority of (conservative) Democrats objected vigorously to the attacks on the banks and, in some states, were able to effect an alliance with the Whig opposition that prevented the hard-money Democrats from achieving their goals. In many states and territories, however, abolition of all banks was official party policy, and, in some, it was actually implemented.

A Changing Agenda: The 1840s

In the 1840s, however, the political agenda shifted decisively, and the nature and priorities of the Democratic Party changed accordingly. Early in the decade, even though the Bank war was still raging in some states, sectional issues resurfaced. For most of the 1840s, the Democratic Party managed to combine a muted version of its original appeal with a new responsiveness to the demands of southern slaveholders. Democratic attacks upon the rich and powerful had been directed against those whose wealth was mercantile, financial, or industrial. Those who had prospered instead by exploiting the labor of African American slaves had escaped censure and indeed were viewed as part of the farming interest that Democrats had pledged to uphold. Nevertheless, in the 1840s, some slaveholders demanded more. Fearing that British antislavery pressure soon would be brought to bear upon the newly independent republic of Texas, some Southerners, with John C. Calhoun once again at their head, urged the immediate annexation of Texas. The Democratic Party succumbed to this pressure, as Northerners and Southerners alike presented this expansionist drive as evidence of the nation's Manifest Destiny to occupy the entire North American continent. Democrats were thus able to call for similar accessions of territory in the North, specifically in Oregon.

The problem was that these accessions of territory, when they could be secured, reopened the question of the extension of slavery. In the 1840s and 1850s, Democrats in the South spearheaded the drive for more slave states, and most Democrats in the North were more willing to countenance these demands than were members of other political parties, whether Whigs, Know-Nothings, or Republicans. In the mid- and late 1840s, Democrats were most keen to wage war with Mexico and most keen to allow slavery into the lands thus acquired, despite the Democratic affiliation of Representative David Wilmot, whose famous Proviso of 1846 sought to prevent the spread of slavery into new areas. Then in 1850, under the leadership of Illinois senator Stephen A. Douglas, Democrats championed the policy of "popular sovereignty," which denied to Congress, but conferred on the inhabitants of the territory in question, the right to determine the fate of slavery there.

These concessions to the South and the slaveholding interest were made only at the expense of a damaging split within the party in the North. Wilmot himself was from Pennsylvania, but the deepest intraparty division was probably in New York. Here the radical Democrats, dubbed "barnburners" by friend and foe alike, led a crusade to prevent the party becoming the vehicle for the expansion of slavery. In 1848 an outright breach occurred when their leader, Martin Van Buren, accepted the Free Soil Party's nomination for president. Van Buren, in common with virtually all Democrats north and south, had traditionally been hostile to abolitionism on the grounds that it threatened national unity. But the extension of slavery awakened fresh concerns that had more to do with the injustices allegedly suffered by white labor than with the iniquities of enslavement itself. Although these northern Democrats repudiated the proslavery pol-

icies of the 1840s, others took their cue from Stephen A. Douglas and acquiesced in them.

Toward the Civil War: 1850–61

Similarly, it was northern Democrats, again under Douglas, who took the lead in extending the policy of popular sovereignty to the territories of Kansas and Nebraska. The Kansas-Nebraska Act of 1854, perhaps the most portentous legislative measure in the history of the republic, repealed the Missouri Compromise and thus created the possibility that Kansas (and Nebraska, though climatic considerations made this highly improbable) might enter the Union as slave states. The Democratic goal here, or at least the northern Democrats' goal, however, was not to spread slavery but instead to open up the West to settlement and to link the existing states of the Midwest to those recently established on the Pacific Coast.

The impact of the Kansas-Nebraska Act was immense. It played a major role in weakening the Democrats in the North while confirming and extending their influence in the South. Moreover, it created in Kansas conditions that were ripe for a rapid descent into near civil war as pro- and antislavery settlers repeatedly clashed.

In the mid-1850s, however, these were not the only issues to achieve prominence. The crusade for a governmental prohibition of alcohol, though focused entirely on state and local governments, polarized many communities, especially in the North. Democrats had traditionally frowned upon such governmental activism, partly on the grounds that it eroded individual liberty, and that it seemed to confer dangerous powers upon a self-constituted moral elite. These attitudes persisted into the 1850s, but some states and localities modified or abandoned them as the temperance movement gained strength. More important was the Know-Nothing crusade, which rose to meteoric prominence in late 1854 and 1855. Once again, traditional Democratic values mandated a defense of the immigrant, and of the right to vote of even the recently arrived immigrant, but those values were modified or even renounced in some localities.

By the time of the presidential election of 1856, however, both the temperance and the anti-immigrant crusades had subsided, leaving the slavery question at the top of the nation's political agenda. By now the political geography of the nation had changed markedly. In the heyday of the Second Party System in the late 1830s and early 1840s, the Democrats had been strong throughout the nation, but especially in the West, the lower North, and the Deep South. By the mid- to late 1850s, on the other hand, the South, apart from the border states, was solidly Democratic, whereas the North as a whole had been lost, apart from Pennsylvania, Illinois, Indiana, and the then underpopulated states of Oregon and California.

By now, too, the agrarian radicalism of Jacksonian times had largely disappeared from view. A financial panic in 1857 allowed it to reemerge but on a much smaller scale and, as far as most of the nation was concerned, for only a matter of months. In contrast, by 1860 the Democrats' southern orientation was more evident than ever and resulted in a split in the party in 1860. Northern Democrats, having been saddled with the defense of unpopular measures or actions like the Kansas-Nebraska Act, the subsequent unrest in Kansas, and the beating of Charles Sumner in the U.S. Senate in 1856, now refused to bend the knee once more in subjection to the southern demand for a slave code in the territories (by which Congress would be required to protect slavery in any territory until the moment of statehood). This Democratic split was probably not responsible for the Republican victory of 1860, but it did reveal the inability of the party to come to terms with the dominant issues of the day.

The Democratic Party Balance Sheet

The Democratic split of 1860 both mirrored and anticipated the split in the nation that would usher in four years of slaughter and carnage. Since the time of Andrew Jackson, the party had enjoyed extraordinary political success, achieving victory in all but two presidential elections between 1828 and 1859. Democrats had controlled Congress for most of this time, and they had also controlled a majority of the states. What had the party accomplished? Its policies had—until the 1850s, at any rate—been crowned with success. As Democratic ideology implied, the federal government had withdrawn from the activities that it had once pursued: a national bank had been dismantled and a low-tariff policy instituted; and Congress had even renounced its control over slavery in the territories. Equally important, the populistic political practices inaugurated in the 1820s by the Jacksonians had become standard by 1860, and were adopted enthusiastically by the Republicans that year. Ironically, this played a major part in bringing about the collapse of Democratic control.

The Democratic balance sheet contains many liabilities. Democratic economic policies were, on the whole,

triumphant. But by midcentury, they resulted not in the triumph of Jeffersonian agrarianism but instead in economic development and diversification that more closely resembled the vision of those in the anti-Democratic tradition. Moreover, the party utterly failed to deal with the slavery question. It increasingly became the vehicle for southern proslavery militancy, and—first in the North, and then in the nation as a whole—paid a high electoral price as a result.

For a generation, the party had claimed to be the party of American democracy and of the republic. In a sense, this claim was still valid in 1860. Within Republican ranks, the former Democrats were famed for their inflexible unionism, their refusal to contemplate any major concessions to the slaveholding interest. Even those who had not defected to the Republican Party rallied to the Union, with few exceptions, once the first shots had been fired at Fort Sumter. But by now northern Democrats were bit players in the great national drama that was unfolding. Southern Democrats, by contrast, were essentially in charge of events south of the Mason-Dixon Line but had little enthusiasm for party forms, little affection for the vast majority of their onetime northern allies, and little pride in the traditions of the Democratic Party. The days of Democratic hegemony were over. But in one sense, this confirmed the connections among the party, American democracy, and the nation itself. The marginalization of the party signaled the failure of the democratic process. It also announced the deepest crisis ever to face the American republic.

See also abolitionism; agrarian politics; banking policy; Jacksonian era, 1828–45; Native Americans and politics; slavery.

FURTHER READING

Ashworth, John. *Slavery Capitalism and Politics in the Antebellum Republic.* 2 vols. New York: Cambridge University Press, 1995, 2007.

Benson, Lee. *The Concept of Jacksonian Democracy: New York as a Test Case.* Princeton, NJ: Princeton University Press, 1961.

Johannsen, Robert W. *Stephen A. Douglas.* New York: Oxford University Press, 1973.

Nichols, Roy F. *The Disruption of American Democracy.* New York: Macmillan, 1948.

Remini, Robert. *Andrew Jackson.* 3 vols. Baltimore, MD: Johns Hopkins University Press, 1977–84.

Schlesinger, Arthur M., Jr. *The Age of Jackson.* Boston: Little, Brown, 1945.

JOHN ASHWORTH

Democratic Party, 1860–96

In 1860 the Democratic Party suffered the most disastrous defeat in its entire history. The party split apart, running two separate tickets, one headed by Senator Stephen Douglas of Illinois and the other by John C. Breckinridge of Kentucky, the sitting vice president. The Democrats lost not just the election but also half of their membership, which left to join the southern Confederacy. From this low point, the party managed to revive and then, by the mid-1870s, return to its former position as the rival of the nation's other major party, the Republicans. How did it manage to achieve such a remarkable recovery?

Throughout the first half of the nineteenth century, the Democratic Party, and its predecessor, the Democratic-Republican Party of Thomas Jefferson and James Madison, had assumed the role of watchdog over American politics, making sure that the power and authority of the federal government were kept under control. To offset federal authority, the Democrats mobilized the power of state and local government and the ideas associated with them, states' rights and localism. To counter attempts by Federalists, or Whigs, or Republicans to impose cultural or religious orthodoxy or to marginalize particular ethnic or social groups, the Democrats insisted on the promotion of cultural and social diversity and the protection of civil liberties. As the *New York Herald* complained in 1860, Democrats had to fight against "the evils of political meddling with morals, religion and the rights of communities." Opposition to federal interference and government meddling, whether in the economic, social, or cultural sphere, was the Democratic Party's assigned role in American party politics. As long as it maintained this oppositional tradition, the party would continue to be both necessary and viable.

But a political party is held together by more than ideology and identity. It also consists of an electoral coalition of interests and groups. By the outbreak of civil war in 1861, the Democrats' base of support was well established. Its geographic center lay in the southern slaveholding states, along with the border states and the lower portions of the Midwest that were populated by migrants from the nearby South. In the northern states, it relied primarily on the immigrant population, mainly Irish and German, as well as the growing numbers of Catholics, most of them Irish. Living in the cities, these religious and ethnic groups tended to be organized by the Democratic bosses and machines that were proliferating there. Also reliably Democratic were New York and New Jersey, both of which contained important economic sectors engaged in commerce and finance. Although one of their hallmarks was a tolerance of ethnic and religious differences, the Democrats were nevertheless hostile toward nonwhite races, African Americans in particular but also Native Americans and later the Chinese. White supremacy, in fact, continued to be a defining feature of Democratic identity after the war. Therefore, those whites who responded to racist appeals and racial fears were a basic component of the Democratic coalition.

Possessing a well-established ideology, or creed, and a broad electoral coalition, the Democrats could probably withstand the calamity of 1860 as long as they hewed to their recognized role in American politics as the party of opposition whose task was to prevent political centralization and cultural homogenization. Abandonment of this traditional stance would risk losing the party's identity and courting electoral disaster.

Phase One: Upheaval, 1861–74

The prospects for the Democratic Party when war broke out looked gloomy indeed. Once the overwhelmingly Democratic Southerners had withdrawn, the party became a distinct minority in Congress. As the party that had collaborated with the men who were now rebels and traitors, the Democrats might have faced extinction. That possibility threatened when the Republican Party renamed itself the Union Party and succeeded in drawing into its inclusive tent a number of what were soon called "War Democrats" when the other wing of the party, consisting of the "Peace Democrats," or "Copperheads," began to oppose the war and call for a negotiated peace. But the main body of the Democratic minority decided to assume the role of a vigorous opposition so as to maintain "the Constitution as it is, the Union as it was," even though it lacked the votes to prevent or change the Republicans' policy initiatives.

In assuming this stand, the regular Democrats opposed the dominant Republican Party in several arenas of public policy during the war. First, they challenged the Republicans when they took advantage of their wartime majority in the Thirty-eighth Congress and promoted their activist, partisan agenda, consisting of a protective tariff, a transcontinental railroad, homestead legislation, land-grant colleges, and a uniform national system of banking and currency. Democrats also reacted strongly to many of the Republicans' civil measures for prosecuting the war, such as their Confiscation Acts of 1861 and 1862, as well as periodic action by the executive branch and the military to curb seditious activities by curtailing civil liberties. Also generating Democratic opposition were the Republicans' efforts to finance the war by means of taxes, loans, and paper money (greenbacks), all involving dangerous economic intervention and change. And, finally, Republican attempts to expand war aims beyond the limited objective of saving the Union provoked Democratic ire, most notably over the introduction of emancipation of the slaves in the fall of 1862.

The Democrats' function as an unwavering opposition and their routine votes against most Republican measures during the war seemed to resonate with an electorate fearful of federal activism and innovation. Party leaders calculated accurately the extent of the electorate's primordial resistance to central authority as well as their own party's ability to benefit politically from it. In the 1864 presidential election, 45 percent of voters cast a ballot for the Democrats, despite their nomination of a failed Union general, George B. McClellan, who ran on a platform calling for a negotiated peace after "four years of failure" to restore the Union through war. New York's governor, Horatio Seymour, hailed this strong Democratic showing as evidence of "our numerous strength."

With the end of the war in April 1865, sectional conflict did not cease, nor did the Democrats become more cooperative. Instead, the formulation of policy for the defeated South became an arena for the Democrats to continue to challenge the Republicans, though they now shifted their stance from instinctive opposition to willful obstruction. If Lincoln's successor, Andrew Johnson, had not chosen to resist the Republicans' determined efforts to introduce a new political order in the South, the Democratic minority in Congress might have taken a different and more pragmatic course. But the ensuing struggle between Johnson and Congress over Reconstruction policy provided the Democrats with an influential and stubborn ally in their attempt to revitalize their party. So they voted solidly, often unanimously, against all the major Reconstruction legislation enacted by the Republicans—the Civil Rights Act of 1866, the Fourteenth Amendment, and the Reconstruction Act of 1867. And they provided eager and reliable support for Johnson's steady stream of truculent vetoes.

Although this strategy of resistance did not prevent the Republicans from enacting their vital measures for reconstructing the South, it still polarized the differences between the parties, giving the Democrats a clearly defined posture that, they were convinced, would ensure their viability as a needed check on radical federal policies. Democrats stood for conciliation toward the former Confederates and a speedy reunion of the divided country, and they objected to an externally imposed reconstruction of the South. They also encouraged white hostility to Republican efforts to provide blacks with legal and physical protection in the South and to guarantee them equal rights and suffrage throughout the nation. Sectional reconciliation and white supremacy would resonate, so the Democrats hoped, with northern voters tired of conflict and eager for stability and order. The sharp contrast between the major parties was dramatized during the 1868 presidential contest, when the Democrats selected a well-known Peace Democrat, Horatio Seymour, whose running mate, Francis Blair Jr., denounced the Reconstruction Acts as "null and void" and made his distaste for African Americans abundantly clear.

During the two-term Grant administration from 1868 to 1876, the Democrats continued to vote as a bloc against further measures to sustain Reconstruction in the South, such as the Enforcement Acts of 1870–71, as well as against additional civil rights legislation like the Fifteenth Amendment and the Civil Rights Act of 1875. But, after 1870, they shifted their position somewhat by pledging formally that, if it should return to power nationally, the Democratic Party would not overturn any federal statute or amendment expanding black rights. This initiative, called the New Departure, prepared the way for the party to move on to other issues, which it did in 1872, when the Democrats endorsed the presidential nominee of the Liberal Republican Party, which had just been formed by a sizable group of Republican dissidents opposed to the renomination of Grant. This maneuver was intended to broaden the Democrats' support as well as to proclaim their changed stance, away from obstruction and back to opposition.

Even though this scheme failed when Horace Greeley lost decisively to President Grant, the party's fortunes revived dramatically over the next few years. The new Republican governments elected and installed in the South after 1868 had encountered difficulties from the outset, and, by the 1870s, they were struggling to stay in control. Simultaneously, their opponents, the former Confederates and their allies who had aligned themselves with the Democrats, were returning to power in the region, sometimes by fair means, usually by foul.

After the nation's economy plunged into a depression in 1873, the Democrats blamed their Republican opponents for the ensuing hard times and were rewarded with a majority in the House a year later. The Republicans' 102-seat majority was replaced by a Democratic majority of 60 seats, the largest electoral swing at the national level in the nineteenth century. Significantly, two-thirds of the South's congressional seats were now held by Democrats. Meanwhile, all but a few states in the Lower South had come under Democratic control as the Reconstruction governments collapsed under their opponents' onslaught. Of course, the national Democrats stood to gain immensely from the return of their southern base. By 1876, when Reconstruction formally ended, they actually enjoyed near parity with the Republicans (149 to 130 in the House and 36 to 39 in the Senate).

Phase Two: Stalemate, 1874–96

After the turmoil of the Civil War and Reconstruction, the political system experienced deadlock for the next 20 years. In sharp contrast with the dramatic growth of large-scale industries and big cities that were transforming American life, the political arena was static. Turnout at elections was extremely high (around 75 percent), but voter efforts proved disappointing because they produced a balance between the two major parties so close and so precarious that neither party was prepared to take risks or act forcefully. For the Democrats, whose traditional approach was oppositional and whose preference was for limited and inactive government, such a situation was almost ideal. Even though the Democrats won the presidency only twice in that period (in 1884 and 1892, each time with Grover Cleveland of New York), they controlled the House for all but eight years. By contrast, they enjoyed only four years of dominance in the Senate. Congress was therefore divided, and the majorities in both houses were razor thin. Similarly in equipoise was the presidency. Despite the Republicans' seeming stranglehold, the executive branch was also closely contested. The popular vote was always so tight that a Democratic victory in New York, or Indiana, or Ohio could prevent the Republicans from winning.

Contributing to the electoral stalemate were the powerful identities each party represented in the minds of voters. As a result, anxiety over expected close elections was compounded by awareness of dire consequences if the enemy were to seize control. Democrats were still tarnished by their identification with the Confederacy, and so their Republican opponents constantly reminded voters of this by "waving the bloody shirt." Moreover, by the 1880s, it was difficult for the Democrats to refute this charge since the party's heartland had once again become the South, while southern Democrats were back in control of most committees in the Democratic-controlled House.

This sharp cleavage was supplemented by several other distinctive differences. Democrats, both northern and southern, could be expected to denounce racial equality and oppose civil rights for blacks, as their party continued to identify itself as the upholder of white supremacy. Further distinguishing the parties was the Democrats' persistent laissez-faire approach to governance. As Thomas "Czar" Reed, the Republican House Speaker in the 1800s, once observed contemptuously, "The Republican party does things; the Democratic party criticizes." And, finally, one policy issue clearly differentiated Republicans from Democrats. The Republicans advocated a protective tariff, and they clung firmly to that issue, claiming that it developed the economy and protected workers' wages. Naturally, Democrats countered with their traditional support for a tariff "for revenue only." But they were not as adamant or consistent about reducing the tariff as their rivals were about maintaining or increasing it.

In fact, the Democrats' stance on a number of prominent issues of the late nineteenth century was more equivocal and imprecise than the Republicans. The primary reason for this was the diversity of the Democratic coalition. Those Democratic districts where manufacturing and mining interests were influential wanted tariff protection against foreign competition. Consequently, when Democrats in both Cleveland administrations tried to lower the tariff, they found themselves having to concede to protectionist demands, and so they failed on each occasion. And while the party generally wanted a more flexible currency and an increased money supply, New England and New York Democrats who were engaged in banking and commerce favored currency contraction and maintenance of the gold standard.

But this alignment of the parties changed dramatically when the electoral equilibrium was suddenly shattered in 1888 and again in 1892. In 1888 the Republicans won the presidency and both houses of Congress and proceeded to enact the party's campaign platform. Four years later, the Democrats did the exact same thing and met with the same result—defeat at the next national election. The Republicans returned to power between 1894 and 1896 and stayed there until 1932.

This definitive outcome occurred for two reasons. First, another depression struck in 1893, soon after Cleveland's second term began, but it was far worse than its predecessor in 1873–74. In response, the president contracted the money supply by getting Congress to repeal the Sherman Silver Purchase Act of 1890 and return the nation to the gold standard, an action that undoubtedly aggravated the economic distress. Also seriously damaged were the Democrats' chances of winning the 1896 election. Second, the 1896 contest forced the Democrats to take a clear-cut position on the money question. Repudiating the sound money/gold standard wing of the party, they aligned decisively with free silver and currency expansion by nominating William Jennings Bryan, a young and popular silverite, for president. Instead of trying to balance its gold and silver factions (as it had also balanced its protectionist/reductionist elements on the tariff), the party committed itself unequivocally to free silver and its determined advocates in the South and West. Simultaneously, the Republicans endorsed gold equally decisively after having tried to appease the pro-silver forces in the West during the Benjamin Harrison administration (1888–92) by means of the Silver Purchase Act. The election of 1896 became a "battle of the standards," gold versus silver, hard money versus soft.

Beset by a serious economic crisis, the two parties had been forced to identify themselves clearly with one or the other of the economic panaceas currently in fashion. In the election, the Republicans won, partly because of their own well-run campaign and partly because of a confusing campaign by the Democrats, whose nominee was also backed by the new, insurgent People's Party. Although it totaled a mere 4 percent of the votes cast, the Republican margin of victory amounted nevertheless to a larger electoral shift than in any presidential election since 1872. As a result, both the electoral stalemate and the policy logjam ended. The lifting of the economic depression a few years later suggested that perhaps the Republican policy, and therefore the Republican Party, had got it right.

Not until another even more severe depression in the 1930s did the Democrats develop a winning alternative. During the intervening 30 years, the party found itself once again defeated and discredited, as it had been after 1860. This time, however, the Democrats would revive, not by preserving their traditional issues and identity, as they had done since 1860, but by transforming themselves into a very different party, one that was predominantly liberal, urban, northern—and barely recognizable.

See also Democratic Party, 1828–60; Gilded Age, 1870s–90s; Reconstruction era, 1865–77; sectional conflict and secession; tariffs and politics.

FURTHER READING

Argersinger, Peter H. "The Transformation of American Politics: Political Institutions and Public Policy, 1865–1910." In *Contesting Democracy: Substance and Structure in American Political History, 1775–2000*, edited by Byron E. Shafer and Anthony J. Badger, 117–47. Lawrence: University of Kansas Press, 2001.

Bensel, Richard Franklin. *The Political Economy of American Industrialization, 1877–1900*. New York: Cambridge University Press, 2000.

Calhoun, Charles W. *The Gilded Age: Essays on the Origins of Modern America*. Wilmington, DE: Scholarly Resources, 1996.

Cherney, Robert W. *American Politics in the Gilded Age, 1868–1900*. Wheeling, IL: Harlan Davidson, 1997.

Donald, David Herbert, Jean Harvey Baker, and Michael F. Holt. *The Civil War and Reconstruction*. New York: Norton, 2001.

Foner, Eric. *Reconstruction: America's Unfinished Revolution, 1863–1877*. New York: Harper and Row, 1988.

Silbey, Joel H. *A Respectable Minority: The Democratic Party in the Civil War Era, 1860–1868*. New York: Norton, 1977.

MICHAEL PERMAN

Democratic Party, 1896–1932

Unlike many other political changes, the modern history of the Democratic Party began with a speech. When William Jennings Bryan gave one of the most famous speeches in American history to the 1896 Democratic convention, he not only boosted his own nomination for president, he also began the reshaping of a party of mixed and murky motivation into a party of persistent themes of activist government, reform, and regulation. Later Democrats might not identify with Bryan's issues and attitudes, but they could recognize his instincts.

Since the Civil War, the Democratic Party had been an outsiders' alliance led by white Southerners and urban machines, often winning control of the House but usually losing the White House and the Senate. The party included some elements challenging the nation's new industrial conditions and corporate power, but it also contained northern leaders close to business and Jeffersonians (frequently southern) committed on principle to weak government, especially weak federal government. The people support the government, explained Grover Cleveland, the only Democratic president between Buchanan and Wilson, but that did not mean the government should support the people.

Bryan's Party

The massive depression of the 1890s, crushing to both farmers and workers, challenged this attitude. Western and southern Democrats echoed the calls of the Populist Party for expanding the money supply with silver (creating inflation and benefiting debtors) and regulating railroads and business. At the 1896 Democratic convention, the long-shot candidate Bryan, a former Nebraska congressman, captured the nomination with a speech warning, "Thou shalt not crucify mankind upon a cross of gold." The speech displayed both the eloquence and passion that would make him a national leader for decades and the heartland Protestant religiosity that would persistently discomfit immigrant and urban voters.

As the voice of the western and southern challenge, Bryan became the Populist as well as the Democratic nominee, taking on former Ohio governor William McKinley in a high-stakes race that was one of the most exciting in U.S. history. Republicans waged a multimillion-dollar campaign in which thousands of speakers warned against the dangers of Bryan, who pioneered modern campaigning by barnstorming the country and making hundreds of speeches. Bryan lost the presidency because he was unable to break into the Northeast and Great Lakes states, a problem for Democratic White House candidates for years to come and an alignment that kept the Democrats in mostly minority status until the Great Depression.

But the party influence of the Commoner, as Bryan came to be called, endured and strengthened. In 1900 he was renominated easily, and in the wake of the Spanish-American War, his opposition to imperialism in the Philippines won back some Cleveland conservatives. An improved national economic situation, however, knocked off enough of his original supporters that he actually lost some ground. Even in 1904, when Cleveland conservatives briefly recaptured the party to nominate New York judge Alton Parker against President Theodore Roosevelt, Bryan controlled the platform process.

By his third unsuccessful run, in 1908, Bryan was clearly the national leader of the party, sweeping convention delegates from every region, as he called for business regulation, an income tax, direct election of senators, the right of labor to organize, and a lower tariff—the issue that bound even Bryan and Cleveland Democrats together. Bryan's campaign also produced a direct endorsement by the American Federation of Labor, an alliance that would shape the Democratic Party ever after.

Partly because of the lack of other national leaders or governors and senators from northern states during this time, Democratic newspapers became particularly influential. The *New York World* was considered a national party voice, even after the death of Joseph Pulitzer in 1911, and William Randolph Hearst, with his chain of newspapers spreading across the country, was perhaps the only powerful party figure throughout the entire 1896–1932 period—even if he never achieved his personal goal of winning high office.

Besides Bryan, the party's foremost negotiable asset during this time was the South. During Bryan's years the region became solidly Democratic, with disfranchisement of African Americans embedded into state constitutions, succeeding—although not entirely ending—the tactics of violence and fraud previously used against blacks (and Populists). From 1900 the 11 states of the former Confederacy would not elect a single Republican senator until 1961. In the earlier part of the century, many southern Democratic leaders combined economic reformism with virulent racism, as the white supremacist South remained the most thoroughly Bryanized part of the country. As late as the 1960s, South Carolina had a congressman named William Jennings Bryan Dorn.

That economic outlook shaped southern Democratic voting in Congress through years when Democrats were out of the White House and during Woodrow Wilson's New Freedom years. Democrats, overwhelmingly from southern and border states, strongly supported Theodore Roosevelt's reform efforts and voted with insurgent Republicans during William Howard Taft's presidency, taking on tariff, regulation, and labor issues in an alliance of mutual mistrust. Progressive Republicans, heavily from west of the Mississippi with old-stock and Scandinavian backgrounds, distrusted both Southerners and urban immigrants, while congressional Democrats felt that progressives, like Roosevelt himself, often used them mostly as leverage to cut deals with the conservative GOP leadership.

After 1910—when Taft's problems and a wave of reform agitation gave the Democrats the House, ten Senate seats, and a raft of governorships in a widely overlooked harbinger of 1912 victory—the House launched widely covered investigations of corporate excesses and passed extensive legislation from the party platform. Most of it died in the Senate, although Democrats and Progressive Republicans did pass through Congress the Seventeenth Amendment for direct election of senators, improving Democrats' chances in many northern states. The record of the House made presidential contenders of its two leaders, Speaker Champ Clark of Missouri, an old Bryanite, and Majority Leader Oscar Underwood of Alabama.

Wilson Recreates the Democrats

Clark and Underwood would lose the 1912 nomination, in 44 ballots, to one of the new Democratic governors, Woodrow Wilson of New Jersey. The former president of Princeton University, Wilson had been a traditional Cleveland Democrat but had moved steadily and repeatedly left to achieve political credibility in his party—first in New Jersey and then nationally. Still, he was about to lose the presidential nomination to Clark, who had a majority of delegates until Bryan broke the Baltimore convention apart, declaring he could not support any candidate backed by New York—a move intended either to enforce progressive purity or to create chaos that might yield him a fourth nomination.

As the Democratic nominee, Wilson faced a shattered Republican Party, with Theodore Roosevelt running on the new Bull Moose Progressive ticket. The GOP split ensured Wilson's victory (and a massively Democratic House), but had historically obscured trends that had been already running in the Democrats' direction.

During the campaign, Wilson advocated a New Freedom, based largely on the thinking of reformist lawyer Louis Brandeis. The Democrat emphasized breaking up combinations of corporate power rather than trying to control them, the goal of Roosevelt's New Nationalism. The campaign was hardly a philosophical exchange, but it did send Democrats into complete control of Washington—for the first time in 20 years and only the second time since the Civil War—with a clear program and mandate.

In office, Wilson and the Democrats compiled an extensive record of reform legislation, including tariff reduction (with an income tax, now permitted by the Sixteenth Amendment); a new antitrust act, including some legal protections for labor unions; and the creation of the Federal Reserve, a distant descendant of the currency question of 1896. Wilson's bonds with the mostly

southern congressional Democrats were bolstered by the Virginia-born president's sympathy for their racial attitudes, as he expanded segregation through the federal government.

Approaching reelection in 1916, Wilson—to the applause of most congressional Democrats—moved to a more aggressively interventionist stance. He backed legislation enforcing an eight-hour day for railroad workers and banning child labor in interstate commerce, and filled a Supreme Court vacancy with Louis Brandeis, the most activist reformer and the first Jew ever named to the high court. Brandeis's appointment was a major step in attracting Jews, previously uncomfortable with Bryan's assertive Protestantism and Irish Catholic city machines, into the Democratic Party. This two-decade evolution was symbolized by Henry Morgenthau, Wilson's fundraiser and ambassador to Turkey, and his son, Henry Jr., Franklin D. Roosevelt's secretary of the treasury.

The strategy worked just well enough; Wilson drew heavily from former Bull Moosers, Socialists, and unionists in the West to win a narrow, improbable reelection and to establish enduring Democratic roots in the Rocky Mountains. Republicans, and some subsequent historians, have argued that only persistent GOP divisions, and the claim that Wilson had kept the country out of World War I, allowed Wilson to slip through. But Democrats could also claim that low-level support among Irish and German voters, angry over friendliness to Great Britain, kept Wilson from a more resounding victory.

The Great War continued to produce great problems for the party. In 1920 anger over the postwar peace agreements, which frustrated the wishes of many immigrants and dismayed other voters, produced a Republican landslide, with Ohio senator Warren Harding smashing the Democratic ticket of Ohio governor James Cox and Assistant Secretary of the Navy Franklin D. Roosevelt. Never again would a Democratic candidate follow Wilson in supporting U.S. membership in the League of Nations.

But Wilson's ideal in foreign affairs, of a U.S. advocacy for democracy exercised through international organizations and alliances, shaped the Democratic view long afterward. Both President Franklin D. Roosevelt and his secretary of state Cordell Hull were Wilsonians—Roosevelt in the administration and Hull in the House—an experience shaping their commitment to a United Nations, spurring a Democratic belief in multilateral efforts extending as far as John F. Kennedy and Bill Clinton. Wilson remained an iconic figure among many

Democrats; Alben Barkley of Kentucky (Franklin D. Roosevelt's Senate majority leader and Harry Truman's vice president) concluded in his memoirs that Wilson was the greatest man he had ever known.

Cultural Clashes and Reconciliation

The ethnic strains in the Democratic Party, reflected in foreign policy issues in 1916 and 1920, exploded across domestic policy throughout the 1920s. Immigrant groups' prominence in the party rose steadily, as urban machines that had for decades nominated old-stock Protestants for statewide offices increasingly claimed governorships and Senate seats for members of their own ethnic groups. Their rise was symbolized by New York governor Alfred E. Smith, who became the first Catholic to contend for the White House. From 1919 to 1929, Smith's success expanding reach, protections, and efficiency in the state government made him one of the great governors in American history, providing concepts and officials to later Democratic national administrations.

But the changing dynamics of the party and of 1920s America, dismayed the party's Bryanite rural and small-town roots in the South and West. The nation's cultural and political conflicts were reflected in the rise of the Ku Klux Klan outside the South during the 1920s, the battle over Prohibition, and congressional struggles over immigration quotas. During the 1920s, especially in presidential politics, cultural strains overshadowed economic interests to a degree not seen again until the 1970s.

The strains exploded at the 1924 convention in New York in a 103-ballot death struggle between Smith's Northeast and Midwest supporters and the southern and western core of former treasury secretary (and Wilson son-in-law) William Gibbs McAdoo. During the weeks-long battle, the convention divided in half over condemning the Ku Klux Klan and an equally divisive final appearance by Bryan. To run against Calvin Coolidge, the convention ultimately issued a by-then worthless nomination to conservative John W. Davis, spurring a third-party run by Senator Robert La Follette, Republican of Wisconsin. The Democratic ticket won less than 30 percent of the vote, running third in much of the West and Midwest.

By 1928 most of the party concluded that Smith was inevitable, but his nomination led to the loss of half of the South to Herbert Hoover and a national GOP landslide, in a time of national prosperity and a blizzard of anti-Catholic agitation. The New York governor also alienated many traditional party supporters with his prominent Wall Street supporters, his opposition to (and personal defiance of) Prohibition, and his difficulty in connecting with rural voters.

Still, Smith ran better than any presidential Democratic candidate in memory among urban voters, a group that would provide the party core for decades to come. Later, pollster Samuel Lubell, in one of the most famous assessments in political history, would pronounce, "Before the Roosevelt Revolution, there was an Al Smith Revolution."

Moreover, quadrennial White House disasters were not the sole indications of the party's strength during the 1920s. In 1922, 1926, and 1930, off-year congressional elections produced sizable gains and displays of party potential. Allied with insurgent Republicans from the Midwest and West, Democrats managed to pass legislation for farm relief and labor protection, frequently vetoed by Republican presidents.

With the stock market crash in 1929 and the ensuing depression, Democratic chances in 1932 seemed highly promising. But the same stresses that had broken apart the Democrats in three previous campaigns surfaced again. New York governor Franklin D. Roosevelt, a former Smith ally, emerged as the leading candidate after his overwhelming 1930 reelection. He arrived at the Chicago convention with a majority of the delegates, but was kept short of the necessary two-thirds by a loose alliance of favorite sons, House Speaker John Nance Garner of Texas and Smith, embittered by the bigoted religious rhetoric of 1928 and his displacement by Roosevelt.

Despite his Albany address, Roosevelt's delegates were largely from southern and western Bryanite territories. A former Wilson subcabinet official, the candidate connected deeply with earlier party roots. In a preconvention message Roosevelt assured delegates, "I am a progressive in deed and word, in the truest and most Democratic sense." He won the nomination by allying with and offering the vice presidency to Garner, whose own House service extended back into Bryan's and Wilson's times.

On a platform vague about plans to treat the Great Depression—but explicit on re-legalizing beer—Roosevelt won the first of four landslide victories that would define the Democrats as the nation's majority party for half a century. To the traditional Democratic alliance of the South and urban ethnic voters, Roosevelt locked in the party's alliance with labor and added Western progressives who had been dubious about Democrats since 1916.

During the course of Roosevelt's New Deal, many of its elements—business regulation, protection of union-organizing rights, federal insurance of bank deposits, and even going off the gold standard—had roots in Bryanism.

The Democratic outsiders' alliance, now a majority, would persist through most of the twentieth century, until over the course of decades it shattered on the entry of the nation's ultimate outsiders, African Americans. But almost a hundred years later, the persistent Democratic themes of activist government at home and multilateralism abroad can still be traced to the party of Bryan, Wilson, and Smith.

See also conservative interregnum, 1920–32; Democratic Party, 1860–96; progressivism and the Progressive Era, 1890s–1920.

FURTHER READING

Burner, David. *The Politics of Provincialism: The Democratic Party in Transition 1918–1932.* New York: Knopf, 1968.

Craig, Douglas B. *After Wilson: The Struggle for the Democratic Party, 1920–1934.* Chapel Hill: University of North Carolina Press, 1992.

Hollingsworth, J. Rogers. *The Whirligig of Politics: The Democracy of Cleveland and Bryan.* Chicago: University of Chicago Press, 1963.

Kazin, Michael. *A Godly Hero: The Life of William Jennings Bryan.* New York: Knopf, 2006.

Link, Arthur. *Wilson.* 5 vols. Princeton, NJ: Princeton University Press, 1947–65.

Murray, Robert K. *The 103rd Ballot: Democrats and the Disaster in Madison Square Garden.* New York: Harper and Row, 1976.

Oulahan, Richard. *The Man Who . . . The Story of the 1932 Democratic National Convention.* New York: Dial Press, 1971.

Perman, Michael. *Struggle for Mastery: Disfranchisement in the South, 1888–1908.* Chapel Hill: University of North Carolina Press, 2001.

Sanders, Elizabeth. *Roots of Reform: Farmers, Workers, and the American State, 1877–1917.* Chicago: University of Chicago Press, 1999.

Sarasohn, David. *Party of Reform: Democrats in the Progressive Era.* Jackson: University Press of Mississippi, 1989.

Slayton, Robert A. *Empire Statesman: The Rise and Redemption of Al Smith.* New York: Free Press, 2001.

DAVID SARASOHN

Democratic Party, 1932–68

On March 4, 1933, in Washington, D.C., standing hatless and coatless on a dreary, windswept inauguration day, Franklin D. Roosevelt placed his hand on an old family Bible and recited the oath of office. Afterward, he turned to face the 100,000 spectators somberly gathered in front of the Capitol. The faces staring back at him were lined with despair. One in four Americans were without a job. Each month, thousands of farmers and business owners went bankrupt. A Roosevelt adviser, Rexford Guy Tugwell, wrote in his diary, "Never in modern times, I should think, has there been so widespread unemployment and such moving distress from cold and hunger."

Roosevelt's first task as president was to restore hope in the future and confidence in government. In a firm and confident voice, he promised to ask Congress for "broad executive power to wage a war against the emergency, as great as the power that would be given to me if we were invaded by a foreign foe." Over the next few years, Roosevelt backed up his words with a bold and ambitious reform agenda designed to revive the economy and the nation's spirit. The New Deal, along with the dozens of alphabet agencies it spawned, redefined the relationship between the federal government and its citizens and forged a new political coalition that would sustain the Democratic Party and dominate American politics for the next three decades.

Roosevelt's landslide victory in 1936 institutionalized the New Deal political coalition. That year Roosevelt swept every state but Maine and Vermont, and carried with him into Congress unprecedented Democratic margins of 331 to 89 in the House and 76 to 16 in the Senate. Six million more people voted in 1936 than had cast ballots in 1932, and the bulk of these new voters supported the Democratic Party. Economic need served as the glue binding together the New Deal coalition. Hardship fused the interests of millions of rural farmers and urban workers, both skilled and unskilled, native-born and foreign-born, white and nonwhite, male and female. The disparate coalition included rural Protestants and urban Catholics; white segregationists and African Americans; liberal intellectuals and tradition-minded conservatives.

The journalist Samuel Lubell argued that the United States had a "sun" party, whose light dominated the landscape, and a "moon" party that reflected the sun's rays. Roosevelt's New Deal, and the coalition that sustained it, provided much of the energy that would illuminate American politics for the next three decades. By the 1960s, however, larger social and demographic changes eroded popular support for government activism, at the same time that a controversial war in Vietnam, combined with racial conflict at home, weakened old loyalties and exposed deep fissures in the New Deal coalition. By 1968 fear and uncertainty had eclipsed much of the light from the Democratic "sun."

The New Deal and Congressional Conservatism: 1938–52

While Roosevelt had created a new coalition in presidential elections, he was less successful in sustaining the congressional majorities needed to support his vision of a more activist federal government. A couple of uncharacteristic Roosevelt blunders—a misconceived plan to reform the Supreme Court and an effort to "purge" the party by campaigning in the 1938 primaries against conservatives who had opposed New Deal measures—allowed Republicans to make major gains in Congress. During the 1940s, wartime prosperity and the emergence of foreign policy issues further diluted the New Deal agenda. By 1944 the Republicans controlled 209 House seats—only 13 fewer than the Democrats. Since most of the Democratic losses came in the North and Midwest, the Republican gains enhanced the southern balance of power within the Democratic Party. In the House, representatives from 15 southern and border states claimed 120 of the 222 Democratic seats; in the Senate they held 29 of 57 seats. This "conservative coalition" placed a break on major new reforms until Lyndon Johnson's landslide in 1964.

Roosevelt's death in April 1945 left behind a powerful but weakened coalition, lacking a clear sense of how to deal with the economic pain of reconversion to a peacetime economy or the growing rift with the Soviet Union. While Republicans fed on public worries about inflation and unemployment, Democrats fought over how to deal with the cold war. When Harry Truman chose a confrontational course with the Soviet Union, many liberals rallied around former vice president Henry Wallace, who advocated maintaining a "popular front" with America's wartime ally. Republicans took advantage of the confusion, making major gains in the 1946 congressional elections and taking control of the House for the first time since 1930.

The cold war was only one of the new questions facing Truman and threatening the Democratic Party. When the Democratic Party included an endorsement of civil rights in its 1948 platform, southern delegates stormed out of the convention, formed the States' Rights Democratic, or "Dixiecrat," Party, and nominated J. Strom Thurmond, governor of South Carolina, for the presidency. "We stand for the segregation of the races and the racial integrity of each race," the platform declared.

In 1948, with his party deeply fractured over both the cold war and civil rights, observers gave Truman little chance of winning against popular New York governor Thomas E. Dewey. While Dewey tried to stay above the partisan fray, Truman waged a tough, bare-knuckled campaign, tying himself to Roosevelt's legacy, reminding voters that the Democratic Party had led the nation through depression and world war.

On Election Day, Truman scored the most dramatic upset victory in the history of presidential elections, winning 24.1 million votes to Dewey's 22 million. The election demonstrated the enduring appeal of the New Deal. "I talked about voting for Dewey all summer, but when the time came I just couldn't do it," confessed one farmer. "I remembered the Depression and all the other things that had come to me under the Democrats." The Democrats, by picking up 9 seats in the Senate and 75 in the House, regained control of Congress. "[T]he party that Roosevelt formed has survived his death," the journalist Walter Lippmann observed, "and is without question the dominant force in American politics."

From the Fair Deal to the New Frontier: 1948–63

Truman had promised the nation a "Fair Deal," and he managed to push some reforms through a reluctant Congress. By 1952, however, public attention had moved away from the economic concerns that had defined the New Deal and carried Truman over the finish line in 1948. With the administration burdened by an unpopular war in Korea, charges of corruption, and accusations of coddling Communists, the public turned to Republican war hero Dwight Eisenhower in 1952. Not only did Eisenhower win in a landslide, Republicans won control of the House and Senate, although by slim margins.

Their poor showing on Election Day revealed that the Democrats faced serious problems as they tried to update the New Deal agenda to a new political environment. During the 1950s, the Democratic Party found itself trapped between the growing aspirations of African Americans and the increased intransigence of the white South. The Supreme Court raised the stakes in 1954, when, in a unanimous decision popularly known as *Brown v. Board of Education of Topeka, Kansas*, the justices declared segregation in public schools to be illegal. The historic decision triggered massive resistance to ending Jim Crow among state and local Democratic politicians in the South. Nineteen southern senators and 77 representatives signed a manifesto in 1956 that bound them to "use all lawful means to bring about a reversal of this decision which is contrary to the Court and to prevent the use of force in its implementation."

Race was dividing the Democrats at the same time that prosperity was eroding the common sense of economic grievance that united the disparate coalition. The United States experienced an unprecedented economic boom following World War II. Between 1940 and 1960, the gross national product (GNP) more than doubled from $227 billion to $488 billion. The median family income rose from $3,083 to $5,657, and real wages rose by almost 30 percent. How could a party born during a period of economic crisis adapt to a new age of prosperity?

In a series of articles written throughout the decade, liberal historian Arthur Schlesinger Jr. argued that liberalism born during the Depression needed to adjust to a new age of abundance. Instead of a quantitative liberalism "dedicated to the struggle to secure the economic basis of life," Schlesinger called for a "qualitative liberalism dedicated to bettering the quality of people's lives and opportunities." The Democratic Party had sowed the seeds of its own demise, he argued, by creating a satiated middle-class society.

Despite these challenges, the party turned anxiety over a struggling economy and worry about Soviet advances into a major victory in 1958. Indicting a failure of leadership in Washington, Democratic congressional candidates won 56 percent of votes cast—the highest figure since 1936. Democrats increased their majority in the House from 235 to 282. Democratic victories on the state level gave them control of 34 governorships, including those in traditional Republican strongholds like South Dakota, Wisconsin, and Nebraska.

Two years later, the Democrats turned to the youthful and attractive John F. Kennedy to head the party's ticket. The 42-year-old Massachusetts senator was the first Catholic to contend for the presidency since Al Smith in 1928. Realizing he needed a running mate who could provide regional balance, Kennedy asked Texas senator Lyndon Johnson to join the ticket. The Democratic ticket won by promising to "get the nation moving again," but Kennedy's razor-thin victory revealed the divisions within the party.

The new president's youthful style and soaring rhetoric inspired the nation, although his actions, especially on the home front, seemed timid by comparison. His tragic assassination in November 1963 turned the party over to Johnson, who used the shock of Kennedy's death to score a decisive victory in 1964. Johnson's percentage of the popular vote, 61.1 percent, matched Roosevelt's in 1936. Congressional Democrats coasted to victory on the president's coattails, providing the administration with large majorities in both houses: 68 to 32 in the Senate and 295 to 140 in the House

The Rise and Fall of the Great Society: 1963–68

Johnson reforged the New Deal coalition and promised to fulfill the unrealized legislative program of the New Deal and Fair Deal. His goal was to emulate his hero, Franklin D. Roosevelt, whom he once described as "like a daddy to me." In the spring of 1964, Johnson coined a phrase meant to define his vision for the presidency, announcing that he hoped to build a "Great Society," "where men are more concerned with the quality of their goals than the quantity of their goods." Johnson had built his vision of a Great Society on the belief that America had forged a new national consensus around shared goals of economic growth, anticommunism, and activist government.

Events over the next four years would expose the fragility of the New Deal coalition. The racial dividing line in the Democratic Party grew wider after Johnson signed into law the Civil Rights Act of 1964 and the Voting Rights Act of 1965. "I think we just gave the South to the Republicans for your lifetime and mine," Johnson confessed to an aide after signing the Civil Rights Act.

The racial rioting that ripped through the nation's cities in the 1960s added to the divisions. Between 1964 and 1968, the United States experienced the most intense period of civil unrest since the Civil War. Most whites responded to the riots and the new black militancy with fear and anger. In 1966 Republicans campaigning on a tough "law-and-order" platform gained 47 House seats and 3 in the Senate. The Democrats lost more seats in 1966 than they had won in 1964. After November 1966, there were 156 northern Democrats in the House, 62 short of a majority.

While the debate over civil rights and riots exposed the racial divide in the Democratic Party, the Vietnam War split it into rival camps of hawks and doves, and pushed millions of young people to take to the streets to protest the war. The draft system, which placed an unfair burden on the poor and working class, added to the frustrations that were tearing the party apart. A large number of working-class Americans opposed the war, but they disliked privileged student protesters even more. "We can't understand," lamented a blue-collar worker, "how all those rich kids—the kids with the beads from the fancy suburbs—how they get off when my son has to go over there and maybe get his head shot off."

The conflicting currents of the decade converged during the 1968 presidential election year. After Minnesota senator Eugene McCarthy, campaigning as an antiwar candidate, scored a symbolic victory in the New Hampshire primary, Senator Robert Kennedy entered the race. Many people believed that Kennedy offered the best opportunity for the party to reforge its tattered coalition. His tragic assassination in June, however, ended that hope and left the nomination to Vice President Hubert Humphrey.

The Democrats who gathered in Chicago that summer for their convention were members of a party in disarray. President Johnson, who did not attend, was determined to see the party support his Vietnam policy, thus denying Humphrey the ability to make peace with the antiwar forces. A small but vocal group of radical activists traveled to Chicago intent on provoking a violent confrontation with the police. The city's powerful mayor, Richard Daley, was just as determined to demonstrate that he was in control of the streets, turning the area around the convention hall into an armed fortress. The combustible mix produced a violent explosion, captured by news cameras and projected into the homes of millions of Americans. The images of baton-wielding police officers clubbing young people in the streets of Chicago contributed to the impression that the Democrats were a party in disorder, incapable of effective governing.

Two other major presidential candidates that year helped reinforce that message. American Independence Party candidate George Wallace, whose symbolic stance in a university doorway had made him a hero to southern whites, appealed to many northern Democrats angry over the party's association with protest and integration. Joining Wallace in pursuit of the hearts and minds of America's angry white voters was the Republican nominee, Richard Nixon, who appealed to the "forgotten Americans."

Nixon achieved a narrow victory on Election Day. While the Democrats maintained healthy majorities in Congress and many statehouses across the nation, the election exposed the deep fault lines in the New Deal coalition. Nearly as many people voted for Wallace and Nixon as had supported Johnson in 1964, revealing a growing conservative trend in American politics. Racial tensions made it difficult for Democrats to sustain a biracial coalition, and geographical differences between North and South threatened the very fabric of the party. Humphrey, who won only 10 percent of the vote among white Southerners, carried just one state in the ex-Confederacy, Texas. Franklin Roosevelt still cast a long shadow over American politics and policy, but the coalition he created was showing its age.

See also conservative interregnum, 1920–32; era of consensus, 1952–64; New Deal Era; presidency, 1932–2008.

FURTHER READING

Edsall, Thomas. *Chain Reaction: The Impact of Race, Rights, and Taxes on American Politics.* New York: Norton, 1992.

Farber, David. *Chicago '68.* Chicago: University of Chicago Press, 1994.

Hamby, Alonzo. *Beyond the New Deal: Harry S Truman and American Liberalism.* New York: Columbia University Press, 1976.

Lubell, Samuel. *The Future of American Politics.* New York: Harper and Row, 1965.

Matusow, Alen J. *The Unraveling of America: A History of Liberalism in the 1960s.* New York: Harper and Row, 1984.

Patterson, James T. *Congressional Conservatism and the New Deal.* Lexington: University Press of Kentucky, 1967.

STEVEN M. GILLON

Democratic Party, 1968–2008

Democratic Crack-up: 1968–76

When Lyndon B. Johnson succeeded to the presidency in November 1963, the Democratic Party was still dominated by a latter-day version of New Deal liberalism and a cold war commitment to the containment of international communism. By the time Johnson declined to seek another term in March 1968, both of these creeds were under attack. The intervening years had brought an overwhelming victory in the 1964 presidential and congressional elections, a major expansion of the welfare state called the Great Society, a less well-funded but still significant War on Poverty, and civil rights legislation that opened the way to full legal equality for African Americans. Starting in early 1965, while offering assurances that the booming economy could provide both "guns and butter," the Johnson administration steadily expanded the war in Vietnam.

These political developments, in confluence with such broader trends as the revival of feminism, increasing violent crime, loosening of sexual mores, and growing black militancy divided the country in general and the Democratic Party in particular. By 1964 there were signs of a "white backlash," a reaction against rising taxes, urban crime, and African American militancy. Segregationist governor George Wallace of Alabama won a large protest vote in three northern presidential primaries. Four years later Wallace ran for president on his own American Independent Party ticket.

The 1968 campaign occurred during the most tumultuous year for Americans since 1919. In January the Communist Tet Offensive in Vietnam undermined the administration's recent predictions of imminent victory. In March Senator Eugene J. McCarthy of Minnesota, an antiwar candidate, won 42 percent of the vote against Johnson in the New Hampshire primary. Then Senator Robert F. Kennedy of New York entered the race as a critic of the war. Vice President Hubert Humphrey became the de facto candidate of the Democratic establishment (even though Johnson dreamed of being drafted to run). After Kennedy's assassination in June, Humphrey received a nomination thought to be worthless. Outside the convention hall, Chicago police beat bystanders as well as angry antiwar demonstrators.

Humphrey ran 500,000 votes behind Republican Richard Nixon, while the Democrats retained control of Congress. He came so close to winning only because the anti-Democratic vote (57 percent) was split; Wallace won 13.6 percent. Humphrey received less than one-third of the southern vote.

The 1968 convention highlighted problems with party structure as well as ideological divisions. The Democrats began searching for a formula that would balance the interests of both party elites and grassroots movements. All factions agreed on the need to democratize the presidential selection process and increase the number of minority, female, and young delegates. The most important of several commissions created to find remedies was headed by Senator George McGovern of South Dakota. In 1971, despite opposition from organized labor, numerous members of Congress, and white Southerners, the Democratic National Committee ad-

opted the McGovern commission "guidelines" and related reforms. Even prominent officials would not be guaranteed seats at the next national convention unless they were selected fairly. Moreover, all delegations had to take "affirmative steps" to include women, minorities, and the young.

McGovern used both the reforms he had recommended and the connections he had cultivated as commission chair to win the presidential nomination in 1972. Skeptical of cold war premises and enthusiastic about expanding the welfare state, McGovern was the most liberal major party nominee in the twentieth century. His closest rivals for the nomination were Hubert Humphrey, who now claimed to represent a responsible center, and Senator Henry Jackson of Washington, an unreconstructed cold warrior. McGovern's nomination was the product of a genuine grassroots movement. Fifteen percent of the convention delegates were black and 40 percent women, triple the percentages in 1968; 21 percent were under 30. Many in McGovern's "new politics" constituency wanted to change prevailing American ways of life as well as government policies. For instance, the convention considered a platform plank supporting abortion rights, which was rejected at McGovern's behest.

Nixon's shrewd combination of grudging liberalism and populist conservatism made him a formidable opponent. As president, he had agreed to expansion of the welfare state, pursued détente with the Soviet Union, normalized relations with the People's Republic of China, removed most ground troops from Vietnam, evaded enforcement of school desegregation, appointed conservative Supreme Court justices, and mobilized "square America" in opposition to cultural liberalization. A likely Democratic defeat was turned into a rout when McGovern chose Senator Thomas Eagleton of Missouri as his running mate. Eagleton was nudged from the ticket after reports surfaced that he had received electroshock treatment for clinical depression. The whole affair made McGovern look incompetent. Nixon won more than 60 percent of the vote, including 75 percent of erstwhile Wallace supporters, a majority of Catholics, and 30 percent of Jews. The Democrats nonetheless retained control of Congress.

The Carter Interlude: 1976–80

The most consequential act of the 1972 campaign did not affect the outcome. Burglars with ties to the White House broke into the Democratic national headquarters at the Watergate office building. This botched exercise in political espionage came to symbolize Nixon's high-handed presidency. He resigned on the verge of impeachment in 1974. Two years later Jimmy Carter, a former governor of Georgia, won the Democratic presidential nomination and general election in large part because the electorate, reeling from the Vietnam War as well as the Watergate scandal, craved an ostentatiously moral "outsider" in the White House. Other decisive factors were less amorphous than Carter's promise of a "government as good as the people": division among his economically more liberal Democratic rivals between chastened cold warriors and unreconstructed cold warriors; support from a growing constituency of evangelical Protestants who embraced this "born-again" Baptist as one of their own; and "stagflation" (a combination of high unemployment and high inflation) that Gerald Ford's administration could not cure. Carter's victory represented no resurrection of a predominantly liberal version of the New Deal coalition. Although Carter carried standard, if sometimes skeptical, Democratic constituencies, his narrow margin over Ford also reflected support from 44 percent of independents and 30 percent of self-described conservatives.

Carter's relations with a Democratic Congress began badly and got worse. Most congressional Democrats wanted to expand the welfare state while Carter, drawing on a pre–New Deal version of liberalism, emphasized efficiency, conservation, and consumer protection. This agenda reflected political calculation as well as the president's worldview. As the blue-collar workforce shrunk along with membership in labor unions, Carter sought to cultivate a new constituency among middle-class suburbanites. Almost all party leaders acknowledged that recent social and political developments made some adaptations necessary. For instance, Senator Edward Kennedy of Massachusetts, the president's foremost Democratic rival, joined forces with Carter to deregulate passenger air travel.

Any rapprochement between congressional welfare-state liberals and efficiency liberals in the White House was doomed by circumstances beyond their control. Indeed, during Carter's presidency, chronic domestic and international problems that had been building for years became acute. The most important of these were the inherent instability of détente combined with fears of the Soviet advances; growing militancy in the third world; economic stagflation exacerbated by the rising cost of petroleum; and the increasing prominence of cultural issues like abortion.

In this context, most of Carter's victories proved to be pyrrhic. Ratification of the treaties that ultimately returned the Canal Zone to Panama revitalized Republican conservatives. Advocacy of human rights in the Third World looked like weakness to Carter's foes at home and abroad. Legislation lifting price controls on oil and natural gas in order to increase supply split the Democrats along ideological, regional, and class lines. Carter's acceptance of abortion as a constitutional right convinced evangelicals that he was more liberal than he had appeared in 1976.

The president's unique coalition was already disintegrating in November 1979 when his decision to admit the deposed Shah of Iran to the United States for medical treatment precipitated the seizure of the American embassy in Tehran. In December the Soviet Union invaded Afghanistan. These events widened another Democratic division—between advocates of international conciliation and proponents of an assertive foreign policy. The latter faction increasingly included the president himself.

After winning a bitter battle for renomination against Edward Kennedy, Carter lost a three-way race to Republican Ronald Reagan in 1980. Frightened liberals in their retrospective analysis emphasized Reagan's strong support among evangelical Protestants, many of whom had been mobilized by a new Christian right. A working-class willingness to become "Reagan Democrats" was at least as significant; a majority of white union members voted for the Republican nominee. Carter barely won a plurality among Jews. The most prominent Jewish defectors were neoconservative "Henry Jackson Democrats," who rejected the conciliatory side of Carter's foreign policy. The Republicans also captured the Senate for the first time since 1952. In sum, Reagan, a former Democrat who had voted for Franklin Roosevelt four times, detached important elements from the residual New Deal coalition.

Defeat and Confusion: 1980–92

President Reagan proved to be more flexible and popular than his opponents anticipated. A few congressional "blue dog" Democrats, most of them from the South, supported his conservative economic program. Seeking ways to forestall the emergence of a national Republican majority, Democratic leaders as a whole spent the Reagan years tinkering with party structure and exploring ideological adjustments. Many inferred from the nominations of McGovern and Carter that presidential selection had become too democratic. In accordance with the recommendation of another rules commission in 1982, members of Congress and other high officials would automatically serve as "superdelegates" to national conventions. Meanwhile, grassroots party organization was allowed to disintegrate in places where Reagan had strong support, including those southern states where native son Carter had run fairly well in 1980.

Throughout the 1980s, many prominent Democrats went along with the Republican caricature of liberalism. Except for the black activist Jesse Jackson, all major presidential contenders said that past Democratic administrations had ignored the merits of the market, wasted taxpayers' money, and slighted national defense. As appeals to the working class ebbed, the party cultivated newly influential constituencies and trendy rhetorical motifs. Women seemed an especially promising bloc because the Reagan administration attacked the welfare state and opposed abortion. To exploit the "gender gap" in 1984, presidential candidate Walter Mondale chose Representative Geraldine Ferraro of New York as his running mate. Trying to reclaim the center in 1988, presidential nominee Michael Dukakis, the governor of Massachusetts, waged his campaign on the basis of "competence" rather than "ideology."

With the possible exception of the Democratic recapture of the Senate in 1986, these tactical shifts rarely worked. Mondale received only 41 percent of the vote against Reagan, who won majorities among working-class whites, Catholics, and women. In 1988 George H. W. Bush, a weaker Republican candidate, turned the election into a referendum on patriotism. Although Dukakis received 46 percent of the vote, he too lost among Catholics, blue-collar workers, and white Southerners.

Governor Bill Clinton of Arkansas joined the effort to re-brand the Democrats as a "centrist" party during the early 1980s. When Clinton defeated President Bush and independent candidate Ross Perot in 1992, a majority of voters polled viewed him as a "new kind of Democrat." He won a plurality of Catholics and carried four southern states. Clinton also profited from evolving cultural attitudes. Many swing voters—especially single women—now favored abortion rights and feared the Christian right's influence among Republicans; four female Democrats were elected to the Senate in 1992. Amid a recession, however, a sign in Clinton's campaign headquarters summarized the main reason for his victory: "It's the economy, stupid."

"A New Kind of Democrat": 1992–2000

Clinton's initial agenda as president mixed old and new Democratic goals. He successfully pushed congressional Democrats to reduce the budget deficit and to promote international commerce by ratifying the North American Free Trade Agreement (NAFTA). Much more liberal on cultural issues than Carter, he tried unsuccessfully to lift the ban on gays in the military. He put his wife, Hillary Rodham Clinton, in charge of a failed effort to pass national health insurance, a liberal Democratic dream since the New Deal. Aided by an economic downturn in 1994, Republican conservatives led by Representative Newt Gingrich of Georgia captured both houses of Congress in a landslide. Clinton fought back effectively with his characteristic ideological mix of new and old. On the one hand, he fulfilled a 1992 campaign promise to "end welfare as we know it" by signing legislation to abolish a New Deal entitlement, Aid to Families with Dependent Children (AFDC). On the other hand, he defended programs popular among swing voters, especially Medicare, environmental protection, gun control, and abortion rights. Running against Republican Robert Dole and Reform Party candidate Ross Perot in 1996, Clinton won 50.1 percent of the three-party vote. The Republicans not only retained control of Congress but also gained two Senate seats.

Whatever small chance Clinton had of turning his personal triumph into further legislative or ideological victories was destroyed by the scandal that dominated national politics from January 1998 to February 1999. Congressional Republicans tried to remove Clinton from office primarily because he lied under oath about having had sex with Monica Lewinsky, a young government employee. Most Americans doubted that Clinton's misbehavior rose to the level of an impeachable offense, as was demonstrated by Democratic gains in the 1998 congressional elections. Even so, the Lewinsky scandal left the party much weaker than it otherwise would have been. Vice President Al Gore, the presidential candidate in 2000, tried to distance himself from Clinton's personal flaws while sharing credit for the administration's successes as well as a revived economy.

Ambiguous Defeat and Revival: 2000–2006

Although Gore led Republican George W. Bush by 540,000 popular votes, the outcome in the Electoral College turned on disputed returns from Florida. In the end, Bush was certified the winner by 537 votes. Gore's loss of Florida had many causes, including support drawn away by Green Party candidate Ralph Nader, confusing ballots in key districts, a U.S. Supreme Court decision halting a recount, and perhaps intimidation of African Americans at the polls. But the Florida situation also reflected the Democrats' long-term inattention to grassroots organization. The old kind of Democrats in the New Deal coalition would have supplied poll watchers to explain confusing ballots and protect party faithful from intimidation.

Foreign policy and military action dominated politics after al-Qaeda terrorists attacked the United States on September 11, 2001. A majority of congressional Democrats favored the war to destroy the al-Qaeda sanctuary in Afghanistan. With greater reservations, they also supported the intervention begun in 2003 to overthrow Saddam Hussein's dictatorship in Iraq. The characteristic inclination of voters in wartime to follow a president's lead helped Republicans to recapture the Senate in 2002 (after a brief interlude under Democratic control because a Republican senator declared himself an Independent).

In 2004 former governor Howard Dean of Vermont sought the Democratic presidential nomination as a strong critic of the Iraq war. The Dean campaign resembled the grassroots movement that had supported Eugene McCarthy in 1968, and it too fell short. The Democrats nominated Senator John Kerry of Massachusetts, who had recently begun to criticize the intervention he had earlier voted to authorize. The electorate's continuing willingness to back a wartime president was the chief reason Bush defeated Kerry by 3 million votes. In an electoral landmark, Kerry, a Catholic, lost the Catholic vote. Still, his relatively narrow defeat by an incumbent president during wartime revealed growing public impatience with the Iraq intervention.

In 2006 the Democrats won a decisive majority in the House of Representatives and, joined by two independents, also gained control of the Senate. Disenchantment with the Iraq War, which had now become widespread, was the main cause of this sweep. Worries about a sagging economy also played an important role. In addition, the Democrats had begun to rebuild their grassroots organization even in conservative areas. The party's worst ideological wounds from the 1960s and 1970s finally had been healed by the passing of cold war issues, defection of conservatives to Republican ranks, and shared dislike of the Bush administration. In 2008 Barack Obama, an African American first-term senator from Illinois, used a brilliantly conceived and geographically extensive campaign to win the presidency. For the first time in 15 years, Democrats controlled the presidency and both houses of Congress.

See also Democratic Party, 1800–2008.

FURTHER READING

Pomper, Gerald M., et al. *The Election of 1984: Reports and Interpretations.* Chatham, NJ: Chatham House, 1985.
———. *The Election of 1988: Reports and Interpretations.* Chatham, NJ: Chatham House, 1989.
———. *The Election of 1992: Reports and Interpretations.* Chatham, NJ: Chatham House, 1993.
———. *The Election of 1996: Reports and Interpretations.* Chatham, NJ: Chatham House, 1997.
———. *The Election of 2000: Reports and Interpretations.* New York: South Bridges Press, 2001.
White, Theodore H. *America in Search of Itself: The Making of the President 1956–1980.* New York: Harper and Row, 1982.
Witcover, Jules. *Party of the People: A History of the Democrats.* New York: Random House, 2003.

LEO P. RIBUFFO

economy and politics to 1860

Before the Civil War, the central impetus for economic development was the growth of markets. Simply put, people bought and sold more on regional, national, and international markets than they had done in the colonial period. In the eighteenth century, high transportation costs, low population densities, and shortages of cash kept many Americans from participating in these markets. A wave of nineteenth-century transportation projects (known to contemporaries as "internal improvements") made it far easier to exchange goods and services with more distant places. Farmers took advantage of turnpikes, canals, river improvements, and railroads and produced greater surpluses of cash crops. Farmers specializing in cash crops demanded more textiles, furniture, clocks, books, and other consumer goods. Demand from the countryside created a large market for merchants and manufacturers that fueled the growth of cities and industries. Scores of newly chartered banks provided capital to entrepreneurs taking advantage of these new opportunities. Historians have called the great expansion of commerce the "market revolution." Economists have labeled the process "Smithian growth," after the famous eighteenth-century economist Adam Smith. Smith argued that economic specialization and the division of labor—the crux of what he called the "wealth of nations," the title of his classic treatise—crucially depended on large markets.

The expansion of markets rested as much on political decisions as on economic actions. Scholars have increasingly viewed "institutions"—what might be thought of as the myriad formal and informal rules that shape economic behavior—as a central component of market exchanges. Nineteenth-century Americans self-consciously adopted rules that favored the creation of markets,

whether these were permissive policies toward corporate chartering or the removal of barriers to interstate trade. The "rules of the game" that Americans chose reflected a consensus that commercial and technological progress generated widespread benefits. If Americans generally agreed that commercial progress was important, they disagreed on precisely how national, state, and local governments would shape commercial markets. Two distinct visions dominated economic policy. One called for large-scale federal involvement—including national banks, national internal improvements, and a high tariff—while the other favored a decentralized approach in which state and local governments would take the lead in encouraging economic development. These two different visions of economic change would help shape political parties and economic policy before the Civil War.

Economic Issues and the First Party System

When ratified in 1788, the Constitution established a favorable framework for the growth of markets. The Constitution prohibited the states from establishing trade barriers and thus established a large internal "free-trade zone" that allowed commerce to flourish. Contracts, including debts, made in one state were enforceable in another, giving businesses confidence to engage in interstate commerce. The Constitution also authorized a patent system that protected the rights of inventors. During the nineteenth century the federal government made patents cheap to obtain and easy to enforce—at least relative to European nations—which encouraged inventive activity among thousands of individuals, from humble mechanics to professional inventors. While generally favorable to development, the Constitution was also ambiguous about the role of the federal government in promoting economic development. Could the federal government establish a central bank to help stabilize the nation's financial system? Could the federal government build roads, canals, and other internal improvements? Could the federal government enact tariffs to protect domestic industry from foreign competition?

The Federalists, led by nationalists such as Alexander Hamilton and John Adams, believed that strong national institutions could bind the fragmented republic together. A large national debt, for example, ensured that the prominent financiers and merchants who owned government securities would have a vested interest in the security and prosperity of the nation. In similar fashion, a national bank that would handle the business of the federal government, including the deposit of tax receipts, would give merchants and manufacturers a source of capital while regulating state and local banks. The Federalist vision of a strong, activist state had an undeniable modernizing element, but it sprang from a decidedly eighteenth-century view of politics and society. The Federalists self-consciously sought to concentrate economic and political power in the hands of a small group of wealthy men with the experience, expertise, and leadership to run the nation's economy. In the Federalist vision ordinary voters would act as a check to ensure that these men did not abuse these powers, but Federalists presumed that most men of modest means would defer to their economic and social superiors.

The Federalists prevailed in the 1790s, and with Hamilton's leadership they nationalized the Revolutionary War debt (some of which had been owed by individual states), levied new taxes, and established a national bank. In the pivotal election of 1800, however, Thomas Jefferson's Republican Party triumphed and would dominate electoral politics for the next quarter century. Republicans advocated a decentralized approach to economic policy, leaving most power in the hands of states and localities. Jefferson and his adherents interpreted the Federalist program as a ploy to centralize power within the hands of a power-hungry cabal of would-be aristocrats. Republicans believed, for example, that a national bank would use its considerable financial resources to reward its friends and punish its enemies, thus setting into motion a cycle of corruption that threatened the very existence of the republic. Republicans tied their support for expanding democracy (at least for white males) with their critique of Federalist economic policies: ordinary farmers and artisans, not elitist financiers, should be the real drivers of economic development. Once in power, Jefferson cut taxes, decreased government spending, and reduced the size of the government debt. President James Madison, a close friend of Jefferson and a stalwart Republican, allowed Hamilton's Bank of the United States to expire in 1811.

Political Economy and the Second Party System

Despite the success of the Jeffersonians in limiting the economic role of the federal government, conflict with Great Britain (culminating in the War of 1812) led some Republicans to embrace elements of economic nationalism, albeit without Hamilton's overt elitism. The fusion of economic nationalism with Jeffersonian democracy is best represented by Henry Clay's "American System." Clay argued that protecting American industry from foreign manufacturers would create large internal markets for cotton, foodstuffs, and other agricultural products. Clay and other advocates of the American System argued that high tariffs would benefit all sectors of the economy. Manufacturers would flourish, safely protected from cheap foreign goods. Farmers and planters would also prosper as a safe, dependable home market replaced uncertain foreign markets as the major outlet of American agricultural products. Merchants who coordinated the exchanges between cities and the countryside would see their business grow as well.

By 1832, Clay added two other major elements to the American System: a government-financed system of transportation improvements and a national bank. As committed nationalists, Clay and his allies—who eventually became known as National Republicans and then Whigs—believed that federal funding of roads, canals, and railroads would connect all American localities to the domestic market. Clay and his allies also vigorously defended the Second Bank of the United States, which they believed would regulate state banks, ensure a stable currency, and supply businesses with much-needed capital. A national system of internal improvements and a national bank would also strengthen commercial ties and provide a shared set of common economic interests that would transcend regional loyalties. The economic and nationalistic appeals of the American System became an important part of Clay's platform during his presidential bids in 1824, 1832, and 1844. The nationalistic wing of the Jeffersonian Party embraced the American System in the 1820s. The National Republicans became a core constituency of the Whig Party, which formed in the early 1830s to oppose Andrew Jackson. Influential editors and writers such as Hezekiah Niles and Henry Carey strongly supported the Whig agenda, which also found considerable support in commercially developed areas with substantial manufacturing interests.

Much as Clay sought to revitalize elements of Hamilton's nationalistic program, Andrew Jackson resuscitated the Jeffersonian critique of activist government. Elected in 1828 on a populist appeal to democracy, Jackson aggressively attacked elements of Clay's American System. In 1830 Jackson vetoed the Maysville Road Bill, which would have provided federal funding for an important project in Clay's own state of Kentucky. Even more important, Jackson vetoed, in 1832, a bill to recharter the Second Bank of the United States. Jackson soundly defeated Clay in the presidential election of 1832, effectively dooming the American System. Most voters (especially those in the South and West) apparently shared Jackson's fears that the Whig economic program, in mixing economic power with political centralization, would invite political corruption. Traditional fears of political corruption reflected concerns that state activism was a zero-sum game in which some interests won and other interests lost. Such a political environment made it especially difficult for the federal government to fund transportation projects. Cities, states, and regions perceived to be on the short end of federal funding became a powerful voting bloc to oppose government investment. Federal funding thus proceeded on an ad hoc basis with little systematic planning.

A distinctly regional critique of activist government developed in the South. High tariffs were especially unpopular there: planters opposed paying higher prices for manufactured goods for the benefit of northeastern manufacturers. Some Southerners also feared that the centralization of power inherent in the American System presented a long-term threat to slavery. If the federal government had the power to protect industry, build canals, and regulate banking, they reasoned, then it might have the power to abolish slavery as well. During the winter of 1832–33, South Carolina took the dramatic step of nullifying the Tariff of 1828, which was known in the state as the "tariff of abominations." South Carolina eventually backed down, but the state's response indicated that Southerners saw an activist national government as a threat to slavery. As debates over slavery became more intense during the 1840s and 1850s, southern opposition to activist policies (at least those emanating from the federal government) hardened, resulting in a legislative deadlock that eliminated any real hope of passing the Whig's economic agenda.

Economic Development at the State Level

Jeffersonians and Jacksonians, however critical of national initiatives, eagerly supported economic development at the state and local level. Leaving most economic policy in the hands of state and local governments, in fact, helped democratize institutions such as the corporation. European nations tended to tightly restrict corporate chartering, often giving established corporations monopoly privileges in return for sweetheart deals with government officials. In the United States, though, intense competition between states and cities worked to loosen corporate chartering, as legislatures sought to please a variety of influential local interests. The more decentralized and democratic political culture in the United States encouraged logrolling rather than legislative monopoly. Banking is an excellent example. The number of state-chartered banks accelerated sharply so that, by 1820, the United States was well ahead of Great Britain and other European nations in bank capital per capita. These state banks were hardly the exclusive domain of wealthy financiers. Tens of thousands of ordinary individuals—including a good many prosperous farmers and artisans—invested in state-chartered banks. Political institutions in the United States, in short, managed to channel powerful "bottom-up" forces into economic development.

The decentralized nature of economic policy in the United States sometimes led to greater government involvement in the economy. Transportation improvements are a case in point. Fearing that private investors would avoid the risk associated with large-scale projects, the New York legislature authorized the construction of the Erie Canal as a state-run enterprise in 1817. The canal, built along a 363-mile route from Albany to Buffalo, promised an all-water route from the Great Lakes region to New York City. Completed in 1825, the Erie Canal was a stunning success. The bonanza of canal revenues allowed New York to finance politically popular branch lines. Prodded by New York's example, state governments in Pennsylvania, Maryland, and Virginia attempted to build their own canal systems to improve links with the Trans-Appalachian West. From 1817 to 1844 Americans invested nearly $131 million to build 3,360 miles of canals. Most of the investment came from state governments eager to spur economic development, either directly from canal revenues or indirectly via property taxes on rapidly appreciating land.

The failure of most canals to meet the grandiose expectations of their supporters led to fiscal retrenchment in many states. Part of the problem was that the Erie Canal proved exceptionally profitable. Most other canals, traversing more mountainous terrain or serving smaller populations, barely covered the cost of upkeep and repairs. Heavy investments in canals created large state debts that led to a backlash against state investment. In the 1840s and 1850s, important northern states such as New York, Pennsylvania, and Ohio adopted constitutional amendments that banned government investment in private corporations. The backlash against state canal investment—combined with the continued development of financial centers such as New York City and Philadelphia—left most railroad construction in private hands. Faster and more flexible than canals, railroads captured the imagination of both private capitalists and the general public. By 1840 Americans had built 2,818 miles of track; by 1860 that figure ballooned to 30,626 miles.

Although private capital financed much of the nation's railroad network, railroads were hardly examples of free enterprise. In the North, municipal and county governments often purchased railroad stock to encourage local companies. In the South, the region's slave economy prevented the growth of large financial centers that might finance railroad construction. State investment thus remained the norm. The public character of railroads, even when they were privately financed, generated a host of disputes that courts and local governments often decided. Should eminent domain compensation be determined by local juries (which often favored landowners) or special commissioners (which often favored companies)? Should railroads compensate farmers when locomotives struck livestock that were crossing tracks? Could cities regulate railroad operations to reduce noise, congestion, and pollution? Judges and legislators typically attempted to strike compromises that mediated the government's considerable interest in encouraging railroad construction with individual and public rights.

For the most part, the federal government played a secondary role to state and local governments in the proliferation of transportation companies. National policies—especially land policy—nevertheless had an important indirect impact. The federal government made land grants to various canals and railroads in the West and South. Although small compared to the investment of state governments, these land grants nevertheless aided individual enterprises, such as Indiana's Wabash and Erie Canal. More important, federal policy regarding land sales affected the rate of western settlement, thus had an important impact on internal improvements and the rest of the economy. Some easterners (including Northerners and Southerners) feared that rapid western expansion would undermine their own political influence. They therefore supported relatively high prices for the vast tracts of western land that the U.S. government owned. Not only did high prices slow western settlement, but they also provided an important source of revenue for the federal government. Popular pressure for cheap western land, though, led to the passage of the Land Act of 1841, which allowed settlers the right to buy a 160-acre homestead for as low as $1.25 per acre.

In the 1850s, the emerging Republican Party embraced the nationalistic ideas of Hamilton and Clay. Abraham Lincoln and many other Republicans had long admired Clay and his ideas. Republicans eagerly supported generous land grants to transcontinental railroads, a highly protective tariff, and a new national bank. Unlike Clay, the Republicans made slavery an economic policy issue. Believing that slavery inevitably discouraged hard work and enterprise, Republicans blamed the institution for the South's lack of development. While southern slaveholders often generated large profits from plantation agriculture, the South lagged behind the North in urbanization, manufacturing, and other benchmarks of economic development. Republicans, fearing that slavery would poison the national economy if allowed to spread, thus opposed the extension of slavery into the West. They instead supported a homestead act that would allow free-labor households to acquire federal land at little or no cost. Debates over federal land policy played a crucial role in the coming of the Civil War.

See also business and politics; economy and politics since 1860.

FURTHER READING

Lamoreaux, Naomi R. *Insider Lending: Banks, Personal Connections, and Economic Development in Industrial New England.* New York: Cambridge University Press, 1994.

Larson, John Lauritz. *Internal Improvement: National Public Works and the Promise of Popular Government in the Early United States.* Chapel Hill: University of North Carolina Press, 2000.

Majewski, John. *A House Dividing: Economic Development in Pennsylvania and Virginia before the Civil War.* New York: Cambridge University Press, 2000.

Meyer, David R. *The Roots of American Industrialization.* Baltimore, MD: Johns Hopkins University Press, 2003.

Rothenberg, Winifred Barr. *From Market-Places to a Market Economy: The Transformation of Rural Massachusetts, 1750–1850.* Chicago: University of Chicago Press, 1992.

Wright, Gavin. *Slavery and American Economic Development.* Baton Rouge: Louisiana State University Press, 2006.

JOHN MAJEWSKI

economy and politics, 1860–1920

Since the founding of the republic, Americans have debated about how to make the economy work for the general welfare. Making it work, however, has always been a means to larger social and political ends. Growing the economy has never been an end in itself.

Liberty was, at the founding, construed as a simple function of property ownership: if you owned property, you were economically independent of others, and thus could be a self-mastering individual—a citizen. Americans have since redefined liberty, equality, and citizenship, but most still conceive of "real politics" in terms of their economic status.

The politics of the period from 1860 to 1920 can be viewed as a debate about how to reorganize or reject an Atlantic economy, then as a way of imagining the political future of a more cosmopolitan, a more inclusive—maybe even a global—economy. Thus conceived, the politics of the period became an argument about how, not whether, to include the federal government in the sponsorship and supervision of economic arrangements.

The nonmilitary legislation of the 1860s, for example, which enacted the Republican platform on which Abraham Lincoln ran for president, was a detailed blueprint for industrialization on a continental scale. It could be implemented only because the South had removed its representatives from the national legislature. The Morrill tariff of 1861 was the first step. It reversed the trend toward free trade, which began under President Andrew Jackson in 1832 and culminated under President James Buchanan in 1857. The new tariff imposed specific duties on imports such as steel rails and thus allowed American manufacturers to undersell their more efficient British competitors.

Other steps included the Homestead Act, which excluded slavery from the territories by encouraging white settlers to head for the new frontier in the trans-Mississippi West; the National Banking Acts of 1863 and 1864, which, by forbidding state and private banks to issue money, created a uniform national currency and a new stratum of bankers with vested interests in manufacturing and transportation; the Immigration Act of 1864, which flooded the late-nineteenth-century American labor market with exactly the kind of ornery, adventurous, and ambitious individuals who might have led the class struggle back home; and the Aid to Railroads Acts of 1864–68, which subsidized the construction of transcontinental trunk lines, thus building the necessary infrastructure of a tightly knit national market for both finished goods and investment capital. Finally, the three "freedom amendments" to the Constitution—the Thirteenth, Fourteenth, and Fifteenth Amendments—abolished slavery, guaranteed due process of law to all persons (regardless of race), and armed the freedmen with the vote. Together they created a unitary labor/property system and prevented the restoration of the South to its prewar political preeminence.

This last step, a result of Radical Reconstruction, was more important than it may seem, because the repeal of the Republican Party's blueprint for modern America was a real possibility. Indeed, it was a programmatic imperative of the Democratic Party in the North. Even moderate Republicans with constituencies in the seaboard cities of the Northeast were anxious to restore, not reconstruct, the abject South, because the merchants and bankers who had organized and financed the antebellum cotton trade from their offices in New York, Philadelphia, and Boston wanted an immediate return to a free-trade Atlantic economy in which the pound sterling and the gold standard ruled. Many thousands of other Northerners who had been employed in and by this trade wanted the same thing.

When a majority of these merchants and bankers realized that there were more lucrative outlets for their capital in the "great and growing West" than in the restoration of the South and the resurrection of the cotton trade, the possibility of a return to a free-trade Atlantic economy was dead. So, too, was the Democratic Party's preference for "do-nothing government" (or "laissez-faire"). So, finally, was the related notion that the future of the American economy would be determined by the scale and scope of British demand for agricultural raw materials. In this sense, the abdication of merchant capital, the political power behind King Cotton's throne, turned agriculture into a mere branch of industry. As a result, the once regnant, even arrogant South had to reinvent itself as a political supplicant and a colonial appendage of the northeastern metropolis.

Politics in the late nineteenth century was mostly a matter of answering the money question, the labor question, and the trust question, as they were then called. Of course, party coalitions were based as much on ethnic loyalties and rivalries as on class allegiances. In the United States, race and ethnicity are never absent, or even distant, from the calculations of politicians. But the public discourse of the period 1860–1920 was a language of class conflict that kept asking not whether but how to use the powers of the state and federal governments to promote *equitable* economic development.

The political stalemate of the post–Civil War period had both a class component and a regional one. The regional component was a continental version of imperial politics. The northeastern metropolis stretching from Boston to Chicago could not simply impose its will on the South or the West in the 1880s and 1890s. Too many states and too many people resisted the juggernaut of industrial capitalism, sometimes with electoral initiatives and sometimes with extra-electoral activity that involved armed struggle, as in the terrorist campaigns of white supremacists in the South during Reconstruction and after.

The class component of the "great stalemate" was more important, however, because it had more profound intellectual as well as political effects. The short version of the argument is that the workers were winning the class struggle of the late nineteenth century, and the capitalists knew it. Certainly the rise of "big business" was a crucial phenomenon in the period, but corporations could not translate their obvious market power into political legitimacy without a struggle. When workers went on strike, for example, local populations usually sided with them.

Many observers of the economic scene proposed, therefore, to change things, so that labor and capital could share more equitably in the benefits of industrial accumulation. From the standpoint of capital, this change would mean that labor relinquished its control over machine production and allowed for greater efficiency and for a more minute division of labor. From the standpoint of labor, this change would mean that capital relinquished or reduced its claim to a share of national income, on the grounds that it produced nothing—that capital merely deducted its income from the sum of value produced by others.

This was the labor question of the late nineteenth century: how to allocate the benefits of economic growth in such a way that all social classes, all social strata—not just capital, not just labor—might benefit. It shaped political discourse because the answers determined where the parties stood but also where other organizations and institutions situated themselves, including state governments and federal courts.

The subtext was a political question: Could republican government survive the eruption of class conflict and the emergence of class society? Arthur T. Hadley, a Yale University economist who was also a member of the Pennsylvania Railroad's finance committee, answered this way: "A republican government is organized on the assumption that all men are free and equal. If the political power is equally distributed while the industrial power is concentrated in the hands of the few, it creates dangers of class struggles and class legislation which menace both our political and our industrial order."

The pacification of the epic class struggle of the late nineteenth century, a struggle that was more open, violent, and sustained in the United States than anywhere else, occurred only when the labor movement accepted capital as a legitimate claimant on a share of national income. This accomplishment was largely, but not only, the result of the American Federation of Labor (AFL), founded in 1886, and it was not complete until 1914, with the Clayton Act (which is usually interpreted as a concession to labor). Even then, labor was still the junior partner of capital, and would remain so until 1935, when the Wagner Act gave the federal government the power to punish businesses for refusing to deal with unions.

The money question was more complicated, and reached more constituencies, but it addressed the same problem: how to equitably allocate the benefits of economic growth. Was the money supply a cause or an effect of economic growth? What did money represent, anyway?

From the standpoint of capital, the money supply had increased in the late nineteenth century because substitutes for cash and coin had supplemented these meager (and shrinking) means of exchange—substitutes like checks, drafts, bills, securities, futures—all the financial devices that people called "credit" and understood as the foundation of a new, corporate economy. From the standpoint of labor and farmer activists, the money supply had shrunk because, after 1873, silver was no longer a precious metal to be treated as the backing for currency or the stuff of coins. The volume of national banknotes did, in fact, decline during and after the 1880s, but the procapitalist position was correct—the money supply had increased in spite of this decline.

For the critics, money was merely a means of exchange. To increase its quantity was to increase demand for goods, thus employing more labor and growing the economy and to make sure that price deflation didn't force borrowers to pay off their loans in money that was worth more than they originally took from the bank. From the standpoint of capital, money was multifarious, mysterious—it was credit, a system unto itself. As Edward Bellamy explained in *Looking Backward* (1888), his best-selling utopian novel that created something of a political cult, "Money was a sign of real commodities, but credit was but the sign of a sign."

Close regulation of the money supply and the ability to manage economic crises with such financial devices as interest rates and reserve requirements were finally accomplished with the creation of the Federal Reserve System in 1913. The answer to the money question, like the resolution of the labor question, was an adjunct to the trust question, for it made the corporation the central problem, and promise, of the politics of the period.

The trust questions went like this: Can we regulate and discipline these large corporations? Are they natural monopolies or unlawful restraints of trade? (The common law made this distinction, and the political discourse of the time seized on it.) Do they signify industrial serfdom? Can we be mere employees of their huge bureaucracies and still be free men and women? If they are artificial persons, fragile artifacts of the law, does that mean we are, too?

The turn of the wheel—the end of the Great Stalemate—came in the late 1890s, when the AFL could provide its new answer to the labor question and when Democrat-Populist William Jennings Bryan lost his bid for the presidency in 1896. "Free silver" became something of a joke, and the money question was resolved in favor of a gold standard.

Progressivism and Imperialism

After 1896, the urban industrial area of the nation was the primary scene of political discourse and party conflict. The relation between the corporations and the larger society was the question that shaped, even dominated, the Progressive Era. Some historians argue that, ironically, procorporate ideologues, executives, intellectuals, and journalists wrote a lot of the legislation that regulated the new corporations— the products of the great merger movement of 1898–1903.

But there is no irony in the simple fact that large business enterprises need stability and predictability, and therefore want regulation of market forces.

The anarchy of the market is anathema for all participants, in capital as well as in labor. The issue was not whether but how to regulate it, through public agencies such as the Federal Reserve and the Federal Trade Commission (FTC) or through private organizations such as trade unions.

The Progressive Era was a time when the corporation was finally "domesticated," to borrow historian Richard Hofstadter's term. It was finally recognized as a normal part of economic and political life in the United States. By 1920 it was subject to close regulation, juridical supervision, and consistent public scrutiny. Woodrow Wilson had successfully split the difference between William Howard Taft and Theodore Roosevelt in the 1912 campaign by rejecting both Roosevelt's program of statist command of the market and Taft's program of fervent trust-busting in the name of renewed competition. The FTC was the emblem of his different answer to the trust question, combining executive power, antitrust law, and regulatory zeal without a trace of nostalgia for the small business owner.

The "domestication" of the large corporation in the Progressive Era also changed the world. For if imperialism was possible in the absence of corporate capitalism, the new corporate order could not survive in the absence of imperialism. The corporations were simply too efficient in reducing costs and increasing output without a comparable increase of labor inputs. Their "scientific" managers redesigned the shop floors to economize on the costs of skilled labor (the advent of electric power helped), and improved productivity to the point where the growth of the industrial working class ceased by 1905. What then? Where would the surplus go?

By the 1880s, the domestic market was saturated with the output of American industry. New overseas markets were imperative. Industry leaders and intellectuals were trying, by the 1890s, to think through an imperial model that would avoid the idiocies of European colonialism. The point was to avoid military conquest and occupation.

At the end of the nineteenth century, U.S. policy makers and a new stratum of such "public intellectuals" as Charles Conant, Arthur T. Hadley, and Jeremiah Jenks were inventing a new kind of imperialism, so new that it inaugurated the "American Century." With the international circulation of John Hay's *Open Door Notes* in 1899–1900, there was a doctrine to go with the new thinking.

The doctrine had six core principles. First, all people, all cultures, were capable of development—there were no racial barriers to advanced civilization. Second, in view of the insurrections staged in the American South and West in the late nineteenth century, as well as the Boxer Rebellion in China, economic development was the key to creating modern social strata where there were none. It was a risky strategy because rapid growth always displaces vested interests and creates new ones, but the alternative was recurrent insurrection on behalf of people deprived of the fruits of development. Third, development meant direct investment in, or transfers of technology to, less-developed parts of the world. Trade was important, but nowhere near as important as investment.

Fourth, the sovereignty of every nation, including China, then a large but crumbling empire, was inviolable. The American experience of the nineteenth century had taught U.S. policy makers like John Hay, the secretary of state under Presidents William McKinley and Theodore Roosevelt, that a nation could absorb enormous quantities of foreign capital and still thrive as long as its political integrity was kept intact. Fifth, the seat of empire was shifting to the United States. The question was, could this shift be accomplished without war?

Yes, Hay and others said, and their answer was the sixth core principle—that of an anticolonial, open-door world. If economic growth was the means to pacify domestic class conflict and avoid international conflict over the allocation of *shares* of world income, they claimed, then a world without barriers to trade and investment was a world of peace. If the *volume* of world income grew quickly enough, there would be no fighting about respective *shares*. An open-door world—without exclusive "spheres of influence," without colonies—was then the way to a *postimperialist* future.

The Politics of War and the Shape of the Future

This is the world for which the United States, under President Woodrow Wilson, went to war in 1917. It was not the world that resulted; the European victors were not about to give up their colonial possessions because the United States asked them to. But it is the world that American policy makers described as their goal until the end of the twentieth century, when neoconservatives proposed to go back to a military definition of power.

American entry into World War I was predicated on the politics of the new imperialism, which would have been almost entirely economic in nature. With U.S. troops in battle, the stalemate between the warring sides would be broken. A socialist revolution could be forestalled and German victory prevented. So, too, would the reinstatement of European colonialism proposed by the Allies, for the United States would no longer be a neutral party and could negotiate an early version of decolonization through a system of mandates.

The results were as good as could be expected in the absence of a prolonged American military presence in Europe, something that was unthinkable in 1919, when the war ended. For that reason, the United States could never have joined the League of Nations: enough senators refused to deploy American military power, such as it was, to sustain empires already in place.

Still, the future was written in the second decade of the twentieth century. An open-door world became the aim of American foreign policy. Organized labor came of age during and after the war; it waned and it waited in the 1920s, to be sure, but it was ready for power when depression struck in the 1930s. Finally, the problem of structural unemployment became crucial to the thinking of economists and politicians alike.

Here, the issue of corporate efficiency was again the driving force. The new corporations could increase output without any increase of inputs—whether of labor or of capital. So the pressing questions became how to employ a growing population and what would happen to the intellectual and political status of profit. If employment can't be provided to a growing population through private investment, what justification is there for profit? And, how else could people be employed? Public spending? These were the questions that surfaced in the second decade of the twentieth century, and we are still trying to answer them.

See also banking policy; business and politics; labor movement and politics; tariffs and politics.

FURTHER READING

Bensel, Richard. *The Political Economy of American Industrialization, 1877–1900.* New York: Cambridge University Press, 2002.

Chandler, Alfred D., Jr. *The Visible Hand: The Managerial Revolution in American Business.* Cambridge, MA: Belknap Press of Harvard University Press, 1977.

Hofstadter, Richard. *The Age of Reform.* New York: Vantage, 1955.

Livingston, James. *Pragmatism and the Political Economy of Cultural Revolution, 1850–1940.* Chapel Hill: University of North Carolina Press, 1994.

McGerr, Michael. *The Decline of Popular Politics: The American North, 1865–1928.* New York: Oxford University Press, 1986.

Sanders, Elizabeth. *Roots of Reform: Farmers, Workers, and the American State, 1877–1917.* Chicago: University of Chicago Press, 1999.

Sklar, Martin J. *The Corporate Reconstruction of American Capitalism, 1890–1916.* New York: Cambridge University Press, 1988.

Wiebe, Robert. *The Search for Order, 1877–1920.* New York: Hill and Wang, 1966.

JAMES LIVINGSTON

economy and politics, 1920–45

In 1920 Republican presidential candidate Warren Harding announced that "America's present need is not heroics, but healing; not nostrums, but normalcy; not revolution, but restoration." Spoken after an alarming year of widespread labor unrest, the vicious Red Scare, and a bruising congressional battle over the country's postwar foreign commitments, the promise of "normalcy" soothed his constituents' jangled nerves and provided them with hope for a swift end to the dislocations stirred up by the Great War. Yet Harding's neologism signaled more than an assurance of domestic peace and a commitment to shut down the international adventures. Not only should Americans put the war and its unsettling aftermath behind them, his words suggested; so, too, should the country dispense with the previous decade of dangerously socialistic economic experimentation.

The Republican Party, as most business conservatives saw it, had been rudely unseated from national power by Democrat Woodrow Wilson's presidency from 1913 to 1921. During that time, an unexpected alliance of rural representatives and urban labor interests had provided the congressional muscle for a sweeping array of federal regulatory legislation, transferring the Progressive reform energy of the states and municipalities to the national level and there consolidating its reach and permanence. Even more jarring to the self-appointed protectors of property and sound money in both parties was the specter of a political coalition of reform-minded Theodore Roosevelt Republicans joined in unholy partnership with agrarian inflationists indoctrinated by the Democratic-populist credos of William Jennings Bryan.

But for the next ten years, party standpatters could put these worries to rest. A decade of unsurpassed prosperity muted the previous era's concerns for economic justice and responsive government. Both Harding and his successor, Calvin Coolidge, brought to the White House a political philosophy oriented toward private accumulation and proud of governmental inaction. "The chief business of the American people is business," Coolidge famously intoned, a dictum perfectly matched to the country's diminished concern with corporate concentration. Big businesses, now depicted in splashy advertisements, provided valuable and essential services that distributed everyday comforts and conveniences, brought families closer together, and satisfied the individual tastes of discerning consumers.

Indeed, after a brief recession that ended in 1921, the American economy certainly appeared capable of raising living standards quickly and dramatically, and without government interference. By 1930 manufacturing output had increased fourfold over 1900 levels. Real industrial wages, which rose almost 25 percent during the 1920s, put a portion of the accompanying productivity gains directly into the worker's pocket. The technological and organizational feats of Fordist mass production turned out low-cost consumer durables at prices average Americans could afford. High wages and low prices most famously brought automobile ownership within the reach of millions; at decade's end, one out every five Americans was driving a car. But they were not only crowding the roads with their modern marvels; by 1930 almost two-thirds of the nation's homes received electric service. Electrical appliances—refrigerators, ovens, radios, and vacuum cleaners—had become regular features of domestic life.

The nation's rapidly growing urban areas, which housed a majority of the population after 1920, provided the primary setting for such dizzying consumption. The decade's very prosperity, in fact, pushed the economic questions of the Progressive Era to the back burner and brought to the political forefront a simmering cultural divide between small-town America and the cities with their bustling immigrant communities, beer-soaked politics, and increasingly cosmopolitan tastes. Nothing showcased these geographical frictions better than the Democratic Party, reduced during the 1920s to infighting between its urban, working-class members and a Protestant, native-born, and prohibitionist wing. Furthermore, the party's rural faction was anchored—even dominated—by the segregationist, antiunion South, whose cotton barons and low-wage employers suppressed the region's populist heritage, warily eyed the big-city machines, and accrued ever more congressional seniority. Fistfights broke out on the 1924 Democratic Party convention floor over a petition to condemn the Ku Klux Klan and brought the proceedings to a days-long standstill. Irish Catholic Alfred E. Smith, backed by New York City's Tammany Hall and an emblem of all the Klan reviled, lost that nomination, only to claim it four years later and to suffer a humiliating national defeat in 1928.

Rural Issues during the 1920s

The culture war falls short as a guiding framework for the political world of the 1920s, however. What separated the town and the country was not merely a mismatch of values and social customs but a gaping economic imbalance. Industrial America had not yet vanquished its agrarian past. Farmers still constituted nearly one-third of the nation's workforce, but earned, on average, one-fourth the income of industrial workers. While other Americans experienced rising wages and dazzling consumer choices, farmers received an unwelcome taste of the Great Depression to come. Emboldened by high prices and government encouragement, they had expanded production during World War I, often pushing into marginal lands where success was far from certain. Agricultural incomes dropped precipitously when overseas demand plummeted after 1920. Besieged by the postwar contraction, farmers found themselves caught between the low prices they received for farm products and the high prices they paid for nonfarm items; wheat and other commodity markets suffered from overproduction throughout the decade.

This agricultural distress prompted urgent calls for national assistance from a new congressional bloc of southern Democrats and farm-state Republicans. Their discontent found concrete expression in the McNary-Haugen Farm Bills, the focal point of farm relief legislation during the 1920s. The legislation proposed to raise domestic prices directly by selling surplus stocks abroad. Its proponents believed that this two-price system would not entail special protection for agriculture; it would simply extend the benefits of the tariff (already enjoyed by American manufacturers) to farmers. New Deal policy makers would soon criticize this export dumping and prescribe a purely domestic agricultural rescue package, but not before the bills faced decisive opposition

from President Coolidge as well as Herbert Hoover, his Republican successor.

The political significance of the agricultural depression, though, lay not in the farm bloc's defeats during the 1920s but in the growing potential to resurrect an alliance between rural Democrats and Progressive Republicans. The absence of farm prosperity and the search for a method to address the economic imbalance kept alive an issue tailor-made for uniting rural representatives of all political stripes: public power. Private utilities and electric companies had decided that most farmers simply did not have the income to put them in the customer class; it was far more profitable to serve more densely populated urban areas. No one represented the progressive's passion for public power more than Nebraska Republican George Norris, who battled to bring the nation's rivers and waterways under state-sponsored, multiple-purpose control. Throughout the 1920s, Senator Norris labored to keep the government's World War I–era hydroelectric facility at Muscle Shoals, Alabama, in public hands and to use it as the starting point for a more ambitious scheme to develop the entire Tennessee River basin—a project realized eventually in the creation of the Tennessee Valley Authority. However, like the proponents of the McNary-Haugen Bills, the proponents of public power also faced decisive presidential opposition before the New Deal.

Onset of the Great Depression

While the agricultural depression aroused Progressive-like calls for government assistance during a decade whose governing ethos rejected such intervention, it also contributed to the Great Depression. Of the many domestic causes of the Depression's length and severity, the inequitable distribution of wealth ranks very high. The maladjustment was not only apparent in the disparity between rural and urban incomes; workers' wages, despite their increase, had failed to rise in step with industrial output or with corporate profits, thus spreading too thinly the purchasing power required to run the motors of mass production. The lower 93 percent of the population actually saw their per-capita incomes drop during the latter part of the 1920s. Furthermore, far too many excited buyers had purchased all of those consumer durables on installment plans. Entire industries balanced precariously on a shaky foundation of consumer debt.

The automobile and construction sectors felt the pinch as early as 1925, and by the end of the decade, businesses struggled with unsold inventories that had nearly quadrupled in value. A speculative frenzy on Wall Street ended with a stock market crash in the autumn of 1929. Less than 5 percent of the population owned securities in 1929, but many more Americans held bank deposits, and lost those in the wave of bank failures that followed. Still, the Depression was not merely the result of income inequality or credit-fueled overexpansion. It also emerged from a complicated tangle of domestic and international circumstances—an undercapitalized banking system with too few branch operations; a Federal Reserve that restricted the money supply instead of easing credit; an unassisted Europe that defaulted on its war debts; and a world trading system that fell prey to fits of economic nationalism. Much of the blame, in fact, could be placed on the doorstep of the United States, which emerged from World War I as the world's leading creditor nation but evaded the responsibilities of this leadership. Instead, during the 1920s, the U.S. government hindered the repayment of European debt and restricted the global movement of labor, goods, and capital by halting immigration and raising tariffs to astronomically high levels—even while aggressively promoting its own products overseas. The president to whose lot the economic emergency first fell was Herbert Hoover, a widely respected engineer who had orchestrated European food relief efforts during World War I and who had served as secretary of commerce under Harding and Coolidge. Unlike his predecessors, Hoover was no orthodox disciple of laissez-faire. He claimed that the increasing complexity of modern society required the federal government to gather information and suggestions for the nation's improvement. He insisted, though, that these tools be used primarily to assist the voluntary activities of those people, businesses, and local governments interested in collective self-help.

By the spring of 1933, nearly 25 percent of the labor force was unemployed, and millions more worked only part-time. Construction had slowed, manufacturing had stalled, and new investment had virtually come to a halt. Traditional sources of assistance—mutual aid societies, municipal treasuries, even national charities—were crippled by such unprecedented need. Unlike his treasury secretary, Andrew Mellon, whom Hoover later criticized as a "leave-it-alone liquidationist," the president at first demonstrated considerable flexibility—he cajoled industrial leaders to resist lowering wages; requested public works funds from the U.S. Congress; persuaded the

Federal Reserve to ease credit (though, as events would prove, not by nearly enough); and set up the Reconstruction Finance Corporation to provide billions of dollars to banks and businesses. On a few critical issues, however, Hoover dug in his heels: he refused to sanction direct federal assistance for either farmers or unemployed people, and he opposed any proposal that required the government to produce and distribute electricity without the assistance of private business.

Franklin D. Roosevelt and the New Deal

Into this political opening marched Franklin D. Roosevelt, the Democratic governor of New York, who challenged Hoover for the presidency in 1932. Roosevelt not only pledged relief to the urban unemployed but—unlike his gubernatorial predecessor Alfred E. Smith—also demonstrated remarkable acuity for rural issues. During his governorship, Roosevelt had begun a statewide program of soil surveys and reforestation, and attempted to provide rural New Yorkers with inexpensive electricity from government-run hydroelectric power facilities. In his lustiest presidential campaign rhetoric, he promised federal development of prime hydroelectric sites across the country. The federal government would not only build the required infrastructure but would distribute the electricity to the surrounding communities at the lowest possible cost. Roosevelt also committed his party to a program of direct farm assistance that would combine production control with higher prices and natural resource conservation.

Roosevelt put rural issues up front in his campaign not simply to distinguish his record from Hoover's but because he and his advisors attributed the Depression to an absence of farm purchasing power. Low agricultural incomes, they argued, kept factories idle and urban workers unemployed. Roosevelt had addressed the question of the urban unemployed as governor by instituting work relief and welfare benefits, anticipating the similar programs of the New Deal as well as the federal government's recognition of organized labor. Still, the model of the Depression that he initially adopted cast the farm sector as the primary problem, with the low purchasing power of the working class a complementary concern. Whatever the genuine economic causes of the Depression—and Roosevelt can certainly be faulted for embracing an exclusively domestic analysis, especially an agrarian fundamentalist one—the underconsumptionist model was political gold. The president intended to use the nation's economic distress to transcend the poisonous cultural divide between the country and the city and to create a more lasting reform coalition within the Democratic Party.

In the election of 1932, Roosevelt won a significant plurality of votes in the nation's major cities, swept the South and the West, and polled his largest majorities in the farm regions. Congress, pressured by constituents at home to do something quickly, submitted to executive leadership and engaged in a remarkable flurry of legislative energy. It first passed measures repairing the country's money and credit. To restore confidence in the financial system, Roosevelt authorized the federal government to reorganize failing banks and to issue more currency. Congress also created the Federal Deposit Insurance Corporation (FDIC) to insure regular Americans' savings accounts. The rural wing of the Democratic Party had historically agitated for inflation so that farm prices might rise and debts be repaid with easier money. Roosevelt moved in this direction by partially severing the currency from the gold standard, which had provided a basis of trust for international financial transactions but impeded domestic growth. Funneling assistance to those in need was an equally urgent task, and the administration set up aid programs that distributed cash grants through state relief agencies, put the unemployed directly to work with government jobs, and employed needy Americans indirectly by investing in public works projects.

The primary new departure in federal policy was the New Deal's attempt to raise prices and wages simultaneously—to get farms and businesses producing again and to supply consumers with the incomes to assist in that recovery. The Agricultural Adjustment Administration (AAA) sought to curb overproduction and raise prices by restricting the acreage planted in key commodities, providing farmers with support payments collected from taxes on agricultural processors. Such intervention was necessary, the AAA argued, to increase farm purchasing power and spur national economic recovery. On the industrial end, the National Recovery Administration (NRA) sought to foster cooperation among government, management, labor, and consumers, empowering planning boards to issue regulatory codes governing wages, prices, and profits. The NRA's enabling act, the National Industrial Recovery Act, also included funds for the Public Works Administration (PWA). The theory was that public works money would operate alongside the AAA's cash benefits to increase the total number of purchases nationwide, while the NRA would see to it that labor and capital shared the fruits of recovery. Policy makers initially embarked on such intricately managerial experiments because they never seriously considered the socialist alternatives—nor, for that matter, other liberal options such as massive government spending or aggressive taxation and redistribution. For most of the 1930s, balanced budgets remained the orthodoxy among New Dealers, including the president, and long-standing traditions of limited government and self-help continued to shape the beliefs of most liberals. Such ideas also continued to shape legal opinion; the Supreme Court overturned the NRA in 1935 and the AAA in 1936.

Rural issues remained central to New Deal policy. Congress enacted the creation of a second AAA, now financed with revenues from the general treasury. The government purchased thousands of acres of marginal and tax-delinquent farmland and added it to the national preserves and forests. Farmers also received cash benefits and technical assistance to halt soil erosion—a cause soon rendered even more urgent after the nation absorbed shocking images of the Dust Bowl—and the government financed construction of massive hydroelectric dams, irrigation facilities, and power distribution systems. Beginning with the Tennessee Valley Authority Act of 1933, every public dam-building agency (such as the TVA, the Bureau of Reclamation, and the Army Corps of Engineers) was required to produce and distribute power to serve surrounding rural areas, a task accomplished with the assistance of other New Deal creations such as the Rural Electrification Administration and the PWA. Such generous financing for rural development especially benefited the South and the West, the "Sunbelt" regions that emerged in the postwar era as economic counterweights to the Northeast and the Midwest.

While agriculture and rural resource policy remained central to New Deal policy, farm politics quickly gave way to a more urban orientation within the Democratic Party. Beginning with Roosevelt's landslide reelection in 1936, urban majorities became decisive in Democratic victories. Roosevelt's urban appeal lay in the federal government's work relief and welfare benefits, and in the New Deal's recognition of formerly marginalized religious and cultural groups. Though some reformers denounced the Democratic Party's ties to city machines, municipal officials and urban constituencies often liberalized the party, pushing to the forefront questions of workplace justice and civil rights. Nothing better signaled the urban liberal turn in national politics than the rise of the labor movement, officially sanctioned in

1935 by the National Labor Relations Act, which guaranteed workers' right to organize, hold elections, and establish closed shops. While business leaders resisted labor organizing, unions won enormous victories in the nation's major industrial centers. Legal recognition and government-mandated bargaining between labor and management put the nation's industrial policy on a more lasting footing: the government would set labor free as a countervailing power to business, rather than attempt to dictate industrial relations or to redistribute wealth directly to the working class.

End of Reform and World War II

The New Deal's initial political partnership between rural and urban America assumed that each party well understood its interdependence and the need to raise purchasing power among both farmers and workers. But the urban liberal tilt in national affairs—especially the rapid escalation of labor strikes and challenges to management—reignited long-standing divisions between countryside and city. Many southern Democrats and western progressives disdained what they viewed as the nonemergency New Deal: public housing experiments, relief for the "shiftless," unnecessary government projects, and programs that helped the rural poor—programs that only occasionally benefited African Americans but nonetheless convinced white Southerners that a direct federal assault on Jim Crow could not be far behind. The rising prices that accompanied the nation's agricultural and industrial policies also irked middle-class consumers. After Roosevelt's ill-judged attempt in 1937 to "pack" the Supreme Court, these tensions crystallized in Congress with the formation of a conservation coalition composed of Republicans and anti–New Deal Democrats (mainly Southerners, whose seniority granted them a disproportionate number of committee chairs). An antilynching bill backed by civil rights leaders and urban representatives drove a wedge further into the Democratic Party. Roosevelt declined to back the bill, citing the irate Southerners' strategic positions in Congress, and instead attempted to "purge" the conservatives from his party by intervening personally in the primary elections of 1938. Not only did this effort fail miserably, but voters all over the country also rebuked the president by replacing a significant number of Democratic representatives and governors with Republicans.

Compounding the political stalemate was an economic downturn that began in the autumn of 1937. Though the economy had never regained pre-Depression levels of employment and investment, enough progress had been made after 1933 that the administration could claim some success, however uncoordinated or dictatorial the New Deal appeared to its critics. But the recession shook this confidence. As in 1929, it began with a crash in the stock market and prompted unwelcome comparisons between Roosevelt's stalled agenda and the political fumbles of Hoover before him. More significant, it set off a debate within the administration over the causes of the downturn and the proper methods for economic revival. Some liberals blamed businesses for failing to invest; others intended to launch new legal actions against corporate monopolies. Still others drew lessons from the previous year's budget cuts, arguing that government spending had shored up consumer purchasing power from 1933 to 1937 and that its recent reduction posed the problem. In a line of economic argument that became known as "Keynesian" after British economist John Maynard Keynes, these liberals put forward the idea that consumption, not investment, drove modern industrial economies, and that public spending was the best vehicle for stimulating demand in a downturn. This analysis probably owed more to domestic champions of consumer purchasing power than to Keynes himself, whose complicated ideas Americans embraced only gradually and partially. Still, the reasoning nudged the New Deal in a different and less reformist direction. Roosevelt authorized increased spending programs in 1938 and justified these as important in their own right rather than as needed benefits for particular groups. No doubt Roosevelt also anticipated the political appeal of fiscal policy, which demanded less government intervention in the private decisions of firms, farmers, or consumers.

Public expenditures in 1938, only 8 percent of the national gross domestic product (GDP), were timid by later standards. Not until World War II, when federal spending reached 40 percent of the GDP, would public funds really ignite economic recovery. Between 1940 and 1944, the United States enjoyed the greatest increase of industrial output in its history—almost overnight, full employment returned and wages rose without government prodding. Clearly, the New Deal alone did not restore prosperity, nor had it substantially reduced income inequality. But it did remove much of the risk from market capitalism, providing a certain measure of security to farmers and businesses, homeowners and financiers, employers and employees.

This security was built along distinctly American lines. The New Deal's signature triumph, Social Security, departed from other models of universal social insurance by financing its benefits with regressive payroll taxes and dividing its assistance into two tiers: the retirement pensions, administered at the national level and pegged to national standards; and the unemployment and supplemental welfare programs administered by the individual states, which set their own eligibility requirements and benefit levels. Along with union recognition, laws regulating hours and wages, and World War II–era support for home purchases and education, Social Security provided a framework for the upward mobility of the postwar American middle class. But this framework also operated along distinctly American lines. African Americans were denied many of these benefits owing to the continued power of southern congressmen, who excluded from protection the occupations in which blacks were most represented, insisted on local administrative control, and prevented the passage of antidiscrimination provisions.

During the Depression, it was not uncommon for Americans to question the national faith in unlimited expansion. Some analysts had even wondered whether the idea of a "mature economy" might not describe the country's predicament; perhaps it was time to come to terms with an economic system that had reached the limits of its capacity to grow. But the lightning-quick recovery generated by World War II altered this mindset fundamentally and permanently. Migrants streamed across the nation to take up work in the booming defense centers in the West and Midwest, many settling in the new suburbs spreading outward from urban cores. African Americans, eager to share in the promise of economic mobility but prevented from joining this workforce on equal terms, threatened a march on Washington to protest the injustice. Emboldened by Roosevelt's subsequent executive order forbidding discrimination in defense industries, blacks launched a "double V" campaign to fight for victory over enemies both at home and abroad. While victory on the home front would remain far more elusive than victory over Germany and Japan, the war energized a new, more assertive generation of civil rights activists.

Wartime mobilization also strengthened the conservative coalition in Congress, which targeted "nonessential" spending and dismantled relief agencies such as the Works Progress Administration, the National Youth Administration, the Civilian Conservation Corps, and the Farm Security Administration. Conservatives combined these attacks with more pointed critiques of government planning, drawing exaggerated parallels between the New Deal and the fascist regimes that had fomented the war. They also grew bolder in challenging organized labor, which faced diminished public and political support owing to unauthorized wildcat strikes. Wartime opportunities had raised labor's hopes for rising wages and perhaps even an equal share of managerial authority, but pressured by government officials, labor lowered its sights and agreed to a "no strike" pledge and to wage increases that rose in step with inflation but not higher. Now on the defensive along with their liberal allies, union leaders adapted to the anti-statism of the war years by more firmly embracing a Keynesian model of government intervention that steered clear of micromanaging private economic institutions and instead used macroeconomic fiscal tools to support mass consumption.

The war not only swept away any lingering doubts about the economy's ability to expand; it also buried the agrarian analysis of the Depression's origins. Suddenly policy makers grappled with commodity shortages, rising prices, and a labor deficit in the countryside—a sharp turnaround from earlier questions of overproduction, low prices, and a potentially permanent labor surplus. Rural policy makers moved away from the idea that the nation's economic health depended on stabilizing the existing rural population and instead defended a less reformist but still aggressive government role in expanding the country's industrial base and increasing its aggregate purchasing power. Clearly the future was in the factories and defense plants that were running at full capacity, not on America's small farms. But if the nation's economic future lay in urban and suburban America, politics at the end of the war still reflected long-standing divisions between the country and the city. The Democratic Party would emerge from the war as the majority party, but one nonetheless destined to rediscover its historic fault lines of region and race.

See also banking policy; business and politics; tariffs and politics; taxation.

FURTHER READING

Badger, Anthony J. *The New Deal: The Depression Years, 1933–1940.* New York: Hill and Wang, 1989.

Brinkley, Alan. *The End of Reform: New Deal Liberalism in Recession and War.* New York: Knopf, 1995.

Cohen, Lizabeth. *Making a New Deal: Industrial Workers in Chicago, 1919–1939.* New York: Cambridge University Press, 1990.

Jacobs, Meg. *Pocketbook Politics: Economic Citizenship in Twentieth-Century America.* Princeton, NJ: Princeton University Press, 2005.

Katznelson, Ira. *When Affirmative Action Was White: An Untold History of Racial Inequality in Twentieth-Century America.* New York: Norton, 2005.

Kennedy, David M. *Freedom from Fear: The American People in Depression and War, 1929–1945.* New York: Oxford University Press, 1999.

Leuchtenberg, William E. *Franklin D. Roosevelt and the New Deal, 1932–1940.* New York: Harper and Row, 1963.

———. *The Perils of Prosperity, 1914–1932.* Chicago: University of Chicago Press, 1958.

Patterson, James T. *Congressional Conservatism and the New Deal: The Growth of the Conservative Coalition in Congress, 1933–1939.* Lexington: University of Kentucky Press, 1967.

Phillips, Sarah T. *This Land, This Nation: Conservation, Rural America, and the New Deal.* New York: Cambridge University Press, 2007.

Rauchway, Eric. *The Great Depression and the New Deal: A Very Short Introduction.* New York: Oxford University Press, 2008.

Schulman, Bruce J. *From Cotton Belt to Sunbelt: Federal Policy, Economic Development, and the Transformation of the South.* New York: Oxford University Press, 1991.

Smith, Jason Scott. *Building New Deal Liberalism: The Political Economy of Public Works, 1933–1956.* New York: Cambridge University Press, 2006.

SARAH T. PHILLIPS

economy and politics, 1945–70

The political economy of the United States during the first three decades after World War II can best be characterized as a liberal Keynesian regime. From the 1940s through the 1970s, the living standards of both the working class and the middle class doubled in an era that also experienced relatively rapid economic growth. This achievement rested on several key pillars: a legal framework favoring strong trade unions, a liberal welfare state entailing government promotion of economic security and labor standards, large expenditures for both the military and civilian infrastructure, and an interventionist state that regulated finance, investment, and trade. These policy initiatives were largely upheld during both Democratic and Republican administrations. As the income gap between the rich and poor narrowed—and social movements successfully extended citizenship rights to African Americans and other excluded groups within the population—the United States became a place of much greater social equality.

The New Deal created the terrain on which all post–World War II political struggles took place. It put *security*—economic security—at the center of American political and economic life. The enactment of federal mortgage assistance, bank deposit insurance, minimum wages, Social Security, and laws bolstering labor's right to organize created social and economic entitlements that legitimized the modern state and vitalized an expansive citizenship within new strata of the population. New Dealers identified economic security as a grand national project, "a great cooperative enterprise" among "the citizens, the economic system, and the government." Security necessarily entailed an element of public power. Though Roosevelt-era policy makers initially excluded many women, Latinos, and African Americans from the new entitlement state, President Lyndon Johnson's Great Society did much to expand the social citizenship concept, even as it engendered a fierce, debilitating backlash.

Moreover, Keynesians believed that such policies would generate high levels of employment by boosting aggregate demand in the economy. Through manipulating government spending and the money supply, the federal government could stimulate the economy when it lagged or slow growth when inflation threatened. The booms and busts that had been a routine feature of American economic life would instead be turned into steady growth and more widely shared benefits.

World War II mobilization policies completed social tasks begun in the Great Depression and set the stage for a postwar social Keynesianism. In exchange for labor's unimpeded participation in continuous war production, the federal government settled labor disputes through a National War Labor Board and facilitated union growth with a "maintenance of membership" policy that required every worker in a unionized workplace to join the union and pay dues. With millions of workers pouring into industrial manufacturing, national union membership soon jumped to 15 million, about 30 percent of nonfarm employment.

For American workers the fight against fascism during World War II had significance at home as well as abroad. As the new union movement, the Congress of Industrial

Organizations (CIO), put it, their hard work and sacrifice could also be seen as a struggle to "Insure Your Future . . . For Peace–Jobs–Security." Urging American workers and their families to "vote for Collective Bargaining and Full Employment, Lasting Peace and Security," the CIO saw the rights of the National Labor Relations Act (NRLA), Social Security, and the international struggle for democracy as inseparable: "The broad problems of world security and the personal problems of individual security seem to merge." President Franklin Roosevelt further legitimized the idea of a right to security when, in 1944, he proposed a Second Bill of Rights, protecting opportunity and security in the realms of housing, education, recreation, medical care, food, and clothing.

During the war the government kept a cap on both wages and prices as part of its anti-inflation strategy. American business flourished and productivity leaped forward, the consequence of nearly five years of government-subsidized investment in plant, machinery, scientific research, and physical infrastructure. Not unexpectedly, workers were ready to demand their share of wartime profits and prosperity. This demand took on particular urgency once it appeared that President Harry Truman planned to end government price controls, thereby unleashing an inflationary pulse that threatened to reduce real income for most working-class wage earners.

A huge strike wave swept through manufacturing industries in 1945 and 1946. America's workers had also gone on strike at the end of World War I, but at that time employers, relying on the armed force of the state, crippled the postwar union movement in steel, meatpacking, and coal mining, and on the railroads. But after World War II, unions were far more secure, with almost 35 percent of nonfarm workers enrolled. The frontier of trade unionism did not advance into agriculture, domestic service, the lower ranks of factory supervision, southern textiles, nor most white-collar occupations. Throughout the manufacturing, transport, utility, and construction sectors, however, legally sanctioned collective bargaining became a permanent feature of the U.S. political economy. Along with the New Dealers now in seemingly permanent command of the government policy-making and regulatory bureaucracy, union leaders contended that the key to economic growth must rest upon a regime of mass consumer purchasing power. Workers throughout the economy should be able to buy all the new goods the economy could produce, including housing, medical care, leisure, and entertainment.

In the late 1940s, labor and its New Deal allies saw the movement for greater purchasing power and security as a battle on two fronts: economic and political. Facing corporate employers, labor demanded not only higher wages, protections against inflation, and job security but also "fringe benefits": paid vacation, sick leave, health insurance, and pensions. The National Labor Relations Board (NLRB), created by the New Deal NLRA in 1935, eventually sustained by the Supreme Court, endorsed this bargaining strategy, thus forcing management to accept a widening sphere for collective bargaining. The strategy proved most successful in oligopolistic sectors of the economy (auto, steel, tire and rubber, airplane manufacturing), where the market power of the corporations and the bargaining clout of the unions made it possible to take wages out of competition. This generated "pattern bargaining": when a leading corporation signed a new contract, the other top companies in the sector agreed to almost all of its main provisions. Moreover, companies that did not want to become unionized but sought to maintain stable workforces, such as Kodak, DuPont, Johnson & Johnson, and Colgate Palmolive, also followed the pattern established by the big unions. Consequently, the presence of a strong, dynamic union movement helped drive wages up in primary labor markets across the economy. As inflation ebbed and women entered the workforce in a proportion that exceeded even that at the height of World War II, median family incomes rose in dramatic fashion, doubling in just over a generation.

Labor had a partner in the New Deal state. The Keynesian approach to economic management was embodied in the 1946 Employment Act. The federal government would be responsible for promoting "maximum employment, production, and purchasing power." Rather than waiting for economic crisis to provoke a government response, a new Council of Economic Advisors would have a continuing role developing macroeconomic policy aimed at these goals. The federal government also drove economic growth through investment in an interstate highway system, hospitals and medical schools, universities, and hydroelectric power. Economic modernization was not to be achieved at the expense of the working class or middle class. Building on the national welfare state of the New Deal, the Servicemen's Readjustment Act of 1944 (known more commonly as the GI Bill) offered veterans government support for home mortgages, vocational or university education, and small business start-up. The act was administered locally, however, and black and female veterans were often passed over for these benefits.

Harry Truman had initially sought to extend the New Deal welfare state as soon as the war was over, pushing forward a comprehensive agenda that included a higher minimum wage, federal commitment to public housing, increased unemployment insurance, and national health insurance. Although the Democrats lost badly during the 1946 congressional elections, Truman and a broad-based coalition of labor, liberals, and small farmers demonstrated the majority status of the Roosevelt coalition during the 1948 elections. Interpreting his surprising reelection as a vindication of the New Deal project, Truman declared early in 1949, "Every segment of our population and every individual has a right to expect from our government a fair deal." But a congressional bloc of Republicans and southern Democrats, known as "Dixiecrats," turned back many Fair Deal proposals. Dixiecrats, increasingly wary that Fair Deal labor policies and civil rights initiatives would threaten white supremacy in the states of the Old Confederacy, formed a generation-long alliance with anti–New Deal Republicans.

In the eyes of American business leaders, Truman's endorsement of a strong alliance between labor and the state smacked of European-style social democracy. They did not want to see further erosion of what they considered "managerial prerogatives," nor a further expansion of the welfare state. American employers recognized the social and political premium placed on security—economic security—as vividly as did the Democratic Party, the labor movement, and the proponents of national Social Security. While they were willing to accede to workers' demands for security, the link between union power and the federal government would have to be severed. As *Business Week* warned in 1950, "management, for the first time, is faced with a broad social demand—the demand for security. But if management does not use it wisely, the worker is likely to transfer his demands from the bargaining table to the ballot box." In order to outflank the political mobilization of labor, especially in its demands for health insurance and greater social security, corporate executives imitated the state: companies would now provide social security through private pensions and insurance benefits. Mimicking the standards set by the state, American business firms and commercial insurance companies became partners in creating and expanding private alternatives to public social insurance and community-controlled social welfare institutions. "The American working man must look to manage-

ment," Ford Motor Company vice president John Bugas told the American Management Association.

This viewpoint reached fruition in 1950, when General Motors (GM) signed an unprecedented five-year contract with the powerful United Automobile Workers, an agreement that *Fortune* magazine dubbed "The Treaty of Detroit." GM agreed to assume health insurance and pension obligations for its workers, blue collar and white collar, forging an employment template that many other U.S. corporations soon followed. Henceforth paid vacations, sick leave, health insurance, and pension became standard features of blue-collar and white-collar employment. GM president Charles Wilson claimed to have achieved "an American solution for the relations of labor and industry." The government agreed. A 1956 Senate report labeled employee benefits programs "a tribute to the free enterprise system." By extending such security to employees, America's largest companies headed off political alternatives, including national health insurance, more progressive public pensions, and even union control of firm-based benefits.

Those elements of the Fair Deal that stayed within the parameters of the welfare state already set—minimum wage, means-tested public housing for the poor, improvements in Social Security pensions—passed into law. Proposals that would expand the welfare state in scope and curtail emerging private markets, like health insurance, went down to permanent defeat.

Also stymied in the immediate postwar years was the government's commitment to racial justice. African Americans had begun to make economic progress during World War II through the CIO, a newly aggressive NAACP, President Franklin D. Roosevelt's nondiscrimination executive order for defense work, and the Fair Employment Practices Committee (FEPC). With the FEPC, the federal government legitimized African American demands for equal opportunity and fairness at work. Although the FEPC itself had little power, African Americans mobilized around it and used it to pry open the previously insulated realms of segregated employment. After the war, CIO leaders and the NAACP pushed for a permanent FEPC. Some states did establish commissions on fair employment, but the Dixiecrats made sure the U.S. Congress never did. Instead, it took a massive, direct-action social movement, sweeping through the South two decades later to force Congress and the president to prohibit employment discrimination, on the basis of sex as well as race, with Civil Rights Act of 1964.

By the time Republican Dwight Eisenhower took office, the New Deal welfare state, labor reforms, and state regulatory policies were firmly established. Although a Republican with strong ties to corporate elites, Eisenhower shared the essential premises of liberal Keynesianism and the New Deal order. He signed a raise in the minimum wage, oversaw new amendments to Social Security that added disability pensions and expanded old-age coverage to new groups, including agricultural and domestic workers, and created a new cabinet department, Health, Education, and Welfare.

Eisenhower, however, viewed with skepticism the rapid expansion of another pillar of the Keynesian state, the military-industrial complex. After a brief period of demobilization at the end of World War II, national security affairs became the largest, fastest growing sector of the American government. Truman not only turned the War Department into the Defense Department but created domestic national security agencies. As tensions with the Soviet Union heightened in the late 1940s, and the United States took on an increasingly interventionist role in Western Europe, Greece, Turkey, Korea, and elsewhere, defense spending became a permanent, rising part of the federal budget. The defense budget hit $50 billion a year—half the total federal budget—when the United States went to war in Korea. For the first time, the United States maintained permanent military bases in over three dozen countries. The militant anti-Communist agenda abroad also translated into political purges of leftists at home.

Liberals and conservatives alike let go of their sacrosanct commitment to balanced budgets and instead came to believe that by pumping money into the economy, Americans could have "guns and butter too." Defense spending in southern California and the Southeast—on military bases, weapons production, scientific research—built up entire local and regional economies. Military spending drove suburbanization, well-paid employment, and mass consumption in places like Orange County, California, during the 1950s and 1960s.

The American South, while eagerly digesting government largesse for military bases, defense contracts, and universities, contested the liberal political economy based on rising wages and labor rights. Through the New Deal and especially the war, Southerners had finally experienced a vast improvement in their standard of living. The Fair Labor Standards Act (which established the national minimum wage and 40-hour workweek), rural electrification, wartime spending, and economic modernization brought southern wages and consumer purchasing closer than ever to northern standards. Southern textiles plants continuously raised wages in order to stay a step ahead of the Textile Workers Union of America, primarily based in the North but seeking to organize the South. After 1948, however, southern states took advantage of the Taft-Hartley Act to ban the union shop through so-called right-to-work laws, while southern employers quickly made use of Taft-Hartley's grant of "free speech" for management during union elections. Within a few years, southern employers had stopped the postwar union movement in its tracks. By the latter half of the 1950s, it was clear the South would remain a lower-wage region. American business took the cue and began moving plants south of the Mason Dixon Line. Over the next decade and a half, leading corporations like Westinghouse, DuPont, and RCA and a wide range of smaller companies making textiles, light fixtures, chemicals, and auto parts relocated production to southern areas where states promised lax regulation, minimal taxation, low wages, and a union-free environment.

For new migrants to American cities, such as African Americans, Puerto Ricans, and Native Americans, capital flight had frustrating and devastating effects. Five million African Americans had migrated from South to North, and now industrial jobs went to precisely the repressive and impoverishing places they had recently fled. Companies like General Motors and Ford Motor relocated plants to suburbs and small communities where African Americans were shut out by racial exclusion. In places such as Detroit, the "arsenal of democracy" that had drawn so many black migrants, black unemployment shot up as high as 18 percent by 1960. Federal "termination" and "relocation" programs moved Indians off reservations to cities like Chicago, while Chicago lost over 90,000 jobs. This new urban working class ended up in low-wage service sector jobs, as janitors, domestics, or hospital workers, or in public sector jobs, as sanitation workers, school custodians, and home-care aides.

Cresting with the civil rights movement of the 1960s, though, public sector workers, long-excluded from the NLRA, began to win union organizing rights. Two decades of public investment had dramatically expanded the government workforce at all levels. President Johnson's War on Poverty and Great Society created even more social service jobs—in health care, education, job training. In a wave of union militancy not seen since the 1930s, public sector workers struck and won unions for teachers, hospital workers, police, social workers, and sanitation workers. These new unions fought for higher wages, better working conditions, dignity, and respect for tens of thousands of female and minority workers but also for expanded public services and social welfare. This movement created 4 million new union members, but it marked the last period of sustained union growth in the twentieth century.

For two generations, the public and private welfare state grew in tandem. Yet critical observers, journalists, liberal economists like John Kenneth Galbraith, civil rights activists, and feminists insisted with increasing urgency in the early 1960s that many Americans had been left out of this postwar prosperity—that poverty persisted amid plenty. John F. Kennedy, a cold warrior, focused his attention on foreign policy, although he had begun to take programmatic steps to address unemployment through job-training programs. Lyndon Johnson, however, was a New Deal liberal. When he became president after Kennedy's death, Johnson saw an opportunity to complete the project of the New Deal—and this time, to ensure that racial justice would not be pushed to the sidelines. Declaring "unconditional war on poverty" in 1964, LBJ oversaw the passage of the Economic Opportunity Act, which established Job Corps, Neighborhood Youth Corps, Adult Education Program, Volunteers in Service to America (VISTA), and Work Experience for those on AFDC. Believing that macroeconomic policy had solved the problems of economic growth, War on Poverty liberals more often sought to reform workers than to restructure the labor market. Poverty and unemployment, they argued, could be overcome through expanding individual opportunity without substantial redistribution. More broadly, Johnson's Great Society program included national health insurance for the elderly, Medicare, and medical assistance for the poor, Medicaid; public housing; Fair Housing to overcome decades of racial discrimination in housing markets; education funding and college grants and loans; and the elimination of national origins quotas for immigrants.

It also stressed a kind of participatory democracy. Through War on Poverty grants, community action agencies pressured city governments for better services, jobs, and housing. The Office of Economic Opportunity's Legal Services mobilized welfare rights activists to press for due process, supplemental grants, and basic citizenship rights for public assistance recipients; in California, it teamed up with United Farm Workers to win civil rights for Mexican Americans. Women and African

Americans acted through collective mobilization and unions to achieve the promises of affirmative action and Title VII of the 1964 Civil Rights Act declaring discrimination based on "race, color, religion, sex, or national origin" to be an "unlawful employment practice," and backed it up with new means for redress. In the following decade, domestic workers won inclusion in the Fair Labor Standards Act. Women's groups used class-action lawsuits to force colleges and universities to change employment and admissions policies. The enactment of the Occupational Safety and Health Act (OSHA) brought the reach of the New Deal regulatory state into toxic and dangerous workplaces where many minorities worked. OSHA represented the last gasp of the New Deal.

The Keynesian New Deal order foundered in the 1970s, as economic growth slowed significantly, corporate profitability stagnated, energy costs soared, and inflation took off unabated. Manufacturing firms, which had already spent two decades shifting production to lower wage areas within the United States, sought yet another spatial fix, moving production out of the country. Unemployment hit levels not seen since the Depression, reaching 8.5 percent in 1975. High oil prices, unemployment, and inflation produced a new toxic brew—"stagflation"—and Keynesian policies of economic stimulus did not seem to work. Thus, in part, the conditions that had sustained the liberal Keynesian order changed.

But there was an increasingly successful political assault on it as well. A new conservative political movement had been taking shape and coalescing throughout the 1960s—in corporate boardrooms, new think tanks and foundations, and churches; among suburban housewives in the Sunbelt and college students in Young Americans for Freedom. Conservative activists began shifting the Republican Party rightward with the presidential nomination of Barry Goldwater in 1964 and the election of Ronald Reagan as California governor in 1966. Inspired by Friedrich Hayek and Milton Friedman, they set out to liberate the free market from the shackles of the welfare state, regulation, and labor unions. In the 1970s, conservatives successfully chipped away at the New Deal. Employers hired anti-labor management "consulting" firms to disestablish unions. The U.S. Chamber of Commerce launched aggressive campaign financing and lobbying operations and, along with new corporate political action committees, stopped liberal reforms in Congress. President Richard Nixon attempted to check the growing tide of welfare state spending. At the same time, wages and incomes stagnated, fueling well-orchestrated tax revolts. A Democratic president, Jimmy Carter, helped set the mold for the "Reagan revolution" of the 1980s—initiating deregulation and workers' concessions at the bargaining table, through the federal rescue plan of the ailing Chrysler Corporation. A path had been cleared for the rise of a new free-market ideology.

See also business and politics; era of confrontation and decline, 1964–80; era of consensus, 1952–64.

FURTHER READING

Biondi, Martha. *To Stand and Fight: The Struggle for Postwar New York City.* Cambridge, MA: Harvard University Press, 2003.

Cobble, Dorothy Sue. *The Other Women's Movement: Workplace Justice and Social Rights in Modern America.* Princeton, NJ: Princeton University Press, 2004.

Freeman, Joshua B. *Working-Class New York: Life and Labor Since World War II.* New York: New Press, 2000.

Jacobs, Meg. *Pocketbook Politics: Economic Citizenship in the Twentieth Century.* Princeton, NJ: Princeton University Press, 2004.

Klein, Jennifer. *For All These Rights: Business, Labor, and the Shaping of America's Public-Private Welfare State.* Princeton, NJ: Princeton University Press, 2003.

Lichtenstein, Nelson. *Walter Reuther: The Most Dangerous Man in Detroit.* Urbana: University of Illinois Press, 1997.

MacLean, Nancy. *Freedom Is Not Enough: The Opening of the American Workplace.* Cambridge, MA: Harvard University Press, 2006.

Minchin, Timothy. *What Do We Need a Union For? The TWUA in the South, 1945–1955.* Chapel Hill: University of North Carolina Press, 1997.

Phillips-Fein, Kimberly. *Visible Hands: The Making of the Conservative Movement from the New Deal to Reagan.* New York: Norton, 2009.

Self, Robert. *American Babylon: Race and the Struggle for Postwar Oakland.* Princeton, NJ: Princeton University Press, 2003.

JENNIFER KLEIN

economy and politics since 1970

The political economy of the United States has been hugely transformed in the years since 1970. In 1970 the United States had a largely insular economy, with trade accounting for just over 10 percent of gross domestic product (GDP). Major sectors of the economy, such as banking and finance, transportation, communications, and energy, were subject to extensive regulation covering both prices and product offerings. Unions were a major force in the economy, with close to one-third of the private sector workforce being represented by a union.

By 2005, trade accounted for almost 30 percent of GDP. Most major industries had been partially or whole deregulated, with corporations free to charge whatever prices the market would bear and enter and exit sectors as they pleased. In 2005, just over 7 percent of the private sector workforce was represented by a union, with membership still declining. These changes in the economy were driven by deliberate policy decisions that in turn transformed the face of politics in the United States.

A number of factors came together to bring about this transformation. In 1970 the United States was still in the midst of its long post–World War II boom. The boom was characterized by rapid productivity growth, which was passed along in rapid wage growth. This led to rising living standards, which sustained demand growth and led to further gains in productivity.

The End of Prosperity

This virtuous circle came to end in the mid-1970s. First higher oil prices, due to the assertiveness of the Middle Eastern countries in OPEC and later a cutoff in oil exports stemming from the Iranian revolution, ended the era of cheap energy. Higher food prices, resulting from large grain sales to the Soviet Union, also added to inflationary pressure. And most importantly, the long postwar productivity boom came to an end. For reasons that are still not fully understood, the annual rate of productivity growth slowed from more than 2.5 percent to less than 1.5 percent. This contributed further to inflation, since slower growth in productivity means that goods and services cost more to produce than if productivity growth was faster.

The economy suffered its worst recession of the postwar period in 1974–75 as the Federal Reserve Board raised interest rates sharply to try to contain inflation. By raising interest rates, the Fed hoped to slow economic growth and thereby reduce the rate of job growth. Slower job growth translates into higher unemployment. The Fed hoped that higher unemployment would slow wage growth, which would in turn slow cost pressures and reduce the rate of price growth. The recession occurred because the Fed went too far, with the unemployment rate eventually rising to 9 percent at the worst of the recession in 1975.

Even though it was painful in terms of throwing people out of work and reducing the rate of wage growth, the Fed's policy did have the desired effect of slowing the rate of inflation. However, this benefit proved to be short-lived. In 1979 the cutoff of oil from Iran again sent oil prices soaring. It also forced car owners to wait in gas lines; price controls often caused shortages, since gas prices could not just rise to their market clearing levels. Inflation went into double digits for the first time since the removal of price controls in the immediate aftermath of World War II. The Fed again slammed on the brakes, bringing on a short but steep recession in the spring of 1980.

This timing proved to be disastrous for the sitting president, Jimmy Carter, who faced reelection that fall. Ronald Reagan, the Republican presidential candidate, highlighted the country's economic problems in making his pitch for the White House. He repeatedly referred to the "misery index," the sum of the inflation rate and the unemployment rate, which reached its highest level in the postwar era in 1980.

The Sharp Right Turn

Reagan promised a new economic policy that would be a sharp departure from the policies pursued by previous administrations of both parties. At the center of this new policy was a 30 percent cut in income taxes. Reagan argued that a tax cut of this size would produce so much economic growth that it would actually pay for itself. For this reason, Reagan claimed that he could both cut taxes and balance the federal budget.

Reagan also promised to cut what he described as wasteful government social programs. In his campaign he repeatedly presented dubious examples of people defrauding welfare programs. He promised to put an end to such "waste, fraud and abuse." This promise had considerable appeal, especially among conservative white voters who perceived the prime welfare abusers to be African Americans.

In addition, Reagan promised to curtail regulation in a wide variety of areas. This agenda included measures like ending price controls on oil. It also meant promoting the deregulation of major industries like airlines, trucking, and banks. Reagan also promised to rein in what he described as abusive environmental and safety regulations.

Reagan's economic agenda, coupled with the promise of a more muscular foreign policy, proved sufficiently popular to earn him a solid victory in the presidential

race and to sweep the Republicans into control of the Senate, the first time that they had controlled a house of Congress for almost three decades.

Reagan quickly sought to implement his agenda. He managed to push a large tax cut through Congress before the end of his first year in office. He also set about fulfilling other campaign promises. He cut back a wide range of social programs, most notably in the areas of job training, housing, and community development. Pushing his deregulatory agenda, Reagan reduced or eliminated regulations in a number of industries, accelerating a process that had begun under Jimmy Carter.

Early in his administration, President Reagan picked a fight with the Professional Air Traffic Controllers Union (PATCO) that proved to have enormous significance for the labor movement. PATCO reached a bargaining impasse with the Transportation Department and went out on strike. Reagan told the workers that if they did not return to work, they would be fired and replaced by military controllers. When the union ignored the warning, Reagan carried through on his threat, firing more than 10,000 striking controllers.

While Reagan had the legal authority to fire the striking controllers (strikes by federal employees are illegal), this marked a sharp departure from past practices. Employers in both the private and government sector almost always sought to negotiate with striking workers. Even when public sector workers were engaged in arguably illegal strikes, a solution to the dispute would usually paper over any legal issues. However, following the PATCO firings, it became routine for employers to use the threat of replacement workers. Suddenly, going out on strike meant that workers risked losing their jobs. This made strikes a far less effective weapon.

This was not the only action by the Reagan administration that weakened unions. President Reagan appointed members to the National Labor Relations Board (NLRB) who were far more supportive of management than appointees of previous administrations. The NLRB also developed a large backlog of cases, which made it far less useful to workers seeking redress for illegal actions by employers, such as firing workers for organizing.

Reagan's policies hit unionized workers in other ways. Following the election, the Federal Reserve Board again began to raise interest rates in an effort to quell inflation. This led to an even worse recession in 1981–82, with the unemployment rate reaching almost 11 percent. Heavily unionized industries like automobiles and construction were especially hard hit.

The Fed's high interest rate policy also led to a sharp rise in the value of the dollar against other major currencies. A higher dollar makes imported goods less expensive for people in the United States, which means that consumers are more likely to buy imported cars, clothes, and other items than goods produced in the United States. For this reason, the high dollar of this period provided yet another source of pain for many of the same industries that were hard hit by the recession.

While most workers did not do very well in the Reagan years (after adjusting for inflation, wages for most workers actually fell in the 1980s), more highly educated workers did see reasonable wage growth. Most workers also benefited from the fall in interest rates from the high inflation years at the end of the 1970s and the beginning of the 1980s. Lower interest rates made it much easier to buy a home or new car.

The big winners from the Reagan era were those who held considerable amounts of stock. The shift from wages to profits, coupled with the decline in both individual and corporate tax rates, sent the stock market soaring. Adjusted for inflation, the stock market rose by more than 90 percent between 1979 and 1989.

The Reagan era also left the country with a serious deficit problem. The size of the federal debt had been falling relative to the size of the economy since the end of World War II. This pattern reversed sharply as a result of President Reagan's tax cuts and military buildup. (The tax cuts did not generate enough growth to increase revenue.) Deficit reduction became a major priority for his immediate successors, George H. W. Bush and Bill Clinton.

The Rise of the Bubble Economy

Under President Bush, a modest tax increase coupled with spending controls helped to contain the deficit, but the 1990–91 recession, coupled with a weak recovery, left a large deficit in place by the time Bill Clinton entered the White House. During his campaign, Clinton had laid out an ambitious platform of public investment in education, job training, and infrastructure. This platform was quickly abandoned after he took office.

Clinton had drawn considerable support from the financial industry and he was determined to pursue policies with which that industry was comfortable, even if this risked alienating unions and other traditional Democratic constituencies. The priority on deficit reduction was very much in keeping with this Wall Street focus.

In addition, Clinton decided to make the inclusion of Mexico in a North American Free Trade Agreement (NAFTA) a top agenda item of his first year in office. A main purpose of NAFTA was to make it as easy as possible for U.S. manufacturers to relocate their operations to Mexico, thereby putting U.S. manufacturing workers into direct competition with much lower paid workers in Mexico. Using the full power of the presidency, including promises to fund pet projects (or threats to block such projects for NAFTA opponents), President Clinton was able to narrowly secure a victory for NAFTA in Congress.

Clinton used similar arm-twisting for approval of the Uruguay Round of the World Trade Organization and later trade agreements with China and other countries. The effect of such deals was to place a major source of downward pressure on the wages of the 70 percent of the U.S. workforce that lacked a college degree. This impact was heightened by the extraordinary run-up in the dollar that began in the mid-1990s. The dollar had drifted lower, partly as the result of conscious policy, since the mid-1980s. However, in the mid-1990s, under Robert Rubin, Clinton's second Treasury secretary, the United States again pursued a "strong dollar" policy.

The immediate force driving the dollar upward was the stock market bubble, which drew in foreign investors at a rapid pace. While the stock market soared, the strong dollar made U.S. goods less competitive in the world economy, leading to the loss of millions of manufacturing jobs. As was the case in the 1980s, the lost manufacturing jobs were disproportionately union jobs in traditional industrial states like Michigan and Ohio.

By 2006, manufacturing employment accounted for just over 10 percent of total employment. This compared to more than 25 percent in 1970. Just over 12 percent of manufacturing workers were unionized in 2006, compared to almost 40 percent in 1970. This means that the once powerful sector of unionized manufacturing workers accounted for just over 1 percent of the workforce.

If unionized manufacturing workers were obvious losers over this period, the financial sector was the most obvious winner. It expanded from just 12 percent of domestic corporate profits in 1970 to almost 30 percent by 2006. Its political power reflected this extraordinary growth as the financial sector could insist that both major parties adopt platforms that reflected its interests.

These policies include a commitment to low inflation, even if this is at the cost of high unemployment. The financial industry also vigorously pursued a policy of deregulation even when this led to instability and government bailouts. The collapse and bailout of the savings-and-loan industry in the 1980s is the most obvious example of poorly planned deregulation. More recently, inadequate regulation allowed hundreds of billions of questionable mortgages to be issued to homeowners who lacked the ability to repay them. This debt was then passed along in secondary markets through a variety of exotic financial instruments.

The financial industry's political agenda also included a willingness to ignore the economic distortions and disruptions associated with financial bubbles. The stock bubble and the housing bubble both led to enormous distortions in the economy. In the case of the stock bubble, tens of billions of dollars were pulled away from potentially productive uses and instead thrown into ill-conceived Internet schemes. The housing bubble led to huge investments in housing that may remain underutilized for many years to come. Both bubbles had the effect of distorting individuals' saving decisions, as many people assumed that the bubble-inflated prices of stock and housing would persist. As a result, they saved far too little for retirement or other needs. Many pension funds made similar mistakes. With the collapse of the housing bubble and the plunge in the stock market in 2008, tens of millions of families approaching retirement had little or no wealth accumulated, and traditional defined benefit pension plans faced enormous shortfalls.

The changes in the country's economy and politics since 1970 had the effect of shifting wealth and power upward. Since World War II, unions had been by far the most important institution supporting the interests of moderate-income and middle-income families. The policies of this period were intended to weaken their influence and were quite successful. Partly as a result, those in the middle and bottom of the income distribution enjoyed less economic security than they had through most of the post–World War II period.

The growing insecurity for those at the middle and the bottom coincided with an upward redistribution of income and wealth to those at the top. By the early twenty-first century, the richest 1 percent of the population owned a larger share of national wealth than at any time since the Great Depression. The sharp downturn brought on by these policies offered President Barack Obama an enormous opportunity to place the economy on a fundamentally different course.

See also business and politics; labor movement and politics.

FURTHER READING

Baker, Dean. *The United States since 1980*. New York: Cambridge University Press, 2007.

Ehrenreich, Barbara. *Nickel and Dimed: On (Not) Getting By in America*. New York: Metropolitan Books, 2001.

Hacker, Jacob. *The Great Risk Shift: New Economic Insecurity and the Decline of the American Dream*. New York: Oxford University Press, 2006.

Mishel, Larry, Jared Bernstein, and Sylvia Allegretto. *The State of Working America, 2006–2007*. Ithaca, NY: Cornell University Press, 2007.

Uchitelle, Louis. *The Disposable American: Layoffs and Their Consequences*. New York: Vintage, 2007.

DEAN BAKER

education and politics

Politics in its various guises has always shaped educational ideals, whether in Plato's *Republic* or in recent federal initiatives such as No Child Left Behind. From the days of the founders to the present, Americans have generally agreed that "knowledge is power," and they have invested considerable time, money, and emotion in educating the young. Since the nineteenth century, they have increasingly focused those efforts on tax-supported public schools, whose nature, character, and quality have long been the subject of political commentary and the object of scorn or favor by the major political parties. When faced with everyday, seemingly intractable problems, from poverty to racial segregation, from poor nutrition to teenage pregnancy, Americans often turn to education and schooling as a panacea. Educational credentials for most decent jobs and careers have also risen considerably over the last half century. So it is not surprising that many governors seeking the presidency (whether Bill Clinton or George W. Bush) helped establish their bona fides as advocates of school improvement.

American Revolution to the Civil War

Education and politics have been intertwined since the birth of the nation. In colonial America, families and churches were the primary educators, supplemented, in

New England, by a range of tax-assisted schools. The leaders of the Protestant Reformation and the majority Protestant population in British North America stressed the importance of literacy to enable everyone to read the Bible, thus liberating individuals from the church authority associated with Roman Catholicism. Independence, however, meant that the new nation had to determine the relative influence of federal, state, and local authority in most aspects of life, including education. Thorny questions about how to ensure good citizenship and nation building loomed large in public discourse.

Many political leaders in the late eighteenth and early nineteenth centuries fretted over the fragility of the republic; historically, most republics were small and short-lived, and, as classical history taught, often fell prey to tyranny. By the early 1800s, white citizens almost enjoyed almost universal literacy, which was applauded as a foundation for good citizenship. Contemporaries believed that literacy and properly trained minds would help ensure that voters would choose wisely at the polls, mothers would rear virtuous children, and commercial transactions based on uniform means of communication and calculation would flourish. But a common faith in education and literacy—unchallenged except with regard to slaves—did not mean that Americans rushed to build a system of free schools for all or agreed about the ultimate purposes of education.

The Constitution, in fact, ignored the subject of education. Instead, newly created states, like some colonies before them, encouraged the spread of knowledge and the establishment of schools. In the early 1800s, schools were a small part of most people's experience, and the options for education included a hodgepodge of one-room schools in the countryside and tuition-dependent schools and academies for those who could afford them. Schools gradually rose in importance in the coming decades, especially in the northern states, serving both ongoing secular concerns such as training for citizenship, exposure to the expanding world of print, and older religious needs, including Bible reading. The federal government also encouraged literacy and learning through generous postal rates, thereby subsidizing the spread of cheap print and newspapers. But the idea that there should be a significant federal role in education on any level ran into strong opposition.

Several Founding Fathers engaged in extended debates on the place of education and schools in the national polity. Advocates of a strong federal government, such as George Washington, called for the establishment of a national university to help train future leaders, an idea that never gained support. In contrast, fellow Virginian and anti-Federalist Thomas Jefferson wrote eloquently on behalf of state-financed schools; in his plan, schools would help identify the best and the brightest, allowing some poor but bright boys to enjoy a subsidized education at his alma mater, William and Mary. But the Virginia legislature rejected his plans, believing that families, churches, and existing educational arrangements sufficed. While some lands were set aside for sale under the provisions of the Northwest Ordinance of 1787 to encourage education, public schools by law and custom would long remain the province of states, whose constitutions encouraged or mandated their establishment. In practice, these schools were largely locally controlled and funded through property taxes and other fees.

Members of the major political parties continued to battle over education and schooling in the antebellum period. The Whig Party, heir to the Federalist ideal of strong centralized authority, led most campaigns to build public school systems in the 1830s and 1840s. Horace Mann, Henry Barnard, and most male school reformers were Whigs, often holding a wide range of political offices. Support for Whigs proved strongest among native-born Protestants and Northerners and especially those living in areas undergoing commercial and industrial development. Writing from Massachusetts, Mann affirmed that public schools trained children in proper moral values, good citizenship, and basic Christian virtues, all taught through the ubiquitous McGuffey Readers and other school texts. Democrats, reflecting the views of southern slaveholders, Irish immigrants, and northern Catholics, typically opposed strong centralized authority; Southerners even opposed the creation of state school systems for all white children, and Catholics often favored state subsidies for their own parochial systems. Public school textbooks were laced with anti-Catholic sentiments. Violent riots in Philadelphia in 1844 over the use of the King James Bible in local schools testified to the intense political world of which education was an integral part. Everywhere, local school committees, elected to office on political tickets, routinely used their patronage positions (from hiring teachers to awarding school contracts for supplies and construction) to enrich party members.

Civil War to World War II

During the Reconstruction period, schooling for African Americans became a major political issue for the Republican Party, especially its radical wing. The Republican and unionist battle cry of free men, free labor, and free soil was joined with the older Whig demand for more free schools. The short-lived federal Freedmen's Bureau helped protect educational initiatives sponsored by blacks themselves and by various northern missionary societies that sent teachers south to teach the freedmen. The very civil rights of black Americans thus became wedded to access to quality education. While federal protection for black civil rights declined in the 1870s, southern states were forced to include provisions in newly written constitutions to establish public schools for all races as a condition of readmission to the Union. Though ex-slaves shared the Republican conception of knowledge as power, the Democratic Party revived to rule the South with a heavy hand, denying many blacks access to any schools and allowing only some to attend inferior, poorly funded, segregated ones.

While public school enrollments, especially on the elementary level, continued to grow in all regions after the Civil War, exclusionary policies toward blacks in the South (and often in the North) and Asian immigrants on the West Coast demonstrated that local politics, based on white supremacy, compromised the ideal of all-inclusive public schools. Republicans not only withdrew federal protection for the ex-slaves, but in the 1870s they also helped rewrite northern state constitutions to tighten restrictions on the use of public monies for parochial schools. Nativist Republican politicians in Illinois and Wisconsin late in the century also tried to require children in all schools to use only English as the language of instruction, which led Catholics and Lutherans to rally at the polls to beat back the draconian measure.

Until the post–World War II era, the Republican Party remained the most important organized political party that endorsed public education. Championing the emergence of a more urban, industrial, corporate America, Republicans often favored political changes that proved influential and enduring. During the early decades of twentieth century, school boards underwent dramatic transformation, especially in urban areas. Urban school boards had traditionally been large, ward-based, and intimately tied to local party politics. But Republicans especially sponsored legislation that dramatically reduced the size of school boards, often eliminating ward-based representation and replacing it with at-large, "nonpartisan" positions, which consolidated power in the hands of elites. This also helped professionalize schooling, since board members, resembling a corporate board of directors, increasingly hired superintendents and other ex-

perts to take more formal control over curricular and other educational programs.

While removing politics from schools was the ostensible aim of these reforms, battles over curriculum and the purposes of education remained contentious. In the early 1900s, labor unions and socialists often fought to elect their own representatives to school boards and lobbied business-dominated boards to expand social services such as free breakfasts and lunches for poor children, playgrounds, and after-school and summer programs. John Dewey and other left-leaning intellectuals also protested the use of intelligence tests to sort working-class children and the poor generally into new, nonacademic vocational programs. Dewey famously criticized the sing-song teaching methods common in most schools and endorsed more democracy in school decision making, in contrast to the prevailing corporate-style models of administration, which emphasized efficiency and testing. As high school enrollments exploded, debates intensified over who should benefit from academic instruction and what should be taught (the biology curriculum became the subject of national attention at the Scopes trial in Dayton, Tennessee, in 1925). About 6 percent of all adolescents entered high school in 1890, while about half attended in 1930.

Schools in the first half of the twentieth century thus were embroiled in numerous political battles. Fundamentalists demanded the exclusion of Darwinian theory from science class, and they successfully eviscerated the teaching of evolution from many classrooms in the coming decades, despite their presumed defeat at Dayton. In the 1920s, reviving an old nativist demand, patriotic groups and the Ku Klux Klan tried without success to force parochial schools to teach pupils in English only. African Americans in turn fought against incredible odds to increase educational opportunities for their children; as late as 1930, 230 counties in the former Confederate states lacked any public high school for blacks, and those who attended any schools were often enrolled in inferior buildings with hand-me-down textbooks. The National Association for the Advancement of Colored People (NAACP), founded in 1909, successfully defeated Jim Crow in several momentous lawsuits, culminating in the famous *Brown v. Board of Education* case in 1954.

World War II to the Present

Throughout the 1950s and 1960s, political conflicts over education and the schools resurfaced on many fronts. Since secondary education had become nearly universal, more citizens had attended high school, and they increasingly voiced opinions on the character and problems of the institution. Rising expectations characteristic of the baby boom era, when the economy grew dramatically and the civil rights movement blossomed, also meant that schools were held accountable for America's failure to provide every citizen with access to the American dream of social mobility and justice for all. Civil rights activists faced uphill struggles against Jim Crow after *Brown*, and President Dwight D. Eisenhower only reluctantly deployed federal troops to help integrate Central High in Little Rock, Arkansas, in 1957. White resistance to racial integration was powerful, often violent, and widespread, and only about 1 percent of all southern blacks attended school with any whites by 1961.

More middle-class parents now expected their children to attend college, and they demanded the elevation of high school standards—especially for their children—an effort that intensified after the passage of the National Defense Education Act (NDEA) in 1958. Following the launching of the Soviet *Sputnik*, the NDEA (which emphasized among other things improved math, science, and foreign language instruction) brought cold war concerns directly to bear upon educational policy. Cold warriors also accused teachers of being too soft, progressive, and child-centered, and many districts demanded that teachers toe the line when it came to loyalty to God and country. Duck-and-cover drills taught children that the world teetered on the precipice of nuclear annihilation.

Modern liberalism flourished in the 1960s, despite the existence of countercurrents of conservatism that grew powerful by the end of the decade. The Great Society of Lyndon B. Johnson represented the new face of the modern Democratic Party, which had coalesced during the New Deal. While Republicans had traditionally been the prime champions of public education, Johnson and his allies, seizing the moment, used the federal government to advance reform in unprecedented ways. Legislation ranging from the Civil Rights Act, which empowered the Justice Department to sue southern districts that refused to desegregate; the Elementary and Secondary Education Act (ESEA), which led to major federal funding of schools; the Economic Opportunity Act, which created Head Start; the Higher Education Act; the Bilingual-Bicultural Act; and numerous other initiatives placed the Democratic Party in the vanguard of educational change. Because of the unpopularity of some of these reforms, especially in the area of civil rights, Johnson

rightly predicted that the South would shift rightward toward the Republican Party. The liberal Warren Court, which ruled state-sponsored prayer and the banning of the teaching of evolution unconstitutional, also proved unpopular, fueling even more political dissent against public education.

Culture wars, an old feature of American society and common enough in the schools, reignited in the 1980s. Following the election of Ronald Reagan to the presidency in 1980, the failures of public education again grabbed the nation's attention, and the liberalism of the 1960s was routinely held accountable for educational failures. Reagan promised to restore prayer in the schools and abolish the new Department of Education (created during the Carter administration in 1979); he did neither, though he dramatically cut federal spending on education. Republicans also weakened federal support for busing to achieve racial integration, adding to their popularity. Ironically, the Department of Education enabled Republicans to regain their traditional eminence in framing debates about education and the schools. The department sponsored a commission that produced the most important educational document of the late twentieth century, *A Nation at Risk* (1983). Permeated with cold war rhetoric, the report claimed that low academic standards in the schools had weakened the American economy. In times of crisis, someone or something is usually held accountable, and instead of corporate boardrooms, it was the schools.

By the 1980s, governors in many states made educational reform integral to their political campaigns. While only roughly 7 percent of school funding came from Washington, Reagan's successor, George H. W. Bush, asserted that he wanted to become the "education president." Working with moderate Democrats, including Bill Clinton, a prominent champion of school reform while governor of Arkansas, Bush organized a major educational conference in 1989 in Charlottesville, Virginia, that led to successive federal initiatives (America 2000, then Goals 2000) that promised to end violence in the schools, improve graduation rates, and raise test scores, especially in math and science.

Very few successful politicians who wore the mantle of school reformer since the Reagan years called for more racial integration or equalization of school funding between city and suburb, showing the clear connections between politics and educational policy. Conservative times led many Democrats to move to the right, downplaying concerns about equality and equity.

In addition, since the 1980s, Republicans in particular have advocated market competition, tax incentives, or vouchers for private schools, enabling tax dollars, in some cases, to flow to religious-based schools. Democrats, with major support from teachers' unions, have tended to favor choice within the public school system, reflected in the spread of magnet schools in the 1970s and 1980s and in charter schools during the early twenty-first century.

Raising standards is the ubiquitous goal of most politicians concerned with educational policy. The revision of ESEA, No Child Left Behind, enjoyed initial bipartisan support when enacted in 2002, and it reflected widespread concerns about low academic standards. But whether in liberal Connecticut or conservative Utah, states sometimes protested against federal intervention, reflecting age-old support for state and local control over the schools. Characteristically, each state set the standard for academic norms under No Child Left Behind. Americans want neither a national curriculum nor federal control, but they do support higher standards.

Politics and education remain inseparable. Schools teach values as well as subjects, and most educational issues concerning race (including court-ordered busing), or religion (including school prayer or the teaching of "intelligent design"), or finance (including redistribution of resources to the poor) inevitably lead to political controversy and dissent. These issues embroil local communities far more than standardized test results. Compared with most western nations, America has weak national authority over its schools (which are still governed by over 13,000 independent school districts), and education remains subjected to various federal, state, and local political pressures.

Most educational policies and practices are rooted in decisions about power and authority, so all education is inherently political. Even if political parties disappeared, every decision facing every teacher in every school would remain in the broadest sense political. Every debate about curriculum, pedagogy, or the values taught to pupils involves questions of whose ideas will triumph.

George Washington discovered how entangled education and politics were when he endorsed the creation of a national university; Thomas Jefferson realized it when he called for free schools for all white children in the slave South; and the intermingling was given broad attention when John T. Scopes became a symbol of the right of teachers to teach evolution. While defending an educational ideal, these men quickly learned that, at least in their lifetime, what seemed desirable and defensible to them lacked widespread political legitimacy and public sanction.

FURTHER READING

Angus, David L., and Jeffrey E. Mirel. *The Failed Promise of the American High School, 1890–1995.* New York: Teachers College Press, 1999.

Hays, Samuel P. "The Politics of Reform in Municipal Government in the Progressive Era." *Pacific Northwest Quarterly* 55 (October 1964), 157–69.

Howe, Daniel Walker. *What Hath God Wrought: The Transformation of America, 1815–1848.* New York: Oxford University Press, 2007.

Kaestle, Carl F. *Pillars of the Republic: Common Schools and American Society, 1780–1860.* New York: Hill and Wang, 1983.

Reese, William J. *America's Public Schools: From the Common Schools to "No Child Left Behind."* Baltimore, MD: Johns Hopkins University Press, 2005.

Tyack, David B. *The One Best System: A History of American Urban Education.* Cambridge, MA: Harvard University Press, 1974.

WILLIAM J. REESE

elections and electoral eras

Scholars have partitioned American history into distinct electoral eras, each of which is marked by stability in competition between political parties, the issues confronting the nation, and the composition of voter blocs. The constant feature of American politics that runs through these historical periods is a relatively stable two-party system, with shifting constellations of third parties introducing new ideas and leaders. Although most other democratic societies developed multiparty systems in the nineteenth and twentieth centuries, several factors account for persistent two-party dominance in the United States. Most critically, American elections are winner take all. Third parties lack the means to win a majority of Electoral College votes or to win the pluralities needed to secure other national, state, or local positions. Third parties also lack financial resources, established local organizations, and experienced leadership. In the twentieth century, restrictive state laws made it difficult for third parties to place their candidates on the ballot, and party primaries have shut members of third parties out of the nominating process in many states.

The First Party System: 1787–1804

In his farewell address of 1797, George Washington warned against the dangerous "spirit of Party," which he said "serves always to distract the Public Councils and enfeeble the Public Administration. It ignites the Community with ill founded Jealousies and false alarms, kindles the animosity of one part against another, foments occasionally riot & insurrection." Yet in opposing the formation of political parties, Washington was voicing a vain hope. During Washington's first term as president, his treasury secretary, Alexander Hamilton, had already formed the Federalist Party and his secretary of state, Thomas Jefferson, had founded the opposition Democratic-Republican Party. Hamilton intended to build a Federalist Party committed to strong central government, sustained by commercial interests. In contrast, Jefferson favored limited central authority, states' rights, and agrarian over commercial interests. Jefferson also opposed Hamilton's objective of building ties with England rather than with revolutionary France. To Jefferson, England was a corrupt, repressive society that still threatened the survival of American liberty.

As early as 1792, party-line voting emerged in Congress, local and national partisan allegiances took shape, and both the ruling and opposition parties cultivated partisan newspapers, with no lines drawn between news and opinion. In 1800 the first turning-point election in U.S. history, Federalist president John Adams—George Washington's successor—lost to Jefferson, and the Democratic-Republicans gained control of Congress. In his later years, Jefferson looked back on this contest as "the Revolution of 1800." He said that the election "was a real a revolution in the principles of our government as that of 1776 was in its form; not effected indeed by the sword, as that, but by the rational and peaceable instrument of reform, the suffrage of the people." Despite the hyperbole, Jefferson was essentially correct. The election of 1800 firmly established the two-party system as the norm in American politics. It set a precedent for the peaceful transfer of political power and changed the course of public policy. As president, Jefferson promoted states' rights, economy in government, a pared-down military establishment, lower taxes, and elimination of the national debt. In foreign policy he tilted more toward France than Britain.

The election also corrected a flaw in the system for electing presidents. Under the Constitution of 1787, members of the Electoral College cast two votes for president. The leading vote-getter, provided that he received a majority of the electoral vote, was elected president. The second leading vote-getter was elected vice president. If no candidate received a majority or if two candidates tied, the House of Representatives would choose the president, with each state casting a single vote. In 1800, Jefferson and his putative running mate, Aaron Burr, each received 73 electoral votes. The House that chose the president was not the new, heavily Jeffersonian House elected in 1800, but the lame-duck House that was closely divided between Federalists and Jeffersonians. It took 36 ballots for the House finally to elect Jefferson as president, with Burr becoming vice president. To avoid the problem of future tied votes, the Twelfth Amendment in 1804 created the modern ticket system, with separate balloting for president and vice president in the Electoral College.

The election of 1800 also set a precedent for two centuries of negative campaigns. Neither Adams nor Jefferson campaigned personally, in deference to George Washington's belief that presidents should be called to service. Still, Adams's Federalist backers attacked Jefferson for his alleged atheism, radicalism, and lack of moral standards. One propagandist warned that, with Jefferson as president, "murder, robbery, rape, adultery, and incest will be openly taught and practiced, the air will be rent with the cries of the distressed, the soil will be soaked with blood, and the nation black with crimes." Jefferson's backers responded with smears of their own, charging that Adams planned to marry one of his sons to the daughter of the king of England, start an American monarchy, and finally reunite America and England.

One-Party Dominance: 1804–24

Although nominal two-party competition persisted after Jefferson's victory, the Federalist Party would never again come close to winning the presidency or to controlling either house of Congress. The Federalists were caught up in the old politics of officeholding as nonpartisan service and of public deference to the nation's supposedly "natural" leaders. They never adjusted to the new era of electioneering and the mobilization of public opinion. To control the process of presidential succession, the Democratic-Republican Party relied on the congressional caucus to sort out the ambitions of competing candidates and nominate a single chosen leader. Nomination by "King Caucus" was tantamount to election, given the weakness of the Federalist opposition. The system worked well until 1824, when it broke down internally and externally. With the end of the administration of James Monroe—the last of the Revolutionary-era presidents—the caucus could not control the ambitions of competing candidates. Moreover, elite control over elections was declining as states eliminated property qualifications for voting and increasingly chose electors by popular vote rather than the vote of state legislatures.

More than in any prior presidential campaign, the supporters of competing candidates in 1824 engaged in efforts to mobilize public opinion. A weak congressional caucus, attended by a minority of Democratic-Republican members of Congress, nominated a weak candidate, an ailing William Crawford, Monroe's secretary of the treasury. Three other candidates also contended for the presidency. The first candidate was John Quincy Adams, James Monroe's eight-year secretary of state and the main author of the Monroe Doctrine. The second candidate was Henry Clay, the Speaker of the House and architect of the Missouri Compromise of 1820, which temporarily quieted sectional conflict over slavery. The final candidate was the war hero Andrew Jackson, the first presidential candidate from the growing West. Jackson ran as an outsider who would clean out the corrupt political establishment that festered in the capital.

Jackson won a plurality of the popular and electoral votes. But his failure to win a majority of electoral votes meant that the House of Representatives would choose the president from among the top three finishers—Jackson, Adams, and Crawford. Jackson's supporters argued that in deference to the mandate of the people, the House should choose the first-place finisher. But the argument failed to convince Speaker of the House Clay, whose lobbying for Adams helped the secretary of state win election by the House. Although Jackson did not challenge the result, he was later outraged when Adams appointed Clay secretary of state, charging that "bargain and corruption" had combined to produce his defeat.

The Second Party System: 1828–56

In 1828, when Jackson made a second bid for the presidency, he began the transition to a new and more balanced system of two-party competition. In another high-stakes election with abusive charges coming from both sides, Jackson easily defeated Adams in both the popular vote and the Electoral College. Jackson inspired

a broad and diverse following—diehard pro-slavery and states' rights advocates like John C. Calhoun of South Carolina, practitioners of the new patronage politics like Martin Van Buren of New York, Tennessee businessmen, western agrarians, and influential editors—that became the core of his new Democratic Party. The centerpiece of Jackson's two terms as president was a war against the Bank of the United States, which he regarded as representing the privileged interests that he had come to Washington to drive out of power. In his 1832 message vetoing legislation that would have granted the bank a new charter, Jackson declared that "we must stand against all new grants of monopolies and exclusive privileges, against any prostitution of our Government to the advancement of the few at the expense of the many."

Although Jackson easily swept to a second term in 1832, that election marked the emergence of America's first significant third party, the Anti-Masonic Party, dedicated to opposing the Masons and other secret societies that the party claimed imposed elite rule on the United States. The Anti-Masons gained a credible 8 percent of the popular vote and held the first national presidential nominating convention. The Anti-Masons represented one of three variants of third parties that would emerge in the United States: the single-issue third party. Other single-issue parties included the antislavery Free Soil of 1848 and the Prohibition Party that anti-alcohol activists founded in 1869. A second type of third party advanced a broad ideology. Examples included the People's Party, which agrarian reformers founded in the late nineteenth century; the Socialist Party of the early twentieth century; and the Libertarian Party of the late twentieth century. Finally, some third parties served primarily as vehicles for the presidential aspirations of particular candidates, such as Theodore Roosevelt in 1912, George Wallace in 1968, and Ross Perot in 1992 and 1996.

In 1834 Jackson's opponents coalesced into a new Whig Party, led by Clay and Senator Daniel Webster of New Hampshire. In contrast to the Democrats' philosophy of limited government and states' rights, the Whigs backed federal intervention to protect domestic industries through tariffs, promote education, build the nation's infrastructure, and enforce moral standards. The Whigs also opposed the Democrats' aggressive approach to the territorial expansion of the United States. Democrats and Whigs would compete on relatively equal terms nationally and in nearly every state of the union. Unlike later party systems, partisan allegiances were not sharply divided along sectional lines. From 1836 to 1852,

Democrats won the presidential elections of 1836, 1845, and 1852, whereas Whigs prevailed in 1840 and 1848. During these years, neither party gained a decisive advantage in Congress. Close partisan competition, a rising number of elected offices, and new forms of popular mobilization greatly increased voter turnout in federal, state, and local elections. The election of 1840 also contributed to the rise of popular politics, with the Whigs shrewdly, if misleadingly, marketing the wealthy planter and war hero William Henry Harrison as the "log cabin and hard cider" candidate, a man of the people from the rough and tumble West. They organized log cabin clubs and distributed log cabin mugs and medallions and flyers showing Harrison seated beside a log cabin and a barrel of cider. The Whigs led songfests that celebrated Harrison as the hero of the common man and lampooned their Democratic opponent, President Martin Van Buren, as an effete eastern dandy addicted to French wine.

The presidential election of 1844 between the Democrat James K. Polk and the Whig Henry Clay was pivotal to the Second Party System. This election was the last contest in which different states held elections on different days. In 1845 Congress passed a law establishing Election Day as the first Tuesday after the first Monday in November. Members of Congress viewed Polk's narrow victory over the anti-expansionist Clay as a mandate for the annexation of Texas, and Congress passed a joint resolution to accomplish that end, which outgoing President John Tyler signed. Polk's election portended additional expansion that he achieved by settling a boundary dispute with Britain over the northwest territory that became Oregon and Washington and acquiring what became California, Utah, Nevada, and parts of other states through war with Mexico. Had Clay prevailed in 1844, American history would likely have followed a profoundly different course.

At the time that Americans were proclaiming their Manifest Destiny to expand across the continent, the United States was also deeply divided by the presence of slavery in the newly acquired territories. The Second Party System unraveled in the 1850s under the pressure of sectional conflict over the expansion of slavery. The Whig Party included moderate but generally proslavery Southerners as well as northern Protestants in the vanguard of the antislavery, temperance, and anti-immigrant movements. This amalgam did not hold. During the 1850s, southern Whigs deserted the party as antislavery Northerners sought, in vain, to keep the party united in their region. After the Whigs decisively lost the presidential

election of 1852, Whig representative Lewis Davis Campbell of Ohio prophetically said, "We are slayed. The party is dead-dead-dead!" By the next presidential election in 1856, the Whigs had disintegrated and two new parties had arisen to compete with the ruling Democrats. The American, or Know Nothing, Party was based on opposition to Catholics and immigrants. The Republican Party opposed the expansion of slavery and, like the defunct Whigs, backed an activist government that promoted industry, commerce, and education. Although the Republican nominee for president, the famed explorer John C. Frémont, lost to Democratic nominee James Buchanan in the presidential election of 1856, he finished in second place, well ahead of the Know Nothing nominee, former president Millard Fillmore. The results of the 1856 elections for the presidency and Congress established the fledgling Republican Party as the alternative to the Democratic Party in a new two-party system.

The Third Party System: 1860–96

The Third Party System marked the first of several distinct eras of competition between Republicans and Democrats. Unlike the Whigs, the Democrats withstood sectional divisions and endured to oppose Republican president Abraham Lincoln's commitment to military victory in the Civil War as well as Republican efforts to establish political and civil rights for the freed slaves during the postwar Reconstruction. Partisan conflict over racial issues in the 1860s would give Republicans a sizable advantage in northern states, create a solidly Democratic South after the demise of Republican-run Reconstruction governments, and define voter loyalties for another 70 years. The Republicans were the party of activist government in the late nineteenth century, whereas Democrats continued to defend limited government and states' rights.

In the pivotal election of 1860, Abraham Lincoln prevailed over a field of candidates that included Senator Stephen Douglas of Illinois, the regular Democratic nominee; Vice President John Breckinridge, the candidate of bolting southern Democrats; and former senator John Bell of Tennessee, the candidate of the compromise Constitutional Union Party. Although Lincoln won only 40 percent of the popular vote, he carried every northern state and gained a substantial majority of Electoral College votes. Just six years after its birth, the new Republican Party had won control over the national government. Abraham Lincoln, elected because of the dissolution of the old political order, would have the cheerless task of presiding over the near dissolution of the nation itself. The selection of a Republican president was unacceptable to many Southerners. Even before Lincoln took the oath of office on March 4, 1861, seven southern states had seceded from the Union. On April 12, 1861, the Civil War began with the bombardment of Fort Sumter in South Carolina.

The war dragged on for four long years and transformed the nation. When Lincoln issued the Emancipation Proclamation, which freed all slaves still held by the Confederacy, he committed the federal government for the first time to a decisive stand against slavery. The Lincoln administration also instituted a graduated income tax, established a national banking system, facilitated the settlement of western lands, and began the nation's first draft of soldiers. Lincoln won reelection in 1864 and, with the South still out of the Union, his Republican Party gained decisive majorities in both houses of Congress and passed the Thirteenth Amendment, which ended slavery in the United States. The election also ensured that the Republicans would dominate the reconstruction of the Union after the guns fell silent. "I earnestly believe that the consequences of this day's work will be to the lasting advantage, if not the very salvation, of the country," Lincoln said. But Lincoln's assassination in April 1865 meant that he would not live to fulfill his prophecy.

At the time of Lincoln's death, the big questions of Reconstruction were still unresolved. Under what terms would the South be restored to the Union? To what extent would the federal government act to provide civil rights, civil liberties, economic security, and political rights to the newly freed slaves? In the face of opposition from Lincoln's successor, the former Democrat Andrew Johnson, Congress enacted a fairly ambitious program of Reconstruction. It included civil rights laws; the Fourteenth Amendment, which guaranteed "equal protection under the law"; and the Fifteenth Amendment, which prohibited the denial of voting rights on grounds of race, religion, or previous servitude. Still, in the late 1860s and 1870s, Republicans would be unable to prevent the unraveling of Reconstruction and the "redemption" of southern states by Democratic leaders committed to white-only government and to the exploitation of cheap black labor.

The disputed presidential election of 1876 marked the end of Reconstruction. Although Democratic candidate Samuel J. Tilden, the governor of New York, won the popular vote against Republican governor Rutherford B. Hayes of Ohio, the outcome of the election turned on disputed Electoral College votes in Florida, South Carolina, and Louisiana. With the Constitution silent on the resolution of such disputes, Congress improvised by forming a special electoral commission of eight Republicans and seven Democrats. The commission voted on party lines to award all disputed electoral votes to Hayes, which handed him the presidency. The years from 1876 to 1892 were marked by a sharp regional division of political power growing out of Civil War alignments and a national stalemate between Republicans, who dominated the North, and Democrats, who controlled the South. White Southerners disenfranchised African Americans and established an all-white one-party system in most of their region. The stalled politics of America's late nineteenth-century Gilded Age resulted in a seesaw series of close elections: with neither party able to gain a firm hold on government or the electorate, the White House would change hands in every contest of the era except 1880, when Republican James A. Garfield won by some 2,000 votes. During this period the difference between Democratic and Republican percentages of the national popular vote for president averaged only about 1 percent, whereas differences in the vote between the North and the South averaged about 25 percent.

This combination of major-party stasis and electoral uncertainty left the nation unable to cope with the deep depression of the mid-1890s, which shattered the second administration of Democratic president Grover Cleveland. In 1884 Cleveland became the first Democrat to win the White House since Buchanan in 1856. Four years later he narrowly prevailed in the popular vote but lost in the Electoral College to Republican Benjamin Harrison. Becoming the only American president to serve two nonconsecutive terms, Cleveland defeated Harrison in 1892. With Cleveland declining to compete for a third term in 1896, the insurgent Democratic candidate William Jennings Bryan was unable to shake off the legacy of Cleveland's failures. With his candidacy endorsed by the People's Party, Bryan embraced such reform proposals as the free coinage of silver to inflate the currency, a graduated income tax, arbitration of labor disputes, and stricter regulation of railroads—policies that were at odds with his party's traditional commitment to hands-off government. Despite Bryan's defeat by Republican William McKinley, his nomination began to transform the political philosophy of the major parties. By vigorously stumping the nation in 1896, Bryan also helped introduce the modern style of presidential campaigns. In turn, the Republicans, who vastly outspent the Democrats, pioneered modern fund-raising techniques.

The Fourth Party System: 1896–1928

The Republican Party dominated American politics from 1896 through 1928. Except for the two administrations of Woodrow Wilson, from 1913 to 1921, the GOP controlled the presidency throughout this period, which was marked by foreign expansionism and the rise and fall of progressive reform. Although William Jennings Bryan emerged as the reformist leader of the Democratic Party, it took the ascendancy of Theodore Roosevelt and a new generation of Republican progressives to add domestic reform to the expansionist policies begun by President McKinley during the Spanish-American War of 1898. Roosevelt became president through four unpredictable turns of fate. First, President William McKinley's vice president, Garret A. Hobart, died in 1899. Second, Republican boss Thomas C. Platt saw his chance to rid New York of its reformer governor, Theodore Roosevelt, by promoting him for vice president on McKinley's ticket in 1900. Third, McKinley defeated Bryan in a rematch of 1896, and fourth, Roosevelt became president six months into his vice presidency when McKinley died of a gunshot wound inflicted by anarchist Leon Czolgosz. During two terms in office, Roosevelt put his progressive stamp on the presidency. His sustained McKinley's expansionist foreign policies and gave concrete expression to his idea that government should operate in the public interest by steering a middle course between unchecked corporate greed and socialistic remedies.

After stepping down from the presidency in 1908, Roosevelt was so disappointed with his hand-picked successor, William Howard Taft, that he sought a third term as president. In 1912 Roosevelt, Taft, and Senator Robert M. La Follette of Wisconsin fought the first primary-election campaign in American history, battling one another in the dozen states that had recently established party primaries. Although Roosevelt garnered more primary votes than Taft and La Follette combined, most convention delegates were selected by party bosses, who overwhelmingly backed Taft. The disgruntled Roosevelt launched an insurgent campaign behind the new Progressive Party that advocated reforms such as women's suffrage, tariff reduction, old-age pensions, and laws prohibiting child labor. Roosevelt siphoned off about half of the voters who had backed Taft in 1908. Democratic candidate Woodrow Wilson, the governor of New Jersey, held the Democrats together and won the election with only 42 percent of the popular vote. Roosevelt finished second in the popular vote with 27 percent, compared to 23 percent for Taft. It was the largest vote ever tallied by a third-party candidate.

During his two terms in office, Wilson pioneered the modern liberal tradition within the Democratic Party. Under his watch, the federal government reduced tariffs, adopted the Federal Reserve System, established the Federal Trade Commission to regulate business, and joined much of the Western world in guaranteeing voting rights for women. Wilson also increased America's involvement abroad and led the nation victoriously through World War I. Wilson had a broad vision of a peaceful postwar world based upon America's moral and material example. He became the first president of any party to advocate a strong internationalist program that centered on America's leadership in a League of Nations. He would not realize this vision, although it would be largely achieved under Franklin Roosevelt and Harry Truman after World War II.

The reaction that followed World War I and Wilson's failed peace plans led to the election of conservative Republican Warren G. Harding in 1920. Republicans won all three presidential elections of the 1920s by landslide margins and maintained control over Congress during the period. Republican presidents and congresses of the 1920s slashed taxes, deregulated industry, restricted immigration, enforced Prohibition, and increased protection tariffs. In 1928, when Commerce Secretary Herbert Hoover decisively defeated Governor Al Smith of New York—the first Catholic presidential candidate on a major party ticket—GOP senator William Borah of Idaho said, "We have an opportunity to put the Republican Party in a position where it can remain in power without much trouble for the next twenty years." But Democratic weakness concealed the party's resilient strength. The Democrats' pluralism, which melded diverse voters from outside America's elite—whites in the South, working-class Catholics and new immigrants in the North, and reformers in Mountain States—helped the party weather adversity, evolve with changing circumstance, and survive in contests for congressional and state offices. The Democrats' 1924 presidential candidate, John W. Davis, said after the election: "I doubt whether a minority party can win as long as the country is in fairly prosperous condition. . . . Some day, I am sure, the tide will turn."

The Fifth Party System: 1932–80

The tide turned after the crash of 1929 began the nation's longest and deepest depression and led to a two-tiered realignment of the American party system. First, between 1930 and 1932 the Democrats benefited from a "depression effect" that swelled the ranks of party voters throughout the United States but neither restored the Democrats to majority status nor reshuffled voter coalitions. Second, after Franklin Roosevelt won the presidential election of 1932, the "Roosevelt effect" completed the realignment process. FDR's liberal New Deal reforms and his inspirational leadership created a positive incentive for loyalty to the Democratic Party.

In 1936, after losing badly in four consecutive presidential and midterm elections, Republicans seemed nearly as obsolete as the Whigs they had displaced in 1854. Since 1928 the party had lost 178 U.S. House seats, 40 Senate seats, and 19 governorships. The GOP retained a meager 89 House members and just 16 senators. As Democrats completed the realignment of party loyalties, they recruited new voters and converted Republicans. From 1928 to 1936, the GOP's share of the two-party registration fell from 69 percent to 45 percent in five northern states and from 64 to 35 percent in major cities. The durable new Democratic majority—the so-called Roosevelt coalition—consisted of white Protestant Southerners, Catholics and Jews, African Americans, and union members.

Republicans recovered sufficiently in the midterm elections of 1938 to regain a critical mass in Congress and to join with conservative southern Democrats to halt the domestic reform phase of the New Deal. However, Republican hopes to regain the presidency and Congress in 1940 were dashed by the outbreak of war in Europe. A nationwide Gallup Poll found that respondents preferred Roosevelt to any challenger, although most said that they would have backed a Republican candidate in the absence of war abroad. Roosevelt won an unprecedented third term and led the nation into a war that largely ended America's traditional isolation from foreign entanglements.

In the first postwar election, held in 1946, the GOP's new slogan, "Had Enough?" evoked scarcity, high prices, and labor strife under Harry Truman, who had become president after Roosevelt's death in April 1945. In postwar Britain, voters defeated Winston Churchill and his conservative majority in Parliament. Americans, however, could not dispatch the Democrats in a single blow.

The midterm elections of 1946 issued no policy mandate to Republicans in Congress, who had to confront a president armed with veto power, the bully pulpit, and the initiative in foreign affairs. After leading America into the cold war against communism, Truman unexpectedly won the election of 1948, and Democrats regained control of Congress.

Four years later, in the midst of disillusionment over a stalled war in Korea and Democratic corruption, the war hero Dwight David Eisenhower became the first Republican president in 20 years. But Eisenhower had no intention of turning back the clock to the 1920s. Instead, he governed as a "modern Republican" who steered a middle course between Democratic liberals and the right wing of the Republican Party. However, modern Republicanism neither stole the thunder of Democrats nor attracted independents to the GOP. Although Eisenhower remained personally popular, Democrats controlled Congress during his last six years in office. When he stepped down in 1960—the Twenty-Second Amendment, ratified in 1951, barred presidents from seeking third terms—a Democrat, John F. Kennedy, became America's first Catholic president by defeating Eisenhowers' vice president, Richard Nixon.

Kennedy and his successor, Lyndon Johnson, presided over a vast expansion of the liberal state. These Democratic presidents embedded the struggle for minority rights within the liberal agenda and, in another departure from the New Deal, targeted needs—housing, health care, nutrition, and education—rather than groups, such as the elderly or the unemployed. Its civil rights agenda would eventually cost the Democratic Party the allegiance of the South, but in the near term the enfranchisement of African Americans under the Voting Rights Act of 1965 offset losses among white Southerners. Still, the Johnson administration unraveled under pressure from a failing war in Vietnam and social unrest at home. In 1968 Richard Nixon became the second Republican to gain the White House since 1932. Although Nixon talked like a conservative, he governed more liberally than Eisenhower. Nixon signed pathbreaking environmental laws, backed affirmative action programs, opened relations with mainland China, and de-escalated the cold war.

The Watergate scandal and Nixon's resignation in 1974 dashed any hopes that Republicans could recapture Congress or pull even with Democrats in party identification. However, conservative Republicans began rebuilding in adversity. They formed the Heritage Foundation to generate ideas, the Eagle Forum to rally women, new business lobbies, and Christian Right groups to inspire evangelical Protestants. Although Democrat Jimmy Carter won the presidential election of 1976, his administration was unable to protect its constituents from the ravages of "stagflation"—an improbable mix of slow growth, high unemployment, high inflation, and high interest rates. Carter also exhibited weakness in foreign affairs by failing to gain the quick release of American hostages seized by militants in Iran or to halt the resurgent expansionism of the Soviet Union.

The Sixth Party System: 1980–2008

After defeating Carter in 1980, Republican Ronald Reagan, the former actor and governor of California, became the first conservative president since the 1920s. The election of 1980 did not match the shattering realignment of 1932. Republicans did not gain durable control of Congress, long-term domination of the presidency, or an edge in the party identification of voters. Nonetheless, the election profoundly changed American politics. It brought Republicans into near parity with Democrats, enabled Reagan to implement his conservative ideas in domestic and foreign policy, and moved the national conversation about politics to the right. In 1980 Republicans gained control of the Senate and held an ideological edge in the House. In his first year as president, Reagan cut taxes, reduced regulation, shifted government spending from domestic programs to the military, and adopted an aggressive approach to fighting communism abroad. Although Reagan won reelection after a troubled economy recovered in 1984, the "Reagan revolution" stalled in his second term. Still, Reagan presided over the beginning of the end of the cold war, a process completed by his vice president, George H. W. Bush, who won the presidency in 1988.

Republican progress stalled when moderate Democrat Bill Clinton of Arkansas defeated Bush in the presidential election of 1992. However, conservatives and Republicans rebounded in 1994, when the GOP regained control of both houses of Congress for the first time in 40 years. Although Republicans failed to enact their most ambitious policy proposals or prevent Clinton's reelection in 1996, the congressional revolution of 1994, no less than the Reagan revolution of 1980, advanced conservative politics in the United States. The elections gave Republicans unified control of Congress for most of the next dozen years, established Republicans as the dominant party in the South, polarized the parties along ideological lines, and forestalled new liberal initiatives by the Clinton administration.

In the disputed presidential election of 2000, Republican George W. Bush, the governor of Texas, trailed Vice President Al Gore in the popular vote by half a percent. But the Electoral College vote turned on contested votes in Florida. On December 12, the U.S. Supreme Court stopped a recount of Florida's votes with Bush ahead by 537 votes out of 6 million cast. Bush won a bare majority of 271 Electoral College votes, including all in the South and about one-third elsewhere. He won overwhelming support from white evangelical Protestants and affluent voters.

Bush's conservative backers in 2000 brushed aside suggestions from media commentators that the president-elect fulfill his promise to be "a uniter, not a divider" and emulate Rutherford B. Hayes, who governed from the center after the disputed election of 1876. Dick Cheney, who was poised to become the most influential vice president in American history, added, "The suggestion that somehow, because this was a close election, we should fundamentally change our beliefs I just think is silly." Bush advanced the conservative agenda by steering major tax cuts and business subsidies through Congress, advancing a Christian conservative agenda through executive orders, and aggressively opposing foreign enemies abroad.

Although Bush won reelection in 2004, under his watch conservatism, like liberalism in the 1970s, faced internal contradictions. Conservatives had long opposed social engineering by government, but in Iraq and Afghanistan the Bush administration assumed two of the largest and most daunting social engineering projects in U.S. history. Conservatives have also defended limited government, fiscal responsibility, states' rights, and individual freedom. Yet the size and scope of the federal government and its authority over the states and individuals greatly expanded during the Bush years. These contradictions, along with the Republicans' loss of Congress in 2006 and Democrat Barack Obama's victory in the 2008 presidential race, suggest that the conservative era that began in 1980 had come to an end.

See also Democratic Party; Republican Party.

FURTHER READING

Burnham, Walter Dean. *Critical Elections and the Mainsprings of American Politics.* New York: Norton, 1970.

Gerring, John. *Party Ideologies in America, 1828–1996.* New York: Cambridge University Press, 1998.

Lichtman, Allan J. *White Protestant Nation: The Rise of the American Conservative Movement.* New York: Grove Atlantic, 2008.

Mayhew, David R. *Electoral Realignments: A Critique of an American Genre.* New Haven, CT: Yale University Press, 2004.

Nelson, Albert J. *Shadow Realignment, Partisan Strength and Competition, 1960 to 2000.* Westport, CT: Praeger, 2002.

Rosenof, Theodore. *Realignment: The Theory That Changed the Way We Think about American Politics.* Lanham, MD: Rowman and Littlefield, 2003.

Shafer, Byron E. *End of Realignment? Interpreting American Electoral Eras.* Madison: University of Wisconsin Press, 1991.

Silbey, Joel. *The American Political Nation, 1838–1893.* Stanford, CA: Stanford University Press, 1991.

ALLAN J. LICHTMAN

Electoral College

In many ways, the history of the Electoral College reflects the evolution of a persistent problem in American politics, one summarized in political scientist Robert Dahl's succinct question "Who governs?" The answers Americans have given have changed throughout the nation's history. The framers of the Constitution believed the college would balance tensions among the various states and protect the authority of the executive from the influence of Congress and the population at large. More recently, however, debates over the college have centered upon whether it performs these functions too well, and, in so doing, hampers democratic values increasingly important to Americans.

Origins

Many of the delegates to the Constitutional Convention in 1787 initially were convinced that the president should be chosen by majority vote of Congress or the state legislatures. Both these options steadily lost popularity as it became clear the Convention did not want to make the presidency beholden to the legislature or to the states. However, many delegates also found distasteful the most viable alternative—direct election by the populace—due to fears that the public would not be able to make an intelligent choice and hence would simply splinter among various regional favorite-son candidates.

On August 31, 1787, toward the end of its third month, the convention created the Committee on Postponed Matters, or the "Committee of Eleven," to solve such problems. Chaired by David Brearley of New Jersey and including Virginia's James Madison, within four days of its organization, the committee proposed that electors, equal in number to each state's congressional delegation and selected in a manner determined by the state legislatures, should choose the president. These electors would each choose two candidates; when Congress tabulated the votes, the candidate with the "greatest Number of Votes" would become president and the runner-up vice president. In the case of a tie, the House of Representatives would choose the president and the Senate the vice president. This plan proved acceptable to the convention because it was a compromise on many of the points that had rendered earlier proposals unworkable—it insulated the president from the various legislatures but preserved the process from undue popular influence. Similarly, in basing its numbers on the bicameral Congress, the college moderated the overwhelming influence of the populous states. Though the phrase "Electoral College" was not included in the Constitution, the plan was encoded in Article II, section I.

The College and the States: Solving Problems

Over the first few presidential elections, states experimented with various means of choosing their electors. In the first presidential election, for example, 11 states participated. Four held popular elections to select electors; in five the legislature made the decision. The remaining two combined these methods; the legislature chose individuals from a field selected by general election.

Despite this carefully constructed compromise, the practicalities of electoral politics gradually overtook the college's system. Most influential was the surprisingly quick emergence of political parties that coalesced around individual candidates. By 1800, the Democratic-Republican Party and its rival Federalist Party had gained control of many state governments and began to manipulate local methods for selecting electors; the Federalist parties of Massachusetts and New Hampshire, for example, were in command of those states' legislatures and reserved to those organizations the right to select electors. In the next presidential election, the legislature, doubting its ability to secure the states' electors for the Federalists, switched to a system in which each congressional district selected one elector, only to revert back to legislative control in 1808. Similarly, in Virginia the Democratic-Republican Party shifted the authority to a winner-take-all general election, where favorite-son candidate Thomas Jefferson was assured to gain a majority and sweep the state's electoral votes. Thus, despite the original expectation that independent electors would gather and deliberate over the most qualified candidate, they were increasingly selected to represent their parties and to cast their votes accordingly.

The 1800 election also revealed perhaps the greatest flaw in the Electoral College as established by the Constitution. The Democratic-Republican electors chosen in 1800 obediently voted for their party's choice for president, Jefferson, and vice president, New York's Aaron Burr. However, the convention had not anticipated such party-line voting, and the tabulation of the electors' votes revealed an inadvertent tie. In accordance with the Constitution, the election was thrown to the House, where Federalist representatives strove to deny their archenemy Jefferson the presidency. It took 36 ballots before the Virginian secured his election. As a result, in 1804 the Twelfth Amendment was added to the Constitution, providing that electors should cast separate ballots for the president and vice president. Despite several recurrences of such crises in the system, only one other constitutional reform of the college has been adopted; in 1961, under pressure from citizens complaining of disenfranchisement, the Twenty-Third Amendment was added to the Constitution; it granted the District of Columbia three electoral votes.

As the nineteenth century progressed, such manipulations as occurred in Massachusetts and New Hampshire gradually faded in favor of assigning electors to the winner of the general election. The combination of new styles of mass politics that presidential contenders like Andrew Jackson embodied and the allure that the winner-take-all system held for confident parties meant that by 1836 South Carolina was the only state in the Union that clung to legislative choice against popular election, and even that state capitulated after the Civil War. Despite the occasional crisis in which states have resorted to legislative choice—such as Massachusetts in 1848, when a powerful bid by the Free Soil Party meant that no party gained a majority of the popular vote, or Florida in 2000, when the legislature selected a slate of electors in case the heated contest over the disputed popular vote was not resolved—this system has remained ever since.

The Problem of the Popular Vote

This does not mean, however, that it has always worked perfectly. As concerns over regional balance and the fitness of the electorate have receded, debate has centered on the awkwardness of the combination of popular ballots and state selection. For example, the winner-take-all system ensures that the minority in each state is disenfranchised when the electors cast their votes. Indeed, despite the universal desire to empower the general electorate, it remains quite possible for the president to be chosen by a minority of the popular vote. In the three-way election of 1912, for example, Democrat Woodrow Wilson won more than 80 percent of the electoral vote despite winning only a plurality of the popular vote— barely 41 percent. Similarly, Democrat Bill Clinton was elected in 1992 when his 43 percent of the popular vote—a plurality—translated into nearly 70 percent in the Electoral College. Though neither of these elections was in danger of being thrown to the House of Representatives, a similar three-way election in 1968 raised such fears; indeed, the independent candidate George Wallace hoped to gain enough electoral votes to force such an event and gain concessions from either Republican Richard Nixon or Democrat Hubert Humphrey. Nixon, however, gained a close majority in the Electoral College.

Despite earning the appellation "minority president" from their weak showing in the popular election, Nixon, Wilson, and Clinton did at least receive pluralities. Several other times, the uneven correlation between the popular vote and the Electoral College resulted in the loser of the former attaining the presidency. In 1888, Republican Benjamin Harrison defeated the incumbent Democrat Grover Cleveland in the Electoral College despite losing the popular vote; Cleveland's graciousness, however, assured a smooth transition of power. The other such elections—1824, 1876, and 2000—were met with discontent and protest from the losing party. Indeed, though correct constitutional procedure was followed in each case, all three elections were tainted with accusations of corruption and manipulation, allegations exacerbated and legitimated by each eventual president's failure to win the majority of the popular vote.

In 1824 the presidential election was a contest among several Democratic candidates, and a situation the Convention had hoped to avert occurred: the nation split along regional lines. Andrew Jackson gained a plurality of the popular and electoral vote, primarily in the South and middle Atlantic. Trailing in both totals was John Quincy Adams, whose base was in New England. The other candidates, Henry Clay and William Crawford, won only three and two states, respectively (though both also won individual electoral votes from states that divided their totals). Despite his plurality, Jackson was unable to gain a majority of the electoral vote, and the election was again, as in 1800, thrown to the House of Representatives. There, Clay threw his support to Adams, who was selected. Despite the fact that correct procedure was followed, Jackson denounced Adams and Clay for thwarting the will of the people and subsequently swept Adams out of office in 1828.

In 1876 Democrat Samuel Tilden led Republican Rutherford B. Hayes by more than a quarter million popular votes. However, the results in four states, Oregon and the southern states of Florida, South Carolina, and Louisiana—all three of which were expected to easily go for Tilden—were disputed. Without the electoral votes of these states, Tilden found himself one vote short of a majority. All four states sent competing slates of electors to the session of Congress that tabulated the votes. In 1865 Congress had adopted the Twenty-Second Joint Rule, which provided that contested electoral votes could be approved by concurrent votes of the House and Senate. However, the rule lapsed in January 1876, leaving Congress with no means to resolve the dispute. In January 1877, therefore, Congress passed the Electoral Commission Law, which established—for only the particular case of the 1876 election—a 15-member commission, consisting of 5 members of the House, 5 of the Senate, and 5 justices of the Supreme Court, which would rule on the 15 disputed electoral votes. Seven seats were held by members of each party; the remaining seat was expected to go to David Davis, an independent justice of the Supreme Court. However, Davis left the commission to take a Senate seat, and his replacement was the Republican justice Joseph Bradley. Unsurprisingly, the commission awarded each disputed vote to Hayes, 8 to 7. Hayes thus edged Tilden in the college, 185 to 184. Though Democrats threatened to filibuster the joint session of Congress called to certify the new electoral vote, they agreed to let the session continue when Hayes agreed to end Reconstruction and withdraw federal troops from the South. The Hayes-Tilden crisis resulted in the 1887 Electoral Count Act, which gave each state authority to determine the legality of its electoral vote but also provided that a concurrent majority of both houses of Congress could reject disputed votes.

The act was invoked to resolve such a dispute in 1969 and again in the first two presidential elections of the twenty-first century. The 2000 election mirrored the Hayes-Tilden crisis; as in 1876, the Democratic candidate, Al Gore, held a clear edge in the popular vote, leading Republican George W. Bush by half a million votes. However, the balance in the Electoral College was close enough that the 25 votes of Florida would decide the election. Initial returns in that state favored Bush by the slimmest of margins but recounts narrowed the gap to within a thousand. Finally, however, the Supreme Court affirmed Bush's appeal to stop the recounts; the Republican was awarded a 537-vote victory in the state and consequently a majority in the Electoral College. Democrats in the House of Representatives attempted to invoke the 1887 law to disqualify Florida's slate of electors but failed to gain the necessary support in the Senate to put the matter to a vote. Bush's successful 2004 reelection campaign against Democrat John Kerry also sparked discontent, and concerns about the balloting in Ohio prompted House Democrats to again invoke the law. This time, though, they were able to gain enough Senate support to force a concurrent vote; it affirmed Ohio's Republican slate of electors by a large margin.

These controversies have highlighted growing discontent with the intent and function of the Electoral College, and the reasoning behind the Constitutional Convention's adoption of the institution has been increasingly marshaled against it. While the founders hoped that electors would select the president based on reasoned discussion, 24 states now have laws to punish "faithless electors" who defy the results of their states' popular election and vote for another candidate, as has occurred eight times since World War II. While the founders hoped the Electoral College would create a presidency relatively independent of public opinion, it has come under fire since Andrew Jackson's time for doing exactly that.

Possible Solutions

Multiple measures have been proposed to more closely align the Electoral College with the popular vote. One of the more commonly mentioned solutions is proportional representation; that is, rather than the winner of the presidential election in each state taking all that state's electoral votes, the state would distribute those votes in proportion to the election results. Such a reform would almost certainly enhance the chances of third parties to gain electoral votes. However, since the Constitution requires a majority of the Electoral College for victory, this solution would most likely throw many more presidential elections to the House of Representatives. For instance, under this system the elections of 1912, 1968, and 1992 would all have been decided by the

House. Thus, proportional representation would undo two of the Framers' wishes, tying the presidency not only closer to the general public but perhaps unintentionally to Congress as well. The Colorado electorate rejected a state constitutional amendment for proportional representation in 2004.

A similar policy is often referred to as the "Maine-Nebraska rule," after the two states that have adopted it: Maine in 1972 and Nebraska in 1996. It is reminiscent of the district policy that states such as Virginia and Massachusetts implemented in the early years of the republic. Maine and Nebraska allot one electoral vote to the winner of each congressional district, and assign the final two (corresponding to each state's two senators) to the overall winner of the state's popular vote. While this technique seems to limit the potential chaos of the proportional method, it does not actually solve the problem: if every state in the Union adopted the Maine-Nebraska rule, it would still be possible for a presidential candidate to lose the election despite winning the popular vote.

A third state-based reform of the Electoral College system gained significant support in April 2007, when the Maryland legislature passed a law calling on the rest of the states to agree to assign their electors to whichever presidential candidate wins the popular vote. This would effectively circumvent the Electoral College, while retaining the elector and Congress's tabulation of the vote as a symbolic, constitutional formality.

Finally, many commentators have called for a constitutional amendment simply eliminating the Electoral College entirely, arguing that, in addition to the possibility of presidential victors who have lost the popular vote, the electoral system artificially inflates the value of votes in small states (due to the constitutionally mandated minimum of three votes to every state), discourages minority parties, and encourages candidates to ignore states they believe they cannot win. However, the college is not universally unpopular; its supporters counter that the system maintains political stability and forces candidates to expend effort on states with small populations that they might otherwise bypass. Additionally, supporters of the Electoral College maintain that it is an important connection to the federal system envisioned by the framers of the Constitution.

Some observers have noted that disputes over the college tend to follow fault lines already existing in American politics. Gore's loss in the 2000 election inspired many Democrats to look at the college with a critical perspective; additionally, more rural states, small in population, that oppose losing the influence the Electoral College gives them tend to support Republican candidates. Heavily urban states with more concentrated populations tend to vote Democratic. Thus, the regional differences the Convention hoped to moderate through the Electoral College have been effectively translated into partisan differences that the college exacerbates. However, the constitutional barriers to removing the college likely ensure it will remain on the American political landscape for the foreseeable future.

See also elections and electoral eras; voting.

FURTHER READING

McCormick, Richard. *The Presidential Game: The Origins of American Presidential Politics.* New York: Oxford University Press, 1982.

Schlesinger, Arthur, Jr. *The History of American Presidential Elections, 1789–1968.* New York: Chelsea House, 1971.

Schumaker, Paul D., and Burdett A. Loomis, eds. *Choosing a President: The Electoral College and Beyond.* Washington, DC: CQ Press, 2002.

MATTHEW BOWMAN

energy and politics

For most of its history, the United States has depended on its own abundant supply of energy resources. If there is a common political theme in the history of American energy and politics, it is the desire to maximize domestic production and to stabilize competition between private firms. Although these imperatives dominated the energy policies of the nineteenth and twentieth centuries, events in the 1970s caused a dramatic reversal of direction. This article traces the development of public policies in the coal and oil industries, since these commodities supplied the bulk of American energy throughout the nation's history and were the primary target of state and federal policy makers. This necessarily excludes important developments in the political history of utilities, electrification, and the development of nuclear power, but it allows for a long-range perspective on American energy policy.

Policy Making and the Rise of Coal

At the time of the American Revolution, the predominant forms of energy came from human or animal power and firewood. Coal was in limited use, but American policy makers viewed the domestic coal trade as vital to the young nation's future. To encourage the growth of a coal industry the federal government moved to protect American colliers from foreign competition. The original tariff on coal imports in 1789 was 2 cents per bushel. It increased gradually over the years, until in 1812 it reached 10 cents a bushel, or about 15 percent of the wholesale price of British coal. After the War of 1812, tariff rates on coal dropped in 1816 to 5 cents a bushel, which ranged between 10 and 25 percent of the price of foreign coal in New York, and remained at about that range until 1842. British imports bounced back after 1815, but they never again exceeded more than 10 percent of American production. Tariff levels did not completely push British coal out of American markets, but they did severely restrict its ability to compete with the domestic product. By the postbellum decades, the federal government had eliminated the tariff on anthracite, and levels on bituminous coal bottomed out at 40 cents a ton in 1895. Domestic production dominated American coal markets, and the United States became a net exporter of coal in the 1870s.

Under the umbrella of federal protection, state governments encouraged the rapid development of coal mining in the antebellum period. First, in the 1830s, Pennsylvania's legislature exempted anthracite coal from taxation and promoted its use in the iron industry through a liberal corporate chartering law. As anthracite use increased, Pennsylvania officials refused to grant exclusive carrying or vending rights to any company engaged in transporting anthracite to urban markets. As a result, a diverse group of canals and railroads served Pennsylvania's relatively compact anthracite fields. Competition between the Schuylkill Navigation Company's all-water route and the Lehigh Coal and Navigation Company's rail and water connections to Philadelphia, for example, ensured that anthracite prices remained low. To expedite the exploitation of new coalfields, many states commissioned geological surveys. North Carolina employed a state geologist to catalog the state's mineral resources in 1823; by 1837, 14 states had followed suit. The annual reports and final compilation of the state geological surveys served to underwrite the cost of finding viable coal seams and marking valuable mineral deposits for entrepreneurs.

In some cases, such as Pennsylvania and Illinois, the state geologist specifically targeted coalfields as the primary emphasis of the survey. In others, a more general assessment of mineral resources occurred. Although state geologists would find, label, and survey the coalfields, it was up to private firms to mine, carry, and sell the coal to domestic and industrial consumers. Pennsylvania's leadership in this field was apparent, as that state boosted coal production levels to nearly 6.5 million tons, or about three-fourths of U.S. production, by 1850.

The period following the Civil War saw a heightened role for railroads in American energy policy. Railroad companies appealed to state legislatures for the right to buy or lease coal lands—a combination of mining and carrying privileges that many antebellum policy makers were unwilling to tolerate. In Pennsylvania an 1869 law authorized railroad and canal companies to purchase the stocks and bonds of mining firms. By the 1870s the Philadelphia and Reading Railroad embarked on an ambitious plan to purchase enough anthracite coal lands to set prices. The Philadelphia and Reading failed in its attempt to monopolize anthracite, but it and other regional railroads became increasingly powerful in the late nineteenth century. The nation's bituminous fields were too large for any significant concentration of power, but in the more compact anthracite fields, a distinct combination of large mining and carrying companies formed during the 1880s to keep prices high even as they forced small-scale colliers to sell their coal at rock-bottom prices. State-level attempts to impose rates on railroads, as well as early attempts by federal authorities to regulate the coal trade under the auspices of the Interstate Commerce Commission (1887) or the Sherman Anti-Trust Act (1890), fell flat, as policy makers at both state and federal levels remained focused on maintaining high production levels, keeping prices low, and bringing new coalfields into production. For example, Congress created the United States Geological Survey in 1879, an agency charged with the topographic and geological mapping of the entire nation. This institution combined several surveys that had been created for military and scientific purposes in order to catalog valuable mineral resources of the nation just as the antebellum surveys did for their respective states.

The relations between labor and capital in energy production also became a concern for policy makers by the late nineteenth century. Prior to the Civil War, coal mining was done on a relatively small scale. Individual proprietorships could survive with a few skilled miners who exerted total control over the hiring of laborers, the construction of the shafts and tunnels, and the cutting and hauling of the coal from the mine. Experienced miners thus acted as independent contractors throughout most of the nineteenth century. The corporate reorganization of coalfields created new pressures on firms; now they needed to increase production and cut costs at every turn. Many mine operators sought to use the autonomy of miners for their own benefit by pressing tonnage rates down, docking miners for sending up coal with too many "impurities," and paying miners in scrip rather than cash. Although the transformation of work at the coal seam itself with the introduction of machine cutters would not occur until the 1890s, labor relations aboveground changed rapidly during and after the Civil War. Small-scale unions formed in individual coalfields and struck, with varying effectiveness, for higher wages. Since the largest variable cost in coal mining is in labor, colliers insisted on the ability to control wages and fought to keep unions from organizing in American coalfields. In 1890, however, a national trade union, the United Mine Workers of America (UMWA), formed in Columbus, Ohio. For the next half century, the UMWA struggled to win collective bargaining rights in the nation's geographically diverse and decentralized coal trade.

Federal authorities were drawn into the regulation of the nation's coal trade during the early twentieth century. In the anthracite fields of Pennsylvania, for example, labor disputes and an attempt by a handful of railroad operators to manipulate prices provoked federal action. When miners in the anthracite fields sought the aid of the UMWA to secure an eight-hour day, decent wages, and safe working conditions, managers of coal companies responded with intimidation, lockouts, and violence. The long and crippling strike of 1902, which threatened energy supplies across the eastern seaboard by shutting down anthracite production, drew President Theodore Roosevelt into the fray. By declaring that he would negotiate a "square deal" between labor and management, Roosevelt set a precedent for federal intervention. A square deal, however, did not create a federal mandate for collective bargaining rights for coal miners; nevertheless, it did offer some modicum of governmental oversight. In 1908 the Justice Department, under the authority of the Interstate Commerce Commission (ICC), filed a major lawsuit against anthracite railroads accused of manipulating prices and intimidating independent colliers. Results were mixed; the Supreme Court upheld the "commodities clause" of the ICC, which banned the direct ownership of coal mines by railroads, but informal relationships between large coal companies and railroads continued to dominate the region. Finally, the U.S. Bureau of Mines, created in 1910, enforced safety regulations on reluctant coal operators. Mine safety remained a concern for the industry, but miners in this period did at least see a modest increase in protection from hazardous working conditions. In all these cases, federal intervention in the nation's coal trade preserved the nineteenth-century focus on high levels of production, even as new legislation and policy decisions produced minor victories for small colliers and mine workers.

The Rise of Federal Policy Making and the American Oil Industry

Throughout most of the nineteenth century, the U.S. government's energy policy consisted of tariff protection and the promotion of new coalfields, either actively by creating agencies like the U.S. Geological Survey or passively by refusing to regulate the coal trade. At the advent of the twentieth century, however, federal policy makers found themselves drawn into major conflicts over competition and labor, as well as the rise of oil and natural gas as new sources of energy. The era between 1880 and 1920 truly was the reign of "King Coal": production soared from 80 million tons to 659 million tons, an increase of more than 800 percent, and coal accounted for 70 percent of the nation's energy consumption. Crude oil production increased seventeenfold, from 26 million barrels in 1880 to 443 million in 1920; yet American refineries still focused on illumination and lubrication products, rather than fuel, throughout the late nineteenth and early twentieth centuries. The discovery of massive reserves in the Spindletop oil field in southeastern Texas, the Mid-Continent Field of Kansas and Oklahoma, and southern California during the decade before World War I all pointed toward American oil's bright future as a source of energy.

Natural gas also became a significant energy source in the early twentieth century. Producers pumped 812 billion cubic feet by 1920, an increase from the 128 billion cubic feet they secured in 1900. As nationwide reserves came into production, interstate railroads and pipelines made state-level oversight difficult, and the bulk of energy policy shifted to the federal level throughout the twentieth century. The rise of oil and gas, moreover, created more challenges for policy makers and forced them

A well at Spindletop field in Beaumont, Texas, strikes oil in January 1901. (Texas Energy Museum, Beaumont, Texas)

the vagaries of the well-organized anthracite and vast decentralized bituminous coal industries; attempts to fix prices failed, and a coal shortage crippled the American economy in the winter of 1917–18. To boost production levels, the USFA encouraged the opening of new mines and restricted coal consumption among non-war-related industries and households. Wartime demand for petroleum boosted production but also created headaches for the USFA's Oil Division. Petroleum shortages during the war were less debilitating, however. The price stability caused by the artificially high demand provoked much needed conservation and storage reforms among private petroleum producers and put new oil fields into production. Some USFA officials advocated a continuation of the command-and-control approach to energy policy after the war ended in November 1918. Pre-war energy markets had faced debilitating gluts and shortages, coupled with unstable prices. Since energy reserves in the United States were still abundant, they argued, public oversight might help stabilize both production and consumption of vital commodities like coal, oil, and natural gas.

Despite calls for a continued presence of federal authority, Congress cut appropriations for the USFA at the war's end. By 1919 the coal trade was experiencing serious problems. Wartime demand had boosted the number of American coal mines from 6,939 in 1917 to 8,994 in 1919. When new orders for coal waned, mine operators reduced wages and laid off miners at the same time that millions of American soldiers returned in search of work. A series of strikes rocked the bituminous and anthracite industries in the 1920s as the UMWA continued its efforts to organize the nation's miners, now 615,000 strong. By 1932 the number of miners dropped to less than 400,000 and the American coal industry was in disarray. The creation of the National Industrial Recovery Act (NIRA) the following year set up price codes for coal and helped stanch the bleeding. The UMWA also benefited from Section 7(a) of the NIRA, which provided for collective bargaining. By 1935 federal support for unionization swelled the ranks of the UMWA to more than half a million. But when the Supreme Court declared the NIRA unconstitutional in that same year, the short-lived stability faded. Federal support for collective bargaining continued, but the American coal trade returned to its old familiar pattern of decentralized, uncoordinated production, which kept prices relatively low for consumers but profit margins razor-thin for mine operators. Labor relations became even more heated, as the UMWA, under the leadership of its forceful president

to regulate production, competition, and price setting in unprecedented ways.

The specific crises brought by World War I created a new kind of regulatory regime and signaled the growing importance of oil in the nation's energy economy. In response to the anticipated coal shortage triggered by the American declaration of war in 1917, the Federal Trade Commission explored the possibility of federal controls over prices and distribution. Although initial attempts to coordinate the nation's coal trade failed when the Council for National Defense's Committee on Coal Production folded in the summer of 1917, Congress granted President Woodrow Wilson broad authority over energy production and consumption, including the right to set the price of coal. This resulted in the creation of the United States Fuel Administration, a wartime agency designed to coordinate coal, petroleum, and railroad operations in both military and civilian sectors of the economy. Its director, Harry Garfield, was unfamiliar with

John L. Lewis, challenged attempts to cut wage rates at every turn.

Oil and gas producers also suffered during the Great Depression, even as production levels reached all-time highs of nearly a billion barrels of crude petroleum in 1935. In Texas, state regulation, under the aegis of the Texas Railroad Commission, helped maintain some price stability by limiting production. Oil producers also had price and production codes under the NIRA, but without the labor conflicts of their counterparts in coal, no controversy over collective bargaining hit the industry. With the termination of the NIRA, no broad regulatory agency appeared in the petroleum industry. Instead, a consortium of six major oil-producing states formed to regulate production and stabilize the industry. The 1935 Interstate Compact to Conserve Oil and Gas joined Colorado, Kansas, Illinois, New Mexico, Oklahoma, and Texas together to replicate the state-level programs of the Texas Railroad Commission in a national setting. Natural gas came under federal control with the passage of the Natural Gas Act of 1938, which regulated interstate trade in gas, including the nation's growing network of pipelines for shipping natural gas. In oil and gas the control of interstate traffic remained an essential, and ultimately effective, way to ensure price stability without radically expanding government oversight.

By the advent of World War II, coal had declined to about 50 percent of the nation's energy consumption, even though reserves of coal showed little sign of depletion. When the UMWA's 400,000 coal miners struck in 1943, federal officials seized some mines and reopened them under government control. Coal remained important, but the increasing popularity of automobiles, oil for heating, and electric motors in industry made petroleum the dominant element of the American fuel economy. The Petroleum Administration for War, under the leadership of Secretary of Interior Harold Ickes, coordinated the flow of oil for civilian and military uses. Some rationing occurred to avoid costly shortages, but most significant for long-term growth were the thousands of miles of new pipelines to connect the oil fields of the Southwest to the rest of the nation. Following the war, the Oil and Gas Division of the Department of the Interior was established to stabilize the oil industry through price data sharing, pipeline policies, and consulting trade organizations such as the National Petroleum Council. The World War II years also introduced nuclear power into the nation's energy future, although the use of nuclear power was not widespread immediately after the war.

As the consumption of energy skyrocketed in the post–World War II decades, oil continued to grow in importance. Most significant for energy policy, the United States became a net importer of oil in 1948. As the booming postwar economy grew, American producers attempted to stem the flow of foreign oil by persuading President Dwight D. Eisenhower to set up mandatory oil import quotas. A year later a cartel of major oil-producing nations such as Saudi Arabia, Iraq, Iran, Kuwait, and Venezuela formed the Organization of Petroleum Exporting Countries (OPEC). OPEC had little impact on American energy markets, and the extent to which the United States depended upon foreign oil remained untested, until the Arab-Israeli conflict of 1973 triggered an embargo by Arab nations on exports to the United States. By early 1974 the price of oil had nearly quadrupled, triggering the first "oil shock" in the American economy. The embargo ended that same year, but throughout the 1970s American dependence on Middle Eastern oil became a political issue, coming to a head with the overthrow of the pro-American regime in Iran in 1979. From that point on, energy policies became intertwined with foreign policy, particularly in the Middle East.

The 1970s brought a major reversal in American energy policy, the repercussions of which are still shaking out today. Nuclear power, once considered a major source of energy for the future, became politically toxic after the 1979 partial meltdown of a reactor core at the Three Mile Island facility in Pennsylvania. The oil shocks of that decade, moreover, suggested that traditional policies directed at maximizing domestic production of energy sources were no longer adequate for the United States. In response to this new challenge, Congress passed the National Energy Act in 1978, which aimed to reduce gasoline consumption by 10 percent, cut imports to make up only one-eighth of American consumption, and increase the use of domestic coal—about one-third of American energy consumption in the early 1970s—to take advantage of abundant reserves. President Jimmy Carter also created the Department of Energy (DOE) in 1978 and promoted the further exploration of alternative energy sources such as solar, wind, and wave power. Although the DOE's emphasis on traditional versus alternative energy sources seemed to wax and wane with changes in presidential administrations, alternatives to the well-established fossil fuel sources of energy have demanded the attention of policy makers in Washington. In this regard, energy policy in the twenty-first century will take a different course from the first two centuries of the nation's history.

See also business and politics; environmental issues and politics; transportation and politics.

FURTHER READING

Adams, Sean Patrick. *Old Dominion, Industrial Commonwealth: Coal, Politics, and Economy in Antebellum America.* Baltimore, MD: Johns Hopkins University Press, 2004.

Childs, William. *The Texas Railroad Commission: Understanding Regulation in America to the Mid-Twentieth Century.* College Station: Texas A&M Press, 2005.

Clark, John. *Energy and the Federal Government: Fossil Fuel Policies, 1900–1946.* Urbana: University of Illinois Press, 1987.

Melosi, Martin. *Coping with Abundance: Energy and Environment in Industrial America.* Philadelphia: Temple University Press, 1985.

Nye, David. *Consuming Power: A Social History of American Energies.* Cambridge, MA: MIT Press, 1997.

Painter, David. *Oil and the American Century: The Political Economy of US Foreign Oil Policy, 1941–1954.* Baltimore, MD: Johns Hopkins University Press, 1986.

Pratt, Joseph A. "The Petroleum Industry in Transition: Anti-Trust and the Decline of Monopoly Control in Oil." *Journal of Economic History* 40 (December 1980), 815–37.

Vietor, Richard. *Energy Policy in America since 1945.* New York: Cambridge University Press, 1984.

SEAN ADAMS

environmental issues and politics

Today, the phrase "environmental issues and politics" invariably refers to debates about problems such as pollution, species extinction, and global warming. But the United States had environmental policies long before the rise of the modern environmental movement. Indeed, the modern movement is partly a rejection of earlier American ideas about government and nature.

From the founding of the nation, government at all levels encouraged the development of land. To promote the real-estate market, New York City created a street grid in 1807. States built canals—"artificial rivers"—to facilitate commerce. Beginning in 1862, the federal government gave land to settlers willing to improve the landscape by establishing farms. In the 1930s, the federal government sought to promote economic development in the South and the West by constructing vast systems of dams. In many ways, state and federal policy has encouraged exploitation of natural resources, from timber to oil. The federal government also has helped individuals and businesses to conquer nature: federal agencies have predicted the weather, controlled wildfires, protected cattle and sheep from predators, and kept floodwaters at bay.

The first challenges to the nation's pro-development spirit came in the decades before the Civil War. A small group of artists and writers began to celebrate the undeveloped countryside as a romantic escape from civilization and a sublime source of national pride. In some states, farmers began to complain about dwindling stocks of fish. Though a few of the fish defenders were concerned about pollution, most argued that the principal threats to fisheries were dams built to power mills. Residents of a few cities also took legal action to rid their neighborhoods of manufacturing smoke and stenches.

The Formative Period

The antebellum questioning of development was limited to a tiny minority. In the period from 1865 to 1915, however, many more Americans sought government action to address what we now call environmental problems. They organized to stop pollution, conserve natural resources, and preserve wild places and wild creatures. Many urban Americans also sought to renew their relationship with nature.

The activism of those formative years was a response to the profound environmental changes brought by unprecedented urbanization, industrialization, and immigration. Hundreds of towns became congested, polluted industrial cities. The vast forests of the Great Lakes region were cut down. Millions of acres of grassland were transformed into farms and ranches. Many creatures that once were important parts of the landscape were driven to the edge of extinction or beyond.

To many Americans, the industrial city seemed to be a great experiment, a new form of civilization that promised much but that might prove unsustainable. Many of the doubts were environmental. The urban environment was far less healthy than the rural or small-town landscape. Would cities ever become places where births exceeded deaths? Many observers also feared the moral and social effects of separating so many millions from contact with nature.

Without remedial action, the rapid transformation of the countryside also portended harm as well as good. Would the United States continue to have the resources necessary to grow richer and more powerful and to take its ordained place on the world stage? The symbolic closing of the frontier in 1890 led many Americans to conclude that the nation no longer could take superabundance for granted.

Municipal governments felt the greatest pressure to assume new responsibilities. In 1865 most cities had no sanitary infrastructure. The explosive concentration of people and industrial activity threatened to turn urban areas into environmental hellholes. The leaders of many cities responded by greatly expanding the power of municipal government. They created boards of health. They also built sewer systems, took responsibility for collecting garbage and cleaning streets, established parks, protected sources of drinking water, and regulated "the smoke nuisance."

The urban environmental reforms of the Gilded Age and Progressive Era had mixed consequences. The new sanitary infrastructure greatly reduced mortality from epidemic diseases, especially cholera and typhoid. In most cities, the parks became valuable oases. But the antismoke regulations did little to improve air quality. Though most cities were able to improve their drinking water, many forms of water pollution continued unabated, and some grew worse: most cities dumped untreated sewage into nearby rivers and harbors.

At the federal level, the concern about the nation's environmental future led to a dramatic change in land policy. After decades of trying to privatize the public domain, the government decided that millions of acres never would be sold or given away. Those lands instead were to be national forests, parks, and wildlife refuges. To manage the forest reserves, the government established a new kind of bureaucracy, run by scientifically trained experts. The parks initially were the responsibility of the U.S. Army, but the government established the National Park Service in 1916, and the agency soon became a powerful promoter of outdoor recreation.

State governments also responded to new environmental demands. Many established boards of public health, fish-and-game departments, and forest commissions. At a time when the federal government had limited capacity, states also took the initiative in studying environmental problems. Massachusetts undertook the first systematic surveys of river pollution in the 1870s. In the 1910s, Illinois pioneered the study of environmental

hazards in the workplace, and these investigations led to a deeper understanding of the health effects of air pollution.

Many of the new laws and agencies met resistance. In debates about pollution, business leaders often argued that environmental degradation was the price of progress. Immigrants sometimes resisted sanitary and conservation regulations. In national parks and forests, officials were challenged by people who no longer could use those areas for subsistence.

The support for environmental initiatives in the Gilded Age and Progressive Era came largely from the well-to-do. Many professional men supported conservation, preservation, and antipollution efforts. To progressives, social and environmental reform went hand-in-hand. The reform cause always had some backing from the business community. In sheer numbers, however, the greatest support came from middle- and upper-class women. Because so many environmental issues involved the traditionally feminine concerns of beauty, health, and the well-being of future generations, women often argued that they were especially equipped to address environmental problems. That argument became a justification for suffrage as well as a rationale for professional careers.

New Deal Conservation

Until recently, scholars paid little attention to environmental issues and politics from the end of the Progressive Era until the first stirrings of the modern environmental movement in the 1950s. But a number of new works make clear that the age of Franklin D. Roosevelt deserves more attention from environmental historians. Though grassroots activism was relatively limited, government and university research on environmental problems in the interwar period provided a foundation for future reform efforts. Federal environmental policy also became much more ambitious in the New Deal years.

Among the many agencies established by New Dealers, several had conservation missions, including the Soil Conservation Service, the Tennessee Valley Authority, and the Civilian Conservation Corps. The new agencies were partly a response to natural disasters. In the 1930s, dust storms devastated the Great Plains, while floods wreaked havoc on much of the eastern third of the continent. In addition to providing relief, the government undertook to prevent a recurrence of such disasters. That preventive effort depended on a new recognition that dust storms and floods were not entirely acts of nature:

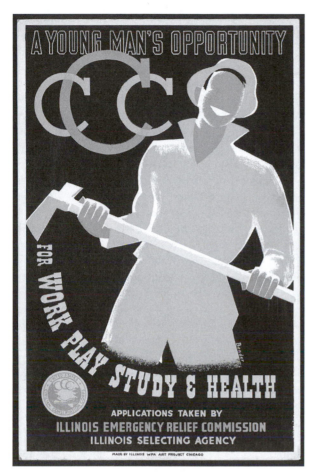

The Illinois WPA Art Project created this poster to advertise the U.S. Civilian Conservation Corps in 1941. (Library of Congress)

The corps reclaimed denuded landscapes by planting trees, worked with farmers to protect soil from erosion, and built outdoor-recreation facilities, including parks, trails, and roads, to attract visitors.

In contrast to the Progressive Era, when the federal government sought to influence private decision making by demonstrating "wise use" of resources in public forest reserves, many of the New Deal conservation initiatives sought to have a direct impact on the management of privately owned land. The Soil Conservation Service encouraged the formation of thousands of county conservation districts and provided financial and technical assistance to millions of farmers. For the first time, the New Dealers sought a role for the government in land-use planning. The Taylor Grazing Act of 1934 greatly strengthened the ability of federal officials to control the way ranchers used millions of acres of the public domain. Though a New Deal effort to plan development on the Great Plains failed, the TVA had a far-reaching impact on the South.

New Dealers also spread the conservation gospel more than any previous adminstration. Government photographs of the dust bowl and the rural South became iconic images. Two government-sponsored films—*The Plow That Broke the Plains* and *The River*—publicized the New Deal argument about the social causes of the period's great natural disasters. The 3 million men who joined the CCC were instructed in conservation principles. Almost all the enrollees came from cities, and the government hoped that CCC work would strengthen their bodies and persuade them that contact with nature had many benefits. Historians now credit the CCC with broadening the constituency for environmental protection.

In other ways, however, New Deal policy left a mixed legacy. Though officials hoped to revitalize rural America, many New Deal measures ultimately encouraged large enterprises rather than small farms. The soil conservation effort checked some of the worst agricultural practices, but few farmers truly accepted a new land ethic. In the decades after World War II, environmentalists often argued that New Deal conservation put economic development ahead of ecological balance.

The Environmental Age

The modern environmental movement became a major political and social force in the 1960s. The great symbol of the movement's emergence was the inaugural Earth Day in 1970, when approximately 20 million Americans

in both cases, federal policy makers concluded, human action had turned climatic extremes into economic and social tragedies.

The new conservation agencies were not conceived together, yet all became part of the New Deal attempt to end the Depression. Like the conservationists of the Progressive Era, the New Dealers believed that conservation would ensure future prosperity. But their joining of environmental and economic goals was more explicit. The Tennessee Valley Authority (TVA) was a development agency for the nation's most destitute region. By controlling the South's rampaging rivers, the TVA would stimulate industry and improve rural life. The Civilian Conservation Corps (CCC) put 3 million men to work on conservation and economic development projects:

gathered in thousands of communities to seek action in addressing "the environmental crisis." It was the biggest demonstration in U.S. history.

Three broad developments explain the rise of environmentalism after World War II. First, the unprecedented affluence of the postwar years encouraged millions of Americans to reject the old argument that pollution was the price of economic progress. Instead, they argued that the citizens of a rich nation should be able to enjoy a healthy and beautiful environment. Second, the development of atomic energy, the chemical revolution in agriculture, the proliferation of synthetic materials, and the increased scale of power-generation and resource-extraction technology created new environmental hazards. From atomic fallout to suburban sprawl, new threats provoked grassroots and expert protest. Third, the insights of ecology gave countless citizens a new appreciation of the risks of transforming nature. Rachel Carson's 1962 best-seller *Silent Spring*—a powerful critique of chemical pesticides—was especially important in popularizing ecological ideas.

Even before the first Earth Day, government at all levels had begun to respond to new environmental demands. In 1964, for example, the federal government created a system of "wilderness" areas. But the explosion came in the 1970s—the environmental decade. A series of landmark federal laws addressed such critical environmental problems as air and water pollution, endangered species, and toxic waste. The federal government and many states established environmental-protection agencies. A "quiet revolution" gave state and local officials unprecedented power to regulate the use of privately owned land. In many communities, Earth Day led to the creation of ecology centers, some short-lived and some enduring. The early 1970s brought new national environmental organizations with different goals than the conservation and preservation groups established in the late nineteenth century. Colleges and universities established environmental studies programs. The 1970s also saw the first attempts to create environmentally friendly ways of organizing daily life, from recycling to efforts to grow organic food.

The sources of support for the new movement were varied. Many Democrats concluded that a liberal agenda for affluent times needed to include environmental protection. Middle-class women often saw environmental problems as threats to home and family. Young critics of the nation's institutions were especially important in the mobilization for Earth Day. To varying degrees, old

resource-conservation and wilderness-preservation organizations took up new environmental issues in the 1950s and 1960s. Many scientists warned the public about the environmental dangers of new technologies. The environmental cause also depended on the institutional support of many professional groups, from public-health officials to landscape architects. Though still based largely among white, well-to-do residents of cities and suburbs, the modern movement was more demographically diverse than its predecessors.

Despite the popularity of the environmental cause in the early 1970s, the new movement had powerful opposition. The coal industry organized a coalition to try to defeat or weaken the Clean Air Act of 1970, while the National Association of Homebuilders led a successful campaign against national land-use legislation. Though a handful of unions supported antipollution initiatives, many labor leaders sided with management in opposing environmental regulation. The successes of environmentalists also provoked a backlash. In the so-called Sagebrush Rebellion, Western timber and cattle interests challenged federal management of forest and grazing lands. The revolution in state and local regulation of land use soon sparked a "property rights" movement.

The opposition grew stronger after the oil crisis of 1973. Because the production and distribution of oil comes at a steep environmental cost, environmentalists already had begun to lobby for the development of alternative forms of energy, and the crisis might have made that case more compelling. But the sudden scarcity of a critical resource instead strengthened the position of those who saw environmentalism as a terrible drag on the economy. The oil crisis was perhaps the final blow to the postwar boom. Both inflation and unemployment worsened, and the hard times brought a revised version of the old argument about jobs and environmental protection: The nation could have one or the other, but not both.

The backlash against environmentalism helped Ronald Reagan win the presidency in 1980. Reagan promised to remove restrictions on energy development, eliminate thousands of environmental regulations, and privatize millions of acres of the public domain. But he was only partly successful. The resurgence of conservatism forced environmentalists to give up any hope of expanding the federal government's power to protect the environment. The Reagan administration was unable, however, to undo the environmental initiatives of the early 1970s. In the 1980s, the membership of environmental organizations reached new highs.

The rise of concern about global warming in the late 1980s did not change the basic political dynamic. The federal government undertook few important environmental initiatives in the generation after Reagan left office. Though scientists, environmentalists, and many others called with increasing urgency for bold action to limit human-induced climate change, their efforts did not break the political stalemate at the federal level. But the environmental movement was more successful in other arenas. Environmental ways of thinking and acting are more common now in many basic American institutions, from schools to corporations.

See also energy and politics.

FURTHER READING

Andrews, Richard N. L. *Managing Nature, Managing Ourselves: A History of American Environmental Policy.* 2nd ed. New Haven, CT: Yale University Press, 2006.

Fox, Stephen. *The American Conservation Movement: John Muir and His Legacy.* Madison: University of Wisconsin Press, 1985.

Gottlieb, Robert. *Forcing the Spring: The Transformation of the American Environmental Movement.* Revised and updated ed. Washington, DC: Island Press, 2005.

Hays, Samuel P. *Beauty, Health, and Permanence: Environmental Politics in the United States, 1955–1985.* New York: Cambridge University Press, 1987.

Melosi, Martin V. *The Sanitary City: Urban Infrastructure in America from Colonial Times to the Present.* Baltimore, MD: Johns Hopkins University Press, 2000.

Merchant, Carolyn. *The Columbia Guide to American Environmental History.* New York: Columbia University Press, 2002.

Rome, Adam. *The Bulldozer in the Countryside: Suburban Sprawl and the Rise of American Environmentalism.* New York: Cambridge University Press, 2001.

Rome, Adam. " 'Give Earth a Chance': The Environmental Movement and the Sixties." *Journal of American History* 90 (September 2003), 525–54.

Steinberg, Ted. *Down to Earth: Nature's Role in American History.* New York: Oxford University Press, 2002.

Wellock, Thomas R. *Preserving the Nation: The Conservation and Environmental Movements, 1870–2000.* Wheeling, IL: Harlan Davidson, 2007.

ADAM ROME

era of a new republic, 1789–1827

In 1789 the United States was a new republic on multiple levels. The new nation represented the first attempt at a continent-sized republic in the history of the world. Regarding organized competition for national power as both immoral and likely to bring on civil war or foreign intervention, the founders designed the constitutional system to prevent the development of political parties, then lined up unanimously behind the country's most revered public figure, General George Washington, as the first occupant of the powerful new presidency.

On a more substantive level, the question of what kind of nation the United States would become was completely open. Despite their commitment to unity, American political leaders turned out to have very different ideas about the future direction of the country. To northeastern nationalists like Alexander Hamilton, America was "Hercules in his cradle," the raw materials out of which they hoped to rapidly build an urban, oceangoing commercial and military empire like Great Britain. Upper South liberals like Thomas Jefferson hoped for a reformed version of their expansive pastoral society, gradually purged of slavery and gross social inequality, and sought to stave off traditional imperial development. Less enlightened planter-politicians in the more economically robust lower South looked forward to building new plantation districts on rich lands just becoming available and to acquiring the slave population they expected to build and work them. Still other Americans who were relatively new to politics—artisans, immigrants, and town dwellers of the middle and lower ranks—held to the radicalism of 1776 and saw America as the seedbed in which the most democratic and egalitarian political visions of the Enlightenment would flower.

"Monarchical Prettinesses"

All these potential futures were predicated on a distinctive role for the American state and different policies. With Alexander Hamilton ensconced as Washington's treasury secretary and de facto prime minister, his option got the first trial. Proceeding on the assumption that ample revenues and stable credit were the "sinews of power," Hamilton set up a British-style system of public finance, with a privately owned national bank and an interest-bearing national debt. Secretary of State Jefferson and Hamilton's old ally Representative James Madison protested the resulting windfall profits for northern financial interests and bristled at the freedom from constitutional restraint with which Hamilton acted—there was no constitutional provision for a national bank or even for creating corporations. Hamilton's reading of the Constitution's "necessary and proper" clause as allowing any government action that was convenient or conducive to its general purposes horrified Jefferson and Madison as tantamount to no constitutional limitations at all.

Despite his own rapid social climb, Hamilton's expansive approach to government power went along with a dismissive attitude toward popular aspirations for political democracy and social equality. This attitude was quite congenial to the wealthiest men in every region, merchants and planters alike, and these elites formed the backbone of what became the Federalist party. As long as they held power, the Federalists did not consider themselves a party at all, but instead the nation's rightful ruling elite. While admitting that republican government was rooted in popular consent, they favored strict limits on where and when consent was exercised. Political contention "out of doors" (outside the halls of government) should stop once the elections did.

Slaveholding democrats such as Jefferson and Madison stood in a more ambiguous relation to popular democratic aspirations than their northern followers realized, but they shared in the distaste aired in the press for the "monarchical prettinesses" built up around President Washington to strengthen respect for the new government. These included official birthday tributes, a magnificent coach and mansion, and the restriction of access to the presidential person to official "levees" at which guests were forbidden the democratic gesture of shaking the president's hand. This monarchical culture sparked the first stirrings of party organization, when Jefferson and Madison recruited poet Philip Freneau to edit the *National Gazette*, a newspaper that first named and defined the Republican (better known as Democratic-Republican) opposition and became the model for the hundreds of partisan newspapers that were the lifeblood of the early party system.

A Postcolonial Politics

From the inward-looking modern American perspective, it may be surprising that the catalyst for full-scale party conflict actually came from outside the republic's borders. Yet the early United States was also a new nation in the global order of its time. The great political upheavals of Europe during the 1790s elicited tremendous passions in America and reached out inexorably to influence the nation's politics, often through the direct manipulations of the great powers.

As was the case in other former colonies, U.S. politics inevitably revolved partly around debates over the nation's relationship with the mother country. Respecting Great Britain's wealth and power, Hamilton and the Federalists generally favored reestablishing a relatively close economic and political relationship with the British; Democratic-Republicans were less quick to forget their revolutionary views and sought to forge some completely independent status based on universal republicanism and free trade.

Then there was the question of the old alliance with France. Initially, the French Revolution was uncontroversial in the United States, but as the French situation became more radical and bloody it divided the rest of the Atlantic World. Just as Washington began his second term, France was declared a republic, King Louis XVI was executed, and Great Britain joined Austria and Prussia's war against France, setting up a conflict that would involve the young United States repeatedly over the next 20 years. Both sides periodically retaliated against neutral American shipping and sought to push American policy in the desired direction.

Hamilton and the Federalists recoiled from the new French republic. Yet, despite its violence and cultural overreach (rewriting the calendar, closing the churches, etc.), the radicalized French Revolution was wildly popular in many American quarters, especially with younger men and women who had been raised on the French alliance and the rhetoric of the American Revolution. When Edmond Genet, the first diplomatic envoy from the French republic, arrived in America in April 1793, he found enthusiastic crowds and willing recruits for various projects to aid the French war effort, including the commissioning of privateers and the planned "liberation" of Louisiana from Spain.

The political response to Genet was even more impressive. A network of radical debating societies sprang up, headed by the Philadelphia-based Democratic Society of Pennsylvania. The societies were modeled on the French Jacobin clubs and opened political participation to artisans and recent immigrants. While not founded as party organizations, they provided a critical base for opposition politics in Philadelphia and other cities. Genet's antics flamed out quickly, but it was the Democratic-Republican Societies that struck fear into the hearts of the constituted authorities.

President Washington denounced the clubs as "self-created"—extra-constitutional and illegitimate—and blamed them for the western troubles known as the Whiskey Rebellion.

The Democratic-Republican Societies as such withered under Washington's frowns, but the opposition grew even stronger when Chief Justice John Jay brought back a submissive new treaty with Great Britain at a time when the British navy was seizing neutral American ships and impressing American sailors by the score. French minister Pierre Adet bought a copy of the secret document from a senator and saw that it fell into the hands of printer and Democratic Society leader Benjamin Franklin Bache. Bache disseminated it widely, helping to evoke the biggest demonstrations America had seen since the Stamp Act crisis. Once Washington reluctantly signed the treaty, the opposition forces shifted their focus to the House of Representatives, where they tried to deny the appropriation of funds needed to implement certain provisions of the treaty. This effort asserted a right of popular majorities to influence foreign policy that the Framers had tried to block by vesting the "advise and consent" power in the Senate only. This tactic narrowly faltered in the face of a wave of pro-treaty petitions and town meetings skillfully orchestrated and funded by the heavily Federalist merchant community—an early example of successful public lobbying by business interest groups.

By the middle of 1796, the only constitutional alternative the opposition seemed to have left was electing a new president. Washington desperately wanted to retire, but with only the unpopular Vice President John Adams available as a plausible replacement, Hamilton convinced Washington to delay his farewell until a month before the 1796 presidential voting was scheduled to take place. Though hampered by a fragmented electoral system in which only a few states actually allowed popular voting for president, the Republicans mounted a furious campaign that framed the election as a choice between British-style monarchy or American republicanism. These efforts propelled Thomas Jefferson to a second-place finish that, under the party-unfriendly rules of the Electoral College, made him Adams's vice president. Unfortunately, Jefferson's victory in the swing state of Pennsylvania was clouded by published French threats of war if Adams was elected.

The Federalist "Reign of Terror"
Federalists were in a vengeful mood and unexpectedly dominant when the next Congress convened. French diplomatic insults and prospective French attacks on American shipping stoked a desire to deal harshly with the new nation's enemies, within and without. Amid the "black cockade fever" for war against France, the Federalists embarked on a sweeping security program that included what would have been a huge expansion of the armed forces. The enemies within were a wave of radical immigrants, especially journalists, who had been driven from Great Britain as the popular constitutional reform movement there, another side effect of the French Revolution, was ruthlessly suppressed.

The Federalists' means of dealing with the new arrivals and the problem of political opposition more generally were the Alien and Sedition Acts. The Alien Acts made it easier for the president to deport noncitizens he deemed threats, such as the aforementioned refugee radicals, and lengthened the delay for immigrants seeking citizenship. The Sedition Act made criticism of the government a criminal offense, imposing penalties of up to $2,000 and two years in prison on anyone who tried to bring the government or its officers "into contempt or disrepute; or to excite against them the hatred of the good people of the United States." Of course, it was almost impossible to engage in the normal activities of a democratic opposition without trying to bring those in power into some degree of public "contempt or disrepute."

The power grab backfired badly. Ignored by his own cabinet, Adams belatedly decided to make peace with France. Despite prosecuting all the major opposition editors, jailing a critical congressman, and backing legal persecution with occasional violence and substantial economic pressure, the Federalists found themselves dealing with more opposition newspapers after the Sedition Act than before, and a clearly faltering electoral position. Leaning heavily on a politicized clergy, Federalists defended their New England stronghold with the first "culture war" in American political history, painting Jefferson as an effete philosopher, coward, and atheist who might be part of the international Illuminati conspiracy to infiltrate and destroy the world's religions and governments. Voters were invited to choose "GOD—AND A RELIGIOUS PRESIDENT; Or impiously declare for JEFFERSON—AND NO GOD!!"

By the end of 1800, all that was left was scheming to avoid the inevitable: Pennsylvania Federalists used the state senate to block any presidential voting in that banner Republican state, while Alexander Hamilton tried to torpedo Adams with a South Carolina stalking horse for the second election in a row. When strenuous partisan campaigning produced exactly equal electoral vote totals for Jefferson and his unofficial running mate, Aaron Burr, congressional Federalists toyed with installing the more pliable Burr as president. As angry Democratic-Republicans prepared for civil war, the Federalists backed down and accepted Jefferson's election after 35 ballots were cast.

After the Revolution of 1800

The 1800 election permanently resolved the question of whether popular democratic politics "out of doors" would be permitted, but Jefferson and his successors did not regard the party conflict itself as permanent or desirable. Jefferson's goal was not so much total unity as a one-party state in which the more moderate Federalists would join the Democratic-Republicans (as John Adams's son soon did) and leave the rest as an irrelevant splinter group. Though Jefferson believed the defeat of the Federalists represented a second American revolution, his policies represented only modest changes. Few of the working-class radicals who campaigned for Jefferson found their way into office. Hamilton's financial system was not abolished but only partially phased out, with the national debt slowly repaid and the national bank preserved until its charter expired.

In contrast, Jefferson's victory had a profound impact on the democratization of American political culture. Though the electoral system had been fragmented and oligarchic in 1800, it became much less so once "the People's Friend" was in power. Jefferson self-consciously dispensed with "monarchical prettinesses" in conducting his presidency, receiving state visitors in casual clothing, inviting congressmen in for "pell-mell" dinner parties, and personally accepting homely tributes from ordinary Americans such as the Mammoth Cheese from the Baptist dairy farmers of Cheshire, Massachusetts. Putting the French machinations of 1796 behind them, the Democratic-Republicans had successfully taken up the mantle of patriotic national leadership, and one of their most successful tactics was promoting the Jefferson- and democracy-oriented Fourth of July as the prime day of national celebration, over competitors that commemorated Washington's birthday or major military victories. Rooted in celebrations and mass meetings knitted together by a network of newspapers, the Jeffersonian politics of patriotic celebration proved a powerful form of democratic campaigning. Using these methods, vibrant though fractious Democratic-Republican parties took control in most of the states, moving to win areas

(such as New England, New Jersey, and Delaware) that Jefferson had not carried in 1800 and posting some of the highest voter turnouts ever recorded.

In response, the Federalists began behaving more like a political party, dropping self-conscious elitism, intensifying their culture war, and putting more money and effort into political organization as they fought to hold on. Hamilton suggested organizing Christian constitutional societies to better promote the idea of a Federalist monopoly on religion. New England Federalists amplified their claims to include the suggestion that Jefferson and his followers were libertines who wanted to destroy the family. From 1802 on, Federalists also began to bring up slavery periodically, not to propose abolishing the institution, but instead to use it as a wedge issue to keep northern voters away from Virginia presidential candidates. The revelations about Jefferson's relationship with his slave Sally Hemings were used as another example of his libertinism and disrespect for social order, while the three-fifths clause of the Constitution was decried as evidence that Southerners wanted to treat northern voters just like their slaves.

While there was no direct foreign interference after 1800, postcoloniality remained the dominant fact of American political life through the end of the War of 1812. Though wildly popular and serving Jefferson's larger agenda of agricultural expansion without heavy taxation or a large military, the Louisiana Purchase owed much to Napoleon's desire to destabilize the United States and set it against Spain and Britain, and he achieved that goal. Jefferson and his two successors lived in fear of territorial dismemberment at the hands of European powers allied with Indians, slaves, and disloyal American politicians, among them Jefferson's first vice president, Aaron Burr, who was courted as a possible leader by both western and eastern disunionists.

Beginning late in Jefferson's second term, the Napoleonic Wars subjected the country to renewed pressures, as both the British and French took countervailing measures against American shipping. It was now the Republicans' turn to clamor for war, this time against Great Britain. Having largely dismantled the Federalist military buildup and loath to violate his small military/low taxation principles, in 1807 Jefferson unleashed a total embargo on all foreign trade. In so doing, he hoped to impel the belligerent powers to treat American ships more fairly by denying them needed raw materials, especially food, and markets for their manufactured goods. The embargo policy failed miserably and brought disproportionate economic suffering to commercial New England, but it proved a godsend for the Federalists.

Beginning in 1808, the Federalist party stormed back to competitiveness in much of the North and stabilized itself as a viable opposition party, despite never managing to field a national candidate who could seriously challenge Madison or Monroe. New York's De Witt Clinton came the closest, but rather than a Federalist he was an independent Democratic-Republican sometimes willing to cooperate with them. State and local Federalists did better once Madison and Congress finally broke down and declared war in 1812. The hapless nature of the American war effort soon lured the Federalists to their death as a national party, or at least the sickness unto death. In 1814 the once-again firmly Federalist New England states called a special convention at Hartford that was widely perceived as disunionist.

Andrew Jackson's shocking, lopsided victory at New Orleans in January 1815 revolutionized the war's public image. The Battle of New Orleans placed the Federalists in a dangerously ignominious light. It also made many of the existing postcolonial issues irrelevant, with Jackson having shown the great European powers that further intervention on the North American mainland would be costly and fruitless. "Hartford Convention Federalist" became a watchword for pusillanimity and treason. Federalist political support retreated to its strongest redoubts and declined even there. In 1818 even Connecticut, a "Land of Steady Habits" that neither Jefferson nor Madison had ever carried, fell to the Democratic-Republicans.

The Era of Mixed Feelings

The Federalists' decline went along with a collapse of the key distinctions of the old party conflict. Most Republican officeholders were gentlemen attorneys and planters who had long since broken with the old Jacobin radicals and joined the ruling elite themselves. At the same time, the war had convinced many younger Republican leaders that a more powerful and prestigious federal government was necessary to keep the country safe and united. During Madison's second term, a second Bank of the United States was created, and ambitious plans were made for federally funded improvements in the nation's transportation facilities and military capabilities. Before leaving office, Madison—citing constitutional qualms—vetoed a Bonus Bill that would have spent some of the money earned from the new bank on the planned internal improvements.

Though once the fiercest of partisans, James Monroe faced only token regional opposition in the 1816 election and arrived in the presidency ready to officially call a halt to party politics. He toured New England, and many former enemies embraced him, but what a Federalist newspaper declared an "Era of Good Feeling" was rather deceptive. While Democratic-Republican officials in Washington accepted a neo-Hamiltonian vision of governing, and squabbled over who would succeed to the presidency, powerful and contrary democratic currents flowed beneath the surface. Popular voting was increasingly the norm for selecting presidential electors and ever more state and local offices, and property qualifications for voting were rapidly disappearing. This change had the side effect of disfranchising a small number of women and African Americans who had hitherto been allowed to vote in some states on the basis of owning property.

Republican radicals in many states, often calling themselves just Democrats or operating under some local label, refused to accept the partisan cease-fire and battled over economic development, religion, the courts, and other issues. Pennsylvania Democrats split into New School and Old School factions, with the former controlling most of the offices but the latter maintaining the Jeffersonian egalitarianism and suspicion of northern capitalism. Divisions over debtor relief following the Panic of 1819 left Kentucky with two competing supreme courts, and civil war a distinct possibility. When Congress tried to upgrade member living standards in 1816 by converting their $6 per diem allowance to a $1,500 yearly salary, backlash among voters and the press forced 80 percent of the members who voted for the pay raise out of office.

The collapse of national party lines also permitted a number of other threatening developments as politicians operated without the need or means to build a national majority. For example, General Andrew Jackson was allowed to seize Spanish territory in Florida to aid the expansion of the southern cotton belt. Jackson's actions were then repudiated by the Monroe administration and pilloried by House Speaker and presidential candidate Henry Clay, only to be vindicated in the end by another contender, Secretary of State John Quincy Adams, and his Transcontinental Treaty with Spain.

Slavery also emerged as a major national issue when the northern majority House of Representatives voted to block Missouri's entry into the union as a slave state. Though slavery had existed in every state at the time of the Revolution, the North had largely, though gradually, abolished it by the 1820s. Coming seemingly out of nowhere, the proposal of New York congressman James Tallmadge (a Clintonian Democrat) sparked one of the fullest and most honest debates on slavery that Congress would ever see, with various members adopting the sectional positions that would eventually bring on the Civil War. Nationalists led by Henry Clay and President Monroe worked out a compromise to the Missouri Crisis, but a group of Democratic leaders centered around New York's Martin Van Buren, already disturbed by the rampant crossing of party lines, concluded that the old Jeffersonian coalition of northern workers and farmers with southern planters would have to be resurrected if the union was to survive. Unfortunately, that meant limiting further congressional discussions of slavery, along with additional national development programs that might break down the constitutional barriers protecting slavery and southern interests.

Van Buren's first try at executing his plan was doomed by the lack of party institutions possessing any semblance of democratic authenticity. Though for many years the congressional caucus system of nominations had been under attack from radical democrats, in 1824, Van Buren and his allies still used it to nominate their favorite, Treasury Secretary William Crawford, despite the fact that Crawford was gravely ill and most members of Congress refused to attend the caucus. In the presidential election, with no clear party distinctions operating, Crawford and fellow southern contender Henry Clay were beaten by surprise candidate Andrew Jackson and Secretary of State John Quincy Adams. Jackson's sudden political rise, launched by cynical western Clayites but then supported by "Old School" Democrats back east, had already swamped the candidacy of John C. Calhoun, who stepped into the vice presidency. Jackson appeared to have attracted the most popular votes, in a light turnout. But with no Electoral College majority, Congress elected the younger Adams in a "corrupt bargain" with Clay that was permissible within the existing constitutional rules but flew in the face of an increasingly democratic political culture.

The "Lurid Administration" and the Origins of the Second Party System

The deal that made Adams president also played into the hands of those looking to resuscitate the old Jeffersonian coalition at his expense. Van Buren and his allies somewhat grudgingly decided that the popular but excitable

General Jackson could supply the electoral vitality they needed. Denied the presidency, Jackson vowed revenge on Clay and Adams, and his supporters in Congress set out to turn the Adams administration into a lurid caricature that would ensure Jackson's election in 1828.

Though among the most far-sighted and conscientious of men, John Quincy Adams was a failure as a president. A useful ally of Jackson and the South before 1824, he assumed that his good intentions toward all sides were understood. So he forged ahead with a continuation and expansion of the Monroe administration's nonpartisan approach and nationalist policies. In his first presidential speeches, Adams urged Congress to literally reach for the skies, proposing not only an integrated system of roads and canals but also federal funding for a national university, a naval academy, and for scientific exploration and research, including geographic expeditions and astronomical observatories—"those light-houses of the skies," as Adams called them in a much-lampooned turn of phrase. Knowing that such an ambitious expansion of government would meet public resistance in a still largely rural nation, Adams made one of the more tone-deaf comments in the history of presidential speechmaking, urging Congress not to be "palsied by the will of our constituents" in pursuing his agenda. This remark, and the imperious attitude behind it, was a gift for enemies who were already bent on depicting Adams's election as a crime against democracy.

After that the Jacksonian onslaught never ceased and Adams's every action was ginned into a scandal by a hostile Congress and a burgeoning Jacksonian press. Adams's decision to send a U.S. delegation to Panama for a meeting of independent American states sparked a congressional fracas that lasted so long the meeting was over before the Americans could arrive. This labored outrage over the Panama Congress was partly racial in nature because diplomats from Haiti would be present. Though Adams undoubtedly ran one of the cleanest, least partisan administrations, refusing to fire even open enemies such as Postmaster General John McLean, Jacksonians also mounted cacophonous investigations of malfeasance and politicization in the president's expenditures and appointments.

Like the election of 1800, the 1828 election was both a democratic upheaval and a nasty culture war. This time the anti-intellectual shoe was on the other foot, as relatively unlettered new voters were urged to identify with Old Hickory's military prowess over Adams's many accomplishments. The slogan was "John Quincy Adams who can write/and Andrew Jackson who can fight." At the same time, Adams drew support from the forces associated with the emerging "benevolent empire" of evangelical Christianity. With an eye on evangelical voters, Adams partisans muckraked Jackson's life relentlessly for moral scandal. The general probably deserved the "coffin handbills" calling him a murderer for his dueling and several incidents of his military career, but the detailed eviscerations of his staid, respectable marriage, in which Jackson was accused of seduction and his dying wife Rachel of wantonness and bigamy, have few equals in the annals of American political campaigning. Such aggressive moralizing failed to save Adams's presidency, but it did help define one of the enduring boundaries of the Second Party System, pitting middle-class evangelicals against more secular-minded democrats, immigrant workers, and slaveholders.

See also anti-Federalists; Democratic Party, 1800–28; federalism; Federalist Party; slavery; War of 1812.

FURTHER READING

Basch, Norma. "Marriage, Morals, and Politics in the Election of 1828." *Journal of American History* 80 (1993), 890–918.

Dangerfield, George. *The Awakening of American Nationalism, 1815–1828.* New York: Harper and Row, 1965.

Elkins, Stanley, and Eric McKitrick. *The Age of Federalism.* New York: Oxford University Press, 1993.

Ellis, Richard E. *The Jeffersonian Crisis: Courts and Politics in the Young Republic.* New York: Norton, 1974.

Foner, Philip S., ed. *The Democratic-Republican Societies, 1790–1800: A Documentary Sourcebook of Constitutions, Declarations, Addresses, Resolutions, and Toasts.* Westport, CT: Greenwood Press, 1976.

Forbes, Robert Pierce. *The Missouri Compromise and Its Aftermath: Slavery and the Meaning of America.* Chapel Hill: University of North Carolina Press, 2007.

Hofstadter, Richard. *The Idea of a Party System: The Rise of Legitimate Opposition in the United States, 1780–1840.* Berkeley: University of California Press, 1969.

Pasley, Jeffrey L. *"The Tyranny of Printers": Newspaper Politics in the Early American Republic.* Charlottesville: University Press of Virginia, 2001.

Pasley, Jeffrey L., Andrew W. Robertson, and David Waldstreicher, eds. *Beyond the Founders: New Approaches to the Political History of the Early American Republic.* Chapel Hill: University of North Carolina Press, 2004.

Phillips, Kim T. "The Pennsylvania Origins of the Jackson Movement." *Political Science Quarterly* 91, no. 3 (Fall 1976), 489–508.

Skeen, C. Edward. "*Vox Populi, Vox Dei*: The Compensation Act of 1816 and the Rise of Popular Politics." *Journal of the Early Republic* 6 (Fall 1986), 253–74.

Taylor, Alan. "From Fathers to Friends of the People: Political Personas in the Early Republic." *Journal of the Early Republic* 11 (1991), 465–91.

Waldstreicher, David. *In the Midst of Perpetual Fetes: The Making of American Nationalism, 1776–1820.* Chapel Hill: University of North Carolina Press for the Omohundro Institute of Early American History and Culture, 1997.

JEFFREY L. PASLEY

era of confrontation and decline, 1964–80

Addressing a grieving nation on November 27, 1963, five days after the assassination of President John F. Kennedy, Lyndon B. Johnson offered a simple message of reassurance. In his inaugural address in January 1961, Kennedy had declared, "Let us begin." President Johnson amended that injunction to "Let us continue." But if there was one quality that characterized neither his presidency nor those that followed over the next decade and a half, it was continuity. The years between 1964 and 1980 brought wrenching political, social, economic, and cultural changes to the United States.

Johnson had sound political reasons to position himself as caretaker of Kennedy's legacy. He feared being seen as an interloper, an illegitimate successor to a martyred hero. Accordingly, he presented his legislative agenda for 1964 as the fulfillment of his predecessor's work. He actually hoped to go far beyond Kennedy's domestic record: "To tell the truth," Johnson confided to a prominent Kennedy associate in early 1964, "John F. Kennedy was a little too conservative to suit my taste."

Liberalism at High Tide

Nineteen sixty-four turned into a year of triumph for Johnson and for a resurgent American liberalism. In his January State of the Union address, the president announced plans for an "unconditional war on poverty." In May, in a speech to students at the University of Michigan, he offered an even more ambitious agenda of reforms, under the slogan "the Great Society," promising "an end to poverty and racial injustice," as well as programs to improve education, protect the environment, and foster the arts. Two days before the Independence Day holiday in July, he signed into law the Civil Rights Act, the most significant federal legislation advancing the rights of black citizens since the Reconstruction era, with provisions outlawing segregation in public facilities and discrimination in employment and education. In August he signed the Economic Opportunity Act, the centerpiece of his war on poverty, funding local antipoverty "community action agencies," and programs like the Job Corps (providing vocational training to unemployed teenagers) and VISTA (a domestic version of the Peace Corps).

Rounding out his triumphant year in November, Johnson soundly defeated conservative challenger Barry Goldwater. Strengthened Democratic majorities in the eighty-ninth Congress gave the president a comfortable margin of support for his reform agenda. Johnson went on to send 87 bills to Congress in 1965, including such landmark measures as Medicare and Medicaid, the Voting Rights Act, the Clean Water Act, and the Immigration Reform Act.

Dark Shadows in Vietnam

But other events in 1964–65 had troubling implications for the future of American liberalism. The war in South Vietnam was another Kennedy legacy that Johnson inherited, and it was not going well. Communists were making military gains in the countryside, and in Saigon one unpopular regime followed another in a series of military coups. On November 22, 1963, just under 17,000 U.S. servicemen were stationed in South Vietnam; a year later, under Johnson, the number had grown to 23,000. During the election campaign, Johnson sought to downplay the war, promising not to send "American boys nine or ten thousand miles away from home to do what Asian boys ought to be doing for themselves." But there was an ominous sign of a widening war in August, when North Vietnamese PT boats allegedly attacked American destroyers in the Gulf of Tonkin, and Johnson authorized a retaliatory air strike against North Vietnamese naval bases. He also secured passage of the Gulf of Tonkin Resolution, a joint congressional resolution providing him open-ended authorization for the use of U.S. military force in Southeast Asia.

Vietnam turned into a major war six months later, in February 1965, when Johnson ordered the start of a massive and continuous bombing campaign against North Vietnam. A month later he began sending ground combat forces to South Vietnam. By the end of 1965, there were close to 185,000 U.S. troops in South Vietnam, and more than 2,000 Americans had died in the war.

Racial Justice and Racial War

At home in 1965, the civil rights movement led by Dr. Martin Luther King Jr. reached its high point in the spring with a campaign for voting rights in Selma, Alabama. Johnson had not originally intended to bring a voting rights bill before Congress in 1965, but public outrage at bloody attacks by Alabama authorities on King's nonviolent followers changed his mind. On August 6, 1965, the President signed the Voting Rights Act, fulfilling the long-deferred promise of democracy for African American citizens in the South, perhaps the greatest achievement of the Johnson administration.

But just five days later, the poverty-stricken black neighborhood of Watts in Los Angeles exploded in rioting. Before police and National Guardsmen were able to suppress the outbreak 34 people were killed and more than 250 buildings burned down. Nineteen sixty-five proved the first of a series of "long hot summers" of similar ghetto conflagrations. America's racial problems were now a national crisis, not simply a southern issue. The political consequences were dramatic. White Southerners were already switching their allegiance to the formerly unthinkable alternative of the Republican Party, in reaction to Democrats' support for civil rights. Now white working-class voters in northern cities were departing the Democratic Party as well, to support candidates who promised to make the restoration of "law and order" their highest priority. The New Deal coalition of the Solid South, the industrial North, and liberal intellectuals that had made the Democratic Party the normal majority party since the 1930s was unraveling.

Thunder on the Left

Liberalism was coming under attack from another and unexpected quarter, the nation's campuses. Inspired by the civil rights movement, a new generation of radical student activists, the New Left, had been growing in influence since the early 1960s. In the Kennedy years New Leftists had regarded liberals as potential allies in tackling issues like racism and poverty. Johnson's escalation of the war in Vietnam now led New Leftists, centered in the rapidly growing Students for a Democratic Society (SDS), to view liberals as part of the problem instead of part of the solution. Within a few years the New Left embraced a politics of militant confrontation that had little in common with traditional liberalism.

Buildings burn during the Watts riot in Los Angeles, August 1965. (Library of Congress)

Young black activists in groups like the Student Non-Violent Coordinating Committee (SNCC) abandoned both nonviolence as a philosophy and integration as a goal, as they raised the slogan "Black Power."

Meanwhile, the war in Vietnam escalated. By the end of 1967, there were almost a half million U.S. troops fighting in South Vietnam and nearly 20,000 Americans killed in action. The U.S. military commander in Vietnam, General William Westmoreland, sought to shore up shaky public support for the war by proclaiming in November 1967 that "the light at the end of the tunnel" was in sight.

Things Fall Apart

Nineteen sixty-eight was the year that many things fell apart, not least the American public's belief that victory was at hand in Vietnam. The Communists' Tet Offensive, launched at the end of January, proved a great psychological victory. At the end of March, following a near defeat at the hands of antiwar challenger Eugene McCarthy in the New Hampshire primary, President Johnson announced a partial halt in the bombing campaign against North Vietnam and coupled that with a declaration that he would not run for reelection in the fall. Five days later, Martin Luther King Jr. was assassinated in Memphis, Tennessee, sparking riots in a hundred cities. In June, after winning the California Democratic

primary, Robert Kennedy was assassinated in Los Angeles. Eugene McCarthy continued a dispirited race for his party's presidential nomination, but Vice President Hubert Humphrey, who did not compete in a single primary, arrived in Chicago at the Democratic National Convention in August with enough delegates to guarantee his nomination. The convention would be remembered chiefly for the rioting that took place outside the hall as antiwar protesters and police clashed in the streets.

In the presidential campaign in the fall, Humphrey was crippled by his inability to distance himself from Johnson's Vietnam policies. Many liberal voters chose to sit out the election or cast their votes for fringe candidates. Former Alabama governor and arch-segregationist George Wallace, running as a third-party candidate, also drained conservative Democratic votes from Humphrey. In the three-way race, Republican candidate Richard Nixon won the White House with a plurality of popular votes.

Thunder on the Right

Following his election Nixon promised Americans that his administration would "bring us together," but that was neither his natural instinct as a politician nor his strategy for building what one adviser called an "emerging Republican majority." George Wallace's strong showing in the election suggested the advantages of pursuing a "southern strategy," raising divisive issues of race and culture to peel off traditional Democratic voters in the South and Southwest and in working-class neighborhoods in the North.

During the 1968 campaign, Nixon had spoken of a "secret plan" to end the war in Vietnam. In private conversations with his closest adviser, Henry Kissinger (national security adviser 1969–72 and thereafter secretary of state), Nixon would speak of the war as a lost cause. But his policies suggested that he hoped against reason that some kind of victory could still be achieved, and he would not become "the first American president to lose a war." His problem was to find a way to prosecute the war while giving the American public the reassurance it sought that the war was in fact winding down. His solution was to begin a gradual withdrawal of American ground combat forces from South Vietnam in 1969, while stepping up the air war, including launching a secret bombing campaign against Cambodia.

Meanwhile, American soldiers continued to die (a total of 22,000 during Nixon's presidency). The antiwar

President Richard M. Nixon hangs tangled in a spider's web. Recording tapes dangle above him. This drawing by Robert Pryor, refers to Nixon's refusal to turn over White House tapes to the House Judiciary Committee, which was investigating the Watergate cover-up. (Library of Congress)

movement grew in size and breadth; in November 1969 half a million Americans marched in Washington, D.C., to protest the war. In May 1970, when Nixon broadened the role of U.S. ground forces, sending them into Cambodia in what he called an "incursion," nationwide protests on and off college campuses forced him to back down, although he argued that a "silent majority" supported his policies.

Nixon Self-Destructs

In the end, Nixon's combative style of governing and his penchant for secrecy proved fatal to his presidency and historical reputation. In the first months after taking office, he ordered the illegal wiretapping of some of Kissinger's aides to find out who had leaked news of the secret bombing of Cambodia to the press. Later he would authorize the creation of an in-house security operation, known as the "Plumbers," to stage break-ins against and play dirty tricks on political opponents. Some of the Plumbers were arrested in a bungled break-in at the Democratic National Committee headquarters in the Watergate complex in June 1972. The subsequent Watergate scandal attracted little attention during the campaign, and Nixon coasted to easy reelection over his Democratic opponent, George McGovern. And in January 1973, with the signing of the Paris Peace Accords, the war in Vietnam was formally ended.

But in the months that followed, as the Watergate burglars were brought to trial, the cover-up initiated by the White House unraveled. The Senate launched a formal investigation of Nixon's campaign abuses. Indictments were handed down against top Nixon aides and associates, including former attorney general John Mitchell. Vice President Spiro Agnew resigned after pleading no contest on unrelated corruption charges and was succeeded in office by House minority leader Gerald Ford. Finally, in August 1974, facing impeachment, Nixon resigned.

Nightmare Ended?

On taking office, President Ford attempted to reassure the nation that "our long national nightmare" had ended, but soon after he saw his own popularity plummet when he offered a blanket pardon to President Nixon for any crimes committed while in the White House. The Democrats did very well in the fall 1974 midterm elections, and liberals hoped that the whole Nixon era would prove an aberration rather than a foretaste of an era of conservative dominance. But the overall mood of the country in the mid-1970s was one of gloom, rather than renewed political enthusiasm, either liberal or conservative. The most striking feature of the 1974 elections had been the marked downturn in voter turnout. The country's mood worsened the following spring, when the Communists in Vietnam launched a final offensive leading to the fall of the U.S.-backed regime in Saigon. It was now apparent to many that 58,000 American lives had been wasted. Some Americans feared that a resurgent Soviet Union had the United States on the run throughout the world, not just in Southeast Asia.

And there now seemed to be new foreign opponents to contend with, among them the Arab oil-producing nations that launched a devastating oil embargo in the aftermath of the 1973 Arab-Israeli War. The subsequent leap in energy prices was but part of the economic woes of the late 1970s, including the loss of manufacturing jobs overseas, rising unemployment, declining real wages, soaring inflation, and a mounting trade deficit. Americans had come to take for granted the long period of prosperity that followed World War II, and now it was clearly coming to an end.

One Last Chance for Democrats

The immediate political beneficiary of this doom and gloom was a self-defined political outsider, Jimmy Carter, a one-term former governor of Georgia, who promised voters in 1976 a "government as good as its people," and beat out a field of better-known rivals for the Democratic presidential nomination. As a Southerner and a born-again Christian, Carter hoped to embody a return to a simpler and more virtuous era; he was deliberately vague in campaign speeches as to his preference in political philosophy and policies. With the economy in tatters and the memory of Watergate still strong, it was a good year to run against an incumbent Republican president, but Carter barely squeaked out a victory in November over Gerald Ford, in an election in which just over 50 percent of eligible voters turned out to vote, the lowest level in nearly 30 years.

Carter's outsider status did not help him govern effectively once in office. He disappointed traditional Democratic interest groups by showing little interest in social welfare issues. And Republicans attacked him for what they regarded as his moralistic and wishy-washy foreign policy. The economic news only worsened in the later 1970s, with increased unemployment and inflation. And in 1979, when Islamic militants seized the American embassy in Teheran and took several dozen embassy staff members as hostages, Carter's political fate was sealed. The hostage taking provided the perfect issue for the Republican presidential nominee in 1980, former movie star and California governor Ronald Reagan, who vowed that in a Reagan administration America would "stand tall" again. In a three-way race that included independent Republican John Anderson, Reagan handily defeated Carter, and the Republicans regained control of the Senate for the first time since 1952. This political landslide was the beginning of a new era known as the "Reagan revolution."

See also civil rights; liberalism; New Left; Vietnam and Indochina wars; voting.

FURTHER READING

Dallek, Robert. *Flawed Giant: Lyndon Johnson and His Times, 1961–1973.* New York: Oxford University Press, 1999.

Herring, George C. *America's Longest War: The United States and Vietnam, 1950–1975.* 4th ed. New York: McGraw-Hill, 2001.

Isserman, Maurice, and Michael Kazin. *America Divided: The Civil War of the 1960s.* 3rd ed. New York: Oxford University Press, 2008.

Patterson, James T. *Grand Expectations: The United States, 1945–1974.* New York: Oxford University Press, 1997.

Perlstein, Rick. *Nixonland: America's Second Civil War and the Divisive Legacy of Richard Nixon, 1965–1972.* New York: Scribner, 2008.

Schulman, Bruce. *The Seventies: The Great Shift in American Culture, Society, and Politics.* New York: Free Press, 2001.

MAURICE ISSERMAN

era of consensus, 1952–64

The years between 1952 and 1964 have long been viewed as an era of consensus. During this period, the fierce struggles over political economy that had dominated the country during the 1930s and 1940s receded, as the Republican Party under the leadership of President Dwight D. Eisenhower accepted the reforms of the New Deal and Fair Deal years. Both political parties agreed about the positive role that government could play in ensuring economic growth and security. Labor unions abandoned radical politics, while most critics of capitalism had been silenced by the anticommunism of the McCarthy years.

And many leading political and intellectual figures celebrated the country's ability to transcend destructive conflicts of ideology or politics.

Yet when we look at the period more closely, it is clear that in many ways the consensus was far from complete. Under the surface, many business leaders and conservative activists already dissented from the New Deal order. Leading industrial companies had begun their migration from northern and midwestern cities to the southern United States. A significant conservative political subculture that organized around a reaction against the New Deal order began to emerge. Long before the turn toward black power, the civil rights movement was already meeting with great hostility, even in the North. Today, many historians see the period as one of continued, if at times submerged, political and economic conflict more than genuine consensus.

Dwight D. Eisenhower, elected in 1952, presided over many of the consensus years. Eisenhower was a genial and popular World War II military leader, and his victory in the Republican primary over Senator Robert Taft of Ohio, who had been a stalwart opponent of the New Deal since the 1930s, seemed to mark a dramatic shift on the part of the Republican Party. Eisenhower viewed fighting the changes of the New Deal as a political dead end; as he wrote to his more conservative brother, "Should any political party attempt to abolish social security, unemployment insurance, and eliminate labor laws and farm programs, you would not hear of that party again in our history." He advocated "modern Republicanism," a new fiscal conservatism that nonetheless accepted the transformations of the 1930s and 1940s. Eisenhower was not a liberal. He generally refused further expansion of the welfare state; he reduced the federal budget, gave oil-rich lands to private companies for development, and opposed national health insurance. But he also maintained and expanded Social Security, raised the minimum wage, and distanced himself from the anti-Communist paranoia of Senator Joseph McCarthy of Wisconsin (although he was reluctant to challenge McCarthy openly). Business and labor, he believed, needed to come together in a common program, united in opposition to communism and confidence in the ability of the state to bring about consensus in areas that, left to the private economy alone, would be fraught with conflict.

The declining opposition of the Republican Party leadership to the New Deal program helped bring the two political parties together. And, more than anything else, what they came to agree about was economic growth. The age of consensus was defined by its leaders' abiding confidence in the idea that the government could and should intervene in the economy in certain circumscribed ways in order to ensure the continued expansion of national wealth. The resulting material abundance, they believed, would permit the resolution of virtually all social problems. Many different thinkers from across the political spectrum argued that economic growth and the constant expansion of material wealth made class conflict obsolete, and that the mass-consumption economy emerging in the decade was fundamentally different from the old, exploitative capitalism of the pre–New Deal years. Government intervention in the economy through fiscal and monetary policies—as suggested by British economist John Maynard Keynes—could tame the frenetic cycle of recession and expansion, ensuring a smooth and steady economic course. Such involvement by the state in economic life did not need to challenge private property or capitalism; on the contrary, by reducing poverty, it would lessen social unrest.

Indeed, the high proportion of the workforce represented by labor unions—over one-third, a high point for the century—caused many commentators to argue that the working class itself no longer existed, having been replaced by a broad middle class. Suburban homeownership, made possible by new federally subsidized loans for veterans and the construction of highways, extended to working-class Americans the possibility of participation in what historian Lizabeth Cohen has called a "consumers' republic." Televisions and movies and the rise of a national mass culture—especially a youth culture—helped create the image of a single, unified middle class. The class divisions of the early years of the century had been transcended by a broad consensus organized around continued material expansion and mass consumption; the old era of economic conflict was over.

If there seemed to be a new consensus around the basic virtue of a capitalism regulated and managed by strategic government intervention, the two political parties and most leading intellectual and economic figures shared an equally powerful hostility to communism and the Soviet Union. Senator McCarthy's mudslinging career came to a close in 1954, when he accused the U.S. Army of harboring spies in a set of televised hearings that made clear to the country that the senator from Wisconsin had lost whatever support he had once had in Washington. But

Soviet foreign deputy minister Valerian A. Zorin, Cuba's Permanent Representative to the United Nations Mario Garcia-Inchaustegui, and U.S. Ambassador Adlai Stevenson attend a United Nations Security Council meeting on the Cuban Missile Crisis, October 23, 1962. (Library of Congress)

the Red Scare that had dominated American politics in the late 1940s and early 1950s—peaking with the electrocution of Julius and Ethel Rosenberg in 1953 for giving the Soviets atomic secrets in the 1940s—had already reshaped the country's political culture.

In this context, the number of people willing to publicly affiliate themselves with the radical left dwindled greatly. Membership in the Communist Party (never very high to begin with) collapsed, and the radical political scene that had flourished in the party's orbit dried up. The liberal establishment, no less than conservatives, joined in making anticommunism central to national politics. In the late 1940s, liberal historian Arthur Schlesinger Jr. identified the struggle against communism as the preeminent issue defining liberalism in the postwar period. Labor unions sought to expel Communists from their ranks. Virtually no one was openly critical of the underlying assumptions of the anti-Communist worldview in the 1950s.

The cold war and fear of nuclear holocaust helped cement the anti-Communist consensus in foreign policy. The threat of a third world war in which nuclear weapons might annihilate all of humanity deepened the broad agreement about the necessity of fighting communism. Even after the Korean War ended in 1953, the United States remained an active supporter of anti-Communist governments throughout the decade. The CIA helped engineer coups against leftist leaders in Guatemala and Iran; the American government supported Ngo Dinh Diem's anti-Communist regime in Vietnam and then later acquiesced in his overthrow. In the atmosphere of broad agreement about the necessity of containing communism, few objected to such actions.

Although many of them viewed the consensus warily, intellectuals during the 1950s did much to create the idea that fundamental political conflicts were a relic of the past in the modern United States. They gave various diagnoses for what they saw as a new quiescence. Some thinkers, like sociologist Daniel Bell and theologian Reinhold Niebuhr, believed that Nazism, Stalinism, and the end of science in the atomic age had all helped to create a sense of the limits of ideas and of reason in guiding human affairs. As Bell put it in his 1960 book *The End of Ideology*, the sharply confrontational political ideas of the 1930s and 1940s—socialism, communism, fascism, traditional conservatism—had been "exhausted" in the America of the 1950s: "In the West, among the intellectuals, the old passions are spent." American historians such as Richard Hofstadter and political scientists like Louis Hartz argued that a basic agreement about the principles of laissez-faire capitalism had endured throughout the nation's past. Others, like sociologist David Riesman, suggested that the rise of a consumer society sustained personality types that sought assimilation to the norm rather than individuality, terrified to stand out and constantly seeking to fit in. And C. Wright Mills wrote that the rise of a "power elite" limited the range of collective action available to the rest of the nation, leading to a stunned apathy in political life.

The election of John F. Kennedy in 1960 over Richard Nixon (Eisenhower's vice president) seemed to mark a new political direction, as his calls to public service contrasted with the private, consumer-oriented society of the 1950s. But in other ways Kennedy's administration did not diverge significantly from the politics of the earlier decade. He delivered the first major tax cuts of the postwar period, and while he justified them by talking about the incentives that they would offer to investment, the cuts were crafted along Keynesian lines in order to stimulate the economy. He continued to advocate a fierce anticommunism, speaking of a struggle between "two conflicting ideologies: freedom under God versus ruthless, godless tyranny." The ill-fated Bay of Pigs invasion of Cuba in 1961 (followed by the showdown with the Soviet Union over the stationing of nuclear weapons on Cuba the next year) showed that he was more than willing to translate such rhetoric into military action.

In all these ways, Kennedy's administration—which was cut short by his assassination in November 1963—was well within the governing framework of the era of consensus.

Yet by the early 1960s, the limits of the consensus were also becoming clear. The most important challenge to consensus politics was the civil rights movement, which called into question the legitimacy of the image of the United States as a land of freedom opposed to totalitarianism and Fascism. The legal victory of the National Association for the Advancement of Colored People in *Brown v. Board of Education*, the 1954 Supreme Court decision that ruled segregation of public schools unconstitutional, helped to expose the harsh inequalities that African Americans faced throughout the country. Starting with the boycott of segregated public buses in Montgomery, Alabama, the following year, African Americans began to engage in new political strategies, most importantly that of nonviolent civil disobedience, which embodied a politics of moral witness and protest that was deeply at odds with the political style of consensus. Martin Luther King Jr. emerged as a national leader out of the bus boycott, and his Southern Christian Leadership Council was the largest organization coordinating the movement's strategy. In the early 1960s, civil rights activists engaged in sit-ins at department store counters that refused to serve black people, registered black voters

in the South, and resisted the system of Jim Crow legislation in countless other ways.

Although the roots of the civil rights movement were in the South, the image of ordinary people taking charge of their lives through direct action also inspired white students and others in the North. In 1962 a small group of students gathered in Port Huron, Michigan, to write the Port Huron Statement, which would become the founding manifesto of Students for a Democratic Society, the largest organization on the New Left. In the same year, Michael Harrington published *The Other America*, a book that called attention to the persistence, despite two decades of economic growth, of deep poverty within the United States—in the inner cities, in Appalachia, and among the elderly.

As the consensus began to fray from the left, it also came under increased criticism from the right. In the business world, many corporate leaders continued to resent the new power of labor unions and the federal government. While the unions and the idea of the legitimacy of the state were too powerful to challenge openly, some corporations did donate money to think tanks and intellectual organizations (such as the American Enterprise Association, later the American Enterprise Institute) that criticized Keynesian liberalism. Others, like General Electric, adopted hard-line bargaining strategies in attempts to resist their labor unions, a tactic that caught on with companies such as U.S. Steel at the end of the 1950s, when a brief recession made labor costs more onerous. And some corporations, including RCA and General Motors as well as countless textile shops, sought to flee the regions where labor unions had made the most dramatic gains in the 1930s and 1940s, leaving the North and Midwest for the southern and southwestern parts of the country, where labor was much weaker.

In the late 1950s, organizations like the John Birch Society and Fred Schwarz's Christian Anti-Communism Schools flourished, especially in regions such as southern California's Orange County, where affluent suburbanites became increasingly critical of liberalism. The civil rights movement met with massive resistance from white Southerners, who removed their children from public schools to start separate all-white private academies, insisted that segregation would endure forever, and turned to violence through the Ku Klux Klan in an attempt to suppress the movement. In the North, too, white people in cities like Chicago and Detroit continued to fight the racial integration of their neighborhoods, revealing the limits of the New Deal electoral coalition.

These varied forms of conservative rebellion came together in the 1964 presidential campaign of Arizona Senator Barry Goldwater. Goldwater, a Phoenix businessman and department store owner, was a leading critic of what he called the "dime store New Deal" of Eisenhower's modern Republicanism. His open attacks on labor unions, especially the United Auto Workers, won him the respect of anti-union businessmen. He had supported a right-to-work statute in Arizona that helped the state attract companies relocating from the North. And his opposition to the Supreme Court decision in *Brown v. Board of Education*, as well as his vote against the Civil Rights Act of 1964, won him the allegiance of whites in the North and South alike who were afraid of the successes of the civil rights movement. Lyndon B. Johnson defeated Goldwater soundly in the 1964 election, which at the time was seen as the last gasp of the old right. In later years, it would become clear that it was in fact the first campaign of a new conservatism, which would be able to take advantage of the crisis that liberalism fell into later in the 1960s and in the 1970s.

The reality of the "era of consensus" was sustained struggle over the terms of the liberal order. But despite such continued conflicts, the two major political parties, along with many intellectual figures, continued to extol the ideal of consensus in ways that would become impossible only a few years later.

See also anticommunism; civil rights; communism; conservatism; foreign policy and domestic politics since 1933; Korean War and cold war; labor movement and politics; liberalism.

FURTHER READING

Branch, Taylor. *Parting the Waters: America in the King Years, 1954–1963.* New York: Simon and Schuster, 1988.

Cohen, Lizabeth. *A Consumer's Republic: The Politics of Mass Consumption in Postwar America.* New York: Knopf, 2003.

Collins, Robert M. *More: The Politics of Economic Growth in Postwar America.* New York: Oxford University Press, 2000.

Fones-Wolf, Elizabeth. *Selling Free Enterprise: The Business Assault on Labor and Liberalism, 1945–1960.* Urbana: University of Illinois Press, 1994.

Gerstle, Gary. "Race and the Myth of the Liberal Consensus." *Journal of American History* 82, no. 2 (September 1995), 579–86.

Griffith, Robert. "Dwight D. Eisenhower and the Corporate Commonwealth." *American Historical Review* 87, no. 1 (February 1982), 87–122.

Halberstam, David. *The Fifties.* New York: Villard Books, 1993.

Hodgson, Godfrey. *America in Our Time.* Garden City, NY: Doubleday, 1976.

McGirr, Lisa. *Suburban Warriors: The Origins of the New American Right.* Princeton, NJ: Princeton University Press, 2001.

Patterson, James. *Grand Expectations: The United States, 1945–1974.* New York: Oxford University Press, 1996.

Pell, Richard. *The Liberal Mind in a Conservative Age: American Intellectuals in the 1940s and 1950s.* New York: Harper and Row, 1985.

Perlstein, Rick. *Before the Storm: Barry Goldwater and the Unmaking of the American Consensus.* New York: Hill and Wang, 2001.

Stebenne, David. *Modern Republican: Arthur Larson and the Eisenhower Years.* Bloomington: University of Indiana Press, 2006.

Sugrue, Thomas. *The Origins of the Urban Crisis: Race and Inequality in Postwar Detroit.* Princeton, NJ: Princeton University Press, 1996.

Wall, Wendy. *Inventing the "American Way": The Politics of Consensus from the New Deal to the Civil Rights Movement.* New York: Oxford University Press, 2008.

KIM PHILLIPS-FEIN

European immigrants and politics

The 13 colonies that became the United States, although dominated by British arrivals and their descendants, were, by the 1770s, ethnic clusters that included Dutch, Swedish, French, Catholics, Protestants, and Sephardic Jews forged into a nation by the Revolutionary War and sustained by a common belief in democratic government and their increasing economic interdependence. After the Revolution, national unity was preserved at least in part by the suspicious eye cast at new immigrants arriving in large numbers from the largely nondemocratic societies of Europe.

Although the African slave trade brought tens of thousands of forced migrants to North American shores, the young country was spared mass immigration from Europe until the third decade of the nineteenth century. Then, the large numbers of newcomers became a perennial and critical element in the evolution of the American political system. As millions of new arrivals poured into American ports and across the nation's borders beginning in the decades prior to the Civil War, politicians calculated the electoral opportunities and obstacles posed by the new arrivals. While some new Americans, such as Mexicans, were engulfed by the United States through the process of conquest and annexation following the Mexican War in 1848, the Atlantic seaports were crowded with European immigrants, mostly from northern and western Europe. In the period between 1840 and 1860, 4.5 million newcomers arrived, mostly from Ireland, the German states, and the Scandinavian countries. By the end of the nineteenth century, the main origin of European migration to the United States shifted from western Europe to eastern and southern Europe. By the end of the twentieth century, European immigration was dwarfed by the flow arriving from Asia, Africa, Latin America, and the Middle East.

Migration and the Shaping of U.S. Political Institutions

European immigration never existed in a vacuum; the nation was created by arrivals from all over the world. Some settled in the eastern and southern states, some pushed on to the Midwest and far West. American politicians vacillated between courting these arrivals or denouncing their presence and playing on the fears of immigration's opponents. Likewise, the reaction of immigrants to American politics has varied greatly over the past two centuries. The nation's founders crafted the Declaration of Independence and the Constitution of 1788 in a manner reflecting their English heritage and the experience of rebelling against king and Parliament. However, their embrace of freedom was not egalitarian; it did not include slaves or women.

In the late eighteenth and early nineteenth centuries, some immigrants arriving from Germany, France, England, and Ireland brought with them the authoritarian tradition of monarchy. Even those who yearned for democracy were at times inexperienced in its practice. Others, such as some antebellum German arrivals and some eastern European Jews who came in the early twentieth century, arrived imbued with radical ideologies, including anarchism, socialism, and communism. Most of these immigrants gradually abandoned dreams of revolution and accepted the pursuit of social justice at the ballot box rather than in the streets. In the twenty-first century, ethnic voting blocs remain part of the American political landscape, with highly paid political consultants

angling for the loyalty of descendants of immigrants who still vote their pasts on Election Day.

Immigrants and American Political Party Formation

Mass immigration nurtured political party development in the antebellum era of the nineteenth century. By the 1840s, there was, for the first time, a competitive two-party system in every state of the nation. State and local party leaders often sought to speed the process of immigrant naturalization, especially around election time, to create a valuable reservoir of new voters who they could actively court. Partisanship was based on fundamentally different sets of attitudes, values, and beliefs. The Democratic Party, which traced its origins to Thomas Jefferson, depicted itself as the "party of personal liberty," denouncing Whigs as the "party of paternalism." Democrats sought to position themselves as opposing state interference in the private lives of citizens, such as sumptuary legislation, and were unwilling to support laws meddling in the daily affairs of people, for example, temperance and Sunday closing laws. Whigs, on the other hand, portrayed themselves as the "Christian Party" and appealed to those groups that supported government regulation designed to fashion a moral society. Whigs favored temperance legislation and laws maintaining a Puritan Sabbath. Politicians competed for power in support of one or the other of these belief systems.

Who voted? In the first third of the nineteenth century, property qualifications for voting were removed state by state, dramatically expanding the size of the electorate. Democratic and Whig politicians began to aggressively court those newly eligible to vote. Political participation exercised an unparalleled power and influence over the imaginations of citizens. Between 1840 and 1860, voter turnout for all elections in the North was 71.3 percent. Turnout for presidential elections averaged 81.1 percent, with a slightly lower but still impressive nonpresidential election average of 69.9 percent.

European immigration helped expand the electorate. The Irish were especially attractive to politicians. One and three-quarter million Irishmen arrived in the United States between 1840 and 1860, almost 40 percent of the total immigration during that time. Most were Roman Catholics from the southern counties, fleeing the potato famine and the oppressiveness of English rule. The Irish tended to vote Democratic because the party advocated a strict separation of church and state. Fearing oppression by a Protestant majority, Irish Catholics hoped to avoid temperance and sabbatarian legislation designed to regulate their personal behavior. They saw the Whigs and third-party abolitionists as Protestant fanatics. German immigrants tended to divide by religion, with German Catholics voting Democratic and German Lutherans supporting Whigs.

The urban political machine was born in antebellum America. Founded in the 1780s, the Tammany Society, or Columbian Order of New York City, became a dominant force for reform in New York and its followers controlled the Democratic Party. To retain power, Tammany politicians turned to the newly arrived immigrants, especially the Irish. In return for food and clothing in times of emergency, patronage jobs, and assistance to those arrested, immigrants overlooked dishonest election practices and voted for Tammany candidates. Their proficiency in English allowed them rapid entry into mainstream politics, and the urban Irish quickly came to dominate the Democratic Party. The pattern was similar in other cities, with bosses such as James McManus in Philadelphia and Christopher Magee and William Finn in Pittsburgh.

By the mid-1850s, the Whig Party was fragmenting. Prior to the rise of the new Republican Party, some voters were attracted to the American, or Know-Nothing, Party. The party's anti-Catholic, anti-immigrant political agenda appealed to those who feared that the foreign-born would take their jobs or change the cultural identity of the country. Many opposed alien ownership of land in the West. In the 1850s, nativist voters turned to the new Republican Party.

The Civil War intensified divisions among ethnic groups. Historians long thought that Abraham Lincoln's victory in the election of 1860 was in part the result of strong German support, especially in the immigrant enclaves of the Midwest. More recent voting analysis has revealed that Germans joined Irish immigrants in the ranks of the Democratic Party; temperance and Sabbatarian legislation affected their lifestyles and values far more than slavery. Alienated by the anti-immigrant inclinations of many Republicans, they voted for Stephen Douglas in 1860.

Immigration and Late Nineteenth-Century American Politics

Immigration from northern and western Europe continued through the 1880s, but between 1880 and the 1920s, 23.5 million newcomers arrived in the United States, largely from the countries of southern and eastern Europe as well as China, Japan, Canada, and Mexico. The

debate over integrating these new foreign-born and their children into American society and culture was often at the base of partisan political battles at the state and local levels. Just as African Americans were kept from the polls by walls of discrimination, many immigrants also found the path to full political participation narrow. Most Asians were denied access to citizenship, and many European immigrants could not pass the required examination.

By 1896 the major parties were deciding what role newcomers might play in their coalitions at the national level. That year, Democrats from the Midwest, including many anti-urban Populists, joined southern Democrats to give the nomination to William Jennings Bryan, who lost to Republican William McKinley. After Bryan's defeat, Democrats turned to European immigrant voters, especially the urban Catholic wing of the party, to resuscitate their prospects. However, immigrant party preferences differed in different parts of the nation. While German Lutherans in the Midwest continued to vote Republican, Russian Jews in the East voted either Democratic or Socialist.

Immigration's Role in Early Twentieth-Century American Politics

Woodrow Wilson's election in 1912 placed in the White House a Progressive reformer who also had won the confidence of many European immigrant voters. In 1915 and 1916, he vetoed bills calling for tests that would deny illiterates admission to the United States. In 1917, Congress passed such a bill and overrode Wilson's veto. As always, events in Europe shaped political behavior in the United States. As war loomed, Irish immigrants supporting Ireland's desire for independence became alienated by Wilson's increasing Anglophilia. Harkening to older loyalties, European immigrants were divided in their support of World War I.

World War I generated an anti-alien emotionalism that would be a catalyst for postwar immigration restrictions. German Americans, especially, were the target of "100 percent Americanism" propaganda. In the spirit of the moment, sauerkraut was renamed "liberty cabbage," the German language was removed from high school and college curricula, and Woodrow Wilson's Committee on Public Information under George Creel recruited 75,000 "Four Minutemen" who could briefly describe German atrocities to community and church groups. German ethnicity and German culture never recovered their prewar prestige in the United States.

The 1917 Russian Revolution and the Red Scare of 1919 resulted in a hysteria that victimized many European immigrants. What historian John Higham called "anti-radical nativism" and the ability of American industry to thrive with the immigrant labor already in the country led to highly restrictive immigration policies. The 1924 Johnson-Reed Immigration Act created the national origins quota system. Each nation received a quota equal to 2 percent of the 1890 population of aliens of that nationality already in the United States. The system was designed to put southern and eastern Europeans at a disadvantage, and it worked. Immigration legislation, however, did not reassure Americans consumed by fears of foreign-born radicals. The Sacco-Vanzetti case ended in the 1927 electrocution of two Italian immigrant anarchists who were convicted of the robbery and murder of a shoe company paymaster in South Braintree, Massachusetts. Despite insufficient evidence, the testimony, charged with nativism, resulted in a guilty verdict.

Non-Protestant immigrants and their children also remained objects of suspicion. Democrat Al Smith had been governor of New York, but his Catholicism and Irish American urban flavor undermined his presidential hopes; in 1928 he lost to Herbert Hoover. However, after the stock market crash of 1929, rural white Protestant Southerners of European heritage joined with urban Irish Catholics and eastern European Jews and an increasing number of African Americans to form the coalition that supported Franklin D. Roosevelt in 1932 and paved the way for the New Deal.

Immigrant Voters, Refugees, and Roosevelt

Fascism in Italy and Germany had political reverberations in the United States. The German American Bund encouraged recent immigrants and those of German heritage to support Adolph Hitler and the German fatherland. Bund members denounced FDR and other European immigrant groups in the United States, especially Jewish newcomers. When war came, most Americans of German heritage remained loyal to the United States, but fears of wartime subversion led federal authorities to intern some German Americans and Italian Americans during the war, although the number was far smaller than the 110,000 West Coast Japanese interned for the war's duration.

Beginning in the early 1930s, Presidents Hoover and Roosevelt, respectively, urged the State Department to rigorously enforce U.S. immigration restrictions by en-

couraging American consular officials abroad to issue fewer visas than were allocated to the country in which they served. No exceptions were made for Jewish refugees in flight from Nazi persecution. Thus, between 1933 and 1945 only a quarter of a million Jews in flight from Nazism made it to the United States. The majority of Jews living in the United States in this period had been in the country fewer than 25 years. Neither the pleas of prominent Jews, such as Louis Brandeis and Felix Frankfurter, nor the protests of those who filled Madison Square Garden for a pro-refugee rally in 1933 could alter FDR's refusal to change American policy. Nor were postwar policies toward displaced persons much more generous. The era of mass European immigration to the United States was definitely over. Cold war hostilities drove down the number of European immigrants seeking admission to the United States, and with the McCarran-Walter Act of 1952, Congress effectively excluded dissident voices from Communist-controlled countries.

An Irish Catholic President and Immigration Reform in the 1960s

In 1960 John F. Kennedy became the first Roman Catholic elected president of the United States. The grandchild of Irish immigrants, Kennedy's election marked a sea change in European immigrant influence in American politics. If an Irish Catholic could be president, then others of different groups could follow. Kennedy drew his strength from the same coalition that had supported Democrats since 1932. He hoped to reform American immigration law and, after his assassination, the more generous 1965 Immigration Act abandoned the national origins quota system for hemispheric quotas.

The half century following Kennedy's election has seen a shift in the role of European immigrants in politics. High rates of ethnic intermarriage, especially among Catholic immigrants from various European countries and their American-born children, weakened ethnic voting bloc discipline. Ethnic-bloc voting is still occasionally in evidence but less frequently than in earlier eras. At times, particular issues, such as relations between Ireland and Great Britain, rally Irish American voters. A politician's Middle Eastern policies can attract or repel the support of Jewish voters whose parents or grandparents came to the United States from Europe in flight from persecution. However, increasingly the children and grandchildren of European immigrants vote with others of their socioeconomic class. And as sociologist Mary Waters has observed, the children of marriages between parents of different backgrounds may choose their identity and their political loyalties.

New Arrivals and New Political Patterns

In the 1990s, the end of the cold war brought millions of eastern European immigrants to the United States, especially from Russia and former Soviet-dominated lands such as Ukraine. Muslims in flight from the murderous "ethnic cleansing" in Bosnia and refugees from the fighting in Kosovo and other zones of ethnic warfare in Europe also sought refuge in the West. Similar to groups from other parts of the world, European immigrants sometimes arrive legally but overstay their visas, or clandestinely enter the United States as unauthorized newcomers.

By the twenty-first century, Americans anxious to preserve their jobs and cultural hegemony had shifted their fears to Latino and Asian immigrants. While the political system remains a product of its European founders, the push and pull between native and newcomer will continue. Predicted to become an ethnic minority by the middle to late twenty-first century, those of European descent will find themselves on an altered political stage but with a democratic form of government that has evolved to accommodate just such demographic change.

See also Americanism; Catholics and politics; immigration policy; Jews and politics; nativism; Protestants and politics.

FURTHER READING

Allswang, John. *Bosses, Machines, and Urban Voters*. Revised ed. Baltimore, MD: Johns Hopkins University Press, 1997.

Anbinder, Tyler. *Nativism and Slavery: The Northern Know Nothings and the Politics of the 1850s*. New York: Oxford University Press, 1992.

Bernstein, Iver. *The New York City Draft Riots: Their Significance for American Society and Politics in the Age of the Civil War*. New York: Oxford University Press, 1991.

Cohen, Lizabeth. *Making a New Deal: Industrial Workers in Chicago, 1919–1939*. Cambridge, UK: Cambridge University Press, 1990.

Daniels, Roger. *Coming to America: A History of Immigration and Ethnicity in American Life*. New York: HarperCollins, 1990.

Gerstle, Gary. *American Crucible: Race and Nation in the Twentieth Century*. Princeton, NJ: Princeton University Press, 2001.

Higham, John. *Strangers in the Land: Patterns of American Nativism, 1860–1925*. New Brunswick, NJ: Rutgers University Press, 1955.

Jacobson, Matthew Frye. *Special Sorrows: The Diasporic Imagination of Irish, Polish, and Jewish Immigrants in the United States*. Cambridge, MA: Harvard University Press, 1995.

Kazin, Michael. *A Godly Hero: The Life of William Jennings Bryan*. New York: Knopf, 2006.

Kraut, Alan M. *The Huddled Masses: The Immigrant in American Society, 1880–1921*. 2nd ed. Wheeling, IL: Harlan Davidson, 2001.

Lichtman, Allan J. *Prejudice and the Old Politics: The Presidential Election of 1928*. Chapel Hill: University of North Carolina Press, 1979.

Lubell, Samuel. *The Future of American Politics*. Revised 3rd ed. New York: Harper and Row, 1965.

Pavlak, Thomas J. *Ethnic Identification and Political Behavior*. San Francisco: R&E Research Associates, 1976.

Wilentz, Sean. *Chants Democratic: New York City and the Rise of the American Working Class, 1788–1850*. New York: Oxford University Press, 1984.

———. *The Rise of American Democracy: Jefferson to Lincoln*. New York: Norton, 2005.

ALAN M. KRAUT

exceptionalism

See liberal consensus and American exceptionalism.

executive branch

See cabinet departments; presidency.

federalism

The foundations of federalism were laid in the colonial period, when power was shared between governments in the American provinces and the British metropolis. The sources and limits of political authority in the empire were increasingly controversial in the years leading up to independence, and the failure to resolve these constitutional issues led to the revolutionary-era outburst of state constitution writing. Abjuring their allegiance to King George III, revolutionary constitutionalists invoked the "sovereignty" of the people. But relocating legitimate authority did not clarify the distribution of authority in an extended republican polity. Pressed by the exigencies of war making on a continental scale, revolutionaries sought to cement the alliance of the states under the Articles of Confederation (drafted by Congress in 1777 and finally ratified when Maryland acceded in 1781) and the Constitution (drafted in 1787 and ratified by 11 states in 1787–88).

In theory, the sovereign people, acting through their state republics, delegated strictly defined powers to a central government exercising sovereign powers in the international system. In practice, however, the location of sovereignty remained controversial. The process of constitution writing taught Americans that the actual distribution of power was subject to their political will. The bitterly contested constitutional politics of the Revolutionary years culminated in the debate over the Constitution between Federalist proponents and anti-Federalist opponents, thus preparing the way for the vicious party battles of the 1790s and subsequent struggles over the character of the federal union. The constitutional ambiguity was never fully resolved before the victory of Union forces in the Civil War and the imposition of a new federal regime through Constitutional amendments and the Reconstruction of the seceding southern states.

The crisis that destroyed the British Empire in North America resulted from a constitutional deficit—from the failure of the British government to negotiate terms of union that would have secured provincial autonomy and guaranteed colonists the rights of Englishmen. Antebellum Americans suffered no such deficit. Quite the contrary, the destruction of their federal union was the result of a contentious, highly polarized political culture—a surfeit of constitutionalism—that inspired politicians and theorists to raise fundamental questions about the sources of legitimate authority and its proper distribution. From crisis to crisis, the union survived only through a series of increasingly tenuous compromises: in 1820–21, over admitting Missouri; in 1832–33, over South Carolina's nullification of the tariff; and in 1850, over the future of the West, the rendition of fugitive slaves, and other related issues. Every compromise left a legacy of bitterness for principled constitutionalists.

Forging the Federal Union

Security issues had prompted the colonists to consider forming intercolonial alliances before the Revolution, most notably in the abortive Albany Plan of Union in 1754, drafted by Benjamin Franklin. His plan to manage Indian relations under the aegis of an American grand council and a crown-appointed governor general was rejected both by provincial governments, wary of curbs on their autonomy, and by imperial authorities. In the subsequent war with France and its Indian allies (1757–63), the British ministry made no further effort to tamper with colonial constitutions, instead promoting colonial cooperation though large-scale spending and generous financial guarantees. Led by provincial assemblies determined to defend traditional privileges and liberties, patriotic Americans thus linked loyalty to king and empire with expansive conceptions of colonial autonomy;

primed to resist postwar reforms that jeopardized the constitutional status quo, defenders of British American rights looked to their king, George III, to protect them against encroachments by the British Parliament.

Before the empire's final rupture, the idea that the American colonies were distinct dominions, or "kingdoms," was embraced by John Adams, Thomas Jefferson, James Wilson, and other forward-looking patriots. Through their allegiance to a common sovereign, the American provinces constituted a federal union. When George III definitively rejected this extraordinary conception of his authority and unleashed massive force against his recalcitrant American subjects, reluctantly independent Americans had to forge bonds of union on an entirely new basis. Although they had improvised ad hoc extraconstitutional structures, from local committees through the Continental Congress and the Continental Army, the protracted mobilization against imperial authority systematically undercut the legitimacy of imperial—or continental—governance. The great challenge for American constitutionalists was to reverse these centrifugal tendencies and find a way to superimpose a strong executive power capable of making war and of securing peace, over a loose federation of independent republics. The first step was for delegates from the respective states to symbolically kill the king and to assert their own authority—or, rather, the authority of the sovereign peoples they represented.

Americans did not resist British imperial authority with the intention of creating unconnected, independent state republics that would exercise full sovereign powers. The Declaration of Independence, Jefferson later recalled, was "the fundamental act of union of these States." But the war effort itself led many Americans to fear they might be creating a monster in their own midst. The drafting and ratification of the Articles of Confederation *followed* the wartime exercise of unprecedented governmental power over the lives of ordinary Americans, imposing strict limits on a central government and securing the residual "sovereignty" of member states. Defenders of the subsequent Constitution attempted to resolve this conceptual incoherence; sovereignty, they claimed, remained in the people—whoever (and wherever) they were. But clever rhetoric could not make the problem go away. Conditioned by the imperial crisis to see a fundamental tension between provincial liberties and imperial authority, Americans struggled to create and preserve a tenuous federal balance among legitimate—that is, sovereign—authorities.

Federal union was supposed to secure the protection that the American colonies had formerly enjoyed under the empire. But Americans feared that an energetic central government would jeopardize their liberties; they also feared that some states would gain the advantage over others, reducing them to subject provinces. State equality was therefore the fundamental premise of the confederation, an alliance that would protect the states from each other as well as from external threats. Though the Constitution introduced the principle of proportional representation in the lower house, the state equality principle survived in the senate as well as in Article IV, Section 3, providing for the equality of new states. Expansion would also stabilize the union by mitigating power imbalances among the original states.

Because the invention of American federalism reflected various—sometimes conflicting—imperatives, the Constitution has been subject to an extraordinary range of interpretations. On one hand, American constitutionalists sought to construct a regime that would secure a place for the United States as an independent nation in the system of Atlantic States. This "nationalist" impulse emphasized energetic administration and state building on the federal level, drawing inspiration from Britain's powerful fiscal-military state. In response, advocates of states' rights harked back to the defense of provincial liberties against imperial reform efforts in the run-up to the American Revolution: the Articles of Confederation struck the original federal balance and remained the benchmark for strict constructionists even after the Constitution's ratification.

Concerns about the new nation's faltering position in the postwar period—the Confederation's inability to raise revenue, service its debts, or negotiate effectively with other powers—led to a new push for energetic government, but reformers had to accommodate widely shared concerns about the dangers of centralized, "consolidated" authority. Federalists thus presented the Constitution as a "peace plan" that would guarantee collective security and protect the states from one another, thus enabling them to enjoy the full benefits of their republican governments. Federalist assurances that the new regime would secure, not destroy, the states constituted the first great exercise in constitutional interpretation (however disingenuous), buttressed by the subsequent implementation of campaign promises to adopt amendments that would protect states and citizens from federal overreach. James Madison pushed ten amendments (collectively known as the Bill of Rights) through the first federal Congress, demonstrating the reformers' good faith and providing skeptical oppositionists with potentially useful lines of defense.

Far from clarifying the character of the new federal regime, the proliferating commentaries on the Constitution initiated by the ratification debate generated massive interpretive confusion. To some extent, controversy over the limits of federal authority had a stabilizing effect, channeling political conflicts into the courts and promoting the formation of broad political party coalitions. But, in the 1790s, clashing views on the constitutionality of the first Bank of the United States and other key planks of Treasury Secretary Alexander Hamilton's ambitious state-building program also gave new life to fundamental questions about the distribution of authority that had destroyed the British Empire and chronically jeopardized the American union. Hamiltonian "loose constructionists" betrayed impatience with—if not contempt for—the Constitution as a mere text, seemingly confirming anti-Federalist skepticism about the Federalists' good faith. For their part, Jeffersonian "strict constructionists" convinced themselves that the whole point of the Constitution was to limit federal authority and secure states' rights, thus turning the original reform impulse on its head.

The party battles of the 1790s thus perpetuated the constitutional politics of the ratification debate, with controversy centering on how to interpret the Constitution and party mobilization focused on maintaining or gaining control of the federal government. Jeffersonian Republicans promoted state sovereignty claims, intimating during the darkest hours of High Federalist oppression during the undeclared war with France of 1798–1800 that liberty-loving states might have to exercise their primal exit rights and leave the union. But their goal was to redeem the union from hypercentralization and reinforce the consensual bonds that, Jefferson later asserted, made the government of the union "the strongest on earth." Meanwhile, High Federalists invoked patriotic sentiments to build a powerful warmaking federal state, implementing direct taxation, curbing seditious speech, and taking controversial steps to contain the alien menace (all in 1798): at best, the states would have only a subordinate, administrative role under the new dispensation. The Republican response, articulated in Jefferson's Kentucky Resolutions (1798), Madison's Virginia Resolutions (1798), and Madison's report to the Virginia legislature (1800), became the new

orthodoxy—"the principles of 1798"—in the wake of Jefferson's "Revolution of 1800." Recognition of the states' foundational role, their original sovereignty and continuing autonomy, was the hallmark of the new orthodoxy. Yet the character of American federalism would remain incoherent and controversial in subsequent decades—until the union finally collapsed in 1861.

Political Economy

Beginning in 1801, Republicans controlled Congress and the presidency but not the federal court system. The Jeffersonians' subsequent campaign to purge the Federalist-dominated judiciary was foiled, as Federalist Chief Justice John Marshall beat a prudent retreat. Marshall went on to establish the Supreme Court's role as the ultimate arbiter of constitutionality under the new regime in *McCulloch v. Maryland* (1819) and other landmark federalism cases. Yet notwithstanding the charges of orthodox Jeffersonians, Marshall was no High Federalist intent on dismantling the states. To the contrary, the thrust of Marshall's jurisprudence, and particularly of his expansive readings of the Commerce Clause (in Article I, Section VIII), was to promote mobility and market exchange in a continentwide free trade zone and so foster the interdependent interests that Republicans agreed were the most durable bonds of union.

Marshall's long tenure as chief justice (1801–35) coincided with a period of extraordinary economic growth in which *state* governments played the most crucial role. Freed from the crippling tax burdens of the confederation years by the new federal government's assumption of Revolutionary War debts, the states responded to popular pressure for internal improvements, banks, and state-sanctioned business enterprises. The "commonwealth" period of mixed enterprise and aggressive state promotion of market development was the heyday of early American federalism, with governments at all levels demonstrating increased capacity in an expanding economy. The federal government guaranteed free trade at home, regulated overseas commerce, acquired new territory, and secured the states against foreign threats; it also subsidized the circulation of news and financial information through the postal service; sponsored a wide range of improvements, from lighthouses to post roads, that were related (sometimes only very loosely) to its primary security functions; removed Indians from their homelands; privatized public lands; and promoted political and economic development in western territories (most importantly by opening the Southwest to slavery).

The federal balance was not well defined in the antebellum decades, though periodic crises would revive old arguments about the source and location of legitimate authority. What is most remarkable about the period is the generally high level of tolerance for theoretical ambiguity and the ability of politicians to foster good working relations between state and federal governments. Intergovernmental cooperation was helped by the circulation of party elites from the local to the national level, from the more or less distant periphery to the center of action in Washington, D.C., the republican metropolis. The overlap and interpenetration of governments through the "corruption" of party politics—loaves and fishes to the politicians, and pork to their constituents—made federalism work, substituting a virtuous circle of expanding benefits for the vicious cycle of escalating threats that periodically threatened the union. Theorizing about federalism, whether in the British Empire or in the antebellum United States, tended to culminate in irreconcilable sovereignty claims.

State Rights and Sectional Nationalisms

The Constitution created a "more perfect union" that periodically threatened to fall apart. Major economic interests vying for advantage were concentrated in particular sections: for example, southern cotton producers sought free trade with foreign trading partners while northern manufacturers pressed for a protected home market. Struggles over national commercial policy led in turn to new controversies over constitutional interpretation. Opponents of protection argued for a narrow construction of the Commerce Clause, insisting high tariffs distributed benefits unequally and thus threatened to subvert the union; protectionists responded that collective security depended on achieving economic independence and balanced development in an expansive home market. Differing assessments of risk and opportunity in a world trading system that had been chronically wracked by war pitted economic "nationalists" who preached preparedness against cosmopolitan free traders who began to question the value of the union. Discounting the threat of foreign war, strict constructionists instead emphasized the danger of concentrated power *within* the union: their Constitution, seen as a more perfect version of the Articles of Confederation, was supposed to guarantee the rights of states against the "foreign" power of a corrupt and despotic central government.

In the federal arena, policy disputes tended to rise (or descend) to fundamental questions about the character of the union. Depending on changing calculations of costs and benefits, combatants shifted grounds, sometimes embracing federal authority, sometimes resisting its supposed encroachments. The "slave power" was notoriously changeable, first using the federal government to guarantee slave property, secure foreign markets, and remove Indians from productive western lands. Then, debates over the tariff transformed John C. Calhoun and other southern "nationalists" into defenders of states' rights who feared that *any* exercise of federal authority jeopardized their peculiar institution. Yet even as they threatened to bolt the union, Southerners pressed for constitutional protections of slavery throughout the union—and a new federal regime strong enough to enforce them.

Radical Southerners, determined to perpetuate the institution of slavery talked about strict construction and state sovereignty in order to justify secession, but they envisioned the creation of a powerful new slaveholding nation that would assume a prominent place in the world. For northern nationalists, America's future greatness depended on preserving and strengthening the union, with or without slavery. Northerners mobilized to block slavery's expansion only when the Republicans emerged as a strictly sectional party, but even then few challenged the institution where it already existed.

Yet, despite the limited appeal of antislavery, slavery proved to be the polarizing, nonnegotiable issue that destroyed American federalism. As Southerners and Northerners embraced incompatible conceptions of American (or southern) nationhood, the founders' provisions for union and collective security seemed less and less compelling. The threat of sectional domination—whether by the slave power or by a prospective antislavery majority—came from within, not from abroad. For growing numbers of alienated or principled Americans, North and South, the intersectional party coalitions that made federal policy making possible increasingly reeked of corruption: majority rule threatened minority rights. The virtuous circle of federal politics, fueled by the growing capacity of governments at all levels to deliver benefits, now lurched into reverse. Efforts to mend the system accelerated its collapse. As the sectional crisis deepened, increasingly desperate unionists proposed to amend or rewrite the Constitution, thus depriving the union of its last shred of legitimacy and preparing the way for disunion and war.

Americans talked themselves into Civil War. Alienated by the tariff and fearful of moves against slavery by Constitutional majorities, Southerners moved from strict construction to first principles, bringing the sovereignty question back to the fore: if sovereign states had made the union, they could also unmake it. In response, Northerners embraced an increasingly robust conception of union as nation, but also moved away from the original understanding of "the union as it was." The destiny of the United States was to be a great nation, humankind's best hope. Pledging to uphold "our national Constitution," Abraham Lincoln thus promised his fellow Americans in his first inaugural address that "the Union will endure forever." Of course, it only endured because the rump Union was finally able to impose its will on the Confederacy.

Before the Civil War, Joseph Story and other nationalists had countered the orthodox Republican claim that the states had exercised their original, sovereign powers in creating the union, insisting instead that the "nation" had come first. The war resolved any lingering ambiguity on the question of origins, confirming a new orthodoxy: the nation had created—and continued to sustain—the union. The Civil War Amendments (1865–70) constitutionalized U.S. rule over the defeated Confederacy. They outlawed slavery, defined national citizenship, and promised to uphold freedmen's voting rights, thus overturning slave state constitutions and transforming the character of the old federal union. In the Supreme Court case *Texas v. White* (1869), Chief Justice Salmon Chase echoed Lincoln in concluding that the Constitution had created "an indestructible Union, composed of indestructible states." The national polity would thus preserve constitutionally subordinate jurisdictions: if the precise distribution of authority sometimes generated controversy, the practical business of federalism now focused on politics, administration, and intergovernmental relations. The sovereignty issue had been definitively resolved.

Yet if the Civil War seemed to resolve the fundamental theoretical questions that had finally destroyed the antebellum Union, the perpetuation of multiple jurisdictions offered subsequent generations of American politicians and lawyers continuing opportunities to promote and protect particular interests, sometimes in apparent defiance of the national will—as in the case of segregated "Jim Crow" regimes in the South. During the early twentieth century, progressive reformers would also seek to recalibrate the federal balance in favor of the states, celebrating them as "laboratories of democracy."

And, during the first year of the Obama administration, some conservative Republicans asserted a right to "state sovereignty," based on their reading of the Tenth Amendment. The legacy of antebellum conflicts over the nature of the Union thus persists in both opportunistic and principled efforts to renew or redefine American federalism.

See also anti-Federalists; Civil War; Constitution, federal; era of new republic, 1789–1827; state constitutions.

FURTHER READING

Edling, Max M. *A Revolution in Favor of Government: Origins of the U.S. Constitution and the Making of the American State.* New York: Oxford University Press, 2003.

Greene, Jack P. *Peripheries and Center: Constitutional Development in the Extended Polities of the British Empire and the United States, 1607–1788.* Athens: University of Georgia Press, 1986.

Handlin, Oscar. *Commonwealth: A Study of the Role of Government in the American Economy: Massachusetts, 1774–1861.* Revised ed. Cambridge, MA: Harvard University Press, 1969.

Hendrickson, David. *Peace Pact: The Lost World of the American Founding.* Lawrence: University Press of Kansas, 2003.

Holt, Michael F. *The Political Crisis of the 1850s.* New York: Wiley, 1978.

Hyman, Harold M. *A More Perfect Union: The Impact of the Civil War and Reconstruction on the Constitution.* New York: Knopf, 1973.

Knupfer, Peter. *The Union As It Is: Constitutional Unionism and Sectional Compromise, 1787–1861.* Chapel Hill: University of North Carolina Press, 1991.

McDonald, Forrest. *States' Rights and Union: Imperium in Imperio, 1776–1876.* Lawrence: University Press of Kansas, 2000.

Morgan, Edmund S. *Inventing the People: The Rise of Popular Sovereignty in England and America.* New York: Norton, 1988.

Onuf, Nicholas, and Peter Onuf. *Nations, Markets, and War: Modern History and the American Civil War.* Charlottesville: University of Virginia Press, 2006.

Onuf, Peter S. "Federalism, Republicanism, and the Origins of American Sectionalism." In *All Over the Map: Rethinking Region and Nation in the United States,* edited by Edward L. Ayers, Patricia Nelson Limerick, and Stephen Nissenbaum, 11–37. Baltimore, MD: Johns Hopkins University Press, 1996.

———. *Jefferson's Empire: The Language of American Nationhood.* Charlottesville: University Press of Virginia, 2000.

White, Edward G. *The Marshall Court and Cultural Change, 1815–1835.* New York: Oxford University Press, 1991.

PETER S. ONUF

Federalist Party

Disagreements over domestic and foreign policy within George Washington's cabinet, then within Congress, brought on the emergence of the first two political parties in the world with recognizably modern attributes. One of those parties was the Federalist Party.

The party was not a product of earlier divisions over ratification of the Constitution. Nor were its adherents, who always championed a vigorous national government, the direct descendants of those, also called "federalists," who had championed the writing and ratification of the new Constitution in 1787 and 1788. To be sure, the party's leaders had led that movement to replace the Articles of Confederation. Yet, so had many others, like James Madison, who, after joining the new government, soon formed the core of the Federalists' opposition, the Democratic-Republican Party. Both original parties thus came into being because of new circumstances of government and new policy issues after 1789.

The Federalist Party as Political Party

What justifies calling the Federalist Party a "party" in the first place, when, considered as a political party, it was a pale image of what have since become continuing, clearly defined popular organizations with large staffs, impressive fund-raising capacities, and office seekers and officeholders at all levels of government? The justification is that the Federalist Party had many of the characteristics possessed by modern parties in nation-states with open societies governed under popular constitutions by freely elected representative assemblies and executive officers. The party put up candidates who engaged in competition for public office. It built the capacity to define public issues, educate the public about its policies, and mobilize people to vote by holding election rallies. By printing political handbills, pamphlets, and sermons; founding newspapers; and raising funds, the party created what we know of as political campaigns. It worked to get out the vote from qualified male voters, and even from women in those few places where, for

a time, women could vote. It developed a rudimentary kind of organization—with a rough leadership hierarchy from congressional and legislative caucuses to state, town, and ward committees and with responsibilities distributed among adherents. It took over existing non-partisan institutions, like volunteer militia companies, to make them accessories of the party. "Membership" was open to anyone who wished to support the party. In that respect, it was a voluntary association, not an emanation of the national state, and it operated under the rule of public law. It also developed a clearly defined political ideology, many of whose elements, like the championship of strong federal intervention in the economy and opposition to the spread of slavery, had enduring consequences in American history.

The Federalist Party was a party in a modern sense. It was not, for instance, a "faction" or "interest," a group of like-minded men—long characteristic of British government, the Continental states, and the colonies—who protected each other's interests and sought preferment on personal, regional, or class grounds rather than for policy ends. Nor was it a closed association—one that required its members to pass a kind of test for entry. No coercion or state sponsorship (like that exhibited in totalitarian, Communist, and some post-Communist nations like Russia) were involved in its creation or development. It was not the expression of a tribal identity or clan affiliation, as in many parts of the Middle East and Africa. Nor was it a kind of family possession, as was the case with some parties in, for example, Pakistan. Instead, the Federalist Party was an institution, recognized as such, with whom anyone could freely associate as compatriots whose principal aim was to put up candidates to contest and win elective offices and thus gain the power to enact legislation and steer bureaucratic policies in particular directions.

But why did the United States and not another nation give birth to modern parties? The Constitution created a national arena in which each contest for the presidency, the principal elective national office, had to be organized and waged. Unlike parliamentary systems, in which the largest party or a coalition of smaller parties elect a prime minister, under the Constitution, a majority of electoral votes cast in all the states was made to decide the presidential contest, and so the electoral outcome in no state could be left to chance. Control of Congress also depended on fielding candidates of like political mind in every state. Under electoral methods prevailing in the nation's early years, state governments usually elected each state's senators, and thus control of the state legislatures themselves was imperative if a party was to gain control of Congress. Finally, since American elections were—as they are today—single winner-take-all contests in which a plurality of votes, not a majority, was necessary for election (with no second-chance, runoff elections as in, for example, France), each contest was a deciding struggle between candidates. It did not, therefore, take long for the generation of the framers and those who staffed the early administrations and served in the early congresses to realize that, despite their dislike of parties, partisanship, and political discord, the realities of the constitutional government they had created and of the world into which they had launched the new constitutional system called for national political organization.

The Federalist Party Emerges

Signs of partisan division appeared soon after the new government came into being in 1789. Washington himself, while disdaining parties and disclaiming party affiliation, was, by political view and personal inclination, a Federalist and the party's great figurehead, and he drew to himself other leading figures—John Adams, Alexander Hamilton, John Jay, and John Marshall—who were of like mind. Policy differences within Washington's cabinet originated after Hamilton, the first secretary of the treasury, in 1790 proposed a set of bold, strategic, precedent-setting steps to stabilize the nation's finances. Hamilton urged the federal government to assume the states' Revolutionary War debts, pay those debts at their par value rather than at their depressed market value, and charter a national bank. Because, if enacted, these proposals would reward speculators in federal and state debt instruments and significantly boost the power of the national government over the nation's financial system, Secretary of State Thomas Jefferson argued vigorously within the cabinet against the initiatives, and Virginia congressman James Madison led opposition to Hamilton's plan in the House of Representatives, where he was then serving. This opposition was confined more or less to circles in the capital (then New York, soon, until 1800, Philadelphia) and did not spread much beyond. Moreover, the opposition failed, and Hamilton's proposals were enacted into law in 1791.

The Federalist Party began to take more organized shape and gain a larger set of adherents within the general public. In 1794 the administration called up troops to quell the "Whiskey Rebellion" in western Pennsylvania, and in 1795 and 1796 Congress debated the ratification and implementation of a new treaty with Great Britain (known as Jay's Treaty, after Chief Justice John Jay, its American negotiator). Under Hamilton's leadership, the party began to gain its historic identity as a champion of strong national government; decisive executive leadership; domestic order, maintained if necessary by military force; wide-ranging judicial oversight of legislation; a preference for commercial links with Britain; and a deep suspicion of French policies (especially after the commencement of the French Revolution in 1789). The classic statement of the party's views, prepared with Hamilton's help, was Washington's celebrated Farewell Address of 1796. The president's valedictory deplored partisan division and urged the avoidance of all permanent alliances with foreign powers (a veiled attack on the 1778 wartime alliance, still in force, with France).

While Washington had avoided openly identifying himself with the Federalist Party, Vice President John Adams, who succeeded Washington in 1797, was the first president to be an avowed partisan. Adams initially maintained Washington's cabinet members and policies, and his administration engaged in a popular undeclared naval war with France, the so-called Quasi War. Adams also supported and implemented the Alien and Sedition Acts after congressional Federalists, having gained control of both the House and Senate in the 1798 elections, enacted them. Their passage marked the Federalists' political high watermark.

Soon the party came under withering attack for implementing these laws, which limited free speech and put immigrants under suspicion of disloyalty. As a result of a popular backlash, never again would the Federalists control both the presidency and Congress. In fact, the party began to splinter in 1799 as Hamilton's wing of the party attacked Adams for opening negotiations with France to end the Quasi War. The Hamiltonians finally broke with Adams when he reorganized the cabinet with men loyal to himself and not to Hamilton. These actions, taken in part to strengthen Adams's own political position, proved insufficient to gain him reelection. Nevertheless, before handing over the presidency to Thomas Jefferson, Adams concluded peace with France and saw his nominee, John Marshall, confirmed as chief justice of the Supreme Court. Through Marshall's court, Federalist principles became the foundation of American constitutional law and extended the party's influence and principles well into the future.

The Federalists in Opposition

In the minority after 1801, Federalists had to accept the need to create a system of state party organizations and adopt more democratic electoral practices to parallel and compete with those of their Democratic-Republican rivals. Even with such a system in place, Federalists remained a minority party whose following was found principally in the commercial Northeast, especially in Massachusetts and Connecticut, and in Delaware and sections of Virginia, North Carolina, and South Carolina among the commercial elite. The party also attracted workingmen attached to commercial interests and adherents of established religious bodies, like Congregationalists and Episcopalians. But it lacked appeal among the nation's largest bloc of voters, small farmers in the South and West, as well as among religious dissenters (like Baptists) and slaveholding plantation owners in the South, especially once the party began to attack the overrepresentation of slave states in Congress and the Electoral College because of the Constitution's three-fifths clause.

Federalist policies appealed principally to those who supported a strong national government to counterbalance state governments, an economic system controlled by a national bank, tariffs to protect American commerce, and a military force capable of protecting the nation and, if necessary, putting down domestic disorders. And, although they were forced by circumstances to adopt popular methods of campaigning and to encourage the gradual broadening of the electorate, the party's leaders, whose style was generally elitist, opposed as long as possible the general spread of political and social democracy. Not surprisingly, Federalist ideology and policies, plus the resulting geographic limitations on the party's support, led to its repeated defeats (save in a few states), its inability to mount successful national candidacies, and its eventual demise.

Jefferson's election in 1800 and the popularity of his administration made the Federalists' chances of regaining the presidency with Charles Cotesworth Pinckney in 1804 difficult at best. But their opposition in 1803 to the popular Louisiana Purchase, because it threatened the influence of northeastern states and was too costly, resulted in Federalists' resounding defeat in that election. Hamilton's death in a duel with Vice President Aaron Burr the same year cost the party its most energetic, if divisive, leader. Those setbacks might have been enough to destroy the party, but the Jeffferson administration's 1807 embargo on all foreign trade, which seriously injured the economy, gave Federalists a new lease on political life. Yet they failed once again to win the presidency when Secretary of State James Madison defeated the Federalist candidate, again Charles Cotesworth Pinckney, in the 1808 presidential election. Even after Madison's administration declared war against Great Britain in 1812, the Federalists could not mount an effective challenge to his reelection that year, when the party carried only New York, New Jersey, and some of Maryland, in addition to New England. The party's days seemed numbered.

With another approach, Federalist leaders might have built upon their renewed popularity after the embargo of 1807 and given the party a fighting chance at a new majority. Instead, by choosing to oppose the War of 1812 and then to obstruct it—the kind of strategy always tempting but usually dangerous for opposition parties in time of war—the Federalists sealed their political doom. Convening in Hartford in 1814 to discuss how to affect the course of the war by legal means, Federalists instead faced charges, however unjust and inaccurate, that they had secessionist and treasonous aims. It did not help that the report of the Hartford Convention appeared just as news of the war-ending Treaty of Ghent arrived in the United States in early 1815. Facing ridicule, the party never recovered. In the 1816 presidential election, Secretary of State James Monroe swamped Federalist candidate Rufus King, who carried only Massachusetts, Connecticut, and Delaware. This was the last time the party would contest a presidential election.

Following that defeat the party could only hold on for a while in Congress and in some states and cities. With Monroe's administration and Congress enacting many measures (such as chartering a second national bank) urged earlier by the Federalists, and with the emergence of new issues in the 1820s that brought about a general reorganization of American politics, the Federalist Party was no more. Finding a home in both the Democratic Party and the Whig Party, Federalists thereafter transferred their energies into civic, charitable, professional, historical, and cultural organizations and into corporations and banks, where in many places, especially in cities, they had lasting influence.

The Federalist Party Assessed

How are we to assess the history of the first American political party to die? Its death surely was due in large part to its inability, despite its adoption of many popular political and electoral methods, to adjust its views, strategies, words, and tone to the nation's increasingly democratic culture. Federalist resistance to democracy, while gaining some support among workingmen in the nation's commercial towns and cities, could not appeal to the majority of Americans who, as farmers, were suspicious of the government and its influence over the economy and were increasingly less inclined to accept the political dominance of members of the wealthy elite. Federalist attacks on slave representation made the party in effect a regional party of the Northeast. In addition, the party's close association with British interests, both commercial and strategic, gradually eroded its popularity. When it then opposed war with Britain, it seemed to be nothing more than an opposition party—one without commitment to the national interest. Not for the last time did a party opposing a popular war cast its future into doubt.

Nevertheless, the Federalist Party left an enduring legacy to the nation. Its principles—an energetic executive, a vigorous federal government, a national economy comparatively free of internal restraint, and a judiciary capable of interpreting law and Constitution —eventually became bedrocks of American government and politics. A reluctance to get involved in troubles overseas, especially in Europe, classically expressed in Washington's Farewell Address, became the fundamental, if not always honored, theme of American foreign policy. By even briefly, if not with full commitment, seeking and accepting the votes of women, the party recognized (more so than the Democratic-Republicans) the political agency of that part of the population that would not be fully enfranchised until the twentieth century. And by introducing into partisan politics many issues about slavery—its immorality, the excess political strength it gave the South, and its further spread westward, issues subsequently taken up by the Whig, and then Republican, parties—the Federalists laid the groundwork for defining northern politics as distinct from those of the South and for the political abolitionism that would ineluctably lead to the Civil War.

See also anti-Federalists; federalism.

FURTHER READING

Banner, James M., Jr. *To the Hartford Convention: The Federalists and the Origins of Party Politics in Massachusetts, 1789–1815*. New York: Knopf, 1970.

Ben-Atar, Doron, and Barbara B. Oberg, eds. *Federalists Reconsidered*. Charlottesville: University Press of Virginia, 1998.

Elkins, Stanley, and Eric McKitrick. *The Age of Federalism: The Early American Republic, 1788–1800*. New York: Oxford University Press, 1993.

Koschnik, Albrecht. *"Let a Common Interest Bind Us Together": Associations, Partisanship, and Culture in Philadelphia, 1775–1840*. Charlottesville: University of Virginia Press, 2007.

Livermore, Shaw, Jr. *The Twilight of Federalism: The Disintegration of the Federalist Party, 1815–1830*. Princeton, NJ: Princeton University Press, 1962.

Mason, Matthew. *Slavery and Politics in the Early American Republic*. Chapel Hill: University of North Carolina Press, 2006.

Sharp, James Roger. *American Politics in the Early Republic: The New Nation in Crisis*. New Haven, CT: Yale University Press, 1993.

Zagarri, Rosemarie. *Revolutionary Backlash: Women and Politics in the Early American Republic*. Philadelphia: University of Pennsylvania Press, 2007.

JAMES M. BANNER JR.

feminism

The word *feminism* comes from the French word *feminisme*, which was coined in the nineteenth century by followers of communitarian socialist Charles Fourier to denote their women's rights stance. By the end of that century, feminism in Europe became associated with an emphasis on enlightened motherhood as a key to social reform and on establishing national welfare programs to provide financial support to unmarried mothers so that they could stay home to raise their children. The word feminism and the ideas associated with it first appeared in the United States in 1910. They especially appealed to younger women who wanted both careers and families and who were critical of older women's rights leaders for not marrying, being antimale, and focusing on political and legal issues above maternal and psychological ones. Until 1910 the terms *woman's rights* and *women's rights* denoted the drive for equality for women in the United States. From this perspective, the use of the word feminism to apply to earlier women's rights endeavors in the United States is technically inaccurate, although the usage has become standard among historians. By the 1960s, feminism was adopted as an umbrella term for a variety of intellectual positions that called for gender equality.

The Wave Metaphor: A Framework

Historians often use the metaphor of a wave to categorize three major periods of feminist advocacy in the history of the United States. Many women in the 1960s and 1970s described their conversion to feminism in terms of an ocean "wave" crashing over and carrying them along in its wake. In the historical framework based on this metaphor, the first wave occurred between 1848 and 1920; the second in the 1960s and 1970s; and the third in the 1970s and 1980s. In 1848 a convention held in Seneca Falls, New York, launched the women's rights movement, and in 1920 the Nineteenth Amendment, giving the vote to women, became law. In the 1960s, groups of women discovered that discriminatory laws and practices against women existed on the local, state, and national levels. They worked to eliminate them, inspired by the civil rights movement of the 1950s and 1960s and the student movement of the 1960s. The term *third wave* is sometimes applied to the "post-feminists" of the 1970s and 1980s who, paralleling their predecessors in the 1910s, launched an attack on the previous generation of feminists as antifamily, antimale, and, in this instance, puritanical about sex.

Within the wave framework, the period from 1920 to 1960 is usually viewed as an interlude between first wave and second wave feminism. According to this interpretation, once the suffrage amendment became law, the energy of the women's movement dissipated and it factionalized into different groups, while the political and social conservatism of the 1920s and the national focus on the sexual revolution of the decade hampered its progress. A revisionist interpretation by younger historians, however, stresses greater continuity between historical periods and questions the use of the wave metaphor.

From the Seneca Falls Convention to the Woman Suffrage Amendment

Even before the Seneca Falls Convention marked the formal beginning of the equal rights movement, individual women—like communitarian socialist reformer Frances Wright—had called for legal and social rights for women equal to those of men. In addition, women had been leaders in antebellum reform groups, such as ones organized to eliminate prostitution and alcoholism, both seen as male vices. Some historians use the term *social feminism* to denote women's participation in general reform movements that advanced women's position. The Seneca Falls Convention, however, focused on gaining legal, political, and social rights for women at a time when married women were defined as legal appendages of their husbands—with no right to their property, their earnings, their children, and even their bodies—and when most colleges and professions were closed to them. They did not have voting rights. The famed Seneca Falls Declaration of Sentiments detailed such wrongs visited on women and called for their elimination.

During the 1850s and 1860s, the women's rights movement took a backseat to the militant antislavery movement and to issues raised by the Civil War. After the war, and especially after antislavery leaders refused to include women under the terms of the Fifteenth Amendment, which enfranchised black men, the women's movement focused on attaining woman suffrage. In 1868 a woman suffrage amendment was introduced into Congress. At the same time, groups of feminist women (and men) in municipalities and states throughout the nation secured women's entry into higher education and into the professions, while significant advances were made in overturning legal codes that discriminated against women. By the end of the nineteenth century, in most states women had rights to their property and earnings, and in cases of divorce, mothers usually were awarded custody of their children.

Women's involvement in social feminism soared in the late nineteenth and early twentieth centuries, as women helped initiate and lead the Progressive reform movement of that era. Women—both black and white—participated in community and state efforts throughout the nation to provide public services like paved roads, sewage systems, playgrounds, and parks. They joined organizations like the many settlement houses located in urban ghettos that were designed to help the impoverished improve the conditions of their lives, and they established local and national organizations like the General Federation of Women's Clubs and the National Association of Black Women. They lobbied for pure food and drug acts, subsidized housing for the poor, and legislation to provide payments to unmarried women with children. To justify these reform endeavors, women used the Victorian argument that they were "morally superior" to men combined with the new "feminist" emphasis on the moral superiority of motherhood and Jane Addams's proposal that women's experiences as domestic managers of homes could translate into an ability to become effective "municipal housekeepers."

Women's reform efforts supported the growing campaign for a woman suffrage amendment to the constitution. That campaign dated from the Reconstruction

Era, when women were excluded from the Fourteenth and Fifteenth Amendments. For more than 40 years, national woman suffrage organizations lobbied legislatures and organized electoral campaigns to achieve women's right to vote. They finally secured that right in 1920 with ratification of the Nineteenth Amendment.

From 1920 through the 1950s

Some historians of women argue that the period between 1920 and 1960 was not static with regard to women's advance. Indeed, organizations like the women's clubs, the National Parent-Teachers Association, and the League of Women Voters had sizable memberships, while all worked to a greater or lesser degree to further a woman's rights agenda. In the face of a strong conservative backlash, however, women's organizations expended considerable energy maintaining the advances that had been won, giving the incorrect impression that they were ineffectual. Both conservatives and the media caricatured feminism as out of date and unnecessary, while the term itself was less and less used. An equal rights amendment guaranteeing women's equality was introduced into Congress in 1923, but it failed to pass either house in the interwar period. The sexual revolution of the 1920s and its flagrant consumerism also gave the false impression that women had achieved all the rights they desired. In the 1930s, the economic depression occupied the attention of the nation, and strong leftist organizations like the Communist Party focused on issues concerning labor and class, and overlooked gender. Yet some historians contend that feminism remained sufficiently strong in the interwar years that the wave metaphor as the paradigm for the history of women in the United States should be abandoned altogether.

During World War II, men joined the armed services and journeyed overseas, while women entered the workforce in large numbers. Yet this participation did not spark a new feminist movement. Once the war ended, many women returned to the home, and the domestic ideal of the 1950s, which drew strong distinctions between masculinity and femininity and viewed women's proper place as in the home, undermined any desire on the part of women to agitate for rights that were still denied them. On the other hand, some historians argue that the women's organizations in existence pursued a proto-feminist agenda, while the very domesticity of many 1950s women may have inspired their daughters in the 1960s to demand equal rights and social participation.

The 1960s

Once the civil rights movement emerged in the 1950s and the student movement followed in the early 1960s, it was probably inevitable that women would follow suit, especially since numerous women involved in the civil rights and student movements found that their male colleagues treated them as second-class citizens. Such treatment led them to identify with the disadvantaged groups whose goals they were furthering and to realize that they also were oppressed. At the same time, a number of women in the leadership ranks of labor unions and in government service grouped around Eleanor Roosevelt to persuade John F. Kennedy to call a presidential commission on the status of women soon after he was elected president. That commission, which identified existing discriminations against women, implicitly publicized the goals of feminists.

Second-wave feminists, doing their own research in books and magazines, studies and reports, found widespread evidence of discrimination against women. Professional schools enforced quotas on the number of women they admitted, as they did on blacks, Hispanics, and Jews. Women in business were relegated to the clerical pool or low-level management, while the entire workforce was segregated by gender into women's and men's occupations, with women's occupations, like airline stewardess, paying less than similar jobs for men. Under the law, women could not serve on juries; they did not have access to credit in their own names; they could not join the regular military forces; and men had control over the family in the case of divorce. Antiabortion laws were strictly enforced, and in the case of rape, women were usually considered the instigators. Men dominated municipal governments, state legislatures, and the federal government.

Feminist Perspective: 1960s and 1970s

In response to discrimination, women formed national and state organizations—like the National Organization for Women, founded in 1966—to right these wrongs. Laws were passed extending government protections to women—like Title VII of the Civil Rights Act of 1964, which extended to women the concept of affirmative action, under which sex discrimination in hiring became illegal. In 1972, under pressure from women marching in the streets and organized in the National Abortion Rights Action League (NARAL), the Supreme Court in *Roe v. Wade* made abortion legal throughout the nation.

With many adherents on college campuses and in radical study groups, the feminist movement of the 1960s and 1970s generated a number of theoretical perspectives. Many of them were grounded in the major male intellectual paradigms of the previous century. Eight dominant strains of feminism emerged: liberal, Marxist, radical, spiritual, psychoanalytic, eco-feminist, women of color feminism, and post-feminism. Liberal feminists, grounded in the equal rights traditions of the eighteenth-century Enlightenment and of John Stuart Mill in the mid-nineteenth century, focused on changing laws, equalizing education, and opening the professions and politics as equally to women as to men. Marxist feminists, whose theories were based on the ideas of Karl Marx, grounded the oppression of women in their economic exploitation, while they related women's oppression to the oppression of social class. Psychoanalytic feminists revised Sigmund Freud's doctrine that women suffered from "penis envy" to argue that men, in fact, had a more difficult time developing an adult identity than did women.

Radical feminists located the oppression of women in the objectification of their bodies under the domination of a male "gaze," while they contended that a male patriarchy controlled both women and the social order. Spiritual feminists who belonged to Christian, Buddhist, Jewish, and Islamic religions worked for the ordination of women as ministers and rabbis and produced feminist versions of traditional liturgies. Other spiritual feminists eschewed traditional religion and developed woman-centered religions like Wicca (witchcraft) and goddess worship. Eco-feminists interpreted both the oppression of women and the oppression of nature as part of the general system of patriarchal oppression. Women of color often sided with black men over white women as their natural allies, attacked the entire feminist enterprise as disregarding their concerns, and accused it of treating women of all races, ethnicities, and sexual orientations as the same, ignoring major differences that existed among them.

The post-feminists of the 1970s and 1980s, influenced by the theoretical perspectives of post-modernism and deconstruction, seconded the critique advanced by women of color, by accusing mainstream feminists of "essentialism"—or of positing the existence of universalizing constructs like patriarchy, which, they argued, varied widely over time and by geographic location. Yet some of them, influenced by the theories of Antonin Gramsci and Michel Foucault, contended that women internalized their oppression and enforced it on their own bodies. At the same time, responding to the fall of communism, the end of the cold war, and the seeming triumph of capitalism, some post-feminists proposed advancing the cause of women by the subversion of cultural styles through dress, music, and behavior, and they argued that women's true freedom lay in reinvigorating femininity by sexualizing their bodies and behaviors in order to attain power through manipulating men.

Conflict Between Generations

Throughout U.S. history, the definition of feminism—whether as a concept or just a word—has changed, as in 1910, when a new generation of women adopted the word to challenge the ideology of the previous generation of women's rights reformers, as did the post-feminists in the 1970s and 1980s. Indeed, changes in the meaning of feminism often have been motivated by conflict between generations. This recurring conflict may provide the grounding for a cyclical interpretation of the history of feminism that might replace the wave concept. Historians have stretched the definition of feminism to cover a variety of historical phenomena. Thus, some historians have identified a "domestic" feminism that grew out of women's attempts to exert themselves through their experiences in the home, as in the dramatically lessened birth rates over the course of the nineteenth century, which may have indicated a drive on the part of women to take control over their lives. Then there is social feminism, which refers to women's involvement in general reform movements. Finally, some historians have coined the term *maternal feminism* to apply to the movement for financial aid to unmarried women with children, which culminated in the Aid to Dependent Children provision of the Social Security Act of 1936.

Backlash

Since the 1980s, the successes of second-wave feminism have occasioned a backlash. Especially troubled by the legalization of abortion, the religious right waged a campaign to overturn *Roe. v. Wade* and to impose constraints on women's bodies. Political conservatives focused on ending affirmative action, and an increasingly conservative Supreme Court decreased its effectiveness. The equal rights amendment finally passed both houses of Congress in 1973, but it subsequently failed to achieve the votes of two-thirds of the state legislatures that were necessary for its passage. Identifying second-wave feminists as "man-haters" and "lesbians," many in the media successfully convinced younger generations of women that the feminists of the 1960s and 1970s were unthinking dissenters whose actions were irrelevant to the opportunities they possessed. Even within the feminist movement, alternatives to the word feminism were proposed, such as "womanist," which many African American activists prefer, or "humanist," which, some individuals argue, might more explicitly include men within any movement for gender equality. Once before in the history of the United States, a major movement for women's rights took a new direction with the aging and then the death of its original members, as first-wave feminists aged and then died. As second-wave feminists undergo the same life cycle realities, feminism itself may once again disappear—or take on new forms.

See also civil rights; woman suffrage; women and politics.

FURTHER READING

Banner, Lois W. *Women in Modern America: A Brief History.* 4th ed. Belmont, CA: Thomson Wadsworth, 2005.

Cott, Nancy. *The Grounding of Modern Feminism.* New Haven, CT: Yale University Press, 1987.

Donovan, Josephine. *Feminist Theory: The Intellectual Traditions of American Feminism.* New York: Continuum, 2006.

Ferree, Myra Marx, and Beth H. Hess. *Controversy and Coalition: The New Feminist Movement Across Four Decades of Change.* New York: Routledge, 2000.

Freedman, Estelle, ed. *The Essential Feminist Reader.* New York: Modern Library, 2007.

Frost-Knappman, Elizabeth. *Women's Suffrage in America.* New York: Facts on File, 2005.

Love, Barbara J. *Feminists Who Changed America, 1963–1975.* Urbana, IL: University of Illinois Press, 2006.

McMillan, Sally. *Seneca Falls and the Origins of the Women's Rights Movement.* New York: Oxford University Press, 2008.

Rosen, Ruth. *The World Split Open: How the Modern Women's Movement Changed America.* New York: Viking, 2000.

LOIS BANNER

foreign observers of U.S. politics

Foreign observers of the United States were preceded by those who developed an idea of America during the Age of Discovery. Indeed, long before the idea of America broke upon the general consciousness of the world, originally as a place to immigrate and eventually as a power whose military, movies, music, and money spanned the globe, European elites were aware of what they called the New World. *Mundis novis* and *de orbe novo* were the terms the educated literate classes in Western Europe used to describe the Americas after Christopher Columbus's voyages of discovery. The idea of America gripped the imaginations of both rulers and thinkers. Rulers envisioned it as a place rich in resources and territory that could add strength and grandeur to their empires; thinkers viewed it as a dramatic challenge to established ways of knowing about the human condition. As J. Martin Evans argues in *America: The View from Europe,* the discovery of the Americas challenged the notion of limitation, which was simply assumed to be a characteristic of the human condition.

The discovery of America not only required that maps of the world be redrawn, but also that ideas about humankind be rethought and recentered. The leading intellectuals of Europe quickly invested the New World with idealistic meaning. It was paradise, a tabula rasa, a place of innocence, regeneration, and new beginnings. After Columbus, it was no longer possible to contemplate the human condition and its possibilities without taking America into account. Before America became a place to be fought over and plundered by the Old World and a destination for its emigrants, it was already an idea. The mythic significance of America to the elite classes preceded its practical significance on the world stage.

For the masses in Europe, however, America represented something different. Emigration on a significant scale did not begin before the early 1600s, and even then it was small compared to the huge migrations of the nineteenth and twentieth centuries. For these millions, the attraction of America had little to do with a philosophical idea of the place and more to do with a dream of opportunity, an exile from misfortune, or flight from religious persecution. It is doubtful that many of the millions who emigrated did so because they had read accounts like St. Jean de Crèvecoeur's "What is an American?" (published in England in 1782 in *Letters from an American Farmer,* and a year later in France). Crèvecoeur extolled the freedom, egalitarian spirit, and opportunities for material betterment and personal dignity that America offered the European masses. Hundreds of European observers visited the United States during the period from the War of Independence to the early twentieth century, a period during which roughly 30 million immigrants arrived. Some, such as Alexis de Tocqueville and James Bryce, published famous accounts of their visits.

Among the hundreds of accounts written by foreign visitors to America during the early decades of the republic, many dealt with the subject of the Indian population. One of the best known and most influential of such accounts was François René de Chateaubriand's *Travels in America* (1827). Chateaubriand did not subscribe to the uninformed romanticism of Jean-Jacques Rousseau, for whom the Indians were "noble savages." Instead, he argued that "The Indian was not savage; the European civilization did not act on the pure of nature; it acted on the rising American civilization . . . it found manners and destroyed them because it was stronger and did not consider it should mix with those manners." The fate of the Indian population in the face of America's expanding western frontier was, Chateaubriand believed, tragic and inevitable. This judgment was shared by his more famous compatriot, Alexis de Tocqueville. In Book I of *Democracy in America* (1835) he observed, "Before the arrival of white men in the New World, the inhabitants of North America lived quietly in their woods, enduring the vicissitudes and practicing the virtues and vices common to savage nations. The Europeans having dispersed the Indian tribes and driven them into the deserts, condemned them to a wandering life, full of inexpressible sufferings." The Scottish writer Robert Louis Stevenson included the Indians with the Chinese as what he called the "despised races" in America. In *Across the Plains* (1892), an account of his journey from New York to San Francisco, Stevenson wrote, "If oppression drives a wise man mad, what should be raging in the hearts of these poor tribes, who have been driven back and back, step after step, their promised reservations torn from them one after another as the States extended westward, until at length they are shut up into these hideous mountain deserts of the centre—and even there find themselves invaded, insulted, and hunted out . . ."

The Civil War that threatened to bring the American union to an end was also a subject of considerable interest for many of Europe's most prominent intellectuals. In a letter written in 1864 to President Lincoln, Karl Marx made clear that he believed the defeat of the Confederacy would be a victory for the working class: "The working men of Europe feel sure that, as the American War of Independence initiated a new era of ascendancy for the middle class, so the American Anti-Slavery War will do for the working classes." Most of the British press

commenting on the Civil War saw in it nothing more than an economic struggle between a protectionist industrializing North and a pro–free trade, agricultural South. Slavery, most British observers argued, had little or nothing to do with the conflict. Charles Dickens, who returned to visit the United States shortly after the war, agreed with this assessment. And, like many of his British contemporaries, he characterized Lincoln as a brutal tyrant. Although British opinion leaders were, in the main, supportive of the South, they opposed the institution of slavery. Harriet Martineau, one of the most prominent British feminists and social reformers of the nineteenth century and a longtime abolitionist, was among the few prominent defenders of Lincoln and the North.

Mass and Elite Perceptions of America

"[W]ithout an image of America," Hannah Arendt observed in 1954, "no European colonist would ever have crossed the ocean." That image, she argued, was never homogeneous across class and ideological lines. Among the lower classes, America represented the dream of opportunity and material betterment. Among liberal and democratic thinkers, it represented the promise of greater freedom and equality. Yet for the traditional European bourgeoisie, the aristocracy, and what might be described as anti-modern intellectuals, America represented a sort of nightmare, the "evening land" of human civilization, as D. H. Lawrence put it in 1923.

Outside of Europe, foreign elites have not always given a great deal of thought to America. The Muslim world paid little attention to the United States before the middle of the twentieth century, and in such parts of the world as China, India, Japan, and Africa, little was written about America before the United States emerged as a world military power at the end of the nineteenth century.

Many Latin American intellectuals, however, at first viewed the independence of the United States with optimism. They saw the Americas, including the United States, as what Greg Grandin calls a "renovating world force distinct from archaic Europe." But by the mid-nineteenth century, a particular form of anti-Americanism arose in reaction to the Mexican-American War, the invasion of Nicaragua, and the growing economic influence of American business in Latin America. It was characterized by mistrust of American motives, disappointment over what was seen as U.S. abandonment of the democratic ideals it had represented only a generation or two earlier, and resentment toward what was perceived as the tendency of the new nation to impose its values, institutions, and preferences on other peoples.

By the middle of the twentieth century, the criticisms Latin American intellectuals had long expressed toward the United States were largely replaced by a more widespread anti-Americanism based on the perception of the nation as an imperialist power. As in other regions of the world, some of this anti-Americanism was the product of what Alan McPherson calls "elite opportunism." But the record of American involvement in Latin American countries, particularly during the cold war era, made it both easy and often plausible to portray the United States as the cause of every problem from political instability to poverty and weak economies. The slogan "Yankee go home!" resonated throughout the region, from Mexico to Argentina, although it did not entirely submerge admiration for some perceived attributes of Americans and American society.

In Europe, the idea of America has long been an obsession among many national elites, for reasons that early on had nothing to do with the military or economic power of the United States. Among French elites, the idea of America has shaped the way they understand their own society, the human condition, and world history since the time of Alexis de Tocqueville, but particularly and less sympathetically since Georges Duhamel's extremely negative portrait of American civilization in *America: the Menace* (1930). Simone de Beauvoir, Jean Baudrillard, Jean-François Revel, Régis Debray, and Bernard-Henri Lévy were among the prominent French thinkers who, since Duhamel, attempted to understand the meaning of America in world history.

There is some disagreement over whether the preponderance of European elite observation and interpretation of America has been, historically, mainly favorable or antipathetic. In a collection of foreign writings on the subject, *America in Perspective* (1947), Henry Steele Commager notes that the European view of America was mainly flattering. But Andrei Markovits argues that European elites have long held a mainly negative image of America. He uses the term *ressentiment*—the French word for resentment, but with connotations of a deeper, more passionate emotion—to characterize the hostility that Western European elites have long expressed toward the United States. Markovits places emphasis on the holders of hostile sentiments rather than their object, arguing that anti-Americanism has long operated as a sort of prejudice in that its holders prejudge the object of their hostility based on what they believe America signifies, rather than on the actual characteristics and actions of the United States and its citizens.

Chinese perceptions of the United States appear to have moved through a number of phases since the mid-nineteenth century, when Chinese visitors first arrived in America and recorded their impressions. These phases, as described by R. David Arkush and Leo Lee, begin with a period of exotic wonder, lasting until roughly 1900, followed by a half century during which admiration of an idealized America was mixed with criticism of what were seen as serious flaws in its culture and social institutions. A long period of state-orchestrated, anti-American propaganda followed (though not in Taiwan, where the United States was viewed as a friend and protector). Since the 1980s and the liberalization of the Chinese economy, both official and popular attitudes toward the United States and American society have lost the virulent and paranoid qualities that continue to characterize North Korean propaganda. Nevertheless, the continued high degree of state censorship and control over the media ensure that Chinese public opinion is strongly influenced by whatever image of the United States the political authorities wish to project.

There is, of course, no single or simple image of America held by opinion leaders from Paris to Beijing. The image of America held by the members of a national population is often quite complex and segmented. In some countries, including Canada and the United Kingdom, the idea- and information-generating class has long been divided in how it portrays and assesses the United States. In a country like South Korea, there is a considerable divide between generations when it comes to public opinion toward America. And in virtually all countries it is important to recognize conflicting ideas, beliefs, and sentiments toward different aspects of America. Admiration for what are thought to be particular American traits, values, historical figures and events, or accomplishments can coexist with a lively dislike or even hatred of other traits or motives ascribed to America or its government, particular policies or actions, and specific influences believed to be exerted by American governments, businesses, culture, or other institutions.

The systematic comparative study of mass perceptions of America may date from William Buchanan and Hadley Cantril's 1953 publication, *How Nations See Each Other*, which drew upon survey data carried out for UNESCO in 1948–49. The images of America that emerged were overwhelmingly positive and were also, in most cases, quite different from the way these populations were inclined to see themselves or other nations. *Progressive, practical, hardworking,* and *generous* were among the words most often selected by foreigners as describing Americans.

As is also true of national elites, the perceptions of mass publics include a mixture of positive and negative beliefs and images. The negative elements have gained influence during certain periods, particularly when American foreign policies were seen as harmful for world peace or inconsistent with the values that its citizens claimed to represent and that other nations expected of American behavior. During the Vietnam War, and again in the 1980s when the Reagan administration accelerated spending on missile defense, mass publics throughout the world followed the lead of their elites in becoming less positive toward the United States. Most commentators suggest that these occasional downdrafts in America's image abroad involve foreign perceptions of the U.S. government or of corporate interests.

Ambivalence and Anti-Americanism

A sharp international decline in popular sympathy for and admiration of the United States occurred in 2002, leading up to and continuing after the invasion of Iraq. But even as the image of the United States was taking a drubbing, a 2003 survey of 11 countries revealed that national populations continued to admire such aspects of America as its scientific and technological innovation, economic opportunities, and, to a lesser degree, its respect for freedom of expression and its democratic institutions. This corroborated the findings of a 43-country survey conducted in 2002 by the Pew Center's Global Attitudes Project, which in addition to reporting widespread admiration for what were seen as America's technological and scientific accomplishments also found that American popular culture and American ideas about democracy were widely admired.

In an empirical analysis of ambivalence in foreign perceptions of America, Giacomo Chiozza observes that "contradictory perceptions coexist in people's minds because America is an inherently multidimensional 'object' to which individuals relate in different manners." Muslim foreign observers of America are often thought to be the least sympathetically disposed toward American values and actions, but, even in this case, Chiozza maintains that a love-hate relationship more accurately describes the Muslim world's perception of America. "Muslim respondents are not systematically opposed to all aspects of America," he asserts. "The appreciation of American

political and societal ideals coexists in the minds of the highly informed with the rejection of America's foreign policy choices in the Middle Eastern political arena."

In Western European populations, Chiozza found that widespread dislike of President George W. Bush and his administration's foreign policies did not produce a corresponding decline in the generally warm sentiments toward American political values and America as a positive symbol. It appeared that in many countries throughout the world, national populations were quite able to separate their perceptions of the American government from those of the American people and society.

Recent attempts to understand what foreigners believe about America have focused on anti-Americanism. This, according to Josef Joffe, is the inevitable result of the United States occupying the role of "Mr. Big" on the world stage and thus being the focus for the resentments, grievances, and criticisms of opinion leaders and populations in societies as diverse as Russia, Iran, and France. Joffe argues that what America actually *does* is less important than what America *is* or is seen to be.

Casting the United States as "the Great Satan" has proved an influential tool for mobilizing public opinion and maintaining popular legitimacy in parts of the Muslim world since the Iranian Revolution of 1979. Bernard Lewis argues that the rise of militant and fundamentalist Islam in the last half century is largely due to resentment over the undeniable decline of Islam's stature in the contemporary world and the effort to locate the source of this deterioration in the actions and values of the West. As the obvious embodiment of what the West is understood to represent, the United States has been the chief target of this anger and resentment.

Anti-Americanism has performed a rather different ideological function in Western Europe, argues Markovits. He contends that the construction of a European identity centered on the institutions of the European Union, a project embraced by most Western European elites, requires a measure of hostility toward America and is built on a foundation of anti-Americanism. "History teaches us," he notes, "that *any* entity—certainly in its developing stages—only attains consciousness and self-awareness by defining itself in opposition to another entity." Anti-Americanism has become a necessary part of the construction of a European identity and the idea of America serves as a measure against which those engaged in this enterprise of identity construction define what they maintain is a more human, civilized, and just alternative.

The View from Abroad

Foreign observers of the United States continue to be gripped by ideas of America, as was the learned elite of Western Europe five centuries ago. Some of the meanings attributed to America during this earlier time—as a place of new beginnings, opportunity, regeneration, and freedom from limits—remain important in foreign perceptions of the United States. But the view from abroad has become much more complex and ambivalent as the characteristics of American society, and the role of America in the world, have changed enormously through history.

See also transnational influences on American politics.

FURTHER READING

Arkush, R. David, and Leo O. Lee, eds. *Land without Ghosts: Chinese Impressions of America from the Mid-Nineteenth Century to the Present*. Berkeley: University of California Press, 1990.

Brooks, Stephen. *As Others See Us: The Causes and Consequences of Foreign Perceptions of America*. Toronto: Broadview Press, 2006.

Bryce, James. *The American Commonwealth*. New York: G. P. Putnam's Sons, 1959. (Originally published in 1888.)

Buchanan, William, and Hadley Cantril. *How Nations See Each Other: A Study in Public Opinion*. Urbana: University of Illinois Press, 1953.

Chateaubriand, François René de. *Travels in America and Italy*. London: H. Colburn, 1828. (Originally published in 1827 as *Voyages en Amérique et en Italie*.)

Chiozza, Giacomo. "Disaggregating Anti-Americanism: An Analysis of Individual Attitudes toward the United States," in Peter J. Katzenstein and Robert O. Keohane, eds. *Anti-Americanism in World Politics*. Ithaca, NY: Cornell University Press, 2007, pp.93-126.

Commager, Henry Steele, ed. *America in Perspective: The United States through Foreign Eyes*. New York: Random House, 1947.

Evans, J. Martin. *America: The View from Europe*. Stanford, CA: Stanford Alumni Association, 1979.

Grandin, Greg. "Your Americanism and Mine: Americanism and Anti-Americanism in the Americas." *American Historical Review* (October 2006), 1042–66.

Hollander, Paul. *Anti-Americanism*. New York: Oxford University Press, 1992.

Joffe, Josef. "Who's Afraid of Mr.Big?" *The National Interest* 64 (Summer 2001), 43–52.

Katzenstein, Peter J., and Robert O. Keohane, eds. *Anti-Americanism in World Politics*. Ithaca, NY: Cornell University Press, 2007.

Lewis, Bernard. *What Went Wrong? The Clash Between Islam and Modernity in the Middle East*. New York: HarperCollins, 2002.

Markovits, Andrei. *Uncouth Nation: Why Europe Dislikes America*. Princeton, NJ: Princeton University Press, 2007.

McPherson, Alan. *Yankee No! Anti-Americanism in U.S.–Latin American Relations*. Cambridge, MA: Harvard University Press, 2003.

Revel, Jean-François. *Anti-Americanism*. New York: Encounter Books, 2003.

Stevenson, Robert Louis. *Across the Plains*. London: Chatto and Windus, 1892.

Tocqueville, Alexis de. *Democracracy in America*. New York: Knopf, 1994. (Originally published as 2 vols., 1835 and 1840.)

STEPHEN BROOKS

foreign policy and domestic politics to 1865

During the first century of its existence, the United States pursued a foreign policy that had three main goals. During the Revolutionary War and its aftermath, it engaged with foreign powers to confirm its existence as an independent nation-state and to preserve this freedom during international crises caused by the French revolutionary wars and the Napoleonic Wars. With independence secure, the United States then pursued two further goals: to ensure prosperity for American elites and the bulk of the enfranchised American public by diplomatically opening foreign markets to American producers and consumers on favorable terms, and to expand the territorial size of the United States on the North American continent through both diplomacy and the use of military force. The desire for expansion culminated in a war with Mexico in the mid-1840s and the acquisition of new territory that vastly increased the size of the United States. This territorial expansion fueled internal debates about the expansion of the institution of slavery, which culminated in the Civil War, during which the United States of America and the Confederate States of America pursued diametrically opposite foreign policies, with the Confederacy seeking international recognition of its independence and the Union doing all it could to prevent such recognition. Keeping foreign powers out the Civil War facilitated the defeat of the Confederacy and allowed the federal government to retain control over the entire nation.

The American Revolution: 1775–83

The primary goals of American foreign policy during the Revolutionary War were straightforward: the United States wanted foreign powers to recognize its independence and to assist materially, financially, and militarily in its war against Great Britain. The Continental Congress began to look for foreign assistance in its resistance to British policy months before the formal Declaration of Independence. On November 29, 1775, the Congress created the Committee of Secret Correspondence, with the stated mission of communicating with the "friends" of the American cause in Britain, Ireland, and "other parts of the world." The committee initially made discreet inquiries to known friends of the American cause in Europe and also made contact with one the few colonial agents (the colonies' lobbyists to Parliament) in Britain who still supported the congressional cause, Virginian Arthur Lee. In December 1775, the committee received a clandestine agent of the French government, Julien-Alexandre Archard de Bonvouloir, dispatched from his official post in the Caribbean by the French foreign minister, Charles Gravier, Comte de Vergennes. Bonvouloir made it clear to the Continental Congress that France was prepared to support the American effort against Britain, at least with some material and financial assistance. In early March 1776, the Continental Congress dispatched Connecticut merchant Silas Deane to Paris to work with Arthur Lee and began to make more formal inquiries for French assistance. Although Vergennes was eager to support the American cause in order to weaken Britain, until the American colonies formally declared independence French assistance had to be secret and, of necessity, small in scope.

With the Declaration of Independence of July 1776, the United States formally sought recognition of its sovereignty from other powers as well as foreign assistance. Although Vergennes was predisposed to direct King Louis XVI to recognize and support the United States, he knew that such recognition meant open war with Great Britain, and he thus wished to wait until an ongoing French military and naval buildup was close to complete. In the interim, Vergennes employed writer Pierre Augustin, Caron de Beaumarchais, to head a dummy corporation, known as Roderigue Hortalez and Company, to funnel arms and other war materiel to the Americans. The arrival in early 1777 of a third American minister

to France, Benjamin Franklin, assisted the American cause in giving the United States a famous public face in that country, and helped sway French public opinion toward favoring the Americans. By the autumn of 1777, the French government was disposed toward formal recognition of the United States. When word of American General Horatio Gates's victory over Britain's General John Burgoyne at Saratoga reached Europe, the negotiations between Vergennes and the American ministers moved into high gear, and two treaties—the Treaty of Alliance and the Treaty of Amity and Commerce—were concluded between the United States and France on February 6, 1778.

The need for a formal alliance with France was disturbing to some of the political leadership in America. Shortly after the Declaration of Independence, the Continental Congress had approved a blueprint for American diplomacy with the European powers, known formally as the Plan of Treaties but sometimes called the Model Treaty. Drafted largely by John Adams, the Plan of Treaties called for the United States to seek out commercial connections with all of the European states but to avoid political connections. America would replicate its colonial economic relationship with Britain with the rest of Europe. The United States would send agricultural produce and other raw materials to Europe and to colonies in the Caribbean in exchange for European manufactured goods. U.S. diplomats were thus called on to negotiate commercial treaties that would open foreign markets but not political alliances that would draw the United States into the European balance of power. The French Alliance—rooted in both a political and a commercial treaty—thus went against this cardinal principle. Diplomatic historians point to the unwillingness of the French to agree to the terms of the Plan of Treaties as a reflection of the foreign policy idealism that informed it. Despite this, American policy makers continued to hope for commercial treaties and relationships with the European powers without committing to formal political alliances.

The French Alliance proved crucial in securing American victory in the Revolutionary War. Many French officers volunteered for service in America even before the alliance had been concluded. In May 1780, the Expeditionary Force under General Jean-Baptise de Vimeur, Comte de Rochambeau departed France and arrived in Newport late the next month. By 1781 Rochambeau and Washington were conducting joint operations around New York City, and in late summer, the forces of both men hurried to Virginia to trap British General Charles Cornwallis at Yorktown, following victory over the British fleet of French Admiral François-Joseph-Paul, Comte de Grasse-Rouville. The Comte de Grasse's victory and the subsequent successful capture of Cornwallis were both products of the French-American alliance and of the larger coalition that Vergennes had built.

After the Treaty of Alliance between France and the United States was concluded, the Comte de Vergennes began to negotiate a treaty of alliance between the kingdoms of Spain and France. Although the Spanish kingdom of Carlos III did not recognize the independence of the United States, Spain joined France in the fight against Britain. A formal alliance was concluded with the Treaty of Aranjuez in April 1779. When Great Britain declared war on the Netherlands in December 1780, it too joined Vergennes's coalition against Great Britain. It would not be until April 1782 that the Dutch would formally recognize American independence, when they received John Adams as minister. Adams was able to negotiate a Treaty of Amity and Commerce between the United States and the Netherlands, which was concluded in October 1782. As diplomatic historian Jonathan Dull has argued, this alliance of France, Spain, and the Netherlands put to sea a combined navy far larger than that of Great Britain. Forced to defend itself against three major European powers, Britain's resources available for returning the former American colonies to its empire were severely diminished. The alliance thus paved the way for the Comte de Grasse's victory, as well as the inability of the British government to send another army to America after Cornwallis's was captured.

The United States commissioned ministers Benjamin Franklin, John Adams, John Jay, and Henry Laurens to negotiate a peace treaty with the British government. After the collapse of Frederick North, Lord North's ministry, and the death of his successor the Marquis of Rockingham, the prime ministership fell to William Petty-Fitzmaurice, Earl of Shelburne, who favored a quick and generous peace treaty with the Americans. Shelburne appointed a Scots merchant, Richard Oswald, to lead the negotiations in Paris with the Americans; they concluded a preliminary peace treaty on November 30, 1782. The Preliminary Peace, as it was known, was generous to the Americans: the United States was given title to North American territory that included not only the first 13 states but land bounded to the west by the Mississippi River, to the north by the Great Lakes, and to the south by the Floridas. Americans were also granted rights to fish the Grand Banks of the Atlantic Ocean. Controversially, the American commissioners agreed to language in the treaty that the Continental Congress would "recommend" to the individual states that they restore the property of loyalists that had been seized. Similarly, the British committed to restoration of property (including slaves) that was taken from American citizens. Neither of these promises were honored in full. An additional controversial element about the treaty between the United States and Great Britain was that it was done without consulting the French government, a violation of the Treaty of Alliance. Vergennes, however, did not publicly voice displeasure with the Americans; France and Spain concluded an armistice with Great Britain on January 30, 1783. The final peace treaties were signed between Britain and the United States on September 3, 1783, in Paris, with Spain and France signing their treaty with Britain the same day at Versailles. The first objective of American foreign policy during the Revolution—recognition of American independence—had been achieved. The second foreign policy goal of the United States—the opening of foreign markets to American commerce—would prove to be much more elusive.

The Confederation Period and the Constitution: 1783–89

The primary goal of American foreign policy during the years under the Articles of Confederation was to negotiate commercial treaties that would open European and colonial markets to American agricultural produce and other raw materials, and in turn secure favorable terms for importing foreign manufactures and other goods. American diplomats had only limited success in achieving these goals, as the United States was seen as having a weak government that could not enforce the treaty provisions it signed. Few European powers were willing to sign commercial agreements with the United States. The weakness of the confederation government in conducting foreign policy was a major impetus behind the moves to reform the Articles of Confederation, a measure that culminated in the Philadelphia Convention of 1787, and the new Constitution.

In the years following the Revolutionary War, securing favorable treaties with foreign powers proved a difficult task for the men charged with managing U.S. diplomacy. Upon his return from negotiating the Treaty of Paris, John Jay was appointed the Continental Congress's secretary for foreign affairs in December 1784. When the Spanish government closed the mouth of the Mississippi

River to American shipping in 1784, Jay opened negotiations with the Spanish minister to the United States, Don Diego de Gardoqui. Conducted during 1785, the Jay-Gardoqui negotiations put forward a controversial compromise: Spain proposed to allow American merchants and shippers open access to commerce with Spain and the Canary Islands (but not Spanish America) in exchange for granting Spain the exclusive right to navigate the Mississippi River for 25 years. Although Jay moved forward with negotiations, delegates to the Continental Congress from the states with western interests (especially in the South) were horrified by the proposal, which promised to retard the growth of western settlements and only benefit northern shipping interests. Congress ordered Jay to suspend negotiations, but word of the proposed treaty inflamed nascent sectional tensions.

The U.S. ministers to Great Britain and France after 1784, John Adams and Thomas Jefferson, respectively, found diplomacy with the European powers equally difficult. After his formal reception as the U.S. minister to the Court of St. James on June 1, 1785, Adams was unsuccessful in negotiating a new commercial treaty with the British government. From the conclusion of the Preliminary Peace Treaty, British policy toward the United States was informed by a set of principles known as neomercantilism. The British government encouraged essentially free trade within the British Empire, but offered most-favored-nation status to only a few other foreign nations. Neomercantilist commentators—most notably, John Holroyd, Lord Sheffield—had posited that the newly independent United States would continue to engage in the majority of its commercial activity with Britain and the British Empire. The British government could therefore withhold most-favored-nation status and still capture the bulk of American commerce. This assessment proved accurate. There was little Adams could do to change British policy.

At the same time, Jefferson faced a difficult situation in France. French commerce was theoretically open to Americans under the terms of the 1778 Treaty of Amity and Commerce, but the realities of the legal regime and economic order of France made trade problematic. The French government's practice of tax farming (delegating the collection of all taxes) resulted in the body with the privilege of collecting most taxes—the farmers-general—having enormous power to decide which goods could enter and leave France and who could engage in this trade.

Jefferson's lobbying to change this system met with little success. Although he won an opening in the French market for American whale oil, he was only able to open the tobacco market for a minority of American planters. Jefferson's greatest success came in late 1788, when he completed negotiations on a new consular convention between France and the United States. Notably, this new convention made consuls subject to the laws of the land in which they operated, not where they were appointed. All told, in dealing with the most powerful nations in Europe in the 1780s—Great Britain and France—U.S. diplomats found themselves with very little power and legitimacy, and their ability to affect positive changes in the position of the United States vis-à-vis these European states was quite limited.

The weakness of the United States in the realm of diplomacy was a primary motive among those who wished to reform and strengthen the Articles of Confederation. Under the articles—although Congress had the power to appoint diplomats and conclude treaties—commercial regulations were left to the individual states. Several states sent delegations to the 1786 Annapolis Convention to discuss new commercial regulations for all of the United States, and the delegates quickly concluded that a full revision of all of the Articles of Confederation would be necessary. This became the Philadelphia Convention of May–September 1787. Of all of the issues that animated debate during the ratification process of the Constitution, among the least controversial was that of foreign policy. The Constitution put all the powers involved in making foreign policy in the hands of the central, or federal, government. Within the federal government, the bulk of foreign policy powers was given to the executive branch. The president had the power to appoint a secretary of state, subordinate diplomats, and to negotiate treaties. Treaties required a two-thirds vote of the Senate in order to be ratified, and the Senate also had to approve presidential diplomatic appointments. The extent to which the Senate's power to provide "advice and consent" to the president allowed it, and Congress as a whole, to participate in the treaty-making process would be a subject of heated debate during the early years of the federal government and beyond.

The Federalist Era: 1789–1801
The Electoral College overwhelmingly chose George Washington as the first president of the United States. After taking the oath of office on April 30, 1789, Washington and his administration were almost immediately confronted with a series of foreign policy crises. With the rechristening of the French Estates General as the

French National Assembly in June 1789, the French Revolution began. The majority of Americans supported the French Revolution during its early years, as the creation of a constitutional monarchy, the abolition of feudalism, and the promulgation of a Declaration of the Rights of Man were all seen as developments either related to, or an extension of, the American Revolution. In September 1792, the government of the National Assembly was replaced by the more radical National Convention. This new government proceeded to abolish the monarchy, and then tried and executed King Louis XVI in January 1793. Already at war with Prussia and Austria, France declared war against Great Britain, the Netherlands, and Spain. The American reaction to the execution of Louis was divided. Also unclear was the question of whether the 1778 Treaty of Alliance bound the United States to assist France in its war against the rest of the European powers. Washington's cabinet was divided on both counts. Representing the emerging pro-administration party known as the Federalists, Secretary of the Treasury Alexander Hamilton did not approve of the radical turn of the French Revolution and believed that the execution of Louis XVI rendered the Treaty of Alliance null and void, since the treaty had been between the United States and him. Speaking for the emerging opposition known as the Republicans, Secretary of State Thomas Jefferson lamented the bloodshed in France but continued to approve of the larger revolution. He believed that treaties existed between nations, and therefore the alliance was still in effect. Washington split the difference between the two viewpoints. He chose to formally receive the new French government's minister, Edmond Genêt, but issued the Proclamation of Neutrality on April 22, 1793, declaring that the United States would remain neutral in the conflict between France and its enemies. The Proclamation of Neutrality was an important milestone—it confirmed the ability of the president to interpret treaties, and the controversy helped coalesce the Federalist and Republican movements into something resembling political "parties"—although historians debate to extent to which this first "party system" resembled that of later, more modern political parties.

The ongoing wars of the French Revolution continued to affect the United States during the remainder of the 1790s. Although the United States maintained its neutrality, Great Britain began seizing American merchant ships bound for the European continent, claiming a broad definition of contraband goods that justified the seizures. Washington dispatched John Jay to Britain to negotiate a compromise, and the resulting Treaty of Amity and Commerce became known as the Jay Treaty. Under the terms of the treaty, commerce between the United States and Great Britain would now exist on a most-favored-nation basis, and Britain would evacuate posts in the American West it continued to occupy. But commerce between the United States and the British islands in the West Indies would be restricted—Americans could only employ vessels of under 70 tons, and the export of several staple crops to the Indies was forbidden. These restrictions promised to affect the planters and farmers of the South and West greatly, and to secure a pro-ratification vote, the Senate struck out the West Indies article. The treaty still barely passed. Before Washington could sign it, public opposition—led by Jefferson and James Madison's Republican Party—grew. Washington ultimately signed the treaty after the British government leaked intercepted French documents that implicated Jefferson's successor as secretary of state, Edmund Randolph, as secretly favoring France over Britain. Although there was nothing substantial to the accusations, the controversy gave Washington political cover to sign the Jay Treaty, which he did on August 18, 1795.

Not all of Washington's diplomatic efforts were controversial. A treaty with Spain negotiated by Thomas Pinckney and ratified in early 1796 clarified the southern boundary of the United States with Spanish Florida, and also gave Americans the right to navigate the Mississippi River and transship their goods onto oceangoing vessels at the Port of New Orleans; this was known as *the right of deposit*. As Washington prepared to leave office at the close of his second term as president, he issued his now-famous Farewell Address, which restated the principle of the Plan of Treaties—that the United States should seek out commercial connections with foreign powers while avoiding political connections.

Avoiding foreign entanglements proved difficult for Washington's successor, John Adams. In the wake of the Jay Treaty's ratification, France (now being governed by an executive council called the Directory) interpreted the new treaty as an American alliance with Britain, and began interdicting American shipping. Adams sent a team of three ministers—John Marshall, Elbridge Gerry, and Charles C. Pinckney—to negotiate with the Directory's foreign minister, Charles Maurice de Talleyrand-Périgord. Before formal negotiations began, agents of Talleyrand solicited bribes from the American ministers and asked them to arrange an American loan for the French government. The commissioners balked at this offer, and when word of the proposed bribes reached the United States and was published (Talleyrand's agents were code-named X, Y, and Z in the public dispatches), a clamor for war with France swept through much of American public opinion. Following the lead of Congress, Adams signed authorization for an expansion of the U.S. Army, the creation of a navy, and the controversial Alien and Sedition Acts. An undeclared naval war—the Quasi-War—between France and the United States ensued. Rather than ask Congress for a formal declaration of war, however, Adams pursued further negotiations that culminated in the September 1800 Convention of Mortefontaine. Word of the peace treaty reached the United States after the presidential election, which Adams lost to Thomas Jefferson.

The Jeffersonian Era and the War of 1812: 1801–15

During his two terms as president, Jefferson sought to keep the United States out of the European wars between Napoleonic France and the various coalitions against it led by Great Britain. During Jefferson's first term, American neutrality, combined with a brief peace between France and Britain, allowed American commerce to flourish. The only exception was American commerce in the Mediterranean, which was subject to seizure by pirates sponsored by the state of Tripoli (one of the "Barbary States" of North Africa). Although he campaigned on drydocking the blue-water force of frigates of the U.S. Navy in favor of relying on smaller, short-range gunboats for coastal defense, Jefferson put aside those plans and dispatched the Navy against the Tripolitan forces. During operations in 1803, a frigate, the USS *Philadelphia*, ran aground in Tripoli harbor and surrendered; its crew was taken hostage. A subsequent operation bombarded Tripoli, and a small force of U.S. Marines captured the smaller Tripolitan port of Derna, forcing the pasha of Tripoli to sign a treaty with the United States and return the prisoners.

Jefferson's pragmatic abandonment of his campaign promises was also evident in his acceptance of Napoleon Bonaparte's 1803 offer to sell the United States the French territory of Louisiane (Louisiana). The offer to purchase Louisiana came after the Spanish intendant of New Orleans suspended the American right of deposit in late 1802. Hearing of the eminent transfer of New Orleans and Louisiana from Spain to France, Jefferson dispatched

James Monroe to assist Robert R. Livingston in negotiating with Napoleon's government and gave both diplomats explicit instructions to offer to buy New Orleans and the Floridas from France. Having lost an army in a futile attempt to reconquer the former French colony of Haiti and build an empire in the Americas, Napoleon responded with an offer of Louisiana (Spain had retained the Floridas), which Monroe and Livingston accepted. Although the diplomats had technically violated their instructions, and Jefferson was uncertain whether the Constitution allowed the annexation of new territories, he sent the treaty to the Senate anyway, where its ratification was approved and the sale confirmed by the end of 1803. Although Haitian military success paved the way for the sale of Louisiana, Jefferson refused to recognize Haiti when it formally declared its independence on New Year's Day, 1804. Not wanting to support an independent nation born of a successful slave rebellion, American administrations would refuse to recognize Haiti until 1862.

The Louisiana Purchase was the final time the events of the Napoleonic Wars would redound to the advantage of the United States. At the end of 1803, war between France and the British-led coalition resumed. Between 1805 and 1807, Napoleon defeated Austria, Prussia, and Russia, leaving Britain and France the only belligerents locked in what both saw as a war for survival. Both countries imposed blockades on the other's trade, and the French and British navies were soon seizing American merchants who attempted to trade with the opposite power. At the same time, the British government extended the use of the policy of impressment, under which the Royal Navy searched American ships looking for deserted British seamen and other British subjects, who when found would be forced into the British service. In addition to the humiliation this practice caused to American honor, many American citizens were inadvertently caught up in this gauntlet and the British government was slow to respond to their complaints, if it did at all. The height of humiliation came in 1807, when the HMS *Leopard*, looking for British deserters, fired on the USS *Chesapeake* within sight of the American shore. Public opinion called for war, but Jefferson demurred, preferring to suspend American commerce altogether in an attempt to force Britain and France to comply with American understandings of neutral rights. The embargo lasted for the final two years of Jefferson's presidency and did little to change the policies of France or Britain.

When James Madison succeeded Jefferson as president in 1809, he convinced the Congress to abandon the embargo and adopt a policy of nonimportation of British and French goods, with the promise that the United States would open its ports to the first power to rescind its restrictions on American commerce. When in late 1810, a back-channel communication from a French diplomat indicated that Napoleon was considering repealing his restrictions (the Berlin and Milan Decrees), Madison removed restraints on American commerce with France, and only nonintercourse with Britain remained. Impressments and interdictions by the British navy continued through 1811. The British were also blamed as tensions rose in the trans-Appalachian West, with the emergence of a large American Indian resistance movement against American expansion, led by the Shawnee war chief Tecumseh. Madison asked Congress for a declaration of war against Great Britain on June 1, 1812, and both the House and Senate voted to declare war, although the votes were very close, with all the Federalists and several Republicans voting against war.

The War of 1812 formally lasted from June 1812 until the Treaty of Ghent of December 24, 1814. The slow speed of communication, however, meant that the war continued into the early months of 1815. The United States attempted multiple invasions of British Canada—the intention being to seize as much of British North America as possible to force concessions in maritime and commercial policy at the bargaining table. The American invasions of 1812 were thwarted by British forces. The American campaigns of 1813 were a little more successful—the United States established naval superiority on the Great Lakes by the end of the year, and Tecumseh was killed at the Battle of the Thames in October 1813. By the summer of 1814, Napoleon had been defeated, and Britain brought its naval superiority to bear on the American coast, capturing and burning Washington in August 1814 and briefly shelling Baltimore's outer fortifications weeks later. By the end of the year, the British Navy was engaged in a similar campaign of harassment on the Gulf of Mexico coast.

The relative stalemate between British and American forces, and a desire on the part of both parties to end the war brought diplomats from both countries together in Ghent, Belgium, in August. The Ghent negotiations came after an 1813 offer by the Russian government to mediate the conflict, which the British government turned down, and an offer in early 1814 by British foreign minister Robert Stewart, Viscount Castlereagh, to engage in direct talks with the Americans. Madison had commissioned John Quincy Adams, Albert Gallatin, Henry Clay, James Bayard, and Jonathan Russell to negotiate for the United States; Britain sent three relatively minor officials: Dr. William Adams, an admiralty lawyer; Lord Gambier, a naval officer; and Henry Goulburn, an undersecretary in the Colonial Office. Goulburn took charge of the British delegation, while Adams, Clay, and Gallatin were the dominant voices for the Americans. The negotiations dragged on for months; although both sides dropped discussion of the issue of impressments, the British negotiators presented a series of demands that infuriated most of the American delegation, including a proposal to create an American Indian buffer state in the Great Lakes region, and a proposed reworking of American rights to the Canadian fisheries.

However, as the talks at the more important Congress of Vienna dragged on, the British government instructed its diplomats to agree to a treaty that simply restored the prewar status quo. The Americans jumped at this opening. British plans for an American Indian buffer state were dropped, and American Indian nations within U.S. borders lost their last major remaining European diplomatic partner, clearing a path for American westward expansion. Other outstanding issues, such as the boundary between the United States and Canada, would be settled by subsequent commissions. The Treaty of Ghent allowed Britain to focus on European diplomacy and the Americans to claim a peace with honor. News of the treaty reached the United States at the same time that word was spreading of Andrew Jackson's victory at New Orleans—allowing the War of 1812 to be remembered as an American victory even though its result was as equivocal as any war in U.S. history.

Antebellum Foreign Policy:
The Monroe Doctrine, the Quest for Markets, and Manifest Destiny: 1815–45

Following the War of 1812, American foreign policy was directed toward opening foreign markets to American commerce, keeping European political interference in the Americas to a minimum, and increasing the territorial size of the United States. The war transformed the domestic political scene. First, it spelled the end of the Federalists as a national political force. Between December 1814 and January 1815, New England Federalists had convened a special Congress called the Hartford Convention to discuss difficulties caused by the war. Although the convention ultimately called for some policy changes by the Madison administration and Congress in the conduct of the war, and proposed seven amendments to the Constitution, the body's secret meetings allowed Republican opponents to smear its activities as treasonous. Outside New England, Federalism had acquired the taint of disloyalty.

Second, the setbacks the United States had faced during the war in terms of mobilization, materiel, transportation, and, most of all, funding prompted a split within the Republican Party. Many, including Henry Clay and John C. Calhoun became known as National Republicans, who advocated federal government funding of a system of internal improvements, coastal fortifications, a standing army, and a national bank. These were measures that the so-called Old Republicans like James Madison and James Monroe balked at, as they had a whiff of the old Hamiltonian program about them. These basic divides would inform the ultimate split of the Republicans into Andrew Jackson's Democrats and Henry Clay's Whigs in the 1830s.

These different visions extended to approaches to foreign policy. Although the embargo and the War of 1812 and the resulting disruptions in trade helped facilitate the growth of an American manufacturing sector (a process that had begun in the 1790s), the United States remained an overwhelmingly agricultural nation in the late 1810s and 1820s. Planters and farmers desired to ship their foodstuffs and staples to Europe and the European colonies in the Americas and wanted diplomacy devoted to ensuring the continued flow of transatlantic commerce. This became the policy position of the Old Republicans and the Jacksonian Democrats. The National Republicans, and then the Whigs, had a different vision: they hoped the federal government could spur the expansion of the American industrial and financial sectors and wanted to develop internal transportation and markets. Under Henry Clay's leadership in Congress, this became known as the "American System." Its most controversial aspect was high protective tariffs, which passed Congress in 1828 during John Quincy Adams's presidency. In 1832 the so-called Tariff of Abominations almost split the Union, as South Carolina threatened nullification of the law. A compromise was reached, but the crisis showed how central commercial and foreign policy was to the domestic political scene.

No matter what the tariff rates, the United States still actively sought to expand its access to world markets during this period. Under the initiative of merchant John Jacob Astor and others, Americans expanded the scope of the fur trade in the American West and Pacific Northwest, and regular shipping to the Pacific Coast soon extended to Hawai'i and across the Pacific to East Asia. American trade with China, begun in the 1790s,

increased in scope in the first half of the nineteenth century, and the U.S. Navy was operating across the Pacific by the late 1840s; under the expedition of Commodore Matthew Perry, the United States forced open trade with Japan with the 1854 Treaty of Kanagawa. American merchants and financiers also seized the opportunities provided by the collapse of the Spanish Empire, and American trade with the newly independent republics of the Americas increased during the 1820s and 1830s as well.

Responding to the end of the Spanish Empire and the various Latin American independence movements provided the United States with its first great diplomatic challenge of the post–War of 1812 world. The bulk of the Spanish colonies had experienced a de facto independence of sorts during Napoleon's occupation of Spain. Although the particulars varied from country to country, Latin American settler elites generally resisted the attempts of the Spanish government to reimpose direct imperial rule after Napoleon's fall.

While many Americans were sympathetic to the various Latin American revolutionaries (especially South America's Simón Bolívar), the Monroe administration held off recognizing Latin American independence while Spain still wielded a modicum of power. This allowed Monroe's secretary of state, John Quincy Adams, to conclude the 1819 Transcontinental Treaty with Spain, which established a firm western border between the United States and New Spain (Mexico), and also to broker the purchase of the Floridas from Spain at the same time. The acquisition of the Gulf Coast was a boon to the states to the Deep South, as it guaranteed their access to Atlantic markets and abetted the ongoing expansion of the Cotton Belt. In 1822, following military successes on the part of Bolívar's forces in South America and a successful revolution in Mexico, the Monroe administration finally recognized the independence of four Latin American republics—Mexico, Peru, Colombia, and Rio de la Plata (Argentina).

When it appeared that Spain's European allies would support an attempt to send another expedition to reconquer the republics, Secretary of State Adams and President Monroe drafted a proclamation declaring that the United States was opposed to any attempts by the European powers to recolonize the Americas, and would resist attempts to draw the Americas into the European balance of power. This statement, issued on December 2, 1823, became known as the Monroe Doctrine, and would be used to justify American diplomacy and military activity in the Western Hemisphere for the rest of the nineteenth century and into the twentieth.

The Monroe Doctrine was also significant in that Monroe and Adams rejected an opportunity to issue a joint declaration on Latin American affairs with the British government, despite the fact that both governments shared the same policy. British-American relations evolved in a generally amicable direction during the 1820s and 1830s, as trade between the two countries remained vital to the economies of both. However, tensions over the U.S.-Canadian border flared in the late 1830s, and the Americans had tended to be recalcitrant in providing naval vessels to assist with British efforts to interdict the African slave trade (which Britain had abolished in 1807, with the United States following in 1808). Both issues were resolved by a treaty negotiated by Secretary of State Daniel Webster and British Minister Alexander Baring, Baron Ashburton, in August 1842. The Webster-Ashburton Treaty formalized the contested boundary between Maine, New Brunswick, and Quebec (the Revolutionary Era maps the boundary had been drawn on in 1783 proved highly inaccurate) and committed the United States to a more robust presence in assisting the British West Africa Squadron in slave trade interdiction.

With the expansion of American access to overseas markets came a desire to increase the amount of American territory under settlement and cultivation and to increase the size of the United States in total. This desire for expansion was felt by most white Americans, but under the term *Manifest Destiny* (coined by a Democratic newspaper editor named John L. O'Sullivan) it became a hallmark of the Democratic Party's platform. The notion that it was the Manifest Destiny of the United States to extend from the Atlantic to the Pacific (and even beyond) informed the presidential election of 1844. Running against Whig Henry Clay, Democrat James K. Polk wanted to follow up the successful Webster-Ashburton Treaty of 1842 with negotiations (or belligerence) that would compel Britain to cede the United States all of the so-called Oregon Country (modern-day Oregon, Washington, and British Columbia). More important, Polk called for the immediate annexation of the Republic of Texas, a breakaway province of Mexico that had declared and won its independence in 1836. Mexico, however, refused to recognize Texas's independence. The issue proved immensely popular in the South and the West, and spurred Polk to victory in 1844. His belligerence, however, put Mexico and the United States on a collision course for war.

The Mexican-American War: 1845–48

Polk's predecessor, John Tyler, had begun to pursue the annexation of Texas as early as 1843, and negotiated an annexation treaty that finally passed in Congress days before Polk took office. Almost immediately after Polk's inauguration, Mexico suspended diplomatic relations with the United States. Polk sent a special envoy with extensive knowledge of Mexico, John Slidell, as a fully accredited minister to negotiate with the Mexican government. Controversy ensued over Slidell's credentials as a normal minister plenipotentiary, which caused Mexican officials to believe that if they received Slidell it would indicate their acquiescence in the Texas annexation. Also factoring into Mexico's response was an ongoing internal political debate between conservative centralizers and liberal federalists that made compromise on Texas very difficult.

As Slidell's mission was failing, Polk dispatched the bulk of the U.S. Army under General Zachary Taylor to the disputed borderland between the Nueces River and the Rio Grande. A violent confrontation ensued between U.S. and Mexican forces, and war formally began in May 1846.

The war dragged on longer than expected. For all his success as a polemicist, Polk proved to be a poor war president. He withheld support for Taylor during the latter part of his successful campaign in northern Mexico, fearing his Whig-leaning general was becoming too popular. Polk then allowed Mexico's exiled president and military leader Antonio Lopez de Santa Anna to return to Mexico; rather than negotiate an end to the conflict, Santa Anna took charge of the Mexican war effort. It fell to General Winfield Scott to defeat Santa Anna, which he did, landing at Veracruz in March 1847 and capturing Mexico City in September of that same year. During the winter of 1847–48, Nicholas Trist, a State Department clerk who had accompanied Scott, negotiated with delegates from the Mexican Congress (now in charge after Santa Anna's resignation).

Although Polk hoped for the acquisition of most, if not all, of Mexico, Trist was less ambitious. The Treaty of Guadalupe Hidalgo confirmed American control of Texas, a boundary at the Rio Grande, and granted the United States the territories of Upper California and New Mexico in exchange for a $15 million payment and the assumption by the United States of the claims of all American citizens against the Mexican government. Polk was unhappy with the treaty but did not want to prolong the war and feared that he could not negotiate a better treaty. The Senate voted to ratify the treaty on March 10, 1848.

The Sectional Crisis and the Civil War: 1848–65

The acquisition of the Mexican Cession moved the question of the extension of the institution of slavery into western territories to the forefront of American political debate. The number of states that would be carved from the new territory and the question of whether they would be slave states or free states vexed American politics until the Compromise of 1850; the desire on the part of Southerners to add territory that could be open to slavery did not abate, however.

The southern cause was pursued by a small number of private adventurers known as filibusters—men who gathered small forces of mercenaries and attempted to conquer several Latin American states and eventually incorporate them into the United States. A Venezualan-born Cuban exile named Narisco López sought American support for his plans to capture Cuba from Spain and annex it to the United States; he led three unsuccessful invasions of Cuba between 1849 and 1851. Another notable filibuster was a Tennessee doctor named William Walker who launched a private invasion of Mexico in 1853 and actually succeeded in controlling Nicaragua during a filibuster between 1855 and 1857. Driven out by the local population, Walker made three more expeditions to Central America before being captured and executed in Honduras in 1860.

More legitimate were attempts by the U.S. government to acquire Cuba, where Spain had remained in charge and where slavery remained legal. President Franklin Pierce made several attempts to purchase Cuba from Spain to placate southern Democrats. Meeting secretly at Ostend, Belgium, the U.S. ministers to Britain, France, and Spain vowed to work together to acquire Cuba by purchase or force. When word of this secret plan (known as the "Ostend Manifesto") leaked, controversy ensued, and Pierce was forced to recall the most controversial of the diplomats, Louisiana's Pierre Soulé.

Attempts to increase American territory did not placate the South and only served to exacerbate sectional tensions. With the formation of the new Republican Party in 1856 (a party committed to halting the extension of slavery and the protection of free labor) and the election of its presidential candidate Abraham Lincoln in 1860, the process of secession began and the United States was at war with itself by April 1861. The Confederate States of America sought foreign recognition of its independence and foreign assistance for its war against the federal government. The United States sought to prevent European powers from recognizing and assisting the Confederacy. The U.S. Navy blockaded the ports of the South. Most controversially, in November 1861, the commander of the USS *San Jacinto* boarded the British mail ship HMS *Trent* and captured two Confederate diplomats bound for Britain. The seizure provoked a minor diplomatic incident, but the U.S. minister to Great Britain, Charles Francis Adams, succeeded in keeping Britain from recognizing the Confederate government and thus out of the war. Starved for materiel and unable to sell its cotton crop abroad, the Confederacy capitulated in April 1865.

See also Articles of Confederation; Civil War and Reconstruction; Constitution, federal; federalism; Mexican-American War; War of 1812; war for independence.

FURTHER READING

Bemis, Samuel Flagg. *The Diplomacy of the American Revolution*. New York: American Historical Association, 1935.

Combs, Jerald A. *The Jay Treaty: Political Battleground of the Founding Fathers*. Berkeley: University of California Press, 1970.

DeConde, Alexander. *Entangling Alliance: Politics and Diplomacy under George Washington*. Durham, NC: Duke University Press, 1958.

———. *The Quasi-War: The Politics and Diplomacy of the Undeclared War with France, 1797–1801*. New York: Scribner, 1966.

———. *This Affair of Louisiana*. Baton Rouge: Louisiana State University Press, 1976.

Dull, Jonathan R. *A Diplomatic History of the American Revolution*. New Haven, CT: Yale University Press, 1985.

———. *The French Navy and American Independence: A Study of Arms and Diplomacy, 1774–1787*. Princeton, NJ: Princeton University Press, 1975.

Hickey, Donald R. *The War of 1812: A Forgotten Conflict*. Urbana: University of Illinois Press, 1989.

Howe, Daniel Walker. *What Hath God Wrought? The Transformation of America, 1815–1848*. Oxford: Oxford University Press, 2007.

Paterson, Thomas G., J. Garry Clifford, and Kenneth J. Hagan. *American Foreign Relations: A History*. Lexington, MA: Heath, 1995.

Perkins, Bradford. *Prologue to War: England and the United States, 1805–1812*. Berkeley: University of California Press, 1968.

Stagg, J.C.A. *Mr. Madison's War: Politics, Diplomacy, and Warfare in the Early American Republic, 1783–1830*. Princeton, NJ: Princeton University Press, 1983.

Stourzh, Gerald. *Benjamin Franklin and American Foreign Policy*. 2nd ed. Chicago: University of Chicago Press, 1969.

LEONARD J. SADOSKY

foreign policy and domestic politics, 1865–1933

In foreign policy as in domestic politics, if the period before the Civil War concerned itself with *whether* the United States would remain a nation, then 1865–1933 helped determine *what kind* of nation it would be. The themes of this contest for national self-definition included the limits to continental and extracontinental expansion; the role of industry in expansion and vice versa; the power of the executive; the debate over "imperialism"; the sharpening markers of race, religion, and gender; and the definition of citizenship.

As presidents, secretaries of state, members of congress, business lobbyists, missionaries, journalists, and other opinion makers wrestled with these themes, patterns emerged. On one hand, a powerful majority of Americans supported expansion beyond the continental limits of the nation as an outlet for commercial and moral energies. On the other, a smaller but not negligible group called for restraint in the exercise of global power. Interestingly, both the dominant expansionists and the so-called isolationists articulated arguments based on similar domestic pressures and ideologies.

Manifest Destiny and Continental Expansion: 1865–90

In the area of westward expansion, there was relatively strong consensus. The ideals of Manifest Destiny gained ever-greater currency after the Civil War. Both political parties sided with President Andrew Johnson's desire to speed up the readmission of the former Confederate states into the Union so as to move on to what they considered the more pressing matter of developing the West. The end of the war also worsened the odds for tribes beyond the Mississippi, because in 1871 the Supreme Court ruled that Congress could override the traditional treaty system and consider tribes "local dependent communities" to be controlled, rather than independent nations. This led to a cycle of violence ending in the confinement of most Native Americans on reservations by the 1890s.

The "winning of the west," as Theodore Roosevelt called it, shaped future U.S. conquests of nonwhites. Starting with the War of 1898, U.S. troops overseas referred to the enemy as "Indians" and called hostile territory "Indian country." Eighty-seven percent of American generals who fought against Filipinos after

1898 were seasoned "Indian chasers." Native American wars also produced land laws that would be redrafted for overseas possessions, drew a blueprint for the "Americanization" of foreign cultures, prepared U.S. military tacticians for guerrilla tactics, and inoculated enlisted men against the brutality of race war. In 1902 Elihu Root, corporate lawyer and soon-to-be secretary of state, justified taking the Philippines thusly: "Without the consent of hundreds of thousands of Indians whom our fathers found in possession of this land," he said, "we have assumed and exercised sovereignty over them." He prescribed the same for "the ignorant and credulous Filipinos."

Early Overseas Acquisitions and Failures: 1865–97

Policy makers after the Civil War were much less united in their desire for overseas possessions. Among the expansionists, Secretary of State William Henry Seward (1861–69) was a visionary. He understood that "political supremacy follows commercial ascendancy," and argued against European-style colonization. His plan, rather, was to secure naval bases in the Pacific and a canal in the Caribbean to create a "highway" for U.S. commerce with Asia. Against those who derided Alaska as "Seward's Icebox," the secretary purchased the barren land from the Russians for $7.2 million in 1867. The same year he annexed the Midway Islands for a possible way station and cable point in the Asian trade.

Those who pressed to end the post–Civil War feud with London shared Seward's imperial optimism. Many Americans remained outraged that British ships used by the Confederacy had destroyed or disabled about 250 Union ships, and they asked for millions in what were called the *Alabama* claims. Anti-British sentiments even ensured a GOP victory in 1872. Against this crowd, expansionists felt that settling these claims would strengthen the bonds of "Anglo-Saxonism." Equally important, it would keep England and America out of each other's empire. Eventually, deals struck in 1872 and 1893 resolved the claims peacefully. "I feel very strongly that the English-speaking peoples are now closer together than for a century and a quarter," wrote a relieved Theodore Roosevelt to a friend.

Other expansionists issued calls for strengthening U.S. military power. After the Civil War, the Union army and navy demobilized and, by the 1880s, they respectively ranked a lowly thirteenth and twelfth in the world. The army was so depleted that even the Pinkerton Detective Agency was larger. In 1890, Captain Alfred Thayer

Mahan published *The Influence of Sea Power upon History, 1660–1783*, which convinced many that the path to global power lay with the military. In response, the navy, described by its secretary, John D. Long, in 1885 as "an alphabet of floating wash-tubs," won appropriation after appropriation from the Congress until, by the end of the century, the United States ranked sixth in the world in battleships commissioned or under construction. All the while, officer colleges sprang up and the diplomatic corps grew more professional, ridding itself of its most embarrassing political appointees and finally using the rank of ambassador, as of 1893.

A countervailing force of antiexpansionists was more powerful in the Gilded Age than at any time since. Few of them, however, cited moral qualms against expansion. Instead, domestic politics motivated many objections. The House, for instance, refused to pass the Alaska appropriations in 1867 until it moved to impeach Johnson. Others thought overseas expansion too expensive. The *New York Evening Post* cited the "unprofitableness" of empire, and, in 1867, the Senate thought $7.5 million to be too steep a price for the Virgin Islands. When Seward moved on Hawai'i, the Senate defeated his treaty on the basis that it would hurt the tariff. Still others used racist arguments *against* empire. In 1869, when President Ulysses S. Grant negotiated the annexation of the Dominican Republic, opponents in the Senate countered that the United States could not absorb such a mixed-race people, and ratification fell short of the two-thirds needed.

Economic Growth and Party Politics

The extraordinary industrial boom of the late nineteenth century fueled an expansionist surge. U.S. share of world trade climbed from 6 percent in 1868 to 16 percent in 1929, producing a century-long trade surplus starting in 1874. Transnational corporations such as Singer Sewing Machines and Eastman Kodak appeared in the 1880s, and industrialists such as John D. Rockefeller, Cyrus McCormick, and J. P. Morgan became shapers of foreign policy. By 1929, with only 6 percent of the world's population, the United States accounted for about half of its industrial goods and gold reserves. The railroad, steamship, telephone, and transatlantic cable eroded the cherished insularity of Americans. In 1901 President William McKinley marveled at "how near one to the other is every part of the world. Modern inventions have brought into close relations widely separated peoples. . . . The world's products are being exchanged as never before . . . isolation is no longer possible or desirable."

Despite booms and busts affecting all regions—at century's end, 70 to 80 percent of the South's cotton was exported—until 1913 Republicans tended to favor Republican foreign policies and Democrats, Democratic ones. Diplomatic posts were largely political footballs. For instance, Republicans defeated an important Canadian fisheries agreement in 1888 because it had been reached by Democrats, and when Grover Cleveland gained the presidency—the only Democrat to do so during the Gilded Age—he rolled back Republican actions on a Nicaraguan canal (1885) and on the Congo (1885), Hawai'i (1893), and Samoa (1894). Regional interests also mattered, as when Republicans from the interior voted against a bigger navy while seacoast Democrats voted in favor.

The tariff was the most divisive partisan issue. High tariffs, erected during the Civil War to raise revenue, remained high afterward for protectionist reasons. Groups interested in the tariff were many and complex, but the general fault lines had the Republicans mostly in favor because they protected infant industries and held workers' wages high, and the Democrats less in favor because high tariffs elicited countertariffs against crops such as cotton. Allegiances ebbed and flowed: industrialist Andrew Carnegie once said he got into the business of steel because its tariff was high, but by 1885 he argued for lowering tariffs to enable the purchase of cheap raw materials. The McKinley Tariff of 1890 and the Dingley Tariff of 1897 lowered rates somewhat, but U.S. rates remained far higher than those in Europe. The power of the tariff was a testament to the hold on foreign policy enjoyed by Congress in the nineteenth century.

Farmers also had their own foreign policies. To be sure, farmers shared in the export boom. But agrarian reformers organized as the Populist Party to protest farmers' shrinking piece of the export pie and the downward pressure on prices exerted by agricultural powerhouses Russia, Canada, Argentina, and India. Populist sympathizers such as Democrat William Jennings Bryan wished to disengage from the world and merely stand as an example of "the glory that can be achieved by a republic," and Populist leader Tom Watson railed that the War of 1898 benefited only the "privileged classes." In the end, Populists faded partly because their signature foreign policy issue—the free coinage of silver—went down in flames with the defeat of Bryan as a presidential candidate in 1896 and the passage of the Gold Standard Act in 1900, which declared the gold dollar the only currency standard.

Crises in the 1890s

The year 1893 witnessed the most serious recession in U.S. history to that point, sparking crises whose solution would be perceived to be more, not less, expansion. Some industrialists reasoned that domestic consumers were too few to buy the nation's output. As a result, many organized in 1895 into the National Association of Manufacturers (NAM) to promote exports. "We have the Anglo-Saxon thirst for wide markets growing upon us," said NAM president Joseph C. Hendrix in 1898. Hendrix, like others, saw mounting threats: the workers might revolt; immigrants multiplied; Europeans raised tariffs; and a new power in the Far East, Japan, defeated China in 1895 and now threatened the greatest potential U.S. market. Fear of a "glut" in exports was exaggerated, but plenty of farmers and factory owners shared it.

Many also believed that land had run out. Although there remained millions of unclaimed acres on the mainland, historian Frederick Jackson Turner's 1893 essay "The Significance of the Frontier in American History" fueled the crisis atmosphere by arguing that the disappearance of the frontier out West threatened the yeoman democracy and rugged individualism that graced American character. The solution, he said in 1896, was "a vigorous foreign policy . . . [and] the extension of American influence to outlying islands and adjoining countries."

Several groups heeded his words, starting with Protestant missionaries. In 1869 there had been only 16 American missionary societies. By 1900 there were 90, and by 1910, Americans outpaced even the British in financing missionaries. With the rise of Darwinian science, Protestant churches feared losing social status and compensated by sending thousands of missionaries abroad, the large majority to China. Their chief propagandist was Josiah Strong, a Congregationalist minister whose 1885 bestseller, *Our Country*, argued that the spread of American religion would advance the cause of American foreign policy. Protestants abroad exposed locals to U.S. goods and preached a morality that helped sell those goods, for instance, covering naked bodies with New England's textiles. Hoping to produce what the Student Volunteers for Foreign Missions called "the Evangelization of the World in This Generation," millions joined missionary societies in the United States. In 1890 women made up 60 percent of the movement. One woman explained that missionary work "should appeal to every broad-minded Christian woman who is interested in education, civics, sanitation, social settlements, hospitals, good literature, and the emancipation of children, the right of women

to health, home and protection; and the coming of the Kingdom of our Lord."

Just as missionary work filled a void in the 1890s, so did a renewed sense of racial superiority that arose from domestic developments. Social Darwinism had already raised the profile of racism in the United States, southern supremacists had encoded racial segregation for African Americans into law, and xenophobes warned of the "yellow peril" in the West. Americans now integrated visions of domestic and foreign race relations in the dozen or so international expositions of the Gilded Age. The World's Colombian Exposition in Chicago in 1893, for instance, displayed all the supposed races of the world on its main strip, from least to most civilized, starting with Africans and moving on to Indonesians, Pacific Islanders, other Asians, on up the ladder to Anglo-Saxons. As the century turned, race justified expansion. "We are a conquering race," argued Senator Albert Beveridge, Republican of Indiana. "We must obey our blood and occupy new markets, and, if necessary, new lands."

But racism was not simply for conquering. The "White Man's Burden," as British poet Rudyard Kipling called it in 1899, posited a moral, paternalistic obligation to uplift inferior races. Theodore Roosevelt shared it fully, explaining "it is our duty toward the people living in barbarism to see that they are freed from their chains." Race and racism, moreover, could be themselves changed by the experience of empire. Americans occupied the Philippines in 1898 with a racial ideology that held that Filipino "niggers" were unredeemable savages but then came out years later with a more subdued view that Filipinos had a "capacity" for self-government if properly directed.

Less obvious was the domestic crisis of gender. Late-century American men felt emasculated by urbanization and modern life. Roosevelt argued that adventures abroad could help men relive "the strenuous life." "Over-sentimentality, oversoftness . . . , and mushiness are the great danger of this age and this people," he complained. He wanted to revive "barbarian virtues" and yearned for a war that would do so. "You and your generation have had your chance from 1861 to 1865," he told Civil War veteran and anti-imperialist Carl Schurz. "Now let us of this generation have ours!"

The War of 1898 and Its Consequences

As if responding on cue to the domestic martial spirit, the United States fought Spain in 1898 and joined the club of great powers. "From a nation of shopkeepers we became a nation of warriors" is how Democratic Party boss Henry Watterson described the transition. However, while between 1870 and 1900 Great Britain added 4.7 million square miles to its empire and France added 3.5 million to its own, the United States annexed only 125,000. This was not because Americans were "reluctant" imperialists but because they preferred informal control of foreign lands rather than formal colonization.

The struggle over Cuba helped define the U.S. preference for informal empire. The explosion of the USS *Maine* and the death of 266 American sailors in February 1898 punctuated an already tense situation in which U.S. observers sympathized with Cubans rebelling against corrupt Spanish rule. Even after this tragedy, however, U.S. opinion was by no means united behind war. The "yellow press" and religious publications wanted war on nationalistic and humanitarian grounds, but others warned against the cost of fighting even a weak empire like Spain. U.S. planters in Cuba and trade journals back home were hawkish, but the American Federation of Labor (AFL) feared the island's cheap labor. President McKinley moved for war in April only after the Congress insisted on a promise of nonannexation though the Teller Amendment, named for Senator Henry Teller of Colorado, who acted to protect his state's beet sugar from Cuba's cane sugar. In the end, McKinley asked for war not to pander to a jingoistic public but to stop a Cuban revolution that could threaten U.S. property and to stem charges of cowardice from Democrats. The "splendid little war," as Rough Rider Theodore Roosevelt called it, ended quickly, prompting the *New York Sun* to declare, "We are all jingoes now," and giving Washington control over Cuba, Puerto Rico, the Philippines, and Guam. The Platt Amendment, strong-armed into the Cuban Constitution of 1901, gave oversight of the island's foreign policy to the United States and confirmed the apparent wisdom of informal empire.

The war in the Philippines—the other major former Spanish colony—garnered far less consensus. Easily defeating Spain, the United States then entered into a years-long brutally racist guerrilla war with Filipino rebels, led by Emilio Aguinaldo. "Civilize 'em with a Krag," went a popular army song, as Americans administered the "water cure" and other tortures to captured Filipinos. "I want no prisoners," General Jacob Smith instructed his troops. "I wish you to kill and burn, the more you kill and burn the better you will please me." The war took 4,165 American lives and more than 200,000 Filipino lives. McKinley justified the carnage with a classic

euphemism: "benevolent assimilation" meant the desire to uplift Filipinos through Americanization, a program that began in earnest after the war.

But while it lasted, the carnage stirred the period's greatest domestic debate about foreign policy. Anti-imperialism made for strange bedfellows: writers and editors such as Mark Twain, E. L. Godkin, and William Dean Howells joined industrialists like Carnegie, social reformers like Jane Addams, the AFL's Samuel Gompers, and politicians of both parties. Opponents formed the Anti-Imperialist League in Boston in June 1898, and its arguments largely reflected domestic politics. Civil rights leader Moorfield Storey, for instance, saw parallels between the treatment of Filipinos and African Americans; and women identified with Aguinaldo's fury at being governed without his consent. Others feared "the incorporation of a mongrel and semibarbarous population into our body politic," as a South Carolina senator expressed it. As one observer noted, all the posturing, abroad like at home, achieved little: "Democrats howling about Republicans shooting negroes in the Philippines and the Republicans objecting to Democrats shooting negroes in the South. This may be good politics, but it is rough on the negroes."

Besides the takeover of Cuba and the Philippines, the War of 1898 had other important consequences. One was the annexation of Hawai'i. By the 1890s, planters, missionaries, navy planners, whalers, and traders on their way to China had long advocated U.S. control of the islands. A treaty from the mid-1870s boosting sugar made Hawaiians "practically members of an American Zollverein in an outlying district of the state of California," said Secretary of State James G. Blaine. A believer in economic imperialism, Blaine championed annexation as "a purely American form of colonization." By 1893 Americans made up only 5 percent of Hawai'i's population but owned 65 percent of its land. That year, they led a coup against a strong-willed Queen Liliuokalani that paved the way for full annexation in the heat of the war with Spain, on August 12, 1898.

Hawai'i foreshadowed another consequence of 1898: the rising power of the executive. When McKinley could not carry two-thirds of the Senate for a Hawaiian treaty, he achieved it through a joint resolution, which required only simple majorities. McKinley and his successor, Theodore Roosevelt, especially overpowered Congress in foreign policy. McKinley was the first chief executive with cabinet officers who had few political bases of their own and so were more loyal to him. He was also first to appoint a "secretary to the president," who assumed the duties of today's press secretary: holding daily meetings with reporters, issuing press releases, and putting together press scrapbooks. During the war, the president imposed harsh rules on war reporting and had three telegraph wires and 25 telephone lines running into the White House. With such expanded powers, McKinley took unprecedented license. He responded to China's Boxer Rebellion of 1900, for instance, by sending troops without congressional permission. Meanwhile, Roosevelt penned several "executive agreements" that could supplant treaties and circumvent Congress. It was not clear, however, if a stronger White House meant an expanded voice for the people in foreign policy. The Oval Office often defied popular sympathies, for instance, when it sided with the British in South Africa's Boer War. And besides, McKinley and Roosevelt believed the president's role was not to follow but to "educate," in the style of the Progressive movement. To Roosevelt, public opinion was "the voice of the devil, or what is still worse, the voice of a fool."

World War I: Wilsonianism Abroad and at Home

The Great War of 1914–18, more commonly known as World War I, sparked yet another debate, this one over U.S. involvement in Europe. Americans greeted the news of war with a reflexive reluctance, and as late as August 1917, one journalist assessed that two-thirds of the nation was still against the war. Antiwar groups included Irish Americans who hated the British Empire and German Americans who disapproved of fighting their *Heimat* (homeland). The Socialist Party made gains with its rhetoric of peace, and the Selective Service Act, or draft, passed the House by a slim margin of 199 to 178, with 52 abstentions. President Woodrow Wilson won reelection in 1916 with the motto "He Kept Us Out of War." In fact, neutrality paid off: before they joined the war, Americans sold some $2.2 billion in arms to the British and their Allies.

Yet the moralistic internationalism advocated by Wilson and fellow progressives led logically to war. Herbert Croly, in his 1909 book *The Promise of American Life*, had linked progressivism to foreign relations by calling for a centralized Hamiltonian state, a stronger military, and lower tariffs that would promote democracy and capitalism abroad. When Wilson called for war in the spring of 1917, he articulated aims in the "fourteen points" speech of January 8, 1918. Its major principles included self-determination for small nations, freedom of the seas, reduction of armaments, adjustment of colonial claims, open

treaties, and a vaguely defined League of Nations. "There are American principles, American policies," explained the president. Wilson presented a democratic alternative to the specter of communism engulfing Russia as of 1917. "The spirit of the Bolsheviki is everywhere," he warned.

Wilson's democratic spirit was a hit with European audiences. Parisians lined their streets under banners that read "*Vive Wilson*" and Italians welcomed him as the *Redentore dell'Humanità* (Redeemer of Humanity). But negotiations over the Treaty of Versailles and the League of Nations faced opposition from European victors and crippling criticism at home. Republicans who now controlled the Senate organized as the "reservationists" and "irreconcilables." The latter wanted nothing to do with the treaty or the league, while the former, headed by Henry Cabot Lodge, the chairman of the Senate Foreign Relations Committee, were wary of surrendering U.S. sovereignty. "Are you willing to put your soldiers and your sailors at the disposition of other nations?" Lodge asked rhetorically. Wilson refused to give Congress oversight over such matters and embarked on an 8,000-mile, 22-day, cross-country speaking tour that worked him into a paralyzing stroke. The tour was in vain. Congress kept the United States out of the treaty and the league.

War also affected domestic groups. African Americans "over here," as the popular song called the homeland, still lived overwhelmingly in a South that lynched 382 of their own from 1914 to 1920, and met with hostility that often boiled over into race riots when they migrated to the North. Four hundred thousand joined the military but were assigned to camps often segregated with "whites only" signs. Leaders such as W.E.B. Du Bois took a respite from encouraging "black nationality" among those of African descent and argued for standing "shoulder to shoulder" with whites in a common struggle for democracy. Du Bois organized a Pan-African Congress in conjunction with the Versailles conference, but his advocacy fell on deaf ears with the Great Powers. Women, too, mobilized for food campaigns, child welfare work, and Liberty bond and loyalty drives. "The Girl Behind the Man Behind the Gun" is how one poster described their influence. For women, patriotism brought concrete political gain: the Nineteenth Amendment securing the vote was ratified in 1920.

For those not deemed patriotic enough, repression came swiftly. Respectively passed in 1917 and 1918, the Espionage Act and the Sedition Act interpreted any criticism of the war as subversive, and as a result some

German-born residents of the United States fell victim to vigilante mobs. In 1919 war's end brought not only racial but labor strife. When terrorists exploded a bomb outside the home of Attorney General A. Mitchell Palmer, the state rounded up thousands of pacifists and labor leaders, leading to the deportation of more than 500 aliens. Even Eugene Debs, the Socialist Party's standard-bearer, was imprisoned under Wilson, against whom he had run for the presidency in 1912.

Empire in the Caribbean and Central America

Despite the rejection of European postwar settlements, the United States did not turn inward. Quite the contrary, it expanded its presence around the world, especially when unopposed by other Great Powers. Cultural and economic radiance were especially intertwined. Marketers spread the "American Dream" of material wealth, and exporters satisfied those urges with the automobile, motion pictures, and the radio. "Foreign lands are feeling the benefit of American progress, our American right thinking," automaker Henry Ford believed. "Both Russia's and China's problems are fundamentally industrial and will be solved by the application of the right methods of thinking, practically applied." Americans also sent themselves abroad; passport holders multiplied almost tenfold in the 1910s and 1920s. Finally, Americans increasingly imported the world's goods. French salons, English libraries, Japanese designs, and folk objects from American Indians or Latin America became de rigueur in chic homes.

In the Caribbean area, however, imposing "right thinking" did not go smoothly. Especially after 1898, president after president sent U.S. troops to occupy Latin American ports, negotiate loans in exchange for financial supervision—an arrangement called "dollar diplomacy"—and remake what they perceived to be unstable political cultures into havens for U.S. security, foreign investment, and moral reform. In 1903, when Theodore Roosevelt encouraged the separation of Panama from Colombia through French and U.S. private promoters, it showed the convergence of the U.S. Navy's need for a canal with American merchants' desire for increased trade. The result was the opening of the Panama Canal in 1914, built by a multinational workforce and managed by thousands of U.S. citizens living in a ten-mile-wide colony bisecting the Central American Isthmus.

The canal engendered another need: securing Caribbean routes leading to it. In 1904, when he signed an agreement with Dominicans to take over their customs houses, Roosevelt declared the need for the United States to exercise "international police power" in its "backyard." Racist paternalism again mixed with security and business interests to send U.S. troops to invade Caribbean countries at least 34 times in the 30 years after 1903. Wilson's interventions in the Mexican Revolution were especially contradictory, since he rejected conquest yet sent soldiers so that the Mexican government could "be founded on a moral basis." A desire to minimize criticism of these adventures, especially by the "peace progressives" in Congress, led Presidents Herbert Hoover and Franklin D. Roosevelt in the late 1920s and early 1930s to call for the end of military interventions, what FDR coined the Good Neighbor Policy.

Puerto Rico fit oddly into this pattern. U.S. troops took it over in 1898 but met no armed resistance. In 1900 the Foraker Act made the island an "unincorporated territory" led by a U.S.-appointed governor and subject to congressional laws, thus taking away Puerto Ricans' independence but not granting them rights as U.S. citizens. In decisions from 1901 to 1910 known as the Insular Cases, the Supreme Court ratified this state of legal limbo. In 1917 the Jones Act gave Puerto Ricans U.S. citizenship—just in time to draft them into the war—but awarded the island neither statehood nor independence.

Citizenship and Immigration

Immigration and foreign policy were closely related in 1865–1933 because defining citizenship was key to U.S. relationships with the world. So while the era was a high point for immigrants from Europe, it was not so for Asians. In 1882 Congress passed the Chinese Exclusion Act, banning practically all Chinese from entering the United States and marking the first such restriction based on race or nationality. In 1907 Roosevelt signed a "Gentlemen's Agreement" with Tokyo, sharply cutting back Japanese immigration in return for putting pressure on the California legislature not to segregate Japanese students. Such xenophobic actions went hand-in-hand with Jim Crow laws in that they relegated nonwhites to a separate, second-class citizenry. Meanwhile, "Americanization" movements aimed to assimilate Europeans into a "melting pot" that allowed them to minimize differences and emphasize their common whiteness.

The Johnson-Reed Immigration Act of 1924 solidified this narrowing of citizenship. It established the first numerical limits for immigrants of every nation, nonwhites such as those from China and India being limited to 100 per year. Supreme Court decisions in the 1920s went further, barring Japanese and Asian Indians from claiming whiteness and therefore citizenship. Hardened racial lines created the "alien citizen," or U.S. citizen now seen as alien by most Americans.

For Mexican Americans—the large majority of Latin American immigrants before the 1960s—the process was different but equally revealing of domestic politics. From 1900 to 1930, more than 1 million Mexicans came into the United States, nearly all to work in the fields of the Southwest. The 1924 law did not apply to Mexicans because farmers needed cheap labor, but by the late 1920s, calls for restriction grew more strident. Mexicans did compete for some jobs and housing with U.S. citizens, and were often called ignorant, dirty, lazy, and criminal. Ominously, the 1930 U.S. Census for the first time defined Mexicans as a separate race. When the Great Depression hit, the U.S. government forced half a million Mexicans in America, nearly one in five, back to their homeland.

Defining America

The Depression caused a sharp downturn in U.S. engagement with the world. Exports declined 60 percent, and Americans virtually stopped investing overseas. In 1930 the protectionist wall, eroded slightly since Wilson, went back up with the Smoot-Hawley Tariff. Two years later, some 25 nations had retaliated. It would take another war in Europe to reinvigorate U.S. leadership in world affairs.

From the Civil War to the Great Depression, proponents and opponents of expansion tied themselves to the word *Americanism*, suggesting that they were expressing the best of the country's values through its behavior abroad. That debate, perhaps more than anything, marked the era. Now that issues such as trade openness, military expansion, and immigration are again debated, the importance of defining America through its foreign relations speaks to the seminal nature of the 1865–1933 period.

See also Alaska and Hawai'i; Americanism; business and politics; Caribbean, Central America, and Mexico, interventions in, 1903–34; immigration policy; Latinos and politics; Native Americans and politics; race and politics; tariffs and politics.

FURTHER READING

Beisner, Robert L. *From the Old Diplomacy to the New, 1865–1900.* 2nd ed. Arlington Heights, IL: Harlan-Davidson, 1986.

———. *Twelve against Empire: The Anti-Imperialists, 1898–1900.* Chicago: Imprint, 1992.

Fry, Joseph A. "Phases of Empire: Late Nineteenth-Century U.S. Foreign Relations." In *The Gilded Age: Essays on the Origins of Modern America,* edited by Charles W. Calhoun, 261–88. Wilmington, DE: Scholarly Resources, 1996.

Gyory, Andrew. *Race, Politics, and the Chinese Exclusion Act.* Chapel Hill: The University of North Carolina Press, 1998.

Hoganson, Kristin L. "Cosmopolitan Domesticity: Importing the American Dream, 1865–1920." *American Historical Review* 107, no. 1 (February 2002), 55–83.

Hutchison, William R. *Errand to the World: American Protestant Thought and Foreign Missions.* Chicago: University of Chicago Press, 1987.

Iriye, Akira. *The Globalizing of America, 1913–1945.* Vol. 3 of *The Cambridge History of American Foreign Relations.* Cambridge, UK: Cambridge University Press, 1993.

Jacobson, Matthew Frye. *Barbarian Virtues: The United States Encounters Foreign Peoples at Home and Abroad, 1876–1917.* New York: Hill and Wang, 2000.

Kramer, Paul. *The Blood of Government: Race, Empire, the United States, and the Philippines.* Chapel Hill: University of North Carolina Press, 2006.

LaFeber, Walter. *The American Search for Opportunity, 1865–1913.* Vol. 2 of *The Cambridge History of American Foreign Relations.* Cambridge, UK: Cambridge University Press, 1993.

Love, Eric T. L. *Race over Empire: Racism and U.S. Imperialism 1865–1900.* Chapel Hill: University of North Carolina Press, 2004.

Ngai, Mae. *Impossible Subjects: Illegal Aliens and the Making of Modern America.* Princeton, NJ: Princeton University Press, 2005.

Offner, John L. "United States Politics and the 1898 War over Cuba." In *The Crisis of 1898: Colonial Redistribution and Nationalist Mobilization,* edited by Angel Smith and Emma Dávila-Cox, 18–44. New York: St. Martin's Press, 1999.

Renda, Mary. *Taking Haiti: Military Occupation and the Culture of U.S. Imperialism, 1915–1940.* Chapel Hill: University of North Carolina Press, 2001.

Ricard, Serge, ed. *An American Empire: Expansionist Cultures and Policies, 1881–1917.* Aix-en-Provence, France: Groupe de Recherche et d'Études Nord-Américaines, 1990.

Rosenberg, Emily S. *Financial Missionaries to the World: The Politics and Culture of Dollar Diplomacy, 1900–1930.* Durham, NC: Duke University Press, 2003.

———. *Spreading the American Dream: American Economic and Cultural Expansion, 1890–1945.* New York: Hill and Wang, 1982.

Rydell, Robert W. *All the World's a Fair: Visions of Empire at American International Expositions, 1876–1916.* Chicago: University of Chicago Press, 1984.

Skinner, Elliott P. *African Americans and U.S. Policy toward Africa, 1850–1924: In Defense of Black Nationality.* Washington, DC: Howard University Press, 1992.

Wynn, Neil A. *From Progressivism to Prosperity: World War I and American Society.* New York: Holmes and Meier, 1986.

ALAN MCPHERSON

foreign policy and domestic politics since 1933

Bookended by moments of far-reaching global and national crisis, the period from 1933 through the early twenty-first century opened with the United States in economic depression and enforced retreat from the bold internationalism espoused by President Woodrow Wilson. The long-standing isolationism that dashed Wilson's global aspirations ended abruptly when the United States entered World War II, and when the country emerged from the war as the ascendant global power, with European colonialism collapsing in the wake of wartime challenges. After the Allied Forces' victory over global fascism, the United States competed for the next 40 years with the Soviet Union for the hearts, minds, and resources of the more than 40 new nations then emerging from decades of European colonial rule. That history of conflict—of the aspirations of formerly colonized peoples seeking national independence, control of their resources, and an independent course for their economic development pitted against cold war policies—remains resonant. By the end of the U.S.-Soviet conflict, both sides had poured millions of dollars and tons of weapons into Africa, Asia, Latin America, and the Middle East, setting the stage for contemporary ethnic conflicts and the rise of al-Qaeda and global terrorist groups. Moreover, by the early twenty-first century, the United States would be engaged in costly protracted wars in Iraq and Afghanistan while facing the greatest national and global crisis since the Great Depression.

Consuming the World

The United States emerged from World War II as the dominant military and economic power amid proclamations of the "American Century." Several decades later, the demise of the Detroit automotive industry that had served as the nation's arsenal during wartime would symbolize the end of American supremacy in manufacturing. Once the world's wealthiest creditor, the United States became a debtor nation (with, in mid-2008, a national debt of $9.5 trillion and a federal budget deficit of $410 billion). The export of manufacturing jobs, the decline of the dollar in relation to foreign currencies, the nation's dependency on foreign-produced oil, and the nation's borrowing from China to finance its deficit spending have made connections between U.S. foreign policy and the nation's domestic life and politics visible to many Americans. Many undoubtedly recall with nostalgia how the U.S. entry into World War II pulled the country out of a prolonged economic crisis. But other aspects of the relationship between foreign policy and the way Americans live have remained mysterious to many Americans. How many know, for example, that the unprecedented expansion of wealth in the 1950s and the benefits of a consumer society depended on U.S. domination of strategic and manufacturing resources?

Conceptualizations of connections between domestic politics and U.S. foreign relations—military, economic, and diplomatic—have changed dramatically over time. At moments defined by national crisis, such as restrictions on civil liberties during the cold war, or more recently, during the "war on terror" after the 9/11 attacks, the connection between domestic and foreign affairs seems abundantly clear. Less well known are the more routine socioeconomic ties that have historically bound the United States to foreign peoples and their societies. The material abundance of a domestic U.S. consumer society founded on cheap energy, industry's access to raw materials, and foreign sweatshop labor has fostered in many Americans an innocence about the relationship between inflated military spending and a neglected national infrastructure and public sphere. Similarly, this innocence of past ties between foreign relations and domestic politics emerges in the unwillingness of anti-immigration forces to consider the impact of past U.S. foreign wars and economic policies as a catalyst for immigration. Yet it is impossible to consider U.S. politics and culture outside of the history of the United States on the world stage.

The relationship between U.S. foreign and domestic policy tends to enter the American political arena and public consciousness primarily in times of war or crisis, while significant realms and operations of U.S. power remain on the periphery of public discourse and awareness. One reason is that some momentous foreign policy actions were carried out covertly, such as the 1953 CIA overthrow of the Iranian elected government of Muhammad Musaddiq and the installation of Shah Reza Pahlevi's U.S.-friendly dictatorship. Beyond this, the actions of powerful nonstate actors who are nonetheless sanctioned or promoted by the government—from the Hollywood film industry in the twentieth century, which accepted State Department guidelines for cinematic content in exchange for the global distribution of films, to corporations contracted to secure the occupation and rebuilding of Iraq—remain hidden to most Americans, and beyond the reach of U.S. legal and regulatory authority.

Although contemporary historians of the United States have vigorously challenged earlier tendencies to separate the foreign and domestic spheres and have raised awareness of America's intricate global connections, the story of the post–World War II economic boom, demographic and social shifts such as the growth of the suburbs, the population shift to the Sun Belt, and the unprecedented material affluence experienced by that generation of Americans is often told without considering how profoundly these shifts depended on U.S. policies that aggressively promoted a globally integrated, U.S.-led capitalist economy. Americans simply would not have had the automobiles, refrigerators, and air conditioning that enabled these massive demographic shifts without ready Western access to resources in southern Africa, the Middle East, and Latin America. The growth of commercial air travel would not have developed without cobalt, an essential material for jet engines. Like uranium, diamonds (without which computers could not operate), and countless other metals, the vast majority of cobalt reserves were in southern Africa. Then, as now, the classic American freedom of the open road depended on Middle Eastern oil production. The 1970s energy crisis exposed U.S. oil dependence, a dependency again well in evidence as the world market price of oil and unprecedented gas prices reached new highs in the aftermath of the U.S. invasion and occupation of Iraq.

Global dependencies structured daily consumption as well as fundamental economic and social shifts. In the 1950s and 1960s, Americans consumed millions of frozen TV dinners, no doubt for the most part unaware of the origins of the aluminum tins in Jamaican bauxite mines, acquired during World War II by the U.S.-based Reynolds Metals corporation; the fried chicken processed under the dismal working and living conditions of the undocumented immigrants in southern poultry farms; and the fruit dessert harvested by migrant farm workers

in the West. Today, the U.S. presence within a web of global labor relations, including past and present wars and global entanglements, is reflected in myriad seemingly mundane consumer decisions such as whether to order Vietnamese or Cambodian food for takeout. Many American cultural and culinary tastes are shaped by the history of the nation's expansive global involvement, as well as its high consumption of energy and natural resources.

Wilsonian Internationalism and the American Century

In 1933 the global economic depression temporarily stalled America's earlier imperial expansions and disrupted the Wilsonian project of making the world safe for American democracy and institutions. During World War I, Wilson had waged explicit and fierce economic competition with America's military allies, and changed the United States from a debtor nation to a creditor nation with legislation that freed U.S. banks and corporations from Progressive Era restrictions. The establishment of the Federal Reserve and its central banking system provided U.S. industries with a competitive global advantage. Wilson's missionary zeal for reshaping the world in America's image was further reflected in his response to the 1917 Russian revolution and Vladimir Lenin's call for a worldwide revolution against imperial powers. In response to Lenin, Wilson's "Fourteen Points" speech offered an anticolonial politics that challenged Europe's privileged access to markets and investment.

Compelled to focus on the domestic crisis of the Great Depression, Franklin D. Roosevelt also looked outward as the first president to recognize the Soviet Union, and through his attempts in the face of isolationist opposition to build new alliances in aiding opponents of Japanese and German aggression. World War II sparked social conflict within the United States, notably in the forced internment of Japanese American citizens and in the widespread white resistance to the movement of African Americans into cities and the West with the opening of factories and jobs. At the same time, the wartime alliance with the Soviet Union enabled a second flowering of the popular front culture of the 1930s, as leftist-inspired labor and social movements vigorously debated the appropriate character of U.S. internationalism. The period of World War II through the early cold war marked the ascendance of the United States as a global superpower at precisely the moment that European colonialism collapsed, and in the midst of a related cold war with the Soviet Union. Both superpowers struggled to win the allegiance and resources of formerly colonized peoples. Many Americans, including such black radicals as Paul Robeson and W.E.B. DuBois, and Roosevelt's first vice president, Henry Wallace (the Progressive Party candidate in the 1948 election), envisioned a worldwide New Deal in which future peace and prosperity hinged on ending colonialism and raising the standard of living of colonized peoples as well as continued cooperation between the United States and the Soviet Union.

Others revived the ambitious Wilsonian internationalism of World War I to argue that the priority in a new American-led internationalism was the safety of American investments and America's access to resources needed for economic growth. For Time-Life publisher Henry Luce and his allies, the "American Century" would usher in a world where American values, culture, and consumer products peacefully conquered the world. This vision profoundly influenced U.S. wartime and postwar objectives, as U.S. policy makers envisioned an American-led, globally integrated capitalist economy. Committed to ensuring the West's privileged access to the world's markets, industrial infrastructure, and raw materials, this group embraced President Harry Truman's ambitious declaration that the United States had the right and responsibility to intervene in external and internal threats everywhere across the globe.

The Cold War and U.S. Global Ambitions

Scholars generally agree that despite Joseph Stalin's notorious brutality toward the Soviet people, the Soviet Union was not expansionist in the early years of the cold war, forced instead to rebuild internally after the enormous casualties and destruction of infrastructure during World War II. (This would change dramatically in the 1960s under Soviet Premier Nikita Khrushchev, who declared support for national liberation movements worldwide.) Yet at the end of World War II, with conservatives throughout Europe tarnished by collaborations with the Nazis, and Communists and Socialists hailed as the core of resistance to fascism, the European left emerged from the war greatly strengthened, and anticapitalist ideologies had enormous appeal for anticolonial movements. In the eyes of many U.S. policy makers, this represented a serious threat to American economic and political objectives.

The Truman Doctrine, announced before Congress on March 12, 1947, specifically funded beleaguered anti-Communist governments in Greece and Turkey but more broadly asked Americans to accept the "great responsibilities" entailed in a global struggle against communism. The Attorney General's List of Subversive Organizations and the Loyalty Oath declared the criticism of American foreign policy beyond the pale of acceptable discourse. The cold war repression of political dissent intensified during the early 1950s, under the leadership of Wisconsin senator Joseph McCarthy, who used the spotlight of nationally televised hearings to promote the idea of a conspiracy of Communists who had infiltrated the nation's foreign policy establishment. McCarthy's witch hunts had a far-reaching, intimidating influence on critical institutions such as the press and education from the elementary to university level, and in setting up a bipartisan cold war foreign policy consensus.

After decades of careful documentation of cold war repression within the United States, some scholars have more recently contended that the cold war's impact on the narrowing of political and cultural expression has been overemphasized. Certainly, some social processes and intellectual and political traditions transcended cold war divides. But a fundamental issue remains: despite sometimes heated debates over strategy, such as Eisenhower's critique of Truman's execution of the Korean war, the United States consolidated its position as the world's dominant power largely without scrutiny of means or ends. For 20 years following the announcement of the Truman Doctrine in 1947, the ruling assumptions and objectives of American foreign policy to contain communism went unopposed in Congress or within any significant sector of the American people. The substantially narrowed anti-Communist political discourse during the 1950s helped account for the episodic nature of American citizens' engagement with foreign affairs, as well as the explosive social conflict that occurred in the 1960s. Most important, the institutional patterns of secrecy and lack of democratic accountability established in the early cold war years posed profound challenges to not only the broader vibrancy of a democratic culture where citizens feel engaged and empowered in matters that affect their lives, but the most basic tenets of liberal procedural democracy.

Anticolonialism, Civil Rights, and the Cold War

The leading international alternative to the cold war's bipolar vision of global politics, the nonaligned movement of newly independent Afro-Asian nations, had little traction within U.S. politics. The most far-reaching demands for political and economic equality of the World War II era, including the linking of civil rights to anticolonial struggles abroad, were abruptly altered and in many cases thoroughly repressed in the early cold war. While such radical advocates of anticolonialism as Robeson and DuBois were prosecuted and had their passports seized, others, such as the NAACP's Walter White, became architects of a new anti-Communist liberalism, promoting an anticolonialism that was justified by anticommunism, arguing that the abuses of colonialism opened the doors to Communists and that Asia and Africa must remain in the Western orbit.

Despite strong rhetoric denouncing the abuses of domestic racism, such as Secretary of State Dean G. Acheson's warning that the United States could not neglect the "international implications of civil rights violations," advocates for civil rights and desegregation found the range of debate sharply constrained, despite the Truman administration's unprecedented endorsement of a civil rights agenda. Truman's embrace of civil rights acknowledged Acheson's understanding of civil rights as a national security issue. But in focusing more on the cold war than on civil rights, Truman presided over the contraction of public debate and the collapse of the left during the early cold war years. As early as 1946, with the formation of Truman's Committee on Civil Rights, White and others began to craft the dominant argument of the anti-Communist civil rights liberals. The new argument seized on international criticism, in the world press, of American racism to argue that antidiscrimination measures were vital for the United States in its struggle against communism. The dominant liberal argument against racial segregation, using anticommunism to justify the fight against racism and for civil rights, conceded the high ground to anticommunism.

Scholars have traced a powerful remobilization of business between 1946 and 1948, which afforded anti-Communist labor leaders power within the circles of the corporate elite and blocked the radical social agenda of labor and civil rights evident during World War II. The growing conservatism of the labor movement and the narrowing of labor's agenda had a critical impact on global politics. As Communists and progressives were expelled from unions in America, American labor supported anti-Communist unions abroad even when that meant collaborating with former Nazis and other fascists. In 1949 CIO unions left the World Federation of Trade Unions (WFTU), and both the AFL and CIO took the lead in setting up the new anti-Communist International Confederation of Free Trade Unions. CIO support for African labor during World War II had been an important feature of the globally inflected civil rights activism that had also supported anticolonial movements. But after the CIO's departure from the WFTU, the role of U.S. labor in Africa, as well as in the well-documented European cases, would be filtered through a close collaboration between the AFL-CIO (under director George Meany) and the State Department—with covert support from the CIA.

The Hot Battle for Hearts and Mines

The debate over the significance of the cold war in shaping American politics rests in part on the very definition of the term *cold war*. To grasp the implications of U.S. cold war policies it is necessary to look beyond the bipolar U.S.-Soviet conflict. From the U.S. entry into World War II through the early cold war, the United States ascended as the hegemonic power while competing with the Soviet Union for the allegiance and resources of formerly colonized peoples. In theory, colonialism had no place in the vision of American democratic capitalism. U.S. policy makers not only objected to the resources and markets that colonialism afforded the European powers but also came to see American race relations as the Achilles' heel in the cold war battle for hearts and minds overseas, and sought to distinguish themselves from European colonizers.

Thus, for the most part, U.S. policy makers did not seek to take over European models of colonialism as they withered in the face of anticolonial challenges and the straitened conditions of wartime. Asserting instead the right of the United States to lead the "free world," they pursued global economic integration through modernization and development. American policy makers committed themselves to making sure that the West had privileged access to the world's markets, industrial infrastructure, and raw materials. And like the Wilsonian promotion of self-determination that had no trouble reconciling the invasions of Haiti and Mexico when U.S. interests and investments were at stake, policy makers in the post-1945 period interpreted democracy to mean capitalism first and foremost, and consistently supported dictatorships friendly to capitalism over democratically elected nationalist governments in Asia, Africa, and the Middle East or U.S. economic imperialism in Latin America.

In the face of persistent attempts by formerly colonized peoples to regain control of their resources, U.S.

policy makers made repeated use of (often covert) military force; the "cold" war was in fact a bloody and protracted conflict for the peoples of Asia, Africa, Latin America, and the Middle East, where democratic challenges often met with violent suppression by either U.S. proxies, covert operatives, or both. By the mid-1950s, the CIA had already carried out covert actions to oust elected leaders in Iran and Guatemala, and by the mid-1960s, had waged counterinsurgencies in Indonesia, Syria, the Congo, Cuba, Guyana, and Vietnam. Certainly many policy makers viewed these actions as a necessary evil. The "common sense" of covert action depended on a worldview of the Soviet Union as a dangerous enemy that fundamentally threatened "the American way of life." But in confronting a seemingly ubiquitous Soviet threat, American policy makers repeatedly conflated nationalism and communism. Moreover, U.S. opposition to leaders throughout the Middle East, Africa, Asia, and Latin America often reflected ethnocentric and paternalistic assessments of non-Western leaders that prohibited American policy makers from viewing them as independent political agents. From the CIA overthrow of Muhammad Musaddiq in Iran to the ouster and assassination of Patrice Lumumba in the Congo in 1961, U.S. officials tended to see leaders in these regions as pawns or potential pawns of the Soviets. Despite the complexity of America's global relationships, when control over crucial strategic resources such as oil and uranium were at stake American officials brooked no ambiguity in assessing the allegiances of national leaders.

The enormous reach of U.S. foreign policy entailed highly porous boundaries between the government and purportedly private corporations and cultural industries. As the Soviet Union sent classical orchestras and ballet companies around the world and the United States responded with jazz, dance, and other cultural forms, the circulation of culture became part of the cold war battle for hearts and minds. The United States Information Agency produced and distributed films, radio programs, and vast numbers of pamphlets and news releases aimed at showing the world the superiority of the American way of life and American democracy. By 1955 the Voice of America brought American music and culture to an estimated 30 million people in more than 80 countries. In the next decade, that number would triple. The State Department sponsored cultural presentations involving a multitude of artists, from jazz musicians Louis Armstrong, Duke Ellington, and Dizzy Gillespie to dancers and choreographers Martha Graham, Alvin Ailey, and Paul Taylor to the Cleveland Orchestra, high school marching bands, and rhythm and blues and soul groups. While such tours were highly publicized, the CIA clandestinely funded cultural institutions from the Museum of Modern Art in New York City to radio, newspapers, and the motion picture industry. Touring jazz ensembles closely followed an itinerary tracking the cold war commodities of oil and uranium; some appearances occurred practically simultaneously with U.S. backed coups and interventions. As the U.S. government courted neocolonial elites, musicians traveled with remarkable frequency to places where the CIA operated, from Iran and Iraq to the Republic of the Congo to other areas of America's northern perimeter defense zone across Afghanistan, Pakistan, and Turkey.

As the U.S. government secured access to oil for American companies by means from coups to concerts, precursors of Texaco, Chevron, Exxon, and Mobil exported U.S. segregationist race relations in their worker-management relations throughout the Western hemisphere. In the segregated workforces the oil companies assembled in Mexico and Venezuela, workers were paid differently according to race. These same companies owned the conglomerate Arabian American Oil Company, which styled itself as a private enterprise version of the Marshall Plan as it extended such arrangements into former parts of the British and French empires, transplanting segregationist labor and housing laws to the oil fields and refineries of Saudi Arabia, where Arab workers labored under Jim Crow–style discrimination.

As these private enterprises thrived throughout Central America and the Middle East, in the many areas where the accelerated anticolonial activity of World War II carried into armed conflict between independence movements and colonial powers, ultimately the United States nearly always backed up its colonial allies when they faced challenges to their rule. Only in rare cases—such as Indonesia, where the United States judged the Dutch to be so intransigent as to be driving the Indonesians into the hands of the Communists, and the 1956 Suez Canal crisis, in which the United States defied Britain and France and eventually forced them to withdraw troops they had amassed to challenge Gamel Abdel Nasser after he nationalized the canal—did the United States directly challenge its European allies in matters of colonial control.

Vietnam and Deepening Militarism

The case of America's longest war, in Vietnam, starkly illustrates the tendency of the United States to ultimately back up its colonial allies. Historians have struggled to explain America's participation in the Vietnam War, a war that would shape the character of American politics and society for decades to come. Scholars have analyzed the war as an inevitable by-product of cold war assumptions and even as an example of the sheer excess of liberal cold war ideology. While both of these views are important, historians have less often considered the war as an ill-advised by-product of the U.S. commitment to colonial France. With the United States initially sympathetic to Ho Chi Minh's revolutionary nationalism, when the French government of General Charles de Gaulle found itself both embattled by the Communist left and incapable of defending its colonial empire, the United States reversed its position and came to its aid, propping up successive South Vietnamese governments tottering precariously atop an inherited colonial state structure.

In his Farewell Address, President Dwight Eisenhower expressed concern that what he labeled "the military industrial complex" might imperil American democratic institutions. Over time, antiwar critics would extend this observation to charge that America had overinvested in military sectors at the expense of basic industry, manufacturing, and infrastructure. The most radical critics of U.S. participation in the Vietnam War linked the war to U.S. imperialism throughout the globe.

Protest and National Nervous Breakdown

Scholars have discussed the irony of a government defending democracy from communism by creating a secret government accountable to no one. Certainly, the fact that so much U.S. foreign policy remained under the radar in the early cold war—such as the order by John F. Kennedy to depose President Ngo Dinh Diem of South Vietnam in 1961, and the 1964 Tonkin Gulf incident that led President Lyndon Johnson to ratchet up U.S. intervention in the war—contributed enormously to the outrage of the 1960s antiwar movement, as many Americans who had generally trusted their government and shared in the hopeful optimism projected by Kennedy began to discover that they did not have the whole story, and indeed, had been lied to. In 1965 high school students in Des Moines, Iowa, braved suspension and even death threats by wearing black armbands in an antiwar demonstration. Four years later the Supreme Court upheld the First Amendment Rights of students (and teachers) at school. Americans inundated by humanitarian appeals to sponsor impoverished children because poverty would lead them to communism now saw those children slaughtered by American troops. In 1967, the year of the My Lai Massacre in Vietnam, Americans also learned that the CIA had illegally funded such American organizations as the National Students Association and the American Society of African Culture, in addition to a multitude of foreign cultural organizations.

By 1968 the violence—whether covert or military—that had become integral to the pursuit of U.S. objectives abroad seemed endemic in U.S. society as well. In February of that year, police fired on African American students protesting segregation in Orangeburg, South Carolina. Domestic and international opposition to U.S. participation in the Vietnam War became a polarizing force, further undermining the liberal consensus for civil rights reform, fracturing the Democratic Party and sowing the seeds for the demise of the New Deal Coalition and the rise of the New Right. Martin Luther King Jr.'s antiwar speech on April 4, 1967, and his opposition to racism, poverty, and militarism divided the civil rights movement. In 1968 the unpopular war had forced President Johnson to withdraw his campaign for reelection. The assassination of King, and shortly afterward of Robert Kennedy, the leading antiwar contender for the Democratic nomination for president, hurled the nation into chaos.

President Richard M. Nixon, who parlayed the nation's racial and antiwar conflicts to gaining the presidency in 1968, ordered the expansion of the conflict to Laos and the secret bombing of Cambodia. The term *imperial presidency* usually refers to Nixon's use of unchecked executive power in his conduct of American involvement in the war, and his disregard for legislative oversight. The Watergate scandal, caused by the administration's cover-up of the burglary of Democratic National Committee offices before the 1972 presidential campaign, proved to be Nixon's undoing. He resigned when his claims of executive privilege on the withholding of evidence related to Watergate were rejected by the Supreme Court. And by firing Archibald Cox, the special prosecutor appointed by Congress, who investigated the scandal, Nixon had outraged critics by causing a constitutional crisis. To be sure, Nixon was a complex figure, a paranoid and mean-spirited politician eager to destroy his critics on the eve of his 1972 reelection campaign, but also an astute statesman whose policy of détente opened up relations with the China and the Soviet Union. But the view of Nixon and his National Security Advisor Henry Kissinger that managing superpower relations was the key to resolving all global conflicts extended the cold war conflation of nationalism and communism and failed its greatest test in Vietnam. The Nixon-Kissinger foreign policy favored aggressive protection of U.S. access to key strategic and economic resources at the expense of democratic governments and movements. The administration supported military dictatorship in Pakistan in its war with India and its genocide in Bangladesh. Nixon supported the right wing dictatorship of Portugal in its colonial war in Angola, and backed white supremacist governments of southern Africa. Nixon and Kissinger also directed CIA support for the bloody 1973 military coup that overthrew Salvador Allende, the democratically elected Socialist president of Chile. The coup, led by General Augusto Pinochet, killed more than 3,000, including Allende himself. Pinochet's military dictatorship, marked by detention, torture, and murder, lasted until 1990.

Debating U.S. Power

Nixon's use of executive power led to demands for transparency and congressional oversight. The War Powers Act (1973), passed over Nixon's veto, called for congressional authorization of the president's deployment of the armed forces. After a series of revelations, including the U.S. Army surveillance of civilians and covert CIA activities reported by Seymour Hersh in 1975, a Senate Select Committee on Intelligence Activities chaired by Senator Frank Church (D-Idaho) unearthed extensive information on covert intelligence and counterinsurgency programs, including FBI domestic surveillance and CIA operations, plots to assassinate foreign leaders ordered by presidents, and a shared CIA-FBI program involving the surveillance of the mail of American citizens. The Church Committee inspired regulatory restraints, including an executive ban on U.S.-sanctioned assassinations of foreign leaders. In addition, the Federal Intelligence Surveillance Act (FISA) established court procedures and oversight for surveillance of foreign intelligence agents. The Church Committee's efforts to impose limits on the CIA and executive authority were strongly resisted by President Gerald Ford's advisors, including Kissinger and Donald Rumsfeld.

The fact that Congress never debated, voted on, or declared an official U.S. war in Vietnam meant that its

financing was concealed from public oversight. The high cost of the war led to the "stagflation" and economic crisis of the 1970s, unveiling longer patterns of global interdependence. The 1973 oil embargo led by the Organization of Petroleum Exporting Countries, the cartel of oil-producing nations, unmasked America's dependence on foreign oil. The triple shocks of the Vietnam War, Watergate, and the oil crisis revealed the Western Fordist industrial economy to be in precipitous decline, with shrinking social welfare benefits for workers in Western industrial societies and the rise of new transnational corporations and financial institutions with rapidly diminishing accountability to states and nations. The long-term U.S. economic dependence on the extraction of raw materials in dangerous and exploitative conditions may not have been apparent to most Americans, but the loss of 500,000 auto jobs between 1978 and 1982, leading to widespread hardship, was highly visible.

Popular discontent at the failure in Vietnam, economic troubles, and the exposure of government improprieties led to the election of Georgia Democrat Jimmy Carter to the presidency in 1978. Carter advocated U.S. foreign policy guided by concern for human rights and urged Americans to accept limits to the easy access to resources that many had taken for granted. Leading by example, Carter promoted energy conservation as a means of reducing America's dependence on foreign oil. Carter's challenges to the American public provoked a backlash. And to many, Carter appeared generally inept at foreign policy, powerless to stop the erosion of the gains of détente and the escalation of the cold war as the Soviets invaded Afghanistan and stepped up support for leftist governments and opposition groups. In 1979 the Iranian Revolution sent the U.S.-backed shah into exile, creating a vacuum filled by the Islamic cleric Ayatollah Ruholla Khomeini. When young Iranian militants seized 52 U.S. diplomats as hostages, Carter staged a military rescue mission that failed. While Carter brokered the hostages' release before the end of his term, the 444-day national ordeal had doomed his reelection campaign.

A Supernova Burning Brightest at the Moment of Its Demise: The Last Years of the Cold War

Republican Ronald Reagan ran on two simple premises: getting the "monkey of government" off people's back and restoring U.S. might and right. Although Reagan ran against big government, his administration increased military spending while scaling back the welfare state.

During the 1980s, with the nation deeply divided over U.S. foreign policy, the Reagan administration accelerated the cold war, particularly through support of anti-Communist counterinsurgencies in Latin America. Through the continuing and new proxy wars of the 1980s, the Reagan administration supported right-wing insurgencies in El Salvador and Nicaragua. When the Boland Amendment blocked Reagan's support of the contras in Nicaragua, the White House, led by National Security Council staff member Lieutenant Oliver L. North, secretly funneled support to the contras as they sought to overthrow the democratically elected Sandinistas. The disclosure of North's "shadow government" led to the Iran-Contra Affair, in which North diverted to the contras the proceeds of arms sales to moderates in Iran in exchange for the release of Americans held hostage there.

Ironically, as a president who presided over a dramatic escalation of the cold war, Reagan ended his second term benefiting from Soviet Premier Mikhail Gorbachev's campaign of Glasnost and Perestroika—political openness and economic reform—and the formal dissolution of the Soviet Union in 1991. The collapse of the Soviet Union and the fall of Communist governments in the Eastern Bloc states led to profound changes in global politics. While activists demanded a "peace dividend" of investment in domestic social programs, in 1989 one commentator, Francis Fukuyama, proclaimed "the end of history" marked by the universal triumph of Western liberal democracy and the demise of all ideological alternatives. Many U.S. policy makers shared Fukuyama's thesis and believed that the fall of Communist states vindicated the values of free-market capitalism. But this triumphalist view of the cold war mitigated against an examination of failed policies on all sides of the conflict. Many have tended to view present dangers with nostalgia for the supposed stability of the cold war era. But one cannot neatly classify the wars and challenges of the twenty-first century as those of a distinct post–cold war moment with entirely new dynamics. State and nonstate wars, the U.S. occupation of Iraq, political violence in Africa, and the "war on terror" all suggest the limitations of Fukuyama's bipolar cold war perspective.

The Reagan administration opposed the Soviet occupation of Afghanistan by supporting the anti-Soviet Mujahadeen fighters in that country (including Osama bin Laden). Reagan also enlisted Iraq and its dictator Saddam Hussein as an ally against Iran after the overthrow of the shah of Iran. The arming of Africa and the Middle East by the United States and Soviet Union, and the dubious alliances between western powers and third world "strongmen," contributed to continued instability in Africa and later electoral victories of leftist governments in Latin America, including those of Brazil, Venezuela, and Bolivia. The alliance with Pakistan in the "war on terror" was part of a longer history of U.S. military support for Pakistan that reaches back to partition and U.S hostility toward India and its nonaligned foreign policy.

Cold War Continuities and the War on Terror

The George W. Bush administration's responses to the terrorist attacks of September 11, 2001, and the U.S. invasion and occupation of Iraq not only marked a return to the government secrecy of the cold war but also deployed U.S. armed forces in the region where the United States first engaged in cold war–era covert operations. Some of the ardent cold warriors of the Reagan era, including Elliot Abrams, Donald Rumsfeld, and Dick Cheney, resurfaced in the administration of George W. Bush, implementing their "ends justify the means" vision of unchecked executive power in the pursuit of war and intelligence gathering. The publication of photographs taken by U.S. troops engaging in the torture of detainees in the Abu Ghraib prison in Iraq sparked public outrage and congressional scrutiny. Further investigations revealed that despite widespread opposition within the administration itself; from members of Congress in both parties; and from people within the Justice Department, the State Department, and the CIA, a small but powerful group led by Vice President Dick Cheney extended a network of secret prisons and secret torture unprecedented in U.S. history in its scope and disregard for both the U.S. Constitution and international law.

In a sense, every presidential election since the end of U.S. participation in the Vietnam War has served as a referendum on American foreign policy and America's place in the world. The crises of the early twenty-first century suggest that the country has yet to overcome the institutionalized patterns of secrecy and lack of democratic accountability established in the early cold war years. Many have argued that such patterns have profoundly damaged democratic institutions within the United States. For many citizens and elected officials, the use of torture, the erosion of civil liberties, and widespread electoral fraud of the 2000 and 2004 elections called into question the legitimacy of the electoral system, the basic functioning of procedural democracy, and the survival of the Constitution. Some hoped that the severity of the crisis would present a historic opportunity to restore transparency and democratic accountability, and to rethink U.S. foreign policy, the country's dependence on global resources, and the future of the United States in a multilateral world.

See also anticommunism; globalization; immigration policy; war and politics.

FURTHER READING

Borstelmann, Thomas. *The Cold War and the Color Line.* Cambridge, MA: Harvard University Press, 2003.

Mamdani, Mahmood. *Good Muslim, Bad Muslim: The Cold War and Roots of Terror.* New York: Pantheon, 2004.

May, Elaine Tyler. *Homeward Bound: American Families in the Cold War Era.* New York: Basic Books, 1988.

Mayer, Jane. *The Dark Side: The Inside Story of How the War on Terror Turned into a War on American Ideals.* New York: Doubleday, 2008.

Saunders, Frances Stoner. *The Cultural Cold War: The CIA and the World of Arts and Letters.* New York: New Press, 1999.

Schmitz, David F. *The United States and Right Wing Dictatorships, 1965–1989.* New York: Cambridge University Press, 2006.

Vitalis, Robert. *America's Kingdom: Mythmaking on the Saudi Oil Frontier.* Stanford, CA: Stanford University Press, 2007.

Von Eschen, Penny. *Race against Empire: Black Americans and Anticolonialism.* Ithaca, NY: Cornell University Press, 1997.

———. *Satchmo Blows Up the World: Jazz Ambassadors Play the Cold War.* Cambridge, MA: Harvard University Press, 2004.

Westad, Odd Arne. *The Global Cold War and the Making of Our Times.* New York: Cambridge University Press, 2005.

PENNY M. VON ESCHEN

Free Soil Party

The Free Soil Party was an organization founded in 1848 to oppose the spread of slavery into the territories the United States had acquired in the recently concluded war against Mexico. Believing that, constitutionally, it could not challenge slavery in the existing slave states, the party supported the Wilmot Proviso, then under debate in Congress, to contain slavery within its existing boundaries. As a third party, it attempted to force Democrats and Whigs to stop catering to the interests of what it called the "Slave Power," which demanded that slavery be legal in all territories.

The treaty ending the Mexican-American War, ratified by the Senate in February 1848, resulted in the acquisition of vast new southwestern territories that included California and expanded American boundaries westward from Texas and the Louisiana Purchase to the Pacific. During the war, Representative David Wilmot, a Democrat from Pennsylvania, had proposed prohibiting slavery in any territory acquired from Mexico. Although approved by the northern-dominated House, the proviso stalled in the Senate and debate raged as the presidential campaign began. When the conventions of both the Democratic and Whig parties refused to include Wilmot Proviso planks in their platforms, factions of both organizations seceded and joined with the small abolitionist Liberty Party to form the Free Soil Party at a mass convention in Buffalo attended by close to 20,000 people.

The Liberty Party, which had formed in 1840, joined the Free Soilers somewhat reluctantly, since its members stood for total abolition and considered joining those who sought only to contain slavery to be a sacrifice of principle. They were especially concerned that the new party was led by a former proslavery Democrat, Martin Van Buren. Yet most in the Liberty Party accepted the decision of their party leaders, knowing that a larger political organization would bring greater influence. Led by Salmon P. Chase and Gamaliel Bailey of Ohio, and joined by Massachusetts and New York Liberty men, the party attracted a more idealistic element and added the support of such leaders as poet John Greenleaf Whittier, Joshua Leavitt, and John P. Hale. Many Liberty women, including editor Jane Grey Swisshelm of Pittsburgh, added their support, even though they were denied the ballot. All worked strenuously and enthusiastically during the campaign. The party received its most enthusiastic support in New York, Massachusetts, and northeastern Ohio.

Under the leadership of Chase, the delegates adopted a platform calling for a host of reforms but stressing the Wilmot Proviso. They also called for a homestead bill, protective tariffs, and federal aid for internal improvements, and concluded with the slogan "FREE SOIL, FREE SPEECH, FREE LABOR, and FREE MEN." The delegates chose a ticket of former president Van Buren and Charles Francis Adams, son of the recently deceased John Quincy Adams, a longtime opponent of the war. The platform was silent on the issue of racial equality because many party members opposed extending civil rights to African Americans; yet many free blacks still endorsed it, including Frederick Douglass.

For them, the Free Soil Party was the only viable alternative to proslavery candidates Zachary Taylor and Lewis Cass and a continuation of Slave Power influence. Despite Liberty reluctance over Van Buren as the candidate, Leavitt concluded, "The Liberty party is not dead, but translated." Many antislavery Democrats and Whigs resisted joining, however, fearing the loss of political influence in a party unlikely to be competitive. This group included Abraham Lincoln, William H. Seward, Hannibal Hamlin, Thaddeus Stevens, and Benjamin Wade.

Late in organizing and low in campaign funds and editorial support, the third party was unable to resist the strength of Democratic and Whig organizations. It faced the inevitable charge that a vote for a third party was not only a wasted vote but in fact aided one of the two major parties by drawing support away from the other. The Free Soil Party gained only 10 percent of the vote in an election that placed Mexican-American War hero General Zachary Taylor in the White House. Although it won a dozen seats in the House and soon placed Chase and Charles Sumner in the Senate, the party proved unable to withstand the lure of political power and the trend toward North-South compromise in 1849 and 1850. Many members returned to their original parties. Especially damaging was the defection of the Van Burenites, who surrendered their antislavery principles and rejoined the New York Democratic Party.

The Free Soilers struggled in 1852 in reduced form with a presidential ticket of John P. Hale of New Hampshire and George W. Julian of Indiana, winning only half of their 1848 total. Without most of its Democratic component, the party was a more principled organization but proved incapable of countering the Democratic and Whig argument that the Compromise of 1850 had settled the important sectional issues.

A lull in sectional agitation, interrupted by fugitive slave rescues and the publication of Harriet Beecher Stowe's *Uncle Tom's Cabin,* was shattered in 1854, when Senator Stephen A. Douglas, Democrat of Illinois, proposed his Kansas-Nebraska bill repealing the Missouri Compromise ban on territorial slavery above 36°30′ north latitude. With their key leaders, Daniel Webster and Henry Clay, dead, the Whigs offered only ineffective opposition to the Douglas bill, and their decline accelerated. Northerners, seeking a new, more effective antislavery party, responded with the Republican Party, with Free Soilers Chase, Sumner, and Joshua Giddings of Ohio in the lead. The new party fought off a challenge from the anti-immigrant American Party (the Know-Nothing Party), and, by 1855, emerged as a member of the two-party system. In its first presidential campaign in 1856, the party platform stressed the Wilmot Proviso concept and succeeded in winning the support of many antislavery politicians who had earlier rejected the Free Soil Party, including Lincoln, Seward, Hamlin, Stevens, and Wade. When the party won its first presidential election four years later, with a ticket headed by Lincoln and Hamlin, it did so with a containment of slavery platform closely resembling that of the Free Soilers in 1848. Thus, as the country teetered on the brink of civil war, the founders of the party could claim with justification that Northerners had finally realized the need to challenge the Slave Power's control over the federal government and prevent the spread of slavery.

See also American (Know-Nothing) Party; Whig Party.

FURTHER READING

Blue, Frederick J. *The Free Soilers: Third Party Politics, 1848–54.* Urbana: University of Illinois Press, 1973.

Foner, Eric. *Free Soil, Free Labor, Free Men: The Ideology of the Republican Party Before the Civil War.* New York: Oxford University Press, 1970.

Morrison, Chaplain W. *Democratic Politics and Sectionalism: The Wilmot Proviso Controversy.* Chapel Hill: University of North Carolina Press, 1967.

Morrison, Michael A. *Slavery and the American West: The Eclipse of Manifest Destiny and the Coming of the Civil War.* Chapel Hill: University of North Carolina Press, 1997.

Rayback, Joseph G. *Free Soil: The Election of 1848.* Lexington: University of Kentucky Press, 1970.

Richards, Leonard L. *The Slave Power: The Free North and Southern Domination, 1780–1860.* Baton Rouge: Louisiana State University Press, 2000.

Sewell, Richard H. *Ballots for Freedom: Antislavery Politics in the United States, 1837–1860.* New York: Oxford University Press, 1976.

FREDERICK J. BLUE

G

gender and sexuality

Debates over gender and sexuality have been central to American politics since the days of the Founding Fathers. At stake have been conflicting definitions of men's and women's proper roles, both in the family and in relation to state and nation. These disputes are significant, in part, for their enduring rhetorical appeal: few politicians have sought to depict themselves as "antifamily," while many have criticized their male opponents as weak and effeminate or, conversely, violent and piratical. In a deeper sense, recurring conflicts over public policy—over the outcome of politics—have also had crucial gender dimensions. Over two centuries, the accepted model of American family life moved from a patriarchal model to one centered on domesticity and women's indirect moral influence, then gradually, in the twentieth century, toward an egalitarian ideal. Political parties and movements not only responded to these long-term shifts, they helped articulate and advance them.

The centrality of aggressive masculinity in U.S. empire building has had a critical impact on the nation's politics at many junctures, from at least the 1840s through the cold war. Masculine "toughness" has served as a potent rallying cry for military mobilization and, at moments of crisis, has proven difficult for both male and female peace advocates to counter. Consistently, calls for manliness have been racially charged, a phenomenon that has had clear domestic racial parallels in, for example, the era of "Redemption," when Southern white supremacists called upon white men to overthrow Reconstruction by armed force, in the name of protecting white womanhood. Women, meanwhile, have steadily gained a place within party organizations and electoral campaigns beginning as early as the antebellum era. But women remain a minority among convention delegates, candidates, and decision makers. Exclusion from power has prompted politically active women to develop a rich array of extrapartisan strategies and organizations. Both inside and outside the parties, women have often cultivated a politics of moral zeal that has drawn upon domestic ideology, perceptions of female purity and selflessness, and women's very real status as political outsiders.

The Revolution and Its Aftermath

The American Revolution, grounded in an Enlightenment vision of human equality, opened new possibilities for both men and women in politics. The victory of the new United States established the world's first modern republic, with political power vested in the individual citizen. Americans viewed voters' "civic virtue" as crucial for the nation's survival. Though the vast majority of Americans considered citizenship a male prerogative, prominent thinkers like Judith Sargent Murray argued that American women had a special role to play in promoting civic virtue. As "republican mothers," they should educate themselves and take an interest in political affairs, in order to raise their sons to be virtuous citizens and their daughters to become republican mothers in the next generation.

With suffrage confined at first to property-holding white men (except for a brief extension of the franchise to propertied women in New Jersey), the very core of American politics lay in a gentlemen's code of honor. Within that code, hierarchies of wealth, family connections, and reputation pitted men against one another. Early American politics relied on personal networks of friendship, obligation, and gossip. When a man's honor was attacked, political duels were not uncommon. While a few women became partisan writers and editors, most who exercised political influence did so informally, through social networks. As parties developed, the more elite-based Federalists proved particularly welcoming to female participation in campaign work. While

365

Democratic-Republicans achieved a more radical vision in class terms, granting full citizenship rights to nonpropertied men by the 1820s, they were hostile to women's participation. The fading of Revolutionary radicalism and the Federalist Party's demise caused women's place in politics to decline by the 1810s.

Militant Manhood in the Antebellum Era

The election of Andrew Jackson in 1828 ushered in a vibrant era of mass-based party politics. Drawing first on Jackson's public persona as a military hero and aggressive Indian fighter, Democrats celebrated a "white man's democracy" with overt gender dimensions as well as racial ones: they defended the authority of white men over all dependents in their households, including wives, children, bound laborers, and slaves. Patriarchal manhood helped unite Democrats across class and regional lines and informed the party's small-government stance. Consistently, Democrats attacked "paternalistic" government policies as intrusions on the rights of white male citizens. During the Jacksonian era, when most states extended suffrage to all white men, politicians gradually began to cultivate a folksy style and depict themselves as "men of the people." Slaveholding complicated this pattern in the South, where political power continued to be equated with mastery, and thus to some extent with wealth. In a region that disciplined labor through direct, brutal violence rather than through the exigencies of survival through wage work, duels and physical violence persisted longer than in the North.

In the meantime, a powerful domestic ideology began to emerge in the growing northern cities and factory towns. Increasingly, prosperous urban men worked outside the home, while wives and mothers, responsible for a domestic space that had allegedly been stripped of its productive role, came to be seen as conservators of morality and noncommercial values. For men, domesticity prescribed temperance, self-control, and deference to womanly moral influence. Political conflicts over such issues emerged as early as 1828, when Jackson's opponents caricatured him as a violent man, prey to the vices of lust and liquor, and alleged that he had seduced his wife Rachel into bigamy. After Rachel's death, Jackson's opponents lamented that she could no longer "control the violence of his temper" or serve as a "restraining and benign influence" over the new president. Domesticity quickly spread beyond the northern urban middle classes to many other sectors of American society. It filtered into politics, predominantly through the vehicles of the Whig

and Republican parties, and it is hard to overemphasize its significance in American politics thereafter. Seeking to build a "benevolent empire" for reform, Whigs embraced an ideal of manly restraint and a cautious acceptance of indirect female influence in the public sphere. Domesticity had overt class dimensions: Whigs criticized undisciplined, poor men who allegedly drank, brawled, and failed to support their families. By the late 1840s, such critiques included a strong streak of anti-Irish prejudice. The Democrats, meanwhile, championed working-class manhood and largely opposed and ridiculed female political participation.

By the 1840s and 1850s, race and gender became intertwined in an array of political issues, as Americans debated Manifest Destiny and the seizure of lands from native peoples. Democrats, in particular, justified military aggression through appeals to manhood, urging "Anglo-Saxon" men to seek their destinies on the frontier and in Latin America. Such arguments had special appeal for Southerners, who sought to expand the empire of slavery, and for white working-class men, many of whom were losing ground in the new commercial economy. On the other hand, proponents of masculine restraint and self-control, who tended to be Whigs, deplored violent conquest and criticized expansionists as bullies and pirates.

Gendered conflicts between an aggressive, racialized manhood on the Democratic side and restrained manhood and domesticity among their opponents also played a central role in debates over slavery. Radical abolitionists, strongly committed to domesticity, emphasized slavery's perversion of both white and black family life. The Liberty Party and Free Soil Party carried these ideas into the electoral arena, with female editors playing a major role in shaping arguments against slavery. While Free Soil men depicted themselves as moderate compromisers who merely sought to prevent the extension of slavery into federal territories, Free Soil women took the role of moral crusaders: outsiders demanding immediate, unconditional abolition. At the same time, the most radical abolitionists began to call for equal rights for women. These women's rights abolitionists began to move beyond domesticity, critiquing its glorification of "women's sphere" and arguing that female citizens had not only a right but a duty to act as public speakers, writers, and voters.

In gender terms, meanwhile, the new Republican Party of the 1850s inherited and expanded the Whigs' passion for domesticity. Republican leaders drew on the gendered rhetoric of Free Soil men, for example, to oppose extension of slavery into the territories. In some areas, Republicans also attacked immigrant men for their supposed violence and intemperance, arguments that were also made in the 1850s by the short-lived American (or Know-Nothing) Party. Across the North, Midwest, and West, Republicans vigorously attacked the Mormon practice of plural marriage. The party's first presidential candidate, John Frémont, was hailed as "Jessie's choice" because his young and attractive wife, Jessie Benton Frémont, was rumored to have antislavery sympathies. Republicans simultaneously denounced Frémont's opponent, James Buchanan, as an aging bachelor and possibly a homosexual.

From Domesticity to Imperialism
During and after the Civil War, the rise to power of the Republican Party brought a revolution in many aspects of national politics, including gendered political values. As part of their commitment to expanded government power, Republicans vested manhood in the state rather than in the authority of autonomous, patriarchal heads of household, as Democrats had done. Party leaders and rank-and-file members celebrated both Union victory and emancipation as defeats for a violent, tyrannical aristocracy of slaveholders. Though few yet conceived of a modern welfare state, they did lay the foundations for that development in a modest "breadwinner" state. For example, Republicans provided generous Union pensions to widows and disabled Union veterans, and after 1890 to all Union veterans, in legislation that modestly prefigured Social Security. Republicans also defended their economic policies—especially high protective tariffs—on the grounds that they extended domesticity to millions of Americans, helping working-class breadwinners earn a family wage to support their wives and children.

Republicans sought to extend or enforce domesticity among African Americans and native peoples, viewing male breadwinning and female domesticity as the keys to "race uplift" and civilization. Many freedmen and freedwomen in fact embraced domesticity, and African American editors and political leaders preached the gospel of homemaking for women and temperance and self-discipline for men. The late nineteenth century thus represented a kind of apex of political domesticity, exemplified by such models of hearthside happiness as First Lady Lucy Webb Hayes, a temperance advocate who was widely viewed as the force behind her husband's ban on

liquor at the White House. The term *first lady* itself, as a semiofficial title for the president's wife, came into use near the end of the Civil War, a sign of the increasing symbolic importance of presidents' wives and families.

But the patriarchal manhood of the antebellum era did not remain defeated after the Civil War, and by 1900 Republicans also proved susceptible to its appeal. It reemerged most obviously in the South, as ex-Confederates and their allies engineered the violent overthrow of Reconstruction. In so doing, they appealed directly to white men in gendered terms, claiming falsely that enfranchised black men were responsible for an epidemic of rape against white women. The extension of voting rights to African American men was frequently cited as the alleged cause of interracial rape, suggesting the continued political and psychological link that many men drew between voting, sexuality, and men's control over their female dependents. (Several historians have observed that the struggle over "long ballots" versus "short ballots" in this era had phallic overtones; party loyalists who organized campaign pole raisings celebrated the rapidity with which they raised their poles, and they often accused opponents of not being able to raise their poles or failing to keep them "in an upright position.")

"Martial manhood" also reemerged in the Spanish-American War, especially in the figure of Theodore Roosevelt. Yet, departing from the antebellum model of martial manhood, turn-of-the-century imperialists also gave prominent attention to the role of white women as civilizers. They argued that inferior races needed to see the example set by white Christian wives and mothers, in order to adopt domesticity and uplift themselves. Such arguments were advanced not only by government agents in the U.S.-occupied Philippines but on Indian reservations, where missionaries and agents tried to force Native Americans to conform to the model of male breadwinning and female domesticity.

Progressive Politics
The era of Republican dominance paved the way for many other uses of domesticity in politics. The mantle of moral and economic reform passed first to the Prohibition and Populist parties, both of which called for women's political rights while appealing for Americans to "protect the home" by increasing government intervention in the economy. Proposals to protect, support, or supplement family incomes abounded between the Civil War and the New Deal, especially during the Progressive Era. These were often championed by coalitions

of politically active women who appealed to their maternal roles as justification to engage in "municipal housekeeping." After the Civil War, these powerful grassroots women's movements became fixtures in national politics. The most popular, the Woman's Christian Temperance Union (WCTU), counted over a million members at its peak and advanced an explicitly nativist, Christian agenda with its appeal for women to work for "God and Home and Native Land." Despite its initial focus on liquor, the WCTU undertook an array of reform activities, from soup kitchens to the creation of kindergartens; its charismatic leader, Frances Willard, became a strong ally of labor and advocate for the eight-hour workday.

Between 1865 and 1920, women's clubs and missionary societies joined the chorus of female-led groups active in politics. Such groups succeeded, for example, in getting legislators to raise the age of sexual consent in many states, which had been as low as 10 years of age in 14 states and 7 in Delaware. They also helped pass laws to restrict women's working hours and grant mothers' pensions for "deserving" women who found themselves bereft of a breadwinner. Reformers succeeded in adding a Women's Bureau and Children's Bureau to the national Department of Labor. The broad scope of these agencies' work is suggested by the mandate Congress gave the Children's Bureau upon its creation in 1912. The bureau was instructed to investigate child labor and working conditions and to make recommendations on "infant mortality, the birth-rate, orphanages, juvenile courts, desertion, dangerous occupations, and accidents and diseases of children."

The woman suffrage movement, still small at the end of the Civil War, flourished in the Gilded Age and Progressive Era. Women began voting in some western states and territories as early as 1869, and by the early 1910s, most women in states west of the Mississippi had achieved full suffrage. By that same decade, suffrage had become a mainstream cause with widespread support across class and regional lines. The exception, unsurprisingly, was in the South, where suffragists made little headway even when they argued that white women's votes would help sustain white supremacy. When the federal woman's suffrage amendment achieved ratification in 1921, it did so with the support of only one legislature in an ex-Confederate state—that of Tennessee.

The Progressive Era thus offered new opportunities for women in the public sphere, including full voting rights, but it also vividly demonstrated the limits of women's power, especially on subjects such as foreign policy, where calls to martial manhood still had a powerful appeal.

When the United States entered World War I, proponents of war mobilization fiercely attacked women who worked for disarmament and arbitration through groups like the Woman's Peace Party. (Theodore Roosevelt, still on the national scene, declared that the place for such women was "in China—or by preference in a harem—and not in the United States.") At the same time, reformers who appealed for government action on the basis of motherhood and domesticity reinscribed the very outsider status that made it hard for women to implement laws in the first place.

Breadwinners and Consumers

With the passage of national woman suffrage after World War I, candidates at all levels faced new pressures to tailor their appeals to both women and men. Anxious party leaders began including women more fully in their organizations and worked for passage of national Prohibition. In cities like Chicago, African American women who had worked for racial justice used their new clout as voters to bring pressure for change. Many candidates appealed to women as housekeepers and shoppers. Herbert Hoover, who had coordinated domestic conservation and food aid during and after World War I appealed directly to female voters. In the 1928 campaign, Republicans recruited "Hoover Hostesses" who invited friends into their homes to hear Hoover's radio campaign speeches.

But equality in voting and representation proved elusive despite the achievement of suffrage. Though women accounted for over half the U.S. population, their voting turnout was low and did not exceed 50 percent until 1980. Those women who did vote were, despite suffragists' hopes, divided along geographic, economic, racial, and religious lines. Advancement of women's rights suffered a serious blow in the 1920s in struggles over the first proposed equal rights amendment (ERA). Progressive reformers who had achieved gender-based protective labor legislation limiting women's working hours, helped defeat the ERA, fearing it would undermine such laws. Meanwhile, despite suffrage, many states refused to permit women to serve on juries, and an array of other discriminatory practices remained legal.

The onset of the Great Depression intensified conflicts between the old ideal of domesticity and the realities of an increasingly urban and industrial society. It became obvious in the 1930s that, through no fault of their own, millions of men could not support their families. The election of Franklin D. Roosevelt in 1932 firmly established Democrats as the party of government activism, and reformers who sought to protect workers and families gained tremendous clout. The substantial welfare initiatives of the New Deal followed earlier gendered patterns. Programs that aided breadwinners, such as Social Security, provided direct entitlements, while mothers who sought government support had to prove their "moral fitness" to receive aid. Gender and racial exclusion moved, again, in tandem: at the insistence of southern Democrats in Congress, the Social Security Act excluded agricultural and domestic workers, who in the South were overwhelmingly black. African American women thus suffered a double exclusion, both from welfare programs that denied coverage to most black workers and from a "breadwinner model" of government aid that refused to recognize women as wage earners with equal status to men.

Despite Americans' continued faith in the domestic ideal and their widespread blindness or indifference to the needs of wage-earning women, industrialization and urbanization kept issues of sexuality and gender in the political arena. The percentage of married women working outside the home rose to 30 percent by 1960, as women entered the paid workforce in enormous numbers. Urban neighborhoods witnessed a day-care crisis. Unequal pay, gender-segregated job markets, glass ceilings, and sexual harassment gained increasing recognition among working women but negligible attention from political leaders. Instead, Americans publicly celebrated women's "return to domesticity" during the baby boom era. But the number of women working outside the home, including married women with children, continued to climb, and grassroots women's organizations, along with their allies in government agencies like the Women's Bureau, kept alive issues of women's rights.

These efforts culminated in President John F. Kennedy's appointment of a Presidential Commission on the Status of Women (PCSW), which played a high-profile role in calling attention to women's issues between 1961 and 1963. The commission, chaired by Eleanor Roosevelt, considered numerous legislative measures to enhance women's rights. Members of the PCSW, galvanized by their experiences on the commission, played a central role in the creation of the National Organization of Women (NOW) in 1966. In the meantime, when Congress debated the 1964 Civil Rights Act, a conservative southern representative tried to derail the bill by adding language that prohibited discrimination on the basis of sex; the law passed with this language included, providing a basis for federal prosecution of both race- and gender-based discrimination. By the time NOW came into existence, most states had created their own commissions to investigate such issues as domestic violence, unequal pay, female poverty, and sexual harassment in the workplace.

The Cold War, Civil Rights, and Feminism
Urgent domestic needs had been long neglected, in part, because the United States had remained on a war footing after the defeat of Germany and Japan. Fear of Soviet power abroad and communism at home had a chilling effect on both political dissent and domestic reform. Cold war politicians, like their predecessors who advocated aggressive exploits on the frontier or overseas, perceived a need for "toughness" in both their public stances and internal decision making. Belligerent anticommunism ran as a connecting thread through a long line of otherwise diverse administrations during the cold war, from that of Harry Truman through those of Richard Nixon and Ronald Reagan. Like the Woman's Peace Party of the 1910s, antinuclear and peace advocates regularly faced charges that they were effeminate or "soft." The civil rights movement offered a strikingly different model of manhood, centered on courageous nonviolence. The movement achieved early successes in the 1960s through appeals to Christian theology and principled civil disobedience. By late in that decade, however, poverty and growing anger among younger, poor urban African Americans, as well as growing unrest over American militarism abroad, led to the rise of a militant Black Power stance. Black Power advocates critiqued America's involvement in Vietnam, identified with postcolonial black nationalists in Africa, and urged black men to engage in aggressive self-defense. Like earlier African American men, civil rights leaders struggled between seeking access to the masculine prerogatives of American politics and critiquing the highly racialized prerogatives and distinctive models of political manhood.

By the 1970s, national grassroots coalitions were pressuring politicians to address the long-deferred issues of day care and workplace equity as well as sex education, contraception, and abortion rights. Despite the political uses of domesticity, a majority of American families had never achieved the "domestic ideal" of a male breadwinner whose earnings enabled his wife to refrain from productive labor. Feminists proposed sweeping measures to address poverty and the needs of families with children, as well as a vigorous campaign to end discrimination against women. Feminism faced its most crucial public test over the second equal rights amendment, which failed to win ratification by a margin of only one state. Opponents of the ERA rallied on the basis of domesticity, arguing that the ERA would weaken families, undermine women's central identities as wives and mothers, usher in a military draft for women, and lead to such unacceptable innovations as unisex toilets.

In the decades that followed, preservation of traditional gender roles remained a central concern of many conservatives who feared a breakdown of older social mores, especially domesticity. These arguments played a critical role in the rise of the New Right, but the women who joined this movement were hardly united. One group, libertarian women, emphasized the protection of individual rights; like patriarchal Democrats of the antebellum years, they mistrusted government intrusion, but they applied that argument to themselves as women, rather than to men's prerogatives as household heads. The second group, evangelical or social conservatives, focused on enforcing traditional marriage laws, ending abortion, and opposing homosexuality. In some ways these two groups recapitulated gendered political divisions that had emerged in the 1920s, over whether government should protect women or leave them alone, and whether "free markets" or antidiscrimination laws would best ensure women a level playing field.

Probably due to the impact of feminism by the 1980s, social scientists began to identify for the first time differences in the voting patterns of women and men. The so-called gender gap actually appeared less often on obviously gender-based issues such as abortion and marriage law and more often on issues of social welfare and national security. From the Reagan era onward, more women than men favored antipoverty initiatives, opposed the death penalty, and sought reductions in military spending. Another long-term change was the growing success of the gay rights movement. Men and women who identified themselves as gay or lesbian not only gained increasing public acceptance, but they began to run as political candidates and win. While the prospect of gay marriage provoked many of the same anxieties and debates that domesticity did in an earlier era, the emergence of gays and lesbians into public life was one of the clear triumphs of the movement for equal gender rights.

Certain themes have emerged repeatedly in the history of gender and sexuality in American politics. On the domestic front, the parties that have sought more robust government intervention in the economy (Federalists, Whigs, and Republicans), and in the twentieth century enhanced social welfare programs (most often Democrats), have tended to seek women's support and participation more eagerly than their opponents—whichever party has been, at that moment, resisting the growth of domestic government power. Meanwhile, defense of the patriarchal family model has consistently been associated with white supremacy and racialized nationalism in both domestic and foreign affairs. With a few notable exceptions, parties that have advocated an aggressive foreign policy have tended to be those less committed to government intervention in the domestic economy and on behalf of social welfare.

This perhaps explains why the cause of women's rights advanced rapidly after the Civil War and World War I, when women demonstrated that, in times of extreme national crisis, they had shown courage and patriotism—a kind of "martial womanhood." In both the Civil War and the civil rights era, proto-feminism and feminism emerged out of grassroots movements for racial justice, and the party more sympathetic to African American rights has tended to show more sympathy to women's rights, as well.

At critical junctures, women have mobilized on behalf of political causes ranging from "free soil" to Prohibition and for and against equal rights amendments in the 1920s and 1970s. As longtime outsiders to formal politics, women frequently adopted the stance of moral crusaders, from Free Soil women's call for immediate and unconditional abolition, to the temperance movement's call to "protect the home." Since 1920, tensions between women's new status as partial insiders and the power they have long drawn from domesticity and their "outsider" status have continued to resonate among both feminists and neoconservatives. Calls to preserve domesticity and "protect the home" still arise in debates over such issues as day-care funding, abortion, and gay marriage.

Among the many implications of gender and sexuality in American politics is the continuing struggle of public officials and their families to reconcile the realities of political life with the domestic ideal handed down from the nineteenth century. Americans still want their political leaders to display normative gender behavior: no unmarried man became a major presidential candidate in the twentieth century, and marital fidelity has long been a presumed measure of a president's character. The public exposure and resignation of New Jersey governor James McGreevy in 2004, when he revealed that he was gay, suggest that old assumptions had not vanished. Even when polls indicate that a majority of voters are not concerned about private sexual matters—as in the celebrated case of President Bill Clinton's affair with White House intern Monica Lewinsky—such perceived misbehavior remains a powerful tool for opponents when it becomes publicly known.

Meanwhile, political wives are pressured to demonstrate proper wifely and motherly qualities, and Americans continue to show profound ambivalence over the appropriate role for First Ladies. Eleanor Roosevelt served as a transitional figure, playing an influential part in internal debates during her husband's presidency but achieving her greatest political impact after his death. Later First Ladies who took outspoken political positions included Betty Ford, who supported the equal rights amendment and was widely admired for her frankness about her personal struggles with drug dependency and breast cancer. Former First Lady Hillary Rodham Clinton pursued a political career, as a U.S. Senator and then as a leading presidential candidate in 2008.

During the Ohio Democratic primary in the 2008 race, Hillary Clinton's campaign produced an advertisement depicting a sleeping white woman and her children, imperiled by an unseen force. Viewers were invited to ask themselves, when such dangers loomed, who should answer the "red telephone" in the White House. It is both ironic and significant that such an ad—a staple of cold war political campaigns, in its appeal to both executive toughness and white female vulnerability—should resurface in the campaign of the first woman to become a major presidential candidate. The episode, like others in recent years, suggests that gender and sexuality, as well as the underlying hopes and fears on which those constructions rest, will continue to play a central role in both political campaigns and public policy.

See also homosexuality; race and politics; woman suffrage; women and politics.

FURTHER READING

Edwards, Rebecca. *Angels in the Machinery: Gender in American Party Politics from the Civil War to the Progressive Era*. New York: Oxford University Press, 1997.

Freeman, Joanne B. *Affairs of Honor: National Politics in the New Republic*. New Haven, CT: Yale University Press, 2001.

Gordon, Linda. *Pitied but Not Entitled: Single Mothers and the History of Welfare, 1890–1935*. Cambridge, MA: Harvard University Press, 1995.

Greenberg, Amy S. *Manifest Manhood and the Antebellum American Empire*. New York: Cambridge University Press, 2005.

Gustafson, Melanie, Kristie Miller, and Elisabeth Israels Perry. *We Have Come to Stay: American Women and Political Parties, 1880–1960*. Albuquerque: University of New Mexico Press, 1999.

Hoganson, Kirstin. *Fighting for American Manhood: How Gender Politics Provoked the Spanish-American and Philippine-American Wars*. New Haven, CT: Yale University Press, 1998.

Muncy, Robyn. *Creating a Female Dominion in American Reform, 1890–1935*. New York: Oxford University Press, 1991.

Pierson, Michael D. *Free Hearts and Free Homes: Gender and American Antislavery Politics*. Chapel Hill: University of North Carolina Press, 2003.

Rymph, Catherine E. *Republican Women: Feminism and Conservatism from Suffrage through the Rise of the New Right*. Chapel Hill: University of North Carolina Press, 2006.

Tilly, Louise A., and Patricia Gurin, eds. *Women, Politics, and Change*. New York: Russell Sage, 1990.

Varon, Elizabeth R. *We Mean to Be Counted: White Women and Politics in Antebellum Virginia*. Chapel Hill: University of North Carolina Press, 1998.

Whitaker, Lois Duke. *Voting the Gender Gap*. Urbana: University of Illinois Press, 2007.

Zagarri, Rosemarie. *Revolutionary Backlash: Women and Politics in the Early American Republic*. Philadelphia: University of Pennsylvania Press, 2007.

REBECCA EDWARDS

Gilded Age, 1870s–90s

The Gilded Age, a descriptive label for the period from the end of Reconstruction to the start of Theodore Roosevelt's presidency in 1901, came into general use during the middle of the twentieth century. In political history these decades carry a pejorative connotation that has persisted despite much scholarly work on the complexity of the period's public life. Broadly speaking, the Gilded Age is regarded as a time when politicians failed to engage the issues of industrialism, urbanization, and agricultural discontent. Instead, so the argument runs, Republicans and Democrats wasted their time and energies on such peripheral issues as the protective tariff and civil service. By 1901, according to this interpretation, the United States was no better off than it had been when Ulysses S. Grant left the presidency in March 1877.

Historical scholarship has challenged this pejorative view of the late nineteenth century, but the stereotype remains powerful. The term *Gilded Age* itself derives from a novel of the same name by Mark Twain and Charles Dudley Warner, published in 1873, that depicted economic life as a speculative excess where fraud and chicanery abounded. More than half a century later, the phrase seemed to capture the essence of the period between Reconstruction and the emergence of the reform spirit called progressivism.

Americans faced daunting challenges in the fast-moving era of the Gilded Age. The United States industrialized, became more urban, settled the West, and expanded overseas. Racism marred the way citizens interacted. Workers, farmers, and city dwellers faced major inequities and struggled to exist on meager salaries. Ample social problems demanded solutions, and politicians struggled to find useful answers to new dilemmas.

But the Gilded Age, in the minds of its critics, had a larger failing. The men in power and the electorate who supported them should have known that future generations would criticize the record of those in authority between 1877 and 1901. The centers of power in the society should have adopted the reform measures of the New Deal half a century before the presidency of Franklin D. Roosevelt. This lack of prescience about the direction of American life created, with deliberation and malice, an unjust society at the end of the nineteenth century.

There is much that is unhistorical about these generalizations. By projecting twentieth-century assumptions back to nineteenth-century Americans, critics have imposed on the Gilded Age the impossible task of correctly predicting the future. In the process, the real contributions and limitations of national politics during these years have become obscured. Much of the way Americans view politics now stems from the evolution of public life after 1877. When the polemical aspects of the era are removed, the political importance of the Gilded Age can be judged with more accuracy.

The Electoral System

The most salient features of this time period were the high degree of voter involvement in politics and the relatively even balance of the two major parties. The figures indicating a substantial level of electoral participation are striking. Turnout in state, congressional, and presidential contests far exceeded what was common during the twentieth century. In 1896, when William McKinley ran against William Jennings Bryan, some 78 percent of eligible voters outside of the South cast ballots. Of course, African Americans, Hispanics, and women were denied the right to vote throughout much of the country. (It is worth noting that African American men had been granted the right to vote by the Fifteenth Amendment, but that right had been stripped away in a campaign of terror and disenfranchisement culminating in the 1890s. Those African American men who managed to continue to vote through the end of the century almost all supported the Republican Party.) Nonetheless, the extent of voter mobilization during the 1870s, 1880s, and 1890s reflected the strong partisan identifications among Americans.

Within this political universe, Democrats and Republicans battled on equal terms. Neither party achieved an absolute majority in the four contests for president from 1880 through 1892. On Capitol Hill, it was rare for a single party to control both houses (though it did occur on four occasions from 1874 to 1896). In the battleground states of the Middle West, elections often turned on a small percentage of the vote, with the outcome hinging on which party's adherents came to the polls on voting day. Participants at the time believed that the fate of the nation turned on the outcome of voting.

During the Gilded Age, Americans debated with passion an issue that had dominated domestic politics for most of the century: the extent to which government should promote the growth of the economy. The question of regulating the economy and society through government action was not yet a mainstream concern. But the two major parties took positions on the questions at odds with modern perceptions of their ideological differences.

The Republicans were then the party of an active government. They believed that protective tariffs to develop native industries could diffuse the benefits of a prosperous economy through all levels of society. In the arguments of men such as James G. Blaine and William McKinley, the tariff fused economic appeals with nationalistic pride. The doctrine served the interests of the business community, but protectionism also appealed to labor, small business, and farmers who faced competition from Mexico and Canada. For some adherents, the tariff acquired an almost religious significance.

Republican activism carried over into other areas of economic and cultural life. The party favored subsidies to railroads, land grants to farmers, and federal support of public education. It put in place an elaborate, expanding, and expensive program of pension payments to Civil

War veterans and their families. Pensions became one of the largest expenditures of the federal government. While there were regional differences about money and banking policy, the Grand Old Party (as it became known) endorsed the gold standard and opposed inflation. On social issues, most Republicans favored laws against entertainment on the Sabbath, supported the prohibition of alcohol, and sought to have public schools teach all students in English. These positions aroused opposition from immigrant groups. Above all, the Republicans saw themselves as the party of progress and the Democrats as advocates of obstruction.

The Democratic Party (or the Democracy as it was often called) still believed in the core principles that Thomas Jefferson and Andrew Jackson had advanced earlier in the century. The smaller the government and the closer to the people in its operations the better off the country would be. Democrats stood for the rights of the states against the power of the federal government. Since the South was a major bastion of Democratic strength in elections, the ability of white Southerners to maintain racial supremacy was a key element in the appeal of "the party of the fathers." Democrats also supported a smaller government role in the cultural issues of Prohibition and Sunday closings that Republicans favored.

On the tariff, the Democrats identified with the interest of consumers, doubted the constitutionality of customs duties, and stood for freer trade. The most that the party would accept as an official doctrine was "a tariff for revenue only." Since Democrats wanted the government to remain small, in practice, they believed that tariff rates should be as low as possible. Some elements of the party in industrial states favored a degree of protection. Nonetheless, the tariff issue represented a major dividing line between the parties throughout these years.

With the Civil War and Reconstruction a tangible memory for most politicians, the two parties reflected the lingering consequences of that conflict. The Republicans stood for political equality for African Americans, although their fervor for that position waned as the years passed. By the 1890s, many members of the Grand Old Party (GOP) believed that the racial issues of the war and its aftermath should be muted or abandoned.

The Democrats, on the other hand, were unapologetic champions of white domination in the South. A belief in states' rights and the rule of white men was a quasi-religious conviction among southern Democrats. These party members tolerated the Fourteenth and the Fifteenth Amendment because they had no choice. In

their true convictions, they believed that all such legislation should be repealed. As a result, African Americans had at most a marginal position in the public life of the Gilded Age.

Both major parties felt the pressure from reform elements in society to professionalize politics and reduce the impact of partisanship. Calls for changing the ways in which public officials were chosen for government offices became known as civil service reform, and the idea gained popularity in the 1870s and early 1880s. The Pendleton Civil Service Act of 1883 began the process of diminishing the role of parties in the appointment process.

The Party Battles

Stalemate characterized the first ten years of the Gilded Age. The Republicans elected Rutherford B. Hayes in 1876 over Samuel J. Tilden in a disputed contest that reflected the even balance between the parties nationally. Hayes served one reasonably successful term and was succeeded by James A. Garfield, who carried the Republicans to victory in 1880. The president's assassination in the summer of 1881 put Chester Alan Arthur in the White House. After 24 years of successful elections to office, the Republicans were losing their ascendancy in national politics. They nominated their most popular leader, James G. Blaine, in 1884. But the taint of scandal that surrounded him put their chances in serious doubt.

The Democrats selected the governor of New York, Grover Cleveland, to oppose Blaine. In an election notable for its emphasis on personal issues, such as whether Cleveland had fathered an illegitimate child and whether Blaine was corrupt, the Democrats won in a close vote. Cleveland served a solid if undistinguished term and faced uncertain prospects for reelection. In late 1887 he made the issue of the tariff the centerpiece of his impending campaign. Delighted Republicans jumped at the opportunity to wage a presidential race on that topic. Making a unified campaign, the GOP nominated Benjamin Harrison of Indiana, who proved effective in delivering the party's message. Although Cleveland prevailed in the popular vote, Harrison triumphed in the electoral count. The Republicans also controlled both houses of Congress.

In the two years that followed, the Republicans implemented a program of governmental activism with the passage of the McKinley Tariff to raise rates and the Sherman Antitrust Act. Their effort to protect the voting rights of African Americans in the South through a federal elections bill failed in the face of opposition from the

Democrats. Most voters turned against the Republicans and repudiated their initiatives.

By the election of 1890, long-simmering discontent among farmers in the South and West produced a third party in the congressional races. Low crop prices and a heavy burden of debt impelled many agrarians to support candidates for the Farmers Alliance and the People's, or Populist, Party. These candidates spoke out for inflating the currency by coining silver into money on an equal basis with gold. This strategy would, they believed, raise prices and make debts easier to pay back. Congress had enacted the Sherman Silver Purchase Act in 1890 to provide support for silver, but Populists argued that the measure did too little to address the problem. In the 1890 elections, the Republicans lost control of the House as the Democrats and the Populists made impressive gains.

The resurgent Democrats continued their success in the presidential contest in 1892. Cleveland won an impressive victory over Harrison, and his party now controlled both the House and the Senate. The Populists had fielded their own presidential ticket, which carried four states in the West. The new third party had produced significant gains in its effort to become a viable alternative to the Republicans and Democrats.

Economic hard times hit in the spring of 1893 with a panic in the banking sector that soon spread across the nation. Cleveland called Congress into special session in August to repeal the Sherman Silver Purchase Act, which the president blamed for the economic crisis. He achieved his goal but split his party into two warring factions. The situation then deteriorated further for the Democrats. Beyond the monetary issue, the Pullman Strike in the summer of 1894 and other examples of social unrest during hard economic times gave both the Republicans and the Populists an opportunity to capitalize on pervasive discontent.

The congressional elections in 1894 brought dramatic Republican gains. The Democrats lost more than 100 seats in the House and lost their majority. The GOP also gained in the Senate. The Populists saw their vote totals rise to a limited extent. The outcome in 1894 signaled a probable Republican victory in 1896 and also suggested that the appeal of the People's Party was limited to the agrarian regions of the South and West. As it turned out, the Republican triumphs in 1894 proved enduring, and the party held control of the House for the next 16 years.

The political climax of Gilded Age politics came in the presidential election of 1896 in the race between William McKinley for the Republicans and William Jennings Bryan for the Democrats and Populists. Bryan stood for free silver; McKinley defended the gold standard. Voter turnout was very high in the North and Middle West. McKinley won a decisive victory with a nearly 600,000-ballot majority in the popular vote. The stalemated politics that had characterized the Gilded Age had come to an end with the Republicans triumphant.

During McKinley's administration, the nation went to war with Spain over the independence of Cuba, and, in the process, acquired the Philippine Islands in 1898. This overseas adventure sparked debate about the nation's future as an imperial power. At the same time, with the return of prosperity after 1897, concerned citizens argued that the growth of big business required expanded government power to regulate the economy. There was a sense that, for all the material achievements of the late nineteenth century, political and economic reform had become imperative. In 1900, McKinley's second victory over Bryan confirmed Republican dominance, even as there were calls for lowering the tariff, addressing the power of big business, and redressing social injustice. In waging the war with Spain and administering the colonial empire that ensued, McKinley became the first president to administer the United States as a world power. His assassination in September 1901 brought his vice president, Theodore Roosevelt, to the White House. Soon there was talk of "progressive" change and a need to depart from the ideas and policies of the late nineteenth century. The reputation of the Gilded Age sagged and has never recovered.

What did these decades mean for American politics? The intensive voter interest in elections of that time has never been repeated. The issues of the tariff and money have survived in other forms but have never again dominated political discourse. Debate over the role of government in regulating the economy has supplanted the controversy over promoting national growth. The processes of choosing candidates became more democratic with woman suffrage, direct election of U.S. senators, and procedural changes such as the direct primary, the initiative, and referendum. In many respects, the Gilded Age seems a lost world in national politics.

But, the period had a significant legacy. Racial segregation, established after the Civil War and solidified in the Gilded Age, took years to address and still shapes voter attitudes in the South. The power of corporations to influence policy and finance politics has survived all attempts at reform. The two-party system that emerged intact from the late nineteenth century still precludes alternatives. While the Gilded Age may seem a receding era in the political history of the United States, its impact endures.

See also banking policy; Democratic Party, 1860–96; economy and politics, 1860–1920; elections and electoral eras; Republican Party to 1896; Spanish-American War and Filipino Insurrection; tariffs and politics.

FURTHER READING

Calhoun, Charles W. *Conceiving a New Republic: The Republican Party and the Southern Question, 1869–1900*. Lawrence: University Press of Kansas, 2006.

Calhoun, Charles W., ed. *The Gilded Age: Perspectives on the Origins of Modern America*. 2nd ed. Lanham, MD: Rowman and Littlefield, 2007.

Cherny, Robert W. *American Politics in the Gilded Age, 1868–1900*. Wheeling, IL: Harlan Davidson, 1997.

Edwards, Rebecca. *New Spirits: Americans in the Gilded Age, 1865–1905*. New York: Oxford University Press, 2006.

Gould, Lewis L. *The Presidency of William McKinley*. Lawrence: University Press of Kansas, 1980.

Morgan, H. Wayne. *From Hayes to McKinley: National Party Politics, 1877–1896*. Syracuse, NY: Syracuse University Press, 1969.

Morgan, H. Wayne, ed. *The Gilded Age: A Reappraisal*. Revised ed. Syracuse, NY: Syracuse University Press, 1970.

Summers, Mark Wahlgren. *The Gilded Age or, the Hazard of New Functions*. Upper Saddle River, NJ: Prentice Hall, 1997.

Wiebe, Robert. *The Search for Order, 1877–1920*. New York: Hill and Wang, 1967.

Williams, R. Hal. *Years of Decision: American Politics in the 1890s*. Prospect Heights, IL: Waveland Press, 1993.

LEWIS L. GOULD

globalization

Globalization refers to the process of increasing the ease with which goods, people, and money move across borders or, in the more precise language of economic historians, the integration of international markets in commodities, labor, and capital. These markets depend on the support of political institutions, and in turn, the operation of these markets affects political institutions—often in such a way as to create a backlash against globalization.

Trade, migration, and investment across borders characterize the modern world, and so *globalization* becomes a useful term of historical analysis only when we can identify a marked increase or decrease in the volume of these international movements during a particular period and track its effects on politics and culture. We might therefore say that globalization meaningfully shaped the Islamic civilizations of the eleventh-century Near East, whose peoples traded spices, silver, and silks to Europe; salt and swords to Africa; and horses and gold to Asia while a similar claim about the eleventh-century civilizations of North America would necessarily rest on much slimmer evidence. So globalization waxes and wanes, and we need to speak as precisely as we can about its magnitude and local influence if we wish meaningfully to discuss its effects.

The Americas first became important to the history of globalization during the era of European discovery, when the flow of riches from the New World affected the shape of the Old World. Despite the early establishment of Iberian empires, the Dutch benefited greatly from colonial loot because their cities served as entrepôts for colonial trade. Likewise, this early process of globalization dramatically affected the peoples of the Americas, who died off in quantity from war and disease, which frequently go along with globalization. Moreover, the arrival of European goods, including horses, swine, and firearms, turned the Americas into what the historian Alfred Crosby identifies as ecological "Neo-Europes," easing the transplantation of European institutions and politics into a new hemisphere.

With the establishment of European colonies in the Americas and the extension of European trade with Africa, the triangle trade in slaves from Africa, finished goods from Europe, and staple products from America—particularly sugar, tobacco, and cotton—altered the arrangement of power on all three continents. The trade fueled British textile mills, enabling the consequent technological innovation so important to the industrial revolution. It accounted for the forcible removal of around 11 million Africans over the two and a half centuries of the Atlantic slave trade. It built up the wealth and power of the southern colonies (later states) in the United States, permitting Virginia to dominate the new nation's politics and planting the seeds of national self-immolation in the contradictions between racism and the republic's professions of devotion to liberty. And these contradictions in turn provided the earliest instance of international skepticism about the new nation's claims to virtue, often repeated in subsequent centuries: How, the British ministry-approved *Answer to the Declaration* asked, could rights be inalienable if "denied to 'these wretched beings'"?

After the American Revolution, the wars of the French Revolution and their attendant blockades and embargoes slowed the processes of globalization considerably and for a period of some decades. Britain and France tried to keep each other from getting precious metals out of the New World. In the United States, the Non-importation, Embargo, and Nonintercourse Acts of 1807–9 cut off trade to the belligerent nations. Thus barred from importing finished European goods, Americans began to manufacture ever more products for themselves. And as U.S. factory owners grew used to doing business without foreign competition, they began to lobby Congress—often successfully—for continued protective tariff legislation. Protectionism prevailed in Europe as well, with French manufacturing interests lobbying for tariffs and the Corn Laws largely keeping grain imports out of Britain until 1846.

A new era of increased globalization opened in the middle of the nineteenth century. Technological improvements pushed steamship costs downward, making it cheaper to ship goods and for people to book passage over oceans; the Suez Canal opened; new populations of migrants began streaming into the New World; and the lure of profitable expansion into frontiers drew investment from overseas, into the canals, roads, and railroads of new nations.

This early era of international investment in the development of America's frontier ended poorly owing to the peculiar federal structure of the United States. Although Albert Gallatin and other statesmen of the early republic envisioned the government in Washington paying for a transportation network tying the country together, their plan foundered on the objections of Southerners and others already eager to promote the doctrine of state sovereignty. And so the states borrowed money—often from international investors—to build out their frontiers, each in their own way. Initial success, as in the case of the Erie Canal, which paid off its millions of dollars in debts to London, yielded to later failure; by 1841, eight states plus the territory of Florida were in default. "U.S. security" became a byword for worthless paper and fodder for jokes in England.

The institution of federalism coupled with the defaults had long-term consequences, including the rise of powerful American banks on Wall Street. As economic historians Lance Davis and Robert Gallman note, "Gov-ernments with good reputations, Australia and Canada for example, did not have to draw on the services of international financial syndicates to underwrite and market their bonds. In the case of the United States such syndicates were required." These syndicates included American banks with close ties to European banks, including Morgans, Brown Brothers, and Kuhn Loeb, and these American banks learned to intervene where American states had failed.

Meanwhile, the many unanticipated consequences of globalization included the chain of events by which the Irish potato famine helped spark the U.S. Civil War. Together with the failed revolutions of 1848, the famine spurred Irish migration to the United States. The nativist reaction and the short-lived American Party split and destroyed the Whig Party, making way for the rise of the antislavery Republican Party. The subsequent election of a Republican president, Abraham Lincoln, led to the secession of the South. Global trade scuttled the hopes of southern leaders that they could bring European countries to heel by choking off their supply of cotton; instead, other cotton-producing nations, like Egypt and India, increased their output and scuttled the thesis that American cotton was king of world trade.

The war itself contributed further to the rise of American investment banks. As is often the case during war, the effects of globalization diminished: few people wished to migrate to a country at war; blockades stopped trade; international investors shied away from betting on the bonds of a nation that might, in a few years' time, have vanished or at least have repudiated the obligations of a war government. American financial syndicates also learned from this experience how to raise money and how to cloak themselves in patriotism: as Jay Cooke romantically insisted, just as the war freed slaves from their masters, so might it free Americans from the punishing "whip" of foreign capitalists.

Americans emerged from their wrenching sectional crisis into a new era of global openness. Money, people, and goods moved with increased freedom across borders. American banking syndicates channeled British pounds into railroads and ranches in the West, nearly unrestricted immigration let European laborers find better wages in American cities than they could at home, and—even considering the continuing pressure for tariff legislation—international trade ensured that the prices of commodities like wheat, bacon, coal, coffee, copper, cotton, hides, pig iron, tin, and wool converged in markets around the world. As open borders begot a global similarity in the basic stuff of commerce, the midcentury predictions of Karl Marx and Friedrich Engels in the *Communist Manifesto* appeared to be coming true: "The need of a constantly expanding market for its products chases the bourgeoisie over the whole surface of the globe. It must nestle everywhere, settle everywhere, establish connexions everywhere. . . . [W]e have intercourse in every direction, universal inter-dependence of nations. . . . National one-sidedness and narrow-mindedness become more and more impossible . . ."

Marx and Engels turned out to be wrong about this; globalization did not proceed smoothly to create cosmopolitan cultures but rather swiftly begot a backlash against it that, translated into policies, encouraged national one-sidedness. As Engels himself later observed with respect to the American working class, great diversity on the shop floor tended to suppress class consciousness and increase tribal feeling. With increasing energy and effectiveness, Americans lobbied for restrictions on immigration, securing the first of a series of Chinese Exclusion Acts in 1882. The second such act, in 1892, instituted a presumption of illegal presence for persons of Chinese appearance and began the process of requiring documentation for apparently racially different peoples. For decades, various groups including the American Federation of Labor lobbied for the restriction of immigrants by class background, finally getting a literacy test—coupled with further Asian exclusions—passed over President Woodrow Wilson's veto in 1917. The economic crisis after World War I strengthened the forces opposing globalization, leading to a rise in tariffs and immigration quotas. This early postwar legislation saw firmer establishment in the Fordney-McCumber and Smoot-Hawley tariffs, as well as the National Origins Act of 1924. In addition, various states passed laws to prevent foreign ownership of land.

Apart from these efforts to shut globalization down and thus shield themselves from foreign competition, Americans reacted in other, less predictable ways. Some moved out of the cities of the East, where immigration from Europe was heaviest, into the new states of the West. The more such internal migrants the new states had, the more likely their voters were to support the Socialist Party of Eugene Debs. In American cities that became home to larger populations of immigrants, taxpayers responded with policies of self-defense, both cultural (through increased support for public education) and material (through increased support for public

health programs). As a result of such investments, particularly in water purification and waste treatment, the American city finally became a healthier place to live than the countryside. Thus, the fear of immigration and its consequences sometimes led indirectly to an overall improvement in well-being.

American policies that slowed globalization in the 1920s must often shoulder at least part of the blame for the Great Depression. The British economist John Maynard Keynes predicted in his 1919 forecast of the *Economic Consequences of the Peace* that a massive depression would result from the failure to reassemble the nineteenth-century global economy, noting that the world before the war, in allowing movement across borders, had helped relieve economic pressures: the unemployed could seek opportunity elsewhere rather than stay and suffer. But, Keynes noted, the postwar settlement included "no provisions for the economic rehabilitation of Europe . . . or to adjust the systems of the Old World and the New." American unwillingness to help rehabilitate Europe or adjust relations to the Old World might not have mattered, had the Old World, in working off wartime debt, not depended so thoroughly on continued loans from the New World. When those loans began to dry up in 1928–29, countries around the world slid into depression, and the United States followed.

During the Depression, globalization stood at low ebb. Immigrants had no place worth going, even if laws permitted them entry. Nations traded within autonomous blocs. Each country acted, as Franklin Roosevelt wrote in his telegram to the London Economic Conference of 1933, as if "[t]he sound internal economic system of a Nation is a greater factor in its well being" than its international economic relations. Barring a few gestures like the Anglo-American Trade agreement of 1938, the United States carried out its New Deal with (as Isaiah Berlin observed about FDR) "a minimum of relationship with the outside world." During this period of relative isolation from the international arena, the Democratic Party put through some of America's most clearly class-conscious legislation. It is possible, some historians suggest, that this correlation represents causation: with immigration restriction (and its attendant racial hierarchy) firmly in place, it might have been easier to appeal to class solidarity.

After World War II, the United States, with some help from Keynes, worked with its allies to create the system the world had lacked in 1919, to rehabilitate Europe and keep the Old World and the New World in balance. The

Bretton Woods institutions—the World Bank and the International Monetary Fund—especially as augmented by the European Recovery Program, (or Marshall Plan) of 1947 created a degree of international stability while allowing countries the freedom to set their own economic policies. They created the conditions for Americans to invest in the reconstruction and development of the war-torn world and promote the sale of U.S.-manufactured goods overseas. They enabled the growth of trade worldwide, and of non-Communist labor movements in industrialized countries. During these institutions' peak period of operations, per-capita incomes around the globe grew more than under previous or subsequent frameworks for international economic affairs.

In the later twentieth century, a new era of accelerated globalization began. After the Hart-Celler immigration act of 1965, the United States saw renewed immigration from non-European nations, and a new wave of anti-immigrant sentiment to greet it. The United States ran large current-account deficits, buying imports from developing countries, contributing to the growth of manufacturing in the historically poorer parts of the world. Central banks in the developing world—particularly in Asia—increasingly financed the U.S. deficit by buying federal debt. Under such circumstances, Americans could afford, at least for the near term, to save little money and run large government deficits. In the early twenty-first century, the dollar dropped in value, creating an incentive for individual investors in American debt to stop financing the United States, even as collectively their interest lay with continued support for the dollar. In the early years of the new century, there came a growing perception that as the Euro grew more attractive as an alternative investment, the long-standing arrangement might fail, and America might shift away from its historically fortunate place in the center of the global economy. While the world has generally favored the United States with a willingness to invest capital and labor within American borders, these inflows have depended more on historical incident—including reigning American policy and circumstances in the rest of the world—than on general laws.

See also banking policy; economy and politics; federalism; tariffs and politics.

FURTHER READING

Bordo, Michael D., Alan M. Taylor, and Jeffrey G. Williamson. "Introduction." In *Globalization in Historical Perspective*, edited by Michael D. Bordo, Alan M. Taylor, and Jeffrey G. Williamson, 1–10. Chicago: University of Chicago Press, 2003.

Crosby, Alfred W. *Ecological Imperialism: The Biological Expansion of Europe, 900–1900.* Cambridge, UK: Cambridge University Press, 1993.

Davis, Lance Edwin, and Robert E. Gallman. *Evolving Financial Markets and International Capital Flows: Britain, the Americas, and Australia, 1870–1914.* Cambridge, UK: Cambridge University Press, 2001.

DeLong, J. Bradford, and Barry Eichengreen. "The Marshall Plan: History's Most Successful Structural Adjustment Programme." In *Postwar Economic Reconstruction and Lessons for the East Today*, edited by Rüdiger Dornbusch, Wilhelm Nölling, and Richard Layard, 189–230. Cambridge, MA: MIT Press, 1993.

Eichengreen, Barry. *Global Imbalances and the Lessons of Bretton Woods.* Cambridge, MA: MIT Press, 2007.

Findlay, Ronald, and Kevin H. O'Rourke. "Commodity Market Integration, 1500–2000." In *Globalization in Historical Perspective*, edited by Michael D. Bordo, Alan M. Taylor, and Jeffrey G. Williamson, 13–62. Chicago: University of Chicago Press, 2003.

———. *Power and Plenty: Trade, War, and the World Economy in the Second Millennium.* Princeton, NJ: Princeton University Press, 2007.

Gerstle, Gary. *American Crucible: Race and Nation in the Twentieth Century.* Princeton, NJ: Princeton University Press, 2001.

O'Rourke, Kevin H., and Jeffrey G. Williamson. *Globalization and History: The Evolution of a Nineteenth-Century Atlantic Economy.* Cambridge, MA: MIT Press, 1999.

Rauchway, Eric. *Blessed among Nations: How the World Made America.* New York: Hill and Wang, 2006.

ERIC RAUCHWAY

Great Depression

See economy and politics, 1920–45; New Deal Era, 1932–52.

Great Plains, the

The Great Plains—a relatively flat, semiarid region along the east side of the Rocky Mountains—include the eastern parts of Montana, Wyoming, Colorado, and New

Mexico, and the western parts of North and South Dakota, Nebraska, Kansas, Oklahoma, and Texas. Though none of these states are wholly in the Great Plains, all will be treated here.

Before Europeans arrived on the Great Plains, politics there were largely local and focused on authority within bands or tribes of Native Americans and with disputes between or among them. Europeans introduced new dimensions. After the United States acquired the plains in the early nineteenth century, politics there evolved into a regional variant of national patterns. The most distinctive aspects of plains politics appeared between 1890 and World War II, in the form first of Populism and then of progressivism. Since 1945 plains politics have moved close to national patterns.

Before Assertion of U.S. Authority

Before the arrival of Europeans and horses, most indigenous people of the plains lived in villages along streams and rivers. A few were nomadic hunters. For most, the basic political unit was the village. The Pawnee, for example, consisted of four independent bands that formed a confederation, with the internal organization of each band based on villages. Village chiefs met periodically as a tribal council.

Patterns of leadership differed among the plains tribes, but the position of village chief was typically hereditary within certain lineages. A chief's actual authority rested on his ability to resolve disputes, deal with traders, distribute goods, allocate farmlands, and negotiate with outsiders. Those from other families could exercise other forms of leadership. Thus, a village might have one or a few main chiefs, several shamans, and separate leaders for war, buffalo-hunting expeditions, and men's societies. Occasionally, a woman became a shaman, but women did not hold other political roles.

In 1541 Vasquez Coronado and his men became the first Europeans to venture onto the Great Plains. French explorers and traders entered the plains by the early eighteenth century. The Treaty of Paris (1763) gave Spain title to the region between the Mississippi River and the crest of the Rocky Mountains, but in 1800 Spain sold to France the entire Louisiana country north of the Red River. Neither Spain nor France sought to exercise real political authority on the plains.

Though few Europeans came to the region, plains Indians experienced the consequences of European settlement elsewhere. The Pueblo Revolt of 1680, in what became New Mexico, brought horses to the plains. Eu-

ropean settlers along the Atlantic traded with nearby Indian peoples, providing guns and manufactured goods. As European expansion pushed Indian people west, they, in turn, armed with guns and iron weapons, pressured the peoples into whose lands they moved. Such pressures bred conflict between plains tribes and westward migrating tribes and among plains tribes themselves. For example several Lakota bands and the Cheyenne moved onto the plains in the late eighteenth century, became nomadic, and came into conflict with the Crows. Horses and guns combined to populate the plains with bands of nomadic buffalo hunters.

Among nomadic plains tribes, the basic political unit was the band, comparable to the villages of the sedentary peoples. The band traveled, camped, hunted, and made war as a unit. Political leadership was typically fluid, with different leaders for different purposes, none with supreme authority. Bands of the same tribe or closely related tribes came together for religious ceremonies, councils, hunting, or war. As of about 1800, for example, the Cheyenne had ten bands, each with four chiefs. All ten came together each spring, and the four chiefs of each band plus a few other elders formed a tribal council.

The experience of Sitting Bull (Tatanka Iyotake) provides both example and exception. In 1857, when Sitting Bull was about 26 years old, the Hunkpapa Lakota named him a war chief in recognition of his bravery and his victories over the Crows. He also gained a reputation as a holy man, given to prophetic visions. In 1869 Sitting Bull's supporters brought together a group of Lakotas and Cheyennes who named him to an unprecedented position: war chief of the Lakota nation. Given the fluidity of leadership among the Lakotas, however, not all Lakotas accepted this action.

After the United States purchased Louisiana from France in 1803, more explorers ventured onto the plains, notably the Lewis and Clark expedition of 1804–6, intended not only to explore but also to assert U.S. authority in the northern plains and lay claim to the region west of it. By the 1820s, the United States had planted small military posts along the Missouri River and had established a limited military presence on the plains. Federal policy makers considered the region a "permanent Indian frontier," however, and political authority there still rested with villages, bands, and tribes. Eastern tribes were moved to the eastern parts of the plains states beginning in the 1830s.

Through the annexation of Texas (1845), war with Mexico (1846–48), and the Treaty of Guadalupe Hidalgo

(1848), the United States acquired territories that included the southern plains. The new state of Texas claimed most of the area, but the residents of New Mexico contested that claim. In 1850 Congress attempted to resolve these and other issues through an elaborate compromise that, among other provisions, set the western boundary of Texas and established territorial government for New Mexico.

The Compromise of 1850 left most of the plains unorganized, even though they formed a vital part of the major land routes to California, Oregon, and New Mexico territories. Stephen Douglas, senator from Illinois, seeking to have a railroad built from Chicago to the Pacific, wanted to establish territorial organization on the plains, but Southerners opposed territorial status anywhere the Missouri Compromise of 1820 banned slavery. Douglas crafted a compromise in 1854, creating Nebraska and Kansas Territories, with each to decide whether to permit slavery. The Kansas-Nebraska Act provoked a great national debate over slavery, precipitated the emergence of the Republican Party, and contributed significantly to a major national political realignment. The organization of Kansas, in turn, initiated a miniature civil war.

From the Civil War to 1890

Kansas became a state in 1861, Nebraska in 1867, and Colorado in 1876. Beginning in 1861, Congress promoted the rapid economic development of the West through land grants to railroads, the Homestead Act, and similar distributive programs. And Congress created Dakota and Colorado Territories in 1861, Montana Territory in 1864, and Wyoming Territory in 1868.

Late into the nineteenth century, much of the plains remained territories, due to sparse population and sometimes also to congressional jockeying for partisan advantage. Montana and the Dakotas became states only in 1889 and Wyoming in 1890. Oklahoma and New Mexico remained territories into the twentieth century. Residents of territories could not elect their governors or participate in presidential elections, and their delegates to Congress commanded little attention. Political patronage often was allocated in faraway Washington. Some historians have suggested that party organizations and loyalties were stunted by the low stakes in territorial politics.

In the plains states, partisanship developed along regional lines. Kansas, Nebraska, and Colorado were initially Republican strongholds, often under the leadership of Union veterans who constantly reminded voters that Republicans promoted western economic develop-

ment. Party politics in Texas followed from that state's participation in the Confederacy, as westward-moving southern whites assisted the Democrats in redeeming the state from Republican rule in 1873 and keeping it securely Democratic until the 1960s.

Advocates of woman suffrage were active on the northern and central plains. In 1867 Kansas became the first state to vote on the issue, but its voters rejected suffrage. The first session of the Wyoming territorial legislature, in 1869, approved suffrage for women—the first state or territory to take such a step and one of the first political entities in the world to do so. Some attributed that decision to Wyoming males' expectation that woman suffrage would attract more women to the plains but others have pointed to diligent lobbying by suffrage advocates. Wyoming achieved statehood in 1890 and became the first state to fully enfranchise women. Colorado, in 1893, became the first state whose male voters approved woman suffrage. Despite repeated agitation and several referenda, the other plains states continued to reject suffrage until the 1910s, even as women won statewide elective office in North Dakota and Oklahoma.

With or without suffrage, plains women helped to lead reform movements, especially Prohibition. In 1878 Kansans banned the importation, manufacture, and sale of alcohol, but the law was widely violated. Despite referenda in several other plains states, before 1907 laws banning liquor passed only in North and South Dakota, and South Dakotans soon reversed that decision.

On the northern plains, the political battle over alcohol reflected broader ethno-religious differences. Old-stock Americans and immigrants affiliated with the Methodist, Baptist, Congregational, or Presbyterian denominations, along with Norwegian and Swedish immigrants and their offspring, usually condemned as sinful any use of alcohol, and often censured gambling and dancing as well. Catholics and many German Protestants found no sin in a stein of beer, a dance, or a lottery. Thus, referenda on Prohibition and woman suffrage (closely connected in many voters' minds) often turned on the ethno-cultural values of voters. Identification with the Democratic Party and Republican Party on the northern plains often had ethnic dimensions, for northern Democrats adamantly opposed Prohibition and courted German and Irish voters. Republicans usually tried to duck the issue but sometimes issued cautious endorsements.

While Prohibition formed a highly divisive political issue on the northern plains, Texas politics sometimes revolved around race. Texas experienced radical reconstruction beginning in 1867, and a coalition of black and white Republicans held control until 1873, when the Democrats won a gubernatorial election characterized by widespread fraud and intimidation of black voters. The Democrats then wrote a new state constitution, severely limiting the legislature but not disfranchising black voters.

In the plains states, as elsewhere, African Americans aligned themselves with the dominant Republicans. In Kansas and Nebraska, some received political patronage in return, and a few were elected to local or state office, including state auditor in Kansas. In Kansas and Nebraska, and later in Oklahoma Territory, black migrants from the South created all-black towns and exercised local political authority.

Only in New Mexico, in the late nineteenth and early twentieth centuries, did Mexican Americans exercise significant political power. There, the long-established *Hispano* communities (most not on the plains), along with the slow pace of in-migration by other groups, meant that Mexican culture dominated many areas. Voters elected Mexican Americans as local officials, territorial legislators, and territorial delegates. Mexican Americans also secured federal patronage posts, including territorial secretary and governor.

In the 1880s, Congress moved toward a new Indian policy with important implications for the plains. The Great Sioux Reservation, in Dakota Territory, was reduced in size in 1877 and broken into smaller units in 1889. Officials of the Bureau of Indian Affairs, committed to a policy of assimilation, sought to eliminate traditional practices, including structures of authority and governance. The Dawes Act of 1887 directed that reservations be divided among Indian families and the land be owned in severalty (i.e., individually). Remaining land was to be taken out of the reservation system.

On the southern plains, much of what is now Oklahoma became home to the "Five Civilized Tribes"—the Cherokee, Chickasaw, Choctaw, Creek, and Seminole—in the 1830s, when they were moved from their previous homes in the Southeast and were promised permanent reservations in the new territory. During the Civil War, some or all of these tribes in the new territory sided with the Confederacy and, as punishment, were deprived of their western lands. Those lands, in turn, became reservations for tribes from the southern plains. In 1890 Congress created Oklahoma Territory in the western part of what is now Oklahoma, leaving the eastern region as Indian Territory.

Populism and Silver

By the 1880s, political agitators on the plains were condemning both Republicans and Democrats for failing to counteract declining prices for farm products and to regulate railroad rates. Most such agitators were on the margins of politics, but not in Texas. John Reagan, a member of Congress from that state, consistently advocated regulation and contributed significantly to passage of the Interstate Commerce Act in 1886. James Hogg, Texas's attorney general and governor in the late 1880s and early 1890s, also built a following by attacking the railroads.

In 1890, in the central and northern plains states, new political parties emerged, claiming to speak for hard-pressed farmers and laborers. First organized as state parties, they came together as the People's Party, or Populists, in 1892. The new party called for federal action to restrict the great corporations that had developed since the Civil War. Those corporations, Populists argued, limited the economic opportunities and political rights of ordinary citizens. On the plains, Populists drew their greatest support from farmers on marginally productive land, often with large mortgages at high interest rates, for whom the prevailing deflation proved especially ruinous.

The Populists called for government ownership of the railroads; sweeping changes in federal monetary and banking policies, especially currency expansion to counteract deflation; structural reforms to make government more responsive to voters, including the secret ballot and the initiative and referendum; the eight-hour workday; a graduated income tax; and other reforms. Populists won election as local officials, state legislators, governors, and members of Congress. In most places in the central and northern plains states, the Democrats were reduced to a tiny third party and often threw their support behind Populist candidates. Such fusions brought gubernatorial victories in 1892 in Colorado, Kansas, and North Dakota, and in Nebraska in 1894.

In 1896 William Jennings Bryan, a Democrat from Nebraska, won the Democratic presidential nomination on a platform that stressed currency inflation through silver coinage and called for an income tax and other reforms. Most western Populists gave Bryan enthusiastic support, and he secured their party's nomination. Leading western Republicans broke with their party, formed the Silver Party (or Silver Republicans), and also nominated Bryan.

Bryan lost the presidency but did well throughout much of the West. The Populist Party and the Silver Republican Party survived only a few more years. For many former Populist voters, however, party loyalties seem to have significantly weakened. Republicans and Democrats were closely competitive in Nebraska, Colorado, and Montana over the next 20 years. Kansas and the Dakotas, however, usually voted Republican.

Racial issues became prominent in Texas politics in the 1890s, when the state's Populists made a strong appeal to black voters and, fusing with the Republicans, registered a strong vote for their gubernatorial candidate in 1896. Texas adopted a poll tax in 1902 but never followed other former Confederate states in creating a more elaborate set of legal or constitutional restrictions on black participation in politics. Texas Democrats accomplished much the same thing extralegally, however, by barring African Americans from Democratic primaries (and eventually writing that provision into law) and by coercing blacks who insisted on exercising the franchise.

Progressivism

Every plains state experienced progressive reform during the two decades before World War I, and those reforms significantly changed most state governments. George W. Norris, a Nebraska Republican, became an important national leader of progressivism, leading the "revolt against Cannonism"—a reduction in the powers of the Speaker of the House, then Joseph Cannon—in 1910 and continuing as a leading progressive in the U.S. Senate until 1943. Other plains progressives also drew national attention.

"Direct democracy"—efforts to increase the role of voters in the political process—flourished on the plains. In 1898 South Dakota Populists adopted the nation's first initiative and referendum process. Most plains states also adopted the initiative and referendum, though not through Populists' efforts. Other widely adopted direct-democracy reforms included the direct primary and recall. States adopted other structural reforms, including nonpartisan offices, limits on political parties, the merit system for appointing state employees, and rationalization of the structure of state government.

Plains progressives added new functions to state government as they promoted regulation of railroads and public utilities, abolition of child labor, employer liability and workers' compensation, and protections for consumers. Four states set up insurance funds for deposits in state-chartered banks. Under Republican governor Peter Norbeck (1917–21), South Dakota launched several state-owned enterprises, including a coal mine, cement plant, hail insurance fund, and hydroelectric plants. When

Oklahoma became a state in 1907, its constitution included many progressive innovations, including restrictions on corporations, a graduated income tax, and the initiative and referendum. Oklahoma Democrats also enacted racial segregation and a literacy test aimed at disfranchising African American voters.

Renewed efforts by woman suffrage and temperance advocates finally brought victories. Kansas adopted woman suffrage in 1912 and Montana followed in 1914. In 1916 Montana elected the first woman to serve in the House of Representatives, Jeannette Rankin, a progressive Republican. South Dakotans and Oklahomans adopted woman suffrage in 1918. Oklahomans voted their state dry in 1907, and, by 1918, all the plains states but Texas had done the same.

Plains progressivism differed in important ways from progressivism in eastern states. Like other western progressives those on the plains were more likely to favor direct democracy, woman suffrage, and Prohibition than their eastern counterparts. Some, like Norbeck, promoted state-owned enterprise, especially those devoted to economic development. Other plains progressives were more isolationist regarding foreign policy.

In some plains states, groups to the left of the progressives attracted a following. In Oklahoma, the Socialist Party, espousing government ownership of key industries, won 21 percent of the vote for governor in 1914. Socialists developed strength elsewhere in the plains states, electing local officials in several places, but failed to win any office higher than state legislator. In North Dakota, Arthur C. Townley, a former socialist organizer, created the Nonpartisan League (NPL), which worked within the Republican Party to win the governorship in 1916 and the state legislature in 1919. They enacted much of its program, including a state-owned bank and terminal grain elevator.

World War I and the Depression

Rankin and Norris were among those in Congress who voted against the declaration of war in 1917. But throughout the plains, World War I stimulated intense patriotism, encouraged by the federal government, state Councils of Defense, and extra-governmental bodies. Suspicion, hostility, and sometimes vigilante action greeted those of German birth or descent, pacifists (including Mennonites, who were also of German ancestry), and radicals, especially the NPL, Socialists, and the Industrial Workers of the World.

The summer of 1919 brought racial conflict in several parts of the nation, as white mobs lynched African

Americans or attacked black sections of cities. Three riots took place in Texas. In Longview a mob killed several people and burned buildings in the black section of town before National Guard troops arrived. In Omaha, Nebraska, some 4,000 whites intent on lynching a black man accused of raping a white woman attacked police and deputy sheriffs guarding the courthouse, set it on fire, nearly lynched the mayor, beat any black people they found on the streets, and finally lynched the accused man. Ultimately U.S. troops put down the riot. In 1921 Tulsa, Oklahoma, was the scene of the worst race riot in U.S. history. As in Omaha, the riot began with an effort to lynch a black man accused of assaulting a white woman. In Tulsa, however, a group of armed African Americans attempted to assist the sheriff, who was determined to prevent a lynching. A gun battle between blacks and whites left several dead. A white mob then attacked the black commercial and residential section of town, called Greenwood. African Americans fought back. Before the National Guard could arrive, an estimated 300 African Americans and 13 whites were killed. Greenwood was destroyed by fire—more than a thousand buildings worth nearly $2 million.

The war had created a huge demand for wheat and meat. At the end of the war, agricultural prices fell, initiating an agricultural depression that persisted when the rest of the economy began to roar with the prosperity of the 1920s. The economic distress of farmers contributed to the development of a congressional "farm bloc" in 1921. Members of Congress from both parties, including many from the plains states, joined to support regulation of stockyards and grain exchanges, exempting farm cooperatives from antitrust laws, and easing credit for farmers. Despite such efforts, the farm economy continued to slump.

In 1922 agricultural distress and reversals for organized labor, especially railroad workers, sparked political protests among farmers and workers. Organized through the Conference on Progressive Political Action (CPPA), protesting voters put Democrats into the governorship in several states and elected Burton K. Wheeler, a progressive Democrat from Montana, to the Senate. In 1924 the independent presidential candidacy of Robert La Follette drew significant support from plains farmers and organized labor. He failed to win any plains state but carried many counties across the northern and central plains.

In 1924 two plains states elected the nation's first female governors. In Wyoming the death of the incumbent shortly before the election led to the nomination and election of his widow, Nellie Tayloe Ross. Miriam A. "Ma" Ferguson won the governorship in Texas but was widely seen as a surrogate for her husband, James E. Ferguson, who was ineligible because he had been impeached from the office in 1917.

Ma Ferguson won the Texas Democratic primary over the opposition of the Ku Klux Klan. Anti-black, anti-Catholic, anti-Semitic, and anti-immigrant, the Klan presented itself as the defender of old-fashioned Protestant morality and became a significant force in plains politics. Klan-endorsed candidates won local and state offices across Colorado, Kansas, Oklahoma, and Texas in the early and mid-1920s. The Klan tried to influence elections elsewhere but its authority swiftly declined by the end of the decade.

The Depression that began in 1929 was a serious blow to farmers, who had not shared in the prosperity of the 1920s. Shortly after, drought turned large areas of the southern plains into the dust bowl. Political repercussions appeared in some plains states as early as 1930, when voters elected governors and senators who promised to solve their economic problems. In 1932 Franklin D. Roosevelt became the first Democrat to sweep every plains state. He also carried Democrats into Congress, statehouses, and state legislatures. In North Dakota, a revived NPL won control of the state government.

Roosevelt's New Deal addressed farmers' problems with the Agricultural Adjustment Act, which included provisions for paying farmers and stock growers to reduce production. Relief rolls, both state and federal, grew to include a quarter or a third of the population in some plains states, and sometimes two-thirds or more of those in dust bowl counties. Other New Deal programs ranged from construction of schools and bridges to rural electrification, from tree planting and flood control to Social Security. One New Deal project, the Fort Peck Dam in Montana, was the largest earthen dam in the world when it was completed in 1939.

By the mid-1930s, several plains states had experienced efforts by Democratic governors and legislatures to create "Little New Deals," but most were modest and unimaginative. Nearly everywhere, governors and legislatures drastically cut state spending to provide property tax relief. Seeking alternatives to property taxes, several states enacted sales taxes or income taxes.

In a few instances in the 1930s, states went beyond budget cutting, tax reform, and participation in New Deal programs. In 1936 Colorado voters approved a pension program for those over 60; the program proved so costly it absorbed most of the new sales tax. In Nebraska, Senator Norris convinced voters in 1934 to amend the state constitution to create a unicameral, nonpartisan legislature. Norris also inspired the development of Nebraska's public power districts, most of which used federal funds to construct electrical generating and distribution systems. By 1945 the state's entire electrical power system was publicly owned.

The New Deal brought important changes to the governance of Indian reservations. Roosevelt appointed John Collier commissioner of Indian affairs. A long-time critic of previous federal Indian policies, Collier closed many boarding schools and ended efforts to suppress traditional religious practices. His "Indian New Deal" included as its centerpiece the Indian Reorganization Act (1934), which promised to end allotments, restore tribal ownership of unalloted lands, and encourage tribal self-government. Not all were persuaded of the value of the new approach, and some tribes rejected the reforms.

In 1936 Republicans nominated Alfred Landon of Kansas for president, but he was defeated in a Roosevelt landslide that continued Democratic dominance in most plains states. Soon after, however, leading Democrats, notably Burton Wheeler, became increasingly critical of Roosevelt. In 1938 and after, plains voters expressed their disaffection from the New Deal, as most of the northern plains states returned to the Republicans and the southern plains states turned to conservative Democrats.

The mid- and late 1930s saw isolationism at high tide on the northern plains. Senator Gerald Nye (Republican) of North Dakota led investigations into the munitions industry and sponsored neutrality legislation. After the 1941 attack on Pearl Harbor isolationism receded, but Senator William Langer of North Dakota (Republican and NPL), was one of the two senators who voted against joining the United Nations, and both North Dakota senators opposed the North Atlantic Treaty Organization.

Plains Politics since 1945

Prosperity returned to the plains during World War II. Then and after the war, liberals continued on the defensive in most places, as conservative Republicans held most governorships in northern and central plains states and equally conservative Democrats held those in Oklahoma and Texas. Except for Montana and sometimes North Dakota, the northern and central plains states usually sent conservative Republicans to represent them

in Washington. Between the late 1950s and the 1980s, however, all the plains states moved toward more competitive two-party systems.

In the late 1950s the nation entered a recession. Economically distressed farmers and urban dwellers elected liberal Democrats in most northern and central plains states. By 1959 George McGovern of South Dakota, Quentin Burdick of North Dakota (elected following a fusion of the Democratic Party with the NPL in 1956), Gale McGee of Wyoming, and Mike Mansfield and Lee Metcalf of Montana made the northern plains appear to be a center of congressional liberalism. Since then, Montana and North Dakota have usually elected Democratic senators. South Dakota, Nebraska, and Colorado have been competitive in senate races, and Wyoming and Kansas have usually elected Republicans. All the northern plains states have been competitive for governor except South Dakota, which has usually elected Republicans. Underneath those highly visible offices, however, significant majorities of the voters of most northern and central plains states identified as Republicans, especially in the counties that are part of the Great Plains.

As Democrats won elections in northern and central plains states, Republicans made gains in the southern ones. In 1961 Texans sent a Republican, John Tower, to the U.S. Senate for the first time since Reconstruction, and Republicans have won both Texas Senate seats since 1990. In 1962 Henry Bellmon became the first Republican ever to win the Oklahoma governorship, and since then that office has often alternated between the parties. Republicans and Democrats also alternated winning senatorial contests in Oklahoma in the 1970s and 1980s; both Oklahoma Senate seats have gone Republican since 1992. Not until 1978 did a Republican, Bill Clements, win the Texas governorship. That office then alternated between the parties until 1994, when Republicans began a winning streak. New Mexico has been competitive for governor since the 1950s, and the two parties have won almost equal numbers of Senate contests.

The plains states usually voted Republican for president between 1952 and 2004. There have been only a few exceptions: New Mexico in 1960, 1992, 1996, and 2000; Texas in 1960, 1968, and 1976; and Colorado and Montana in 1992. In 2008, Colorado and New Mexico voted Democratic, and Montana and North Dakota were considered "battleground" states. Nebraska law provides that a candidate who carries a congressional district receives one electoral vote, and the candidate who carries the state wins two votes in addition to those earned in the congressional districts. In 2008, for the first time, this law resulted in Nebraska splitting its electoral votes when Barack Obama carried the second congressional district (Omaha and its suburbs to the south).

Republican gains in southern plains states, like Republican gains in the South more generally, came in part in response to Democratic support for civil rights. The civil rights movement had its most direct impact in the southern plains, even though *Brown v. Board of Education* (1954) concerned Topeka, Kansas. Earlier, the Supreme Court had struck down the Texas white primary law (1944) and had ordered Oklahoma and Texas to integrate their state graduate and professional schools (1950). There were, however, relatively few African Americans in most plains counties, so the direct political impact of the civil rights movement was more pronounced in the eastern, non-plains portions of those states. One important exception was Colorado, where Denver residents fought a brutal and occasionally violent battle over school integration between 1969 and 1974. Earlier, Latino veterans returning from World War II had organized the American GI Forum and the Mexican American Legal Defense and Education Fund. These groups took the lead in fighting discrimination against Latinos and made important gains.

The 1970s saw increased politicization of ethnic groups on the plains. In South Dakota, the American Indian Movement, first organized in Minneapolis in 1968, demanded equal treatment and autonomy and challenged existing tribal leadership. A confrontation at Wounded Knee in 1973 resulted in two deaths. In New Mexico a violent, but not deadly, confrontation in 1967 brought the end to the Alianza, a group seeking the return of land grants. In the early 1970s in Texas, Mexican Americans formed the Raza Unida party and won a number of local offices.

During the last quarter of the twentieth century, politics in several plains states achieved a greater measure of racial and gender diversity. New Mexicans, to be certain, have elected Mexican Americans throughout their history. In 1978 Nancy Landon Kassebaum of Kansas won the first of three terms in the U.S. Senate. That same year, Coloradians elected the nation's first black lieutenant governor since Reconstruction, and, in 1992, they sent Ben Nighthorse Campbell, an American Indian, to the U.S. Senate. Patricia Schroeder, member of Congress from Colorado, established a national reputation. In Nebraska in 1986, two women faced each other as the major party candidates for governor.

Throughout most of the Great Plains counties, net out-migration began after World War II and has persisted in most rural places. States consequently became more urban, though most cities were located on the fringe of the Great Plains. Local and state governments faced a variety of problems resulting from a diminishing population base, but education often drew the greatest attention. Declining population and increasing accreditation standards caught rural schools in their pincers. Although school consolidation often proved politically divisive, most plains states witnessed sharp reductions in the number of school districts—by 72 percent in Wyoming between 1952 and 1984 and by 67 percent in Nebraska between 1949 and 1965. In 2008, Arthur County, Nebraska, with an estimated population of 372, had fewer than 70 students in all grades in the entire county. In such places population decline has sometimes made it difficult to fill county and local offices.

Since the 1980s, preachers in evangelical Christian megachurches in such places as Wichita, Tulsa, and Colorado Springs have allied themselves closely with the Republicans and have pushed the party in those states toward the Christian Right by focusing on issues like abortion and gay rights. By the early twenty-first century, however, the evangelical tide within the region's Republican Party seemed to be receding. In Kansas between 1999 and 2007, the state board of education reversed itself repeatedly on the teaching of evolution in the public schools, as first one side then the other won majorities in elections for board members. In South Dakota in 2006, a referendum on a state law banning abortions voided the law by a margin of 52 to 48 percent, and a similar statewide vote in 2008 failed by a slightly larger margin.

The political history of the Great Plains has much in common with its surrounding regions. Many, even most, of its distinctive features are shared with other western or middle-western states. One feature, federal policies aimed at promoting economic development, has been common throughout much of the West. Populism, early approval of woman suffrage, and the western variety of progressivism were, perhaps, the most distinctive aspects of plains political development, but they were not unique to plains states. Populism and progressivism left most plains states with a legacy of direct democracy and a few plains states with state-owned enterprises. Populism and western progressivism, born of agricultural adversity and, in the 1920s at least, nurtured by a political alliance of farmers and labor, grew out of a social and economic situation now largely vanished. The substantial decline in the proportion of farmers and stock growers on the plains has reduced the potential base for such politics, and the emergence of an agribusiness attitude among many of the survivors seems to have given them a different political outlook.

The emergence of two-party competition throughout most of the plains states since the late 1950s suggests that plains political subcultures are being homogenized into larger national patterns. Similarly, the half-century pattern of support for most Republican presidential candidates throughout much of the plains suggests a blending into larger patterns of western politics. Finally, the decline in party loyalty in the East and South suggests that even that aspect of western politics is no longer unique.

See also Latinos and politics; Native Americans and politics; Pacific Coast; populism; progressivism and the Progressive Era, 1890s–1920; race and politics; Rocky Mountain region; taxation; woman suffrage.

FURTHER READING

Brown, Norman D. *Hood, Bonnet, and Little Brown Jug: Texas Politics, 1921–1928*. College Station: Texas A&M University Press, 1984.

Cherny, Robert W. *Populism, Progressivism, and the Transformation of Nebraska Politics, 1885–1915*. Lincoln: University of Nebraska Press, 1981.

Clanton, Gene. *Kansas Populism: Ideas and Men*. Lawrence: University Press of Kansas, 1969.

Davidson, Chandler. *Race and Class in Texas Politics*. Princeton, NJ: Princeton University Press, 1990.

Gómez-Quiñones, Juan. *Chicano Politics, Reality and Promise, 1940–1990*. Albuquerque: University of New Mexico Press, 1990.

Gould, Lewis L. *Progressives and Prohibitionists: Texas Democrats in the Wilson Era*. Austin: University of Texas Press, 1973.

Kleppner, Paul. "Politics without Parties: The Western States, 1900–1984." In *The Twentieth-Century West, Historical Interpretations*, edited by Gerald D. Nash and Richard W. Etulain, 317–21. Albuquerque: University of New Mexico Press, 1989.

Lowitt, Richard. *The New Deal and the West*. Bloomington: Indiana University Press, 1984.

Morlan, Robert L. *Political Prairie Fire: The Nonpartisan League, 1915–1922*. Minneapolis: University of Minnesota Press, 1955.

Saloutos, Theodore, and John D. Hicks. *Agricultural Discontent in the Middle West, 1900–1939*. Madison: University of Wisconsin Press, 1951.

Wright, James E. *The Politics of Populism: Dissent in Colorado*. New Haven, CT: Yale University Press, 1974.

ROBERT W. CHERNY

Greenback-Labor Party

The social tensions engendered by the Civil War gave rise to the Greenback movement. By the late 1860s, some New England affiliates of the new National Labor Union (NLU) launched independent Labor Reform parties, and the NLU nominated a National Labor Reform ticket in 1872 in alliance with Democrats who favored issuing paper currency to relieve debt. Thereafter, Grangers in the new Patrons of Husbandry urged state regulation of railroad rates through independent parties in Illinois, Indiana, Missouri, Michigan, Nebraska, Iowa, Minnesota, Kansas, and Wisconsin.

Currency became a central question for such formations after the Panic of 1873 and the passage of the Specie Resumption Act. The latter replaced the wartime circulation of paper "greenbacks" with "hard money," such as gold or silver, upon which local banks would issue promissory paper, in whatever quantity suited them. The Illinois and Indiana parties held simultaneous state conventions in June 1874 that demanded government control over the money supply. In November, these parties met in Indianapolis with veterans of the National Labor Reform Party from Connecticut, Illinois, New York, Ohio, Pennsylvania, and West Virginia to launch a national Independent, or Greenback, Party, also called the National Party—as opposed to its state affiliates.

Shaping of the Greenback-Labor Party

Dominated by rural Midwesterners, the Greenbackers reached out to the cities and the Northeast. In May 1876, they nominated Peter Cooper of New York and Senator Newton Booth of California, who was later replaced by Samuel F. Cary of Ohio. The ticket offered a pro forma protest, though likely winning much more than the official count of 75,973 in a notoriously "stolen election." In its wake, Greenbackers revived hopes of a coalition with workers' organizations.

The potential scale and power of the labor movement became apparent in July 1877, when major railroads announced pay cuts. This sparked what became a national general strike of roughly 100,000 workers, and strike committees briefly came to power in St. Louis and Toledo. As federal authorities withdrew the last soldiers stationed to enforce civil rights in the former Confederacy, they almost immediately sent troops to break the strikes.

Angry voters responded with the largest unsuccessful third-party insurgency in American history (the Republicans being the result of a successful one a generation before). They voted Greenback where the party existed, and where it did not, formed a number of local labor and Grange parties. The more radical labor reformers already had a distinct socialist organization, the Social Democratic Workingmen's Party of North America (1874), which regrouped with various local organizations into the Workingmen's Party of the United States (1876), and, in the wake of the strike, renamed itself the Socialistic Labor Party. Voters elected some Socialist candidates from Maine to California and from Wisconsin to Kentucky. In February 1878, leaders of the old Greenback Party drew many leaders of these other currents to a national convention at Toledo that launched the Greenback-Labor Party (GLP).

The Peak of the Insurgency and Its Limits

The 1878 congressional elections demonstrated mass interest in an alternative to the two parties. Exclusively Greenback, Independent, Independent Greenback, or National candidates garnered between 802,000 and 852,000 votes, but almost as many voted for independents running with some local Democratic or Republican support, or for independent Democratic or independent Republican candidates running against regular party candidates, or for Socialist and Prohibitionist tickets. Numbering as high as 1,600,000, these voters sent 22 independents to Congress, including General James Baird Weaver of Iowa. The election revealed pockets of GLP strength beyond the Midwest, from rural Maine to northern Alabama.

The GLP sought to unite these currents into a permanent new party that might replace one of the existing major parties, as the Republicans had done only a generation earlier. The Socialists proved receptive, as did the new National Liberal Party of religious freethinkers facing prosecutions by federal officials. Related currents resisting the GLP appeals for unity included various Democratic-organized Greenback Clubs and local "independent" splinters; the Readjusters' Party of Virginia; the Workingmen's Party of California, which focused on the exclusion of the Chinese; and woman suffragists,

who remained hopeful for Republican assistance. Success in creating a permanent national party turned on the 1880 elections.

Demise and Legacy

The 1880 presidential campaign of Weaver and Barzalai J. Chambers of Texas led directly to the destruction of the GLP. In pursuing an initially southern strategy on key states voting earlier, Weaver confronted and protested disenfranchisement and fraud perpetrated by the Democratic "Redeemer" governments. In response, the partisan Democratic press claimed the GLP to be recipients of money from the Republican campaign. Based on this, they simply dropped coverage of the GLP campaign, which allowed Republican papers to do the same. In an election characterized by fraud in the wake of this press blackout, the official count acknowledged only 306,867 votes nationally. Shattered by recriminations, the GLP largely disintegrated.

The party retained strength in some localities, and survived as a national body to endorse the National Antimonopoly Party ticket in 1884 and finally dissolved into the Union Labor Party in 1887–88. In part, the Populist, or Peoples', Party grew out of the ULP and took up much of the GLP agenda, and even ran Weaver for president a second time in 1892. Progressives later adopted some of what the GLP advocated, but much remained the domain of insurgent radicals.

See also banking policy; labor parties; radicalism; socialism.

FURTHER READING

Destler, Chester M. *American Radicalism, 1865–1901.* New London: Connecticut College, 1946.

Fine, Nathan. *Labor and Farmer Parties in the United States, 1828–1928.* New York: Rand School of Social Science, 1928.

Lause, Mark A. *The Civil War's Last Campaign: James B. Weaver, the Greenback-Labor Party and the Politics of Race and Section.* Lanham, MD: University Press of America, 2001.

Montgomery, David. *Beyond Equality.* New York: Knopf, 1967.

Ritter, Gretchen. *Goldbugs and Greenbacks: The Antimonopoly Tradition and the Politics of Finance in America, 1865–1900.* Cambridge, UK: Cambridge University Press, 1997.

MARK LAUSE

health and illness

For much of American history, matters of disease prevention and health promotion were neither the concerns of the national government nor matters of political discourse. One of the critical tropes of American political history is the evolving sense of government authority and responsibility at the local, state, and federal levels for protecting society from disease and promoting individual and community health in the context of an increasingly pluralistic society. Government interventions in different eras have included quarantining the sick, conducting medical inspections of immigrants, sterilizing those defined as mentally defective, providing the public clean water and air, regulating the contents of food and drugs, seeking cures and therapies for disease through medical research and epidemiology, creating institutions for the care of the ill, and preventing disease through inoculation and education. Politicians rarely spoke of such matters until the early years of the Progressive Era, when the pressures of urbanization, industrialization, and immigration threatened to undermine the health and vitality of American citizens and stymie local economic development. In the decades to come, and especially following World War II, battling disease and improving the public's health and access to medical care increasingly became federal priorities and the stuff of national political debate.

What Makes People Sick?

Governments have long acted to protect their communities from foreign diseases. Regulations in medieval Venice required returning seamen who were ill to remain isolated from their neighbors for 40 days. The Italian word for 40, *quarentenaria,* was the origin of the word *quarantine*, the practice of separating the ill from the well for a specified time. In eighteenth-century North America, each colony had quarantine procedures that became state statutes after the American Revolution.

In the eighteenth century, aside from quarantine enforcement and local regulations designed to promote public hygiene, government officials could offer physicians little assistance. A 1744 New York City ordinance stated that "the health of the Inhabitants of any City Does in Great measure Depend upon the Purity of the Air of that City and that when the air of that City is by Noisome smells Corrupted, Distempers of many kinds are thereby Occasioned." The ordinance reflects physicians' beliefs that disease resulted from effluvia or miasmas, noxious gases arising from decaying organic matter. In the mid-nineteenth century, sanitarians would argue that filth caused disease, leaving public sanitation the best form of prevention. In the 1880s, Germany's Robert Koch and France's Louis Pasteur demonstrated that specific diseases were not simply the result of filth but were caused by specific microorganisms, or germs that invaded the body.

Disease and Therapy in Colonial America

Long before most physicians accepted germ theory, however, many understood that contact with a disease, if not fatal, often rewarded victims with immunity. Inducing smallpox immunity via inoculation by placing some diseased matter under the skin was likely taught to the Puritans in the seventeenth century by African slaves. Some thought the procedure the practice of the devil because the slaves were heathens, but others, including the influential minister Cotton Mather, believed in its efficacy and inoculated his family members. Such injections were not without their dangers, because an inoculated individual, even if immune, could still pass smallpox to another who was uninoculated. By 1760, laws regulated the practice and provided for a minimum quarantine period for those inoculated.

Colonial Americans also sought to protect patients from irresponsible medical practitioners. In 1736 the Virginia legislature enacted a law specifying fees for medical services. University-trained physicians could charge more than apprentice-trained doctors. Physicians' bills had to specify what drugs they had prescribed. However, the measure lapsed after two years and was never repassed. True regulation began in New York in the 1750s. By 1760 New York's Provincial Assembly passed the first colonial medical licensure law for New York City, requiring that applicants for a medical license be examined by government officials assisted by respected physicians. Still, quacks and charlatans were ubiquitous.

Government Power in Support of Public Health

Under the U.S. Constitution the new government possessed powers to "promote the general Welfare," powers hardly ever invoked in matters of health and disease. Seamen's health was the exception. Merchant seamen, often without families or permanent abodes, created a burden on public hospitals where they existed and aroused public sympathies. On July 16, 1798, Congress passed and President John Adams signed a bill establishing the United States Marine Hospital Service (USMHS, renamed the U.S. Public Health Service in 1912), a uniformed service for "the temporary relief and maintenance of sick or disabled seamen in the hospitals or other proper institutions . . . in ports where no such institutions exist. . . ." The first hospital built with Marine Hospital funds was in Boston. Soon, America's westward expansion prompted the building of hospitals near rivers in ports such as New Orleans, Chicago, Cleveland, St. Louis, and Louisville. In these hospitals all the surgeons, stewards, matrons, and nurses were political appointees.

In the nineteenth century, state and local governments and private voluntary organizations protected community health with limited funding. Most well-off individuals loathed spending money on the health of strangers, especially those who were nonwhite or from other countries. However, two great epidemic diseases, yellow fever and Asiatic cholera, demanded a cohesive public response. In the South, yellow fever epidemics in the 1850s aroused state legislatures to use their quarantine regulations to keep ships with sick passengers or crew out of their ports. The wealthy could temporarily flee stricken cities, but yellow fever was bad for business. There were passionate political debates over how to keep cities fit for investment and trade. Because of yellow fever, Louisiana became the first state with a permanent board of health. After 1900, when Dr. Walter Reed and his U.S. Army Commission in Havana, Cuba, discovered that yellow fever was spread by a mosquito vector, states funded mosquito control.

In northern cities, Asiatic cholera and poor immigrants, especially the Irish, often arrived simultaneously. In 1832, 1849, and 1866, major cholera epidemics swept the East Coast of the United States. Nativists blamed the immorality and ignorance of Irish Catholic newcomers for the cholera epidemic of 1832. In New York, a Special Medical Council was formed by the politically appointed Board of Health and manned by seven of the city's leading physicians. However, when the epidemic receded in the autumn, the Board of Health regressed into its apathetic state. When New York clergy petitioned President Andrew Jackson to appoint a day of national fasting, prayer, and humiliation to mark the devastation of the epidemic, he refused, affirming his belief in the efficacy of prayer but citing the separation of church and state. Not until 1866 did New York finally launch a permanent Municipal Board of Health removed from the choke hold of politicians and given over to physicians. New York gradually improved urban sanitation and hygiene, the price of industrialization and population congestion.

After the Civil War, the Bureau of Refugees, Freedmen and Abandoned Lands, popularly known as the Freedmen's Bureau, offered medical attention and constructed hospitals to serve newly emancipated black slaves and displaced whites. By 1872 racism and corruption within the bureau had undermined these efforts. Medical research did not become a routine federal endeavor until 1887, when Surgeon General John Hamilton opened the Hygienic Laboratory in one room of the Marine Hospital on Staten Island. There, director Dr. Joseph Kinyoun studied cholera, yellow fever, and the bacterial content of the waters in New York Bay. In 1891 the laboratory moved to Washington, evolving into the National Institutes of Health under the Public Health Service in the next century.

Doctors at the Gate: Immigration, Industrialization, and Disease Prevention in Progressive America

When the federal government assumed responsibility for immigration in 1891, USMHS physicians examined all newcomers at depots such as New York's Ellis Island. Those deemed physically or mentally unfit to support themselves were not admitted. In San Francisco Bay, a depot on Angel Island was the entrance for many Chinese and Japanese arrivals as well as some Europeans, all of whom also underwent physician inspection. An 1893 law gradually transferred quarantine authority from state to federal officials. At Ellis, there were two hospitals to treat newcomers, one a contagious disease facility. Immigrants who recovered were eventually allowed to leave the island and enter the country.

These safeguards proved insufficient for immigration's critics. Nativists, including many eugenicists seeking to improve human stock by encouraging some individuals to procreate while discouraging others, advocated the 1924 Johnson-Reed Immigration Act and its highly restrictive quota system. A broader eugenical concern about the number of children born to those defined as mentally defective, especially retarded persons, criminals, and the insane, resulted in passage of state laws permitting involuntary sterilization of institutionalized persons. These laws were found to be constitutional by the Supreme Court in *Buck v. Bell* (1927), and many remained in force until the late twentieth century.

In unhealthy, congested cities, immigrant workers were felled by such infectious diseases as tuberculosis. Illnesses and injuries from unsafe working conditions abounded. Progressive reformer Dr. Alice Hamilton investigated conditions in tenements and factories where lead in paints and phosphorus on matches were poisoning workers and their families. In public schools, the children of the poor received health education and sometimes even health care, including minor surgeries. Often only labor union agitation or tragedies, such as the 1911 Triangle Shirtwaist factory fire, resulted in state legislation improving health and safety. At the federal level, the Food and Drug Act of 1906 defined food adulteration and the misbranding of products and regulated the interstate shipment of food, penalizing violators. The act was superseded in 1938 by the stricter Food, Drug, and Cosmetics Act.

Government intervention was at times tainted by racism and ethnocentrism. In 1900 several cases of bubonic plague were identified in San Francisco's Chinatown. Local citizens blamed immigrants for their unsanitary living conditions. The government response smacked of anti-Chinese bias, including San Francisco's imposition of quarantine on all Asian residents of Chinatown but not Caucasians and, at the suggestion of USMHS officials, the state's forced inoculation of Asians with an experimental serum. The courts offered relief, lifting the quarantine under the equal protection clause of the Fourteenth Amendment.

Federal Power, Prejudice, and the Public Health

When they had nowhere else to go for assistance, urban immigrants often turned to political machines, such as the New York Democratic Party's Tammany Hall. Tammany, dominated by Irish political bosses, pushed for municipal hospitals and helped individuals gain access to physicians or hospital admission in exchange for votes. In the 1930s, President Franklin Roosevelt's New Deal sounded urban bossism's death knell. Government agencies began to offer health services once obtainable only as political patronage, increasing the federal role in health care. The American Medical Association (AMA), founded in 1847, continued its long-standing opposition to government involvement in such matters. However, the Farm Security Administration's rural health programs provided more than a million migrant workers and some 650,000 others in rural America with medical care. Republicans condemned it as "socialized medicine."

The 1930s was also the time when the U.S. Public Health Service's efforts to treat syphilis in African American communities of the South had to be abandoned because of the economic pressures of the Depression. Instead, in 1932, the PHS, in collaboration with the Tuskegee Institute, embarked on an investigation of untreated syphilis involving hundreds of Alabama blacks that lasted until 1972, long after the discovery that syphilis could be treated with penicillin and long after any medically useful results had been produced. The episode remains synonymous with American medical racism.

A more benign episode of federal investigation and experimentation was the PHS pellagra study under federal physician Dr. Joseph Goldberger, who established that pellagra was a dietary disease. By the 1930s, researchers identified niacin as the missing element in pellagrins' diets. Bread and dairy products were enriched with niacin by presidential order during the war and by state law afterwards.

Federal Aid Improves Health Care in Postwar America

Following World War II, federal funds and regulation had a major impact on research and the provision of health care. The Hospital Survey and Construction Act of 1946 (Hill-Burton Act) funded hospital construction in underserved communities, largely rural and suburban, creating a proportion of 4.5 hospital beds per 1,000 individuals. Prior to the war, Vannevar Bush, director of the Office of Scientific Research and Development, had recommended $15 million for medical research to investigate the therapeutic value of penicillin, the development of insect repellents and insecticides, and the use of serum albumin as a blood substitute—all valuable in wartime. His 1945 report, *Science, the Endless Frontier*, pressed for more funding in science and medicine to establish the National Science Foundation and energize agencies such as the Public Health Service at the National Institutes of Health. Extramural federal funding supported research at medical schools and universities.

Soon a vast federal health bureaucracy developed. In 1953 the Department of Health, Education, and Welfare was created, redesignated the Department of Health and Human Services in 1979. It oversees the Public Health Service, which itself has 42 divisions, including NIH for medical research, Food and Drug Administration (FDA) to implement public health measures, and the Centers for Disease Control and Prevention (CDC), which battle the spread of disease.

Health care became more accessible when President Lyndon Johnson and a Democratic Congress passed Medicare and Medicaid legislation in 1966 to assist elderly and poor citizens, respectively, with medical bills driven higher by an increasing array of drugs and sophisticated medical technologies. However, along with these programs came red tape and regulations that contributed to the escalating cost of medical care.

The Politics of Health Care in the Twenty-First Century

At the beginning of the twenty-first century, issues of health and illness occupied center stage in American politics. Immigration amplified demands for political action in the name of public health. Concern about swine flu crossing the Mexican border increased demand for government expenditures to develop new influenza vaccines. Data collected by the New York City Board of Health tracing spikes in drug resistant tuberculosis to migrants from China and Mexico raised concern about the adequacy of federal health restrictions and immigration procedures. Health care for racial and ethnic minorities and the native-born poor remained inadequate. State governments increasingly offered free DPT vaccinations to children whose parents could not afford them and provided other health care services, as well.

The HIV-AIDS crisis occasioned virulent debates over cultural values but also increased levels of federal funding for research on this disease as well as on cancer, heart disease, and obesity. The federal genome project redefined the future of medical research, stimulating the search for the genetic origins of various diseases. Debates over the morality of stem cell research divided conservatives, especially those on the Christian Right, from their opponents on the liberal left.

Issues of health and disease have long been debated in the political arena. Until the twentieth century, partisan conflict over such matters was largely state and local, but the expanded use of federal power in the twentieth century allowed some Americans to argue that promoting "the general Welfare" should include battling disease, promoting preventive public health measures, and perhaps providing health insurance to every American. The degree of responsibility the federal government ought to assume to conquer disease and in defense of the public's health has become a political perennial.

See also cities and politics; nativism.

FURTHER READING

Duffy, John. *From Humors to Medical Science: A History of American Medicine.* Urbana: University of Illinois Press, 1993.

Grey, Michael. *New Deal Medicine: The Rural Health Programs of the Farm Security Administration.* Baltimore, MD: Johns Hopkins University Press, 1999.

Grob, Gerald N. *The Deadly Truth: A History of Disease in America.* Cambridge, MA: Harvard University Press, 2002.

Harden, Victoria A. *Inventing the NIH.* Baltimore, MD: Johns Hopkins University Press, 1986.

Jones, James H. *Bad Blood: The Tuskegee Syphilis Experiment.* Revised ed. New York: Free Press, 1993.

Kevles, Daniel J. *In the Name of Eugenics: Genetics and the Uses of Human Heredity.* Berkeley: University of California Press, 1985.

Kraut, Alan M. *Silent Travelers: Germs, Genes, and the "Immigrant Menace."* New York: Basic Books, 1994.

Porter, Roy. *Blood and Guts: A Short History of Medicine.* New York: Norton, 2002.

Rosen, George. *A History of Public Health.* Revised ed. Baltimore, MD: Johns Hopkins University Press, 1993.

Rosenberg, Charles E. *The Cholera Years: The United States in 1832, 1849, and 1866.* Revised ed. Chicago University of Chicago Press, 1987.

Starr, Paul. *The Social Transformation of American Medicine: The Rise of a Sovereign Profession and the Making of a Vast Industry.* New York: Basic Books, 1982.

Stevens, Rosemary. *The Public-Private Health Care State: Essays on the History of American Health Care Policy.* New Brunswick, NJ: Transaction Publishers, 2007.

ALAN M. KRAUT

homosexuality

Although the modern concept of "homosexuality" did not emerge until the late nineteenth century, characteristics associated with this category—same-sex desire, same-sex sexual acts, and nonconformist gender performance—have been contested within American political culture since the colonial period in two critical ways. The first involves political struggles over policy, including the legality of same-sex sexual acts, and, by the latter half of the twentieth century, civil rights protections for those who identify as gay, lesbian, bisexual, and transgendered. Second, homosexuality has served a powerful function within American political discourse. Especially in the arena of electoral politics, sodomy and homosexuality have functioned as rhetorical markers of weakness and subversion to social order and American values.

The Politics of Sodomy in Early America

In the seventeenth century, all American colonies adopted sodomy—or "buggery"—laws that prohibited nonprocreative sexual acts between men, as well as between men and women and between men and animals. However, not all forms of nonprocreative sex met with the same level of condemnation or prohibition; in New England, for example, governmental and ministerial officials characterized such sexual acts between men as more sinful and socially dangerous than those committed between men and women. Although religious authorities also condemned sex between women, the crime of sodomy typically required evidence of penetration, so such acts were rarely prosecuted in colonial courts (the sodomy code of the New Haven Colony proved exceptional in its explicit prohibition of sex between women). Colonies imposed a range of punishments for sodomy, from the imposition of fines to execution. However, sodomy laws were unevenly enforced, and severe forms of punishment were relatively rare; historical evidence suggests that American colonists responded to sodomy in more pragmatic ways, carefully weighing their religious opprobrium against the social disruption of legal prosecution.

This disinclination to prosecute sodomy, even more pronounced in the eighteenth century, did not evince true tolerance, however. Indeed, colonial authorities interpreted evidence of male same-sex acts and other forms of sexual "deviance" as grave threats to social and political order. In 1642 Plymouth governor William Bradford ascribed an outbreak of "sodomy and buggery (things fearful to name)" to the arrival of migrants to New England who did not share the Puritan goal of establishing a shining and moral "city on the hill." The linking of sodomy to political subversion became more common in the 1700s when the "sodomite"—a male person who desired sex with other men—emerged as a category of personhood in the transatlantic world. In 1726, for example, a Boston newspaper, reporting on the raids of a number of "sodomitical clubs" in London, linked sodomy to the dangers of a growing and threatening urban commercialism; sodomites and financiers alike conducted secretive and illegal deals that threatened social stability. Sodomy and commercial exchange also evinced European dissoluteness and corruption, as did Freemasonry. Anti-Masonic Massachusetts satirists used phallic homoerotic imagery to recast ostensibly civic-minded Masonic fraternal rituals as corrupt and emasculating. Such aspersions were intended to counter the political prominence of Freemasons in the colony.

This predilection for defining both the practice of sodomy and effeminate gender performance as distinctly foreign—as violating the foundations of American character—continued into the Revolutionary and early national eras. An ascendant Enlightenment ethos was manifested in the revocation of capital punishment for sodomy, but it also produced a model of white American national manhood that emphasized independence and self-governance, a hallmark of which was the control of sexual desire and intensified stigmatization of nonmarital sexual practices. This prescriptive model, espoused by northern elites, took as a foil the stereotype of the decadent and corrupt European "fop," a figure associated with sexual profligacy if not always sodomy. The sodomitical qualities of this figure grew more explicit in the middle of the nineteenth century when American newspapers began to report on groups of urban men who engaged in same-sex relations. The first such known report, appearing in the New York paper *The Whip* in 1842, attributed the appearance of a sodomitical subculture to foreign influences and condemned this development as antithetical to the purity of the young American nation.

Homosexuality and Political Subversion

By the end of the nineteenth century, the figure of the sodomite had been replaced by the "homosexual," a modern category defined by an inversion of gender role and by same-sex desire. The homosexual—alternatively referred to as someone of the "third sex" or an "invert"—emerged from sexology, a new field of medical science that had originated in Europe. Yet, antecedents to this modern figure can be found in nineteenth-century American political culture. Critics of those who advocated radical reforms of the American political system, such as abolitionism and woman suffrage, had been pilloried as improperly gendered. The pejorative name "Miss Nancy" was applied to male abolitionists and male prostitutes alike, for example. Proponents of civil service reform and of third-party movements acquired such descriptors as "third sex" and "political hermaphrodite." This conflation of sexual and political subversion is evinced by the first published American analysis of homosexuality, neurologist Edward Spitzka's "A Historical Case of Sexual Perversion" (1881), which retroactively diagnosed Lord Cornbury, the colonial governor of New York and New Jersey who was alleged to have dressed as a woman, as sexually inverted, anathema to the American ethos of masculine individualism, and as a threat to national strength.

The negative political meanings attached to homosexuality grew more vociferous in the twentieth century, as homosexual men and women were pathologized by medical professionals and further criminalized within the law. In the 1920s, critics used a stigmatizing psychological model of homosexuality to impugn politically active "New Women" who had formed lifelong intimate relationships with other women—including the leading social reformer Jane Addams—as unnatural and perverted "short-haired women." During World War II, homosexuality functioned as grounds for exclusion or discharge from military service; more than 10,000 lesbians and gay men were discharged for "undesirable habits or traits of character" between 1941 and 1945. The policing and persecution of homosexuality intensified after the war. In 1953 President Dwight D. Eisenhower signed Executive Order 10450, which excluded those deemed to be homosexual from federal employment on the grounds that they represented a threat to national security. An array of American thinkers and politicians, including liberal historian Arthur Schlesinger Jr., conflated homosexuality and communism, interpreting both as threats to a masculinist tradition of American pragmatic centrism. Zealous cold warriors, including Senator Joseph McCarthy, viewed both homosexuality and communism as anti-American and embarked on a systematic effort to root out gay men and women from the civil service

and to smear their political opponents on the left. The resulting "lavender scare" ruined careers and lives and undermined the 1952 presidential candidacy of Democrat Adlai Stevenson.

Homosexual Rights and Conservative Backlash

The postwar period also saw the rise of the modern American homosexual rights movement, beginning with the founding of homophile organizations in the postwar years. Although the first to form a sustained movement, homophile leaders drew on an older leftist political discourse that resisted a dominant pejorative American conception of same-sex desire. An array of late-nineteenth-century intellectuals and bohemians, influenced by the poet Walt Whitman's vision of homoerotic democratic "adhesiveness" and the sex radicalism of European freethinkers like Edward Carpenter, had maintained that same-sex desire might be directed toward the civic good. This position was argued most forcefully by American anarchists, including Leonard Abbott and Emma Goldman, who viewed state efforts to regulate homosexuality as a violation of individual freedom and an unjust expression of state power. Early homophile leaders—notably, Harry Hay, who founded the Mattachine Society in 1950—spoke for this tradition within the Communist Party in the 1930s. Although American Communists ultimately proved hostile to homosexuality, Hay and others brought the organizational skills and political commitments developed within the Communist Party to the cause of "homosexual liberation."

Influenced by the civil rights movement, Hay and his homophile comrades conceptualized homosexuals as a minority group "imprisoned within a dominant culture." The 1950s saw the formation of similar groups, including the first lesbian political organization in the United States, the Daughters of Bilitis, in 1955. Although homophile activists struggled over organizational strategies, and many sought to distance themselves from the early leaders' Communist roots, the movement gained strength and engaged in more militant forms of activism by the 1960s. In 1964 members of the East Coast Homophile Organizations coalition staged a demonstration in New York City to protest military policy toward homosexuals. In 1965 the Washington, D.C., Mattachine chapter, led by Frank Kameny, a scientist who had been fired from his government post during the lavender scare, picketed the White House, Pentagon, and Civil Service Commission to protest antigay employment practices.

By the late 1960s, members of the growing homophile movement allied themselves with black power and other radical liberation movements as well as with New Left student and anti–Vietnam War efforts. This radicalization found expression in new slogans like "Gay Power" as well as in more confrontational forms of protest, especially in relation to police harassment in burgeoning urban gay enclaves like New York City's Greenwich Village and the Tenderloin and Castro neighborhoods of San Francisco. Two such dramatic and spontaneous acts of rebellion catalyzed a more radical movement: the 1966 Compton's Cafeteria riot in San Francisco, led by transgender women and gay hustlers, and the more famous 1969 Stonewall rebellion in New York City. These pivotal events set the stage for a dizzying proliferation of gay and lesbian activism, including the 1969 founding of the Gay Liberation Front, inspired by third-world liberation movements, and the lesbian feminist groups Radicalesbians (1970) and Salsa Soul Sisters (1974), which protested both the misogyny of gay male activists and the antilesbian positions of the National Organization for Women.

The mid-1970s saw two key developments in the politics of homosexuality. First, a reform-oriented model of gay activism began to dominate the movement, finding institutional expression in such organizations as the National Gay Task Force (founded in 1973); these organizations achieved significant successes in the legal arena, including the repeal of state sodomy statutes and the passage of antidiscrimination legislation at the local level. Reformist efforts also led to the election of gay and lesbian candidates, notably Harvey Milk as San Francisco city supervisor in 1977. However, the successes of the gay rights movement also engendered a political backlash led by religious conservatives who, calling on the established trope of homosexuality as subversive to American values, waged a vociferous and well-funded battle against "the gay agenda." In 1977 religious singer and orange juice pitchwoman Anita Bryant, arguing that homosexuality posed a threat to American children and families, led an effort to repeal a gay rights ordinance in Dade County, Florida. Her campaign found significant national support, especially among evangelicals, and laid the foundation for the antigay activism of New Right organizations like the Moral Majority, established by Jerry Falwell in 1979.

With the election of Ronald Reagan as president in 1980, culture warriors like Jerry Falwell and Pat Robertson attained considerable influence in the Republican Party, which identified homosexuality as an effective wedge issue in state and national elections. In the 1980s, when the Reagan administration all but ignored the suffering and devastation of the new AIDS epidemic, some gay activists turned to a more confrontational and performative mode of activism, exemplified by ACT UP (the Aids Coalition to Unleash Power), which charged that federal neglect amounted to complicity in the suffering and deaths of those afflicted with AIDS. With the availability of medications that mitigated the effects of HIV (at least for those with access to health care) in the 1990s, the political struggle over gay rights shifted to issues of marriage and military service. Although many had viewed the presidential election of Democrat Bill Clinton in 1992 as a favorable development for the gay rights movement, the failure of the administration to implement a nondiscriminatory military service policy and Clinton's endorsement of the 1996 Defense of Marriage Act, which prohibited federal recognition of same-sex marriages, attested to the continued political opposition to the aims of the movement.

The politics of marriage rights have remained especially contentious into the twenty-first century; by 2008, judicial gains had been countered by restrictive legislation and ballot referenda at the state level. That opponents of same-sex marriage framed their position as "defending" a foundational social institution points to the resilience of an understanding of homosexuality as threatening to social order.

See also gender and sexuality.

FURTHER READING

Adam, Barry D. *The Rise of a Gay and Lesbian Movement.* Boston: Twayne, 1987.

D'Emilio, John. *Sexual Politics, Sexual Communities: The Making of a Homosexual Minority in the United States, 1940–1970.* Chicago: University of Chicago Press, 1983.

Duggan, Lisa, and Nan Hunter. *Sex Wars: Sexual Dissent and Political Culture.* New York: Routledge, 1995.

Foster, Thomas A., ed. *Long Before Stonewall: Histories of Same-Sex Sexuality in Early America.* New York: New York University Press, 2007.

Johnson, David K. *The Lavender Scare: The Cold War Persecution of Gays and Lesbians in the Federal Government.* Chicago: University of Chicago Press, 2004.

Katz, Jonathan. *Gay American History: Lesbians and Gay Men in the U.S.A.* New York: Thomas Y. Crowell, 1976.

Kissack, Terence. *Free Comrades: Anarchism and Homosexuality in the United States, 1895–1917.* Oakland, CA: AK Press, 2008.

McGarry, Molly, and Fred Wasserman. *Becoming Visible: An Illustrated History of Lesbian and Gay Life in Twentieth-Century America*. New York: Penguin Studio, 1998.

Murphy, Kevin P. *Political Manhood: Red Bloods, Mollycoddles and the Politics of Progressive Era Reform*. New York: Columbia University Press, 2008.

Sears, James T. *Behind the Mask of Mattachine: The Hall Call Chronicles and the Early Movement for Homosexual Emancipation*. New York: Harrington Park Press, 2006.

Smith-Rosenberg, Carroll. *Disorderly Conduct: Visions of Gender in Victorian America*. New York: Oxford University Press, 1985.

KEVIN P. MURPHY

House of Representatives

The House of Representatives is often considered to be America's most democratic institution. Since the founding of the American government in 1789, the House has been populated by a more diverse range of individuals than the Senate or the White House. Legislators have been required to face reelection every two years. To win election to the House, the Constitution requires only that a candidate be a minimum of 25 years of age and a U.S. citizen for 7 years. Candidates also have to reside in their district. The founders decided that membership in the House would be proportionate to the size of the population so that the delegations from each state corresponded, albeit imperfectly, to demographic realities. The sheer number of members has required negotiation and compromise. In this respect, the House lived up to George Mason's aspiration that it would be the "grand depository of the democratic principle of the government."

The Constitution bestowed three important responsibilities on the House: the power over revenue and spending, the power to impeach an elected official, and the power to elect the president if the Electoral College was deadlocked. This authority reflected how highly the nation's founders valued the House as an antidote to the British monarchy.

There are four different eras in the history of the House of Representatives, each defined by the procedural framework—the informal and formal rules—through which legislators operated.

The Founding Period

The first three decades of the House were the founding period, during which legislators established the basic mechanisms through which decision making would take place.

In the founding period, legislators developed the committee system and party organizations, as well as procedures that enabled individual legislators to influence decision making from the floor. Initially, the relative importance of each procedure remained unclear. Most legislation would be worked out on the floor and then given to a committee that was temporarily convened to deal with the issue. But some committees became regular components of the House, such as the Rules Committee (created in 1789), which made decisions about scheduling legislation and about the rules through which bills would be debated. Procedural decisions had a big impact on the character of the House. In 1811, for example, an important rules change ensured that the House would become a majoritarian institution by allowing half of the chamber to end debate. This procedural change limited the potential for minority obstruction (in contrast to the Senate filibuster).

One of the most influential legislators in the founding period was Henry Clay of Kentucky. During his tenure as Speaker, Clay, first a Democratic-Republican and later a Whig, elevated the institutional status of the Speaker by using his power to keep members in line. While the speakership was the only position mentioned in the Constitution, its actual status in the House had remained unclear. When he became Speaker at the start of the congressional session in 1812, just after being elected to the House, Clay headed a coalition of war hawks who mounted pressure for military action against Great Britain. Clay also pushed for an expanded role of government in promoting the economy through public works, tariffs, and road construction. To achieve his objectives, Clay took responsibility for deciding which committees would deal with legislation, and he made appointments to key committees.

Even as legislators tried to determine how the House would function, they confronted a series of major challenges. In 1801, for example, the House had to decide a deadlocked presidential election after the electors cast an equal number of votes for Thomas Jefferson and Aaron Burr. The vote went to Jefferson. In 1825 the House was required again to settle a presidential election when none of the candidates received a majority from the Electoral

College. The House then chose John Quincy Adams to be the next president of the nation.

In the era, house majorities also voted for a significant expansion of the federal government. Through the Alien and Sedition Acts (1798), the House strengthened the authority of government to crack down on the political activity of aliens and to prosecute opponents of the Federalists. Although Democratic-Republicans such as Albert Gallatin of Pennsylvania and Edward Livingston of New York derided the Alien and Sedition Acts as a violation of state and individual rights, Federalists pushed the bills through the House by narrow margins. Additional legislation strengthened the administrative capacity of government to conduct war, regulate banking and currency, and improve networks of internal communication. Pork barrel spending was central to financing the construction of roads, railroads, and canals. Tariffs protected industrial goods such as cotton and iron.

Even when not explicitly discussed, slavery was extremely influential throughout the founding period. When considering most issues—as wide ranging as direct taxation, territorial expansion, and diplomacy—legislators always weighed the potential impact of a decision on the slaveholding economy. This was not surprising. Between 1788 and 1850, according to the historian Robin Einhorn, a slaveholder served as Speaker 66 percent of the time and as chairman of the powerful Ways and Means Committee, which controlled revenue and trade, 68 percent of the time.

The Party Period

Despite the fear that the founders expressed about the dangers of political parties and partisanship, a party system slowly took form. In the founding period, Federalists faced off against the Democratic-Republicans. Parties became even more important during the second era in the history of the House—the party period—which lasted from the 1830s to the 1900s. Even though the formal organization of parties remained tenuous before the Civil War, parties influenced House politics in a number of ways, as was evident from the large number of party-line roll call votes in this period. Partisan electorates and state legislators weighed heavily on the decision making of congressmen. Informal norms discouraged mavericks from challenging party leaders. Subsequent speakers followed Henry Clay's precedent by making committee assignments on the basis of party loyalty in voting and sometimes punished those who defied them.

Speakers controlled floor debate to protect their party. Party bosses relied on patronage to ensure that lower-ranking legislators remained loyal.

From the 1830s to the 1850s, Whigs competed against the Democrats. The Whigs supported national programs to promote economic growth, protective tariffs, the creation of a national bank, and moral reform. In contrast, Democrats championed presidential power, protection for southern slaveholders, territorial expansion, and local and state over federal power. Third parties, such as the Anti-Masons, the Liberty Party, and the Know-Nothings, formed to promote issues when neither the Whigs nor Democrats seemed responsive.

By the 1850s, the pull of section in the House became stronger than the pull of party. Each time that the federal government acquired a new territory, legislators fought over whether slavery should be allowed. The tension worsened with congressional passage of the Kansas-Nebraska Act (1854). Whigs and Democrats divided along sectional lines. Although a coalition of northern Whigs, northern Democrats, and Free-Soilers had attempted to block the measure, southern Whigs helped remove the bill from committee. In May 1856, sectional tension became so severe that Representative Preston Brooks of South Carolina beat Senator Charles Sumner of Massachusetts with his walking stick. Brooks was furious about a statement that Sumner, an opponent of slavery, had made about his uncle.

The Civil War of 1861–65 severed the nation. The secession of southern states and the departure of southern politicians were followed by brutal battles on the home front. Toward the end of the conflict, Congress responded to the crisis through legislation. In 1865 the House passed the Thirteenth Amendment (approved by the Senate the previous year), which abolished slavery within the United States. Throughout the war the Republican House remained active on a number of fronts in addition to slavery. For example, the House passed the Pacific Railway Act, created land-grant colleges, and enacted a national income tax. House Republicans also conducted investigations into how the Lincoln administration handled the war.

During Reconstruction, House Republicans pushed for an expanded role for the federal government to rebuild the nation and improve race relations, although the party divided between moderates and radicals over how far the policies should go. In 1866 the House passed the Fourteenth Amendment, which guaranteed due process and equal treatment before the law to all Americans, and, in 1869, the House passed the Fifteenth Amendment, which protected the right of every male citizen to vote. Congress also created the Freedmen's Bureau, which provided food, education, and other forms of assistance to freed African Americans. During Reconstruction a significant number of African Americans were elected to the House. President Andrew Johnson, who opposed most Reconstruction initiatives, attempted to capitalize on divisions among congressional Republicans. His efforts to split moderate and Radical Republicans, however, backfired. In February 1868, the House voted to impeach Johnson. Following a lengthy trial in the chamber, the Senate acquitted him by one vote. Support for Reconstruction diminished by the 1870s.

After Reconstruction the parties regained their strength. Republican legislators captured support in the northern industrial sector by promoting policies to expand national markets, preserve the gold standard, and provide generous Civil War pensions. Meanwhile, Democratic legislators retained their hold on the South by pushing farm assistance, inflationary monetary policies, free trade, and states' rights. These years were competitive for the parties. Republicans tended to control the Senate and Democrats the House between 1875 and 1897. Majorities in both chambers were razor thin. Congress passed legislation in 1872 that required all elections for the House to be held the same day.

Parties were important because they offered platforms to members, but also because they provided some organizational coherence in an era of high turnover. According to *Congressional Quarterly*, 145 out of 243 members of the House were new in 1869.

Members of the House were at the forefront of efforts to expand the federal government beyond policies related to Reconstruction. Democratic House representative John Reagan of Texas, for example, headed attacks against the railroads throughout the 1870s. Reagan's main goal was to protect the interests of farmers, whose distrust of national corporations he shared. He called on the House to impose regulations through legislation rather than rely on independent commissions. He feared that corporations would capture control of a regulatory commission and subvert agrarian interests. This was a widespread fear among southern Democrats. In 1876 Reagan used his seat on the House Commerce Committee to expose the activities of railroad magnates and build support for legislation. He introduced a bill that would prohibit pooling—where the railroads

pooled their revenue so that no individual company would have an incentive to lower its charges and be able to undercut competition—and guarantee fair rates for shippers. Teaming up with the moderate Shelby Cullom of Illinois, Reagan won the support of southern and western legislators, who voted for his bill in 1885. Although the final legislation in 1887 created the Independent Commerce Commission rather than relying on legislative regulations, Reagan's efforts had spearheaded one of the biggest expansions of federal power into the economy.

Toward the end of the party period, the Republican leadership in the House added procedural muscle to their influence. In 1890 Republican speaker Thomas Bracket Reed of Maine won support from his caucus for a rules change that allowed the majority party to block obstructive tactics of the minority. The most important was the "disappearing quorum," whereby Democrats in the House had refused to answer roll calls even while present in order to prevent a quorum. Reed ended this practice by announcing that those physically present were in attendance. After becoming Speaker in 1903, Republican Joseph Cannon of Illinois further strengthened the office. He used his power to stifle progressive legislation and frustrate President Theodore Roosevelt.

However, just as legislative parties started to gain more organizational cohesion, the strength of parties as national political institutions weakened. While parties remained a crucial component of American political life, their influenced vastly diminished. Electoral reforms increased the prevalence of split-ticket voting and precluded many of the tactics that parties had traditionally used to influence voters. National and state civil service reforms, such as the Pendleton Act of 1883, sharply curtailed the parties' ability to ensure loyalty through patronage. Moreover, both parties were forced to compete with organized interest groups, whose leaders promised they could deliver solid votes and ample campaign assistance. The partisan press disintegrated as a new medium arose, a system of professional journalists with an adversarial outlook who maintained weaker allegiances to elected officials. Americans did not vote as much, and electoral politics lost its salience with many citizens, who were more enthralled with amusement parks than with campaigns. Dramatic scandals in the Gilded Age that involved the parties had also spurred reforms that weakened the hold of parties. Partisan roll calls declined.

The high turnover in House membership on which parties had thrived diminished as rates of incumbency increased and legislators started to conceive of serving in the House as a full-time occupation. Seniority took hold as legislators obtained committee assignments by remaining in office for the longest amount of time rather than by displaying party loyalty. Committees themselves gained greater autonomy. Strong party leaders came under attack. In 1909 and 1910, a coalition of insurgent Republicans and Democrats who were unhappy about repeated failures in the legislative process—and about how Cannon had treated them—revolted against the Speaker. Representative George Norris of Nebraska led the attack for the Republicans, working closely with Victor Murdock and Edmund Madison of Kansas as well as John Nelson and Irvine Lenroot of Wisconsin. Missouri's Champ Clark and Alabama's Oscar Underwood led the Democratic part of the team. The coalition removed the Speaker from the Rules Committee and ended his control over committee assignments. It also passed reforms that allowed chairs to bring bills directly to the floor if they were bottled up in the Rules Committee. Finally, legislators agreed to delegate more governance responsibilities to independent commissions. Further reforms in the 1910s facilitated this trend. In 1911, for instance, the Democratic caucus empowered the Ways and Means Committee to handle committee assignments, thereby taking this responsibility away from the Speaker. Promotions in the chamber revolved around seniority. Formal rules and informal norms discouraged younger members from challenging committee chairmen.

The Committee Period

The committee period constituted the next stage in the evolution of the House and lasted from the 1910s through the early 1970s. The committee chairs retained tight control over proceedings. Access to information was restricted to the chairs and a few select senior members. Most deliberations were closed to the public. Legislative negotiations were dominated by tight-knit policy communities composed of committee chairs, representatives from the executive branch and agencies, powerful interest groups, and policy experts. Committee chairs rarely spoke to the national media.

The committee period had several pillars beyond the sheer power and autonomy of chairmen. At the electoral level, states preserved outdated district lines that favored rural constituencies and failed to reflect the growth of urban and suburban populations. The campaign finance system required legislators to cultivate a handful of prominent families, corporations, and unions that were willing to make large contributions. As parties with strong ties to the electorate weakened, interest groups offered legislators a resource to deliver blocs of voters and money. Striving to be objective, the media generally did not adopt an adversarial stance toward the House leadership.

During the committee period, party caucuses refrained from removing committee members for party disloyalty or incompetence. The weak Democratic and Republican caucuses rarely met, and they avoided taking strong positions or imposing them on members. The most influential party leaders were successful because they deferred to committee chairs rather than dominating them.

The committee process did not take hold automatically. Even after the historic revolt against Speaker Cannon, party caucuses remained influential throughout most of the 1910s. During World War I, to the frustration of Republicans, President Woodrow Wilson operated through a partisan alliance with congressional Democrats. He depended on Ways and Means Chairman Claude Kitchen of North Carolina, a progressive who initially opposed American intervention, to move much of the wartime legislation through the House in exchange for reforms. Yet by the Great Depression, the committee system was in place.

By the advent of the New Deal, southern Democrats and the committee process came to be seen as inseparable. While some Northerners, such as New York's Emanuel Celler, thrived in the committee process, Southerners claimed the greatest rewards in the House since they came from noncompetitive districts and thus retained their seats for longer periods of time. Southerners also constituted a disproportionate part of the Democratic Party. Southern Democrats held over 50 percent of the key committee chairs after the party regained control in 1933.

At the height of the New Deal, Congress responded to the Great Depression and often initiated policies before President Franklin D. Roosevelt did. House Democrats crafted legislation that preserved the alliance between Southerners and Northerners in the party who agreed on many areas of economic policy but disagreed on race relations and unionization. The House leadership included Speaker Henry Rainey of Illinois and Majority Leader Joseph Byrnes of Tennessee. Legislators such as Sam Rayburn of Texas and David Lewis of Maryland were instrumental in passing New Deal legislation.

But the committee process became a subject of contention for New Deal liberals. President Roosevelt had taken the unusual step of campaigning against five conservative Democrats in the 1938 election. He was able to unseat only one of those Democrats: New York representative John O'Connor, chairman of the House Rules Committee. Republicans also scored major victories in 1938. Conservative Democrats replaced liberals and moderates in a number of southern districts. Following the election, tensions escalated between southern chairs and northern Democrats. Southerners were not opposed to the expansion of government in general, but they did oppose unionization in their region and civil rights protection for African Americans.

When northern liberals began to support these issues in the 1940s, the committee process in the House became a major obstacle to twentieth-century liberalism. Southern Democrats, allied with Republicans, could rely on procedures to influence the House. Besides procedural power, southern Democrats and Republicans formed a potent voting bloc on the floor of the House. They could also count on southern Democrats in the Senate to use the filibuster, as they did with an antilynching bill in 1937, to block any civil rights legislation that the House passed.

Throughout World War II and the cold war, the committee-period House continued to produce legislation that expanded government. During World War II, the House agreed to a vast expansion of the tax base as well as a withholding system that enabled the government to collect taxes directly from paychecks. A decade later, the House voted to fund scientific research, highway construction, and civil defense. The House Un-American Activities Committee, founded in 1939, was at the forefront of the congressional investigations of suspected Communists.

By the 1950s, there were enough proponents of civil rights to produce legislation in the House, even though southern power in the Senate remained formidable. House liberals became pivotal players as they continued to force senators to grapple publicly with racial issues many preferred to ignore. The 1960s offered another burst of government activity. Almost 90 years after the end of Reconstruction, the House passed the Civil Rights Act of 1964 and the Voting Rights Act of 1965. Under the banner of the Great Society, the House passed legislation dealing with the environment, health care for the elderly, urban decay, and the War on Poverty.

A majority of Democrats and Republicans in the House also agreed to an expanded international role for the United States. During World War II and the cold war, the House supported a vast mobilization of resources and manpower in the effort to combat fascism and communism. But the Vietnam War broke that concensus apart. Although many members of the House voiced their doubts about intervention in 1964 and early 1965, they allowed President Lyndon Johnson to expand America's involvement in Vietnam. The vote for the 1964 Gulf of Tonkin Resolution was unanimous. By the late 1960s, however, many Democrats and Republicans joined colleagues in the Senate to build pressure on President Richard Nixon for a gradual withdrawal.

Many liberals came to believe that success could only occur if northern legislators worked around the committee system. One of the foils of the 1960s House was Virginia's Howard Smith. Elected in 1938, Smith had taken over the House Rules Committee in 1955 and used the power of his chairmanship to stifle liberal legislation.

As the federal government expanded, so too did the executive branch. Some observers believed this was the period of the "imperial presidency." But many legislators felt differently. Congress continued to exert influence on national politics. In the creation of domestic and international programs, committee chairs retained a tight grip over the government. Wilbur Mills, the Arkansas Democrat who chaired the Ways and Means Committee, caused enormous problems for President Johnson in 1968, when he forced the president to accept domestic spending cuts in exchange for higher taxes.

The Supreme Court had made a series of decisions between 1962 and 1964 that affected the composition of the House because they forced it and state legislatures to create voting districts with equal populations. In *Wesberry v. Sanders* (1964) the Court ruled that Georgia's federal districting system was unconstitutional. Plaintiffs from Georgia's district alleged that they were unjustly treated, since their population was three times as large as the population of the ninth, the smallest district in the state. The fifth district was the most underrepresented in the nation. The Court ruled 6 to 3 that populations in each congressional district must be roughly equal so that the vote of each citizen carried the same weight. In the short term, the decisions put conservative Democrats on notice. One of the earliest victims was Howard Smith. He lost in the 1966 primaries to a Democrat who was more popular in the suburbs but who became part of Smith's district as a result of the "one man-one vote" Supreme Court rulings. In the long term, the Court decisions opened up the opportunity for Republicans to make gains in the South and end the region's one-party monopoly.

Public hostility toward the House intensified in the 1960s, as did the frustration with all government institutions. Liberals denounced Congress for being too timid in its support for the Great Society and for allowing Presidents Kennedy, Johnson, and Nixon to fight the Vietnam War. At the same time, conservatives attacked the House for being inefficient and corrupt. Public interest reformers attacked Congress for failing to represent average citizens and stifling democratic participation. Although the Watergate scandal focused on the abuses of the presidency, reformers believed that Congress could only regain its stature by dismantling the committee process.

During the early 1970s, congressional reformers obtained support for procedures that aimed to weaken committee chairs. The reforms simultaneously centralized power by granting more decision-making authority to the party caucuses and decentralized power through the Subcommittee Bill of Rights in 1973. The House voted for reforms that constrained the power of the president in budgeting and war making. After the 1974 midterm elections, the "Watergate babies" (an influx of newly elected Democrats following Nixon's resignation) deposed four powerful House committee chairs, further weakened the autonomy of committees, and opened more proceedings to the public.

As the committee period ended, the House became fractured and unstable. Freed from the dominance of committee chairs, individual legislators, specialized caucuses, subcommittees, and the congressional minority pursued their own electoral and ideological interests. Although committee chairs lost power, party leaders were not yet able to impose order on the House. For instance, legislators constantly amended committee bills after they reached the floor, in contrast to the previous period when such activity was rare. Several scandals also shook the House, including sexual scandals that brought down Democratic congressmen Wilbur Mills and Wayne Hays as well as the ABSCAM scandal in 1980, when legislators were videotaped accepting bribes. The House reprimanded its first member since the Civil War.

The Partisan Period

In the most recent period, elite partisanship took hold of the House. Although most Americans were not strongly partisan, party caucuses became more influential in the House in two ways. First, Democrats and Republicans became more homogenous ideologically. As the number of southern conservative Democrats diminished and moderates lost power in the Republican Party, Democrats moved to the left and Republicans to the right. Fac-

ing more cohesive membership, party leaders were more willing to use procedural tools that they had gained in the 1970s to expand their role. Between 1987 and 1989, for instance, Speaker James Wright of Texas intimidated members of his own party and manhandled Republicans. On one occasion, he extended the time for voting after Democrats could not find a sufficient number of members to vote for a tax package. Democrats used the extra time to round up more legislators outside the chamber. Younger Republicans such as Newt Gingrich of Georgia rejected the bias of older moderates who favored compromise. Gingrich publicly broke with President George H. W. Bush in 1990 who broke his campaign pledge by agreeing to a tax hike. When Republicans elected Gingrich Speaker after the GOP gained control of the House, he excluded Democrats from deliberations and enhanced the power of party leaders.

The new partisanship in the House differed from that of the nineteenth century. The nineteenth-century parties lacked strong centralized organization in the House but maintained deep roots in the electorate. But after the 1980s, political parties were organizationally strong within the House but lacked meaningful connections to the electorate. American voters thus witnessed a more partisan institution to which they did not feel connected. Instead of mechanisms of political participation, parties increasingly became fund-raising devices and organizational tools.

Partisan fighting was fierce in the partisan period, since neither Republicans nor Democrats were able to maintain solid control over Congress, and the leadership passed back and forth several times. In 1980 Democrats retained control of the House but Republicans gained control of the Senate until 1986. Republicans won both chambers of Congress in 1994, lost the Senate in 2001, and regained control of both chambers in the 2002 midterm elections. In 2006 Democrats regained control of both chambers. Although control of the House remained relatively stable after 1994, razor-thin margins during much of the 1990s fostered insecurity among those in power.

While the reforms of the 1970s had promised to make Congress the dominant branch of government, legislators were still working under tremendous constraints. There were multiple and competing centers of legislative power, with none achieving absolute dominance and none conducive to producing legislative compromise. Many reformers had hoped to ensure that no part of Congress developed the kind of singular strength that committee chairs had; the reformers succeeded in this respect. The proliferation and empowerment of subcommittees and specialized caucuses produced small fiefdoms that became obstacles to party leaders and committee chairs. Furthermore, new rules and norms encouraged mavericks and freshmen to take action when they felt an issue was being ignored by the party leadership. Every legislator from senior party leaders to lower-ranking representatives was subject to new ethics regulations and norms. Scandals brought down powerful leaders, including Speakers Wright, Gingrich, and Tom DeLay.

Public policy was a second constraint on legislators in the partisan period. Since the 1970s, the federal budget loomed large over every congressional decision. The tremendous increase in pre-committed spending, as well as sizable federal deficits and debt, meant there was less money for legislators who wanted to construct new types of government programs outside of national emergencies. By the 1980s and 1990s, almost half of the federal budget went to entitlement programs such as Social Security and Medicare. For most of these years, the federal government spent more than it took in in taxes. In an environment of fiscal constraint, it was hard to create new programs. The nature of the federal budget also made it difficult to dismantle programs.

When conservatives took power in the 1980s, culminating in the 1994 congressional elections, they discovered it was hard to alter most programs, except for federal taxation. Republicans could not touch items like Social Security without severe electoral consequences. This left conservatives with the unattractive option of cutting modestly priced programs like welfare that came with the high cost of antagonizing active interest groups or attacking programs important to their own supporters. Even after the 2000 election, with a staunchly conservative president in office, federal spending grew. The war on terrorism increased the size of government. Conservatives railed against Republicans by 2006, accusing the party of having accepted "big government." In reality, however, cutting the size of the state was virtually impossible.

The news media constituted a third constraint on the power of representatives. In contrast to the committee period, the news media had a hostile relationship with elected officials. Trust and cooperation evaporated. The rise of adversarial journalism in the 1960s and 1970s had produced a new generation of reporters and editors determined to expose corruption. This outlook would continue to shape the print media as well as television. Cable television added to this volatile environment. Producers worked on exposés to attract large television audiences. Even though ownership became concentrated, the number of stations multiplied. Cable television created a 24-hour news cycle, which made controlling the flow of news more difficult since stories could go on the airwaves within seconds. Media organizations looked for shocking material to fill the airwaves and generate high ratings. In a period when most Americans distrusted government, scandals became a favorite topic. Legislators responded by honing their media skills. Some relied on C-SPAN, created in 1979, two years after the House authorized televised proceedings, to communicate directly to voters without the filter of reporters.

It was not just that the media had changed. Another challenge facing legislators in the partisan period was the fractious world of interest groups, think tanks, and political activists. While all these organizations were present throughout the twentieth century, their numbers grew after the 1960s. The expansion of federal regulations and domestic policies since the 1960s increased the incentive for them to lobby legislators. Moreover, campaign finance reforms of the 1970s required legislators to expand their base of financial support. Public interest groups also formed lobbying organizations. The number of think tanks proliferated. This hyper-competitive environment resulted in a situation in which legislators were constantly scrambling to secure their links to a greater number of interest groups, none of which was dominant.

Divided government through much of this era made it difficult for legislators who sought dramatic policy change. Although divided government did not prevent Congress from passing legislation, it no longer offered a hospitable climate for major innovations like the Great Society.

The Supreme Court and the president also remained strong. The Court continued to take an active stand on issues such as legislative redistricting and states' rights. The presidency continued to remain a dominant institution, as when Ronald Reagan used his office to advance conservative aims. The War Powers Act seemed almost irrelevant when Reagan authorized military operations in Nicaragua and El Salvador without congressional approval. Presidents relied on international bodies to legitimate military action. While Congress responded with litigation, investigation, and legislation, the president usually had his way.

Despite all these obstacles, the House still passed significant legislation. In 1990, the House agreed to a deficit reduction plan that increased taxes and lowered spending. Following the terrorist attacks of September 11, 2001, Congress restructured airline security, put money into public health research, and created the Department of Homeland Security. Congress also created a prescription drug benefit for Medicare.

With all the uncertainties that legislators faced, a high rate of incumbency provided a form of personal security. The trend toward incumbency that started in the late nineteenth century never abated. While the Supreme Court had forced the elimination of congressional districts with unequal populations, it never tackled political gerrymandering. As a result, state legislatures were able to draw district lines to protect incumbents. After 1949, the majority of elections brought only 80 new members to the House. Campaign finance rules, moreover, favored those who already held office, since they could raise large sums of money quickly and receive free media exposure. Citizens also tended to like their representatives, even though they disliked Congress as an institution.

As George Mason hoped, the House has energized and preserved America's democratic aspirations. Commentators like to joke that legislation resembles sausage in that the taste may be good, but people do not want to see how the product was made. Yet the messiness and complexity of deliberations in the House, which are often criticized, reflect tensions and divisions that exist in the country. The House has struggled to forge compromises in response to the nation's biggest challenges. Sometimes the institution has failed in this task, but, at other times, the House has sent the Senate legislation that ended up transforming America. At the same time, the history of the House reminds us of some of democracy's biggest weaknesses, including corruption, destructive partisanship, and the lack of accountability on the part of elected officials.

See also Senate; state government.

FURTHER READING

Congressional Quarterly Press Electronic Library, http://library.cqpress.com/.

Einhorn, Robin L. *American Taxation, American Slavery.* Chicago: University of Chicago Press, 2008.

Gould, Lewis L. *The Most Exclusive Club: A History of the United States Senate.* New York: Basic Books, 2006.

Remini, Robert V. *The House: The History of the House of Representatives.* New York: HarperCollins, 2006.

Schickler, Eric. *Disjointed Pluralism: Institutional Innovation and the Development of the U.S. Congress.* Princeton, NJ: Princeton University Press, 2001.

Zelizer, Julian E. *On Capitol Hill: The Struggle to Reform Congress and Its Consequences, 1945–2000.* New York: Cambridge University Press, 2004.

———, ed. *The American Congress: The Building of Democracy.* Boston: Houghton Mifflin, 2004.

JULIAN E. ZELIZER

immigration policy

Immigration policy has long been one of the most contentious and ultimately transformative issues on the American public agenda, evoking intense political struggles over how to regulate the flow of newcomers. Rival interests and ideals lie at the heart of these profound political conflicts. For more than two centuries, Americans have argued about the impact of new immigrants on jobs and economic growth, demography, culture, social welfare, the distribution of political power, foreign relations, and national security.

The United States may be a nation built upon immigration, but it has long been ambivalent about new arrivals. From Benjamin Franklin's eighteenth-century fears that Pennsylvania Germans would never assimilate to Samuel Huntington's more recent warnings that a growing Latino population imperils cultural harmony, many Americans have celebrated their sojourner past while dreading the immigrant present and future. For others, especially those in the labor movement, fresh waves of immigration have been perceived as anathema to workplace standards and economic security. By contrast, cosmopolitans such as Jane Addams and John F. Kennedy have championed broad immigrant admissions and rights as consistent with the American Creed, while capitalists like Andrew Carnegie have praised immigration as "a golden stream" that fortifies U.S. prosperity. In short, the choices raised by immigration policy have spurred vibrant debate since the founding and have served as a bellwether for larger political conflicts over changing economic opportunities, the status of ethnic, religious, and racial minorities, and the nation's evolving role in international diplomacy and warfare.

The polarizing politics of immigration reform, both past and present, has made policy making arduous but not impossible. Indeed, it has produced strange political bedfellows over time and yielded marked shifts from one period to the next between national policies that have significantly stimulated or discouraged immigration. The federal government only gradually and reluctantly took control of regulating immigrant admissions over the course of the nineteenth century. Since then, American immigration policy has assumed both restrictive and expansive forms. Whereas the creation of national origins quotas and an Asiatic Barred Zone in the 1920s effectively closed the gates, immigration reforms since 1965 helped trigger the nation's fourth major wave of migration, predominantly originating in Latin America, the Caribbean, and Asia. Few policy areas have left a more profound mark on the development and present character of American social, economic, political, and cultural life. Even when immigration reform has had unintended results or when the best-laid plans of lawmakers have been defied by migratory behavior—such as dramatic increases in both unauthorized immigration and undocumented populations living in the United States—the policy outcomes have reshaped the nation.

At the time of the founding, due to early waves of immigration and the importation of slaves, the United States was already a remarkably diverse country in terms of religion, race, and ethnicity. Less than half of the new republic's white population could be described as English when the Revolution began. Anglo-Americans remained the dominant group in the former English colonies, but British newcomers increasingly came from Scotland, Wales, and Ireland. Moreover, one-third of the country's white inhabitants claimed German, Swedish, French, Swiss, or Dutch origins. Southern importation of African slaves was the principal engine of racial diversity in the early American republic. Finally, the United States was more religiously diverse than any country in Europe. Although immigration slowed to a trickle during the era of the American Revolution (no more than a few thousand per year), some national leaders remained wary of future inflows. In his *Notes on the State of Virginia* (1781), Thomas Jefferson criticized the new nation's member states for their "present desire to produce rapid population by as great importations of foreigners as possible." Most newcomers, he feared, would prove incapable of shedding their loyalties to the "absolute monarchy" of the Old World, or prone to material and anarchical temptations of the new one. The French Revolution and subsequent Napoleonic warfare in Europe delayed robust immigration to the United States until well after the 1820s. Nevertheless, new state governments wasted little time in establishing their own immigration and naturalization policies soon after the nation's founding. Most of these policies were designed to entice new European settlers and to extend broad membership rights to white male newcomers.

Immigration and the New Republic

With the ratification of the Constitution, the young nation embraced a laissez-faire federal policy toward European immigration and authorized Congress "to establish a uniform Rule of Naturalization." During Philadelphia deliberations in 1787, James Madison observed that those states which most encouraged European immigration were the strongest in population, agriculture, and the arts, and he warned against restrictions on immigrant rights that might "give a tincture of illiberality" to the new republic. The first Congress in 1790 enacted a naturalization law that granted citizenship to "free white persons" who lived in the United States for as little as two years.

During the 1790s, support for immigration was eroded by the Anglo-French conflict and partisan polarization at home. For the dominant Federalists, new French and Irish immigrants were untrustworthy because of their celebration of French revolutionary ideals and their support for the Democratic-Republican opposition. Federalist majorities in Congress passed a new naturalization law in 1795 that increased the residency requirement for citizenship to five years. Responding to security jitters in 1798 associated with the French conflict, Federalist lawmakers enacted the Alien and Sedition Acts. The legislation made immigrants eligible for citizenship only after 14 years of residency, and all aliens were required to register with federal officials. The Alien Act empowered the president to arrest and deport any alien "whom he shall judge dangerous to the peace and safety of the United States." The Alien Enemies Act, passed the same year, au-

thorized the president to confine or remove male enemy aliens age 14 years or older during times of war. The Alien and Sedition Acts proved to be short-lived, as the victory of Jeffersonian Republicans in 1800 led to a repeal of alien registration requirements and the restoration of a five-year residency requirement for naturalization. With future elections and economic development in mind, Jefferson proclaimed that the United States represented a New Canaan where "those whom the misrule of Europe may compel to seek happiness in other climes" would "be received as brothers."

Immigrants, Nativists, and Nation Building: 1820–60

From the 1820s until the start of the Civil War, roughly 5 million European immigrants came to the United States. During the 1820s, immigration accounted for only 4 percent of the steady increase in American population; by the 1850s, immigration accounted for nearly one-third of U.S. population growth. The national government remained all but silent on European immigration during this period. Federal law required that new arrivals be counted after 1819 to maintain uniform statistics, and it mandated minimum living standards for vessels carrying immigrant passengers to the country. However, the task of regulating immigration continued to fall to state and local governments. In practice, the modest structures governing immigrant traffic in antebellum America were the creation and responsibility of a few states with large ports, such as New York (where most immigrants landed), Maryland, Massachusetts, Pennsylvania, and South Carolina. State immigration laws authorized exclusion of immigrants with criminal records, contagious illnesses, or other undesirable qualities, but few were turned away. Coastal states charged ship masters small head taxes on their immigrant passengers, a practice affirmed by the Supreme Court in 1837. The 1848 *Passenger Cases* reversed this holding, asserting that state head taxes violated federal prerogatives, but states made minor adjustments and maintained primacy in this area.

The dramatic expansion of U.S. territory with the Louisiana Purchase and the Mexican-American War created a strong demand for new immigrants to settle a large frontier. Territorial governments actively recruited European newcomers, hiring agents to recruit immigrants overseas or as they landed in port cities. The rise of an industrial economy also required an expanded labor force that European immigration helped realize. Grassroots nativism accompanied the unprecedented immigration of the antebellum decades, with Irish Catholic newcomers the most frequent targets of xenophobic hostility. Whereas Germans, who dominated immigration in these years. exemplified religious, class, and ideological diversity, the Irish were almost invariably poor and Roman Catholic. Anglo-American angst over the Irish Catholic influx, which soared during the Irish potato famine of the 1840s, was exacerbated by competition for jobs and housing in northeastern cities, struggles over public and parochial education, and the marriage of powerful urban party machines and Irish voters. Anti-Catholic books, newspapers, and magazines flourished in the antebellum period, offering lurid accounts of sinister Roman Catholic crimes and plots that fed Protestant antipathy. Sometimes the dark tales promulgated by this anti-Catholic literature spurred mob violence, from the 1834 burning of the Ursuline convent near Boston to the 1844 Bible Riots in Philadelphia that led to 20 deaths and the destruction of more than 100 Catholic churches, schools, and homes. The ranks of secret anti-Catholic associations swelled in seaboard cities. The nativist leader Samuel Morse, a newspaper editor and future inventor of the telegraph, organized an anti-immigrant party and ran for New York City mayor in 1836. He also fed anti-Catholic venom through popular and incendiary writings such as *Foreign Conspiracy* (1841), warning readers that "the evil of immigration brings to these shores illiterate Roman Catholics, the obedient instruments of their more knowing priestly leaders."

Because of the nation's insatiable appetite for immigrant labor and the clout of Irish voters, political nativists enjoyed little success until the 1850s. In 1849 secret nativist societies formed the Order of the Star Spangled Banner to furtively organize electoral support for its anti-Catholic and anti-immigrant agenda in cities around the country. The movement's rank and file included Anglo-American workers, artisans, and small entrepreneurs. Their secrecy led Horace Greeley to mock their members in *New York Tribune* as "know-nothings"—a label soon applied to political nativists who sought to restrict immigration and Catholic influence. The Know-Nothing movement formed a new American Party in the 1850s devoted to strict limits on immigrant admissions, 21-year waiting periods for citizenship, and restricting voting rights and officeholding to the native-born.

The Know-Nothings benefited enormously from a political vacuum created by the gradual demise of the Whig Party and balkanization of the Democrats. During the 1854 and 1855 elections, the American Party elected seven Know-Nothing governors, controlled eight state legislatures, and established a strong presence in Congress. In 1856, the party nominated Millard Fillmore for president, and he won 22 percent of the popular vote. The movement's meteoric rise transcended the ballot box. Know-Nothing candy, tea, and other merchandise were successfully marketed, while buses, stagecoaches and clipper ships soon bore the popular name. The decline of the American Party was as swift and dramatic as its ascent. The new Republican Party siphoned away nativist voters more devoted to excluding slavery from the territories than the Know-Nothings' "war to the hilt on Romanism." By 1860 the movement had collapsed. Ironically, the same slavery controversy that helped elevate anti-Catholic xenophobia in antebellum America was the driving force behind its rapid demise.

Expansion and Exclusion in the Gilded Age

To the chagrin of nativists, European immigration flourished in the last half of the nineteenth century. Fueled by federal recruitment efforts in Europe, the Homestead Act, and industrialization, inflows from Europe reached record levels in the post–Civil War decades. Immigration soared to 2.3 million in the 1860s, 2.8 million in the 1870s, 5.2 million in the 1880s, 3.6 million in the 1890s, and 8.8 million in the first decade of the twentieth century. The vast majority of new arrivals landed in New York, where they were channeled through a central immigration depot, Manhattan's Castle Garden. The nationalization of U.S. immigration policy began in 1875, when the Supreme Court nullified state efforts to regulate alien inflows as unconstitutional encroachments on exclusive congressional power. The Immigration Act of 1882 essentially legitimized state policies governing immigration that had been struck down by the Court. It excluded "any convict, lunatic, idiot" or anyone deemed likely to become a public charge, while assessing head taxes on each entrant to fund inspections and welfare provision for needy arrivals. In 1885 the Knights of Labor persuaded Democratic majorities in Congress to enact a ban on the importation of foreign contract labor. Legislation in 1891 created a new federal bureaucracy in the Treasury Department to supervise the screening of immigrants, with a corps of federal immigration inspectors stationed at the nation's major ports of entry. Within the year, Castle Garden was replaced by a new federal facility in New York harbor, Ellis Island. Screening nearly three-quarters of new arrivals, Ellis Island became the largest and busiest inspection station for years to come.

Compared to its European counterparts, Chinese immigration of the late nineteenth century was miniscule (4 percent of all immigration at its zenith), but it inspired one of the most brutal and successful nativist movements in U.S. history. Official and popular racism made Chinese newcomers especially vulnerable; their lack of numbers, political power, or legal protections gave them none of the weapons that enabled Irish Catholics to counterattack nativists. Chinese workers were first recruited to California from the 1850s through the 1870s as cheap contract labor for mining, railroad construction, manufacturing, and farming. They inspired hostility among white workers for allegedly lowering wages and working conditions, while newspapers and magazines portrayed the Chinese as a race of godless opium addicts, prostitutes, and gamblers. Labor leaders in San Francisco organized large anti-Chinese clubs in every ward of the city during the 1860s, and comparable associations followed in cities and towns throughout the state. California politicians also learned that anti-Chinese speeches and policies translated into votes. The state's first Republican governor in 1862, Leland Stanford, promised "to protect free white labor" from the "degraded" Chinese while, at the same time, his own farming and railroad enterprises employed them.

Economic distress inflamed the anti-Chinese movement in the 1870s, as the closing of unproductive mines, the completion of the transcontinental railroad, and a flood of new settlers to the Pacific Coast led to rampant unemployment. San Francisco union leaders again spearheaded Sinophobic organizational efforts, initiating a grassroots network of Chinese Exclusion Leagues that spread across California and the Far West to elect sympathetic candidates. From 1871 onward, California politicians raced to claim credit for a steady stream of anti-Chinese reforms that included state-level barriers to Chinese entry, segregation laws, and special taxes on Chinese businesses. One of the anti-Chinese movement's most effective firebrands was Denis Kearney, an Irish immigrant who blamed Chinese immigrants for his personal failure at mining. His demagogic campaign, which began with race-baiting speeches in the San Francisco sandlots, drew white laborers into a new Workingmen's Party of California, dedicated to the proposition that "the Chinese must go!" Kearney spurred a state constitutional convention in 1878 targeting the "Chinese menace," as well as an 1879 state referendum that endorsed Chinese exclusion by a 150,000-to-900 vote.

When the Supreme Court struck down state-level efforts to restrict Chinese immigration, the Sinophobic movement pressed Congress to enact sweeping exclusions.

Fierce party competition in presidential elections of the post-Reconstruction era transformed the anti-Chinese movement into a national political juggernaut. As the *New York Times* queried in 1880, "Which great political party is foolish enough to risk losing the votes of the Pacific States by undertaking to do justice to the Chinese?"—neither, as it turned out. Large bipartisan majorities in Congress suspended Chinese admissions for ten years with passage of the Chinese Exclusion Act of 1882. Some of the worst anti-Chinese riots erupted in subsequent years, as Sinophobes sought to purge Chinese communities altogether across the Far West. Forced expulsions were initiated almost wherever Chinese numbered in the hundreds in cities and towns of the Pacific Northwest and Mountain States. During the 1885 Rock Springs, Wyoming, massacre, 28 Chinese were murdered and every Chinese-owned building except one was destroyed. In Tacoma and Seattle during 1885 and 1886, Chinese residents were given "deportation" deadlines. They suffered looting, arson, and violent riots until few remained. In subsequent election years, national Democrats and Republicans curried favor with the Sinophobic movement by enacting increasingly draconian restrictions on the "Chinese race." The 1888 Scott Act, for instance, denied readmission of Chinese who left U.S. territory; 20,000 were not allowed to return under the law and many were separated from their families. The Sinophobic fervor did not subside until the early 1900s, when a significantly reduced Chinese population was concentrated in a few self-sufficient Chinatowns.

As western nativists put their final touches on Chinese exclusion, a new anti-Catholic movement emerged in the nation's heartland. The American Protective Association (APA) was founded in Clinton, Iowa, in 1887 by Henry Bowers, an attorney aggrieved by a friend's mayoral defeat and the decline of public schools, both of which he attributed to malevolent Catholic influence. An ardent Mason, Bowers made the APA into a secret fraternal order with an anti-Catholic political agenda that drew heavily upon the rituals, organization, and membership of Masonic lodges. The APA spread in the early 1890s to larger midwestern and Rocky Mountain communities where Catholics were gaining political and social clout; its support came primarily from Protestant businessmen,

Immigrants exit a pier onto Ellis Island, New York, in the early 1900s. (Library of Congress)

disaffected union workers, and those competing with cheap Irish labor.

In 1893 the ranks of APA faithful surged to more than a half million. Its growth owed much to new leadership by William "Whiskey Bill" Traynor, a former saloon owner with considerable experience promoting anti-Catholic causes and publishing nativist newspapers. During the depression of 1893, he and his APA lieutenants roused crowds by blaming the economic crisis on Irish Catholic immigrants who allegedly stole jobs, started a run on the banks, and encouraged labor militancy.

Rather than form a third party, APA organizers established local and state "advisory boards" to endorse candidates, almost invariably Republican, who demonstrated strong anti-Catholic credentials. In 1893 and 1894, APA voters were credited with electing anti-Catholic Republicans in municipal, school board, and congressional elections in midwestern and Rocky Mountain States. Yet the importance of immigrant labor and votes led many national Republican leaders to challenge the APA's nativist agenda. In 1896 William McKinley's presidential campaign actively courted immigrant and Roman Catholic voters while purging the APA from Republican ranks. Cut loose from its partisan moorings, the APA quickly faded from the political landscape.

Closing the Gates: 1917–44

As the APA crusade dissipated, a new anti-immigrant movement led by the upper-class Immigration Restriction League (IRL), the American Federation of Labor,

and patriotic societies distanced itself from anti-Catholic nativism. Embracing the scientific racism of Social Darwinism and the eugenics movement, these reformers argued that southern and eastern Europeans arriving in record numbers from countries like Italy, Greece, Russia, Hungary, and Poland were biologically inferior to immigrants from Western and Northern Europe. Their chief goal was a literacy test for admission, based on the presumption that most immigrants lacking Anglo-Saxon lineage were unable to read. They enjoyed a prominent champion in Massachusetts senator Henry Cabot Lodge, who warned that "new" European immigration posed "nothing less than the possibility of a great and perilous change in the fabric of our race." Progressive Era nativists also spurned party politics in favor of mass publicity campaigns, biased research, and full-time Washington lobbying. Their efforts paid dividends when the 1911 Dillingham Commission, led by IRL allies, including Lodge, produced 42 volumes of findings that purportedly vindicated nativist claims about southern and eastern Europeans. Despite these inroads, a countermobilization of immigration defenders led by employer and ethnic groups yielded policy stalemate. President Woodrow Wilson denounced the nativist agenda as inconsistent with "the humane ardors of our republic."

The onset of World War I broke the logjam. Immigration restrictionists seized upon wartime anxieties to win passage of an immigration literacy test in 1917, arguing that southern and eastern Europeans were inherently disloyal and dangerous. While the IRL and its allies were closing the gates, an Americanization movement attacked any hint of divided loyalties among the foreign-born already in the country. Theodore Roosevelt led the charge for "100% Americanism," denouncing "hyphenated" Americans as guilty of no less then "moral treason." Patriotic conformity was pursued by a government-sponsored network of local defense and patriotic associations, including 250,000 badge-wearing volunteers of the American Protective League (APL). German Americans, celebrated for decades as the model ethnic group, endured the harshest treatment. They were targets of vandalism, mob violence, surveillance, and harassment by APL watchdogs; job discrimination; and arrest for unpatriotic speech. By 1918 public burnings of German books were common, dozens of German American newspapers and organizations were forced to dissolve, and several states prohibited speaking German or playing German-composed music in public.

After the war, the immigration restriction movement mobilized for new reforms when the literacy test failed to curb southern and eastern European inflows. As European immigration soared to 800,000 in 1920, a sharp leap from the meager numbers of the war years, a State Department report warned that the country faced an inundation of "filthy" and "unassimilable" Jews, displaced by persecution in eastern and central Europe. At the same time, the House Immigration Committee employed its own "expert eugenics agent," Harry Laughlin, to illuminate racial differences among immigrants. "We in this country have been so imbued with the idea of democracy, or the equality of all men," Laughlin testified, "that we have left out of consideration the matter of blood or natural inborn hereditary mental and moral differences. No man who breeds pedigreed plants and animals can afford to neglect this thing." During the first "Red scare," immigration restrictionists pressed for "emergency" legislation to fend off a foreign influx that would compromise national security. The Quota Act of 1921 established annual limits of 3 percent of each nationality living in the United States at the time of the 1910 census. These quotas were applied to immigration from all countries except those of the Western Hemisphere. The free flow of Western Hemisphere immigration was a concession that lawmakers made to southwestern growers who lobbied vigorously to retain access to cheap Mexican farm labor. Southern and eastern European inflows were the chief target of the new law, restricted by quotas to less than one-fourth of annual admissions before World War I.

The Immigration Act of 1924 marked the crowning achievement of the immigration restriction movement. It created a 165,000 ceiling on annual immigrant admissions, refined national origins quotas to reserve 84 percent of annual visas for northern and western Europeans, and reaffirmed an Asiatic Barred Zone that excluded virtually all Asian immigrants and most other nonwhites. "To the national dishonor of the 'assisted' immigration of slave trade days," Jane Addams sadly noted, "we are adding another chapter." But immigration restrictionists exalted as southern and eastern European immigration slowed to a trickle. "The United States is our land," Congressman Albert Johnson proclaimed. "The day of unalloyed welcome to all peoples, the day of indiscriminate acceptance of all races, has definitely ended." Legislation in 1928 made the national origins quota system fully operative, but it also continued to allow unfettered Western Hemisphere migration as a bow to powerful southern and western lawmakers and economic interests. The result was a bifurcated system imposing draconian restrictions on European and Asian immigration while remaining open and flexible toward labor inflows from Mexico and other Western Hemisphere countries.

Mexican immigration increased substantially during the 1920s, but neither legal nor illegal Mexican inflows prompted great concern among national policy makers. Efforts by the American Federation of Labor to impose 1,500 annual quotas on Mexican immigration went nowhere because of resistance from southwestern growers and their supporters in Congress. The onset of the Great Depression changed public perceptions of Mexican labor migration considerably, leading to a mass deportation campaign that reinforced notions of Latino workers as a "returnable" labor force. At the same time, U.S. consular offices denied visas to those deemed "likely to become a public charge," with the effect that many quota slots went unfilled. During the 1930s, immigration reached the lowest levels in a century and the total number of people leaving the country exceeded those entering for the first time in its history. From the rise of the Nazi regime until the end of World War II, powerful members of Congress and State Department officials blocked efforts to grant refuge to European Jews and others fleeing fascist regimes. In the early 1940s, by contrast, agribusinesses and other employer groups won White House support for a new Mexican temporary worker program, the Bracero Program, to address wartime labor shortages. This guest worker program would bring 4.2 million temporary Mexican laborers to the United States before it was terminated at the urging of organized labor in 1963.

Refugees, Cold War, and Reform: 1945–65

During the 1940s and 1950s, pro-immigration reformers attempted to chip away at the national origins quota system. Eager to strengthen a wartime alliance with China, Congress repealed Chinese exclusion statutes in favor of a token annual quota. Symbolic quotas were extended to other Asian nations a few years later. Lawmakers also enacted the War Brides Act in 1946 that waived quota limits for the alien wives and children of U.S. servicemen. The cold war imperatives of global leadership and anticommunism led to other departures from the quota restrictions. President Harry Truman took unilateral action in 1945 to give 40,000 people from various European countries displaced by the war preferential consideration for visas. At Truman's urging, Congress later passed the Displaced Persons acts of 1948 and 1950 to permit European refugees from countries with severe visa limits to be included in future quotas.

Despite these modest breaks in the restrictionist wall, cold war anxieties fueled passage of the Internal Security Act of 1950, which authorized the exclusion or deportation of aliens who had ever been Communists or members of any group deemed to be a "front" organization. In a nation that had fallen under the spell of McCarthyism, immigration restriction continued to enjoy a deep reservoir of both popular and congressional support. The McCarran-Walter Act of 1952 retained national origins quotas as the cornerstone of U.S. immigration policy and expanded the government's alien surveillance and deportation powers. Receiving solid backing from southern and western members of Congress, it is little wonder that the 1952 law also contained a "Texas proviso" that exempted employers of undocumented aliens from any form of legal sanction. A year later, the Eisenhower administration persuaded lawmakers to open the door temporarily for 200,000 European refugees. In 1956 the White House used emergency powers to admit refugees from the failed Hungarian Revolution. During the same period, the federal government cracked down on illegal immigration. Supported by local police and federal troops, the Immigration and Naturalization Service (INS) launched "Operation Wetback" in 1954 to quiet public concerns about a growing population of undocumented aliens. Dragnet raids led to the capture and summary expulsion of more than a million Mexican noncitizens.

The postwar decades witnessed the rise of a new movement for immigration reform that included a broad array of ethnic, human rights, religious, business, and even labor groups like the Congress of Industrial Organizations. During the early 1960s these reformers found champions in Presidents John Kennedy and Lyndon Johnson. In 1964 Johnson called on Congress to "lift by legislation the bars of discrimination against those who seek entry into our country." A product of the Great Society, the Immigration Reform Act of 1965 dismantled the national origins quota system in favor of a new preference system that gave primacy to reuniting families while reserving a limited number of visas for skilled workers and refugees. In its aftermath, an unexpected wave of Asian, Latin American, and Caribbean immigrants came to the United States, with European immigration falling by the early 1970s to only 10 percent of all legal admissions. The 1965 law also placed a 120,000 annual ceiling on Western Hemisphere visas that, along with the 1963 termination of the Bracero Program, spurred illegal Mexican inflows.

Reopening the Golden Door: 1966–present

The issue of illegal immigration inspired more media attention, public concern, and remedial proposals by policy makers than did any other migratory issue of the 1970s. At the heart of early efforts to control porous borders was a proposal by organized labor and congressional Democrats like Peter Rodino to penalize employers who knowingly hired undocumented aliens. Employer sanctions bills met staunch resistance, however, from southwestern growers and various business groups opposed to new regulation as well as Latino and civil rights groups concerned that sanctions would lead employers to discriminate against anyone who looked or sounded foreign. An effort by the Carter White House to enact a compromise reform package in 1977 drew fire from all sides and ultimately died.

As efforts to address illegal immigration became mired in rancorous debate in the late 1970s, Congress created a Select Commission on Immigration and Refugee Policy to broadly review U.S. immigration policy. Its 1982 report endorsed large-scale legal immigration, highlighting the social benefits of family reunification, the economic value of immigrant laborers and taxpayers, and the diplomatic and moral imperatives of admitting refugees. It also concluded that illegal immigration had an adverse affect on American society and recommended a reform package of employer sanctions,

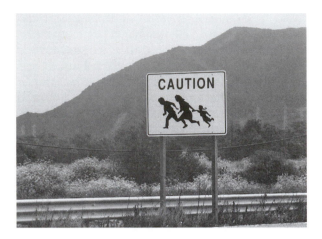

Signs alert drivers in areas of Southern California where illegal immigrants have tried to cross multilane freeways to evade border patrols. (James Steidl/Shutterstock)

enhanced Border Patrol resources, and a legalization program for most of the undocumented population already living in the country. After protracted legislative wrangling, Congress finally took action to curb illegal immigration with enactment of the Immigration Reform and Control Act of 1986 (IRCA). The new law was a compromise package of watered-down employer sanctions, legalization for undocumented aliens living in the country since 1982, and a new Seasonal Agricultural Worker Program to appease growers. The measure proved highly successful in granting legal status to nearly 3 million undocumented aliens, but employer sanctions proved to be a "toothless tiger."

By the late 1980s, it was clear to national policy makers that the IRCA had done virtually nothing to discourage illegal immigration. But legislators were eager to shift their attention to the politically painless task of expanding legal immigration. A welter of advocacy groups clamored for specific expansions in legal immigration opportunities. A "family coalition" of Asian, Latino, and other ethnic and human rights groups won an increase in the number of visas available for family reunification. A "business coalition" secured new preferences and visa allocations for employer-sponsored and skills-based immigration. At the end of the day, the Immigration Act of 1990 unified cosmopolitans and free market expansionists behind a 40 percent increase in annual visa allocations that benefited both family-based and employment-based immigration.

During the early 1990s, a grassroots movement in California mobilized against illegal immigration by advancing a measure, Proposition 187, that was designed to deny unauthorized migrants and their children welfare benefits, health care, and public education. Republican governor Pete Wilson and the state Republican organization threw their support behind the measure during the 1994 campaign, transforming it into a partisan issue. Proposition 187 carried the state with 59 percent of the vote. For the first time since 1952, Republicans gained control of both houses of Congress in 1994. New immigration subcommittee leadership and a special task force on immigration reform, chaired by California Republican Elton Gallegly, called for restrictive policy challenges. Their agenda included new crackdowns on criminal aliens and illegal immigration, denial of welfare benefits to immigrants, and new limits on legal admissions. The first two of these goals were secured in 1996 with passage of the Illegal Immigration Reform and Immigrant Responsibility Act (IIRIRA) and the Personal Responsibility and Work Opportunity Act (PRWOA). Efforts to reduce legal immigration were defeated in the Senate by a cross-party alliance of cosmopolitans and free market expansionists.

In 1995 several prominent Republican congressional leaders expressed optimism behind closed doors that the immigration issue would cost Democrats blue-collar votes. At the start of the 1996 election, Pete Wilson made immigration control the defining issue of his short-lived presidential campaign; Pat Buchanan assailed third world immigration as a source of economic and cultural insecurity at home; and Bob Dole, the eventual Republican standard-bearer, associated himself with the stringent immigrant measures then working their way through Congress. The 1996 Republican platform pledged support for national legislation barring children of undocumented aliens from public schools.

Yet the results of the 1996 election left little doubt about two crucial developments: immigrants comprised the nation's fastest growing voting bloc and Democrats were the immediate beneficiaries of their unanticipated electoral clout. Naturalization rates soared after 1995, as record numbers of aliens became citizens. More than 1 million people became naturalized in 1996 alone. At the same time as unprecedented numbers of aliens petitioned for naturalization in the mid-1990s, President Clinton instructed the INS to implement the so-called Citizenship USA initiative. In the words of the agency, the initiative "was designed to streamline the naturalization process and greatly increase naturalizations during 1996." Voter registrations among Latinos grew by 1.3 million, or 28.7 percent, between 1992 and 1996; the percentage of Latinos on the voter rolls rose from 59 percent of those eligible in 1992 to 65 percent in 1996. The Latino Democratic vote increased from 60 percent in the 1992 presidential election to 72 percent in 1996. Asian voters, a smaller yet important swing bloc, increased their support for the Democratic ticket in the same years from 29 to 43 percent. Dole became the first Republican presidential candidate to lose Florida since Gerald Ford in 1976.

In the 2000 election, Republican national and state organizations drew up plans to attract new Asian and Latino voters. Texas governor George W. Bush was hailed by party leaders as the ideal candidate to court new immigrant voters, and he reminded Latinos throughout the campaign that early on he had "rejected the spirit of Prop 187," opposed "English-only" proposals, and refused "to bash immigrants" when it was popular. Once in the White House, Bush created a special task force, led by Secretary of State Colin Powell, to address illegal immigration anew. These efforts were preempted by the terrorist attacks of September 11, which created a new sense of urgency about the security risks posed by newcomers and porous borders. Soon after the attacks, the Justice Department prescribed special registration requirements for male noncitizens aged 14 years or older from Arab and Muslim countries. The USA Patriot Act of 2001 eased deportations and restricted admission for those with potential ties to terrorist organizations or those who may have the intention of committing a terrorist act. Bush's efforts to relaunch comprehensive immigration reform in his second term, including a guest worker program, earned legalization, employer sanctions, and strengthened border enforcement—went nowhere. While the proposal was assailed by labor leaders and immigrant advocacy groups, the harshest attacks came from fellow conservatives both in Washington and at the grassroots who saw undocumented aliens as threats to national sovereignty, security, and identity.

In the winter of 2005, a punitive bill focused on border enforcement narrowly passed the Republican-controlled House of Representatives. It proposed for the first time to make illegal presence in the United States a felony, and made it a crime for any persons or organizations to lend support to undocumented immigrants. The bill was also a direct attack on day laborer centers. From March through May 2006, demonstrations against the bill by largely Latino immigrants and their supporters, unprecedented in number and size, took place in cities and towns across the United States. These nationwide rallies, protests, and boycotts drew negative reactions from most Americans: just 24 percent had a favorable view of people who marched and protested for immigrant rights in major cities while 52 percent expressed unfavorable opinions. Overall, however, public opinion remained open to varied policy solutions: majorities favored legal status and earned citizenship for undocumented immigrants, stricter employer penalties, and tougher enforcement.

In the spring and summer of 2007, the Bush administration and a bipartisan Senate coalition led by Edward Kennedy negotiated "a grand bargain" that included significant new funding for border security and other interior enforcement measures. It imposed criminal penalties for illegal entry, which had previously been a misdemeanor offense, and proposed to replace the current family and employment–based admissions system with a "merit-based" system. The bill provided a new Z visa for undocumented immigrants that covered "a principal or employed alien, the spouse or elderly parent of that alien, and the minor children of that alien" currently living in the United States. The visa provided they pay fees and penalties that could total as much as $8,000 and a "touchback provision" requiring the leader of the household to return home before applying for legal permanent residency status. The bill also contained a temporary Y worker program that would allow about 200,000 workers to be admitted for a two-year period that could be renewed twice, as long as the worker spent a period of one year outside of the United States between each admission.

The compromise Senate immigration plan was subject to intense media scrutiny and commentary, and the public response ranged from hostile to tepid. Many members of Congress were deluged with angry phone calls, emails, and letters from constituents and other activists. Surveys indicated that most Republicans, Democrats, and Independents opposed the measure, with only 23 percent in favor. Significantly, most Americans opposed the initiative not because they opposed "amnesty" or other proposals for legalizing millions of undocumented immigrants in the country (roughly two-thirds supported earned citizenship options over deportation), but rather because they had little trust that it would provide genuine border security. More than 80 percent in surveys said that they did not believe that the Bush-Senate compromise bill would reduce illegal immigration or enhance border control. Ultimately, the forces arrayed against this last-ditch reform effort were overwhelming, from the grassroots to the halls of Congress. The political minefield of immigration reform was shelved until after the 2008 election.

In the early twentieth century, the United States was in the midst of a "fourth wave" of immigration unprecedented in terms of its extraordinarily diverse origins and the dominance of newcomers from Latin America, the Caribbean, and Asia. Wealthy democracies all face thorny policy challenges when they try to stimulate or restrict the flow of people across their borders. For Americans, immigration policy has long stirred ambivalence and political conflicts that defy the standard liberal-conservative divide, inspire battles among fellow partisans, and produce strange and fleeting bedfellows. The laissez-faire, restrictive, and expansive policies that have emerged from these political struggles over the course of U.S. history have had profound implications for the character and development of the nation.

See also anticommunism; Asian immigrants and politics; citizenship; European immigrants and politics; Latinos and politics; nativism.

FURTHER READING

Calavita, Kitty. *Inside the State: The Bracero Program, Immigration and the I.N.S.* New York: Routledge, 1992.

Daniels, Roger. *Coming to America: A History of Immigration and Ethnicity in American Life.* New York: Harper Perennial, 2002.

Gutierrez, David. *Walls and Mirrors: Mexican Americans, Mexican Immigrants, and the Politics of Ethnicity.* Berkeley: University of California Press, 1985.

Higham, John. *Strangers in the Land: Patterns of American Nativism, 1860–1925.* New Brunswick, NJ: Rutgers University Press, 2002.

Motomura, Hiroshi. *Americans in Waiting: The Lost Story of Immigration and Citizenship in the United States.* New York: Oxford University Press, 2007.

Reimers, David. *Still the Golden Door: The Third World Comes to America.* New York: Columbia University Press, 1985.

Tichenor, Daniel. *Dividing Lines: The Politics of Immigration Control in America.* Princeton, NJ: Princeton University Press, 2002.

Zolberg, Aristide. *A Nation by Design: Immigration Policy in the Fashioning of America.* Cambridge, MA: Harvard University Press, 2006.

DANIEL J. TICHENOR

impeachment

Impeachment is one of the most potent and sharply debated powers of Congress. It is formidable because it is the principal, if not only, means through which Congress may remove presidents, Supreme Court justices, and certain other high-ranking federal officials for misconduct. While the popular understanding of this power has largely been shaped by the notable impeachment efforts against Presidents Andrew Johnson, Richard Nixon, and Bill Clinton and Associate Justice Samuel Chase, it is not possible to understand impeachment generally, much less its high-profile deployments, without analyzing the distinctive features of its application throughout U.S. history.

Impeachment Clauses: Text and Original Meaning

The text and original meaning of the Constitution illuminate the distinctive features of the federal impeachment process. In designing it, the founders distinguished the Constitution's federal impeachment process from that which had been in existence in Britain and the colonies. Whereas the king was not subject to impeachment or removal, Article II, section IV of the Constitution explicitly makes the president, among others, subject to the impeachment process. Article II expressly narrows the range of people subject to impeachment from what it had been in England, where any citizen (other than a member of the royal family) could be impeached. This article explicitly restricts impeachment to "[t]he President, Vice-President and all civil officers of the United States."

Article II further narrows the range of impeachable offenses to "Treason, Bribery, or other high Crimes or Misdemeanors." Although the framers of the Constitution discussed "high Crimes or Misdemeanors" only in abstract terms as referring to political crimes or "great offenses" or "breaches of the public trust," they hoped to restrict the scope of impeachable offenses to deviate from the parliamentary practice, which recognized no limit to the grounds for which people could be removed from office.

Conviction became more difficult than it had been in Great Britain, where the House of Lords could convict with a bare majority. In contrast, the founders divided the impeachment authority between the House and the Senate; gave the House the "sole power to impeach," which required majority approval; and required at least two-thirds concurrence of the Senate for conviction and removal. The Senate was vested with trial authority, because the founders believed that senators would be better educated and more virtuous, well suited to making difficult judgments about procedures and removal, and resistant to majoritarian pressures than members of the House of Representatives.

Whereas the British Parliament could impose any punishment upon conviction, including death, Article I of the Constitution restricts the Senate's power in impeachment trials "to removal from Office, and disqualification to hold and enjoy any Office of honor, Trust, or Profit under the United States." Article II expressly forbids the president from pardoning an individual for the offenses committed, while the king could have pardoned any person convicted in an impeachment trial. In contrast to Great Britain, where impeachment was understood to be a criminal proceeding, Article I provides that "the Party convicted [in an impeachment trial] shall nevertheless be liable and subject to Indictment, Trial, Judgment and Punishment, according to law." Article III explicitly grants federal judges the special tenure of serving "during good Behavior." The founders required the chief justice to preside over presidential impeachment trials to avoid a potential conflict of interest for the vice president, who usually presided over the Senate, in presiding over the trial of the one person standing between him and the presidency. The Constitution further requires senators to be "on oath or affirmation" when sitting in presidential impeachment trials. These requirements underscore the solemnity of such proceedings.

Impeachment Practice

The founders left the scope of the federal impeachment power to be worked out by Congress over time. Since ratification, the House of Representatives has formally impeached 16 officials, including one Supreme Court justice (Samuel Chase) and two presidents (Andrew Johnson and Bill Clinton). President Richard Nixon resigned shortly after the House Judiciary Committee approved three impeachment articles against him. In the course of these proceedings and other occasions on which the House has conducted or considered initiating impeachment inquiries, Congress has faced several significant constitutional questions. Historical patterns are important because they illuminate Congress's deliberate judgments on the major constitutional questions arising

in impeachment proceedings. Indeed, the impeachment judgments of Congress are effectively final, because they are not subject to judicial review—as held by the Supreme Court unanimously in *Walter Nixon v. United States* (1993)—or presidential veto. The realization that they have the final word on impeachment matters encourages most if not all members of Congress to make impeachment judgments that will withstand the scrutiny of history.

The first noteworthy pattern in Congress's impeachment practices clarifies the meaning of "other high Crimes and Misdemeanors" as the basis for removal. Most scholars believe that this language refers to "political crimes" or abuses of power or injuries to the Republic. While they agree that not all indictable crimes are "political crimes" and vice versa, they disagree over how to identify which breaches of the public trust ought to qualify as grounds for removing high-ranking officials from office.

It is suggestive that, of the 16 men whom the House formally impeached, only five were impeached primarily or solely for indictable crimes, and one of the five (Alcee Hastings) had been formally acquitted of bribery prior to his impeachment and removal for that crime and for perjury. The House's impeachment articles against the other 11 included misconduct for which anyone could be criminally punished. Four of the seven impeached officials convicted by the Senate were charged with nonindictable offenses. The remaining three (Harry Claiborne, Alcee Hastings, and Walter Nixon) were charged with indictable crimes. Both Claiborne and Nixon had been indicted, convicted in federal court, and exhausted their criminal appeals prior to their impeachment proceedings.

A second significant pattern in historical practices clarifies the related questions of whether impeachment is the exclusive means for removing judges and justices and whether Article III conditions judicial tenure on "good Behavior" and therefore allows judges or justices to be removed not only for "Treason, Bribery, or other high Crimes and Misdemeanors" but also for any misbehavior, including bad or erroneous decisions. A minority of scholars and members of Congress have argued that the "good Behavior" clause may also establish an alternative mechanism to impeachment for disciplining judges. But most scholars and members of Congress have maintained that a natural inference from the structure of the Constitution, backed by original meaning, is that the impeachment process is the exclusive means by which

Congress may remove judges or justices. The "good Behavior" clause vests Article III judges with life tenure and thus protection from political retaliation for their judicial decisions, and impeaching and removing justices and judges for mistaken decisions would completely undermine their judicial independence.

The principle of judicial independence was vindicated in the only impeachment of a Supreme Court justice to date. In 1804, the House, controlled by Democrat-Republicans, impeached Associate Justice Samuel Chase, a fiercely partisan Federalist, based on claims that he had rendered flagrantly partisan rulings in the trials of two Republicans charged with violating the Federalist-backed Alien and Sedition Acts. A bare majority vote in the Senate to convict Chase fell short of the required two-thirds for conviction and removal. Much later, Chief Justice William Rehnquist construed Chase's acquittal as a seminal decision upholding the "complete independence of federal judges from removal because of their judicial decisions."

Subsequently, impeachment resolutions have been introduced in the House against two other Supreme Court justices: Chief Justice Earl Warren and Associate Justice William O. Douglas. In quickly dismissing inquiries against both justices, the House followed the principle initially laid down by Chase's acquittal. On another occasion, President Nixon's attorney general John Mitchell and other White House aides successfully managed in 1969 to force Justice Abe Fortas to resign from the Supreme Court rather than face public embarrassment and possible impeachment because of a contract into which he briefly entered after joining the Court to provide legal counsel to a former client who had been subsequently convicted for securities fraud.

A third pattern in past impeachment practices suggests that the paradigmatic case for impeachment and removal has three elements: (1) a bad act such as serious abuse of power, (2) a bad or malicious intent, and (3) a link between the official's misconduct and his official duties. Though Richard Nixon was not formally impeached, convicted, and removed from office, scholars agree that all these elements were evident in the misconduct charged against him by the House Judiciary Committee—using the powers of his office to obstruct investigations into his involvement in authorizing or covering up a burglary of the Democratic National Committee headquarters; ordering the FBI and IRS to harass his political enemies; and refusing to comply with a legislative subpoena requesting taped White House conversations, which the Supreme Court had unanimously ordered him to turn over to a special prosecutor. In contrast, many commentators and several senators explained President Clinton's acquittal in 1998 on the absence of one or more of these three elements. Most historians also agree that in acquitting President Andrew Johnson on charges he had abused his powers by not complying with a federal

This illustration of Andrew Jackson's impeachment trial appeared in *Harper's Weekly*, April 11, 1868. (Theodore R. Davis/ Library of Congress)

law requiring him to get Senate approval before firing a cabinet member whom it had confirmed, the Senate had determined that Johnson's misconduct was merely a policy difference with Congress for which removal was inappropriate.

A fourth pattern of impeachment practices reinforces the inference, derived from the specific requirement of at least two-thirds concurrence of the Senate for removal, that removal is only possible with widespread bipartisan support in the Senate. A supermajority is difficult to achieve in the Senate, particularly when the stakes are high, as they were in the impeachment trials of Presidents Johnson and Clinton and Justice Chase. Statistics bear this out, given that most people impeached by the House have been acquitted by the Senate (the 16 House impeachments have resulted in only seven Senate convictions). Indeed, the uniform opposition of all 45 Senate Democrats to President Clinton's conviction for perjury and obstruction of justice highlights the enormous difficulty of securing a conviction in a presidential impeachment trial as long as the senators from the president's party unanimously, or largely, support him. Since a political party rarely controls more than two-thirds of the Senate, presidential removal is only possible if the misconduct is sufficiently compelling to draw support for conviction from senators from both parties.

Fifth, historical practices supplement other sources of constitutional meaning to support the constitutionality of censure as an alternative to impeachment. For instance, the provision that "Judgment in Cases of Impeachment shall not extend further than to" removal from office or disqualification suggests that Congress may take any action against impeachable officials falling short of either of these sanctions, as seems to be the case with censure. Indeed, the House passed resolutions criticizing John Tyler, James Polk, James Buchanan, and several other high-ranking officials, while the Senate passed two resolutions critical of officials other than the president in the nineteenth century and censured Andrew Jackson for firing his treasury secretary for refusing to take actions undermining the national bank. While the Senate later expunged its censure of Jackson, neither the censure nor its subsequent expunging is binding authority on whether senators today may censure impeachable officials.

The historical records further suggest that impeachment is a relatively ineffective check against a popular president's misconduct, particularly in the age of the 24-hour news cycle. If the enormous ramifications of removing a president dissuaded a hostile Senate from doing so with the hugely unpopular Andrew Johnson, as was the case, it should not be surprising that a later Senate would hesitate before removing a popular one who used the bully pulpit of the presidency to defend himself, as was the case with Bill Clinton. The congressional investigation into Watergate took more than two years before the discovery of the "smoking gun"—taped White House conversations—that led to Nixon's resignation. The Clinton impeachment proceedings took roughly six months, among the shortest in history. Yet, throughout the constant media coverage of the proceedings, Clinton's popularity increased while the popularity of, and support for, the Republican majority in the House and Senate seeking his ouster declined.

Indeed, Clinton's case raises the issue of how serious the misconduct of a popular president must be to convince a majority of Americans or a supermajority in the Senate to support his ouster from office. Future members of Congress could hesitate before engaging in a prolonged investigation of a president's misconduct for fear of alienating the public. They might further believe that the failure of the House to do any independent fact-finding prior to impeaching Clinton (one of only three instances when the House failed to do so) was a mistake that cost the House a valuable opportunity to cultivate the public's confidence in its nonpartisan intent. Consequently, what Clinton's acquittal may show is that, in the future, impeachment will be effective only in the rare circumstances in which the wrongdoing is so severe (and so clearly proven) as to galvanize the public and demand the president's ouster or resignation.

A seventh significant pattern in impeachment practices concerns the nonreviewable decisions by the House and Senate on critical procedural issues. In its proceedings against President Clinton, the House held a final vote on the impeachment articles in a lame-duck session, to forego adopting a uniform standard for defining the impeachability of certain misconduct, and not to call witnesses or otherwise engage in independent fact-finding. In Clinton's impeachment trial, senators resolved that each could decide for himself or herself on the applicability of the Fifth Amendment due process clause, burden of proof, rules of evidence, and the propriety of closed-door meetings. The senators also allowed three colleagues to vote on Clinton's removal even though they had voted on his impeachment in the House before being elected to the Senate.

A final set of historical practices is the two instances in which the chief justice presided over presidential impeachment trials. In 1867 the House impeached President Andrew Johnson for illegally obstructing Reconstruction and the Tenure of Office Act, which required Senate approval prior to dismissal by the president of any officials whom he had nominated and the Senate had confirmed. Chief Justice Salmon Chase declared, at the outset, that "the Constitution has charged the Chief Justice with an important function in the [impeachment] trial . . . of the President." Chase helped shape the rules adopted by the Senate to govern the president's impeachment trial, which continue to this day and which include one that empowered him to rule initially on every procedural issue, subject to override by a majority of the Senate. Subsequently, the Senate overrode Chase's evidentiary rulings 17 times. But most of his procedural rulings were upheld by the Senate even though they usually favored Johnson's defense.

In 1999 Chief Justice Rehnquist presided over President Clinton's trial. Whereas many senators had questioned Chief Justice Chase's impartiality (and suspected he wanted to use the proceedings to further his presidential ambitions), Rehnquist commanded the respect of all senators, and there were no Senate challenges to or overrides of any of his procedural rulings.

Since President Clinton's acquittal, the House has not initiated any impeachment proceedings. Some members of Congress and scholars insist justices may be impeached and removed for their decisions. And some insisted that President George W. Bush and Vice President Dick Cheney should have been impeached and removed for their aggressive actions in the wake of the terrorist attacks against the United States on September 11, 2001. But Congress does not appear eager to use its impeachment power. Instead, it seems resigned to employ it, as many founders expected, only as a last resort to deal with severe presidential and judicial misconduct.

See also House of Representatives; Senate; Supreme Court.

FURTHER READING

Berger, Raoul. *Impeachment: The Constitutional Problems.* Cambridge, MA: Harvard University Press, 1973.

Black, Charles L. *Impeachment: A Handbook.* Revised ed. New Haven, CT: Yale University Press, 1998.

Gerhardt, Michael J. *The Federal Impeachment Process: A Constitutional and Historical Analysis.* 2nd ed. Chicago: University of Chicago Press, 2000.

Hoffer, Peter Charles, and N.E.H. Hull. *Impeachment in America, 1635–1801.* New Haven, CT: Yale University Press, 1984.

Rehnquist, William H. *Grand Inquests: The Impeachment Trials of Justice Samuel Chase and President Andrew Johnson.* New York: William Morrow, 1992.

MICHAEL GERHARDT

inaugural addresses of U.S. presidents

The Constitution mandates that a new president of the United States utter only a single sentence upon taking office. Article II, Section I, states: "Before he enter on the Execution of his Office, he shall take the following Oath or Affirmation: 'I do solemnly swear (or affirm) that I will faithfully execute the Office of President of the United States, and will to the best of my Ability, preserve, protect, and defend the Constitution of the United States.'"

History

Traditionally, however, the new chief executive has delivered a speech at the ceremony, which has come to be known as the inaugural address. As Martin Van Buren declared in his own contribution to the genre in 1837, "The practice of all my predecessors imposes on me an obligation I cheerfully fulfill—to accompany the first and solemn act of my public trust with an avowal of the principles that will guide me." In total, 37 presidents have delivered 55 inaugural addresses. Five presidents—John Tyler, Millard Fillmore, Andrew Johnson, Chester A. Arthur, and Gerald R. Ford—never delivered an inaugural address. All these men were vice presidents who succeeded in the midst of a presidential term, the first four due to death of the preceding president, the last due to the resignation of Richard M. Nixon, and none gained election in his own right.

The Twentieth Amendment to the Constitution, ratified in 1933, set the date and time of each inauguration for noon on the January 20 following the presidential election. To that point, inaugurations usually had been held on March 4, the date originally set by the Constitution. Several times, when either of these dates fell on a Sunday, the president (such as Zachary Taylor) put off the inauguration until the following Monday or (for example, Rutherford B. Hayes) took the oath of office privately before delivering an address at a larger celebration the next day.

Only the first inauguration ceremony, that of George Washington in 1789, was held on a different date. Washington was inaugurated on April 30, at a ceremony that set several precedents—most notably, that of giving an address immediately following the oath of office ceremony. Additionally, Washington's first inauguration was held outdoors, before the public and Congress assembled, though this tradition was not resumed until 1817, when James Monroe was inaugurated in front of the Old Brick Capitol at 1st and A Streets, NW, in Washington, D.C. Between Monroe's administration and Ronald Reagan's first inauguration in 1981, virtually all inaugurations took place on the East Portico of the Capitol. Reagan, while continuing to uphold Washington's decision to be inaugurated in public, chose to move the event to the west side of the Capitol, overlooking the Mall, and his successors have done so as well. Washington also added the phrase "So help me God" to the end of the oath of office, a precedent most presidents, and every one since Franklin Roosevelt in his 1933 inauguration, have followed.

George Washington, Father of the Inaugural Address

Several of these traditions—the desire for a public ceremony, the acknowledgment of divine providence in both word and action—reflect another, thematic precedent George Washington set, one powerful enough that his successors have strived to match it. This was Washington's sense of the inaugural address as a uniquely republican ritual, one primarily concerned with a particular understanding of civic virtue and participatory government. The initial draft of Washington's first inaugural was 73 pages long; it included an extensive discussion of the various topics Washington felt were important to lay before the people of the nation. He explained the various economic problems the American Revolution left before the new nation, the failures that the weakness of the Articles of Confederation had caused, and the solutions that the new Constitution might offer. But the education he wished to impress upon his listeners was not merely one of policy or law; he also stressed the importance of selfless acceptance of public duty, the importance of morality and civic virtue, and the dangers of monarchy. Along these lines, he promised Americans that it was not ambition for himself or his family that drew him to office: "I have no child for whom I could wish to make provision—no family to build in greatness upon my country's ruins."

The draft, however, was revised extensively with the help of James Madison, and while much of the policy detail was jettisoned, the key ideas Washington wished to convey remained. Beginning with an acknowledgment that the office was given him by the will of the people, he laid out a plea for public virtue, lauded the high merits of republican government, and emphasized the role of providential favor in the preservation of American liberties. These themes dominated the final version of the address. In the most famous passage, Washington stressed that "the preservation of the sacred fire of liberty and the destiny of the republican model of government are justly considered, perhaps, as deeply, as finally, staked on the experiment entrusted to the hands of the American people." He closed by again invoking the favor of God, tying it deeply to the functioning of American government; praying that "His divine blessing may be equally conspicuous in the enlarged views, the temperate consultations, and the wise measures on which the success of this Government must depend." These lines were the heart of Washington's address and firmly established the inaugural address as a central form of American political discourse. Washington understood the address not as a policy talk but instead as an opportunity for a president to contribute to and shape the nation's political culture.

The Inauguration as Republican Ritual: Civic Religion

Reflecting the transformations between Washington's first and his final draft, the most memorable inaugural addresses have focused less upon particular policy proposals and instead meditate upon and celebrate larger themes of American ideology. They often invoke civic duty, American exceptionalism, or the nation's presumed unique relationship with God. Indeed, Washington taught Americans to expect a pattern from the remarks of their new presidents—a confession of humility, of solidarity with "my fellow Americans"; a denial of ambition; a confirmation of the exceptional virtue of the American people and their form of government; and genuflection to a generic God. Inaugural addresses that have resonated most deeply with the American people captured these themes in memorable ways, binding their abstractions to the particularities of individual time and place, and using promises to confront new problems. It is no coincidence that the most remembered and cited addresses came at times of crisis, when presidential rhetoric reshaped old ideas and symbols in new and effective ways to cope with the challenges of new situations.

Some of the most powerful of these symbols have been religious ones. Washington, for example, not only added "So help me God" to the end of the presidential oath but also began the tradition of taking the oath while resting one hand on a Bible, investing the inauguration ceremony with a sort of civic Christianity, understood to be intimately related to the character of the nation. Every president since, except for John Quincy Adams, who swore with a hand on a volume of federal law, has followed this tradition. More recently, some presidents have opened the Bible to a particular passage, reflecting themes they desired to address not only in their inauguration but also in the presidency itself. In 1905 the activist Theodore Roosevelt placed his hand on James 1:22: "Be ye doers of the word, and not hearers only," while Franklin Roosevelt, father of the New Deal, selected 1 Corinthians 13:13 in 1933: "And now abideth faith, hope, charity, these three; but the greatest of these is charity." Richard Nixon, famed for his interest in and skill at foreign policy, opened the Bible at his first inauguration in 1969 to Isaiah 2:4: "And he shall judge among the nations, and shall rebuke many people: and they shall beat their swords into plowshares, and their spears into pruning hooks: nation shall not lift up sword against nation, neither shall they learn war any more."

But the importance of religion in inaugural rhetoric has frequently gone beyond merely its mute presence on the page. While only three inaugural addresses used the words "Christian" or "Christianity" (William Henry Harrison's 1841 address, James Buchanan's 1857 plea for "a spirit of Christian benevolence," and Lincoln's 1861 call for "intelligence, patriotism, Christianity") and none have mentioned Jesus, appeals for divine guidance and aid appear in virtually every address. Even the deist Thomas Jefferson felt compelled to follow Washington's example, and called upon the "Infinite Power" to give "favorable issue for your peace and prosperity." Jimmy Carter began his own address by reciting the verse the Bible he swore upon was open to: Micah 6:8, "What does the Lord require of thee, but to do justly, and to love mercy, and to walk humbly with thy God."

Some historians have claimed that the Bible at Abraham Lincoln's second inaugural was open to Revelation 16:7: "And I heard another out of the altar say, Even so, Lord God Almighty, true and righteous are thy judgments." Though Chief Justice Salmon Chase later marked a passage from Isaiah as the page Lincoln kissed, that Lincoln paraphrased the verse from Revelation in his address (telling the nation that to the extent the suffering of the Civil War was born of slavery, then, "the judgments of the Lord are true and righteous altogether") demonstrates how presidents have used the symbolic power of religion to lend weight and legitimacy to their visions of the nation.

Although the humility that Lincoln drew from the Bible may be the most profound use of that text in an inaugural address, he is far from the only president to paraphrase its verses or borrow its imagery. In 1965 Lyndon Johnson echoed King Solomon's cry to God for "wisdom and knowledge"; in 1933 Franklin Roosevelt assailed wealthy "money changers," reminiscent of those expelled from the temple by Christ; in 2005 George W. Bush borrowed from the Book of Job when he spoke of a voice in the whirlwind. Most dramatically, perhaps, in 1989 his father George H. W. Bush began his own inaugural address with a prayer.

The Inauguration as Republican Ritual: Virtuous Self-Government

Next to this strong sense of divine providence and purpose for the nation, presidents have used inaugural addresses to appeal to the virtuous ideals associated with the democratic principles of American self-government. Washington, for example, was reluctant to hold another public ceremony at his second inaugural, grieved by the political infighting of his cabinet secretaries Thomas Jefferson and Alexander Hamilton. He ultimately chose to appear in public again and to use his inauguration as a symbol of civic unity. His second address was the shortest in inaugural history, only 135 words, and the second paragraph contained a biting but subtle message: Washington vowed that if his administration "in any instance violated willingly or knowingly the injunction" in his oath of office, he, personally, would "be subject to the upbraiding of all who are now witnesses." Thus did Washington use his address to throw the considerable weight of his personal honor behind the political harmony that he deemed so essential and remind the nation of the public accountability of his government.

The persistent strength of this theme was revealed when Jefferson famously sought to heal political divisions, declaring, "We are all Republicans, we are all Federalists" in his 1801 inaugural address. It is questionable whether this plea was sincere, but the symbolic importance of the ideal was paramount. Lincoln faced perhaps the greatest threat to this ideal of unity; in his 1861 inauguration, he pleaded with the intransigent South: "We are not enemies, but friends. We must not be enemies," and made a powerful argument for the permanence of the Union, ascribing an almost mystical democratic authority to the higher will of the American people.

Unity is not the only virtue associated with democracy, however. Presidents also have celebrated the participation of citizens in the nation's public life. Most memorable in this regard was John F. Kennedy's 1961 inaugural address, in which he challenged the American people: "Ask not what your country can do for you; ask what you can do for your country," reminding them, "In your hands, fellow citizens, more than in mine, will rest the final success or failure of our course." Similarly, Franklin Roosevelt sought to mobilize a dispirited nation in 1933, maintaining, "Nor need we shrink from honestly facing conditions in our country today. This great nation will endure as it has endured, will revive and will prosper. So, first of all, let me assert my firm belief that the only thing we have to fear is fear itself." Later, he noted that "our common difficulties . . . concern, thank God, only material things," avowing a continued confidence in American ability. Through clever rhetoric, FDR rallied the nation by repeatedly referring to "our task" and "our problems," using "we" to the exclusion of "I" when discussing the plans of his administration, and, finally, reminding Americans that "our true destiny is not to be ministered unto but to minister. . . ." Jimmy Carter, in a rare departure, acknowledged that "even our great nation has recognized limits"—a concession that later came to haunt his administration—but then claimed, "Within us, the people of the United States, there is evident a serious and purposeful rekindling of confidence."

While Washington's second inaugural address was the shortest in inaugural history, the longest echoed similar themes of national character. The two hours it took William Henry Harrison to read his 8,445 words in March 1841 bored his audience—and the time spent in the bitter Washington weather of Inauguration Day was thought to have contributed to the pneumonia that killed him only a month later. But Harrison, at great length, expounded upon Washington's celebration of republicanism, drawing vivid and numerous comparisons between Greek liberty and Roman law and their inheritance in the democratic republic of the United States.

While few contemporary presidents make historical references as particular as Harrison did, presidential enthusiasm for celebrating American "liberty" has never ceased. Ronald Reagan fused this passion with Frank-lin Roosevelt's strong sense of confidence, arguing at his first inaugural that the United States had become powerful and prosperous because "freedom and the dignity of the individual have been more available and assured here than in any other place on earth." For Reagan, "no weapon in the arsenals of the world is so formidable as the will and moral courage of free men and women." In his second inaugural, he claimed that "America must remain freedom's staunchest friend, for freedom is our best ally. And it is the world's only hope. . . ." Reagan linked the domestic characteristics of the United States to the sort of providential destiny that Lincoln and Washington had seen.

As time has passed, presidents have increasingly echoed the words of their predecessors. Both George H. W. Bush and his successor, Bill Clinton, quoted George Washington by name in their inaugural addresses; Clinton also quoted Thomas Jefferson and Franklin Roosevelt. Clinton's first address was a model, if not of uniqueness, then of the sentiments that Americans expect of an inaugural. Clinton praised his predecessor, acknowledged the will of the people, declared faith in the American spirit, and called upon the nation to "revitalize democracy." He cited scripture and summoned God's aid, and finally, promised to lead the nation into the twenty-first century. His address demonstrated that the rhetorical tools of two centuries remained the same.

See also political culture; presidency.

FURTHER READING

Boller, Paul F. *Presidential Inaugurations*. New York: Harcourt, 2001.

Hunt, John Gabriel, ed. *The Inaugural Addresses of the Presidents*. New York: Random House, 1997.

Lomask, Milton. *"I Do Solemnly Swear": The Story of the Presidential Inauguration*. New York: Ariel Books, 1966.

MATTHEW BOWMAN

interest groups

The U.S. Constitution designated voting as the primary link between citizens and government, yet it also protected the politically salient rights of free speech, a free press, free assembly, and the right to petition. This framework recognized a broad arena of political activity outside of formal governmental institutions—one that would be funneled through individual voting in periodic elections to select legislators and presidential electors. Yet even before the Constitution was adopted, commentators were well aware that citizens' political activity with formal government was not likely to be limited to the casting of ballots. In Federalist Paper number 10, James Madison famously warned of the dangers of faction, by which he meant "a number of citizens, whether amounting to a majority or minority of the whole, who are united and actuated by some common impulse of passion, or of interest, adverse to the rights of other citizens, or to the permanent and aggregate interest of the community."

The Problem of Faction

Faction was not defined by the character of the group but by the relationship of its interest or passion to the rights of others or to the public good. Under Madison's formulation, a majority could constitute a faction and, therefore, protections against the tyranny of the majority were also protections against these large factions. Although one could not extinguish the causes of faction without extinguishing liberty itself, Madison argued that a system of representative government within a large republic offered the best protection from the dangers of faction, a protection that would be impossible in a pure democracy. Consequently, the lineage from Madison's "factions" to contemporary interest group politics is entwined with a succession of efforts by citizens, firms, and all varieties of organized interests to influence decisions made by representative institutions and executive agencies.

New Forms of Group Politics

The historical development of interest group politics may be traced by following each element of this threefold name: *politics* is modified by *group*, *group* by *interest*. By extension, *group politics* differ in some important way from other kinds of politics, just as *interest groups* are distinct from other sorts of social groups. The emergence of recognizably modern interest group politics required the mobilization of groups outside of electoral politics, the development of methods by which such groups could influence policy outcomes, and the legitimation of these interests as recognized elements of a political system that extended beyond the boundaries of the formal political institutions themselves. Although the presence of organized interests near to government has steadily expanded throughout American history, opinions differ over whether these groups support democracy by ex-

panding citizens' access to politics or undermine it by allowing representatives of narrow interests to control policy making.

For the first half century of the nation's existence, much political energy focused on the invention of "group politics." One important stream of developments gave rise to political parties; another produced the distinctive breed of "private organizations with public purposes" that are the ancestors of the modern nonprofit sector. Yet, as discussed by Alexis de Tocqueville, voluntary associations were particularly intriguing as a vehicle for "shadow government" and for the shaping and mobilization of political opinion. Tocqueville arrived in the United States in 1831, when such large-scale voluntary associations were a relatively novel phenomenon. Fueled by religious revivals, large-scale missionary movements had forged a new "confessional politics" in which individual sins were linked to the sins of the nation. Focused on moral issues from the protection of the Sabbath through temperance and, most consequentially, abolition, this fusing of religious revival to national policy created a powerful template for doing politics not only outside of formal institutions but also outside political parties. Even where the specifically religious impulse was muted, such popular movements made use of the protected freedoms of speech, press, petition, and assembly to mobilize popular support and bring pressure on elected representatives. These new forms of "group politics" remained controversial, exemplified in the 1830s and 1840s by congressional refusal to accept petitions in support of the abolition of slavery.

The People's Lobby

While the abolitionist movement itself eventually entered party politics, for the remainder of the nineteenth century, mobilized groups continued their efforts to influence the outcomes of formal governmental processes. Often, the most direct path led directly into electoral politics, so state and local campaigns saw periodic insurgencies by new parties that championed the concerns of labor, of farmers, of anti-Catholics, or of anti-Masons, along with many other causes. "Group politics" could become "third-party politics" with relative ease, but there was not yet a model for a stable, legitimate, nonelectoral alignment of extrapartisan groups with formal governmental institutions.

That model was elaborated at the turn of the twentieth century, in part by activists who were veterans of the failed third-party efforts of the 1870s and 1880s. While the Populist Party led another surge along the path from social movements to political parties, fusing with the Democratic Party in the elections of 1896, other organized groups explored different kinds of alignments with legislatures and government officials. Some of these efforts centered on influencing those who ran for office, notably by supporting the introduction of primary elections and then seeking to "pledge" candidates to support specific policies if elected. Incumbents were also subjected to new forms of accountability as labor and agrarian groups developed the technology of "roll call vote" scoring, a process that required a group to determine which issues were specifically in its interest and then to identify the precise vote that would provide the most meaningful evidence of a candidate's position. To accomplish this, labor unionists, clubwomen, and agrarian activists immersed themselves in the intricacies of parliamentary rules, recognizing that seemingly obscure procedural votes were often the most consequential ones. As pledges were extracted and votes tabulated, organized movements would then make use of speeches and publications to educate their members about which politicians were most worthy of support and which should be opposed.

This educational component of popular politics did not end with elections. As organized groups became more familiar with the process of policy making they also recognized the advantages of expertise that could be used in the context of legislative hearings or as support for drafting bills. The intensification of interest group activity is evident in the numbers of groups testifying in congressional hearings. According to Daniel Tichenor and Richard Harris, the number of interest groups and private corporations grew almost fourfold in the first decade of the 1900s, from roughly 800 to 3,000. Beyond the growth in numbers, the differences between corporation and interest group representatives was also striking: corporations tended to present narrow, local concerns while other groups were more attuned to broad policy issues. Even with the growing presence of trade associations representing industrywide concerns, various kinds of citizens groups and trade unions continued to account for roughly half of congressional appearances through 1917.

During the Progressive Era, a wide variety of groups developed new methods for influencing political outcomes, both through new provisions for primary elections and direct democracy (initiative, referendum, and recall), and by inserting themselves within legislative investigations and deliberations. The rise of this seem-

ingly new kind of "pressure politics" was linked to the declining role of political parties. This popular mode of policy making reached a zenith with the adoption of constitutional amendments establishing prohibition and enfranchising women. Yet for all these accomplishments, the legitimacy of these extrainstitutional interventions in political decision making was far from established.

The Problem of Legitimacy
Madison's original definition of the term *faction* turned on the issue of whether collective pursuit of interests or passions was "adverse to the rights of other citizens, or to the permanent and aggregate interest of the community." Even movement activists had hesitated in the face of this concern; in 1892, for example, the California State Grange explicitly rejected a proposal that the convention consider proposed amendments to the state constitution and that it inform the state's farmers of where their interests lay in these matters. Such matters were to be left to the consciences of individual voters who, at least according to republican theory, were to vote for "the best man" who would then make legislative decisions in light of the common good rather than in terms of the consequences for his own constituents. Organized groups were thus reluctant to move into pressure politics, particularly when they could not make encompassing moral claims grounded in moral virtue or national destiny. The efforts of individuals and companies to secure favorable legislative action were often enmeshed with the "old lobby" of the nineteenth century, which later commentators portrayed as a web of corruption and, at times, seduction. Not surprisingly, some legislatures responded by adopting policies to limit these extralegislative influences, often appealing to the *Trist v. Child* (1874) ruling in which the Supreme Court declined to enforce a contractual claim for a contingency fee for lobbying Congress for relief related to the Mexican-American War. By the late nineteenth century, some state legislatures began to adopt laws requiring lobbyists to register and regulating campaign contributions, indeed prohibiting such contributions from corporations in some cases.

By the early twentieth century, facts on the ground had outrun theory. Political scientists were staking a disciplinary claim to "group politics," arguing, as Arthur F. Bentley did, that "if a law is in question, we find that our statement of it in terms of the group of men it affects . . . we can state its actual value in the social process at the given time in terms of the groups of men for whose sake it is there: a group of politicians and a number of groups of voters holding the prominent places." Others distinguished the "new lobby" from the old, noting, as E. Pendleton Herring expressed it, the "Washington offices of the associations, societies, leagues, institutes, boards, and federations organized on a nationwide scale to-day for the great lobbies in the capital. By comparison the representatives of corporations, the patronage brokers, the 'wire-pullers,' the crows of old-style lobbyists pale in significance. The men with the power are these spokesmen of organized groups."

As business relationships with the federal government were increasingly mediated by industry associations, the lineages of group politics and the business lobby began to merge into what would come to be labeled *interest group politics*. With the intensification of the federal government's role in the economy, driven by both Depression-era regulatory politics and mobilization for World War II, these ties would grow still stronger. They inspired new labels such as "iron triangles" and President Dwight D. Eisenhower's "military-industrial complex" (which, in its first formulation, was the "military-industrial-congressional complex").

Yet, if political scientists had begun to normalize this development, these groups still drew considerable condemnation. Congressional efforts to regulate lobbyists repeatedly failed and their numbers continued to multiply to an estimated 6,000 by the late 1930s. This "small army," in the words of journalist Kenneth Crawford, was "busy in Washington burning the bridges between the voter and what he voted for." This contrast between interest groups that advanced selfish corporate interests and those that promoted public interests bedeviled the efforts of postwar political science to develop a general theory of interest group politics.

Following the Second World War, political scientists mounted repeated efforts to document both the population of organized interests and their implications for democratic politics. These studies addressed questions of which interests became organized and which remained latent, which techniques were used by organized groups to influence policy outcomes, and whether such efforts actually had political consequences. Particular attention focused on if and how the expansion of government led either to increases in the numbers of organized interests or changes in their character. Although the precise magnitude of these changes depended heavily on the sources and methods used by researchers—directories of groups headquartered in Washington, D.C., or records of congressional testimony—there was consensus that the numbers of organized groups were increasing. One analysis found that the total (listed) population of associations had increased from 5,843 in 1959 to 23,298 in 1995. Within this total, trade associations had accounted for 39 percent in 1959 but only 18 percent by 1995. In the interim, categories such as those of public affairs and social welfare had increased their share of the total interest group population. Studies also explored the consequences of organized business interests, large membership organizations, and advocacy organizations for policy formation. Policy domains were documented as distinctive networks of elected officials, public agencies, organized interests, and private organizations.

The diversity of organized interests, as well as the divergent assessments of their role in American democracy, remains an obstacle to the development of either systematic evidence or theoretical consensus. The relationship between interest groups and political decision making continues to be closely—and often ineffectively—policed, with new variations on lobbyist registration, limits on campaign contributions, and time-limited prohibitions on former officials lobbying their own agencies or one-time colleagues. Yet because the constitutional framework of elections and legislatures provides no institutionalized access for "faction"—mobilized groups with shared yet less than universal interests or passions—interest group politics will continue to function as an "extralegal" mode of political activity.

See also campaign law and finance.

FURTHER READING

Baumgartner, Frank R., and Beth L. Leech. *Basic Interests: The Importance of Groups in Politics and in Political Science.* Princeton, NJ: Princeton University Press, 1998.

Bentley, Arthur F. *The Process of Government: A Study of Social Pressures.* Chicago: University of Chicago Press, 1908.

Clemens, Elisabeth S. *The People's Lobby: Organizational Innovation and the Rise of Interest Group Politics in the United States, 1890–1925.* Chicago: University of Chicago Press, 1997.

Crawford, Kenneth G. *The Pressure Boys: The Inside Story of Lobbying in America.* New York: Julian Messner, 1939.

Hamilton, Alexander, James Madison, and John Jay. *The Federalist Papers.* New York: New American Library, 1961.

Herring, E. Pendleton. "Group Representation before Congress." Ph.D diss, Johns Hopkins University, 1929.

Laumann, Edward O., and David Knoke. *The Organizational State: Social Choice in National Policy Domains.* Madison: University of Wisconsin Press, 1987.

Schlozman, Kay Lehman, and John T. Tierney. *Organized Interests and American Democracy.* New York: Harper and Row, 1986.

Tichenor, Daniel J., and Richard A. Harris. "Organized Interests and American Political Development." *Political Science Quarterly* 117 (2002–3), 587–612.

Truman, David B. *The Governmental Process: Political Interests and Public Opinion.* New York: Knopf, 1951.

Walker, Jack L., Jr. *Mobilizing Interest Groups in America: Patrons, Professions, and Social Movements.* Ann Arbor: University of Michigan Press, 1991.

Young, Michael P. *Bearing Witness against Sin: The Evangelical Birth of the American Social Movement.* Chicago: University of Chicago Press, 2006.

ELISABETH S. CLEMENS

Internet and politics

Among technological innovations with impacts on political history, the Internet counts as a recent entry of major importance. This network of computerized communication channels and devices has given rise to popular new social practices (the search query and e-mail, to name the top two) and constituted a distinctive platform for politicking. Since the early 1990s, the Internet has affected power relations among citizens, candidates, advocacy groups, elected officials, and the news media, mainly by increasing the number of activists attempting to influence election and policy outcomes. Where once dozens of lobbyists enveloped lawmakers as they made decisions, now thousands exert pressure via Internet access, including mobile devices. Where once hundreds of journalists reported and commented on presidential campaigns, now hundreds of thousands of voices chime in via the blogosphere and other Web site forums. The Internet also houses the first genuinely international public space, where individuals in one country can see and respond to political messages from people in other nations, relatively free of state and nationally situated media controls. Of course, not all nations permit such communicative autonomy, China being the most notorious censor of online global discourse. But the participatory capacity and desire exist worldwide.

A gap between expectations and realities is a striking feature of the short history of online politics. High expectations have derived, in part, from the spectacu-lar presence of Microsoft, Amazon, Google, eBay, and other companies that have reaped vast fortunes by marketing information technology products. Surely, some have contended, a communication system capable of linking individuals throughout the world by the pairs, hundreds, thousands, and millions—of connecting any and all to a storehouse of information on the basis of typing a few words into an electronic box—portends the possibility of epic changes in politics as well. Grand expectations also stem from myths about technological power similar to those that surfaced during the social debuts of earlier modes of media and transportation. Those arguing that the Internet can spark a renaissance in freedom and democracy echo idealists beholding the early days of the steamboat and television. Dystopian myths have circulated as well, in which the Internet is viewed as a breeding ground for an anarchic, extremist, and fragmented public discourse where truth cannot be authoritatively differentiated from rumor and propaganda.

So, to recall the first words tapped into a public telegraph line, what hath God wrought in online politics?

What Internet Users Do

The Internet has not yet attained universal social usage, like the television and telephone. In the United States approximately half the population goes online every day (daily use being a better indication of adoption than access), and most other countries have smaller connectivity rates. Studies show that Internet regulars tend to become devotees. As their experience online grows, they increase the hours per day they spend there and, if they can afford it, keep pace with technological improvements. And as they ramp up in time and equipment, their communicative behavior changes. They become accustomed to on-demand access. They join communities devoted to specialized topics, including politics. They don masks of identity and flout conventions of social intercourse. They establish "weak ties" with people they scarcely know. They create and distribute content for public circulation. The resulting population of Internet sophisticates, estimated in the tens of millions in the United States alone, diverges from the conformist consumer model of audience behavior typical of the mass media era. For rising numbers of Internet users, politics is more than a spectacle posing occasional choices for response. Rather, it is a continually involving aspect of communal life.

Inveterate Internet users are more than simply audiences. As receivers of political information, they are smaller in number than their mass media counterparts because they consume political messages voluntarily instead of as a byproduct of their waiting for entertainment programming to resume. Smaller size, however, is offset somewhat by greater intensity. The transition from audience member to active participant is much easier online than in any other communication setting. Those who make the transition are more readily combined into timely, targeted, inexpensive, and persistent pressure groups. Therein lies the much-anticipated dynamic through which Internet users will make political good (if the advocates are reasonable and representative) or ill (if they are wild and extremist).

The record of online political activism to date has been neither good nor bad so much as slow to develop. Online social practices are being adopted in the public square, but not on the scale seen in commerce, leisure, education, and even government services. This relative slowness, another source of the expectation-reality gap, has several causes. First, casting a vote is a much rarer activity than making a date, paying a bill, answering a trivia question, or filling out a form, and thus the political innovators offering new ways to win votes online encounter a smaller demand and shorter and less frequent opportunities to test their wares and win clients for them. Second, to many of those campaign clients, the assets of online communication (raising money, uploading messages at low cost, and next to no editorial limitations) are still outweighed by the liabilities (not being able to reach the entire electorate, not being able to control message contents and distribution circumstances after others download them). Third, there is an age factor: because politicking is harder to relearn than to learn, the data show greater online usage and enthusiasm among the young, while political influentials tend to be older people.

The Evolving Campaign Web Site

These expectations, behaviors, and records are illustrated by the brief history of Web sites opened by candidates for elective office. Since the first campaign Web site appeared in the United States in 1994 (promoting Senator Dianne Feinstein of California), there have been six discernible waves of innovation, cresting roughly every two to three years. That would seem fast in any medium other than the Net, where software can go from version 1.0 to 6.0 in a third of that time, and where the amount of computer power purchasable by a dollar doubles every 18 months. The first generation of campaign Web

sites consisted of veritable brochures, combinations of promotional photos and texts in which the only sign of animation was a waving flag. Campaigners in the late 1990s soon embellished these sites with press releases and policy papers.

In order to hold site visitors' attention and lure them into returning, the second generation resorted to interactive features such as games, quizzes, and, most popularly, polls. These instant surveys were anything but scientific; their value to campaigners lay not in what the aggregate results said about the views of the constituency, but in the capacity of the questions to impart campaign messages, and what individual answers indicated about the issue interests of the visitors. Campaigners learned from marketers to extract e-mail addresses in exchange for the privilege of interacting, and then to send customized e-mail based on the information gleaned from those interactions.

Around the turn of the millennium, the third wave brought campaign Web sites into the business of raising money: the "contribute here" box, the campaign store, the sign-up for e-mail alerts with solicitation links embedded in the text. The blogosphere was the chief innovation of the fourth wave; although few campaigns dared to post links to outside blogs or permit outside comments on their own blogs, they gradually began to hold conference calls with selected bloggers, much as they did with reporters. Fifth, the creation of YouTube, with its peerless capacity to upload and index videos for public access, brought campaigners into the practice of issuing visual messages much more frequently and somewhat more creatively than they did for television. Most recently, the sixth wave has broken with the rise of social networking sites such as MySpace and Facebook. The heavy traffic at these sites has led campaigns to break a precedent stretching back to the inception of the Web by posting outbound links on their pages. The campaigns at the edge of this wave not only encourage visitors to go elsewhere but to take bits of software code known as "widgets" with them, the better to conduct their own, decentralized, campaign operations. For example, a Google widget enables someone to search Google without having to be on the Google Web site. Similarly, a fund-raising widget enables someone to raise money for a campaign from a personal Web site or blog. Today's most advanced campaign Web sites serve as the hubs of a mini-network dedicated to independently run fund-raising, phone-banking, event-staging, canvassing, and vote-mobilizing efforts.

This layered progression (as late as 2004, one in five major party candidates for the U.S. House had yet to reach stage one and open a campaign Web site) marks steps in a steep climb against the prevalent presumption among professional politicians that winning office depends on one-way communication: advertising, speechifying, news making. The idea that there can be continuous give-and-take between an organization and its constituencies remains rare in politics, even as full-fledged blogs and Webinars (online seminars) flood business and higher education. Among the pioneers of campaign conversation have been Howard Dean of the U.S. Democratic Party, David Cameron of the U.K. Conservative Party, and Segolene Royal of the French Socialists. Perhaps the high point to date of online-aided campaign dialogue was the 2007 incorporation of YouTube videos as questions put to presidential candidates in a televised debate. People were invited to submit video questions to CNN and YouTube. Editors selected a few such questions, which were posed to the candidates by the debate anchor. In a handful of instances, the videomaker was in the audience and allowed to react live to the candidates' answers. Both partisans and journalists were part of this conversation with the online citizenry.

Institutional Impacts

Yet even as politics lags behind other social domains and its own envisioned potential, we can already see the impact of the Internet on several political institutions: from elections to journalism and, most recently, government offices. The Internet has been integrated into institutional processes. It also has become the host for alternatives to what institutions provide. The "invisible primary" phase of private meetings among candidates and elites that opened the presidential selection process is now a highly visible public drama, and, prompted by the involvement of online interest groups, a massively multiplayer online game. "Flash mobs" of coordinated activists have tilted the policy-making process at international trade summits, stymied U.S. immigration reform, and, in South Korea and Indonesia, acted as agents of regime change. New tactics for influence have carried particular causes and candidates further than an assessment of conventional political resources and the logic of collective action would have predicted: these tactics include the bundling of small donations, blogger buzz, amateur videography, and the gaming of search engine returns (aka "Google-bombing").

A milestone of sorts was passed in 2006, when U.S. Senator George Allen of Virginia, a presidential hopeful strongly favored for reelection, lost his seat and his national stature, and contributed to his party's loss of its Senate majority position, after failing to respond promptly and honestly to a YouTube video that caught him uttering a racial slur to the camera wielder, a young campaign volunteer of Indian American descent. The lesson of Allen's defeat (his successor, James Webb, raised half his campaign funds online) was swiftly absorbed throughout public life, accelerating the fifth wave. By 2007 the Web video had moved from the avant-garde and amateur provinces into a universally accepted form for public affairs communication.

No political institution has been affected more by the Internet than journalism. Newspapers, magazines, radio, and television face serious threats to their revenues as advertising and consumer loyalties migrate to the Internet. To be sure, the favored Web sites for news tend to be operated by "old media" companies (Yahoo! being the exception), but the business side of journalism has been thrown out of whack. Some worry that, while the Net provides the public with breaking news and instant opinions and analysis as well as the mass media, it may not subsidize investigative and political-beat journalism, a crucial service to democracy. Net enthusiasts counter that the watchdog function will be borne by nonprofits and peer-produced methods such as "crowd-sourcing," wherein individuals contribute pieces of local knowledge to a Web hub so as to supply pooled surveillance of corporate and elective government.

Online politics has yet to make the transition from journalism, elections, and petition/protest to become an instrument of change wielded by an established leader in concert with supporters. Streamlined government services are a far cry from citizen participation in governance or, for that matter, corporate responses to market opportunities. Who will be the first historical figure to marshal online activists on matters of war, economics, social conflict, or the future structure of the Internet itself (where there already exists, as one might expect, a good deal of social activism)? Executives have thus far eschewed the summoning of online ties on behalf of their agendas. A brief preview of such an alliance occurred in 2003, when Roh Moo-hyun ascended to the South Korean presidency in league with the online grassroots newspaper *OhMyNews*. The newspaper surfaced as an alternative source of information about the election, enabling critics of the existing government to reach voters instead of being stymied by establishment media filters.

Obama and the Net

In the 2008 U.S. elections, more than one hundred candidates for federal office distributed videos to the public via YouTube, bypassing the constraints of broadcast and cable television. No videos had greater importance than those by and about Barack Obama. From a music video produced independently by entertainment celebrities to a 37-minute speech explaining his views on race in the wake of a scandal involving his former preacher, Obama-related videos attracted 889 million views, according to an industry metrics study. The Illinois senator masterfully blended online communication with principles and practices drawn from community organizing. Obama's campaign raised hundreds of millions of dollars through the Internet, enough for him to become the first presidential candidate to opt out of the public financing system in the general election. By Election Day, Obama's campaign database held contact information and intelligence for more than 13 million voters, nearly one out of every five who cast a ballot for him in November.

The new president immediately took steps toward becoming an online activist-in-chief. The Saturday radio address, a staple of presidential communication since Ronald Reagan, was now also delivered through Web video. Outside the government, Obama set up a grassroots lobbying arm to influence congressional votes by tapping the campaign database. Inside the government, the new president ordered greater and faster disclosure of executive branch information, and set up Web sites and online forums for citizens to use as instruments of holding officials accountable. The effects of these moves have yet to emerge. But the three-pronged approach—a Web-visible president, a political action unit, and government accountability measures—seems a plausible route by which the Internet may have as strong an impact on political history as it has on other realms of social life, including our political imagination.

See also campaigning; political advertising; television and politics.

FURTHER READING

Benkler, Yochai. *The Wealth of Networks: How Social Networks Transform Markets and Freedom.* New Haven, CT: Yale University Press, 2006.

Bimber, Bruce. *Information and American Democracy: Technology in the Evolution of Political Power.* New York: Cambridge University Press, 2003.

Chadwick, Andrew. *Internet Politics: States, Citizens, and New Communication Technologies.* New York: Oxford University Press, 2006.

Cornfield, Michael. "Game-Changers: New Technology and the 2008 Presidential Election." In *The Year of Obama: How Barack Obama Won the White House*, edited by Larry J. Sabato, 205–30. New York: Longman, 2009.

Lessig, Lawrence. *Code: Version 2.0.* New York: Basic Books, 2006.

Lupia, Arthur, and Gisela Sin. "Which Public Goods Are Endangered? How Evolving Communication Technologies Affect the Logic of Collective Action." *Public Choice* 117 (2003), 315 –31.

Mossberger, Karen, Caroline J. Tolbert, and Ramona S. McNeal. *Digital Citizenship: The Internet, Society, and Participation.* Cambridge, MA: MIT Press, 2007.

Norris, Pippa. *A Virtuous Circle: Political Communications in PostIndustrial Societies.* New York: Cambridge University Press, 2000.

Prior, Markus. *Post-Broadcast Democracy: How Media Choice Increases Inequality in Political Involvement and Polarizes Elections.* New York: Cambridge University Press, 2007.

Rogers, Everett M. *Diffusion of Innovations.* 4th ed. New York: Free Press, 1995.

Teachout, Zephyr, and Thomas Streeter. *Mouse Pads, Shoe Leather, and Hope: Lessons from the Howard Dean Campaign for the Future of Internet Politics.* Kent, WA: Paradigm Press, 2007.

Winner, Langdon. "The Internet and Dreams of Democratic Renewal." In *The Civic Web: Online Politics and Democratic Values*, edited by David M. Anderson and Michael Cornfield. Lanham, MD: Rowman and Littlefield, 2003.

MICHAEL CORNFIELD

Iraq wars of 1991 and 2003

In 1990, following an eight-year war against Iran, Iraq President Saddam Hussein sought to rebuild his battered nation by pressuring neighboring Sunni Arab states into raising international oil prices and forgiving Iraq's substantial war debts. Hussein's attention focused primarily on Kuwait. The Iraqis had long coveted Kuwait, both for its oil and access to the Persian Gulf. Furthermore, Hussein alleged that the Kuwaitis had stolen oil from Iraq through illegal "slant-drilling" in the Rumaila oil field and by exceeding production quotas established by Organization of Petroleum Exporting Countries. When the Kuwaitis rejected Iraqi demands for compensation, Iraq began massing troops along its border with Kuwait.

Previously, the administration of President George H. W. Bush had attempted to maintain friendly relations with Iraq by providing, in the words of National Security Directive (NSD) 26, "economic and political incentives for Iraq to moderate its behavior and to increase our influence with Iraq." During a meeting with Hussein on July 25, 1990, U.S. Ambassador April Glaspie conveyed the U.S. desire for peaceful resolution of Iraq's differences with Kuwait. The United States did not take additional steps to prevent an invasion of Kuwait because other Arab leaders and the Central Intelligence Agency had assured President Bush that Iraq would not invade Kuwait. Consequently, the United States was caught completely unprepared when Iraqi troops overran Kuwait on August 2 and annexed it six days later.

President Bush's national security team agreed that Iraq could not be allowed to remain in Kuwait, since that would give Iraq control of approximately 20 percent of the world's total oil reserves and leave it in a position to threaten Saudi Arabia. This affirmed the Carter Doctrine of 1980, which committed the United States to preventing any power from dominating the Persian Gulf and its oil reserves. After securing the consent of the Saudi royal family, the Bush administation initiated Operation Desert Shield on August 7 and immediately began deploying the first of 250,000 U.S. troops and their equipment to Saudi Arabia.

Disagreement arose over the question of using force to evict Iraq from Kuwait. The chairman of the Joint Chiefs of Staff, General Colin Powell, initially opposed military action and argued that UN sanctions could achieve the same end. Bush's national security advisor, Brent Scowcroft, and his secretary of defense, Richard Cheney, disagreed with Powell and convinced the president not to accept "another Munich." Bush warned Iraq on August 5 (the day before the United Nations imposed a complete embargo on Iraq), "This will not stand, this aggression against Kuwait." On August 20, the president signed NSD 45, which, in light of U.S. "vital" interests in the Persian Gulf (most notably "access to oil and the security and stability of key friendly states in the region"),

called for the "immediate, complete, and unconditional withdrawal of all Iraqi forces from Kuwait." By October, Powell and the commander of U.S. Central Command (CENTCOM, which is responsible for planning and conducting U.S. military operations in the Middle East), General Norman Schwarzkopf, had developed Operation Desert Storm, an ambitious air, land, and sea plan that called for more than 500,000 U.S. troops to evict Iraq from Kuwait.

On November 29, 1991, the UN Security Council passed Resolution 678, giving Iraq a deadline of January 15, 1991, to evacuate Kuwait and authorizing the U.S.-led multinational coalition of over 30 nations (many of which, such as Saudi Arabia, Great Britain, Egypt, and France, provided large numbers of combat troops; others, such as Germany and Japan, provided financial assistance) to use any measures it deemed necessary to enforce compliance. The only remaining obstacle for the Bush administration was the U.S. Senate, which was controlled by the Democratic Party. Scarred by the experience of the Vietnam War and reluctant to give the president carte blanche, most Democrats supported a policy of coercive diplomacy, as embodied by Security Council Resolution 661, adopted on August 6, which imposed a total embargo against Iraq. Such sanctions, Democrats hoped, would eventually compel Iraq to abandon Kuwait without the need for force.

In spite of such opposition and Cheney's insistence that the administration did not need legislative authorization to proceed, the president was determined to secure congressional approval. Following three days of debate, a resolution authorizing the use of force narrowly passed both houses of Congress, thanks largely to the support of Democrats such as Senator Al Gore (Tennessee). Eleven years later, Gore would again make headlines when he condemned the administration of George W. Bush's march to war. The 2004 presidential campaign of Democratic Senator John Kerry (Massachusetts), on the other hand, would be hamstrung by the fact that he opposed the 1991 Gulf War but voted in favor of the use of force in 2003.

Desert Storm commenced on January 17, 1991, with a bombing campaign against Iraqi military and civilian targets and was followed by a land invasion on February 24. After coalition forces outflanked the Iraqi military and threatened to cut off their line of retreat, the Iraqis began falling back on February 26, setting fire to Kuwaiti oil wells along the way. Lacking air cover, however, large numbers of Iraqis were slaughtered by coalition planes along the "highway of death" toward Iraq. At the urging of General Powell, President Bush declared a unilateral ceasefire the following day. By war's end, the United States had suffered a total of 293 dead, while Iraq suffered well over 20,000 military and civilian fatalities. Although coalition casualties during the fighting were light, tens of thousands of veterans later suffered from a variety of aliments that are collectively known as Gulf War Syndrome.

The postwar situation presented problems for the United States. For one thing, the Iraqis used the ceasefire to evacuate substantial portions of their elite Republican Guard divisions from Kuwait. Schwarzkopf also assented to an Iraqi request that they be allowed to use helicopters to ferry troops from Kuwait. In fact, the Iraqis used their remaining army units and aircraft to brutally suppress an uprising by Iraqi Shiites, who had been urged to rebel by the United States. While many in the U.S. government wanted to use the Shiites to destabilize the Ba'ath regime, leading figures such as Scowcroft, Powell, and Cheney opposed any move to assist the Shiites or march on Baghdad, since they did not want to responsible for establishing a new government in Iraq and rebuilding the country. Furthermore, they feared that if Hussein were toppled, Iraq would break apart. The main beneficiary of that situation would be Iran, which would extend its influence into the primarily Shiite provinces of southern Iraq, an area that contained most of Iraq's oil reserves and bordered both Kuwait and Saudi Arabia.

In one of the war's great ironies, Hussein, despite his catastrophic military defeat, managed to remain in power for another 12 years. His primary opponent, President Bush, fared less well. Although he enjoyed high approval ratings for his handling of the Gulf War, Bush's popularity sagged due to a stagnating economy. As a result, he was defeated in the 1992 presidential election by Bill Clinton, whose campaign revolved around the memorable expression, "It's the economy, stupid."

The Interlude of Sanctions: 1991–2001

For the next 12 years, the United States pursued a policy containing Iraq. U.S. and British warplanes enforced "no fly zones" over northern and southern Iraq and the UN Special Commission on Iraq (UNSCOM) was established to verify that the nation had dismantled its substantial programs for weapons of mass destruction (WMD). Despite Iraqi interference, UN weapons inspectors managed to dismantle most of Iraq's WMD infrastructure before withdrawing in December 1998, after

the chief of UNSCOM reported that Iraq was not complying with inspections. Shortly thereafter, the United States and Britain launched Operation Desert Fox, a three-day campaign of aerial bombardment and cruise missile attacks against suspected Iraqi WMD sites and military installations. Although the Clinton administration was criticized for taking only limited action against Iraq in 1998, following the conclusion of the second Iraq war, the Iraq Survey Group (an Anglo-American-Australian team of weapons inspectors established in 2003 to find Iraq's WMD) discovered that UN weapons inspections had been more successful than previously thought. Since Western intelligence services lacked an effective espionage network within Iraq, they had no way of knowing this.

Throughout the 1990s, the consensus of U.S. policy makers was that containment was the most effective policy for dealing with Iraq. Some outspoken opponents, such as Paul Wolfowitz (one of Cheney's deputies at the Pentagon in 1991), however, argued strongly in favor of regime change. In January 1998, an organization called the Project for a New American Century sent a letter to President Clinton asserting that the United States could no longer rely on UN inspections or containment to prevent Hussein from threatening the Middle East. Among the signatories of the letter were numerous prominent "neoconservatives" and future members of the second Bush administration. Their recommendations did not receive significant support within the American foreign policy establishment, however, and when the second Bush administration came to power in January 2001, it initially pursued a policy of "smart sanctions" designed to ease the humanitarian burden on Iraq's civilian population.

A New Administration and a New War: 2001–8

The U.S. government's attitude changed completely following the terrorist attacks of September 11, 2001. The attacks proved to be the catalyst for the invasion of Iraq for fear that state sponsors of terrorism—such as Iraq—could provide radical Islamic terrorists with WMD. Accordingly, by the summer of 2002, the administration of George W. Bush publicly embraced the concept of preventive war. In a speech that June at the United States Military Academy at West Point, the president stated that the United States would "confront the worst threats before they emerge." Furthermore, even before the 2001 terrorist attacks, proponents of regime change in Iraq had argued that prior U.S. foreign policy in the Middle

East had created the popular basis for the rise of terrorist organization such as al-Qaeda through its support for authoritarian regimes, and that the United States needed to aggressively promote democratization in the Middle East.

The administration formally unveiled its new foreign policy on September 20, 2002, when it published the *National Security Strategy of the United States*, whose tenets came to be known as the Bush Doctrine. Among its highlights was an explicit repudiation of the cold war concept of deterrence in favor of "preemptive" and, if necessary, unilateral military action.

The Bush administration began warning of the threat posed by Iraqi WMD before the 2001 military campaign in Afghanistan had even ended, and throughout 2002. In his 2002 State of the Union address, President Bush named three nations—Iran, Iraq, and North Korea, which he collectively called the "axis of evil"—that were actively developing WMD and might supply such weapons to terrorists. In August, Vice President Richard Cheney unequivocally stated that "there is no doubt that Saddam Hussein now has weapons of mass destruction; there is no doubt that he is amassing them to use against our friends, against our allies, and against us." Quoting President Bush, Cheney warned, "Time is not on our side," and that the "risks of inaction are far greater than the risks of action."

The tipping point came in October, when the government distributed a national intelligence estimate concerning Iraq's "continuing" WMD programs. With a majority in the Senate, congressional Democrats could have derailed the president's plans, but the terrorist attacks of the previous year had left them on the defensive. With midterm elections quickly approaching, and the president's popularity soaring in the wake of the terrorist attacks and the seemingly successful war in Afghanistan, congressional Democrats reckoned that they could not wage an effective campaign on national security and sought to shift the emphasis back to domestic issues such as health care and corporate scandals by supporting the Bush administration's stance on Iraq. Consequently, on October 16, 2002, Congress authorized Bush to "defend the national security of the United States against the continuing threat posed by Iraq." This electoral gambit failed, however, and Democrats were defeated in the 2002 midterm elections.

The Bush administration faced a stiffer challenge at the United Nations. The Security Council unanimously passed Resolution 1441 in November 2002, which de-

clared that Iraq was in material breach of previous resolutions and that it had 30 days to accept the reentry of weapons inspectors. Months of inspections failed, however, to turn up evidence of an illicit Iraqi WMD program. In spite of Secretary of State Colin Powell's speech before the Security Council on February 5, 2003, describing alleged Iraqi violations of existing Security Council resolutions and cooperation with Islamist terrorist groups, several members, most notably France and Germany, remained opposed to military action. Consequently, the United States and the 48 other nations that comprised the "coalition of the willing" (of which only four actually provided combat troops for the invasion) moved to the next stage. On March 16, the United States ordered all UN weapons inspectors to leave Iraq and, the following day, gave Hussein and his family 48 hours to seek exile. On the morning of March 20, the United States and its allies began Operation Iraqi Freedom with a massive aerial bombardment of Baghdad and a land invasion from Kuwait.

It soon became apparent that U.S. war planning was flawed for two reasons: it relied on too few troops to occupy Iraq, and it ignored the question of postwar planning. As early as November 2001, CENTCOM had been charged with drawing up a plan. At the time, Secretary of Defense Donald Rumsfeld pushed for a small, highly mobile invasion force, over the objections of senior officers such as Army Chief of Staff General Eric Shinseki, who warned that the United States would require a large presence in Iraq for an indefinite period in order to guarantee postwar peace and security. Deputy Secretary of Defense Wolfowitz publicly ridiculed such concerns and asserted that the U.S. occupation of Iraq would be self-financing through Iraqi oil exports. In fact, U.S. government expenditures during the first four years of the war exceeded $2 billion per week.

Although the small force envisaged by Rumsfeld (145,000 U.S. and British soldiers) quickly routed the Iraqi Army, it was unable to stabilize the country after the collapse of Hussein's Ba'ath regime. Following the fall of Baghdad on April 9, widespread looting broke out across the city in front of helpless U.S. troops. The scene was repeated across the country, with dire consequences for U.S. forces, since insurgents looted arms depots and secured large supplies of small arms and explosives.

After President Bush declared an end to "major combat operations" on May 1, 2003, the United States created a Coalition Provisional Authority to govern Iraq. The original head of the CPA was retired General Jay

Garner, who planned to quickly transfer the responsibility for governing Iraq to local authorities and rely on the Iraqi Army to maintain order. Garner also clashed with Ahmed Chalabi, the leader of a prominent Iraqi exile group (the Iraqi National Congress) that had provided much of the flawed evidence of Iraqi WMD to the U.S. government who aspired to high political office in post-Ba'ath Iraq. Garner soon fell afoul of the leadership in Washington and was replaced by a former diplomat, L. Paul Bremer, in May. Bremer subsequently made two momentous decisions. On May 16, he issued an order expelling all Ba'ath Party members from Iraqi civil service. One week later, he demobilized the Iraqi Army and laid off the staff of the Interior Ministry and Hussein's personal security forces. These disgruntled soldiers and Ba'ath Party members provided the nucleus for an insurgency that claimed the lives of thousands of coalition soldiers and untold numbers of Iraqi soldiers, police, and civilians.

While it was hoped that the capture of Hussein in December 2003 would stabilize Iraq, two events in early 2004 shattered any such illusions. First, on March 31, a convoy carrying four private U.S. military contractors was ambushed by insurgents in Fallujah, and the contractors' charred remains were later hung from a nearby bridge. Much of the city was subsequently destroyed, and its population displaced, when U.S. Marines stormed it at great cost in November. Second, at the end of April, reporter Seymour Hersh revealed the torture of Iraqi detainees by U.S. Army guards at the Abu Ghraib prison. The U.S. government claimed that the excesses had been committed by only a handful of soldiers and were not the result of official policy. Nevertheless, the sexually explicit nature of the offenses, as well as the fact that they took place in a prison that had been used by the Ba'ath regime, stripped away much of the U.S. occupation's moral legitimacy, both in Iraq and abroad.

Despite the deteriorating the situation in Iraq, President Bush won reelection against John Kerry in 2004 by the narrowest margin for a sitting president since Woodrow Wilson in 1916. The war in Iraq was probably not the decisive issue during the campaign, since matters such as terrorism, same-sex marriage, the economy, and health care also received much attention. Furthermore, Kerry did not advocate a withdrawal from Iraq. Rather, he criticized the president for poor management of postwar Iraq and argued that the United States needed allies to help stabilize that nation. Kerry's initial

support of the resolution authorizing the use of force, and the fact that he continued to argue as late as August 2004 that "it was the right authority" for a president to have, left him vulnerable to withering attacks by the Republicans, who derided him as an opportunistic "flip-flopper."

The political costs of the war for the Republican Party only became evident during the 2006 congressional midterm elections. In November 2005, Democrat John Murtha (Pennsylvania), a senior congressman with close ties to the U.S. military, withdrew his support for the war and offered a plan to withdraw U.S. troops from Iraq at the "earliest practicable date." Although Democrats remained divided over how quickly any withdrawal should proceed, most rallied around Murtha's call for a "strategic redeployment." Sagging popular support for the war, combined with a series of scandals involving high-ranking Republicans and Bush's unpopularity following his failed bid to privatize Social Security and his administration's botched response to Hurricane Katrina, handed the Democrats an electoral triumph as spectacular as that of the Republicans in 1994.

Although President Bush acknowledged that the results of the 2006 election reflected substantial public discontent over his handling of the war and accepted the resignation of Defense Secretary Rumsfeld, he remained adamantly opposed to withdrawal from Iraq. Consequently, in May 2007, Bush vetoed a bill funding U.S. military operations in Iraq and Afghanistan because it included a timeline for withdrawal. It was only the second time he had used that power since becoming president.

As an alternative to the "redeployment" plans advocated by Democrats and the Iraq Study Group (a bipartisan panel created by Congress in 2006 to provide recommendations on future policy concerning Iraq), in January 2007, Bush unveiled a new counterinsurgency strategy that featured the deployment of an additional 20,000 troops to Iraq to "clear and secure" insurgent-controlled areas in Baghdad, under the direction of the newly installed commander of Multi-National Force–Iraq, General David Petraeus, a noted expert on counterinsurgency warfare and author of the U.S. Army/Marine Corps *Counterinsurgency Field Manual*. The aim of the 2007 "troop surge" was not, however, to achieve a decisive military victory over the Sunni insurgency. Rather, it was to provide enough stability within Baghdad to promote political reconciliation between rival sectarian and ethnic factions within the Iraqi government and prevent a civil war. Since congressional Democrats lacked the votes either to override a presidential veto concerning withdrawal or to cut off spending for the war, the questions of when and how the United States would eventually withdraw from Iraq were left to be settled after the 2008 presidential election.

See also foreign policy and domestic politics since 1933; war and politics.

FURTHER READING

Bacevich, Andrew J., and Efraim Inbar, eds. *The Gulf War of 1991 Reconsidered*. London; Portland: Frank Cass, 2003.

Chandrasekaran, Rajiv. *Imperial Life in the Emerald City: Inside Iraq's Green Zone*. New York: Knopf, 2006.

Cleveland, William. *A History of the Modern Middle East*. Boulder, CO: Westview Press, 2004.

Fallows, James. *Blind into Baghdad: America's War in Iraq*. New York: Vintage Books, 2006.

Freedman, Lawrence. *A Choice of Enemies: American Confronts the Middle East*. New York: Public Affairs, 2008.

Freedman, Lawrence, and Efraim Karsh. *The Gulf Conflict, 1990–1991: Diplomacy and War in the New World Order*. Princeton, NJ: Princeton University Press, 1993.

Gardner, Lloyd C., and Marilyn B. Young, eds. *The New American Empire: A 21st Century Teach-In on U.S. Foreign Policy*. New York: New Press, 2005.

Gordon, Michael R., and Bernard E. Trainor. *Cobra 2: The Inside Story of the Invasion and Occupation of Iraq*. New York: Pantheon Books, 2006.

Hess, Gary R. *Presidential Decisions for War: Korea, Vietnam, the Persian Gulf, and Iraq*. Baltimore, MD: Johns Hopkins University Press, 2009.

Klare, Michael. *Blood and Oil: The Dangers and Consequences of America's Growing Petroleum Dependency*. New York: Metropolitan Books, 2004.

Little, Douglas. *American Orientalism: The United States and the Middle East since 1945*. Chapel Hill: University of North Carolina Press, 2008.

Mann, James. *Rise of the Vulcans: The History of Bush's War Cabinet*. New York: Penguin Books, 2004.

National Security Council. *The National Security Strategy of the United States of America*. Downloadable from http://georgewbush-whitehouse.archives.gov/nsc/nss/2002/index.html.

Newell, Clayton R. *The A to Z of the Persian Gulf War, 1990–1991*. Lanham, MD: Scarecrow Press, 2007.

Packer, George. *The Assassins' Gate: America in Iraq*. New York: Farrar, Straus and Giroux, 2005.

Ricks, Thomas E. *Fiasco: The American Military Adventure in Iraq*. New York: Penguin Press, 2006.

Rutledge, Ian. *Addicted to Oil: America's Relentless Drive for Energy Security*. London: I.B. Tauris, 2005.

Sifry, Micah L., and Christopher Cerf, eds. *The Gulf War Reader: History, Documents, Opinions*. New York: Times Books, 1991.

Weiner, Tim. *Legacy of Ashes: The History of the CIA*. New York: Doubleday, 2007.

Woodward, Bob. *Plan of Attack*. New York: Simon and Schuster, 2004.

———. *State of Denial*. New York: Simon and Schuster, 2006.

———. *The War Within: A Secret White House History, 2006–2008*. New York: Simon and Schuster, 2008.

Yetiv, Steve A. *The Persian Gulf Crisis*. Westport, CT: Greenwood Press, 1997.

ANAND TOPRANI

Jacksonian era, 1828–45

The Jacksonian era was the period in American political history dominated by the influence of the seventh president, General Andrew Jackson (1767–1846), who served two terms between 1825 and 1837. An exuberantly egalitarian political culture for white men, divisive political reactions to economic change, the development of a mass-based two-party electoral system, and the growing importance of the slavery issue in national politics all marked the period. Jackson and his associates pushed American politics from an older republican tradition in the direction of democracy but saw their work as restoration rather than innovation.

A Changing Society

From the end of the eighteenth century, a series of linked economic and technological changes, sometimes referred to as the Market Revolution, framed the social and economic context of the Jacksonian era. Faster and cheaper forms of transportation, including turnpike roads, steamboats, canals, and ultimately railroads, spread from the Northeast across the country, hastening passenger travel and cutting freight costs. This made it much more feasible to make goods in one place while selling them in another. Once-isolated farmers increased their production of staples like wheat, corn, and pork for the world market, while entrepreneurs replaced traditional artisanal manufactures with new means for making and distributing cheap consumer goods like shoes, hats, and clothing. The invention of the cotton gin (1793) opened the way for large-scale cotton production in the southern interior, fed the movement of planters and slaves to the Southwest, and furnished raw material to a generation of newly mechanized textile factories in Britain and New England.

A rapid increase in the number and size of chartered banks facilitated this active commerce. The first American bank opened in 1782 (Robert Morris's Bank of North America), and the numbers of banks grew to 28 in 1800 and 729 by 1837. Often operating on slender capital reserves, these banks provided credit-hungry borrowers with loans in the form of paper notes that served as the medium of exchange for an increasingly monetized economy. Eager to foster economic development, state governments frequently protected banks and internal improvement companies with the privilege of corporate charters. The largest and most privileged corporation of all was the second Bank of the United States, chartered for 30 years in 1816, with a capital of \$35 million, a monopoly of the banking business of the federal government, and the size and strength to discipline the note issue of the state banks.

Americans reacted to commercial growth with a mixture of optimism and anxiety. Farmers who profited from the sale of commodities welcomed the changes, unless the purchase of new lands and new equipment for market production put them perilously in debt and subjected them to market swings. Customers certainly welcomed cheaper consumer goods, but new forms of inequality, including new class structures and new gender roles, also accompanied the new economy. Cultural tension was reflected in the so-called Second Great Awakening, a wave of religious revivals that offered reformed ways of life to converts who suffered from social and spiritual upheaval from frontiers to big cities.

State decisions to relax property requirements and other restrictions on white men's right to vote amplified political reactions to economic, social, and cultural change. The new voters did not cast their ballots consistently along class lines, and many did not vote at all initially, but the broadened franchise created a mass electorate that skilled political operatives would soon learn to mobilize. Roused by compelling rhetoric and public spectacles, the new voters would form the mass membership for Jacksonian-era political parties.

Jackson's Life

Andrew Jackson's dramatic personal story greatly contributed to his popular appeal and sharply contrasted with the privileged upbringings of earlier presidents. He was born under modest circumstances in a backcountry settlement on the border of the two Carolinas. Jackson's father died before his birth, so his mother raised her three sons with relatives. The future president received some schooling in the neighborhood but never attended college.

During the war for independence, 13-year-old Andrew Jackson was captured as an American messenger when the British invaded the Carolina backcountry in 1780. He received lifelong scars when he refused to clean his captor's boots and the furious officer slashed him with a saber. Jackson also survived an attack of smallpox he contracted in captivity, but war took the lives of his mother and two brothers, leaving the youth seemingly marked by providence as the only member of his immediate family to survive the American Revolution. He would become the last U.S. president to have served in that conflict.

With iron determination, Jackson managed to overcome his difficult adolescence by reading law, moving to Nashville, Tennessee, and rapidly rising in his profession. There he married Rachel Donelson Robards, leading to a later scandal when enemies revealed that the couple had married before the bride was divorced from her first husband. Jackson also succeeded in land speculation, won a duel, and joined the region's nascent planter elite. Entering politics, he briefly served in the U.S. House, the U.S. Senate, and the Tennessee Supreme Court, but he preferred his work as major general of the state militia.

Military distinction brought the frontier general to national attention. During the War of 1812, Jackson's troops honored his toughness with the nickname "Old Hickory," as he crushed an uprising of the Creek Indians, occupied Spanish Florida in pursuit of the survivors, executed their British advisors, and repelled the British invasion of New Orleans. At war's end, Jackson pursued warring Seminoles into Florida again, which provoked international outrage but also pressured Spain to sell the vulnerable province to the United States in 1819. After cementing U.S. rule as first territorial governor of Florida, Jackson retired to the Hermitage, his plantation outside Nashville.

Jackson's rise coincided with serious national stress. In 1819 a postwar boom collapsed in a disastrous "panic," or depression. Collapsing prices for land and crops bankrupted countless farmers and speculators who had borrowed heavily to purchase public lands. Banks, especially the Bank of the United States, roused widespread resentment when they pressed their borrowers relentlessly but refused to honor their obligations to pay specie (gold or silver) for their notes. The federal government could not act in the crisis but plunged into bitter sectional controversy when northern congressmen tried to limit the growth of slavery as a condition for the admission of Missouri to the union. Temporarily eased by the Missouri Compromise, the slavery dispute threatened serious long-term disruption and frightened the aging Thomas Jefferson "like a fire-bell in the night."

Seeming to ignore these dangers, national leaders intrigued instead to succeed retiring President James Monroe in the election of 1824. Four major candidates emerged, three of them from Monroe's own cabinet: Secretary of State John Quincy Adams, Secretary of the Treasury William H. Crawford, and Secretary of War John C. Calhoun. A fourth, Speaker of the House Henry Clay of Kentucky, supposedly led the administration's friends in Congress.

The triumphant Tennessean seemed to offer a stark contrast to these bickering and self-interested insiders. While government insiders scoffed at his inexperience, lack of polish, and pugnacious, high-handed temperament, Jackson appealed to ordinary voters, especially in the West and South, as the embodiment of bold action and old-fashioned republican virtue.

Nominated by the Tennessee legislature, Jackson led in both the popular and electoral vote without gaining a majority, so the House of Representatives had to choose between Jackson, Adams, and Crawford, the three highest vote-getters. Jackson believed that his plurality, plus state legislative instructions in his favor, gave him the moral right to win. Instead, Henry Clay threw his support to Adams and gave him the victory. Soon afterward, Adams made Clay his secretary of state, rousing furious charges by Jacksonians of a "corrupt bargain" to defeat the "will of the people." Determined on vindication, Jackson and his supporters launched an immediate and ultimately successful campaign to gain the White House in 1828, putting claims for majority rule and the moral superiority of "the people" over "aristocrats" at the ideological core of his movement.

Jackson's Presidency

As president, Jackson repeatedly invoked the republican principles of the Revolution, but he actually turned American political culture toward democracy by identifying the people themselves, not an enlightened elite, as the greatest source of public virtue. Seeing his movement as the majority's legitimate voice, however, Jackson rarely saw a difference between the people's welfare and the good of his own party. His first major initiative, for example, was to replace long-established federal officeholders with his own supporters, insisting that the incumbents were often incompetent or corrupt, but also arguing that holdovers from previous administrations were out of step with the people's will. Jacksonians strongly defended this so-called spoils system, but advocates of an independent civil service struggled against it for most of the nineteenth century.

Jackson also took office determined to remove the eastern Indian tribes to lands beyond the Missisippi. The Indian Removal Act of 1830 authorized the president to exchange lands in modern Oklahoma for tribal lands within existing states. Occupying extensive tracts in Georgia, Alabama, Mississippi, and Florida, the Cherokees, Creeks, Choctaws, Chickasaws, and Seminoles were quite unwilling to move. The Cherokees were promised partial protection in two Supreme Court decisions, *Cherokee Nation v. Georgia* and *Worcester v. Georgia*, but the decisions proved unenforceable. All the major eastern tribes, with as many as 100,000 members, were eventually deported by a combination of bribery, fraud, intimidation, and coercion. Corruption and neglect led to the death of about one Indian in four along the so-called Trail of Tears.

When South Carolina, worried about the viability of its slave-based economy, followed John C. Calhoun's proposal to nullify the federal tariff in 1832, Jackson threatened military action to restore federal supremacy, arguing that the state's actions were an intolerable rejection of majority rule. In 1835 South Carolinians defied federal law again when a mob seized and burned a shipment of abolitionist tracts from the Charleston post office. Supporting the mob's goals but opposing its methods, Jackson called for federal legislation to exclude "incendiary" materials from the U.S. mail. The proposal foundered, so the administration tolerated informal mail censorship by local vigilance committees.

Andrew Jackson's war against the Bank of the United States (BUS) was the central political struggle of his presidency. Partly inspired by the eighteenth-century British radicals who underpinned the republican tradition and also denounced privileged corporations like the Bank of England and the South Sea Company, Jackson distrusted all banks. He especially distrusted the Bank of the United States for allegedly using its immense powers and legal privileges for private gain at public expense. Drawing energy from Americans' ambivalent feelings about the new economy that banks had abetted, the Bank War revived the two-party system and defined American politics for the decade following Jackson's presidency.

When Congress granted the bank a new charter in the summer of 1832, Jackson vetoed the bill with a ringing denunciation of wealthy men who misused government "to make the rich richer and the potent more powerful." Supporters denounced the veto as ignorant madness, but the message was wildly popular among voters who shared Jackson's misgivings about unrestrained private power, and Jackson was resoundingly reelected with a larger majority than before. Soon after, Jackson went further and pulled the government's funds from the bank, an arguably illegal move that crippled it both politically and financially. In a related policy, Jackson favored state control of internal improvements and vetoed the use of federal funds for local transportation projects.

The Second Party System

Deposit removal galvanized the president's opponents, who argued that his high-handed actions defied Congress and threatened a dictatorship. Denouncing Jackson as "King Andrew I," they organized themselves as the Whig Party, adopting the name from the British opponents of centralized royal power. Led by congressional magnates like Henry Clay and Daniel Webster, the Whigs became a formidable political force after Jackson left office and another powerful panic swept the United States in 1837. Jacksonians responded by reviving Jeffersonian party lines, shortening the older name "Democratic-Republicans" to "Democratic Party," and portraying the Whigs as resurrected Federalists. Each party solidified its identity and its organization by blaming its opponents for the panic of 1837, creating a competitive political structure that scholars have called the Second American Party System, to distinguish it from the First Party System of Federalists and Democratic-Republicans.

Both parties became national institutions that contested elections at the federal and local level in every state except South Carolina, which remained aloof from both. Democrats generally embraced party organization with vigor and finesse; Whigs retained more antipartisan principles and weaker gifts for organization. A Washington newspaper spelled out doctrine for each party—*The Globe* for the Democrats and *The National Intelligencer* for the Whigs—while a host of state-level prints adapted the message to local conditions. Each party also embraced an ascending network of local, district, state, and national party conventions to convey opinions and decisions between bottom and top, to adopt platforms, and to nominate candidates for public office.

For presidential elections, each party organized a national campaign committee to distribute pamphlets and special campaign newspapers to corresponding networks of state, county, and local committees. Successful office seekers rewarded followers with government patronage and enforced party discipline by threatening to revoke it if crossed. Historians Glenn C. Altschuler and Stuart M. Blumin have questioned voters' genuine emotional involvement in Jacksonian elections, but most scholars note that voting turnout rates often approached and sometimes exceeded 80 percent, and conclude that colorful spectacles and lively debates between rival candidates successfully drew the connections between party doctrines and local concerns.

In their platforms, Democrats typically denounced federal measures to promote the new economy, including the national bank, high tariffs, and public funding for internal improvements, and all restraints on the liberty of common white men, including moral reforms favored by revivalists, like Sunday blue laws and restrictions on the sale of alcohol. After the panic of 1837, many Democrats shared Jackson's own desire to prohibit paper money banking altogether and return the country to an all-metallic currency. Party rhetoric denounced class privilege and stressed the equality of all white men, sometimes underscored with a fierce antiblack racism. Whigs were more likely to champion personal and public improvement over unrestrained liberty, and favored banks, internal improvements, the rights of corporations, evangelical moral reforms, and philanthropic causes like public schools and benevolent institutions. Though business conservatism often sent the largest southern planters into Whig ranks, Whigs across the nation were somewhat more tolerant of black rights and antislavery opinions than their rivals. Some Whigs and Democrats were found within all social classes, but voting studies have found that leading urban businessmen were more likely to be Whigs, while working-class wards usually leaned to the Democrats, and Whig counties were more

closely linked to the market economy than their Democratic counterparts.

The Democratic Party and the Whig Party did not monopolize contemporary Americans' political reactions to the challenges of their era. An Anti-Masonic Party channeled popular resentment in northeastern states before absorption by the Whigs. Trade union movements and workingmen's parties briefly flared in large cities, before succumbing to hard times and Democratic blandishments after the panic of 1837. Women entered public life through allegedly nonpartisan religious and reform movements and also found supportive partisan roles, especially among Whigs. Rebuffed by mainstream politicians, radical black and white abolitionists agitated outside party structures, though some eventually embraced politics through the Liberty Party and its successors. The example of Jacksonian politics proved irresistibly attractive, even to those it rigorously excluded.

Jackson's immediate successors competed within the political and ideological framework established during his presidency. In 1836 Vice President Martin Van Buren succeeded Jackson in the presidency but struggled unsuccessfully with the panic of 1837 and its aftermath. In 1840, the Whigs created a storm of popular enthusiasm for William Henry Harrison of Indiana, their own popular frontier general. Soon after being inaugurated, Harrison died and his vice president, John Tyler of Virginia, alienated both parties and proved that party support had become essential to a functional presidency. By 1844, however, the opportunity for western expansion through the acquisition of Texas and Oregon had eclipsed older issues. Martin Van Buren lost the Democratic nomination to James K. Polk of Tennessee when he fumbled the territorial issue. As president, Polk echoed Jacksonian themes in his veto of the Rivers and Harbors Bill, but the Mexican War dominated his term, and the territorial expansion of slavery preoccupied his successors.

Polk's election sent American politics in new and dangerous directions. In 1845 the annexation of Texas led to war with Mexico, conquest of the Far West, and a steadily intensifying national quarrel over the future of slavery there. That controversy would eventually destroy the Whig Party and other specific features of the Jacksonian political system, but subsequent generations of Americans would find the strong presidency, the rhetoric of democracy, and the institutions of party politics that Jacksonians had introduced to be indispensable to public life.

See also banking policy; Democratic Party, 1828–60; economy and politics to 1860; Republican Party to 1896; Whig Party.

FURTHER READING

Altschuler, Glenn C., and Stuart M. Blumin. *Rude Republic: Americans and Their Politics in the Nineteenth Century.* Princeton, NJ: Princeton University Press, 2000.

Holt, Michael F. *The Rise and Fall of the American Whig Party: Jacksonian Politics and the Onset of the Civil War.* New York: Oxford University Press, 1999.

Howe, Daniel Walker. *What Hath God Wrought: The Transformation of America, 1815–1848.* New York: Oxford University Press, 2008.

Larson, John Lauritz. *Internal Improvement: National Public Works and the Promise of Popular Government in the Early United States.* Chapel Hill: University of North Carolina Press, 2001.

Remini, Robert V. *Andrew Jackson and the Course of American Democracy, 1833–1845.* New York: Harper and Row, 1984.

———. *Andrew Jackson and the Course of American Empire, 1767–1821.* New York: Harper and Row, 1977.

———. *Andrew Jackson and the Course of American Freedom, 1822–1832.* New York: Harper and Row, 1981.

Ryan, Mary P. *Women in Public: Between Banners and Ballots, 1825–1880.* Baltimore, MD: Johns Hopkins University Press, 1990.

Sellers, Charles. *The Market Revolution: Jacksonian America, 1815–1846.* New York: Oxford University Press, 1991.

Shade, William G. "Political Pluralism and Party Development: The Creation of the Modern Party System, 1815–1852." In *The Evolution of American Political Systems*, edited by Paul Kleppner, 77–112. Westport, CT: Greenwood Press, 1981.

Watson, Harry L. *Liberty and Power: The Politics of Jacksonian America.* 2nd revised ed., New York: Hill and Wang, 1990, 2006.

Wilentz, Sean. *The Rise of American Democracy: Jefferson to Lincoln.* New York: Norton, 2005.

HARRY L. WATSON

Jews and politics

In the twentieth century and thereafter, Jewish public culture has been peculiar in the extent to which ethical idealism has trumped material interest. The result has been a persistent progressivism uncharacteristic of any comparable group of white Americans. Devotion to the liberal wing of the Democratic Party has shaped the political profile of American Jewry in ways that no other ethnic or religious minority has matched.

Antecedents of Liberalism

During the colonial period and until the end of the nineteenth century, Jews were neither numerous enough nor conspicuous enough to have constituted a singular political force. Their cohesiveness would await two events: mass migration from Eastern Europe in the aftermath of czarist pogroms and the response of Franklin D. Roosevelt's administration to the Great Depression. For nearly four decades prior to World War I, well over 2 million Jews arrived in the metropolises of the East Coast and the Midwest in particular. These immigrants were so impoverished that, according to one government report, $9 was the average sum in their pockets. Because eastern European Jews were fleeing not only worsening destitution but also religious persecution, their politics tended to be more dissident and desperate than the stance of the much smaller, prosperous, established Sephardic and German Jewish communities. Co-religionists who were already entrenched in the United States tended to be conservative in their political views.

Membership in the working and lower classes made the new Jewish immigrants and their children receptive to the appeal of varieties of radicalism, which elicited sympathy longer among Jews than among other Americans. Jews were long overrepresented in the various socialist and Communist parties and in the anarchist movement and were often in their leadership. The penury that was commonplace in the Jewish community also made it especially vulnerable to the crisis of capitalism that erupted in 1929, though most Jews turned not to extreme solutions but rather (like most Americans) to the New Deal. Its promise to meet the systemic challenge of the Great Depression, and the elusive goals of recovery, relief, and regulation that President Roosevelt enunciated lured Jews into the Democratic Party in overwhelming numbers, forming a pattern that has endured to the present. The four elections that FDR won set the standard against which subsequent Jewish allegiance to the liberalism of the Democratic Party has come to be measured. In the 1936 election, for example, the nation's most densely Jewish ward—located in Chicago—gave the incumbent a margin of 96 percent (the sort of near unanimity otherwise enjoyed by dictators, who prefer to run unopposed). The depth of the fervor for FDR was signified by the Schechter brothers, whose beleaguered kosher poultry business in Brooklyn led them to challenge the constitutionality of the National Recovery Administration (NRA), a keystone of New Deal economic regulation. In a landmark 1935 decision, the Supreme Court agreed with the Schechters and ruled the NRA unconstitutional. The following year all 16 votes in the Schechter family were nevertheless cast for the very candidate whose NRA had presumably damaged their business.

After Roosevelt's 1936 electoral landslide, he could not keep intact a precarious coalition that ranged all the way from southern segregationists to northern blacks. Other voters had suffered at least as much as the Jews during the Great Depression. Yet no group would cling more tenaciously to the Democratic Party—and especially its reformist wing—than American Jewry, which gave Roosevelt a staggering 90 percent of its vote in 1940 and again in 1944. To be sure, such loyalty to the New Deal could be read as the gratitude of a disadvantaged group that its economic needs were being satisfied.

But other factors must be summoned to account for FDR's popularity among Jews. He symbolized the progressive spirit of communal claims against the nation's sweet tooth for a rampant individualism that was foreign to historic Judaism. The president had also admirably prevailed over the snobbery of his patrician origins. His close associates included Secretary of the Treasury Henry Morgenthau Jr., legislative draftsman and advisor Benjamin V. Cohen, and speechwriter Sam Rosenman, as well as Justice Felix Frankfurter, whom FDR appointed to the U.S. Supreme Court in 1939. Beginning in 1941, the commander in chief also helped personify the Allied war against the Third Reich and offered in his articulation of the Four Freedoms a democratic riposte to Nazism. No wonder then that a Republican judge, Jonah Goldstein, ruefully remarked that his co-religionists belonged to three *velten* (Yiddish for "worlds"): *de velt* ("this world"), *yene velt* ("the world to come"), and Roosevelt.

After the New Deal

The election of 1948 was not a fair test of the enduring Jewish attachment to liberalism. The Fair Deal was, after all, a continuation of the New Deal, and President Harry S. Truman had recognized the state of Israel only 11 minutes after its birth. Consider instead the 1950s, when large segments of the Jewish community were enjoying unprecedented prosperity in suburbia and were abandoning their proletarian origins for good. Running against Dwight D. Eisenhower, the enormously popular former general who had led the crusade in Europe, Democrat Adlai Stevenson nevertheless attracted almost two out of every three Jewish votes. By 1960 puzzled political scientists were obliged to explain why the Democratic nominee, Senator John F. Kennedy, the first and only Roman Catholic ever elected to the presidency, won a higher proportion of votes among Jews than he did among his co-religionists. In 1964 his successor campaigned against a fiercely conservative Republican nominee. Lyndon B. Johnson received almost nine out of ten Jewish votes—in no small measure because the Great Society was packaged as a completion of the unfinished agenda of the New Deal.

The ballots cast for Vice President Hubert Humphrey in middle-class Jewish neighborhoods in 1968 closely paralleled the Democratic nominee's popularity in the inner cities. This anomaly inspired Milton Himmelfarb of the American Jewish Committee to quip that Jews lived like Episcopalians but voted like Puerto Ricans. Soon this generalization would prove shaky, however, because Jewish income levels became higher than the earnings of the Episcopalians and Congregationalists, whose ancestors had settled in the New World over three centuries earlier. Around 1970 the income gap that had opened up between Jews and Christians became wider than that between whites and blacks; soon the gap between Jews and Christians would double. (According to a 2000 poll, long after the axis of American politics had shifted dramatically to the right, proportionally more Jews even than blacks defined themselves as liberal—and a higher percentage of African Americans called themselves conservative than did Jews. Even as progressivism appeared at the dawn of the new century to be on the defensive, Jews were twice as likely to designate themselves as liberal as were other Americans—and certainly as other white Americans.)

Richard M. Nixon's overwhelming reelection in 1972 looks in retrospect like the pivot of the political realignment to the right. Three out of every four voters living in high socioeconomic areas gave him their support, as did the majority of every white ethnic group—except one. His Democratic opponent was the son of a preacher: Senator George McGovern was a Methodist from the Great Plains whose isolationist undertones ("Come Home, America") implied softness toward a militarily robust Israel. He even blundered during a campaign stop in New York's Garment

District by ordering milk with his chopped chicken liver. Not since FDR was a major-party candidate more liberal than McGovern, who consequently garnered a whopping two-thirds of the Jewish vote. Indeed, had the rest of the electorate voted as Jews did, Nixon would have been buried in the greatest landslide in American history. Even after Nixon resigned from office in the summer of 1974 to avoid impeachment, over a quarter of the populace had a favorable opinion of the unindicted co-conspirator and regretted his resignation. The proportion of Jews expressing such sentiments was 6 percent.

How could political scientists account for 1976? A white Southerner was much less likely to vote for former governor Jimmy Carter of Georgia than was a northern Jew. Four years later, the president's support among Jewish voters dropped from 72 percent to 44 percent, five points ahead of former governor Ronald Reagan. The plurality that Carter achieved from Jewish voters in 1980 marked the first time since the New Deal era that a Democratic nominee for the White House had failed to secure a majority of Jewish ballots (because Congressman John Anderson—running as an independent—received about 15 percent of the Jewish vote). Four years later, the GOP spent four times as much as did the Democrats in making direct pitches to Jewish voters, who nevertheless gave Reagan 8 percent less of their support in 1984, even as his percentage of the popular vote increased by the same figure. Electoral analysts discovered that the only categories of the populace that bestowed upon former vice president Walter Mondale two-thirds of their votes—other than the Jews—were blacks and the unemployed. In 1988 Governor Michael Dukakis ran badly against Reagan's vice president, George H. W. Bush, but did better among Jews than even among Greek Americans.

The Durability of Progressivism

This voting pattern has if anything solidified into something akin to industrial strength, impervious to Republican attack. Take the four presidential elections before 2008. Four out of every five Jewish voters chose the Democratic nominee: Governor Bill Clinton in 1992 and again in 1996, Vice President Al Gore in 2000, and Senator John F. Kerry in 2004. In 1999 President Clinton's popularity among Jews held steady even during his impeachment ordeal. His chosen successor not only beat his opponent, Governor George W. Bush of Texas, by half a million votes in the general election but did significantly better among Jews as well, attracting 79

percent of their ballots. Though about one in five Jews reliably vote Republican (and that number can double in special circumstances), the commitment of Jews to the Democratic column has remained so intractable that the selection of Senator Joseph I. Lieberman as Gore's running mate in 2000 made no appreciable difference in their totals.

Perhaps even more noteworthy is that the prominence of a Jew on the Democratic ticket stirred no evident anti-Semitism. Informal religious tests are still applied for public office—for example, against atheists and agnostics. But in 2000 no such test was imposed on Lieberman, an Orthodox Jew. This expansion of political opportunity marked a remarkable transformation since the mid-1930s, when pollsters learned that two out of every five Americans would not vote for an otherwise qualified Jewish candidate for the presidency. Half a century later, that proportion fell to less than one in ten—which was statistically insignificant. One measure of the decline of bigotry occurred in 1992, which was the first time that the number of Jews serving in the U.S. Senate reached ten, the minimum necessary for a prayer quorum, or *minyan*. If the number of Jews serving in the Senate were to reflect the proportion of their co-religionists in the general population, there would be only two members of the upper house eligible for a *minyan*. Instead, in the Congress of the early twenty-first century, roughly a dozen senators were eligible. More Jews served in the Senate than adherents of any single Protestant denomination. The voters of two states, California and Wisconsin, each elected two Jewish Democrats to the Senate: Barbara Boxer and Dianne Feinstein, and Russ Feingold and Herb Kohl, respectively. Only two Jews serving in the Senate in 2008 were Republicans, Norm Coleman and Arlen Specter; and one senator aligned with the Democrats, Bernie Sanders, was actually a socialist. When the 30 Jews elected to the House of Representatives in the 110th Congress were added to the equation, a minority group long associated with marginality and persecution outnumbered Episcopalians and ranked just behind Presbyterians.

Ideology over Income

The Jewish vote in itself cannot account for such disproportionate representation and has been cast in states and districts too tiny to constitute a "bloc" favoring Jewish candidates. Because of the dominance of ideology, Jewish voters have tended to exempt themselves from the allure of identity politics. Unlike, for example, Irish Americans in the past or African Americans in the present, Jews have not been especially receptive to candidates of their own ethnicity and faith—unless they also promise to activate the liberal imagination. Not only arguments of immediate expediency but also appeals to ethnic loyalty—while not negligible—have found Jews less receptive than other minorities when stepping inside the polling booth. Perhaps that is because of historic charges of "dual loyalty," which raised the specter of unreliable patriotism, and of bloc voting, which insinuated the unwholesome and excessive influence of a minority. Often yearning to surmount the narrowness of parochial interest, Jewish voters have generally voted for non-Jewish candidates who were liberal rather than Jewish office seekers who were conservative.

But then, very few such candidates are conservative. The first two Jews to serve in the Senate ended up championing the Confederacy cause: Democrat David Levy Yulee of antebellum Florida and Whig Judah P. Benjamin of antebellum Louisiana. (Benjamin served in the secessionist cabinet as attorney general, secretary of war, and secretary of state.) Two-thirds of their successors in the twentieth and early twenty-first centuries have been Democrats, often left of center, exemplified by Herbert H. Lehman of New York, Abraham A. Ribicoff of Connecticut, Carl Levin of Michigan, Paul Wellstone of Minnesota, and Charles Schumer of New York. In the 2007–9 House of Representatives, for instance, the chief deputy minority whip was Eric Cantor of Virginia. But he was the only Republican representative who was Jewish. (In 2009 the only congressional caucus consisting of fewer Republicans was African American, because every black member of the House of Representatives was a Democrat.) How durable this one-sidedness among Jews will prove to be is not clear. Consider, though, the willingness in 2008 of only one in ten Jews under the age of 35 to call themselves Republicans.

In their relative indifference to pocketbook considerations, Jewish voters since the New Deal have violated one of the few axioms of political science: the higher the income, the greater the enthusiasm for the GOP. What then accounts for the distinctiveness of this political orientation? In the body-contact sport that American political operatives play, the most convincing explanation is quite eccentric: Jews have harbored a thirst for justice, often expressed in a moralistic idiom. They have envisioned politics to be the means by which unfairness and oppression might be challenged. An interpretation that highlights the quest for social justice hardly implies that Jews hold a monopoly on such motives. But what supports such an analysis are the voting patterns and the polling data and questionnaires that admit no other interpretation. In 1940, when W.E.B. Du Bois hailed the chairman of the NAACP's board of directors, Joel Spingarn, as "one of those vivid, enthusiastic but clear-thinking idealists which from age to age the Jewish race has given the world," the editor of *The Crisis* was hinting at the impulse that has set Jews apart from other participants in the nation's politics.

Impact

Perhaps no minority group has taken more seriously the ideal of popular sovereignty or has been more inspired by the rhetoric of civic responsibility. Jews have been twice as likely to vote as other citizens, sometimes constituting as much as 6 percent of the electorate. Such faith in the suffrage has paid off because of the unrepresentative character of the Electoral College, which the framers unintentionally tilted to favor Jewish residential patterns. That is why the political culture of so small a minority actually matters. Take 1976: in the state of New York, about a quarter of the voters were Jewish. They swung about 80 percent for Carter over incumbent Gerald Ford, enabling the Democratic challenger to carry the state and, with it, the presidency. Had Carter and President Ford evenly split the Jewish vote of New York, Carter would have lost the state and with it the White House. Even more consequential was the freakish 2000 election, which was decided in Palm Beach County, in the battleground state of Florida, by several hundred elderly Jews, a constituency to which the highly conservative independent candidate Patrick J. Buchanan would have been unable to pander. Confused by the "butterfly" ballot, this handful of Jewish senior citizens inadvertently voted for Buchanan and swung the election to Bush in the winner-take-all system devised in 1787.

Because Jews happen to be concentrated in states of high urban density, the impact of this minority group is magnified. That is why, ever since the political alignment that was forged in 1932, the attitudes and values of Jewish voters have been integral not only to the fate of liberalism in the United States but also to the vicissitudes of its democratic experiment.

See also European immigrants and politics; religion and politics since 1945.

FURTHER READING

Dollinger, Marc. *Quest for Inclusion: Jews and Liberalism in Modern America.* Princeton, NJ: Princeton University Press, 2000.

Fuchs, Lawrence H. *The Political Behavior of American Jews.* Glencoe, IL: Free Press, 1956.

Goren, Arthur A. *The Politics and Public Culture of American Jews.* Bloomington: Indiana University Press, 1999.

Greenberg, Cheryl Lynn. *Troubling the Waters: Black-Jewish Relations in the American Century.* Princeton, NJ: Princeton University Press, 2006.

Himmelfarb, Milton. *The Jews of Modernity.* New York: Basic Books, 1973.

Howe, Irving. *World of Our Fathers.* New York: Harcourt Brace Jovanovich, 1976.

Isaacs, Stephen D. *Jews and American Politics.* Garden City, NY: Doubleday, 1974.

Liebman, Arthur. *Jews and the Left.* New York: Wiley, 1979.

Maisel, L. Sandy, and Ira N. Forman, eds. *Jews in American Politics.* Lanham, MD: Rowman and Littlefield, 2001.

Shapiro, Edward S. *We Are Many: Reflections on American Jewish History and Identity.* Syracuse, NY: Syracuse University Press, 2005.

Whitfield, Stephen J. *American Space, Jewish Time.* Hamden, CT: Shoe String Press, 1988.

STEPHEN J. WHITFIELD

judicial branch

See Supreme Court.

Korean War and cold war

The Korean War (1950–53), sometimes considered the forgotten war, was the first military confrontation between U.S. and Communist forces in the cold war era. It began on June 25, 1950, when armed forces of the People's Democratic Republic of Korea (PDRK, or North Korea) attacked across the thirty-eighth parallel, the line that divided Communist North Korea, led by Kim Il Sung, from the non-Communist Republic of Korea (ROK, or South Korea), led by Syngman Rhee.

North Korea's objective was to unify the two Koreas as a single Communist state. The United States led a military force under the auspices of the United Nations to repel North Korea's assault on the South. The UN troops successfully cleared North Korean troops from South Korea by October. Thereafter, the Truman administration changed its war aims. The U.S. commander of the UN forces, General Douglas MacArthur, led his army across the thirty-eighth parallel in order to unify Korea under the leadership of the Rhee government. In November the Communist-led People's Republic of China (PRC) entered the war to counter the advance of UN forces toward the Yalu River, the border between China and North Korea. The war continued for another two-and-a-half years until July 27, 1953, when the United States and the United Nations signed an armistice with China and North Korea.

Origins of the War
The Korean peninsula had a long history of invasion and war. Japan occupied Korea from 1910 until its defeat in 1945 in World War II. U.S. forces replaced the Japanese south of the thirty-eighth parallel, and Soviet troops occupied the northern part of the country. These occupations ended in 1947, when the United States and the Soviet Union withdrew their military forces. The United States installed Rhee as president of South Korea, and the Soviets sponsored Kim Il Sung as the leader of North Korea. Both Rhee and Kim declared that there was a single Korean state, of which he was the legitimate leader.

The political climate and geopolitical balance of power in East Asia changed dramatically in 1949, when the Chinese Communist Party, under the leadership of Chairman Mao Zedong, won the Chinese civil war against the Nationalists, led by Jiang Jieshi, and founded the People's Republic of China. Mao's victory represented a serious challenge to the U.S. political and military position in East Asia. U.S. policy makers had hoped that Chiang's Republic of China (ROC) would help the United States impose regional stability. President Harry Truman and Secretary of State Dean Acheson considered Mao a partner of Soviet leader Joseph Stalin, interested in fomenting Communist-inspired revolutions throughout East Asia. Faced with the new reality of the PRC in control of the Chinese mainland and a greatly diminished ROC on the island of Taiwan, Acheson, in January 1950, defined a defense perimeter for the United States in East Asia running through the Philippines, Taiwan, and Japan. South Korea was not included under this shield, because Acheson believed only the three island states he had mentioned were of paramount strategic importance to the United States.

The situation on the Korean peninsula became increasingly tense. After the creation of South Korea and North Korea in 1947, armed forces on each side conducted raids across the thirty-eighth parallel to harass and destabilize the other regime. Early in 1950, Kim asked Mao for support should the North Korean leader decide on a full-scale attack against South Korea. Mao did not explicitly warn Kim against an attack; instead, he offered vague assurances of future support. Mao consulted with Stalin about potential Soviet backing for a North Korean attack on the South Koreans. Stalin urged restraint but promised Mao military support should the United States threaten the PRC.

Outbreak of the War

North Korean forces attacked across the thirty-eighth parallel on June 25. They quickly overcame the poorly armed and outmanned South Korean army and captured Seoul, the capital of South Korea, within days. The Truman administration was shocked by the assault. Truman was already under severe political attack: his critics accused him of having allowed the Communists to win the Chinese civil war. North Korea's attack appeared to be another sign of Communist power in Asia. The Truman administration had not expected North Korea to move, but when it did, U.S. officials believed Stalin was behind the assault. The president ordered General Douglas MacArthur, the commander of U.S. armed forces stationed in Japan, to send troops to Korea to reinforce the battered South Korean army.

The United States brought the issue of North Korea's attack before the UN Security Council. Within days, the Security Council labeled North Korea's actions unacceptable aggression, called on it to withdraw north of the thirty-eighth parallel, and authorized member states to use armed force to help South Korea repel the invasion. The resolution passed without an expected Soviet veto, because the Soviet Union had boycotted the Security Council meetings over the UN refusal to seat the Communist PRC as the official representative of China.

Truman's firm response to the North Korean attack led to a sharp increase in his public approval, from 36 percent to 46 percent, in early July. Yet the military situation in South Korea was bleak throughout the summer. North Korean forces continued to push South Korean, United States, and allied forces fighting under UN auspices southward until they held only a small semicircle of territory around the southern port of Pusan. Then, on September 15, UN forces under MacArthur landed by sea at Inchon, northwest of Seoul. They surprised and quickly overwhelmed the North Koreans. The UN forces quickly recaptured Seoul, and by early October, they crossed the thirty-eighth parallel and marched into North Korea.

The Truman administration now changed its war aims from repelling aggression from the North to unifying Korea as a non-Communist state. As the UN forces continued their advance into North Korea, Kim be-

came desperate for his future and Mao worried that the United States intended to attack China. The Chinese warned the United States not to approach the Yalu River separating Korea and China, or China would enter the war. MacArthur dismissed these warnings and assured Truman that China would not intervene. The president allowed UN troops to proceed north. As the UN forces approached the Yalu in mid-November, China sent an army of more than 300,000 across the river to attack the approaching troops. The Chinese outnumbered the UN forces and made them retreat south of the thirty-eighth parallel. North Korean troops once more occupied Seoul.

On November 30, Truman stated that the use of atomic weapons in Korea had "always been" under consideration. Such speculation alarmed British leaders whose troops fought alongside the Americans. After Prime Minister Clement Attlee complained, Truman backed away from the threat to use atomic weapons against Chinese or North Korean forces.

In the first three months of 1951, UN forces regrouped, retook Seoul, and advanced to positions near where the war had begun. Truman and his principal foreign policy and military advisors now favored pursuing a limited war in Korea, one that would assure the future of South Korea without sparking a larger conflagration with the Soviet Union.

MacArthur, on the other hand, continued his provocative rhetoric toward North Korea and China. Truman became increasingly angry and frustrated with MacArthur's belligerent tone. In April MacArthur telegraphed Republican House minority leader Joseph Martin, demanding that Truman "open a second front in Asia" by permitting him to attack China. Truman called this "rank insubordination" the last straw in his tense relationship with the general, and he fired MacArthur. The dismissal ignited a firestorm of public protest against the president, whose approval rating fell to an abysmal 23 percent. MacArthur received a hero's welcome in Washington and New York when he returned home. Truman's opponents called for the president's impeachment, but the political storm subsided. More people came to believe that MacArthur's incessant demands for victory over North Korea and China might lead to a third world war.

Peace Talks

Peace talks between the UN and North Korea began in July 1951, but the war continued unabated. U.S. in-

Legend:
- ||||||||||||| Communist Chinese offensive
- ·–·–·–· U.N. offensive Sept.–Nov. 1950
- ——— North Korean invasion June–Sept. 1950

CHINA

USSR

Farthest U.N. advance Nov. 1950

Yalu River

Chosin Reservoir

NORTH KOREA

Pyongyang

Wonsan

KOREA BAY

Armistice Line 1953

38th Parallel

YELLOW SEA

Inchon

Seoul

U.N. Landing Sept. 15, 1950

SOUTH KOREA

SEA OF JAPAN

U.N. defensive line Sept. 1950

Kunsan

Pohang-dong

Masan

Pusan

TSUSHIMA

JAPAN

HONSHU

KOREA STRAIT

KYUSHU

CHEJU

CHINA

MATSU

QUEMOY

TAIWAN

SOUTH CHINA SEA

Scale:
0   50   100 miles
0   50   100 kilometers

The Korean War

volvement in a stalemated conflict became increasingly unpopular at home, and Truman announced, in March 1952, that he would not seek reelection. The Korean War became a major issue in the 1952 presidential election campaign. Democratic presidential nominee Adlai Stevenson, the governor of Illinois, supported Truman's policy of containment and waging limited war in Korea. General Dwight Eisenhower, the Republican nominee, criticized Truman's handling of a war that had gone on for too long. His campaign adopted a slogan, K1C2 (Korea, Communism, and Corruption), as a way to tap popular discontent with the stalemate in Korea, the fear of communism, and anger at scandals involving administration officials. Eisenhower promised that, if elected, he would go to Korea, survey the state of the war, and recommend ways to end it.

Eisenhower, the popular victorious commander in the European theater during World War II, easily defeated Stevenson. The public was looking for a change of parties after 20 years of Democratic control in the White House and eagerly awaited an end to the Korean War. Eisenhower did go to Korea after the election and returned convinced that the war needed to end quickly. He concluded that both North and South Korea were intransigent in their demands, and that the United States needed to apply pressure on both sides to end the fighting.

After Eisenhower became president, the world political environment changed. Soviet leader Stalin died in March 1953, and his passing offered the promise of reducing cold war tensions. The new U.S. administration threatened both North and South Korea in order to produce movement in the stalled peace negotiations. Washington again hinted that it might use atomic weapons against North Korea, and American officials demanded that South Korea drop its requirement that North Korean prisoners of war held in South Korea be permitted to remain there after the war if they chose. The pace of negotiations quickened.

South Korea released more than 100,000 North Korean POWs rather than forcibly repatriate them. The United States, the United Nations, China, and North Korea signed an armistice on July 27, but South Korea refused to join on the grounds that North Korea had not acknowledged its aggression. The armistice divided North and South Korea by a line between the opposing military forces, roughly along the thirty-eighth parallel. A 10-kilometer-wide demilitarized zone separated the two Koreas. Over the next half-century, this border became the most heavily fortified area in the world.

Armed with artillery and tanks, hundreds of thousands of troops from North and South Korea and the United States faced each other. Intermittent negotiations failed to transform the temporary armistice into a full peace agreement.

Aftermath of War

Cold war tensions between the United States and the PRC remained high during and after the Korean War. The question of "who lost China" became a powerful and divisive issue in American politics. Anti-Communists accused Foreign Service officers, who had reported on the strength of Mao and the Communists and the weakness of Chiang and the Nationalists, of having contributed to the Communists' victory in the civil war. Between 1951 and 1953, many of these "China Hands" were fired from the State Department.

The Eisenhower administration provided more support for the Nationalist government of Taiwan than Truman had done. Early in the Korean War, the Truman administration had sent the U.S. Navy's Seventh Fleet into the Strait of Taiwan separating the island from the mainland. The aim was to protect Taiwan from a Communist attack but also to discourage the Nationalists from attacking the mainland. Eisenhower lifted the naval defense of Taiwan in 1953. A year later, Jiang sent 70,000 troops to the islands of Quemoy and Matsu, three miles off the coast of mainland China. In September the Chinese Communists began shelling these islands, and in November Communists planes bombed the Tachen Islands in the Taiwan Strait.

During this first Taiwan Strait Crisis, the Joint Chiefs of Staff recommended using atomic weapons against the mainland, and political pressure mounted on Eisenhower to send U.S. troops to protect the offshore islands. In the fall of 1954, the president decided against direct U.S. military involvement in the crisis. Instead, the United States signed a defense treaty with the Republic of China. Under this agreement, the United States promised to protect the island of Taiwan but was silent about the offshore islands. The first Taiwan Strait Crisis intensified in April 1955 when the president said that "A-bombs might be used . . . as you would use a bullet." China said it was willing to negotiate with the United States over the islands and the future of Taiwan. On May 1 China stopped shelling the islands.

Ambassadorial talks between the United States and Communist China began in the summer of 1955 and continued, off and on, mostly in Warsaw, for the next

16 years, until President Richard Nixon announced that he would visit Beijing. These conversations made no progress on the future of the Republic of China in Taiwan, but they did lead to the repatriation of U.S. and Chinese citizens who had been stranded in China or the United States, respectively, during the Chinese civil war and the Korean War. A second Taiwan Strait Crisis began in August 1958, when the Communists resumed shelling Quemoy and Matsu. Eisenhower asserted that the shelling was part of a plan "to liquidate all of the free world positions in the Western Pacific." China stopped shelling the offshore islands on January 1, 1959.

Tensions persisted, and the United States continued to see Communist China as a major threat. During the 1960 presidential campaign, Democratic candidate John F. Kennedy accused the Eisenhower administration of sending mixed signals to China, which had encouraged its aggressive moves in the Taiwan Strait. The growing split between Mao and the Soviet Union, under the leadership of Nikita Khrushchev, ratcheted up the cold war competition. In January 1961, Khrushchev, responding to Mao's accusation that the Soviet Union had retreated from its earlier revolutionary fervor, pledged his country's support for "wars of national liberation" around the world. The new Kennedy administration considered Khrushchev's promise a direct challenge to the United States and its support of pro-western governments. Kennedy increased U.S. support to the government of the Republic of Vietnam, or South Vietnam, as a way to counter Soviet and Communist Chinese influence in Southeast Asia.

The memory of the Korean War and Chinese intervention in it was ever present as the United States deepened its involvement in the Vietnam War during Kennedy's administration and the first 18 months of Lyndon Johnson's presidency. Democratic presidents were haunted by fear that their opponents would resurrect the cry "who lost China?" and charge them with "losing" Vietnam to the Communists. U.S. policy makers believed that the preservation of South Vietnam as an anti-Communist bulwark against what they considered to be a newly aggressive Communist North Vietnam was essential. Kennedy and Johnson administration officials both drew analogies between South Vietnam and South Korea and between North Vietnam and North Korea. They also drew sobering lessons from the Korean War and wished, at all costs, to avoid Chinese intervention in Vietnam.

See also era of consensus, 1952–64; Vietnam and Indochina wars.

FURTHER READING

Chen, Jian. *China's Road to the Korean War: The Making of Sino-American Confrontation.* New York: Columbia University Press, 1994.

Foot, Rosemary. *The Wrong War: American Policy and the Dimensions of the Korean Conflict.* Ithaca, NY: Cornell University Press, 1985.

Gaddis, John Lewis. *The Cold War: A New History.* New York: Penguin, 2006.

Halberstam, David. *The Coldest Winter: America and the Korean War.* New York: Hyperion, 2007.

Khong, Yuen Foong. *Analogies at War: Korean, Munich, Dien Bien Phu and the Vietnam Decision of 1965.* Princeton, NJ: Princeton University Press, 1992.

Schaller, Michael. *Douglas MacArthur: The Far Eastern General.* New York: Oxford University Press, 1989.

Stueck, William. *The Korean War: An International History.* Princeton, NJ: Princeton University Press, 1995.

———. *Rethinking the Korean War: A New Diplomatic and Strategic History.* Princeton, NJ: Princeton University Press, 2002.

Tucker, Nancy Bernkopf. *Taiwan, Hong Kong, and the United States, 1945–1992: Uncertain Friendships.* New York: Twayne, 1994.

Westad, Odd Arne. *The Global Cold War Third World Interventions and the Making of Our Times.* Cambridge, UK: Cambridge University Press, 2005.

ROBERT SCHULZINGER

labor movement and politics

On July 23, 1788, New York City artisans organized a parade to support the ratification of the U.S. Constitution. Marching behind banners of their crafts, artisans mobilized to defend their interests in the nation's emerging political order. As this episode suggests, organized workers have been active in American politics since the founding of the republic. More than 200 years after the New York parade, Web sites, phone banks, campaign contributions, and sophisticated canvassing operations had become labor's favored methods of political mobilization, but the aims of workers' organizations were unchanged: organized labor still mobilized politically around policies in the interest of wage earners.

The 200-year history of labor's political activism reveals a paradox. No nation produced a labor movement with a longer history of concerted electoral activity than the United States. Yet no labor movement had expended as much electoral energy without institutionalizing its political experience in a labor party. Indeed, it was the failure of American workers to develop an enduring labor party that led scholars to periodically ruminate on American exceptionalism.

Many factors worked against a successful American labor party. Some were political: a federal system that dispersed power among federal, state, and local jurisdictions and made it difficult for workers to win enough power to enact policies; winner-take-all elections that undercut minority representation; a court system that often undermined workers' legislative gains. Other factors were social: slavery and its legacy, a racial caste system that made it difficult to unite white and nonwhite workers behind a common political program; and waves of immigration that made the American working class unusually fractious along religious and ethnic lines. Other factors were economic: a vast and competitive national market that fostered an exceptionally anti-union ethic among employers; and a perennial shortage of skilled labor that created opportunities for skilled workers at the expense of working-class solidarity. Still other factors were cultural: in no industrializing nation did an ethic of individualism and social mobility sink deeper roots than in the United States. Together these factors created profound obstacles to the institutionalization of labor's political voice.

Yet despite the factors that inhibited the formation of a labor party, political activism was a continuous theme in the history of organized labor in America. Over two centuries, the form of workers' organization changed from journeymen's societies to craft unions, then to industrial unions, and ultimately to huge organizations encompassing public sector, service, and industrial workers in one union. Over time, union membership expanded beyond its original base among skilled, male, native-born whites and western European immigrants to include women and previously excluded groups of blacks, Asians, and Latinos. Labor's political philosophy moved from an early-nineteenth-century emphasis on anti-monopoly to a late-nineteenth-century brand of anti-statist voluntarism, and it ultimately evolved into support for a welfare state in the twentieth century. Yet in every era, the vast majority of organized workers believed that no matter what form their organizations took, what demographics characterized their membership, or what goals they sought to achieve, if they were to advance their interests they would have to engage in political action as well as workplace organization.

Indeed, if there was a form of "exceptionalism" in the American labor movement, it was represented by those few organizations like the Industrial Workers of the World (IWW) that rejected political action. The case of the ephemeral IWW, founded in 1905 and largely destroyed by combined government and employer repression in 1918, was not atypical: labor organizations that rejected politics altogether tended to have short histories. Thus, while the perennial frustrations and disappointments of American politics nursed a disdain for parties and politicians that waxed and waned among labor's activists from age to age, few labor leaders or organizations ever believed they would gain more by rejecting politics than by engaging in it. Most unions thus constantly sought to maximize their influence on the shifting terrain of American politics.

An analysis of labor's political strategies over the course of two centuries permits three generalizations. First, unions tended to find it more difficult to achieve solidarity at the ballot box than on the job. Not only did labor fail to create its own party, but for much of their history, unions also found it difficult to deliver their members as coherent blocs to one of the mainstream political parties. Second, in part due to the difficulty of constructing political solidarity, unions tended toward pragmatism and opportunism rather than ideological clarity and unity, especially in local and state politics. And third, labor organizations found that their political fortunes rarely rested in their own hands alone. Labor required coalitions, and the success or failure of those efforts was often outside of labor's control alone.

Despite these problems, labor continually found ways to express its political voice, and often exerted political influence that far exceeded its membership. Labor activism helped turn crucial elections, generate popular reform ideas, and mobilize new constituencies. If labor's political power operated under significant constraints, unions nonetheless helped shape American political history, as an examination of labor's activism in four distinct periods illustrates.

The Era of Party and Union Formation: 1780s–1880s

The formation of unions in the United States actually preceded the formation of parties. Philadelphia journeymen's societies began to negotiate with master craftsmen in the 1780s, even before Hamiltonians and Jeffersonians created the first party system. Yet parties grew faster and soon outstripped unions in scope and sophistication. By the mid-1880s, the United States had a well-established two-party system in which political professionals fused local machines into statewide and national coalitions to vie for power. Workers were only then beginning to construct their first broad-based national union federation capable of withstanding an economic downturn.

The unequal development of parties and unions over this century was crucial: it meant that no matter how avidly labor experimented with independent political action, workers were never organized well enough to match party professionals in the creation of national organizations.

Nonetheless, workers were politically active in the early nineteenth century. Indeed, labor's first partisan political activity can be traced to the Jeffersonian Democratic-Republicans, a movement in which New York and Philadelphia artisans played a significant role. Yet before the 1820s, labor's political activism was limited. It was the upsurge of union organization during the economic boom of 1824–37 that saw the first great experiments with labor-based political activism. During the union upsurge of these years, roughly 44,000 workers joined unions. This unionization led to the first city-wide labor federations, a necessary precursor to significant political activism. In 1827 Philadelphia tradesmen founded the Mechanics' Union of Trade Associations, through which they advocated for a ten-hour workday, argued that wealth belonged to those who produced it, and demanded equal rights for workers. The Philadelphia organization inspired the creation of "city central" federations in 13 other cities by 1836, including New York, where the General Trades' Union included 52 organizations. This organizational impulse eventually led to the creation of the National Trades' Union, a short-lived national labor federation.

As Andrew Jackson was consolidating his Democratic Party during these years, workers also turned to politics. Jackson found allies among trade unionists in cities like New York. But the agitation of the 1820s also produced the first instances of independent labor political action as the trades helped form "workingmen's parties" in several states. The first was launched in New York City in 1829, where it attracted talented leaders like labor editor George Henry Evans, reformer Thomas Skidmore, and radicals Robert Dale Owen and Fanny Wright. The workingmen's parties were short-lived, often succumbing to factionalism or absorption into the emerging two-party system, but they succeeded in making a number of issues—including the demand for free universal public education—central to the politics of the Jacksonian era.

When the depression of 1837 struck, labor's thriving organizational structures suddenly collapsed. During the 1840s, unions played an insignificant role in mobilizing workers, as Whigs and Democrats fought increasingly sophisticated campaigns against each other. Instead, the locus of labor activism shifted to the National Reform Association, established in 1845, and the "industrial congresses" that convened in several states. These initiatives helped to put land reform and homesteading on the national political agenda but yielded no independent political vehicle for workers. Such vehicles would not re-emerge until after the Civil War.

It was the emergence of national trades unions that made post–Civil War political action possible. The first national unions, the National Typographical Union and the National Molders' Union, arose in the 1850s. By the 1860s, railroad workers, stonecutters, machinists, shoemakers, and plumbers had formed unions and begun to collect dues and establish strike funds. When the Civil War ended in 1865, some 200,000 workers had been unionized, and by 1872 at least 30 national trade unions had been set up.

This upsurge allowed labor to revive independent political action through a national union federation called the National Labor Union (NLU), formed in 1866. The NLU advocated the eventual replacement of waged labor by a cooperative commonwealth, the exclusion of Chinese contract labor from the United States, and the enactment of eight-hour workday laws. In 1868 iron molder William Sylvis led the NLU's effort to create a national political party to realize this vision. But like the workingmen's parties, the NLU was short-lived. Sylvis's death in 1869, the NLU's abortive attempt to field a presidential candidate in 1872, and the economic depression that struck the next year combined to destroy the NLU.

The social turbulence unleashed by the depression of 1873 soon gave rise to several labor-backed political initiatives. In the space of a few years, three different parties were launched around appeals to labor: the Greenback-Labor Party (1874) advocated currency reform and appealed to farmers and workers alike; the Socialist Labor Party (1877) advocated Marxian socialism and drew support from European immigrant communities; and the Workingmen's Party of California (1877) campaigned for Chinese exclusion. All three parties left a mark: California's workingmen helped bring about the Chinese Exclusion Act of 1882; the Greenback-Labor Party helped win some modifications in the nation's monetary policy and sowed the seeds for the later Populist movement; and the SLP helped incubate the more popular Socialist Party of America (founded in 1901), which would become America's most successful socialist party.

Yet by the 1890s, organized labor began to pull back from independent political action. Labor's reluctance to

Social turbulence in the 1870s gave rise to several labor-backed political initiatives. The Workingmen's Party of California campaigned against Chinese labor immigration, which helped bring about the Chinese Exclusion Act of 1882. (Carl Albert Browne, "Regular Ticket Workingmen's Party California. The Chinese Must Go! 11th Senatorial District," 1878, lithograph. California Historical Society, FN-30623.)

launch its own party became clear in the aftermath of a great contest between two divergent union tendencies: one represented by the Noble and Holy Order of the Knights of Labor, an inclusive union that organized women and men, skilled and unskilled, black and white, founded in 1869; the other by the American Federation of Labor (AFL), founded in 1886 by a group of skilled craft unions, whose members were overwhelmingly white and male. Like the NLU, the Knights hoped to supplant the wage system with a cooperative commonwealth; its local assemblies often engaged in political activity and, in many locations, made alliances with Greenbackers and other third parties. Indeed, Terence V. Powderly, who served as Grand Master Workman of the Knights during its peak years of 1879–93, was elected to three terms as mayor of Scranton on the Greenback-Labor ticket beginning in 1878. The AFL, by contrast, favored the organization of workers by craft and the improvement of their wages, hours, and working conditions through collective bargaining, strikes, and union control of access to jobs. AFL leaders tended to have less faith in political action than did most Knights. AFL president Samuel Gompers, for one, had experienced firsthand the frustrations of political action when legislative compromises and judicial hostility undermined a multiyear campaign by his union, the Cigar Makers International Union, to eliminate tenement-house cigar production. Gompers believed that workers could not count on the state or political parties to deliver reform, and that only strong unions could win lasting gains for workers.

As the AFL grew and the Knights declined by the 1890s, a discernable pattern emerged in organized labor's political practice. The range of independent political initiatives that characterized labor activism in the 1870s gradually gave way to a system of "political collective bargaining" in which unions increasingly forsook independent political action in favor of pragmatic alliances with Democratic or Republican candidates.

The Emergence of Political Collective Bargaining: 1880s–1932

The period between the mid-1880s and the late-1890s saw decisive shifts in both the national party system and the labor movement, the results of which reinforced the new pattern in labor's political activism. If Republicans and Democrats competed on a relatively equal footing in the 1880s, Republicans achieved a decisive national advantage following the election of 1896, in which William McKinley defeated the Democratic-Populist fusion ticket headed by William Jennings Bryan. As Republicans consolidated their power, the AFL's trade unionism supplanted the failing Knights of Labor. The AFL's political approach soon became labor's predominant strategy.

The AFL steered clear of formal alliances with parties. Most of its leaders believed that the loyalties of many workers were already cemented to the Democratic or Republican parties by family tradition, regional or religious affiliations. These leaders never believed that workers would unite in a third party and thus resisted the two significant third parties that tried to attract workers in the years between the 1890s and World War I: the People's (Populist) Party and the Socialist Party of America. Populists tried hard to cultivate ties to labor: the Southern Farmers' Alliance rechristened itself the National Farmers' Alliance and Industrial Union in an effort to link farmers and workers, and Populists organized food shipments from farmers to striking steelworkers in Homestead, Pennsylvania, in 1892. Nonetheless, the AFL rejected populism. "Party politics, whether they be Democratic, Republican, Socialistic, Populistic, Prohibition, or any other shall have no place in the conventions of the American Federation of Labor," resolved the AFL at the height of the Populist agitation. Nor did the AFL reconsider during the climactic 1896 election. "Let the watchword be: No political party domination over the trade unions; no political party influence over trade union action," Gompers announced.

The AFL was equally opposed to an alliance with the Socialist Party of America. Although the Socialists built a strong following among workers, elected mayors in dozens of smaller cities, claimed the support of a significant minority of delegates to AFL national conventions, and perennially nominated the beloved former railroad union leader Eugene V. Debs as a presidential candidate, the AFL steadfastly rejected them.

AFL nonpartisanship did not mean that the organization was nonpolitical. Unlike the syndicalist radicals of the IWW, AFL members were active in partisan politics, especially on the local level. Rather than allying with one party, however, they tended to follow Gompers's dictum that unions should "reward our friends and punish our enemies." Local unions thus tended to engage in political collective bargaining in which they helped those politicians who offered them support on key issues—regardless of their party affiliation.

Even the AFL's nonpartisan approach was flexible. Indeed, in the decade before World War I, the AFL slowly revised its nonpartisanship without ever formally renouncing it. The impetus for this change was the increasing harassment of unions by the courts. In the early twentieth century, judicial injunctions became the bane of trade unionists. Judges' orders regularly barred unions from picketing and disrupted their boycotts and sympathy strikes. In frustration, the AFL drew up a Bill of Grievances in 1906 demanding an anti-injunction law and other measures. In 1908 the AFL presented its demands to both major party conventions. When the Democrats and their presidential nominee, again William Jennings Bryan, responded more favorably, the AFL inched toward an alliance with the Democrats. Still, important elements of the AFL's leadership and membership continued to vote Republican. Given this resistance, and Republican William H. Taft's 1908 election to the presidency, the consummation of an alliance between the AFL and the Democratic party was postponed until Democrat Woodrow Wilson unseated Taft in the 1912 election.

As Wilson took office, both he and AFL leaders saw much to be gained from an alliance. Wilson took the advice of Gompers in making appointments to the U.S. Commission on Industrial Relations, which recommended reforms in the nation's labor practices. Wilson also signed legislation granting an eight-hour workday for the nation's train crews and labor rights to the nation's merchant seamen, as well as the Clayton Anti-Trust Act, which Gompers mistakenly hoped would protect unions from injunctions. By the time Wilson ran for reelection in 1916, the AFL unions were actively working for him. Indeed, labor's help was instrumental in helping Wilson retain control of the White House in that close election.

But the Wilson-AFL alliance was itself cut short by the fallout from World War I. The war initially seemed to strengthen the relationship between labor and the Democratic Party. Even before the United States declared war, the AFL pledged to support Wilson's war policy. In return, the administration created war labor policies that encouraged collective bargaining and repressed the Socialists and the IWW, the AFL's chief rivals. With tacit federal support, the AFL saw its membership nearly double between 1916 and 1919. Yet these gains were fleeting: once the armistice was declared, federal support was withdrawn, and a ferocious anti-union backlash gathered strength. Democrats lost control of Congress in the 1918 elections—in part due to dissatisfaction with Wilson's wartime labor and economic policies—and unions lost a series of strikes in steel, coal, and textiles amid the rising fears of the "Red Scare" of 1919. In the 1920 elections, Republicans regained the White House, leaving the AFL-Democratic alliance in disarray.

The political backlash led to a brief revival of interest in independent labor political action. In 1922 a number of union leaders formed the Conference for Progressive Political Action (CPPA). The CPPA claimed credit for the defeat of dozens of anti-labor U.S. representatives that year, and hoped to launch a national party in 1924. But factional differences frustrated this vision. Senator Robert M. La Follette ran for president as a Progressive in 1924, with support from many unions. However, La Follette's defeat and the death of Samuel Gompers after the election left labor without a clear political strategy. In the 1928 elections, labor divided: Democrat Al Smith garnered the support of some union leaders, while others, including John L. Lewis, president of the United Mine Workers of America (UMW), supported Republican Herbert Hoover. American labor may have distanced itself from the independent political initiatives so prevalent in the nineteenth century, but labor still lacked a coherent political program as the 1920s came to an end. It would take a major economic calamity and political upheaval for labor to fashion an alternative.

The Heyday of the Labor-Democratic Alliance: 1932–72

The 1932 election of Democrat Franklin D. Roosevelt in the midst of the Depression transformed labor's politics.

Roosevelt's election allowed labor and the Democrats to rebuild a national political alliance, this time on a more solid footing. Labor support for Roosevelt in 1932 had not been unanimous; Herbert Hoover still commanded the allegiance of William Hutcheson of the Carpenters and other Republican-leaning union leaders. But once in office, Roosevelt cultivated ties with labor more assiduously than any previous president and his legislative programs earned him the enduring loyalty of rank-and-file unionists. The Wagner Act of 1935 guaranteed most private-sector workers the right to organize, gave the National Labor Relations Board (NLRB) the power to enforce that right, and compelled employers to recognize unions when the majority of their workers wanted to be represented by a union. The 1935 Social Security Act, which created a national retirement program and funded state programs of unemployment insurance and aid to dependent children, laid the basis of an American welfare state (and swept away most lingering resistance to state-administered welfare among the nation's unions). The Fair Labor Standards Act of 1938 finally banned child labor and created a minimum wage.

The enactment of such policies not only transformed labor's orientation to national politics and the state, but changed the union movement. By 1935 the legal and political context for union organizing had improved profoundly, forcing to the surface a long-simmering disagreement within the AFL between craft unionists and industrial unionists over how best to organize in this favorable environment. Led by Gompers's successor, William Green, craft unionists favored continuing the traditional AFL model. But an emerging faction led by UMW president Lewis, Sidney Hillman of the Amalgamated Clothing Workers, and others called for big new industrial unions in each of the nation's basic industries. When the AFL balked at this plan, Lewis and allies plunged ahead. In 1935 they formed the Committee for Industrial Organization, an initiative that soon evolved into a rival labor federation: the Congress of Industrial Organizations (CIO). These unions began recruiting thousands of auto, steel, and rubber workers in 1936.

Although labor was divided on the best method for organizing, the movement remained united politically behind the effort to reelect Roosevelt in 1936. Teamster union leader Daniel Tobin, a CIO opponent, helped coordinate Roosevelt's reelection campaign, even as the CIO also supported Roosevelt. Indeed, John L. Lewis transferred $500,000 from the UMW treasury to Roosevelt's campaign (the largest single contribution to a political campaign in that era). In 1936 Lewis and Hillman also helped launch Labor's Non-Partisan League in an effort to unify labor behind Roosevelt's reelection. George Berry of the AFL's Printing Pressmen's union ran the initiative, which raised $1.5 million for Roosevelt's reelection. Developments on the left aided the budding labor-Democratic alliance. New York labor leaders launched the American Labor Party in 1936, nominating Roosevelt as its presidential standard-bearer, and thus providing lifelong Socialists with a way to vote for Roosevelt without becoming Democrats. Meanwhile, the Communist Party of the United States, which had vocally opposed Roosevelt's policies before 1935, entered its Popular Front phase and encouraged members to support the CIO and New Deal initiatives.

Roosevelt's victory over Republican governor Alf Landon of Kansas in 1936 seemed to seal the emerging alliance between labor and the Democrats on the national level. Labor played a crucial role in the "New Deal political coalition" that emerged in these years. Unions proved especially important in mobilizing millions of second-generation immigrant urban voters.

Yet the national-level labor-Democratic alliance was not without tensions, and it was put to the test repeatedly in its formative years, 1936–48. While Roosevelt's administration relied on labor support in its conflicts with Republicans and conservative Democrats, Roosevelt viewed labor as just one component in a broad governing coalition. He was reluctant to expend political capital for labor. Thus, the president remained neutral during the CIO's failed 1937 "Little Steel" strike even as he asked John L. Lewis to support his failed "court-packing" initiative. Lewis came to mistrust Roosevelt's intentions and later broke with the president on foreign policy. Meanwhile, some anti-Communist trade unionists became suspicious of radical influences in the CIO and New Deal agencies. Still, most labor voters remained Roosevelt loyalists, as Lewis learned in 1940. When Lewis unsuccessfully opposed Roosevelt's election to a third term, he was compelled to turn over leadership of the CIO to Roosevelt ally Philip Murray of the Steelworkers.

American entry into World War II reinforced labor's alliance with Roosevelt while creating new problems for that alliance. Both the AFL and the CIO offered "no strike pledges" and cooperated with the war mobilization; the administration, in turn, supported unionization through the policies of the National War Labor Board.

The union movement emerged from the war larger and more powerful. In turn, labor lent its help to Roosevelt's effort to win an unprecedented fourth term. In 1944 Sidney Hillman helped launch the CIO's Political Action Committee (arguably the first modern PAC). The AFL followed suit, creating a PAC called Labor's League for Political Education in 1947. Yet as labor emerged as a key organizational component of Roosevelt's Democratic party, it also became a target for political attacks. In 1944 an invigorated Republican Party ran its best campaign against Roosevelt by arguing that labor had too much influence in his administration. Although Roosevelt prevailed, the results of the vote indicated that Republicans and conservative southern Democrats had begun to contain the labor wing of the party.

The real test of the labor-Democratic alliance, though, was whether it could weather three transitions that came in rapid succession between 1945 and 1948: the elevation of Roosevelt's successor, Harry S. Truman; conversion to a peacetime economy; and the emergence of the cold war. After Roosevelt's death and the end of World War II, a strike wave swept the nation as unions fought to make up ground lost to wartime inflation. Many labor leaders felt that President Truman, a moderate Missourian, offered tepid support to labor during this tumultuous period, and they resented Truman's threat to draft railroad strikers into the Army during one particularly bitter postwar battle. When Republicans recaptured control of Congress in 1946 and passed the anti-union Taft-Hartley Act over Truman's veto in 1947, labor's dissatisfaction with Truman flared. Left-wing unionists opted to abandon the Democrats and support the Progressive Party candidacy of Henry Wallace, a labor ally and a critic of Truman's emerging anti-Communist foreign policy. Most unions, however, stuck with Truman. Two factors ensured this. First, unions feared that Wallace would divide the Democratic vote and help elect Republican Thomas E. Dewey, a defender of Taft-Hartley. Second, most union leaders and members shared Truman's anticommunism stance and rejected Wallace's contention that the Soviet Union posed no threat to the United States. Ultimately, the AFL and most CIO unions and their members rallied behind Truman and helped him defeat Dewey. There was much truth in Truman's often-quoted reaction to the surprising election results: "Labor did it." Labor's support of Truman in 1948 sealed the national-level alliance between unions and the Democratic Party. But the alliance exacted a high price: the unions that supported

Wallace were expelled from the CIO for alleged Communist domination of their leadership.

The postwar labor-Democratic alliance was founded on the principles of cold war liberalism, the belief that the extension of the New Deal and resistance to Soviet communism were inseparable. Between 1948 and 1972, this shared commitment held the alliance together despite the opposition of southern Democrats, who fought unions and liberal social programs, and liberal Republicans, who courted (and occasionally won) union support, especially on the state or local level.

As the postwar Red Scare faded, labor liberalism emerged as a fragile juggernaut. The AFL and CIO reunited in 1955 to form the AFL-CIO and created the Committee on Political Education (COPE) to channel their political activism. COPE soon became a major source of political contributions and experienced campaign volunteers. Its support was instrumental in electing John F. Kennedy in 1960 and lobbying on behalf of the social programs of Kennedy's successor, Lyndon B. Johnson. The mid-1960s marked a high point for labor's political influence as the AFL-CIO became a powerful force in Lyndon Johnson's Democratic Party. Yet southern Democrats continued to act as a counterweight to labor's influence. Moreover, liberal Democrats, like Walter Reuther of the United Automobile Workers, were reluctant to appear to hold too much sway within the party. Any threatened labor "takeover" of the party, Reuther believed, would instigate a backlash, destroy the party's broad base, and leave labor politically isolated. Moreover, Reuther understood that no union could "deliver" its rank and file as a unified voting bloc. Indeed, Reuther was disturbed to find that a significant minority of his union's white members supported segregationist George Wallace's third-party campaign for the presidency in 1968. Ever conscious of the limited nature of electoral solidarity, unions thus pressed their political agenda without trying to control the Democratic Party, occasionally supporting sympathetic Republicans when it was advantageous. Overall, labor made important strides in the 1960s, including winning local, state, and federal policies that allowed government workers to unionize (government union membership grew tenfold between 1955 and 1975).

Labor in the Era of Post-Liberal Politics: 1972–2008

Before the 1960s ended, the Vietnam War and the civil rights movement—both of which labor supported—divided the Democratic coalition. Labor lobbyists helped pass the Civil Rights Act (1964) and Voting Rights Act (1965), but these laws accelerated the mass departure of southern whites from the Democratic Party over the next 20 years. Nor did labor's influence within the party grow as conservatives departed. In part this was due to labor's support of the Vietnam War. The staunchly anti-Communist AFL-CIO and its president George Meany favored U.S. military intervention in Vietnam in 1965. However, the disastrous war that resulted triggered a Democratic Party rebellion that brought down the Johnson presidency in 1968 and left labor isolated from the growing ranks of antiwar Democrats. Tensions between the AFL-CIO and advocates of the New Politics were exacerbated when the AFL-CIO refused to endorse the presidential candidacy of George McGovern in 1972, helping to ensure the liberal Democrat's crushing defeat by incumbent Richard M. Nixon.

The economic crises of the 1970s helped prevent labor-liberalism from rebounding in that decade as "stagflation" (the simultaneous surge of inflation and unemployment), plant closings, and declining union membership sapped labor's strength. Although unions and the Democrats revived their alliance in Jimmy Carter's successful 1976 campaign, the Carter administration disappointed labor. Carter was too concerned about inflation to back the aggressive economic stimulus programs unions desired and was weak in his support for labor law reform. Thus, several unions endorsed Senator Edward Kennedy's unsuccessful primary challenge to Carter in 1980. Even though labor reunified behind Carter in the general election, many union members voted for Republican Ronald Reagan.

Ironically, labor experienced a nadir of its influence under the administration of the only union leader ever to become president (Reagan had once headed the Screen Actors Guild). Reagan undercut union power by breaking a nationwide strike of air traffic controllers, appointing anti-unionists to the NLRB, and implementing a host of policies inimical to labor. The AFL-CIO fought back by working to rehabilitate the Democratic Party. Labor officials helped redesign the Democratic nominating process in 1984 in a way that created unelected "super-delegates"—including union leaders—who would be empowered to cast votes for the party's presidential nominee. Yet when the AFL-CIO tried to exert its influence by endorsing of Walter Mondale in 1984, the former vice president was attacked for being the candidate of "special interests." Mondale won the nomination only to be trounced by Reagan in 1984.

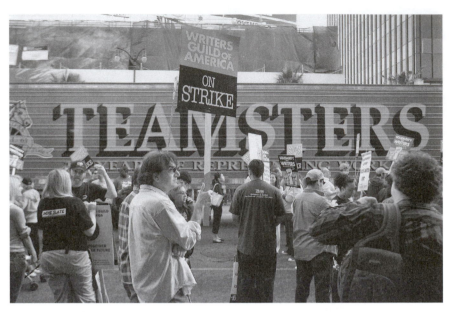

Unions such as the International Brotherhood of Teamsters join striking writers for a march down Hollywood Boulevard. The dispute between the Writers Guild of America and television producers over future revenue from shows distributed over the Internet and other new media started on November 5, 2007, four days after the contract expired and negotiations between the WGA and the Alliance of Motion Picture and Television Producers stalled. (David McNew/Getty)

Labor's influence slipped further when centrist Democrats created the Democratic Leadership Council (DLC) in 1985 in an effort to distance the party from its labor and liberal wings.

The ascendance of conservative politics forced labor to become increasingly adept at political action and to search more pragmatically for allies. In 1992 labor helped elect Arkansas governor Bill Clinton, a charter member of the DLC, to the presidency. Clinton rewarded union allies by supporting a higher minimum wage and stricter occupational health and safety policies. But he also defied labor by signing the North American Free Trade Agreement. When Republicans won control of Congress in 1994, internal dissatisfaction with labor's waning influence resulted in the first contested election for the AFL-CIO presidency in 1995. John Sweeney won that election, promising to retool labor's political operation and revive union organizing.

Sweeney's record was mixed during his first ten years in office. Despite their development of increasingly sophisticated voter mobilization techniques, unions were unable to help the Democrats recapture Congress or help

Vice President Al Gore defeat Republican George W. Bush in the controversial 2000 presidential election. At the same time, the share of workers organized continued to fall, reaching 13 percent by 2005. These failures contributed to the most significant labor schism since the 1930s, when five unions, led by the Service Employees International Union (SEIU) and the Teamsters, left the AFL-CIO in 2005 to form a new federation, Change to Win (CTW), promising to shift their emphasis from political action to workplace organizing. Such promises notwithstanding, CTW unions devoted significant resources to politics. Like the founders of the AFL, CTW concluded that it had no choice but to do so. Indeed, no union spent more on political action during 2005–8 than the SEIU. Although they continued to squabble, the AFL-CIO and CTW devoted millions of dollars and mobilized thousands of volunteers to help Democrats recapture Congress in 2006. Unions also played a vital role in the victory of Democratic presidential candidate Barack Obama in 2008.

The 2006 congressional victory and Obama's election heartened labor activists. Yet, tellingly, most unions discounted predictions of the dawn of a new era of liberalism and labor influence amid the economic turmoil of 2008. A century of labor history since the AFL's Bill of Grievances had taught union leaders to temper their expectations. They knew that no labor movement had a longer history of electoral success. American labor had undeniably left its mark on U.S. political development, but no labor movement anywhere had found the mobilization of working-class political power to be a more Sisyphean task.

See also Democratic Party, 1932–68; interest groups; labor parties; liberalism.

FURTHER READING

Archer, Robin. *Why Is There No Labor Party in the United States?* Princeton, NJ: Princeton University Press, 2007.

Boyle, Kevin, ed. *Organized Labor in American Politics: The Labor-Liberal Alliance 1894–1994.* Albany, NY: SUNY Press, 1998.

———. *The UAW and the Heyday of American Liberalism, 1945–1968.* Ithaca, NY: Cornell University Press, 1995.

Brody, David. *Workers in Industrial America: Essays on the Twentieth Century Struggle.* New York: Oxford University Press, 1980.

Dawley, Alan. *Class and Community: The Industrial Revolution in Lynn.* Cambridge, MA: Harvard University Press, 1976.

Dubofsky, Melvyn. *The State and Labor in Modern America.* Chapel Hill: University of North Carolina Press, 1994.

Fink, Leon. *Workingmen's Democracy: The Knights of Labor and American Politics.* Urbana: University of Illinois Press, 1983.

Francia, Peter L. *The Future of Organized Labor in American Politics.* New York: Columbia University Press, 2006.

Greene, Julie. *Pure and Simple Politics: The American Federation of Labor and Political Activism, 1881–1917.* New York: Cambridge University Press, 1998.

Karson, Marc. *Labor Unions and Politics, 1900–1918.* Carbondale: University of Southern Illinois Press, 1958.

Kazin, Michael. *Barons of Labor: The San Francisco Building Trades and Union Power in the Progressive Era.* Urbana: University of Illinois Press, 1987.

Laslett, John H. M., and Seymour Martin Lipset, eds. *Failure of a Dream? Essays in the History of American Socialism.* Revised ed. Berkeley: University of California Press, 1984.

Lichtenstein, Nelson. *State of the Union: A Century of American Labor.* Princeton, NJ: Princeton University Press, 2002.

Lipset, Seymour Martin. *American Exceptionalism: A Double-Edged Sword.* New York: Norton, 1996.

Lowi, Theodore J. "Why Is There No Socialism in the United States? A Federal Analysis." In *The Costs of Federalism*, edited by Robert T. Golembiewski and Aaron Wildavsky. New Brunswick, NJ: Transaction Books.

Marks, Gary. *Unions in Politics: Britain, Germany, and the United State in the Nineteenth and Early Twentieth Centuries.* Princeton, NJ: Princeton University Press, 1989.

Mink, Gwendolyn. *Old Labor and New Immigrants in American Political Development: Union, Party, and State, 1875–1920.* Ithaca, NY: Cornell University Press, 1986.

Montgomery, David. *The Fall of the House of Labor: The Workplace, the State, and American Labor Activism, 1865–1925.* New York: Cambridge University Press, 1987.

Orren, Karen. *Belated Feudalism: Labor, Law, and Political Development in the United States.* New York: Cambridge University Press, 1991.

Rock, Howard, Paul A. Gilje, and Robert Asher, eds. *American Artisans: Crafting Social Identity, 1750–1850.* Baltimore, MD: Johns Hopkins University Press, 1995.

Rogin, Michael. "Voluntarism: The Political Functions of an Antipolitical Doctrine." *Industrial and Labor Relations Review* 15, no. 4 (July 1962), 521–35.

Schneirov, Richard. *Labor and Urban Politics: Class Conflict and the Origins of Modern Liberalism in Chicago, 1864–97.* Urbana: University of Illinois Press, 1998.

Voss, Kim. *The Making of American Exceptionalism: The Knights of Labor and Class Formation in the Nineteenth Century.* Ithaca, NY: Cornell University Press, 1993.

Wilentz, Sean. *Chants Democratic: New York City and the Rise of the American Working Class, 1788–1850.* New York: Oxford University Press, 1984.

Zieger, Robert. *Republicans and Labor, 1919–1929.* Lexington: University of Kentucky Press, 1969.

JOSEPH A. McCARTIN

labor parties

Beginning with the Workingmen's parties of the 1820s and 1830s and extending into the New Deal era of the 1930s and 1940s, American workers repeatedly organized independent labor parties to enact reforms that could not be won though the unionization of the shop floor alone. Most of these labor parties survived just a few years before being co-opted by the two-party system or collapsing as a result of internal organizational weakness. And yet, while the specific platforms and voting constituencies varied over time, all labor parties shared a common goal of reforming the nation's economy and society to ensure labor's access to the basic rights of American citizenship as defined by workers themselves: an honest chance for upward mobility, a guarantee of basic economic security, the preservation of the dignity of labor in an industrial economy, and meaningful participation in the democratic process. Examining the notable examples of labor party organization case by case provides a glimpse at the changes industrialization brought to both the composition of the American working class and also to American workers' understanding of the rights inherent in American citizenship. Where, when, and why did labor parties emerge? What economic, social, and political reforms did these parties champion?

The Workingmen's Parties

The first labor parties in American history were the Workingmen's parties that appeared in more than 50 cities and towns throughout the mid-Atlantic and Northeast during the late 1820s and early 1830s. The Workingmen attracted support from the ranks of artisans anxious about the downward pressure on wages and the overall threat to skilled work posed by the revolutions in transportation, commerce, and manufacturing then sweeping through the American economy. Events in Philadelphia were typical. Organized following an unsuccessful strike for the ten-hour day, Philadelphia's building tradesmen formed a Workingmen's Party in 1828 and promptly nominated labor-friendly candidates for city and county offices. Their platform clearly reflected the economic anxieties of the city's skilled tradesmen and included demands for the ten-hour day, a mechanics' lien law, and prohibitions on the use of inexpensive convict labor. But the Workingmen in Philadelphia and elsewhere also lobbied for a broad slate of civic reforms designed to ensure for themselves the ability to fully participate in nineteenth-century civic life, including demands for free, universal, tax-supported public schools and for improvements in such basic public health measures as street cleaning and water and sewage works. This approach yielded quick but ultimately short-lived electoral success. In Philadelphia, the Workingmen controlled city government as early as 1829, but by 1832, their party had collapsed. Targeted for co-optation by the major parties and dismissed as the "Dirty Shirt Party" by self-proclaimed respectable middle- and upper-class voters, the Workingmen's parties everywhere disappeared as rapidly as they emerged, and the movement collapsed entirely by the mid-1830s. The meteoric trajectory of the Workingmen's movement foreshadowed the advantages and difficulties awaiting future labor parties: they succeeded during times of labor unrest and in regions where labor enjoyed strong organizational advantages but proved unable to sustain their electoral successes when faced with co-optation by the major parties and the hostility of middle- and upper-class voters.

Free Labor Ideology, Wage Labor Reality

The decades between the decline of the Workingmen's parties and the end of the Civil War proved inauspicious for labor party organization. This was due in part to the consolidation of the two-party system in American politics and its division of working-class voters along ethnocultural lines: the Democratic Party appealed to working-class immigrants of Irish and German descent; the emergent Republican Party attracted support from native-born workers. But above all else it was the development of what historians have labeled *free labor ideology* that curbed independent labor politics at midcentury. First articulated during the mid-1850s by the fledgling Republicans, free labor ideology emphasized the nobility of all labor in a free society, favorably juxtaposed the North's labor system with the slave labor regime in the South, and maintained that even unskilled industrial wage labor could be reconciled with traditional notions of the United States as a nation of independent producers because upward social mobility remained open to any sufficiently hard-working wage earner. For northern workers, the preservation of the Union thus became conjoined with the rhetorical defense of free labor and fealty to the Republican Party. All this discouraged the formation of independent labor parties, but no ideology could long obscure the harsh realities of industrialization during the decades following the Civil War. Free labor ideology had convinced many in the working class that their needs could be met within the two-party system, but the harsh realities of work in late-nineteenth-century industrial America led many to question that notion. Labor parties emerged during the decades following the Civil War whenever workers took measure of the distance between the promises of free labor ideology and the realities of wage labor in industrial America.

Labor Parties during the Age of Industrialization

The depth of working-class discontent caused by industrialization can be gauged by the sheer number of labor parties to emerge during the last four decades of the nineteenth century—the heyday of labor party organization. But the fact that many labor parties emerged during these decades demonstrated that not all workers embraced the same set of reforms and underscored the degree to which industrialization divided the American working class along lines of ethnicity and skill.

The earliest labor parties organized during this era grew out of the eight-hour movement of the late 1860s and clung to a vision of an America full of native-born, independent, republican artisans. Advocates fought to limit a legal day's work to eight hours as a way to ensure for workers enough leisure time for the self-improvement and education necessary for full republican citizenship, a message that appealed directly to northern native-born skilled workers worried that industrialization would leave no place in the American political economy for self-employed artisans. By contrast, other labor party organizers embraced the onrush of industrialization and appealed directly to immigrant wage earners then flooding into America's factories as unskilled laborers.

Founded in 1877, the Socialist Labor Party (SLP) was mainly composed of foreign-born German, Polish, and other Eastern European immigrants. Steeped in Marxist ideology, SLP organizers welcomed the development of a permanent wage-earning working class as the necessary precursor to socialism, demanded the "abolition of the wages system" and the "industrial emancipation of labor" and dismissed the eight-hour movement's idolization of the independent producer. They looked forward to the day when class-conscious wage-earners seized the means of production from their employers.

A third group of labor party activists argued that—given the long-standing agrarian discontent with railroads and eastern financial institutions—building a successful labor party meant forging an effective political coalition with the nation's disgruntled farmers. The National Labor Reform Party of 1872 marked an early attempt at a national-level alliance of farmers and labor. Its organizers tried to balance working-class demands—support for the eight-hour day and a national bureau of labor statistics—with agrarian demands for currency and land reforms.

None of these labor parties achieved much electoral success. The eight-hour movement inspired only short-lived state labor parties in 1869 and 1870. The doctrinaire SLP lasted two decades but experienced success only in immigrant-rich cities such as Milwaukee, Wisconsin, and Chicago, failed to field a presidential ticket until 1892, and never claimed more than a few thousand members.

Abandoned by workers suspicious of aligning themselves with farmers and dominated by agrarian concerns, the Labor Reform Party mustered only 18,600 votes in the 1872 presidential election out of the more than 6 million votes cast. A credible third-party farmer-labor alliance remained elusive until the People's (Populist) Party emerged in the early 1890s.

Episodes of industrial upheaval allowed late-nineteenth-century labor parties to transcend such internal divisions, forge effective coalitions with nonlabor reform movements, and win elections. Unlike the earlier Labor Reform Party, the Greenback-Labor Party (1878–88) was a farmer-labor coalition that actually enjoyed significant working-class support—but only in 1878, when the Great Railroad Strike of 1877 remained fresh in the minds of working-class voters. Running on a platform that included demands for the eight-hour day, mandatory safety inspections for mines and factories, restrictions on the use of child labor, and a national bureau of labor statistics, the Greenback-Labor Party polled better than 50 percent throughout eastern coal-mining regions, performed well in union strongholds such as Pittsburgh, and elected a series of labor-friendly mayors in such medium-sized industrial cities as Scranton, Pennsylvania, and Utica, New York. Working-class support quickly withered, however, and agrarians dominated the party during the 1880s.

The rise of the Knights of Labor during the Great Upheaval of 1886 provided a second occasion for labor party success—this time in over 200 city-level labor parties. In Chicago, the United Labor Party emerged following a crackdown on organized labor that began with the infamous May 1886 Haymarket Square incident. In Milwaukee, the People's Party emerged after striking ironworkers were met with violence. In New York, workers joined an eclectic coalition of reformers in support of the mayoral candidacy of Henry George. These local-level labor parties articulated demands designed to protect the dignity of working-class life in the nation's industrializing cities: they demanded public ownership for transit lines; relief for the urban poor; public works programs to reduce unemployment; the establishment of public libraries, recreation centers, and parks; and improved urban sanitation systems. Enough working-class voters were drawn to the Milwaukee People's Party to elect a mayor, a congressman, and a handful of state assemblymen. Chicago's United Labor Party appeared so strong that Republicans and Democrats fielded a coalition candidate to defeat it. In New York, Henry George finished an impressive second in the city's mayoral contest, ahead of the young Theodore Roosevelt, then running on the Republican ticket. These city-level parties declined quickly, however, and an effort to build a national party based on the localized successes of 1886 proved disastrous. The national United Labor Party, for example, polled fewer than 5,000 votes during the 1888 presidential election.

Conditions favored independent labor politics during the 1890s. Even by the harsh standards of the late nineteenth century, nationwide economic depression and industrial violence meant that these were years of intense suffering for workers. At the same time, moreover, many of the differences that separated previous labor parties had disappeared. Demands for the eight-hour day remained at the top of labor's agenda, for example, but gone was the eight-hour movement's desire to resurrect the era of the skilled republican artisan. By the 1890s, industrial wage labor was recognized as an entrenched reality. And socialism, once the domain of the immigrant-dominated SLP, had become "Americanized" thanks in part to the popularity of reform tracts such as Edward Bellamy's *Looking Backward*, but also due to workers' own brushes with antilabor repression. The emergence of the Social Democratic Party (SDP; 1898–1901) clearly signaled the homegrown nature of labor radicalism. Led by Eugene V. Debs—a charismatic yet previously obscure Midwestern politician transformed by his experiences as a union leader during the early 1890s—the SDP argued that socialism in America could be achieved using nonviolent, democratic means, but only through the organization of an independent labor party.

And yet, just as these conditions seemed auspicious for labor party success another schism emerged within labor's ranks. The American Federation of Labor (AFL) became the dominant labor organization during the 1880s and 1890s by pursuing a strategy of "pure and simple" unionism: it organized trade unions mostly among skilled workers, focused exclusively on workplace demands for better wages and hours, avoided all alliances with political radicals, and—after a contentious 1894 convention—expressly prohibited its membership from participating in any labor party effort. This stance eliminated an important potential source of votes at a critical time. The ideological struggle between "pure and simple" trade unionism and the political socialism of Debs and other activists defined the labor party argument during the Progressive Era.

Trade Unionism and Socialism during the Progressive Era

During the Progressive Era, many middle-class Americans embraced an expanded role for the state in order to resolve the social and economic problems that accompanied industrialization. In this context, the AFL's "pure and simple" trade unionism proved neither illogical nor inflexible. The prohibition against independent labor parties continued, but AFL leaders nevertheless recognized that Progressive Era expansions in the power of government underscored the importance of politics to labor's cause. In 1906 the AFL circulated labor's "Bill of Grievances"—a list of desired reforms—to both the Republican and Democratic parties, and quickly forged informal political alliances with progressives from both parties.

This alliance between progressives and the AFL was facilitated by the fear in both camps that the Socialist Party (founded in 1901) would inspire American workers to demand even more radical reforms. The dominant labor party during the Progressive Era and also the longest-lasting, best-organized, and most successful working-class third party in U.S. history, the SP flatly declared that "pure and simple" trade unionism left the majority of semiskilled and unskilled workers in mass production industries out in the cold. True reform, SP organizers argued, required an independent labor party encompassing workers of all ethnicities and skill levels. "The socialist or cooperative system," these organizers declared in a resolution adopted at the SP's 1901 convention, "can only be brought about by the independent political organization and the united action of the wage working class." To this end, the SP adopted a flexible platform and built a diverse national coalition. SP candidates often employed radical rhetoric evocative of the earlier Socialist Labor Party, but the party platform advocated a series of incremental reforms including—public ownership of the nation's railroads, mines, oil and gas wells, and utility companies; improved hours and wages; public works programs to mitigate periods of high unemployment; and political reforms such as the initiative and referendum. The ranks of the SP, moreover, included not just doctrinaire activists but also coal miners, hard-rock miners, radical farmers, and industrial workers of all ethnicities and skill levels. Based on this diverse coalition and the appeal of its platform, the Socialists achieved a string of electoral victories. By 1912—the height of the SP's electoral fortunes—1,200 Socialists held elective office across the country. Seventy-nine socialist mayors had been elected in such cities as Berkeley, California; Butte, Montana; Flint, Michigan; Milwaukee, Wisconsin; and Schenectady, New York. Eugene Debs—a five-time candidate for president under the SP banner—received nearly 1 million votes (6 percent) in the 1912 presidential election.

The labor-friendly reforms enacted during the Progressive Era can be understood within the context of this surge in Socialist Party support, but World War I brought an abrupt end to the party's influence. Meeting the needs of a wartime economy solidified the alliance between the AFL and the administration of President Woodrow Wilson: workers received better wages and working conditions, and the administration received assurances that AFL leadership would crack down on labor radicalism. Government authorities quickly concluded that the Socialist Party's antiwar stance and its radical critiques of American society jeopardized the war effort. The U.S. Postal Service barred Socialist Party periodicals from the mail, crippling party organization in distant rural areas. Justice Department officials hurt the party everywhere else by throwing its leaders in jail and disrupting party events. Debs himself was arrested and sentenced to ten years in jail following a 1918 antiwar speech. By the end of World War I, the Socialist Party was in a state of disrepair.

Labor Parties after World War I

The same forces that crushed the Socialist Party, however, also produced the next surge in labor party organization. The wartime bargain between labor and the state enhanced workers' stature in American society and encouraged them to approach the postwar world with a sense of anticipation. Having helped the nation fight for democracy abroad, workers began to demand "industrial democracy" at home—a call for workers to have an increased say in the management of industry. But this new sense of purpose within labor's ranks was matched by a decidedly conservative turn in domestic politics that not only jeopardized labor's postwar hopes but also threatened to roll back workers' wartime gains. Labor parties emerged to fight for the workers' vision of the postwar political economy in the face of this rightward shift in American politics.

Labor parties surfaced in nearly 50 cities during 1918 and 1919—an early indication of the vigilance with which workers protected their vision for the postwar world. In November 1919, at the end of a year in which over 4 million workers struck for better wages, shorter hours, and industrial democracy, delegates from these local-level labor parties met in Chicago to create the National Labor Party. In an attempt to capitalize on agrarian unrest stemming from the ongoing postwar agricultural depression, in mid-1920, organizers rechristened their effort the Farmer-Labor Party and wrote arguably the most militant platform in the history of U.S. labor parties. Proclaiming that "political democracy is only an empty phrase without industrial democracy," the 1920 platform explicitly connected labor's struggles with broader reform currents in American society. Farmer-Laborites called for the eight-hour day, the right to organize and bargain collectively, and the right to strike; championed government ownership of key industries; demanded the repeal of the wartime Espionage and Sedition Acts that had crippled the SP; reaffirmed the rights of free speech and assembly; supported democratic reforms such as the initiative, referendum, and recall; and demanded a federal department of education "to the end that the children of workers . . . may have maximum opportunities of training to become unafraid, well-informed citizens of a free country." This ambitious platform, though, did not spare the Farmer-Labor Party of 1920 from disaster at the ballot box. The party won just 265,000 votes in the presidential election of 1920, the result of reactionary postwar politics and yet one more illustration of the elusiveness of effective farmer-labor alliances. Only in Minnesota—a state in which movements among workers and farmers were equally strong—was the farmer-labor effort a lasting success. The state-level Minnesota Farmer-Labor Party sent elected officials to the state legislature, the Minnesota governor's mansion, and the U.S. Congress.

The New Deal Era and Beyond

Labor party politics changed decisively as a result of the Great Depression and the New Deal. Just as the free labor ideology of the mid-nineteenth century preempted the emergence of labor parties for a generation, the New Deal coalition built by Franklin D. Roosevelt curbed independent labor politics and channeled labor's political energies into the Democratic Party from the 1930s onward. Although revisionist scholars often dismiss labor's alliance with the Democratic Party since the 1930s as a "barren marriage," in fact this partnership proved a productive one: the New Deal guaranteed to working Americans the right to organize and collectively bargain for higher wages and better conditions, enacted a broad set of economic reforms designed to make working- and middle-class life more secure, and—like the free labor ideology before it—affirmed the dignity of work in America by offering a full-throated rhetorical veneration of labor's place in society. With the advent of the New Deal, labor moved closer than ever before to the center of American politics. It did so as an appendage of the Democratic Party.

The fortunes of independent labor parties during the long New Deal era—from the 1930s through the 1960s—demonstrates the power of this alliance between labor and the Democratic Party. Labor parties did emerge during this time, but they ultimately *contributed* to the hold that the Democratic Party and the New Deal came to have on working-class voters. A series of grassroots labor parties, for example, sprung up during 1934 and 1935 in cities hit hard by the Great Depression and labor unrest. Each of these parties demanded workers' right to unionize and each pleaded for economic relief. But in so doing, they underscored the enormity of the economic problems caused by the Depression, drove Roosevelt's New Deal to the left, and therefore helped to cement the New Deal–labor alliance. The history of the one major independent labor party to emerge during the New Deal era—New York's American Labor Party (ALP; 1936–56)—is emblematic of the fate of labor parties during these decades. Composed of left-wing activists, radical unionists, African Americans, Hispanics, and Italian Americans, the ALP was created in July 1936 expressly as a way for Socialists and other radicals to cast a ballot *supporting* Franklin Roosevelt's reelection. Although the ALP platform included specific demands for the municipal ownership of utilities and price controls for key food commodities, in effect, the party offered a blanket endorsement of the New Deal. Roosevelt gave the ALP his tacit blessing and in 1936, he received 275,000 on the party's ballot line. The ALP was in this sense not an independent labor party. Its electoral success depended in large part on its support for the Democrats' New Deal.

During the late 1940s, ALP activists—dismayed by what they considered to be President Harry Truman's abandonment of the liberal housing, health care, education, and social security programs called for by Roosevelt in his 1944 "economic bill of rights"—attempted to organize a new national labor party. But this independent effort only showcased the continuing strength of the New Deal–labor alliance. When the ALP supported Henry A. Wallace's third-party challenge to Truman in 1948, both the AFL and the Congress of Industrial Organizations sanctioned neither Wallace's candidacy nor the calls for an independent labor party—a clear indication that organized labor believed that the reelection of New Deal–style Democrats must not be jeopardized by third-party activity. Given Wallace's anemic showing, the collapse of the ALP shortly thereafter, and the lack of significant labor parties since, it appears that working-class voters received the message. The election of 1948 arguably marked the end of independent labor party politics for a generation. Only with the waning of the New Deal order and the rise of the New Right during the 1980s and 1990s did labor activists begin to question their alliance with the Democratic Party and revisit the idea of independent labor politics. A new generation of labor party activists did emerge during the mid-1990s to argue that centrist Democrats had abandoned workers and that a new labor party effort was needed to push for issues such as the living wage, universal health care, and environmental protection. But these labor party advocates ultimately balked when it came to running candidates, a testament to their own acknowledgement of the dim outlook for independent labor politics at the end of the twentieth century.

The Labor Party: An Enduring but Elusive Goal

In every era, the emergence of independent labor parties reflected the desire among workers to win not just better wages and working conditions but also a broader set of reforms designed to ensure access to the full benefits of American citizenship. But while a distinguishing feature of the labor party impulse, this pursuit of reform outside of the workplace paradoxically hindered labor party success. During much of the nineteenth century, labor party activists articulated wildly different visions of what kind of laborer belonged in a labor party; this reflected the heterogeneity of the working class and made political consensus elusive. At other times, the pursuit of broad reforms made labor parties readily susceptible to co-optation by the major parties, particularly when the parties made direct overtures to labor in the form of free labor ideology and New Deal liberalism.

See also Greenback-Labor Party; labor movement and politics; populism; socialism.

FURTHER READING

Archer, Robin. *Why Is There No Labor Party in the United States?* Princeton, NJ: Princeton University Press, 2007.

Brody, David. "The Course of American Labor Politics." In *In Labor's Cause: Main Themes on the History of the American Worker*. New York: Oxford University Press, 1993.

———. "On the Failure of U.S. Radical Politics: A Farmer-Labor Analysis." *Industrial Relations* 22, no. 2 (1983), 141–63.

———. *Workers in Industrial America: Essays on the Twentieth Century Struggle*. New York: Oxford University Press, 1980.

Davin, Eric Leif, and Staughton Lynd. "'Picket Line and Ballot Box': The Forgotten Legacy of the Local Labor Party Movement, 1932–1936." *Radical History Review* 22 (1979–80), 43–63.

Fine, Nathan. *Farmer and Labor Parties in the United States, 1828–1928*. New York: Rand School of Social Science, 1928.

Fink, Leon. *Workingmen's Democracy: The Knights of Labor and American Politics*. Chicago: University of Illinois Press, 1983.

Greene, Julie. *Pure and Simple Politics: The American Federation of Labor and Political Activism, 1881–1917*. New York: Cambridge University Press, 1998.

Greenstone, J. David. *Labor in American Politics*. New York: Knopf, 1969.

Montgomery, David. *Beyond Equality: Labor and the Radical Republicans*. New York: Knopf, 1967.

Shapiro, Stanley. "'Hand and Brain': The Farmer-Labor Party of 1920." *Labor History* 26 (1985), 405–22.

Weinstein, James. *The Decline of Socialism in America, 1912–1925*. New York: Monthly Review Press, 1967.

KEVIN POWERS

Latinos and politics

The term *Latino* refers broadly and inclusively to that portion of the U.S. population that traces its heritage to the Spanish-speaking countries of the Caribbean and Latin America. The currency of the term points to the recent realization that the increase of the U.S.-Latino population, along with its dispersal throughout the country, has transformed Latinos into a significant *national* population group. It also suggests that Latinos have amassed visible political influence in the United States. They constitute key voting blocs in the southwestern states as well as in Florida, New York, and Illinois. Latinos are generally well represented in these state legislatures. Latino mayors have led the major cities of Los Angeles, Denver, San Antonio, and Miami. At the national level, both the Democratic and Republican parties have become acutely aware that Latinos may hold the key to a majority of the 270 electoral votes needed to win the presidency. Accordingly, recent administrations have included at least two high-profile cabinet-level Hispanic appointments. Thus the phrase "Latinos and politics" has a contemporary ring.

But such a view is quite ahistorical. The notable presence of Latinos *as U.S. citizens* dates back to the mid-nineteenth century. An expanding United States, imbued with the spirit of Manifest Destiny, warred with Mexico (1846–47), and acquired the northern half of its territory. Half a century later, after the Spanish-American War (1898), the United States acquired Puerto Rico (and the Philippines). Along with the territorial acquisitions came long-established Latino populations. These populations were accorded citizenship rights, however tentative and restricted in practice.

This "early" experience of Latino political incorporation is a neglected subject in U.S. political history, but it offers a much-needed perspective on current affairs. One learns, for example, that fears about "Latinization" and calls for "Americanization" have a long and prominent place in discussions about Latinos in the United States. In short, one cannot "remember the Alamo" or the Maine, for that matter, and simultaneously think of Latinos as a recent presence.

The phrase "Latino politics" may be misleading if it implies unity among the various national-origin groupings that make up the category "Latino." Significant social and political differences distinguish the three largest and oldest subpopulations: Mexicans (64 percent of all Latinos), Puerto Ricans (9 percent), and Cubans (3.4 percent). Moreover, any putative pan-ethnic identity remains geographically fragmented along distinct national origin lines, with Mexican Americans concentrated in the Southwest, Puerto Ricans in the Northeast, and Cubans in south Florida. Where they comingle, as in New York City, Chicago, or Houston, there is as much tension as solidarity. In fact, the identifier "Latino" may derive its coherence mainly from the perspective of English-speaking non-Latinos.

This article focuses on the three main Latino subpopulations—Mexicans, Puerto Ricans, and Cubans—and describes the manner in which they have become active U.S. citizens. Each group has become part of American society at different times and in different ways.

Mexican Americans

1850–1910: The Experience of Annexation

A comprehensive historical assessment of the Mexican-American experience must deal with the Mexican-American War (1845–47) and the resulting annexation of the northern half of Mexico. An estimated 100,000 Mexicans resided in the annexed territories, with the core settled along the length of the Rio Grande. Although the Treaty of Guadalupe Hidalgo of 1848 was intended to secure the citizenship and property rights of the former Mexican citizens in the new order, regional history for the next 50 years was dominated by conflict around these two sets of rights.

The first major question involved the exercise of American citizenship by the vanquished Mexicans. In both Texas and California, their right to vote was tentative and subject to local review. Some members of the Mexican landed elite remained active in the politics of the new states, such as Jose Antonio Navarro of San Antonio, J. T. Canales of Brownsville, Texas, and Romualdo Pacheco from Santa Barbara, California. Yet even the elite could be subjected to humiliating restrictions, as in the case of Manuel Dominguez of Los Angeles, who in 1857 was prevented from testifying in court because of his "Indianness." Dominguez had been a delegate to the California Constitutional Convention of 1849.

The most telling mechanism of control was the status of New Mexico. Although it had sufficient population to have merited statehood along with California in 1850, New Mexico was not admitted into the Union until 1912. For 64 years after the signing of the Treaty of Guadalupe Hidalgo, New Mexico remained a territory whose governor was appointed by the president and whose territorial legislature could be overridden by the U.S. Congress. As far as Congress was concerned, the statehood matter was inextricably tied with "uplifting" and "Americanizing" the Mexican American citizenry. In the territorial politics of New Mexico, this statehood issue, along with the land question, dominated the discourse of the day. The conscious shift in the 1870s from a Mexican identity to a "Hispano" identity that emphasized European origins was a reframing maneuver that reflected the campaign for statehood and effective citizenship by the Mexican American citizenry.

The next area of tension in the Southwest involved the question of land ownership. Within a generation, most of the better lands changed hands from Mexican owners to "American" ones through distressed sales or outright seizure. Much displacement came about as a result of railroad-induced modernization in the 1870s and 1880s. Such modernization generally increased pressure on traditional subsistence farmers and ranchers in densely settled Mexican communities. The result was a number of "wars"—the El Paso Salt Wars of 1877, the "white cap" (gorras blancas) movement of the 1880s in northern New Mexico, and an explosion in 1915–16 in deep South Texas. All reflected the conflict between "prodevelopment" interests, usually newcomers, and "antidevelopment" old timers, of whom Mexicans were a major component. As the old Spanish-Mexican elite of the annexed territories lost their land base, they also lost whatever political influence they had retained in the new American order. Partial exceptions existed in a few counties in northern New Mexico and along the Texas-Mexican border.

1910–45: Political Incorporation through Segregation

When Mexican immigrants repopulated the Southwest and expanded their old settlements in the early twentieth century, labor-intensive commercial agriculture had already swept aside the centuries-old Mexican class order based on ranching. Now most Mexicans in the region—descendants of the original settlers as well as recent immigrants—constituted the critical farm labor force for an "agricultural revolution." In the 1920s, the sharp increase in the Mexican population sparked a contentious debate in Congress and in the region about the "Mexican problem." In general, Mexicans were seen as another race problem to be handled in much the same way as the African American was handled, through segregationist policies and institutions. The U.S. Census designation of the Mexican-origin population as "other race" in 1930 reflected the racial attitudes of this time. The Great Depression, which led social service agencies and law enforcement officers to organize "voluntary" repatriations, settled the "Mexican problem" temporarily. An estimated 400,000 Mexicans and Mexican Americans—one-fifth of the Mexican population in the country—were repatriated during the 1930s.

New Mexico, finally granted statehood in 1912, remained an exception to the regional pattern of de jure segregation and political exclusion. The presence of a landed elite and merchant class acted to contain such exclusion and separation. Their political representatives also pressed their claims to a Hispanic-European identity. Dennis Chavez, elected to the House of Representatives (1930–34) and later to the Senate (1935–62), came from such a background and was the first Latino senator in the history of the country.

Outside of New Mexico, however, the politics of the Mexican American community was framed by its position as a segregated farm-working class. Addressing working-class issues were mutual aid societies (*mutualistas*) and fledging labor unions. The latter, in particular, were the source of much political activism, as evident in major agricultural strikes in California in the 1930s, the pecan shellers strike of the same period in Texas, and mining strikes in Arizona and New Mexico in the 1940s. Emma Tenayuca of San Antonio, known for her fiery speeches, was perhaps the most prominent labor organizer of the period.

The small but aspiring middle class, many of them World War I veterans, was more concerned with segregation than with labor issues. In Texas and later throughout the Southwest, they organized themselves as the League of United Latin American Citizens (LULAC) in the late 1920s and early 1930s. LULAC was a civic organization dedicated to making its members into "the best and purest" American citizens. The organization distanced itself from militant labor and immigrant organizations; in fact, it often denounced strikes and supported repatriation. LULAC members claimed to be Caucasian, and this was the basis for their legal argument in several court challenges to segregation. (LULAC would change its position on these issues in the early 1950s.) Another organization similar in orientation was the Mexican American Movement in Los Angeles of the 1940s. Such groups reflected emerging class and citizenship divisions within the Mexican community in the United States.

World War II broke the grip of growers on their Mexican American labor force, which either entered the armed forces or went to work in defense plants. An estimated 500,000 Mexican Americans performed military service. After their service, most did not return to the fields but moved to nearby cities. The primary political arena for negotiating Anglo-Mexican relations now became urban areas.

1945–75: Challenging Segregation

As a result of their service during World War II, returning Mexican American veterans mobilized to demand first-class citizenship. Various patriotic groups formed to challenge segregation. The most notable of these was the American GI Forum, which spread rapidly from Texas throughout the Southwest and Midwest after it challenged a funeral home that had refused to handle the body of a decorated Mexican American veteran. In California, the Community Services Organization also began to challenge segregation aggressively in courts and in local urban politics.

Due to pressure from this World War II and the Korean War generation, most city facilities in the Southwest were officially desegregated in the 1950s. In electoral politics, this veteran-driven generation would make important breakthroughs. Raymond Telles was elected mayor of El Paso in 1957. Elected to Congress was Henry B. Gonzalez of San Antonio (1961–99) and Edward Roybal of Los Angeles (1963–93). Representing New Mexico was the second Latino senator in U.S. history, Joseph Montoya (1964–77).

The high watermark of this veteran-driven political movement came with the "Viva Kennedy" campaign of 1960 that focused on Mexican American voters. Its great success was the first indication that Mexican Americans might become important players in national elections. Concretely, the campaign provided the impetus for the creation of two activist political organizations: the Political Association of Spanish-Speaking Organizations (PASSO) in Texas and the Mexican American Political Association (MAPA) in California.

In the 1960s, farm worker strikes in California and Texas in 1965–66 set off organizing energies that quickly reverberated throughout the Southwest and the Midwest. Inspired by the black civil rights movement, youthful activists took the pejorative lower-class labels of *Chicano* and *Chicana* and transformed them into powerful political identities. The Chicano movement scored a few notable successes. It won a handful of rural county and town governments in Texas (under the banner of La Raza Unida Party), fueled a land-grant reclamation movement in New Mexico, secured labor rights for farm workers in California, and opened up universities throughout the region to Chicano youth. The movement also set the stage for considerable reform, both nationally and locally. It left its imprint in the creation of new advocacy organizations: the Mexican American Legal Defense and Educational Fund (MALDEF), the Southwest Voter Registration and Education Project (SVREP), Communities Organized for Public Services (COPS), and the National Council of La Raza (NCLR). Through a combination of lobbying efforts, legal pressure, and voter mobilization campaigns, these organizations laid the groundwork for the full political inclusion of Mexican Americans.

1976–Present: The Rise of a Political Elite

Since the mid-1970s, Mexican Americans have played key political roles in all southwestern states and in several urban areas outside the region. The growth in Mexican American political participation in the Southwest has been dramatic: between 1976 and 1988, the number of Latino registered voters doubled to more than 3 million, while the number of Latino elected officials also doubled to more than 3,000. The watershed elections of Henry Cisneros as mayor of San Antonio (1981–89), of Federico Peña as mayor of Denver (1983–91), of Gloria Molina as Los Angeles city councilwoman (1987–1991) and later as county supervisor (1991–present), as well as the gubernatorial elections of Jerry Apodaca (1975–79) and Tony Anaya (1983–87) in New Mexico, signified an exponential increase in political representation for the Mexican American community.

The makeup of state legislatures has also reflected this newfound influence. In Texas, since the late 1990s, at least 30 of the 150 representatives in the lower chamber and 7 of 31 senators in the upper have belonged to a Mexican American caucus. In California, in spite of an anti-Latino climate—or perhaps because of it—Mexican Americans in 1996 gained 13 seats in the 80-member state assembly, making Cruz Bustamante the first Latino speaker of the lower house. Since then, Bustamante has been followed in that office by Marco Antonio Firebaugh and Fabian Nuñez.

Despite the Democratic leanings of most Mexican Americans, the Republican Party has attempted to make inroads with appeals to "family values" and business development. The result has been a sporadic competition between the two parties for the Mexican American vote. President George H. W. Bush's appointment of Lauro Cavazos as secretary of education (1988–90) and Manuel Lujan as secretary of the interior (1989–93) represented a serious bid to enlist Mexican Americans in the Republican fold. The Democratic Party response was seen in President Bill Clinton's appointments of Henry Cisneros as secretary of housing and urban development (1993–97), of Federico Peña as secretary of transportation (1993–97) and later as secretary of energy (1997–98), and of Congressman Bill Richardson of New Mexico as United Nations ambassador (1997–98) and later as secretary of energy (1998–2001). Attorney General Alberto Gonzalez (2005–07) was appointed by President George W. Bush. These appointments suggest that Mexican American representation at the highest levels have become institutionalized in partisan politics.

Puerto Ricans

1898–1945: Annexation without Incorporation

The Puerto Ricans' path to U.S. citizenship has also involved the experience of annexation and migration. In some aspects, their experience mirrors that of the New Mexicans. In 1898, as a result of the Spanish-American War, Spain ceded Puerto Rico and the Philippines to the United States in the Treaty of Paris. In 1900 the U.S. Congress passed the Foraker Act to set up civil government in Puerto Rico, following the territorial model of New Mexico. From 1900 to 1948, the governor of Puerto Rico was appointed by the president of the United States, and any bill passed by the Puerto Rican legislature was subject to review and veto by the U.S. Congress. In 1917 the Jones Act granted Puerto Ricans U.S. citizenship, but the U.S. Supreme Court ruled, the following year, that the Jones Act did not extend the full protection of the Constitution to Puerto Ricans and that Puerto Rico was an "unincorporated" territory belonging to—but not forming part of—the United States.

This limbo status shaped Puerto Rican politics much as it had earlier shaped New Mexican politics. The Puerto Rican elite chafed under U.S. rule and protested the island's lack of political autonomy. The substitution of English for Spanish as the language of instruction, for example, was a subject of great controversy. Unwilling to accept the colonialism represented by the Foraker Act, the elite organized new political parties based on alternative solutions to the problem of its colonial status. The Republican Party campaigned for eventual statehood, while the Unionist Party proposed greater autonomy and eventual independence. The names and makeup of the main political parties would change over the next 50 years, but a constant question was a party's position on independence or statehood.

As U.S. citizens, Puerto Ricans were not subject to immigration controls and could visit or stay on the mainland at will. The immigration restrictions of 1924 aimed at southern and eastern Europeans sparked the first notable wave of Puerto Rican migrants to the mainland. In New York City, tensions between Puerto Rican migrants and older Jewish residents erupted in "Harlem riots" in 1926. Protection for the growing Puerto Rican *colonias* in New York City came from the Porto Rican Brotherhood of America, a mutual aid and political organization, which evolved in the 1930s into a federation of neighborhood and hometown groups: La Liga Puertorriqueña e Hispana.

For the incoming migrants, neighborhood and hometown groups were the links to both local New York politics and island politics. Given the circular migration between island and mainland, events in Puerto Rico heavily influenced the politics of the migrants. In 1937, for example, over 10,000 Puerto Ricans assembled in Central Park to protest a massacre in Ponce, where police had killed and wounded hundreds of nationalists who had gathered for a rally and march.

1945–75: Migration to the Mainland

The immediate post–World War II period was marked by political and economic upheaval. On the political front, the status question became increasingly violent, as *independentistas* and the colonial government engaged in armed attacks and reprisals. Under pressure to resolve the issue, the U.S. Congress passed legislation in 1947 and 1950 allowing Puerto Ricans to elect their own governor and to draft their own constitution within the colonial framework. This lent support to the first elected governor of Puerto Rico, Luis Muñoz Marín, who had advocated a third, middle-of-the-road option between independence and statehood—that of commonwealth status. The response of *independentistas* to these actions came in the form of an uprising on the island and an attempted assassination of President Harry S. Truman in Washington, D.C., in October 1950. In 1954 four nationalists opened fire inside the U.S. House of Representatives, wounding five congressmen. In response to such actions, the U.S. and Puerto Rican governments carried out a severe repression of the nationalist movement. Since then, the statehood option has emerged as the primary alternative to commonwealth status.

On the economic front, the island government, in an effort to deal with serious chronic unemployment, began to encourage migration to the mainland, opening a Migration Division Bureau in New York City to facilitate the work and adjustment experience of migrants. The Puerto Rican population on the mainland rose from 70,000 in 1940 to 900,000 in 1960. An estimated one-third of the island's population had migrated to the mainland by 1960.

In the 1950s, the political orientation of Puerto Ricans on the mainland was still focused on the island, a reflection of a belief that they would eventually return. Nonetheless, Puerto Ricans gradually began to focus more on mainland politics as opposed to island concerns. This nuanced shift became evident in the organizations that emerged in the late 1950s and early 1960s. The Puerto Rican Forum, modeled after the NAACP and the American Jewish Committee, aimed to become the power broker for the Puerto Rican community, challenging the domination of the Migration Division Bureau. The main objective of the Puerto Rican Association for Community Affairs (PRACA) was the development of a grassroots leadership for the statewide Puerto Rican community. ASPIRA was organized in 1961 to encourage and assist in the educational advancement of Puerto Rican youth. These three organizations were among the most influential in the city. By 1965 New York office-holders included a Puerto Rican city councilman, a justice of the civil court, a state senator, and three state assemblymen.

The late 1960s witnessed the emergence of a Nuyoriqueño identity among the second-generation Puerto Rican youth. In struggles that paralleled those of the African American and the Chicano, organizations ranging from the Young Lords to the Puerto Rican Legal Defense and Education Fund sprang up to call attention to the needs of the Puerto Rican community in New York and Chicago. Such organizations successfully pressured city government, hospital boards, school boards, and universities to increase representation and service.

Since 1976: The Rise of a Mainland Citizenry

The migration from the island and the growth of second- and third-generation Nuyorqueños (and Nu-ingleses, or Puerto Rican New Englanders) gradually shifted the locus of power from the island to the mainland. By 1980, counting second and third generations, the Puerto Rican population on the mainland had doubled to slightly more than 2 million. The number living in New York City was 860,000. Their politicization laid the groundwork in the 1970s and 1980s for the election of several city officials and as many as two state senators and five assemblypersons in the state legislature. Since the 1970s, the congressional representative from the south Bronx has been Puerto Rican. Herman Badillo was the first (1971–77), followed by Robert Garcia (1978–90), and José Serrano (1990–present). Since 1993 Congresswoman Nydia Velázquez has represented a district encompassing parts of Brooklyn and Queens. Congressman Luis Gutiérrez, representing Chicago's Fourth Congressional District, has also been in the House of Representatives since 1993. The three congressional representatives not only speak for their various districts but also concern themselves with the needs of the island.

Thus, the political interests of the commonwealth are now served and protected by Puerto Rican political participation and representation on the mainland. Puerto Rico has no electoral votes and thus has no real say in presidential elections; on the other hand, the northeastern states where mainland Puerto Ricans are concentrated—New York, New Jersey, Pennsylvania, Connecticut, and Massachusetts—represent a critical electoral bloc. Likewise, Puerto Rico is represented in Congress by a nonvoting commissioner, while the mainland communities have three congressional representatives.

During the 1960s, many political activists believed that the problems of the mainland Puerto Rican community would be resolved once the island was granted independence. Today some believe that these problems will disappear once the island is granted statehood. Since 1967, however, a majority of island Puerto Ricans has consistently chosen commonwealth status over the options of statehood and independence in a series of referenda. The status of Puerto Rico remains a recurring issue in party politics on the island.

Ironically, mainland Puerto Ricans may have more say about the future status of Puerto Rico than those on the island. In 2008 the stateside population was estimated to equal the island population of 4 million. It is clear that the second and third generations have become a permanent mainland citizenry. The island's future will be shaped within the context of American mainland politics.

Cuban Americans

1959–79: The Formation of an Exile Community

Except for the cigar-making community of Ybor, Florida, and a community of exiles and merchants in New York and New Orleans, there was no significant Cuban presence in the United States until the 1959 revolution of Fidel Castro. The first wave of about 200,000, mainly Cuba's upper classes, took place in 1959–62. They were granted refugee status and allowed to enter the country without the restrictions imposed on other groups. A program was implemented to assist in their resettlement and economic adjustment. This wave has been called the "Golden Exile" because its refugees have been so economically successful in their adopted country. A second wave of about 260,000, representing the middle sectors of Cuban society, came to the United States during the "freedom flights" of 1965–73. Finally, the Mariel boatlift of 1980 added another 125,000 refugees from a cross-section of Cuban society. Since then, the United

States has admitted approximately 20,000 Cubans annually through a regularized immigration process. Cubans who do not follow this process and who are intercepted in open water are returned to Cuba, while those who touch land are accepted as refugees. This is known as the "wet feet, dry feet" policy. At the close of the twentieth century, there were approximately 1.2 million persons of Cuban origin in the country. The great majority, some 65 percent, live in southern Florida.

The 1960s were dominated by the many exile political organizations concentrated in Miami. By the end of 1963, there were at least four different "provisional governments" and many more paramilitary organizations. These militants, trained by the CIA, limited their actions to Cuba in a barely disguised "secret war." But in the 1970s, they expanded their targets to include those in the exile community who disagreed with their goal of overthrowing Castro. Between 1973 and 1976, more than 100 bombs exploded in the Miami area alone. The FBI nicknamed Miami "the terrorist capital" of the country. Organized crime, especially in drug trafficking, was said to involve those with CIA connections. Three of the Watergate burglars were Cuban exiles with CIA ties.

The persistence of an anti-Castro exile ideology is an important part of Cuban American politics. The desire to recover the homeland has been the focus of much political discourse and the source of most mobilization in the Cuban American community. This primacy of homeland issues explains the preference for the Republican Party, which is seen as more staunchly anti-Communist than the Democratic Party. But young Cuban Americans have begun to split their votes more equally.

Since 1980: Becoming Cuban American

If the Viva Kennedy campaign of 1960 was the clarion call for Mexican Americans, the campaign of Ronald Reagan in 1980 played a similar role for Cuban Americans. Until then, many Cubans had been slow to naturalize as U.S. citizens and register to vote. Reagan's candidacy, however, made participation in the U.S. electoral system consistent with the exile agenda of recovering the homeland. Reagan promised a hard line and even possible overthrow of Castro. Becoming U.S. citizens and voting, far from being an indication of political assimilation, was actually a strategy for advancing the exile agenda. In 1980 and 1984 Miami Cubans voted for Reagan by an overwhelming 90 percent.

Reagan's candidacy and election dramatically increased the participation of Cuban Americans in U.S.

politics. Rather than continue to direct their energies to paramilitary activities, in 1981 the exile leadership created the Cuban American National Foundation (CANF) and a Free Cuba political action committee to help the Reagan administration and Congress formulate foreign policy toward Cuba. CANF was the principal lobbyist for Radio Martí and later TV Martí, as well as for successive measures to tighten the embargo.

Thus, Cubans became influential players in domestic U.S. politics because of their intense interest in shaping policy toward Cuba. In 1976 they only comprised 8 percent of registered voters in Dade County. By 1983 they made up 20 percent of registered voters, and their high turnout made them a critical swing vote in Florida elections. Since 1996 Cuban Americans have been the largest voting bloc (over 40 percent) in Dade County. This produced a boom in the number of Cubans in elected positions at all levels of government. By the late 1980s, the mayor, city manager, and county manager of Miami-Dade were all Cubans. By the early 1990s, Cubans held seven seats in the Florida House of Representatives and three in the Florida Senate. Two émigrés, Ileana Ros-Lehtinen and Lincoln Diaz-Balart, and U.S.-born Mario Diaz-Balart had been elected to Congress. Mel Martinez, formerly Housing and Urban Development secretary in the George W. Bush administration, was elected as U.S. senator in 2005. Carlos Gutierrez served as secretary of commerce (2005–08) in the Bush administration. The acquisition of such political influence by first-generation immigrants is unprecedented in American history.

The passage of time has reduced the proportion of early exiles among the Cuban community in the United States. While they comprised two-thirds of the Cuban-origin population in 1970, by the end of the century, they accounted for less than a third of the Cuban American community. Generational differences have begun to appear, with the U.S.-born second generation more likely to favor a diplomatic solution to the problems in Cuba rather than continued military or economic aggression. Some Cuban Americans have joined pan-Latino organizations such as LULAC, an indication of an emerging ethnic identity. New organizations such as the National Coalition of Cuban Americans are focused on voting rights, employment, housing, education, and other domestic concerns. What is clear is that regardless of what happens on the island, a significant number of the Cuban community will remain in the United States. Nonetheless, the exile ideology still exerts considerable emotion. Witness the Elián González episode of 1999–2000—a controversy over whether six-year-old Elián, survivor of a tragic crossing of the Florida Straits, should be returned to his father in Cuba. For the foreseeable future, the homeland concerns of Cuban Americans will continue to be injected into local and national politics.

The Rise of Latino Politics?

The results of the 2008 national elections illustrate the heightened political influence of Latinos in the United States. Thirty years ago there were only four Latino congressmen—two from Texas, one from California, and one from New York. In 2008, 25 Latinos and Latinas—18 from the Southwest, three from the Northeast, one from the Midwest, and three from Florida—were elected to the 111th Congress. All but four were Democrats. The election of three Latino senators—Ken Salazar, Democrat of Colorado; Robert Menendez, Democrat of New Jersey; and Mel Martinez, Republican of Florida—was also a "first" in American political history. Even the unsuccessful presidential campaign of New Mexico Governor Bill Richardson underscored the increasing prominence of Latinos in national politics. In short, in the early twenty-first century, the presence of Latinos in high office has become an accepted fact of American politics.

Such incorporation does not signify a cohesive Latino political bloc or agenda. Anyone harboring the illusion that there are no significant differences among Latinos need only look at the identity politics of the Cuban-origin community in the United States. Most Cuban Americans consider themselves to be political refugees and draw a sharp distinction between their experience and that of Latino economic immigrants. They object to being placed under the pan-ethnic label of *Hispanic* or *Latino*. Even within specific national groupings, one finds important identity differences, as, for example, between Nuyoricans and Puerto Ricans or between Mexican Americans and Mexican immigrants.

There are, of course, areas of political agreement among Latino groups. Policies concerning education, language use, and immigration may affect all Latino communities. Often, what brings these distinct groups together in common cause is simply the nativist response of non-Latinos. Yet, aside from a natural interest in their respective homelands, the interests and problems of Latinos are basically the same as those of non-Latinos of similar class rank. As it stands, Latino identity remains a general identity rather than the basis for political solidarity.

In the near future, with the dispersal of Puerto Ricans, Cubans, and Mexicans throughout the United

States, along with the relatively recent immigration of Dominicans and Central Americans, it is conceivable that a pan-Latino identity may arise. The vision of such a unity is not new. During his 15-year exile in New York City in the late nineteenth century, Cuban lawyer-intellectual José Martí wrote about "Nuestra America" and a pan-American "Latinidad." Martí envisioned a hemispheric unity of the Spanish-speaking peoples of Latin America. Given the long and difficult history of U.S.–Latin American relations, the possibility that such a pan-Latino identity might in fact be achieved within the United States would be most ironic.

See also immigration policy.

FURTHER READING

De la Garza, Rodolfo L. Desipio, F. C. García, J. A. García, and A. Falcón. *Latino Voices: Mexican, Puerto Rican, and Cuban Perspectives on American Politics.* Boulder, CO: Westview Press, 1993.

García, María Cristina. *Havana USA.* Berkeley: University of California Press, 1996.

Gómez, Laura E. *Manifest Destinies: The Making of the Mexican American Race.* New York: New York University Press, 2007.

Grenier, Guillermo, and Lisandro Pérez. *The Legacy of Exile: Cubans in the United States.* Boston: Allyn and Bacon, 2003.

López, Adalberto, and James Petras, eds. *Puerto Rico and Puerto Ricans.* New York: Wiley, 1974.

Montejano, David, ed. *Chicano Politics and Society in the Late Twentieth Century.* Austin: University of Texas Press, 1999.

Pitt, Leonard. *The Decline of the Californios: A Social History of the Spanish-Speaking Californians, 1846–1890.* Berkeley: University of California Press, 1970.

Sánchez Korrol, Virginia E. *From Colonia to Community: The History of Puerto Ricans in New York City.* Berkeley: University of California Press, 1994.

Weber, David, ed. *Foreigners in Their Native Land: Historical Roots of the Mexican Americans.* Albuquerque: University of New Mexico Press, 1973.

DAVID MONTEJANO

legislative branch

See House of Representatives; Senate.

liberal consensus and American exceptionalism

The idea of liberal consensus took hold of the historiography of the 1950s and in some ways reflected the apparent tranquility of the Eisenhower years. After the tumultuous 1930s, which saw the radicalization of American intellectual life, and the arduous 1940s, in which the American people endured World War II, the 1950s seemed to welcome a healthy return to the sane and normal. The moderation in politics matched the homogenization in historical scholarship, which denied all that had been contentious and conflictual in the American past in order to uphold the "the vital center" that the poet W. B. Yeats once wrote "cannot hold."

Liberal consensus had also been associated with the cold war, and here the chronology needs to be questioned. The first major book that launched the consensus school of thought, Richard Hofstadter's *The American Political Tradition,* appeared in 1948, and the author had been composing it years earlier, before the cold war surfaced with the Soviet invasion of Czechoslovakia and the fall of China toward the end of the decade. But consensus theory did have something to do with communism. Hofstadter, Daniel J. Boorstin, and Louis Hartz had all been Communists or Trotskyists in their college years in the 1930s, and they became convinced that American capitalism would most likely not survive the stresses of the war against Adolf Hitler and the Third Reich. The assumption was that the United States must move toward the left by collectivizing the economy or risk succumbing to some form of fascism in which the U.S. Constitution would be scrapped and liberty lost. When America survived World War II with its political and economic institutions intact, historians Hofstadter, Boorstin, and Hartz, together with the sociologists Daniel Bell and Seymour Martin Lipset, set out to explain what it was that kept the country together when many intellectuals believed it would fall apart. The idea of conflict, especially class conflict, no longer seemed a viable concept, and out of such reconsiderations was born the idea of consensus.

Closely related to consensus was the idea of American exceptionalism, and this, too, had its origins in the 1930s. The term was first coined by the followers of Jay Lovestone, a Communist leader who opposed the official Communist Party of the USA and claimed, against those willing to take orders from Moscow, that America had a different historical experience from Europe and thus had a right to formulate its own policies independently of the Comintern. Among the realities America had to deal with that set it apart from Europe and the rest of the world were the absence of a revolutionary proletariat and a strong socialist tradition, the influx of immigrant populations, and the presence of African Americans, which meant that ethnic cultures and race must be dealt with apart from the class question. Such issues that America had to face confounded Marxism and rendered the country unique and exceptional.

The idea of exceptionalism now has various meanings in different fields, sometimes with disastrous consequences. Political leaders like to invoke America as the "city upon a hill" to claim that their country enjoys the blessings of providence and is somehow morally superior to the rest of the world—forgetting that the seventeenth-century Puritan who first uttered the phrase, John Winthrop, saw the New World as corruptible as the Old World unless it shunned "the sins of the flesh." The idea of exceptionalism has also been invoked in recent discussions of international relations, especially to argue that America has a right to be exempted from rulings of the United Nations and the Geneva Convention.

In the buildup to the war in Iraq in 2003, the idea was also cited to persuade the American people that they had a responsibility to bring democracy to the Middle East. Here the concept of exceptionalism turned into a misleading conceit. Advocates of the war quoted Abraham Lincoln describing his country as the "last best hope" for liberty, as though America could bring its message to any other country for which it wanted a "regime change." But Lincoln was warning, in the 1860s, that if the Union broke apart, liberty would die on native ground. In opposing the war with Mexico in 1848, Lincoln could not believe that America could bring democracy beyond its borders even to its next-door neighbors. Properly understood, the idea of American exceptionalism could reinforce isolationism far more than interventionism.

The three exponents of liberal consensus, the historians Hofstadter, Boorstin, and Hartz, rarely wrote about diplomatic history as they sought to explain the unique structure of American society where many of the conditions of the Old World were lacking. But in the final passage of Hartz's *The Liberal Tradition in America*, the reader may appreciate the connection between liberal consensus and American exceptionalism. America had experienced no great social conflicts in its history, including even the Civil War, which was more a sectional struggle

over the issue of slavery and state sovereignty than of a class conflict between labor and capital that would be solved by revolution. Thus Americans, Hartz pointed out, are unprepared to sympathize with the need for radical change at home and revolutions abroad because they have enjoyed freedom almost as a birthright: "Can a people 'born equal' ever understand peoples elsewhere that have to become so? Can it ever understand itself?" To those who regard liberal consensus as part of what sociologist C. Wright Mills called the "great American celebration," Hartz must represent an exception, a historian who saw little to praise about the past. America offered few answers to the problems facing the country because the pervasiveness of consensus soothed over issues and left people untroubled, completely contented with a life of bovine consumption. In the 1950s, with the "end of ideology" proclaimed, historians began to argue whether there was anything to argue about. Not so Hartz, who wondered how Americans could ever become conscious of themselves as a people with a coherent identity rather than a series of aimless desires. "Instead of recapturing our past, we have got to transcend it," he exhorted. "There is no going home for America."

Hartz followed his own advice. Teaching at Harvard University, he suffered a mental breakdown in the 1960s and, upon retiring, left America, never to return. He set out to discover the third world and spent years studying the non-Western religions of Islam, Confuscious, Buddhism, and Hinduism. He died in Ankara, Turkey, in 1986. His last book, *A Synthesis of World History*, verges on mysticism as it advocated humankind to "be free to be Chinese one day, Indian the next, and European the next."

The three historians of consensus each approached their subject differently. Hofstadter dealt with the unrelenting continuity of the American value system expressed by political leaders and presidents. Hartz examined the structural implications of a country that lacked clear-cut class divisions in society and ideological divisions in the American mind. Boorstin, in contrast, was happy to report that historians need not deal with the American mind since the American people had successfully lived without big ideas or ideologies. In reasoning somewhat like the pragmatists and contemporary neopragmatists, Boorstin argued that it was the philosophy of America to have no philosophy, no metaphysical foundations, no grounding in first principles, no truths upon which beliefs depend. Americans, Boorstin insisted, lived more by doing than by thinking.

Hofstadter, one of the bright "New York intellectuals," lived by thinking, and his *The American Political Tradition and the Men Who Made It* came to a conclusion that Boorstin reached by other means. As evidenced by the positions and speeches taken by their political leaders, the American people did think, but all they thought about was their own materialistic concerns that viewed liberty as the "pursuit of happiness." In the preface to the book, Hofstadter specified the values Americans live by: "The sanctity of private property, the right of the individual to dispose and invest it, the value of opportunity, and the natural evolution of self-interest and self-assertion, within broad legal limits, into a beneficent social order." The conflicts and antagonisms in American history should not be allowed to mislead us, he argued, for individuals and groups compete for the same ends even with different means, whether it be wages or profits, or land prices or financial investment, or the modern trade union or the corporate law firm: "Even when some property right has been challenged—as it was by the followers of Jefferson or Jackson—in the name of the rights of man or the rights of the community, the challenge, when translated into practical policy, has actually been urged on behalf of some other kinds of property." Hofstadter traced this mentality from Thomas Jefferson to Franklin D. Roosevelt, with each and every president committed to bourgeois values that frustrated any possibility for the success of socialism in America. Hofstadter wrote the book as a democratic socialist, and he made readers aware of Wendell Phillips, the New England radical who believed that the abolition of slavery required the redistribution of property in the South to assure that free blacks would enjoy self-sufficiency. But in capitalist America, property remained sacrosanct, the very foundation of the liberal consensus.

In *The Liberal Tradition in America*, Hartz traced that consensus to two factors, the absence of feudalism and the presence of Lockeanism. In the 1830s, Alexis de Tocqueville visited America and was astonished to discover (erroneously) that, in their revolution, all Americans fought on the same side, and he attributed this to the absence of class traditions in an America that had skipped the feudal stage of history and thus had no aristocracy to struggle against and no proletariat to worry about. Hartz drew upon Tocqueville, as did Bell, Lipset, and other sociologists, to explain the implications of a consensual political culture that lacked class tensions.

He also delineated the implications of John Locke's political philosophy that had pervaded America in the colonial era. Whereas the classical and Christian traditions of the past had condemned self-interest as betraying the ideals of civic virtue or the laws of God, Locke hailed it as liberating, giving men the right to property and women the right to divorce, and making labor the source of value in a new environment of possessive individualism. Americans, Hartz observed, had little respect for history and tradition and, unlike the British conservative Edmund Burke, rarely looked to custom to bind generations together in an organic compact with the dead, the living, and those about to be born.

Yet what Hartz discovered within American liberalism turned out to be a conservative time bomb. Although his book was written in the 1950s, it anticipated the President Ronald Reagan of the 1980s, especially the conservative exhortation that Americans should not look to government for a solution to their problems since government itself is the problem. The message would be repeated by Democratic president Bill Clinton, who declared in his second inaugural address, "The era of big government is over." Such stances are what political philosophers call "negative liberty," the Lockean assumption that humankind is free to the extent that the government is diminished—or, as Jefferson put it, "That government is best which governs least"; or, as Henry David Thoreau added, "which governs not at all."

The most intriguing of the consensus historians may have been Boorstin, an uncanny thinker who was a member of a Communist cell while at Harvard University as an undergraduate, a barrister in England after studying law at Oxford University, a "friendly witness" who testified before the House Un-American Activities Committee about his political activities, and then became an eminent scholar at the University of Chicago and later the Librarian of Congress. Perhaps because Boorstin had been seduced by communism's sparkling glitter of ideas, he decided to write a history to argue that America had no need of ideas, especially ideologies and abstract concepts that deflected the mind from the practical tasks of the day. In *The Genius of American Politics*, he insisted that Americans had always been guided by the "givenness" of ideas and values, by thoughts that required no reflection or mediation but were simply acted upon as the country encountered problems to be solved. Boorstin believed that America has almost instinctively resolved one of the greatest issues in philosophy, how to get from factual detail to moral knowledge, from the "is" to the "ought." He argued that moral values were embedded in everyday existence, and thus life as it is "gave the outlines of life as it ought to be, that values were implicit in experience."

One wonders what Lincoln would have thought about Boorstin's explanation of America's "genius." Lincoln insisted that experience itself was the problem, especially the experience of slavery, and, to deal with it, America must look to the Bible and return to the values of the Declaration of Independence, the "sheet anchor" of the republic. But the amazing aspect of Boorstin's conservative position of the 1950s is that it anticipated radical positions taken in the 1980s, especially the neopragmatism of the literary scholar Stanley Fish and the philosopher Richard Rorty. They, too, insisted that history and society have no foundation in philosophy or reason, that we are not what we think in any deep reflective sense but simply what we do, and what we do we do culturally not intellectually, simply following the contingencies of convention. That conservatives and radicals can partake of the same mental outlook could very well be called the cunning of consensus.

The consensus school of history was challenged during the 1960s as students took to the streets to protest the Vietnam War; a decade or so later, after the same radical students went to graduate school and received PhDs, they challenged the idea of consensus in the classroom and in their scholarship. Everywhere in American history they found enclaves of resistance and episodes of opposition, continuing moments of conflict that discredited the idea that America could have ever been held together by a set of core values, especially capitalist values. Everything from a labor strike to a hip-hop album was interpreted as subversive and transgressive, as though the worker had no desire for higher wages and the musician could hardly be motivated by money. While professors told their students how radical America was, the polls continually proved how conservative the country was. Professors proved conflict by teaching it; the masses of people proved consensus by heading for the shopping mall.

See also era of consensus, 1952–64; liberalism.

FURTHER READING

Boorstin, Daniel. J. *The Genius of American Politics.* Chicago: University of Chicago Press, 1953.

Brown, David S. *Richard Hofstadter.* Chicago: University of Chicago Press, 2006.

Diggins, John Patrick. *On Hallowed Grounds: Abraham Lincoln and the Foundations of American History.* New Haven, CT: Yale University Press, 2000.

Hartz, Louis. *The Liberal Tradition in America: An Interpretation of American Political Thought since the Revolution.* New York: Harcourt, Brace, Javonovich, 1955.

———. *A Synthesis of World History.* Zurich: Humanity, 1984.

Higham, John. *Writing American History.* Bloomington: Indiana University Press, 1970.

Hofstadter, Richard. *The American Political Tradition: And the Men Who Made It.* New York: Vintage, 1989.

Lipset, Seymour Martin. *American Exceptionalism: A Double-Edged Sword.* New York: Norton, 1996.

JOHN PATRICK DIGGINS

liberalism

Liberalism has been a word of multiple meanings and valences ever since the late medieval introduction of the word *liberal* to English from Latin. On the one hand, liberal has indicated an inclination toward freedom, open-mindedness, generosity, and the cultivation of intellect; on the other, a shortage of discipline and practicality. As that cluster of disparate meanings suggests, liberalism has been an essentially contested concept, a problem made even more nettlesome for historians by its constantly changing significance over the last four centuries.

Puritan Origins

The Puritans bound for America on the *Arbella* in 1630 heard John Winthrop urge them to practice a "liberality" of spirit consistent with the Hebrew prophet Nehemiah's exhortations and St. Matthew's rendering of the Christian ideal of benevolence. Winthrop instructed his flock, as God's chosen people, to balance a prudent concern for their families with an unrestrained generosity toward those in need of help. Against the temptation of "selfishness," he counterposed Christ's injunction of unrestrained love and cheerful "liberality" to the poor as the surest sign of God's grace. The Puritans must be "knitted together in this work" and "must be willing to abridge ourselves of our superfluities for the supply of others' necessities." If instead they were "seduced" and served "other Gods," such as "our pleasures and profits," Winthrop warned, they would "surely perish."

Thus began the American liberal project. The tensions between the narrow concern for kin and a broader interest in the community, between the sin of selfishness and the divine injunction to generosity, have persisted ever since. Puritans left England to escape religious constraints and to establish communities governed by rules devised according to their understanding of God's will. In laying those foundations, they demonstrated the inextricable ties between liberality and democracy in America. They also showed the artificiality of separating "negative" from "positive" freedom, an empty and misleading but influential distinction made familiar in recent decades after its introduction in 1958 by the Russian-émigré English philosopher Isaiah Berlin. The Puritans fled from the constraints of Anglicanism, but their escape was meaningful only because it enabled them to establish their own religious and civic institutions. As astute American advocates of liberality from Winthrop until today have understood, freedom from restraint exists only when individuals possess a real opportunity to exercise that freedom within self-governing communities. Fantasies of individual rights independent of the capacity of people to exercise them, or outside the boundaries of law that both constitute and constrain their use, have no foundation in American history.

The tensions between selfishness and generosity marked American colonial development up and down the Atlantic seaboard. Everywhere in Europe's American colonies—as everywhere in Europe—women, the poor, and members of racial and religious minorities were subjected to harsh discipline and excluded from decision-making processes. In this world, hierarchy was taken for granted as God's will. Despite his injunctions to generosity, even Winthrop assumed that there would continue to be rich and poor, powerful and powerless. Free men with property existed at one end of a spectrum; slaves at the other; women, children, artisans, servants, religious minorities, native peoples, and the few free people of color fell somewhere in between. Open-mindedness toward those unlike oneself marked a liberal sensibility, but in the seventeenth and early eighteenth centuries, such toleration existed within rigid frameworks that dictated what types of treatment suited what sorts of people. Sharp distinctions, enforced between slave and free, nonwhite and white, women and men, members of religious minorities and majorities, and those without and with property, curtailed the exercise of the benevolence enjoined by Winthrop.

Rights and Duties in the Age of Democratic Revolutions

Beginning with the Revolution of 1688 in England and continuing through the ratification of the U.S. Constitution a century later, a whirlwind of cultural change uprooted many of these hierarchical patterns and transformed others. These ideas, which provided the ammunition for Americans to construct a new national political culture on the foundations of earlier colonial thought and practice, derived from multiple sources.

In American writers' contributions to transatlantic debates during the age of democratic revolutions, diverse traditions of dissenting Protestantism blended with arguments by Samuel Pufendorf and John Locke concerning the relation between individual rights and God's will, with eighteenth-century Scottish common sense moral philosophy, and with varieties of republican political theory drawn from the ancient world and updated by Renaissance humanists. Attempts to disentangle the religious, liberal, and republican strands of the arguments woven during the eighteenth century are futile and counterproductive. Americans involved in these furious debates cited authorities promiscuously, hijacked arguments for their own particular purposes, and did not always see the differences between traditions that now seem evident to many scholars.

The American discourses of independence and constitution making displayed the full range of meanings contained in the idea of a liberal disposition. A passionate commitment to freedom from British rule inspired the local and state declarations of independence on which Thomas Jefferson drew. Versions of that commitment also surfaced in the early rumblings of antislavery sentiment among African Americans, Quakers, and New Englanders and in the scattered calls for women's rights from writers such as Abigail Adams and Judith Sargent Murray. A commitment to open-mindedness manifested itself in the distinctive American idea of amendable constitutions, a federal structure, independent branches of limited government that quickly contested each other's authority, and provisions to protect personal property and the freedom of speech and religious belief. Reminders of the importance of benevolence and generosity coursed through countless speeches, learned treatises aimed at persuading an international reading audience, and informal pamphlets directed toward ordinary people. In their efforts to balance the unquestionable desire to prosper and the equally genuine concern with advancing what they called the "general interest," Americans drew on the Hebrew Bible and the Christian scriptures, philosophical and legal tracts on history and ethics, and new-fangled British and French economic ideas about a self-regulating market.

Among the state constitutions that appeared during the war for independence, the Massachusetts constitution drafted by John Adams in 1779 proved the most influential; it manifests impulses persisting in the American colonies from their early seventeenth-century origins. Adams proclaimed the rights to life, liberty, property, free expression, and trial by jury; he balanced those rights against citizens' duty to worship God, obey the law, and contribute to an educational system that extended from elementary schools to the university in Cambridge. In a republic, Adams insisted, duties matter as much as rights, because "good morals are necessary to the preservation of civil society." A government founded on popular sovereignty could flourish only through the general diffusion of "wisdom and knowledge, as well as virtue." Without "the principles of humanity and general benevolence, public and private charity, industry and frugality," some individuals would be tempted to look to their own "private interest" instead of the proper end of government, "the common good." Unself-consciously echoing John Winthrop, Adams concluded that republican government must "inculcate the principles of humanity and general benevolence" and inspire "generous sentiments among the people."

Easy agreement on a few principles, however, including the rights to self-government and to life, liberty, and the pursuit of happiness, masked deeper divisions. No sooner had Americans won their independence than citizens of the new nation began to squabble. Those who invoked "justice and the general good," or "the common good of society" against the dangers of selfish factions, as James Madison did in *The Federalist*, were charged with elitist leanings poorly masked by their genuflections to popular government. Many of those who resisted the U.S. Constitution claimed it would empower a rising metropolitan elite. But the backwoodsmen and farmers in western regions, who joined with some urban artisans to oppose the new Constitution, were themselves accused of advancing their own narrow self-interest against the broadly shared goals of political stability and commercial expansion. Thus, the multiple meanings of a "liberal" sensibility became apparent as early as the debates that raged over proposed state and national constitutions in the 1780s.

The Puzzle of Parties

With the outbreak of the French Revolution in 1789, centuries-old charges that self-government might prove undisciplined and ultimately impractical persuaded increasing numbers of anxious Americans. The first U.S. party system resulted from the contrasting reactions of Americans to their erstwhile ally's dramatically different experience with democracy. Federalists reacted in horror to the assault on individual rights they saw in the Reign of Terror, whereas Jeffersonian Republicans embraced the cause of *liberté*, *égalité*, and *fraternité* as their own and saw their enemies' embrace of England as treasonous. Both groups embraced ideals of liberality such as freedom, equality, and national self-determination. But only a few years after George Washington warned that political parties would erode Americans' shared commitments to the general good, Jefferson ascended to the presidency in a bitterly contested election that was dubbed a Second American Revolution by his partisans—and by their enemies.

Were either the Federalists or the Jeffersonian Republicans, or were the Whigs or the Jacksonian Democrats that followed them several decades later, more "liberal" than the other? For nearly two centuries, ever since the word *liberal* itself entered Anglo-American discourse with a specifically political meaning during the early nineteenth century, American historians have debated that question. If liberalism is thought to involve generous support for the disfranchised, including African Americans, Indians, and women, and to involve extending educational opportunities and enforcing public authority in the economic sphere for the sake of the common good, then first the Federalists and later the Whigs might deserve to be designated liberals. But if liberalism instead means advancing farmers' and workers' interests against the plutocracy and asserting decentralized local authority against national elites threatening to monopolize political and economic power, then the followers of Jefferson and Jackson ought to be considered the liberals of the antebellum years. To complicate matters even further, many Federalists and Whigs worried about the danger of lawlessness and defended the principle of privilege, hardly a liberal quality, whereas many Jeffersonians and Jacksonians exhibited antiliberal tendencies of their own, ignoring the rights of blacks, Indians, and women as they trumpeted their commitment to white-male democracy.

As those contrasts make clear, both sets of early-nineteenth-century American parties invoked principles and championed programs that drew on some of the original meanings—both favorable and pejorative—of liberality. Only by shoehorning these parties anachronistically into categories that emerged later in American history can either group be made to embody liberal sensibilities, as these were later understood, more fully than the other. The solution to this problem is not to invoke a "liberal" litmus test but to concede that different Americans understood the constellation of liberal commitments toward freedom, toleration, benevolence, cultivation, and popular government in strikingly different ways. Perhaps the French visitor Alexis de Tocqueville's idea of "self-interest properly understood," capturing both Americans' concern with individual rights and the robust sense of social responsibility that inspired them to create countless voluntary organizations, best conveyed the unstable amalgam of American values.

At no time did a unitary "liberal tradition" ever exist in America. The dynamics of antebellum American public life reflected instead racial, gendered, economic, religious, and ethnocultural tensions that increasingly divided the nation along sectional lines. That process culminated in the emergence of Abraham Lincoln, the towering figure of nineteenth-century American politics, the individual who cemented the nation's enduring commitment to the ideals of liberty, equality, and democracy.

Lincoln's Legacies

Only after the Civil War did some American writers and politicians enthusiastically and self-consciously embrace the designation *liberal*. Those who called themselves liberals first clustered around Lincoln's party, the Republican Party that formed in the 1850s from the ashes of the Whigs, an awkward fact for those committed to the idea that Jackson's Democratic Party was the authentic carrier of a continuous American liberal tradition that began with Jefferson and culminated in Franklin Roosevelt. Post–Civil War Republicans called themselves liberals to signal several commitments. First, they embraced and even extended Lincoln's plans for reconstructing the South. They fought to secure the Fourteenth and the Fifteenth Amendments because they judged the extension of social, economic, and political rights to the freedmen crucial to consolidate the triumph of the Union and transform race relations forever. The unyielding force of racism, a tragic legacy of centuries of slavery, doomed their plans to failure.

Second, they embraced the cause of education and aesthetic cultivation. Together with English liberals such as John Stuart Mill, American liberals reasoned that the promise of democracy could be redeemed only if all citizens, black and white, women and men, ordinary workers and college-educated professionals, could read and write and participate in public deliberation. Charges of elitism limited the effectiveness of their program of cultural uplift.

Third, many of those who embraced liberalism sought to exchange the strident sectarianism of American religious denominations with a less doctrinaire and more open-minded emphasis on spirituality. Fierce loyalties to particular religious traditions persisted, however, and manifested themselves in fervent critiques of liberalism as a new species of godlessness masquerading as broadmindedness.

Fourth, liberals championed civil service reform. Liberals worked to end the spoils system and the reign of party bosses and urban machines, not because they hated immigrants but because they judged political corruption among the gravest sins of the republic, a flaw that some of them hyperbolically equated with slavery as an abomination of democracy. But the Democratic Party loyalty of immigrants in northern cities—and of Southerners who hated Lincoln as deeply as these liberals revered him—combined to thwart their efforts.

Finally, liberals imported the British and French idea of laissez-faire. Opposing the legacies of feudal practices and the stifling mercantilist policies of the nation-state on behalf of a free-market economy made sense in Europe in the eighteenth and early nineteenth centuries. But in the United States, economic regulation had been practiced primarily by local and state authorities for the benefit of ordinary people, whether by protecting their neighborhoods against "noxious trades" or by regulating the flow of goods according to the principle *salus populi* (the people's welfare). So the late-nineteenth-century American campaign to restrict government authority did not liberate the energies of shackled entrepreneurs from the stranglehold of monarchies and landed aristocracies, as British and French liberals had sought to do decades earlier. Only in the economic sphere did late-nineteenth-century American liberals succeed, thereby unleashing a wave of unregulated economic activity that soon swamped agricultural and industrial workers alike.

The New Liberalism

Given the failure of liberals to achieve color-blind democracy in the South or defeat bosses in the North, and given the success of their campaign for laissez-faire, the aging liberal Republicans of the Gilded Age came under fire from a new generation of political and social reformers at the end of the nineteenth century. Emerging first in the radicalism of the Knights of Labor, then in diverse forms of rural discontent that assumed the name of populism, these forms of insurgency gave way to a new coalition of reformers who gradually coalesced around the label *progressives*. Allied as their liberal Republican predecessors had been with like-minded English reformers, these progressives likewise adopted a program similar to that advanced by their early-twentieth-century English counterparts, which they dubbed the "new liberalism."

The new liberalism shared with the older version a commitment to cultural reforms such as education, temperance, and campaigns against prostitution. American new liberals also called for democratic reforms like a nonpartisan civil service, the initiative, referendum, recall, and the direct election of U.S. senators. Some new liberals—though not all—favored woman suffrage. As new liberals continued their predecessors' calls for democratic reform, some understood that commitment to mean the elevation of the electorate's judgment rather than the expansion of its size. In the American South, self-styled progressives sold the exclusionary practices of Jim Crow legislation as a form of democratic "purification," just as some English "liberal imperialists" justified the expansion of empire and the denial of home rule to Ireland as versions of the "White Man's Burden." On the question of extending American power in the Spanish-American War, American liberals old and new divided bitterly. Some, including aging veterans of the Civil War and radical Reconstruction such as New England reformer Thomas Wentworth Higginson and cultural critic Charles Eliot Norton, and others, including the writer Samuel Clemens and the philosopher William James, condemned American expansionism as a repudiation of the nation's most precious democratic ideals. Certain liberals, such as Theodore Roosevelt, interpreted American empire as the natural extension of Americans' reformist energies. The Spanish-American War would not be the last time liberals would divide over the issues of war and peace.

The sharpest departure of the new liberalism from the old, however, came in the domain of economic regulation. Empowered by a conception of economics brought back from Germany by a new generation of scholars such as Richard T. Ely and his student John Commons, reformers denied the timelessness of classical economics and asserted that economic ideas, like all others, develop

historically and must be scrutinized critically. The rise of the social gospel shifted the emphasis of prominent Protestant clergymen such as Washington Gladden and Walter Rauschenbusch from the afterlife to the injustices endured by the poor in this life. A new generation of women, often college-educated, sought to exert pressure in various domains. Some justified their reformist activities as a form of "social housekeeping" for which women were uniquely well suited. Others, such as Jane Addams in the settlement house movement, Florence Kelley in the realms of industrial regulation and consumer protection, and Charlotte Perkins Gilman in the broader campaign for women's equality, worked to reconceive and expand women's roles by reassessing their capacities.

In place of laissez-faire, most new liberals called for the federal government to intervene in order to restrain corporate power and restore the rights and freedoms ostensibly secured by law but effectively limited by economic inequality. Progressives created a new apparatus, the regulatory agency, with procedures patterned on the model of scientific inquiry. The officials who staffed regulatory agencies were expected to use their expertise to find and enforce a nonpartisan public interest. Inspired (or shamed) by muckrakers such as Lincoln Steffens, Upton Sinclair, and Ida Tarbell, prominent legislators experimented with new forms of government authority designed to address particular economic and social problems.

Many members of the judiciary abandoned the doctrine of laissez-faire and embraced a conception of law as a flexible instrument, an orientation that jurists like Oliver Wendell Holmes Jr. and Louis Brandeis developed from the premises of the philosophy of pragmatism developed by William James and John Dewey. The principle animating these reforms descended from the eighteenth-century conception of balancing rights and duties. As Theodore Roosevelt put it in 1910, "Every man holds his property subject to the general right of the community to regulate its use to whatever degree the public welfare may require it." These programs were to be financed by the graduated income tax, which many considered the quintessential progressive reform because it tied the obligation owed to the capacity to contribute. The implementation of these programs, however, left much to be desired. Both legislators and regulatory commissions proved susceptible to capture by those they were empowered to restrain. Business interests proved as creative in eluding government oversight as they were in exploiting new resources and new markets.

Despite its failures, the new liberalism permanently transformed American politics. Affirming the principle that government may intervene in the economy to protect the interest of consumers, workers, and other disadvantaged groups remained a pillar of liberal doctrine throughout the twentieth century, as did a more or less self-consciously pragmatist commitment to flexible experimentation in public policy. Whereas the old liberalism had calcified by 1900 around an unyielding commitment to laissez-faire, the new liberalism substituted what Walter Lippmann called "mastery" for now-discredited "drift." Many new liberals saw in the open-endedness of pragmatism not a threat to stability but the key to fulfilling what another central theorist, Herbert Croly, called "the promise of American life," the use of democratic means to attain a great national end of active government devoted to serving the common good.

Toward a Second Bill of Rights

World War I constituted a cultural watershed in American life, but politically the changes were more subtle. The war and its aftermath, especially the failure of the United States to join the League of Nations, soured many progressives such as Lippmann on the possibilities of democracy. So did the fracturing of the progressive coalition between its urban and rural factions. Many evangelical Christians supported the prohibition of alcohol and opposed new ideas such as evolution; those passionate commitments divided them sharply from many of their erstwhile progressive allies and opened a new rift between increasingly secular and enduringly religious Americans previously linked by a shared commitment to principles both groups considered liberal. An equally fateful rift opened between those who embraced government power and sought to silence critics of Woodrow Wilson's war effort and those who, like the founding members of the American Civil Liberties Union, considered freedom of speech inviolable. Both the division between progressive and conservative religious groups and the division between civil libertarians and those wary of unregulated speech and behavior have become increasingly deep—and more debilitating both politically and culturally for liberalism—over the last century.

In the 1920s, liberals' pre–World War I interest in bringing scientific expertise to government continued unabated. The most celebrated hero of the war, the "great engineer" Herbert Hoover, abandoned Woodrow Wilson's internationalism but continued to think of himself as a progressive keen on efficient management. First as secretary of commerce and then as president, Hoover oversaw a modified regulatory regime that purported to extend the progressives' approach to government-business relations while surrendering decision making to the private sector. When that experiment in corporatism failed dramatically and the nation sank into depression, Franklin D. Roosevelt stumbled into half-hearted versions of progressive economic regulation while forging a coalition of voters that sustained his unstable brand of liberalism for several decades. Some members of Roosevelt's administration embraced much more aggressive schemes of economic planning that would have expanded public control over the private sector to an unprecedented degree. But their efforts, like those of the most ambitious new liberals before them, crumpled in Congress under the assault of critics who characterized such plans as utopian, medieval, Communist, or Fascist.

When the United States was forced into World War II by Pearl Harbor, doctrinal disagreements no longer mattered as much. Spurred by the urgent need to produce military supplies as fast as possible, informal arrangements between government and business facilitated unprecedented economic growth. In the face of never before seen military dangers, government authorities curtailed the civil liberties of many Americans, particularly those of Japanese descent. At the end of the war, the United States faced a new world. Now the richest economy as well as the most powerful military in the world, the nation had to decide how to use its wealth and power. For several years Roosevelt had been developing a plan to meet that challenge, which he outlined in his 1944 State of the Union address and on which he campaigned for reelection that fall.

The Second Bill of Rights, as Roosevelt called his plan, was to include the right of every American to a job at a living wage, adequate food, clothing, housing, medical care, education, and "protection from the economic fears of old age, sickness, accident, and unemployment." Similar programs of social provision took shape throughout the industrialized world. In almost all western European nations, through the efforts of liberal and social democratic coalitions, they came to fruition. Roosevelt griped to Secretary of Labor Frances Perkins that the most visible of these schemes, England's Beveridge Plan, which served as the blueprint for Clement Atlee's postwar Labour government, should have been called the Roosevelt

Plan. But the same forces that had stymied earlier liberal programs did the same to the Second Bill of Rights, which Congress dismantled in the wake of Roosevelt's death. Only a remnant of the plan survived in the form of the G.I. Bill. The benefits provided by even that limited measure fueled a sustained wave of prosperity that lasted three decades, and scholars of the Second Bill of Rights have been left wondering about its effect had Roosevelt lived to shepherd it into law.

Cold War Transformations

The postwar period never saw the resurrection of Roosevelt's ambitious plan, the unrealized ideal of one strand of twentieth-century liberalism. The onset of the cold war transformed American politics even more dramatically than had the Red Scare after World War I. Harry Truman presented his Fair Deal as the culmination of Roosevelt's liberal plan for generous social provision, a benevolent discharging of comfortable Americans' duties to their less fortunate fellow citizens. But, given the perceived threat from an expansionist Soviet Union, such programs were vulnerable to the charge that they had become un-American. After three centuries in which Americans had worked to balance their rights against their responsibilities and the sin of selfishness against the divine command of benevolence, property rights metamorphosed under the shadow of communism into the essence of America and concern with the poor into almost a sign of disloyalty. Consumption replaced generosity in the national pantheon. New Dealers shifted from redistributionist schemes to the stabilizing ideas of English economist John Maynard Keynes; conservatives embraced the free-market principles of Ludwig von Mises and Friedrich Hayek. Confusingly, both Keynesians who emphasized government intervention through monetary and especially fiscal policy and conservatives who prized laissez-faire called themselves liberals, as European champions of free-market capitalism do to this day. But whereas the heirs of FDR continued to invoke the principle of equality alongside their commitment to liberty, American conservatives increasingly branded egalitarian ideals as socialist and exchanged the term *liberal*, which they rejected as tainted by its association with progressives' and New Dealers' economic programs, for the new label *libertarian*.

Not all American liberals retreated before the widespread enthusiasm for salvation by consumption. Many followed the neo-orthodox Protestant minister Reinhold Niebuhr. Counterposing a newly chastened realism to

the ostensibly naïve reformism of earlier liberals such as Dewey and his followers in the New Deal (many of whom remained committed to the possibilities of radical democracy), Niebuhr urged Americans to acknowledge the pervasiveness of sin and the ubiquity of evil. Tough opponents called for tough-mindedness, and although Niebuhr did not entirely renounce Rauschenbusch's social gospel, many liberals' shift in emphasis from possibilities to dangers, and from pragmatic problem solving to ironies and tragedies, was unmistakable. Whereas Roosevelt had called Americans to an expansive egalitarian mission, liberals such as Arthur Schlesinger Jr. instead urged them to cluster around "the vital center." For many liberals, as well as most libertarians, ambitious egalitarian plans took a backseat to hard-headed geopolitical maneuvering.

Beneath the tone of cold war realism, though, a more subtle shift in liberal focus was taking place. Despite a rhetoric of free-market triumphalism, many ostensibly conservative mid-century Republicans shared liberals' belief that some version of a government-business alliance was in the interest of all Americans. Just as informal gentlemen's agreements had enabled war production to go forward, so new treaties were struck with labor unions, interest groups, and government regulatory agencies in the hope that some new American hybrid would emerge to dissolve the tensions between labor and management. Many liberals shared the confidence that a new, university-trained, non- or post-ideological managerial elite could staff the ramparts of the private and public sectors. Where earlier progressives had seen inevitable conflict, new corporate liberals trumpeted a professionally engineered consensus forged by voluntary accommodation.

So placid (or constricted) did such visions seem that some American observers projected them backward across American history. Many scholars argued that Americans had always agreed on basic principles, but they disagreed in evaluating that consensus. Historian Daniel Boorstin deemed it "the genius of American politics." Political scientist Louis Hartz considered it a tragedy. Unfortunately, one of the most influential books ever written about American politics, Hartz's *The Liberal Tradition in America*, was also among the most misleading. Not only did Hartz's account minimize the significance of the nonwhites and women who were still ignored by many white male writers in the 1950s, it also papered over the fierce battles that had characterized public life in America ever since the founding of the English colonies. Hartz's portrait of a one-dimensional and stifling consensus flattened a much more conflictual and dynamic record of constant struggles. Liberals grappled with their opponents over the meanings and purposes of American democracy, a conflict that flared into violence and culminated in a bloody Civil War, and even those who assumed the mantle of liberalism frequently disagreed about its meaning.

Indeed, no sooner had sociologist Daniel Bell and other liberals proclaimed "the end of ideology" than dramatic conflicts began breaking out over competing principles. The first battleground was the South. African Americans radicalized by the rhetoric of democracy, by the experience of military life, or by knowledge of a world outside the segregated South mobilized to challenge the stifling regime of Jim Crow. This racial crusade began decades earlier, as signaled by the founding of the National Association for the Advancement of Colored People (NAACP) in 1909. Booker T. Washington had already emerged by then as a prominent educator and writer, and his critic W.E.B. DuBois, the only African American among the founders of the NAACP, had offered profound analyses of "the problem of the color line" as the central challenge of the twentieth century. After simmering for decades without attracting the attention of the mainstream press, the African American campaign for civil rights at last awakened the consciences of white liberals. When the combustible combination of post–World War II agitation, the Supreme Court's 1954 decision in *Brown v. Board of Education of Topeka, Kansas* (which declared segregation of public facilities unconstitutional), and the Montgomery, Alabama, bus boycott inspired by Rosa Parks and led by Martin Luther King Jr. came together, the scattered efforts of many activists ignited into a national movement.

Earlier accounts, which centered on the heroic struggles of King and a few visible leaders, have been replaced by broader histories of a "long civil rights movement" that stretched unbroken from the early twentieth century and extended through the efforts of countless foot soldiers who challenged norms of racial subjugation across the nation. Coming as it did at the same time that social scientists and literary scholars were constructing a new paradigm of "human"—as opposed to "national" or "racial" or "ethnic" or "gendered"—characteristics, the civil rights movement rode a wave of universalism that most American liberals took as the harbinger of a transformed set of social relations across earlier chasms of race, class, and gender. From linguistics to sociology,

from anthropology to the study of sexuality, from biology to philosophy, liberal scholarly investigators joined the quest for a common denominator that would link all humans.

These heady ambitions fueled forms of liberal social and political activity that left a permanent imprint on American culture and American law. Under pressure from liberal and radical reformers, race, gender, and labor relations gradually shifted. These changes—piecemeal, partial, and incremental—rarely satisfied impatient liberal activists, yet they nevertheless transformed the American cultural landscape. Campaigns in the 1960s and 1970s on behalf of American women, workers, prisoners, and those who were poor, mentally or physically disabled, gay, lesbian, or aged changed the ways in which employers, police, judges, school officials, architects, engineers, social workers, and physicians worked. In another domain, a chorus of environmentalists assailed smug assumptions about the consequences of Americans' profligate use of natural resources and worked to nurture alternative environmentalist sensibilities. Visionaries saw the dawn of a new age.

Challenges from Right and Left

Within little more than a decade, however, such hopes had evaporated. Struggles within the movements for black liberation, women's liberation, the labor movement, and against the war in Vietnam began to seem almost as bitter as the struggles fought by the partisans in those conflicts against their conservative foes. By the time the prolonged economic expansion of the postwar decades ended with the oil crisis of 1973–74, liberals' cultural confidence had been shattered. They found themselves assailed not only from the right but from a new, and more radical, left. A newly energized conservative movement found a modern leader in the governor of California, Ronald Reagan, and additional support from disgruntled white ethnics, suburbanites anxious about their cultural and religious values and their future, and an increasingly vocal segment of Americans antagonized by blacks, women, and gay and lesbian Americans demanding equal rights. Critics on the left began to assail liberals for their alleged complicity in the forms of racism, sexism, and exclusion practiced internally and in the nation's imperialist atrocities abroad, all of which were said to derive from the Enlightenment's shallow confidence in a narrow form of "reason" that promised liberating fulfillment but delivered only confinement. By the time Reagan was elected president in 1980, liberalism had become a term of opprobrium for critics on the left as well as the right.

In recent decades liberals have struggled to escape the dismissive caricatures of both radicals and conservatives. Liberals' egalitarian dreams were judged unrealistic and their cultural leanings elitist, their generosity counterproductive and their confidence in reasoned debate faintly comic. Liberals' commitment to freedom of expression also came under attack. By excluding religion and tolerating obscenity, critics charged, liberals made possible a degrading competition between pornography and banality in the value-free zone of popular culture. According to critics left and right, liberals were responsible for all that was wrong with America—even though those groups offered diametrically opposite diagnoses of the nation's maladies.

When the Soviet Union and its satellite states collapsed in 1989–91, and when the domestic U.S. economy began to lose ground relative to both the industrialized and the developing world, liberal confidence was shaken. Without a Communist menace or a socialist alternative, which had provided the fixed points against which many liberals could measure their economic policies, navigating the new terrain of domestic and international politics became more treacherous. Free-market champions and their allies in academic disciplines who were attracted to models proclaiming self-interested behavior as the consequence of "rational choice" increasingly set the terms of social scientific debate. The particularistic agendas of identity politics challenged the integrationist programs of the civil rights movement and the post–World War II wave of feminism. The earlier liberal emphasis on freedom and toleration remained, but in the absence of a compelling agenda of economic reforms premised on the ideal of equality or the older virtue of benevolence, the new liberal critique of a naturalized and thus unassailable free-market model seemed vulnerable to libertarians' charges of impracticality.

By the twenty-first century, few candidates for public office embraced the label of liberalism—not surprising given that fewer than 25 percent of voters identified themselves as liberals. Clearly the momentum had shifted: 50 years earlier Boorstin and Hartz had declared all of American history a species of the genus liberalism, and liberals confidently proclaimed that the future belonged to them as well. Partisan squabbles seemed to be subsiding. New nations were emerging from colonial childhood into full membership in the United Nations. As partialities and particularities appeared to be giving way to a new universalism, a reign of liberal toleration, benevolence, generosity, and cultural cultivation seemed visible on the horizon. One decade into the twenty-first century, that world seemed very far away.

Opposition to the war in Vietnam had prompted liberals to associate flag-waving patriotism with their hawkish opponents, a strategic disaster that enabled conservatives to identify their own aggressive foreign policy with the national interest and to portray liberals as traitors. Particularly after September 11, 2001—and with disastrous consequences—the charge stuck, which was odd given the commitments of earlier American liberals. From the birth of the nation through the Civil War to World War II, most liberals had rallied to legitimate assertions of American power. Relinquishing that tradition proved catastrophic, both culturally and politically. Likewise from the dawn of the United States through the height of the civil rights movement and the opposition to the Vietnam War, liberals mobilized alongside—not against—people of faith. Surrendering religion to the right proved as damaging to the political prospects of liberalism as the widespread concern that liberals were insufficiently patriotic because they disagreed with conservatives over issues of foreign policy.

Yet if liberals were able to recover from those strategic blunders or correct those misperceptions, they might find their fortunes changing in the twenty-first century. Opinion polls demonstrate that the ideals associated with liberalism for the last four centuries retain a grip on the American imagination. If liberals could regain the confidence to embrace and reassert those ideals, and if they could abandon commitments to failed policies and programs and construct a new cultural and political agenda to advance the principles they embrace, they might yet see a brighter horizon. From the early seventeenth century until the present, many of those attuned to liberality have distrusted selfishness and parochialism and embraced the idea that popular sovereignty could enable Americans to replace inherited practices of oppression and hierarchy with open-mindedness and generosity. Achieving those goals remains the challenge facing liberals today.

See also conservatism; democracy, radicalism.

FURTHER READING

Appleby, Joyce. *Liberalism and Republicanism in the Historical Imagination*. Cambridge, MA: Harvard University Press, 1992.

Berlin, Isaiah. *Four Essays on Liberty*. Oxford: Oxford University Press, 1969.

Borgwardt, Elizabeth. *A New Deal for the World: America's Vision for Human Rights*. Cambridge, MA: Harvard University Press, 2005.

Brick, Howard. *Transcending Capitalism: Visions of a New Society in Modern American Thought*. Ithaca, NY: Cornell University Press, 2006.

Brinkley, Alan. *The End of Reform: New Deal Liberalism in Recession and War*. New York: Knopf, 1995.

Butler, Leslie. *Critical Americans: Victorian Intellectuals and Transatlantic Liberal Reform*. Chapel Hill: University of North Carolina Press, 2006.

Cohen, Lizabeth. *A Consumers' Republic: The Politics of Mass Consumption in Postwar America*. New York: Knopf, 2003.

Foner, Eric. *The Story of American Freedom*. New York: Norton, 1998.

Greenstone, J. David. *The Lincoln Persuasion: Remaking American Liberalism*. Princeton, NJ: Princeton University Press, 1993.

Hartz, Louis. *The Liberal Tradition in America*. New York: Harcourt, Brace, 1955.

Hollinger, David A. *Postethnic America: Beyond Multiculturalism*. 3rd ed. New York: Basic Books, 2006.

Howe, Daniel Walker. *What Hath God Wrought: The Transformation of America, 1815–1848*. Oxford, UK: Oxford University Press, 2007.

Jacobs, Meg, Julian E. Zelizer, and William J. Novak, eds. *The Democratic Experiment: New Directions in American Political History*. Princeton, NJ: Princeton University Press, 2003.

Jumonville, Neil, and Kevin Mattson, eds. *Liberalism for a New Century*. Berkeley: University of California Press, 2007.

Kalman, Laura. *The Strange Career of Legal Liberalism*. New Haven, CT: Yale University Press, 1996.

Kazin, Michael. *The Populist Persuasion: An American History*. Revised ed. Ithaca, NY: Cornell University Press, 1998.

Kerber, Linda. *No Constitutional Right to Be Ladies: Women and the Obligations of Citizenship*. New York: Hill and Wang, 1998.

Keyssar, Alexander. *The Right to Vote: The Contested History of Democracy in America*. New York: Basic Books, 2000.

King, Richard. *Civil Rights and the Idea of Freedom*. Oxford, UK: Oxford University Press, 1992.

Kloppenberg, James T. *The Virtues of Liberalism*. Oxford, UK: Oxford University Press, 1998.

———. *Uncertain Victory: Social Democracy and Progressivism in European and American Thought*. Oxford, UK: Oxford University Press, 1986.

Rawls, John. *Political Liberalism: The John Dewey Essays in Philosophy*. New York: Columbia University Press, 1993.

Rodgers, Daniel. *Contested Truths: Keywords in American Politics since Independence*. New York: Basic Books, 1987.

Sandel, Michael. *Democracy's Discontent: America in Search of a Public Philosophy*. Cambridge, MA: Harvard University Press, 1996.

Smith, Rogers. *Civic Ideals: Conflicting Visions of Citizenship in U. S. History*. New Haven, CT: Yale University Press, 1997.

Wilentz, Sean. *The Rise of American Democracy: Jefferson to Lincoln*. New York: Norton, 2005.

Winthrop, John. "Christian Charity, A Model Hereof." In *Puritans in the New World, A Critical Anthology*, edited by David D. Hall, 165–80. Princeton, NJ: Princeton University Press, 2004.

Wood, Gordon. *The Creation of the American Republic, 1776–1787*. 2nd ed. Chapel Hill: University of North Carolina Press, 1998.

JAMES T. KLOPPENBERG

Libertarian Party

The Libertarian Party was organized on December 11, 1971, in Denver, Colorado, at the home of David Nolan by a circle of conservative activists furious with the Nixon administration's Keynesian economic policies. In addition to Nolan, a former Republican activist, its leaders included the prominent economist Murray Rothbard, philosophy professor John Hospers, and businessman Edward Crane (later founder of the Cato Institute, a libertarian think tank). The party quickly became one of the most successful alternative entities in twentieth-century American politics. It gained a place on the presidential ballot of every state by 1980, and as of 2005 had elected a total of more than 600 members to public office on various levels across the country. By July 2006, 235,500 Americans were registered Libertarian Party members. Despite these achievements, however, like many independent political organizations the Libertarian Party has had a greater impact on American political language and ideology than on practical policy—a phenomenon particularly evident in its troubled relationship with the Republican Party.

Members of the Libertarian Party understand individual liberty to be the fundamental and necessary basis of a moral and just society. The "guiding principle" of libertarianism as defined by the founders of the party is "mutual respect for rights." To that end, libertarians argue, the primary role of the government should be greatly narrowed, and ultimately, merely twofold: to provide protection of property rights domestically and a national defense abroad. Libertarians would greatly reduce governmental bureaucracy, eliminating social programs, regulation of the economy, and prosecution of "victimless crimes" while taking a strong stand in favor of broad civil liberties and free trade and isolationism abroad. This political philosophy has a long pedigree. It has roots in the classical liberalism of eighteenth- and nineteenth-century British thinkers such as John Stuart Mill, and, more recently, in the Austrian school of economics represented most powerfully in the United States by Ludwig von Mises and Friedrich Hayek. On a more popular level, the novelists Ayn Rand and Robert Heinlein proved effective propagators of a radical anti-statist, individualist ethos, and, according to historian Brian Doherty, more than half of the earliest Libertarians cited one of these two authors as their primary ideological influence.

While the platform of the Libertarian Party accepted the system of government as laid out in the U.S. Constitution as the best means to achieve its goals, the party often was beset with internal dissent and schism. The most prominent of these was the anarcho-capitalism movement Rothbard eventually championed, which maintained that the state itself should be eliminated. The Libertarian Party periodically was torn between these advocates of anarchism and supporters of "minarchism" (acceptance of a minimal state). Though a truce between these groups was negotiated in 1974, in 1983 another internal war broke out over the party's presidential nomination. A purist faction led by Rothbard revolted against Edward Crane's "machine," which had led the party to win the most votes it had ever received for president in the 1980 election but which Rothbard accused of ideological compromise. Crane's candidate, Earl Ravenal, lost at the 1983 convention, and Crane led an exodus from the party, taking many resources and wealthy supporters with him.

The year of the party's founding, 1971, was the year the Republican administration of Richard Nixon abandoned the gold standard and implemented price controls in an attempt to curb rampant inflation—this, coming from a party that only seven years earlier had nominated the fiscal conservative Barry Goldwater for president, convinced Nolan and his adherents that neither major political party could be trusted to protect the liberties of Americans. The next year, after Rothbard declined the nomination, a convention of 89 delegates in Denver named Hospers and Oregon activist Tonie Nathan as the Libertarian candidates for the presidency and vice presidency. Though the Hospers-Nathan ticket gained only 2,691 votes, the Virginia Republican elector Roger MacBride, disillusioned with Richard Nixon, gave the Libertarians their first—and to date, only—electoral vote. Since then, the Libertarian Party has nominated a candidate for the presidency every year, but only once—in 1980, behind the ticket of Ed Clark and David Koch—has it gained more than 1 percent of the popular vote: Clark's 921,299 votes far outpaced the second most successful campaign, the 1996 Harry Browne–Jo Jorgensen ticket, which garnered 485,798 votes. Despite such promising initial success in presidential politics, after Clark's campaign, the party stagnated on the presidential level. Between 1984 and 2008, every Libertarian presidential candidate won between roughly a quarter and a half million votes, one-third to one-half of one percent of the total votes cast in a given election.

On the local level, Libertarians have achieved more success. In 1978 Richard Randolph became the first Libertarian elected to state office, gaining a seat in the Alaska House of Representatives. Three years later, Richard Siano won a three-way race, defeating both Republican and Democratic candidates to gain a city council seat in Kingwood Township, New Jersey. As of 2008, 12 Libertarians have gained seats in state legislatures. While a Libertarian candidate has never won election to national office (with the debatable exception of Ron Paul, the 1988 Libertarian presidential candidate who gained a seat in the House of Representatives as a Republican in 1996), the party's rhetoric has to some extent penetrated national politics. Many Libertarians were optimistic about the election of Ronald Reagan, who skillfully invoked libertarian rhetoric during the 1980 presidential campaign. Movement figures such as Milton Friedman and Alan Greenspan (an admirer of Rand), held places in Reagan's circle, and much was made of a 1980 photograph of Reagan reading the libertarian journal *Freeman*. The Cato Institute moved to Washington in 1981, hoping to influence the administration. However, by 1982, Edward Crane had lost faith in Reagan for supporting Social Security and engaging in economic protectionism. Other Libertarians were disappointed with the president's endorsement of restrictive policies on social issues such as abortion and drug use. Similarly, the Contract with America, the banner under which Republicans, led by Georgia Representative Newt Gingrich, reclaimed Congress in 1994, raised libertarian expectations; several of its proposals, such as term limits and deregulation of industry, gained strong libertarian support. However, hopes were again dashed when the Republican-led Congress ultimately failed to reverse trends toward government spending and increased federal power.

In 2007 Ron Paul mounted an essentially libertarian campaign for the Republican presidential nomination and gained a surprising amount of media attention. Despite his membership in the Republican Party, Paul's opposition to the war in Iraq (a position largely, though not universally, supported in the libertarian mainstream, such as in the Cato Institute) gained him criticism from many in the GOP, suggesting that the ideological differences that had motivated former Republicans to found the Libertarian Party had persisted. The swirl of interest around Paul's candidacy provided a jolt to a movement that had flagged in the late 1990s, when its electoral influence declined and the party suffered internal dissension. Paul's campaign revealed that the ideological influence of libertarianism was far from dead.

See also liberalism; Republican Party, 1968–2008.

FURTHER READING

Boaz, David. *Libertarianism: A Primer*. New York: Free Press, 1997.

Doherty, Brian. *Radicals for Capitalism: A Freewheeling History of the Modern American Libertarian Movement*. New York: Public Affairs, 2007.

Hazlett, Joseph. *The Libertarian Party and Other Minor Political Parties in the United States*. Jefferson, NC: McFarland, 1992.

MATTHEW BOWMAN

Liberty Party

A small group of abolitionists formed the Liberty Party in Albany, New York, in April 1840. For eight years, the party asked antislavery Northerners to "vote as you pray and pray as you vote." Few did. The party's presidential candidate, James Birney, won 7,000 votes in the election of 1840 and 62,000 in 1844, with more than half of the 1844 vote coming from New York, Massachusetts, and Ohio. Despite its tepid electoral support, the Liberty Party broke the two major parties' stranglehold on Jacksonian politics and gave the antislavery movement an independent political voice.

The Liberty Party grew out of the radical abolitionist movement of the 1830s. While eschewing partisan politics, abolitionists engaged in such activities as flooding Congress with petitions calling for the abolition of slavery in the District of Columbia. But abolitionists failed to sway the two major parties toward more vigorous opposition to slavery, since both needed southern slaveholders to build a coalition capable of winning national elections. The gag rule instituted in the House of Representatives in 1836 to silence debate over antislavery petitions to Congress exemplified the two parties' hostility to antislavery agitation.

Many abolitionists saw the Democrats and the Whigs as beholden to the "Slave Power," but they disagreed over what to do about it. Faced with a stubborn political system, the abolitionist movement split over principles and tactics. One faction, led by William Lloyd Garrison, decried politics as inherently corrupt and focused instead on the task of swaying northern public opinion against slavery. An anti-Garrisonian faction backed by the wealthy New York philanthropist Gerrit Smith, equally devoted to abolition but more open to politics, organized a new political party with the single goal of advancing an antislavery agenda.

The Liberty Party (as it was soon called) mirrored the radical abolitionists' "come-outer" tendency of breaking free from existing organizations tainted by slavery—especially churches—and creating new ones with an antislavery core. Indeed, many of the Liberty Party's strongest supporters were members of antislavery Protestant denominations like the Congregationalists, Free Will Baptists, Wesleyan Methodists, and Quakers. Geographically, support for the party was strongest in New England, the "burnt-over" district of intense evangelical activity in upstate New York, and in areas of the old northwest (Ohio, Illinois, Michigan, etc.) settled by New Englanders.

The party advocated the "absolute and unqualified divorce of the General Government from slavery." Although some Liberty supporters denied that slavery was constitutional anywhere in the Union, the party platform did not call for the abolition of slavery in the states where it already existed. It did demand the abolition of slavery and the slave trade in the District of Columbia and in other federal territory, a prohibition on the inter-state slave trade, and a ban on the admission of new slave states. It also regarded the fugitive slave clause of the U.S. Constitution as "null and void" and disavowed any obligation on the part of northern citizens or state officials to help in the capture and return of escaped slaves.

Boldly standing for equal rights for African Americans, the Liberty Party challenged northern racism at a time when black Northerners faced disenfranchisement, legal discrimination, prejudice, and violence. It welcomed African Americans into its ranks, and many prominent black abolitionists, including Henry Highland Garnet, actively supported the party. The National Convention of Colored Men in Buffalo endorsed the Liberty Party in 1843.

The party took a less radical stand on women's rights, especially compared with the Garrisonians. Still, many abolitionist women worked actively for the Liberty Party, contributing essays to party newspapers and forming auxiliary committees. Some women's rights activists received valuable training in Liberty Party circles. Elizabeth Cady Stanton's exposure to a broad network of political activists through her husband, Liberty Party bigwig Henry Stanton, helped prepare her for a leadership role at the Seneca Falls convention in 1848.

As third parties usually discover, peeling voters from established parties is difficult, and the fierce partisan loyalties of Jacksonian America made the task even harder for the Liberty Party. The single-minded spokesmen for the party had to find a way to shift voters' attention away from the economic issues that had dominated the 1830s and toward slavery. Since northern Whig voters were more likely than northern Democrats to sympathize with abolition, the Liberty Party's biggest hurdle was convincing antislavery Whigs that voting for Liberty would not ultimately help the Democrats.

Taking the Liberty Party threat seriously, Whigs fought back by alleging (and even fabricating documents to prove) that the party was a secret Democratic plot to weaken the Whigs. After the 1844 presidential election, many Whigs bitterly complained that the Liberty Party's more than 15,000 votes in New York had catapulted the Democratic candidate, James Polk, to the presidency. The Democratic Party took the Liberty Party threat seriously too, lambasting the party as disunionist and pro-black.

Liberty strength grew somewhat in the early 1840s, bolstered by victories at state levels and the revival of territorial expansion as a hot political issue. The par-

ty's greatest success came in Vermont in 1845, when John P. Hale, an antislavery Democratic congressman, was dumped by his party for criticizing the annexation of Texas. Hale's Democratic supporters joined with conscience Whigs and the Liberty Party to capture the state legislature early in 1846 and send Hale to the U.S. Senate as a champion of what was essentially the Liberty Party's agenda.

Hale's success signaled the prospect of a broader antislavery alliance that appealed to some of the Liberty Party's more pragmatic leaders, most notably Salmon P. Chase of Ohio. A Cincinnati lawyer who had been instrumental in developing the concept of an antislavery Constitution, Chase helped to fold the Liberty Party into the newly formed Free Soil Party in 1848—a remarkable turn of events given that the Free Soil candidate for president, the Barnburner Democrat Martin Van Buren, had been the abolitionists' chief political nemesis a decade earlier. (One vicious political cartoon from 1848 depicted the union of the Free Soil and Liberty parties as a marriage between Van Buren and an African American woman.)

Abolitionist editor Joshua Leavitt told his fellow Liberty Party supporters that their movement had been "translated" into the Free Soil Party, but some diehards thought essential principles were lost in translation. They formed the Liberty League to carry on not just the Liberty Party's opposition to slavery but also its concern for black equality. The election of 1848 handed down a harsh judgment against them: the Liberty League's candidate for president, Gerrit Smith, won a mere 2,500 votes, while Van Buren won more than 291,000.

The Liberty Party advanced the antislavery cause in the United States by developing new constitutional and legal strategies and adopting the tactics of a mass party organization. Its supporters hoped to build an independent northern party committed to racial egalitarianism and to pressure the two major parties to resist the southern "slave power." Though an electoral failure, the party helped to catalyze the epic realignment of the political system that culminated in the Civil War.

See also abolitionism; Democratic Party, 1828–60; Free Soil Party; Jacksonian era, 1828–45; Whig Party; women and politics, 1828–65.

FURTHER READING

Blue, Frederick J. *Salmon P. Chase: A Life in Politics*. Kent, OH: Kent State University Press, 1987.

Fladeland, Betty. *James Gillespie Birney: Slaveholder to Abolitionist*. New York: Greenwood Press, 1969.

Pierson, Michael. *Free Hearts and Free Homes: Gender and American Antislavery Politics*. Chapel Hill: University of North Carolina Press, 2003.

Stewart, James Brewer. *Holy Warriors: The Abolitionists and American Slavery*. New York: Hill and Wang, 1996.

Strong, Douglas M. *Perfectionist Politics: Abolitionism and the Religious Tensions of American Democracy*. Syracuse, NY: Syracuse University Press, 1999.

Volpe, Vernon L. *Forlorn Hope of Freedom: The Liberty Party in the Old Northwest, 1838–1848*. Kent, OH: Kent State University Press, 1990.

ADAM ROTHMAN

lobbying

See interest groups.

local government

For four centuries Americans have remained devoted to grassroots rule and organs of local government. They have deemed that government closest to the people as most representative of the popular will and thus have jealously protected and perpetuated local power. In Canada and Great Britain as well as the continental European nations, central lawmakers have been able to revise and reform local government without submitting their measures to the veto of local referenda. In the United States, however, voters have repeatedly blocked the path to change, fearful that the destruction of inherited local units would diminish their political voice and open the door to dreaded centralization. Perhaps more than any other nation, the United States is a land of local satrapies, a prevailing fear of big, distant government preserving a complex structure of local rule. State governments have increasingly imposed a degree of supervision over localities. But local institutions persist as perceived bulwarks against central authority, and the defensive instincts of the local electorate remain strong.

Local Rule 1607–1900

During the colonial era, Americans fashioned the primary units of the future nation's structure of local rule. In New England the town was the chief governing unit, exercising responsibility for schools, poor relief, and roads. Policy-making power rested with the town meeting, a conclave of all enfranchised townspeople, though popularly elected selectmen assumed primary authority for day-to-day governance. In the South the county court and parish vestry of the established Church of England were the chief units of local government. Dominated by the local gentry, the county courts served both judicial and administrative functions, hearing legal suits as well as maintaining county roads. The parish vestry was generally responsible for poor relief. The middle colonies of Pennsylvania, New Jersey, and New York combined the governmental forms of New England and the South, assigning a large share of local responsibility to counties but also maintaining town or township governments. In this hybrid mix, counties were less powerful than in the South, but towns or townships exercised less authority than their New England counterparts.

To govern their emerging cities, the middle and southern colonies applied the institution of the municipal corporation inherited from Great Britain. Some municipalities such as Philadelphia, Williamsburg, and Norfolk were closed corporations in which the incumbent board of aldermen filled any vacancies in their governing body; the local citizenry had no voice in the selection of city officials. In Albany, New York City, and the municipal corporations of New Jersey, however, popular election of the governing aldermen prevailed. New England eschewed the institution of the municipal corporation, its more populous communities retaining the town form of rule and the town meeting.

The American Revolution wrought some changes in the system of local government. New municipal charters granted by state legislatures replaced the closed corporations ruled by a self-chosen elite, with government by popularly elected city councils. The disestablishment of the Church of England also deprived the parish vestry of its responsibility for poor relief; henceforth, secular overseers of the poor assumed charge of the least fortunate members of society. Yet there was also great continuity in the forms of local rule. The town remained the principal unit of local government in New England, though in the 1780s five communities in Connecticut, including Hartford and New Haven as well as Newport in Rhode Island, accepted city charters. Not until 1822 did Boston finally abandon town rule and the town meeting, accepting a city form of government with a mayor and municipal legislature. In the middle states, counties and towns continued to exercise local authority, and the county courts remained supreme in the South.

The new western states adopted the established forms of their eastern neighbors. Ohio, Indiana, Illinois, Michigan, and Wisconsin embraced the hybrid form of county-township rule characteristic of Pennsylvania and New York, whereas in the new southern states of Kentucky, Tennessee, Alabama, and Mississippi the county was the focus of local authority. The town or township never took root in the South. During the late nineteenth century, the states west of the Rockies also found diminutive township units unsuited for their sparsely settled rural areas. Consequently, the town or township remained primarily a northeastern and midwestern unit. In these regions, it administered local roads, cemeteries, and poor relief while township justices of the peace handled minor offenses and disputes.

One new unit of local government that proliferated during the nineteenth century was the school district. Elected school boards administered education in miniscule districts across America. For example, the number of school districts in Michigan rose from 3,097 in 1850 to 7,168 in 1890. By the latter date, there was one school district for every 60 pupils enrolled in the state. Over 1,000 districts could claim less than 25 pupils. In many areas of the nation, there was a unit of school government for every one-room schoolhouse, each a diminutive educational republic charged with bringing reading, writing, and arithmetic to its youth.

Meanwhile, municipal corporations had to adapt to burgeoning centers of urban population. As New York City, Philadelphia, Chicago, and scores of lesser metropolises attracted millions of migrants from Europe and rural America, their city governments assumed new and expanded duties. In the mid-nineteenth century professional fire departments supplanted the volunteer forces of the past, and a professional police bureaucracy developed to preserve the urban peace. An emerging corps of professional engineers applied their expertise to water supply and sewerage, constructing elaborate systems of aqueducts, reservoirs, and drainage tunnels. A body of pioneering landscape architects led by Frederick Law Olmsted laid out great urban parks, the most notable being New York City's Central Park.

The adoption of universal manhood suffrage in the early nineteenth century shifted the political advantage to plebeian leaders who cultivated the loyalty of the immigrant masses flooding the cities. Tammany Hall, New York City's Democratic organization, became known for its steadfast support among Irish immigrants who benefited from the public jobs and favors that Tammany could bestow. Sober citizens who deemed themselves the respectable class grew increasingly troubled by the rising power of such partisan organizations and launched repeated campaigns to reform the structure of municipal rule. Consequently, in the latter half of the nineteenth century, city councils dominated by neighborhood leaders, some of them local saloonkeepers, lost power to mayors who were generally respected businessmen.

Twentieth-Century Reform

Reform demands mounted in the early twentieth century, resulting in a major restructuring of many city governments. In 1901 Galveston, Texas, pioneered the commission form of government, which lodged all executive and legislative authority in a small board of elected commissioners, each commissioner charged with responsibility for one area of municipal administration. This city commission plan eliminated the ward-based councils deemed the source of much local corruption; by carefully defining the responsibilities of each commissioner, the plan also heightened official accountability. By the end of 1913, 337 American municipalities had adopted the commission plan.

The commission scheme, however, did not ensure professional, expert administration of municipal services. Consequently, during the second decade of the twentieth century reformers increasingly turned to another alternative, the city manager plan. First adopted in Staunton, Virginia, in 1908, the city manager plan lodged policy-making authority in an elected city council, but the execution of policy and administration of the city was the job of an appointed city manager. Expected to be nonpartisan professional administrators, city managers were supposed to apply their expertise and guarantee optimal efficiency in the operation of their municipalities. By the close of 1923, 269 cities employed city managers, and the number would increase throughout the twentieth century, as the manager plan supplanted commission rule as the preferred reform alternative.

Meanwhile, some reformers were also turning their attention to the antiquated structure of county government. Traditionally, elected boards of supervisors or county commissioners had exercised both executive and legislative authority at the county level, and a long list of elected officials such as county treasurer, auditor, clerk of courts, and sheriff had performed specific administrative functions. The concept of separation of powers did not exist at the county level, and popularity at the polls rather than professional credentials determined who would administer these local units. Proponents of the manager plan proposed extending it to counties, but not until 1927 did Iredell County, North Carolina, appoint the nation's first county manager. By 1950 only 16 of the nation's more than 3,000 counties had hired administrators with duties akin to those of the city manager. In the 1930s two populous New York counties, Nassau and Westchester, sought to rationalize local rule by creating the elected office of county executive to serve basically as mayor of the county. Not until the late twentieth century, however, did large numbers of counties create the post of elected executive or hire a professional administrator charged with broad managerial supervision of county affairs.

Structural reformers also targeted New England's venerable town meetings. By the early twentieth century, only a small proportion of those eligible actually attended the meetings in New England's largest towns. Consequently, an unrepresentative and self-interested minority appeared to be determining town policies. To correct this problem, in 1915 reformers in the populous suburban town of Brookline, Massachusetts, secured adoption of the representative town meeting form of government. Henceforth, Brookline voters would elect 240 town meeting members who were to represent them at the meetings. Every town voter could attend the meetings and participate in discussion, but only the elected members could vote. By 1930, 18 Massachusetts towns had opted for the representative town meeting form.

Local Rule in Metropolitan America

Rationalization of local government attracted increasing attention from the 1920s onward, as rapid suburbanization produced a bewildering array of new governmental units in metropolitan areas throughout the nation. During the nineteenth century, states had adopted permissive incorporation procedures, allowing virtually any community to become an independent municipality. As Americans moved to the suburbs, they took advantage of this to create a mass of new municipalities tailormade to serve the interests of their residents. In the 1920s American municipalities acquired zoning powers in order to protect the interests of homeowners and

upscale-housing developers. Now municipalities not only could provide traditional policing, ensure street maintenance, and offer water and sewer services, they could also restrict who and what moved into a community. For the growing corps of home-owning suburbanites, this constituted a strong incentive to incorporate. In suburbanizing Nassau County on Long Island, the number of municipalities soared from 20 in 1920 to 65 in 1940, and in suburban Saint Louis County, Missouri, the municipal head count rose from 20 in 1930 to 84 in 1950.

Meanwhile, Americans organized thousands of special district governments to provide certain services. Unlike multipurpose municipalities or townships, special districts usually provided only a single service. From 1920 to 1933, the number of such units in Nassau County climbed from 87 to 173; this latter figure included 38 districts charged with water supply, 52 fire protection districts, and 53 lighting districts responsible for the provision of street lights. Each special district had separate taxing powers, and their proliferation markedly augmented the number of hands reaching into taxpayers' pockets.

Some metropolitan residents deplored the confusion and fragmentation of authority resulting from this multitude of counties, townships, municipalities, and special districts. But in the 1920s and early 1930s campaigns for the consolidation or federation of local units failed in the seriously divided Pittsburgh, Cleveland, and Saint Louis metropolitan areas. Localism posed a formidable barrier to unification, and a renewal of metropolitan government crusades in the 1950s again produced no significant results. Any consolidation or federation of units in the United States required voter approval, and this was not forthcoming. Repackaged as the new regionalism, in the 1990s metropolitan cooperation stirred renewed interest among scholars and civic reformers but yielded few results. During the latter half of the twentieth century in a few metropolitan areas such as Jacksonville, Nashville, and Indianapolis, civic leaders secured a consolidation of city and county governments, thereby attempting to streamline local administration and achieve some unity in policy making. But consolidation was the exception, not the rule. A myriad of township, village, and city governments survived, and the number of special districts soared.

In contrast, states were successful in reducing the number of school districts. Whereas village and township governments could adapt and provide minimal services for twentieth-century small towns and rural areas, school districts designed to govern one-room schools were outmoded in a nation where a good education was perceived as necessary to personal success. Claiming that consolidation of districts would improve schooling and offer rural residents advantages formerly enjoyed only in city schools, state departments of education coerced or cajoled Americans to eschew the miniscule districts of the past. The number of school districts in the United States thus dropped from 127,531 in 1932 to 15,781 in 1972.

By the last decades of the twentieth century, states were also forced to intervene and prop up some faltering central-city municipal regimes as well as distressed inner-city school governments. As business investment abandoned aging central cities for the suburbs, tax bases shrank; at the same time, the expense of providing services for the remaining impoverished residents increased. In 1975, New York State took charge of the finances of a virtually bankrupt New York City, and, until the mid-1980s, the state carefully monitored fiscal decision making in the nation's largest city. Cleveland, Philadelphia, Buffalo, and Pittsburgh also became fiscal wards of their state governments. Financial difficulties as well as poor academic performance resulted in state takeovers of some city school systems, with state-appointed administrators superseding the authority of locally elected school board members.

Yet such heavy-handed state intervention was not the norm. Americans continued to place their faith in local elected officials, preferring grassroots rule to centralized dictation. At the beginning of the twenty-first century, there were 87,849 units of local government in the United States. In the late twentieth century the number of counties remained stable, whereas the figure for municipalities increased slowly. For decades so-called experts had criticized townships as unnecessary relics of the horse-and-buggy era, yet there remained 16,506 of these units in 2002, the number falling only 2 percent in the previous quarter-century. The traditional New England town meeting survived, with only 38 of

the 300 Massachusetts towns opting for the representative town meeting. The last half of the twentieth century also witnessed a sharp rise in special districts, their number almost tripling from 12,340 in 1952 to 35,356 in 2002. Owing to innovations in transportation and communication, the lives of most Americans were no longer confined to the narrow boundaries of localities. In this increasingly cosmopolitan nation, however, the government of the village and town remained a jealously guarded political legacy.

See also cities and politics; suburbs and politics.

FURTHER READING

Berman, David R., ed. *County Governments in an Era of Change.* Westport, CT: Greenwood Press, 1993.

Bollens, John C. *Special District Governments in the United States.* Berkeley: University California Press, 1957.

Callow, Alexander B. *The Tweed Ring.* New York: Oxford University Press, 1966.

Gilbertson, H. S. *The County: The "Dark Continent" of American Politics.* New York: National Short Ballot Organization, 1917.

Ireland, Robert M. *The County Courts in Antebellum Kentucky.* Lexington: University Press of Kentucky, 1972.

Rice, Bradley R. *Progressive Cities: The Commission Government Movement in America, 1901–1920.* Austin: University of Texas Press, 1977.

Sly, John Fairfield. *Town Government in Massachusetts, 1620–1930.* Cambridge, MA: Harvard University Press, 1930.

Teaford, Jon C. *City and Suburb: The Political Fragmentation of Metropolitan America, 1850–1970.* Baltimore, MD: Johns Hopkins University Press, 1979.

———. *The Municipal Revolution in America: Origins of Modern Urban Government, 1650–1825.* Chicago: University of Chicago Press, 1975.

———. *The Unheralded Triumph: City Government in America, 1870–1900.* Baltimore, MD: Johns Hopkins University Press, 1984.

JON C. TEAFORD